KEY TO WORLD M… GES

PHILIP'S

INTERNATIONAL WORLD ATLAS

CONTENTS

WORLD STATISTICS

Countries vi
Physical Dimensions vii
Philip's World Maps viii

THE WORLD OF NATIONS

A Gazetteer of Countries, Continent by Continent

Europe 1
Asia 12
Africa 24
Australia and Oceania 36
North America 38
South America 44
Index and Notes 48

PROFILE OF THE EARTH

Geology and Climate 50-51
Environment 52-53
Population 54-55
The Human Family 56-57
Standards of Living 58-59
Energy 60-61
Production 62-63
Time and the Seasons 64

WORLD MAPS

Map Symbols
1

The World: Political 1:80 000 000
2-3

Arctic Ocean 1:35 000 000
4

Antarctica 1:35 000 000
5

EUROPE

Europe: Physical 1:20 000 000
6

Europe: Political 1:20 000 000
7

Scandinavia and the Baltic Lands 1:5 000 000

8-9

England and Wales 1:2 000 000

10-11

Scotland 1:2 000 000

12

Ireland 1:2 000 000

13

British Isles 1:4 000 000

14

Netherlands, Belgium and Luxembourg 1:2 500 000

15

Central Europe 1:5 000 000

16-17

France 1:5 000 000

18

Spain and Portugal 1:5 000 000

19

Italy and the Balkan States 1:5 000 000

20-21

Balearics, Canaries and Madeira 1:1 000 000/1:2 000 000

22

Malta, Crete, Corfu, Rhodes and Cyprus 1:1 000 000/1:1 300 000

23

Eastern Europe and Turkey 1:10 000 000

24-25

ASIA

Russia and Central Asia 1:20 000 000

26-27

Asia: Physical 1:50 000 000
28

Asia: Political 1:50 000 000
29

Japan 1:5 000 000

30-31

China and Korea 1:15 000 000

32-33

Northern China and Korea 1:6 000 000

34-35

Indonesia and the Philippines 1:12 500 000

36-37

Mainland South-East Asia 1:6 000 000

38-39

South Asia 1:10 000 000

40-41

The Indo-Gangetic Plain 1:6 000 000

42-43

The Middle East
1:7 000 000

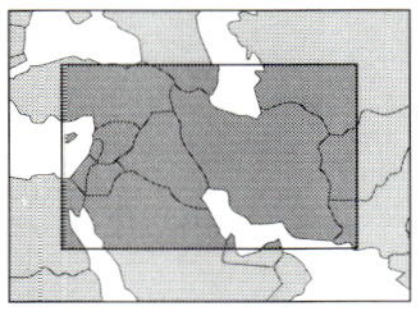

44-45

Arabia and the Horn of Africa 1:15 000 000

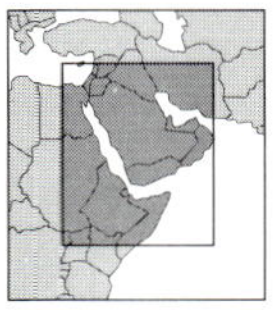

46

The Near East
1:2 500 000

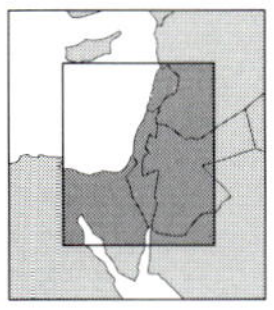

47

AFRICA

Africa: Physical
1:40 000 000
48

Africa: Political
1:40 000 000
49

Northern Africa
1:15 000 000

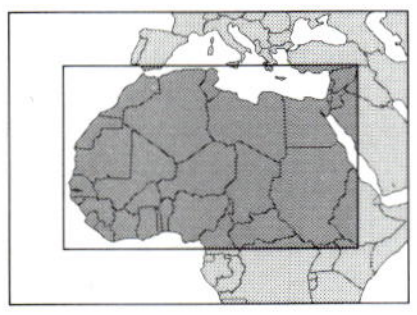

50-51

Central and Southern Africa 1:15 000 000

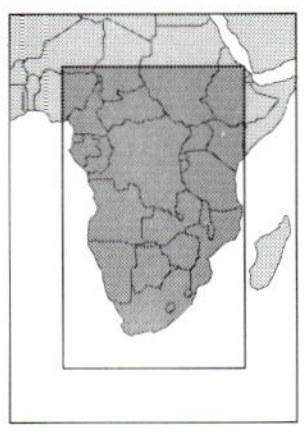

52-53

East Africa 1:8 000 000

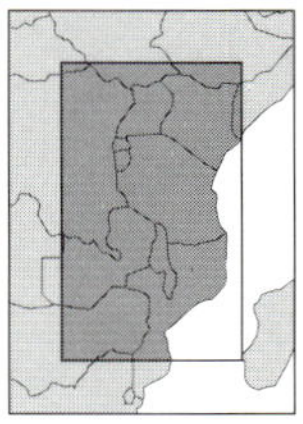

54-55

Southern Africa
1:8 000 000
Madagascar 1:8 000 000

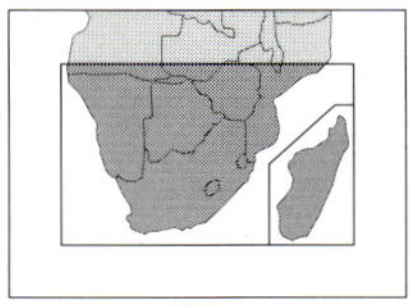

56-57

AUSTRALIA AND OCEANIA

Australia and Oceania: Physical and Political 1:40 000 000
58

New Zealand
1:6 000 000

59

Western Australia
1:8 000 000

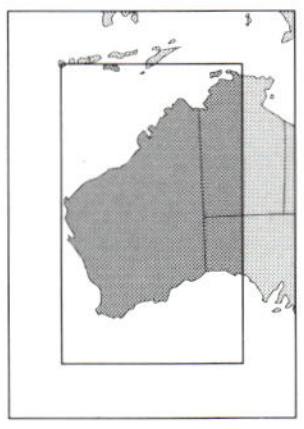

60-61

Eastern Australia
1:8 000 000

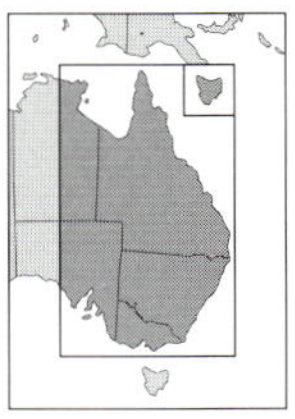

62-63

Pacific Ocean
1:54 000 000
64-65

NORTH AMERICA

North America: Physical 1:35 000 000
66

North America: Political 1:35 000 000
67

Canada 1:15 000 000
Alaska 1:30 000 000

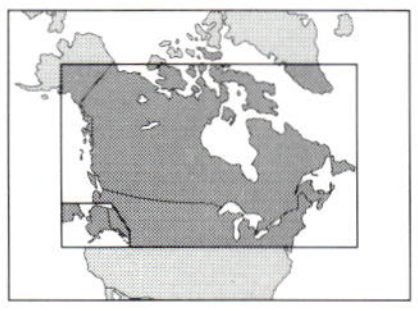

68-69

Eastern Canada
1:7 000 000

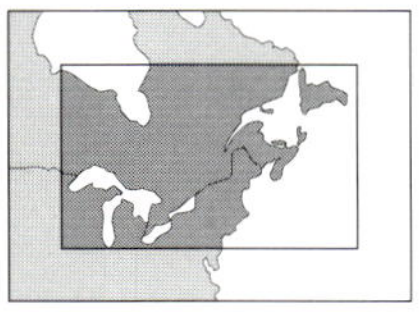

70-71

Western Canada
1:7 000 000

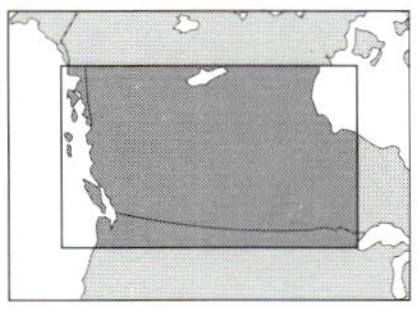

72-73

United States
1:12 000 000
Hawaii 1:10 000 000

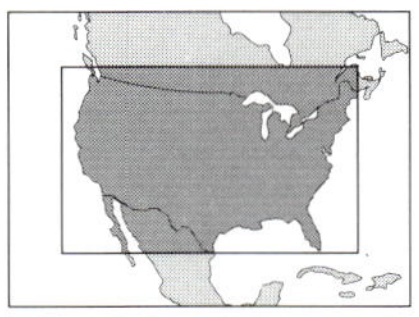

74-75

Eastern United States
1:6 000 000

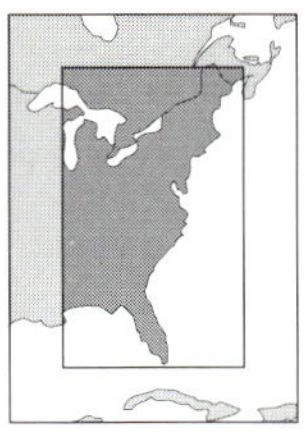

76-77

North-Eastern United States 1:2 500 000

78-79

Middle United States
1:6 000 000

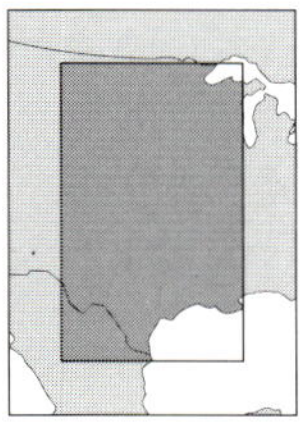

80-81

Western United States
1:6 000 000

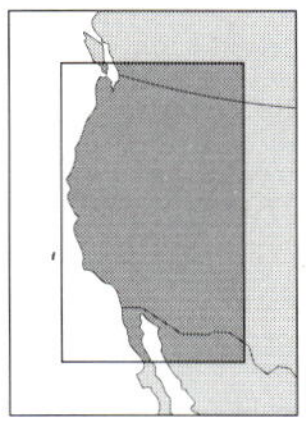

82-83

Central and Southern California and Washington 1:2 500 000

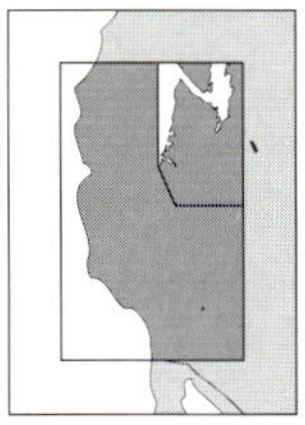

84-85

Mexico 1:8 000 000

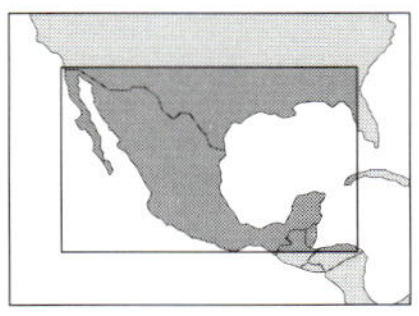

86-87

Central America and the West Indies
1:8 000 000

88-89

SOUTH AMERICA

South America: Physical 1:30 000 000
90

South America: Political 1:30 000 000
91

South America - North
1:16 000 000

92-93

Central South America 1:8 000 000

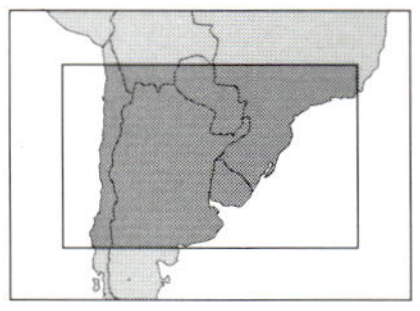

94-95

South America - South
1:16 000 000

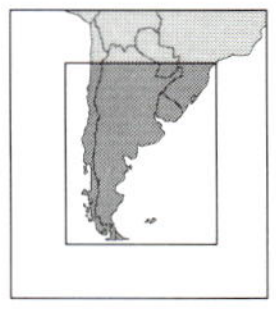

96

INDEX TO WORLD MAPS

World Statistics: Countries

This alphabetical list includes the principal countries and territories of the world. If a territory is not completely independent, then the country it is associated with is named. The area figures give the total area of land, inland water and ice. Units for areas and populations are thousands. The annual income is the Gross National Product per capita in US dollars. The figures are the latest available, usually 1989-91.

Country/Territory	**Area** km^2 *Thousands*	**Area** miles^2 *Thousands*	**Population** *Thousands*	**Capital**	**Annual Income** US $
Afghanistan	652	25	16,433	Kabul	450
Albania	28.8	11.1	3,250	Tiranë	1,000
Algeria	2,382	920	24,960	Algiers	2,060
American Samoa (US)	0.20	0.08	39	Pago Pago	6,000
Andorra (Fr/Spain)	0.45	0.17	52	Andorre-la-Vella	
Angola	1,247	481	10,020	Luanda	620
Anguilla (UK)	0.40	0.09	8	The Valley	
Antigua & Barbuda	0.44	0.17	77	St. John's	4,600
Argentina	2,767	1,068	32,322	Buenos Aires	2,370
Armenia	29.8	11.5	3,300	Yerevan	
Aruba (Neths)	0.19	0.07	60	Oranjestad	6,000
Australia	7,687	2,968	17,086	Canberra	17,080
Austria	83.9	32.4	7,712	Vienna	19,240
Azerbaijan	86.6	33.4	7,100	Baku	
Azores (Port)	2.2	0.87	260	Ponta Delgada	
Bahamas	13.9	5.4	253	Nassau	11,510
Bahrain	0.68	0.26	503	Manama	6,500
Bangladesh	144	56	115,594	Dacca	200
Barbados	0.43	0.17	255	Bridgetown	6,540
Belau (US)	0.46	0.18	15	Koror	
Belgium	30.5	11.8	9,845	Brussels	15,440
Belize	23.0	8.9	188	Belmopan	1,970
Belorussia	208	80.1	10,300	Minsk	
Benin	113	43	4,736	Porto-Novo	360
Bermuda (UK)	0.05	0.02	61	Hamilton	25,000
Bhutan (India)	47.0	18.1	1,517	Thimphu	190
Bolivia	1,099	424	7,400	La Paz/Sucre	620
Botswana	582	225	1,291	Gaborone	2,040
Brazil	8,512	3,286	153,322	Brasilia	2,680
Brit. Antarctic Terr. (UK)	1,709	660	0.3	Stanley	
Brit. Ind. Oc. Terr (UK)	0.08	0.03	3	-	
Brunei	5.8	2.2	266	Bandar Seri Begawan	6,000
Bulgaria	111	43	9,011	Sofia	2,210
Burkina Faso	274	106	9,001	Ouagadougou	330
Burma (Myanmar)	677	261	41,675	Rangoon	500
Burundi	27.8	10.7	5,438	Bujumbura	210
Cambodia	181	70	8,246	Phnom Penh	300
Cameroon	475	184	11,834	Yaoundé	940
Canada	9,976	3,852	26,522	Ottawa	20,450
Canary Is. (Spain)	7.3	2.8	1,700	Las Palmas/S.Cruz	
Cape Verde Is.	4.0	1.6	370	Praia	890
Cayman Is. (UK)	0.26	0.10	27	Georgetown	
Cent. African Rep.	623	241	3,039	Bangui	390
Chad	1,284	496	5,679	Ndjamena	190
Chile	757	292	13,386	Santiago	1,940
China	9,597	3,682	1,139,060	Beijing	370
Colombia	1,139	440	32,987	Bogotá	1,240
Comoros	2.2	0.86	551	Moroni	480
Congo	342	132	2,271	Brazzaville	1,010
Costa Rica	51.1	19.7	2,994	San José	1,910
Croatia	56.5	21.8	4,680	Zagreb	
Cuba	111	43	10,609	Havana	3,000
Cyprus	9.3	3.6	702	Nicosia	8,040
Czechoslovakia	128	49	15,678	Prague	3,140
Denmark	43.1	16.6	5,140	Copenhagen	22,090
Djibouti	23.2	9.0	409	Djibouti	1,000
Dominica	0.75	0.29	83	Roseau	1,940
Dominican Rep.	48.7	18.8	7,170	Santo Domingo	820
Ecuador	284	109	10,782	Quito	960
Egypt	1,001	387	53,153	Cairo	600
El Salvador	21.0	8.1	5,252	San Salvador	1,100
Equatorial Guinea	28.1	10.8	348	Malabo	330
Estonia	44.7	17.3	1,600	Tallinn	
Ethiopia	1,222	472	50,974	Addis Ababa	120
Falkland Is. (UK)	12.2	4.7	2	Stanley	
Faroe Is. (Den)	1.4	0.54	47	Tórshavn	22,090
Fiji	18.3	7.1	765	Suva	1,770
Finland	338	131	4,986	Helsinki	26,070
France	552	213	56,440	Paris	19,480
French Guiana (Fr)	90.0	34.7	99	Cayenne	2,500
French Polynesia (Fr)	4.0	1.5	206	Papeete	6,000
Gabon	268	103	1,172	Libreville	3,220
Gambia, The	11.3	4.4	861	Banjul	260
Georgia	69.7	26.9	5,500	Tbilisi	
Germany	357	138	79,479	Berlin/Bonn	17,000
Ghana	239	92	15,028	Accra	390
Gibraltar (UK)	0.007	0.003	31	-	4,000
Greece	132	51	10,269	Athens	6,000
Greenland (Den)	2,176	840	60	Godthåb	6,000
Grenada	0.34	0.13	85	St. George's	2,120
Guadeloupe (Fr)	1.7	0.66	344	Basse-Terre	7,000
Guam (US)	0.55	0.21	119	Agana	6,000
Guatemala	109	42	9,197	Guatemala City	900
Guinea	246	95	5,756	Conakry	480
Guinea-Bissau	36.1	13.9	965	Bissau	180
Guyana	215	83	796	Georgetown	370
Haiti	27.8	10.7	6,486	Port-au-Prince	370
Honduras	112	43	5,105	Tegucigalpa	590
Hong Kong (UK)	1.1	0.40	5,801	-	11,540
Hungary	93.0	35.9	10,344	Budapest	2,780
Iceland	103	40	255	Reykjavik	21,150
India	3,288	1,269	843,931	Delhi	350
Indonesia	1,905	735	179,300	Jakarta	560
Iran	1,648	636	58,031	Tehran	2,450
Iraq	438	169	18,920	Baghdad	2,000
Ireland	70.3	27.1	3,523	Dublin	9,550
Israel	27.0	10.4	4,659	Jerusalem	10,970
Italy	301	116	57,663	Rome	16,850
Ivory Coast	322	125	11,998	Abidjan	730
Jamaica	11.0	4.2	2,420	Kingston	1,510
Japan	378	146	123,537	Tokyo	25,430
Jordan	89.2	34.4	4,009	Amman	1,240
Kazakhstan	2,717	1,049	16,700	Alma Ata	
Kenya	580	224	24,032	Nairobi	370
Kirghizia	199	76.9	4,400	Bishkek	
Kiribati	0.72	0.28	66	Tarawa	760
Korea, North	121	47	21,773	Pyongyang	900
Korea, South	99.0	38.2	43,302	Seoul	5,400
Kuwait	17.8	6.9	2,143	Kuwait City	16,380
Laos	237	91	4,139	Vientiane	200
Latvia	63.1	24.4	2,700	Riga	
Lebanon	10.4	4.0	2,701	Beirut	2,000
Lesotho	30.4	11.7	1,774	Maseru	470
Liberia	111	43	2,607	Monrovia	500
Libya	1,760	679	4,545	Tripoli	5,800
Liechtenstein	0.16	0.06	29	Vaduz	33,000
Lithuania	65.2	25.2	3,751	Vilnius	
Luxembourg	2.6	1.0	384	Luxembourg	28,770
Macau (Port)	0.02	0.006	479	-	2,000
Madagascar	587	227	11,197	Antananarivo	230
Malawi	118	46	8,556	Lilongwe	200
Malaysia	330	127	17,861	Kuala Lumpur	2,340
Maldives	0.30	0.12	215	Malé	440
Mali	1,240	479	8,156	Bamako	270
Malta	0.32	0.12	354	Valletta	6,630
Martinique (Fr)	1.1	0.42	341	Fort-de-France	4,000
Mauritania	1,025	396	2,050	Nouakchott	500
Mauritius	1.9	0.72	1,075	Port Louis	2,250
Mexico	1,958	756	86,154	Mexico City	2,490
Micronesia, Fed. Stat (US)	0.70	0.27	103	Kolonia	
Moldavia	33.7	13.0	4,400	Kishinev	
Monaco	0.002	0.0001	29	-	20,000
Mongolia	1,567	605	2,190	Ulan Bator	400
Montserrat (UK)	0.10	0.04	13	Plymouth	
Morocco	447	172	25,061	Rabat	950
Mozambique	802	309	15,656	Maputo	80
Namibia	824	318	1,781	Windhoek	1,000
Nauru	0.02	0.008	10	Domaneab	
Nepal	141	54	18,916	Katmandu	170
Netherlands	41.9	16.2	15,019	Amsterdam	17,330
Neths. Antilles (Neths)	0.99	0.38	189	Willemstad	6,000
New Caledonia (Fr)	19.0	7.3	168	Nouméa	4,000
New Zealand	269	104	3,429	Wellington	12,680
Nicaragua	130	50	3,871	Managua	800
Niger	1,267	489	7,732	Niamey	310
Nigeria	924	357	108,542	Lagos (Abuja)	270
Norway	324	125	4,242	Oslo	23,120
Oman	212	82	1,502	Muscat	5,220
Pakistan	796	307	112,050	Islamabad	380
Panama	77.1	29.8	2,418	Panama City	1,830
Papua New Guinea	463	179	3,699	Port Moresby	860
Paraguay	407	157	4,277	Asunción	1,110
Peru	1,285	496	22,332	Lima	1,160
Philippines	300	116	61,480	Manila	730
Poland	313	121	38,180	Warsaw	1,700
Portugal	92.4	35.7	10,525	Lisbon	4,890
Puerto Rico (US)	8.9	3.4	3,599	San Juan	6,470
Qatar	11.0	4.2	368	Doha	15,860
Réunion (Fr)	2.5	0.97	599	St.-Denis	
Romania	238	92	23,200	Bucharest	1,640
Russia	17,068	6,593	147,400	Moscow	
Rwanda	26.3	10.2	7,181	Kigali	310
St. Christopher/Nevis	0.36	0.14	44	Basseterre	3,330
St. Lucia	0.62	0.24	151	Castries	1,900
St. Pierre & Miquelon (Fr)	0.24	0.09	6	St. Pierre	
St. Vincent/Grenadines	0.39	0.15	116	Kingstown	1,610
San Marino	0.06	0.02	24	San Marino	
São Tomé & Príncipe	0.96	0.37	121	São Tomé	380
Saudi Arabia	2,150	830	14,870	Riyadh	6,230
Senegal	197	76	7,327	Dakar	710
Seychelles	0.28	0.11	67	Victoria	4,670
Sierra Leone	71.7	27.7	4,151	Freetown	240
Singapore	0.62	0.24	3,003	Singapore	12,310
Slovenia	20.3	7.8	1,940	Ljubljana	
Solomon Is.	28.9	11.2	321	Honiara	580
Somalia	638	246	7,497	Mogadishu	150
South Africa	1,221	471	35,282	Pretoria	2,520
Spain	505	195	38,959	Madrid	10,920
Sri Lanka	65.6	25.3	16,993	Colombo	470
Sudan	2,506	967	25,204	Khartoum	450
Surinam	163	63	422	Paramaribo	3,050
Swaziland	17.4	6.7	768	Mbabane	820
Sweden	450	174	8,618	Stockholm	23,680
Switzerland	41.3	15.9	6,712	Bern	32,790
Syria	185	71	12,116	Damascus	990
Taiwan	36.0	13.9	20,300	Taipei	6,600
Tajikistan	143	55.2	5,300	Dushanbe	
Taiwan	36.0	13.9	20,300	Taipei	6,600
Tanzania	945	365	25,635	Dar es Salaam	120
Thailand	513	198	57,196	Bangkok	1,420
Togo	56.8	21.9	3,531	Lome	410
Tokelau (NZ)	0.01	0.005	2	Nukunonu	
Tonga	0.75	0.29	95	Nuku'alofa	1,010
Trinidad & Tobago	5.1	2.0	1,227	Port of Spain	3,470
Tunisia	164	63	8,180	Tunis	1,420
Turkey	779	301	57,326	Ankara	1,630
Turkmenistan	488	188	3,600	Ashkhabad	
Turks & Caicos Is. (UK)	0.43	0.17	10	Grand Turk	
Tuvalu	0.03	0.01	10	Funafuti	600
Uganda	236	91	18,795	Kampala	220
Ukraine	604	233	51,800	Kiev	
United Arab Emirates	83.6	32.3	1,589	Abu Dhabi	19,860
United Kingdom	244	94	57,405	London	16,070
United States	9,373	3,619	249,928	Washington	21,700
Uruguay	177	68	3,094	Montevideo	2,560
Uzbekistan	447	173	20,300	Tashkent	
Vanuatu	12.2	4.7	147	Port Vila	1,060
Vatican City	0.0004	0.0002	1.0	-	
Venezuela	912	352	19,735	Caracas	2,560
Vietnam	332	127	66,200	Hanoi	300
Virgin Is. (UK)	0.15	0.06	13	Road Town	
Virgin Is. (US)	0.34	0.13	117	Charlotte Amalie	12,000
Western Sahara (Mor)	266	103	179	El Aiun	
Western Samoa	2.8	1.1	164	Apia	730
Yemen	528	204	11,282	San'a	640
Yugoslavia (ex. Croatia/Slov.)	179	69	17,144	Belgrade	3,060
Zaïre	2,345	906	35,562	Kinshasa	230
Zambia	753	291	8,073	Lusaka	420

World Statistics: Physical Dimensions

Each topic list is divided into continents and within a continent the items are listed in size order. The order of the continents is as in the atlas, Europe through to South America. The bottom part of many of the lists are selective. The world top ten are shown in square brackets; in the case of mountains this has not been done because the world top thirty are all in Asia. The figures are rounded as appropriate.

World, Continents, Oceans

	km²	miles²	%
The World	509,450,000	196,672,000	
Land	149,450,000	57,688,000	29.3
Water	360,000,000	138,984,000	70.7
Asia	44,500,000	17,177,000	29.8
Africa	30,302,000	11,697,000	20.3
North America	24,241,000	9,357,000	16.2
South America	17,793,000	6,868,000	11.9
Antarctica	14,100,000	5,443,000	9.4
Europe	9,957,000	3,843,000	6.7
Australia & Oceania	8,557,000	3,303,000	5.7
Pacific Ocean	179,679,000	69,356,000	49.9
Atlantic Ocean	92,373,000	35,657,000	25.7
Indian Ocean	73,917,000	28,532,000	20.5
Arctic Ocean	14,090,000	5,439,000	3.9

Mountains

Europe		m	ft
Mont Blanc	*France/Italy*	4,807	15,771
Monte Rosa	*Italy/Switz.*	4,634	15,203
Dom	*Switzerland*	4,545	14,911
Weisshorn	*Switzerland*	4,505	14,780
Matterhorn/Cervino	*Italy/Switz.*	4,478	14,691
Mt. Maudit	*France/Italy*	4,465	14,649
Finsteraarhorn	*Switzerland*	4,275	14,025
Aletschhorn	*Switzerland*	4,182	13,720
Jungfrau	*Switzerland*	4,158	13,642
Barre des Ecrins	*France*	4,103	13,461
Gran Paradiso	*Italy*	4,061	13,323
Piz Bernina	*Italy/Switz.*	4,052	13,294
Ortles	*Italy*	3,899	12,792
Monte Viso	*Italy*	3,841	12,602
Grossglockner	*Austria*	3,797	12,457
Mulhacén	*Spain*	3,478	11,411
Pico de Aneto	*Spain*	3,404	11,168
Etna	*Italy*	3,340	10,958
Galdhöpiggen	*Norway*	2,469	8,100
Hvannadalshnúkur	*Iceland*	2,119	6,952
Ben Nevis	*UK*	1,343	4,406
Asia			
Everest	*China/Nepal*	8,848	29,029
Godwin Austen (K2)	*China/Kashmir*	8,611	28,251
Kanchenjunga	*India/Nepal*	8,598	28,208
Lhotse	*China/Nepal*	8,516	27,939
Makalu	*China/Nepal*	8,481	27,824
Cho Oyu	*China/Nepal*	8,201	26,906
Dhaulagiri	*Nepal*	8,172	26,811
Manaslu	*Nepal*	8,156	26,758
Nanga Parbat	*Kashmir*	8,126	26,660
Annapurna	*Nepal*	8,078	26,502
Gasherbrum	*China/Kashmir*	8,068	26,469
Broad Peak	*India*	8,051	26,414
Gosainthan	*China*	8,012	26,286
Disteghil Sar	*Kashmir*	7,885	25,869
Nuptse	*Nepal*	7,879	25,849
Elbrus	*Russia*	5,633	18,481
Fuji-san	*Japan*	3,776	12,388
Pidurutalagala	*Sri Lanka*	2,524	8,281
Africa			
Kilimanjaro	*Tanzania*	5,895	19,340
Mt. Kenya	*Kenya*	5,199	17,057
Ruwenzori	*Uganda/Zaïre*	5,109	16,762
Ras Dashan	*Ethiopia*	4,620	15,157
Meru	*Tanzania*	4,565	14,977
Karisimbi	*Rwanda/Zaïre*	4,507	14,787
Mt. Elgon	*Kenya/Uganda*	4,321	14,176
Batu	*Ethiopia*	4,307	14,130
Gughe	*Ethiopia*	4,200	13,779
Toubkal	*Morocco*	4,165	13,665
Oceania			
Puncak Jaya	*Indonesia*	5,029	16,499
Puncak Mandala	*Indonesia*	4,760	15,617
Puncak Trikora	*Indonesia*	4,750	15,584
Mt. Wilhelm	*Papua N. Guinea*	4,508	14,790
Mauna Kea	*USA (Hawaii)*	4,208	13,806
Mauna Loa	*USA (Hawaii)*	4,169	13,678
Mt. Cook	*New Zealand*	3,753	12,313
Kosciusko	*Australia*	2,230	7,316
North America			
Mt. McKinley	*USA (Alaska)*	6,194	20,321
Mt. Logan	*Canada*	6,050	19,849
Citlaltepetl	*Mexico*	5,700	18,701
Mt. St.Elias	*USA/Canada*	5,489	18,008
Popocatepetl	*Mexico*	5,452	17,887
Mt. Foraker	*USA (Alaska)*	5,304	17,401
Ixtaccihuatl	*Mexico*	5,286	17,342
Lucania	*USA (Alaska)*	5,226	17,145
Mt. Steele	*Canada*	5,011	16,440
Mt. Bona	*USA (Alaska)*	5,005	16,420
South America			
Aconcagua	*Argentina*	6,960	22,834
Illimani	*Bolivia*	6,882	22,578
Bonete	*Argentina*	6,872	22,546
Ojos del Salado	*Argentina/Chile*	6,863	22,516
Tupungato	*Argentina/Chile*	6,800	22,309
Pissis	*Argentina*	6,779	22,241
Mercedario	*Argentina/Chile*	6,770	22,211
Huascaran	*Peru*	6,768	22,204
Llullaillaco	*Argentina/Chile*	6,723	22,057
Nudo de Cachi	*Argentina*	6,720	22,047
Antarctica			
Vinson Massif		4,897	16,066

Ocean Depths

Atlantic Ocean	m	ft
Puerto Rico (Milwaukee) Deep [7]	9,200	30,183
Cayman Trench [10]	7,680	25,197
Gulf of Mexico	5,203	17,070
Mediterranean	5,121	16,801
Black Sea	2,211	7,254
North Sea	310	1,017
Baltic Sea	294	965
Hudson Bay	111	364
Indian Ocean		
Java Trench	7,450	24,442
Red Sea	2,266	7,434
Persian Gulf	73	239
Pacific Ocean		
Mariana Trench [1]	11,022	36,161
Tonga Trench [2]	10,822	35,505
Japan Trench [3]	10,554	34,626
Kuril Trench [4]	10,542	34,586
Mindanao Trench [5]	10,497	34,439
Kermadec Trench [6]	10,047	32,962
Peru-Chile Trench [8]	8,050	26,410
Aleutian Trench [9]	7,822	25,662
Middle American Trench	6,662	21,857
Arctic Ocean		
Molloy Deep	5,608	18,399

Land Lows

		m	ft
Caspian Sea	*Europe*	-28	-92
Dead Sea	*Asia*	-400	-1,312
Lake Assal	*Africa*	-156	-512
Lake Eyre North	*Oceania*	-16	-52
Death Valley	*N. America*	-86	-282
Valdés Peninsula	*S. America*	-40	-131

Rivers

Europe		km	miles
Volga	*Caspian Sea*	3,700	2,300
Danube	*Black Sea*	2,850	1,770
Ural	*Caspian Sea*	2,535	1,574
Dnieper	*Volga*	2,285	1,420
Kama	*Volga*	2,030	1,260
Don	*Volga*	1,990	1,240
Petchora	*Arctic*	1,790	1,110
Dniester	*Black Sea*	1,400	870
Rhine	*North Sea*	1,320	820
Elbe	*North Sea*	1,145	710
Vistula	*Baltic Sea*	1,090	675
Loire	*Atlantic*	1,020	635
Thames	*North Sea*	335	210
Asia			
Yangtse [3]	*Pacific*	6,380	3,960
Yenisei-Angara [5]	*Arctic*	5,550	3,445
Ob-Irtysh [6]	*Arctic*	5,410	3,360
Hwang Ho [7]	*Pacific*	4,840	3,005
Amur [9]	*Pacific*	4,510	2,800
Mekong [10]	*Pacific*	4,500	2,795
Lena	*Arctic*	4,400	2,730
Irtysh	*Ob*	4,250	2,640
Yenisei	*Arctic*	4,090	2,540
Ob	*Arctic*	3,680	2,285
Indus	*Indian*	3,100	1,925
Brahmaputra	*Indian*	2,900	1,800
Syr Darya	*Aral Sea*	2,860	1,775
Salween	*Indian*	2,800	1,740
Euphrates	*Indian*	2,700	1,675
Vilyuy	*Lena*	2,650	1,645
Kolyma	*Arctic*	2,600	1,615
Amu Darya	*Aral Sea*	2,540	1,575
Ural	*Caspian Sea*	2,535	1,575
Ganges	*Indian*	2,510	1,560
Si Kiang	*Pacific*	2,100	1,305
Irrawaddy	*Indian*	2,010	1,250
Tigris	*Indian*	1,900	1,180
Africa			
Nile [1]	*Mediterranean*	6,670	4,140
Zaïre/Congo [8]	*Atlantic*	4,670	2,900
Niger	*Atlantic*	4,180	2,595
Zambezi	*Indian*	2,740	1,700
Oubangi/Uele	*Zaïre*	2,250	1,400
Kasai	*Zaïre*	1,950	1,210
Shaballe	*Indian*	1,930	1,200
Orange	*Atlantic*	1,860	1,155
Australia			
Murray-Darling	*Indian*	3,720	2,310
Darling	*Murray*	3,070	1,905
Murray	*Indian*	2,575	1,600
Murrumbidgee	*Murray*	1,690	1,050
North America			
Mississippi-Missouri [4]	*Gulf of Mexico*	6,020	3,740
Mackenzie	*Arctic*	4,240	2,630
Mississippi	*Gulf of Mexico*	3,780	2,350
Missouri	*Mississippi*	3,725	2,310
Yukon	*Pacific*	3,185	1,980
Rio Grande	*Gulf of Mexico*	3,030	1,880
Arkansas	*Mississippi*	2,340	1,450
Colorado	*Pacific*	2,330	1,445
Red	*Mississippi*	2,040	1,270
Columbia	*Pacific*	1,950	1,210
Saskatchewan	*L Winnipeg*	1,940	1,205
Snake	*Columbia*	1,670	1,040
South America			
Amazon [2]	*Atlantic*	6,430	3,990
Paraná-Plate	*Atlantic*	4,000	2,480
Purus	*Amazon*	3,350	2,080
Madeira	*Amazon*	3,200	1,990
São Francisco	*Atlantic*	2,900	1,800
Paraná	*Plate*	2,800	1,740
Tocantins	*Atlantic*	2,640	1,640
Paraguay	*Paraná*	2,550	1,580
Orinoco	*Atlantic*	2,500	1,550
Pilcomayo	*Paraná*	2,500	1,550

Lakes

Europe		km²	miles²
Lake Ladoga	*Russia*	18,400	7,100
Lake Onega	*Russia*	9,700	3,700
Saimaa system	*Finland*	8,000	3,100
Asia			
Caspian Sea [1]	*Asia*	371,000	143,000
Aral Sea [6]	*Kazakh/Uzbek*	36,000	13,900
Lake Baikal [9]	*Russia*	31,500	12,200
Tonlé Sap	*Cambodia*	20,000	7,700
Lake Balkhash	*Kazakhstan*	18,500	7,100
Africa			
Lake Victoria [3]	*E. Africa*	68,000	26,000
Lake Tanganyika [7]	*C. Africa*	33,000	13,000
Lake Malawi [10]	*E. Africa*	29,000	11,000
Lake Chad	*C. Africa*	25,000	9,700
Australia			
Lake Eyre	*Australia*	9,000	3,500
North America			
Lake Superior [2]	*Canada/USA*	82,200	31,700
Lake Huron [4]	*Canada/USA*	59,600	23,000
Lake Michigan [5]	*USA*	58,000	22,400
Great Bear Lake [8]	*Canada*	31,500	12,200
Great Slave Lake	*Canada*	28,700	11,100
Lake Erie	*Canada/USA*	25,700	9,900
Lake Winnipeg	*Canada*	24,400	9,400
Lake Ontario	*Canada/USA*	19,500	7,500
South America			
Lake Titicaca	*Bolivia/Peru*	8,200	3,200

Islands

Europe		km²	miles²
Great Britain [8]	*UK*	229,880	88,700
Iceland	*Atlantic Ocean*	103,000	39,800
Ireland	*Ireland/UK*	84,400	32,600
Asia			
Borneo [3]	*S E. Asia*	737,000	284,000
Sumatra [6]	*Indonesia*	425,000	164,000
Honshu [7]	*Japan*	230,000	88,800
Celebes	*Indonesia*	189,000	73,000
Java	*Indonesia*	126,700	48,900
Luzon	*Philippines*	104,700	40,400
Mindanao	*Philippines*	95,000	36,700
Hokkaido	*Japan*	78,400	30,300
Sakhalin	*Russia*	76,400	29,500
Sri Lanka	*Indian Ocean*	65,600	25,300
Africa			
Madagascar [4]	*Indian Ocean*	587,000	226,600
Oceania			
New Guinea [2]	*Indon./Pap. NG*	780,000	301,080
New Zealand (S)	*New Zealand*	150,500	58,100
New Zealand (N)	*New Zealand*	114,400	44,200
Tasmania	*Australia*	67,800	26,200
North America			
Greenland [1]	*Greenland*	2,175,600	839,800
Baffin I. [5]	*Canada*	508,000	196,100
Victoria I. [9]	*Canada*	212,200	81,900
Ellesmere I. [10]	*Canada*	212,000	81,800
Cuba	*Cuba*	114,500	44,200
Newfoundland	*Canada*	96,000	37,100
Hispaniola	*Atlantic Ocean*	76,200	29,400
South America			
Tierra del Fuego	*Argentina/Chile*	47,000	18,100

PHILIP'S WORLD MAPS

The reference maps which form the main body of this atlas have been prepared in accordance with the highest standards of international cartography to provide an accurate and detailed representation of the earth. The scales and projections used have been carefully chosen to give balanced coverage of the world, while emphasizing the most densely populated and economically significant regions. A hallmark of Philip's mapping is the use of hill shading and relief colouring to create a graphic impression of landforms: this makes the maps exceptionally easy to read. However, knowledge of the key features employed in the construction and presentation of the maps will enable the reader to derive the fullest benefit from the atlas.

Map sequence

The atlas covers the earth continent by continent: first Europe; then its land neighbour Asia (mapped north before south, in a clockwise sequence), then Africa, Australia and Oceania, North America and South America. This is the classic arrangement adopted by most cartographers since the 16th century. For each continent, there are maps at a variety of scales. First, physical relief and political maps of the whole continent. Then a series of larger-scale maps of the regions within the continent, each followed, where required, by still larger-scale maps of the most important or densely populated areas. The governing principle is that by turning the pages of the atlas, the reader moves steadily from north to south through each continent, with each map overlapping its neighbours. A key map showing this sequence, and the area covered by each map, can be found on the endpapers of the atlas.

Map presentation

With very few exceptions (eg for the Arctic and Antarctic), the maps are drawn with north at the top, regardless of whether they are presented upright or sideways on the page. In the borders will be found the map title; a locator diagram showing the area covered and the page numbers for maps of adjacent areas; the scale; the projection used; the degrees of latitude and longitude; and the letters and figures used in the index for locating place names and geographical features. Physical relief maps also have a height reference panel identifying the colours used for each layer of contouring.

Map symbols

Each map contains a vast amount of detail which can only be conveyed clearly and accurately by the use of symbols. Points and circles of varying sizes locate and identify the relative importance of towns and cities; different styles of type are employed for administrative, geographical and regional place names. A variety of pictorial symbols denote landscape features such as glaciers, marshes and reefs, and man-made structures including roads, railways, airports, canals and dams. International borders are shown by red lines. Where neighbouring countries are in dispute, for example in the Middle East, the maps show the *de facto* boundary between nations, regardless of the legal or historical situation. The symbols are explained on the first page of the World Maps section of the atlas.

Map scales

The scale of each map is given in the numerical form known as the 'representative fraction'. The first figure is always one, signifying one unit of distance on the map; the second figure, usually in millions, is the number by which the map unit must be multiplied to give the equivalent distance on the earth's surface. Calculations can easily be made in centimetres and kilometres, by dividing the earth units figure by 100 000 (ie deleting the last five 0s). Thus 1:1 000 000 means 1 cm = 10 km. The calculation for inches and miles is more laborious, but 1 000 000 divided by 63 360 (the number of inches in a mile) shows that 1:1 000 000 means approximately 1 inch = 16 miles. The table below provides distance equivalents for scales down to 1:50 000 000.

LARGE SCALE

1: 1 000 000	1 cm = 10 km	1 inch = 16 miles
1: 2 500 000	1 cm = 25 km	1 inch = 39.5 miles
1: 5 000 000	1 cm = 50 km	1 inch = 79 miles
1: 6 000 000	1 cm = 60 km	1 inch = 95 miles
1: 8 000 000	1 cm = 80 km	1 inch = 126 miles
1: 10 000 000	1 cm = 100 km	1 inch = 158 miles
1: 12 000 000	1 cm = 120 km	1 inch = 189 miles
1: 15 000 000	1 cm = 150 km	1 inch = 237 miles
1: 20 000 000	1 cm = 200 km	1 inch = 316 miles
1: 50 000 000	1 cm = 500 km	1 inch = 790 miles

SMALL SCALE

Measuring distances

Although each map is accompanied by a scale bar, distances cannot always be measured with confidence because of the distortions involved in portraying the curved surface of the earth on a flat page. As a general rule, the larger the map scale (ie the lower the number of earth units in the representative fraction), the more accurate and reliable will be the distance measured. On small-scale maps such as those of the world and of entire continents, measurement may only be accurate along the 'standard parallels', or central axes, and should not be attempted without first considering the map projection used.

Latitude and longitude

Accurate positioning of individual points on the earth's surface is made possible by reference to the geometrical system of latitude and longitude. Latitude *parallels* are drawn west-east around the earth and numbered by degrees north and south of the Equator, which is designated 0° of latitude. Longitude *meridians* are drawn north-south and numbered by degrees east and west of the *prime meridian,* 0° of longitude, which passes through Greenwich in England. By referring to these co-ordinates and their sub-divisions of minutes (1/60th of a degree) and seconds (1/60th of a minute), any place on earth can be located to within a few hundred yards. Latitude and longitude are indicated by blue lines on the maps; they are straight or curved according to the projection employed. Reference to these lines is the easiest way of determining the relative positions of places on different large-scale maps, and for plotting compass directions.

Name forms

For ease of reference, both English and local name forms appear in the atlas. Oceans, seas and countries are shown in English throughout the atlas; country names may be abbreviated to their commonly accepted form (eg Germany, not The Federal Republic of Germany). Conventional English forms are also used for place names on the smaller-scale maps of the continents. However, local name forms are used on all large-scale and regional maps, with the English form given in brackets only for important cities – the large-scale map of European Russia thus shows Moskva (Moscow). For countries which do not use a Roman script, place names have been transcribed according to the systems adopted by the British and US Geographic Names Authorities. For China, the Pin Yin system has been used, with some more widely known forms appearing in brackets, as with Beijing (Peking). Both English and local names appear in the index to the world maps.

THE WORLD OF NATIONS

A Gazetteer of Countries, Continent by Continent

Europe 1, Asia 12, Africa 24, Australia and Oceania 36,
North America 38, South America 44
Index and Notes 48

EUROPE – NORTH

ICELAND

Iceland's traditional colours are blue and white. The flag's colours are a combination of those of Denmark, Norway and the coat of arms. Dating from 1915, it became the official flag on independence from Denmark in 1944.

COUNTRY: Republic of Iceland
AREA: 103,000 sq km [39,768 sq mls]
POPULATION: 255,000
CAPITAL (Population): Reykjavik (96,000)
GOVERNMENT: Democratic republic with a bicameral Parliament
ETHNIC GROUPS: Icelanders (97%)
LANGUAGES: Icelandic (official)
RELIGIONS: Christian (Lutheran 96%, Roman Catholic 1%)
NATIONAL DAY: 17 June
CURRENCY: Króna = 100 aurar

ANNUAL INCOME PER PERSON: $21,150
MAIN PRIMARY PRODUCT: Fish
MAIN INDUSTRIES: Freezing, salting, drying and smoking fish, cement and unwrought aluminium
MAIN EXPORTS: Fish products and unwrought aluminium
MAIN IMPORTS: Food and live animals, crude materials and petroleum, basic manufactures
DEFENCE: Iceland has no defence force
POPULATION DENSITY: 2.5 per sq km [6.5 per sq ml]
LIFE EXPECTANCY: Female 81 yrs, Male 75 yrs
ADULT LITERACY: 99%

■ Over 700 hot springs provide 75% of pop. with central heating ■ World's lowest infant mortality & West's highest life expectancy ■ World's highest literacy rate ■ World's first parliament (930AD)

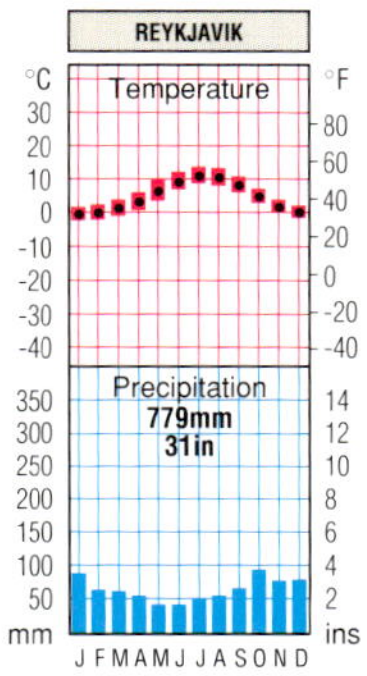

Although the northern tip of Iceland touches the Arctic Circle, thanks to the Gulf Stream, it is quite warm. The coldest month at Reykjavik, January, is normally 0°C [32°F], the same as Copenhagen. Rain falls on 200 days a year, 40 of them as snow. There is very high rainfall on the south coast. Gales are frequent.

SVALBARD

COUNTRY: Norwegian possession

AREA: 62,000 sq km [24,000 sq mls]
POPULATION: 4,000
CAPITAL (Population): Longyearbyen

■ Also known by name of main island, Spitzbergen ■ Name means Cold Coast ■ Whaling base until 19th century, now coal mining by Russia and Norway

NORWAY

Norway's flag has been used since 1898, though its use as a merchant flag dates back to 1821. The design is based on the Dannebrog flag of Denmark, which ruled Norway from the 14th century to the early 19th century.

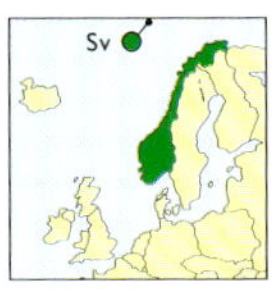

COUNTRY: Kingdom of Norway
AREA: 323,900 sq km [125,050 sq mls]
POPULATION: 4,242,000
CAPITAL (Population): Oslo (455,000)
GOVERNMENT: Constitutional monarchy with a unicameral legislature
ETHNIC GROUPS: Norwegian 97%
LANGUAGES: Norwegian (official), Lappish, Finnish
RELIGIONS: Lutheran 88%
NATIONAL DAY: 17 May; National Independence Day (1905)
CURRENCY: Norwegian krone = 100 øre
ANNUAL INCOME PER PERSON: $23,120
MAIN PRIMARY PRODUCTS: Cereals, potatoes, livestock, fruit, timber, fish, crude oil, gas, coal, copper, iron, lead, nickel, titanium, quartz
MAIN INDUSTRIES: Mining, oil refining, minerals, shipbuilding, food processing, fishing, forestry
EXPORTS: $6,397 per person
MAIN EXPORTS: Crude petroleum 23%, metal products 18%, natural gas 11%, machinery and transport equipment 10%, foodstuffs 8%

MAIN EXPORT PARTNERS: UK 27%, Germany 15%, Sweden 11%, Netherlands 7%
IMPORTS: $5,597 per person
MAIN IMPORTS: Machinery and transport equipment 28%, metal and metal products 12%, raw materials including fuel 11%, foodstuffs 6%
MAIN IMPORT PARTNERS: Sweden 19%, Germany 16%, UK 9%, Denmark 8%
DEFENCE: 6.7% of national budget
TOURISM: 1,782,000 visitors
POPULATION DENSITY: 13 per sq km [34 per sq ml]
INFANT MORTALITY: 6 per 1,000 live births
LIFE EXPECTANCY: Female 81 yrs, Male 75 yrs
ADULT LITERACY: 99%
PRINCIPAL CITIES (Population): Oslo 455,000 Bergen 211,000 Trondheim 137,000

■ Europe's longest coastline: 21,000 km [13,000 mls], excluding the 50,000 islands ■ Width varies from 400 km [250 mls] in south to only 6.5 km [4 mls] near Narvik ■ Border with Sweden 1,619 km [1,017 mls] long, with Oslo closer to Italy than to North Cape ■ Longest fjord, Sognefjord (184 km [115 mls]), is Europe's longest inlet ■ Hornindalsvatn is Europe's deepest lake (500 m [1,640 ft]) ■ Has 5 of world's 10 highest waterfalls ■ Majority of Lapps (25,000) live in Norway ■ Oil & gas comprise over $^1/_2$ export earnings, & world's largest oil platform is Statfjord B, (816,000 tonnes) ■ All electricity comes from water power ■ World's biggest aid donors per capita (1.1% of GNP, against OECD target 0.7%)

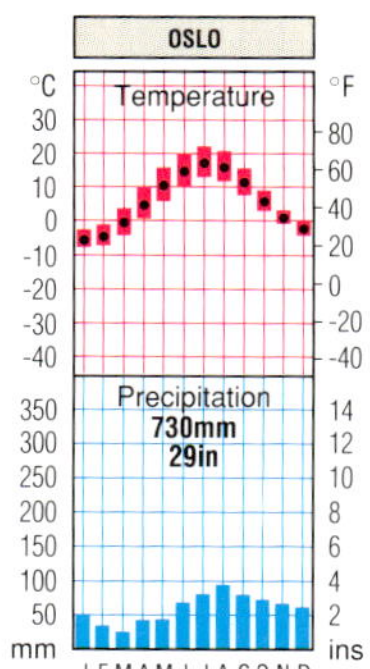

The warm waters and cyclones of the northern Atlantic give the western coastlands of Norway a warm maritime climate of mild winters and cool summers, although wet. The rainfall is heavy on the coast but gets much drier inland and northwards. Inland the winters are more severe and the summers warmer.

FINLAND

Finland became an independent republic only in 1917 after separation from Russia, then in the throes of the Revolution, and the present flag was adopted soon after. The colours symbolise Finland's blue lakes and white snow.

COUNTRY: Republic of Finland
AREA: 338,130 sq km [130,552 sq mls]
POPULATION: 4,986,000
CAPITAL (Population): Helsinki (491,000)
GOVERNMENT: Multi-party parliamentary republic with a unicameral legislature
ETHNIC GROUPS: Finnish 93%, Swedish 6%
LANGUAGES: Finnish and Swedish (official)
RELIGIONS: Lutheran 89%, Greek Orthodox 1%
NATIONAL DAY: 6 December; Independence Day (1917)
CURRENCY: Markka = 100 pennia
ANNUAL INCOME PER PERSON: $26,070
MAIN PRIMARY PRODUCTS: Timber, livestock, copper, lead, iron, zinc, fish
MAIN INDUSTRIES: Forestry, wood pulp, paper machinery, shipbuilding, chemicals, fertilizers
EXPORTS: $4,695 per person
MAIN EXPORTS: Machinery 27%, paper and paperboard 26%,wood, lumber, cork, wastepaper 10%
MAIN EXPORT PARTNERS: Russia and other CIS nations 16%, Sweden 15%, UK 11%, Germany 11%
IMPORTS: $4,964 per person
MAIN IMPORTS: Machinery and transport equipment 44%, basic manufactures, textiles and metals 16%, petroleum and petroleum products 10%, chemicals 10%, foodstuffs 5%
MAIN IMPORT PARTNERS: Germany 17%, Russia and other CIS nations14%, Sweden13%
DEFENCE: 5.7% of national budget
TOURISM: 436,000 visitors
POPULATION DENSITY: 15 per sq km [38 per sq ml]
INFANT MORTALITY: 5 per 1,000 live births
LIFE EXPECTANCY: Female 80 yrs, Male 72 yrs
ADULT LITERACY: 99%
PRINCIPAL CITIES (Population): Helsinki 987,000 Turku 263,000 Tampere 260,000 Espoo 168,000 Vantaa 151,000

■ 1/3 of Finland lies inside the Arctic Circle ■ The land is rising by as much as 800 mm per century which gives 1 sq km above sea level every 10 years ■ More than 185,000 lakes cover nearly 10% of country, forests cover 65% ■ Saimaa lake area Europe's largest inland water system ■ 22 national parks & over 1,000 protected areas ■ About 30,000 islands off Finnish coast, with Baltic province of Ahvenanmaa consisting of 6,554 islands ■ Åland self-governing island province ■ Helsinki only 300 km [190 mls]) from St Petersburg ■ Russia Finland's principal trading partner, paper its main export (world no. 2) ■ Economic growth rate surpassed Japan in 1980s ■ World's best hospital provision (no. of beds per capita) ■ The Finnish language, like neighbouring Estonian and distantly related Hungarian, is not Indo-European ■ In the north there are 2,500 Lapps, a majority of whom are reindeer herders ■ Finnish women first in Europe to gain vote (1906) ■ Officially bilingual, though only 6% speak second language Swedish ■ More coffee drunk per head than by any nation

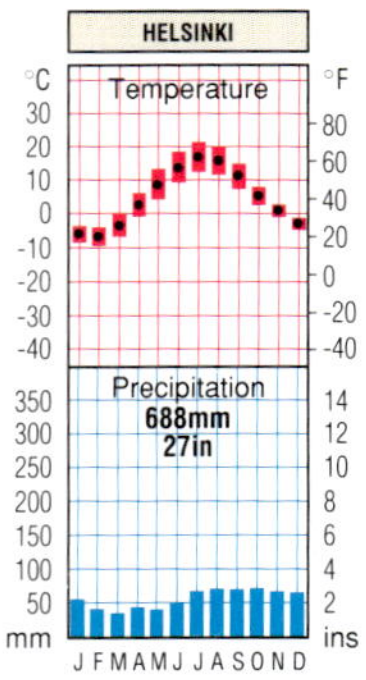

The dominating feature of Finland's climate is the severity of the winter. A third of Finland is north of the Arctic Circle and here temperatures can reach -30°C [-22°F]. Snow can lie for 6 months, never clearing from the north-facing slopes. Helsinki has 4 - 5 months below 0°C [32°F]. The seas and lakes nearly always freeze in winter. The summers can be hot. Rainfall is low, falling late summer to winter, often as snow.

ESTONIA

Used for the independent republic of 1918-20, the Estonian flag was readopted in June, 1988. The colours are said to symbolise the country's blue skies, its black earth, and the snows of its long winter.

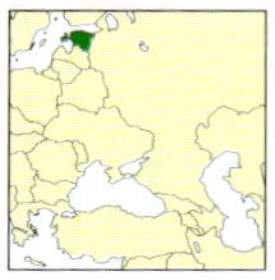

COUNTRY: Estonia
AREA: 44,680 sq km [17,413 sq mls]
POPULATION: 1,600,000
CAPITAL (Population): Tallinn (478,000)
GOVERNMENT: Democratic republic
ETHNIC GROUPS: Estonian 65%, Russian 27%
LANGUAGES: Estonian
MAIN PRIMARY PRODUCTS: Cereals, vegetables, livestock
MAIN INDUSTRIES: Agricultural machinery, electric motors
POPULATION DENSITY: 35.8 per sq km [91.9 per sq ml]
ADULT LITERACY: 99%

■ Estonian language is a non-Indo-European tongue related to Finnish ■ Like the other newly independent Baltic states, has large Russian speaking minority

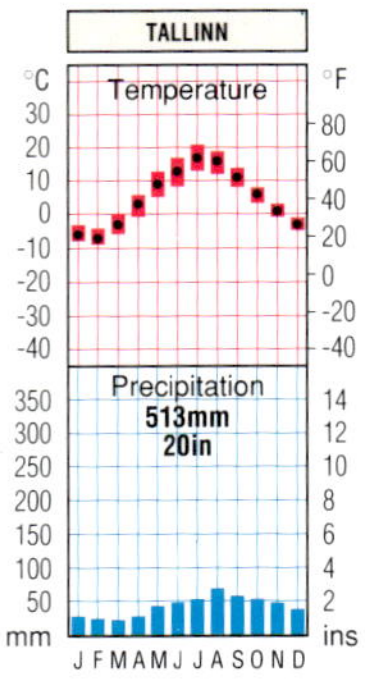

The influences on the climate of Estonia are maritime rather than continental, with warm air masses in the winter and cool in the summer moving in from the west. Night temperatures are sub-zero from November to April, though never lower than -10°C [14°F], and July is the only month where the day temperature rises above 20°C [68°F]. Precipitation is light, late summer and autumn being the wettest period, and is registered on only around 100 days per year.

LATVIA

The burgundy and white Latvian flag, revived after independence from the USSR in 1991, dates back to at least 1280; according to an even older legend, it was first made from a white sheet stained with the blood of a Latvian hero who was wrapped in it.

COUNTRY: Republic of Latvia
area: 63,110 sq km [24,595 sq mls]
POPULATION: 2,700,000
CAPITAL (Population): Riga (915,000)
GOVERNMENT: Single-chamber legislature; executive Council of Ministers
ETHNIC GROUPS: Latvian (52%), Russian, Belorussian, Ukrainian, Polish
LANGUAGES: Latvian (official)
RELIGION: Atheist, Christian (Lutheran and Catholic), small minority Latvian folk belief.
NATIONAL DAY: 18 November, Independence Day (1918)
MAIN PRIMARY PRODUCTS: Timber, dairy products, meat and fisheries
MAIN INDUSTRIES: Railway rolling stock, machinery, telecommunications equipment
DEFENCE: Defence forces still being established
POPULATION DENSITY: 42.8 per sq km [109.77 per sq ml)
LIFE EXPECTANCY: Female 75.2 years, Male 65.3 years
ADULT LITERACY: 99%

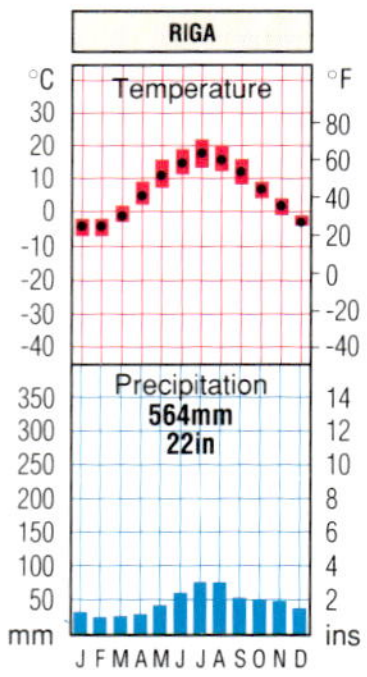

Riga has warm summers and cold winters, with rain or snow in all months. June-August are the warmest months with temperatures over 15°C [59°F], and averages that are sub-zero, December-March.The temperature extremes are only just over 34°C [93°F] and -29°C [-20°F]. On average, rain will fall on a third of the days in the second half of the year, but the total is relatively light. The weather can be overcast for long periods. Snow cover is light, with many thaws.

LITHUANIA

The flag was created in 1918, at the birth of the independent republic. The colours represent Lithuania's rich forests and agricultural wealth. The flag was suppressed after the Soviet annexation in 1940, and restored in November, 1988.

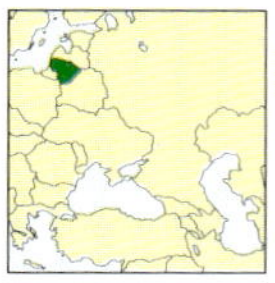

COUNTRY: Republic of Lithuania
AREA: 65,200 sq km [25,400 sq mls]
POPULATION: 3,751,000
CAPITAL (Population): Vilnius (600,000)
GOVERNMENT: Multi-party parliamentary republic with unicameral legislature
ETHNIC GROUPS: Lithuanian 80%, Russian 9%, Polish 7%
LANGUAGES: Lithuanian (official)
RELIGION: Roman Catholic 80%, Orthodox, Lutherans Calvinist
NATIONAL DAY: 16 February, Independence Day (1918)
MAIN PRIMARY PRODUCTS: Livestock
MAIN INDUSTRIES: Machinery & metal processing
MAIN EXPORTS: Foodstuffs, machinery
MAIN IMPORTS: Machinery & transport equipment
DEFENCE: Defence forces still being established
POPULATION DENSITY: 57.4 per sq km [145 per sq ml]
LIFE EXPECTANCY: Female 76.6 years, Male 67.7 years
ADULT LITERACY: 99%

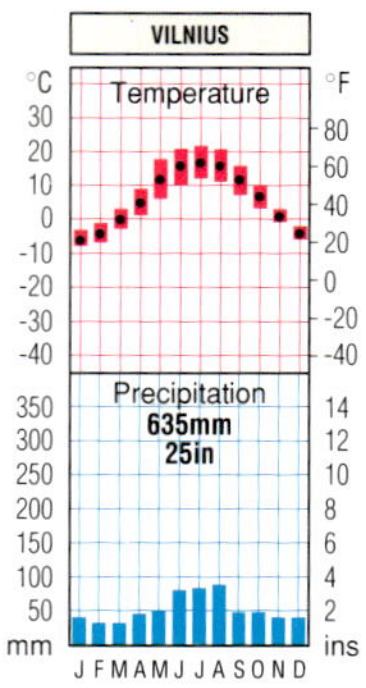

The climate of Lithuania is transitional between the maritime of the west and the continental of eastern Europe. Winters are quite cold with sub-zero temperatures on the nights of November-March, and the summers not too warm, the normal daily maxima June-August being only 20-21°C [68-70°F]. The warmest months are also the wettest and over 40% of the year's low rainfall of around 600 mm [24 in] falls in these months. Rain is recorded on nearly every other day.

SWEDEN

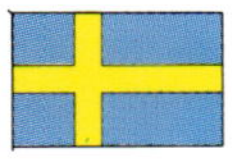

While Sweden's national flag has been flown since the reign of King Gustavus Vasa in the early 16th century, it was not officially adopted until 1906. The colours were derived from the ancient state coat of arms dating from 1364.

COUNTRY: Kingdom of Sweden
AREA: 449,960 sq km [173,730 sq mls]
POPULATION: 8,618,000
CAPITAL (Population): Stockholm (669,000)
GOVERNMENT: Constitutional monarchy and parliamentary state with a unicameral legislature
ETHNIC GROUPS: Swedish 91%, Finnish 3%
LANGUAGES: Swedish (official), Finnish
RELIGIONS: Protestant 89%, Roman Catholic 2%
NATIONAL DAY: 6 June
CURRENCY: Swedish krona = 100 ore
ANNUAL INCOME PER PERSON: $23,680
MAIN PRIMARY PRODUCTS: Cereals, cattle, sugar beet, potatoes, timber, iron ore, copper, lead, zinc
MAIN INDUSTRIES: Engineering, electrical goods, vehicles, mining, timber, paper, wood pulp
EXPORTS: $ 6,071 per person
MAIN EXPORTS: Mach. and trans. equip. 43%, paper prods 11%, elec. mach.8%, wood pulp 7%, chemicals 7%
MAIN EXPORT PARTNERS: Germany 12%, UK 11%, USA 10%, Norway 9%, Denmark 7%, Finland 7%,
IMPORTS: $5,759 per person
MAIN IMPORTS: Mach. and transp. equip. 36%, chem. 10%
MAIN IMPORT PARTNERS: As for exports
DEFENCE: 8.8% of national budget
TOURISM: 814,000 visitors
POPULATION DENSITY: 19 per sq km [50 per sq ml]
INFANT MORTALITY: 6 per 1,000 live births
LIFE EXPECTANCY: Female 81 yrs, Male 75 yrs
ADULT LITERACY: 99%
PRINCIPAL CITIES (Population): Stockholm 669,000 Gothenburg 431,000 Malmö 232,000 Uppsala 162,000

■ Half country is covered in forest, & more trees are planted each year than cut ■ Sareks – Europe's largest national park (1,940 sq km [750 sq mls]) ■ Europe's biggest softwood producer ■ Highest figures for public spending, taxes, social services & individual share ownership in OECD ■ World's heaviest tax burden (welfare services account for 70% of national budget) ■ Not fought a war since 1814 ■ In Arctic Sweden street lighting never extinguished during 7-month winter

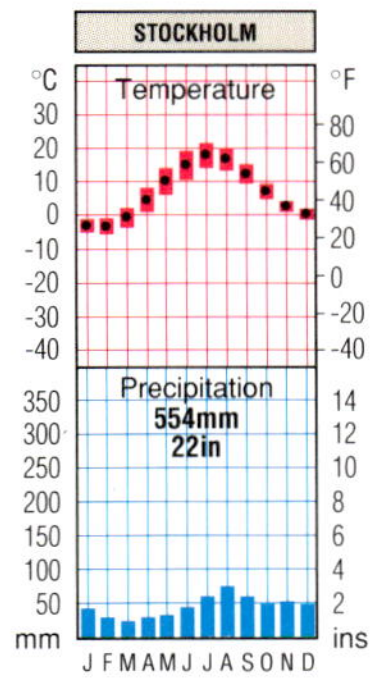

The Gulf Stream warms the southern coastlands, but to the north continentality takes over. The February temperature in the south is just below freezing, but in the north it is -15°C [5°F]. There is low rainfall throughout Sweden, but it lies as snow for over six months in the north. The Baltic is usually frozen for at least five months, but there is rarely any ice on the western coast.

DENMARK

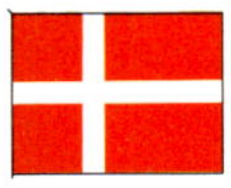

The Dannebrog ('the spirit of Denmark') flag is said to represent King Waldemar II's vision of a white cross against a red sky before the Battle of Lyndanisse in 1219, and is possibly the oldest national flag in continuous use.

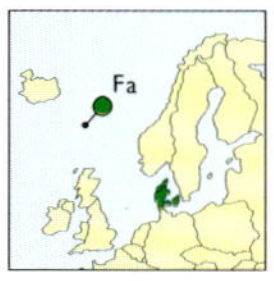

COUNTRY: Kingdom of Denmark
AREA: 43,070 sq km [16,629 sq mls]
POPULATION: 5,140,000
CAPITAL (Population): Copenhagen (1,339,000)
GOVERNMENT: Parliamentary monarchy with a bicameral legislature
ETHNIC GROUPS: Danish 97%
LANGUAGES: Danish (official)
RELIGIONS: Lutheran 91%, Roman Catholic 1%
NATIONAL DAY: 16 April; Birthday of HM the Queen
CURRENCY: Krone = 100 øre
ANNUAL INCOME PER PERSON: $22,090
MAIN PRIMARY PRODUCTS: Livestock, cereals, oil and natural gas
MAIN INDUSTRIES: Agriculture and food processing, shipbuilding, chemicals, petroleum refining
EXPORTS: $5,475 per person
MAIN EXPORTS: Meat, dairy produce, fish 27%, machinery and electronic equipment 24%, chemicals 9%
MAIN EXPORT PARTNERS: Germany 17%, UK 12%, Sweden 11%, USA 8%, Norway 8%
IMPORTS: $5,198 per person
MAIN IMPORTS: Machinery and transport equipment 31%, chemicals 10%, foodstuffs 10%, mineral fuels 9%
MAIN IMPORT PARTNERS: Germany 24%, Sweden 12%, UK 7%, Japan 5%, USA 5%, Netherlands 5%, France 5%
DEFENCE: 7.4% of national budget
TOURISM: 1,171,000 visitors
POPULATION DENSITY: 119 per sq km [308 per sq ml]
INFANT MORTALITY: 6 per 1,000 live births
LIFE EXPECTANCY: Female 79 yrs, Male 73 yrs
ADULT LITERACY: 99%
PRINCIPAL CITIES (Population): Copenhagen 1,339,000 Århus 258,000 Odense 174,000 Ålborg 155,000

■ Eastern archipelago comprises 406 islands, with 89 populated ■ Highest point 171 m [561 ft] above sea level ■ 75% of land cultivated; only 5% of pop. engaged in farming ■ Best known products bacon (12 million pigs) and butter (2.8 million cows) ■ World's chief exporter of insulin ■ Europe's highest rate of suicide & highest no. of deaths from lung cancer in Europe ■ Lego, children's construction toys, created in Danish carpenter's workshop ■ Denmark has a minister for Pollution, with water resources a prime concern

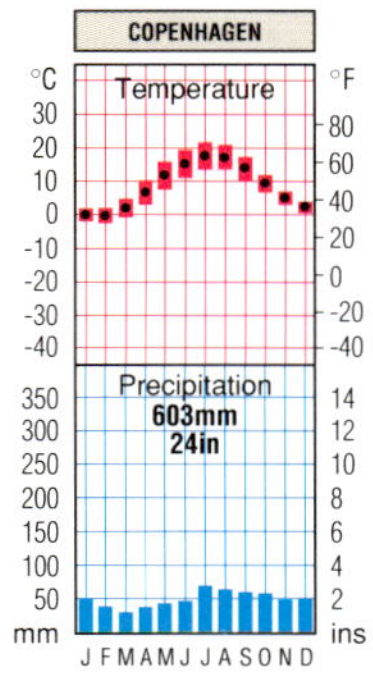

The climate of Denmark reflects that the country is at the meeting of Arctic, continental and maritime influences. The winters, thanks to the warm Atlantic waters, are not too cold, although there may be many nights that are below freezing. The summers are warm. The rainfall is reasonable, falling in all months with a maximum July - Sept. It is drier in the east. With no highland, winds have free play over the peninsula and islands.

FAROES

COUNTRY: Danish self-governing region
AREA: 1,400 sq km [541 sq mls]
POPULATION: 47,000
CAPITAL (Population): Tórshavn (15,000)

IRELAND

The Irish flag was first used by nationalists in 1848 in the struggle for freedom from Britain and adopted in 1922 after independence. Green represents the Roman Catholics, Orange the Protestants and white stands for peace.

COUNTRY: Republic of Ireland
AREA: 70,280 sq km [27,135 sq mls]
POPULATION: 3,523,000
CAPITAL (Population): Dublin (921,000)
GOVERNMENT: Unitary multi-party republic with a bicameral legislature
ETHNIC GROUPS: Irish 94%
LANGUAGES: Irish and English (official)
RELIGIONS: Roman Catholic 93%, Protestant 3%
NATIONAL DAY: 17 March; St Patrick's Day
CURRENCY: Irish pound = 100 new pence
ANNUAL INCOME PER PERSON: $9,550
MAIN PRIMARY PRODUCTS: Cereals, potatoes, vegetables, peat, fish, natural gas
MAIN INDUSTRIES: Agriculture, food processing, tourism, textiles, clothing, machinery
EXPORTS: $5,894 per person
MAIN EXPORTS: Machinery and transport equipment 32%, food and live animals 24%, chemicals 12%
MAIN EXPORT PARTNERS: UK 35%, Germany 11%, France 9%, USA 7%, Netherlands 7%
IMPORTS: $4,965 per person
MAIN IMPORTS: Machinery and transport equipment 34%, chemicals and related products 12%, foodstuffs 11%, petroleum 5%, clothing 4%
MAIN IMPORT PARTNERS: UK 42%, USA 18%, Germany 9%, France 5%, Japan 5%, Netherlands 3%
DEFENCE: 3.5% of national budget
TOURISM: 2,662,000 visitors
POPULATION DENSITY: 50 per sq km [130 per sq ml]
INFANT MORTALITY: 8 per 1,000 live births
LIFE EXPECTANCY: Female 78 yrs, Male 73 yrs
ADULT LITERACY: 99%
PRINCIPAL CITIES (Population): Dublin 921,000 Cork 174,000 Limerick 56,000 Galway 47,000 Waterford 40,000

■ Republic occupies 80% of island of Ireland ■ Peat main indigenous fuel source, but present reserves may last only 20 years ■ Claims highest rate of reforestation in developed world ■ Among least industrialised countries in Europe, but about 25% of the pop. live in Dublin & suburbs ■ Europe's highest number of heart attacks: 89.25 per 100,000 pop. ■ Roman Catholic faith enshrined in constitution ■ 1845-48 Ireland lost 1 million of 8 million pop. by starvation (potato famine), typhoid & emigration ■ Over 2 million people emigrated 1900-1980 ■ Over 1 million people visit from Britain each year

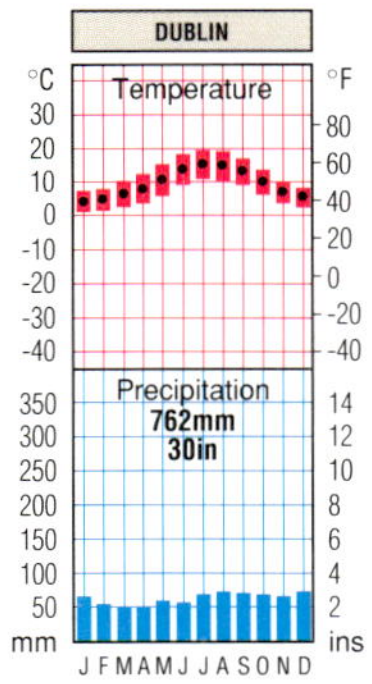

Ireland, open to the Atlantic Ocean, has a mild, damp climate. Humidity is high with frequent fog and low cloud throughout the year. The declining influence of the ocean eastward is most marked in winter when temperatures in Dublin are several degrees colder than in the west, and rainfall which is very uniformly distributed throughout the year, is about half that of western coasts.

UNITED KINGDOM

The first Union flag, combining England's cross of St George and Scotland's cross of St Andrew, dates from 1603 when James VI became James I of England. The Irish emblem, the cross of St Patrick, was added in 1801 to form the present flag.

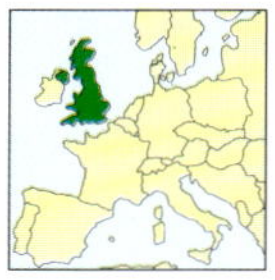

COUNTRY: United Kingdom of Great Britain and Northern Ireland
AREA: 244,046 sq km [94,202 sq mls]
POPULATION: 57,237,000
CAPITAL (Population): London (6,735,000)
GOVERNMENT: Constitutional monarchy with bicameral legislature
ETHNIC GROUPS: White 94%, Asian Indian 1%, West Indian 1%, Pakistani 1%
LANGUAGES: English (official), Welsh, Scots-Gaelic
RELIGIONS: Anglican 57%, Roman Catholic 13%, Presbyterian 7%, Methodist 4%, Baptist 1%, Muslim 1%, Jewish, Hindu, Sikh
NATIONAL DAY: 16 June (1990); HM Queen's Official Birthday
CURRENCY: £ sterling = 100 pence
ANNUAL INCOME PER PERSON: $16,070
SOURCE OF INCOME: Agriculture 2%, Industry 25%, Services 19%
MAIN PRIMARY PRODUCTS: Oil and natural gas, coal, wheat, fish, sugar
MAIN INDUSTRIES: Oil and gas, agriculture, machinery, iron and steel, vehicle manufacture, food processing, textiles, paper, clothing, chemicals, tourism, financial services
EXPORTS: $2,665 per person
MAIN EXPORTS: Machinery and transport equipment 35%, rubber, paper, textile manufactures etc. 15%, chemicals and related products 13%, manufactured items 12%, mineral fuels 11%, food, beverages and tobacco 7%
MAIN EXPORT PARTNERS: USA 14%, Germany 11%, France 10%, Netherlands 8%, Italy 5%, Belgium/Luxembourg 5%, Ireland 5%
IMPORTS: $3,457 per person
MAIN IMPORTS: Machinery and transport equipment 35%, rubber, paper, textile manufactures etc. 18%, manufactured items 14%, chemicals 9%, food and live animals 9%, mineral fuels 6%
MAIN IMPORT PARTNERS: Germany 17%, USA 10%, France 9%, New Zealand 7%, South Korea 5%, Japan 5%
EDUCATIONAL EXPENDITURE: 11.7% of national budget
DEFENCE: 12% of national budget
TOTAL ARMED FORCES: 311,650
TOURISM: 15,445,000 visitors
ROADS: 350,407 km [217,733 mls]
RAILWAYS: 38,053 km [23,645 mls]
POPULATION DENSITY: 235 per sq km [607 per sq ml]
URBAN POPULATION: 93%
POPULATION GROWTH: 0.1% per year
BIRTHS: 13.3 per 1,000 population
DEATHS: 11.6 per 1,000 population
INFANT MORTALITY: 8 per 1,000 live births
LIFE EXPECTANCY: Female 79 yrs, Male 73 yrs
POPULATION PER DOCTOR: 611
ADULT LITERACY: 100%
PRINCIPAL CITIES (Population): Greater London 6,378,000 Manchester 1,669,000 Birmingham 1,400,000 Liverpool 1,060,000 Glasgow 730,000 Newcastle 617,000 Sheffield 445,000 Leeds 432,000 Edinburgh 404,000 Bristol 367,000 Teeside 363,000 Coventry 293,000 Belfast 281,000 Leicester 280,000 Bradford 274,000 Cardiff 273,000 Nottingham 262,000

■ Britain is Europe's largest island - area 229,880 sq km [88,700 sq mls] ■ World's oldest continuous system of government ■ Over 90% of pop. is urban ■ Once centre of largest empire in history, over 25% of world pop. owing allegiance to Britain ■ Major oil exporter ■ World's most powerful wind turbine, started up in Burgar Hill (Orkneys) 1987 ■ London Heathrow world's busiest international airport ■ UK has greatest number of civil aircraft in Europe and highest total of passenger -km flown (83 million annually) ■ Europe's longest bridge span (2nd longest in world) is Humber Estuary Bridge (1,410 m across [4,625 ft]), opened 1981 ■ Network South East world's largest commuter network ■ London Underground most extensive subway system in world, with 400 km [248 mls] of track ■ World's first public railway opened 1826 between Stockton and Darlington ■ Birmingham, Britain's second city, has 35 more km [22 mls] of canal than Venice ■ National Health Service among world's top ten employers & biggest single employer in Europe (1.3 million) ■ World's first postage stamp was Penny Black, issued 1840 ■ British Library largest in Europe (2nd in world) with 18 million books ■ Biggest circulation of daily newspapers in Europe with 23.2 million average of 108 papers ■ Faversham Oyster Fishery world's oldest company, founded 1189 ■ Highest spending per head in world on records, tapes & CDs ■ UK drinks more tea per head than any nation ■ World's biggest importer of champagne 20,648,226 bottles in 1985 ■ Lawn tennis, golf, rugby, soccer, squash & cricket all first played in Britain

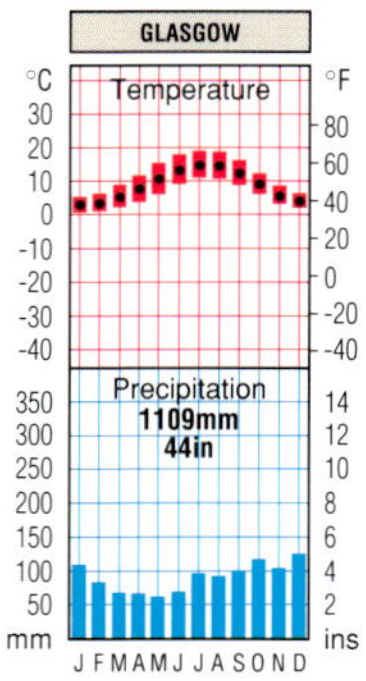

Like most of north-west Europe, Glasgow has a maritime climate with cool summers, mild winters and well distributed rainfall with an autumn maximum. Variations to the general pattern occur with changes in altitude and proximity to the sea. The Clyde valley is more sheltered than the estuary where Greenock receives more than 1,500 mm [590 in] of rain annually.

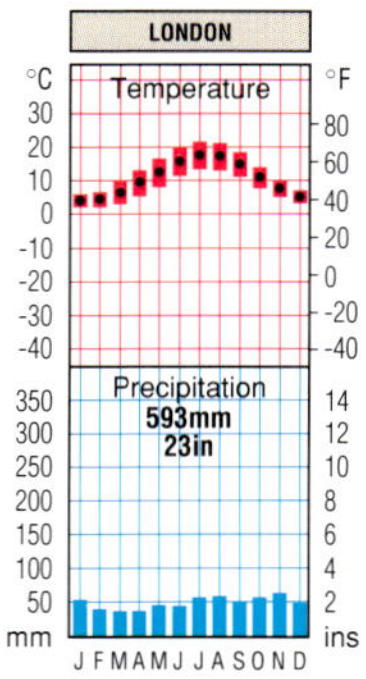

South-eastern England, sheltered from the ocean to the west, is one of the driest parts of the British Isles. Although rainfall varies little throughout the year, greater evaporation creates a deficit between May and August. Like other parts of north-west Europe, London has a small annual temperature range. The metropolis creates its own local climate and nights are generally warmer than in the surrounding countryside.

NETHERLANDS

The Dutch national flag dates from 1630, during the long war of independence from Spain that began in 1568. The tricolour became a symbol of liberty and inspired many other revolutionary flags around the world.

COUNTRY: Kingdom of the Netherlands
AREA: 41,863 sq km [16,163 sq mls]
POPULATION: 15,019,000
CAPITAL (Population): Amsterdam (1,038,000); Seat of Government, The Hague (684,000)
GOVERNMENT: Constitutional monarchy with a bicameral legislature
ETHNIC GROUPS: Netherlander 96%, Turkish 1%, Moroccan 1%
LANGUAGES: Dutch (official)
RELIGIONS: Roman Catholic 36%, Dutch Reformed Church19%, Reformed Churches 8%
NATIONAL DAY: 30 April; Official birthday of HM The Queen
CURRENCY: Netherlands guilder = 100 cents
ANNUAL INCOME PER PERSON: $17,330
SOURCE OF INCOME: Agriculture 4%, Industry 22%, Services 19%
MAIN PRIMARY PRODUCTS: Cereals, fruit, vegetables, sugar beet, livestock, fish, oil, gas, salt
MAIN INDUSTRIES: Agriculture, food processing chemicals, iron and steel, clothing and textiles, shipbuilding, printing, diamond cutting, fish, oil refining
EXPORTS: $7,274 per person
MAIN EXPORTS: Machinery and transport equipment 21%, foodstuffs 20%, chemicals and chemical products 19%
MAIN EXPORT PARTNERS: Germany 26%, Belgium-Luxembourg 15%, France 11%, UK 11%, Italy 6%
IMPORTS: $7,031 per person
MAIN IMPORTS: Machinery and transport equipment 28%, foodstuffs 14%, chemicals 11%, mineral fuels 9%
MAIN IMPORT PARTNERS: Germany 26%, Belgium-Luxembourg 15%, UK 8%, France 8%
DEFENCE: 9.1% of national budget
TOTAL ARMED FORCES: 106,000
TOURISM: 3,189,000 visitors
ROADS: 111,891 km [69,528 mls]
RAILWAYS: 2,867 km [1,782 mls]
POPULATION DENSITY: 359 per sq km [929 per sq ml]
URBAN POPULATION: 89%
POPULATION GROWTH: 0.37% per year
BIRTHS: 11.8 per 1,000 population
DEATHS: 8.9 per 1,000 population
INFANT MORTALITY: 7 per 1000 live births
LIFE EXPECTANCY: Female 81 yrs, Male 74 yrs
POPULATION PER DOCTOR: 450
ADULT LITERACY: 99%
PRINCIPAL CITIES (Population): Rotterdam 1,040,000 Amsterdam 1,038,000 The Hague 684,000 Utrecht 526,000 Eindhoven 381,000 Arnhem 299,000

■ Most densely populated major country in world ■ Randstad Holland - name given to almost unknown joined cities in centre-west has some of highest densities in Europe ■ More than 30% of country lies below sea level ■ Land reclamation has added 2,500 sq km [965 sq mls] since 1900 ■ Without intensive-land protection schemes, nearly 50% of total area would be inundated with sea water twice a day ■ Dutch grow & sell about 3,000 million flowers a year: 80,000 per sq km ■ Has 5,597 km [3,478 mls] of canals ■ The Rhine flows into sea in Netherlands and with canals gives greatest amount of freight carried on inland waterways in Europe ■ The trading and seafaring heritage continues - Rotterdam-Europoort world's biggest port complex ■ Heineken NV Europe's largest brewery (3rd in world) ■ International Court of Justice in The Hague ■ Amsterdam world's oldest stock exchange ■ Has world's most concentrated motorway network ■ Still a monarchy and has been ruled by Queens and female Regents for 100 years ■ Belgium formed from slice of Netherlands in 1830 ■ Glorious flowering of art and cartography - Rembrandt and Mercator in 16 and 17 cent. ■ In 16 cent. part of the Habsburg Empire which included Spain and Austria and over half of the known world; ■ Noted for liberal and progressive attitude to crime and prison

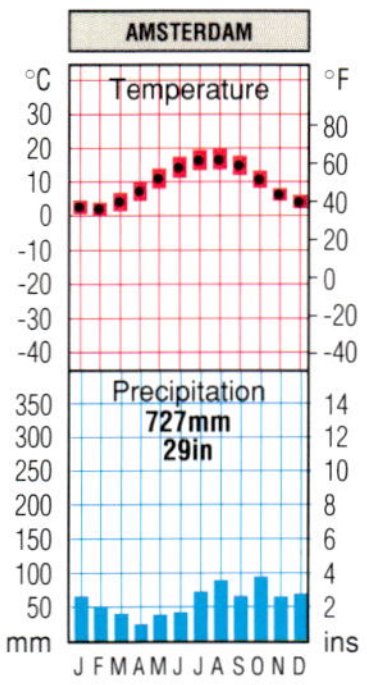

Amsterdam has a climate typical of the coastal margins of north-west Europe. The range of temperature, both daily and annual, is small. Winters are mild with frequent wind and rain from Atlantic depressions. The prevailing westerly winds which once powered the Dutch windmills keep summers cool. Rainfall increases from a spring minimum to a maximum in late summer and autumn.

BELGIUM

The colours of Belgium's flag derive from the arms of the province of Brabant which rebelled against Austrian rule in 1787. It was adopted as the national flag in 1830 when Belgium gained independence from the Netherlands.

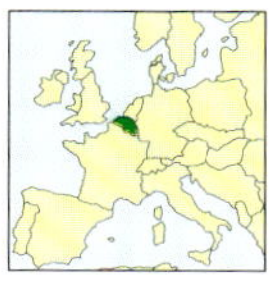

■ Highest urban pop. (97%) among major nations ■ World's highest proportion of total land under 'protection' (44.2% – figure includes Luxembourg) ■ Less than 3% of workforce in agriculture ■ 70% of GDP is exported – highest proportion among OECD countries ■ Imports nearly all fuel and raw materials ■ Close economic links with Luxembourg ■ Brussels is administrative HQ of European Economic Community's government ■ Antwerp has world's oldest diamond market

COUNTRY: Kingdom of Belgium
AREA: 30,510 sq km [11,780 sq mls]
POPULATION: 9,845,000
CAPITAL (Population): Brussels (970,000)
GOVERNMENT: Constitutional monarchy with a bicameral legislature
ETHNIC GROUPS: Belgian 91%, Italian 3%, Moroccan 1%, French 1%, Dutch, Turkish
LANGUAGES: Flemish (57%), French
RELIGIONS: Roman Catholic 90%, Muslim, Protestant
NATIONAL DAY: 21 July; Independent kingdom (1839)
CURRENCY: Belgian franc = 100 centimes
ANNUAL INCOME PER PERSON: $15,440
MAIN PRIMARY PRODUCTS: Sugar beet, potatoes, livestock, timber, coal
MAIN INDUSTRIES: Engineering, iron and steel, petroleum refining, food processing, chemicals, coal
EXPORTS: $10,200 per person
MAIN EXPORTS: Vehicles 15%, chemicals 13%, foodstuffs 9%, iron and steel 7%, pearls, precious and semi-precious stones 6%, petroleum products 3%
MAIN EXPORT PARTNERS: France 20%, Germany 20%, Netherlands 15%, UK 8%, USA 5%
IMPORTS: $10,040 per person
MAIN IMPORTS: Vehicles and parts 14%, chemicals 10%, foodstuffs 9%, petroleum and petroleum products 7%, non-industrial diamonds 6%, electrical machinery 4%
MAIN IMPORT PARTNERS: Germany 24%, Netherlands 17%, France 16%, UK 8%, USA 5%, Italy 4%
DEFENCE: 7.1% of national budget
TOURISM: 2,516,000 visitors
POPULATION DENSITY: 323 per sq km [837 per sq ml]
INFANT MORTALITY: 8 per 1,000 live births
LIFE EXPECTANCY: Female 79 yrs, Male 72 yrs
ADULT LITERACY: 99%
PRINCIPAL CITIES (Population): Brussels 970,000 Antwerp 500,000 Ghent 233,000 Charleroi 209,000 Liège 200,000

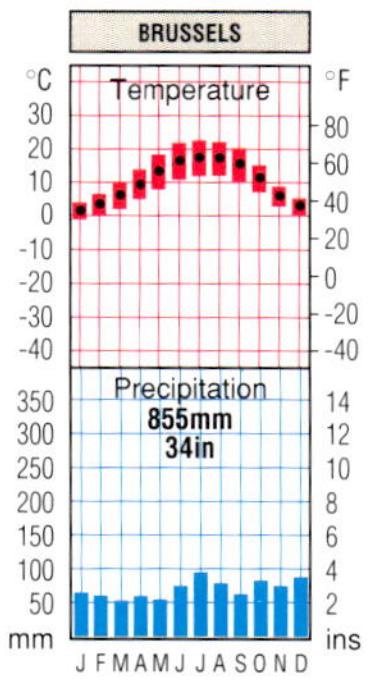

Belgium has a cool temperate maritime climate with the weather systems moving eastwards from the Atlantic. Rainfall is quite heavy in the higher Ardennes plateau with much snow Jan-Feb. The hottest and driest regions are along the coast. At Brussels, no month has a mean temperature below freezing and the summer is pleasantly warm. The temperatures are lower at all seasons in the highlands.

LUXEMBOURG

Luxembourg's colours are taken from the Grand Duke's 14th century coat of arms. The Grand Duchy's flag is almost identical to that of the Netherlands, but the blue stripe is a lighter shade and the flag itself is longer.

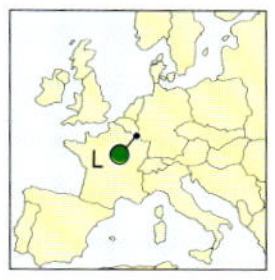

■ Europe's last independent duchy ■ Foreign workers make up nearly 25% of population ■ Seat of European Court of Justice and Secretariat of European Parliament ■ Highest rate of car ownership in Europe (365 cars per 1000 people) & highest no. of car accidents per capita in OECD ■ 114 different banks

COUNTRY: Grand Duchy of Luxembourg
AREA: 2,590 sq km [1,000 sq mls]
POPULATION: 384,000
CAPITAL (Population): Luxembourg (76,000)
GOVERNMENT: Constitutional monarchy with a bicameral legislature
ETHNIC GROUPS: Luxemburger 70%, Portuguese 8%, Italian 5%, French 4%, German 3%
LANGUAGES: Letzeburgish (official), French, German,
RELIGIONS: Christian (Roman Catholic 93%)
NATIONAL DAY: 23 June; Official birthday of the Grand Duke
CURRENCY: Luxembourg franc = 100 centimes
ANNUAL INCOME PER PERSON: $28,770
MAIN PRIMARY PRODUCTS: Iron ore
MAIN INDUSTRIES: Iron and steel, banking and financial services, chemicals, agriculture
MAIN EXPORTS: Base metals, plastic and rubber manufactures
MAIN IMPORTS: Mineral products, base metals and manufactures, machinery, transport equipment
DEFENCE: 3% of national budget
POPULATION DENSITY: 148 per sq km [384 per sq ml]
LIFE EXPECTANCY: Female 79 yrs, Male 72 yrs

GERMANY

The red, black and gold, dating back to the Holy Roman Empire, are associated with the struggle for a united Germany from the 1830s. The horizontal design was officially adopted in 1949, and accepted by 'East Germany' on reunification.

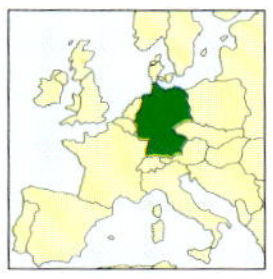

COUNTRY: Germany
AREA: 356,910 sq km [137,803 sq mls]
POPULATION: 79,479,000
CAPITAL (Population): Berlin (3,301,000), Bonn (291,000)
GOVERNMENT: Federal multi-party republic with bicameral legislature
ETHNIC GROUPS: Former GDR: 90% German, Former FRG: 93% German, Turk 2%, Yugoslav 1%, Italian 1%
LANGUAGES: German (official)
RELIGIONS: Roman Catholic, Lutheran
CURRENCY: Deutsche Mark = 100 Pfennige
ANNUAL INCOME PER PERSON: $17,000
SOURCE OF INCOME: Agriculture 2%, Industry 51%, Services 47%
MAIN PRIMARY PRODUCTS: Brown coal, coal, timber, pigs, cattle, natural gas, salt, silver
MAIN INDUSTRIES: Motor vehicles, ship construction, iron, cotton yarn, forestry, aluminium, beer, synthetic fibres and rubber, petroleum products
EXPORTS: $4,764 per person
MAIN EXPORTS: Machinery and transport equipment 48%, chemicals 13%, manufactured articles 11%, textile yarn 3%
MAIN EXPORT PARTNERS: France 12%, Italy 9%, Netherlands 9%, UK 9%, USA 9%, Belgium 7%, Switzerland 6%, Austria 5%, Japan 2%
IMPORTS: $3,829 per person
MAIN IMPORTS: Machinery and transport equipment 28%, food and live animals 10%, chemicals 10%, petroleum and petroleum products 7%, clothing 6%, textile yarn 4%, iron and steel 3%
MAIN IMPORT PARTNERS: France 11%, Netherlands 11%, Italy 10%, Belgium 7%, UK 7%, USA 7%, Japan 6%, Switzerland 5%
EDUCATIONAL EXPENDITURE: 7.8% of national budget
DEFENCE: 22.6% of national budget
TOTAL ARMED FORCES: 494,300
TOURISM: 14,200,000 visitors
ROADS: 491,240 km [305,242 mls]
RAILWAYS: 67,536 km [41,965 mls]
POPULATION DENSITY: 223 per sq km [577 per sq ml]
URBAN POPULATION: 85%
POPULATION GROWTH: -0.1% per year
BIRTHS: 11.1 per 1,000 population
DEATHS: 11.9 per 1,000 population
INFANT MORTALITY: 8 per 1,000 live births
LIFE EXPECTANCY: Female 78 yrs, Male 72 yrs
POPULATION PER DOCTOR: 390
ADULT LITERACY: 99%
PRINCIPAL CITIES (Population): Berlin 3,301,000 Hamburg 1,594,000 Munich 1,189,000 Cologne 928,000 Essen 623,000 Frankfurt/Main 619,000 Dortmund 584,000 Düsseldorf 563,000 Stuttgart 552,000 Leipzig 545,000 Bremen 533,000 Duisburg 525,000 Dresden 518,000 Hanover 495,000 Nuremburg 472,000

■ European country with most international borders ■ Federal Republic of Germany united with German Democratic Republic in 1990 after separation at end of WWII in 1945 ■ Leading country of origin of immigrants to USA, 1820-1987 (7,051,000) ■ Highest GNP in Europe ■ Overtook USA as world's largest exporter in 1986 ■ Europe's biggest producer of iron, steel & cars ■ European country with most cars (3rd in world) ■ Rivers and canals carry almost as much freight as road ■ Greatest tourists in terms of spending (16% of world total) ■ World's highest consumption of beer per head (143 litres [251.6 pints])

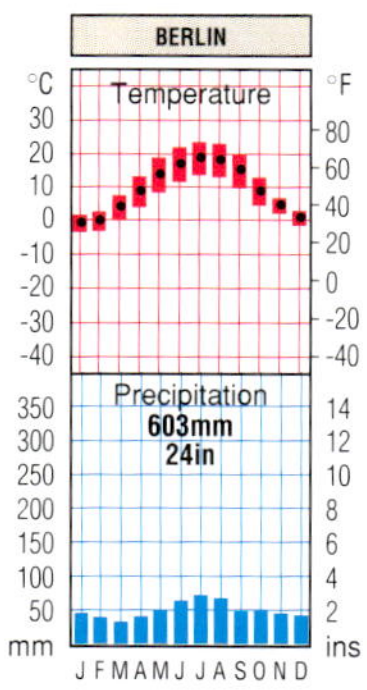

The climate of northern Germany is due mainly to the weather coming in from the Atlantic. Jan. and Feb. are the only months with mean temperatures just below 0°C [32°F], and the summers are warm. Rainfall is moderate, 500 - 750 mm [20 - 30 in], falling in all months, with a maximum in summer. Humidity is always high with fog and the autumn and winter can be overcast for long periods. Snow lies for long periods inland and in the hills. When the winds blow from Scandinavia very cold weather follows.

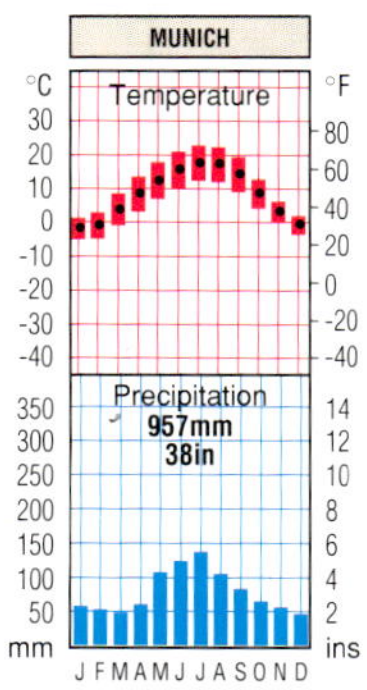

In the south the climate is a little warmer in the summer and a little colder in winter. It is also wetter, Munich receiving nearly twice as much rain as Berlin. Further south it is even wetter with more snow. The rainfall is much heavier in the summer months. The coming of spring is much earlier in the Rhine Valley and the south. The Föhn wind gets its name from this area. It is a dry warm wind that blows northwards from the Alps, mainly in the summer.

EUROPE – CENTRAL

POLAND

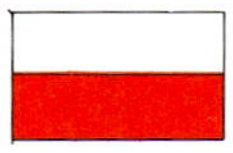

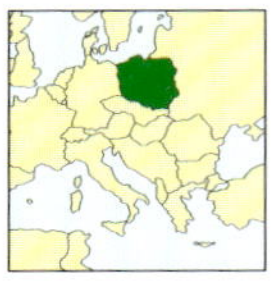

The colours of Poland's flag were derived from the 13th century coat of arms of a white eagle on a red field, which still appears on the Polish merchant flag. The flag's simple design was adopted when Poland became a republic in 1919.

COUNTRY: Republic of Poland
AREA: 312,680 sq km [120,726 sq mls]
POPULATION: 38,180,000
CAPITAL (Population): Warsaw (1,671,000)
GOVERNMENT: Republic with bi-cameral legislature
ETHNIC GROUPS: Polish 98%, Ukrainian 1%
LANGUAGES: Polish (official)
RELIGIONS: Roman Catholic 95%
NATIONAL DAY: 22 July
CURRENCY: Zloty = 100 groszy
ANNUAL INCOME PER PERSON: $1,700
MAIN PRIMARY PRODUCTS: Cereals, potatoes, sugar beet, fish, timber, copper, iron ore, sulphur, zinc
MAIN INDUSTRIES: Machinery, iron and steel, mining, shipbuilding, agriculture, food processing, oil refining, forestry, fishing
EXPORTS: $348 per person
MAIN EXPORTS: Machinery and transport equipment 39%, chemicals 11%, fuel and power 10%, metal 10%, textiles and clothing 7%
MAIN EXPORT PARTNERS: CIS nations 25%, Germany 16%, Czechoslovakia 6%, UK 5%, Yugoslavia 3%
IMPORTS: $266 per person
MAIN IMPORTS: Machinery and transport equipment 36%, chemicals 16%, fuel and power 15%, consumer products 9%, iron and steel products 8%
MAIN IMPORT PARTNERS: CIS nations 23%, Germany 18%, Czechoslovakia 6%, UK 4%, Yugoslavia 3%
DEFENCE: 7.3% of national budget
TOURISM: 3,100,000 visitors
POPULATION DENSITY: 122 per sq km [316 per sq ml]
INFANT MORTALITY: 17 per 1,000 live births
LIFE EXPECTANCY: Female 76 yrs, Male 68 yrs
ADULT LITERACY: 99%
PRINCIPAL CITIES (Population) : Warsaw 1,671,000 Lodz 852,000 Krakow 744,000 Wroclaw 640,000 Poznan 586,000

■ Country which suffered most in WWII, losing 6 million people (17.2% of pop.) ■ Pop. has increased by 50% since 1946 ■ Some 10 million people of Polish descent live abroad ■ Silesia contains richest coal reserves in Europe ■ Opened in 1796, world's thickest surface coal seam at Dabrowa Gornicza; 20 m [66 ft] thick, it's preserved as geological spectacle ■ Europe's largest copper deposits ■ World's 2nd biggest potato grower after Russia ■ World's tallest structure is Warszawa Radio Mast (646.38 m [2,120.6 ft]) ■ 'Solidarity' first free trade union in postwar Eastern Europe (1980)

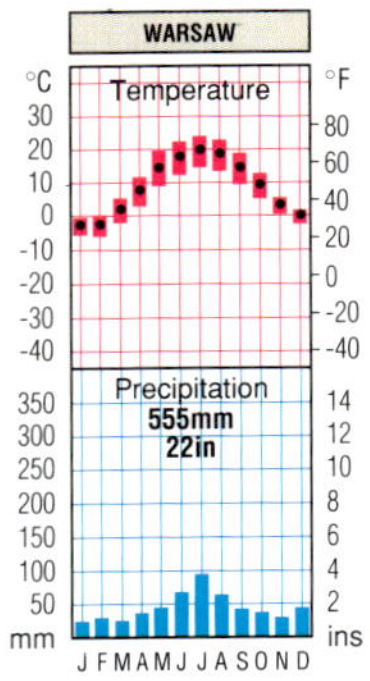

The weather and climate of Poland are transitional between maritime and continental. Warm, humid air masses come in from the west, cold Arctic air from the north and east and warm air from the south. There is a cold snowy winter becoming colder southwards and eastwards, and a warm summer with plenty of rain. The southern mountains have a lot of rain. The driest region of the country is the central lowlands.

CZECHOSLOVAKIA

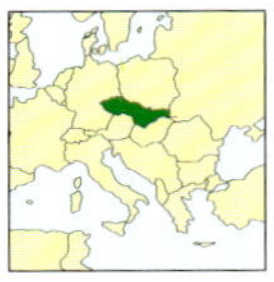

Czechoslovakia's flag, officially adopted in 1920, features the red and white of Bohemia with the blue of Moravia and Slovakia, the colours of Pan-Slavic liberation. They were first used in a horizontal tricolour by Slovakia in 1848.

COUNTRY: Czech and Slovak Federative Republic
AREA: 127,870 sq km [49,371 sq mls]
POPULATION: 15,678,000
CAPITAL (Population): Prague (1,194,000)
GOVERNMENT: Federal republic with a bicameral legislature
ETHNIC GROUPS: Czech 63%, Slovak 32%, Hungarian 4%, Polish and German
LANGUAGES: Czech, Slovak (official), Hungarian
RELIGIONS: Roman Catholic 66%, Czechoslovak Church 4%
NATIONAL DAY: 9 May; Liberation Day (1945)
CURRENCY: Koruna = 100 halura
ANNUAL INCOME PER PERSON: $3,140
MAIN PRIMARY PRODUCTS: Coal, iron ore, lignite, uranium, sugar beet, potatoes, cereals, livestock
MAIN INDUSTRIES: Transport equipment, iron and steel, machinery, chemicals, textiles
EXPORTS: $924 per person
MAIN EXPORTS: Machinery 45%, road vehicles and parts 9%, iron and steel 7%, chemicals 6%
MAIN EXPORT PARTNERS: CIS nations 41%, Germany 9%, Poland 9%
IMPORTS: $913 per person
MAIN IMPORTS: Machinery and transport equipment 32%, mineral fuels and lubricants 30%
MAIN IMPORT PARTNERS: CIS nations 46%, Germany 10%, Poland 9%
DEFENCE: 7.6% of national budget
TOURISM: 6,126,000 visitors
POPULATION DENSITY: 123 per sq km [318 per sq ml]
INFANT MORTALITY: 13 per 1,000 live births
LIFE EXPECTANCY: Female 76 yrs, Male 69 yrs
LITERACY: 99%
PRINCIPAL CITIES (Population): Prague 1,194,000 Bratislava 417,000 Brno 385,000 Ostrava 328,000 Kosice 222,000

■ Europe's largest landlocked country ■ Dense forests cover 40% of Slovakia ■ Two distinct peoples, Czechs in West (Bohemia & Moravia) and Slovaks in East (Slovakia) ■ Czechs and Slovaks have different national characteristics, languages & (since 1968) parliaments ■ President Vaclav Havel one of nation's best-known playwrights ■ Czechoslovakia's patron saint is St Wenceslas, the 'Good King' ■ Greatest users of contraception in the world (British are second) ■ Czechs are Protestant, urban & progressive; Slovaks tend to be rural, Catholic & traditional

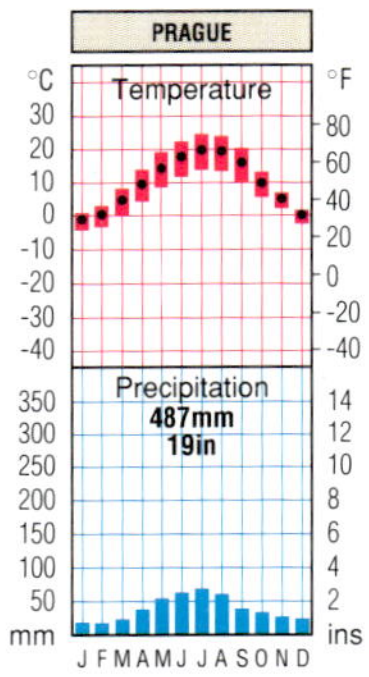

The mountains around the edges of the country cause the largest variations in the country's climate - lower temperatures, higher rainfall and snowfall. The winters in the lowlands are not very cold and the summers quite warm. The lowlands have a relatively low rainfall with a maximum in the summer, May - Aug.

HUNGARY

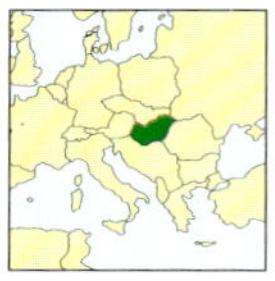

The tricolour became popular in the revolution of 1848, though the colours had been in the Hungarian arms since the 15th century. Adopted in 1919, the design was amended in 1957 to remove the state emblem, which had been added in 1949.

COUNTRY: Republic of Hungary
AREA: 93,030 sq km [35,919 sq mls]
POPULATION: 10,344,000
CAPITAL (Population): Budapest (2,115,000)
GOVERNMENT: Unitary single-party republic with a unicameral legislature
ETHNIC GROUPS: Magyar 97%, German, Slovak
LANGUAGES: Hungarian (official), Slovak, German
RELIGIONS: Roman Catholic 62%, Protestant 23%
NATIONAL DAY: 15 March; Uprising against Austrian rule, 1848
CURRENCY: Forint = 100 filler
ANNUAL INCOME PER PERSON: $2,780
MAIN PRIMARY PRODUCTS: Cereals, sugar beet, potatoes, livestock, fruit, timber, coal, lignite, oil and natural gas
MAIN INDUSTRIES: Agriculture, iron, steel, mining, transport equipment, timber products
EXPORTS: $910 per person
MAIN EXPORTS: Machinery and transport equipment 33%, foodstuffs 21%, semi-finished products 19%, industrial consumer goods 16%
MAIN EXPORT PARTNERS: CIS nations 28%, Germany 16%, Austria 6%, Czechoslovakia 5%, Italy 4%, Poland 3%
IMPORTS: $832 per person
MAIN IMPORTS: Machinery and transport equipment 29%, semi-finished products 26%, fuel and electricity 13%, consumer goods 12%, foodstuffs 8%
MAIN IMPORT PARTNERS: CIS nations 25%, Germany 20%, Austria 7%, Czechoslovakia 5%, Poland 4%, Italy 3%, Yugoslavia 3%
DEFENCE: 7.0% of national budget
TOURISM: 11,826,000 visitors
POPULATION DENSITY: 111 per sq km [288 per sq ml]
INFANT MORTALITY: 17 per 1,000 live births
LIFE EXPECTANCY: Female 75 yrs, Male 68 yrs
ADULT LITERACY: 99%
PRINCIPAL CITIES (Population): Budapest 2,115,000 Debrecen 220,000 Miskolc 208,000 Szeged 189,000 Pécs 183,000

■ Great Alföld, the plain east of the Danube, covers 51,800 sq km [19,995 sq mls], more than 1/2 of country ■ Lake Balaton largest lake in Central Europe (601 sq km [232 sq mls]) ■ Hortobagy is Europe's only surviving area of steppe outside USSR, covering 10,000 sq km [3,900 sq mls] west of Debrecen ■ Budapest is home to 20% of the country's population ■ Foreign trade accounts for 50% of GDP (1989) ■ Before political upheavals in 1989, Hungary had gone furthest of all Communist bloc countries in decentralising and deregulating economy ■ Most doctors per head of population in world

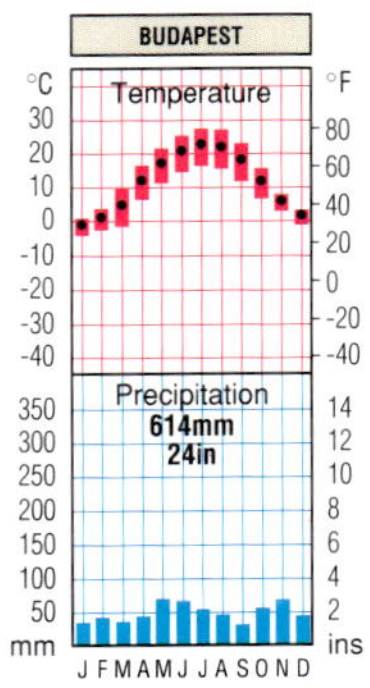

The plains of Hungary have warm, sunny summers and cold winters with snow lying on between 30 and 40 days. There is a double maximum of rainfall, the first in early summer when convectional storms are most active. A second maximum in November becomes an increasingly marked feature of the climate towards the south-west where the Mediterranean Sea exerts its influence.

AUSTRIA

According to legend, the colours of the Austrian flag date from the battle of Ptolemais in 1191, when the only part of the Duke of Bebenberg's tunic not bloodstained was under his swordbelt. The design was officially adopted in 1918.

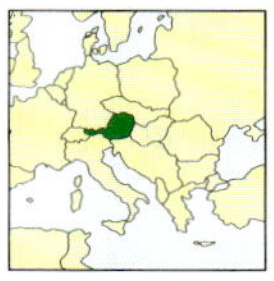

COUNTRY: Republic of Austria
AREA: 83,850 sq km [32,374 sq mls]
POPULATION: 7,712,000
CAPITAL (Population): Vienna (1,483,000)
GOVERNMENT: Federal multi-party republic with bicameral legislature
ETHNIC GROUPS: Austrian 96%, Yugoslav 2%, Turkish, German
LANGUAGES: German (official)
RELIGIONS: Roman Catholic 84%, Protestant 6%
NATIONAL DAY: 26 October; Proclamation of neutrality (1955)
CURRENCY: Schilling = 100 Groschen
ANNUAL INCOME PER PERSON: $19,240
MAIN PRIMARY PRODUCTS: Iron ore, lignite, oil and natural gas, graphite, timber, cattle, wheat
MAIN INDUSTRIES: Agriculture, tourism, iron and steel, wood products, wine, food processing
EXPORTS: $4,256 per person
MAIN EXPORTS: Machinery and transport equipment 34%, iron and steel 7%, paper and board 6%, cork, wood and other crude materials 5%, food stuffs 3%
MAIN EXPORT PARTNERS: Germany 35%, Italy 10%, Switzerland 7%, UK 5%, France 4%
IMPORTS: $5,101 per person
MAIN IMPORTS: Machinery and transport equipment 35%, chemicals and pharmaceuticals 10%, mineral fuels and lubricants 7%, food stuffs 5%
MAIN IMPORT PARTNERS: Germany 44%, Italy 9%, Switzerland 5%, Japan 4%, France 4%
DEFENCE: 2.9% of national budget
TOURISM: 15,761,000 visitors
POPULATION DENSITY: 92 per sq km [238 per sq ml]
INFANT MORTALITY: 9 per 1,000 live births
LIFE EXPECTANCY: Female 79 yrs, Male 72 yrs
ADULT LITERACY: 99%
PRINCIPAL CITIES (Population): Vienna 1,483,000 Graz 243,000 Linz 200,000 Salzburg 139,000 Innsbruck 117,000

■ Forests cover 37% of the country, greater % than any European nation except Sweden & Finland ■ 3,000 sq km [1,200 sq mls] of Alps set aside as protected areas ■ Smallest pop. increase in Europe 1950-86 (9%) ■ Highest tourist receipts in OECD as % of GNP ■ Austrians eat more veal per head than any nation ■ Only state pledged by both law and treaties to neutrality ■ Hapsburg's power lasted over 600 years ■ Only 77 companies employ more than 1000 people ■ Only nuclear power station has been demolished; completed in 1978 at Zwentendorf, it was prevented from going into production by public ballot

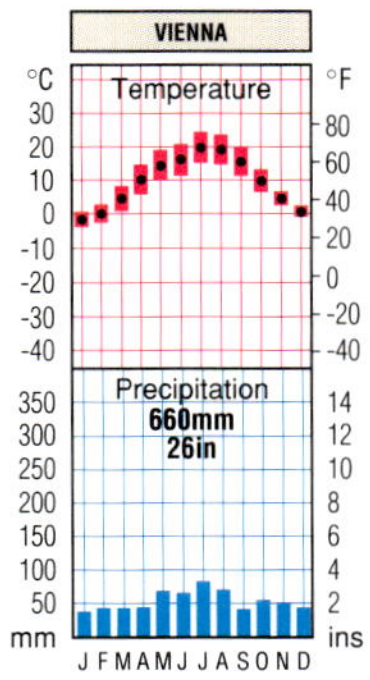

The western Alpine regions have an Atlantic-type climate, while the eastern lowlands are continental. The air-flow is mainly from the west, which has twice the rainfall of the east at over 1,000mm [40 in]. The winters are cold with snow and on the mountains there are glaciers and permanent snow in great depths. In Vienna the Jan. temperature is below freezing and is around 20°C [68°F] in July. There is rain throughout the year but the wettest months, June-Aug., are also the warmest.

LIECHTENSTEIN

COUNTRY: Principality of Liechtenstein
AREA: 157 sq km [61 sq mls]
POPULATION: 29,000
CAPITAL (Population): Vaduz (4,919)

■ Richest country (GNP per head of pop.) in world ■ Currency is Swiss franc ■ Top country in Europe for newspaper sales: 558 per 1000 ■ Some European companies have HQs in Liechtenstein to benefit from country's lenient tax laws

SWITZERLAND

Switzerland's square flag was officially adopted in 1848, though the white cross on a red shield has been the Swiss emblem since the 14th century. The flag of the International Red Cross, based in Geneva, derives from this Swiss flag.

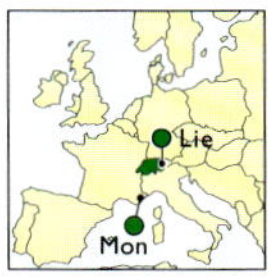

COUNTRY: Swiss Confederation
AREA: 41,290 sq km [15,942 sq mls]
POPULATION: 6,712,000
CAPITAL (Population): Bern (299,000)
GOVERNMENT: Federal state with a bicameral legislature
ETHNIC GROUPS: German 65%, French 18%, Italian 10%, Spanish 2%, Romansch 1%, Turkish 1%
LANGUAGES: French, German and Italian (official)
RELIGIONS: Roman Catholic 48%, Protestant 44%
NATIONAL DAY: 1 August
CURRENCY: Swiss franc = 100 centimes
ANNUAL INCOME PER PERSON: $32,790
MAIN PRIMARY PRODUCTS: Cereals, grapes, potatoes, cattle, timber
MAIN INDUSTRIES: Tourism, banking and financial services, machinery, chemicals, instruments, clocks and watches, textiles, iron and steel
EXPORTS: $7,752 per person
MAIN EXPORTS: Non-electrical machinery 20%, electrical machinery 12%, pharmaceuticals 8%, jewellery 7%, watches 6%
MAIN EXPORT PARTNERS: Germany 21%, France 9%, USA 9%, Italy 8%, UK 8%, Japan 4%
IMPORTS: $8,755 per person
MAIN IMPORTS: Machinery 20%, chemical products 11%, textiles and clothing 10%, precious metals and jewellery 7%
MAIN IMPORT PARTNERS: Germany 34%, France 11%, Italy 10%, UK 6%, USA 5%, Japan 5%
DEFENCE: 19.7% of national budget
TOURISM: 11,600,000 visitors
POPULATION DENSITY: 163 per sq km [421 per sq ml]
INFANT MORTALITY: 7 per 1,000 live births
LIFE EXPECTANCY: Female 81 yrs, Male 75 yrs
ADULT LITERACY: 99%
PRINCIPAL CITIES (Population): Zürich 839,000 Geneva 389,000 Basle 359,000 Bern 299,000 Lausanne 263,000

■ 1,750 banks and financial institutions ■ Unemployment rate has been below 1% for many years ■ Lowest no. of strikes in Europe ■ Europe's biggest spenders on health ■ Most letters posted per capita in world ■ Highest no. of international phone calls per head in world ■ World's biggest producer of chocolate ■ World's tallest dam, Grande Dixence, is 285 m [935 ft] high ■ 15% of population is foreign ■ 100,000 workers cross the border each day, mainly from Italy ■ All Swiss males serve in army or reserve, until 50 (55 for officers) ■ Government intends to provide nuclear shelters for entire population by 2000

■ One of 26 countries without a coastline, but has merchant fleet ■ Highest railway in Europe climbs to Jungfraujoch ■ Nation comprises 23 cantons or local divisions ■ Independence and neutrality guaranteed in perpetuity by international treaty, 1815 ■ Does not belong to UN or any other international organisations, though several UN bodies based there (eg WHO in Geneva) & more than 150 international bodies have HQs there from International Red Cross to WWF ■ Biggest GNP per head in OECD

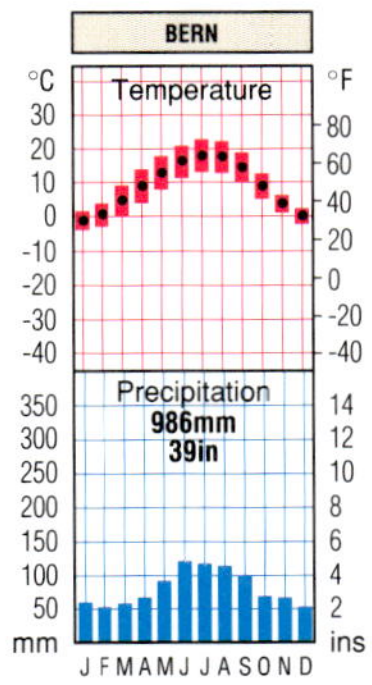

The Alpine foreland of northern Switzerland has a central European climate with a marked summer maximum of rainfall. In winter the region is often blanketed in low cloud resulting in a small diurnal range of temperature in contrast with the mountain resorts which lie above the cloud. Precipitation falls mainly as snow between December and March. Summers are warm with a daily average of 8 hrs. sunshine in July.

MONACO

COUNTRY: Principality of Monaco
AREA: 1.5 sq km [0.6 sq mls]
POPULATION: 29,000
CAPITAL (Population): Monaco-Ville

■ Europe's most densely populated country (2nd in world, after Macau) ■ Only 4,500 of pop. Monégasque citizens ■ Monégasques pay no taxes but not allowed to gamble in casino ■ More telephones per capita than any nation (1,071 per 1,000 pop.)

ANDORRA

COUNTRY: Co-Principality of Andorra
AREA: 453 sq km [175 sq mls]
POPULATION: 52,000
CAPITAL: Andorra la Vella

■ Principality governed by French and Spanish delegations (joint heads of state are President of France and Bishop of Urgel) ■ Catalan is official language but spoken by only 30% of pop.: 59% speak Spanish, 6% French

EUROPE – SOUTH, SOUTH-WEST

FRANCE

The colours of the French flag originated during the Revolution of 1789. The red and blue are said to represent Paris and the white the monarchy. The present design, adopted in 1794, is meant to symbolise republican principles.

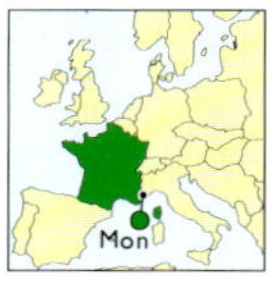

COUNTRY: French Republic
AREA: 551,500 sq km [212,934 sq mls]
POPULATION: 56,440,000
CAPITAL (Population): Paris (8,510,000)
GOVERNMENT: Republic with bicameral legislature
ETHNIC GROUPS: French 93%, Arab 3%, German 2%, Breton 1%, Catalan 1%
LANGUAGES: French (official), Basque, Breton, Arabic
RELIGIONS: Roman Catholic 76%, other Christian 4%, Muslim 3%
NATIONAL DAY: 14 July; Fall of the Bastille
CURRENCY: Franc = 100 centimes
ANNUAL INCOME PER PERSON: $19,480 per person
SOURCE OF INCOME: Agriculture 4%, Industry 37%, Services 59%
MAIN PRIMARY PRODUCTS: Crude petroleum, natural gas, bauxite, iron ore, agricultural products, lead, zinc, potash
MAIN INDUSTRIES: Aluminium, plastics, synthetic fibres and rubber, agriculture, wool, yarn, forestry, fishing, vehicles, steel, cement, paper, petroleum products
EXPORTS: $3,185 per person
MAIN EXPORTS: Machinery and transport equipment 35%, basic manufactures 18%, chemicals and related products 14%, food and live animals 11%
MAIN EXPORT PARTNERS: Germany 17%, Italy 12%, Belgium 9%, UK 9%, USA 7%, Netherlands 5%, Spain 5%, Switzerland 4%
IMPORTS: $3,427 per person
MAIN IMPORTS: Machinery and transport equipment 32%, chemicals 11%, food and live animals 10%, petroleum and petroleum products 8%, textile yarns and fabrics 3%, iron and steel 3%
MAIN IMPORT PARTNERS: Germany 20%, Italy 12%, Belgium 9%, UK 7%, USA 7%, Netherlands 6%, Japan 4%, Spain 4%
EDUCATIONAL EXPENDITURE: 23% of national budget
DEFENCE: 18.7% of national budget
TOTAL ARMED FORCES: 466,300
TOURISM: 36,818,000 visitors
ROADS: 804,765 km [500,055 mls]
RAILWAYS: 34,647 km [211,528 mls]
POPULATION DENSITY: 102 per sq km [263 per sq ml]
URBAN POPULATION: 74%
POPULATION GROWTH: 0.4% per year
BIRTHS: 13.6 per 1,000 population
DEATHS: 10.0 per 1,000 population
INFANT MORTALITY: 7 per 1,000 live births
LIFE EXPECTANCY: Female 81 yrs, Male 73 yrs
POPULATION PER DOCTOR: 320
ADULT LITERACY: 98%
PRINCIPAL CITIES (Population): Paris 8,510,000 Lyons 1,170,000 Marseilles 1,080,000 Lille 935,000 Bordeaux 628,000 Toulouse 523,000 Nantes 465,000 Nice 449,000 Toulon 410,000 Grenoble 392,000 Rouen 380,000 Strasbourg 373,000

■ Europe's largest country outside Russia) ■ Mont Blanc, on Italian border, Europe's highest mountain at 4,807 m [15,770 ft] ■ World's deepest cave Résneau Gouffe Jean Bernard at 1,535 m [5,036 ft] ■ St Malo has Europe's greatest tidal range (15.25 m [50ft]) ■ Most extensive inland waterways in Europe (6,409 km [3982 mls] in use 1986) ■ Still has number of overseas territories (departments) ■ Nearly 1 in 6 of population is over 65 ■ Largest Jewish population after USA & Russia ■ Europe's biggest producer of maize & cheese ■ Europe's biggest uranium producer (6th in world) & biggest producer of nuclear energy (13% of world total) ■ Western Europe's biggest defence spender & biggest arms exporter (3rd in world) ■ Europe's biggest aid donor (Norway biggest per capita) ■ Europe's fastest passenger train (TGV) runs between Paris & Lyon at average speed of 212.5 km/h [132 mph] ■ Highest no. road deaths in Europe (3rd in world) ■ 20% of average household budget spent on food ■ Consumes more alcohol per person than any nation; 20,000 deaths each year from alcohol-related diseases ■ 86% Catholic, but only 14% regularly attend Mass ■ About 3 million people visit Lourdes each year ■ 1 in 4 marriages ends in divorce ■ Gourdon, in central southern France, most polluted town in Europe (WHO figures, sulphur dioxide emissions only)

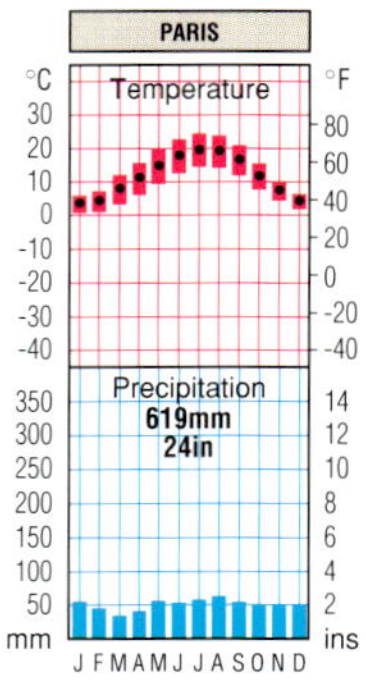

The climate of France is formed from three influences, the Atlantic, the Mediterranean and the continent. With no mountain barriers to affect it the Atlantic regime extends far inland giving mild weather with appreciable wind and rain, but little snow. Eastwards the climate gets warmer but with colder winters. Towards the mountains and to the south the rainfall increases. Rain falls throughout the year, with a maximum May - June. In the Alps and Pyrenees snow lies permanently above 3,000m [12,000ft].

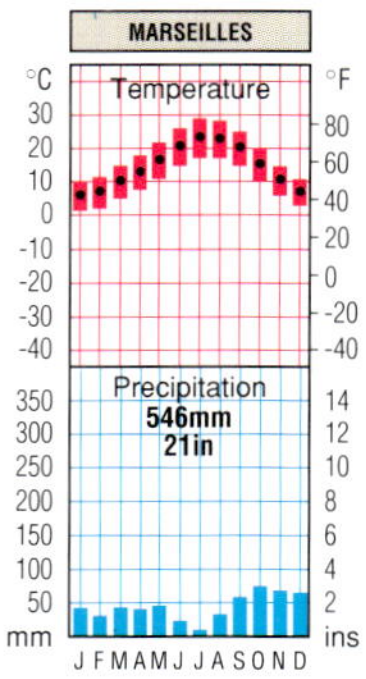

The Mediterranean climate extends over the south-east, pushes northwards into the Rhône valley and into the mountain foothills, and over Corsica. The winters are very mild, with snow and frost a rarity. The summers are dry and the rain falls Sept. - March. One feature of the area is its peculiar winds, notably the Mistral, a cold, dry and strong wind which blows southwards during winter and spring causing crop damage.

SPAIN

The colours of the Spanish flag date back to the old Kingdom of Aragon in the 12th century. The present design, in which the central yellow stripe is twice as wide as each of the red stripes, was adopted during the Civil War in 1938.

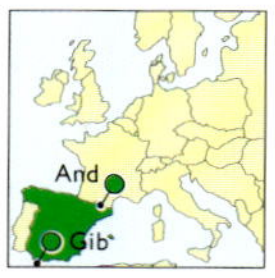

COUNTRY: Kingdom of Spain
AREA: 504,780 sq km [194,896 sq mls]
POPULATION: 38,959,000
CAPITAL (Population): Madrid (3,123,000)
GOVERNMENT: Constitutional monarchy with bicameral legislature
ETHNIC GROUPS: Spanish 73%, Catalan 16%, Galician 8%, Basque 2%
LANGUAGES: Spanish (official), Basque, Catalan, Galician
RELIGIONS: Roman Catholic 97%
NATIONAL DAY: 12 October; Discovery of America (1492)
CURRENCY: Peseta = 100 céntimos
ANNUAL INCOME PER PERSON: $10,920
MAIN PRIMARY PRODUCTS: Cereals, sugar cane, grapes, fruit, timber, olives, fish, cork, lignite, iron, coal, lead, copper, mercury, tungsten, zinc, tin
MAIN INDUSTRIES: Agriculture, wine, food processing, mining, iron and steel, textiles, chemicals, cement, oil refining, engineering, transport equipment, timber, fishing
EXPORTS: $1,146 per person
MAIN EXPORTS: Transport equipment 17%, machinery and electrical equipment 13%, vegetables and fruit 9%, cast iron, iron and steel 9%, chemicals 7%, mineral fuels 6%, food stuffs 5%
MAIN EXPORT PARTNERS: France 15%, USA 10%, Germany 10%, UK 9%, Benelux 8%, Italy 7%
IMPORTS: $1,841 per person
MAIN IMPORTS: Machinery and electrical equipment 20%, mineral fuels and petrol products 19%, chemicals 9%, transport equipment 8%
MAIN IMPORT PARTNERS: USA 11%, Germany 11%, France 9%, UK 7%, Mexico 6%, Italy 5%
DEFENCE: 9.5% of national budget
TOURISM: 32,900,000 visitors
POPULATION DENSITY: 77 per sq km [200 per sq ml]
INFANT MORTALITY: 9 per 1,000 live births
LIFE EXPECTANCY: Female 80 yrs, Male 74 yrs
ADULT LITERACY: 94%
PRINCIPAL CITIES (Population): Madrid 3,123,000 Barcelona 1,694,000 Valencia 739,000 Seville 668,000 Saragossa 596,000 Malaga 595,000 Bilbao 378,000 Las Palmas 372,000 Valladolid 341,000

■ Punto Marroqui, at 36° N latitude, most southerly point on European mainland ■ Europe's second largest country (excl. Russia), & separated from rest of continent by Pyrenees, where peaks rise to 3,400 m [over 11,000 ft] ■ Europe's highest temperature (51°C [124°F]) recorded at Seville ■ Until discovery of the Americas, Galicia known as Finisterre – 'end of the earth' ■ First ship to circumnavigate the globe, Magellan's Victoria, left Spain 1519 & returned in 1522 ■ Tomb of Columbus in Spain's largest cathedral (Seville) ■ World's most visited country: 9% of international travellers go to Spain each year more people than its own population ■ Biggest grower of oranges in Europe and 3rd in world ■ Highest unemployment rate in OECD ■ Euskera language of Basque people of N. Spain may be oldest in world ■ General Francisco Franco's regime was longest lived of European Fascist dictatorships ■ One of few countries where the monarchy was revived with the succession of Franco by King Juan Carlos ■ Since Franco the country has been divided into 17 autonomous regions ■ Still has small enclaves in Africa - the towns of Ceuta and Melilla, the last remnants of a once vast empire ■ Gibraltar still a colony of the UK is actively claimed by Spain ■ Jerez de la Frontera gave sherry its English name ■ Pablo Picasso, who died at 91 in 1973, thought to be world's most productive painter: over 13,000 paintings plus engravings, illustrations & sculptures ■ The relics of St James the Apostle are kept in the cathedral of Santiago de Compostela

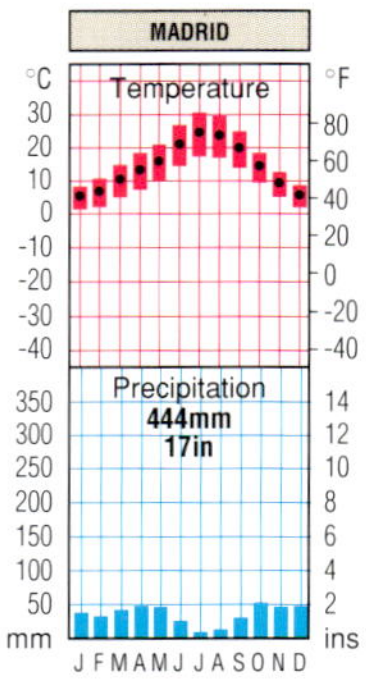

The interior of Spain is a high plateau, isolated from the seas which surround the Iberian Peninsula. Summer days are very hot despite the altitude but at night temperatures fall sharply. Winters are much colder than in coastal districts and frost is not uncommon. Rain is fairly evenly distributed from September to May but the summer drought is broken only by occasional storms. Madrid has an average of 8 hours sunshine a day.

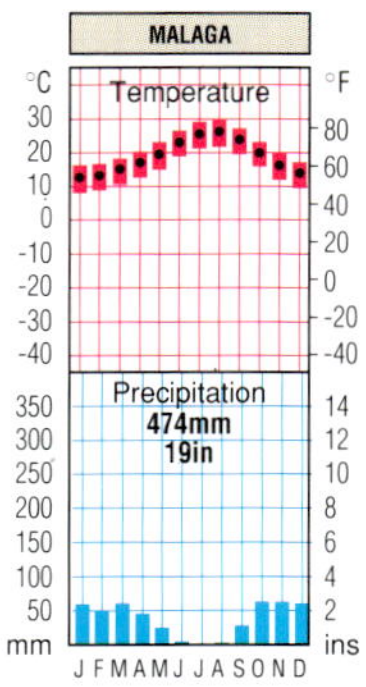

The narrow coastal plain of southern Spain, sheltered by the Sierra Nevada, is noted for its very hot and sunny summers. Rainfall at Malaga is sparse and, like much of the western Mediterranean region, evenly distributed throughout the winter half of the year in contrast to the more prominent winter maximum further east. With an average of only 52 rainy days a year, Malaga is one of the most reliable holiday resorts.

PORTUGAL

Portugal' s colours, adopted in 1910 when it became a republic, represent Henry the Navigator (green) and the monarchy (red). The armillary shield – an early navigational instrument – reflects Portugal's leading role in world exploration.

COUNTRY: Republic of Portugal
AREA: 92,390 sq km [35,672 sq mls]
POPULATION: 10,525,000
CAPITAL (Population): Lisbon (831,000)
GOVERNMENT: Parliamentary state with a unicameral legislature
ETHNIC GROUPS: Portuguese 99%, Cape Verdean, Brazilian, Spanish, British
LANGUAGES: Portuguese (official)
RELIGIONS: Roman Catholic 95%
NATIONAL DAY: 10 June; Portugal Day
CURRENCY: Escudo = 100 centavos
ANNUAL INCOME PER PERSON: $4,890
MAIN PRIMARY PRODUCTS: Cereals, olives, rice, timber, fruit, vegetables, cork, fish, copper, iron, tungsten, tin, salt
MAIN INDUSTRIES: Agriculture, textiles, food processing, wine, chemicals, fishing, mining, tourism
EXPORTS: $1,210 per person
MAIN EXPORTS: Clothing 26%, machinery and transport equipment 20%, footwear 8%, paper and paper products 8%
MAIN EXPORT PARTNERS: France 15%, Germany 15%, UK 14%, Spain 11%
IMPORTS: $1,803 per person
MAIN IMPORTS: Machinery 22%, road vehicles 15%, crude petroleum 9%, iron and steel products 4%, chemicals 4%
MAIN IMPORT PARTNERS: Germany 14%, Spain 14%, France 12%, Italy 9%, UK 8%
DEFENCE: 8.4% of national budget
TOURISM: 6,102,000 visitors
POPULATION DENSITY: 114 per sq km [295 per sq ml]
INFANT MORTALITY: 13 per 1,000 live births
LIFE EXPECTANCY: Female 78 yrs, Male 71 yrs
ADULT LITERACY: 84%
PRINCIPAL CITIES (Population): Lisbon 831,000 Oporto 350,000

■ Cabo da Roca, at 9°31' W longitude, most westerly point on European mainland ■ Probably world's most powerful earthquake took place in Lisbon in 1755 (8.75-9.00 on Richter Scale) ■ First European country to have major overseas empire (14th & 15th centuries) ■ 200 million people speak Portuguese, mostly in Brazil ■ Poorest country in W. Europe ■ 20% of workforce engaged in agriculture ■ Port has been produced in Douro valley for 400 years ■ Every second wine bottle in world sealed with Portuguese cork ■ Highest rate of household savings in OECD

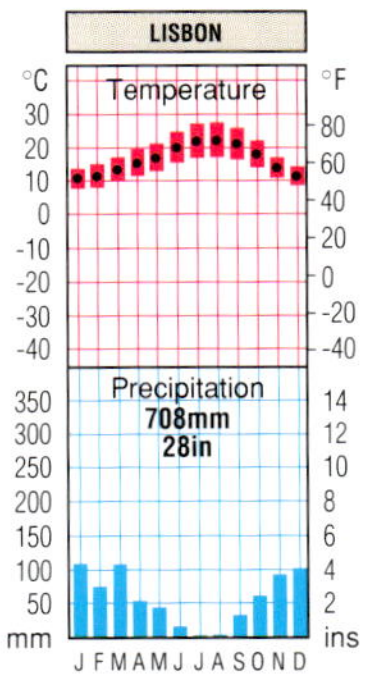

The west coast of the Iberian Peninsula has the oceanic variety of Mediterranean climate with cooler summers, milder winters and a smaller temperature range than in true Mediterranean lands. Sunshine at Lisbon is abundant, averaging 7.5 hours a day throughout the year. Most of the rain falls in the winter half of the year with July and August virtually rainless.

MADEIRA

COUNTRY: Portuguese Autonomous Region
AREA: 813 sq km [314 sq mls]
POPULATION: 280,000
CAPITAL: Funchal

AZORES

COUNTRY: Portuguese Autonomous Region
AREA: 2,390 sq km [921 sq mls]
POPULATION: 260,000
CAPITAL: Ponta Delgada

GIBRALTAR

COUNTRY: British Crown Colony
AREA: 6.5 sq km [2.5 sq mls]
POPULATION: 31,000

■ British since 1713; thorn in the flesh of UK/Spanish relations ■ British and NATO base ■ Barbary apes on 'the Rock' Europe's only wild monkeys

ITALY

When Napoleon invaded Italy in 1796, the French Republican National Guard carried a military standard of vertical green, white and red stripes. After many changes, it was finally adopted as the national flag after the unification of Italy in 1861.

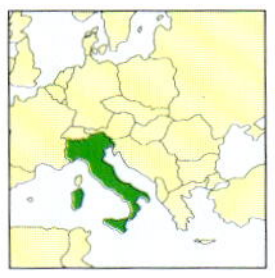

COUNTRY: Italian Republic
AREA: 301,270 sq km [116,320 sq mls]
POPULATION: 57,663,000
CAPITAL (Population): Rome (2,817,000)
GOVERNMENT: Democratic republic with bicameral legislature
ETHNIC GROUPS: Italian 94%, German 2%
LANGUAGES: Italian (official) 94%, German
RELIGIONS: Roman Catholic 83%
NATIONAL DAY: 2 June; Republic (1946)
CURRENCY: Lira (no smaller units)
ANNUAL INCOME PER PERSON: $16,850
SOURCE OF INCOME: Agriculture 4%, Industry 40%, Services 56%
MAIN PRIMARY PRODUCTS: Wheat, barley, vegetables, grapes, fruit, olives, fish oil, iron ore, mercury, zinc, lignite, sulphur, marble
MAIN INDUSTRIES: Iron and steel, chemicals, food processing, oil refining, vehicles, textiles and clothing, wine, tourism
EXPORTS: $2,410 per person
MAIN EXPORTS: Machinery 26%, textiles and clothing 13%, vehicles 9%, chemicals 7%, footwear 5%, petroleum products 3%, iron and steel 3%
MAIN EXPORT PARTNERS: Germany, 19%, France 17%, USA 9%, UK 7%, Switzerland 5%, Belgium 3%, Spain 3%
IMPORTS: $2,658 per person
MAIN IMPORTS: Machinery 17%, textiles and clothing 13%, vehicles 9%, chemicals 7%, footwear 5%, petroleum products 3%, iron and steel 3%
MAIN IMPORT PARTNERS: Germany 21%, France 15%, Saudi Arabia 6%, USA 16%, UK 6%, Belgium 5%
EDUCATIONAL EXPENDITURE: 8% of national budget
DEFENCE: 5.4% of national budget
TOTAL ARMED FORCES: 390,000
TOURISM: 25,749,000 visitors
ROADS: 300,292 [187,683 mls]
RAILWAYS: 15,983 km [9,989 mls]
POPULATION DENSITY: 191 per sq km [496 per sq ml]
URBAN POPULATION: 69%
POPULATION GROWTH: 0.1% per year
BIRTHS: 11.5 per 1,000 population
DEATHS: 10.5 per 1,000 population
INFANT MORTALITY: 9 per 1,000 live births
LIFE EXPECTANCY: Female 80 yrs, Male 73 yrs
POPULATION PER DOCTOR: 234
ADULT LITERACY: 97%
PRINCIPAL CITIES (Population): Rome 2,817,000 Milan 1,464,000 Naples 1,203,000 Turin 1,012,000 Palermo 731,000 Genoa 715,000 Bologna 422,000 Florence 417,000 Catania 371,000 Bari 357,000 Venice 324,000 Messina 272,000 Verona 259,000 Taranto 245,000 Trieste 235,000

■ Country made up of mainland peninsula and the two large islands of Sardinia and Sicily ■ One of world's most active volcanoes & Europe's largest, Mount Etna rises to 3,340 m [10,958 ft] and has about 200 volcanic vents on its slopes ■ Worst earthquake this century in 1908 at Messina (77,000 people killed) ■ Pompeii, ancient ruined city near foot of volcanic Mount Vesuvius, was destroyed by eruption in 79AD ■ Lowest fertility rate in world (1.3 children per woman) ■ World's biggest grape grower & biggest wine producer ■ Europe's largest producer of vegetables & tobacco (1985-87) ■ All crude oil and most raw materials imported ■ GNP doubled 1950 to 1962; in 1950s & 1960s rate of expansion second only to Japan's ■ Makers of more gold jewellery than any nation ■ Has one of highest proportions of university students among EC countries, & by 1985 50% were of working class or peasant background ■ Some of its universities oldest in Europe dating from 13th cent. ■ Most public telephones in Europe (3rd in world), with 7.7 per 1,000 people ■ Reputedly has world's highest rate of tax evasion ■ Largest Greek theatre in existence is on island of Ortygia at Syracuse, Sicily ■ Although Italy has had political stability in recent years, since World War II has had an average of one government per year ■ Late formation of modern state in late 19th cent. ■ Fascist state 1923 - World War II ■ A few bears & wolves still live in hills of the Abruzzi

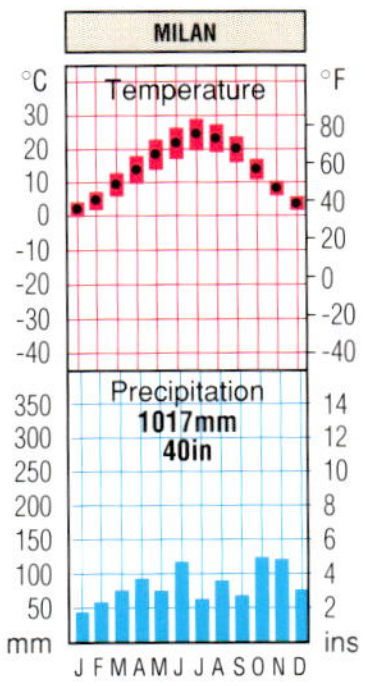

Although the plains of Lombardy lie within the Mediterranean basin they have a climate more like that of central Europe, though with hotter summers. Sunshine averages under 5 hours a day, far less than that of southern Italy. Winter is relatively dry and cold with occasional frost and snow. Rainfall is plentiful, with a double maximum in spring and autumn.

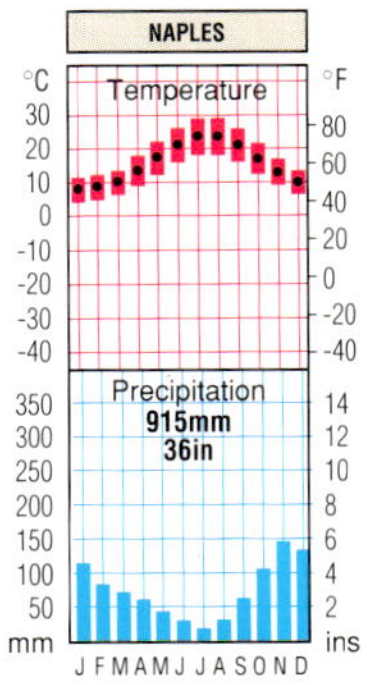

Naples lies in the north of the Mezzogiorno, the most typically Mediterranean region in Italy. Summers are hot and very sunny with occasional thunderstorms providing the only rain. Winters are mild and virtually free from frost with westerly winds bringing abundant rain to the western slopes of the Apennines. November is the wettest month throughout the region.

EUROPE – SOUTH, SOUTH-EAST

SAN MARINO

COUNTRY: Most Serene Republic of San Marino
AREA: 61 sq km [24 sq mls]
POPULATION: 24,000
CAPITAL: San Marino

■ Europe's smallest republic ■ Police are hired from Italy which surrounds state ■ World's lowest birthrate (9.3 per 1,000 in 1985) ■ Named after Marino, the stonemason saint, who settled in 300AD ■ Tourism & agriculture are chief industries

VATICAN CITY

COUNTRY: Vatican City State
AREA: 0.44 sq km [0.17 sq mls]
POPULATION: 1,000
CAPITAL: Vatican City

■ St Peter's Basilica is mother church for world's 700 million Roman Catholics ■ No births – no married inhabitants ■ Popes have lived here since 5th century except for brief period in Avignon in 14th century ■ 100 people are Swiss guards

MALTA

The colours of Malta's flag, adopted on independence in 1964, are those of the Knights of Malta, who ruled the islands from 1530 to 1798. The George Cross was added in 1943 to commemorate the heroism of the Maltese people during World War II.

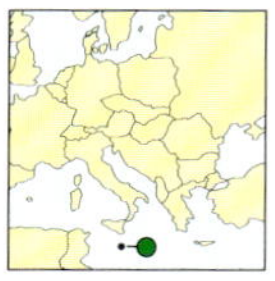

■ Malta is 93 km [58 mls] S. of Sicily and 290 km [180 mls] from N. Africa ■ Has no mountains or rivers ■ Nearly half of working population engaged in agriculture ■ Valletta conurbation has over $^{2}/_{3}$ of population ■ Has been an important strategic base since earliest days of navigation ■ Maltese only became written language this century

COUNTRY: Republic of Malta
AREA: 316 sq km [122 sq mls]
POPULATION: 354,000
CAPITAL (Population): Valletta (101,000)
GOVERNMENT: Multi-party republic with unicameral legislature
ETHNIC GROUPS: Maltese 95%, British 2%
LANGUAGES: Maltese and English
RELIGIONS: Christian (Roman Catholic 96%)
NATIONAL DAY: 31 March; National Day
CURRENCY: Maltese lira = 100 cents = 1,000 mils
ANNUAL INCOME PER PERSON: $6,630
MAIN PRIMARY PRODUCTS: Stone and sand
MAIN INDUSTRIES: Tourism, light industry and agriculture
MAIN EXPORTS: Manufactured articles, clothing, machinery and transport equipment
MAIN IMPORTS: Food and live animals, mineral fuels, textile yarn and machinery
DEFENCE: 4% of national budget
POPULATION DENSITY: 1,120 per sq km [2,901 per sq ml]
LIFE EXPECTANCY: Female 76 yrs, Male 72 yrs
ADULT LITERACY: 84%

GREECE

Blue and white became Greece's national colours during the war of independence. Finally adopted in 1970, the flag's design represents the battle cry 'Freedom or Death' during the struggle against Ottoman (Turkish) domination in the 1820s.

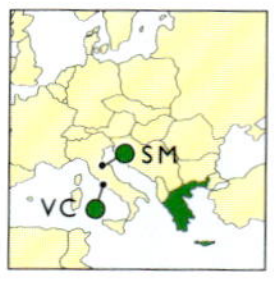

COUNTRY: Hellenic Republic
AREA: 131,990 sq km [50,961 sq mls]
POPULATION: 10,269,000
CAPITAL (Population): Athens (3,072,000)
GOVERNMENT: Unitary multi-party republic with a unicameral legislature
ETHNIC GROUPS: Greek 95%, Macedonian 2%, Turkish 1%
LANGUAGES: Greek (official)
RELIGIONS: Greek Orthodox 97%, Muslim 1%, Roman Catholic
NATIONAL DAY: 25 March; Independence Day (1830)
CURRENCY: Drachma = 100 lepta
ANNUAL INCOME PER PERSON: $5,340
MAIN PRIMARY PRODUCTS: Wheat, tobacco, cotton, olives, grapes, bauxite, iron, chrome, crude oil, barytes
MAIN INDUSTRIES: Agriculture, tourism, chemicals, steel, aluminium, shipbuilding
EXPORTS: $752 per person
MAIN EXPORTS: Foodstuffs, olive oil, tobacco 28%, textiles 23%, petroleum products 8%
MAIN EXPORT PARTNERS: Germany 21%, USA 14%, Italy 14%, UK 9%, France 7%, Netherlands 3%
IMPORTS: $1,610 per person
MAIN IMPORTS: Machinery and transport equipment 23%, foodstuffs and beverages 17%, crude petroleum 9%, chemicals 9%
MAIN IMPORT PARTNERS: Germany 19%, Italy 13%, USA 10%, France 8%, Netherlands 7%, UK 6%, Japan 3%
DEFENCE: 16.9% of national budget
TOURISM: 7,564,000 visitors
POPULATION DENSITY: 78 per sq km [202 per sq ml]
INFANT MORTALITY: 13 per 1,000 live births
LIFE EXPECTANCY: Female 79 yrs, Male 74 yrs
ADULT LITERACY: 92%
PRINCIPAL CITIES (Population): Athens 3,072,000 Thessalonika 872,000 Pátrai 142,000

■ Islands account for $^{1}/_{5}$ of total land area ■ 11.3% of pop. lives on islands, though less than 200 of the 2,000 in Aegean and Ionian Seas inhabited ■ No place more than 70 km [45 mls] from sea ■ Birthplace of European civilization & was centre of Western world 2,500 years ago ■ Athens has increased its population sixfold since 1945; now has 30% of total population and 60% of manufacturing capacity ■ Athens was home of ancient Olympics and host of the first modern games in 1896 ■ Highest smoking nation - about 3,500 cigarettes per adult per year ■ Ancient Greek is incomprehensible to the Greek layman ■ World's biggest merchant fleet (by ownership, not registry) ■ 90% of imports and exports are carried by water ■ Biggest budget deficit in OECD as % of GNP ■ Over 50% of working pop. engaged in agriculture ■ Income per head is about half that of most EC countries ■ Biggest budget deficit in OECD as % of GNP ■ 3 out of 4 of the 5 million tourists each year come from Western Europe

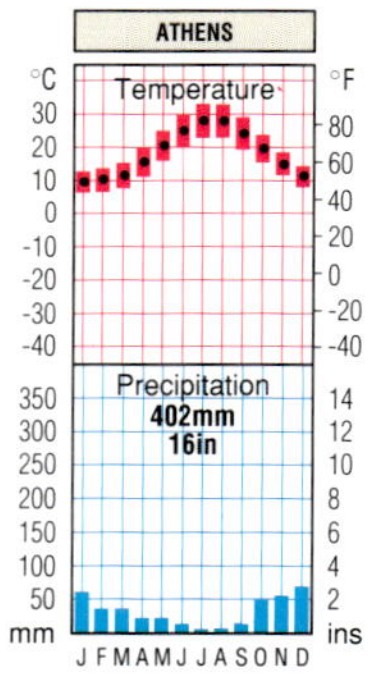

Athens has a climate typical of the eastern Mediterranean basin. A single maximum of rainfall occurs in winter and summers are dry, no rain falling in July or August on an average of one year in three. On hot summer days the calina, a dusty heat haze, is common. The east coast of Greece is sunny with over 2,700 hours of sunshine a year and has only about half the rainfall of the west. Winters are less mild than in the west.

ALBANIA

In the Albanian language the name of the country means 'land of the eagle' and the two-headed black eagle has been on the nation's flag since independence in 1912. The Communist star above the eagle was added in 1945.

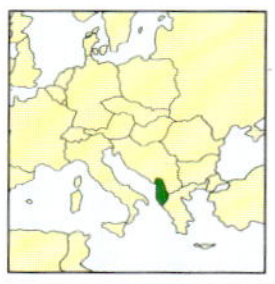

COUNTRY: People's Socialist Republic of Albania
AREA: 28,750 sq km [11,100 sq mls]
POPULATION: 3,250,000
CAPITAL (Population): Tirana (226,000)
GOVERNMENT: Unitary single-party socialist republic with unicameral legislature
ETHNIC GROUPS: Albanian 96%, Greek 2%, Romanian, Macedonian, Montenegrin, Gypsy
LANGUAGES: Albanian (official)
RELIGIONS: Muslim 21%, Christian 5%
NATIONAL DAY: 28 November; Independence Day (1912)
CURRENCY: Lek = 100 qindars
ANNUAL INCOME PER PERSON: $1,000
MAIN PRIMARY PRODUCTS: Copper, chrome, petroleum and natural gas, cereals, fruit, timber, tobacco
MAIN INDUSTRIES: Agriculture, petroleum refining, mining, food and tobacco processing, textiles
DEFENCE: 11.5% of national budget
POPULATION DENSITY: 113 per sq km [293 per sq ml]
LIFE EXPECTANCY: Female 75 yrs, Male 70 yrs
ADULT LITERACY: 63%
PRINCIPAL CITIES (Population): Tirana 226,000 Durrës 79,000 Elbasan 78,000 Shkoder 68,000 Vlorë 62,000

■ Rigid Communist state run by Enver Hoxha 1944-85 & virtually cut off from outside world until 1990 ■ Prices hardly changed for 30 years from 1950s ■ No official religions, though estimated 70% of population Muslim ■ Continuing dispute with Yugoslavia over province of Kosovo which has large Albanian population ■ No private cars ■ $^{2}/_{3}$ of population live in villages ■ On average Albanian women produce more children than any European country ■ Mother Theresa of Calcutta Albania's most famous citizen

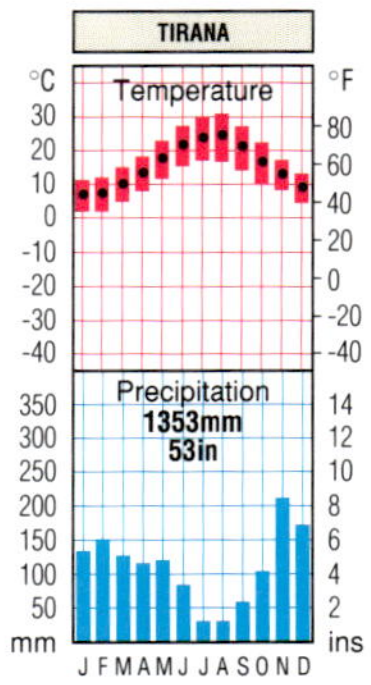

The Mediterranean type climate in the west, with hot and dry summers and cooler winters, changes in the mountains and valleys of the east and north, to become much wetter, with snow. All the country is hot and dry in the summer. In the coastal lowlands, the temperature rarely drops below freezing.

YUGOSLAVIA

The flag dates from the 1918 union of Serbia and Croatia with Slovenia and other Balkan provinces of the old Austro-Hungarian Empire. Yugoslavia began to fall apart in civil war when Croatia and Slovenia opted for independence in 1991.

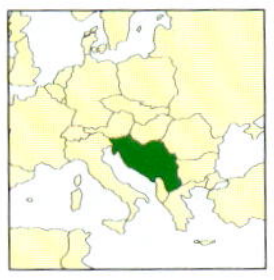

COUNTRY: Socialist Federal Republic of Yugoslavia
AREA: 255,800 sq km [98,764 sq mls]
POPULATION: 23,898,000
CAPITAL (Population): Belgrade (1,470,000)
GOVERNMENT: Federal socialist republic with a bicameral legislature
ETHNIC GROUPS: Serb 36%, Croat 20%, Bosnian Muslim 9%, Slovenian 8%, Albanian 8%, Macedonian 6%
LANGUAGES: Macedonian, Serbo-Croatian and Slovene (official)
RELIGIONS: Serbian Orthodox 35%, Roman Catholic 26%, Other-Christian 11%, Muslim 10%

■ Pre-civil war Yugoslavia had 2 alphabets, 3 languages, 4 religions, 5 nationalities & 6 provinces ■ Country was created after WWI by the union of Bosnia, Herzegovina, Slovenia, Croatia, Serbia, Montenegro and Macedonia ■ Population and area figures show pre-1991 status; final peace settlement likely to leave independent Croatia substantially smaller ■ Ethnic composition of much of country undergoing violent change ■ Old port of Dubrovnik and other historic cities badly damaged in fighting

CROATIA

The red, white and blue flag dates from 1848. During the Communist period a red star was set in its centre, to be replaced by the present coat of arms in 1990.

AREA: 56,500 sq km [21,800 sq mls]
POPULATION: 4,680,000
CAPITAL (Population): Zagreb (1,175,000)
ETHNIC GROUPS: Croats 75.1%, Serbs 11.5%

SLOVENIA

The Slovene flag based on that of Imperial Russia was adopted in 1848. As with Croatia, a red star adorned the flag throughout the Communist years. The present emblem appeared in 1991.

AREA: 20,300 sq km [7,800 sq mls]
POPULATION: 1,940,000
CAPITAL (Population): Ljubljana (305,000)
ETHNIC GROUPS: Slovenes 90.5%

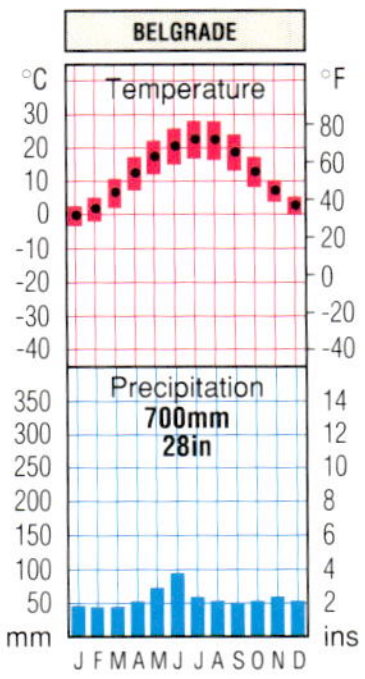

The mountains running parallel with the Adriatic coast restrict the Mediterranean-type climate of warm winters and hot dry summers to the narrow coastal strip. The mountains themselves, with the Alps in the north, have cold winters with snow. They also have local fierce winds, such as the Bora. Further inland there is a continental climate of hot summers and very cold winters. There is a range of temperature of over 20 degrees C [36 degrees F].

BULGARIA

The Slav colours of white, green and red were used in the Bulgarian flag from 1878. The national emblem, incorporating a lion (a symbol of Bulgaria since the 14th century), was first added to the flag in 1947.

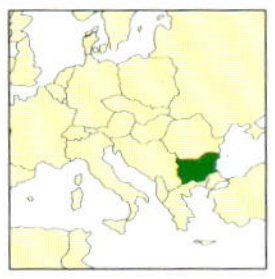

COUNTRY: Republic of Bulgaria
AREA: 110,910 sq km [42,822 sq mls]
POPULATION: 9,011,000
CAPITAL (Population): Sofia (1,129,000)
GOVERNMENT: Unitary single-party socialist republic with a unicameral legislature
ETHNIC GROUPS: Bulgaria 85%, Turkish 9%, Gypsy 3%
LANGUAGES: Bulgarian (official)
RELIGIONS: Eastern Orthodox 27%, Muslim 7%, Protestant 1%, Roman Catholic 1%
NATIONAL DAY: 3 March; Liberation from Ottoman rule (1878)
CURRENCY: Lev (leva) = 100 stotinki
ANNUAL INCOME PER PERSON: $2,210
MAIN PRIMARY PRODUCTS: Coal, oil and natural gas, lignite, cereals, fruit, cattle, sheep
MAIN INDUSTRIES: Agriculture, tobacco, iron and steel, textiles, chemicals, forestry, wine, oil and gas refining
EXPORTS: $1,779 per person
MAIN EXPORTS: Machinery and equipment 57%, foodstuffs, wine and tobacco 14%
MAIN EXPORT PARTNERS: CIS nations 57%, Germany 7%, Czechoslovakia 7%, Poland 7%, Libya 7%
IMPORTS: $1,653 per person
MAIN IMPORTS: Machinery and equipment 43%, fuels, mineral raw materials and metals 43%, chemicals and rubber 7%
MAIN IMPORT PARTNERS: CIS nations 57%, Germany 7%, Czechoslovakia 7%, Italy 7%, Poland 7%
DEFENCE: 6.1% of national budget
TOURISM: 7,594,000 visitors
POPULATION DENSITY: 81 per sq km [210 per sq ml]
INFANT MORTALITY: 14 per 1,000 live births
LIFE EXPECTANCY: Female 76 yrs, Male 70 yrs
ADULT LITERACY: 96%
PRINCIPAL CITIES (Population): Sofia 1,129,000 Plovdiv 357,000 Varna 306,000 Burgas 198,000 Ruse 190,000

■ Urban population increased from 1 in 5 in 1946 to 3 in 5 by 1990 ■ More than 7 million tourists visit every year, mostly the Black Sea coast ■ Became independent state (from Ottoman Empire) in 1908 ■ Unique among E. Europe's democratised former Soviet 'satellites' in re-electing Communist Party to power in April 1990 (under title of Socialists) ■ Bulgarian Cabernet Sauvignon was UK's biggest selling red wine in 1990 ■ Food output quadrupled since the 1950s

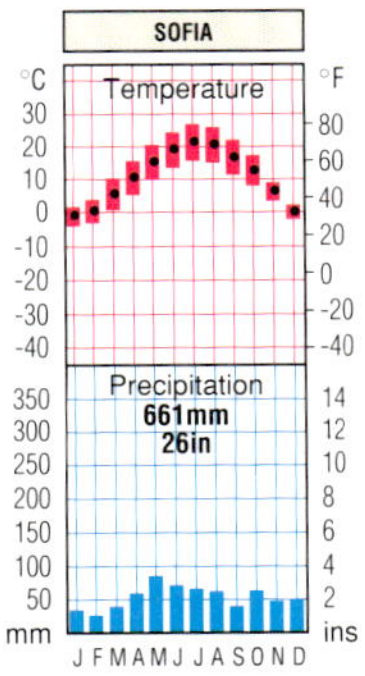

The climate of Bulgaria is one of hot summers, cold, but not severe winters and moderate rainfall, with a maximum April-Aug. This is changed by the influence of the nearby seas and the western mountains. The lowlands of the east and south have a much drier and warmer summer. The Danube lowlands are colder in winter with winds coming in from the continental interior. The temperatures are lower and the rain- and snowfall higher in the mountains of the west.

ROMANIA

Romania's colours come from the arms of the provinces that united to form the country in 1861, and the design was adopted in 1948. The central state coat of arms, added in 1965, was deleted in 1990 after the fall of the Ceaucescu regime.

COUNTRY: Romania
AREA: 237,500 sq km [91,699 sq mls]
POPULATION: 23,200,000
CAPITAL (Population): Bucharest (2,014,400)
GOVERNMENT: Following 1989 revolution, Council of National Salvation
ETHNIC GROUPS: Romanian 88%, Hungarian 8%
LANGUAGES: Romanian (official), Hungarian, German
RELIGIONS: Romanian Orthodox 70%, Greek Orthodox 10%, Muslim 1%
NATIONAL DAY: 23 August; Liberation Day (1945)
CURRENCY: Romanian leu = 100 bani
ANNUAL INCOME PER PERSON: $1,640
MAIN PRIMARY PRODUCTS: Cereals, sugar, fruit, vegetables, grapes, timber, livestock, fish, oil, natural gas, coal, lignite, iron ore, copper, salt, silver, gold, lead
MAIN INDUSTRIES: Agriculture, mining, iron and steel, chemicals, forestry, textiles, food processing
EXPORTS: $542 per person
MAIN EXPORTS: Machinery and transport equipment 38%, fuels 23%, chemicals 9%
MAIN EXPORT PARTNERS: CIS nations 24%, Italy 7%, Germany 1%, USA 6%, France 4%, Egypt 4%, Poland 4%, China 4%
IMPORTS: $458 per person
MAIN IMPORTS: Mineral fuels 53%, machinery 28%, chemicals 5%
MAIN IMPORT PARTNERS: CIS nations 26%, Egypt 12%, Germany 11%, Iran 7%, Poland 6%, China 4%
DEFENCE: 2.7% of national budget
TOURISM: 5,142,000 visitors
POPULATION DENSITY: 98 per sq km [253 per sq ml]
INFANT MORTALITY: 19 per 1,000 live births
LIFE EXPECTANCY: Female 74 yrs, Male 69 yrs
ADULT LITERACY: 96%
PRINCIPAL CITIES (Population): Bucharest 2,014,000 Brasov 351,000 Constanta 328,000 Timisoara 325,000 Iasi 313,000

■ Carpathian Mountains cover about 30% of land area ■ Iron Gates Gorge is 160 km [100 ml] stretch of River Danube ■ Around 3,500 glaciated lakes in Danube's delta region on Black Sea ■ Europe's largest Romany gypsy population ■ Agricultural workforce fell from 75% in 1950 to 30% in 1984 ■ Nicolae Ceaucescu only E. European head of state to receive knighthood from Queen of England; after 24 years of Socialist dictatorship he was executed on Christmas Day 1989 ■ Largest oil producer in E. Europe (exc. CIS nations) ■ Vlad Tepes (1456 –75), known as The Impaler, was immortalised by Bram Stoker as Dracula, the Transylvanian vampire count of the famous horror story

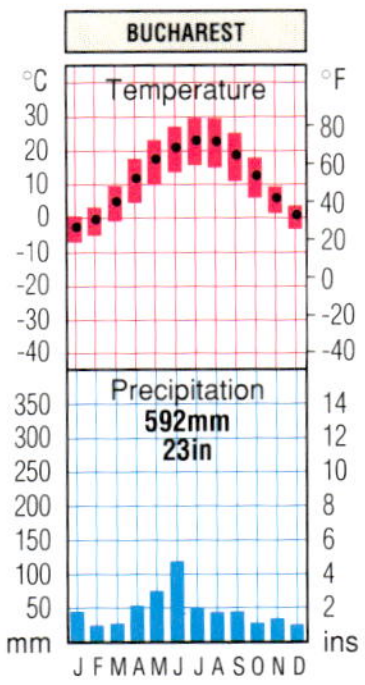

In general, central Europe has a large seasonal range of temperature and a summer rainfall maximum. Winter depressions which bring so much rain to north-west Europe are mostly prevented from reaching the east by persistent high pressure. At Bucharest the heaviest rains fall as thundery showers in spring and early summer when the air warms rapidly. With over 2,000 hours annually, Romania is one of the sunniest parts of Europe.

EURASIA – NORTH

CIS NATIONS

Formed in December 1991 on the formal dissolution of the USSR, the Commonwealth of Independent States is a loose and vaguely defined association that in 1992 included 12 of the old USSR's 15 republics. With no central authority, it seemed unlikely to be a durable institution.

■ Russia world's largest country; extends over 13% of world's land surface ■ Russians and Ukrainians form large minorities in most of the other 10 CIS nations ■ More than 100 languages spoken in the CIS

RUSSIA

The red, white and blue Russian flag was first adopted in 1799 but was suppressed after the 1917 Revolution. It was reintroduced on 22 August 1991.

AREA: 17,068,000 sq km [6,592,800 sq mls]
POPULATION: 147,400,000
CAPITAL (Population): Moscow (8,967,000)
CURRENCY: Ruble = 100 kopecks
POPULATION DENSITY: 8.6 per sq km [22 per sq ml]
PRINCIPAL CITIES (Population): Moscow 8,967,000 St Petersburg 5,020,000 Nizhni Novgorod 1,438,000 Novosibirsk 1,436,000 Yekaterinburg 1,367,000

UKRAINE

The Ukrainian national colours, of heraldic origin, first appeared in 1848. The flag was used briefly in 1918-20 before gaining official status in 1991.

AREA: 604,000 sq km [233,300 sq mls]
POPULATION: 51,800,000
CAPITAL (Population): Kiev (2,587000)
POPULATION DENSITY: 86 per sq km [222 per sq ml]
PRINCIPAL CITIES (Population): Kiev 2,587,000 Kharkhov 1,611,000 Dnepropetrovsk 1,179,000 Donetsk 1,110,000

ARMENIA

AREA: 30,000 sq km [11,600 sq mls]
POPULATION: 3,300,000
CAPITAL (Population): Yerevan (1,199,000)

AZERBAIJAN

AREA: 87,000 sq km [33,600 sq mls]
POPULATION: 7,100,000
CAPITAL (Population): Baku (1,757,000)

BELORUSSIA

AREA: 208,000 sq km [80,350 sq mls]
POPULATION: 10,300,000
CAPITAL (Population): Minsk (1,589,000)

GEORGIA

AREA: 70,000 sq km [27,000 sq mls]
POPULATION: 5,500,000
CAPITAL (Population): Tbilisi (1,194,000)

KAZAKHSTAN

AREA: 2,717,000 sq km [1,049,500 sq mls]
POPULATION: 16,700,000
CAPITAL (Population): Alma-Ata (1,108,000)

KIRGHIZIA

AREA: 199,000 sq km [76,900 sq mls]
POPULATION: 4,400,000
CAPITAL (Population): Bishkek (616,000)

MOLDAVIA

AREA: 34,000 sq km [13,100 sq mls]
POPULATION: 4,400,000
CAPITAL (Population): Kishinev (663,000)

TAJIKISTAN

AREA: 143,000 sq km [55,250 sq mls]
POPULATION: 5,300,000
CAPITAL (Population): Dushanbe (595,000)

TURKMENISTAN

AREA: 488,000 sq km [188,500 sq mls]
POPULATION: 3,600,000
CAPITAL (Population): Ashkhabad (382,000)

UZBEKISTAN

AREA: 447,000 sq km [172,500 sq mls]
POPULATION: 20,300,000
CAPITAL (Population): Tashkent (2,073,000)

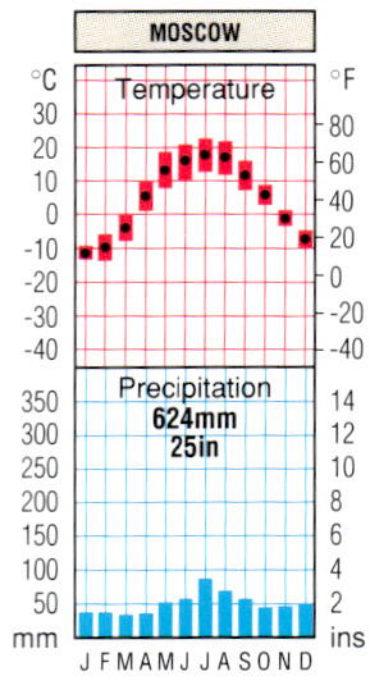

Despite a large temperature range and cold winters, Moscow has a less extreme continental climate than more easterly parts of Russia or Belorussia. Prevailing westerly winds and absence of mountains allow the Atlantic Ocean to extend its influence deep into the continent. Rainfall is well distributed with a slight summer maximum. Winters are cloudy with frequent snow and a very small daily variation in temperature.

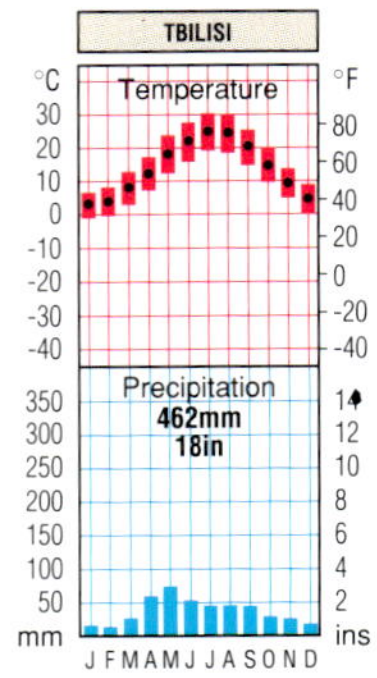

Nestling between the Caucasus and the mountains of Armenia, the Georgian capital Tbilisi is sheltered both from the winter cold of central Asia and the heavy rain of the Black Sea coast. The rather sparse rainfall is effective in spring but mostly evaporates quickly in the heat of summer when conditions resemble those of the Mediterranean region. Winters are less severe than might be expected in a continental location.

JAPAN

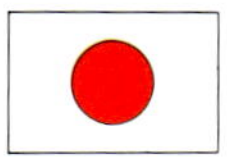

The geographical position of Japan in the East is expressed in the name of the country, Nihon-Koku (Land of the Rising Sun) and in the flag. Officially adopted in 1870, the design had been used by Japanese emperors for many centuries.

COUNTRY: Japan
AREA: 377,800 sq km [145,869 sq mls]
POPULATION: 123,537,000
CAPITAL (Population): Tokyo (11,829,000)
GOVERNMENT: Constitutional monarchy with a bicameral legislature
ETHNIC GROUPS: Japanese 99%, Korean, Chinese
LANGUAGES: Japanese (official), Korean, Chinese
RELIGIONS: Shinto 93%, Buddhism 74%, Christian 1% (Most Japanese consider themselves to be both Shinto and Buddhist)
NATIONAL DAY: 23 December; the Emperor's birthday
CURRENCY: Yen = 100 sen
ANNUAL INCOME PER PERSON: $25,430
SOURCE OF INCOME: Agriculture 3%, Industry 41%, Services 57%
MAIN PRIMARY PRODUCTS: Rice, vegetables, timber, fish, copper, gold, sulphur, natural gas, coal, lead
MAIN INDUSTRIES: Iron and steel, electrical and electronic equipment, cars, ships, textiles, chemicals, food processing, forestry, petroleum refining
EXPORTS: $2,235 per person
MAIN EXPORTS: Machinery, electrical, electronic equipment 36%, vehicles and transport equipment 20%, iron and steel 6%, chemicals 6%, textiles 3%, ships 2%
MAIN EXPORT PARTNERS: USA 84%, South Korea 6%, Germany 6%, Taiwan 5%, Hong Kong 4%, UK 3%, China 3%
IMPORTS: $1,713 per person
MAIN IMPORTS: Petrol and petroleum products 18%, food and live animals 14%, machinery and transport equipment 11%, metals 10%, chemicals 8%, timber and cork 4%, textile fibres 2%
MAIN IMPORT PARTNERS: USA 21%, Indonesia 5%, South Korea 5%, Australia 5%, China 4%, Saudi Arabia 4%, Taiwan 4%
EDUCATIONAL EXPENDITURE: 9% of national budget
DEFENCE: 6.6% of national budget
TOTAL ARMED FORCES: 247,000
TOURISM: 1,939,000 visitors
ROADS: 1,127,500 km [700,600 mls]
RAILWAYS: 25,776 km [16,016 mls]
POPULATION DENSITY: 327 per sq km [847 per sq ml]
URBAN POPULATION: 77%
POPULATION GROWTH: 0.4% per year
BIRTHS: 10 per 1,000 population
DEATHS: 6 per 1,000 population
INFANT MORTALITY: 5 per 1,000 live births
LIFE EXPECTANCY: Female 82 yrs, Male 76 yrs
POPULATION PER DOCTOR: 663
ADULT LITERACY: 99%
PRINCIPAL CITIES (Population): Tokyo 11,829,000 Yokohama 2,993,000 Osaka 2,636,000 Nagoya 2,116,000 Fukuoka 1,160,000 Sapporo 1,543,000 Kyoto 1,479,000 Kobe 1,411,000 Kawasaki 1,089,000 Kitakyushu 1,056,000 Hiroshima 1,044,000

■ Average farm size only 1.4 hectares [3.5 acres] ■ Rice yields among world's highest; nearly half of all farmland devoted to rice ■ World's greatest fishing nation and biggest fish-eating nation ■ World's longest rail tunnel (54 km [33.5 mls]), links islands of Hokkaido and Honshu ■ Economic phenomenon of the late 20th century, now world's 2nd most powerful economy after USA ■ Exports represent only about 10% of GDP ■ Tokyo Stock Exchange world's largest in terms of value of shares traded ■ World's largest merchant shipping fleet with 9,830 ships ■ Less than 3% of world pop., but 10% of world's income ■ Dominate world markets in audio, video, photographic equipment & many areas of microelectronics ■ Income per head higher and more equitably distributed than in many European countries ■ Average Japanese worker takes 101 days off per year (including weekends) compared with 140 in Europe ■ Asia's biggest aid donor ■ Emperor's dynasty dates from about 200AD ■ Asia's highest divorce rate ■ Japanese writing has thousands of characters

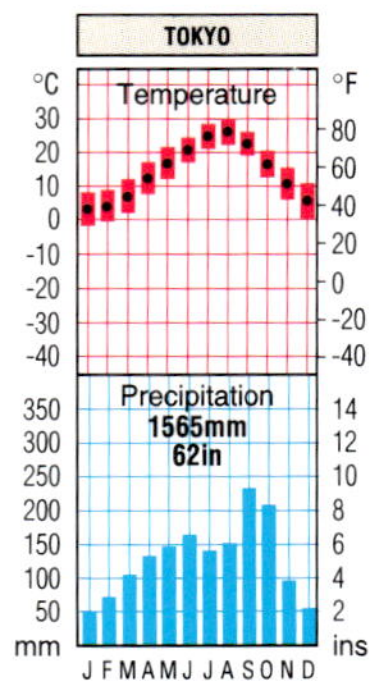

Despite its maritime location, Tokyo has a large annual range of temperature due to the seasonal reversal of wind, blowing from the cold heart of Asia in winter and from the warm Pacific in summer. Winter weather is usually fine and sunny but cold dry north-westerly winds often blow and frost may occur as late as April. Further north, in Hokkaido, snow is frequent. Summer in Tokyo is hot and humid with abundant rainfall.

KOREA, NORTH

The Korean Democratic People's Republic has flown this flag since the country was split into two separate states in 1948. The colours are those of the traditional Korean standard, but in a new Communist design with a red star.

COUNTRY: Democratic People's Republic of Korea
AREA: 120,540 sq km [46,540 sq mls]
POPULATION: 21,773,000
CAPITAL (Population): Pyongyang (2,639,000)
GOVERNMENT: Constitutional monarchy with a bicameral legislature
ETHNIC GROUPS: Korean 99%
LANGUAGES: Korean (official), Chinese
RELIGIONS: Traditional beliefs 16%, Chondogyo 14%, Buddhist 2%, Christian 1%
NATIONAL DAY: 15 August; Independence Day (1945)
CURRENCY: North Korean won = 100 chon
ANNUAL INCOME PER PERSON: $900
MAIN PRIMARY PRODUCTS: Coal, rice, iron ore
MAIN INDUSTRIES: Agriculture, iron and steel, chemicals, engineering, cement
MAIN EXPORTS: Iron and other metals, agricultural products, textiles
MAIN EXPORT PARTNERS: CIS nations 44%, Japan 15%, China 13%
MAIN IMPORTS: Crude petroleum, coal, machinery, transport equipment, chemicals, grain
MAIN IMPORT PARTNERS: CIS nations 35%, China 19%, Japan 13%
DEFENCE: 24% of national budget
POPULATION DENSITY: 181 per sq km [468 per sq ml]
INFANT MORTALITY: 36 per 1,000 live births
LIFE EXPECTANCY: Female 74 yrs, Male 68 yrs
ADULT LITERACY: 90%
PRINCIPAL CITIES (Population): Pyongyang 2,639,000 Hamhung 775,000 Chongjin 754,000

■ Separated from southern part of Korea in 1948 ■ Only 18% of land cultivated ■ Has rich mineral deposits: most major base metals & gold, silver & tungsten ■ Coal supplies 70% of energy needs ■ Economically lags far behind South Korea ■ Defence spending 15% of total state spending ■ Ruled by Kim Il-Sung since 1948 ■ Few western visitors allowed entry

KOREA, SOUTH

Adopted in 1950, South Korea's flag is the traditional white of peace. The central emblem signifies nature's opposing forces: the black symbols stand for the four seasons, the points of the compass and the sun, moon, Earth and heaven.

COUNTRY: Republic of Korea
AREA: 99,020 sq km [38,232 sq mls]
POPULATION: 43,302,000
CAPITAL (Population): Seoul (10,513,000)
GOVERNMENT: Unitary multi-party republic with a unicameral legislature
ETHNIC GROUPS: Korean 99%
LANGUAGES: Korean (official)
RELIGIONS: Buddhist 20%, Protestant 16%, Roman Catholic 5%, Confucian 1%
NATIONAL DAY: 15 August; Independence Day (1945)
CURRENCY: South Korean won = 100 chon
ANNUAL INCOME PER PERSON: $5,400
MAIN PRIMARY PRODUCTS: Tungsten, rice, fish
MAIN INDUSTRIES: Agriculture, chemicals, electronic and electrical goods, shipbuilding, iron and steel
EXPORTS: $1,472 per person
MAIN EXPORTS: Transport equipment 11%, electrical machinery 9%, footwear 6%, textile fabrics 5%
MAIN EXPORT PARTNERS: USA 39%, Japan 18%, Hong Kong 5%, Germany 4%, UK 3%, Canada 3%
IMPORTS: $1,450 per person
MAIN IMPORTS: Petroleum and petroleum products 11%, electronic components 6%, chemicals 5%
MAIN IMPORT PARTNERS: Japan 33%, USA 21%, Germany 4%, Australia 3%
DEFENCE: 32.5% of national budget
TOURISM: 1,875,000 visitors
POPULATION DENSITY: 437 per sq km [1,133 per sq ml]
INFANT MORTALITY: 21 per 1,000 live births
LIFE EXPECTANCY: Female 74 yrs, Male 68 yrs
ADULT LITERACY: 93%
PRINCIPAL CITIES (Population): Seoul 10,513,000 Pusan 3,754,000 Taegu 2,206,000 Inchon 1,604,000 Kwangju 1,165,000

■ Used to be called 'Land of the Morning Calm' ■ Only 23% of land cultivated ■ First records of country date back to 1st century AD ■ Oldest surviving printed work is Dharani Scroll or Sutra from wooden printing blocks found in foundations of Pulguk Sa Pagoda, Kyongju ■ Economic miracle has, like Japan's, been achieved on basis of very slender natural resources ■ Major presence in world export markets, strength of economy in shipbuilding, steel and consumer electronics ■ Imported fuel meets 75% of energy needs ■ Korean language uses phonetic alphabet, unlike picture writing of China and Japan

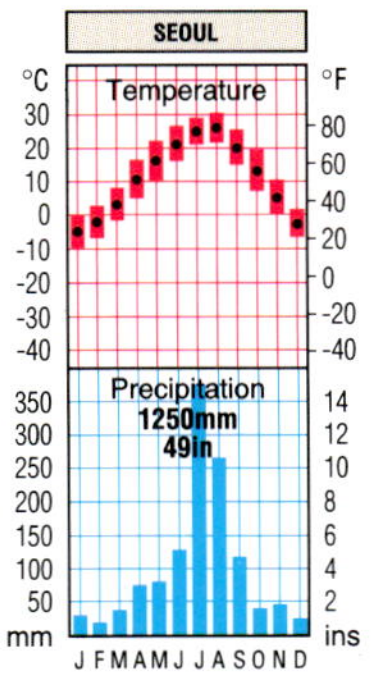

Strong north-westerly winds from central Asia give cold, dry weather in winter. Snow occurs on the western slopes of the mountains to the east of Seoul. In total contrast, summer is hot and wet, the rapid transition giving rise to sea fog around the coasts of Korea in spring as warmer air from the south moves over the cold water surface. Most of the rain falls in the summer half of the year.

CHINA

Red, the traditional colour of both China and Communism, was chosen for the People's Republic flag in 1949. The large star represents the Communist Party programme, the small stars represent the four principal social classes.

COUNTRY: People's Republic of China
AREA: 9,596,960 sq km [3,705,386 sq mls]
POPULATION: 1,139,060,000
CAPITAL (Population): Beijing (9,750,000)
GOVERNMENT: Single-party People's Republic with unicameral legislature
ETHNIC GROUPS: Han (Chinese) 93%, Chuang 1.3%
LANGUAGES: Mandarin Chinese (official); in the south and west, local dialects are spoken
RELIGIONS: Chinese folk-religionist 20%, Buddhist 6%, Muslim 2%, Christian 0.2%
NATIONAL DAY: 1 October; Proclamation of People's Republic (1949)
CURRENCY: Renminbi (yuan) = 10 jiao = 100 fen
ANNUAL INCOME PER PERSON: $370
MAIN PRIMARY PRODUCTS: Antimony, coal, fish, gold, iron ore, manganese, natural gas, petroleum, phosphates, pigs, salt, sheep, timber, tungsten
MAIN INDUSTRIES: Agriculture, cement, forestry, textiles, steel, bicycles, petroleum, newsprint, fertilizers
EXPORTS: $46 per person
MAIN EXPORTS: Manufactured goods 19%, food and live animals 16%, mineral fuels 13%, chemicals 6%
MAIN EXPORT PARTNERS: Hong Kong 32%, Japan 16%, USA 10%, Singapore 1%, UK 1%
IMPORTS: $52 per person
MAIN IMPORTS: Machinery and transport equipment 40%, chemicals 9%, raw materials 7%, food and live animals 5%
MAIN IMPORT PARTNERS: Japan 28%, Hong Kong 14%, USA 12%, Germany 4%
DEFENCE: 7.7% of national budget
TOTAL ARMED FORCES: 3,030,000
TOURISM: 10,760,000 visitors
ROADS: 942,000 km [588,750 mls]
RAILWAYS: 52,487 km [32,804 mls]
POPULATION DENSITY: 119 per sq km [307 per sq ml]
URBAN POPULATION: 21%
POPULATION GROWTH: 1.4% per year
BIRTHS: 21 per 1,000 population
DEATHS: 7 per 1,000 population
INFANT MORTALITY: 27 per 1,000 live births
LIFE EXPECTANCY: Female 73 yrs, Male 69 yrs
POPULATION PER DOCTOR: 1,000
ADULT LITERACY: 69%
PRINCIPAL CITIES (Population): Shanghai 12,320,000 Beijing 9,750,000 Tianjin 5,459,000 Shenyang 4,285,000 Wuhan 3,493,000 Guangzhou 3,359,000 Chongqing 2,832,000 Harbin 2,668,000 Chengdu 2,642,000 Xi'an 2,387,000 Zibo 2,329,000 Nanjing 2,290,000 Nanchang 2,289,000 Lupanshui 2,247,000

■ World's most populous country; pop. of over 1,000 million represents 25% of world total ■ World's third largest country, after Russia and Canada ■ Greatest number of international frontiers in world - 15 neighbouring countries ■ Turfan depression one of lowest areas on Earth (-154 m [-508 ft]) ■ Everest is on border ■ Yellow River, second longest in China, flowing for 4,840 km [3,005 mls], so called because of huge quantities of silt it carries; also called China's sorrow because of flooding, but this has been curbed by dykes ■ Only 10% of land suitable for agriculture but farmers & their families make up 75% of pop. ■ World's largest producer of rice ■ World's leading producer of cotton textiles ■ World's biggest fish farmers ■ Self-sufficient in oil ■ Great Wall, world's longest fortification, runs for 3,460 km [2,150 mls] with branches adding further 2,865 km [1,780 mls]; original structure completed 221-206BC, but present fabric built 1368-1644 ■ Imperial palace in Beijing covers 72 hectares [178 acres] & surrounded by world's largest moat ■ Over 30 cities have pop. of over 1 million ■ Life expectancy more than doubled since 1949 ■ Income per capita 1.5% that of Japan's ■ About 12 million people were killed in 1947-9 civil war ■ Officially atheist but large numbers of Buddhists, Muslims & Christians as well as followers of two home-grown faiths, Taoism & Confucianism ■ More than 100 million bicycles in use

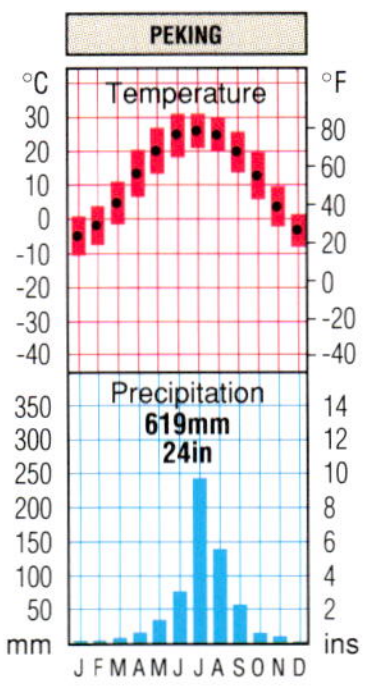

The climate of China is controlled by the air-masses of Asia and the Pacific, and the mountains in the western half of the country. In the winter the cold, dry Siberian air blows southwards giving low temperatures in Peking. In the summer the tropical Pacific air dominates, bring high temperatures and rainfall. In summer the temperature in eastern China is high with little difference between north and south; in winter there is over 20°C [36°F] difference. The annual rain total decreases from over 2,000 mm [80 in] in the south to the desert conditions of the north-west.

ASIA – EAST

MONGOLIA

On Mongolia's flag the red for Communism appears with blue, the country's national colour. The gold star stands for endurance and the Communist Party and the traditional Mongolian soyonbo symbol under the star represents freedom.

■ World's largest landlocked country ■ Most of country 1,500 m [4,900 ft] above sea level ■ 25% of country occupied by Gobi desert; cultivated land less than 1% of land ■ 25% of pop. live in Ulan Bator, world's coldest capital ■ Leading role of Communist Party erased from constitution in 1990

COUNTRY: Mongolian People's Republic
AREA: 1,566,500 sq km [604,826 sq mls]
POPULATION: 2,190,000
CAPITAL (Population): Ulan Bator (500,000)
GOVERNMENT: Single-party republic with unicam. legisl.
ETHNIC GROUPS: Khalkha Mongol 77%, Kazakh 5%
LANGUAGES: Mongolian (official)
RELIGIONS: Traces of Buddhist Lamaism and Shamanism
NATIONAL DAY: 11 July; Independence Day (1921)
CURRENCY: Tugrik = 100 möngös
ANNUAL INCOME PER PERSON: $500
MAIN PRIMARY PRODUCTS: Coal, lignite and fluorspar
MAIN INDUSTRIES: Animal herding, textiles, cement, coal
DEFENCE: 12% of national budget
POPULATION DENSITY: 1.4 per sq km [3.6 per sq ml]
LIFE EXPECTANCY: Female 67 yrs, Male 63 yrs
ADULT LITERACY: 90%

TAIWAN

In 1928 the Nationalists adopted this design as China's national flag and used it in the long struggle against Mao Tse-tung's Communist army. When they were forced to retreat to Taiwan (then Formosa) in 1949, the flag went with them.

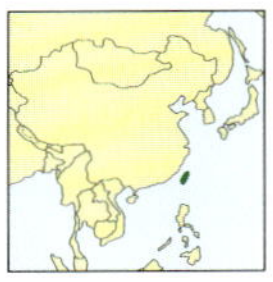

■ Formerly known by Portuguese as Isla Formosa, meaning beautiful island ■ Predominantly Chinese pop. originated from mainland China ■ General Chiang Kai Shek's Nationalist Chinese army, & its supporters, together numbering 2 million, took refuge in 1949 in Taiwan, after defeat by Mao Tse-tung's Communist army ■ 40% of electricity nuclear generated ■ In 1980, joined world's top 20 trading nations ■ Highest standard of living in East Asia outside Japan

COUNTRY: Taiwan (Republic of China)
AREA: 36,000 sq km [13,900 sq mls]
POPULATION: 20,300,000
CAPITAL (Population): Taipei (2,680,000)
GOVERNMENT: Unitary republic with a unicameral legisl.
ETHNIC GROUPS: Taiwanese 84%, Chinese (mainland) 14%, Aborigine 2%
LANGUAGES: Mandarin Chinese
RELIGIONS: Chinese folk-religionist 48%, Buddhist 43%, Christian 7%, Muslim 1%
NATIONAL DAY: 10 October; Republic proclaimed (1911)
CURRENCY: New Taiwan $ = 100 cents
ANNUAL INCOME PER PERSON: $6,600
MAIN INDUSTRIES: Textiles, electrical and electronic goods, chemicals and fertilizers, plastics, agriculture, fishing
MAIN EXPORTS: Plastic goods 9%, calculating machines 7%, clothing 6%, thermionic goods and transistors 3%
MAIN IMPORTS: Petroleum and petroleum products 7%, raw cotton 2%, electrical switchgear 2%
DEFENCE: 7.7% of national budget
POPULATION DENSITY: 554 per sq km [1,435 per sq ml]
INFANT MORTALITY: 7 per 1,000 live births
LIFE EXPECTANCY: Female 76 yrs, Male 71 yrs
ADULT LITERACY: 91%
PRINCIPAL CITIES (Population): Taipei 2,680,000 Kaohsiung 1,343,000 Tai-chung 715,000 Tainan 657,000 Chilung 349,000

HONG KONG

Hong Kong has flown the Blue Ensign since 1841 when it became a British dependent territory. The coat of arms dates from 1959, and includes the British lion and the Chinese dragon. In 1997 Hong Kong will revert to Chinese government control.

■ In 1898 British signed 99-year lease with Chinese government; country will revert to Chinese rule in 1997 ■ Mainstays of economy light manufac-turing, financial services & shipping ■ No natural resources & most water comes from reservoirs in China

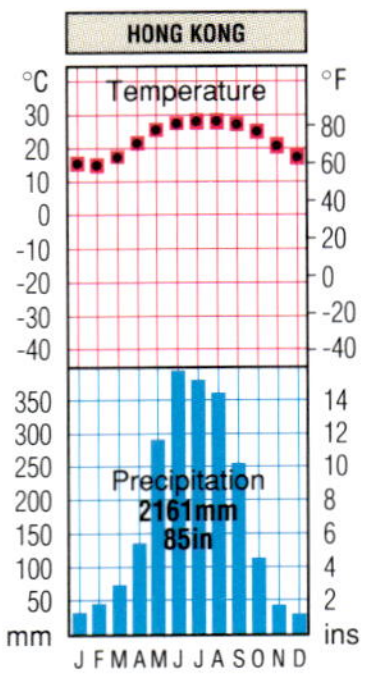

Situated on the south coast of China and within the tropics, Hong Kong experiences the full power of the south-east Asian monsoon. Winter is mild and has enough rain to keep the land green. The long summer is hot and humid with heavy rain, particularly between May and September. Typhoons occur mainly between June and October. Many swing northwards towards Japan but those which cross the coast can do great damage.

COUNTRY: Crown Colony of Hong Kong
AREA: 1,071 sq km [413 sq mls]
POPULATION: 5,801,000
GOVERNMENT: UK appointed governor with bicameral legislative assembly
ETHNIC GROUPS: Chinese 98%, Others, incl. European 2%
LANGUAGES: English and Chinese (official)
RELIGIONS: Buddhist, Confucianist, Taoist, 90%, Christian 8%, Muslim, Hindu Sikh
NATIONAL DAY: Christian and Chinese festivals, Queen's official birthday, 29 Aug., Liberation Day
CURRENCY: Hong Kong $ = 100 cents
ANNUAL INCOME PER PERSON: $11,540
MAIN PRIMARY PRODUCTS: Pigs, poultry, fish, vegetables
MAIN INDUSTRIES: Textiles, electronics, watches, plastic goods, engineering, agric. and fishing
MAIN EXPORTS: Textiles, clothing, plastic and light metal prod., electronic goods
MAIN IMPORTS: Machinery, manufactures, chemicals
DEFENCE: UK responsibility
POPULATION DENSITY: 5,416 per sq km [14,029 per sq ml]
LIFE EXPECTANCY: Female 80 yrs, Male 74 yrs
ADULT LITERACY: 85%

MACAU

COUNTRY: Chinese territory under Portuguese administration
AREA: 16 sq km [6 sq mls]
POPULATION: 479,000

PHILIPPINES

The eight rays of the large sun represent the eight provinces that led the revolt against Spanish rule in 1898 and the three smaller stars stand for the three main island groups of the country. The flag was formally adopted in 1946.

■ 7,107 islands stretch for 1,800 km [1,120 mls]; together their coastline is longer than that of USA ■ Only predominantly Christian country in Asia, named after Philip II of Spain ■ Ocean trench near Mindanao one of world's deepest (10,540 m [34,578 ft or 6.5 mls]) ■ Over 100 cultural & racial groups, each with own language or dialect ■ Most westernised Asian country ■ Mining (of copper, gold & nickel) main source of export earnings ■ Spanish ruled country 1565-1898 USA 'bought' Philippines from Spain at end of 19th century. US ruled 1898-1946 ■ Estimated 40% of Philipino doctors practising abroad, mostly in USA

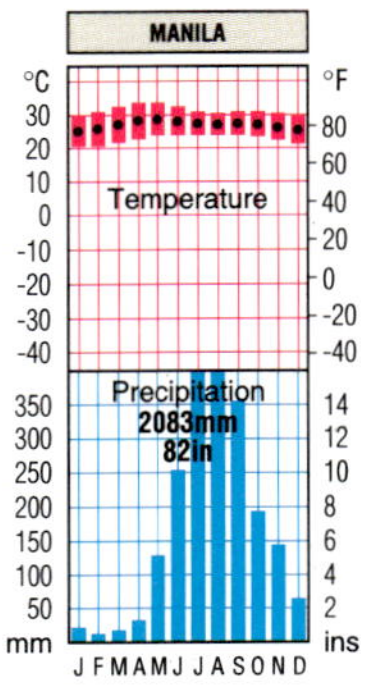

The climate of the Philippines is tropical, the temperature, except in the mountains, rarely dropping below 20°C [68°F]. There is a dry season between about Dec.- April, but there is very high rainfall often associated with typhoons in the rest of the year, especially July and Aug. The latter is particularly true in the eastern Pacific-facing islands and coastlands. The cooler and drier seasons usually coincide.

COUNTRY: Republic of the Philippines
AREA: 300,000 sq km [115,300 sq mls]
POPULATION: 61,480,000
CAPITAL (Population): Manila (1,728,000)
GOVERNMENT: Unitary republic with a bicameral legisl.
ETHNIC GROUPS: Tagalog 30%, Cebuano 24%, Ilocano 10%, Hiligaynon Ilongo 9%, Bicol 6%, Samar-Leyte 4%
LANGUAGES: Philipino and English (official), Spanish
RELIGIONS: Roman Catholic 84%, Aglipayan 6%, Muslim 4%, Protestant 4%
NATIONAL DAY: 12 June; Independence Day (1946)
CURRENCY: Philippine peso = 100 centavos
ANNUAL INCOME PER PERSON: $730
MAIN PRIMARY PRODUCTS: Copper, coal, iron, nickel, chrome, rice, maize, sugar cane, coconuts, abaca, tobacco, rubber, coffee, pineapples
MAIN INDUSTRIES: Agriculture, food processing, textiles, chemicals, mining, timber, fishing
MAIN EXPORTS: Semiconductor devices 10%, clothing 10%, coconut oil 7%, electronic goods 6%, copper metal 3%, fish 3%, timber 3%
MAIN EXPORT PARTNERS: USA 35%, Japan 17%, Neths. 5%, Germany 5%, Hong Kong 5%, UK 5%
MAIN IMPORTS: Mineral fuels 19%, parts for electrical equipment 11%, machinery 8%, electrical machinery 7%, base metals 6%, chemicals 5%, transport equipment 2%
MAIN IMPORT PARTNERS: USA 22%, Japan 17%, Taiwan 6%, Kuwait 5%, Hong Kong 5%, Germany 4%
DEFENCE: 14.7% of national budget
POPULATION DENSITY: 205 per sq km [531 per sq ml]
INFANT MORTALITY: 40 per 1,000 live births
LIFE EXPECTANCY: Female 67 yrs, Male 63 yrs
ADULT LITERACY: 86%
PRINCIPAL CITIES (Population): Manila 1,728,000 Quezon City 1,326,000 Cebu 552,000 Caloocan 525,000

INDONESIA

While the colours date back to the Middle Ages, they were adopted by political groups in the struggle against the Netherlands in the 1920s and became the national flag in 1945, when Indonesia finally proclaimed its independence.

COUNTRY: Republic of Indonesia
AREA: 1,904,570 sq km [735,354 sq mls]
POPULATION: 179,300,000
CAPITAL (Population): Jakarta (7,348,000)
GOVERNMENT: Unitary multi-party republic with bicameral legislature
ETHNIC GROUPS: Javanese 40%, Sundanese 15%, Bahasa Indonesian 12%, Madurese 5%
LANGUAGES: Bahasa Indonesia (official), Javanese, Sundanese, Dutch
RELIGIONS: Muslim 87%, Christian 10%, Hindu 2%, Buddhist 1%
NATIONAL DAY: 17 August; Anniversary of the Proclamation of Independence (1945)
CURRENCY: Indonesian rupiah = 100 sen
ANNUAL INCOME PER PERSON: $560
MAIN PRIMARY PRODUCTS: Rice, cassava, sweet potatoes, sugar cane, soya beans, coffee, tobacco, tea, rubber, timber, fish, oil and natural gas, bauxite, silver, copper
MAIN INDUSTRIES: Agriculture, mining, oil refining, fishing, textiles, cement, fertilizers, chemicals, forestry
MAIN EXPORTS: Crude petroleum 35%, natural gas 14%, wood and cork manufacture 11%, coffee, tea, cocoa, spices 6%, rubber 6%, timber 2%, metals 2%
MAIN IMPORTS: Machinery 30%, chemicals 19%, iron and steel 15%, petroleum and petroleum products 9%, transport equipment 8%, crude materials 8%, food and live animals 5%
EDUCATIONAL EXPENDITURE: 9% of national budget
DEFENCE: 8% of national budget
TOTAL ARMED FORCES: 285,000
TOURISM: 900,000 visitors
POPULATION DENSITY: 94 per sq km [244 per sq ml]
URBAN POPULATION: 29%
POPULATION GROWTH: 1.6% per year
BIRTHS: 28 per 1,000 population
DEATHS: 11 per 1,000 population
INFANT MORTALITY: 74 per 1,000 live births
LIFE EXPECTANCY: Female 60 yrs, Male 57 yrs
POPULATION PER DOCTOR: 9,464
ADULT LITERACY: 74%
PRINCIPAL CITIES (Population): Jakarta 7,348,000 Surabaya 2,224,000 Medan 1,806,000 Bandung 1,567,000 Semarang 1,206,000

■ World's largest island chain with about 13,000 islands, of which less than half are inhabited ■ Over 100 active volcanoes; eruption of Krakatau in 1883 killed 30,000 people - world's most violent & loudest recorded explosion could be heard 5,000 km [3,000 mls] away ■ Java world's most densely pop. island (690 per sq km [1,790 per sq ml]) ■ Java only 7% of land yet contains 60% of pop. ■ Jakarta largest city in S.E. Asia with over 7 million pop. ■ World's most populous Muslim country ■ Oil & gas 50% of domestic product & export earnings ■ One of world's leading producers of rubber & major source of tea & coffee ■ 360 ethnic groups & over 250 languages & dialects spoken ■ Javanese dominate most spheres of Indonesian life ■ Home of world's longest insect, giant stick insect - *Pharnacia serratipes* - females have measured up to 330 mm [13 in] long ■ World's largest flower found in Sumatra. Named *Rafflesia* after Sir Stamford Raffles, up to 1 m across

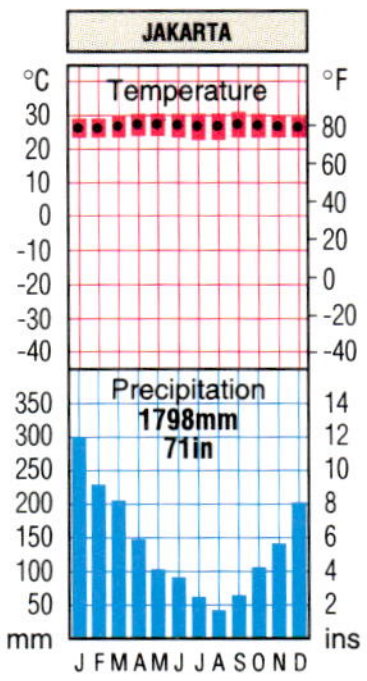

The most remarkable feature of Jakarta's climate is the almost constant high temperature throughout the year. This is due to its location on the shores of the hot Java Sea and the uniform intensity of the midday sun and duration of daylight with an average of over 6 hours of sunshine a day. Rainfall is heaviest in the southern summer, most of it falling in thunderstorms which occur on average 136 days a year.

SINGAPORE

Adopted in 1959, this flag was retained when Singapore broke away from the Federation of Malaysia in 1963. The crescent stands for the nation's ascent and the stars for its aims of democracy, peace, progress, justice and equality.

COUNTRY: Republic of Singapore
AREA: 618 sq km [239 sq mls]
POPULATION: 3,003,000
CAPITAL (Population): Singapore (2,680,000)
GOVERNMENT: Unitary multi-party republic with a unicameral legislature
ETHNIC GROUPS: Chinese 76%, Malay 15%, Indian 7%
LANGUAGES: Chinese, Malay, Tamil, English (all official)
RELIGIONS: Buddhist 28%, Christian 19%, Muslim 16%, Taoist 13%, Hindu 5%
NATIONAL DAY: 9 August; Independence Day (1965)
CURRENCY: Singapore dollar = 100 cents
ANNUAL INCOME PER PERSON: $12,310
MAIN PRIMARY PRODUCTS: Rubber, coconuts, fruit, fish
MAIN INDUSTRIES: Oil refining, oil drilling equipment, chemicals, textiles, shipbuilding, electronic goods
EXPORTS: $16,671 per person
MAIN EXPORTS: Office machines 14%, petroleum products 12%, telecommunications apparatus 10%, clothing 3%, scientific instruments 2%
MAIN EXPORT PARTNERS: USA 24%, Malaysia 14%, Japan 9%, Hong Kong 6%, Thailand 6%, Germany 4%
IMPORTS: $18,536 per person
MAIN IMPORTS: Crude petroleum 9%, office machines 5%, telecommunications equipment 5%, petroleum products 5%, electric power machinery 4%
MAIN IMPORT PARTNERS: Japan 22%, USA 16%, Malaysia 15%, Taiwan 5%, Saudi Arabia 4%
DEFENCE: 20.7% of national budget
TOURISM: 3,373,000 visitors
POPULATION DENSITY: 4,859 per sq km [12,585 per sq ml]
INFANT MORTALITY: 8 per 1,000 live births
LIFE EXPECTANCY: Female 77 yrs, Male 71 yrs
ADULT LITERACY: 86%

■ Name means 'Lion City ■ 76% of pop. Chinese; 80% live in government high-rise flats; 90% of pop. live in capital ■ One of world's smallest yet most successful countries; per capita income 2nd in region to Japan ■ World's 2nd busiest port, after Rotterdam ■ All foodstuffs & raw materials imported, water imported from Malaysia ■ Many companies relocating operations from Hong Kong in view of 1997 reversion to China ■ Leased by Sir Stamford Raffles in 1819 it became Straits Settlements in 1826

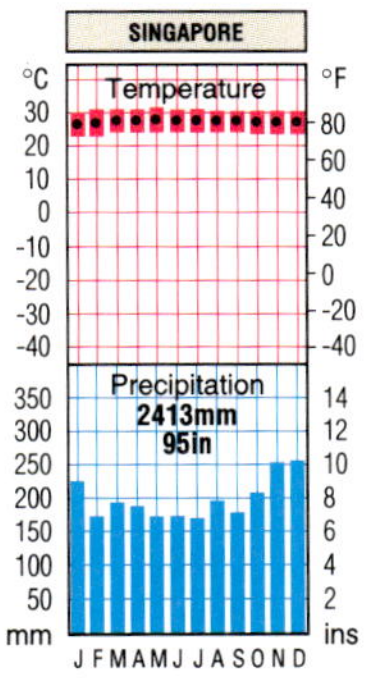

Uniformly high temperature, average 27°C [80°F], and humidity and heavy rain in all months of the year are typical of a place situated very close to the Equator and surrounded by water. Rain is usually intense and thunder occurs on an average of 40 days a year. As in much of the tropics, rainfall varies greatly from year to year, the highest recorded being more than twice the lowest.

MALAYSIA

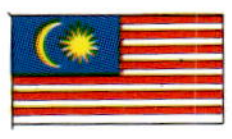

The red and white bands date back to a celebrated revolt in the thirteenth century. The star and crescent are symbols of Islam; the blue represents Malaysia's role in the Commonwealth. This version of the flag was first flown after federation in 1963.

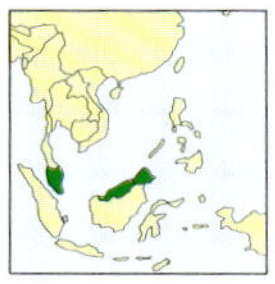

COUNTRY: Malaysia
AREA: 329,750 sq km [127,316 sq mls]
POPULATION: 17,861,000
CAPITAL (Population): Kuala Lumpur (1,103,000)
GOVERNMENT: Federal constitutional monarchy with a bicameral legislature
ETHNIC GROUPS: Malay 61%, Chinese 30%, Indian 8%
LANGUAGES: Malay (official), Chinese, Tamil, Iban, Dusan, English
RELIGIONS: Muslim 53%, Buddhist 17%, Chinese folk religionist 12%, Hindu 7%, Christian 6%
NATIONAL DAY: 31 August; Independence Day (1957)
CURRENCY: Ringgit (Malaysian dollar) = 100 cents
ANNUAL INCOME PER PERSON: $2,340
MAIN PRIMARY PRODUCTS: Rice, timber, palm oil, rubber, cocoa, fish, crude oil, natural gas, bauxite, tin, copper
MAIN INDUSTRIES: Agriculture, crude oil production, mining, fishing, forestry, food processing, rubber products, chemicals, textiles
EXPORTS: $1,479 per person
MAIN EXPORTS: Electronic components 15%, crude petroleum 14%, timber 13%, rubber 9%, palm oil 7%, liquefied natural gas 4%
MAIN EXPORT PARTNERS: Japan 20%, Singapore 18%, US 17%, South Korea 5%, Netherlands 4%,
MAIN IMPORTS: Electronic components 18%, petroleum products 5%, steel sheets 2%, grain 2%, crude petroleum 2%, sugar 1%
IMPORTS: $1,330 per person
DEFENCE: 15.3% of national budget
TOURISM: 3,146,000 visitors
POPULATION DENSITY: 54 per sq km [140 per sq ml]
LIFE EXPECTANCY: Female 73 yrs, Male 69 yrs
ADULT LITERACY: 73%
PRINCIPAL CITIES (Population): Kuala Lumpur 1,103,000 Ipoh 294,000 Penang 248,000 Johor Baharu 246,000 Petaling Jaya 208,000

■ Comprises peninsula states & Sabah & Sarawak on island of Borneo ■ Malays politically dominant, Chinese most powerful economic group ■ World's largest producer of tin, rubber & palm oil ■ Rubber introduced in 1877 from Brazil ■ Forests in Sabah & Sarawak heavily depleted by felling & overcutting ■ One of world's most successful developing countries ■ Manufacturing represents 25% of GNP

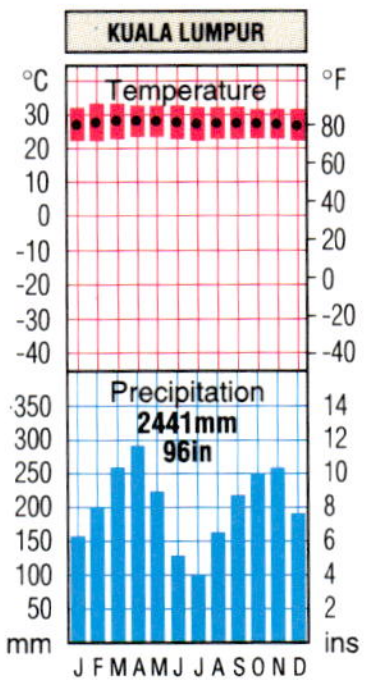

In common with many coastal places close to the Equator, Kuala Lumpur has very uniform temperature throughout the year. The length of daylight and the intensity of the noonday sun varies little from one season to another and the sea is always very warm. Rainfall is abundant at all seasons but with a distinct double maximum around the equinoxes when the tropical rain belt lies close to the Equator.

ASIA – SOUTH-EAST

BRUNEI

The yellow background represents the Sultan, the black and white stripes stand for his two main advisers (wazirs). The arms contain the inscription in Arabic "Brunei, Gate of Peace" and a crescent, symbol of Islam.

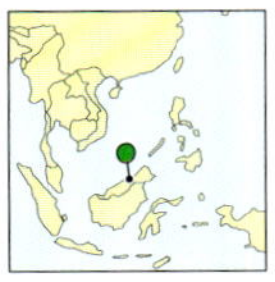

COUNTRY: The Islamic Sultanate of Brunei
AREA: 5,770 sq km [2,228 sq mls]
POPULATION: 266,000
CAPITAL (Population): Bandar Seri Begawan 58,000
GOVERNMENT: Monarchy with an advisory legislative body
ETHNIC GROUPS: Malay 69%, Chinese 18%, Indian
LANGUAGES: Malay and English (official), Chinese
RELIGIONS: Muslim 63%, Buddhist 14%, Christian 10%
NATIONAL DAY: 23 February
CURRENCY: Brunei $ = 100 cents
ANNUAL INCOME PER PERSON: $6,000
POPULATION DENSITY: 46 per sq km [119 per sq ml]
LIFE EXPECTANCY: Female 73 yrs, Male 70 yrs
ADULT LITERACY: 80%

■ Oil & natural gas account for almost all exports ■ Major investor of oil revenues in Western property & Stock Exchanges ■ Key foreign relationship with Britain ■ No income tax; free education & health services; housing loans available at 0.5% interest ■ Sultan & his family rule by hereditary rights stretching back centuries ■ Present Sultan said to be world's 3rd richest man ■ No parliament

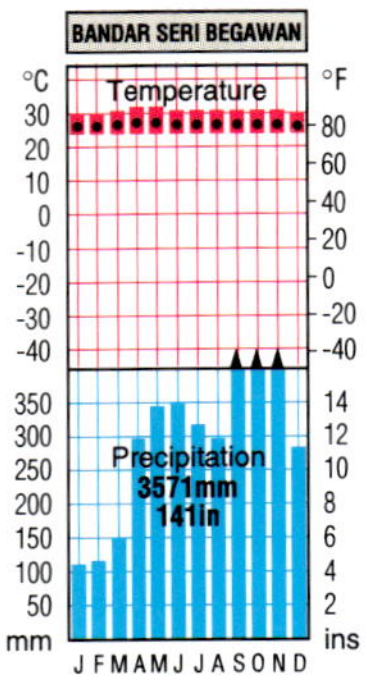

The climate is hot and humid, the temperatures varying little over the year from a minimum of 24°C (75°F) to a maximum of 30°C (86°F). Rainfall is heaviest in Nov. and March when the Equatorial monsoon blows onshore. When the monsoon is offshore June-Aug. the weather is drier and brighter. Rainfall can exceed 5,000 mm [200 ins.] in the mountainous interior.

VIETNAM

First used by the forces of Ho Chi Minh in the liberation struggle against Japan in World War II, the design was adopted as the national flag of North Vietnam in 1945. It was retained when the two parts of the country were reunited in 1975.

COUNTRY: Socialist Republic of Vietnam
AREA: 331,689 sq km [128,065 sq mls]
POPULATION: 66,200,000
CAPITAL (Population): Hanoi (3,100,000)
GOVERNMENT: Unitary single-party socialist republic with one legislative house (National Assembly)
ETHNIC GROUPS: Vietnamese 87.3%, Chinese (Hoa) 1.8%, Tai 1.7%, Thai 1.5%, Khmer 1.4%, Muong 1.3%, Nung 1.1%
LANGUAGES: Vietnamese (official), Chinese, Tho (Tay), Khmer, Muong, Thai, Nung, Miao, Jarai, Rhadé, Hre, Bahnar
RELIGIONS: Buddhist 55.3%, Roman Catholic 7%, Muslim 1%
NATIONAL DAY: 2-3 September
CURRENCY: Dong = 10 hao = 100 xu
ANNUAL INCOME PER PERSON: $300
MAIN PRIMARY PRODUCTS: Coal, anthracite, lignite, cereals, timber
MAIN INDUSTRIES: Mining, food processing, textiles, agriculture
MAIN EXPORTS: Raw materials 46%, handicrafts 24.1%, agricultural products 9.5%
MAIN EXPORT PARTNERS: CIS nations 51.1%, Hong Kong 13.8%, Japan 9.1%, Singapore 8.6%, Czechoslovakia 4.6%, EC countries 3.1%, Poland 2.3%, Hungary 1.5%
MAIN IMPORTS: Fuel and raw materials 44.7%, machinery 23.2%, wheat flour and food products 17.2%
MAIN IMPORT PARTNERS: CIS nations 69.2%, Japan 8.2%, Singapore 7%, Hong Kong 3%, EC countries 3%, Czechoslovakia 3%, Hungary 1%
POPULATION DENSITY: 200 per sq km [517 per sq ml]
INFANT MORTALITY: 54 per 1,000 live births
LIFE EXPECTANCY: Female 66 yrs, Male 62 yrs
ADULT LITERACY: 94%
PRINCIPAL CITIES (Population): Ho Chi Minh City 3,900,000 Hanoi 3,100,000 Haiphong 1,279,000 Da Nang 319,000 Bien Hoa 190,000

■ Country primarily comprises two river plains (Red River & Mekong) separated by narrow hilly central zone ■ Hong (Red) River so called from heavy load of silt it carries; over the years this silt has built up its bed to 12 m [40 ft] above height of surrounding plain ■ Throughout history, Vietnamese have faced danger from flooding, particularly from Red River ■ Highest parts of Mekong delta have been drained & land turned into large rice-producing estates ■ French colony and protectorate 1867-1954, French rule ending with famous battle of Dien Bien Phu ■ Has known a century of war against the Japanese, Chinese, various neighbours, civil war and the US ■ Was divided along 17th parallel in 1954; formally unified under Communist control in 1976 ■ During war US dropped 7 million tonnes of bombs & sprayed defoliant chemicals on 16,200 sq km [6,250 sq mls] ■ About 2 million Vietnamese killed during war ■ 2.8 million Americans served & 57,000 died in Vietnam between 1965-73 ■ Much of country's industry was damaged or destroyed ■ Several hundred thousand Vietnamese left country in 1978 and 1979; many of these 'Boat People' perished in storms or at hands of pirates ■ Standing army of over 1.2 million, with 3 million reserves ■ Southern capital Saigon renamed Ho Chi Minh City after the leader of the North ■ Involved in Cambodian affairs, deposed Pol Pot communists régime 1978 ■ Over 65% of the population supported by agriculture

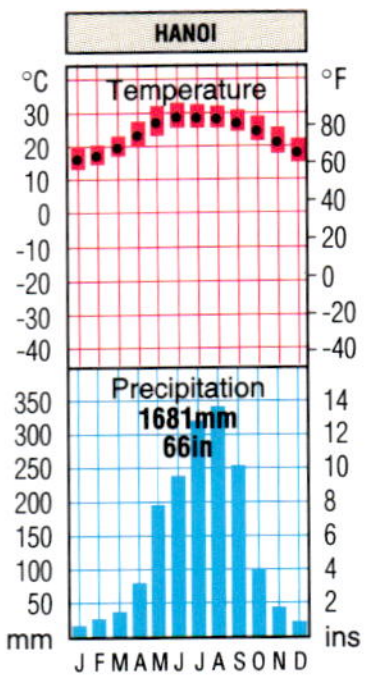

The hottest months are April- Aug., but no month is lower than 15°C [59°F]. The cold months of Jan. and Feb. are colder than in the south. From May-Oct. the south-east monsoon brings heavy rainfall, very heavy in the mountains. The dry season around Jan. is less pronounced than in the south and no month has less than 20 mm [1in].

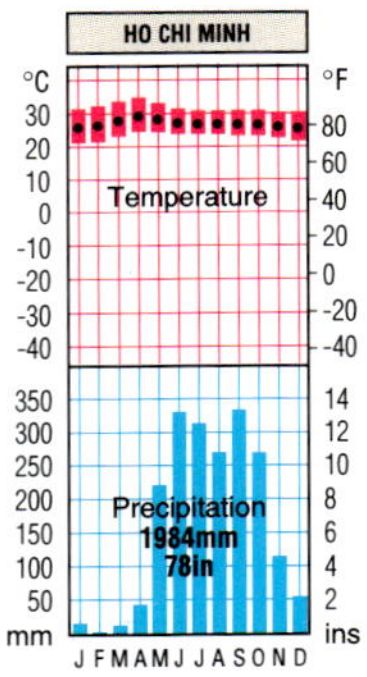

Temperature variation throughout the year is not great. April-May are the hottest months, Nov.-Jan. the coolest, but never falling below 25°C [77°F]. There are lower temperatures in the inland mountains. There is heavy rainfall throughout the year, except Jan-March which are drier. Typhoons can hit the coastal areas.

CAMBODIA

As well as being associated with Communism and revolution, red is the traditional colour of Cambodia. The silhouette is the historic temple of Angkor Wat. The blue symbolises the water resources which are so vital to the people of Cambodia.

COUNTRY: Cambodia
AREA: 181,040 sq km [69,900 sq mls]
POPULATION: 8,246,000
CAPITAL (Population): Phnom Penh (500,000)
GOVERNMENT: Single-party republic with one legislative assembly
ETHNIC GROUPS: Khmer 88%, Chinese 5%, Vietnamese 5%
LANGUAGES: Khmer (official)
RELIGIONS: Buddhist 88%, Muslim 2%
CURRENCY: 1 riel = 100 sen
ANNUAL INCOME PER PERSON: $300
MAIN PRIMARY PRODUCTS: Salt, iron ore, phosphates
MAIN INDUSTRIES: Agriculture
MAIN EXPORTS: Iron, steel and rubber. Before 1970 rice was exported; now Cambodia is a net importer
MAIN IMPORTS: Machinery and equipment, transport, chemicals
POPULATION DENSITY: 46 per sq km [118 per sq ml]
LIFE EXPECTANCY: Female 52 yrs, Male 50 yrs
ADULT LITERACY: 48%

■ Tonle Sap (Great Lake) in centre of Mekong quadruples in size in rain season to become one of world's greatest inland fisheries ■ Highest agricultural share of GNP in Asia ■ Rubber largest export ■ Khmers represent over 85% of pop. ■ World's largest single group of religious buildings, which includes more than 600 Hindu temples, is at Angkor Wat (see flag) & Angkor Thom ■ Language with most letters in alphabet - 72 ■ Worst genocide as percentage of pop. - more than $^1/_3$ of 8 million Khmers killed by Pol Pot régime (April 1975 to Jan 1979) ■ UN recognises régime ousted in 1979 ■ Many Cambodians live in refugee camps in Thailand

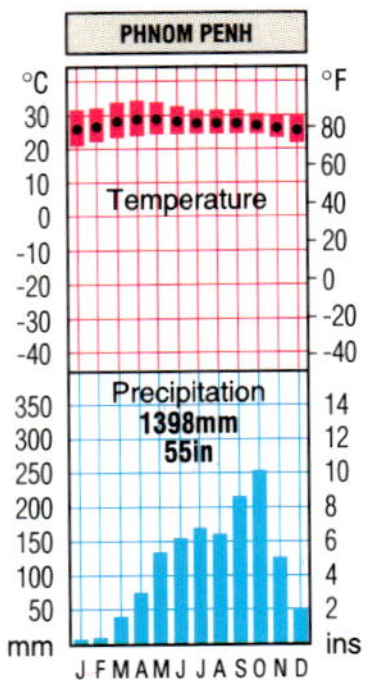

With no mountains and facing the Gulf of Thailand, the climate of Cambodia is dominated by the monsoon which brings heavy rainfall from May-Oct. This will be as high as 5,000 mm [200 in] on the coast but inland it declines to around 1,400 mm [55 in]. The winds reverse in direction Nov.- March and there is a marked dry-season centred on Jan. Temperatures are high throughout the year, with April-May being the hottest and Dec.-Jan. the coolest.

THAILAND

The two red and white stripes are all that remains of Thailand's traditional red-on-white elephant emblem, removed from the flag in 1916. The blue stripe was added in 1917 to show solidarity with the Allies in World War I.

COUNTRY: Kingdom of Thailand
AREA: 513,120 sq km [198,116 sq mls]
POPULATION: 57,196,000
CAPITAL (Population): Bangkok (5,609,000)
GOVERNMENT: Constitutional monarchy with a multi-party bicameral legislature
ETHNIC GROUPS: Thai 80%, Chinese 12%, Malay 4%, Khmer 3%
LANGUAGES: Thai (official), Chinese, Malay
RELIGIONS: Buddhist 95%, Muslim 4%, Christian 1%
NATIONAL DAY: 5 December; Birthday of HM the King
CURRENCY: Thai Baht = 100 stangs
ANNUAL INCOME PER PERSON: $1,420
MAIN PRIMARY PRODUCTS: Rice, rubber, maize, sugar cane, cassava, timber, fish, fruit, tin, iron, tungsten, manganese
MAIN INDUSTRIES: Agriculture, food processing, paper, cement, clothing, mining, forestry
EXPORTS: $362 per person
MAIN EXPORTS: Food and live animals 37%, basic manufactures 20%, machinery and transport equipment 12%
MAIN EXPORT PARTNERS: USA 19%, Japan 15%, Singapore 9%, Netherlands 7%, Germany 5%, Hong Kong 4%, UK 4%
IMPORTS: $465 per person
MAIN IMPORTS: Machinery and transport equipment 34%, basic manufactures 20%, chemicals 15%, fuels and lubricants 13%, inedible crude materials 8%, foodstuffs 4%
MAIN IMPORT PARTNERS: Japan 26%, USA 12%, Singapore 8%, Germany 6%, Malaysia 4%, China 4%, Taiwan 4%, UK 3%
DEFENCE: 19.0% of national budget
TOURISM: 3,483,000 visitors
POPULATION DENSITY: 111 per sq km [289 per sq ml]
INFANT MORTALITY: 32 per 1,000 live births
LIFE EXPECTANCY: Female 69 yrs, Male 65 yrs
ADULT LITERACY: 91%
PRINCIPAL CITIES (Population): Bangkok 5,609,000 Nakhon Ratchasima 191,000 Chiang Mai 151,000

■ 'Thai' means free ■ Known as Siam until 1939 ■ Bangkok known to Thais as Krung Thep, 'City of Angels' ■ Country's forests have shrunk from being 60% of land 25 years ago to 25% ■ World's largest rice exporter & 3rd largest rubber producer ■ Natural gas recently discovered offshore ■ Major source of heroin ■ Thais are descended from tribes that came south from China about 1,000 years ago ■ 50% of Bangkok pop. said to have some Chinese blood ■ 27,000 Buddhist temples & 250,000 monks ■ Only S.E. Asian country never to have been European colony

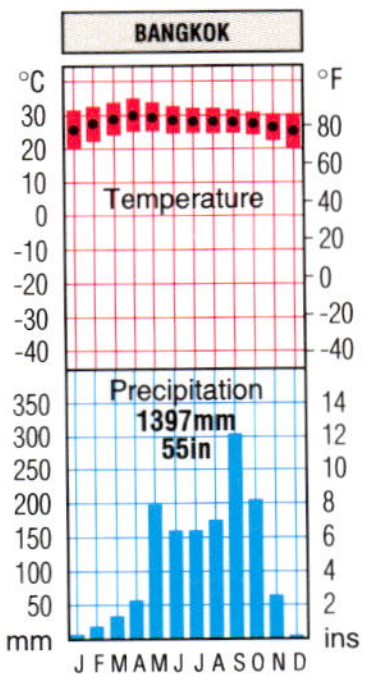

Mountains shelter Bangkok from the rain-bearing south-westerly winds in summer and although the distribution of rainfall is similar to much of south-east Asia, the total is relatively small, being less than half that of the other side of the mountains, a short distance to the west. The warm waters of the Gulf of Thailand to the south sustain uniformly high temperatures throughout the year.

LAOS

Since 1975 Laos has flown the flag of the Pathet Lao, the Communist movement which won the long struggle for control of the country. The blue stands for the Mekong, the white disc the moon, the red the unity and purpose of the people.

COUNTRY: Lao People's Democratic Republic
AREA: 236,800 sq km [91,428 sq mls]
POPULATION: 4,139,000
CAPITAL (Population): Vientiane (377,000)
GOVERNMENT: Single-party republic with a unicameral legislature
ETHNIC GROUPS: Lao 67%, Palaung-Wa 12%, Thai 8%, Man 5%
LANGUAGES: Laotian (official), French
RELIGIONS: Buddhist 58%, tribal religionist 34%, Christian 2%, Muslim 1%
NATIONAL DAY: 2 December
CURRENCY: New Kip = 100 cents
ANNUAL INCOME PER PERSON: $200
MAIN PRIMARY PRODUCTS: Rice, tin, gypsum
MAIN INDUSTRIES: Subsistent farmers
MAIN EXPORTS: Coffee, tea, cocoa, spices, cork and wood
MAIN IMPORTS: Machinery and vehicles, petroleum, woven cotton fabrics
POPULATION DENSITY: 17 per sq km [45 per sq ml]
LIFE EXPECTANCY: Female 53 yrs, Male 50 yrs
ADULT LITERACY: 45%

■ Landlocked country with no railways - Mekong river principal route of communication ■ One of world's poorest countries; its mostly agricultural economy has been only at subsistence level since 1970s ■ Tourist visas limited to 1,000 per year and travel outside capital severely restricted for foreigners

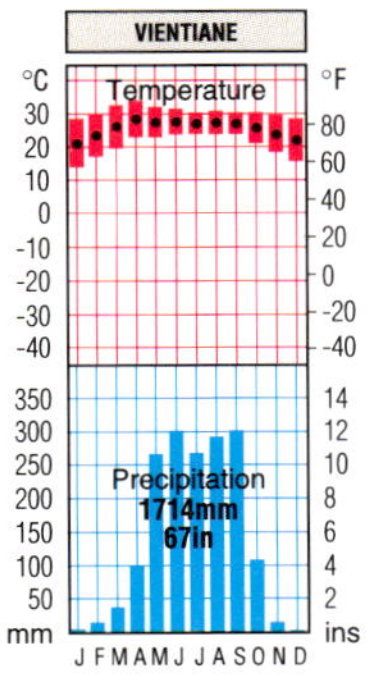

In common with much of south-east Asia, Laos experiences the seasonal reversal of winds associated with the monsoon. In winter Vientiane is sheltered from the north-east winds by mountains and the weather is sunny and dry. The temperature increases steadily until April when the onset of south-westerly winds marks the beginning of the wet season which lasts through to September.

BURMA

The colours were adopted following independence from Britain in 1948. The Socialist symbol, added in 1974, includes a ring of 14 stars for the country's states. The gearwheel represents industry and the rice plant agriculture.

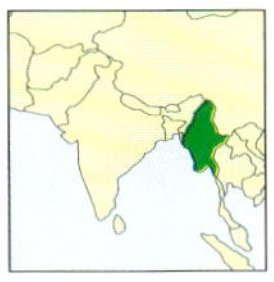

COUNTRY: Union of Myanmar (Burma)
AREA: 676,550 sq km [261,216 sq mls]
POPULATION: 41,675,000
CAPITAL (Population): Rangoon (2,459,000)
GOVERNMENT: Military regime
ETHNIC GROUPS: Burman 69%, Shan 9%, Karen 6%, Rakhine 5%, Mon 2%, Chin 2%, Kachin 1%
LANGUAGES: Burmese (official), English
RELIGIONS: Buddhist 39%, Christian 5%, Muslim 4%
NATIONAL DAY: 4 January; Independence Day (1948)
CURRENCY: Burmese kyat = 100 pyas
ANNUAL INCOME PER PERSON: $500
MAIN PRIMARY PRODUCTS: Zinc, tungsten, nickel, natural gas, oil, rubber, timber, cotton, groundnuts
MAIN INDUSTRIES: Forestry, mining, fishing, oil production
EXPORTS: $5 per person
MAIN EXPORTS: Rice 41%, teak 24%, metals and ores 9%
MAIN EXPORT PARTNERS: India 12%, EC Countries 12%, African Countries 9%, Japan 6%, Middle East 6%
IMPORTS: $5 per person
MAIN IMPORTS: Machinery 18%, base metals 10%, transport equipment 8%
MAIN IMPORT PARTNERS: Japan 33%, EC Countries 13%, Eastern Europe 16%
DEFENCE: 35.5% of national budget
TOURISM: 47,000 visitors
POPULATION DENSITY: 62 per sq km [160 per sq ml]
INFANT MORTALITY: 59 per 1,000 live births
LIFE EXPECTANCY: Female 64 yrs, Male 61 yrs
ADULT LITERACY: 79%
PRINCIPAL CITIES (Population): Rangoon 2,459,000 Mandalay 533,000 Moulmein 220,000 Pegu 150,000 Bassein 144,000

■ In 1989 adopted new name, the Union of Myanmar; however old name will continue to be used, except in official communications ■ Second largest country in S.E. Asia after Indonesia ■ About ²/₃ of country covered by trees ■ Has about 8,000 km [5,000 mls] of navigable rivers ■ Over 100 different languages & dialects spoken ■ One of world's ten poorest countries ■ Was world's largest rice exporter until 1964; rice still accounts for 50% of exports ■ Virtually self-sufficient in oil and gas ■ Rebel groups control 1/3 of country ■ Hill-dwelling Karens have waged 30-year war for independence ■ Burmese Communist Party controls 15,000 sq km [5,800 sq mls] of land adjoining China ■ Business & tourist visas granted for maximum stay of 7 days ■ Showing soles of feet, when sitting, considered offensive

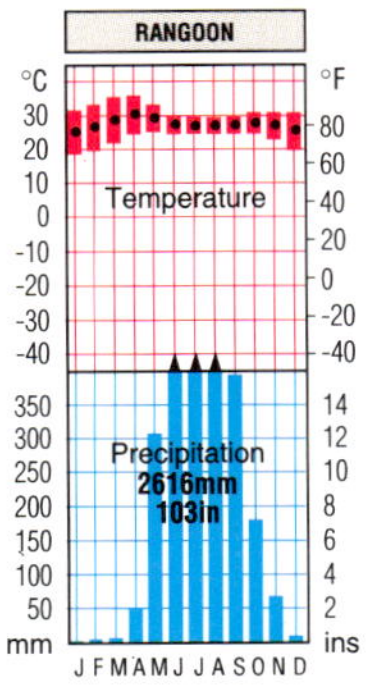

The rain associated with the south-east monsoon affects all the Burmese coastlands (4,000 mm [160 in]), but the rainfall is less in the shadows of the mountain ranges, with a dry zone in the middle Irrawaddy (400 mm [16 in]). The rainy season is May-Oct. and a dry period is centred on Dec.-Jan. Snow falls on the mountains of the north and east, but they do act as a barrier to the colder northern winter winds. Temperatures are high with little annual variation, the hottest period being May-April.

ASIA – SOUTH

BANGLADESH

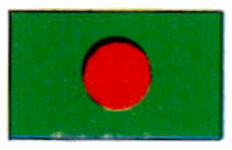

Bangladesh adopted this flag in 1971 following the break from Pakistan. The green is said to represent the fertility of the land, while the red disc commemorates the blood shed in the struggle for freedom.

COUNTRY: People's Republic of Bangladesh
AREA: 144,000 sq km [55,598 sq mls]
POPULATION: 115,594,000
CAPITAL (Population): Dacca (4,770,000)
GOVERNMENT: Unitary multi-party republic with a unicameral legislature
ETHNIC GROUPS: Bengali 98%, Bihari, Tribal
LANGUAGES: Bengali (official)
RELIGIONS: Muslim 87%, Hindu 12%, Buddhist, Christian
NATIONAL DAY: 26 March; Independence Day (1971)
CURRENCY: Taka = 100 paisa
ANNUAL INCOME PER PERSON: $200
MAIN PRIMARY PRODUCTS: Rice, jute, natural gas, sugar cane, cattle, fish, timber
MAIN INDUSTRIES: Jute spinning, textiles, sugar, fishing
EXPORTS: $12 per person
MAIN EXPORTS: Jute goods and raw jute 33%, fish and fish preparations 12%, hides and skins 12%
MAIN EXPORT PARTNERS: USA 30%, Italy 9%, Japan 6%, Singapore 6%, UK 6%
IMPORTS: $33 per person
MAIN IMPORTS: Machinery and basic manufactures 24%, food 16%, petroleum and petroleum products 15%
MAIN IMPORT PARTNERS: Japan 13%, Canada 10%, Singapore 9%, USA 7%, Germany 6%
DEFENCE: 14% of national budget
POPULATION DENSITY: 803 per sq km [2,080 per sq ml]
INFANT MORTALITY: 108 per 1,000 live births
LIFE EXPECTANCY: Female 53 yrs, Male 53 yrs
ADULT LITERACY: 33%
PRINCIPAL CITIES (Population): Dacca 4,770,000 Chittagong 1,840,000 Khulna 860,000

■ Was known for centuries as Golden Bengal (Sonar Bangla) ■ Apart from hills covered in bamboo forest in south- east, country is almost one huge delta formed by Ganges, Brahmaputra & Meghna rivers ■ Combination of this water volume and cyclones have led to great disasters, for example 1970 and 1991 when loss of life was in hundreds of thousands ■ Of countries larger than city/island states, Bangladesh is most densely populated, over 750 persons per sq km [1,000 per sq ml] ■ High pop. growth - above 3% per year ■ Rainfall, sun & silt make land highly productive; often possible to grow two or three crops a year ■ Was world famous for its cotton in 18th century; muslin named after Muslims of Dhaka who wore it ■ Was East Pakistan from 1947 to 1971 ■ One of world's poorest countries ■ More than 60% of country's internal trade carried by boat; few villages served by roads ■ Many households greatly assisted by funds from family members who live abroad, especially in Britain ■ Linguistically, culturally & geographically, Bangladesh & Indian state of Bengal are single region ■ Work in ricefields done by men and boys, not by women

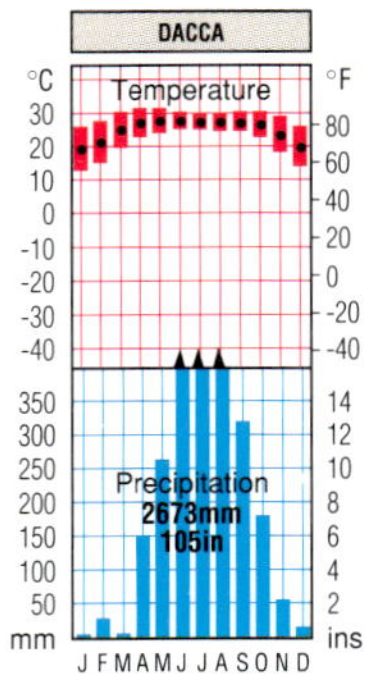

The Ganges delta has a classic monsoon climate. From June-Sept. the winds blow from the south over the Bay of Bengal bringing very heavy rain, over 240 mm [10 in] per month. On occasions, the winds are so strong they pile the sea water up against the outflowing river bringing flood devastation. April is the hottest month and the temperatures remain high throughout the monsoon season. January, with winds blowing from the continental north, is the coldest month of the winter season.

BHUTAN

COUNTRY: Kingdom of Bhutan
AREA: 47,000 sq km [18,147 sq mls]
POPULATION: 1,517,000
CAPITAL (Population): Thimphu (60,000)

MALDIVES

COUNTRY: Republic of the Maldives
AREA: 298 sq km [115 sq mls]
POPULATION: 215,000
CAPITAL (Population): Malé (46,000)

INDIA

India's flag evolved during the struggle for freedom from British rule. The orange represents the Hindu majority, green the country's Muslims and white peace. The Buddhist wheel symbol was added on independence in 1947.

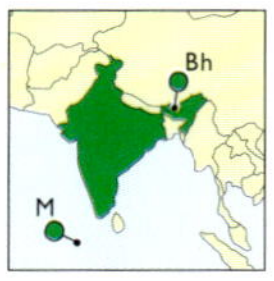

COUNTRY: Republic of India
AREA: 3,287,590 sq km [1,269,338 sq mls]
POPULATION: 843,931,000
CAPITAL: New Delhi (part of Delhi)
GOVERNMENT: Multi-party federal republic with bicameral legislature
ETHNIC GROUPS: (See religions)
LANGUAGES: Hindi and English (official) and over 70 other languages
RELIGIONS: Hindu 83%, Muslim 11%, Christian 2%, Sikh 2%, Buddhist 1%
NATIONAL DAY: 26 January; Republic Day (1950)
CURRENCY: Indian rupee = 100 paisa
ANNUAL INCOME PER PERSON: $350
SOURCE OF INCOME: Agriculture 32%, Industry 30%, Services 38%
MAIN PRIMARY PRODUCTS: Wheat, sugar cane, rice, millet, sorghum, jute, barley, tea, cattle, coal, iron ore, lead, zinc, diamonds, oil and natural gas, bauxite, chromite, copper manganese
MAIN INDUSTRIES: Textiles, chemicals, petroleum products, oil refining, jute, cement, fertilizers, food processing, diesel engines, beverages, iron and steel
EXPORTS: $19 per person
MAIN EXPORTS: Gems and jewellery 17%, clothing 9%, leather and leather manufactures 6%, machinery and transport equipment 6%, cotton fabrics 5%, tea and maté 4%
MAIN EXPORT PARTNERS: USA 19%, CIS nations 15%, Japan 10%, Germany 6%, UK 6%
IMPORTS: $24 per person
MAIN IMPORTS: Non-electrical machinery 18%, mineral fuels 13%, iron and steel 7%, pearls, precious and semi-precious stones 7%, electrical machinery 4%, transport equipment 3%, edible vegetable oil 3%
MAIN IMPORT PARTNERS: Japan 13%, USA 10%, Germany 9%, UK 8%, CIS nations 5%
EDUCATIONAL EXPENDITURE: 14% of national budget
DEFENCE: 27.6% of national budget
TOTAL ARMED FORCES: 1,260,000
TOURISM: 1,164,000 visitors
ROADS: 1,772,000 km [1,101,000 mls]
RAILWAYS: 61,810 km [38,407 mls]
POPULATION DENSITY: 257 per sq km [665 per sq ml]
URBAN POPULATION: 28%
POPULATION GROWTH: 1.9% per year
BIRTHS: 30 per 1,000 population
DEATHS: 10 per 1,000 population
INFANT MORTALITY: 88 per 1,000 live births
LIFE EXPECTANCY: Female 61 yrs, Male 60 yrs
POPULATION PER DOCTOR: 2,521
ADULT LITERACY: 43%
PRINCIPAL CITIES (Population): Calcutta 9,194,000 Bombay 8,243,000 Delhi 5,729,000 Madras 4,289,000 Bangalore 2,922,000 Ahmadabad 2,548,000 Hyderabad 2,546,000 Poona 1,686,000 Kanpur 1,639,000 Nagpur 1,302,000 Jaipur 1,015,000 Lucknow 1,008,000

■ Himalayas world's youngest & tallest mountains ■ Rajasthan canal one of world's longest irrigation canals; flows for 216 km [134 mls] across Punjab without distributing water, then has working length of 469 km [291 mls], branches of 837 km [520 mls] & total length of minor distributaries of 5,474 km [3,400 mls] ■ Some states bigger in pop. than any European country ■ World's biggest masonry dam on Tungabhadra river is 2,441 m [8,008 ft] long & 49 m [162 ft] high ■ World's highest home on Tibet border at Basisa ■ World's largest democracy, over 500 million strong electorate ■ Area around Darjeeling is world's best tea growing region ■ Offshore oil wells account for 75% of country's oil needs ■ 80% of total energy needs home-produced ■ 10th most important industrial power in world ■ World's largest employer is Indian Railways with 1,617,613 staff (1987) ■ Has more Muslims than any nation ■ 75% of pop. live in villages ■ 70% of employment in agriculture ■ 200 million people live below poverty line, mainly in rural areas ■ Density of human settlement in some towns is higher than in Western skyscraper cities ■ Nearly all marriages arranged ■ Mahatma ('Great Soul') Ghandi led 50-year struggle to help poor of India, especially 'untouchables' ■ Cow is sacred animal of Hinduism & never slaughtered ■ Has more cows per capita & per sq km than any country ■ Golden Temple at Amritsar is Sikh religion's most holy place ■ Taj Mahal has been called world's most beautiful building ■ Vedas (religious texts) recited by Hindu priests (Brahmins) are 4,000 years old ■ Produces more feature-films per year than any nation ■ Gir Forest game reserve main home of Indian lion, only species of lion in Asia ■ Indian cities have developed some of world's worst noise pollution ■ Even very poor families buy jewellery as investment & as insurance against starvation ■ Hundreds of different languages spoken ■ Has never suffered a military coup nor a transfer of power between parties except by general election ■ More than 30% of Calcutta's electricity stolen

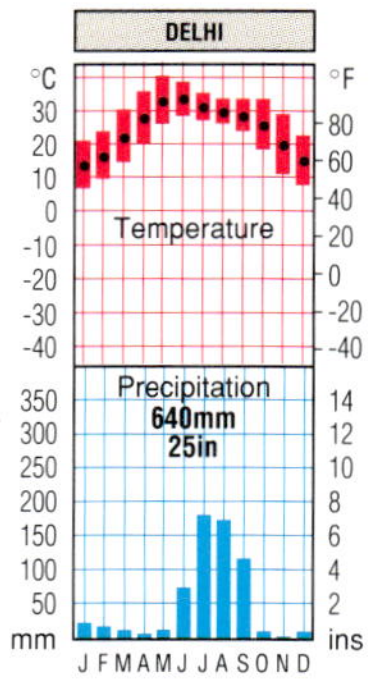

The summer rains, typical of the Indian monsoon, arrive later and are less intense at Delhi than in the lower parts of the Ganges valley. From January to May, the dry season, there is abundant sunshine and temperature increases rapidly until the arrival of the rains in June. During the rainy season the temperature is uniformly hot with little diurnal variation. The latter part of the year is sunny, dry and much cooler.

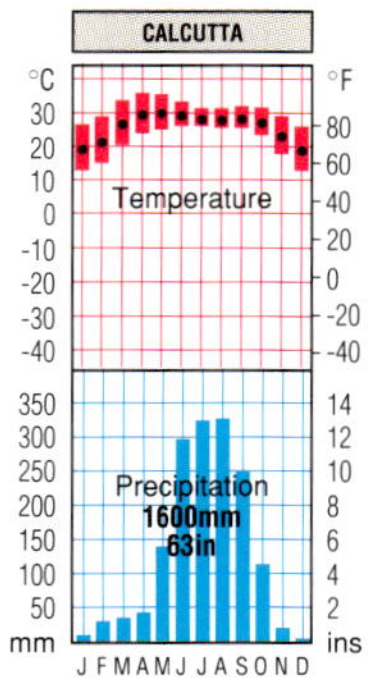

Calcutta has a tropical monsoon climate with wind flow in winter the reverse of that in summer. In winter, north-westerlies bring dry, sunny weather with a large daily range of temperature. By May, the increasing intensity of the sun gives rise to thunderstorms which precede the northwards sweep of the summer monsoon across the Bay of Bengal bringing four months of heavy rain and constant high temperature and humidity.

SRI LANKA

This unusual flag was adopted in 1951, three years after 'Ceylon' gained independence from Britain. The lion banner represents the ancient Buddhist kingdom and the stripes the island's minorities – Muslims (green) and Hindus (orange).

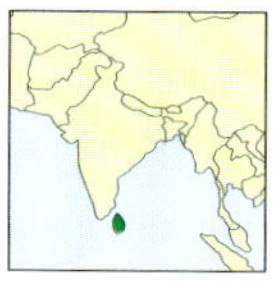

COUNTRY: Democratic Socialist Republic of Sri Lanka
AREA: 65,610 sq km [25,332 sq mls]
POPULATION: 16,993,000
CAPITAL (Population): Colombo (1,412,000)
GOVERNMENT: Unitary multi-party republic with a unicameral legislature
ETHNIC GROUPS: Sinhalese 74%, Tamil 18%, Sri Lankan Moor 7%
LANGUAGES: Sinhalese and Tamil (official), English
RELIGIONS: Buddhist 69%, Hindu 16%, Muslim 8%, Christian 7%
NATIONAL DAY: 4 February; Independence and National Day (1948)
CURRENCY: Sri Lanka rupee = 100 cents
ANNUAL INCOME PER PERSON: $470
MAIN PRIMARY PRODUCTS: Rice, coconuts, rubber, tea, fish, timber, iron ore, precious and semi-precious stones, graphite
MAIN INDUSTRIES: Agriculture, mining, forestry, fishing, textiles, oil refining
EXPORTS: $91 per person
MAIN EXPORTS: Tea 27%, rubber 7%, precious and semi-precious stones 6%, coconuts 3%
MAIN EXPORT PARTNERS: USA 27%, Germany 8%, UK 6%, Japan 5%, Pakistan 2%
IMPORTS: $179 per person
MAIN IMPORTS: Petroleum 15%, machinery and transport equipment 13%, sugar 4%, vehicles and cycles 4%, paper and paperboard 3%
MAIN IMPORT PARTNERS: Japan 15%, UK 7%, USA 6%, Iran 5%, India 4%, China 3%
DEFENCE: 26.6% of national budget
TOURISM: 183,000 visitors
POPULATION DENSITY: 259 per sq km [671 per sq ml]
INFANT MORTALITY: 28 per 1,000 live births
LIFE EXPECTANCY: Female 74 yrs, Male 70 yrs
ADULT LITERACY: 87%
PRINCIPAL CITIES (Population): Colombo 1,412,000 Dehivala-Mt. Lavinia 191,000 Moratuwa 143,000 Jaffna 138,000

■ Name means 'resplendent island' ■ Known by Arab merchants as 'Serendip'; it gave the word serendipity - the making of happy discoveries ■ Other names for country were Taprobane (Romans), Ceilas (Portuguese) & Ceylon (British) ■ 60% of population under 25 ■ First inhabitants, the Veddas, lived there from about 3000BC ■ Present civil strife results from divisions between two of oldest races on island - Tamils and Sinhalese ■ Sinhalese mostly Buddhist, Tamils mostly Hindu ■ Highest literacy rate of any Asian country except Japan ■ Had one of highest living standards in Asia on independence in 1948 ■ World's first woman Prime Minister was Mrs Sirimavo Bandaranaike in July 1960 ■ Has a refuge for orphan elephants

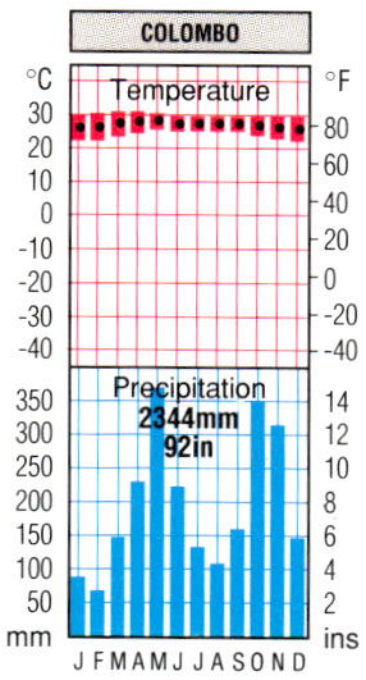

The western side of Sri Lanka has an equatorial climate with a double maximum of rainfall in May and October and very uniform high temperatures throughout the year. The periods of heaviest rain at Colombo mark the advance and retreat of the summer monsoon which gives a single wet season over the Indian sub-continent to the north. The eastern side of the island, sheltered from the south-west, is drier.

NEPAL

This Himalayan kingdom's uniquely shaped flag was adopted in 1962. It came from the joining together in the 19th century of two triangular pennants – the royal family's crescent moon emblem and the powerful Rana family's sun symbol.

COUNTRY: Kingdom of Nepal
AREA: 140,800 sq km [54,363 sq mls]
POPULATION: 18,916,000
CAPITAL (Population): Katmandu (235,000)
GOVERNMENT: Constitutional monarchy with a bicameral legislature
ETHNIC GROUPS: Nepalese 58%, Bihari 19%, Tharu 4%, Tamang 4%, Newar 3%
LANGUAGES: Nepali (official), Maithili, Bhojpuri
RELIGIONS: Hindu 90%, Buddhist 5%, Muslim 3%
NATIONAL DAY: 28 December; Birthday of HM the King
CURRENCY: Nepalese rupee = 100 paisa
ANNUAL INCOME PER PERSON: $170
MAIN PRIMARY PRODUCTS: Rice, cereals, timber, sugar cane, jute, fruit
MAIN INDUSTRIES: Agriculture, sugar, jute, forestry, textiles, tourism
EXPORTS: $9 per person
MAIN EXPORTS: Basic manufactures 35%, foodstuffs 23%, machinery and transport equipment 22%
MAIN EXPORT PARTNERS: India 40%, US 27%, Germany 8%, Singapore 7%, UK 4%
IMPORTS: $32 per person
MAIN IMPORTS: Basic manufactured goods 30%, machinery and transport equipment 23%, chemicals 13%, mineral fuels 11%, foodstuffs 10%

■ Northern border area known as 'Roof of the World' including Everest 8,848 m [29,028 ft]; southern border with India only 300 m [1,000 ft] in altitude ■ Only 20% of pop. literate ■ 90% of pop. work as peasant farmers or labourers ■ Lumbini, grove in village of Rummindei, formerly Kapilavastu, birthplace of Prince Siddhartha Gautama (c. 563-488BC) who came to be known as Buddha, the 'Enlightened One' ■ Closed to outside world until 1951 ■ Home of famous Gurkha warriors

MAIN IMPORT PARTNERS: India 43%, Japan 17%, South Korea 5%, Singapore 4%, China 3%, Germany 3%
DEFENCE: 6.8% of national budget
TOURISM: 248,000 visitors
POPULATION DENSITY: 134 per sq km [348 per sq ml]
INFANT MORTALITY: 118 per 1,000 live births
LIFE EXPECTANCY: Female 53 yrs, Male 54 yrs
ADULT LITERACY: 26%
PRINCIPAL CITIES (Population): Katmandu 235,000 Biratnagar 94,000 Latitpur 80,000

PAKISTAN

Pakistan's flag was adopted when the country gained independence from Britain in 1947. The green, the crescent moon and five-pointed star are traditionally associated with Islam. The white stripe represents Pakistan's other religions.

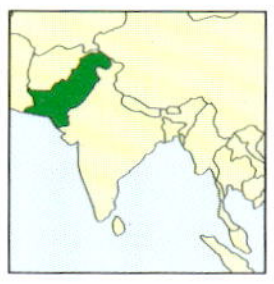

COUNTRY: Islamic Republic of Pakistan
AREA: 796,100 sq km [307,374 sq mls]
POPULATION: 112,050,000
CAPITAL (Population): Islamabad (204,000)
GOVERNMENT: Federal republic with a bicameral legislature
ETHNIC GROUPS: See languages
LANGUAGES: Urdu 8% (official), Punjabi 48%, Pashto 13%, Sinahi 12%, Saraki 10%
RELIGIONS: Muslim 96%, Christian 2%, Hindu 2%
NATIONAL DAY: 23 March; Republic Day (1956)
CURRENCY: Pakistan rupee = 100 paisa
ANNUAL INCOME PER PERSON: $380
MAIN PRIMARY PRODUCTS: Cotton, rice, sugar cane, cereals, dates, tobacco, natural gas, iron ore and unexploited reserves of phosphates, bauxite
MAIN INDUSTRIES: Agriculture, cotton yarn and fabrics, petroleum refining, food processing
EXPORTS: $43 per person
MAIN EXPORTS: Raw cotton 14%, cotton yarn 12%, cotton fabrics 11%, rice 8%, leather 6%, carpets 6%
MAIN EXPORT PARTNERS: Japan 11%, US 11%, Germany 7%, UK 7%, Italy 6%, Saudi Arabia 5%
IMPORTS: $66 per person
MAIN IMPORTS: Machinery 18%, mineral oils 16%, chemicals 9%, transport equipment 9%, edible oils 7%, iron and steel 4%
MAIN IMPORT PARTNERS: Japan 15%, US 11%, Germany 8%, Kuwait 7%, UK 7%, Saudi Arabia 5%, France 4%, China 3%
DEFENCE: 35% of national budget
TOURISM: 425,000 visitors
POPULATION DENSITY: 137 per sq km [354 per sq ml]
INFANT MORTALITY: 98 per 1,000 live births
LIFE EXPECTANCY: Female 59 yrs, Male 59 yrs
ADULT LITERACY: 30%
PRINCIPAL CITIES (Population): Karachi 5,208,000 Lahore 2,953,000 Faisalabad 1,104,000 Rawalpindi 795,000 Islamabad 204,000

■ K2, on China-Pakistan border, world's second largest mountain after Everest at 8,611 m [28,250 ft]; first climbed by Indian team in 1954 ■ Dams on Indus at Tarbela and on Jhelum at Mangla are among world's largest earth- & rock-filled dams ■ About 2/3 of country's energy requirements home-produced ■ Achieved great industrial growth in 1960s largely as a result of aid from USA & rich Arab nations ■ Manufacturing employs less than 16% of workforce ■ Population 96% Muslim with small Hindu & Christian minorities ■ About 20 rich & powerful families control economy ■ Largest recorded women shortage with only about 900 females to every 1,000 males ■ Benazir Bhutto was the Muslim world's first woman Premier

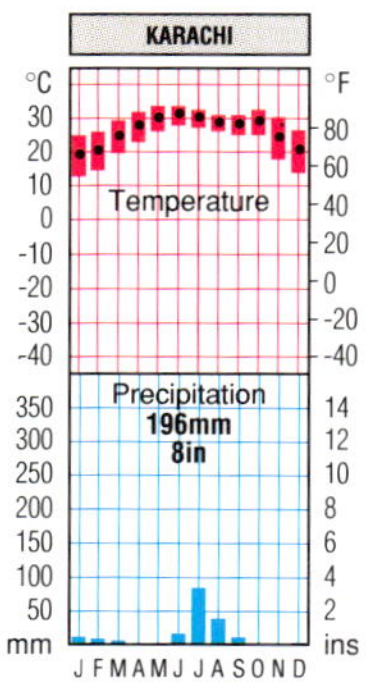

The summer monsoon rains decrease rapidly in intensity from the Indian penisula westwards into Pakistan, leaving much of the Indus lowland arid. Karachi is hot throughout the year but, being on the coast, has a smaller range of temperature than inland. The summer rains are thundery and vary greatly in intensity from year to year. Small amounts of winter rain are brought by low-pressure systems from the west.

AFGHANISTAN

After many design changes in the late 1970s, Afghanistan readopted its traditional colours in 1980 and added the new state emblem. This includes a pulpit, sheaves of wheat, a rising sun and red star, and a copy of the Koran.

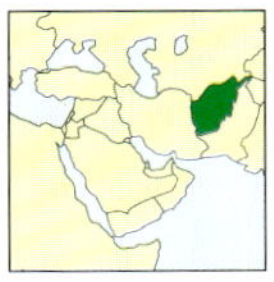

COUNTRY: Republic of Afghanistan
AREA: 652,090 sq km [251,772 sq mls]
POPULATION: 16,433,000
CAPITAL (Population): Kabul (1,127,000)
GOVERNMENT: Unitary single-party People's Republic with a bicameral legislature
ETHNIC GROUPS: Pashtun 52%, Tadzhik 20%, Uzbek 9%, Hazara 9%, Chahar, Turkmen, Baluchi
LANGUAGES: Pashto and Dari Persian (official)
RELIGIONS: Sunni Muslim 74%, Shiite Muslim 25%
NATIONAL DAY: 27 April; Anniversary of Saur Revolution
CURRENCY: Afghani = 100 puls
ANNUAL INCOME PER PERSON: $450
MAIN PRIMARY PRODUCTS: Iron, copper, natural gas, sheep, goats, wheat, cotton
MAIN INDUSTRIES: Agriculture, carpets, textiles
EXPORTS: $15 per person
MAIN EXPORTS: Natural gas 42%, dried fruit 26%, fresh fruit 9%, carpets and rugs 7%
MAIN EXPORT PARTNERS: CIS nations 55%, Pakistan 16%, India 12%
IMPORTS: $51 per person
MAIN IMPORTS: Wheat 5%, vegetable oil 4%, sugar 3%, tyres and tubes 3%, tea 3%
MAIN IMPORT PARTNERS: CIS nations 62%, Japan 13%
DEFENCE: 37% of national budget
POPULATION DENSITY: 25 per sq km [65 per sq ml]
INFANT MORTALITY: 162 per 1,000 live births
LIFE EXPECTANCY: Female 44 yrs, Male 43 yrs
ADULT LITERACY: 20%
PRINCIPAL CITIES (Population): Kabul 1,127,000 Qandahar 198,000 Herat 156,000

■ Hindu Kush 2nd highest mountain system in world; many peaks rise to over 7,000 m [23,000 ft] ■ Among world's lowest recorded life expectancy: up to 50% of children die before age of 5 ■ $2\frac{1}{2}$ million nomads, and millions of refugees in Pakistan ■ 70% of workforce peasant farmers ■ Kabul once capital of Mongol Empire ■ Tribal rivalries have always made country difficult to govern ■ There are 3 rare domestic animals: the yak, the two-humped Bactrian camel and the Karakul lamb, whose curly fleece is used for the prized Persian lamb furs

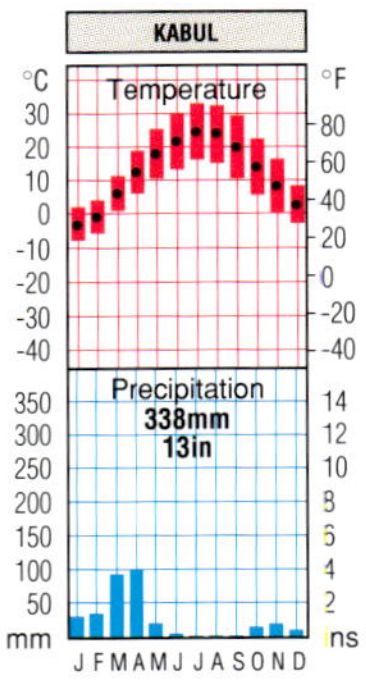

The climate of Afghanistan is made more by its high altitude and being cut off by mountain ranges than by its latitude. From Dec. to March the air masses come from the cold continental north and bring very cold weather and snow on the mountains. June to Sept. is very hot and dry with the east getting some rain from a weakened monsoon. Kabul, at 2,000 m [6,000 ft], has a range of temperature from -5°C to 25°C [23-77°F].

IRAN

Iran's flag has been in use since July 1980 after the fall of the Shah and the rise of Ayatollah Khomeini. Along the edges of the stripes is the legend 'Allah Akbar' (God is Great) repeated 22 times; in the centre is the new national emblem.

COUNTRY: Islamic Republic of Iran
AREA: 1,648,000 sq km [636,293 sq mls]
POPULATION: 58,031,000
CAPITAL (Population): Tehran (6,043,000)
GOVERNMENT: Unitary Islamic republic with a unicameral legislature
ETHNIC GROUPS: Persian 46%, Azerbaijani 17%, Kurdish 9%, Gilaki 5%, Luri, Mazandarani, Baluchi, Arab
LANGUAGES: Farsi (Persian) official; Kurdish, Baluchi, Turkic
RELIGIONS: Shiite Muslim 91%, Sunni Muslim 8%
NATIONAL DAY: 1 April; Islamic Republic Day (1979)
CURRENCY: Rial = 100 dinars
ANNUAL INCOME PER PERSON: $2,450
MAIN PRIMARY PRODUCTS: Crude oil, natural gas, lead, chrome, copper, iron, sheep, cattle, goats, cereals, timber
MAIN INDUSTRIES: Oil refining, gas, steel, textiles, electrical goods, fishing, sugar, flour milling
MAIN EXPORTS: Petroleum and petroleum products 98%
MAIN EXPORT PARTNERS: USA 15%, Japan 13%, Italy 9%, Netherlands 8%, India 6%, Turkey 6%, Spain 6%, Romania 6%
MAIN IMPORTS: Machinery and transport equipment 33%, iron and steel 15%, foodstuffs 13%, chemicals 10%
MAIN IMPORT PARTNERS: Germany 19%, Japan 13%, UK 6%, Italy 6%, Turkey 5%, CIS nations 4%, Netherlands 4%, Australia 3%
DEFENCE: 12% of national budget
TOURISM: 69,000 visitors
POPULATION DENSITY: 35 per sq km [91 per sq ml]
INFANT MORTALITY: 53 per 1,000 live births
LIFE EXPECTANCY: Female 68 yrs, Male 67 yrs
ADULT LITERACY: 51%
PRINCIPAL CITIES (Population): Tehran 6,043,000 Mashhad 1,464,000 Esfahan 987,000 Tabriz 971,000 Shiraz 848,000

■ The word Iran comes from Persian name for country, 'Arian', & was adopted in 1935; before that was known as Persia ■ N. Iran subject to earthquakes; most recent took place in 1990, with estimated death toll of 35,000 ■ Natural gas reserves 2nd only to Russia ■ $\frac{2}{3}$ of pop. descended from ancient Persians; 25% of pop. of Turkish stock ■ Most of pop. live in mountainous north & west of country ■ Became Islamic Republic after fall of Shah & return of Ayatollah Khomeini (1979) ■ Oil discovered in 1908 by Anglo-Persian oil company (later BP) ■ Iran's casualties in Iran-Iraq war (1980-88) variously estimated at between 150,000 - 630,000

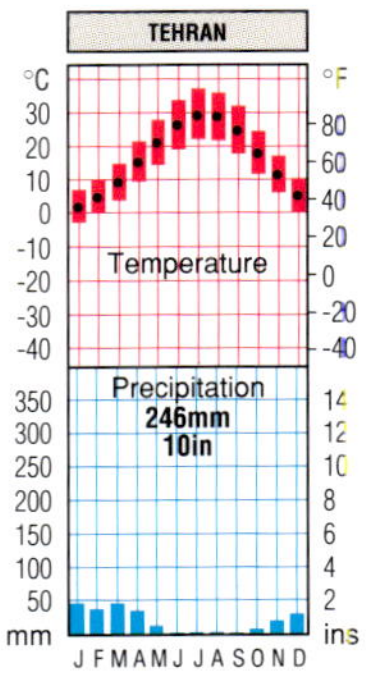

Tehran lies at over 1,200 m [4,000 ft] on the high Iranian plateau, enclosed on all sides by mountains, and experiences the dryness and extreme temperatures of a continental climate. Summers are hot, sunny and dry with low humidity. Most of the rain falls in winter and spring. Winters are cold with strong north-west winds. Snow and frost occur in most years.

KUWAIT

Kuwait's national flag dates from 1961 when the country ceased to be a British protectorate and gained its independence. The flag features the four Pan-Arab colours, the black portion having an unusual trapezium shape.

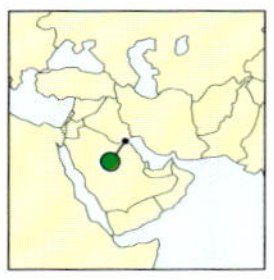

COUNTRY: State of Kuwait
AREA: 17,820 sq km [6,880 sq mls]
POPULATION: 2,143,000
CAPITAL (Population): Kuwait City (189,000)
GOVERNMENT: Constitutional monarchy with unicameral legislature
ETHNIC GROUPS: Kuwaiti Arab 40%, non-Kuwaiti Arab 38%, Asian 21%
LANGUAGES: Arabic 78%, Kurdish 10%, Farsi 4%
RELIGIONS: Muslim 92% (Sunni 80%), Christian 6%
NATIONAL DAY: 25 February
CURRENCY: Kuwaiti dinar = 1,000 fils
ANNUAL INCOME PER PERSON: $16,380
MAIN INDUSTRIES: Petroleum, natural gas
MAIN EXPORTS: Petroleum, petroleum products, fertilizers, natural gas
MAIN IMPORTS: Electrical machinery, transport equipment, chemicals, iron and steel
DEFENCE: 21% of national budget
POPULATION DENSITY: 120 per sq km [311 per sq ml]
LIFE EXPECTANCY: Female 76 yrs, Male 72 yrs
ADULT LITERACY: 75%

■ Oil discovered in 1938; reserves 3rd largest in world ■ World's largest saltwater desalination plants ■ Ruling Al Sabah family came to power in 1756 ■ Overseas investments have now surpassed oil as revenue earner ■ Comprehensive welfare systems ■ Invaded by Iraq in August 1990; liberated 1991

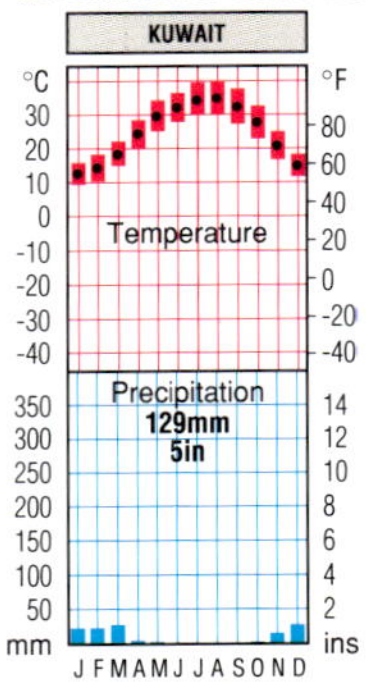

In winter the northern end of the Gulf comes under the influence of low pressure systems moving eastwards from the Mediterranean and rainfall is more reliable than that further down the Gulf. In the wake of low pressure, winds blowing from the north-west bring cooler air to the region. Summers are hot and dry. The frequent shamal winds which blow steadily by day give way to calm, sultry nights.

QATAR

The maroon colour of the Qatari flag is said to result from the natural effect of the sun on the traditional red banner. The proportions of the flag, which dates back to the mid 19th century (though it was not adopted until 1971), are unique.

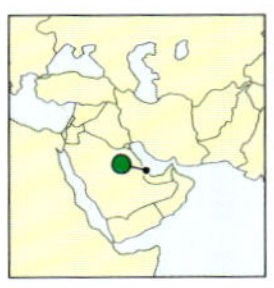

■ More than $\frac{2}{3}$ of pop. foreign workers ■ Oil first exported in 1949 ■ North Field, one of world's largest gas fields, has estimated reserves of 8.5 million million million cu m ■ Every citizen offered free plot of land & interest-free loan ■ Camels from Qatar, bred by Bedouins, considered to be finest in world

COUNTRY: State of Qatar
AREA: 11,000 sq km [4,247 sq mls]
POPULATION: 368,000
CAPITAL (Population): Doha (217,000)
GOVERNMENT: Constitutional monarchy
ETHNIC GROUPS: Southern Asia 34%, Qatari 20%, other Arab 25%, Iranian 16%
LANGUAGES: Arabic
RELIGIONS: Muslim 92%, Christian, Hindu
NATIONAL DAY: 3 September; Independence Day (1971)
CURRENCY: Riyal = 100 dirhams
ANNUAL INCOME PER PERSON: $15,860
POPULATION DENSITY: 33 per sq km [87 per sq ml]
LIFE EXPECTANCY: Female 73 yrs, Male 68 yrs
ADULT LITERACY: 75%

BAHRAIN

The white on Bahrain's flag is a result of the British request in 1820 that it be included in the flags of all friendly Arab states around the Persian Gulf. Red is the traditional colour of Kharijite Muslims. The flag dates from about 1932.

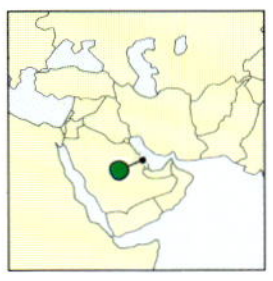

COUNTRY: Emirate of Bahrain
AREA: 678 sq km [262 sq mls]
POPULATION: 503,000
CAPITAL (Population): Manama (152,000)
GOVERNMENT: Monarchy (emirate) with a cabinet appointed by the emir
ETHNIC GROUPS: Bahraini Arab 68%, Persian, Indian and Pakistani 24.7%, other Arab 4.1%, European 2.5%
LANGUAGES: Arabic
RELIGIONS: Muslim 85%, Christian 7.3%
NATIONAL DAY: 16 December

CURRENCY: Bahrain dinar = 1,000 fils
ANNUAL INCOME PER PERSON: $6,500
POPULATION DENSITY: 741 per sq km [1,921 per sq ml]
LIFE EXPECTANCY: Female 74 yrs, Male 70 yrs
ADULT LITERACY: 75%

■ Emirate comprises 33 low-lying islands of which Bahrain Island is largest ■ Third of pop. immigrant workers, attracted by tax-free incomes ■ First Arab country to strike oil (1931) ■ Oil revenue represents 75% of GNP ■ Has aluminium smelting & processing plant which is largest non-oil industrial complex in Gulf

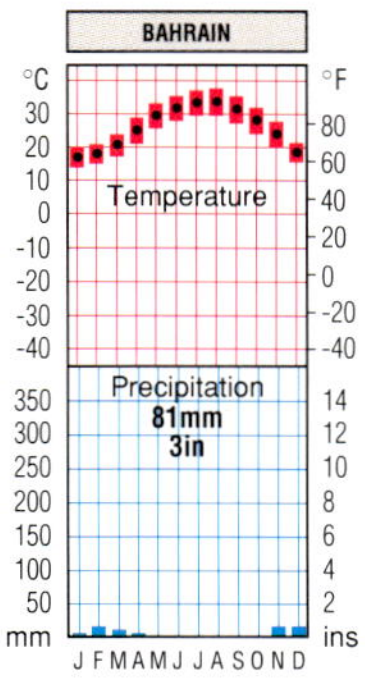

Bahrain island is more humid and has a smaller diurnal range of temperature than other parts of the southern Gulf. The island is noted for extreme heat and humidity in summer, particularly at Muharraq in the north-east. A hot, dry wind, the shamal, sometimes blows from the north. Winter nights are relatively chilly and heavy dew may occur. The small and variable rainfall occurs mainly as winter thunderstorms.

UNITED ARAB EMIRATES

When seven small states around the Persian Gulf combined to form the United Arab Emirates in 1971, this flag was agreed for the new nation. It features the Pan-Arab colours, first used in the Arab revolt against the Turks from 1916.

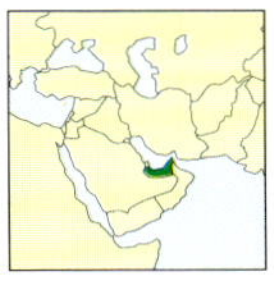

COUNTRY: United Arab Emirates
AREA: 83,600 sq km [32,278 sq mls]
POPULATION: 1,589,000
CAPITAL (Population): Abu Dhabi (293,000)
GOVERNMENT: Monarchy with an advisory Federal National Council
ETHNIC GROUPS: Arab 87%, Indo-Pakistani 9%, Iranian 2%
LANGUAGES: Arabic
RELIGIONS: Muslim (Sunni 80%)
NATIONAL DAY: 2 December; National Day, UAE established (1971)
CURRENCY: UAE dirham = 100 fils
ANNUAL INCOME PER PERSON: $19,860

MAIN PRIMARY PRODUCTS: Crude petroleum and natural gas
MAIN INDUSTRIES: Petroleum, natural gas, agriculture
MAIN EXPORTS: Petroleum
MAIN IMPORTS: Machinery and transport equipment, manufactured goods, food and live animals
DEFENCE: 37% of national budget
POPULATION DENSITY: 19 per sq km [49 per sq ml]
LIFE EXPECTANCY: Female 74 yrs, Male 70 yrs
ADULT LITERACY: 73%

■ Federation, formed in 1971, of seven former Sheikdoms ■ Formerly called Trucial States ■ Abu Dhabi largest & richest of Emirates ■ 80% of pop. foreign workers ■ Only 15% of workforce are UAE nationals ■ Gulf's tallest building is International Trade Centre in Dubai

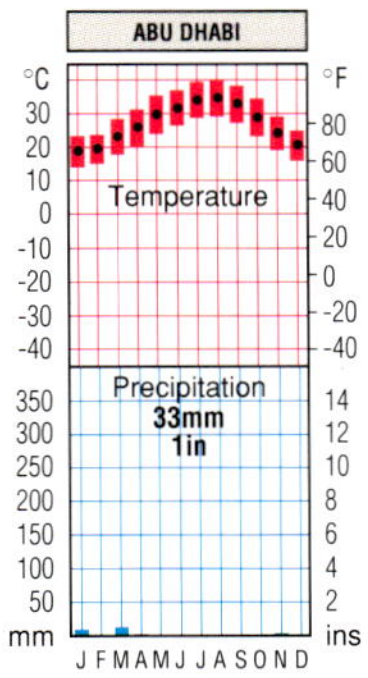

The climate of the southern shores of the Gulf is similar to that of the Gulf of Oman though with a greater temperature range. The cloudless summer days often exceed 40°C [100°F] while winter nights descend to a chilly 15°C [59°F]. The small amount of rain varies greatly from year to year and occurs mainly as thundery downpours in winter.

OMAN

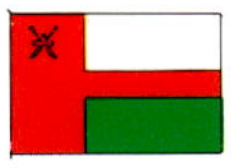

Formerly Muscat and Oman, the state's flag was plain red – the traditional colour of the people who lived in the area. When Oman was established in 1970, the state arms of sword and dagger were added with stripes of white and green.

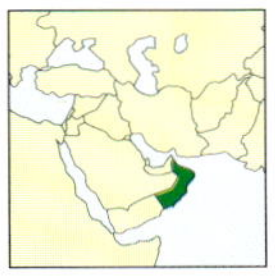

COUNTRY: Sultanate of Oman
AREA: 212,460 sq km [82,031 sq mls]
POPULATION: 1,502,000
CAPITAL (Population): Muscat (250,000)
GOVERNMENT: Monarchy with a consultative council
ETHNIC GROUPS: Omani Arab 77%, Indian 15%
LANGUAGES: Arabic
RELIGIONS: Muslim 86%, Hindu 13%
NATIONAL DAY: 18 November

CURRENCY: Omani rial = 1,000 baizas
ANNUAL INCOME PER PERSON: $5,220
MAIN PRIMARY PRODUCTS: Crude petroleum and natural gas
MAIN INDUSTRIES: Petroleum and natural gas
MAIN EXPORTS: Petroleum
MAIN IMPORTS: Machinery, vehicles, foodstuffs, basic manufactures

■ Known as Muscat and Oman until 1970 ■ 70% of pop. engaged in agriculture and fishery ■ Over 250,000 immigrant workers ■ Exports of oil account for over 90% of GNP ■ Port of Muscat flourishing trade centre since 5th century BC ■ Present Sultan's family have been in power since 18th century ■ Close military links with UK and USA

DEFENCE: 33% of national budget
POPULATION DENSITY: 7 per sq km [18 per sq ml]
LIFE EXPECTANCY: Female 60 yrs, Male 57 yrs

YEMEN

The new straightforward design of Yemen's flag, incorporating the Pan-Arab colours, dates from 1990 when the Yemen Arab Republic (in the north) united with the People's Democratic Republic of Yemen (in the south).

COUNTRY: Yemen
AREA: 527,970 sq km [203,849 sq mls]
POPULATION: 11,282,000
CAPITAL (Population): San'a (500,000)
GOVERNMENT: Multi-party democracy with 301-seat Parliament
ETHNIC GROUPS: Arab (96%)
LANGUAGES: Arabic
RELIGIONS: Moslem
CURRENCY: Northern riyal = 100 fils and Southern dinar = 1000 fils co-exist during transitional period
ANNUAL INCOME PER PERSON: $500
MAIN PRIMARY PRODUCTS: Oil, gas, salt, cotton
MAIN INDUSTRIES: Agriculture, fishing, textiles, plastics, rubber, aluminium goods, paint and matches
EXPORTS: $71 per person

MAIN EXPORTS: Cotton, coffee, fish
IMPORTS: $400 per person
MAIN IMPORTS: Food and live animals
POPULATION DENSITY: 21 per sq km [55 per sq ml]
INFANT MORTALITY: 105 per 1,000 live births
LIFE EXPECTANCY: Female 55 yrs, Male 52 yrs
ADULT LITERACY: 20%
PRINCIPAL CITIES (Population): San'a 500,000 Aden 417,000

■ Until May 1990 was two separate countries: Yemen Arab Republic (North) & People's Democratic Republic of Yemen (South) ■ Roman name for Yemen, Arabia Felix, means 'happy Arabia' ■ 75% of pop. engaged in agriculture ■ 1½ million Yemenis work elsewhere in Arab world ■ Only country to claim 100% adherence to Islam ■ Oil discovered as recently as 1983

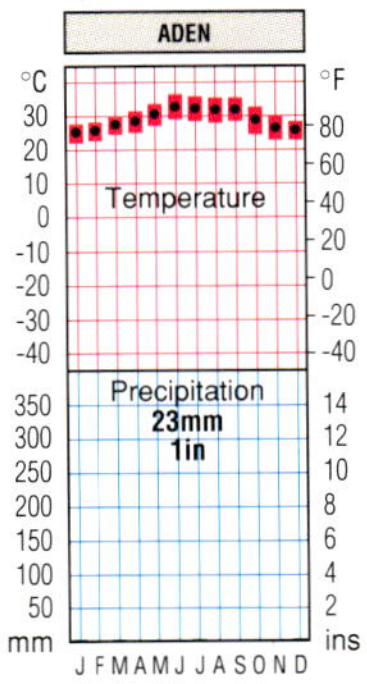

During winter, when rain occurs throughout much of the Middle East, Aden lies under the influence of the dry north-east trade winds which blow from the Arabian desert. In summer the south-west monsoon blows from Africa, raising dust and sand but bringing no rainfall. The prevailing on-shore winds moderate the summer heat and temperatures are several degrees cooler than on the African shore of the Gulf of Aden.

ASIA – SOUTH-WEST

SAUDI ARABIA

The inscription on the Saudi flag above the sword means 'There is no God but Allah, and Mohammed is the Prophet of Allah'. The only national flag with an inscription as its main feature, the design was adopted in 1938.

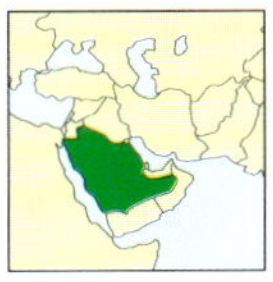

COUNTRY: Kingdom of Saudi Arabia
AREA: 2,149,690 sq km [829,995 sq mls]
POPULATION: 14,870,000
CAPITAL (Population): Riyadh (2,000,000)
GOVERNMENT: Absolute monarchy with advisory councils
ETHNIC GROUPS: Saudi 82%, Yemeni 10%
LANGUAGES: Arabic (official)
RELIGIONS: Muslim (mainly Sunni) 98%, Christian 1%
NATIONAL DAY: 23 September; Unification of the Kingdom (1932)
CURRENCY: Saudi riyal = 100 malalah
ANNUAL INCOME PER PERSON: $6,230
MAIN PRIMARY PRODUCTS: Cattle, sheep, fruit, crude oil and natural gas
MAIN INDUSTRIES: Crude oil, natural gas, chemicals, fertilizers, steel
EXPORTS: $1,966 per person
MAIN EXPORTS: Crude petroleum 94%
MAIN EXPORT PARTNERS: Japan 22%, USA 19%, Netherlands 6%, Bahrain 5%, Singapore 5%, Taiwan 4%
IMPORTS: $1,466 per person
MAIN IMPORTS: Machinery 19%, foodstuffs 17%, transport equipment 14%, textiles and clothing 13%, metals and metal products 8%, chemicals 4%
MAIN IMPORT PARTNERS: Japan 17%, USA 15%, UK 8%, Germany 8%, Italy 7%, France 5%, South Korea 5%
DEFENCE: 36.0% of national budget
TOURISM: 960,000 pilgrims
POPULATION DENSITY: 7 per sq km [18 per sq ml]
INFANT MORTALITY: 58 per 1,000 live births
LIFE EXPECTANCY: Female 68 yrs, Male 64 yrs
ADULT LITERACY: 57%
PRINCIPAL CITIES (Population): Riyadh 2,000,000 Jedda 1,400,000 Mecca 618,000 Medina 500,000

■ Less than 1% of land suitable for agriculture ■ No permanent rivers with outlets to sea ■ Contains more oil than any nation, world's top oil exporter - 1/3 of world output ■ Mecca birthplace of Muhammad, born c. 570, & Islam's most holy city ■ Non-Muslims banned from Mecca & Medina ■ Saudi form of Islam based on 18th-century movement of Najdi leader, Shaikh Mohammed Ibn Abdel-Wahhab ■ About 5,000 princes in Saudi royal family ■ Less than 1% of women employed ■ Alcohol, drugs & pornography are strictly prohibited ■ No tourists allowed entry – only pilgrims

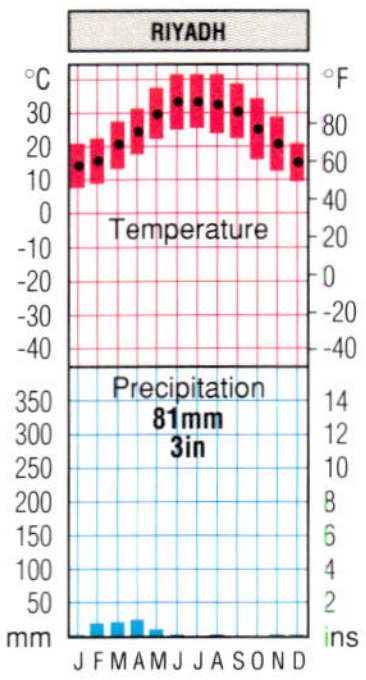

In the interior of Saudi Arabia the diurnal temperature range is much greater than in coastal regions. In the glaring heat of summer, daytime temperatures frequently exceed 40°C [100°F], but fall sharply at night. At over 400 m [1,300 ft] above sea level Riyadh has unusually cold winters for its latitude. Most of the rain falls as short but heavy showers in spring.

IRAQ

Using the four Pan-Arab colours, Iraq's flag was adopted in 1963 at the time of the proposed federation with Egypt and Syria. Iraq retained the three green stars, symbolising the three countries, even though the union failed to materialise.

■ Landlocked country except for its outlet to Gulf at Shatt Al Arab Waterway ■ In normal times oil represents 95% of export earnings ■ Sunni Muslim minority have always held political power ■ Was engaged in war with Iran for most of 1980s ■ Invaded neighbouring Kuwait in Aug. 1990 but was ejected by multi-national forces in Feb. 1991

COUNTRY: Republic of Iraq
AREA: 438,320 sq km [169,235 sq mls]
POPULATION: 18,920,000
CAPITAL (Population): Baghdad (4,649,000)
GOVERNMENT: Unitary single-party republic with a unicameral legislature
ETHNIC GROUPS: Arab 79%, Kurd 16%, Turkmen 2%, Persian 2%
NATIONAL DAY: 17 July; Military revolution (1958) and proclamation of republic
LANGUAGES: Arabic (official), Kurdish, Turkish
RELIGIONS: Shiite Muslim 54%, Sunni Muslim 42%, Christian 2%
CURRENCY: Iraqi dinar = 20 dirhams = 1,000 fils
ANNUAL INCOME PER PERSON: $2,000
MAIN PRIMARY PRODUCTS: Crude oil, natural gas, dates, cattle, sheep, cereals, goats, camels
MAIN INDUSTRIES: Oil and gas production, food processing, textiles
MAIN EXPORTS: Fuels and other energy 98%
MAIN IMPORTS: Machinery and transport equipment 40%, manufactured goods 27%, foodstuffs 16%, chemicals 8%
POPULATION DENSITY: 43 per sq km [112 per sq ml]
LIFE EXPECTANCY: Female 67 yrs, Male 65 yrs
ADULT LITERACY: 60%
PRINCIPAL CITIES (Population): Baghdad 4,649,000 Basra 617,000 Mosul 571,000

TURKEY

Although the crescent moon and the five-pointed star are symbols of Islam, Turkey's religion, their presence on the flag does not denote an Islamic state. The flag was officially adopted when the modern, secular republic was founded in 1923.

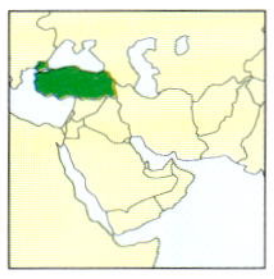

COUNTRY: Republic of Turkey
AREA: 779,450 sq km [300,946 sq mls]
POPULATION: 57,326,000
CAPITAL (Population): Ankara (2,252,000)
GOVERNMENT: Multi-party republic with a unicameral legislature
ETHNIC GROUPS: Turkish 86%, Kurdish 11%, Arab 2%
LANGUAGES: Turkish (official), Kurdish
RELIGIONS: Sunni Muslim 99%, Eastern Orthodox
NATIONAL DAY: 29 October; Republic Day (1923)
CURRENCY: Turkish lira = 100 kurual
ANNUAL INCOME PER PERSON: $1,630
MAIN PRIMARY PRODUCTS: Cereals, cotton, pulses, sugar beet, cattle, sheep, tobacco, fruit, vegetables, coal, lignite, crude oil, iron, boron, copper, chrome
MAIN INDUSTRIES: Agriculture, steel, food processing, textiles, oil, chemicals, fishing, mining
MAIN EXPORTS: Textiles 24%, agricultural products 20%, metals 14%, foodstuffs 7%
MAIN EXPORT PARTNERS: Germany 18%, Iraq 8%, Italy 7%, USA 7%, UK 5%, France 4%, Saudi Arabia 3%
MAIN IMPORTS: Fuels 19%, machinery 17%, chemicals 14%, iron and steel 12%, pharmaceuticals 7%
MAIN IMPORT PARTNERS: Germany 14%, USA 11%, Iraq 10%, Italy 7%, UK 6%, France 5%
DEFENCE: 17.5% of national budget
TOURISM: 2,468,000 visitors
POPULATION DENSITY: 74 per sq km [190 per sq ml]
INFANT MORTALITY: 62 per 1,000 live births
LIFE EXPECTANCY: Female 68 yrs, Male 65 yrs
ADULT LITERACY: 74%
PRINCIPAL CITIES (Population): Istanbul 5,495,000 Ankara 2,252,000 Izmir 1,490,000 Adana 776,000 Bursa 614,000

■ Small area (3% of total) of country on European 'mainland' (Thrace) ■ Europe linked to Asia by suspension bridges spanning Bosphorus, which separates Mediterranean from Black Sea ■ Tigris and Euphrates rivers rise in Turkey ■ 25% of country covered in state-owned forest ■ Was hub of Byzantine Empire & for nearly 500 years was centre of Ottoman Empire, at one time controlling 25% of Europe ■ Istanbul was formerly known as Byzantium and Constantinople ■ Over 1½ million Turks work in Germany ■ Military coup 3 times since 1960

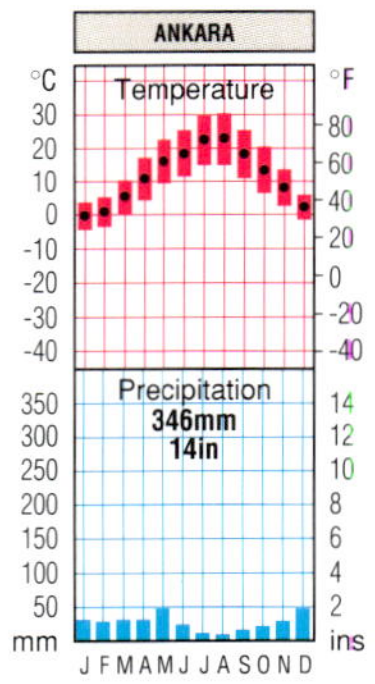

The plateau of Anatolia is a region of continental extremes and scanty precipitation. Ankara lies just to the north of the driest part of the plateau which is situated around the large saltwater Lake Tuz. Summer days are hot and sunny and nights pleasantly cool. Winters are cold with the mean temperature in January close to freezing. Snow falls on average on 20 to 30 days a year.

CYPRUS

The design, featuring a map of the island with two olive branches, has been the official state flag since independence from Britain in 1960. However, Cyprus is now divided and the separate communities fly the Greek and Turkish flags.

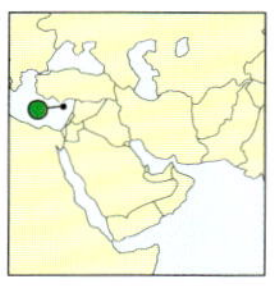

■ Name in Greek (Kypros) means copper ■ Partitioned since 1974 when Turkey invaded the island ■ UN forces maintain truce ■ Has been famous for its wines, sherries and brandies since classical times ■ Christianity was brought to island by St Paul & St Barnabas in 1st century AD

COUNTRY: Cyprus
AREA: 9,250 sq km [3,571 sq mls]
POPULATION: 702,000
CAPITAL (Population): Nicosia (167,000)
GOVERNMENT: Multi-party republic with unicameral legislature
ETHNIC GROUPS: Greek Cyp. 81%; Turkish Cyp. 19%
LANGUAGES: Greek and Turkish
RELIGIONS: Greek Orthodox and Muslim
NATIONAL DAY: 1 October; Independence Day (1960)
CURRENCY: Cyprus £ = 1,000 mils
ANNUAL INCOME PER PERSON: $8,040
MAIN INDUSTRIES: Cement, mosaic tiles, wine making, footwear, cigarettes
MAIN PRIMARY PRODUCTS: Asbestos, pyrites, copper
MAIN EXPORTS: Vegetables, fruit, clothing and footwear
MAIN IMPORTS: Food, petroleum, chemicals
DEFENCE: 1% of national budget
POPULATION DENSITY: 76 per sq km [197 per sq ml]
LIFE EXPECTANCY: Female 80 yrs, Male 74 yrs
ADULT LITERACY: 93%

SYRIA

The flag of Syria is the one adopted in 1958 by the former United Arab Republic (which included Syria, Egypt and Yemen). At various times in their history Egypt and Syria have shared the same flag, but since 1980 Syria has used this design.

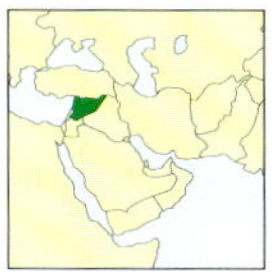

COUNTRY: Syrian Arab Republic
AREA: 185,180 sq km [71,498 sq mls]
POPULATION: 12,116,000
CAPITAL (Population): Damascus (1,361,000)
GOVERNMENT: Unitary multi-party republic with a unicameral legislature
ETHNIC GROUPS: Arab 89%, Kurdish 6%
LANGUAGES: Arabic (official), Kurdish, Armenian
RELIGIONS: Muslim (mostly Sunni) 90%, Christian 9%
NATIONAL DAY: 17 April
CURRENCY: Syrian £ = 100 piastres
ANNUAL INCOME PER PERSON: $990
MAIN PRIMARY PRODUCTS: Sheep, goats, cattle, cotton, sugar, fruit, cereals, crude oil, natural gas, phosphates, manganese, salt
MAIN INDUSTRIES: Agriculture, oil and gas, cotton, wool, metal goods, glass, flour, soap
MAIN EXPORTS: Crude petroleum and natural gas 33%, chemicals 29%, textiles and clothing 26%, foodstuffs 4%
MAIN EXPORT PARTNERS: Italy 31%, CIS nations 21%, France 10%, Romania 9%, Iran 5%, Germany 5%
MAIN IMPORTS: Machinery and equipment 30%, chemicals 21%, foodstuffs 12%, basic metal products 8%, textiles 3%
MAIN IMPORT PARTNERS: France 10%, CIS nations 8%, Iran 8%, Germany 8%, Italy 7%, Libya 6%, USA 5%
DEFENCE: 34.9% of national budget
POPULATION DENSITY: 65 per sq km [169 per sq ml]
LIFE EXPECTANCY: Female 69 yrs, Male 65 yrs
ADULT LITERACY: 61%
PRINCIPAL CITIES (Population): Damascus 1,361,000 Aleppo 1,308,000 Homs 464,000 Latakia 258,000

■ Damascus world's oldest capital & world's longest continually inhabited city (since 2500BC) ■ Most of E. part of country desert or semi-desert ■ 50% of workforce engaged in agriculture ■ Hydroelectric power from dam on Euphrates at Al-Thaura produces 70% of electricity ■ Oil production only $^{1}/_{16}$ of neighbouring Iraq's, but provides 75% of Syria's export earnings ■ World's oldest surviving Christian church is converted house in Syria 232AD; St Paul's refuge, Honania's house, still standing in Damascus

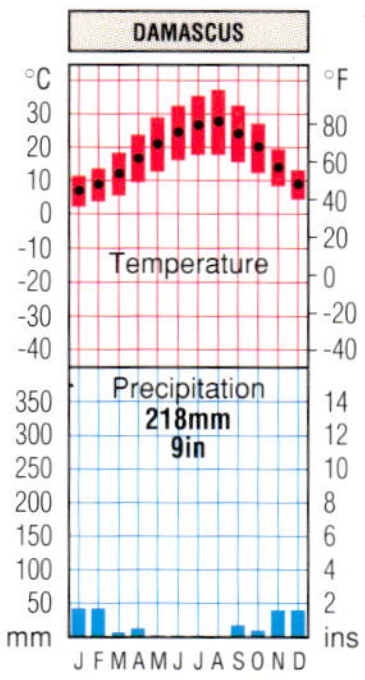

Damascus is isolated from the maritime influence of the Mediterranean by the Lebanon Mts. Rainfall, confined to winter, is less than on the coast and more variable. The Syrian winter becomes colder the further east one travels and frost and snow are not uncommon. On the higher mountains, patches of snow persist throughout the year. Summers are very hot and dry with a large diurnal range of temperature.

LEBANON

Adopted in 1943, Lebanon's colours are those of the Lebanese Legion in World War I. The cedar tree, many of which grow in the country's mountains, has been a Lebanese symbol since biblical times.

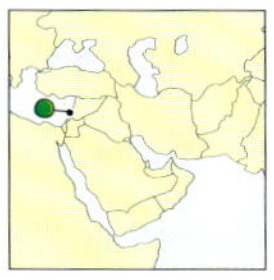

COUNTRY: Republic of Lebanon
AREA: 10,400 sq km [4,015 sq mls]
POPULATION: 2,701,000
CAPITAL (Population): Beirut (702,000)
GOVERNMENT: Multi-party republic with a unicameral legislature
ETHNIC GROUPS: Lebanese 83%, Palestinian 10%, Armenian 5%
LANGUAGES: Arabic (official), French and English
RELIGIONS: Muslim 57%, Christian 43%
NATIONAL DAY: 22 November; Independence Day (1941)
CURRENCY: Lebanese £ = 100 piastres
ANNUAL INCOME PER PERSON: $2,000
MAIN PRIMARY PRODUCTS: Salt, gypsum, tin
MAIN INDUSTRIES: Agriculture, fishing, manufacture of rubber tyres and tubes
MAIN EXPORTS: Clothing, jewellery, aluminium and pharmaceutical products, food production, machinery
MAIN IMPORTS: Cereals, petroleum products, machinery
DEFENCE: 21% of national budget
POPULATION DENSITY: 260 per sq km [673 per sq ml]
LIFE EXPECTANCY: Female 71 yrs, Male 67 yrs
ADULT LITERACY: 77%

■ Until mid 1970s, Beirut was major financial & commercial centre for Middle East ■ Has been in state of civil war since 1975 ■ Israeli troops occupy 'security zone' in south, Syrians control much of Beirut ■ UN peacekeeping force since 1977

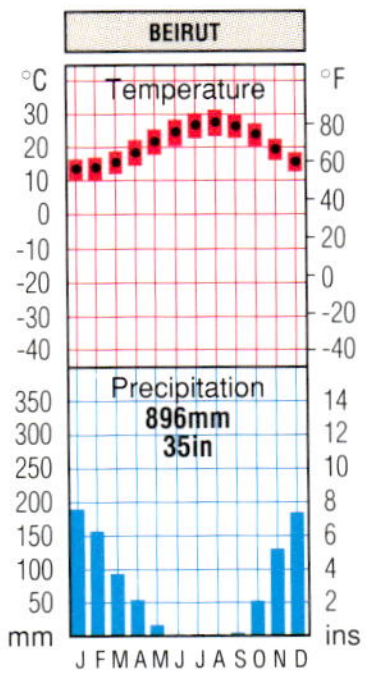

The coast of Lebanon has the hot, dry summers and mild, wet winters characteristic of much of the Mediterranean basin. The four months, June to September, are almost completely dry. In winter, onshore winds rise against the steep western edge of the Lebanon mountains bringing heavy rain at sea level with snow at high altitude. Close to the sea, there is a small daily range of temperature.

JORDAN

Green, white and black are the colours of the three tribes who led the Arab Revolt against the Turks in 1917, while red is the colour of the Husain dynasty. The points of the star represent the first seven verses of the Koran.

COUNTRY: Hashemite Kingdom of Jordan
AREA: 89,210 sq km [34,444 sq mls]
POPULATION: 4,009,000
CAPITAL (Population): Amman (1,160,000)
ETHNIC GROUPS: Arab 99%
GOVERNMENT: Constitutional monarchy with a bicameral legislature
LANGUAGES: Arabic
RELIGIONS: Sunni Muslim 93%, Christian 5%
NATIONAL DAY: 25 May; Independence Day (1948)

■ Has very small stretch of Red Sea coast centred on important port of Aqaba ■ Over 50% of pop. is Palestinian ■ 10 UN refugee camps for Palestinians ■ 1967 Middle East war deprived Jordan of 80% of its fruit growing area (i.e. West Bank) ■ King Hussein has ruled since 1952, making him Middle East's longest serving ruler

CURRENCY: Jordan dinar = 1000 fils
ANNUAL INCOME PER PERSON: $1,240
POPULATION DENSITY: 45 per sq km [116 per sq ml]
LIFE EXPECTANCY: Female 70 yrs, Male 66 yrs
ADULT LITERACY: 75%

ISRAEL

The blue and white stripes on Israel's flag are based on a Hebrew prayer shawl. In the centre is the ancient six-pointed Star of David. The flag was designed in America in 1891 and officially adopted by the new Jewish state in 1948.

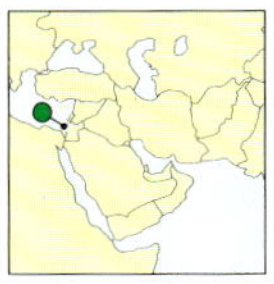

COUNTRY: State of Israel
AREA: 26,650 sq km [10,290 sq mls]
POPULATION: 4,659,000
CAPITAL (Population): Jerusalem (483,000)
GOVERNMENT: Multi-party republic with unicameral legislature
ETHNIC GROUPS: Jewish 83%, Arab 16%
LANGUAGES: Hebrew and Arabic (official)
RELIGIONS: Jewish 82%, Muslim 14%, Christian 2%
NATIONAL DAY: 10 May (variable each year); Independence Day (1948)
CURRENCY: Israeli sheqel = 100 agorat
ANNUAL INCOME PER PERSON: $10,970
MAIN PRIMARY PRODUCTS: Livestock, natural gas, fruit, vegetables
MAIN INDUSTRIES: Agriculture, mining, food processing, textiles, clothing, fertilizers, cement, diamond cutting
EXPORTS: $2,288 per person
MAIN EXPORTS: Machinery 29%, diamonds 29%, chemicals 22%, textiles 8%, foodstuffs 5%
MAIN EXPORT PARTNERS: USA 31%, UK 8%, Japan 7%, Germany 5%, Hong Kong 5%, Netherlands 5%
IMPORTS: $2,817 per person
MAIN IMPORTS: Diamonds 20%, capital goods 15%, consumer goods 11%, fuels and lubricants 8%
MAIN IMPORT PARTNERS: USA 16%, Belgium - Lux. 15%, Germany 11%, UK 9%, Switzerland 9%, Ireland 6%, France 4%
DEFENCE: 18.2% of national budget
TOURISM: 1,379,000 visitors
POPULATION DENSITY: 175 per sq km [453 per sq ml]
INFANT MORTALITY: 10 per 1,000 live births
LIFE EXPECTANCY: Female 78 yrs, Male 74 yrs
ADULT LITERACY: 92%
PRINCIPAL CITIES (Population): Jerusalem 483,000 Tel Aviv-Jaffa 323,000 Haifa 225,000

■ Dead Sea is world's lowest point (396 m [1,279 ft] below sea level) ■ Sea of Galilee Israel's main reservoir of fresh water ■ State of Israel created in 1948; return of Jews to their historic homeland marked 18 centuries of exile ■ 5 wars since 1948 in which Arab nations & Palestinians fought against Israel ■ Nearly 25% of national budget spent on defence ■ Men do 3 years national service, single women 2 years ■ World's top recipient of aid, mainly from US

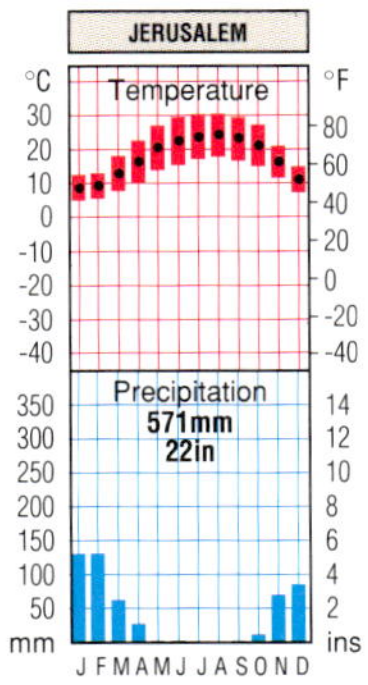

East of the Mediterranean Sea the annual rainfall decreases inland and the length of the summer dry season increases to more than five months. At over 700 m [2,250 ft], Jerusalem has lower temperatures and a greater range than coastal regions of Israel. To the south, rainfall decreases rapidly to only 70 mm [2.5 in] in the rocky desert around the Dead Sea.

AFRICA – NORTH

EGYPT

Egypt has flown a flag of red, white and black (the Pan-Arab colours) since 1958 but with various emblems in the centre. The present design, with the gold eagle emblem symbolising the Arab hero Saladin, was introduced in 1984.

COUNTRY: Arab Republic of Egypt
AREA: 1,001,450 sq km [386,660 sq mls]
POPULATION: 53,153,000
CAPITAL (Population): Cairo (6,325,000)
GOVERNMENT: Republic with a unicameral legislature
ETHNIC GROUPS: Egyptian 99%
LANGUAGES: Arabic (official), French, English
RELIGIONS: Sunni Muslim 94%, Christian
NATIONAL DAY: 23 July; Anniversary of the Revolution (1952)
CURRENCY: Egyptian pound = 100 piastres = 1,000 milièmes
ANNUAL INCOME PER PERSON: $600
MAIN PRIMARY PRODUCTS: Cotton, rice, maize, sugar, sheep, goats, phosphates, oil and natural gas
MAIN INDUSTRIES: Oil refining, cement, textiles, fertilizers, iron and steel, tourism
EXPORTS: $48 per person
MAIN EXPORTS: Mineral products including crude petroleum 65%, textiles 19%
MAIN EXPORT PARTNERS: Italy 19%, France 12%, Romania 12%
IMPORTS: $140 per person
MAIN IMPORTS: Foodstuffs 30%, machinery and electrical equipment 20%
MAIN IMPORT PARTNERS: USA 14%, Germany 9%, Italy 7%
DEFENCE: 14% of national budget
TOURISM: 1,795,000 visitors
POPULATION DENSITY: 53 per sq km [138 per sq ml]
INFANT MORTALITY: 71 per 1,000 live births
LIFE EXPECTANCY: Female 65 yrs, Male 62 yrs
ADULT LITERACY: 45%
PRINCIPAL CITIES (Population): Cairo 6,325,000 Alexandria 2,893,000 Giza 1,858,000 Shubra el Kheima 711,000 El Mahalla el Kubra 385,000

■ Mostly flat desert devoid of vegetation except Nile Delta, borders of Nile, Red Sea coastal strip & few oases in Western Desert ■ Africa's second most populous country, after Nigeria ■ Suez Canal (opened 1869, 173 km [107 mls] long) links Mediterranean with Red Sea, carrying more than 20,000 vessels per year ■ Aswan High Dam controls annual floods that once put most of Nile Valley under water; also produces hydo-electricity ■ 2nd largest industrial African nation, after S. Africa ■ Major recipient of US aid ■ Tourism one of main industries ■ Rural peasant farmers make up ²/₃ of pop. ■ Over 90% of pop. live in Nile Delta ■ 90% Muslim, with Coptic Christian minority ■ Women more emancipated than anywhere else in Arab world ■ Since 525BC, has often been dominated by foreign powers ■ Egyptian pyramids, at El Giza near Cairo, built more than 4,000 years ago; oldest & only surviving of Seven Wonders of Ancient World ■ Has fought 4 wars with Israel since 1948, but in 1979 became only Arab country to sign peace agreement with Israel (Camp David Accord)

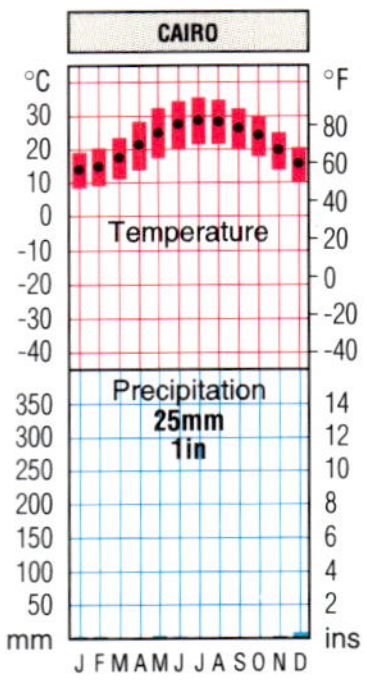

The rainfall of Egypt is very low, falling, if at all, in the winter months, Nov.- Feb. The Nile, carrying tropical rainfall northwards to the Mediterranean, is the lifeline of the land. In the south and on the Red Sea coast no rain falls for many years. The winters are cool but the summers very hot, getting hotter north to south. Hot dusty winds can blow into the Nile from the surrounding deserts during March-July.

LIBYA

The simplest of all world flags, Libya's represents the nation's quest for a green revolution in agriculture. Libya flew the flag of the Federation of Arab Republics until 1977 when it left the organisation.

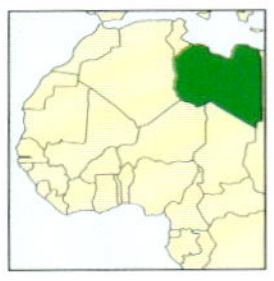

COUNTRY: Socialist People's Libyan Arab Jamahiriya
AREA: 1,759,540 sq km [679,358 sq mls]
POPULATION: 4,545,000
CAPITAL (Population): Tripoli (980,000)
GOVERNMENT: Socialist state with one policy-making body
ETHNIC GROUPS: Libyan Arab and Berber 89%
LANGUAGES: Arabic (official), Berber
RELIGIONS: Sunni Muslim 97%
NATIONAL DAY: 1 September; Revolution Day (1969)
CURRENCY: Libyan dinar = 1,000 dirhams
ANNUAL INCOME PER PERSON: $5,800
MAIN PRIMARY PRODUCTS: Cereals, fruit, olives, dates, groundnuts, oil, natural gas
MAIN INDUSTRIES: Oil and gas production and refining, cement, agriculture, food processing, textiles, fishing
EXPORTS: $2,001 per person
MAIN EXPORTS: Crude petroleum 96%, natural gas
MAIN EXPORT PARTNERS: Italy 39%, Germany 19%, Spain 13%, CIS nations 8%, France 7%
IMPORTS: $1,078 per person
MAIN IMPORTS: Machinery and transport equipment 37%, consumer goods 27%, foodstuffs 14%
MAIN IMPORT PARTNERS: Italy 20%, Germany 9%, UK 6%, France 4%
DEFENCE: 36% of national budget
TOURISM: 120,000 visitors
POPULATION DENSITY: 2.6 per sq km [6.7 per sq ml]
INFANT MORTALITY: 68 per 1,000 live births
LIFE EXPECTANCY: Female 65 yrs, Male 62 yrs
ADULT LITERACY: 74%
PRINCIPAL CITIES (Population): Tripoli 980,000 Benghazi 650,000 Misratah 285,000

■ Formed in 1949 by uniting Tripolitania, Cyrenia & Fezzan ■ One of world's poorest countries until discovery of oil in 1958 ■ Oil accounts for 98% of exports ■ Huge irrigation projects creating fertile land from desert ■ One of world's highest pop. growth rates ■ Spends more % on education than any other African country ■ Possibly finest Roman ruins in Africa at Leptis Magna ■ Military coup in 1969 brought Moamar al Gaddafi to power ■ Anything vaguely connected with Israel confiscated from arriving traveller

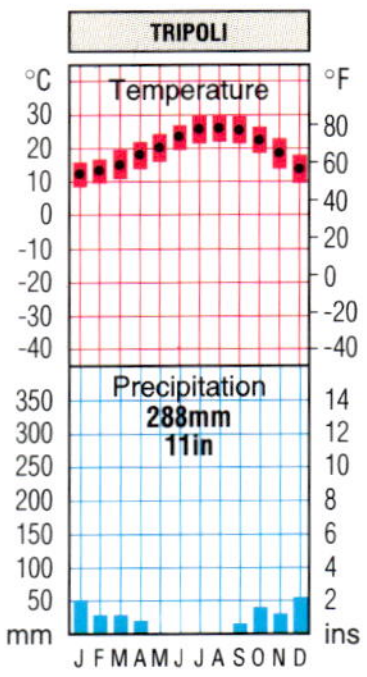

The climate of the Libyan coast is transitional between the Mediterranean region and the Sahara Desert. Proximity to the sea results in less extreme temperatures and higher rainfall than is found even a short distance further south. The winter rains occur when low pressure systems pass eastward across the Mediterranean. The hot, dry Scirocco wind from off the desert is particularly frequent in spring.

TUNISIA

The Tunisian flag features the crescent and the star, traditional symbols of Islam. It originated in about 1835 when the country was still officially under Turkish rule and was adopted after independence from France in 1956.

COUNTRY: Republic of Tunisia
AREA: 163,610 sq km [63,170 sq mls]
POPULATION: 8,180,000
CAPITAL (Population): Tunis (774,000)
GOVERNMENT: Multi-party republic with a unicameral legislature
ETHNIC GROUPS: Arab 98%, Berber 1%, French
LANGUAGES: Arabic (official), French
RELIGIONS: Sunni Muslim 99%
NATIONAL DAY: 20 March; Independence Day (1956)
CURRENCY: Dinar = 1,000 millimes
ANNUAL INCOME PER PERSON: $1,420
MAIN PRIMARY PRODUCTS: Crude oil and natural gas, phosphates, salt, lead, iron, timber, fruit, wheat, olives, barley, tomatoes
MAIN INDUSTRIES: Tourism, mining, oil refining, food processing, phosphate processing, textiles
EXPORTS: $367 per person
MAIN EXPORTS: Petroleum and derivatives 24%, clothing 20%, fertilizers 12%
MAIN EXPORT PARTNERS: France 22%, Germany 20%, Italy 17%, Belgium 7%
IMPORTS: $548 per person
MAIN IMPORTS: Machinery 17%, petroleum and derivatives 8%, raw cotton, cotton yarn and fabrics 6%, iron and steel 6%
MAIN IMPORT PARTNERS: France 27%, Germany 13%, Italy 11%, USA 6%
DEFENCE: 15% of national budget
TOURISM: 1,875,000 visitors
POPULATION DENSITY: 50 per sq km [129 per sq ml]
INFANT MORTALITY: 47 per 1,000 live births
LIFE EXPECTANCY: Female 68 yrs, Male 67 yrs
ADULT LITERACY: 54%
PRINCIPAL CITIES (Population): Tunis 774,000 Sfax 232,000

■ Chotts - salt pans - sometimes lower than sea level ■ Kairouan, holiest Muslim city in Africa; 7 trips to this city considered by faithful equivalent to 1 visit to Mecca ■ Oil in Sahara, near Algerian border, represents 30% of export earnings ■ World's 2nd largest exporter of olive oil, 15% of export earnings ■ N. Africa's largest Jewish community around Tunis & Jerba ■ Though Muslim country, women do not wear veil ■ One of Africa's best educational systems, free from primary level to university ■ Site of ancient Carthage ■ Romans built 180 cities in Tunisia during 400-year stay

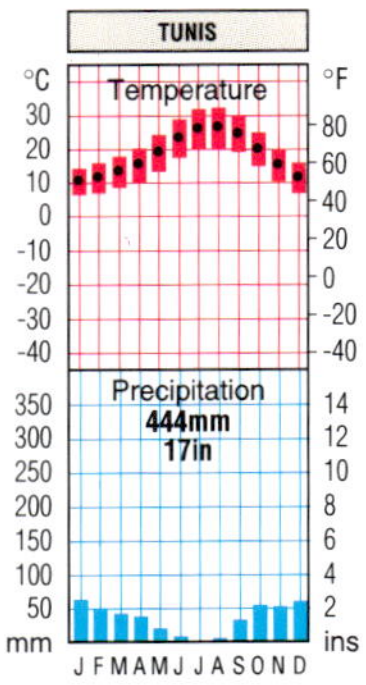

Although most of the rain in Tunisia falls in winter when the region is affected by low pressure, prevailing north-easterly winds from the sea in summer result in a shorter dry season than is found in many parts of the Mediterranean basin. The influence of the sea also helps to moderate extremes of temperature and although they are mostly sunny, summer days are seldom oppressive.

ALGERIA

Algeria's flag features traditional Islamic symbols and colours and the design dates back to the early 19th century. Used by the liberation movement that fought against French rule after 1954, it was adopted on independence in 1962.

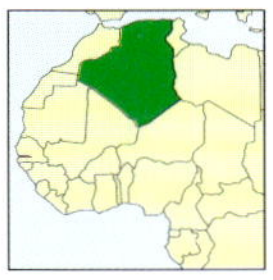

COUNTRY: Democratic and Popular Republic of Algeria
AREA: 2,381,700 sq km [919,590 sq mls]
POPULATION: 24,960,000
CAPITAL (Population): Algiers (1,722,000)
GOVERNMENT: Socialist republic with unicameral legislature
ETHNIC GROUPS: Arab 83%, Berber 17%, French
LANGUAGES: Arabic
RELIGIONS: Sunni Muslim 98%, Roman Catholic
NATIONAL DAY: 1 November; Anniversary of the Revolution (1954)
CURRENCY: Algerian dinar = 100 centimes
ANNUAL INCOME PER PERSON: $2,060
MAIN PRIMARY PRODUCTS: Oil and natural gas, phosphates, iron ore, lead, copper, cereals, fruit, olives, timber, livestock
MAIN INDUSTRIES: Oil refining, natural gas, petrochemicals, mining, agriculture, wine, food processing
EXPORTS: $333 per person
MAIN EXPORTS: Crude oil, petroleum products, natural gas 97%, wine, vegetables and fruit
MAIN EXPORT PARTNERS: France 29%, USA 22%, Italy 19%
IMPORTS: $286 per person
MAIN IMPORTS: Machinery and transport equipment 29%, semi-finished products 29%, foodstuffs 18%
MAIN IMPORT PARTNERS: France 24%, Germany 10%, Italy 8%, USA 6%, Spain 4%, Belgium 4%
DEFENCE: 9.6% of national budget
TOURISM: 800,000 visitors
POPULATION DENSITY: 10 per sq km [27 per sq ml]
INFANT MORTALITY: 61 per 1,000 live births
LIFE EXPECTANCY: Female 67 yrs, Male 63 yrs
ADULT LITERACY: 50%
PRINCIPAL CITIES (Population): Algiers 1,722,000 Oran 664,000 Constantine 449,000 Annaba 348,000 Blida 191,000

■ Africa's 2nd largest country, after Sudan, & 10th in world ■ Sahara desert covers 80% of country ■ One of world's largest reserves of natural gas ■ Africa's largest crude oil refining capacity and 3rd largest oil producer ■ Oil & gas account for 98% of all exports & provide 65% of revenue ■ Arable land is 3% of area; 30% of pop. are farmers ■ 90% of pop. live along coastal strip ■ 60% of pop. urban ■ 1 million French settlers left for France after 1962 independence ■ One of few African countries to have car manufacturing capacity; makes $\frac{1}{3}$ of its commercial vehicles ■ French Foreign Legion formed in 1831 to subdue tribesmen

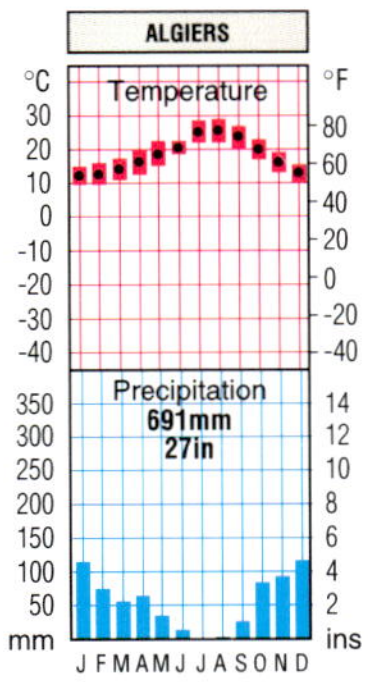

Algiers is exposed to the maritime influences of the Mediterranean Sea but is sheltered from the Sahara to the south by the Atlas mountains. The temperature range, both annual and diurnal is remarkably small. Rainfall has a winter maximum typical of the Mediterranean region and amounts vary greatly from year to year. The mountains to the south are often snow-covered in winter.

MOROCCO

A red flag had been flown in Morocco since the 16th century and the star-shaped green pentagram, the Seal of Solomon, was added in 1915. This design was retained when Morocco gained independence from French and Spanish rule in 1956.

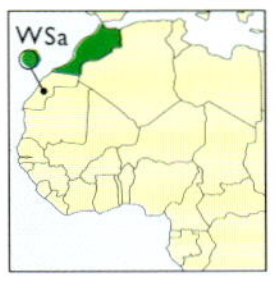

COUNTRY: Kingdom of Morocco
AREA: 446,550 sq km [172,413 sq mls]
POPULATION: 25,061,000
CAPITAL (Population): Rabat (893,000)
GOVERNMENT: Constitutional monarchy with a unicameral legislature
ETHNIC GROUPS: Arab-Berber 99%
LANGUAGES: Arabic (official), Berber
RELIGIONS: Muslim (mainly Sunni) 99%
NATIONAL DAY: 3 March; Accession of King Hassan II to the throne (1961)
CURRENCY: Moroccan dirham = 100 Moroccan francs
ANNUAL INCOME PER PERSON: $950
MAIN PRIMARY PRODUCTS: Cereals, fruit, vegetables, sheep, goats, dates, fish, timber, phosphates, manganese, lead, iron
MAIN INDUSTRIES: Agriculture, wine, food processing, textiles, leather goods, fertilizers, mining, forestry, fishing
EXPORTS: $135 per person
MAIN EXPORTS: Food and beverages 27%, phosphoric acid 15%, phosphates 13%, clothing 10%
MAIN EXPORT PARTNERS: France 30%, Spain 7%, West Germany 6%, Italy 6%
IMPORTS: $224 per person
MAIN IMPORTS: Capital goods 21%, crude oil 15%, consumer goods 12%, foodstuffs 11%, sulphur 6%
MAIN IMPORT PARTNERS: France 22%, USA 9%, Spain 9%
DEFENCE: 14% of national budget
TOURISM: 2,248,000 visitors
POPULATION DENSITY: 56 per sq km [145 per sq ml]
INFANT MORTALITY: 68 per 1,000 live births
LIFE EXPECTANCY: Female 65 yrs, Male 62 yrs
ADULT LITERACY: 70%
PRINCIPAL CITIES (Population): Casablanca 2,158,000 Rabat-Salé 893,000 Fès 548,000 Marrakech 482,000 Oujda 479,000 Kénitra 450,000

■ One of only 3 kingdoms left in Africa ■ Since 1976 has been fighting Polisario Front & W. Sahara government in exile (Sahrawi Arab Democratic Republic) over former W. Sahara ■ Agricultural production has not kept pace with rising pop.; therefore much food imported ■ World's largest reserves of phosphates & third largest producer, after USA & Russia ■ One of best infrastructures on African continent ■ Occupied parts of Spain & S.W. France from early 8th to end of 15th century ■ Oldest educational institution in world, University of Kairaouin founded in 859AD in Fès

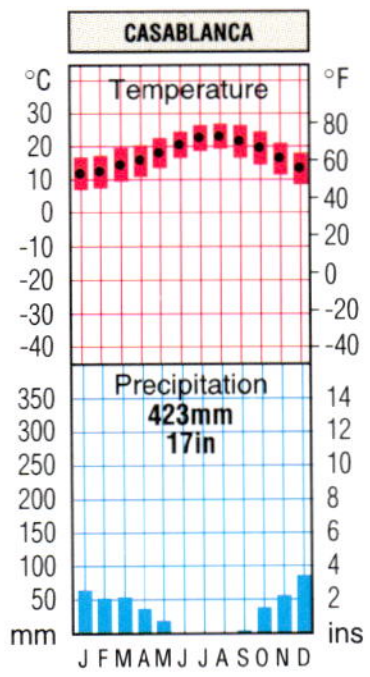

The Atlantic coast of Morocco is washed by the cool Canaries current which keeps summers notably cool for the latitude. Inland, summers are hot and dry with bright sunshine but near the coast low cloud and fog are not infrequent. In winter the prevailing winds are westerly bringing rain from the Atlantic and often heavy snow over the High Atlas mountains of the interior.

WESTERN SAHARA

COUNTRY: Occupied by Morocco
AREA: 266,000 sq km [102,703 sq mls]
POPULATION: 179,000
CAPITAL (Population): El Aaiún (97,000)

CAPE VERDE ISLANDS

COUNTRY: Republic of Cape Verde
AREA: 4,030 sq km [1,556 sq mls]
POPULATION: 370,000
CAPITAL (Population): Praia (58,000)
ETHNIC GROUPS: Mixed 71%, black 28%, white 1%
LANGUAGES: Portuguese
RELIGIONS: Roman Catholic 97%, Protestant 2%
NATIONAL DAY: 5 July; Independence Day (1975)
CURRENCY: Cape Verde escudo = 100 centavos
ANNUAL INCOME PER PERSON: $890
POPULATION DENSITY: 92 per sq km [238 per sq ml]
LIFE EXPECTANCY: Female 65 yrs, Male 61 yrs
ADULT LITERACY: 47%

MAURITANIA

The Mauritanian Islamic Republic's flag features the star and the crescent, traditional symbols of the Muslim religion. It was adopted in 1959, the year before the country gained its independence from France.

COUNTRY: Islamic Republic of Mauritania
AREA: 1,025,520 sq km [395,953 sq mls]
POPULATION: 2,025,000
CAPITAL (Population): Nouakchott (500,000)
GOVERNMENT: Military regime
ETHNIC GROUPS: Moor (Arab-Berber) 81%, Wolof 7%, Tukulor 5%
LANGUAGES: Arabic and French (official), Fulfulde, Fulani
RELIGIONS: Muslim 99%
NATIONAL DAY: 28 November; Independence Day (1960)
CURRENCY: Ouguiya = 5 khoums
ANNUAL INCOME PER PERSON: $500
MAIN PRIMARY PRODUCTS: Iron ore
MAIN INDUSTRIES: Fishing and iron ore
MAIN EXPORTS: Iron, fish and fish products
MAIN IMPORTS: Food, vehicles and fuels
DEFENCE: 14% of national budget
POPULATION DENSITY: 1.9 per sq km [5.0 per sq ml]
LIFE EXPECTANCY: Female 50 yrs, Male 46 yrs
ADULT LITERACY: 28%

■ $\frac{2}{3}$ of pop. Moorish (Arab/Berber) or mixed Moorish & black descent ■ Severe drought since 1970s has killed 50-70% of nation's animals ■ Iron ore main export ■ Heavily reliant on foreign aid, especially from Arab countries ■ In 1979 withdrew its claim to W. Sahara, currently claimed & occupied by Morocco

AFRICA – WEST

GAMBIA, THE

The blue stripe in the Republic of The Gambia's flag represents the Gambia river that flows through the country while the red stands for the sun overhead and the green for the land. The design was adopted on independence from Britain in 1965.

COUNTRY: Republic of The Gambia
AREA: 11,300 sq km [4,363 sq mls]
POPULATION: 861,000
CAPITAL (Population): Banjul (146,000)
GOVERNMENT: Multi-party republic with unicameral legislature
ETHNIC GROUPS: Malinke 40%, Fulani 19%, Wolof 15%, Dyolo 10%, Soninke 8%
LANGUAGES: English (official), Mandinka, Fula, Wolof
RELIGIONS: Muslim 95%, Christian 4%

NATIONAL DAY: 18 February; Independence Day (1965)
CURRENCY: Dalisi = 100 butut
ANNUAL INCOME PER PERSON: $260
POPULATION DENSITY: 76 per sq km [197 per sq ml]
LIFE EXPECTANCY: Female 47 yrs, Male 43 yrs
ADULT LITERACY: 75%

■ Smallest, most westerly mainland African country ■ At no point wider than 50 km [30 mls] ■ Added 'The' to its name to further distinguish it from Zambia

■ Groundnuts main exports ■ Britain's first & last African colony (colonised in 1765 - independence 1965)

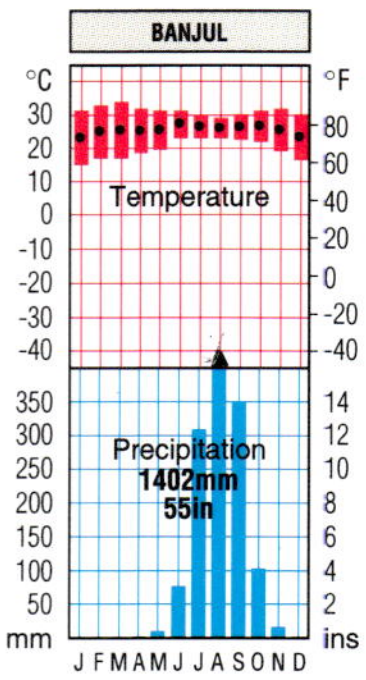

Winds along the west African coast alternate seasonally between dry north-easterlies in winter and moist south- westerlies in summer. The proportion of the year for which the south-westerlies blow and hence the length of the rainy season decreases northwards. At Banjul it lasts from June to October during which period the temperature is very uniform. In the dry season skies are clear and the temperature range is much greater.

SENEGAL

Apart from the green five-pointed star, which symbolises the Muslim faith of the majority of the population, Senegal's flag is identical to that of Mali. It was adopted in 1960 when the country gained its independence from France.

■ Named after Zenega Berbers who invaded from Mauritania in 14th century bringing Islamic faith ■ C. Verde African mainland's most westerly point ■ Most land less than 100 m [330 ft] above sea level ■ Only colony where French citizenship granted to Africans ■ 1st university, museum & cathedral in W. Africa

COUNTRY: Republic of Senegal
AREA: 196,720 sq km [75,954 sq mls]
POPULATION: 7,327,000
CAPITAL (Population): Dakar (1,382,000)
GOVERNMENT: Republic with unicameral legislature
ETHNIC GROUPS: Wolof 36%, Fulani 18%, Serer 17%
LANGUAGES: French (official)

RELIGIONS: Muslim 91%, Christian, traditional beliefs
NATIONAL DAY: 4 April
CURRENCY: CFA franc = 100 centimes
ANNUAL INCOME PER PERSON: $710
MAIN PRIMARY PRODUCTS: Phosphates, fish
MAIN INDUSTRIES: Agriculture, fishing, seed cotton, textiles
MAIN EXPORTS: Groundnuts, phosphates and textiles

MAIN IMPORTS: Crude petroleum, cereals, vehicles, chemicals
DEFENCE: 6% of national budget
POPULATION DENSITY: 37 per sq km [97 per sq ml]
LIFE EXPECTANCY: Female 50 yrs, Male 46 yrs
ADULT LITERACY: 35%

MALI

Mali's flag uses the Pan-African colours employed by the African Democratic Rally before the French colony (then called French Sudan) won independence from France in 1960.

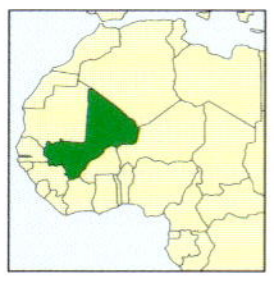

■ ½ country covered by Sahara which is encroaching southwards ■ Less than 2% of land can be cultivated ■ Droughts of 1970s & 1980s have brought crop failure, famine & death ■ No significant industry & virtually all non-agricultural products imported

COUNTRY: Republic of Mali
AREA: 1,240,190 sq km [478,837 sq mls]
POPULATION: 8,156,000
CAPITAL (Population): Bamako (646,000)
GOVERNMENT: Multi-party republic with a unicameral legislature
ETHNIC GROUPS: Bambara 31%, Fulani 13%, Senufo 12%, Soninke 8%
LANGUAGES: French (official) and languages of the Mande group
RELIGIONS: Muslim 90%, traditional beliefs 9%, Christian 1%
NATIONAL DAY: 22 September; Independence Day (1960)

CURRENCY: Franc CFA = 100 centimes
ANNUAL INCOME PER PERSON: $270
MAIN PRIMARY PRODUCTS: Gold and salt
MAIN INDUSTRIES: Agriculture and mining
MAIN EXPORTS: Ginned cotton and live animals
MAIN IMPORTS: Industrial products and refined petroleum products
DEFENCE: 11% of national budget
POPULATION DENSITY: 6.5 per sq km [16.9 per sq ml]
LIFE EXPECTANCY: Female 48 yrs, Male 44 yrs
ADULT LITERACY: 17%

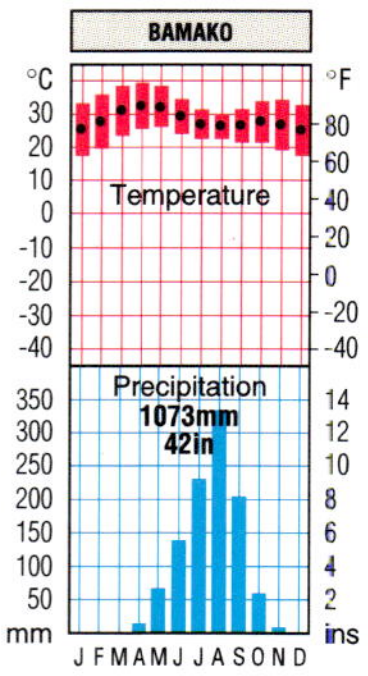

The interior of West Africa has seasonal variations of climate similar to those of the Indian subcontinent. In winter, the dry season, the north-east Harmattan wind brings hot, dry air from the Sahara. In summer the south- west monsoon brings rain from the Gulf of Guinea, the amount of rain decreasing rapidly northwards. The annual temperature range is quite small, the highest temperatures occuring in spring when skies are clear.

GUINEA-BISSAU

The Republic of Guinea-Bissau adopted this flag, using the Pan-African colours, on gaining independence from Portugal in 1973. The five-pointed black star represents the PAIGC political party that led the struggle from 1962.

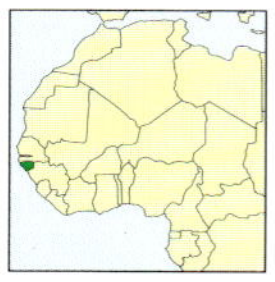

■ Ruled by Portugal for 500 years; formerly known as Portuguese Guinea ■ Thick forest & mangrove swamps cover area nearest Atlantic, savannah covers inland area ■ Timber only significant industry

COUNTRY: Republic of Guinea-Bissau
AREA: 36,120 sq km [13,946 sq mls]
POPULATION: 965,000
CAPITAL (Population): Bissau (125,000)
GOVERNMENT: Single-party republic with unicameral legislature

ETHNIC GROUPS: Balante 39%, Malinke 23%, Mandyako 11%, Pepel 10%
LANGUAGES: Portuguese (official), Crioulo
RELIGIONS: Traditional beliefs 65%, Muslim 30%, Christian 4%
NATIONAL DAY: 24 September; National Day

CURRENCY: Peso = 100 centavos
ANNUAL INCOME PER PERSON: $180
POPULATION DENSITY: 27 per sq km [77 per sq ml]
LIFE EXPECTANCY: Female 49 yrs, Male 45 yrs
ADULT LITERACY: 31%

GUINEA

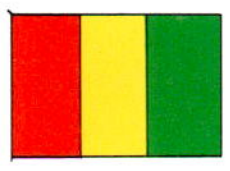

Guinea's Pan-African colours, adopted on independence from France in 1958, represent the three words of the national motto: work (red), justice (yellow) and solidarity (green). The design is based on the French tricolour.

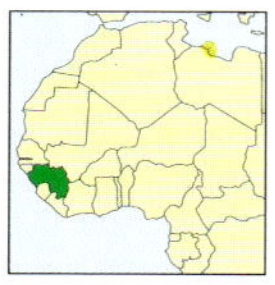

■ Some of world's biggest reserves of high-grade bauxite (90% of export earnings) ■ First independent state of French-speaking Africa ■ Only French protectorate to refuse to join French community on independence ■ 25% of pop. left country 1958-1983

COUNTRY: Republic of Guinea
AREA: 245,860 sq km [94,927 sq mls]
POPULATION: 5,756,000
CAPITAL (Population): Conakry (705,000)
GOVERNMENT: Military state ruled by a Military Committee for National Recovery

ETHNIC GROUPS: Fulani 39%, Malinka 23%, Susu 11%, Kissi 6%
LANGUAGES: French (official), Soussou and Manika
RELIGIONS: Muslim 69%, traditional beliefs 30%, Christian 1%
NATIONAL DAY: 3 April; Independence Day (1958)

CURRENCY: Guinean franc = 100 cauris
ANNUAL INCOME PER PERSON: $480
MAIN INDUSTRIES: Agriculture, mining
POPULATION DENSITY: 27 per sq km [71 per sq ml]
LIFE EXPECTANCY: Female 46 yrs, Male 43 yrs
ADULT LITERACY: 28%

SIERRA LEONE

The colours of Sierra Leone's flag, adopted on independence from Britain in 1961, come from the coat of arms. Green represents the country's agriculture, white stands for peace and blue for the Atlantic Ocean.

■ Name means 'lion mountain' ■ Freetown Bay one of Africa's finest natural harbours ■ Capital, Freetown, created as refuge for liberated slaves in 1792 ■ Supplies 25% of world's diamonds ■ One of highest death rates in world

COUNTRY: Republic of Sierra Leone
AREA: 71,740 sq km [27,699 sq mls]
POPULATION: 4,151,000
CAPITAL (Population): Freetown (470,000)
GOVERNMENT: Single-party republic with unicameral legislature
ETHNIC GROUPS: Mende 34%, Temne 31%, Limba 8%
LANGUAGES: English (official), Creole, Mende, Limba and Temne
RELIGIONS: Traditional beliefs 51%, Muslim 39%, Christian
NATIONAL DAY: 27 April; Independence Day (1961)
CURRENCY: Leone = 100 cents
ANNUAL INCOME PER PERSON: $240
MAIN PRIMARY PRODUCTS: Iron ore, bauxite, diamonds, rutile concentrates
MAIN INDUSTRIES: Mining
MAIN EXPORTS: Diamonds, rutile, coffee, bauxite, cocoa beans
MAIN IMPORTS: Food and live animals, mineral fuels, machinery and transport equipment
DEFENCE: 4% of national budget
POPULATION DENSITY: 58 per sq km [150 per sq ml]
LIFE EXPECTANCY: Female 45 yrs, Male 41 yrs
ADULT LITERACY: 29%

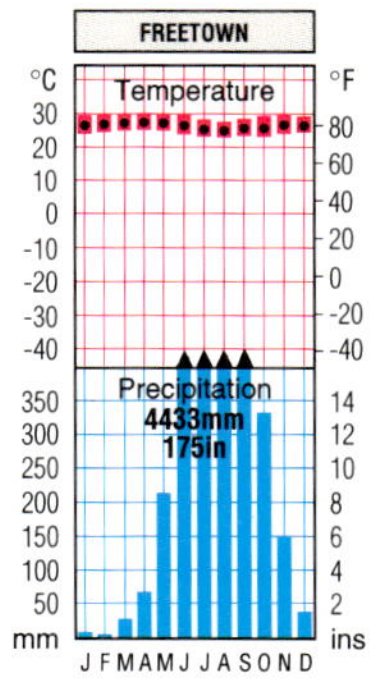

The coast of Sierra Leone faces directly into the rain-bearing south-west monsoon and is backed by the high Fouta Djalon plateau which forces the air to ascend and release moisture. For 7 months of the year rainfall is heavy, reaching a maximum in July of nearly 1,200 mm [47 in]. Temperature and humidity along the coast are uniformly high. In winter the wind is offshore and there is little rain for 4 months.

LIBERIA

Liberia was founded in the early 19th century as an American colony for freed black slaves wanting to return to Africa from the United States. The flag, based on the American 'Stars and Stripes', was adopted on independence in 1847.

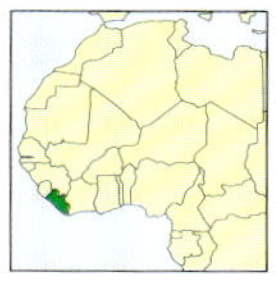

■ Oldest African independent republic; ■ Bought from tribal chiefs in 1822 by American Colonization Society to settle freed slaves ■ Africa's 2nd largest miner of iron ore, after S. Africa; 50% of export earnings ■ Much of economy under US control ■ World's biggest merchant shipping fleet; 'flag of convenience'

COUNTRY: Republic of Liberia
AREA: 111,370 sq km [43,000 sq mls]
POPULATION: 2,607,000
CAPITAL (Population): Monrovia (425,000)
GOVERNMENT: Multi-party republic with a bicameral legisl.
ETHNIC GROUPS: Kpelle 19%, Bassa 14%, Grebo 9%, Gio 8%, Kru 7%, Mano 7%
LANGUAGES: English (official), Mande, West Atlantic and Kwa
RELIGIONS: Christian 68%, Muslim 14%, traditional beliefs 18%
NATIONAL DAY: 26 July; Independence Day (1847)
CURRENCY: Liberian $ = 100 cents
ANNUAL INCOME PER PERSON: $500
MAIN PRIMARY PRODUCTS: Iron ore, diamonds, gold
MAIN INDUSTRIES: Rubber, agriculture, forestry, fishing, mining
MAIN EXPORTS: Iron ore and concentrates, natural rubber, coffee, timber, cocoa
MAIN IMPORTS: Food, machinery and transport equipment, mineral fuels, chemicals
DEFENCE: 12% of national budget
POPULATION DENSITY: 23 per sq km [61 per sq ml]
LIFE EXPECTANCY: Female 58 yrs, Male 55 yrs
ADULT LITERACY: 35%

IVORY COAST

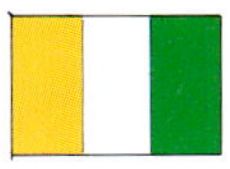

On independence from France in 1960 this former colony adopted a compromise between the French tricolour and the colours of the Pan-African movement. Orange represents the northern savannas, white peace and unity and green the forests.

COUNTRY: Republic of Côte d'Ivoire
AREA: 322,460 sq km [124,502 sq mls]
POPULATION: 11,998,000
CAPITAL (Population): Abidjan (1,850,000)
GOVERNMENT: Single-party republic with unicameral legislature
ETHNIC GROUPS: Akan 41%, Kru 18%, Voltaic 16%, Malinke 15%, Southern Mande 10%
LANGUAGES: French (official) but many African languages are spoken
RELIGIONS: Traditional beliefs 44%, Christian 32%, Muslim 24%
NATIONAL DAY: 7 December; Independence Day (1960)
CURRENCY: Franc CFA = 100 centimes
ANNUAL INCOME PER PERSON: $730
MAIN PRIMARY PRODUCTS: Petroleum, timber
MAIN INDUSTRIES: Agriculture, timber, petroleum
MAIN EXPORTS: Coffee, cocoa, fuels, timber, canned fish and fruit
MAIN IMPORTS: Crude petroleum, machinery and transport equipment, chemicals, vehicles
DEFENCE: 6% of national budget
POPULATION DENSITY: 37 per sq km [96 per sq ml]
LIFE EXPECTANCY: Female 56 yrs, Male 53 yrs
ADULT LITERACY: 43%

■ Name derives from ivory trade which flourished from 15th to 19th century ■ World's largest producer of cocoa ■ Africa's biggest producer of coffee ■ Offshore oil discovered in late 1970s ■ Has car assembly plant ■ Abidjan one of world's most expensive cities; capital to move to Yamoussoukro ■ Basilica of Our Lady of Peace in Yamoussoukro, world's biggest church; consecrated by Pope John Paul II in 1990

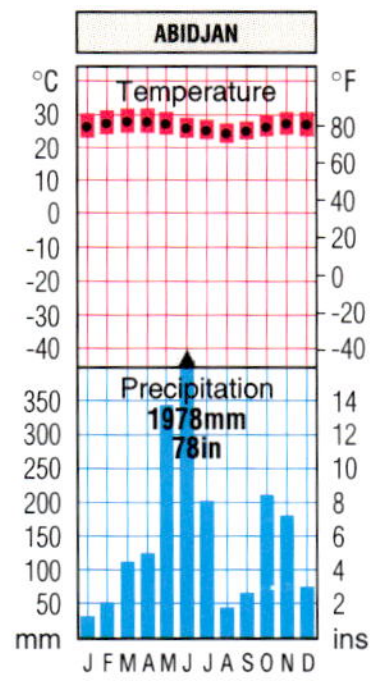

The uniform high temperature and humidity and the double rainfall maxima are a distinctive feature of the climate of the west African coast as far west as Liberia (see Accra). The total rainfall increases steadily westwards as the south-west monsoon winds of summer have a longer sea track. The heaviest and most prolonged rainfall is in May and June when inter-tropical rain belt moves northwards ahead of the monsoon.

GHANA

Adopted on independence from Britain in 1957, Ghana's flag features the colours first used by Ethiopia, Africa's oldest independent nation. Following Ghana's lead, other ex-colonies adopted them as a symbol of black Pan-African unity.

■ Known as Gold Coast prior to independence from Britain ■ 1st black African state to achieve independence from European power ■ Lake Volta one of world's largest artificial lakes ■ Cocoa, most important crop, introduced by African blacksmith in 1879 ■ Kwame Nkrumah, first post-independence ruler, inspired 'African Socialism'

COUNTRY: Republic of Ghana
AREA: 238,540 sq km [92,100 sq mls]
POPULATION: 15,028,000
CAPITAL (Population): Accra (965,000)
GOVERNMENT: Republic with military-civilian council
ETHNIC GROUPS: (as languages)
LANGUAGES: English (official), Akan 52%, Mossi 16%, Ewe 12%, Ga-Adangme 8%, Gurma 3%, Yoruba 1%
RELIGIONS: Protestant 28%, Traditional beliefs 21%, Roman Catholic 19%, Muslim 16%
NATIONAL DAY: 6 March; Independence Day (1957)
CURRENCY: Cedi = 100 pesewas
ANNUAL INCOME PER PERSON: $390
MAIN PRIMARY PRODUCTS: Maize, cassava, cocoa, bananas, sorghum, timber, diamonds, gold, manganese, bauxite
MAIN INDUSTRIES: Agriculture, mining, bauxite and oil refining, food processing, forestry
MAIN EXPORTS: Cocoa 59%, gold 15%, timber 4%, manganese ore 2%, industrial diamonds 1%
MAIN IMPORTS: Mineral fuels and lubricants 29%, machinery and transport equipment 26%, chemicals 13%, basic manufactures 11%, foodstuffs 4%
DEFENCE: 8% of national budget
POPULATION DENSITY: 63 per sq km [163 per sq ml]
INFANT MORTALITY: 81 per 1,000 live births
LIFE EXPECTANCY: Female 58 yrs, Male 54 yrs
ADULT LITERACY: 53%
PRINCIPAL CITIES (Population): Accra 965,000 Kumasi 385,000 Tema 191,000 Tamale 168,000

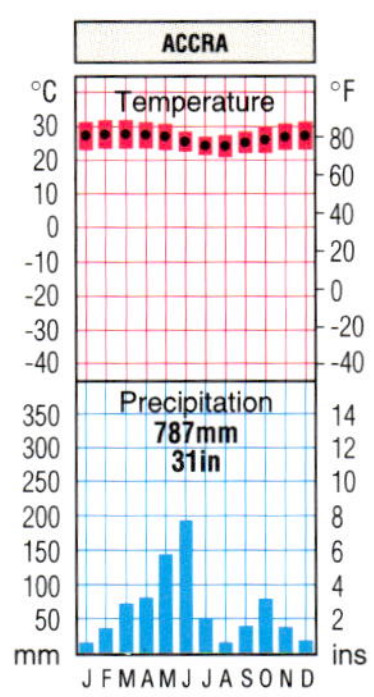

The climate of the coastal regions of Ghana is similar to much of the Guinea coast with uniformly high temperatures, high humidity and a marked double maximum of rainfall associated with the two passages of the inter-tropical rain belt. However, the total rainfall is less than that of coastal regions to the east and west of Ghana, a feature which is attributed to the presence of a local upwell of cooler water offshore.

AFRICA – WEST, CENTRAL

BURKINA FASO

Formerly Upper Volta, this country adopted a new name and flag in 1984, replacing those used since independence from France in 1960. The colours are the Pan-African shades of Burkina Faso's neighbours.

■ Known as 'Upper Volta' till 1984 ■ Sahara Desert encroaching in northern areas ■ 90% of pop. live in rural areas, 80% engaged in agriculture which contributes 45% of GDP ■ Heavily dependent on overseas aid; world's 6th poorest country according to World Bank assessments

COUNTRY: Burkina Faso
AREA: 274,200 sq km [105,869 sq mls]
POPULATION: 9,001,000
CAPITAL (Population): Ouagadougou (422,000)
GOVERNMENT: Military state
ETHNIC GROUPS: Mossi 48%, Mande 8%, Fulani 8%
LANGUAGES: French (official)
RELIGIONS: Traditional beliefs 45%, Muslim 43%, Christian 12%
NATIONAL DAY: 4 August; Independence Day (1960)
CURRENCY: Franc CFA = 100 centimes
ANNUAL INCOME PER PERSON: $330
MAIN PRIMARY PRODUCTS: Sorghum, millet, maize
MAIN INDUSTRIES: Agriculture, mining, food processing
MAIN EXPORTS: Ginned cotton, livestock and livestock products
MAIN IMPORTS: Transport equipment, non-electrical machinery, petroleum products and cereals
DEFENCE: 17% of national budget
POPULATION DENSITY: 33 per sq km [85 per sq ml]
LIFE EXPECTANCY: Female 51 yrs, Male 48 yrs
ADULT LITERACY: 13%

TOGO

Togo's Pan-African colours stand for agriculture and the future (green), mineral wealth and the value of hard work (yellow), and the blood shed in the struggle for independence from France in 1960 (red), with the white star for national purity.

■ Great geographical diversity for such small area ■ Colonised by Germans, then by French & British ■ Part of country colonised by British merged with Ghana in 1956 ■ 80% of pop. engaged in agriculture ■ Port of Lomé, capital, handles trade for landlocked Niger & Burkina Faso ■ Phosphate ores principal export earner

COUNTRY: Republic of Togo
AREA: 56,790 sq km [21,927 sq mls]
POPULATION: 3,531,000
CAPITAL (Population): Lomé (366,000)
GOVERNMENT: Single-party republic with a unicameral legislature
ETHNIC GROUPS: Ewe-Adja 43%, Tem-Kabre 26%, Gurma 16%
LANGUAGES: French, Ewe and Kabiye
RELIGIONS: Traditional beliefs 58%, Christian 27%, Muslim 12%
NATIONAL DAY: 27 April; Independence Day (1960)
CURRENCY: Franc CFA = 100 cents
ANNUAL INCOME PER PERSON: $410
MAIN PRIMARY PRODUCTS: Natural phosphates
MAIN INDUSTRIES: Agriculture, phosphate extraction, manufacturing
MAIN EXPORTS: Calcium phosphates, ginned cotton, coffee, cocoa
MAIN IMPORTS: Food, fuels, machinery and transport equipment
DEFENCE: 7% of national budget
POPULATION DENSITY: 62 per sq km [161 per sq ml]
LIFE EXPECTANCY: Female 57 yrs, Male 53 yrs
ADULT LITERACY: 40%

BENIN

On independence from France in 1960 the country (then called Dahomey) flew the red, yellow and green Pan-African colours, but on becoming the People's Republic of Benin in 1975, the yellow was dropped and the present design adopted.

■ Known as Dahomey until 1975 ■ Ancient kingdom of Dahomey already centuries old when Portuguese landed in 16th century ■ Offshore oil; petroleum products largest export earner ■ Major trading point for pepper & ivory during 18th & 19th centuries

COUNTRY: People's Republic of Benin
AREA: 112,620 sq km [43,483 sq mls]
POPULATION: 4,736,000
CAPITAL (Population): Porto-Novo (208,000)
GOVERNMENT: Multi-party republic with unicameral legislature
ETHNIC GROUPS: Fon 66%, Bariba 10%, Yoruba 9%, Somba 5%
LANGUAGES: French (official); Fon spoken by 47%
RELIGIONS: Traditional beliefs 61%, Christian 23%, Muslim 15%
NATIONAL DAY: 30 November; Independence Day (1960)
CURRENCY: Franc = 100 centimes
ANNUAL INCOME PER PERSON: $360
MAIN PRIMARY PRODUCTS: Palm oil and palm kernel oil
MAIN INDUSTRIES: Mainly agriculture employing 63% of the labour force
MAIN EXPORTS: Fuels, raw cotton, palm products
MAIN IMPORTS: Manufactured goods, textiles, non-electrical machinery
DEFENCE: 18% of national budget
POPULATION DENSITY: 42 per sq km [109 per sq ml]
LIFE EXPECTANCY: Female 50 yrs, Male 47 yrs
ADULT LITERACY: 26%

NIGERIA

The design of Nigeria's flag was selected after a competition to find a new national flag in time for independence from Britain in 1960. The green represents the country's forests and the white is for peace.

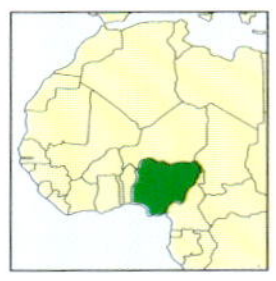

■ Africa's most populous nation ■ Great contrast between landscape & livelihood of people in north with those in south ■ Kainji Reservoir, one of Africa's largest man-made lakes ■ Variety of crops & vegetables grown in south; cereals, nuts & cotton grown & livestock reared in north ■ Between 1973 & 1981, transformed from rural country with agricultural economy to one in which oil accounted for 90% of revenues ■ Large untapped reserves of gas & coal ■ Africa's biggest foreign debt ■ Muslim majority, especially in north & west ■ Deep-rooted conflict between Muslim north & Christian south ■ Present government mostly Muslim ■ Military government; first elections for nearly 10 years scheduled for 1992 ■ Over 1 million died in Biafran civil war 1967-70 ■ In Yoruba areas, considered sign of respect to curtsey ■ Lagos renowned for traffic congestion

COUNTRY: Federal Republic of Nigeria
AREA: 923,770 sq km [356,668 sq mls]
POPULATION: 108,542,000
CAPITAL (Population): Lagos (1,097,000)
GOVERNMENT: Federal republic; at this time military ruling council
ETHNIC GROUPS: Hausa 21%, Yoruba 20%, Ibo 17%, Fulani 9%
LANGUAGES: English (official), Hausa, Yoruba, Ibo
RELIGIONS: Muslim 45%, Protestant 26%, Roman Catholic 12%, African indigenous 11%
NATIONAL DAY: 1 October; Republic Day (1963)
CURRENCY: Nigerian Naira = 100 kobo
ANNUAL INCOME PER PERSON: $270
SOURCE OF INCOME: Agriculture 34%, Industry 36%, Services 29%
MAIN PRIMARY PRODUCTS: Groundnuts, maize, cocoa, cotton, millet, cassava, livestock, rice, timber, iron ore, oil and natural gas, tin coal
MAIN INDUSTRIES: Mining, oil and natural gas, agriculture, fertilizers, vehicles, food processing
EXPORTS: $68 per person
MAIN EXPORTS: Mineral fuels and lubricants 96%, foodstuffs 2%
MAIN EXPORT PARTNERS: USA 18%, Italy 16%, France 16%, Netherlands 12%, Germany 7%, UK 4%
IMPORTS: $36 per person
MAIN IMPORTS: Machinery and transport equipment 35%, basic manufactures 24%, food and live animals 16%
MAIN IMPORT PARTNERS: UK 20%, USA 13%, Germany 13%, France 9%, Japan 7%
EDUCATIONAL EXPENDITURE: 2.4% of national budget
DEFENCE: 5.2% of national budget
TOTAL ARMED FORCES: 94,500
TOURISM: 340,000 visitors
ROADS: 124,000 km [77,500 mls]
RAILWAYS: 3,505 km [2,191 mls]
POPULATION DENSITY: 117 per sq km [304 per sq ml]
URBAN POPULATION: 35%
POPULATION GROWTH: 3.43% per year
BIRTHS: 50 per 1,000 population
DEATHS: 17 per 1,000 population
INFANT MORTALITY: 96 per 1,000 live births
LIFE EXPECTANCY: Female 54 yrs, Male 51 yrs
POPULATION PER DOCTOR: 7,978
ADULT LITERACY: 42%
PRINCIPAL CITIES (Population): Lagos 1,097,000 Ibadan 1,060,000 Ogbomosho 527,000 Kano 487,000 Oshogbo 345,000 Ilorin 344,000 Abeokuta 309,000 Port Harcourt 296,00

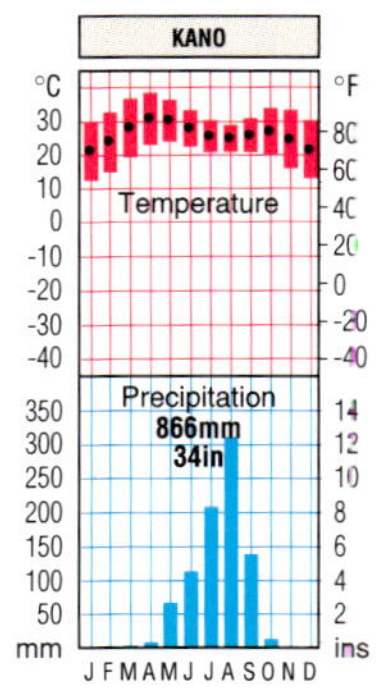

The north of Nigeria extends into the great belt of tropical grassland known as the Sudan which extends across north Africa from the Red Sea to the Atlantic. The climate is markedly seasonal with hot, dry winters and hot, wet summers. In winter the hot, dry Harmattan blows from the Sahara. With clear skies and no rain, the daily range of temperature is large. In June, rain approaches from the south, often preceded by tornadoes.

NIGER

Niger's flag was adopted shortly before independence from France in 1960. The circle represents the sun, the orange stripe the Sahara Desert in the north, the green stripe the grasslands of the south and the white goodness and purity.

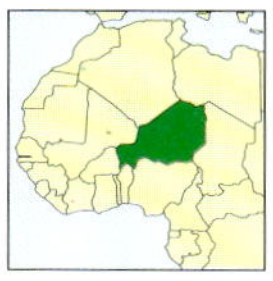

COUNTRY: Republic of Niger
AREA: 1,267,000 sq km [489,189 sq mls]
POPULATION: 7,732,000
CAPITAL (Population): Niamey (399,000)
GOVERNMENT: Single-party republic with an advisory National Development Council
ETHNIC GROUPS: Hausa 52%, Djerma 14%, Fulani 10%
LANGUAGES: French (official) and Hausa
RELIGIONS: Sunni Muslim 97%
NATIONAL DAY: 18 December; Republic Day (1958)
CURRENCY: Franc CFA = 100 centimes
ANNUAL INCOME PER PERSON: $310
MAIN PRIMARY PRODUCTS: Uranium, tin, coal, gypsum and salt
MAIN INDUSTRIES: Agriculture, mining
MAIN EXPORTS: Uranium ore, live animals, vegetables
MAIN IMPORTS: Cereals, machinery, vehicles, refined petroleum products
DEFENCE: 5% of national budget
POPULATION DENSITY: 6 per sq km [16 per sq ml]
LIFE EXPECTANCY: Female 48 yrs, Male 45 yrs
ADULT LITERACY: 14%

■ Encroaching Sahara desert in north & drought-stricken Sahel in south ■ 90% of pop. work on land, yet less than 5% cultivated ■ Only 10% of agriculture cash crops ■ Many nomadic Tuareg in north wiped out by drought in 1970s & 80s ■ One of world's poorest countries

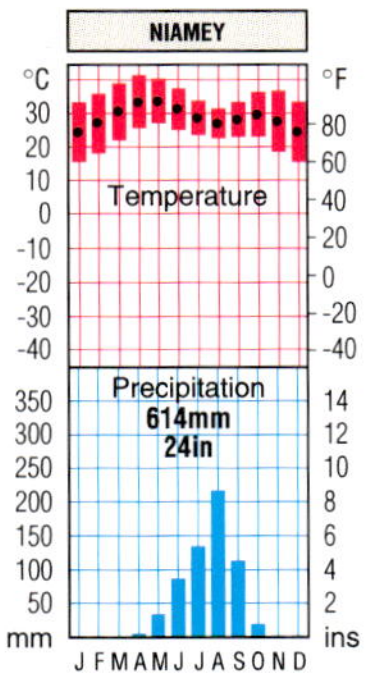

The climate of southern Niger is very similar to other places within the vast tropical grassland belt of northern Africa. From November to April the hot, dry Harmattan wind blows from the Sahara, skies are clear and there is no rain. From March to May is the hot season when the intensity of the sun increases rapidly. In June the inter-tropical rain belt reaches the region and increasing cloud and rain give cooler conditions.

CHAD

Adopted in 1959, Chad's colours are a compromise between the French and Pan-African flags. Blue represents the sky, the streams of the south and hope, yellow the sun and the Sahara Desert in the north, and red national sacrifice.

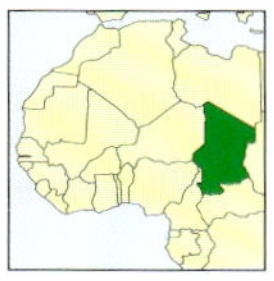

COUNTRY: Republic of Chad
AREA: 1,284,000 sq km [495,752 sq mls]
POPULATION: 5,679,000
CAPITAL (Population): Ndjamena (512,000)
GOVERNMENT: Single- party republic
ETHNIC GROUPS: Bagirmi, Sara and Kreish 31%, Sudanic Arab 26%, Teda 7%
LANGUAGES: French (official) but more than 100 languages and dialects spoken
RELIGIONS: Muslim 44%, Christian 33%
NATIONAL DAY: 11 August; Independence Day (1960)
CURRENCY: Franc CFA = 100 centimes
ANNUAL INCOME PER PERSON: $190
MAIN PRIMARY PRODUCTS: Salt. Uranium, gold and bauxite have still to be exploited.
MAIN INDUSTRIES: Cotton ginning, sugar refining and textiles
MAIN EXPORTS: Cotton, live cattle
MAIN IMPORTS: Cereals, petroleum products, chemicals, transport equipment
DEFENCE: 40% of national budget
POPULATION DENSITY: 4.5 per sq km [11.5 per sq ml]
LIFE EXPECTANCY: Female 44 yrs, Male 42 yrs
ADULT LITERACY: 25%

■ More than twice size of France, its former colonial ruler ■ Cotton main cash crop, providing 90% of export earnings ■ Shores of Lake Chad were for centuries important marshalling yard for several major trans- Saharan caravan routes ■ Libyan & French military forces involved in fighting during civil war in 1980s

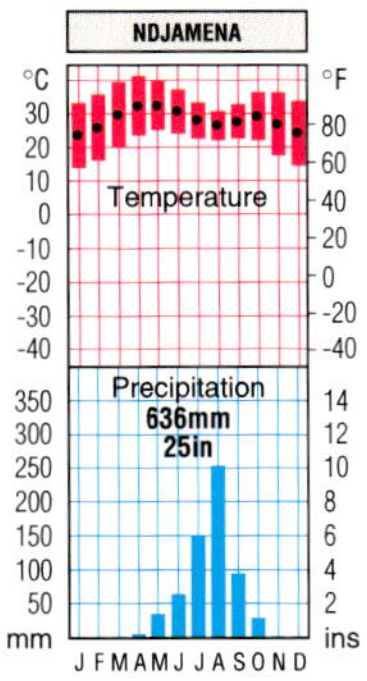

The central regions of Chad lie within the tropical grassland belt known as the Sudan which extends across north Africa. The climate is markedly seasonal. A dry season with north-easterly winds extends from November to April. The sky is clear and the daily range of temperature large. The heat increases until the beginning of the rainy season in June when cloud and rain bring cooler but more humid conditions.

CAMEROON

Cameroon's flag employs the Pan-African colours, as used by many former African colonies. The design, with the yellow liberty star, dates from 1975 and is based on the tricolour adopted in 1957 before independence from France in 1960.

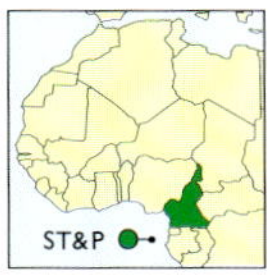

COUNTRY: Republic of Cameroon
AREA: 475,440 sq km [183,567 sq mls]
POPULATION: 11,834,000
CAPITAL (Population): Yaoundé (654,000)
GOVERNMENT: Republic with a unicameral legislative assembly
ETHNIC GROUPS: Fang 20%, Bamileke and Mamum 19%, Duala, Luanda and Basa 15%, Fulani 10%
LANGUAGES: French and English (both official), Sudanic and Bantu
RELIGIONS: Christian 53%, Animist 25%, Muslim 22%
NATIONAL DAY: 20 May; National Day
CURRENCY: Franc CFA = 100 centimes
ANNUAL INCOME PER PERSON: $940
MAIN PRIMARY PRODUCTS: Bauxite, kyanite, oil
MAIN INDUSTRIES: Aluminium, cement, rubber, palm-oil, sugar
MAIN EXPORTS: Aluminium products, coffee, cocoa, cotton fibre, logs
MAIN IMPORTS: Transport equipment, iron and steel, medicine, textiles
DEFENCE: 7% of national budget
POPULATION DENSITY: 25 per sq km [64 per sq ml]
INFANT MORTALITY: 86 per 1,000 live births
LIFE EXPECTANCY: Female 55 yrs, Male 51 yrs
ADULT LITERACY: 56%

■ Name 'Cameroon' comes from Portuguese word 'cameroes' (prawns) found in Wouri River ■ One of Africa's most successful economies due to consistent agricultural performance & rapid growth of oil industry ■ One of world's largest producers of cocoa ■ Self-sufficient in oil & exports crude & refined oil

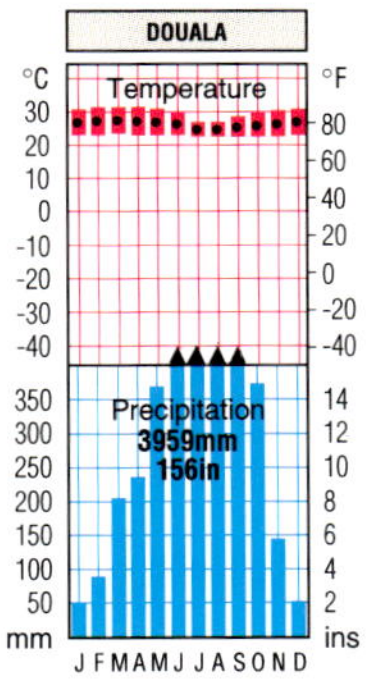

The north-east corner of the Gulf of Guinea is a region of very high rainfall and uniformly high temperature and humidity. The rain is at its heaviest during July, August and September when the south-west monsoon is at its strongest and steadiest and the temperature hardly varies at all. The rainfall on the seaward slopes of Cameroon Peak is even heavier and exceeds 9,000 mm [350 in] in places.

SÃO TOMÉ & PRÍNCIPE

COUNTRY: Republic of São Tomé and Príncipe
AREA: 964 sq km [372 sq mls]
POPULATION: 121,000
CAPITAL (Population): Sao Tomé 35,000

ST HELENA AND DEPENDENCIES UK COLONY

COUNTRY: Ascension
AREA: 88 sq km [34 sq ml]
POPULATION: 1,500
CAPITAL: Georgetown

COUNTRY: St. Helena
AREA: 122 sq km [47 sq mls]
POPULATION: 7,000
CAPITAL: Jamestown

COUNTRY: Tristan da Cunha
AREA: 104 sq km [44 sq mls]
POPULATION: 330
CAPITAL: Edinburgh

EQUATORIAL GUINEA

Equatorial Guinea's flag dates from independence from Spain in 1968. Green represents the country's natural resources, blue the sea, red the nation's struggle for independence and the white stands for peace.

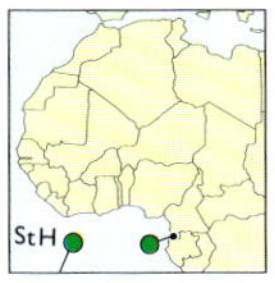

■ Comprises mainland region, Mbini (Rio Muni), main island region Bioko (Fernando Po) & 4 smaller islands. Bioko contains country's capital, Malabo, which stands beside volcanic crater flooded by the sea ■ Bioko has Creole descendants of slaves freed by Britain in 19th century

COUNTRY: Republic of Equatorial Guinea
AREA: 28,050 sq km [10,830 sq mls]
POPULATION: 348,000
CAPITAL (Population): Malabo (37,000)
GOVERNMENT: Single party republic with unicameral legisl.
ETHNIC GROUPS: Fang 82%, Bubi 15%, Duala 3%
LANGUAGES: Spanish, Fang, Bubi
RELIGIONS: Christian (mainly Roman Catholic) 89%, traditional beliefs 5%
NATIONAL DAY: 12 October; Independence Day (1968)
CURRENCY: Franc CFA = 100 centimes
ANNUAL INCOME PER PERSON: $330
POPULATION DENSITY: 12 per sq km [32 per sq ml]
LIFE EXPECTANCY: Female 50 yrs, Male 47 yrs
ADULT LITERACY: 37%

AFRICA – CENTRAL, NORTH-EAST

GABON

Gabon's tricolour was adopted on independence from France in 1960. The yellow, now representing the sun, used to be thinner to symbolise the equator on which the country lies. The green stands for Gabon's forests and blue for the sea.

COUNTRY: Gabonese Republic
AREA: 267,670 sq km [103,347 sq mls]
POPULATION: 1,172,000
CAPITAL (Population): Libreville (350,000)
GOVERNMENT: Single-party republic with unicameral legislature
ETHNIC GROUPS: Fang 36%, Mpongwe 15%, Mbete 14%
LANGUAGES: French (official)
RELIGIONS: Christian 96%, traditional beliefs 3%
NATIONAL DAY: 17 August; Independence Day (1960)
CURRENCY: Franc CFA = 100 cents

ANNUAL INCOME PER PERSON: $3,220
MAIN PRIMARY PRODUCTS: Manganese, oil, uranium
MAIN INDUSTRIES: Agriculture, forestry, petroleum
MAIN EXPORTS: Petroleum and petroleum products, manganese, timber, uranium
MAIN IMPORTS: Machinery, transport equipment, food products, metal and metal products
DEFENCE: 12% of national budget
POPULATION DENSITY: 4.4 per sq km [11.4 per sq ml]
LIFE EXPECTANCY: Female 55 yrs, Male 52 yrs
ADULT LITERACY: 62%

■ Lowest birth rate in Africa ■ Albert Schweitzer set up Lambaréné hospital in 1913, for which he won 1952 Nobel Peace Prize ■ Capital Libreville founded in 1849 by French as home for slaves rescued from illegal slaving ships

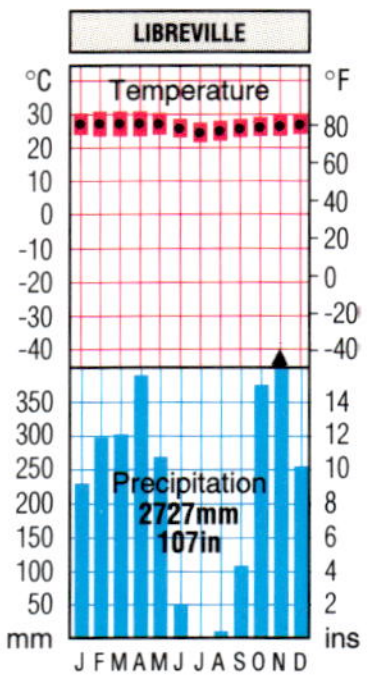

The climate of Gabon is mainly equatorial with uniform heat and humidity throughout the year and very high rainfall. At Libreville the rains last from September to May with maxima in November and April following the passage of the sun across the Equator at the equinoxes. From June to August winds blow offshore and it is almost rainless.

CONGO

The People's Republic of the Congo was created ten years after independence in 1960 and adopted this new flag, which shows the country's Socialist beliefs. The hammer and hoe represent industry and agriculture and the palm branches stand for peace.

COUNTRY: People's Republic of the Congo
AREA: 342,000 sq km [132,046 sq mls]
POPULATION: 2,271,000
CAPITAL (Population): Brazzaville (596,000)
GOVERNMENT: Republic with a unicameral legisl. assem.
ETHNIC GROUPS: Kongo 52%, Teke 17%, Mboshi 12%, Mbete 5%
LANGUAGES: French (official), Kongo, Teke, Ubangi and Sanka
RELIGIONS: Christian 82%, traditional beliefs 5%
NATIONAL DAY: 15 August; Independence Day (1960)

CURRENCY: Franc CFA = 100 centimes
ANNUAL INCOME PER PERSON: $1,010
MAIN PRIMARY PRODUCTS: Timber, petroleum, copper
MAIN INDUSTRIES: Petroleum and forestry
MAIN EXPORTS: Petroleum, timber, diamonds
MAIN IMPORTS: Machinery, iron, steel, transport equipment, food
DEFENCE: 15% of national budget
POPULATION DENSITY: 6.6 per sq km [17.2 per sq ml]
LIFE EXPECTANCY: Female 52 yrs, Male 49 yrs
ADULT LITERACY: 63%

■ Over 50% of country forest ■ Less than 2% of land cultivated, yet 1/3 of pop. engaged in agriculture ■ Vast offshore oil deposits discovered in 1969 ■ Oil & related products generate almost 90% of export earnings , 60% to USA ■ Africa's first declared Communist state

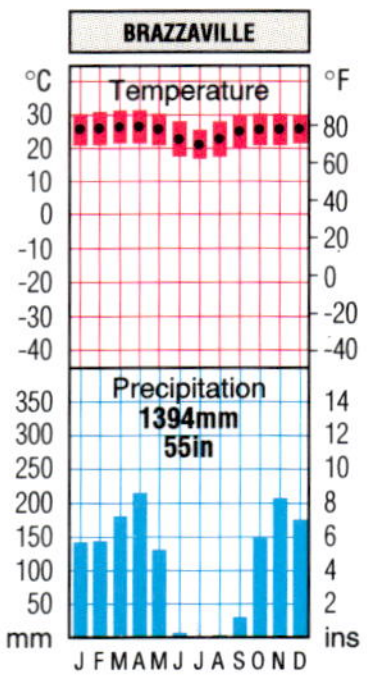

The Equator passes through the centre of the country. There is a tropical climate of high temperatures and high rainfall. There is little variation in the temperature through the year, but it is slightly cooler near the Atlantic coast. There is a marked dry season.

CENTRAL AFRICAN REPUBLIC

The national flag of the Central African Republic, adopted in 1958, combines the green, yellow and red of Pan-African unity with the blue, white and red of the flag of the country's former colonial ruler, France.

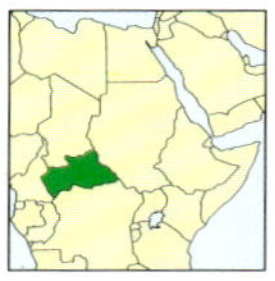

COUNTRY: Central African Republic
AREA: 622,980 sq km [240,533 sq mls]
POPULATION: 3,039,000
CAPITAL (Population): Bangui (597,000)
GOVERNMENT: Single-party republic with unicameral legisative assembly
ETHNIC GROUPS: Banda 29%, Baya 25%, Ngbandi 11%, Azande 10%
LANGUAGES: French (official)
RELIGIONS: Christian 83%, traditional beliefs 12%, Muslim 3%
NATIONAL DAY: 1 December

CURRENCY: Franc CFA = 100 centimes
ANNUAL INCOME PER PERSON: $390
MAIN PRIMARY PRODUCTS: Diamonds, cotton, timber
MAIN INDUSTRIES: Agriculture
MAIN EXPORTS: Coffee, cotton, cork, wood and diamonds
MAIN IMPORTS: Cereals, machinery and transport equipment, medicines
DEFENCE: 6.6% of national budget
POPULATION DENSITY: 4.9 per sq km [12.6 per sq ml]
LIFE EXPECTANCY: Female 49 yrs, Male 46 yrs
ADULT LITERACY: 40%

■ Over 60 species of valuable trees ■ Only 5% of land cultivated yet 90% of pop. engaged in agriculture ■ Diamonds account for 50% of foreign earnings ■ French military garrisons at Bangui & Bouar ■ Elephant pop. reduced by 75% (1966-80)

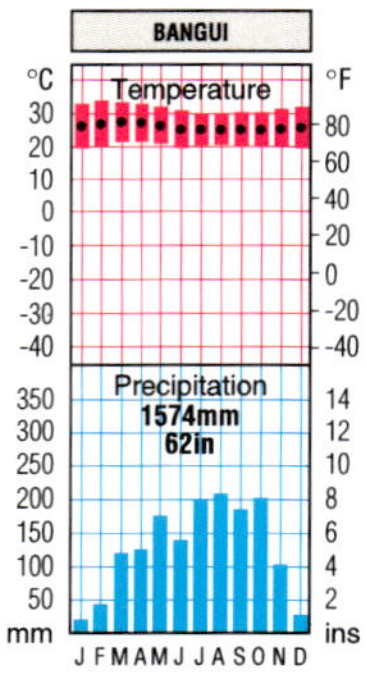

The climate of this land-locked country is tropical. The northeast trade winds blow Nov.-Feb. from the Sahara causing a dry season with high temperatures. There are no appreciable mountains to affect this air flow. The south-west winds bring a slightly cooler régime and a wet season from July-Oct. Annual rainfall is high with some rain in all months.

SUDAN

The design of Sudan's flag is based on the flag of the Arab revolt used in Syria, Iraq and Jordan after 1918. Adopted in 1969, it features the Pan-Arab colours and an Islamic green triangle symbolising material prosperity and spiritual wealth.

COUNTRY: Republic of the Sudan
AREA: 2,505,810 sq km [967,493 sq mls]
POPULATION: 25,204,000
CAPITAL (Population): Khartoum (476,000)
GOVERNMENT: Multi-party republic with a unicameral legislature
ETHNIC GROUPS: Sudanese Arab 49%, Dinka 12%, Nuba 8%, Beja 6%, Nuer 5%, Azande 3%
LANGUAGES: Arabic (official), English, Nubian and other local languages
RELIGIONS: Sunni Muslim 73%, traditional beliefs 17%, Roman Catholic 6%, Protestant 2%
NATIONAL DAY: 1 January; Independence Day (1956)
CURRENCY: Sudanese pound = 100 piastres
ANNUAL INCOME PER PERSON: $450
MAIN PRIMARY PRODUCTS: Cotton, dates, livestock, gum arabic, wheat, beans, chromium, crude oil, natural gas

MAIN INDUSTRIES: Agriculture, oil, food processing
MAIN EXPORTS: Cotton 30%, gum arabic 18%, sesame seeds 9%
MAIN IMPORTS: Machinery and transport equipment 33%, manufactured goods 19%, petroleum products 19%, food and tobacco 16%, chemicals 10%, textiles 3%
DEFENCE: 32% of national budget
TOURISM: 52,000 visitors
POPULATION DENSITY: 10 per sq km [26 per sq ml]
INFANT MORTALITY: 99 per 1,000 live births
LIFE EXPECTANCY: Female 53 yrs, Male 51 yrs
ADULT LITERACY: 22%
PRINCIPAL CITIES (Population): Omdurman 526,000 Khartoum 476,000 Khartoum North 341,000 Port Sudan 207,000

■ Largest African country ■ Has major problems: drought, famine, economic crisis, political instability & civil war ■ One of world's largest sugar complexes at Kenana where state-run plantations produced over 300,000 tonnes of sugar in 1984-5 ■ Racial melting pot - Arab & Muslim in north; black Africans - some Christian, most traditional religions - in south ■ Many northern people nomadic ■ Many skilled Sudanese work in Gulf states ■ 1 million refugees from Ethiopia ■ Civil war (1955-72) restarted 1983 after government introduced Muslim laws ■ Khartoum streets laid out in pattern of British flag

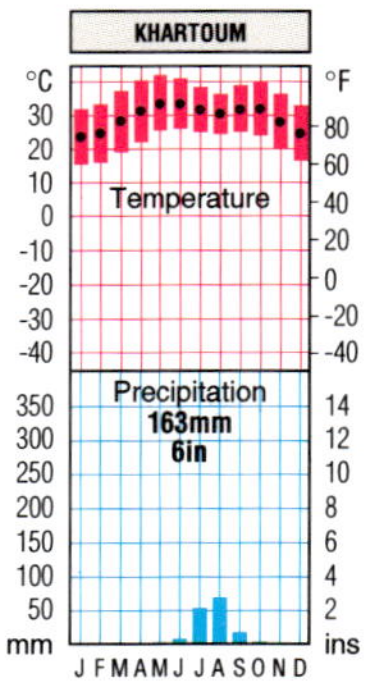

Sudan extends from the Sahara almost to the Equator and the climate changes from desert to equatorial as the influence of the inter-tropical rain belt increases southwards. At Khartoum rain falls during 3 summer months when the rain belt is at its most northerly extent. The rain may be squally and accompanied by dust storms called haboobs. There is a large daily range of temperature and summer days are particularly hot.

ETHIOPIA

Ethiopia's tricolour was first flown as three separate pennants, one above the other. The combination of red, yellow and green dates from the late 19th century and appeared in flag form in 1897. The present sequence was adopted in 1941.

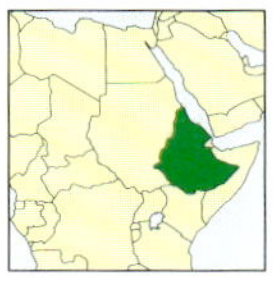

COUNTRY: People's Democratic Republic of Ethiopia
AREA: 1,221,900 sq km [471,776 sq mls]
POPULATION: 50,974,000
CAPITAL (Population): Addis Ababa (1,686,000)
GOVERNMENT: Unitary single-party people's republic with a unicameral legislature
ETHNIC GROUPS: Amharic 38%, Galla 35%, Tigre 9%, Gurage 3%
LANGUAGES: Amharic (official), Galla, Tigre
RELIGIONS: Ethiopian Orthodox 53%, Muslim 31%, traditional beliefs 11%
NATIONAL DAY: 12 September; People's Revolution Day (1974)
CURRENCY: Ethiopian Birr = 100 cents
ANNUAL INCOME PER PERSON: $120
MAIN PRIMARY PRODUCTS: Cattle, cereals, sorghum, coffee, cotton, timber, sugar cane, salt
MAIN INDUSTRIES: Agriculture, textiles, food processing
EXPORTS: $9 per person
MAIN EXPORTS: Coffee 56%, hides and skins 11%
MAIN EXPORT PARTNERS: Germany 18%, Netherlands 13%, Japan 11%, USA 10%
IMPORTS: $22 per person
MAIN IMPORTS: Machinery and transport equipment 39%, petroleum 17%, textile yarn 17%, chemicals 11%
MAIN IMPORT PARTNERS: CIS nations 20%, USA 15%, Germany 10%, UK 10%, Japan 1%
DEFENCE: 18% of national budget
POPULATION DENSITY: 42 per sq km [108 per sq ml]
INFANT MORTALITY: 143 per 1,000 live births
LIFE EXPECTANCY: Female 45 yrs, Male 41 yrs
ADULT LITERACY: 62%
PRINCIPAL CITIES (Population): Addis Ababa 1,686,000 Asmera 319,000

■ Long-running civil wars in northern provinces of Tigre & Eritrea ended in 1991 after flight of President Mengistu & former rebels took power ■ Severe droughts in 1980s created widespread famine ■ As ancient Abyssinian Empire, country dates from biblical times; last monarchy traced its origin to Queen of Sheba & King Solomon ■ Ethiopian calendar is based on traditional calendar of Ethiopian Church; year divided into 13 months

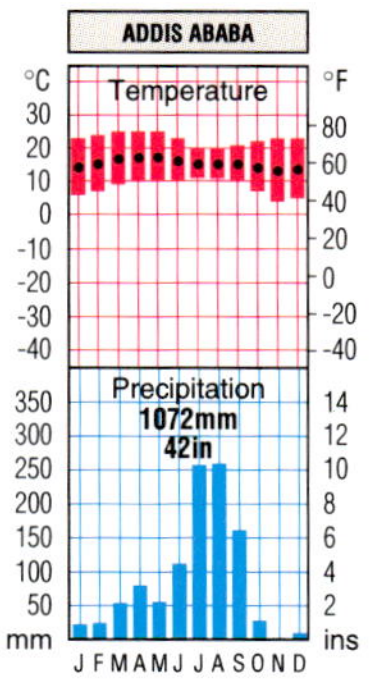

Located at the centre of the Shewan Plateau, at an altitude of 2,450 m [8,000 ft], Addis Ababa experiences an average annual temperature of 20°C [68°F], the altitude lowering the expected temperatures for these latitudes. The highest temperatures are recorded in October 22°C [72°F], with June and July the coolest months at about 18°C [64°F]. As much as 1,151 mm [45 ins] of rain falls throughout the year, with December-March the wettest months. The rainy season tends to lower temperatures.

DJIBOUTI

Djibouti's flag was adopted on independence from France in 1977, though its use by the independence movement had begun five years earlier. The colours represent the two principal peoples in the country: the Issas (blue) and the Afars (green).

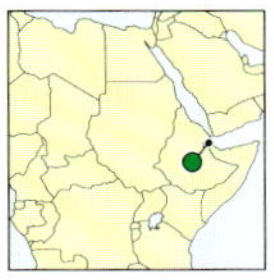

COUNTRY: Republic of Djibouti
AREA: 23,200 sq km [8,958 sq mls]
POPULATION: 409,000
CAPITAL (Population): Djibouti (290,000)
GOVERNMENT: Unitary single-party republic with a unicameral legislature
ETHNIC GROUPS: Issa 47%, Afar 38%, Arab 6%
LANGUAGES: Arabic and French (official), Cushitic
RELIGIONS: Sunni Muslim 94%, Roman Catholic 4%
NATIONAL DAY: 4 July; Independence Day (1977)
CURRENCY: Djibouti franc = 100 centimes
ANNUAL INCOME PER PERSON: $1,000
POPULATION DENSITY: 18 per sq km [46 per sq ml]
LIFE EXPECTANCY: Female 51 yrs, Male 47 yrs
ADULT LITERACY: 12%

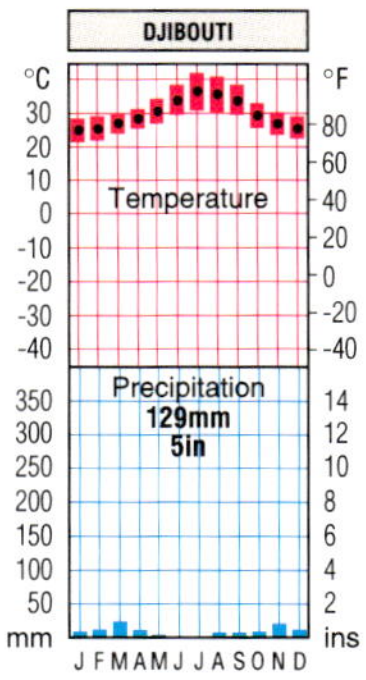

■ Desert land where Gulf of Aden meets Red Sea ■ Known as French Somaliland until 1945 and as "Land of The Afars & The Issas", (1967-77)

Along the western shores of the Gulf of Aden is a narrow strip of hot, arid lowland between the Gulf and the Ethiopian highlands. The temperature is high throughout the year and summer days are cloudless and exceptionally hot, regularly exceeding 40°C [100°F]. The sparse and variable rainfall occurs in winter when northerly winds bring moisture from the Red Sea and the Gulf of Aden

SOMALIA

In 1960 British Somaliland (in the north) united with Italian Somalia (in the south) to form present-day Somalia and the flag of the southern region was adopted. The points of the star represent the five regions of East Africa where Somalis live.

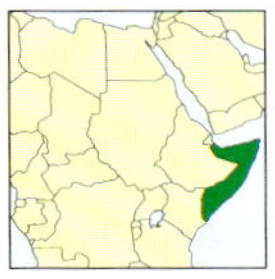

■ Arid country with only 2 rivers; along banks lie most of agricultural land ■ Among longest beaches in world ■ Many Somalis in Kenya, Ethiopia & Djibouti ■ Economy severely affected by drought ■ Large foreign debt; heavily reliant on foreign aid ■ High infant mortality, low life expectancy

COUNTRY: Somali Democratic Republic
AREA: 637,660 sq km [246,201 sq mls]
POPULATION: 7,497,000
CAPITAL (Population): Mogadishu (1,000,000)
GOVERNMENT: Single-party republic, military dominated with a unicameral legislature
ETHNIC GROUPS: Somali 98%, Arab 1%
LANGUAGES: Somali and Arabic (official), English and Italian
RELIGIONS: Muslim
NATIONAL DAY: 21 October; Anniversary of coup (1969)
CURRENCY: Somali shilling = 100 cents
ANNUAL INCOME PER PERSON: $150
MAIN PRIMARY PRODUCTS: Salt
MAIN INDUSTRIES: Raising livestock and subsistence agriculture
MAIN EXPORTS: Livestock, bananas, myrrh
MAIN IMPORTS: Petroleum, foodstuffs, construction materials, machinery and parts
DEFENCE: 40% of national budget
POPULATION DENSITY: 12 per sq km [30 per sq ml]
LIFE EXPECTANCY: Female 49 yrs, Male 45 yrs
ADULT LITERACY: 12%

KENYA

The Kenyan flag, which dates from independence from Britain in 1963, is based on the flag of the Kenya African National Union, which led the colonial struggle. The Masai warrior's shield and crossed spears represent the defence of freedom.

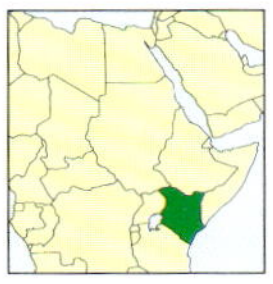

COUNTRY: Republic of Kenya
AREA: 580,370 sq km [224,081 sq mls]
POPULATION: 24,032,000
CAPITAL (Population): Nairobi (1,429,000)
GOVERNMENT: Single-party republic with a unicameral legislature
ETHNIC GROUPS: Kikuyu 21%, Luhya 14%, Luo 13%, Kamba 11%, Kalenjin 11%
LANGUAGES: Swahili and English (official)
RELIGIONS: Protestant 26%, Roman Catholic 26%, African indigenous 18%
NATIONAL DAY: 12 December; Independence Day (1963)
CURRENCY: Kenyan shilling = 100 cents
ANNUAL INCOME PER PERSON: $370
MAIN PRIMARY PRODUCTS: Maize, millet, cassava, beans, pyrethrum, tea, coffee, sugar, cattle, sisal
MAIN INDUSTRIES: Agriculture, oil refining, food processing, tourism, cement
MAIN EXPORTS: Coffee 26%, tea 22%, petroleum products 13%, vegetables and fruit 10%
MAIN EXPORT PARTNERS: UK 17%, Germany 10%, Uganda 9%, The Netherlands 7%, USA 5%
MAIN IMPORTS: Machinery and transport equipment 34%, crude petroleum 20%, chemicals 18%
MAIN IMPORT PARTNERS: UK 17%, Japan 11%, Germany 8%, USA 7%, France 7%
TOURISM: 662,000 visitors
POPULATION DENSITY: 41 per sq km [107 per sq ml]
INFANT MORTALITY: 64 per 1,000 live births
LIFE EXPECTANCY: Female 63 yrs, Male 59 yrs
ADULT LITERACY: 69%
PRINCIPAL CITIES (Population): Nairobi 1,429,000 Mombasa 426,000 Kisumu 198,000 Nakuru 112,000

■ Named after Mount Kenya ■ 'Cradle of Mankind': earliest bones found on shores of Lake Turkana ■ World's highest birth rate: 55 per 1,000 ■ 50% of pop. under 15 ■ 85% of pop. engaged in agriculture ■ Kikuyu dominate national affairs ■ Largest recipient of British aid in Africa & 3rd in world ■ Nairobi originally railway depot for East African Railway now among largest E. African cities ■ Tourism 3rd most important source of foreign exchange

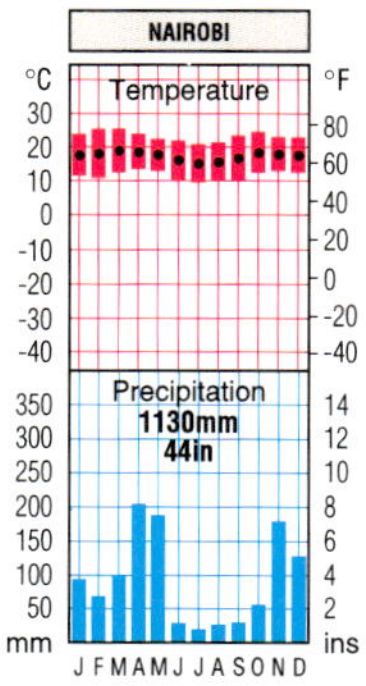

The Equator passes through the centre of Kenya and while the climate is tropical it is very much affected by altitude, the western half of the country being over 1,000m [3,250 ft]. Mount Kenya is over 5,000m [16,000 ft] with glaciers. In summer, Nairobi is 10° [18°F] cooler than Mombasa on the coast. There are two temperature maxima associated with the passage of the sun. The rains fall April-May with a lesser period, Nov. -Dec.

AFRICA – EAST, SOUTH

UGANDA

Adopted on independence from Britain in 1962, Uganda's flag is that of the party which won the first national election. The colours represent the people (black), the sun (yellow), and brotherhood (red); the country's emblem is a crested crane.

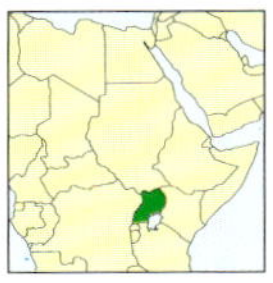

COUNTRY: Republic of Uganda
AREA: 235,880 sq km [91,073 sq mls]
POPULATION: 18,795,000
CAPITAL (Population): Kampala (459,000)
GOVERNMENT: Military régime with a unicameral legisl.
ETHNIC GROUPS: Ganda 18%, Teso 9%, Nkole 8%, Soga 8%, Gisu 7%, Chiga 7%, Lango 6%, Rwanda 6%, Acholi 6%
LANGUAGES: English and Swahili (official)
RELIGIONS: Roman Catholic 50%, Protestant 29%, Muslim 7%
NATIONAL DAY: 9 October; Independence Day (1962)
CURRENCY: Uganda shilling = 100 cents
ANNUAL INCOME PER PERSON: $220
MAIN PRIMARY PRODUCTS: Coffee, cotton, tea, livestock, sugar, copper, phosphates, timber
MAIN INDUSTRIES: Agriculture, food processing, textiles, metal processing, mining, cement

■ Mostly rich fertile land, well watered & with kindly climate; described by Winston Churchill as 'Pearl of Africa' ■ Country of source lakes of Nile ■ Top of Mount Elgon often snow-covered despite country's position on Equator ■ Coffee most important export ■ Culturally, linguistically & racially, ethnic groups very diverse ■ Estimated that up to 300,000 killed during Idi Amin's rule (1971-1979) & over 200,000 in subsequent troubles

MAIN EXPORTS: Unroasted coffee 97%, cotton, tea
MAIN IMPORTS: Sugar 16%, vehicles 11%, clothing 10%, construction materials 8%, food 5%
DEFENCE: 13% of national budget
POPULATION DENSITY: 80 per sq km [206 per sq ml]
LIFE EXPECTANCY: Female 55 yrs, Male 51 yrs
ADULT LITERACY: 57%

ZAÏRE

The Pan-African colours of red, yellow and green were adopted for Zaïre's flag in 1971. The central emblem symbolises the revolutionary spirit of the nation and was used by the Popular Movement of the Revolution, formed in 1967.

COUNTRY: Republic of Zaïre
AREA: 2,345,095 sq km [905,441 sq mls]
POPULATION: 35,562,000
CAPITAL (Population): Kinshasa (2,654,000)
GOVERNMENT: Single-party republic with a unicam. legisl.
ETHNIC GROUPS: Luba 18%, Kongo 16%, Mongo 14%, Rwanda 10%, Azandi 6%, Bangi and Ngale 6%
LANGUAGES: French (official), Lingala, Swahili, Kikongo, Tshiluba
RELIGIONS: Roman Catholic 48%, Protestant 29%, Indigenous Christian 17%, tradit. beliefs 3%, Muslim 1%
NATIONAL DAY: 24 November; Anniversary of the Second Republic (1965)
CURRENCY: Zaïre = 100 makuta = 10,000 sengi
ANNUAL INCOME PER PERSON: $230
MAIN INDUSTRIES: Agriculture, food processing, oil refining, textiles and clothing, mining, forestry
MAIN PRIMARY PRODUCTS: Cassava, plantains and bananas, groundnuts, sugar cane, coffee, rubber, cotton, palm oil, cocoa, tea, timber, oil, gas, copper, cobalt, tin, zinc, gold
MAIN EXPORTS: Copper 52%, coffee 16%, diamonds 11%, crude petroleum 8%, cobalt 5%, zinc 1%
MAIN IMPORTS: Mining equipment 32%, foodstuffs 15%, energy 14%, transport equipment 8%, consumer goods 7%
DEFENCE: 3.9% of national budget
POPULATION DENSITY: 15 per sq km [39 per sq ml]
INFANT MORTALITY: 90 per 1,000 live births
LIFE EXPECTANCY: Female 56 yrs, Male 53 yrs
ADULT LITERACY: 61%
PRINCIPAL CITIES (Population): Kinshasa 2,654,000 Lubumbashi 543,000 Mbuji Mayi 423,000 Kananga 291,000 Kisangani 283,000

■ Africa's 3rd largest country, 77 times larger than Belgium by whom it was ruled for over 50 years ■ Coastline only 27 km [17 mls] at outlet of Zaïre river into Atlantic ■ Africa's most active volcano is Nyiragongo (3,520 m [11,541 ft]) ■ On basis of average annual flow, Boyoma (formerly Stanley) Falls are world's greatest waterfalls ■ 55% of country rainforest; national parks & reserves comprise 15%, cultivated land 3% ■ Copper represents nearly 50% country's total value of exports ■ World's leading cobalt producer ■ World's 2nd largest diamond producer

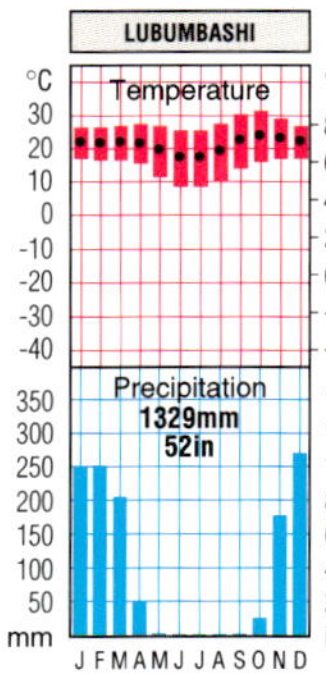

Equator passes through the northern half of Zaïre, and in this zone the rainfall and temperature are high throughout the year. To the north and south is a sub-tropical zone with slightly lower temperatures and a marked wet and dry season. The climate near the coast, because of a cold ocean current, is cooler and drier. In the east there is a mountain climate.

RWANDA

Adopted in 1961, Rwanda's tricolour in the Pan-African colours features the letter 'R' to distinguish it from Guinea's flag. Red represents the blood shed in the 1959 revolution, yellow for victory over tyranny and green for hope.

■ Until 1962, linked to Burundi under name of Ruanda-Urundi; administered by Belgium ■ 96% of pop. live in rural areas ■ One of world's least developed countries ■ Members of Tutsi tribe among world's tallest peoples, often over 2 m [6.5 ft] tall ■ Has some of last mountain gorillas

COUNTRY: Republic of Rwanda
AREA: 26,340 sq km [10,170 sq mls]
POPULATION: 7,181,000
CAPITAL (Population): Kigali (157,000)
GOVERNMENT: Single-party republic with unicam. legisl.
ETHNIC GROUPS: Hutu 85%, Tuti 14%, Twal 1%
LANGUAGES: French and Kinyarwanda (official)
RELIGIONS: Christian, Muslim and traditional beliefs
NATIONAL DAY: 1 July; Independence Day (1962)
CURRENCY: Rwanda franc
ANNUAL INCOME PER PERSON: $310
POPULATION DENSITY: 272 per sq km [706 per sq ml]
LIFE EXPECTANCY: Female 52 yrs, Male 49 yrs
ADULT LITERACY: 47%

BURUNDI

The three stars in Burundi's flag symbolise the nation's motto 'Unity, Work, Progress'. Green represents hope, red the struggle for independence, and white peace. Burundi adopted this unusual design when it became a republic in 1966.

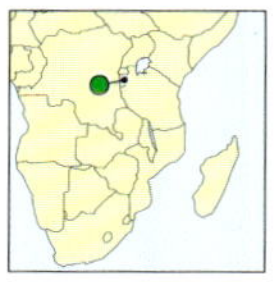

■ Small densely populated country, intensively cultivated despite mountainous terrain ■ Pygmy Twa, original inhabitants, now less than 1% of pop. ■ Centuries old enmities between Hutu & Tutsi peoples; estimated 100,000 Hutu killed by Tutsi in 1972 & 20,000 in 1988

COUNTRY: Republic of Burundi
AREA: 27,830 sq km [10,745 sq mls]
POPULATION: 5,458,000
CAPITAL (Population): Bujumbura (273,000)
GOVERNMENT: Military state
ETHNIC GROUPS: Rundi 97%
LANGUAGES: French and Kirundi (both official)
RELIGIONS: Christian 86% (Roman Catholic 78%), traditional beliefs 14%
NATIONAL DAY: 1 July; Independence Day (1962)
CURRENCY: Burundi franc = 100 centimes
ANNUAL INCOME PER PERSON: $210
POPULATION DENSITY: 196 per sq km [508 per sq ml]
LIFE EXPECTANCY: Female 53 yrs, Male 49 yrs
ADULT LITERACY: 34%

TANZANIA

In 1964 Tanganyika united with the island of Zanzibar to form the United Republic of Tanzania and a new flag was adopted. The colours represent agriculture (green), minerals (yellow), the people (black), water and Zanzibar (blue).

■ Earliest known human structure found at Lower Palaeolithic site at Olduvai Gorge in 1964 ■ Mount Kilimanjaro - Africa's highest mountain (5,895 m [19,340 ft]) snow-capped all year although only 3° south of Equator ■ Selous Game Reserve covering 50,000 sq km [19,000 sq mls], world's largest game reserve - over 1 million large animals

COUNTRY: United Republic of Tanzania
AREA: 945,090 sq km [364,899 sq mls]
POPULATION: 25,635,000
CAPITAL (Population): Dar es Salaam (1,100,000)
GOVERNMENT: Single party republic with a unicam. legisl.
ETHNIC GROUPS: Nyamwezi and Sukama 21%, Swahili 9%, Hehet and Bena 7%, Makonde 6%, Haya 6%
LANGUAGES: Swahili (official), English
RELIGIONS: Christian 34%, Muslim 33%, tradit. beliefs
NATIONAL DAY: 26 April; Union Day (1964)
CURRENCY: Tanzanian shilling = 100 cents
ANNUAL INCOME PER PERSON: $120
MAIN PRIMARY PRODUCTS: Agricultural and diamonds
MAIN INDUSTRIES: Agriculture, food processing, cement
MAIN EXPORTS: Coffee 26%, cotton 24%, sisal 1%
MAIN IMPORTS: Machinery and industrial goods 73%
DEFENCE: 20% of national budget
POPULATION DENSITY: 27 per sq km [70 per sq ml]
INFANT MORTALITY: 97 per 1,000 live births
LIFE EXPECTANCY: Female 57 yrs, Male 53 yrs
ADULT LITERACY: 85%

MALAWI

The colours in Malawi's flag come from the flag adopted by the Malawi Congress Party in 1953. The rising sun symbol, representing the beginning of a new era for Africa, was added when the country gained independence from Britain in 1964.

■ Name means 'The lake where sun-haze is reflected in the water like fire' ■ Narrow strip, at no point over 160 km [100 mls] wide ■ Lake Malawi Africa's 3rd biggest lake ■ Economy almost entirely agricultural ■ Self-sufficient in food but heavily dependent on foreign aid ■ Dr Hastings Banda, President since independence

COUNTRY: Republic of Malawi
AREA: 118,480 sq km [45,745 sq mls]
POPULATION: 8,556,000
CAPITAL (Population): Lilongwe (187,000)
GOVERNMENT: Single-party republic with unicam. legisl.
ETHNIC GROUPS: Maravi 58%, Lomwe 18%, Yao 13%, Ngoni 7%

LANGUAGES: Chichewa and English
RELIGIONS: Christian 64%, traditional beliefs 19%, Muslim 16%
NATIONAL DAY: 6 July; Independence Day (1966)
CURRENCY: Kwacha = 100 tambala
ANNUAL INCOME PER PERSON: $200
MAIN PRIMARY PRODUCTS: Limestone and timber

MAIN INDUSTRIES: Agriculture, fishing
MAIN EXPORTS: Tobacco, tea and sugar
MAIN IMPORTS: Fuel, vehicles and clothing
DEFENCE: 5% of national budget
POPULATION DENSITY: 72 per sq km [187 per sq ml]
LIFE EXPECTANCY: Female 50 yrs, Male 48 yrs
ADULT LITERACY: 41%

ZAMBIA

The colours of Zambia's distinctive national flag are those of the United Nationalist Independence Party, which led the struggle against Britain. The flying eagle represents freedom. The design was adopted on independence in 1964.

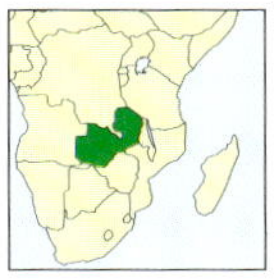

■ Africa's largest, & world's 5th largest, copper producer provides 95% of exports & 55% of all government revenues ■ Collapse of world copper prices in 1970s severely damaged economy ■ Kariba hydro-electric dam on Zambesi river has created lake covering 5,300 sq km [2,046 sq mls]

COUNTRY: Republic of Zambia
AREA: 752,614 sq km [290,586 sq mls]
POPULATION: 8,073,000
CAPITAL (Population): Lusaka (900,000)
GOVERNMENT: Republic with a unicameral legislature
ETHNIC GROUPS: Bemba 34%, Tonga 16%, Malawi 14%, Lozi 9%

LANGUAGES: English (official), Bemba, Nyanja, Lozi, Lunda, Luvale and Tonga
RELIGIONS: Christian 44%, Animist 40%
CURRENCY: Kwacha = 100 negwee
ANNUAL INCOME PER PERSON: $420
MAIN PRIMARY PRODUCTS: Copper, coal, zinc, lead, gold
MAIN INDUSTRIES: Mining, agriculture

MAIN EXPORTS: Copper, cobalt, zinc, tobacco
MAIN IMPORTS: Machinery, transport, chemical, fuel and electricity
DEFENCE: 2% of national budget
POPULATION DENSITY: 11 per sq km [28 per sq ml]
LIFE EXPECTANCY: Female 57 yrs, Male 54 yrs
ADULT LITERACY: 76%

ANGOLA

The flag is based on that of the Popular Movement for the Liberation of Angola during the struggle for independence from Portugal (1975). The emblem, incorporating a half gearwheel and a machete, symbolises Angola's Socialist ideology.

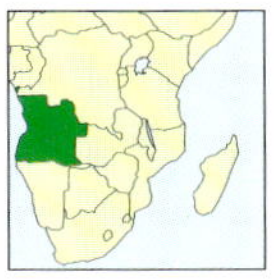

■ Name derives from King N'gola, who led West African kingdom before European immigration ■ 14 times bigger than Portugal, its former colonial master ■ Large unexploited mineral reserves (manganese, copper & phosphates) ■ More than 2 decades of civil war between Government MPLA & UNITA forces ceased mid-1991

COUNTRY: People's Republic of Angola
AREA: 1,246,700 sq km [481,351 sq mls]
POPULATION: 10,020,000
CAPITAL (Population): Luanda (1,200,000)
GOVERNMENT: One party socialist republic with a unicameral House of Assembly
ETHNIC GROUPS: Ovimbundu 37%, Mbundu 23%, Kongo, Luimbe, Humbe, Chokwe
LANGUAGES: Portuguese (official), but Ovimbundu, Kimbundu, Bakango and Chokwe in common use

RELIGIONS: Christian (mainly Roman Catholic) 64%; Animist 34%
NATIONAL DAY: 11 November; Independence Day (1975)
CURRENCY: Kwanza = 100 lwei
ANNUAL INCOME PER PERSON: $620
MAIN PRIMARY PRODUCTS: Coffee, cassava, crude petroleum, diamonds
MAIN INDUSTRIES: Agriculture, oil-related products
MAIN EXPORTS: Mineral products, pearls, gemstones, precious metals

MAIN IMPORTS: Base metals, electrical and transport equipment
DEFENCE: 38% of national budget
POPULATION DENSITY: 8 per sq km [21 per sq ml]
LIFE EXPECTANCY: Female 48 yrs, Male 45 yrs
ADULT LITERACY: 28%

NAMIBIA

One of the world's newest states, Namibia adopted its flag after independence in 1990. The red and white colours symbolise the country's human resources while the green, blue and the gold sun emblem represent the natural resources, mostly minerals.

■ Formerly known as South West Africa ■ One of world's driest countries ■ Mining contributes 35% of GDP ■ Some of world's richest fishing grounds (fed by Benguela current) ■ One of world's richest offshore diamond beds

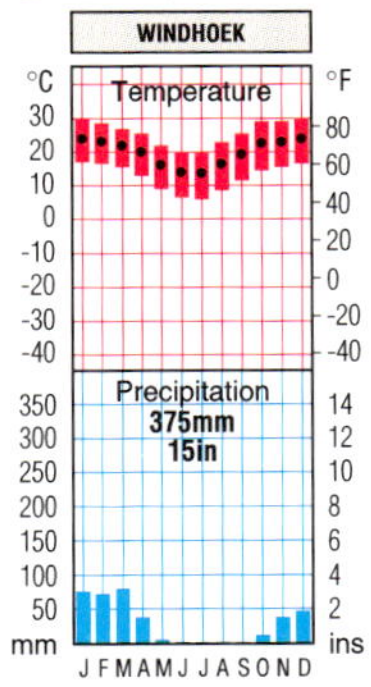

Windhoek lies at 1,700 m [5,500 ft] on the Namibian plateau and is isolated from the effects of the cold Benguela current which washes the coast to the west. With little cloud and clear, dry air the daily range of temperature is much larger than on the coast. Summer days are hot and frost may occur on winter nights. Thundery rain in summer provides enough water to support vegetation, in contrast to the deserts to the east and west.

COUNTRY: Namibia
AREA: 824,290 sq km [318,258 sq mls]
POPULATION: 1,781,000
CAPITAL (Population): Windhoek (115,000)
GOVERNMENT: In transition to an independent state
ETHNIC GROUPS: Ovambo 50%, Kavango 9%, Herero 7%, Damara 7%, White 6%
LANGUAGES: English and Afrikaans
RELIGIONS: Christian (Lutheran 51%)
CURRENCY: South African Rand = 100 cents

ANNUAL INCOME PER PERSON: $1,000
MAIN PRIMARY PRODUCTS: Uranium, tin, copper, lead, zinc, silver and diamonds
MAIN INDUSTRIES: Mining and agriculture
MAIN EXPORTS: Minerals
MAIN IMPORTS: Food, transport equipment
DEFENCE: 19% of national budget
POPULATION DENSITY: 2.2 per sq km [5.7 per sq ml]
LIFE EXPECTANCY: Female 60 yrs, Male 58 yrs
ADULT LITERACY: 73%

BOTSWANA

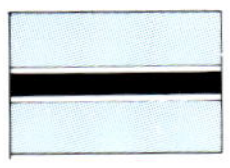

Botswana's flag dates from independence from Britain in 1966. The black and white zebra stripe represents the racial harmony of the people and blue symbolises the country's most vital need – rainwater.

■ Known as Bechuanaland until 1966 ■ Much of north, west & south form part of Kalahari Desert ■ Jwaneng diamond mine said to be world's richest after Kimberley ■ Export of cattle produces large proportion of foreign exchange ■ 17% of land set aside for wildlife conservation

COUNTRY: Botswana
AREA: 581,730 sq km [224,606 sq mls]
POPULATION: 1,291,000
CAPITAL (Population): Gaborone (120,000)
GOVERNMENT: Multi-party republic with a unicameral legislative assembly
ETHNIC GROUPS: Tswana 76%, Shana 12%, San (Bushmen) 3%

LANGUAGES: English (official) and Tswana
RELIGIONS: Christian 50%, traditional beliefs 49%
NATIONAL DAY: 30 September; Independence Day (1966)
CURRENCY: Pula = 100 thebe
ANNUAL INCOME PER PERSON: $2,040
MAIN PRIMARY PRODUCTS: Coal, diamonds, copper, nickel, cobalt, sorghum and pulses
MAIN INDUSTRIES: Agricultural and mining

MAIN EXPORTS: Diamonds, copper-nickel matte, meat and meat products
MAIN IMPORTS: Food, beverages, tobacco, machinery, electrical goods and transport
DEFENCE: 4% of national budget
POPULATION DENSITY: 2.2 per sq km [5.7 per sq ml]
LIFE EXPECTANCY: Female 64 yrs, Male 58 yrs
ADULT LITERACY: 71%

AFRICA – SOUTH, INDIAN OCEAN

SOUTH AFRICA

The design of South Africa's flag, adopted in 1928, is based on one brought by the first Dutch settlers in the 17th century. On the central stripe are the British Union flag and the flags of the Orange Free State and the Transvaal.

COUNTRY: Republic of South Africa
AREA: 1,221,040 sq km [471,444 sq mls]
POPULATION: 35,282,000
CAPITAL (Population): Pretoria (823,000)
GOVERNMENT: Multi-party republic with tricameral legislature
ETHNIC GROUPS: Black 68%, White 18%, Coloured 11%, Asian 3%
LANGUAGES: Afrikaans and English (official), Xhosa, Zulu
RELIGIONS: Black Christian churches 31%, Dutch Reform 23%, Roman Catholic 15%, Hindu 3%, Muslim 2%
NATIONAL DAY: 31 May; Republic Day (1961)
CURRENCY: Rand = 100 cents
ANNUAL INCOME PER PERSON: $2,520
SOURCE OF INCOME: Agriculture 6%, Industry 45%, Services 49%
MAIN PRIMARY PRODUCTS: Gold, iron ore, copper, uranium, diamonds, coal, zinc, tin, phosphates, vermiculite, cereals, fruit, sugar, tobacco, timber, fish, cotton
MAIN INDUSTRIES: Mining, iron and steel, vehicles, food processing, oil refining, agriculture, clothing, paper, wine, fishing, forestry
EXPORTS: $439 per person
MAIN EXPORTS: Gold 39%, base metals 14%, mineral products 10%, pearls, precious and semi-precious stones and precious metals 8%, chemical products 3%, textiles 3%
MAIN EXPORT PARTNERS: USA 10%, Japan 8%, UK 6%, Netherlands 4%, Switzerland 4%
IMPORTS: $491 per person
MAIN IMPORTS: Machinery and mechanical equipment 31%, transport equipment 14%, chemical products 11%
MAIN IMPORT PARTNERS: USA 17%, Germany 17%, UK 12%, Japan 10%
EDUCATIONAL EXPENDITURE: 19% of national budget
DEFENCE: 18% of national budget
TOTAL ARMED FORCES: 103,000
TOURISM: 703,000 visitors
ROADS: 183,851 km [114,243 mls]
RAILWAYS: 23,607 km [14,669 mls]
POPULATION DENSITY: 29 per sq km [75 per sq ml]
URBAN POPULATION: 59%
POPULATION GROWTH: 2.2% per year
BIRTHS: 33 per 1,000 population
DEATHS: 10 per 1,000 population
INFANT MORTALITY: 62 per 1,000 live births
LIFE EXPECTANCY: Female 66 yrs, Male 60 yrs
POPULATION PER DOCTOR: 1,900
ADULT LITERACY: White 93%, Asian 69%, Black 32%
PRINCIPAL CITIES (Population): Cape Town 1,912,000 Johannesburg 1,726,000 East Rand 1,038,000 Durban 982,000 Pretoria 823,000 Port Elizabeth 652,000 West Rand 647,000

■ Johannesburg largest city, Cape Town legislative capital, Pretoria administrative capital ■ World's largest producer & exporter of gold & diamonds ■ World's highest concentration of chromium, manganese, vanadium & platinum ■ One of world's strongest economies & dominates southern part of African continent ■ Mining accounts for about 15% of GDP ■ Almost self-sufficient in foodstuffs though agriculture provides less than 10% GDP ■ Large defence industry, established as result of world arms embargo ■ 50% of cars run on fuel derived from 'liquid coal' ■ Dutch settlers first arrived in 1652 ■ National Party in power since 1948 ■ Politically isolated from most of world due to apartheid (separate racial development) policies ■ Until 1984, parliament drawn from & elected by whites only; Asian & Coloured communities then allowed representation but still with built-in white majority vote; blacks have no vote ■ Country's financial position & political isolation prompted landmark concessions in 1990 ■ Nelson Mandela, deputy leader of African National Congress, released from prison in 1990 after 26 years ■ Apartheid system being dismantled from 1991 onwards

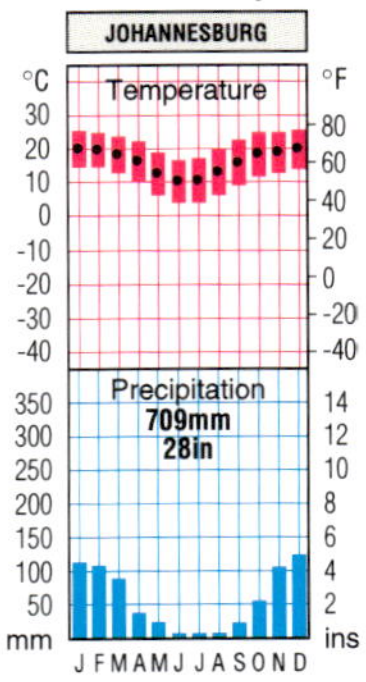

In winter the air is very dry and the sky almost cloudless on the High Veld. The large diurnal range of temperature resembles that of other places on the high plateaus of southern Africa. Summer is the rainy season when north-easterly winds bring moist air from the Indian Ocean. Rainfall is more abundant and the winter dry season shorter than in western areas at the same latitude.

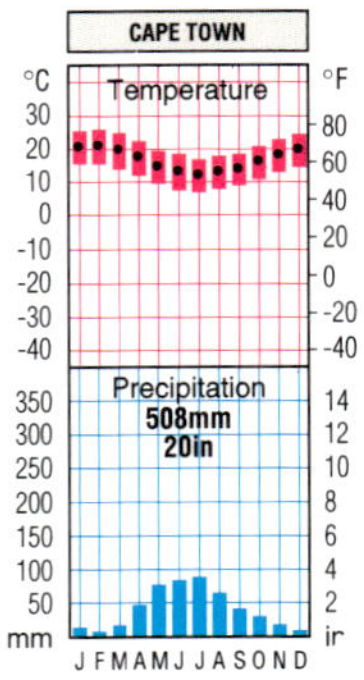

The south-western corner of South Africa has a very different climate from the rest of the country. It lies far enough south to be affected by westerly winds which blow across the Southern Ocean in winter bringing cloud and rain. The dry, sunny summers and wet winters resemble those of the Mediterranean region but it is less hot in summer due to the cold Benguela current flowing southward along the coast.

ZIMBABWE

Adopted when legal independence was secured in 1980, Zimbabwe's flag is based on the colours of the ruling Patriotic Front. Within the white triangle is the soapstone bird national emblem and a red star, symbolising Socialist policy.

COUNTRY: Republic of Zimbabwe
AREA: 390,579 sq km [150,873 sq mls]
POPULATION: 9,369,000
CAPITAL (Population): Harare 681,100
GOVERNMENT: Single-party republic with bicameral legisl.
ETHNIC GROUPS: Bantu 70%, Ndebele
LANGUAGES: English (official), Chichona and Sindebele
RELIGIONS: Christian 44%, Animist 40%
CURRENCY: Zimbabwe $ = 100 cents
NATIONAL DAY: 18 April; Independence Day (1980)
ANNUAL INCOME PER PERSON: $640
MAIN PRIMARY PRODUCTS: Nickel, copper, coal, cobalt, asbestos, gold, iron ore, silver, tin
MAIN INDUSTRIES: Agriculture, mining, manufacturing
EXPORTS: $156 per person
MAIN EXPORTS: Food, tobacco, cotton lint, asbestos, copper, nickel, iron and steel bars
IMPORTS: $115 per person
MAIN IMPORTS: Food, tobacco, cotton lint, asbestos, copper, nickel, iron and steel bars
DEFENCE: 8% of national budget
POPULATION DENSITY: 24 per sq km [62 per sq ml]
LIFE EXPECTANCY: Female 63 yrs, Male 59 yrs

■ Named after Great Zimbabwe, largest of dry stone village sites occupied by Shona-Karanga civilisation ■ Almost all country over 300 m [1,000 ft] above sea level ■ Rich in minerals & wealth of farmland ■ Tobacco, most important crop, accounts for 20% of export earnings ■ Tourism major growth industry ■ White pop. less than 2% still own bulk of resources ■ Known as Southern Rhodesia (after Cecil Rhodes) till independence in 1980 ■ White settlers issued UDI in 1965 to resist decolonisation; this triggered civil war which finally ended in 1980

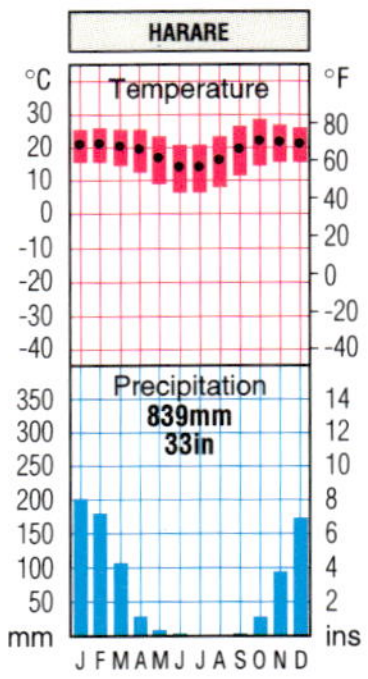

In common with other places on the high interior plateau of southern Africa, Harare has a large diurnal range of temperature, particularly in the dry, sunny winter and is much cooler than lowlands at the same latitude. The main rains of summer are brought by south-easterly winds from the Indian Ocean. They are usually preceded by isolated thundery outbreaks which extend the rainy season from late October to March.

MOZAMBIQUE

The green stripe represents the fertile land, the black stripe Africa and the yellow stripe mineral wealth. The badge on the red triangle contains a rifle, hoe, cogwheel and book which are all Marxist symbols of the struggle against colonialism.

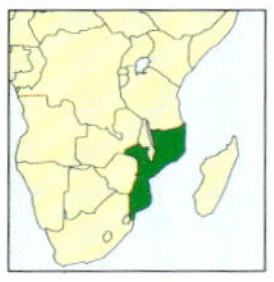

COUNTRY: People's Republic of Mozambique
AREA: 801,590 sq km [309,494 sq mls]
POPULATION: 15,656,000
CAPITAL (Population): Maputo (1,070,000)
GOVERNMENT: People's republic with a unicameral legislature
ETHNIC GROUPS: Makua 47%, Tsonga 23%, Malawi 12%, Shona 11%, Yao 4%, Swahili 1%, Makonde 1%
LANGUAGES: Portuguese (official), other Bantu languages as ethnic groups above
RELIGIONS: Traditional beliefs 48%, Roman Catholic 31%, Muslim 13%
NATIONAL DAY: 25 June; Independence Day (1975)
CURRENCY: Metical = 100 centavos
ANNUAL INCOME PER PERSON: $80
MAIN PRIMARY PRODUCTS: Cotton, cereals, cashew nuts, sugar, tea, fruit, sisal, groundnuts, coal
MAIN INDUSTRIES: Agriculture, textiles, chemicals, mining, food processing, fishing
MAIN EXPORTS: Shrimps 39%, cashew nuts 32%, cotton 7%, sugar 3%, copra 3%
MAIN IMPORTS: Foodstuffs 38%, capital equipment 19%, machinery and spare parts 15%, petroleum 10%, chemicals 5%, metals 4%
DEFENCE: 38% of national budget
POPULATION DENSITY: 20 per sq km [51 per sq ml]
LIFE EXPECTANCY: Female 50 yrs, Male 47 yrs
ADULT LITERACY: 38%

■ Huge mineral reserves unexploited - coal, copper, bauxite & offshore gas deposits ■ Officially designated as world's poorest country ■ Major source of revenue is charges for freight carried on Beira railway for landlocked states of Southern Africa ■ Right-wing guerrilla movement (Renamo) have been fighting against government since early 1980s, peace talks between Government & Renamo began in 1991 ■ Most Portuguese former residents refused entry

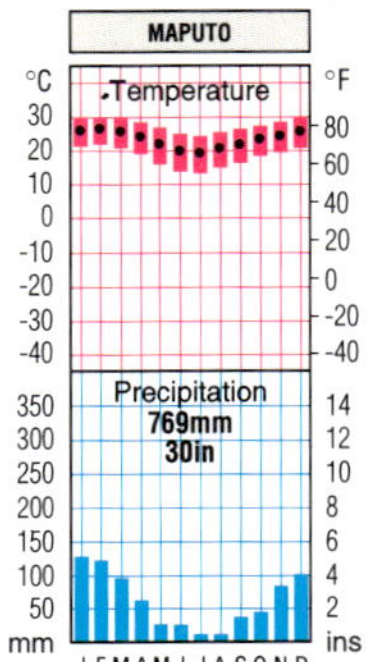

Maputo is located on the coast of Mozambique at the southern end of an extensive lowland. The range of temperature is less than that of the interior plateaus and summers are hot and humid, partly due to the warm Agulhas Current which flows southward along the coast. Most of the rain falls in summer when the inter-tropical rain belt is at its furthest south. There is a not entirely rainless dry season in winter.

LESOTHO

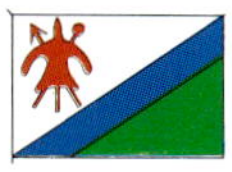

In 1987 this succeeded the flag adopted on independence from Britain in 1966. The white, blue and green represent peace, rain and prosperity – the words of the national motto. The emblem comprises shield, knobkerrie and ostrich feather sceptre.

COUNTRY: Kingdom of Lesotho
AREA: 30,350 sq km [11,718 sq mls]
POPULATION: 1,774,000
CAPITAL (Population): Maseru (109,000)
GOVERNMENT: Military-dominated monarchy
ETHNIC GROUPS: Sotho
LANGUAGES: Sotho and English
RELIGIONS: Christian (of which Roman Catholic 44%)
NATIONAL DAY: 4 October; Independence Day (1966)
CURRENCY: Loti = 100 lisente

ANNUAL INCOME PER PERSON: $470
POPULATION DENSITY: 58 per sq km [151 per sq ml]
LIFE EXPECTANCY: Female 63 yrs, Male 54 yrs
ADULT LITERACY: 74%

■ Formerly known as Basutoland ■ 80% of pop. engaged in agriculture ■ Only 1/8 of land cultivatable; main crop maize ■ About 60% of working age males work in S. Africa ■ S. Africa provides over 95% of imports

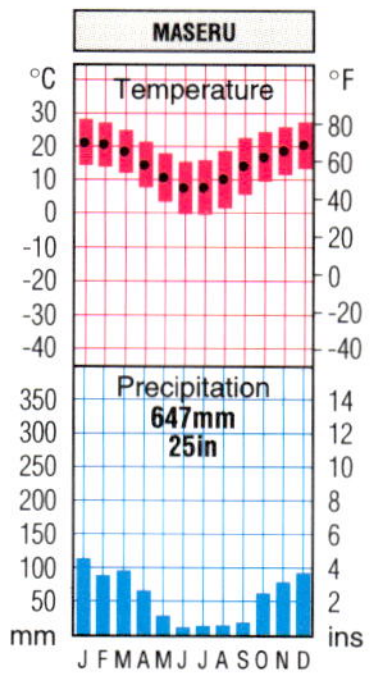

Lesotho includes most of the highest land in southern Africa, reaching over 3,000 metres [10,000 ft] in the Drakensberg. Average temperatures are greatly reduced by altitude and the daily range is large, often falling below freezing on winter nights. Although most of the rain falls in summer, winter is not as dry as other parts of the high plateaus and snow may occur.

SWAZILAND

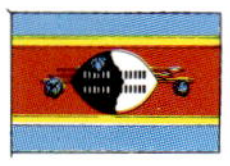

The Kingdom has flown this distinctive flag, which is based on that of the Swazi Pioneer Corps of World War II, since independence from Britain in 1968. The emblem has the weapons of a warrior – ox-hide shield, two assegai and a fighting stick.

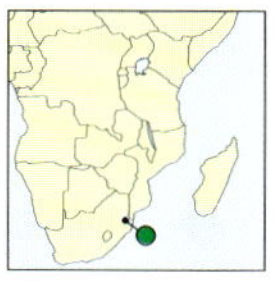

■ One of best-watered areas in southern Africa ■ Surrounded on 3 sides by S. Africa ■ One of 3 remaining African monarchies ■ Parts of original tribal homelands, with 1 million Swazi people, in S. Africa ■ 75% of working pop. engaged in agriculture ■ Economy dominated by - & closely linked to - S. Afr.

COUNTRY: Kingdom of Swaziland
AREA: 17,360 sq km [6,703 sq mls]
POPULATION: 768,000
CAPITAL (Population): Mbabane (38,000)
GOVERNMENT: Monarchy with bicameral legislature

ETHNIC GROUPS: Swazi 84%, Zulu 10%, Tsonga 3%
LANGUAGES: Swazi and English (official)
RELIGIONS: Christian 77%, traditional beliefs 20%
NATIONAL DAY: 6 September; Independence Day (1968)
CURRENCY: Lilangeni = 100 cents

ANNUAL INCOME PER PERSON: $820
POPULATION DENSITY: 44 per sq km [115 per sq ml]
LIFE EXPECTANCY: Female 60 yrs, Male 56 yrs
ADULT LITERACY: 68%

MADAGASCAR

Madagascar's colours are those of historical flags of South-East Asia, from where the island's first inhabitants came before 1000 AD. The present flag was adopted in 1958 when the country first became a republic after French rule.

■ World's fourth largest island; largest off African mainland ■ Known as Malagasy Republic (1960-75) ■ Much fauna & flora unique to island ■ Only about 5% of land cultivated ■ Produces 2/3 of world's supply of vanilla

COUNTRY: Democratic Republic of Madagascar
AREA: 587,040 sq km [226,656 sq mls]
POPULATION: 11,197,000
CAPITAL (Population): Antananarivo (703,000)
GOVERNMENT: Single-party republic with unicameral legislature
ETHNIC GROUPS: Merina 26%, Betsimisaraka 15%, Betsileo 12%
LANGUAGES: Malagasy and French
RELIGIONS: Christian 51%, traditional beliefs 47%, Muslim 2%
NATIONAL DAY: 26 June; Independence Day (1960)
CURRENCY: Franc (FMG) = 100 centimes

ANNUAL INCOME PER PERSON: $230
MAIN PRIMARY PRODUCTS: Chromite, graphite and salt
MAIN INDUSTRIES: Agriculture, fishing, mining
MAIN EXPORTS: Coffee, vanilla, sugar and cloves
MAIN IMPORTS: Petroleum, chemicals, machinery and vehicles
DEFENCE: 11% of national budget
POPULATION DENSITY: 19 per sq km [49 per sq ml]
LIFE EXPECTANCY: Female 57 yrs, Male 54 yrs
ADULT LITERACY: 66%

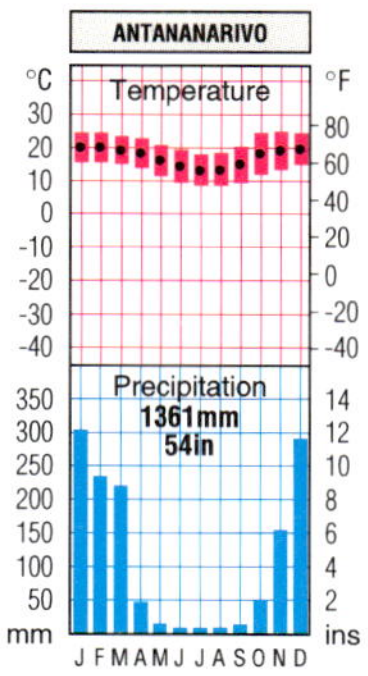

Apart from the east coast which has rain at all seasons, Madagascar has a summer rainy season and a marked winter dry season. Antananarivo lies in the central highlands and temperatures are considerably moderated by its altitude. The island, especially the north- west, is reputed to be one of the most thundery regions on Earth. In February tropical cyclones from the Indian Ocean may affect the island.

MAURITIUS

The flag of this small island state was adopted on independence from Britain in 1968. Red stands for the struggle for independence, blue for the Indian Ocean, yellow for the bright future and green for the lush vegetation.

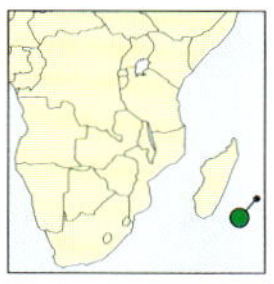

COUNTRY: Mauritius
AREA: 1,860 sq km [718 sq mls]
POPULATION: 1,075,000
CAPITAL (Population): Port Louis (139,000)
GOVERNMENT: Constitutional monarchy with a unicameral legislature
ETHNIC GROUPS: Creole 56%, Indian 40%, European 3%
LANGUAGES: English (official), French Creole, Bhoipuri, Hindi
RELIGIONS: Hindu 53%, Roman Catholic 26%, Muslim 13%, Protestant 4%
NATIONAL DAY: 12 March; Independence Day (1968)

CURRENCY: Mauritian rupee = 100 cents
ANNUAL INCOME PER PERSON: $2,250
POPULATION DENSITY: 578 per sq km [1,497 per sq ml]
LIFE EXPECTANCY: Female 73 yrs, Male 68 yrs
ADULT LITERACY: 82%

■ Volcanic island state in Indian Ocean off S.E. African coast ■ Includes Rodriguez Island to the E. ■ Named by Dutch after their ruler, Prince Maurice of Nassau ■ Sugar cane plantations cover 45% of land ■ Economy heavily dependent on sugar, 60% of exports 1/3 of labour force ■ In relation to size, no land on earth has as many different languages spoken by so many different ethnic groups ■ Pop. has increased rapidly over past decade because eradication of malaria ■ Home of now extinct dodo - destroyed by European sailors & their domestic animals ■ Colonised first by French and, from 1810 to independence, by British

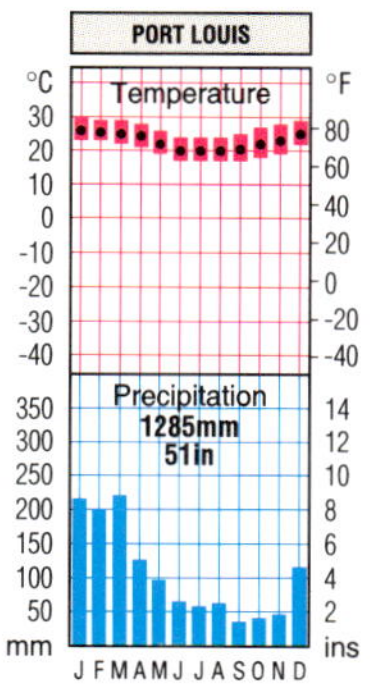

Bathed by the warm waters of the Indian Ocean the climate is mild and humid. There are two seasons; hot Nov.-Apr., with temperatures reaching 31°C (88°F) and cool May-Oct., 25°C (77°F). The central plateau is cooler and wetter receiving over 5,000 mm [200 ins.] rainfall. The prevailing south-east trades bring heavier rain to the eastern slopes.

COMOROS

COUNTRY: French Islamic Republic of the Comoros
AREA: 2,230 sq km [861 sq mls]
POPULATION: 551,000
CAPITAL (Population): Moroni (21,000)

BIOT

COUNTRY: British Indian Ocean Territory. (UK dependent territory)
AREA: 80 sq km [31 sq mls]
POPULATION: 3,000

RÉUNION

COUNTRY: French overseas department
AREA: 2,510 sq km [969 sq mls]
POPULATION: 599,000
CAPITAL (Population): St.-Denis (109,000)

SEYCHELLES

COUNTRY: Republic of Seychelles
AREA: 110 sq km [453 sq mls]
POPULATION: 67,000
CAPITAL (Population): Victoria (23,000)

AUSTRALIA AND OCEANIA

AUSTRALIA

Showing its historical link with Britain, Australia's flag, adopted in 1901, features the British Blue Ensign. The five stars represent the Southern Cross constellation and the larger star symbolises the Federal Commonwealth.

COUNTRY: Commonwealth of Australia
AREA: 7,686,850 sq km [2,967,893 sq mls]
POPULATION: 17,086,000
CAPITAL (Population): Canberra (289,000)
GOVERNMENT: Federal parliamentary state with bicameral legislature
ETHNIC GROUPS: White 94%, Asian 2%, Aboriginal 1%
LANGUAGES: English
RELIGIONS: Roman Catholic 24%, Anglican 24%, Orthodox, Muslim, Jewish, Buddhist
NATIONAL DAY: 26 January; Australia Day
CURRENCY: Australian $ = 100 cents
ANNUAL INCOME PER PERSON: $17,080
SOURCE OF INCOME: Agriculture 4%, Industry 34%, Services 61%
MAIN PRIMARY PRODUCTS: Coal, crude petroleum, bauxite, sheep, cattle, timber, zircon, natural gas, gold, silver, nickel
MAIN INDUSTRIES: Metal fabrication, mining, construction of vehicles and aircraft, agriculture, petrol refining, chemicals, electronics, general manufactures
EXPORTS: $2,181 per person
MAIN EXPORTS: Food and live animals 22%, oil and gas 19%, metallic ores 14%, textile fibres 11%, machinery 6%, transport equipment 3%
MAIN EXPORT PARTNERS: Japan 25%, USA 12%, New Zealand 5%, South Korea 4%, UK 4%, Germany 3%, Hong Kong 3%, Taiwan 3%
IMPORTS: $2,381 per person
MAIN IMPORTS: Machinery and transport equipment 40%, basic manufactures 16%, chemicals 8%, petroleum and petroleum products 5%, food and live animals 5%
MAIN IMPORT PARTNERS: USA 22%, Japan 21%, Germany 8%, UK 7%, New Zealand 4%, Taiwan 4%
EDUCATIONAL EXPENDITURE: 6.4% of national budget
DEFENCE: 9.3% of national budget
TOTAL ARMED FORCES: 69,600
TOURISM: 1,785,000 visitors
ROADS: 840,000 km [525,000 mls]
RAILWAYS: 39,251 km [22,657 mls]
POPULATION DENSITY: 2.2 per sq km [5.7 per sq ml]
URBAN POPULATION: 86%
POPULATION GROWTH: 1.2%
BIRTHS: 14.2 per 1,000 population
DEATHS: 7.6 per 1,000 population
INFANT MORTALITY: 7 per 1,000 live births
LIFE EXPECTANCY: Female 80 yrs, Male 74 yrs
POPULATION PER DOCTOR: 388
ADULT LITERACY: 99%
PRINCIPAL CITIES (Population): Sydney 3,531,000 Melbourne 2,965,000 Brisbane 1,215,000 Perth 1,083,000 Adelaide 1,013,000

■ World's largest island - or smallest continent ■ Great Artesian Basin, world's largest underground natural reservoir, lying beneath area of about 1.7 million sq km [656,000 sq mls] & discharging 1,500 million litres [330 million gallons] per day ■ Ayers Rock, one of world's largest monoliths, sacred to aborigines who have recovered its ownership & renamed it Uluru ■ Great Barrier Reef world's largest coral reef, stretching about 2,000 km [1,250 mls] ■ Centre of Australia occupied by number of distinct deserts which together comprise vast arid area of 3.8 million sq km [1.5 million sq mls] ■ Sydney has world's largest 'natural' harbour ■ Many unique species of plants & animals ■ Home to 70% of world's poisonous insects ■ Home to world's only wild camels ■ 140 million sheep produce 25% of world's wool, generating nearly 9% of export earnings ■ World's biggest producer of bauxite ■ Self-sufficient in energy ■ In 1986, overtook USA to become world's leading coal exporter; 15% export earnings ■ Only about 40% of Aboriginal pop. still live in rural areas

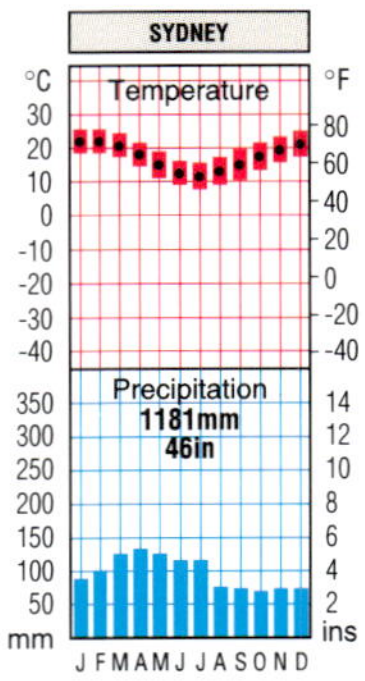

In the south-east, the annual rainfall total is reasonably high and distributed throughout the year, with maxima April-June. The vast valleys inland of the Great Divide, in the lee of the rain-bearing winds, are drier. The temperatures are moderate with winter night frosts throughout the south and the interior. Snow falls on the uplands of the south-east and Tasmania.

NEW ZEALAND

Like Australia, New Zealand flies a flag based on the design of the British Blue Ensign. Designed in 1869 and adopted in 1907 on acquiring Dominion status, it displays four of the five stars of the Southern Cross constellation.

COUNTRY: New Zealand
AREA: 268,680 sq km [103,737 sq mls]
POPULATION: 3,429,000
CAPITAL (Population): Wellington (325,000)
GOVERNMENT: Constitutional monarchy with a unicameral legislature
ETHNIC GROUPS: European 81%, Maori 9%, Polynesian 3%
LANGUAGES: English (official) and Maori
RELIGIONS: Anglican 24%, Presbyterian 18%, Roman Catholic 15%, Methodist 5%
NATIONAL DAY: 6 February; Treaty of Waitangi (1840)
CURRENCY: New Zealand $ = 100 cents
ANNUAL INCOME PER PERSON: $12,680
MAIN PRIMARY PRODUCTS: Sheep, cereals, fruit and vegetables, cattle, fish, coal, natural gas, iron and silica sands
MAIN INDUSTRIES: Iron and steel, agriculture, wine, timber, tourism, aluminium, natural gas and petroleum
EXPORTS: $2,679 per person
MAIN EXPORTS: Meat and meat preparations 20%, wool 14%, fruit and vegetables 7%, forest products 7%, hides, skins and pelts 4%, butter 4%
MAIN EXPORT PARTNERS: USA 17%, Japan 15%, Australia 15%, UK 9%
IMPORTS: $2,651 per person
MAIN IMPORTS: Machinery and electrical goods 26%, transport equipment 15%, chemicals 12%, textiles, clothing and footwear 7%
MAIN IMPORT PARTNERS: Japan 20%, Australia 18%, USA 16%, UK 10%
DEFENCE: 4.3% of national budget
TOURISM: 901,000 visitors
POPULATION DENSITY: 12.8 per sq km [33 per sq ml]
INFANT MORTALITY: 9 per 1,000 live births
LIFE EXPECTANCY: Female 79 yrs, Male 73 yrs
ADULT LITERACY: 99%
PRINCIPAL CITIES (Population): Auckland 885,377 Wellington 325,000 Hamilton 148,000 Napier-Hastings 110,000 Dunedin 109,000

■ 20 peaks over 3,000 m [10,000 ft] high ■ No place more than 110 km [70 mls] from sea ■ Kaingaroa Forest one of world's largest man-made forests, covers some 200,000 hectares [495,000 acres] ■ Wellington world's most southerly capital ■ Livestock outnumber people 24 to 1 ■ World's largest exporter of lamb & dairy products; 2nd largest exporter of wool ■ 50% of pop. under 30 ■ 10% of school leavers attend university ■ Polynesian Maoris were first settlers at least 1,000 years ago ■ 1st modern democracy to give women vote (in 1893), with Australia 2nd ■ In 1985 barred nuclear powered or nuclear armed ships from its ports

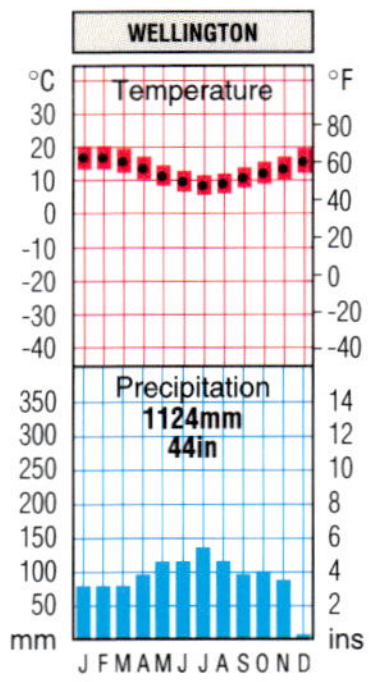

New Zealand lies within the influence of westerly winds throughout the year and has a well distributed rainfall with a winter maximum. The islands are set in a vast ocean which moderates the temperatures and although Wellington is at the same latitude as Rome, summers are 8°C [14°F] cooler. Despite its high rainfall, New Zealand with over 2,000 hours of sunshine per year is sunnier than comparable parts of Europe.

PAPUA NEW GUINEA

When Papua New Guinea became independent from Australia in 1975 it adopted a flag which had been used for the country since 1971. The design includes a bird of paradise in flight and the stars of the Southern Cross constellation.

COUNTRY: Papua New Guinea
AREA: 462,840 sq km [178,703 sq mls]
POPULATION: 3,699,000
CAPITAL (Population): Port Moresby (152,000)
GOVERNMENT: Parliamentary monarchy with a unicameral legislature
ETHNIC GROUPS: Papuan 84%, Melanesian 15%
LANGUAGES: Motu and English
RELIGIONS: Christian and traditional beliefs
NATIONAL DAY: 16 September; Independence Day (1975)
CURRENCY: Kina = 100 toea
ANNUAL INCOME PER PERSON: $860
MAIN PRIMARY PRODUCTS: Copper, silver and gold
MAIN INDUSTRIES: Mining, agriculture and forestry
MAIN EXPORTS: Copper ore and concentrates, coffee, timber, cocoa beans
MAIN IMPORTS: Machinery and vehicles, manufactured goods, mineral fuels, foodstuffs

■ Includes eastern half of New Guinea, world's second biggest non-continental island ■ Over 600 islands ■ Line of active volcanoes stretches along N. coast of mainland through island of New Britain ■ Greatest concentration of separate languages in world - over 700 languages & dialects spoken ■ Pidgin is common language of whole country ■ One of last outposts of Stone Age peoples ■ Major recipient of Australian aid

DEFENCE: 4.7% of national budget
POPULATION DENSITY: 7.9 per sq km [20.6 per sq ml]
LIFE EXPECTANCY: Female 57 yrs, Male 55 yrs
ADULT LITERACY: 45%

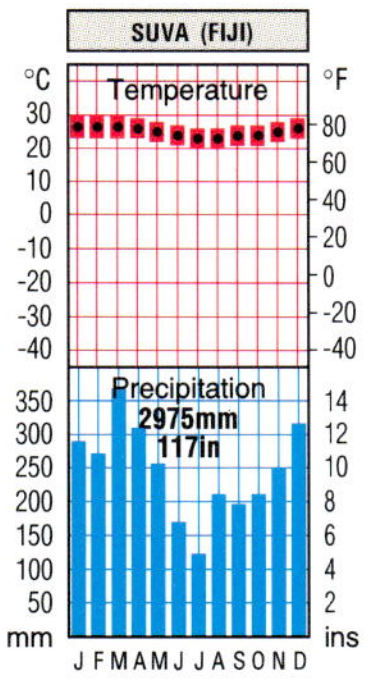

The south-east trades blow all year round, producing local contrasts; windward slopes are cloudier and wetter with rainfall exceeding 3,000 mm [120 ins]. Rainfall varies greatly from year to year. Hurricanes can cause great damage Dec.-Apr. Temperatures are uniformly high throughout the year, rising to 32°C [90°F] in the hot season (Dec.-Apr.).

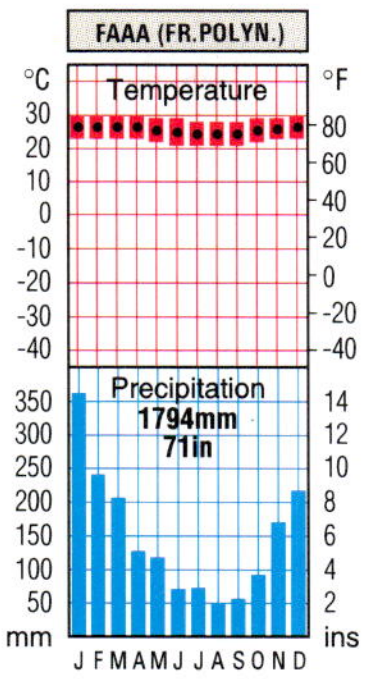

The climate is warm and humid with nearly continuous cloud cover over the mountain peaks. Temperatures remain high throughout the year with a slight maximum in March, during the warm rainy season. Rainfall is abundant and heaviest on the windward slopes (north and east facing). There are long periods of calm Apr.-June when the weather is brighter and drier.

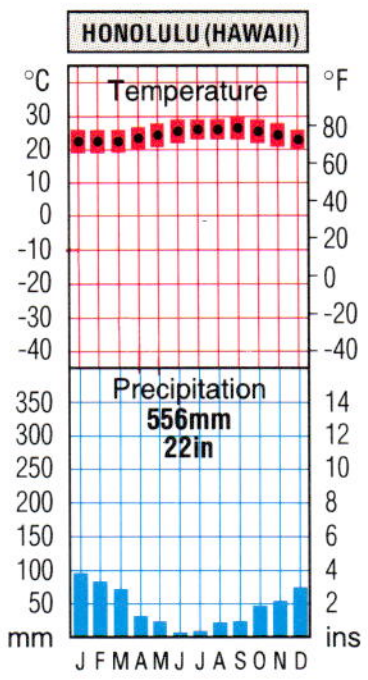

These sub-tropical islands are cooled by the moisture-laden north-east trades. Temperatures remain high throughout the year, ranging from 26°C [79°F] in the warmest month to 22°C [72°F] in the coolest. Rainfall varies greatly throughout these mountainous islands. Mt. Waialeale on Kauai has a rainfall of 12,000 mm [472 ins], whilst Puako on the leeward side of Hawaii receives less than 250 m [10 ins]. The lofty volcanoes Mauna Kea and Mauna Loa are frequently snow covered.

AMERICAN SAMOA

COUNTRY: Territory of American Samoa
AREA: 200 sq km [77 sq mls]
POPULATION: 39,000
CAPITAL: Pago Pago

BELAU

COUNTRY: US Trusteeship Territory
AREA: 458 sq km [177 sq mls]
POPULATION: 15,000
CAPITAL: Koror

COOK ISLANDS

COUNTRY: Self-governing in association with New Zealand
AREA: 236 sq km [91 sq mls]
POPULATION: 18,000
CAPITAL: Avarua

FIJI

COUNTRY: Republic of Fiji
AREA: 18,270 sq km [7,054 sq mls]
POPULATION: 765,000
CAPITAL (Population): Suva (141,000)

FRENCH POLYNESIA

COUNTRY: French Overseas Territory
AREA: 4,000 sq km [1,544 sq mls]
POPULATION: 206,000
CAPITAL: Papeete

GUAM

COUNTRY: Guam - US territory
AREA: 541 sq km [209 sq mls]
POPULATION: 119,000
CAPITAL (Population): Agana (29,000)

KIRIBATI

COUNTRY: Republic of Kiribati
AREA: 728 sq km [281 sq mls]
POPULATION: 66,000
CAPITAL (Population): Tarawa (24,000)

MARIANA ISLANDS

COUNTRY: Commonwealth of the Northern Mariana Islands
AREA: 477 sq km [184 sq mls]
POPULATION: 22,000
CAPITAL: Saipan

MARSHALL ISLANDS

COUNTRY: Territory in association with US
AREA: 181 sq km [70 sq mls]
POPULATION: 42,000
CAPITAL: Majuro

MICRONESIA

COUNTRY: Federal States of Micronesia
AREA: 705 sq km [272 sq mls]
POPULATION: 103,000
CAPITAL: Kolonia

NAURU

COUNTRY: Republic of Nauru
AREA: 21 sq km [8 sq mls]
POPULATION: 10,000
CAPITAL (Population): Domaneab (8,000)

NEW CALEDONIA

COUNTRY: French Overseas Territory
AREA: 19,000 sq km [7,334 sq mls]
POPULATION: 168,000
CAPITAL: Nouméa (60,000)

NIUE

COUNTRY: Self-governing in association with New Zealand
AREA: 260 sq km [100 sq mls]
POPULATION: 3,000
CAPITAL: Alofi

NORFOLK ISLAND

COUNTRY: Australian territory
AREA: 36 sq km [14 sq mls]
POPULATION: 2,000
CAPITAL: Kingston

PITCAIRN ISLANDS

COUNTRY: British Crown Colony
AREA: 27 sq km [10 sq mls]
POPULATION: 60
CAPITAL: Adamstown

SOLOMON ISLANDS

COUNTRY: Commonwealth Constitutional Monarchy
AREA: 28,900 sq km [11,158 sq mls]
POPULATION: 321,000
CAPITAL: Honiara (34,000)

TOKELAU ISLANDS

COUNTRY: New Zealand external territory
AREA: 12 sq km [5 sq mls]
POPULATION: 2,000
CAPITAL: Nukunonu

TONGA

COUNTRY: Kingdom of Tonga
AREA: 750 sq km [290 sq mls]
POPULATION: 95,000
CAPITAL: Nuku'alofa (29,000)

TUVALU

COUNTRY: Commonwealth const. monarchy
AREA: 24 sq km [9 sq mls]
POPULATION: 10,000
CAPITAL: Funafuti (3,000)

VANUATU

COUNTRY: Republic of Vanuatu
AREA: 12,190 sq km [4,707 sq mls]
POPULATION: 147,000
CAPITAL: Port Vila (18,000)

WALLIS AND FUTUNA ISLANDS

COUNTRY: French Overseas Territory
AREA: 200 sq km [77 sq mls]
POPULATION: 18,000
CAPITAL: Mata Utu (800)

WESTERN SAMOA

COUNTRY: Independent state of Western Samoa
AREA: 2,840 sq km [1,097 sq mls]
POPULATION: 164,000
CAPITAL: Apia (33,000)

CHRISTMAS ISLANDS (INDIAN OCEAN)

COUNTRY: Administered by Australia
AREA: 135 sq km [52 sq mls]
POPULATION: 2,300
CAPITAL: The Settlement

COCOS ISLANDS (INDIAN OCEAN)

COUNTRY: Cocos (Keeling) Is. are an Australian territory
AREA: 14 sq km [5.4 sq mls]
POPULATION: 700

NORTH AMERICA

GREENLAND

COUNTRY: Self-governing division of Denmark
AREA: 2,175,600 sq km [839,999 sq mls]
POPULATION: 57,000
CAPITAL: Godthåb

ST PIERRE ET MIQUELON

COUNTRY: Territorial Collectivity of France
AREA: 242 sq km [93 sq mls]
POPULATION: 7,000
CAPITAL: St-Pierre

CANADA

The British Red Ensign was used from 1892 but became unpopular with Canada's French community. After many attempts to find a more acceptable design, the present flag featuring the simple maple leaf emblem was finally adopted in 1965.

COUNTRY: Canada
AREA: 9,976,140 sq km [3,851,788 sq mls]
POPULATION: 26,522,000
CAPITAL (Population): Ottawa (819,000)
GOVERNMENT: Federal multi-party parliamentary state with bicameral legislature
ETHNIC GROUPS: British 40%, French 27%, other European 20%, Asiatic 2%, Inuit (Eskimo)
LANGUAGES: English 57%, French 23%
RELIGIONS: Roman Catholic 47%, Protestant 41%, Eastern Orthodox, Jewish, Muslim, Hindu
NATIONAL DAY: 1 July
CURRENCY: Canadian $ = 100 cents
ANNUAL INCOME PER PERSON: $20,450
SOURCE OF INCOME: Agriculture 4%, Industry 40%, Services 56%
MAIN PRIMARY PRODUCTS: Coal, cobalt, copper, fish, furs, gold, iron ore, lead, molybdenum, natural gas, nickel, platinum, petroleum, silver, timber, wheat
MAIN INDUSTRIES: Transport equipment, food, paper and allied products, primary metal, fabricated metal, electrical and electronic, wood and timber, rubber and plastics
EXPORTS: $4,426 per person
MAIN EXPORTS: Passenger vehicles, trucks and parts 26%, food, feed, beverages and tobacco 6%, timber 5%, newspaper print 5%, wood pulp 4%, petroleum 4%, natural gas 3%, industrial machinery 3%
MAIN EXPORT PARTNERS: USA 75%, Japan 6%, UK 2%
IMPORTS: $4,348 per person
MAIN IMPORTS: Vehicles and parts 26%, machinery 9%, food, feed, beverages and tobacco 6%, chemicals 5%, computers 4%, petroleum 3%, iron and steel 2%
MAIN IMPORT PARTNERS: USA 68%, Japan 7%, Germany 4%
EDUCATIONAL EXPENDITURE: Controlled by provinces
DEFENCE: 10% of national budget
TOTAL ARMED FORCES: 89,000
TOURISM: 39,253,000 visitors
ROADS: 280,251 km [175,157 mls]
RAILWAYS: 93,544 km [58,465 mls]
POPULATION DENSITY: 2.7 per sq km [6.9 per sq ml]
URBAN POPULATION: 76%
POPULATION GROWTH: 0.9% per year
BIRTHS: 15 per 1,000 population
DEATHS: 7 per 1,000 population
INFANT MORTALITY: 8 per 1,000 live births
LIFE EXPECTANCY: Female 81 yrs, Male 74 yrs
POPULATION PER DOCTOR: 515
ADULT LITERACY: 96%
PRINCIPAL CITIES (Population): Toronto 3,427,000 Montréal 2,921,000 Vancouver 1,381,000 Ottawa-Hull 819,000 Edmonton 785,000 Calgary 631,000 Winnipeg 623,000, Québec 603,000 Hamilton 557,000

■ World's second-largest country, after Russia ■ World's longest coastline (250,000 km [155,000 mls] ■ 80% of land uninhabited ■ More lakes than any other country ■ Trans-Canada Highway spans 8,000 km [5,000 mls] from Newfoundland to British Columbia ■ Forests cover over 50% of total land area ■ St Lawrence Seaway, completed 1959, enables ocean-going vessels (28,000 tonnes) to sail into Great Lakes ■ St Lawrence river closed to traffic for 3 or 4 winter months ■ Most rivers frozen for much of year ■ Spans 6 time zones ■ Prairies, from Alberta to Manitoba, represent 80% of farmland & $^{2}/_{3}$ of farm income ■ Exports over 50% of agricultural produce ■ World's leading exporter of fish, wood pulp & paper ■ Almost all forests owned by provincial or federal governments; 1 job in 10 depends on wood ■ World's biggest producer of uranium, nickel & zinc ■ Hydroelectric power generates 70% of electricity ■ World's longest oil pipeline stretches from Edmonton to Buffalo, New York State, USA (2,856 km [1,775 mls]) ■ Alberta produces 90% of oil output & nearly 50% of coal ■ Trade with USA represents world's largest single bilateral trade route, 68% imports, 76% exports ■ Native Indian pop. lives mostly in 2,250 reserves covering 2.6 million hectares [6.4 million acres], widely spread across country, & speak 60 different languages ■ Inuit live in Mackenzie river delta, on Arctic islands & on mainland Labrador coast

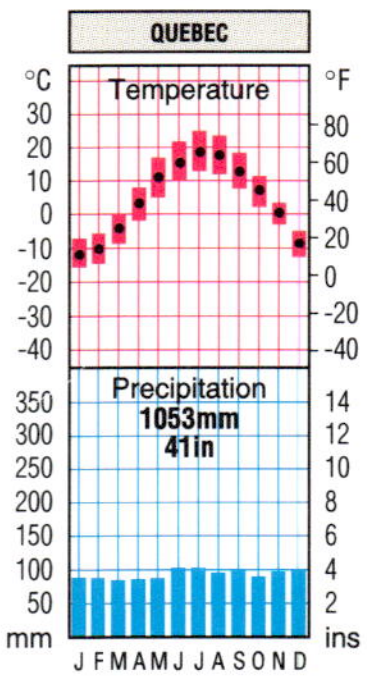

The effect of the Great Lakes is felt in the Ontario Peninsula with slightly warmer winters than in Québec. The temperatures in northern Canada are violent; along the Arctic circle the mean monthly temperatures for over seven months are below freezing. Rainfall is moderate throughout the year with no marked peak and a reasonable amount of snow. In the mid-west the July temperature is about 17°C [63°F], but the cold of December is nearly -14°C [6°F], an annual range of over 30°C [54°F].

UNITED STATES

The 'Stars and Stripes' has had the same basic design since 1777 during the War of Independence. The 13 stripes represent the original colonies that rebelled against British rule, the 50 stars the present states of the Union.

COUNTRY: United States of America
AREA: 9,372,610 sq km [3,618,765 sq mls]
POPULATION: 249,975,000
CAPITAL (Population): Washington, D.C. (3,734,000)
GOVERNMENT: Federal republic with a bicameral legislature
ETHNIC GROUPS: White 85%, Black 12%, other races 3%
LANGUAGES: English (official), Spanish and over 30 others
RELIGIONS: Protestant 55%, Roman Catholic 30%, Jewish 3%, Eastern Orthodox 2%, Muslim 2%
NATIONAL DAY: 4 July; Declaration of Independence by Congress (1776)
CURRENCY: United States $ = 100 cents
ANNUAL INCOME PER PERSON: $21,700
SOURCE OF INCOME: Agriculture 2%, Industry 33%, Services 65%
MAIN PRIMARY PRODUCTS: Cereals, cotton, tobacco, soya beans, fruit, potatoes, oilseeds, sugar cane, livestock, timber, oil and natural gas, coal, copper, lead, iron ore, zinc, molybdenum, silver, gold
MAIN INDUSTRIES: Iron and steel, vehicles, chemicals, telecommunications, aeronautics and space, electronics, computers, textiles, paper, fishing, agriculture, mining
EXPORTS: $1,463 per person
MAIN EXPORTS: Machinery and transport equipment 43%, chemicals 10%, food, beverages and tobacco 9%, crude materials 8%
MAIN EXPORT PARTNERS: Canada 24%, Japan 11%, Mexico 6%, UK 6%, Germany 5%
IMPORTS: $1,983 per person
MAIN IMPORTS: Machinery and transport equipment 44%, clothing, footwear and manufactured articles 16%, paper, textiles, diamonds, iron and steel, non-ferrous metals 13%, mineral fuels 11%, food, beverages and tobacco 6%
MAIN IMPORT PARTNERS: Japan 21%, Canada 18%, Germany 7%, Taiwan 6%, Mexico 5%, UK 4%
EDUCATIONAL EXPENDITURE: 7% of national budget
DEFENCE: 27.1% of national budget
TOTAL ARMED FORCES: 2,124,900
TOURISM: 28,787,000 visitors
ROADS: 6,243,340 km [3,879,538 mls]
RAILWAYS: 296,497 km [184,235 mls]
POPULATION DENSITY: 27 per sq km [70 per sq ml]
URBAN POPULATION: 74%
POPULATION GROWTH: 0.8% per year
BIRTHS: 16 per 1,000 population
DEATHS: 9 per 1,000 population
INFANT MORTALITY: 8 per 1,000 live births
LIFE EXPECTANCY: Female 80 yrs, Male 73 yrs
POPULATION PER DOCTOR: 473
ADULT LITERACY: 96%
PRINCIPAL CITIES (Population): New York 18,087,000 Los Angeles 14,532,000 Chicago 8,066,000 San Francisco 6,253,000 Philadelphia 5,899,000 Detroit 4,665,000 Boston 4,172,000 Washington 3,924,000 Dallas 3,885,000 Houston 3,711,000 Miami 3,193,000 Atlanta 2,834,000 Cleveland 2,760,000 Seattle 2,559,000 San Diego 2,498,000 Minneapolis 2,464,000 St Louis 2,444,000 Baltimore 2,382,000

■ World's 4th largest country, after Russia, Canada & China ■ World's 3rd most populous country, after China & India ■ Dawn comes 8 hours later to Alaska than Maine ■ Yellowstone National Park country's oldest national park, established 1872, & largest outside Alaska ■ World's tallest trees, 110 m [365 ft] grow in redwood forests of California ■ Death Valley, California, lowest point in Western Hemisphere, 86 m [282 ft] below sea level ■ World's largest producer of beef, poultry & cheese & biggest exporter of wheat ■ Produces $^{1}/_{2}$ world's maize, $^{2}/_{3}$ world's soya beans, $^{1}/_{7}$ world's tomatoes, $^{1}/_{5}$ world's peaches ■ World's most powerful & diverse economy - US interests dominate world markets in almost every sector ■ Average US citizen uses about 1,000 times as much fuel in lifetime as average Nepalese citizen ■ World's largest producer of lead, paper, hardwood, beer, copper, gypsum, kaolin, mica, salt, phosphates & sulphur ■ World's largest oil refining capacity ■ World's 2nd largest oil producer, but 2nd largest oil importer ■ World-leading manufacturing country in many areas including steel, vehicles, aerospace, telecommunications, chemicals, electronics & consumer goods ■ Income of Exxon Oil Corporation about equal to national income of Belgium ■ World's biggest spender on military defence ■ World's largest library, Library of Congress in Washington (22 million books) ■ One of world's worst crime rates ■ Serious drug problems ■ In 1984, 27% in 18-24 age group attended higher education ■ Americans have won twice as many Nobel prizes as people of any other nation ■ Bought Alaska from Russia for $7,200,000 in 1867 ■ Estimated 7 million illegal Mexican immigrants ■ 20-25% of teenagers designated 'fundamentally illiterate' ■ Less than 50% of registered voters vote in presidential elections

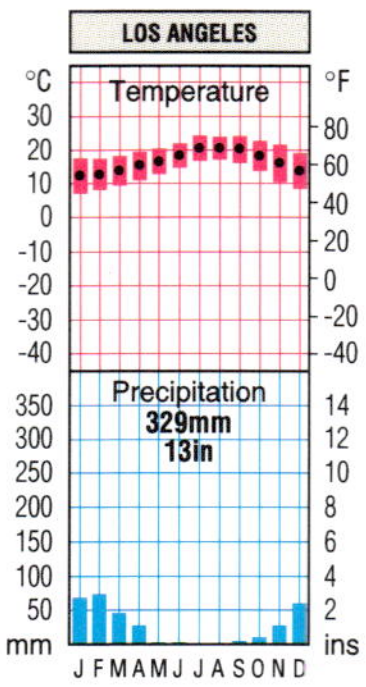

The climate of Los Angeles is similar in some respects to that of the Mediterranean with dry summers and rain in winter. However, the cool Californian current in the Pacific with high pressure and light winds throughout the year reduces the heat of summer and inhibits cloud and rain giving an ideal climate for outdoor activities such as sport and film-making but also encouraging the notorious 'smog' to form. In the east there are much greater extremes of temperature. Rainfall is evenly distributed throughout the year with heavy winter snowfall, particularly inland.

MEXICO

The stripes on the Mexican flag were inspired by the French tricolour and date from 1821. The emblem of the eagle, snake and cactus is based on an ancient Aztec legend about the founding of Mexico City. The design was adopted in 1968.

COUNTRY: United Mexican States
AREA: 1,958,200 sq km [756,061 sq mls]
POPULATION: 86,154,000
CAPITAL (Population): Mexico City (18,748,000)
GOVERNMENT: Federal republic with a bicameral legisl.
ETHNIC GROUPS: Mestizo 55%, Amerindian 29%, Caucasian 15%
LANGUAGES: Spanish (official), Nahuati, Maya, Zapotec, Otomi, Mixtec
RELIGIONS: Roman Catholic 93%, Protestant 3%
NATIONAL DAY: 16 September; Proclamation of Independence (1821)
CURRENCY: Peso = 100 centavos
ANNUAL INCOME PER PERSON: $2,490
SOURCE OF INCOME: Agriculture 9%, Industry 35%, Services 56%
MAIN PRIMARY PRODUCTS: Wheat, maize, coffee, sorghum, cattle, sugar, cotton, copper, sulphur, coal, lead, iron, gold, silver, oil, natural gas, phosphates
MAIN INDUSTRIES: Oil refining, natural gas, mining, agriculture, aluminium, vehicle manufacture, textiles, machinery, pottery
EXPORTS: $271 per person
MAIN EXPORTS: Crude petroleum 38%, engines, vehicle parts 7%, machinery 3%, coffee 2%, shrimps 2%
MAIN EXPORT PARTNERS: USA 64%, Japan 6%, Germany 3%
IMPORTS: $280 per person
MAIN IMPORTS: Parts for car assembly 6%, machinery 5%, maize 2%
MAIN IMPORT PARTNERS: USA 62%, Japan 6%, Germany 6%
EDUCATIONAL EXPENDITURE: 12% of national budget
DEFENCE: 1.4% of national budget
TOTAL ARMED FORCES: 141,500
TOURISM: 5,407,000 visitors
ROADS: 225,684 km (151,053 miles)
RAILWAYS: 19,906 km (12,441 miles)
POPULATION DENSITY: 44 per sq km [114 per sq ml]
URBAN POPULATION: 73%
POPULATION GROWTH: 2.2% per year
BIRTHS: 32 per 1,000 population
DEATHS: 5 per 1,000 population
INFANT MORTALITY: 41 per 1,000 live births
LIFE EXPECTANCY: Female 74 yrs, Male 67 yrs
POPULATION PER DOCTOR: 1,242
ADULT LITERACY: 90%
PRINCIPAL CITIES (Population): Mexico City 18,748,000 Guadalajara 2,587,000 Monterrey 2,335,000 Puebla de Zaragoza 1,218,000 León de los Aldamas 947,000 Torreón 730,000 San Luis Potosí 602,000 Ciudad Juàrez 596,000 Mérida 580,000 Culiacàn Rosales 560,000

■ Over 50% of country more than 1,000 m [3,300 ft] above sea level ■ California, Texas, Arizona & New Mexico in USA used to be part of Mexico (until 1848) ■ Only 1/6 of land suitable for cultivation ■ 1/3 of pop. engaged in agriculture ■ World's 4th largest producer of crude oil ■ 2nd largest oil reserves ■ Car assembly, steel, textiles, food processing & breweries main industries ■ Self-sufficient in almost all semi-manufactured goods ■ About 65% of pop. live in urban areas ■ Mexico City, world's largest city (pop. 18.75 million) ■ 59 different dialects spoken by over 3 million of country's 25 million native Indians who form about 30% of pop. ■ Frontier with USA world's busiest - over 120 million cross border each year ■ More people emigrate from Mexico than from any other country: estimated 800,000 entered USA from Mexico in 1980; estimated 10 million legal residents in USA ■ 10,000 monuments to ancient civilisations (Olmec, Maya, Aztec etc) ■ One political party (PRI) has controlled politics & government since 1929

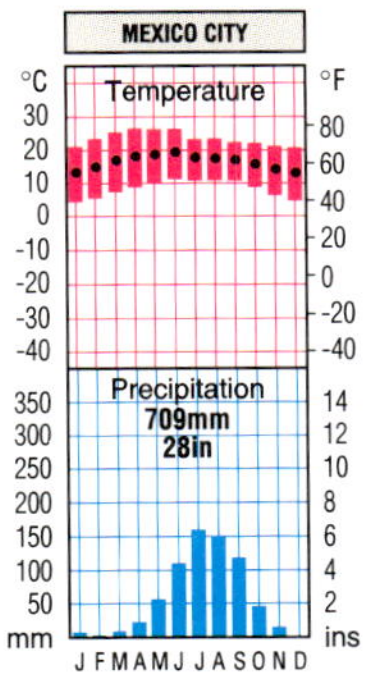

Due to its elevation of over 2,000 m [6,500 ft], temperatures at Mexico City are some 9°C [16°F] lower than on the Gulf coast though the annual range is about the same. But the daily range of temperature is far greater on the plateau and frost and snow are not unknown. Rainfall on the plateau is markedly seasonal and decreases northwards to under 250 mm [10 in] where the country widens.

BELIZE

The badge shows loggers bearing axes and oars, tools employed in the industry responsible for developing Belize. The flag is commonly displayed without the badge - a simple white disc on a royal blue background.

■ Previously known as British Honduras ■ Offshore coral reef, world's 2nd largest after Great Barrier reef ■ Belmopan capital since 1970, after former capital, Belize City, damaged by hurricane in 1961 ■ Tourism fastest growing sector of economy ■ Border disputes with Guatemala; British troop presence since 1970s

COUNTRY: Belize
AREA: 22,960 sq km [8,865 sq mls]
POPULATION: 188,000
CAPITAL (Population): Belmopan (4,500)
GOVERNMENT: Constitutional monarchy with a bicameral National Assembly
ETHNIC GROUPS: Creole 40%, Mestizo (Spanish Maya) 33%, Caribs 8%
LANGUAGES: English (official) but Spanish is spoken by 50%
RELIGIONS: Roman Catholic 68%, Protestants 29%
NATIONAL DAY: 21 September; Independence Day (1981)
CURRENCY: Belize $ = 100 cents
ANNUAL INCOME PER PERSON: $1,970
POPULATION DENSITY: 8 per sq km [21 per sq ml]
LIFE EXPECTANCY: Female 75 yrs, Male 68 yrs
ADULT LITERACY: 93%

GUATEMALA

The simple design of Guatemala's flag was adopted in 1871, but its origins date back to the Central American Federation (1825-39) formed with Honduras, El Salvador, Nicaragua and Costa Rica after the break from Spanish rule in 1821.

■ Highest point in C. America, peak of Tajumulco volcano ■ Capital, Guatemala City, hit by earthquakes 3 times this century ■ Coffee production & trading dominate economy; 1/3 of foreign earnings ■ Largest manufacturing centre in C. America ■ Remains of largest of pre-Columbian Maya Indian cities in Central America at Tikal ■ One of C. America's most militarised countries

COUNTRY: Republic of Guatemala
AREA: 108,890 sq km [42,042 sq mls]
POPULATION: 9,197,000
CAPITAL (Population): Guatemala City (2,000,000)
GOVERNMENT: Republic with a unicameral legislature
ETHNIC GROUPS: Amerindian 55%, Ladiono 42%
LANGUAGES: Spanish
RELIGIONS: Christian (Roman Catholic 75%)
NATIONAL DAY: 15 September; Independence Day (1821)
CURRENCY: Guatemalean quetzel = 100 centavos
ANNUAL INCOME PER PERSON: $900
MAIN PRIMARY PRODUCTS: Petroleum, iron, lead and nickel ore
MAIN INDUSTRIES: Agriculture, forestry, fishing, food processing, rubber, textiles and pharmaceuticals
MAIN EXPORTS: Coffee, bananas, sugar, cardamom
MAIN IMPORTS: Mineral fuels, chemicals, machinery and transport equipment, manufactured goods, food products
DEFENCE: 15% of national budget
POPULATION DENSITY: 84 per sq km [219 per sq ml]
LIFE EXPECTANCY: Female 67 yrs, Male 62 yrs
ADULT LITERACY: 55%

HONDURAS

Officially adopted in 1949, the flag of Honduras is based on that of the Central American Federation (see Guatemala). Honduras left the organisation in 1838 but in 1866 added the five stars to the flag to express a hope for a future federation.

■ Name (given by Columbus in 1502) means 'depths' in Spanish, possibly referring to deep coastal waters ■ 5 times larger than neighbouring El Salvador but smaller pop. ■ Original 'banana republic' - was world's leading banana exporter from 1920s - 1940s ■ Only 22% of land cultivated ■ 1/3 of pop. urban ■ Education free, yet 40% of pop. illiterate

COUNTRY: Honduras
AREA: 112,090 sq km [43,278 sq mls]
POPULATION: 5,105,000
CAPITAL (Population): Tegucigalpa (605,000)
GOVERNMENT: Multi-party republic with one legislative house (Congress)
ETHNIC GROUPS: Mestizo 89.9%, Amerindian 6.7%, Black (including Black Carib) 2.1%, White 1.3%
LANGUAGES: Spanish (official), Black Carib (Garifuna), English Creole, Miskito
RELIGIONS: Roman Catholic
NATIONAL DAY: 15 September; Independence Day (1821)
CURRENCY: Honduran lempira = 100 centavos
ANNUAL INCOME PER PERSON: $590
MAIN PRIMARY PRODUCTS: Bananas, coffee, sugar, tobacco, meat, shrimp and lobster, timber
MAIN INDUSTRIES: Agriculture, forestry, fishing, cement, sugar
MAIN EXPORTS: Coffee, bananas, shrimp and lobsters, roundwood, frozen meat
MAIN IMPORTS: Machinery and transport equipment, chemical products, basic manufactures, mineral fuels, food products
DEFENCE: 12% of national budget
POPULATION DENSITY: 46 per sq km [118 per sq ml]
LIFE EXPECTANCY: Female 68 yrs, Male 64 yrs
ADULT LITERACY: 60%

CENTRAL AMERICA AND CARIBBEAN

EL SALVADOR

The original flag, the "Stars and Stripes" was replaced in 1912 by the current one. The blue and white stripes are a common feature of the flags of Central American countries who gained their independence from Spain at the same time in 1821.

COUNTRY: Republic of El Salvador
AREA: 21,040 sq km [8,124 sq mls]
POPULATION: 5,252,000
CAPITAL (Population): San Salvador (973,000)
GOVERNMENT: Republic with a unicameral legislature
ETHNIC GROUPS: Mestizo 94%, Indian 5%, White 1%
LANGUAGES: Spanish (official)
RELIGIONS: Christian (Roman Catholic 92%)
NATIONAL DAY: 15 September; Independence Day (1821)
CURRENCY: Colón = 100 centavos

■ Most densely populated country in C. America ■ Coffee represents about 40% of exports ■ Government receives $2 million per day in aid from US government ■ Extensive Indian civilisation has existed in area since 3000 BC ■ Was only Latin American country to request US statehood (in 1822) ■ Thousands have died each year since 1979 due to civil war; 50,000 refugees in camps

ANNUAL INCOME PER PERSON: $1,100
POPULATION DENSITY: 250 per sq km [647 per sq ml]
LIFE EXPECTANCY: Female 69 yrs, Male 64 yrs
ADULT LITERACY: 72%

NICARAGUA

Nicaragua's flag, adopted in 1908, is identical to that of the Central American Federation (see Guatemala) to which it once belonged. Except for a difference in the shading of the blue, it is also the same as the flag of El Salvador.

(see Guatemala)

COUNTRY: Republic of Nicaragua
AREA: 130,000 sq km [50,193 sq mls]
POPULATION: 3,871,000
CAPITAL (Population): Managua (682,000)
GOVERNMENT: Multi-party republic with a unicam. legisl.
ETHNIC GROUPS: Mestizo 69%, White 14%, Black 8%
LANGUAGES: Spanish
RELIGIONS: Christian (Roman Catholic 87%)
NATIONAL DAY: 15 September; Independence Day (1838)
CURRENCY: New córdoba = 100 centavos
ANNUAL INCOME PER PERSON: $800
MAIN PRIMARY PRODUCTS: Silver, gold, gypsum, lead, zinc
MAIN INDUSTRIES: Agriculture, mining, textiles
MAIN EXPORTS: Coffee, cotton, sugar and bananas
MAIN IMPORTS: Agricultural capital goods, petroleum products, vehicles and machinery
DEFENCE: 6% of national budget
POPULATION DENSITY: 30 per sq km [77 per sq ml]
LIFE EXPECTANCY: Female 68 yrs, Male 65 yrs
ADULT LITERACY: 87%

■ Capital, Managua, destroyed by earthquakes 1931 & 1972 ■ Somoza family dominated government from 1930s until overthrown by Sandanistas in 1979 ■ US Government financed 'Contra' rebellion against Sandanistan Government in 1980s

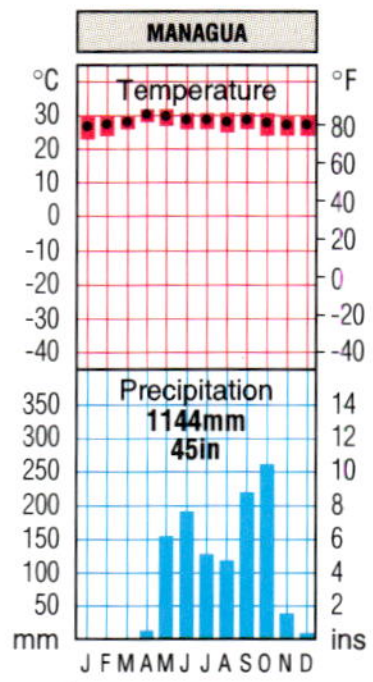

The west coast of Nicaragua is sheltered by mountains from the north-easterly winds which prevail in winter and therefore has an extensive dry season and far less rain than falls on the Mosquito Coast to the east. The very uniform temperature and the thundery nature of the summer rains is typical of a coastal climate within the tropics.

COSTA RICA

Dating from 1848, Costa Rica's national flag is based on the blue/white/blue sequence of the flag of the Central American Federation (see Guatemala) but with an additional red stripe.

COUNTRY: Republic of Costa Rica
AREA: 51,100 sq km [19,730 sq mls]
POPULATION: 2,994,000
CAPITAL (Population): San José (284,000)
GOVERNMENT: Multi-party republic with one legisl. assem.
ETHNIC GROUPS: European 87%, Mestizo 7%
LANGUAGES: Spanish
RELIGIONS: Christian (Roman Catholic 92%)
NATIONAL DAY: 15 September; Independence (1821)
CURRENCY: Costa Rican colón = 100 céntimos
ANNUAL INCOME PER PERSON: $1,910
MAIN INDUSTRIES: Agriculture, food processing, textiles, fertilizers, pharmaceuticals, electrical equipment
MAIN EXPORTS: Manufactured goods, agri. products

■ First C. American country to grow coffee & bananas commercially ■ Wealth & land more evenly distributed than in any other C. American country ■ Most stable & liberal C. American state ■ High literacy rate & high standard of living ■ Voting compulsory for all citizens over 18 ■ No armed forces since 1948

MAIN PRIMARY PRODUCTS: Gold, salt, haematite, maize
MAIN IMPORTS: Machinery, transport equipment, chemicals, fuel and mineral oils
DEFENCE: No armed forces since 1948
POPULATION DENSITY: 59 per sq km [152 per sq ml]
LIFE EXPECTANCY: Female 78 yrs, Male 73 yrs
ADULT LITERACY: 94%

PANAMA

The Panamanian flag dates from the break with Colombia in 1903. Blue stands for the Conservative Party, red for the Liberal Party and white for the hope of peace. The red star represents law and order and the blue star 'public honesty'.

COUNTRY: Republic of Panama
AREA: 77,080 sq km [29,761 sq mls]
POPULATION: 2,418,000
CAPITAL (Population): Panama City (625,000)
GOVERNMENT: Multi-party republic with a unicam. legisl.
ETHNIC GROUPS: Mentizo/Mulatto 59%, Black 14%, White 12%, Amerindian 7%
LANGUAGES: Spanish (official)
RELIGIONS: Christian 93%, Muslim 4%
NATIONAL DAY: 3 November; Independence Day (1821)
CURRENCY: Balboa = 100 cents
ANNUAL INCOME PER PERSON: $1,830
MAIN INDUSTRIES: Finance, the Canal, agriculture and fishing, petroleum refining
MAIN EXPORTS: Bananas, shrimps, coffee and sugar
MAIN IMPORTS: Mineral products, electrical, electric and transport equipment, metal and metal manufacture
DEFENCE: 6% of national budget
POPULATION DENSITY: 31 per sq km [81 per sq ml]
LIFE EXPECTANCY: Female 75 yrs, Male 71 yrs
ADULT LITERACY: 88%

■ Canal cuts across isthmus of Panama, linking Pacific & Atlantic Oceans; completed in 1914 ■ 12,000 ships sail under Panamian flag, due to low fees & lenient labour laws ■ Until 1979, US had sovereign control of Canal ■ Panamanian government takes full control 1999

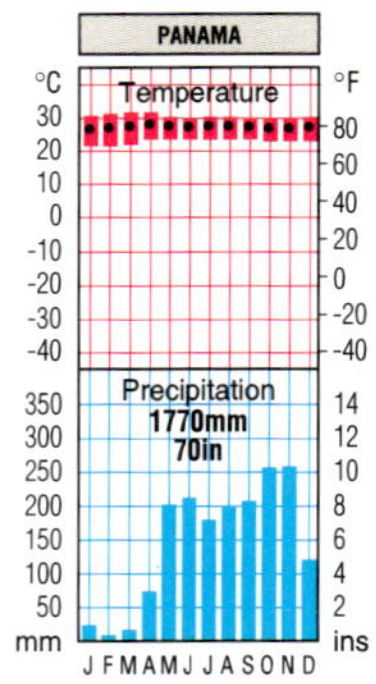

Panama has a marked dry season from January to March when the inter-tropical rain belt is at its furthest south and the north-east trade winds blow steadily. The narrowness of the isthmus of Panama and its position between the warm waters of the Caribbean Sea and the Pacific Ocean contribute to the constancy of temperature, high humidity and rainfall during the summer months.

CUBA

First designed in 1849, Cuba's flag, the 'Lone Star' banner, was not officially adopted until the island finally gained its independence from Spain in 1902. The red triangle represents the Cuban people's bloody struggle for independence.

■ State-controlled economy ■ World's largest sugar exporter & 3rd largest producer ■ Free education & health service & guaranteed basic wage ■ ⅔ of pop. urban ■ Last right wing dictator, Fulgencio Batista, overthrown in 1959 revolution led by Fidel Castro & Che Guevara ■ US military base at Guantánamo

COUNTRY: Republic of Cuba
AREA: 110,860 sq km [42,803 sq mls]
POPULATION: 10,609,000
CAPITAL (Population): Havana (2,059,000)
GOVERNMENT: Socialist republic with a unicam. legisl.
ETHNIC GROUPS: White 66%, Mulatto 22%, Black 12%
LANGUAGES: Spanish
RELIGIONS: Roman Catholic 40%, Protestant 3%
NATIONAL DAY: 1 January; Day of Liberation (1959)
CURRENCY: Peso = 100 centavos
ANNUAL INCOME PER PERSON: $3,000
MAIN PRIMARY PRODUCTS: Sugar cane, nickel, cobalt, copper, chrome, tobacco, citrus fruits, rice
MAIN INDUSTRIES: Agriculture, mining, food processing, tobacco, fishing, textiles, chemicals
MAIN EXPORTS: Sugar and sugar products 77%, copper and nickel 7%, agricultural products 4%, tobacco 1%
MAIN IMPORTS: Mineral fuels and lubricants 34%, machinery and transport equipment 31%, foodstuffs 9%
DEFENCE: 10% of national budget
POPULATION DENSITY: 96 per sq km [248 per sq ml]
INFANT MORTALITY: 13 per 1,000 live births
LIFE EXPECTANCY: Female 77 yrs, Male 73 yrs
ADULT LITERACY: 91%
PRINCIPAL CITIES (Population): Havana 2,059,000 Santiago de Cuba 380,000 Camagüey 275,000 Holguín 218,000 Guatánamo 193,000 Santa Clara 188,000

JAMAICA

Jamaica's distinctive flag dates from independence from Britain in 1962. The gold stands for the country's natural resources and sunshine, the green for its agriculture and hope for the future and black for the nation's hardships.

COUNTRY: Jamaica
AREA: 10,990 sq km [4,243 sq mls]
POPULATION: 2,420,000
CAPITAL (Population): Kingston (525,000)
GOVERNMENT: Constitutional monarchy with a bicameral legislature
ETHNIC GROUPS: Black 76%, Afro-European 15%, East Indian and Afro-East Indian 3%, White 3%
LANGUAGES: English (official), English Creole, Hindi, Chinese, Spanish
RELIGIONS: Protestant 56%, Roman Catholic 5%
NATIONAL DAY: 7 August; Independence Day (1962)
CURRENCY: Jamaican $ = 100 cents
ANNUAL INCOME PER PERSON: $1,510
MAIN PRIMARY PRODUCTS: Bauxite, sugar, bananas, coffee
MAIN INDUSTRIES: Mining, agriculture, tourism, sugar, cement, petrol refining
MAIN EXPORTS: Alumina, bauxite, clothing, sugar, bananas
MAIN IMPORTS: Mineral fuels, food, construction materials, transport equipment
DEFENCE: 2% of national budget
POPULATION DENSITY: 220 per sq km [570 per sq ml]
LIFE EXPECTANCY: Female 78 yrs, Male 72 yrs
ADULT LITERACY: 89%

■ Luxuriant tropical & sub-tropical vegetation unsurpassed elsewhere in Caribbean ■ World's 3rd largest producer of bauxite ■ Marijuana thought to be 3rd largest export, after bauxite & bananas ■ Nearly 1 million tourists each year ■ Large foreign debts - interest payments in 1984 equalled 40% of total export revenues ■ Arawak Indians called country Xaymaca - land of wood & water

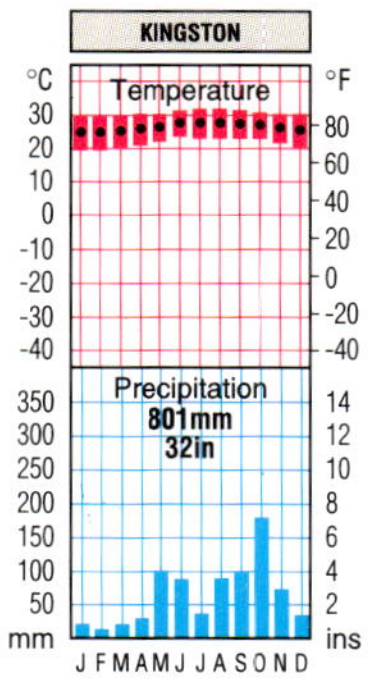

The mountains of eastern Jamaica exert a strong influence on rainfall. Kingston on the south coast and in the lee of the mountains has 800 mm [31 in] and a dry season from December to April, while Port Antonio on the windward north-east coast, has 3500 mm [138 in] and no dry season. The annual total is very variable, mainly due to the irregularity of hurricane rains in August and September.

HAITI

Although the colours, first used in 1803, are said to represent the country's African heritage, the design of Haiti's flag derives from that of France, to which it once belonged. The present version was first used in 1843 and restored in 1986.

COUNTRY: Republic of Haiti
AREA: 27,750 sq km [10,714 sq mls]
POPULATION: 6,486,000
CAPITAL (Population): Port-au-Prince (1,144,000)
GOVERNMENT: Military régime
ETHNIC GROUPS: Black 95%, Mulatto 5%
LANGUAGES: French and Haitian Creole (official)
RELIGIONS: Christian (Roman Catholic 80%), Voodoo
NATIONAL DAY: 1 January; Independence Day (1804)
CURRENCY: Gourde = 100 centimes
ANNUAL INCOME PER PERSON: $370
MAIN PRIMARY PRODUCTS: Bauxite, timber
MAIN EXPORTS: Coffee, cocoa, essential oils, leather and wood handicrafts
MAIN IMPORTS: Food, machinery, transport equipment, mineral fuels, chemicals

■ Occupies western 1/3 of island of Hispaniola ■ Once richest country in Caribbean, now lowest average income per capita in W. Hemisphere ■ 2/3 of working pop. engaged in agriculture, mostly in coffee plantations which generate 25% of country's export earnings ■ Recipient of US aid ■ 80% of pop. rural ■ Less than 50% of children attend school ■ Only 3% have electricity ■ Voodoo widely practised ■ Toussaint L'Ouverture, freed slave who led slave revolt of 1791, first Caribbean revolutionary leader

MAIN INDUSTRIES: Agriculture, forestry, fishing, mining
DEFENCE: 9% of national budget
POPULATION DENSITY: 234 per sq km [605 per sq ml]
LIFE EXPECTANCY: Female 58 yrs, Male 55 yrs
ADULT LITERACY: 38%

DOMINICAN REPUBLIC

The Dominican Republic's flag dates from 1844, when the country finally gained its independence from both Spain and Haiti. The design developed from Haiti's flag, adding a white cross and rearranging the position of the colours.

COUNTRY: Dominican Republic
AREA: 48,730 sq km [18,815 sq mls]
POPULATION: 7,170,000
CAPITAL (Population): Santo Domingo (1,313,000)
GOVERNMENT: Multi-party republic with bicameral legislature
ETHNIC GROUPS: Mulatto 73%, White 16%, Black 11%
LANGUAGES: Spanish
RELIGIONS: Christian (Roman Catholic 93%)
NATIONAL DAY: 27 February; Independence Day (1844)
CURRENCY: Dominican peso = 100 centavos
ANNUAL INCOME PER PERSON: $820
MAIN PRIMARY PRODUCTS: Gold, ferro-nickel, sugar and silver
MAIN INDUSTRIES: Agriculture, textiles, mining
MAIN EXPORTS: Raw sugar, coffee, alloys of gold and silver

■ Pico Duarte highest point in West Indies (3,175 m [10,417 ft]) ■ Only 1/3 of cultivable area farmed ■ Sugar principal export ■ Ferro-nickel, gold & silver important exports ■ Largest operating gold mine in Caribbean ■ 72-hour divorces may be obtained, despite country's R. Catholicism ■ 1st European settlement in Americas Santa Domingo, founded 1496, oldest city in Americas & cathedral, built 1512-40

MAIN IMPORTS: Foodstuffs, petroleum and petroleum products, machinery, vehicles and chemicals
DEFENCE: 9% of national budget
POPULATION DENSITY: 147 per sq km [381 per sq ml]
LIFE EXPECTANCY: Female 70 yrs, Male 65 yrs
ADULT LITERACY: 77%

BAHAMAS

The black hoist triangle symbolises the unity of the Bahamian people and their resolve to develop the island's natural resources. The golden sand and blue sea of the islands are depicted by the yellow and aquamarine stripes.

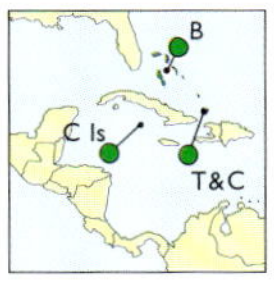

COUNTRY: The Commonwealth of the Bahamas
AREA: 13,880 sq km [5,359 sq mls]
POPULATION: 253,000
CAPITAL (Population): Nassau (135,000)
GOVERNMENT: Free and democratic sovereign state with a bicameral parliament
ETHNIC GROUPS: Black 73%, Mixed 14%, White 13%
LANGUAGES: English
RELIGIONS: Non-Anglican Protestant 48%, Roman Catholic 26%, Anglican 21%
NATIONAL DAY: 10 July; Independence Day (1973)
CURRENCY: Bahamian $ = 100 cents
ANNUAL INCOME PER PERSON: $11,510
POPULATION DENSITY: 18 per sq km [47 per sq ml]
LIFE EXPECTANCY: Female 74 yrs, Male 68 yrs
ADULT LITERACY: 89%

■ Comprises 700 islands & 2,000 coral islets ■ Economy almost entirely dependent on tourism; over 2 million tourists per year (90% from USA); 2/3 of workforce engaged in tourism ■ Freeport City/Lucaya largest single resort complex in W. Indies ■ Inagua, southernmost island, has 1 of world's largest complexes for producing salt by solar evaporation ■ Island of San Salvador thought to be place where Christopher Columbus first set foot in New World in 1492

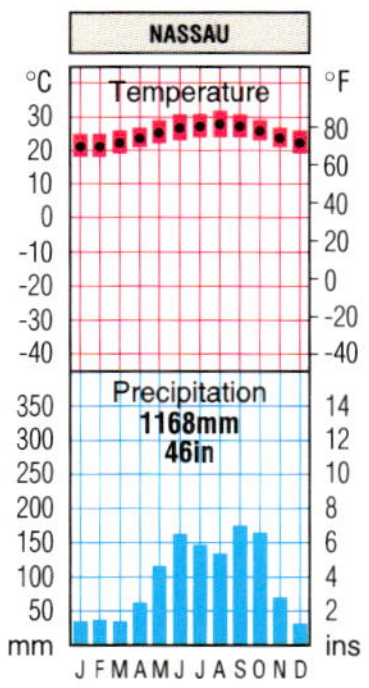

The pleasant sub-tropical climate is the tourist attraction of the region. Sea breezes keep the temperatures below 30°C [86°F] but they seldom fall below 15°C [59°F]. In the summer the average temperature is around 27°C [80°F] and in the winter 21°C [70°F]. There is moderate rainfall of about 1,270 mm [50 ins] falling with a maximum in the summer months from May to October. Hurricanes which have in the past been disastrous occur July-November. There are no mountains to markedly affect the climate.

BERMUDA

COUNTRY: British colony
AREA: 53 sq km [20 sq mls]
POPULATION: 61,000
CAPITAL (Population): Hamilton (3,000)

CAYMAN ISLANDS

COUNTRY: British possession
AREA: 259 sq km [100 sq mls]
POPULATION: 27,000
CAPITAL (Population): Georgetown (12,000)

TURKS/CAICOS

COUNTRY: British colony
AREA: 430 sq km [166 sq mls]
POPULATION: 10,000
CAPITAL (Population): Grand Turk (3,000)

CENTRAL AMERICA AND CARIBBEAN

PUERTO RICO

Puerto Rico fought with Cuba for independence from Spain and their flags are almost identical. The island is a dependent territory of the United States and the flag, adopted in 1952, is flown only with the American 'Stars and Stripes'.

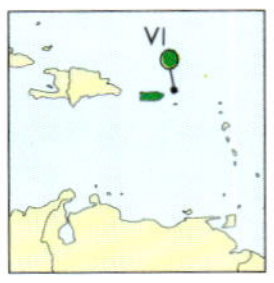

■ Spanish for "rich port" ■ Manufacturing overtaken agriculture as main source of income ■ US corporations dominate economy ■ Inhabitants US citizens (since 1917) but may not vote in US elections ■ World's biggest radiotelescope (NASA) built into rock at Arecibo

COUNTRY: 'Commonwealth state' of USA
AREA: 8,900 sq km [3,436 sq mls]
POPULATION: 3,599,000
CAPITAL (Population): San Juan (1,816,000)
GOVERNMENT: Republic with bicameral legislature

ETHNIC GROUPS: Spanish, Negro, Indian
LANGUAGES: Spanish, English (official)
RELIGIONS: Christian, mainly Roman Catholic
NATIONAL DAY: 25 July; Constitution Day
CURRENCY: US$ = 100 cents

ANNUAL INCOME PER PERSON: $6,470
POPULATION DENSITY: 404 per sq km [1,047 per sq ml]
LIFE EXPECTANCY: Female 79 yrs, Male 73 yrs
ADULT LITERACY: 95%

BRITISH VIRGIN ISLANDS

COUNTRY: British Dependent Territory
AREA: 153 sq km [59 sq mls]

POPULATION: 13,000
CAPITAL (Population): Road Town (4,000)

■ 4 main islands: Tortola, Virgin Gorda, Anegada & Jost Van Dyke ■ Tourism main economic activity ■ Rum largest export ■ British Dependent Territory; large measure of internal self-government since 1967

US VIRGIN ISLANDS

COUNTRY: US Territory
AREA: 130 sq km [340 sq mls]

POPULATION: 117,000
CAPITAL: Charlotte Amalie

■ 3 main islands: St Croix, St John & St Thomas ■ Tourism by far most important industry ■ More hotels per km/ml than anywhere else in Caribbean ■ US government purchased islands in 1917 from Dutch

ST CHRISTOPHER AND NEVIS

The colours represent fertility (green), sunshine (yellow), the independence struggle (red) and the African heritage (black); the stars stand for hope and liberty. The flag was adopted on independence from Britain in 1983.

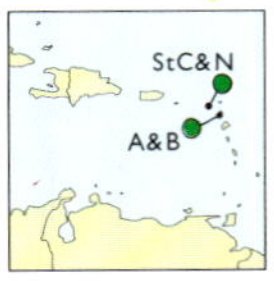

■ St Kitts comprises 3 groups of rugged volcano peaks split by deep ravines ■ Sugar main export of St Kitts; sugar industry nationalised in 1975 ■ Tourism main source of income for Nevis ■ Nevis named by Columbus after snow-covered peaks of Spain (Spanish word for snows: nieves)

COUNTRY: Federation of Saint Christopher (Kitts) and Nevis
AREA: 360 sq km [139 sq mls]
POPULATION: 44,000
CAPITAL (Population): Basseterre (15,000)

GOVERNMENT: Constitutional monarchy with a unicameral legislature
ETHNIC GROUPS: Black 91%, mixed 5%, Indo-Pakistani 3%, White 1%
LANGUAGES: English (official)
RELIGIONS: Protestant 83%, Roman Catholic 7%

NATIONAL DAY: 19 September; Independence Day (1983)
CURRENCY: Eastern Caribbean $ = 100 cents
ANNUAL INCOME PER PERSON: $3,330
POPULATION DENSITY: 122 per sq km [317 per sq ml]
LIFE EXPECTANCY: Female 70 yrs, Male 64 yrs
ADULT LITERACY: 90%

ANTIGUA & BARBUDA

COUNTRY: Antigua and Barbuda
AREA: 440 sq km [170 sq mls]

POPULATION: 77,000
CAPITAL (Population): Saint John's (30,000)

■ Part of Leeward Islands ■ One of lowest rainfalls in Caribbean ■ Lack of water resources ■ Over 365 sandy beaches on Antigua ■ One of 1st Caribbean islands to actively encourage tourism, beginning in late 1960s

ANGUILLA

COUNTRY: Dependent Territory of UK
AREA: 96 sq km [37 sq mls]

POPULATION: 8,000
CAPITAL (Population): The Valley (2,000)

■ Most northerly of Leewards ■ Columbus landed 1493 (anguil (Span) = "eel") ■ British colony from 1650 ■ Population mainly of black African descent ■ Unsuccessfully joined with St Kitts and Antigua

MONTSERRAT

COUNTRY: Dependent territory of UK
AREA: 102 sq km [39 sq mls]

POPULATION: 13,000
CAPITAL (Population): Plymouth (3,000)

■ Columbus named the island after Santa Maria de Montserrat (Spanish monastery) ■ Descendants of African slaves and British/Irish settlers from 1632 ■ Economy - tourism, fruit and vegetables and cotton

DOMINICA

The Caribbean island of Dominica adopted its flag on independence from Britain in 1978 and slightly amended it in 1981. The parrot from the coat of arms, is the national bird, the sisserou, and the stars represent the ten island parishes.

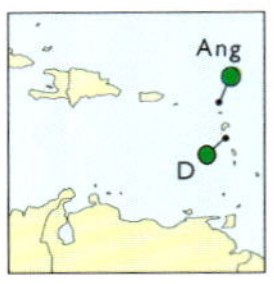

■ 75% of land forested ■ Named by Christopher Columbus in 1493 because he discovered it on Sunday (Spanish: Domingo) ■ Lower density of pop. & poorer standard of living than most W. Indian countries ■ Agriculture provides almost all exports ■ Major recipient of overseas aid ■ Less tourism than elsewhere in Caribbean ■ English official language, though majority of pop. speak French patois

COUNTRY: Commonwealth of Dominica
AREA: 751 sq km [290 sq mls]
POPULATION: 83,000
CAPITAL (Population): Roseau (20,000)
GOVERNMENT: Multi-party republic with unicam. legisl.
ETHNIC GROUPS: Black 91%, mixed race 6%, Amerindian 1.5%

LANGUAGES: English (official)
RELIGIONS: Christian (80% Roman Catholic)
NATIONAL DAY: 3 November; Independence Day (1978)
CURRENCY: East Caribbean dollar = 100 cents
ANNUAL INCOME PER PERSON: $1,940

POPULATION DENSITY: 110 per sq km [286 per sq ml]
EXPECTANCY: Female 77 yrs, Male 73 yrs
ADULT LITERACY: 95%

ST LUCIA

This Caribbean island became an Associated State of Great Britain in 1967 and adopted this modern-looking flag. It is a symbolic representation of St Lucia itself: the black volcanic hills of the island rising from the blue ocean.

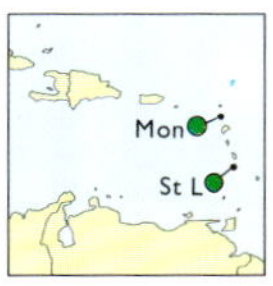

■ Island of extinct volcanoes ■ Great variety of plant & animal life; indigenous wildlife includes species of ground lizard, unique to island ■ Bananas main crop & chief export ■ Grande Cul de Sac Bay, S. of capital, Castries, one of deepest & most modern tanker ports in Americas for oil trans-shipment ■ Ownership changed 14 times between English & French from 1660 to 1814

COUNTRY: Saint Lucia
AREA: 622 sq km [240 sq mls]
POPULATION: 151,000
CAPITAL (Population): Castries (53,000)
GOVERNMENT: Constitutional monarchy with a bicameral legislature

ETHNIC GROUPS: Black 87%, mixed 9%, East Indian 3%, White 1%
LANGUAGES: English (official), French patois
RELIGIONS: Roman Catholic 86%, Protestant 11%
NATIONAL DAY: 22 February; Independence Day (1979)
CURRENCY: East Caribbean $ = 100 cents

ANNUAL INCOME PER PERSON: $1,900
POPULATION DENSITY: 243 per sq km [628 per sq ml]
LIFE EXPECTANCY: Female 75 yrs, Male 68 yrs
ADULT LITERACY: 90%

GUADELOUPE

COUNTRY: Overseas department of France
AREA: 1,710 sq km [660 sq mls]
POPULATION: 344,000
CAPITAL (Population): Basse-Terre (14,000)

■ La Soufrière-active volcano and highest point in Caribbean ■ Columbus 1493, French settlers arrived 1635, some British and Swedish occupation in 18 c, descendants of French settlers and negro slaves ■ Economy - French subsidy, tourism, bananas, aubergines and rum ■ Basse-Terre capital, but Pointe-à-Pitre largest town

MARTINIQUE

The appearance of the French Flag here is a reminder that there are three overseas departments of France in this region, Martinique, Guadeloupe and French Guiana.

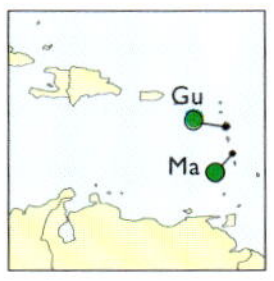

COUNTRY: Overseas department of France
AREA: 1,100 sq km [425 sq mls]
POPULATION: 341,000
CAPITAL (Population): Fort-de-France (100,000)

■ Most northerly of Windwards ■ Named by Columbus in honour of St. Martin ■ On average, suffers some sort of natural disaster every 4 years ■ Active volcano Mount Pelée erupted 1902 killing all 28,000 inhabitants of St Pierre in 3 minutes; only 1 man in jail survived ■ Economy relies almost exclusively on tourism & agriculture

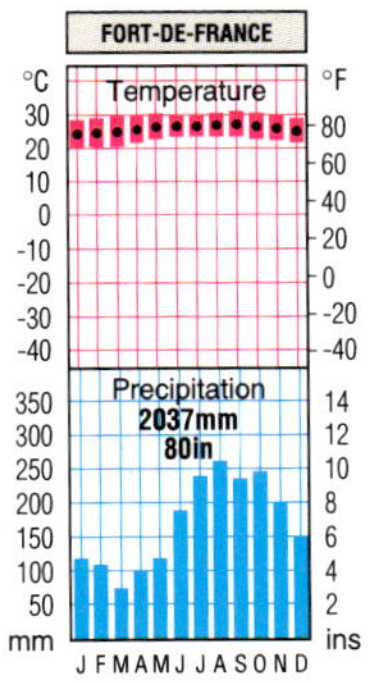

The small islands of the Caribbean all have very similar climates with a small range of temperature, high humidity, especially in summer, and a high annual rainfall with a summer maximum. The summer rainfall is mainly in the form of thundery showers which build up in the afternoon but in winter the rain tends to be lighter and more prolonged. Hurricanes may occur in August and September when the sea is at its warmest.

BARBADOS

The flag was adopted on independence from Britain in 1960. The trident had been part of the colonial badge of Barbados and was retained as the centre to its flag. The gold stripe represents the beaches of the Island and the two blue stripes the sea and sky.

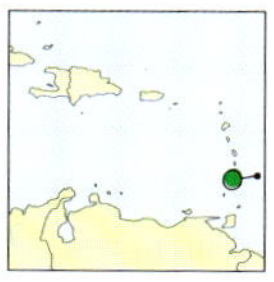

■ Claims highest literacy rate in region ■ Sometimes called Little England or 'Bimshire' (Bim is slang for Barbados) ■ Capital, Bridgetown, has Trafalgar Square, like London, with statue of Nelson, erected in 1813

COUNTRY: Barbados
AREA: 430 sq km [166 sq mls]
POPULATION: 255,000
CAPITAL (Population): Bridgetown (7,466)
GOVERNMENT: Constitutional monarchy with a bicameral legislature
ETHNIC GROUPS: Black 92%, White 3%, Mulatto 3%, East Indian 1%
LANGUAGES: English (official)
RELIGIONS: Protestant 65%, Roman Catholic 4%
NATIONAL DAY: 30 November; Independence Day (1966)
CURRENCY: Barbados $ = 100 cents
ANNUAL INCOME PER PERSON: $6,540
POPULATION DENSITY: 593 per sq km [1,536 per sq ml]
LIFE EXPECTANCY: Female 78 yrs, Male 72 yrs
ADULT LITERACY: 98%

■ Easternmost island of W. Indies ■ Island's coral structure acts as natural filter, making Barbadian water among world's purest ■ Sugar principal export; 60% of island given over to cultivation of sugar cane ■ Tourism overtook sugar as main source of foreign currency in 1968 ■ Densely populated - many people emigrate

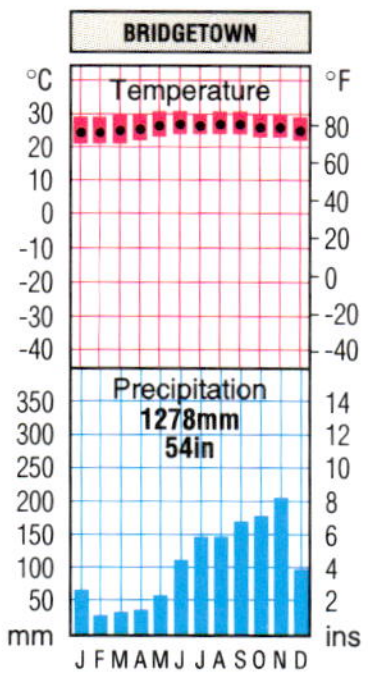

Bridgetown is situated on the drier side of the island where it is sheltered from the prevailing north easterly winds by the Central Uplands. About three-quarters of the rainfall occurs during the humid wet season which lasts from June to November. Rainfall can vary greatly from year to year; a dry year can drastically affect the island's sugar cane yield. Hurricanes are most likely in August and September when they can bring great devastation and loss of life.

ST VINCENT AND THE GRENADINES

On independence from Britain in 1979, St Vincent adopted this tricolour but with the islands' coat of arms in the centre. In 1985 this was replaced by the present three green diamonds representing the islands as the 'gems of the Antilles'.

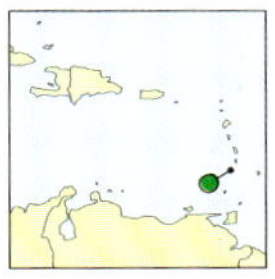

■ Sometimes called 'Tahiti of Caribbean' on account of productive soil & luxuriant vegetation ■ Soufrière still active volcano - last erupted in 1979 ■ Agriculture main source of income & export earnings; bananas main crop ■ World's leading producer of arrowroot ■ 1783 Treaty of Versailles restored country to Britain, after over 100 years of wars & disputes between British & Carib inhabitants supported by French

COUNTRY: Saint Vincent and the Grenadines
AREA: 388 sq km [150 sq mls]
POPULATION: 116,000
CAPITAL (Population): Kingstown (34,000)
GOVERNMENT: Constitutional monarchy with a unicameral legislature
ETHNIC GROUPS: Black 74%, Mulatto 19%, White 3%, American Indian/Black 2%, East Indian 2%
LANGUAGES: English (official)
RELIGIONS: Protestant 77%, Roman Catholic 19%
NATIONAL DAY: 27 October; Independence Day (1979)
CURRENCY: Eastern Caribbean $ = 100 cents
ANNUAL INCOME PER PERSON: $1,610
POPULATION DENSITY: 299 per sq km [774 per sq ml]
LIFE EXPECTANCY: Female 74 yrs, Male 69 yrs
ADULT LITERACY: 85%

GRENADA

Each star represents one of Grenada's seven parishes. The country's traditional cash crop, nutmeg, is depicted in the hoist triangle. The Grenadian people are represented by the colours red (for unity) and yellow (for friendliness), the island by the colour green.

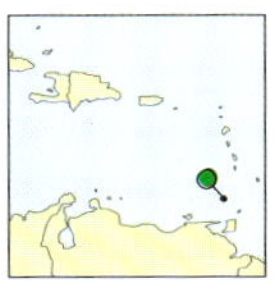

■ Southernmost of Windward Islands ■ Consists of remains of extinct volcanoes; only flat land is along rivers' lower courses & part of coast ■ World's largest producer of nutmeg ■ Tourism single most important economic activity ■ Reliant on foreign aid ■ Radical politics hallmark of society since early 1950s ■ Hurricane virtually destroyed capital, St. George's, in 1955 ■ Military forces from US & several Caribbean countries invaded in 1983 to topple Marxist government

COUNTRY: Grenada
AREA: 344 sq km [133 sq mls]
POPULATION: 85,000
CAPITAL (Population): St George's (29,000)
GOVERNMENT: Constitutional monarchy with a bicameral legislature
ETHNIC GROUPS: Black 84%, mixed 12%, East Indian 3%, White 1%
LANGUAGES: English (official)
RELIGIONS: Roman Catholic 64%, Protestant 34%
NATIONAL DAY: 7 February; Independence Day (1974)
CURRENCY: East Caribbean $ = 100 cents
ANNUAL INCOME PER PERSON: $2,120
POPULATION DENSITY: 247 per sq km [640 per sq ml]
LIFE EXPECTANCY: Female 69 yrs, Male 65 yrs
ADULT LITERACY: 85%

SOUTH AMERICA – NORTH

TRINIDAD & TOBAGO

The islands of Trinidad and Tobago have flown this flag since independence from Britain in 1962. Red stands for the people's warmth and vitality, black for their strength, and white for their hopes and the surf of the sea.

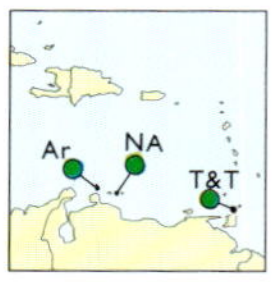

COUNTRY: Republic of Trinidad and Tobago
AREA: 5,130 sq km [1,981 sq mls]
POPULATION: 1,227,000
CAPITAL (Population): Port-of-Spain (60,000)
GOVERNMENT: Republic with a bicameral legislature
ETHNIC GROUPS: Black 40%, East Indian 40%, mixed 16%, White 1%
LANGUAGES: English
RELIGIONS: Christian 62%, Hindu 24%, Muslim 9%
NATIONAL DAY: 31 August; Independence Day (1962)
CURRENCY: Trinidad and Tobago $ = 100 cents
ANNUAL INCOME PER PERSON: $3,470
MAIN PRIMARY PRODUCTS: Crude petroleum, natural gas, asphalt
MAIN INDUSTRIES: Petroleum, natural gas, asphalt, tourism and agriculture
MAIN EXPORTS: Mineral fuels, lubricants, chemicals, food and live animals
MAIN IMPORTS: Machinery and transport equipment, foodstuffs, chemicals
DEFENCE: 2.3% of national budget
POPULATION DENSITY: 239 per sq km [619 per sq ml]
LIFE EXPECTANCY: Female 74 yrs, Male 69 yrs
ADULT LITERACY: 96%

■ Extensive forests on Trinidad, parts of which now made into nature reserves & national parks ■ Trinidad pop. has highest standard of living of W. Indies Commonwealth countries ■ Trinidad one of world's oldest oil-producing countries; 1st well drilled in 1867, only 8 years after 1st US oil well ■ Sugar & cocoa principal crops though agriculture has declined in economic importance ■ National gas reserves have provided raw material for fast developing petrochemical industry ■ Tobago depends almost entirely on tourism ■ World's main source of natural asphalt ■ 43% of pop. descendants of African slaves, 40% of Asian origin

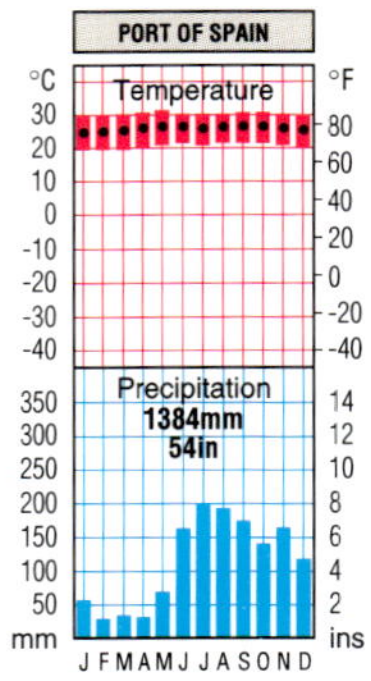

The annual temperature range is very small as would be expected of a coastal location only 10° from the Equator. By day the temperature rises rapidly, setting off heavy showers during the afternoon in the rainy season, but the sky clears in the evenings which feel pleasantly cool. The wettest months are in summer when the inter-tropical rain belt reaches its most northerly extent and lies close to Trinidad.

NETHERLANDS ANTILLES

COUNTRY: Self-governing Dutch territory
AREA: 993 sq km [383 sq mls]
POPULATION: 189,000
CAPITAL (Population): Willemstad (94,000)

ARUBA

COUNTRY: Self-governing Dutch territory
AREA: 193 sq km [75 sq mls]
POPULATION: 60,000
CAPITAL: Oranjestad

COLOMBIA

Colombia's colours – showing the (yellow) land of the nation separated by the (blue) sea from the tyranny of Spain, whose rule the people fought with their (red) blood – are shared by Ecuador and Venezuela. The blue is darker than her neighbours'.

COUNTRY: Republic of Colombia
AREA: 1,138,910 sq km [439,733 sq mls]
POPULATION: 32,987,000
CAPITAL (Population): Bogotá (4,185,000)
GOVERNMENT: Unitary republic with bicameral legislature
ETHNIC GROUPS: Mestizo 68%, White 20%, Amerindian 7%, Black 5%
LANGUAGES: Spanish (official)
RELIGIONS: Roman Catholic 95%
NATIONAL DAY: 20 July; Independence Day (1819)
CURRENCY: Peso = 100 centavos
ANNUAL INCOME PER PERSON: $1,240
MAIN PRIMARY PRODUCTS: Coal, natural gas, petroleum, silver, gold, iron ore
MAIN INDUSTRIES: Iron, cement, petroleum industries, vehicles, food processing, paper
EXPORTS: $184 per person
MAIN EXPORTS: Coffee 43%, crude petroleum 8%, bananas 6%, cotton 3%
MAIN EXPORT PARTNERS: USA (40%), Germany, Netherlands, Japan
IMPORTS: $161 per person
MAIN IMPORTS: Machinery 28%, chemicals 18%, vehicles 13%
MAIN IMPORT PARTNERS: USA (36%), Japan, Venezuela, Germany
TOURISM: 732,000 visitors
POPULATION DENSITY: 29 per sq km [75 per sq ml]
INFANT MORTALITY: 42 per 1,000 live births
LIFE EXPECTANCY: Female 68 yrs, Male 64 yrs
ADULT LITERACY: 88% (Indians 60%)
PRINCIPAL CITIES (Population): Bogotá 4,185,000 Medellín 1,506,000 Cali 1,397,000 Barranquilla 920,000 Cartagena 560,000

■ World's 2nd biggest producer & leading exporter of coffee ■ Agriculture accounts for 75% of export earnings ■ S. America's biggest coal exporter & largest reserves (18 billion tonnes) ■ Produces 90% of world's emeralds ■ 70% of pop. urban ■ National flower 1 of many species of orchid ■ Home to world's largest cockroach *(Megaloblatta Longipennis)* ■ Reputed to have more species of birds than anywhere else in world (1500 including N. American immigrants) ■ Panama was part of country until 1903 ■ Chibchas civilization round Bogotá gave rise to legend of El Dorado, 'the gilded one' ■ Cities notorious for street crime, especially drug related ■ Medellín centre of coca producing area, cocaine production & trafficking ■ Education accounts for nearly 20% of national budget

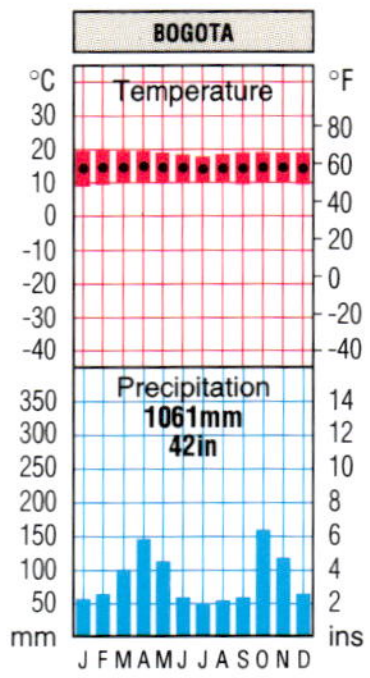

Colombia is split by the northern Andes. Their altitude fundamentally changes the tropical climate of the country, lowering temperatures and increasing rainfall and with permanent snow at the higher levels. Temperatures are high with little annual variation. Rainfall is high, very high on the Pacific coast, but it is drier on the Caribbean coast and in the Magdalena valley, with dry seasons.

VENEZUELA

The seven stars on the tricolour (see Colombia and Ecuador) represent the provinces forming the Venezuelan Federation in 1811. The shield in the coat of arms depicts a wheatsheaf (for unity), weapons (for victory) and a wild horse (for liberty).

COUNTRY: Republic of Venezuela
AREA: 912,050 sq km [352,143 sq mls]
POPULATION: 19,735,000
CAPITAL (Population): Caracas (3,247,000)
GOVERNMENT: Republic with bicameral legislature
ETHNIC GROUPS: Mestizo 67%, White 21%, Black 10%, Indian 2%
LANGUAGES: Spanish (official), Amerindian languages
RELIGIONS: Christian (Roman Catholic)
NATIONAL DAY: 5 July; Independence Day (1811)
CURRENCY: Bolívar = 100 centivos
ANNUAL INCOME PER PERSON: $2,560
MAIN PRIMARY PRODUCTS: Food, oil, bauxite
MAIN INDUSTRIES: Oil refining, steel manufacture, food processing, textiles, vehicles
EXPORTS: $670 per person
MAIN EXPORTS: Petroleum, bauxite, iron ore
MAIN EXPORT PARTNERS: US, Germany, Japan, Italy, Brazil
IMPORTS: $407 per person
MAIN IMPORTS: Food, chemicals, manufactured goods
MAIN IMPORT PARTNERS: US, Germany, Japan, Netherlands
DEFENCE: 5.8% of national budget
TOURISM: 317,300 visitors
POPULATION DENSITY: 22 per sq km [56 per sq ml]
INFANT MORTALITY: 33 per 1,000 live births
LIFE EXPECTANCY: Female 74 yrs, Male 68 yrs
ADULT LITERACY: 86%
PRINCIPAL CITIES (Population): Caracas 3,247,000 Maracaibo 1,295,000 Valencia 1,135,000 Maracay 857,000 Barquisimeto 718,000 Ciudad Guyana 466,000

■ Name means 'Little Venice', coined by Italian explorer Amerigo Vespucci (1499) ■ Angel Falls, named after American airman Jimmy Angel who 'discovered' them, world's highest (979 m [3,212 ft]), 10 times height of Niagara ■ World's longest (12 km [7.5 mls]) & highest (4765 m [15,633 ft]) cablecar ride runs from Merida to Pico Espijo ■ Ciudad Guayana, huge new city based on HEP generated at confluence of Orinoco & Caroní rivers ■ S. America's richest country ■ Less than 25% of workforce engaged in agriculture ■ S. America's biggest oil producer ■ Bolivar currency named after Simon Bolivar ■ Motorcycles banned in Caracas after 22.00 hrs.

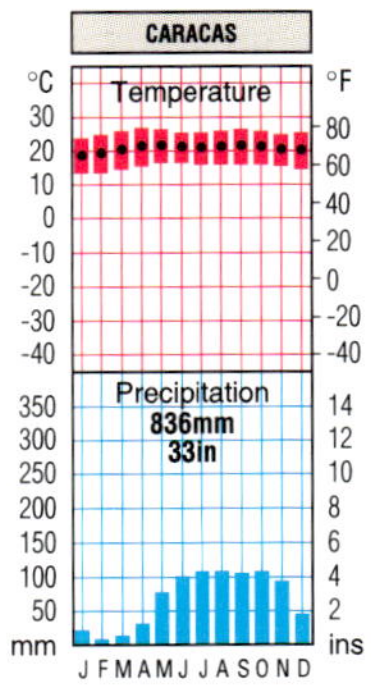

There is a tropical climate throughout the country. There is little variation in temperature from month to month, but there are marked wet and dry seasons, the rain falling from May - Nov. The north-east trade winds leave little rain in the coastal lowlands, but the total increases when they hit the mountains. The monthly temperature of Caracas on the northern coast is between 19 and 22°C [66-72°F], but this is much lower on the higher land. Some of the northern Andean peaks have permanent snow.

GUYANA

This striking design, adopted by Guyana on independence from Britain in 1966, has colours representing the people's energy building a new nation (red), their perseverance (black), minerals (yellow), rivers (white) and forests (green).

COUNTRY: Cooperative Republic of Guyana
AREA: 214,970 sq km [83,000 sq mls]
POPULATION: 796,000
CAPITAL (Population): Georgetown (188,000)
GOVERNMENT: Republic with unicameral legislature
ETHNIC GROUPS: Asian Indian 51%, Black 29%, Mulatto 13%, Amerindian 4%

LANGUAGES: English (official), Hindi, Urdu and Amerindian dialects
RELIGIONS: Hindu 34%, Protestant 34%, Roman Catholic 18%, Muslim 9%
NATIONAL DAY: 23 February; Republic Day (1970)
CURRENCY: Guyana $ = 100 cents
ANNUAL INCOME PER PERSON: $370

■ Name means 'land of many waters' ■ Kaieteur Falls, spectacular waterfall on Pokaro river with uninterrupted drop of 226 m [741 ft], more than 4 times height of Niagara ■ Only English-speaking country in S. America ■ Asian Indians largest ethnic group ■ Bauxite mining principal economic activity ■ Long-standing border dispute with Venezuela ■ Known as British Guiana until independence in 1966

POPULATION DENSITY: 3.7 per sq km [9.6 per sq ml]
LIFE EXPECTANCY: Female 74 yrs, Male 69 yrs
ADULT LITERACY: 75%

SURINAM

Adopted on independence from the Dutch in 1975, Surinam's flag features the colours of the main political parties, the yellow star symbolising unity and a golden future. The red is twice the width of the green, four times that of the white.

COUNTRY: Republic of Suriname
AREA: 163,270 sq km [63,039 sq mls]
POPULATION: 422,000
CAPITAL (Population): Paramaribo (192,000)
GOVERNMENT: Republic with unicameral legislature
ETHNIC GROUPS: Asian Indian 37%, Creole 31%, Indonesian 14%, Black 9%, Amerindian 3%

LANGUAGES: Dutch (official), English
RELIGIONS: Hindu 27%, Roman Catholic 23%, Muslim 20%, Protestant 19%
NATIONAL DAY: 25 November
CURRENCY: Surinam guilder = 100 cents
ANNUAL INCOME PER PERSON: $3,050
POPULATION DENSITY: 2.6 per sq km [6.7 per sq ml]

■ During 1970s, between 1/3 & 1/2 of entire pop. emigrated, mainly to Netherlands ■ Originally populated by Arawak & Carib Indians, who now represent under 3% of pop. ■ Formerly known as Willoughbyland & Dutch Guiana ■ Country 'given' to Netherlands by Britain in 1667 in exchange for Nieuw Amsterdam (now New York) ■ Bauxite exports represent 80% of total ■ Civil war in 1980s severely damaged economy

LIFE EXPECTANCY: Female 73 yrs, Male 68 yrs
ADULT LITERACY: 65%

FRENCH GUIANA

The official flag flown over 'Guyane' is the French tricolour. A French possession since 1676 (apart from 1809-1817), the territory is treated as part of mainland France and its citizens send representatives to the Paris parliament.

COUNTRY: Department of French Guiana
AREA: 90,000 sq km [34,749 sq mls]
POPULATION: 99,000
CAPITAL (Population): Cayenne (38,000)
GOVERNMENT: French Overseas Department of France
ETHNIC GROUPS: Creole 42%, Chinese 14%, French 10%, Haitian 7%

LANGUAGES: French (official)
RELIGIONS: Roman Catholic 80%, Protestant 4%
NATIONAL DAY: 14 July; National Day - Storming of the Bastille (1789)
CURRENCY: Franc = 100 centimes
ANNUAL INCOME PER PERSON: $2,500
POPULATION DENSITY: 1 per sq km [2.6 per sq ml]

■ Smallest S. American country ■ Over 80% of land forested ■ Overseas Department of France ■ Most food & manufactured goods imported; 60% of imports from France ■ Kourou European Space Agency's rocket-launching site; site's equatorial position enables rockets to reach orbit with less fuel ■ Over 50% of pop. live in capital Cayenne (from which cayenne pepper's name derives) ■ 2/3 of pop. descendants of African slaves from Guyana & Surinam ■ Devil's Island, notorious convict settlement, closed in 1945 ■ Government biggest employer

LIFE EXPECTANCY: Female 75 yrs, Male 68 yrs
ADULT LITERACY: 80%

BRAZIL

The sphere bears the motto 'Order and Progress' and its 23 stars, arranged in the pattern of the night sky over Brazil, represent the states and federal district. Green symbolises the nation's forests, the yellow diamond its mineral wealth.

COUNTRY: Federative Republic of Brazil
AREA: 8,511,970 sq km [3,286,472 sq mls]
POPULATION: 153,322,000
CAPITAL (Population): Brasilia (1,577,000)
GOVERNMENT: Federal republic with bicameral legislature
ETHNIC GROUPS: White 53%, Mulatto 22%, Mestizo 12%, Black 11%
LANGUAGES: Portuguese (official), others
RELIGIONS: Roman Catholic 87%, Protestant 8%
NATIONAL DAY: 7 September; Independence Day (1822)
CURRENCY: Cruzado = 100 centavos
ANNUAL INCOME PER PERSON: $2,680
SOURCE OF INCOME: Agriculture 9%, Industry 43%, Services 49%
MAIN PRIMARY PRODUCTS: Coal, iron ore, manganese, gold, bauxite, copper, diamonds, petroleum, natural gas
MAIN INDUSTRIES: Steel, petro-chemicals, vehicles, chemicals, machinery, consumer goods, cement, offshore oil, shipping, timber
EXPORTS: $233 per person
MAIN EXPORTS: Transport equipment 12%, soya beans 9%, coffee 8%, iron ore 7%, machinery 6%, footwear 5%
MAIN EXPORT PARTNERS: USA 27%, Japan 6%, Netherlands 6%, Germany 4%, Italy 5%
IMPORTS: $124 per person
MAIN IMPORTS: Primary products 33%, capital goods 26%, oil and oil products 25%
MAIN IMPORT PARTNERS: USA 20%, Germany 9%, Japan 6%, Saudi Arabia 6%
TOTAL ARMED FORCES: 320,000

TOURISM: 1,800,000 visitors
ROADS: 1,675,040 km [1,046,900 mls]
RAILWAYS: 29,901 km [18,688 mls]
POPULATION DENSITY: 18 per sq km [45 per sq ml]
URBAN POPULATION: 77%
POPULATION GROWTH: 2.1 % per year
BIRTHS: 28 per 1,000 population
DEATHS: 8 per 1,000 population
INFANT MORTALITY: 57 per 1,000 live births
LIFE EXPECTANCY: Female 69 yrs, Male 64 yrs
POPULATION PER DOCTOR: 1,080
ADULT LITERACY: 80%
PRINCIPAL CITIES (Population): São Paulo 16,832,000 Rio de Janeiro 11,141,000 Belo Horizonte 3,446,000 Recife 2,945,000 Pôrto Alegre 2,924,000 Salvador 2,362,000 Fortaleza 2,169,000 Curitiba 1,926,000 Brasilia 1,577,000 Nova Iguaçu 1,325,000 Belém 1,296,000 Santos 1,200,000 Goiânia 928,000 Campinas 845,000 Manaus 834,000

■ S. America's largest country; world's 5th largest ■ S. America's longest coastline (7,400 km [4,600mls]) ■ Amazon, world's most voluminous river & drains largest area; Amazon basin represents 1/3 of Brazil ■ Navigable waterways of 43,000 km [27,000 mls] ■ Panatal wildlife reserve 1 of world's richest areas for freshwater fish; 350 species of fish & 600 species of bird ■ World's biggest producer of coffee, sugar cane, bananas, oranges, cassava, sisal & castor oil ■ 30% of pop. engaged in farming, forestry or fishing ■ Generates 93% of electricity by HEP, including world's largest plant on Paraná river ■ 80% of oil imported ■ World's greatest exporter of iron ore & greatest reserves at Carajas ■ Country most heavily in debt at 1.1.89 ($120.1 billion) ■ Over 25% of cars run on fuel made from sugar cane & cassava ■ 4 million African slaves shipped in between 16th century & abolition of slavery in 1888 ■ Only S. American country to have Portuguese as national language ■ World's largest R. Catholic pop. ■ Name comes from 'brassa', high-quality red dye extracted from local trees by Portuguese explorer Cabral ■ Brazilian troops fought on Allied side against Germany in WWs I & II

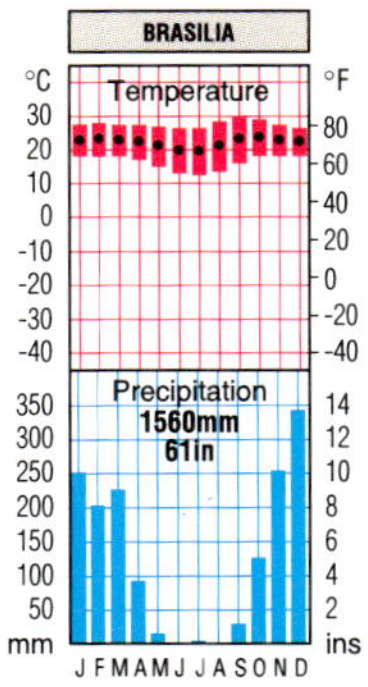

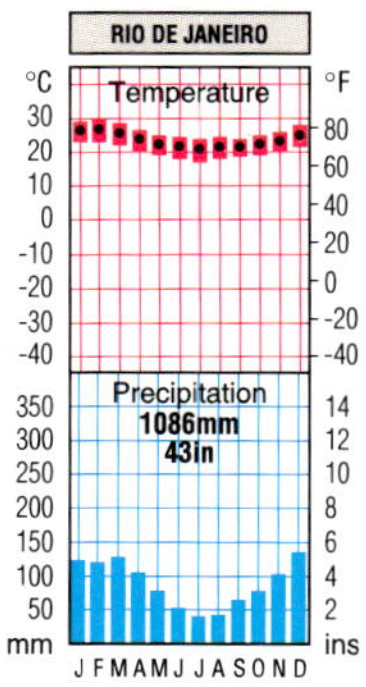

Brazil lies almost entirely within the tropics. The northern half of the country is dominated by the Amazon basin and except for the highlands in the south-east, there are no mountains. The monthly temperatures are high - over 25°C [77°F] - and there is little annual variation. Brasilia has only a 4°C [7°F] difference between July and Oct; Rio has twice this range. The hottest part of the country is in the north-east. Frosts do occur in the eastern highlands and the extreme south of the country. There is heavy rain, but inland a marked dry-season May-Aug. In Rio there is high rainfall and a dry season, but not so marked as inland. Most of Brazil has moderate rainfall, but there are very heavy totals at the mouth and in the headwaters of the Amazon and on the south-east coast below the highlands. There is an arid zone in the north-east.

SOUTH AMERICA – SOUTH

ECUADOR

Shared in different proportions by Colombia and Venezuela, Ecuador's colours were used in the flag created by the patriot Francisco de Miranda in 1806 and flown by Simon Bolivar, whose armies also liberated Peru and Bolivia.

COUNTRY: Republic of Ecuador
AREA: 283,560 sq km [109,483 sq mls]
POPULATION: 10,782,000
CAPITAL (Population): Quito (1,110,248)
GOVERNMENT: Unitary republic with unicameral legislature
ETHNIC GROUPS: Mestizo 55%, Amerindians 25%, White 10%, Black 10%
LANGUAGES: Spanish (official), Quechua
RELIGIONS: Roman Catholic 92%, Protestant 6%
NATIONAL DAY: 10 August, Independence of Quito (1809)
CURRENCY: Sucre = 100 centavos
ANNUAL INCOME PER PERSON: $960

MAIN PRIMARY PRODUCTS: Silver, gold, copper, zinc
MAIN INDUSTRIES: Petroleum, agriculture, textiles
MAIN EXPORTS: Petroleum, seafood, bananas, cocoa, coffee
MAIN IMPORTS: Fuels, lubricants, transport equipment, inputs and capital equipment for industry
DEFENCE: 12% of national budget
POPULATION DENSITY: 38 per sq km [98 per sq ml]
LIFE EXPECTANCY: Female 69 yrs, Male 65 yrs
ADULT LITERACY: 85%

■ Name means 'equator' in Spanish ■ World's highest active volcano, Cotopaxi, 5,897 m [19,347 ft], last erupted 1877 ■ Over 30 active volcanoes ■ Over 60% of exports go to USA ■ World's largest exporter of bananas ■ Crude oil single largest export earner ■ Largest city, Guayaquil (1,301,000), country's main port ■ One of S. America's most stable & democratic countries

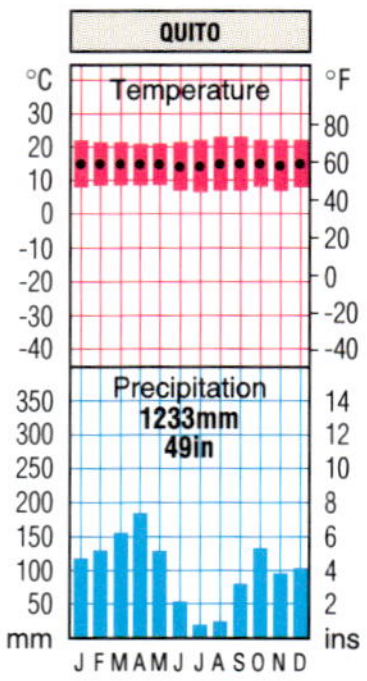

Ecuador lies on the Equator, but it is bisected by the high Andes which significantly lower the expected high temperatures. Although off-shore there is the cold Peruvian current, the coastal temperatures are 23-25°C [73-77°F] throughout the year. At Quito, inland at 2,500m [8,200 ft] this drops to 14-15°C [57-59°F]. There are permanent snowfields and glaciers nearby. Rainfall is low in the extreme south- west, but generally rainfall is heavy, and very heavy in the eastern, Amazonian side of the country. There is a dry season June-Sept.

PERU

Flown since 1825, the flag's colours are said to have come about when the Argentine patriot General Jos de San Martin, arriving to liberate Peru from Spain in 1820, saw a flock of red and white flamingoes flying over his marching army.

COUNTRY: Republic of Peru
AREA: 1,285,220 sq km [496,223 sq mls]
POPULATION: 22,332,000
CAPITAL (Population): Lima (4,605,000)
GOVERNMENT: Unitary republic with bicameral legislature
ETHNIC GROUPS: Quechua 47%, Mestizo 32%, White 12%
LANGUAGES: Spanish and Quechua (official), Aymara
RELIGIONS: Roman Catholic 92%
NATIONAL DAY: 28 July; Independence Day (1821)
CURRENCY: Inti = 100 céntimos = 1,000 soles
ANNUAL INCOME PER PERSON: $1,160
MAIN PRIMARY PRODUCTS: Iron ore, silver, zinc, tungsten, petroleum, gold, copper, lead, tin, molybdenum
MAIN INDUSTRIES: Food processing, textiles, copper smelting, forestry

EXPORTS: $170 per person
MAIN EXPORTS: Copper 19%, petroleum and derivatives 10%, lead 9%, zinc 8%, fishmeal 8%, coffee 5%
MAIN EXPORT PARTNERS: USA 34%, Japan 10%, Belgium 4%, Germany 4%
IMPORTS: $84 per person
MAIN IMPORTS: Fuels, machinery, chemicals, food, tobacco
MAIN IMPORT PARTNERS: USA 27%, Argentina 9%, Brazil 6%
TOURISM: 350,000 visitors
POPULATION DENSITY: 17 per sq km [45 per sq ml]
INFANT MORTALITY: 76 per 1,000 live births
LIFE EXPECTANCY: Female 67 yrs, Male 63 yrs
ADULT LITERACY: 80%
PRINCIPAL CITIES (Population): Lima 4,605,000 Arequipa 592,000 Trujillo 491,000 Chiclayo 395,000

■ Only S. American country with official Amerindian language ■ World's highest railway climbs to 4817 m [15,806 ft] above sea level at La Cuia ■ World's largest producer of coca; government attempting to eliminate crop ■ Once world's largest fish catches; declined due to overfishing & climatic changes ■ Ruined Inca city of Machu Picchu, in Cuzco region, stands 2,270 m [7,480 ft] above Urabamba river; destroyed in 16th century by Spaniards, its ruins lay undicovered until 1911 ■ S. America's heaviest defence spender per head of pop.

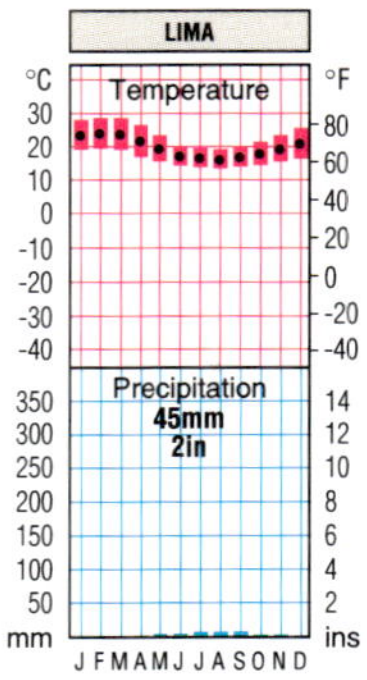

Peru has a great variety of climates; its northern border touches the Equator, over half the country is astride the high Andes and the prevailing winds from the south-west blow over the cold Peruvian current of the Pacific. Desert conditions prevail along the foothills of the Andes. The rainfall increases with altitude, with snow-covered peaks. In the tropical north-eastern lowlands there are high temperatures and rainfall.

BOLIVIA

Dating from liberation in 1825, the tricolour has been used as both national and merchant flag since 1888. The red stands for Bolivia's animals and the army's courage, the yellow for mineral resources and the green for agriculture.

COUNTRY: Republic of Bolivia
AREA: 1,098,580 sq km [424,162 sq mls]
POPULATION: 7,400,000
CAPITAL (Population): La Paz (993,000)
GOVERNMENT: Unitary republic with bicameral legislature
ETHNIC GROUPS: Mestizo 31%, Quechua 25%, Aymara 17%, White 15%
LANGUAGES: Spanish (official), Aymara, Quechua
RELIGIONS: Roman Catholic 94%
NATIONAL DAY: 6 August; Independence Day (1825)
CURRENCY: Boliviano = 100 centavos

ANNUAL INCOME PER PERSON: $620
MAIN PRIMARY PRODUCTS: Tin, sugar cane, rice, cotton
MAIN INDUSTRIES: Agriculture, manufacturing, tin mining
MAIN EXPORTS: Tin, zinc, antimony, natural gas
MAIN IMPORTS: Consumer goods, transport equipment
POPULATION DENSITY: 6.7 per sq km [17.4 per sq ml]
LIFE EXPECTANCY: Female 58 yrs, Male 54 yrs
ADULT LITERACY: 63%

■ 1 of S. America's 2 landlocked countries (other is Paraguay) ■ La Paz (The Peace) world's highest capital (3,625 m [11,893 ft]) ■ Estimated that trade in cocaine, from coca plant, may account for $^2/_3$ of country's exports ■ Rate of inflation in 1985 reached 24,000% ■ Native Indian peasants form 50% of pop. ■ Nearly $^1/_3$ of pop. urban ■ Country with most coups: 192 in 156 years from independence to 1981

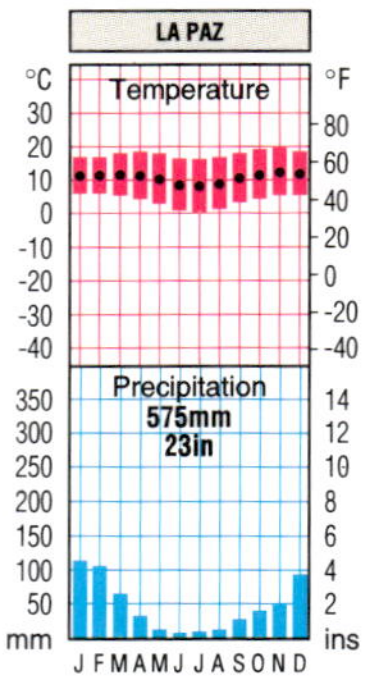

Although within the tropics, La Paz lies at 3,625 m [11,893 ft] on the Bolivian plateau and temperatures are clearly affected by altitude. The annual range is very small but temperatures rise rapidly by day and fall sharply at night in the clear air and the diurnal range is very large with frequent night frost in winter. Rainfall, which is often thundery, occurs mainly in summer.

PARAGUAY

Paraguay's tricolour is the only national flag with different sides. On the obverse the state emblem, illustrated here, displays the May Star to commemorate liberation from Spain (1811); the reverse shows the treasury seal – a lion and staff.

COUNTRY: Republic of Paraguay
AREA: 406,750 sq km [157,046 sq mls]
POPULATION: 4,277,000
CAPITAL (Population): Asunción (729,000)
GOVERNMENT: Unitary republic with bicameral legislature
ETHNIC GROUPS: Mestizo 90%, Amerindian 3%
LANGUAGES: Spanish (official), Guarani
RELIGIONS: Roman Catholic 96%, Protestant 2%
NATIONAL DAY: 14 May (Independence Day - 1811)
CURRENCY: Guarani = 100 centimos
ANNUAL INCOME PER PERSON: $1,110

MAIN PRIMARY PRODUCTS: Timber, cattle, limestone, kaolin, gypsum
MAIN INDUSTRIES: Agriculture, manufacturing
MAIN EXPORTS: Cotton, oil-seeds, oilcake etc, timber
MAIN IMPORTS: Petroleum and petroleum products, chemicals, machinery, transport and electrical equipment
POPULATION DENSITY: 11 per sq km [27 per sq ml]
LIFE EXPECTANCY: Female 70 yrs, Male 65 yrs
ADULT LITERACY: 81%

■ No coastline, therefore no ports but vessels up to 1700 tonnes can sail up Paraguay River to Asuncion, distance of 1610 km [1000 mls] ■ Agriculture supplies $^1/_3$ of GDP & almost all export earnings ■ Self-sufficient in energy ■ World's biggest HEP plant on Paraná river at Itaipu on Brazilian border ■ Low foreign debts, unlike most of S. America ■ 60% of pop. rural ■ 70% of pop. under 30 years old

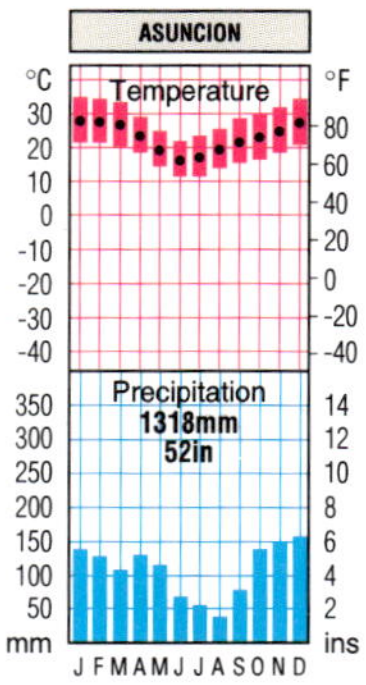

In S. America between 20° and 30°S there is a prominent summer wet season. The rain is often heavy and can yield as much as 20 mm [0.8 in] a day in Asunción. Summers throughout the plains of Paraguay are very hot and humid. Winters are mild and relatively dry. Much of the winter rain is associated with surges of cold air from the Southern Ocean which can give surprisingly low temperatures, especially in the south of the country.

URUGUAY

Displayed since 1830, the stripes represent the nine provinces of Uruguay on independence from Spain two years earlier. The blue and white and the May Sun derive from the flag originally employed by Argentina in the colonial struggle.

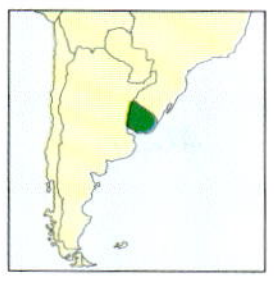

COUNTRY: Eastern Republic of Uruguay
AREA: 177,410 sq km [68,498 sq mls]
POPULATION: 3,094,000
CAPITAL (Population): Montevideo (1,248,000)
GOVERNMENT: Unitary state with bicameral legislature
ETHNIC GROUPS: White 88%, Mestizo 8%, Black 4%
LANGUAGES: Spanish (official)
RELIGIONS: Christian (Roman Catholic) 66%, Protestant 2%, Jewish 2%
NATIONAL DAY: 25 August; National Independence Day
CURRENCY: Peso = 100 centisimos
ANNUAL INCOME PER PERSON: $2,560
MAIN PRIMARY PRODUCTS: Rice, meat, fruit, fish
MAIN INDUSTRIES: Meat processing
MAIN EXPORTS: Hides and leather, meat, wool
MAIN IMPORTS: Fuels, metals, machinery, cars and lorries
DEFENCE: 10% of national budget
POPULATION DENSITY: 17 per sq km [45 per sq ml]
LIFE EXPECTANCY: Female 75 yrs, Male 68 yrs
ADULT LITERACY: 94%

■ 'Oriental' of official name means 'east' (of River Plate) ■ 90% of land suitable for agriculture but only 10% cultivated ■ Cows & sheep outnumber people by about 9:1 ■ Highest literacy rate, one of smallest pop. growth rates & one of most even distributions of wealth among Latin American republics ■ Montevideo nearly 20 times size of next largest city (Salto) ■ First hosts & winners of soccer's World Cup (1930); also won in Brazil, 1930 ■ In 1976 had world's highest no. of political prisoners per head of pop.

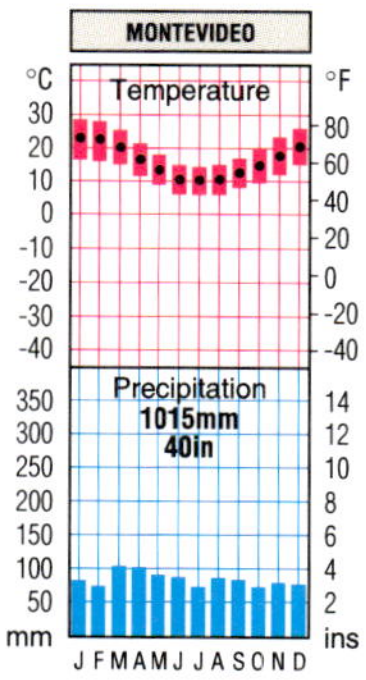

The plains around the Plate estuary have a very even distribution of rainfall throughout the year. Much of the rain is associated with the advance of cold air from the Southern Ocean which may be accompanied by a Pampero Sucio, a violent squall with rain and thunder followed by cooler, sunny weather. Near to the ocean, summers are pleasantly warm and winters less cold than at similar latitudes in the northern hemisphere.

ARGENTINA

The 'celeste' and white stripes, symbol of independence since 1810 around Buenos Aires, became the national flag in 1816 and influenced other Latin American countries. A May Sun, not in general use, was added two years later.

COUNTRY: Argentine Republic
AREA: 2,766,890 sq km [1,068,296 sq mls]
POPULATION: 32,322,000
CAPITAL (Population): Buenos Aires (10,728,000)
GOVERNMENT: Federal republic with bicameral legislature
ETHNIC GROUPS: European 85%, Amerindian, Mestizo
LANGUAGES: Spanish (official), Italian, Guarani
RELIGIONS: Roman Catholic 93%, Protestant 2%
NATIONAL DAY: 10 July, Independence Day (1816)
CURRENCY: Austral = 1,000 pesos
ANNUAL INCOME PER PERSON: $2,370
MAIN PRIMARY PRODUCTS: Coal, cattle, petroleum, natural gas, zinc, lead, silver
MAIN INDUSTRIES: Food processing, wine, cotton yarn, cement, iron and steel, vehicles
EXPORTS: $286 per person
MAIN EXPORTS: Vegetable products 43%, textiles and manufactures 4%
MAIN EXPORT PARTNERS: Netherlands 10%, Brazil 9%, USA 8%
IMPORTS: $167 per person
MAIN IMPORTS: Machinery 23%, chemicals and petrochemicals 21%, mineral products 13%
MAIN IMPORT PARTNERS: USA 17%, Brazil 14%, Germany 11%, Bolivia 7%, Japan 7%
DEFENCE: 6% of national budget
TOURISM: 1,600,000 visitors
POPULATION DENSITY: 12 per sq km [30 per sq ml]
INFANT MORTALITY: 29 per 1000 live births
LIFE EXPECTANCY: Female 75 yrs, Male 68 yrs
ADULT LITERACY: 95%
PRINCIPAL CITIES (Population): Buenos Aires 10,728,000 Córdoba 1,055,000 Rosario 1,016,000 Mendoza 668,000 La Plata 611,000 San Miguel de Tucumán 571,000

■ World's 8th largest country ■ Aconcagua (6,960 m [22,834 ft] highest mountain outside Central Asia ■ Agriculture accounts for 70% of export earnings ■ 1 of world's biggest wheat exporters ■ Largest wine producer (5th) outside Europe ■ Most of pop. descendants of European immigrants ■ Nearly 1/3 of pop. live in Greater Buenos Aires ■ S. America's largest rail network (over 35,000 km [21,000 mls]) ■ Great economic growth, 1850 to 1930 - source of much of world's meat & cereals until 1914 ■ Estimated that 9000 killed, 9000 tortured & 2 million fled country during 'dirty war' of military regime, 1976-1982 ■ Invaded British Falkland Islands in 1982 but ejected after 10 weeks by British forces ■ Welsh-speaking sheep farmers in Patagonia, descendants of settlers in 1865 ■ Federal capital scheduled to move from Buenos Aires to Viedma-Carmen de Patagones before 1995

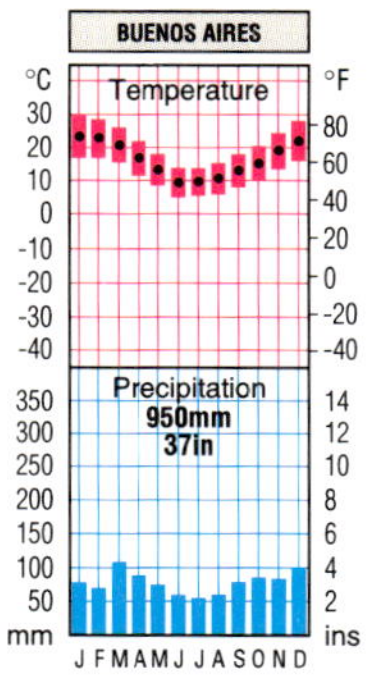

Argentina, stretching from the tropics almost into Antarctica, with the high Andes to the west and lying in the narrow neck of land between the two oceans, experiences many climates. The north is tropical with temperatures around 20°C [68°F] in June and 25°C [77°F] in Jan. The south is temperate with May-Aug. about freezing and 10°C [50°F] in Jan. or Feb. Rainfall is heaviest in the sub-tropical north-east and in Patagonia, but quite arid in the west in the lee of the Andes.

CHILE

Inspired by the US Stars and Stripes, the flag was designed by an American serving with the Chilean Army in 1817 and adopted that year. White represents the snow-capped Andes (to the east), blue the sky and red the blood of patriots.

COUNTRY: Republic of Chile
AREA: 756,950 sq km [292,258 sq mls]
POPULATION: 13,386,000
CAPITAL (Population): Santiago (4,858,000)
GOVERNMENT: Return to civilian rule following military control
ETHNIC GROUPS: Mestizo 92%, Amerindian 7%
LANGUAGES: Spanish (official)
RELIGIONS: Roman Catholic 80%, Protestant 6%
NATIONAL DAY: 18 September; Independence Day (1810)
CURRENCY: Peso = 100 centavos
ANNUAL INCOME PER PERSON: $1,940
MAIN PRIMARY PRODUCTS: Coal, petroleum, natural gas, gold, lead, iron ore, copper
MAIN INDUSTRIES: Food processing, wine, forestry, iron and steel, copper, cement
EXPORTS: $632 per person
MAIN EXPORTS: Copper 46%, fresh fruit 9%, fishmeal 3%, iron ore 2%
MAIN EXPORT PARTNERS: USA 22%, Japan 11%, Germany 9%, Brazil 7%
IMPORTS: $504 per person
MAIN IMPORTS: Machinery 24%, mineral products 20%, chemicals 13%, food 8%
MAIN IMPORT PARTNERS: USA 19%, Japan 10%, Brazil 9%, Germany 8%
DEFENCE: 11% of national budget
TOURISM: 560,000 visitors
POPULATION DENSITY: 18 per sq km [46 per sq ml]
INFANT MORTALITY: 19 per 1,000 live births
LIFE EXPECTANCY: Female 76 yrs, Male 69 yrs
PRINCIPAL CITIES (Population): Santiago 4,858,000 Concepción 394,000 Viña del Mar 316,000 Valparaiso 279,000 Talcahuano 221,000 Antofagasta 205,000

■ World's thinnest country - 25 times long as wide ■ Owns Easter Island, 3780 km [2350 mls] away in Pacific Ocean & home to famous 50-tonne 'Moai' statues ■ Robinson Crusoe Island part of Juan Fernández Islands about 640 km [400 mls] W. of Santiago ■ Every kind of climate from desert to icy wastes ■ 1 place in Atacama Desert recorded no rainfall for nearly 400 years ■ Magellanes, southernmost region of country including Cape Horn & Tierra del Fuego, contains oil fields which produce about 1/2 of country's needs ■ World's leading producer of copper (1987), with mining products nearly 1/2 of exports ■ 60% of pop. live in 800 km [300 ml] stretch of land in central valley region ■ 1970 election produced world's 1st democratically elected Marxist government; overthrown 1973 in right-wing coup supported by CIA

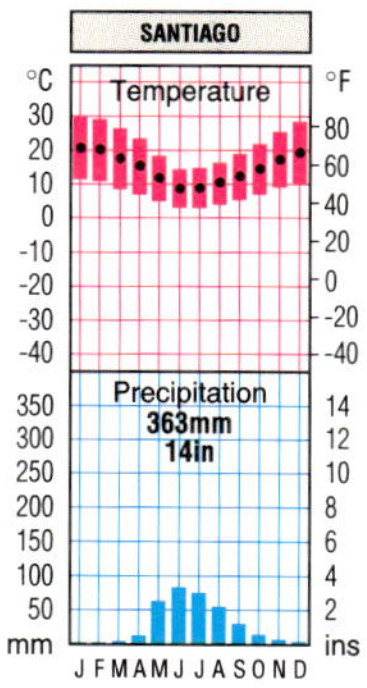

Chile has nearly every type of climate because of its latitudinal extent and the Andes in the east. In northern Chile is the Atacama desert. Rainfall increases southwards and central Chile has a Mediterranean type climate of a dry season, Nov.-March, a hot summer and warm winter. Monthly temperatures are never below 5°C [41°F]. In the south, westerly winds all the year bring storms and high rainfall. Except in the mountains there are no very low temperatures in Chile.

FALKLAND ISLANDS

COUNTRY: British Dependent Territory
AREA: 12,170 sq km [4,699 sq mls]
POPULATION: 2,000
CAPITAL (Population): Stanley (1,000)

World of Nations: Index to Countries

Afghanistan 20
Albania 10
Algeria 25
American Samoa 37
Andorra 7
Angola 33
Anguilla 42
Antigua and Barbuda 42
Argentina 47
Armenia 12
Aruba 44
Ascension Island 29
Australia 36
Austria 7
Azerbaijan 12
Azores 9

Bahamas 41
Bahrain 21
Bangladesh 18
Barbados 43
Belau 37
Belgium 5
Belize 39
Belorussia 12
Benin 28
Bermuda 41
Bhutan 18
Bolivia 46
Botswana 33
Brazil 45
British Indian Ocean Territory 35
Brunei 16
Bulgaria 11
Burkina Faso 28
Burma (Myanmar) 17
Burundi 32

Cambodia 16
Cameroon 29
Canada 38
Cape Verde Islands 25
Cayman Islands 41
Central African Republic 30
Chad 29
Chile 47
China 13
Christmas Island 37
CIS Nations 12
Cocos (Keeling) Islands 37
Colombia 44
Comoros 35
Congo 30
Cook Islands 37
Costa Rica 40
Croatia 11
Cuba 40
Cyprus 22
Czechoslovakia 6

Denmark 3
Djibouti 31
Dominica 42
Dominican Republic 41

Ecuador 46
Egypt 24
Equatorial Guinea 29
El Salvador 40
Estonia 2
Ethiopia 31

Falkland Islands 47
Faroes 3
Fiji 37
Finland 2
France 8
French Guiana 45
French Polynesia 37

Gabon 30
Gambia, The 26
Georgia 12
Germany 5
Ghana 27
Gibraltar 9
Greece 10
Greenland 38
Grenada 43
Guadeloupe 43
Guam 37
Guatemala 39
Guinea 26
Guinea-Bissau 26
Guyana 45

Haiti 41
Honduras 39
Hong Kong 14
Hungary 6

Iceland 1
India 18
Indonesia 15
Iran 20
Iraq 22
Ireland 3
Israel 23
Italy 9
Ivory Coast 27

Jamaica 41
Japan 12
Jordan 23

Kazakhstan 12
Kenya 31
Kirghizia 12
Kiribati 37
Korea, North 13
Korea, South 13
Kuwait 20

Laos 17
Latvia 2
Lebanon 23
Lesotho 35
Liberia 27
Libya 24
Liechtenstein 7
Lithuania 2
Luxembourg 5

Macau 14
Madagascar 35
Madeira 9
Malawi 33
Malaysia 15
Maldives 18
Mali 26
Malta 10
Mariana Islands 37
Marshall Islands 37
Martinique 43
Mauritania 25
Mauritius 35
Mexico 39
Micronesia Fed. Stat 37
Moldavia 12
Monaco 7
Mongolia 14
Montserrat 42
Morocco 25
Mozambique 34

Namibia 33
Nauru 37
Nepal 19
Netherlands 4
Netherlands Antilles 44
New Caledonia 37
New Zealand 36
Nicaragua 40
Niger 29
Nigeria 28
Niue 37
Norfolk Island 37
Norway 1

Oman 21

Pakistan 19
Panama 40
Papua New Guinea 36
Paraguay 46
Peru 46
Philippines 14
Pitcairn Islands 37
Poland 6
Portugal 9
Puerto Rico 42

Qatar 21

Réunion 35
Romania 11
Russia 12
Rwanda 32

St Christopher/ Nevis 42
St Helena 29
St Lucia 42
St Pierre and Miquelon 38
St Vincent/ Grenadines 43
San Marino 10
São Tomé and Príncipe 29
Saudi Arabia 22
Senegal 26
Seychelles 35
Sierra Leone 27
Singapore 15
Slovenia 11
Solomon Islands 37
Somalia 31
South Africa 34
Spain 8
Sri Lanka 19
Sudan 30
Surinam 45
Svalbard 1
Swaziland 35
Sweden 3
Switzerland 7
Syria 23

Taiwan 14
Tajikistan 12
Tanzania 32
Thailand 17
Togo 28
Tokelau 37
Tonga 37
Trinidad and Tobago 44
Tristan da Cunha 29
Tunisia 24
Turkey 22
Turkmenistan 12
Turks and Caicos Islands 41
Tuvalu 37

Uganda 32
Ukraine 12
United Arab Emirates 21
United Kingdom 4
United States 38
Uruguay 47
Uzbekistan 12

Vanuatu 37
Vatican City 10
Venezuela 44
Vietnam 16
Virgin Islands (Br.) 42
Virgin Islands (US) 42

Wallis and Futuna Islands 37
Western Sahara 25
Western Samoa 37

Yemen 21
Yugoslavia 11

Zaïre 32
Zambia 33
Zimbabwe 34

Notes

The order of countries in the gazetteer follows the same sequence as the World Maps, beginning in North West Europe and proceeding through Europe and Asia into Africa, then via the Indian Ocean to Australia and Oceania, and through the Pacific to North and South America. The last territory listed is the Falkland Islands.

The gazetteer gives information for all countries and territories of the world, but for the smallest territories, often islands, only the basic data of area, population and capital town are shown. A few small and near/uninhabited islands are not listed.

The statistical data is the latest available, usually for 1989-90, or within the period 1987-89.

Country area includes inland water, and land areas covered in ice, as in Greenland and Canada, for example.

City populations are usually those of the 'urban agglomerations' rather than within the legal city boundaries.

Annual income, given in US $, is the Gross National Product (GNP) divided by the population.

GNP is the value of a country's production plus the balance of foreign financial transactions. For the larger countries the origin of this income is divided between the major categories of agriculture, mining and manufacturing, and the service sector.

Foreign trade. The total value of the imports and exports have been divided by the population to give a relative measure of a nation's trading activity. The figures are in US $ per person.

Population growth, where quoted, is the average yearly growth in the period 1985-90.

Infant mortality is the number of deaths of children under the age of one year measured against each thousand live births.

Life expectancy is the number of years a girl or boy can expect to live if born today.

PROFILE OF THE EARTH

Geology and Climate 50, Environment 52, Population 54, The Human Family 56, Standards of Living 58, Energy 60, Production 62, Time and the Seasons 64

GEOLOGY & CLIMATE

The origin of the Earth is still open to conjecture, although the most widely accepted theory is that it was formed from a solar cloud consisting mainly of hydrogen. Under gravitation the cloud condensed and shrank to form the planets orbiting around the Sun. Gravitation forced the lighter elements to the surface of the Earth, where they cooled to form a crust - while the inner material remained hot and molten. The Earth's first rocks were formed over 3,500 million years ago, but the surface has since been constantly altered.

The Earth's surface is slowly but continually being rearranged. Some changes, such as erosion and deposition, are extremely slow, in marked contrast to other more abrupt changes often originating deep within the Earth's interior. The constant movements there vary in intensity, often with stresses building up to volcanic eruptions or earthquakes.

The outer layer or crust of the Earth consists of a comparatively brittle, low-density material varying from 5 to 50 kilometres deep beneath the continents. This consists predominately of silica and aluminium; hence its name, 'sial'. Extending under the ocean floors and below the sial is a basaltic layer known as 'sima', comprising mainly silica and magnesium.

Immediately below the crust, at he mohorovicic discontinuity line, there is a distinct change in density and chemical properties. This is the mantle - made up of iron and magnesium silicates - where temperatures reach 1,600°C. The rigid upper mantle extends down to a depth of about 1,000 kilometres, below which is a more viscous lower mantle which about 1,900 kilometres wide.

The outer core, measuring about 2,100 kilometres thick, consists of molten iron and nickel at 2,100°C to 5,000°C, possibly separated from the less dense mantle by an oxidised shell. About 5,000 kilometres below the surface is liquid transition zone, below which is the solid inner core, a sphere of about 2,700 kilometres diameter where rock is three times as dense as in the crust.

Volcanoes occur when hot liquefied rock beneath the crust reaches the surface as lava. An accumulation of ash and cinders around a vent forms a crater. Successive layers of thin lava flows creates an acid lava volcano, while thick lava flows produce a basic lava volcano. A caldera forms when a particularly violent eruption blows off the top of an already existing cone. Krakatau, scene of Indonesia's famous 1883 eruption, was an underwater caldera.

THE EARTH'S STRUCTURE

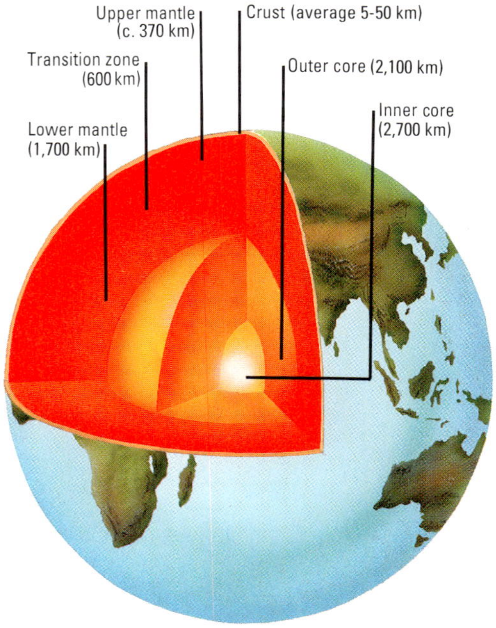

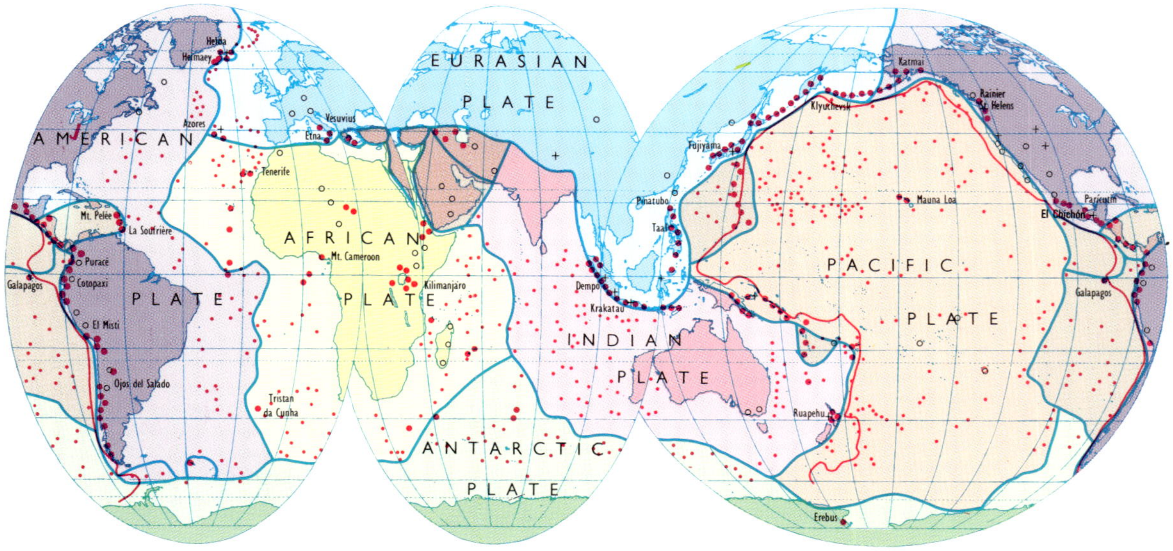

VOLCANOES

- Land volcanoes active since 1700
- Land volcanoes inactive since 1700
- Submarine volcanoes
- Geysers
- Plate boundaries
- Andesite line (boundary between sial continental crust & sima oceanic crust in the Pacific)

Volcanoes can suddenly erupt after lying dormant for centuries: in 1991 Mount Pinatubo, in the Philippines, burst into life after sleeping for more than 600 years.

EARTHQUAKES

- Mobile land areas
- Submarine zones of mobile land areas
- Stable land platforms
- Submarine extensions of stable land platforms
- Mid-oceanic volcanic ridges
- Oceanic platforms
- Principal earthquakes & dates • 1906
- Oceanic marginal troughs

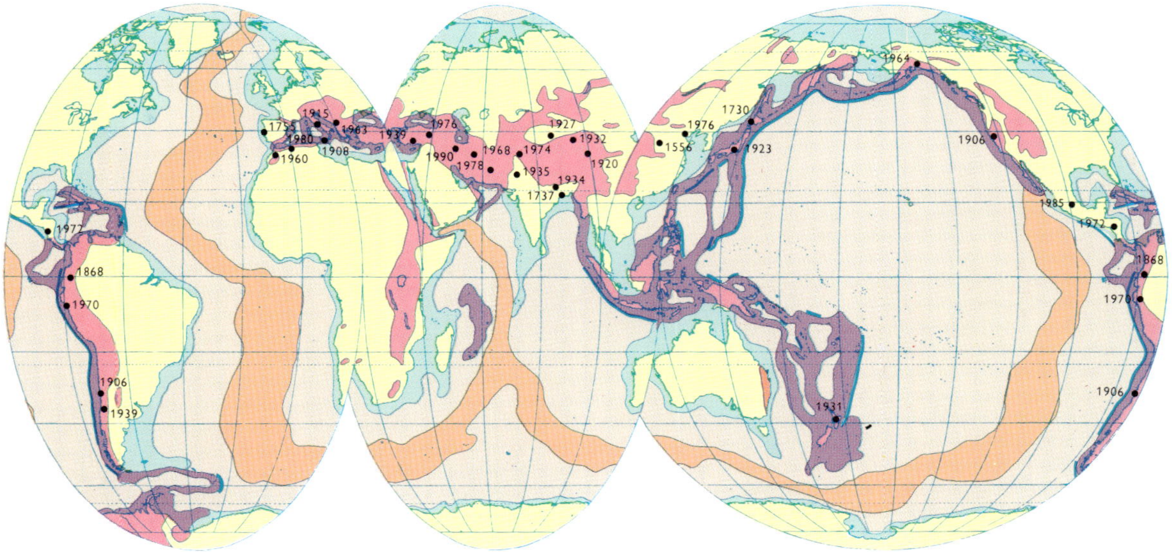

The highest magnitude recorded on the Richter scale was 8.9, in Japan on 2 March 1933 (2,990 deaths). The most devastating quake ever was in Shaanxi (Shensi) province, central China, on 24 January 1566, when an estimated 830,000 people were killed.

CLIMATIC REGIONS

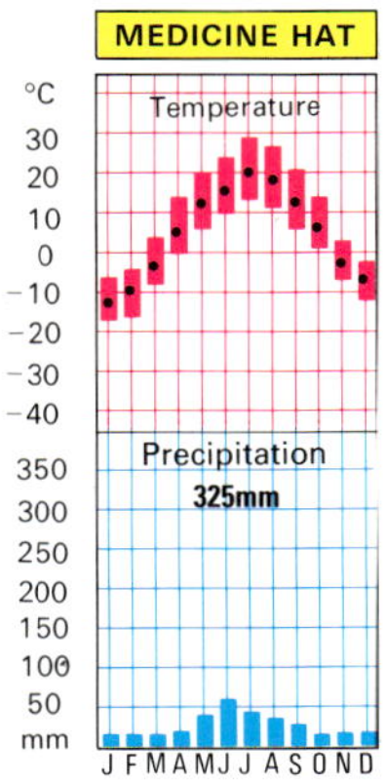

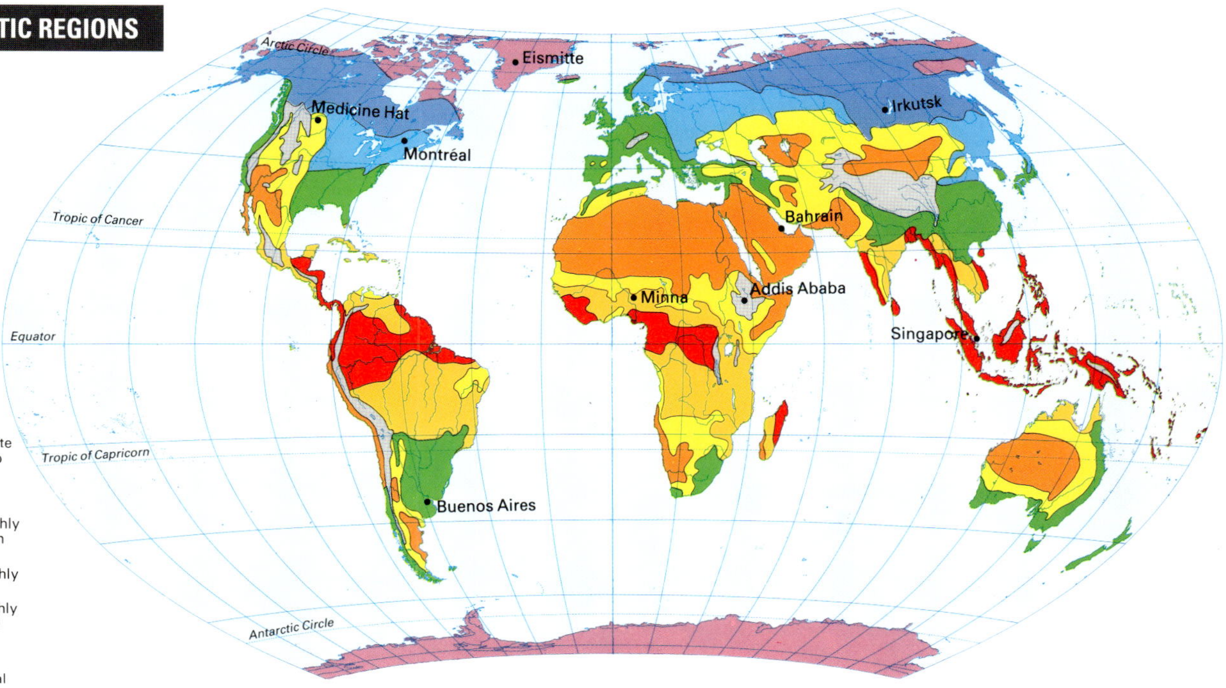

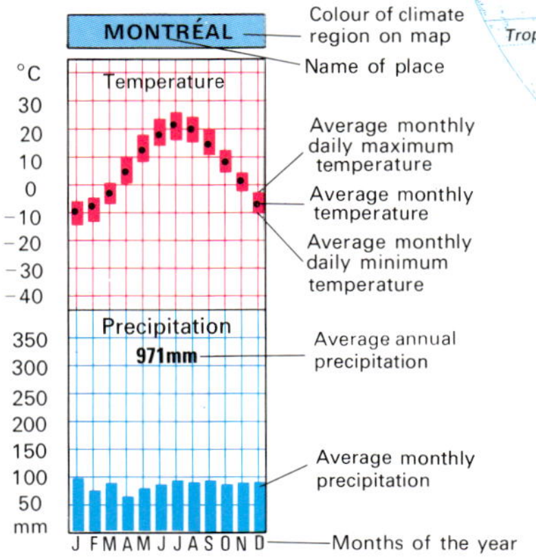

Tropical climate (hot with rain all year)

Savanna climate (hot with dry season)

Steppe climate (warm and dry)

Desert climate (hot and very dry)

Mild climate (warm and wet)

Continental climate (wet with cold winter)

Subarctic climate (very cold winter)

Polar climate (very cold and dry)

Mountainous climate (altitude affects climate)

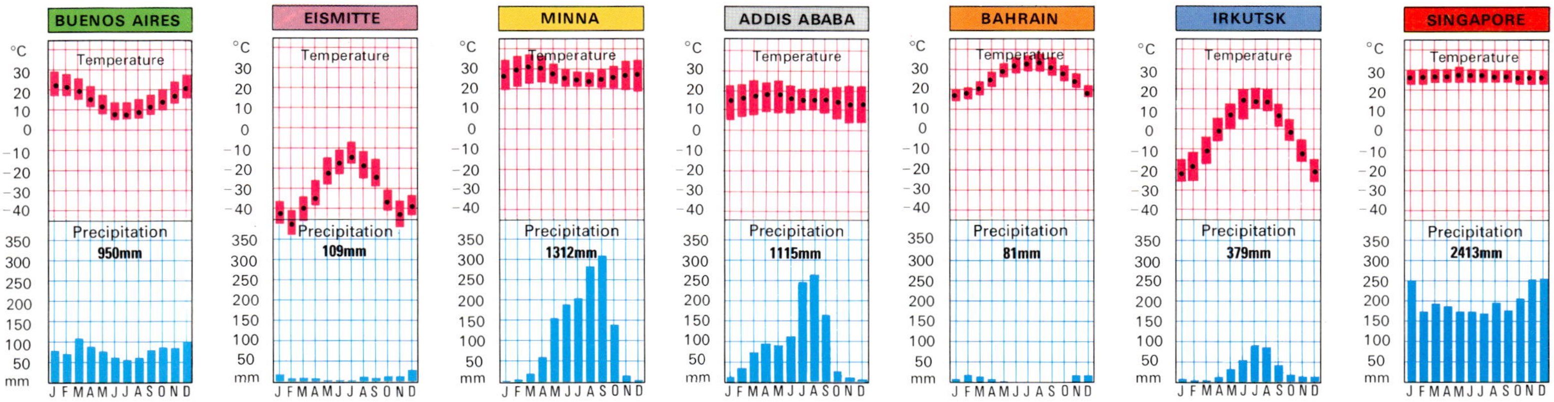

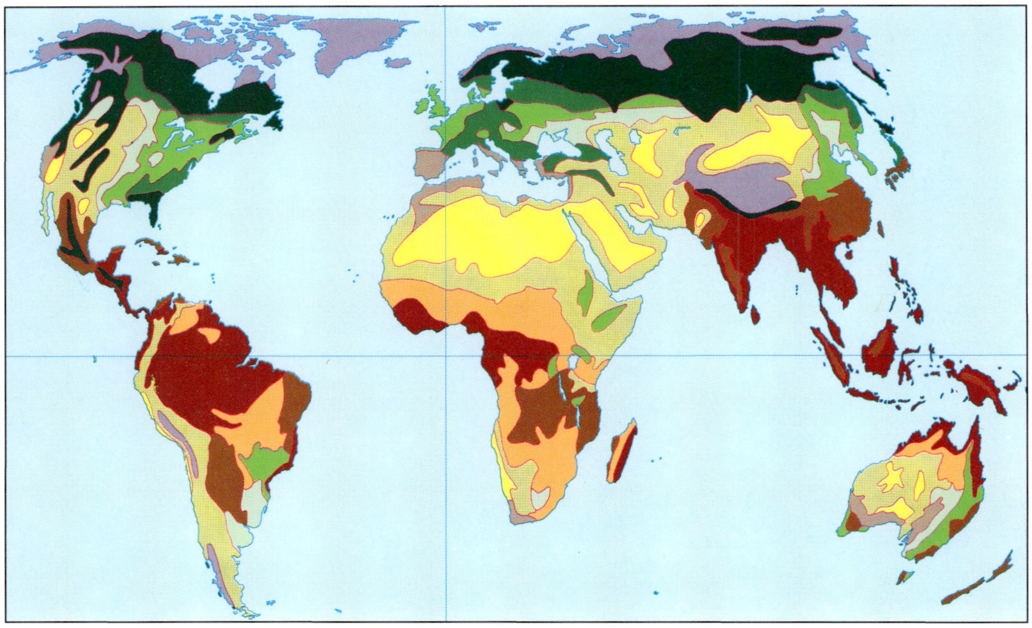

NATURAL VEGETATION

Regional variation in vegetation

- Tundra & mountain vegetation
- Needleleaf evergreen forest
- Mixed needleleaf evergreen & broadleaf deciduous trees
- Broadleaf deciduous woodland
- Mid-latitude grassland
- Evergreen broadleaf & deciduous trees & shrubs
- Semi-desert scrub
- Desert
- Tropical grassland (savanna)
- Tropical broadleaf rainforest & monsoon forest
- Sub-tropical broadleaf & needleleaf forest

ENVIRONMENT

Humans have always had a dramatic effect on their environment, at least since the invention of agriculture almost 10,000 years ago. Generally, the Earth has accepted human interference without obvious ill effects: the complex systems that regulate the global environment have been able to absorb substantial damage while maintaining a stable and comfortable home for the planet's trillions of lifeforms. But advancing human technology and the rapidly-expanding populations it supports are now threatening to overwhelm the Earth's ability to compensate.

Industrial wastes, acid rainfall, desertification and large-scale deforestation: all combine to create environmental change at a rate far faster than the slow cycles of planetary evolution can accommodate. Equipped with chain-saws and flamethrowers, humans can now destroy more forest in a day than their ancestors could in a century, upsetting the balance between plant and animal, carbon dioxide and oxygen, on which all life ultimately depends.

The fossil fuels that power industrial civilisation have pumped enough carbon dioxide and other so-called greenhouse gases into the atmosphere to make climatic change a near-certainty. Chlorofluorocarbons - CFCs - and other man-made chemicals are rapidly eroding the ozone layer, the atmosphere's screen against ultra-violet radiation.

As a result, the Earth's average temperature has risen by approximately 0.5°C since the beginning of the 20th century, and is still rising.

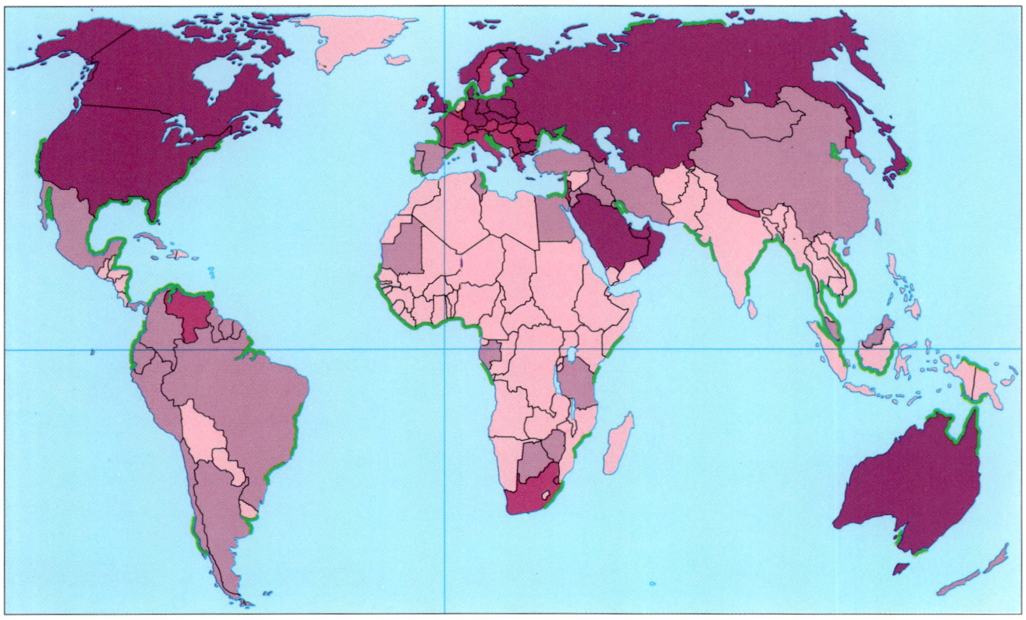

CLIMATIC CHANGE

Carbon dioxide emissions in tonnes per person per year (1980s)

High atmospheric concentrations of heat-absorbing gases, especially carbon dioxide, appear to be causing a steady rise in average temperatures worldwide - up to 1.5°C by the year 2020, according to some estimates. Global warming is likely to bring with it a rise in sea-levels that may flood some of the Earth's most densely populated coastlines.

- Over 10 tonnes of CO_2
- 5 - 10 tonnes of CO_2
- 1 - 5 tonnes of CO_2
- Under 1 tonne of CO_2

- Coastal areas in danger of flooding from rising sea levels caused by global warming

GREENHOUSE POWER

Relative contributions to the Greenhouse Effect by the major heat-absorbing gases in the atmosphere

The chart combines greenhouse potency and volume. Carbon dioxide has a greenhouse potential of only 1 but its concentration of 350 parts per million, makes it predominate. CFC 12 , with 25,000 times the absorption capacity of CO_2, is present only as 0.00044 ppm.

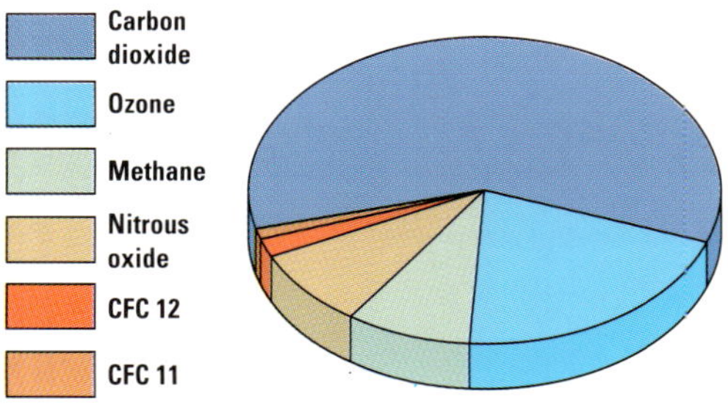

CARBON DIOXIDE

Carbon dioxide released in millions of tonnes (1980s)

Although most of the net increase in atmospheric carbon dioxide comes from fossil fuel combustion, deforestation and changing land use also contribute.

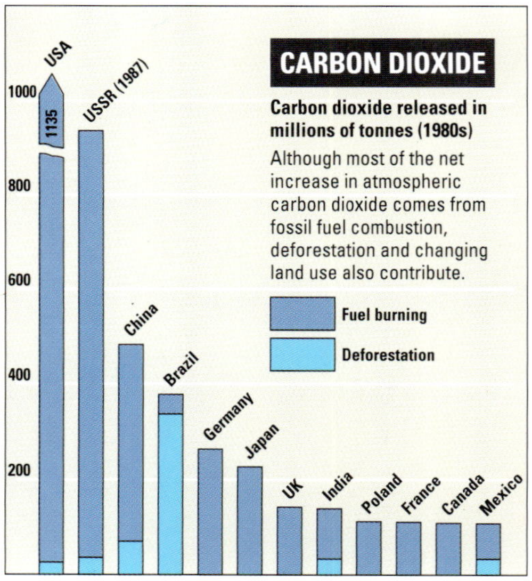

GLOBAL WARMING

The rise in average temperatures caused by carbon dioxide and other greenhouse gases (1960-2020)

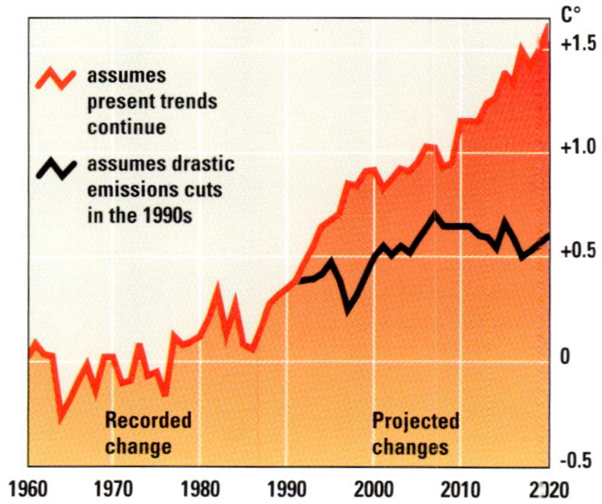

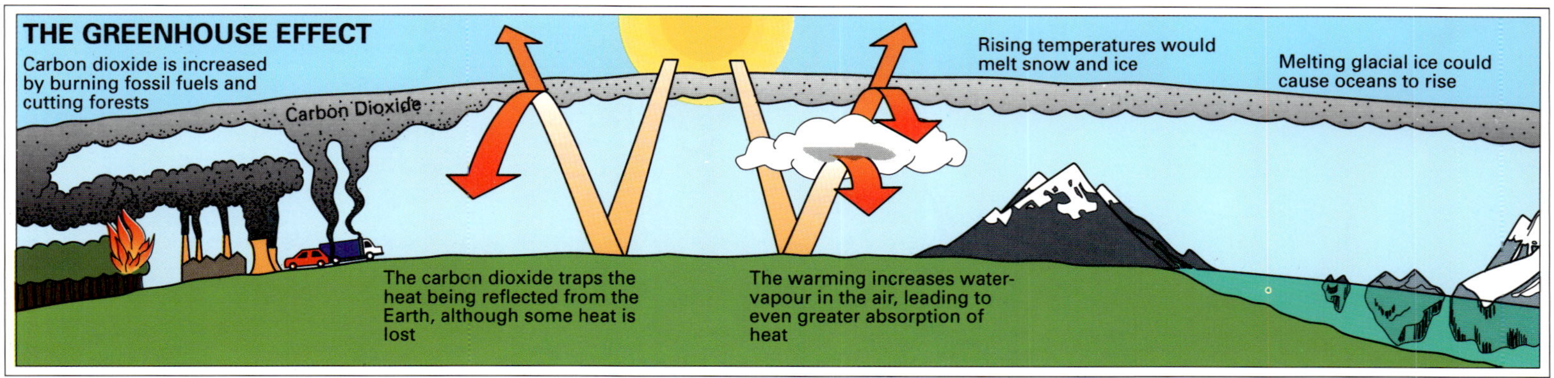

DESERTIFICATION

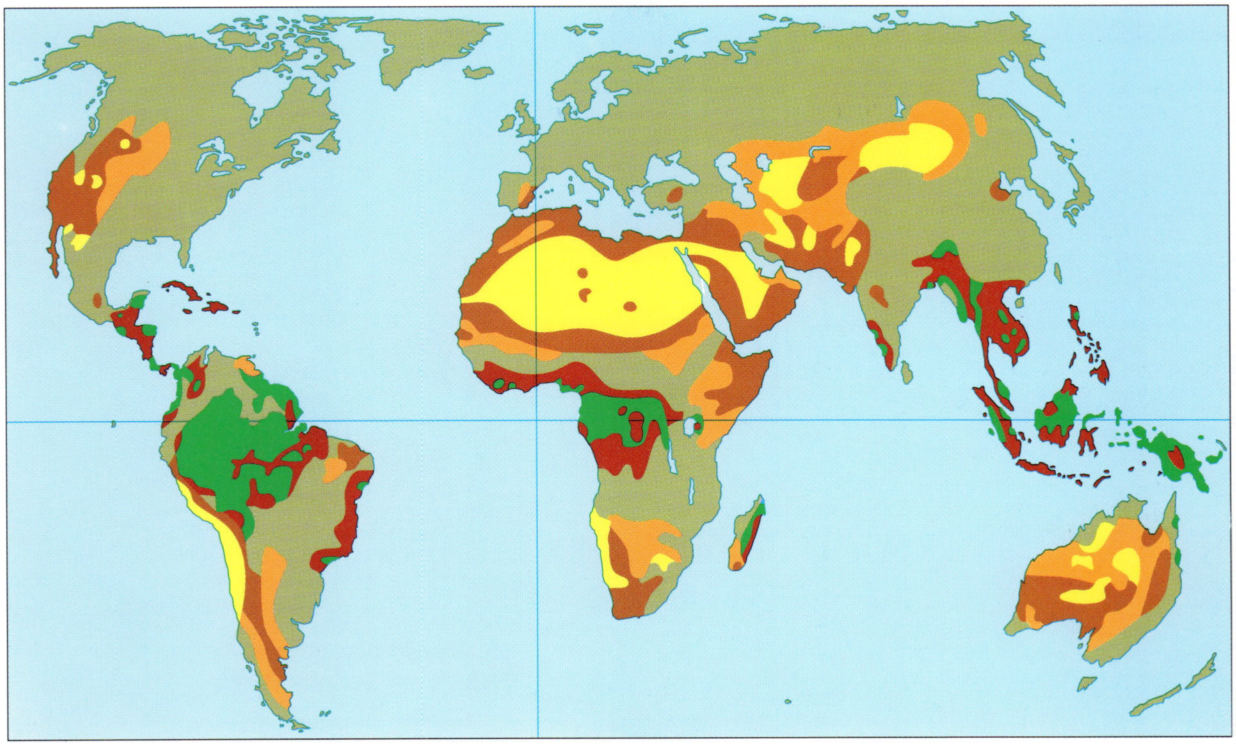

DEFORESTATION

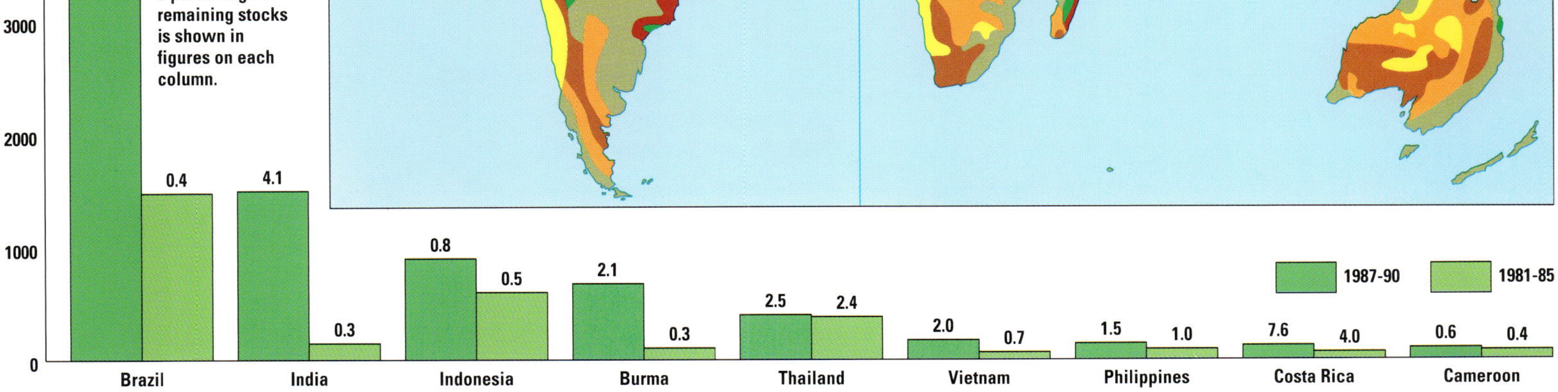

DESERTIFICATION

The result of overcultivation, overgrazing, and overcutting of ground cover for firewood, desertification is also caused by faulty irrigation techniques that leave land too saline or alkaline to support viable crops. Changing rainfall patterns or prolonged droughts exacerbate the process. As much as 60% of the world's croplands and rangelands are in some danger, with 6 million hectares lost altogether every year and a further 21 million rendered agriculturally worthless. Africa is especially badly hit: in Mali the Sahara advanced 350 kilometres southwards in only 20 years.

DEFORESTATION

The Earth's remaining forests are under attack from three directions: expanding agriculture, logging, and growing consumption of fuelwood, often in combination. Sometimes deforestation is the direct result of government policy, as in the efforts made to resettle the urban poor in some parts of Brazil; just as often, it comes about despite state attempts at conservation. Loggers, licensed or unlicensed, blaze a trail into virgin forest, often destroying twice as many trees as they harvest. Landless farmers follow, burning away most of what remains to plant their crops, completing the destruction.

ACID RAIN

Killing trees, poisoning lakes and rivers and eating away buildings, acid rain is mostly produced by sulphur dioxide emissions from industry, although the burning of savanna lands by African farmers has also caused acid downpours on tropical rainforests. By the late 1980s, acid rain had sterilised 4,000 or more of Sweden's lakes and left 45% of Switzerland's alpine conifers dead or dying, while the monuments of Greece were dissolving in Athens' smog. Prevailing wind patterns mean that the acids often fall many hundred kilometres from where the original pollutants were discharged.

ACID RAIN

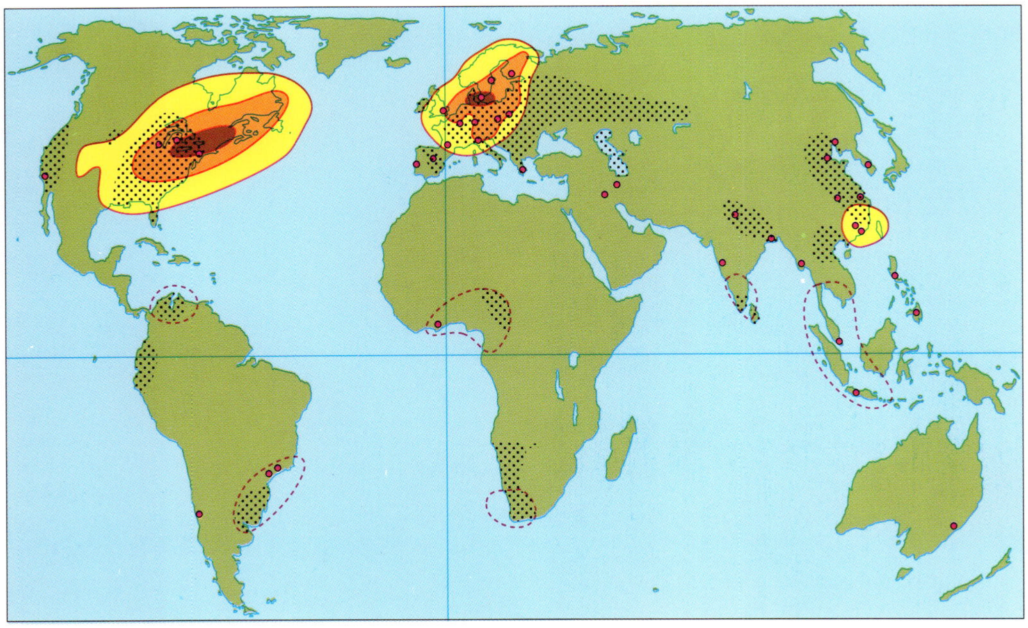

Acid rainfall & sources of acidic emissions (1980s)

Acid rain is caused when sulphur & nitrogen oxides in the air combine with water vapour to form sulphuric, nitric & other acids.

Regions where sulphur and nitrogen oxides are released in high concentrations, mainly from fossil fuel combustion.

Major cities with high levels of air pollution (including nitrogen & sulphur emissions)

Areas of heavy acid deposition

pH numbers indicate acidity, decreasing from a neutral 7. Normal rain, slightly acid from dissolved carbon dioxide, never exceeds a pH of 5.6.

pH less than 4.0 (most acidic)

pH 4.0 to 4.5

pH 4.5 to 5.0

Areas where acid rain is a potential danger

POPULATION

DEMOGRAPHIC PROFILES

Developed nations such as the US have populations evenly spread across age groups and, usually, a growing proportion of elderly people. Developing nations fall into a pattern somewhere between that of Kenya and the world model: the great majority of their people are in the younger age groups, about to enter their most fertile years. In time, even Kenya's population profile should resemble the world profile, but the transition will come about only after a few more generations of rapid population growth.

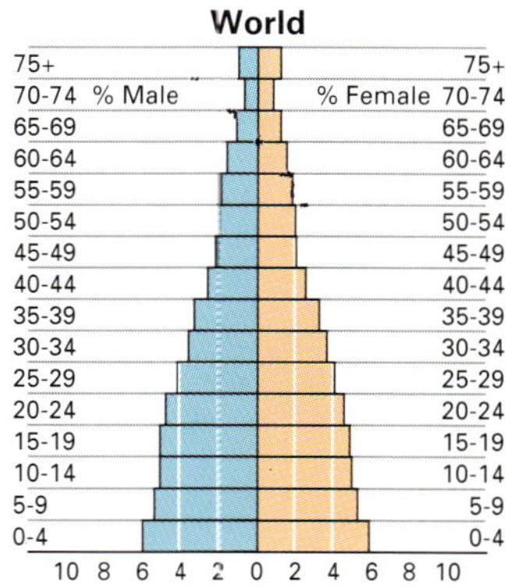

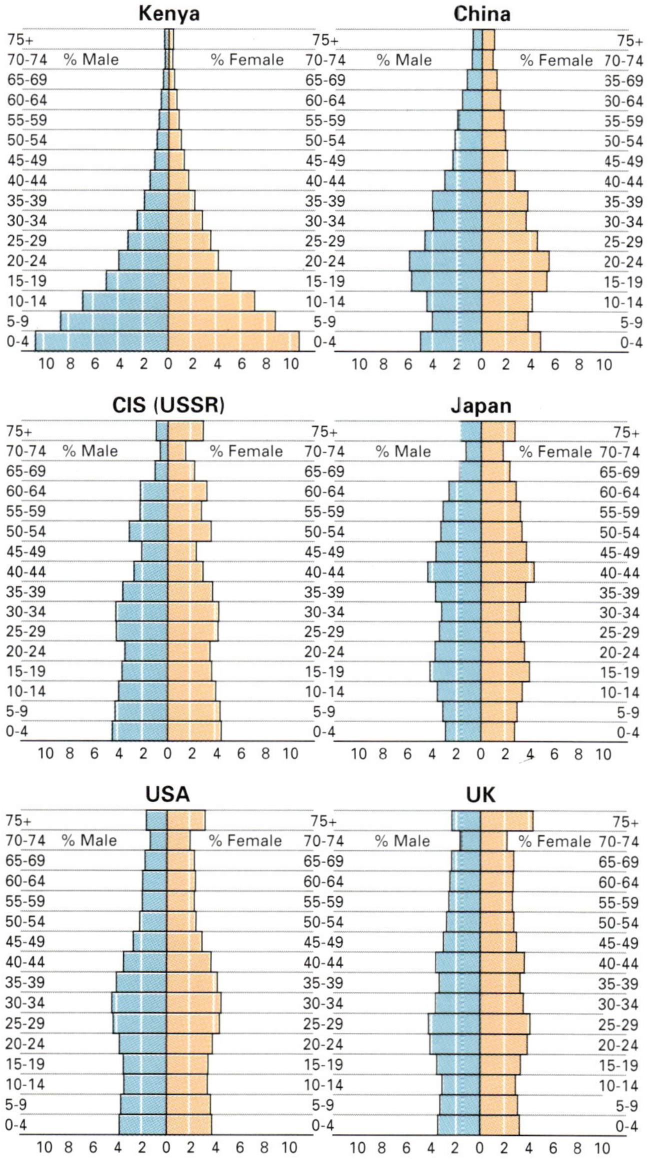

MOST POPULOUS NATIONS [in millions (1989)]

1. China	1120	9. Pakistan	109	17. Turkey	57
2. India	812	10. Bangladesh	107	18. France	56
3. USA	250	11. Mexico	84	19. Thailand	55
4. Indonesia	179	12. Germany	79	20. Iran	55
5. Brazil	148	13. Vietnam	66	21. Egypt	53
6. Russia	147	14. Philippines	60	22. Ukraine	52
7. Japan	123	15. Italy	58	23. Ethiopia	51
8. Nigeria	109	16. UK	57	24. S. Korea	43

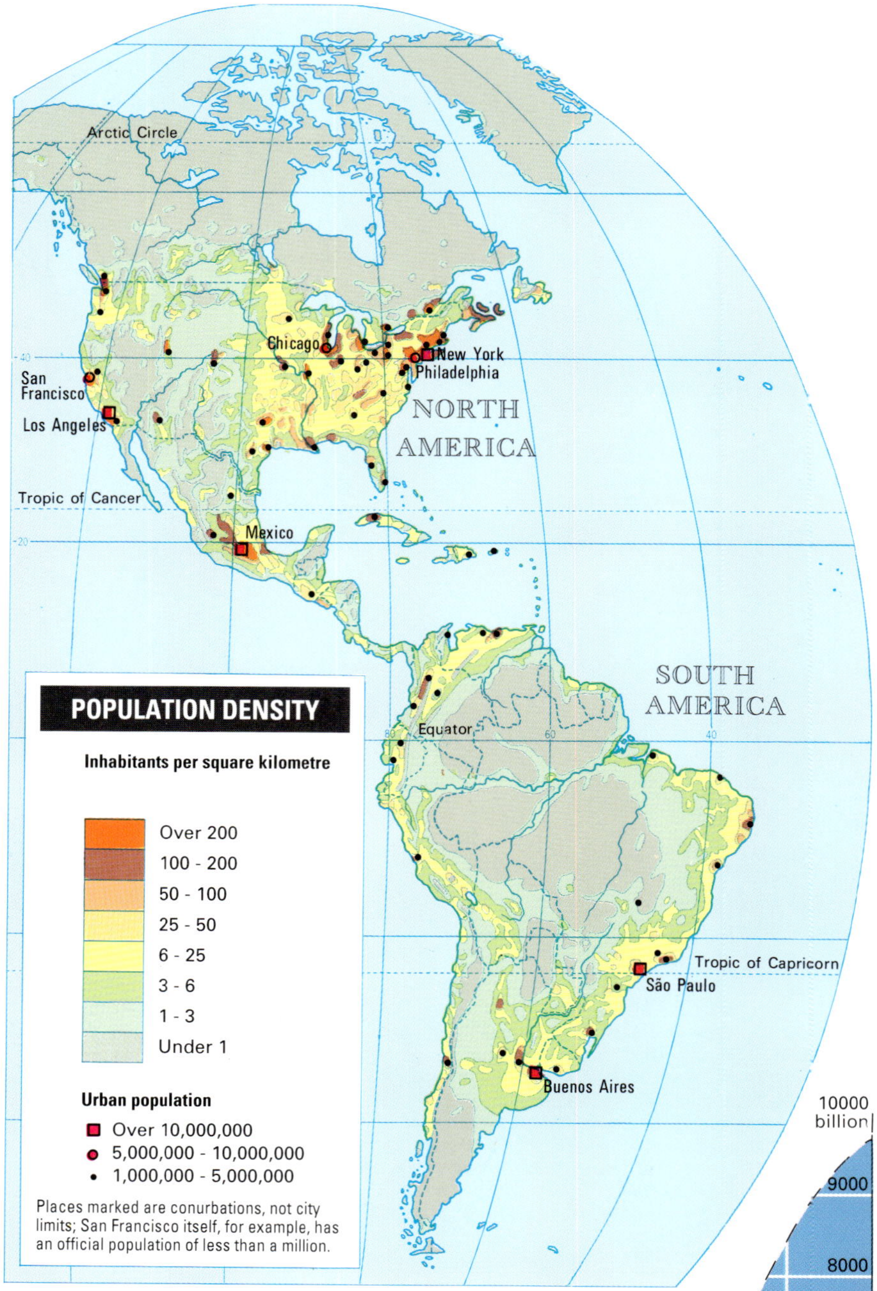

CONTINENTAL COMPARISONS

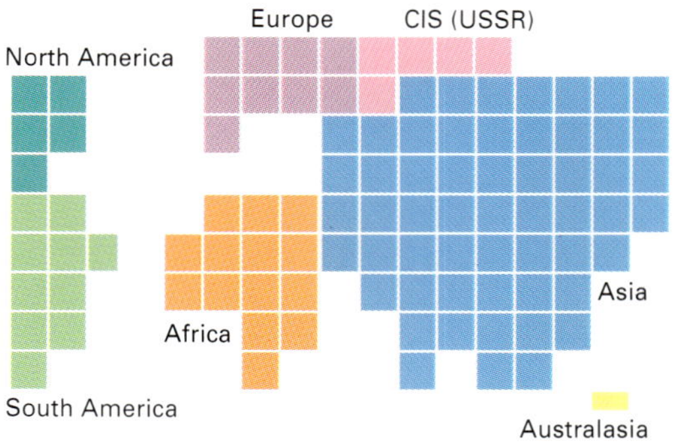

Each square in the diagram above represents 1% of the world total (1990)

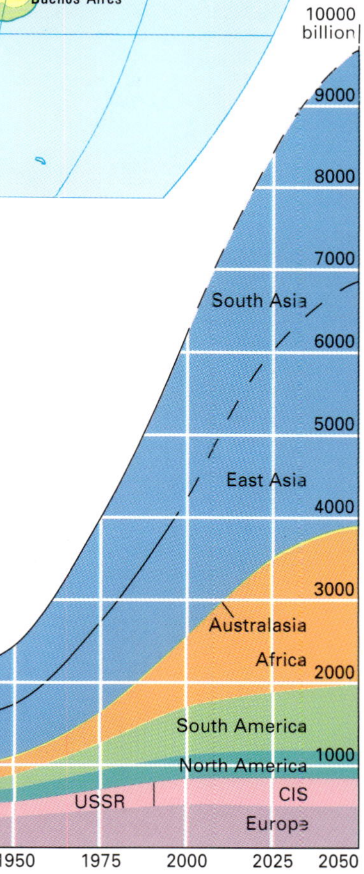

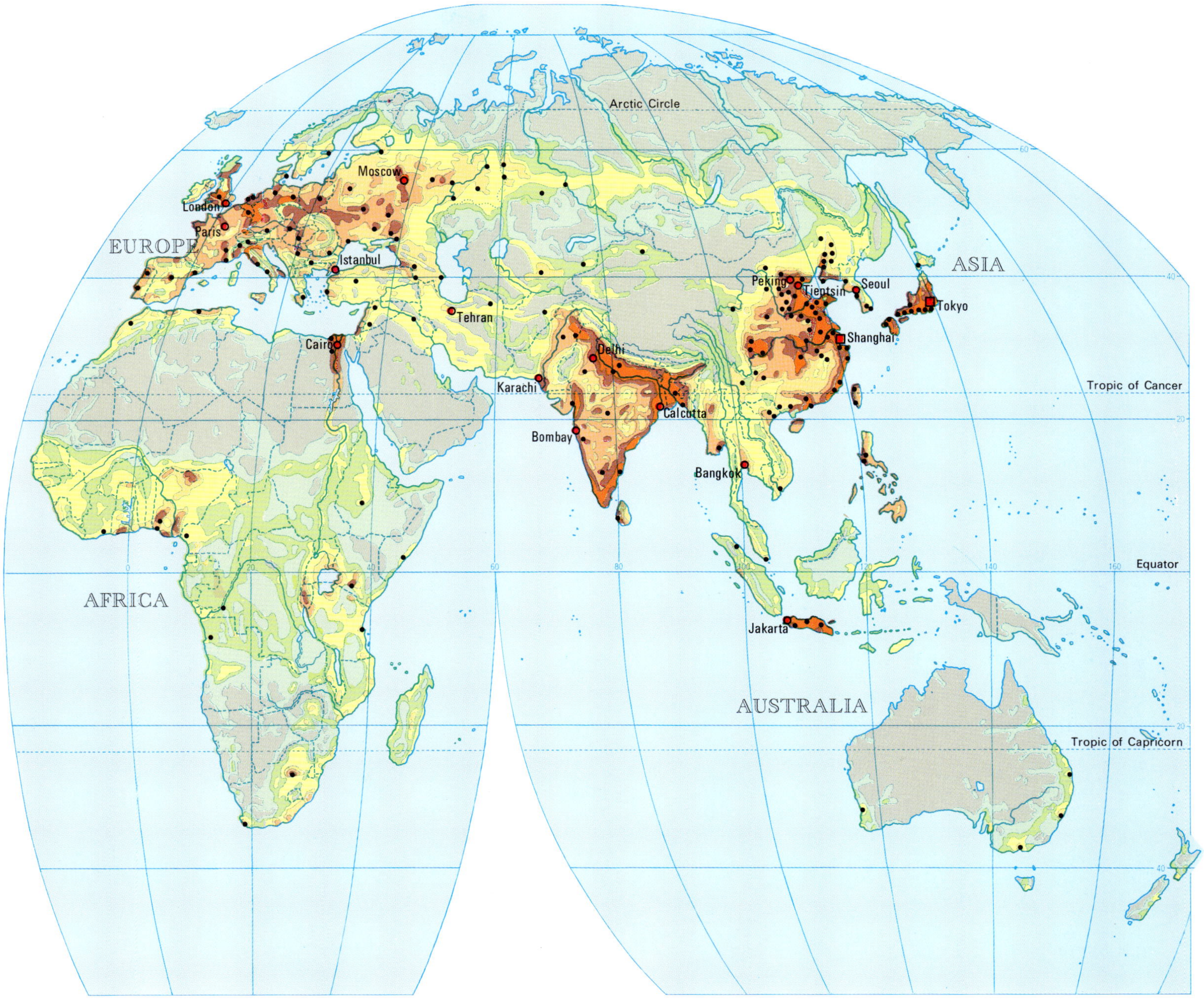

URBAN POPULATION

Percentage of total population living in towns & cities (1990)

Over 75%
50 - 75%
25 - 50%
10 - 25%
Under 10%

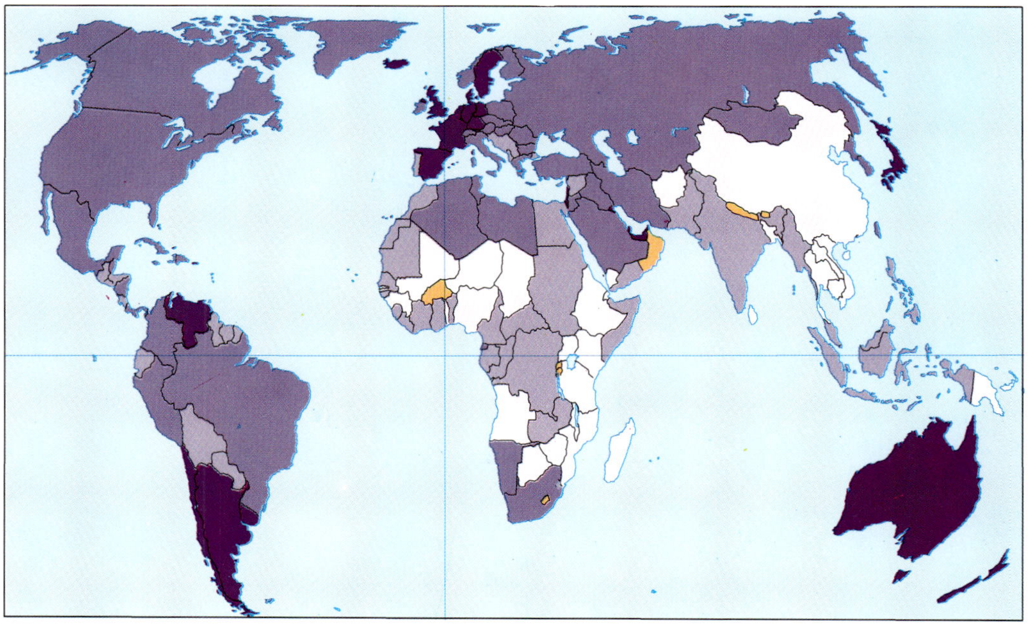

Highest urban population*		**Lowest urban population**	
Macau	98.7%	Bhutan	5.3%
Belgium	96.9%	Burundi	7.3%
Kuwait	95.6%	Rwanda	7.7%
Hong Kong	93.2%	Burkina Faso	9.0%
UK	92.5%	Nepal	9.6%
Israel	91.6%	Oman	10.0%
Iceland	90.5%	Uganda	10.4%

* Several small countries, including Bermuda, Monaco, Singapore & Vatican City, are designated as '100% urban'

The Human Family

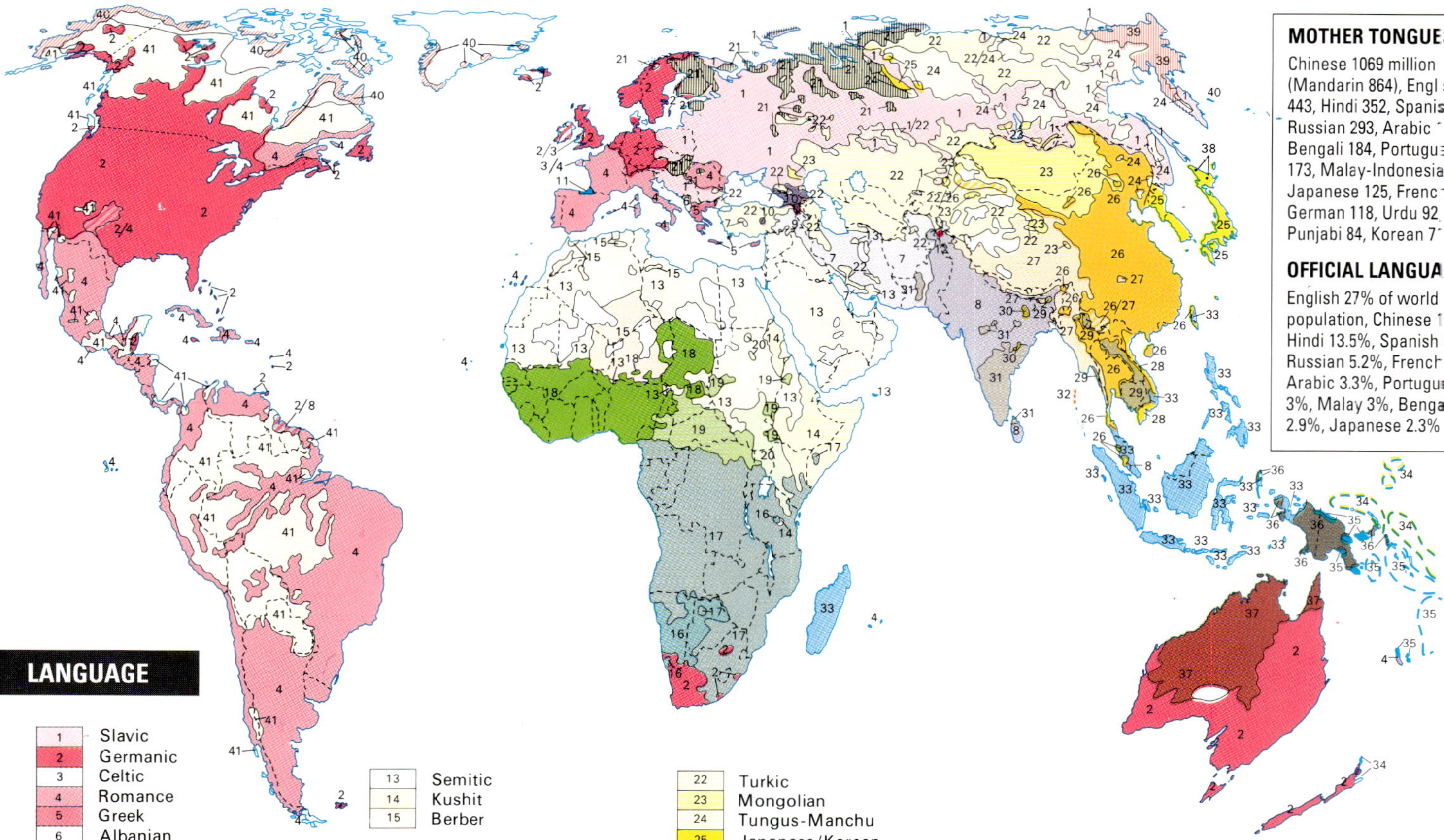

LANGUAGE

Key	Language family
1	Slavic
2	Germanic
3	Celtic
4	Romance
5	Greek
6	Albanian
7	Iranian
8	Indo-Aryan
9	Armenian
10	Caucasian
11	Basque
12	Burushaskis
13	Semitic
14	Kushit
15	Berber
16	Khoisan
17	Bantu
18	Sudanese
19	E & C Sudan
20	Nilotic
21	Ural
22	Turkic
23	Mongolian
24	Tungus-Manchu
25	Japanese/Korean
26	Sinitic and other
27	Tibeto-Burman
28	Vietnamese
29	Mon-Khmer
30	Munda
31	Dravidian
32	Andamanese
33	Indonesian
34	Polynesian
35	Melanesian
36	Papuan
37	Australian Abor.
•38•	Ainu
39	Paleoasiatic
40	Eskimo-Aleut
41	Amerindian

MOTHER TONGUES

Chinese 1069 million (Mandarin 864), English 443, Hindi 352, Spanish 341, Russian 293, Arabic 197, Bengali 184, Portuguese 173, Malay-Indonesian 142, Japanese 125, French 121, German 118, Urdu 92, Punjabi 84, Korean 71.

OFFICIAL LANGUAGES

English 27% of world population, Chinese 19%, Hindi 13.5%, Spanish 5.4%, Russian 5.2%, French 4.2%, Arabic 3.3%, Portuguese 3%, Malay 3%, Bengali 2.9%, Japanese 2.3%

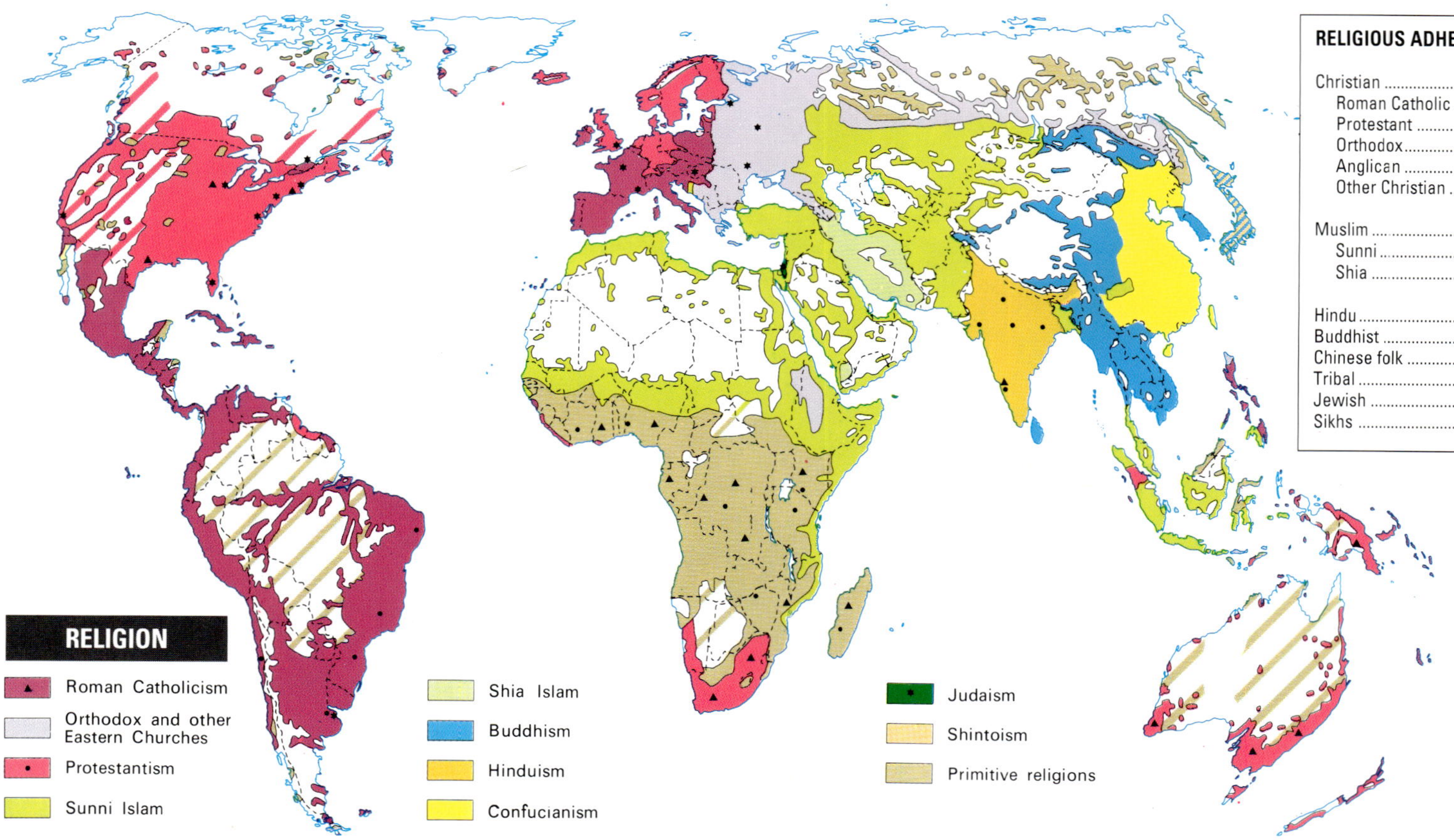

RELIGION

- Roman Catholicism
- Orthodox and other Eastern Churches
- Protestantism
- Sunni Islam
- Shia Islam
- Buddhism
- Hinduism
- Confucianism
- Judaism
- Shintoism
- Primitive religions

RELIGIOUS ADHERENTS

Christian	1667m
Roman Catholic	952m
Protestant	337m
Orthodox	162m
Anglican	70m
Other Christian	148m
Muslim	881m
Sunni	841m
Shia	40m
Hindu	663m
Buddhist	312m
Chinese folk	172m
Tribal	92m
Jewish	18m
Sikhs	17m

UNITED NATIONS

Created in 1945 to promote peace and cooperation and based in New York, the United Nations is the world's largest international organization, with over 160 members and an annual budget exceeding two billion US dollars. Each member of the General Assembly has one vote, while the permanent members of the 15-nation Security Council - USA, Russia, China, UK and France - hold a veto. The 54 members of the Economic and Social Council are responsible for economic, social, cultural, educational, health and related matters. The Secretariat is the UN's chief administrative arm; the only territory now administered by the Trusteeship Council is Belau (by the USA). The UN has 24 specialized agencies - based in Canada, France, Switzerland and Italy as well as the USA - which help members in fields such as economic development (UNDP), education (UNESCO), agriculture (FAO) and medicine (WHO).

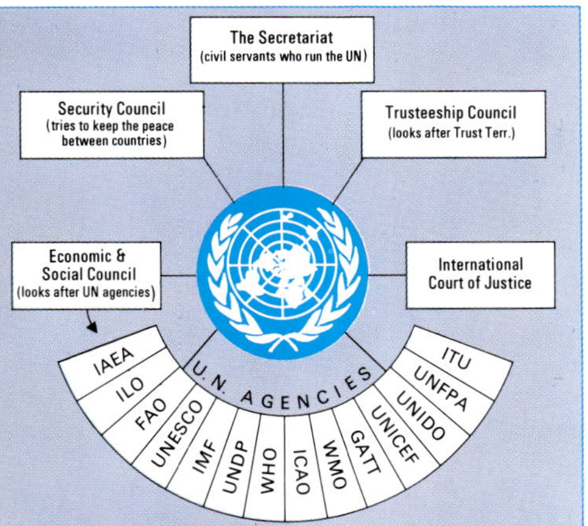

[The International Court of Justice is based in The Hague]

Membership: There are 13 independent states who are not members of the UN - Andorra, Kiribati, Liechtenstein, N. Korea, S. Korea, Monaco, Nauru, San Marino, Switzerland, Taiwan, Tonga, Tuvalu and Vatican City. By 1992, the successor states of the former USSR had either joined or planned to. There were 51 members in 1945. Official languages are Chinese, English, French, Russian, Spanish and Arabic.
Funding: The UN budget for 1988-1989 was US $ 1,788,746,000. Contributions are assessed by members' ability to pay, with the maximum 25% of the total, the minimum 0.01%. Contributions for 1988-1989 were: USA 25%, Japan 11.38%, USSR 9.99%, W. Germany 8.08%, France 6.25%, UK 4.86%, Italy 3.99%, Canada 3.09%, Spain 1.95%, Netherlands 1.65% (others 23.75%).
Peacekeeping: The UN has been involved in 18 peacekeeping operations worldwide since 1945, five of which (Afghanistan/Pakistan, Iran/Iraq, Angola, Namibia and Honduras) were initiated in 1988-1989. In June 1991 UN personnel totalling over 11,000 were working in eight separate areas.

EFTA: European Free Trade Association (formed in 1960). Portugal left the 'Seven' in 1989 to join the EEC.
ACP: African-Caribbean-Pacific (1963).
COMECON: Council for Mutual Economic Assistance. Founded in 1949 by Joseph Stalin, it has been largely moribund since the political upheavals of 1989-92.

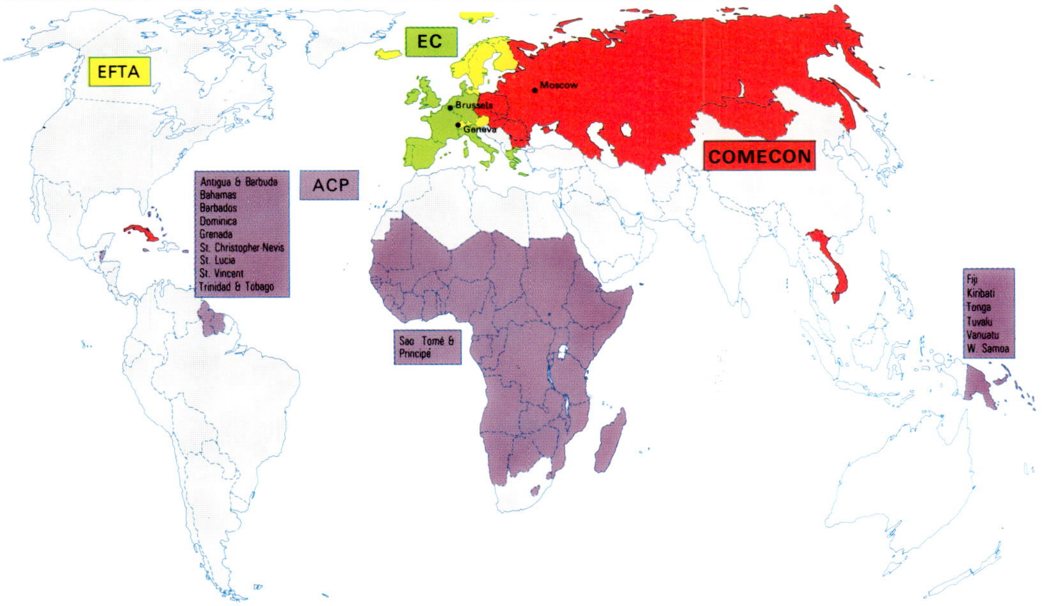

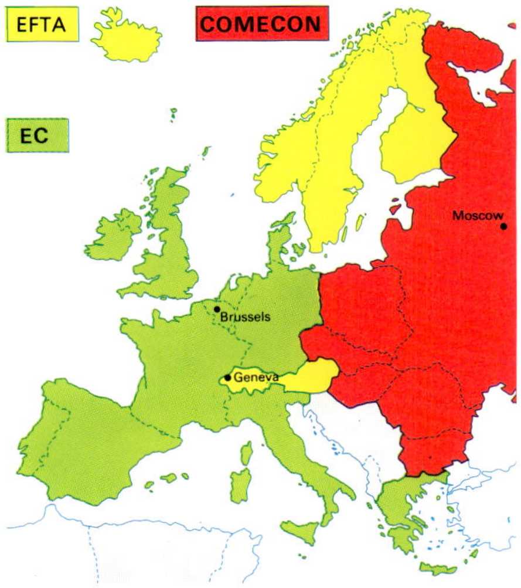

EC: European Community (1957). The original 'Common Market' now aims to integrate economies, coordinate social developments and bring about political union. Members of what is now the world's biggest market share agricultural and industrial policies and tariffs on trade. Over 60 ACP nations are affiliated under the Lomé Convention of 1975.

NATO: North Atlantic Treaty Organization (formed 1949). It continues after 1991 despite the winding up of the Warsaw Pact.
OAU: Organization of African Unity (1963). Its 52 members represent over 90% of Africa's population.
ASEAN: Association of South-East Asian Nations (1967).
OAS: Organization of American States (1949). It aims to promote social and economic cooperation between developed countries of North America and developing nations of Latin America.
LAIA: Latin American Integration Association (1980).
OECD: Organization for Economic Cooperation and Development (1961). The 24 major Western free-market economies plus Yugoslavia as associate member. 'G7' is its 'inner group' of USA, Canada, Japan, UK, Germany, Italy and France.
COMMONWEALTH: The Commonwealth of Nations evolved from the British Empire; it comprises 18 nations recognizing the British monarch as head of state and 32 with their own heads of state.
OPEC: Organization of Petroleum Exporting Countries (1960). It controls about three-quarters of the world's oil supply.

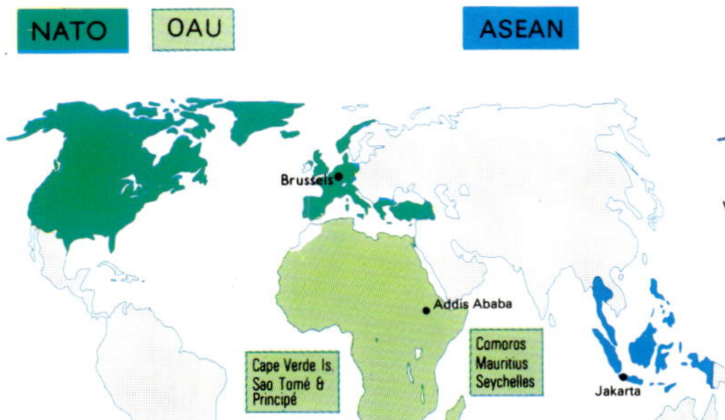

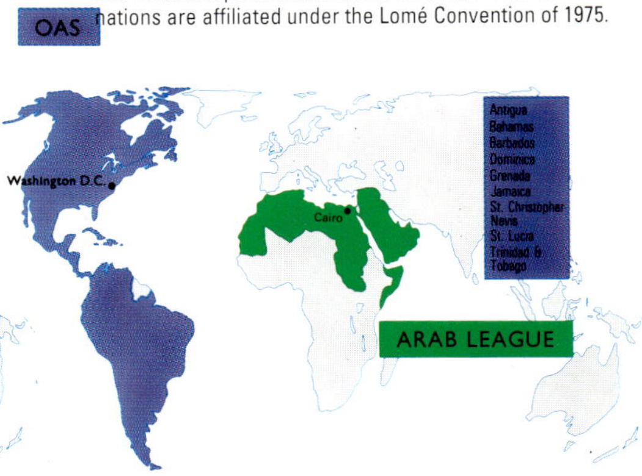

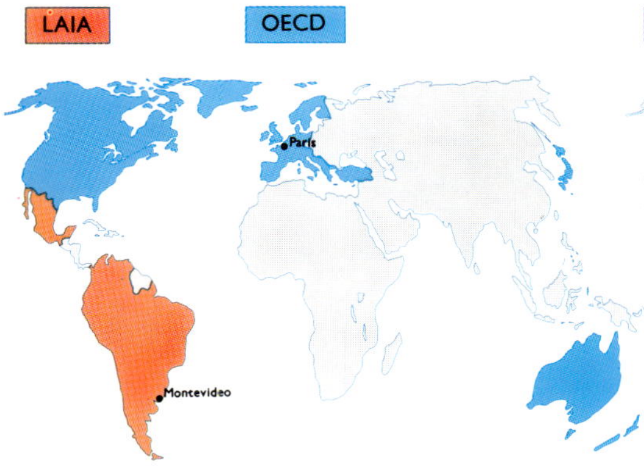

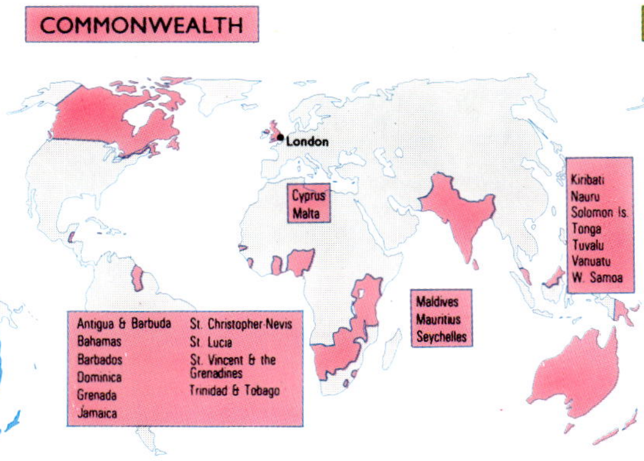

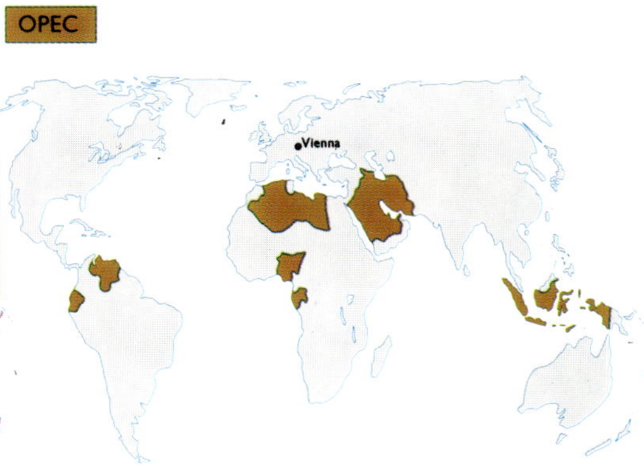

Standards of Living

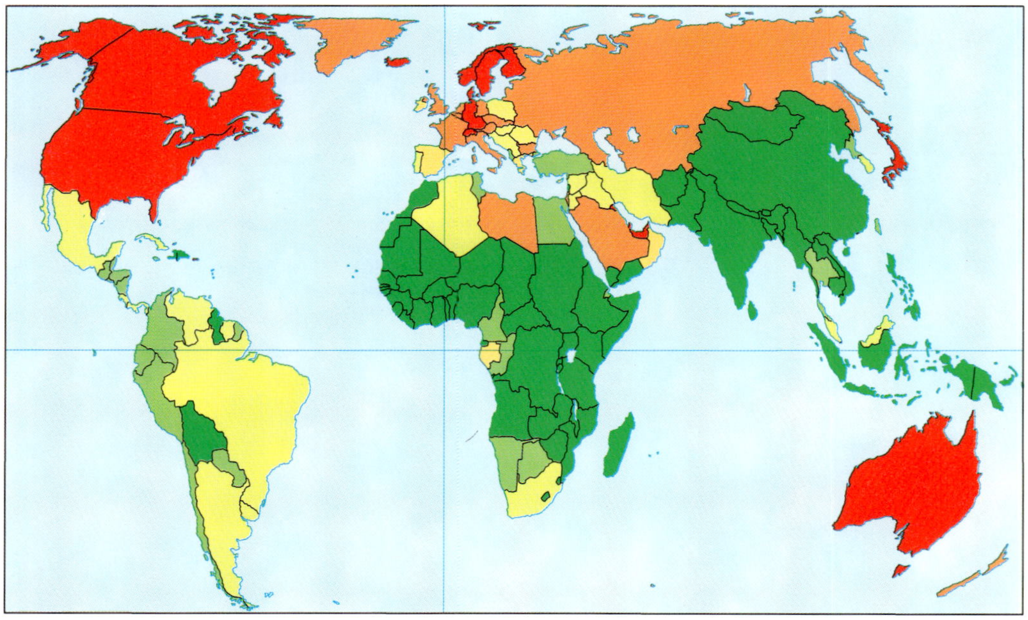

LEVELS OF INCOME

Gross National Product : the value of total production divided by population (1986)

- Over 400% of world average
- 200 - 400% of world average
- 100 - 200% of world average

[World average wealth per person US $2,940]

- 50 - 100% of world average
- 25 - 50% of world average
- Under 25% of world average

WEALTH CREATION

The Gross National Product (GNP) of the world's largest economies, US $ billion (1989)

1. USA	5,237,707	21. Denmark	105,263
2. Japan	2,920,310	22. Norway	92,097
3. Germany	1,272,959	23. Saudi Arabia	89,986
4. France	1,000,866	24. Indonesia	87,936
5. Italy	871,955	25. South Africa	86,029
6. UK	834,166	26. Turkey	74,731
7. Canada	500,337	27. Argentina	68,780
8. China	393,006	28. Poland	66,974
9. Brazil	375,146	29. Thailand	64,437
10. Spain	358,352	30. Hong Kong	59,202
11. India	287,383	31. Yugoslavia	59,080
12. Australia	242,131	32. Greece	53,626
13. Netherlands	237,451	33. Algeria	53,116
14. Switzerland	197,984	34. Venezuela	47,164
15. South Korea	186,467	35. Israel	44,131
16. Sweden	184,230	36. Portugal	44,058
17. Mexico	170,053	37. Philippines	42,754
18. Belgium	162,026	38. Pakistan	40,134
19. Austria	131,899	39. New Zealand	39,437
20. Finland	109,705	40. Colombia	38,607

There are no accurate figures available for either the USSR or its successor nations.

THE WEALTH GAP

The world's richest & poorest countries, by Gross National Product per capita in US $ (1989)

1. Liechtenstein	33,000	1. Mozambique	80
2. Switzerland	30,270	2. Ethiopia	120
3. Bermuda	25,000	3. Tanzania	120
4. Luxembourg	24,860	4. Laos	170
5. Japan	23,730	5. Nepal	170
6. Finland	22,060	6. Somalia	170
7. Norway	21,850	7. Bangladesh	180
8. Sweden	21,710	8. Malawi	180
9. Iceland	21,240	9. Bhutan	190
10. USA	21,100	10. Chad	190
11. Denmark	20,510	11. Sierra Leone	200
12. Canada	19,020	12. Burundi	220
13. UAE	18,430	13. Gambia	230
14. France	17,830	14. Madagascar	230
15. Austria	17,360	15. Nigeria	250
16. Germany	16,500	16. Uganda	250
17. Belgium	16,390	17. Mali	260
18. Kuwait	16,380	18. Zaire	260
19. Netherlands	16,010	19. Niger	290
20. Italy	15,150	20. Burkina Faso	310

GNP per capita is calculated by dividing a country's Gross National Product by its population. The UK ranks 21st, with US $14,570.

CONTINENTAL SHARES

Shares of population and of wealth (GNP) by continent

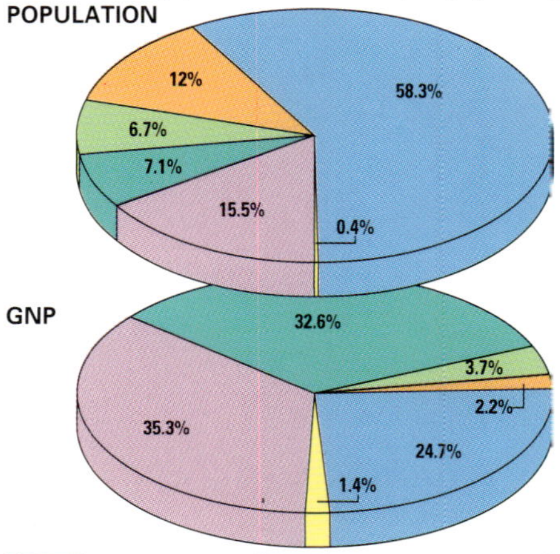

Europe · Asia · South America · Australia · Africa · North America

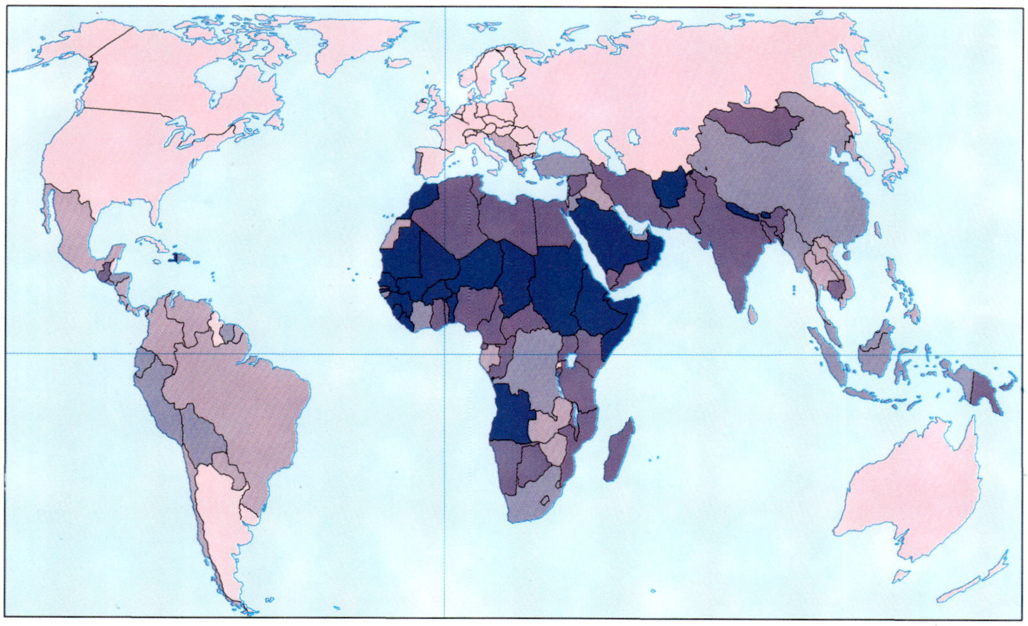

LITERACY

Percentage of adult population unable to read or write (1988)

- Over 75%
- 50 - 75%
- 25 - 50%
- 10 - 15%
- Under 10%

Highest illiteracy

Somalia	88%
Burkina Faso	87%
Niger	86%
Mali	83%
Mauritania	83%
Yemen	82%
Chad	78%
Benin	76%
Nepal	76%

Highest female illiteracy

Yemen	97%
Burkina Faso	94%
Somalia	94%
Niger	91%
Chad	89%
Mali	89%
Nepal	88%
Benin	84%
Guinea	83%

DISTRIBUTION OF SPENDING

Percentage share of household spending

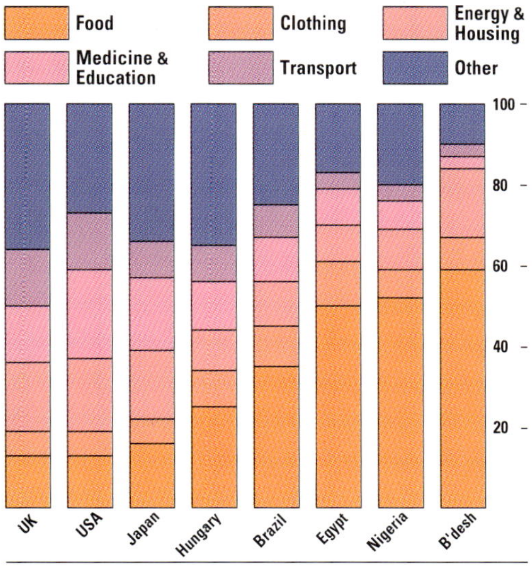

AIDS

Cases reported up to 1990, per 100,000 population, selected countries

[UK: 5.7]

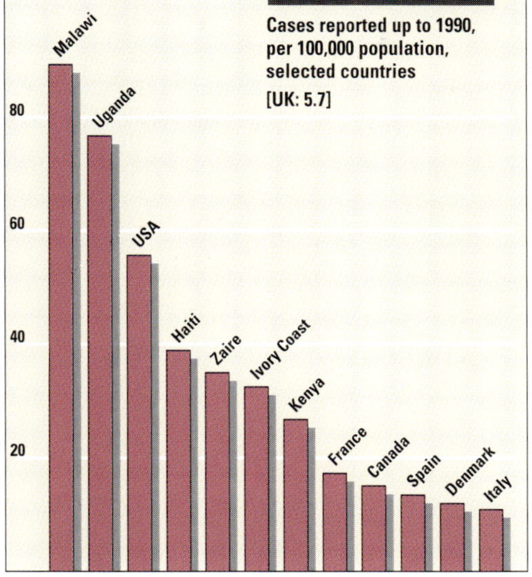

INFECTIOUS DISEASE

Deaths from infectious disease, per 100,000 people, selected countries (latest figures, 1983-88)

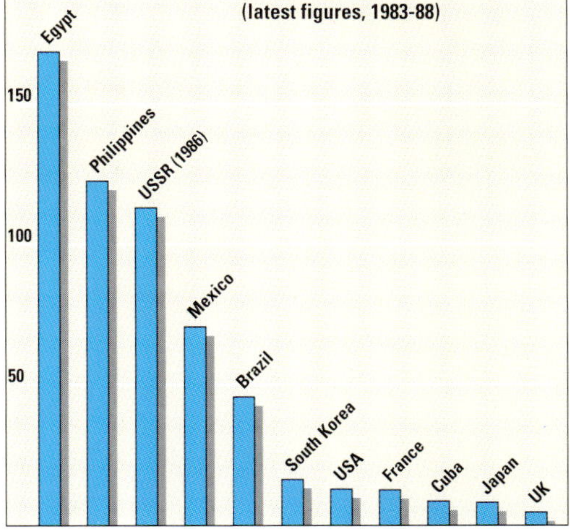

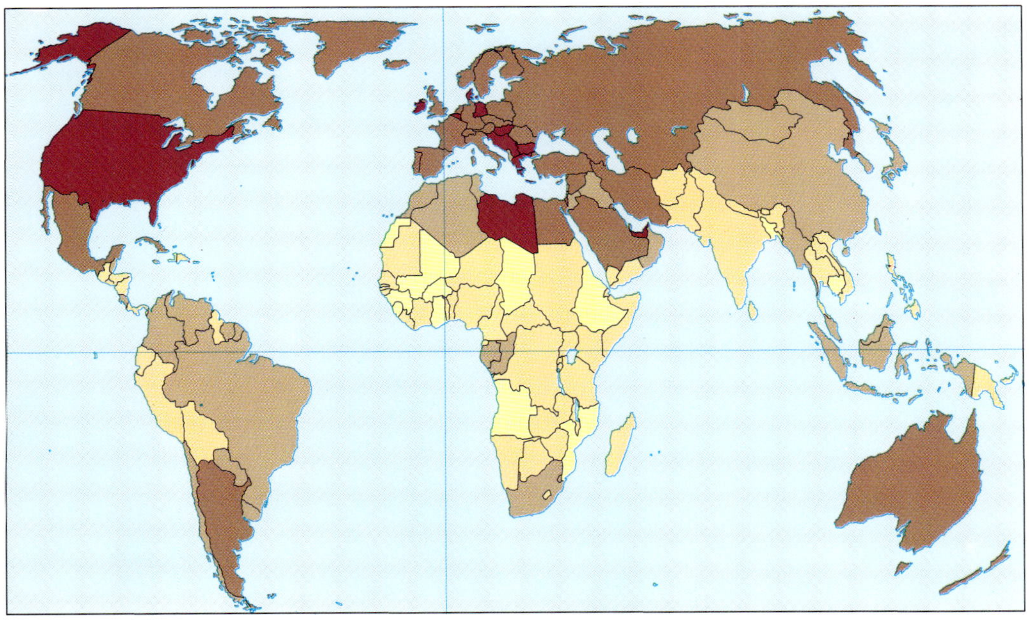

FOOD CONSUMPTION

Average daily food intake per person in kilocalories (1988)

Over 3,500

3,000 - 3,500

2,500 - 3,000

2,000 - 2,500

Under 2,000

Highest intake		Lowest intake	
Germany	3,814	C. African Rep.	1,040
UAE	3,733	Mozambique	1,595
Greece	3,688	Chad	1,717
USA	3,645	Ethiopia	1,749
Bulgaria	3,642	Guinea	1,776
Denmark	3,633	Rwanda	1,830
Ireland	3,632	Sierra Leone	1,854
Libya	3,601	Angola	1,880
Hungary	3,569	Haiti	1,902

EDUCATION

Percentage of age group in secondary school, selected countries (1987)

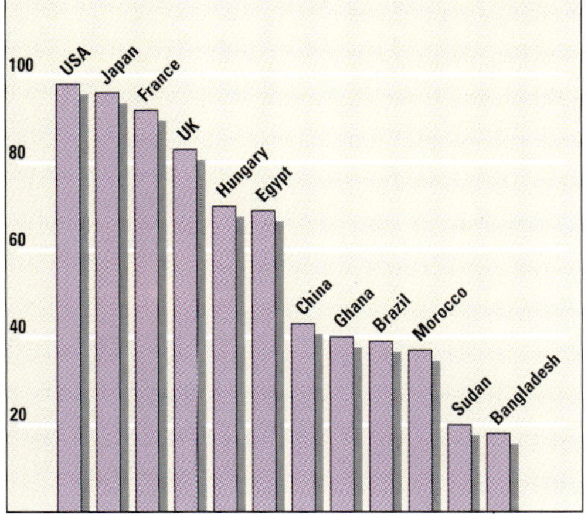

HOSPITAL CAPACITY

Hospital beds available for each 1000 people, (latest available year (1983-1988)

Highest capacity		Lowest capacity	
Finland	14.9	Bangladesh	0.2
Sweden	13.2	Nepal	0.2
France	12.9	Ethiopia	0.3
USSR (1986)	12.8	Mauritania	0.4
Netherlands	12.0	Mali	0.5
North Korea	11.7	Burkina Faso	0.6
Switzerland	11.3	Pakistan	0.6
Austria	10.4	Niger	0.7
Czechoslovakia	10.1	Haiti	0.8
Hungary	9.1	Chad	0.8

[UK 8] [USA 5.9]

Although the ratio of people to hospital beds gives a good approximation of a country's health provision, it is not an absolute indicator. Raw numbers may mask inefficiency and other weaknesses: the high availability of beds in North Korea, for example, has not prevented infant mortality rates almost three times as high as in the United Kingdom.

LIFE EXPECTANCY

Years of life expectancy at birth, selected countries (1988-89)

The chart shows combined data for both sexes. On average, women live longer than men worldwide, even in developing countries with high maternal mortality rates. Overall, life expectancy is steadily rising, though the difference between rich and poor nations remains dramatic.

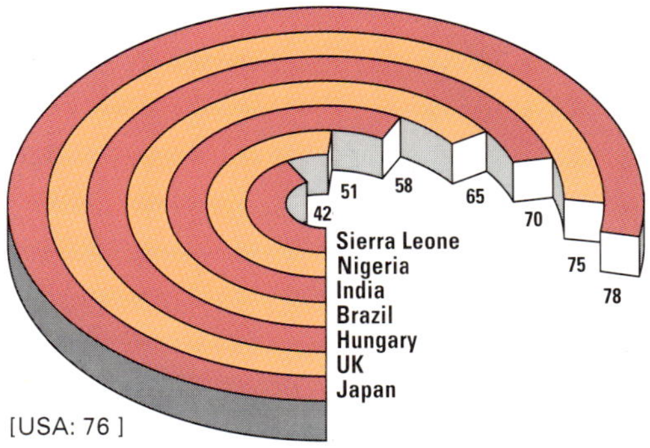

[USA: 76]

ENERGY

PRODUCTION

[Each square represents 1% of world energy production]

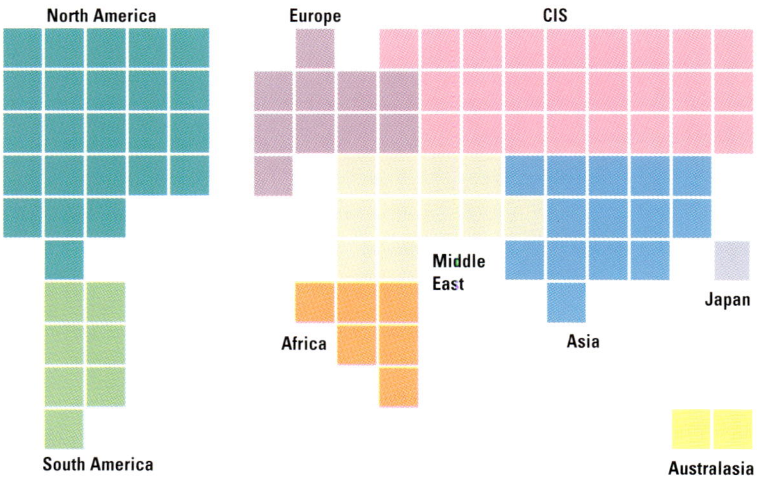

CONSUMPTION

[Each square represents 1% of world energy consumption]

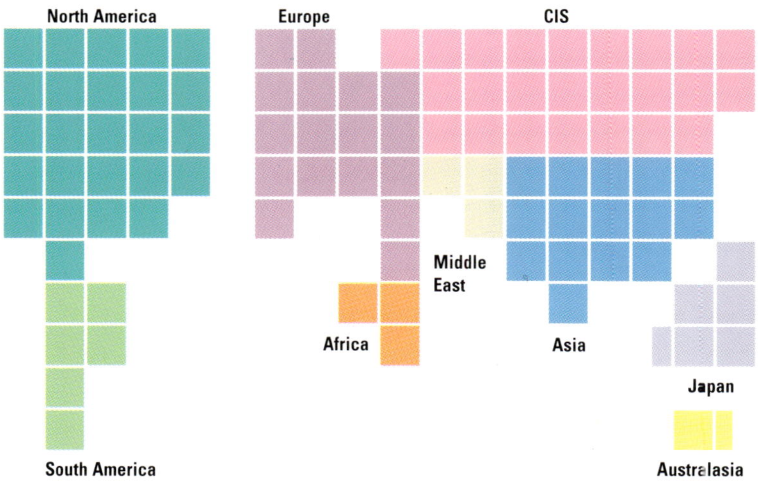

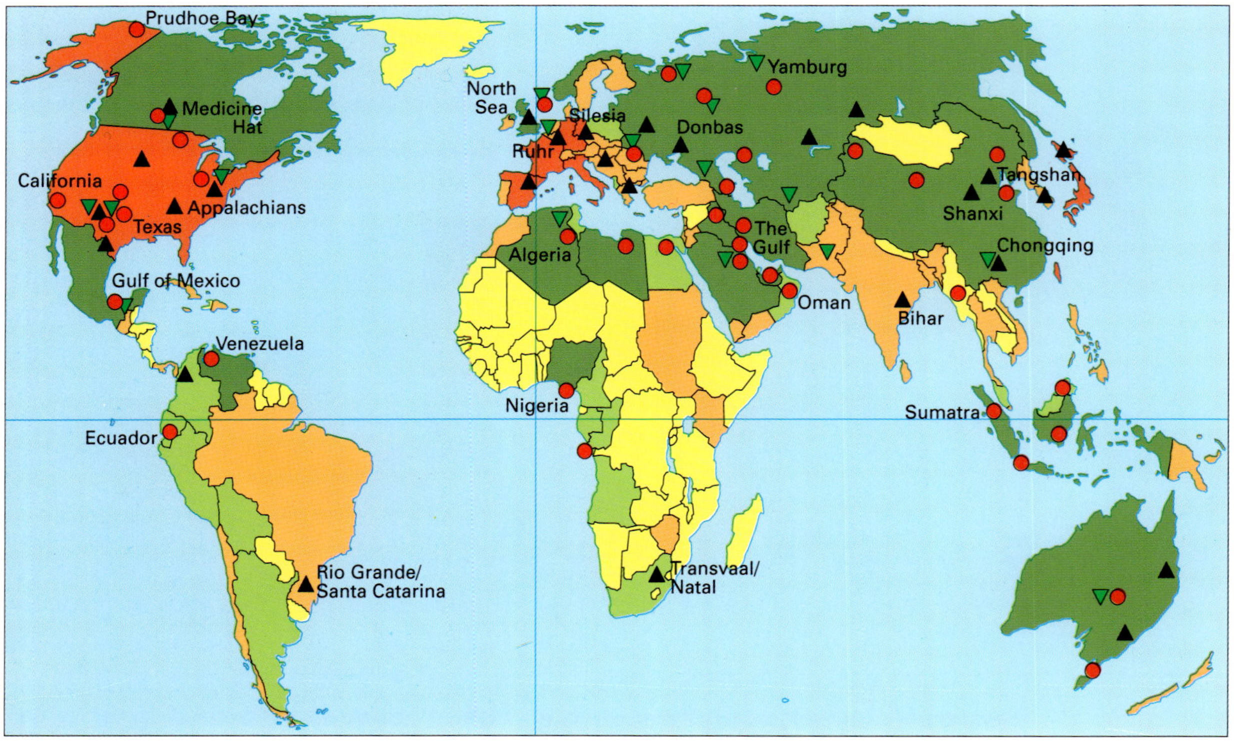

ENERGY BALANCE

Difference between energy production & consumption in millions of tonnes of oil equivalent (1989)

Energy deficit ↑

- Over 35 MtOe
- 1 - 35 MtOe
- Approx. balance
- 1 - 35 MtOe
- Over 35 MtOe

Energy surplus ↓

- Major oilfields
- Major gasfields
- Major coalfields

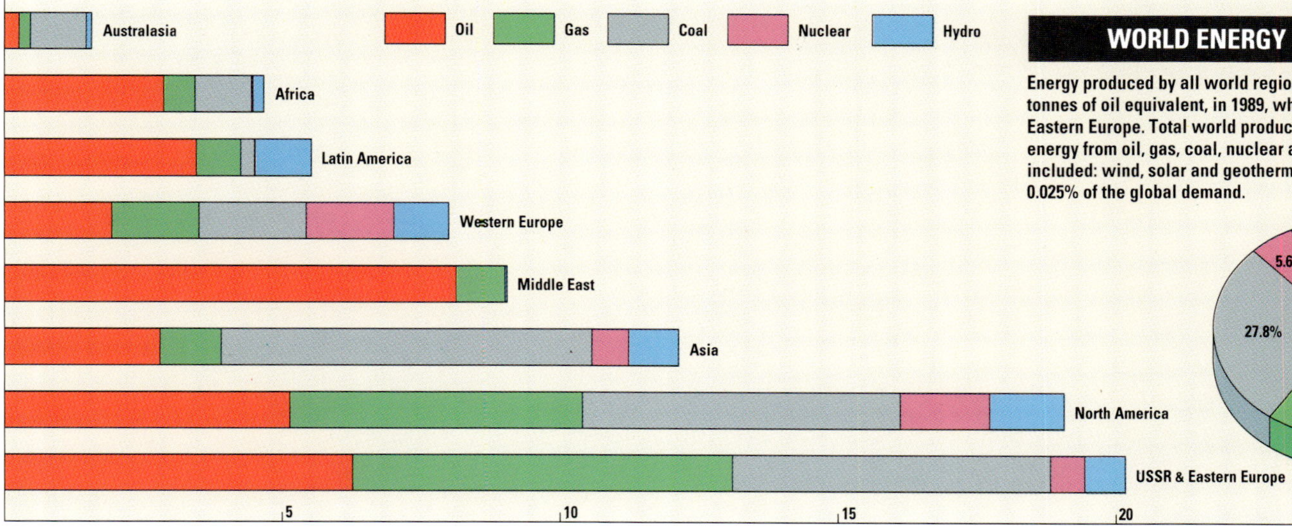

WORLD ENERGY PRODUCTION

Energy produced by all world regions, measured in million tonnes of oil equivalent, in 1989, when the USSR still dominated Eastern Europe. Total world production was 8019 mtoe. Only energy from oil, gas, coal, nuclear and hydro-electric sources is included: wind, solar and geothermal power together met only 0.025% of the global demand.

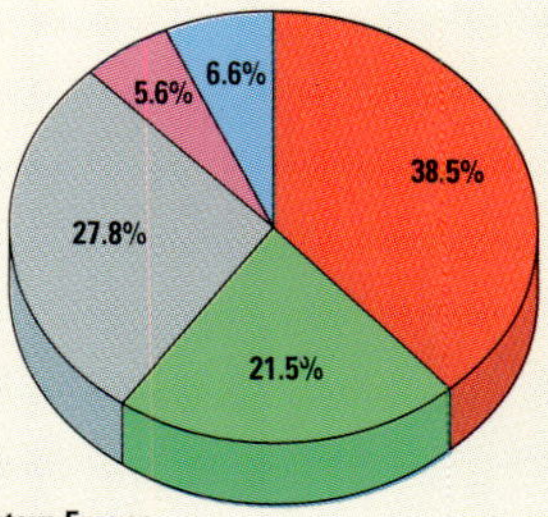

NUCLEAR POWER

Percentage of electricity generated by nuclear power stations, leading nations (1988)

1. France	70%	11. Germany (W)	34%
2. Belgium	66%	12. Japan	28%
3. Hungary	49%	13. Czechoslovakia	27%
4. South Korea	47%	14. UK	18%
5. Sweden	46%	15. USA	17%
6. Taiwan	41%	16. Canada	16%
7. Switzerland	37%	17. Argentina	12%
8. Finland	36%	18. USSR (1989)	11%
9. Spain	36%	19. Yugoslavia	6%
10. Bulgaria	36%	20. Netherlands	5%

The decade 1980-1990 was a bad time for the nuclear power industry. Major projects regularly ran vastly over-budget, and fears of long-term environmental damage were heavily reinforced by the 1986 Soviet disaster at Chernobyl. Although the number of reactors in service continued to increase throughout the period, orders for new plant shrank dramatically, and most countries cut back on their nuclear programmes.

HYDRO-ELECTRICITY

Percentage of electricity generated by hydro-electrical power stations, leading nations (1988)

1. Paraguay	99.9%	11. Laos	95.5%
2. Zambia	99.6%	12. Nepal	95.2%
3. Norway	99.5%	13. Iceland	94.0%
4. Congo	99.1%	14. Uruguay	93.0%
5. Costa Rica	98.3%	15. Brazil	91.7%
6. Uganda	98.3%	16. Albania	87.2%
7. Rwanda	97.7%	17. Fiji	81.4%
8. Malawi	97.6%	18. Ecuador	80.7%
9. Zaïre	97.4%	19. C. African Rep.	80.4%
10. Cameroon	97.2%	20. Sri Lanka	80.4%

Countries heavily reliant on hydro-electricity are usually small and non-industrial: a high proportion of hydro-electric power more often reflects a modest energy budget than vast hydro-electric resources. The USA, for instance, produces only 8% of power requirements from hydro-electricity; yet that 8% amounts to more than three times the hydro-power generated by all of Africa.

ALTERNATIVE ENERGY SOURCES

Solar: Each year the sun bestows upon the Earth almost a million times as much energy as is locked up in all the planet's oil reserves, but only an insignificant fraction is trapped and used commercially. In some experimental installations, mirrors focus the sun's rays on to boilers, whose steam generates electricity by spinning conventional turbines. Solar cells turn sunlight into electricity directly. Efficiencies are still low, but advancing technology could make the sun a major electricity source by 2100.
Wind: Caused by the uneven heating of the spinning Earth, winds are themselves the product of solar energy. Traditional windmills turn wind power into mechanical work; recent models usually generate electricity. But efficient windmills are expensive to build, and suitable locations are few.
Tidal: The energy from tides is potentially enormous, although only a few installations have been built to exploit it. In theory at least, waves and currents could also provide almost unimaginable power, and the thermal differences in the ocean depths are another huge well of potential energy.

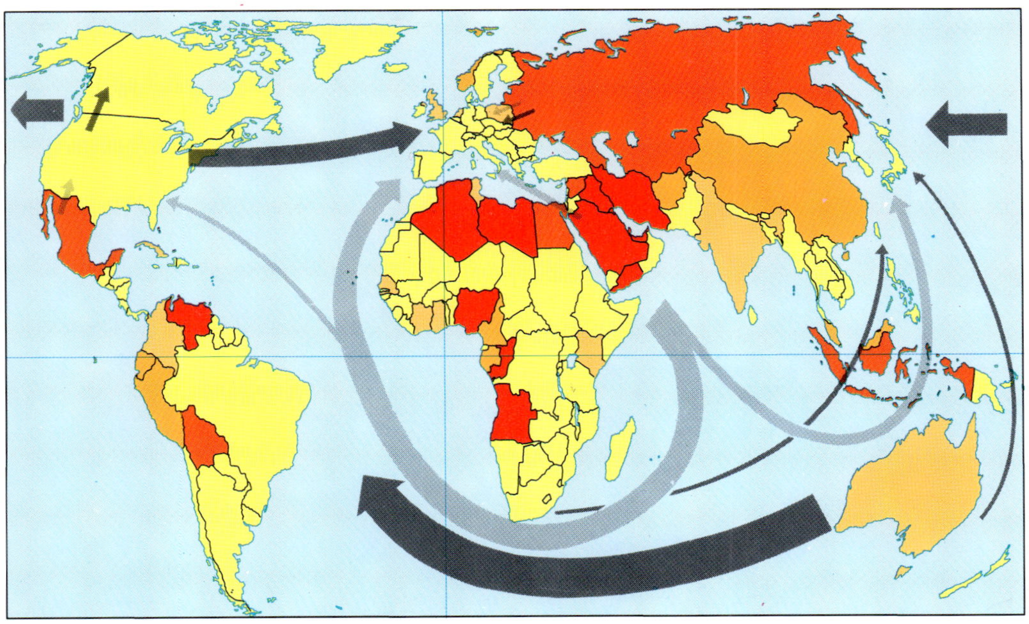

FUEL EXPORTS

Fuels as a percentage of total value of all exports (1986)

- Over 75%
- 50 - 75%
- 25 - 50%
- 10 - 25%
- Under 10%

Direction of trade

- Major movements of coal
- Major movements of oil

Arrows show the major trade direction of selected fuels, & are proportional to export value

CONVERSIONS

For historical reasons, oil is still traded in 'barrels'. The weight and volume equivalents shown below are all based on average density 'Arabian light' crude oil.

The energy equivalents given for a tonne of oil are also somewhat imprecise: oil and coal of different qualities will have varying energy contents, a fact usually reflected in their price on world markets.

1 barrel: 0.136 tonnes/159 litres/35 Imperial gallons/ 42 US gallons. **1 tonne:** 7.33 barrels/1185 litres/ 256 Imperial gallons/261 US gallons. **1 tonne oil:** 1.5 tonnes hard coal/3.0 tonnes lignite/12,000 kWh.

COAL RESERVES

World coal reserves by region and country, thousand million tonnes (1988)

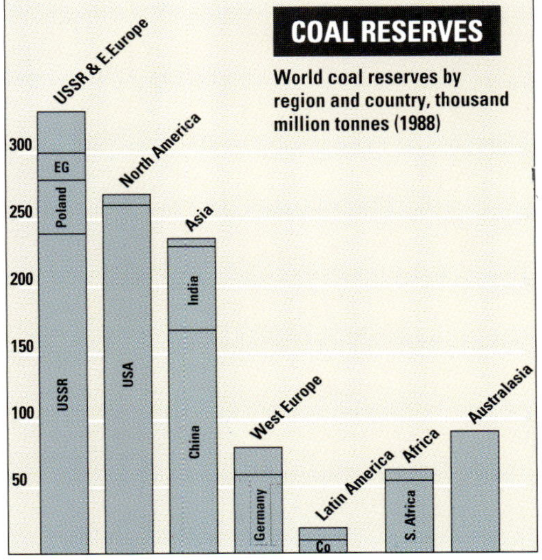

GAS RESERVES

World natural gas reserves by region and country, thousand million tonnes (1988)

Ca: Canada
In: Indonesia
Ma: Malaysia
AD: Abu Dhabi
SA: Saudi Arabia
Qa: Qatar
Iq: Iraq
No: Norway
Ne: Netherlands
Ve: Venezuela
Mx: Mexico
Al: Algeria
Ni: Nigeria

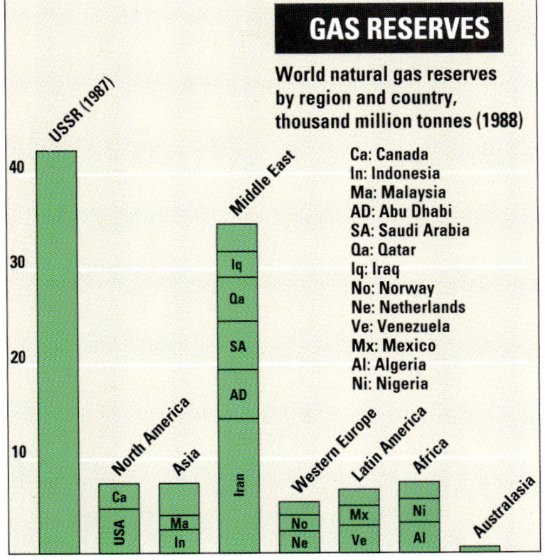

OIL RESERVES

World oil reserves by region and country, thousand million tonnes (1988)

AD: Abu Dhabi
Ve: Venezuela
Mx: Mexico

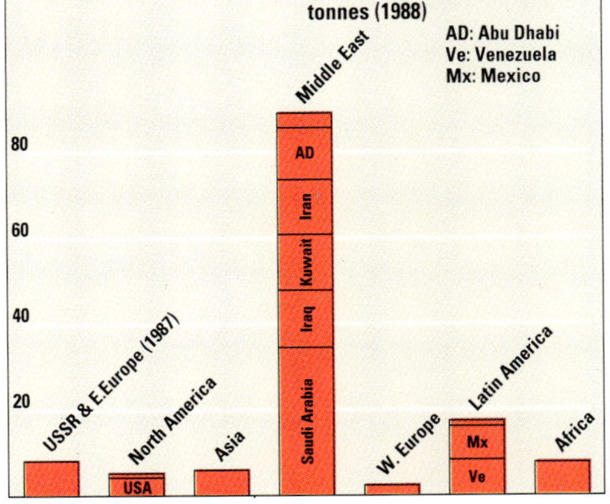

PRODUCTION

AGRICULTURE

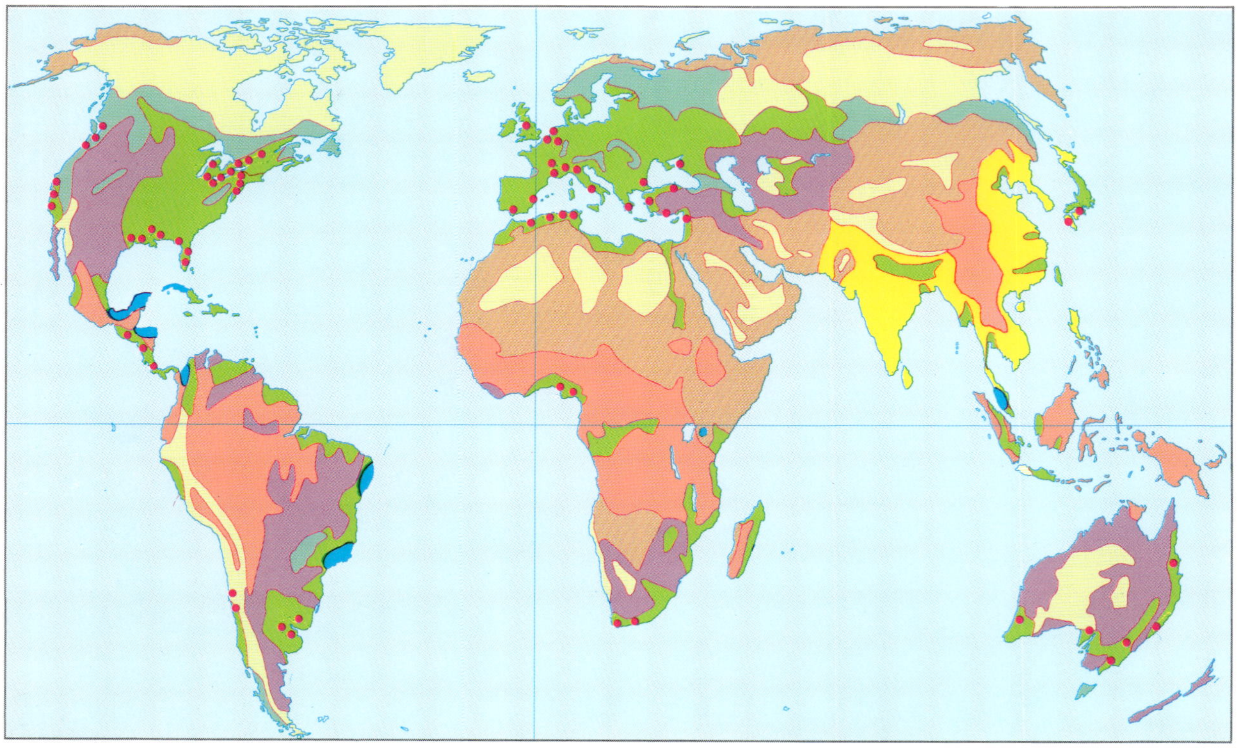

- Nomadic herding
- Primitive subsistence farming
- Intensive subsistence farming
- Tropical plantation agriculture
- Commercial ranching
- Commercial livestock & grain farming
- Commercial fruit growing & market gardening
- Forestry
- Land of little or no agricultural value

STAPLE CROPS

Separate figures for Russia, Ukraine and the other successors of the defunct USSR are not yet available

Wheat

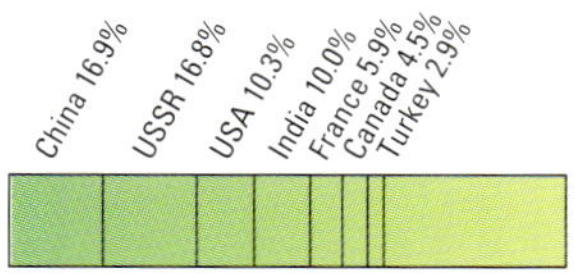

World total (1989): 538,056,000 tonnes

Rice

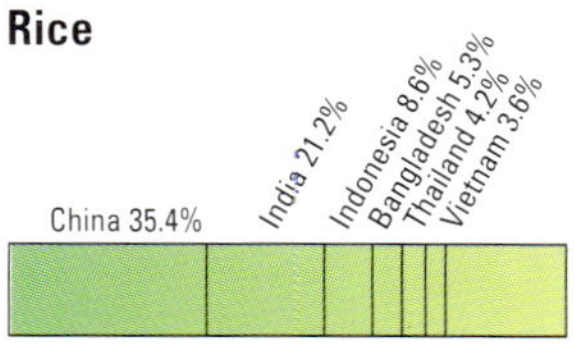

World total (1989): 506,291,000 tonnes

Maize

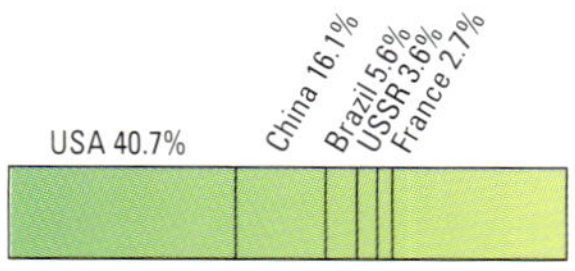

World total (1989): 470,318,000 tonnes

Potatoes

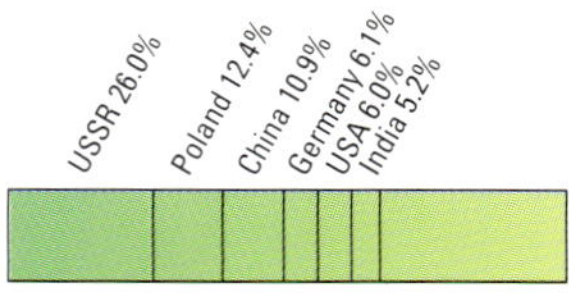

World total (1989): 276,740,000 tonnes

Millet

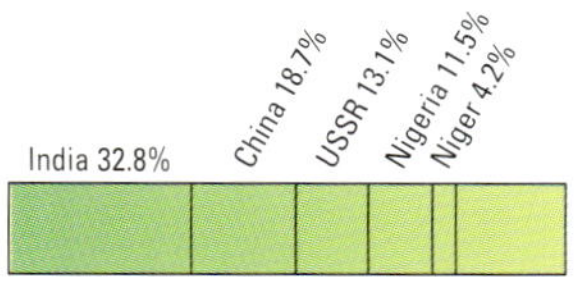

World total (1989): 30,512,000 tonnes

Rye

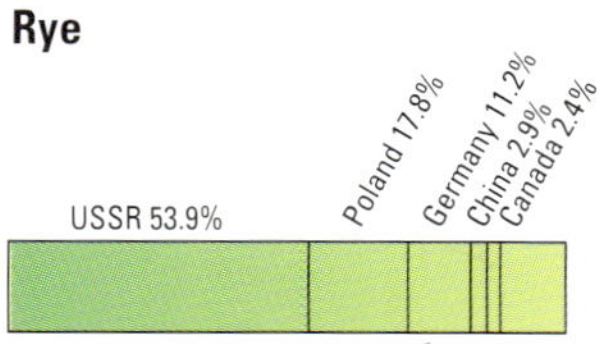

World total (1989): 34,893,000 tonnes

Soya

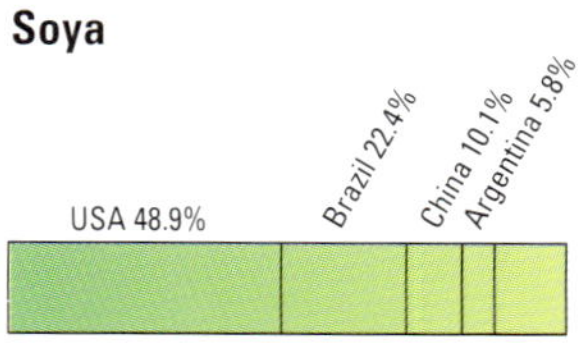

World total (1989): 107,350,000 tonnes

Cassava

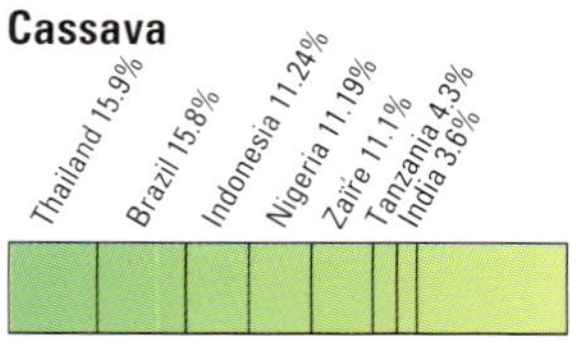

World total (1989): 147,500,000 tonnes

SUGARS

Sugar cane

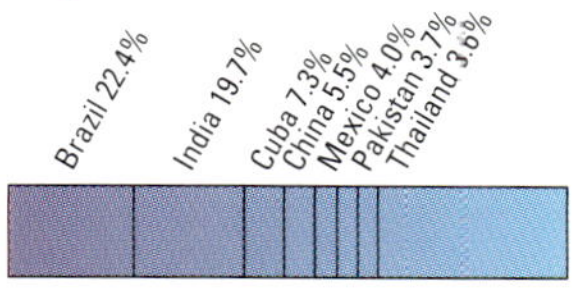

World total (1989): 1,007,184,000 tonnes

Sugar beet

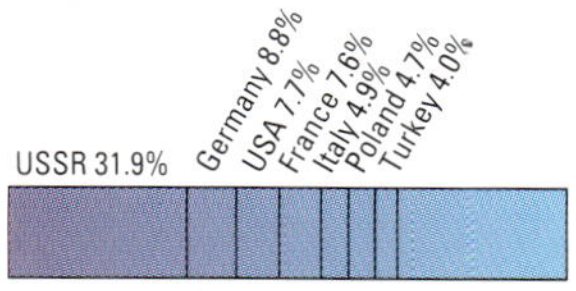

World total (1989): 305,882,000 tonnes

BALANCE OF EMPLOYMENT

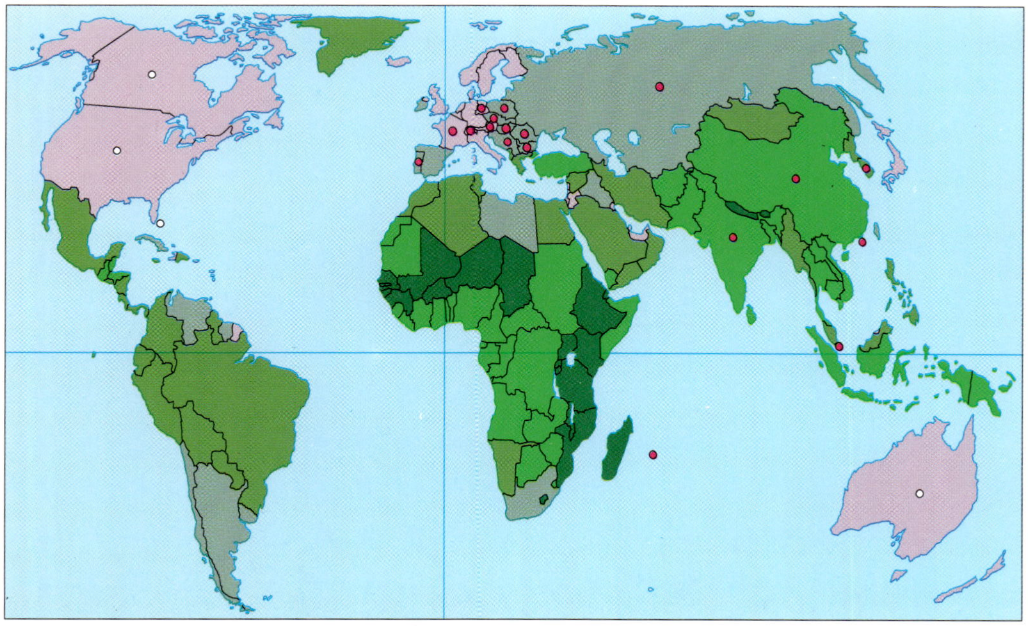

Percentage of total workforce employed in agriculture, forestry & fishing (latest available year)

- Over 75%
- 50 - 75%
- 25 - 50%
- 10 - 25%
- Under 10%

- Over 25% of total workforce employed in manufacturing
- Over 75% of total workforce employed in service industries (e.g. work in offices, shops, tourism, transport, entertainment & administration)

MINERAL PRODUCTION

Separate figures for Russia, Ukraine and the other successors of the defunct USSR are not yet available

Copper

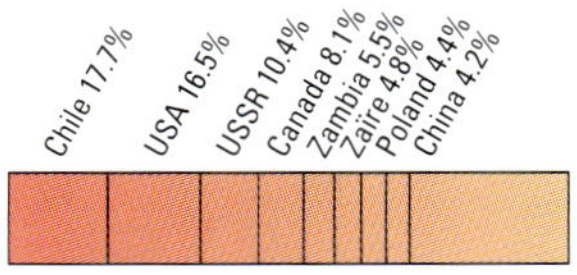

World total (1989): 9,100,000 tonnes

Iron

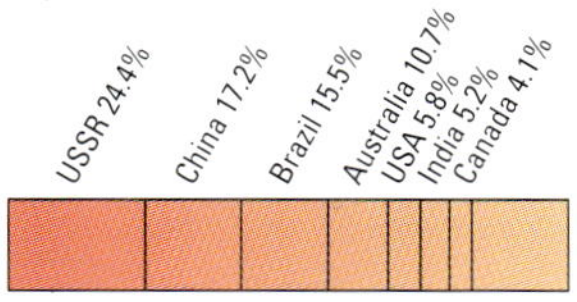

World total (1989): 989,000,000 tonnes

Chromium

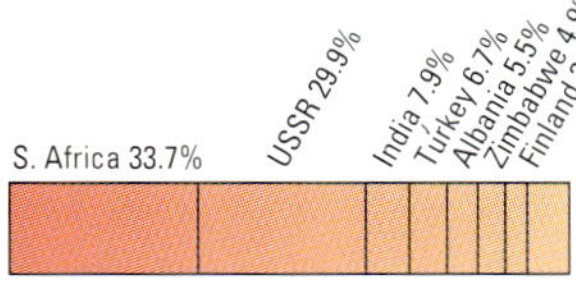

World total (1989): 12,700,000 tonnes

Gold

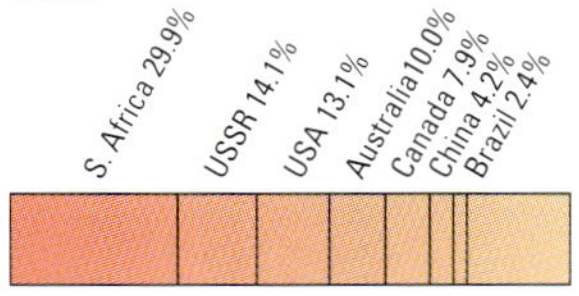

World total (1989): 2,026,000 kilograms

Uranium

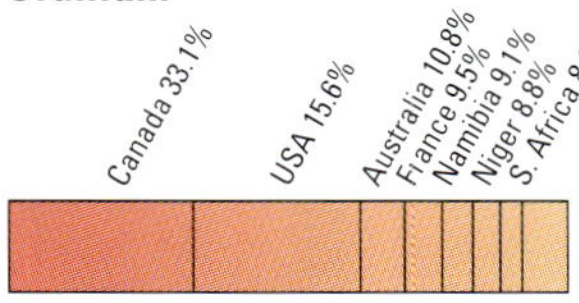

World total (1989): 34,000 tonnes

Lead

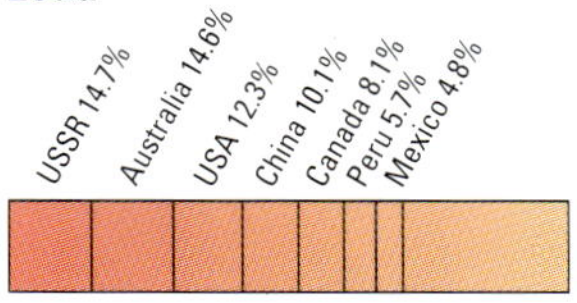

World total (1989): 3,400,000 tonnes

Tin

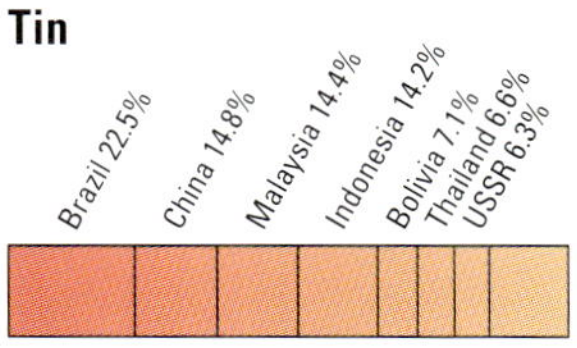

World total (1989): 223,000 tonnes

Manganese

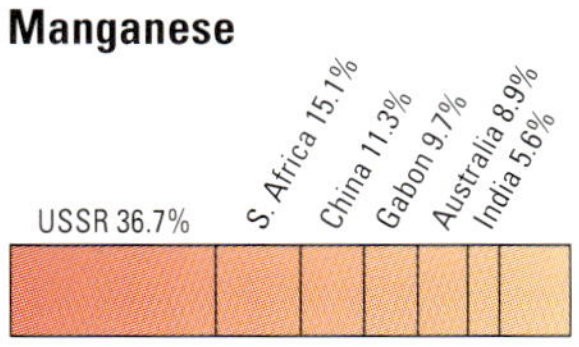

World total (1989): 24,000,000 tonnes

Silver

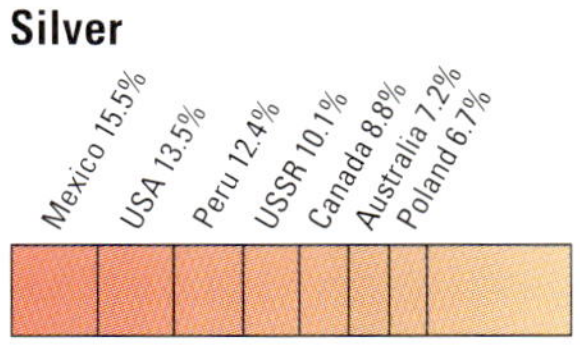

World total (1989): 14,896,000 kilograms

Aluminium

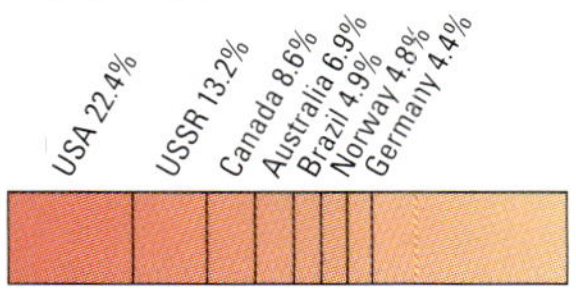

World total (1989): 18,000,000 tonnes

Mercury

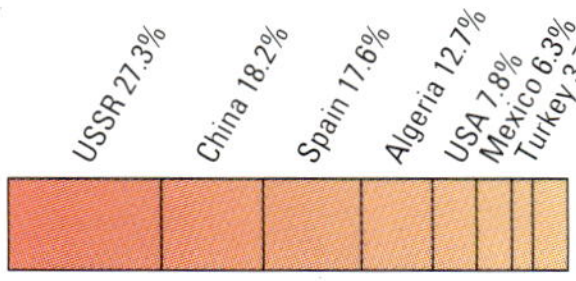

World total (1989): 5,500,000 kilograms

Zinc

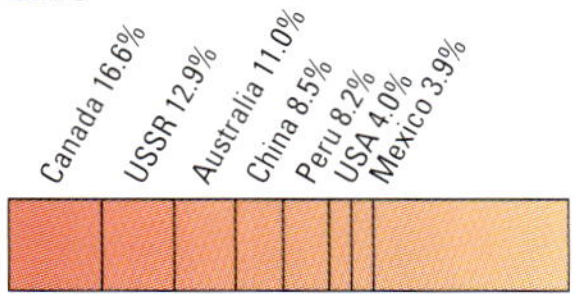

World total (1989): 7,300,000 tonnes

Nickel

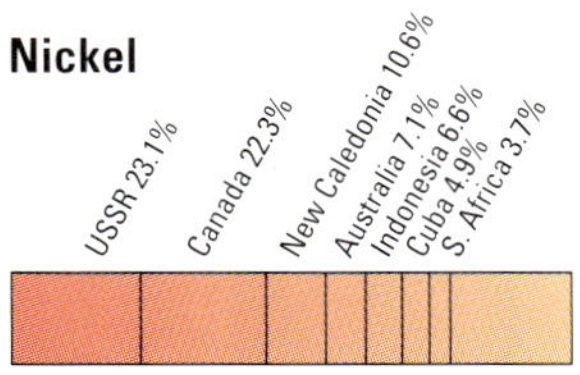

World total (1989): 910,000 tonnes

Diamonds

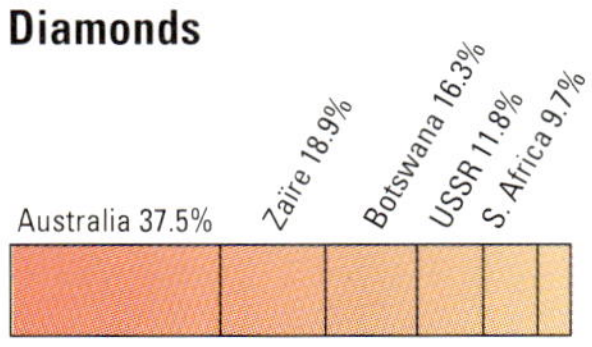

World total (1989): 96,600,000 carats

MINERAL DISTRIBUTION

Light metals
- Bauxite

Base metals
- Copper
- Lead
- Mercury
- Tin
- Zinc

Iron and ferro-alloys
- Iron
- Chrome
- Manganese
- Nickel

Precious metals
- Gold
- Silver

Precious stones
- Diamonds

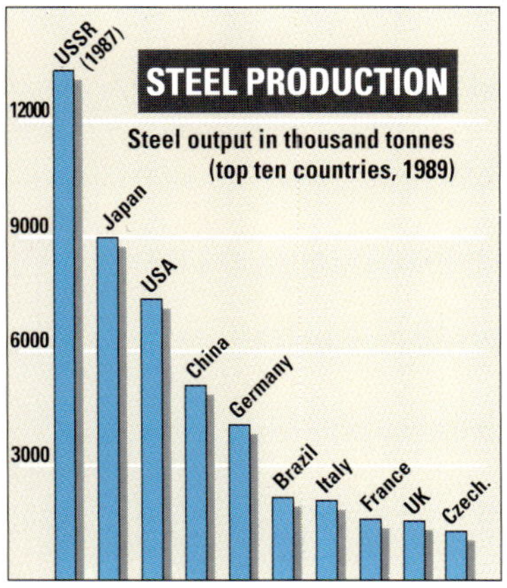

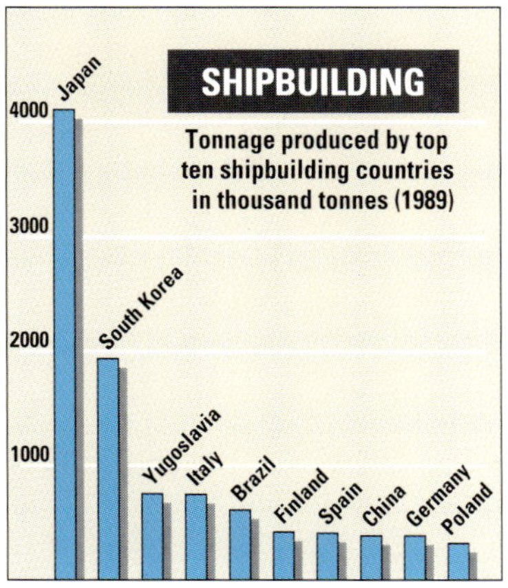

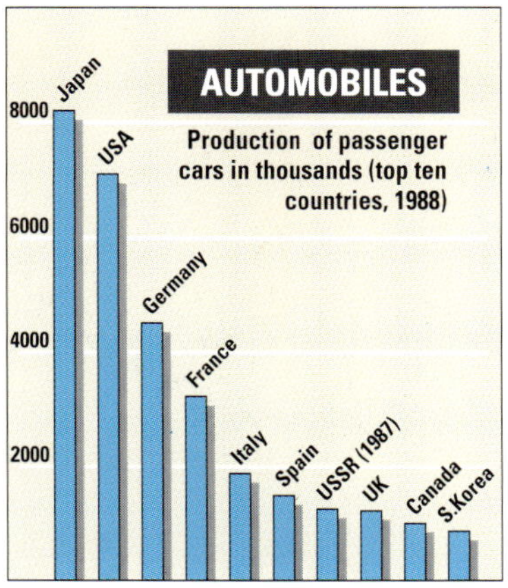

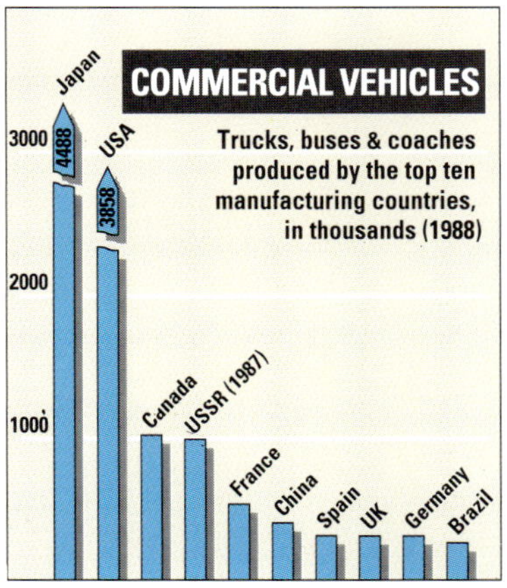

TIME & THE SEASONS

THE SEASONS

The Earth revolves around the Sun once a year in an 'anti-clockwise' direction, tilted at a constant angle 66½°. In June, the northern hemisphere is tilted towards the Sun: as a result it receives more hours of sunshine in a day and therefore has its warmest season, summer. By December, the Earth has rotated halfway round the Sun so that the southern hemisphere is tilted towards the Sun and has its summer; the hemisphere that is tilted away from the Sun has winter. On 21 June the Sun is directly overhead at the Tropic of Cancer (23½° N), and this is midsummer in the northern hemisphere. Midsummer in the southern hemisphere occurs on 21 December, when the Sun is overhead at the Tropic of Capricorn (23½° S).

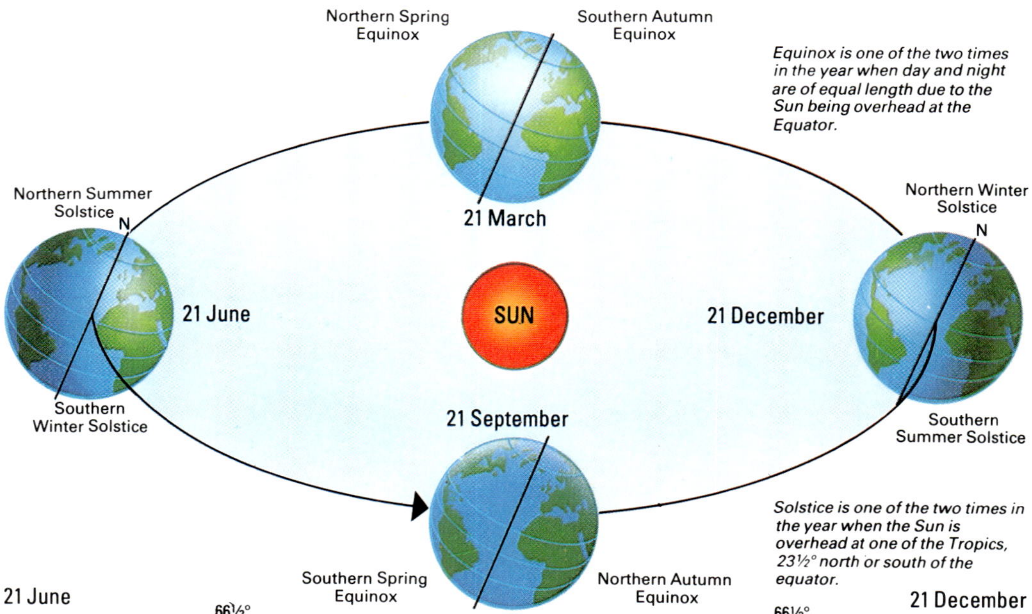

DAY & NIGHT

The Sun appears to rise in the east, reach its highest point at noon, and then set in the west, to be followed by night. In reality it is not the Sun that is moving but the Earth revolving from west to east. Due to the tilting of the Earth the length of day and night varies from place to place and month to month.

At the summer solstice in the northern hemisphere (21 June), the Arctic has total daylight and the Antarctic total darkness. The opposite occurs at the winter solstice (21 December). At the equator, the length of day and night are almost equal all year, at latitude 30° the length of day varies from about 14 hours to 10 hours, and at latitude 50° from about 16 hours to about 8 hours.

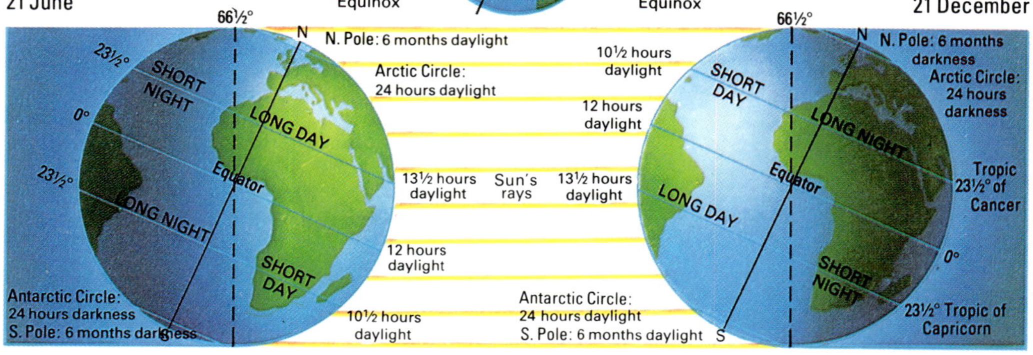

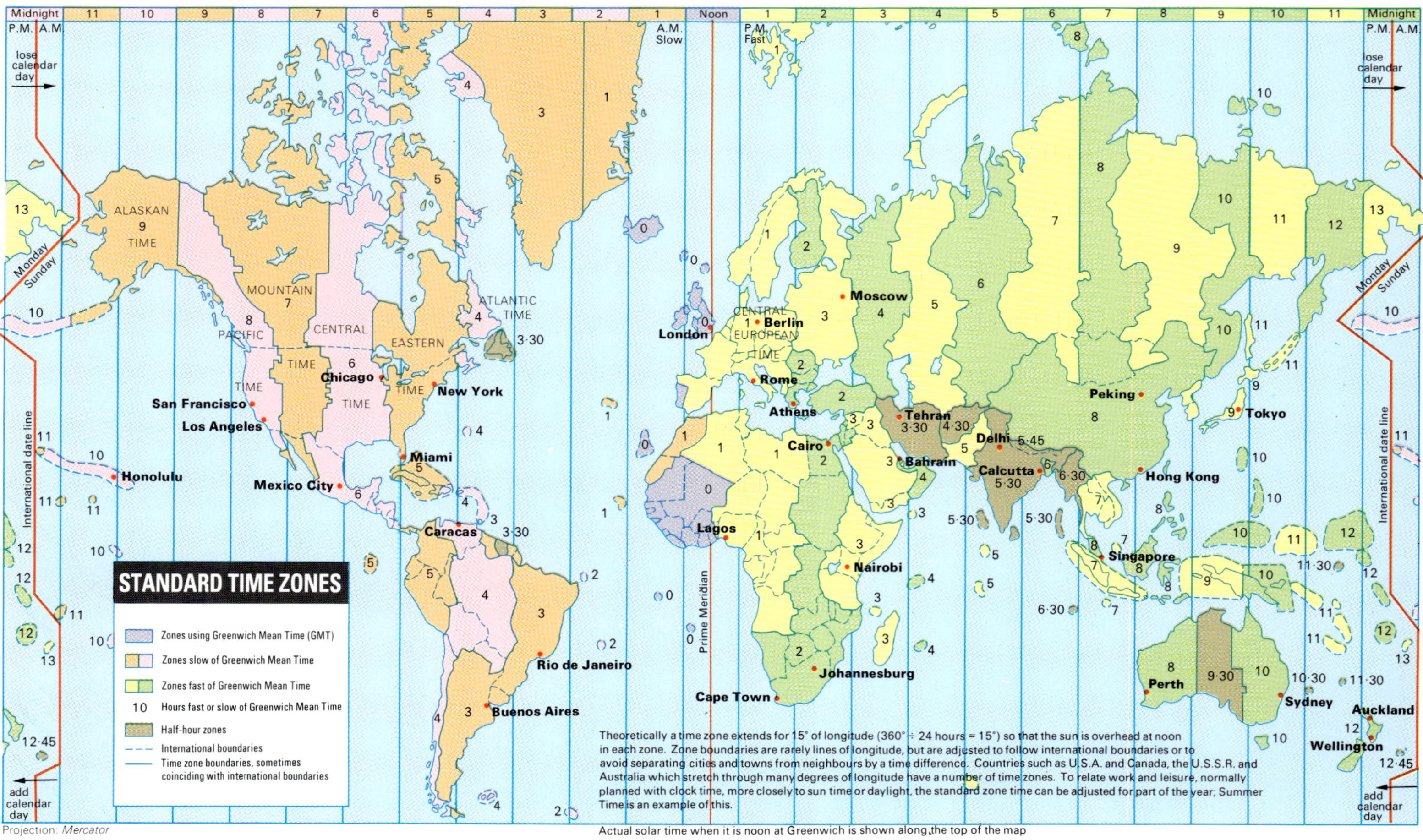

Projection: Mercator

Actual solar time when it is noon at Greenwich is shown along the top of the map

WORLD MAPS

SETTLEMENTS

PARIS **Berne** **Livorno** Brugge *Algeciras* *Fréjus* *Oberammergau* *Thira*

Settlement symbols and type styles vary according to the scale of each map and indicate the importance of towns on the map rather than specific population figures

∴ Ruins or Archæological Sites

Wells in Desert

ADMINISTRATION

International Boundaries

International Boundaries (Undefined or Disputed)

Internal Boundaries

National Parks

Country Names

NICARAGUA

Administrative Area Names

KENT

CALABRIA

International boundaries show the *de facto* situation where there are rival claims to territory

COMMUNICATIONS

Principal Roads

Other Roads

Trails and Seasonal Roads

Passes

Airfields

Principal Railways

Railways Under Construction

Other Railways

Railway Tunnels

Principal Canals

PHYSICAL FEATURES

Perennial Streams

Intermittent Streams

Perennial Lakes

Intermittent Lakes

Swamps and Marshes

Permanent Ice and Glaciers

▲ 8848 Elevations in metres

▼ 8050 Sea Depths in metres

1134 Height of Lake Surface Above Sea Level in metres

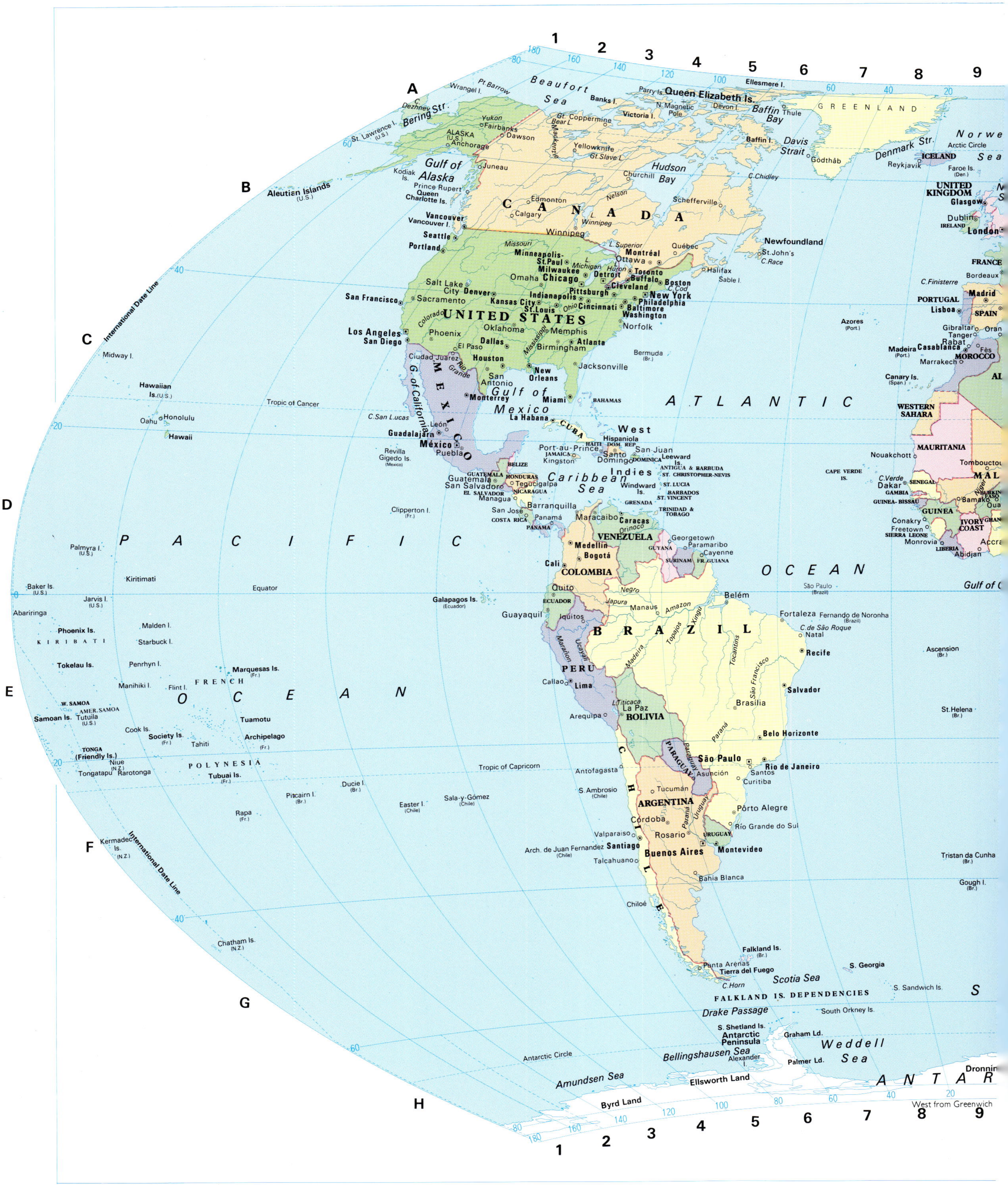

Projection: *Hammer Equal Area*

ARCTIC OCEAN
Svalbard (Norway)
Zemlya Frantsa Iosifa
Novaya Zemlya
Severnaya Zemlya
Barents Sea
Kara Sea
Laptev Sea
New Siberian Is.
East Siberian Sea
Arctic Circle
Bering Sea
Sea of Okhotsk
RUSSIAN FEDERATION
KAZAKHSTAN
MONGOLIA
CHINA
XIZANG (TIBET)
INDIA
PAKISTAN
IRAN
TURKEY
SAUDI ARABIA
EGYPT
LIBYA
NIGER
CHAD
SUDAN
ETHIOPIA
ZAÏRE (CONGO)
ANGOLA
ZAMBIA
ZIMBABWE
NAMIBIA
BOTSWANA
SOUTH AFRICA
MADAGASCAR
TANZANIA
KENYA
NIGERIA
CENTRAL AFRICAN REPUBLIC
Mediterranean Sea
Black Sea
Caspian Sea
Aral Sea
Red Sea
Gulf of Aden
The Gulf
Arabian Sea
Bay of Bengal
South China Sea
East China Sea
Sea of Japan
JAPAN
KOREA
PHILIPPINES
MALAYSIA
INDONESIA
THAILAND
BURMA (MYANMAR)
PAPUA NEW GUINEA
AUSTRALIA
NORTHERN TERRITORY
WESTERN AUSTRALIA
SOUTH AUSTRALIA
QUEENSLAND
NEW SOUTH WALES
VICTORIA
TASMANIA
NEW ZEALAND
Tasman Sea
Arafura Sea
Timor Sea
Great Australian Bight
PACIFIC OCEAN
FEDERATED STATES OF MICRONESIA
INDIAN OCEAN
SOUTHERN OCEAN
Antarctic Circle
Tropic of Cancer
Tropic of Capricorn
Equator
Enderby Land
Wilkes Land
S. Magnetic Pole
Ross Sea
ANTARCTICA
East from Greenwich
A B C D E F G H
10 11 12 13 14 15 16 17 18

ARCTIC OCEAN

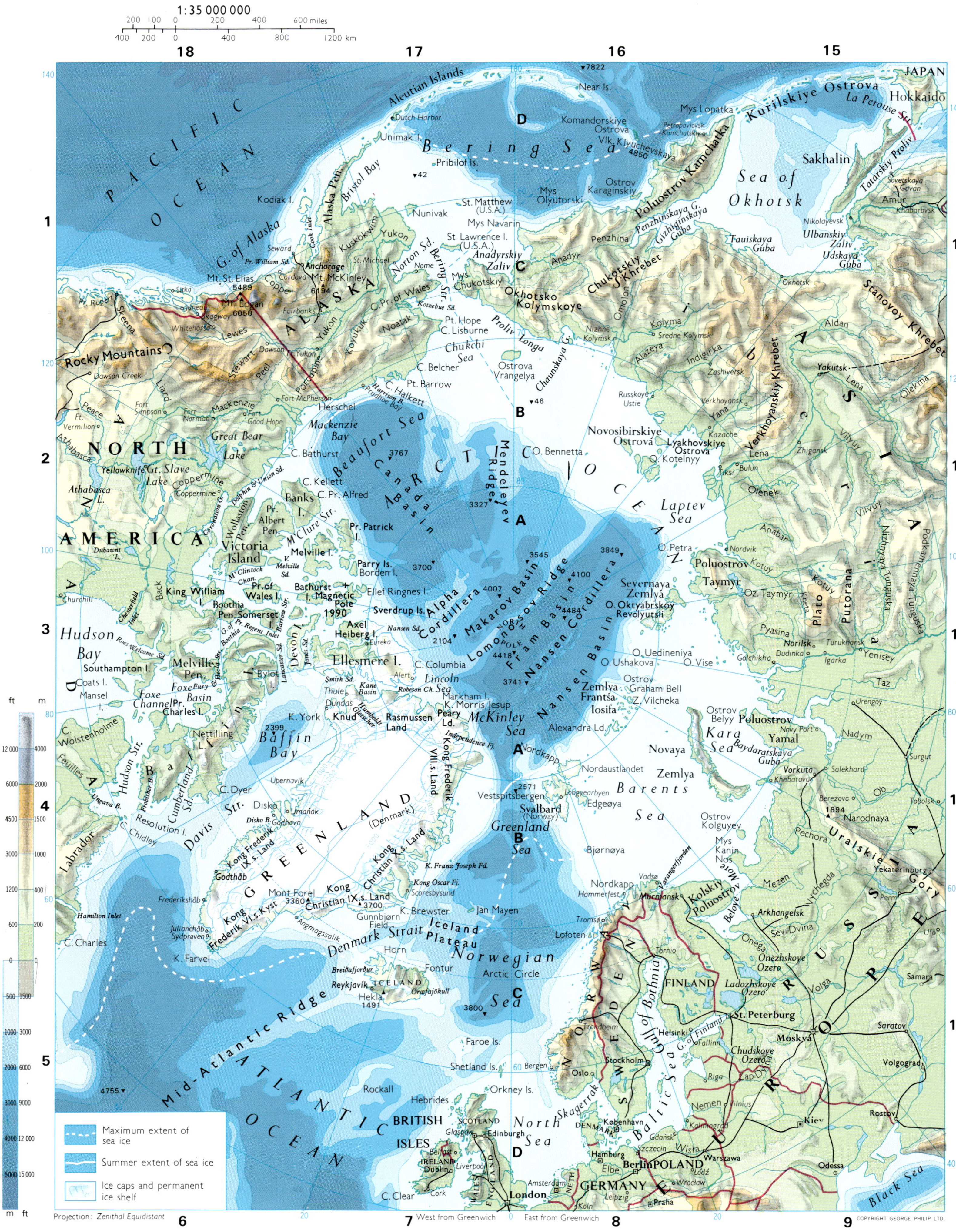

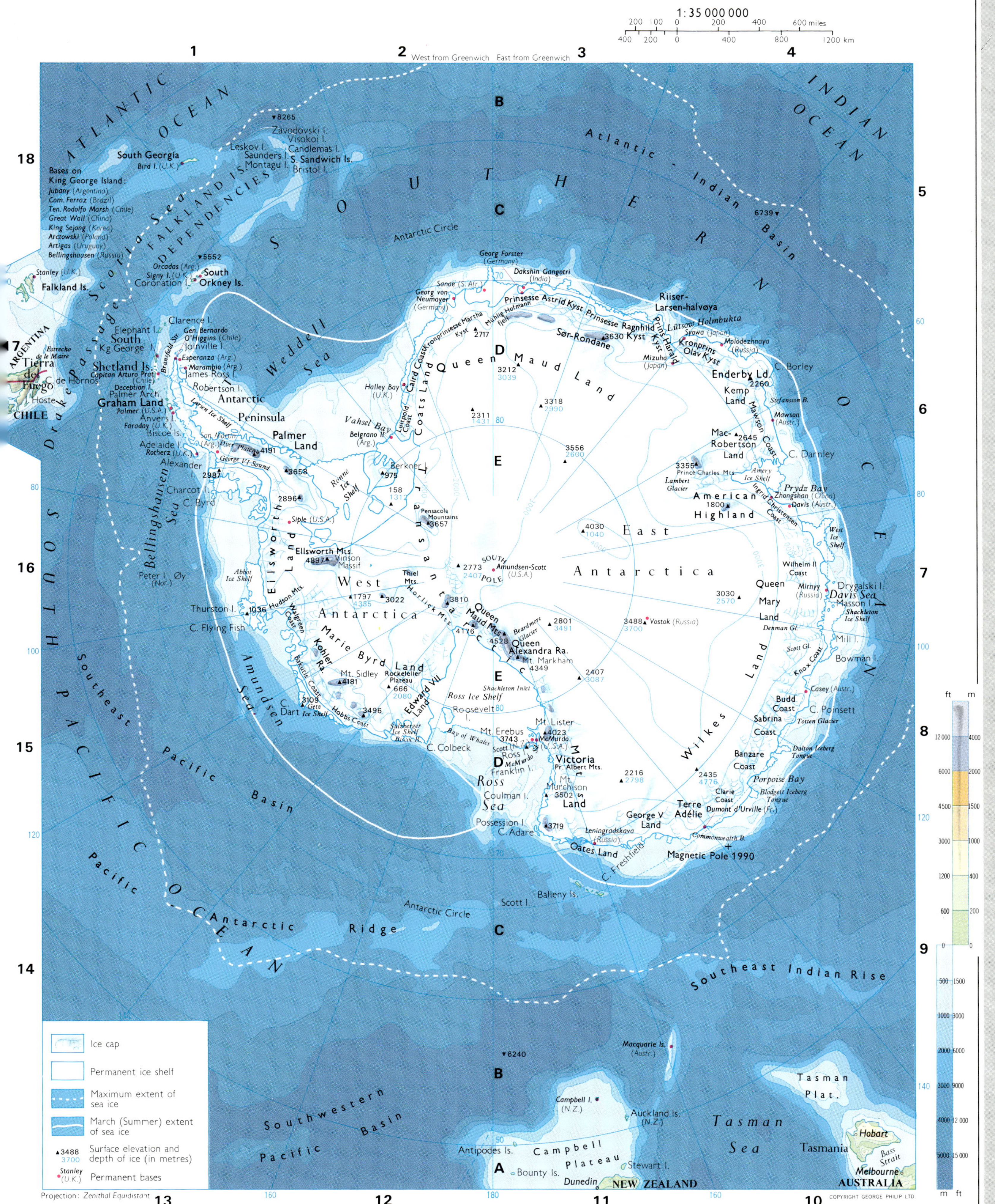

Projection: Zenithal Equidistant

The Antarctic Treaty was signed in Washington in 1959 so that scientific and technical research could continue unhampered by international politics.

All territorial claims covering land areas south of latitude 60°S have been suspended. Those claims were:

Norwegian claim	45°E - 20°W	French claim	136°E - 142°E	British claim	80°W - 20°W
Australian claims	45°E - 136°E, 142°E - 160°E	New Zealand claim	160°E - 150°W	Argentine claim	74°W - 53°W
		Chilean claim	90°W - 53°W		

1:20 000 000
miles
km
NORWEGIAN SEA
NORTH SEA
BALTIC SEA
BLACK SEA
CASPIAN SEA
ADRIATIC SEA
MEDITERRANEAN SEA
ATLANTIC OCEAN
Bay of Biscay
English Channel
Irish Sea
Dogger Bank
Tyrrhenian Sea
Ionian Sea
Aegean Sea
Ligurian Sea
G. of Bothnia
G. of Finland
G. of Riga
G. of Lions
White Sea
Sea of Azov
Iceland
Ireland
Great Britain
British Isles
Faroe Is.
Shetland Is.
Orkney Is.
Hebrides
Corsica
Sardinia
Sicily
Crete
Cyprus
Malta
Balearic Is.
Scandinavia
Lapland
Finland
Kola Peninsula
Kanin Peninsula
Jutland
Brittany
Central Massif
Pyrenees
Iberian Peninsula
Old Castile
New Castile
Andalusia
Sierra Morena
Sa. Nevada
Alps
Apennines
Carpathians
Transylvanian Alps
Dinaric Alps
Balkan Peninsula
Balkans
Rhodope
Pindus
Morea
Plain of Hungary
Wallachia
Pripyat Marshes
Ukraine
Central Russian Uplands
Volga Uplands
Obshchiy Syrt
Ural Mountains
Caucasus
Crimea
Anatolia
Taurus
Kurdistan
Armenia
Atlas
Plateau of the Shotts
Volga
Don
Danube
Dnepr (Dnieper)
Dnestr (Dniester)
Wisła (Vistula)
Odra (Oder)
Elbe
Rhine
Weser
Loire
Seine
Garonne
Rhône
Po
Tiber
Ural
Str. of Gibraltar
Str. of Otranto
Str. of Messina
Bosporus
Projection: Bonne West from Greenwich 0 East from Greenwich
COPYRIGHT, GEORGE PHILIP & SON, LTD.

1: 20 000 000

100 0 100 200 300 400 miles

100 0 100 200 300 400 500 600 km

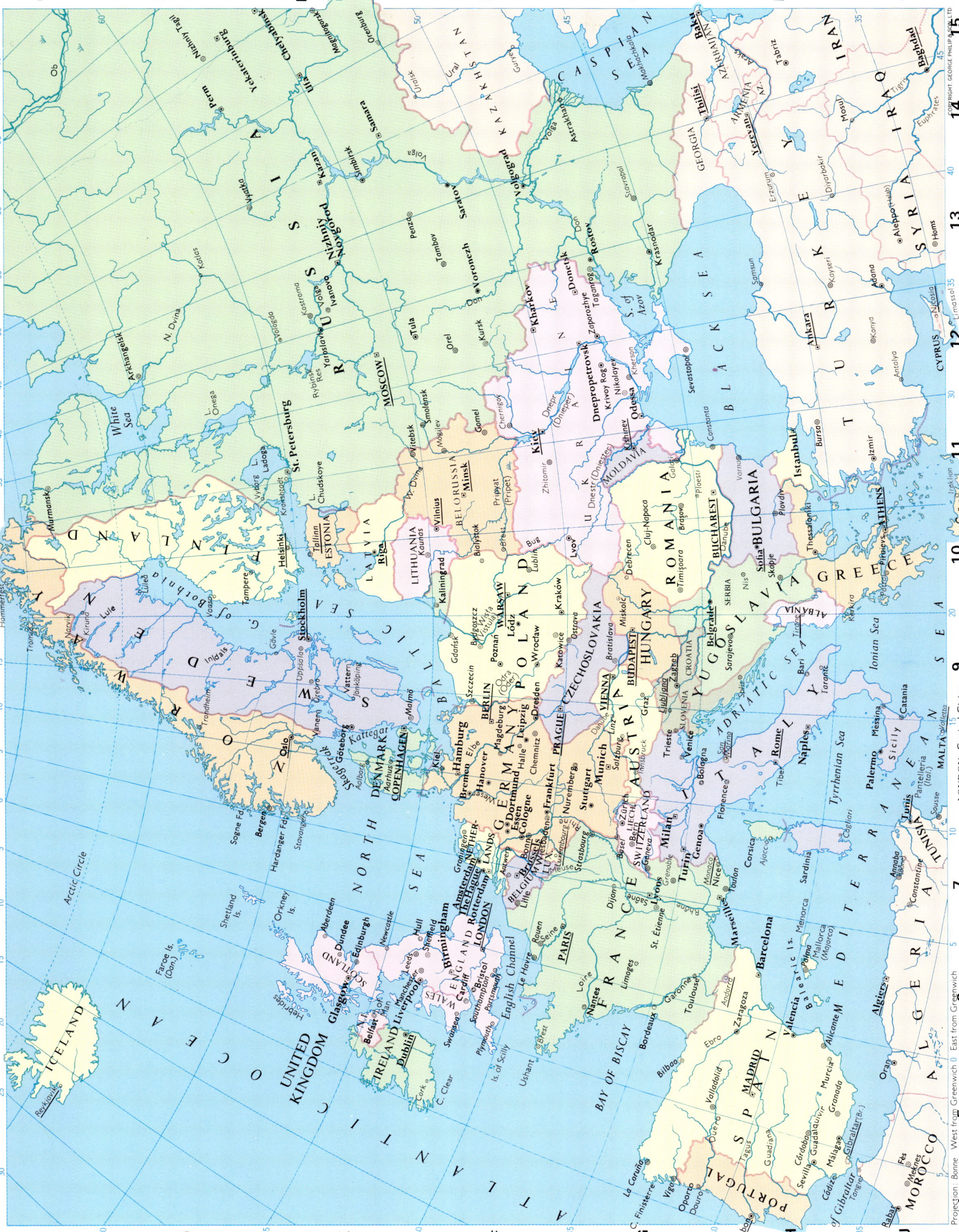

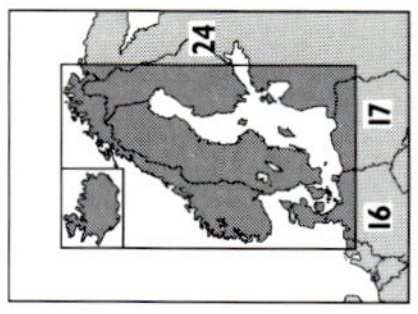
24
17
16

NORWEGIAN SEA
ICELAND
on the same scale as general map
Vatnajökull
Lofoten
Vesterålen
Arctic Circle
Reykjavík
Keflavík
Akureyri
Húsavík
Sauðárkrókur
Ísafjörður
Tromsø
Narvik
Kiruna
Gällivare
Bodø
Mo
Mosjøen
Namsos
Steinkjer
Levanger
Trondheim
Kristiansund
Molde
Ålesund
Hammerfest
Vadsø
Inari
Oulu
Kemi
Tornio
Haparanda
Luleå
Boden
Piteå
Skellefteå
Umeå
Örnsköldsvik
Härnösand
Sundsvall
Östersund
Vaasa
Jakobstad
Kokkola
Jyväskylä
Kajaani
Rovaniemi
Sorsele
Storuman
Lycksele
Arvidsjaur
Jokkmokk
Kvarken
Hekla
Westmannaeyjar
Surtsey
Reykjanes

1:5 000 000
miles
km
DENMARK
ESTONIA
LATVIA
LITHUANIA
RUSSIA
BELO-RUSSIA
POLAND
GERMANY
BALTIC SEA
G. OF FINLAND
GULF
Skagerrak
Kattegat
The Sound
Gotland
Öland
Bornholm
Rīgas Jūras Līcis (Gulf of Riga)
Zatoka Gdańska
STOCKHOLM
OSLO
HELSINKI (Helsingfors)
KØBENHAVN
Tallinn
Riga
Göteborg
Malmö
Gdańsk
Kaliningrad
Vilnius
Kaunas
Hamburg
Kiel
Lübeck
Rostock
Szczecin (Stettin)
Bergen
Stavanger
Kristiansand
Turku (Åbo)
Tampere
Uppsala
Norrköping
Linköping
Karlstad
Örebro
Jönköping
Visby
Klaipėda
Liepaja
Ventspils
Projection: Conical with two standard parallels
East from Greenwich
COPYRIGHT GEORGE PHILIP & SON, LTD.

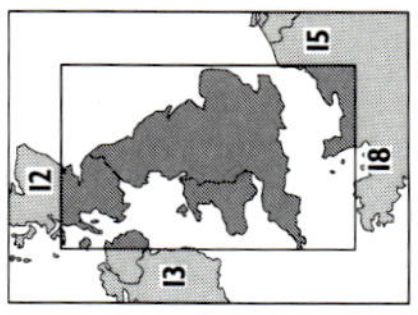
12
13
15
18

NORTH SEA
IRISH SEA
SCOTLAND
Southern Uplands
Pennines
North Channel
Firth of Clyde
Solway Firth
Firth of Forth
ISLE OF MAN
Anglesey
NORTHUMBERLAND
DURHAM
CLEVELAND
CUMBRIA
NORTH YORKSHIRE
W. YORKSHIRE
SOUTH YORKSHIRE
HUMBERSIDE
LANCASHIRE
GREATER MANCHESTER
MERSEYSIDE
CHESHIRE
DERBY
NOTTS
LINCOLN
NORFOLK
STAFFORD
CLWYD
GWYNEDD
TYNE & WEAR
Cumbrian Mts.
Cheviot Hills
N. York Moors
Edinburgh
Glasgow
Newcastle
Sunderland
Middlesbrough
Carlisle
Leeds
Bradford
Manchester
Liverpool
Sheffield
Hull
York
Nottingham
Derby
Lincoln
Belfast
Douglas
Blackpool
Preston
Stoke-on-Trent
A
B
C
D
E
2
3
4
5
6
7
8
9

1:2 000 000
50 miles
80 km
SCILLY ISLES
On same Scale
Isles of Scilly
St. Mary's
Land's End
Penzance
St. Ives
ENGLISH CHANNEL
Bristol Channel
Channel Islands
Guernsey
Alderney
Sark
St. Peter Port
Jersey
St. Helier
FRANCE
Cherbourg
Le Havre
Rouen
Dieppe
Caen
Bayeux
St. Lô
Honfleur
Trouville
Fécamp
CORNWALL
DEVON
DORSET
SOMERSET
AVON
WILTS
HANTS
BERKS
OXFORD
BUCKS
BEDFORD
HERTFORD
ESSEX
SUFFOLK
CAMBRIDGE
NORTHAMPTON
WARWICK
WORCESTER
GLOUCESTER
HEREFORD & WORCESTER
SHROPSHIRE
POWYS
DYFED
GWENT
MID GLAMORGAN
WEST GLAMORGAN
SURREY
KENT
WEST SUSSEX
EAST SUSSEX
ISLE OF WIGHT
LONDON
Birmingham
Coventry
Leicester
Peterborough
Cambridge
Northampton
Bedford
Milton Keynes
Luton
Oxford
Reading
Swindon
Bristol
Bath
Cardiff
Newport
Swansea
Gloucester
Cheltenham
Worcester
Hereford
Exeter
Plymouth
Devonport
Torquay (Torbay)
Paignton
Taunton
Yeovil
Weymouth
Poole
Bournemouth
Southampton
Portsmouth
Brighton
Worthing
Eastbourne
Hastings
Folkestone
Dover
Canterbury
Margate
Ramsgate
Maidstone
Southend
Basildon
Chelmsford
Colchester
Ipswich
Lowestoft
Exmoor
Dartmoor
Lundy
Lizard
Start Pt.
Portland Bill
West from Greenwich
East from Greenwich
COPYRIGHT. GEORGE PHILIP & SON, LTD.
Projection: Conical with two standard parallels.

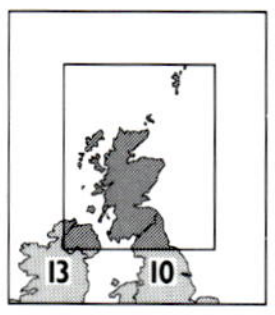

1:2 000 000

Projection: Conical with two standard parallels.

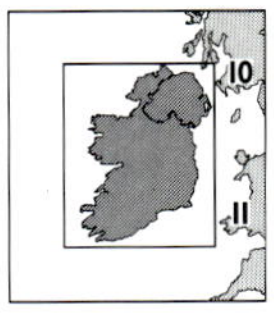

1:2 000 000

10 0 10 20 30 40 50 miles

10 0 10 20 30 40 50 60 70 80 km

Towns underlined in Northern Ireland give their names to the Districts in which they stand

The remaining Districts are:—

1	Fermanagh	5	Castlereagh
2	Moyle	6	Ards
3	Newtownabbey	7	Down
4	North Down	8	Newry & Mourne

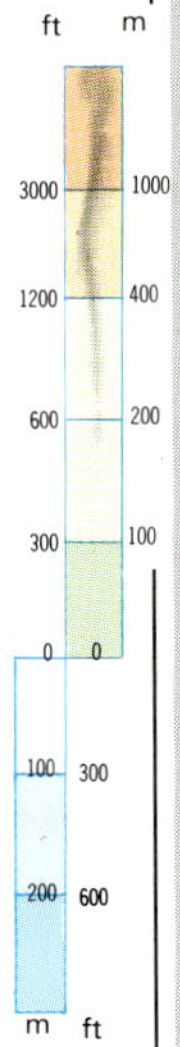

Projection: *Conical with two standard parallels.*

Projection: Conical with two standard parallels

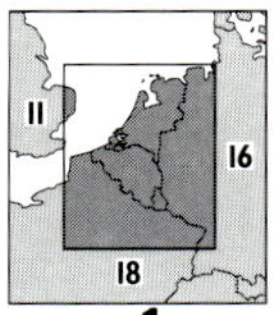
11
16
18

1:2 500 000

N O R T H S E A
ENGLAND
NETHERLANDS
BELGIUM
LUXEMBOURG
FRANCE
GERMANY
AMSTERDAM
'S-GRAVENHAGE
(The Hague)
ROTTERDAM
BRUSSEL
(Bruxelles)
PARIS
KÖLN
DÜSSELDORF
DORTMUND
ESSEN
DUISBURG
Antwerpen
Gent
Liège
Luxembourg
Utrecht
Eindhoven
Groningen
Bremerhaven
Oldenburg
Osnabrück
Münster
Wiesbaden
Mainz
Koblenz
Bonn
Aachen
Saarbrücken
Metz
Nancy
Strasbourg
Reims
Lille
Calais
Dunkerque
Brugge
Oostende
Amiens
Laon
Charleville-Mézières
Verdun
Trier
Kaiserslautern
Arnhem
Nijmegen
Zwolle
Enschede
Leeuwarden
Den Helder
Texel
Vlieland
Terschelling
Ameland
Schiermonnikoog
WADDENEILANDEN
OSTFRIESISCHE INSELN
ARDENNES
Projection: Conical with two standard parallels
East from Greenwich
COPYRIGHT. GEORGE PHILIP & SON. LTD.

NORTH SEA
BALTIC
NETHERLANDS
BELGIUM
LUX.
GERMANY
CZECHOSL
FRANCE
SWITZERLAND
AUSTRIA
ITALY
SLOVENIA
CROA
ADRIATIC SEA
Golfo di Génova
Golfo di Venézia
Amsterdam
'S-Gravenhage (The Hague)
Rotterdam
Brussel
Luxembourg
Hamburg
Bremen
Hannover
BERLIN
Köln
Düsseldorf
Frankfurt
Stuttgart
München
Nürnberg
Leipzig
Dresden
Praha
Wien
Zürich
Bern
Genève
Milano
Torino
Venézia
Ljubljana
Zagreb
Lyon
Strasbourg
Dijon
Marseille
Projection: Conical with two standard parallels
East from Greenwich

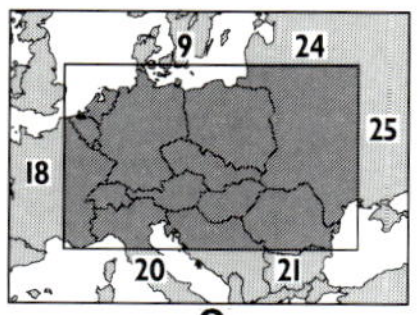

1:5 000 000

50 0 50 100 miles

50 0 50 100 150 km

9 10 11 12 13

9 10 11 12 13 14

1:5 000 000

50 0 50 100 miles

50 0 50 100 150 km

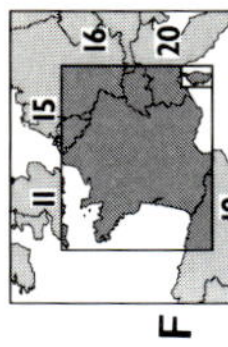

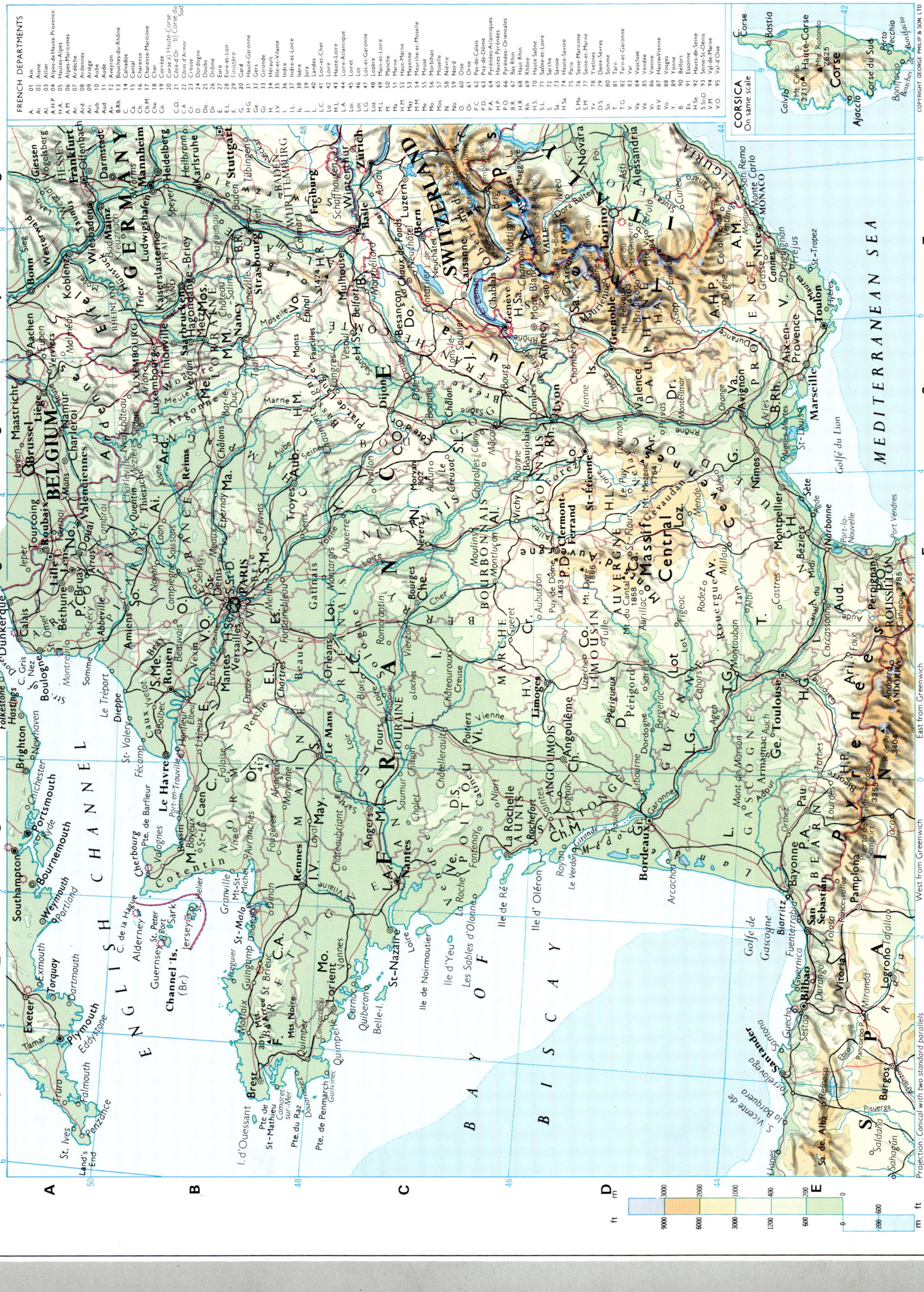

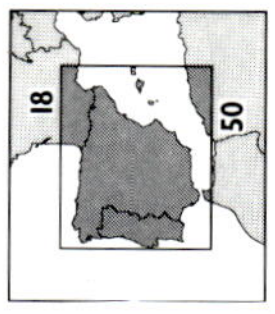

1:5 000 000

SPAIN AND PORTUGAL
ESPAÑA
PORTUGAL
FRANCE
ALGERIA
MOROCCO
ISLAS BALEARES
MEDITERRANEAN SEA
ATLANTIC OCEAN
Bay of Biscay
Golfe du Lion
Golfo de Cádiz
Strait of Gibraltar
MADRID
Lisboa
Barcelona
Valencia
Sevilla
Zaragoza
Bilbao
Málaga
Porto
Palma
Alger
Oran
Pyrénées
Cordillera Cantábrica
Sierra Nevada
Sierra Morena
Meseta
Projection: Conical with two standard parallels
West from Greenwich
East from Greenwich
COPYRIGHT GEORGE PHILIP & SON, LTD.

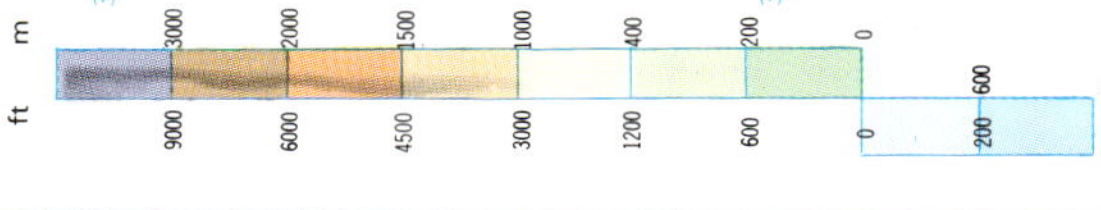

m
ft
3000
2000
1500
1000
400
200
0
9000
6000
4500
3000
1200
600
200
600

Projection: Conical with two standard parallels

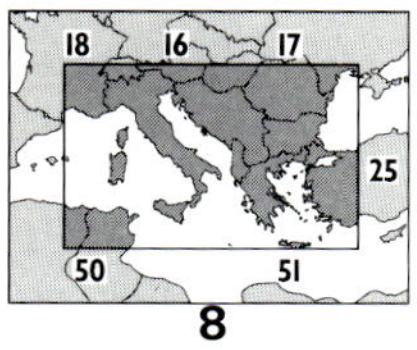

1:5 000 000

50 0 50 100 miles

50 0 50 100 150 km

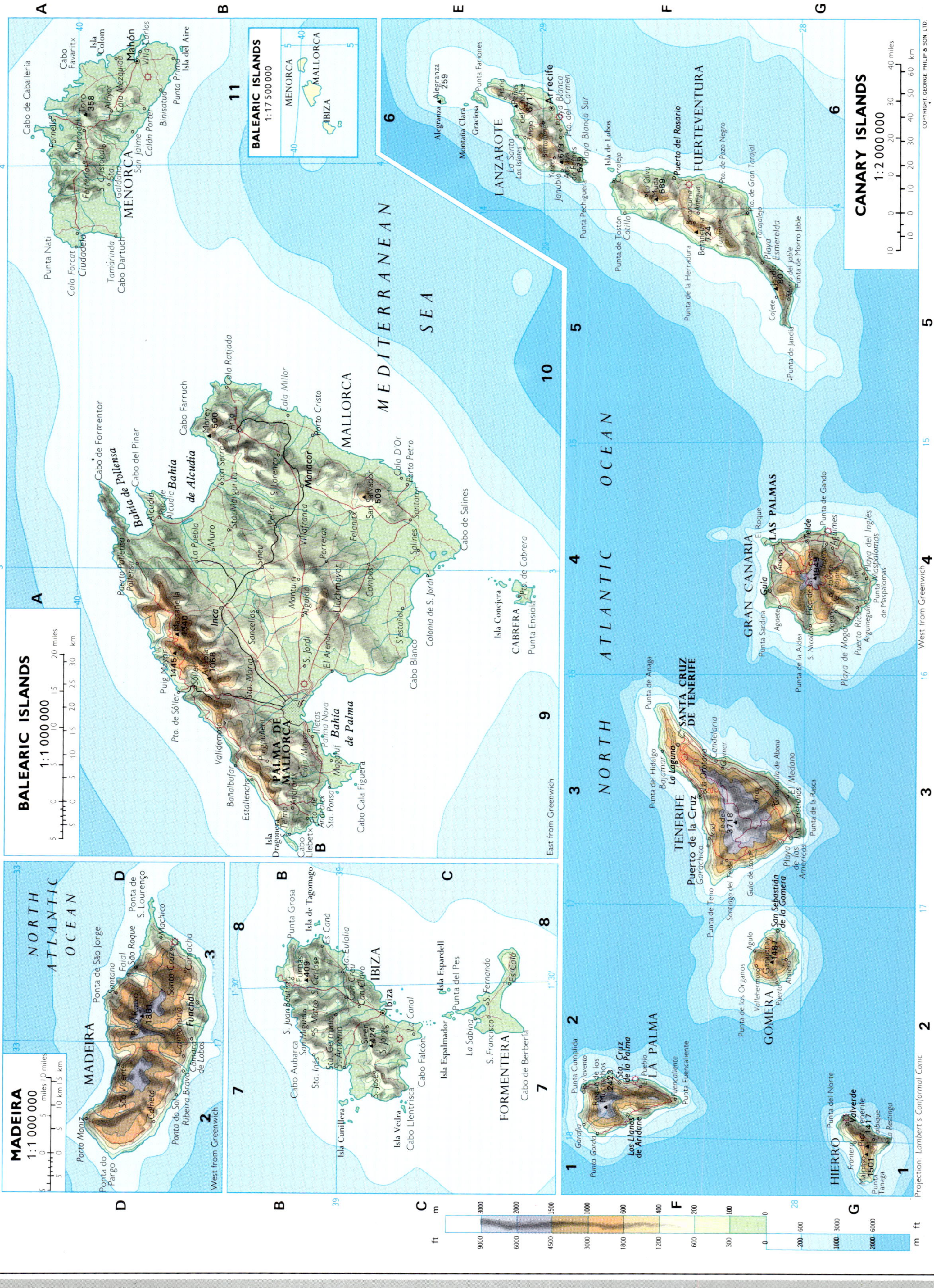
BALEARIC ISLANDS
1:1 000 000
BALEARIC ISLANDS
1:17 500 000
MENORCA
MALLORCA
IBIZA
FORMENTERA
CABRERA
PALMA DE MALLORCA
MEDITERRANEAN SEA
MADEIRA
1:1 000 000
NORTH ATLANTIC OCEAN
Funchal
CANARY ISLANDS
1:2 000 000
LANZAROTE
FUERTEVENTURA
GRAN CANARIA
LAS PALMAS
TENERIFE
SANTA CRUZ DE TENERIFE
GOMERA
LA PALMA
HIERRO
Projection: Lambert's Conformal Conic
COPYRIGHT GEORGE PHILIP & SON LTD

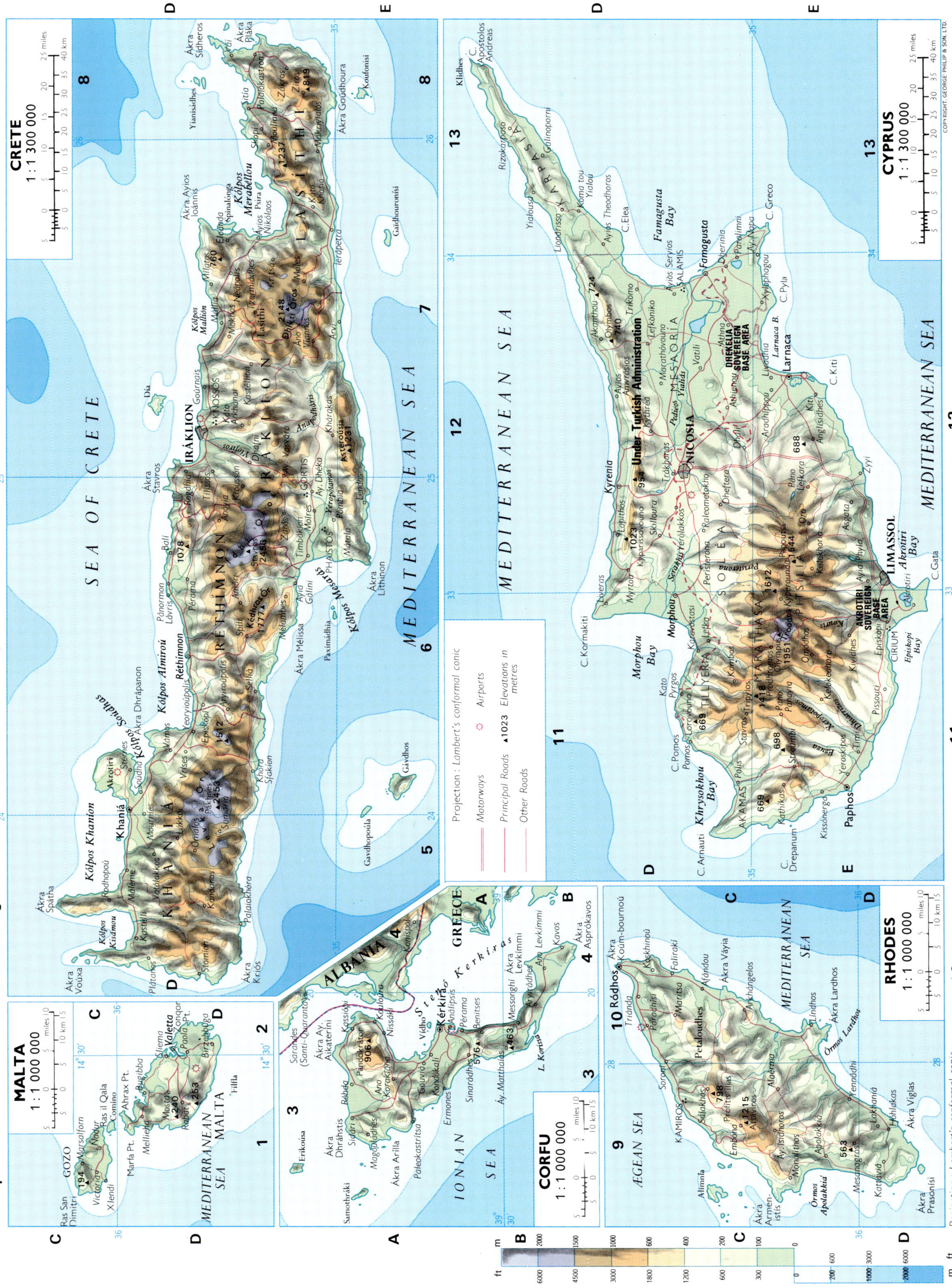
CRETE
1 : 1 300 000
SEA OF CRETE
MEDITERRANEAN SEA
CYPRUS
1 : 1 300 000
MEDITERRANEAN SEA
MALTA
1 : 1 000 000
CORFU
1 : 1 000 000
IONIAN SEA
RHODES
1 : 1 000 000
ÆGEAN SEA
Projection : Lambert's conformal conic
Motorways
Principal Roads
Other Roads
Airports
Elevations in metres
COPYRIGHT GEORGE PHILIP & SON, LTD.

Kolguyev
P-ov. Kanin
Timanskiy Kryazh
Bolshezemelskaya Tundra
Arkhangelsk
Beloye More (White Sea)
Kolskiy Poluostrov
Murmansk
Syktyvkar
Perm
Kirov
Kazan
Ufa
Nizhniy Novgorod
Yaroslavl
Vologda
Kostroma
Ivanovo
Vladimir
Ryazan
MOSKVA (Moscow)
Tula
Kaluga
Smolensk
Bryansk
Orel
Kursk
Voronezh
Tambov
Penza
Saratov
Samara
Orenburg
Tver
Novgorod
Pskov
ST. PETERBURG (Leningrad)
Ladozhskoye Ozero
Onezhskoye Ozero
Petrozavodsk
FINLAND
Helsinki
Tampere
Turku
Oulu
Gulf of Bothnia
Stockholm
ESTONIA
Tallinn
LATVIA
Riga
LITHUANIA
Vilnius
Kaunas
BELORUSSIA
Minsk
Gomel
Mogilev
Vitebsk
Brest
POLAND
WARSZAWA (Warsaw)
Kaliningrad
(RUSSIA)
Severnyye Uvaly
MORDOVIAN REP.
TATAR REP.
UDMURT REP.
MARI REP.
CHUVASH REP.
BASHKIR REP.
KARELIAN REP.

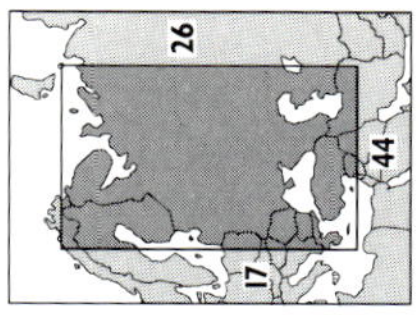

1:10 000 000
miles
km
BLACK SEA
CASPIAN SEA
MEDITERRANEAN SEA
Levant
Azovskoye More (Sea of Azov)
UKRAINE
KAZAKHSTAN
KALMYK REP.
GEORGIA
ARMENIA
AZERBAIJAN
TURKEY
SYRIA
IRAQ
IRAN
ROMANIA
BULGARIA
MOLDAVIA
CYPRUS
LEBANON
Kirgiz Step
Prikaspiyskaya Nizmennost
Bol'shoy Kavkaz
Anadolu Dağları
Toros Dağları
Kuzey Anadolu Dağları
Alborz
Zagros
Bādiyat ash Sham
KIYEV
KHARKOV
Volgograd
Rostov
Krasnodar
Novorossiysk
Sevastopol
Simferopol
Odessa
Kishinev
Dnepropetrovsk
Zaporozhye
Donetsk
Astrakhan
Makhachkala
Tbilisi
Yerevan
BAKU
Sumgait
TEHRAN
Tabrīz
Rasht
Qazvin
Hamadān
Qom
Baghdād
Kirkūk
Al Mawşil
Halab
Ḥamāh
Ḥimş
Dimashq (Damascus)
Bayrūt (Beirut)
Adana
Mersin
Konya
Kayseri
Ankara
Samsun
Trabzon
Erzurum
Sivas
Malatya
Diyarbakir
İzmir (Smyrna)
Bursa
ISTANBUL
Varna
Burgas
Constanța
BUCUREȘTI (Bucharest)
Brașov
Ploiești
Brăila
Galați
Lvov
Rodhos
Dhodhekanisos
Kara Bogaz Gol
Volga
Don
Dnepr
Ural
Kura
Nahr al Furāt (Euphrates)
Nahr Dijlah (Tigris)
Projection: Conical with two standard parallels
Division between Greeks and Turks in Cyprus; Turks to the North.
1 Kabardino-Balkar Rep.
2 North Ossetian Rep. (Azer.)
3 Nakhichevan Rep. (Azer.)
4 Checheno-Ingush Rep.
East from Greenwich
COPYRIGHT GEORGE PHILIP & SON LTD

1:20 000 000

6 7 8 9

A
B
C
D
E
F
10
11
12
13
14
OCEAN
Laptev Sea
East Siberian Sea
Sea of Okhotsk
Bering Sea
Sea of Japan
Severnaya Zemlya
Ostrov Komsomolets
Ostrov Oktyabrskoy Revolyutsii
Ostrov Bolshevik
Proliv Vilkitskogo
Poluostrov Taymyr
Gory Byrranga
Novosibirskiye Ostrova
Ostrov Kotelnyy
Ostrov Faddeyevskiy
Ostrov Novaya Sibir
Ostrova De Longa
Lyakhovskiye Ostrova
Proliv Dmitriya Lapteva
Ostrov Vrangelya
Ostrova Medvezhi
Chukotskoye More
Mys Dezhneva (East C.)
St. Lawrence I. (U.S.A.)
Anadyrskiy Zaliv
Chukotskiy Khrebet
Koryakskiy Khrebet
Penzhinskaya Guba
Gizhiginskaya Guba
Zaliv Shelikhova
Poluostrov Kamchatka
Petropavlovsk-Kamchatskiy
Komandorskiye Ostrova
Kurilskiye Ostrova
Verkhoyanskiy Khrebet
Khrebet Cherskogo
Kolymskoye
Khrebet Dzhugdzhur
Stanovoy Khrebet
Yablonovyy Khrebet
Sikhote Alin
Sakhalin
Tatarskiy Proliv
Zaliv Sakhalinskiy
Yakutsk
Tiksi
Magadan
Okhotsk
Olekminsk
Nordvik
Norilsk
Krasnoyarsk
Bratsk
Irkutsk
Angarsk
Ulan Ude
Chita
Kirensk
Vitim
Blagoveshchensk
Khabarovsk
Komsomolsk
Nikolayevsk-na-Amure
Vladivostok
Nakhodka
Ussuriysk
Yuzhno-Sakhalinsk
Ostrov Iturup
Ostrov Kunashir
Hokkaidō
Sapporo
Hakodate
Honshū
Niigata
Kanazawa
Toyama
Qiqihar
Harbin
Jiamusi
Jilin
Changchun
Shenyang
Fushun
Anshan
Dalian
Beijing
Hohhot
Baotou
Zhangjiakou
Ulaanbaatar (Ulan Bator)
Chongjin
Pyongyang
Wŏnsan
Sŏul
Inch'on
Taegu
Pusan
NORTH KOREA
SOUTH KOREA
MONGOLIA
GOBI
Hentiyn Nuruu
Hangayn Nuruu
Da Hinggan Ling
Arctic Circle
Ozero Baykal
Lena
Amur
Boundaries of Autonomous Republics
COPYRIGHT. GEORGE PHILIP & SON. LTD.

1:50 000 000
miles
km
ARCTIC OCEAN
PACIFIC OCEAN
INDIAN OCEAN
Barents Sea
Kara Sea
Laptev Sea
Bering Sea
Sea of Okhotsk
Sea of Japan
Yellow Sea
East China Sea
South China Sea
Sulu Sea
Celebes Sea
Banda Sea
Arafura Sea
Java Sea
Bay of Bengal
Arabian Sea
Caspian Sea
Aral Sea
Black Sea
Mediterranean Sea
Red Sea
The Gulf
G. of Oman
G. of Aden
Baltic Sea
North Sea
Adriatic Sea
White Sea
Novaya Zemlya
Severnaya Zemlya
New Siberian Is.
Wrangel I.
Taimyr Peninsula
Kamchatka Peninsula
Sakhalin
Kuril Is.
Hokkaido
Honshu
Kyushu
Shikoku
Ryukyu Is.
Formosa
Hainan
Philippine Is.
Luzon
Mindanao
Borneo
Celebes
Sumatra
Java
Timor
New Guinea
Australia
Ceylon
Andaman Is.
Nicobar Is.
Maldive Is.
Laccadive Is.
Socotra
Seychelles
Cyprus
Iceland
Greenland
British Isles
Scandinavia
Finland
Svalbard
Ural Mountains
West Siberian Plain
Central Siberian Plateau
Verkhoyansk Range
Gydan Ra. (Kolyma)
Stanovoy Ra.
Yablonovy Ra.
Sayan Mts.
Altai
Plateau of Mongolia
Gobi
Great Khingan Mts.
Manchurian Plain
Tien Shan
Kunlun Shan
Plateau of Tibet
Himalaya
Karakoram Ra.
Hindu Kush
Pamir
Plateau of Iran
Elburz Mts.
Caucasus
Turanian Plain
Steppe
Arabia
Mesopotamia
Syrian Desert
Anatolia
Deccan
India
Thar
Eastern Ghats
Western Ghats
Malay Peninsula
Somali Peninsula
Libyan Desert
Lake Victoria
Everest 8848
Kinabalu 4101
Elbrus 5633
Ararat 5165
Demavend 5604
Belukha 4506
Communism Pk. 7495
Narodnaya 1894
Lena
Yenisei
Ob
Irtysh
Amur
Kolyma
Indigirka
Angara
Selenga
Volga
Ural
Don
Dnepr
Danube
Vistula
Oder
Elbe
Rhine
Syr Darya
Amu Darya
Indus
Ganga
Brahmaputra
Irrawaddy
Salween
Mekong
Chao Phraya
Hwang Ho
Yangtze
Sikiang
Tigris
Euphrates
Nile
Tropic of Cancer
Arctic Circle
Equator
East from Greenwich
Projection: Bonne
COPYRIGHT, GEORGE PHILIP & SON, LTD.

1:50 000 000
miles
km
ARCTIC OCEAN
PACIFIC OCEAN
INDIAN OCEAN
RUSSIA
CHINA
MONGOLIA
KAZAKHSTAN
INDIA
PAKISTAN
AFGHANISTAN
IRAN
IRAQ
SAUDI ARABIA
TURKEY
EUROPE
AFRICA
THAILAND
BURMA (MYANMAR)
PHILIPPINES
INDONESIA
MALAYSIA
AUSTRALIA
Peking
Tokyo
Moscow
Delhi
Calcutta
Bombay
Shanghai
Hong Kong
Manila
Jakarta
Tehran
Baghdad
Bangkok
Karachi
Tashkent
Ulan Bator
Seoul
Peking Capital Cities
East from Greenwich
Projection: Bonne
COPYRIGHT GEORGE PHILIP & SON, LTD

SEA OF OKHOTSK
SEA OF JAPAN
RUSSIA
CHINA
NORTH KOREA
HOKKAIDO
TŌHOKU
CHŪBU
Sakhalin
La Pérouse Strait
(Sōya-Kaikyō)
Nemuro-Kaikyō
Ostrov Kunashir
Abashiri-Wan
Ishikari-Wan
(Otaru-Wan)
Uchiura-Wan
Tsugaru-Kaikyō
Mutsu-Wan
Sendai-Wan
Ozero Khanka
Zaliv Petra Velikogo
Sikhote Alin
Wakkanai
Rishiri-Tō
Rebun-Tō
Kitami
Asahikawa
Abashiri
Kushiro
Nemuro
Obihiro
SAPPORO
Otaru
Ebetsu
Tomakomai
Muroran
Hakodate
Okushiri-Tō
Aomori
Hachinohe
Hirosaki
Noshiro
Akita
Morioka
Miyako
Kamaishi
Ichinoseki
Kesennuma
Ishinomaki
Shiogama
Sendai
Yamagata
Sakata
Tsuruoka
Yonezawa
Fukushima
Kōriyama
Niigata
Shibata
Sado
Vladivostok
Nakhodka
Ussuriysk
Artem
Spassk-Dalniy
Lesozavodsk
Dalnerechensk
Dalnegorsk
Kavalerovo
Preobrazheniye
Bikin
Jiamusi
Chongjin
Najin
Khasan
Kraskino
Slavyanka
Pogranichnyy
Lipovcy
Manzovka
Svetlaya
Amgu
Terney
Plastun
Olga
Suchan
Lazo
Trudovoye
Nakhodka
1745
1855
1498
2290
2077
2052
1661
1914
2280
1980
1819
A
B
C
D
E
F
5
6
7
8
9
10
11
12
46
44
42
40
132
134
136
138
140
142
144

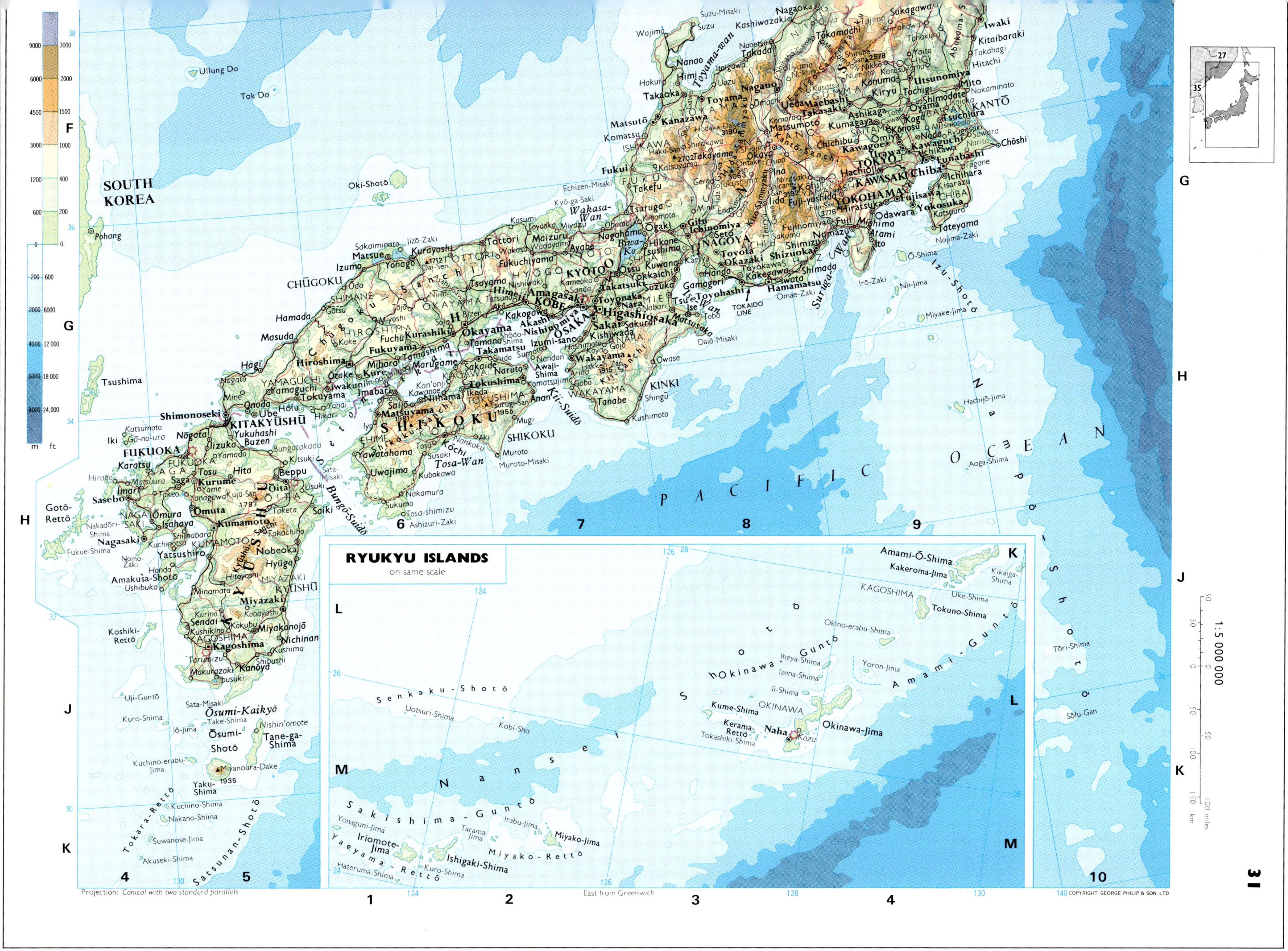

1:5 000 000
50 0 50 100 miles
50 0 50 100 150 km
SOUTH KOREA
Pohang
Ullung Do
Tok Do
Tsushima
Oki-Shotō
CHŪGOKU
SHIKOKU
KINKI
KANTŌ
KYŪSHŪ
Shimonoseki
KITAKYŪSHŪ
FUKUOKA
Nagasaki
Sasebo
Kumamoto
Kagoshima
Miyazaki
Ōita
Beppu
Hiroshima
Okayama
Matsuyama
Takamatsu
Kōchi
Tokushima
KŌBE
ŌSAKA
KYŌTO
NAGOYA
Shizuoka
Hamamatsu
YOKOHAMA
KAWASAKI
TŌKYŌ
Chiba
Nagano
Niigata
Toyama
Kanazawa
Fukui
Utsunomiya
Mito
Iwaki
Chōshi
Izu-Shotō
Hachijō-Jima
Miyake-Jima
P A C I F I C   O C E A N
Bungo-Suidō
Kii-Suidō
Tosa-Wan
Ōsumi-Kaikyō
Tane-ga-Shima
Yaku-Shima
Tokara-Rettō
Satsunan-Shotō
Gotō-Rettō
Koshiki-Rettō
RYUKYU ISLANDS
on same scale
Amami-Ō-Shima
Tokuno-Shima
Okino-erabu-Shima
Amami-Guntō
Okinawa-Guntō
Okinawa-Jima
Naha
Kume-Shima
Kerama-Rettō
Senkaku-Shotō
Sakishima-Guntō
Miyako-Jima
Ishigaki-Shima
Iriomote-Jima
Yonaguni-Jima
Yaeyama-Rettō
Miyako-Rettō
Nansei-Shotō
Tōri-Shima
Sōfu-Gan
Projection: Conical with two standard parallels
East from Greenwich
© COPYRIGHT GEORGE PHILIP & SON LTD.

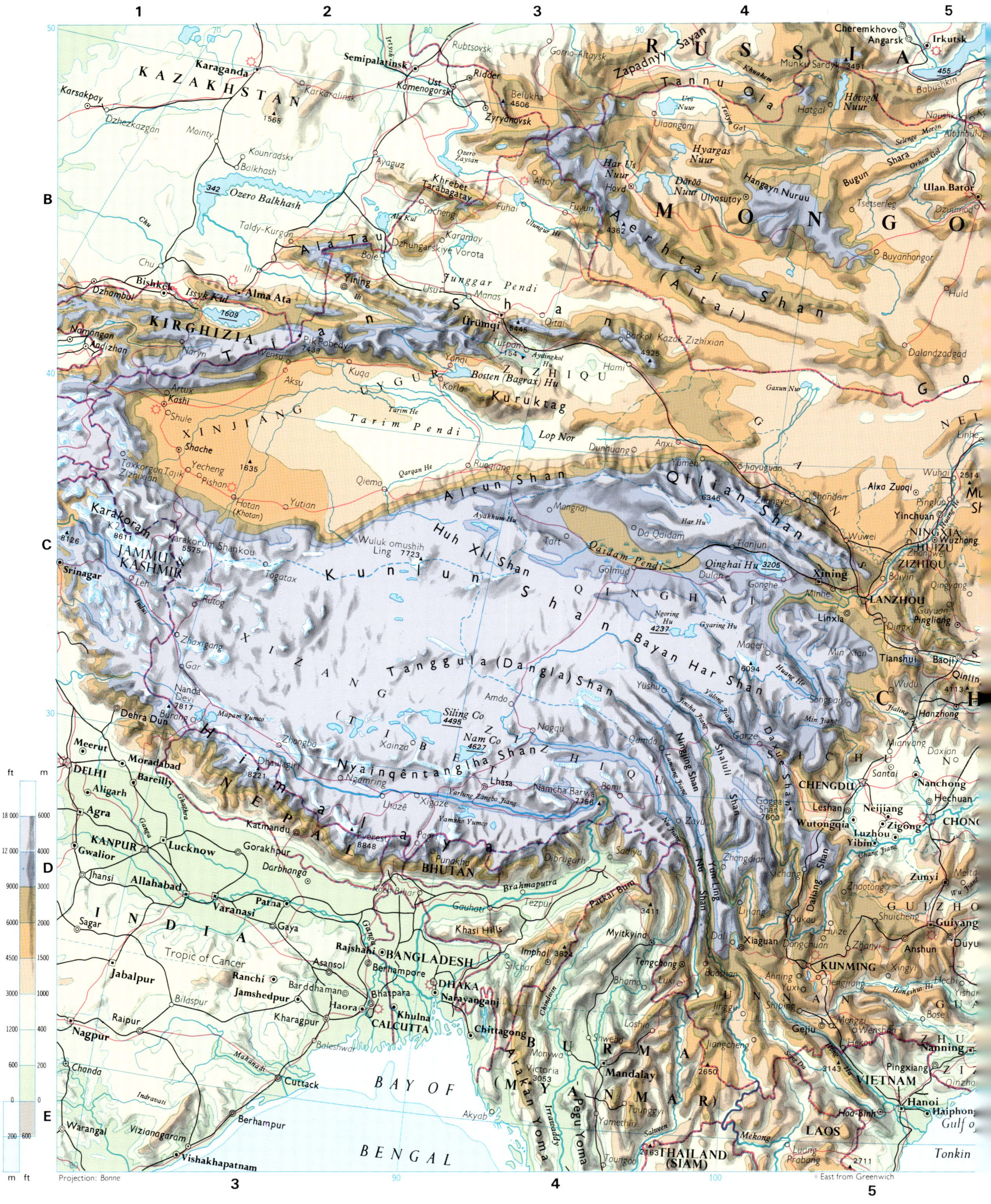

KAZAKHSTAN
RUSSIA
MONGOLIA
KIRGHIZIA
XINJIANG UYGUR ZIZHIQU
QINGHAI
XIZANG (TIBET) ZIZHIQU
SICHUAN
YUNNAN
INDIA
NEPAL
BHUTAN
BANGLADESH
BURMA (MYANMAR)
THAILAND (SIAM)
LAOS
VIETNAM
BAY OF BENGAL
Tropic of Cancer
Tarim Pendi
Junggar Pendi
Tian Shan
Altun Shan
Kunlun Shan
Qilian Shan
Tanggula (Dangla) Shan
Bayan Har Shan
Himalaya
Nyainqêntanglha Shan
Karakoram
JAMMU & KASHMIR
Aerhtai Shan (Altai)
Hangayn Nuruu
Ozero Balkhash
Lop Nor
Qinghai Hu
Ürümqi
Lhasa
Kashi
Xining
LANZHOU
CHENGDU
KUNMING
Alma Ata
Bishkek
Karaganda
Semipalatinsk
Irkutsk
Ulan Bator
DELHI
Agra
KANPUR
Lucknow
Allahabad
Varanasi
Patna
Katmandu
DHAKA
CALCUTTA
Chittagong
Mandalay
Hanoi
Haiphong
Nanning
Guiyang
Everest 8848
Projection: Bonne
East from Greenwich

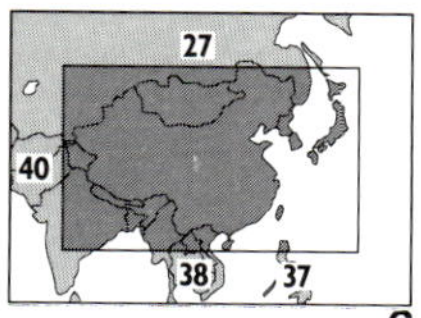

1:15 000 000

100 0 100 200 300 400 miles

100 0 100 200 300 400 500 600 km

NORTHERN CHINA AND KOREA

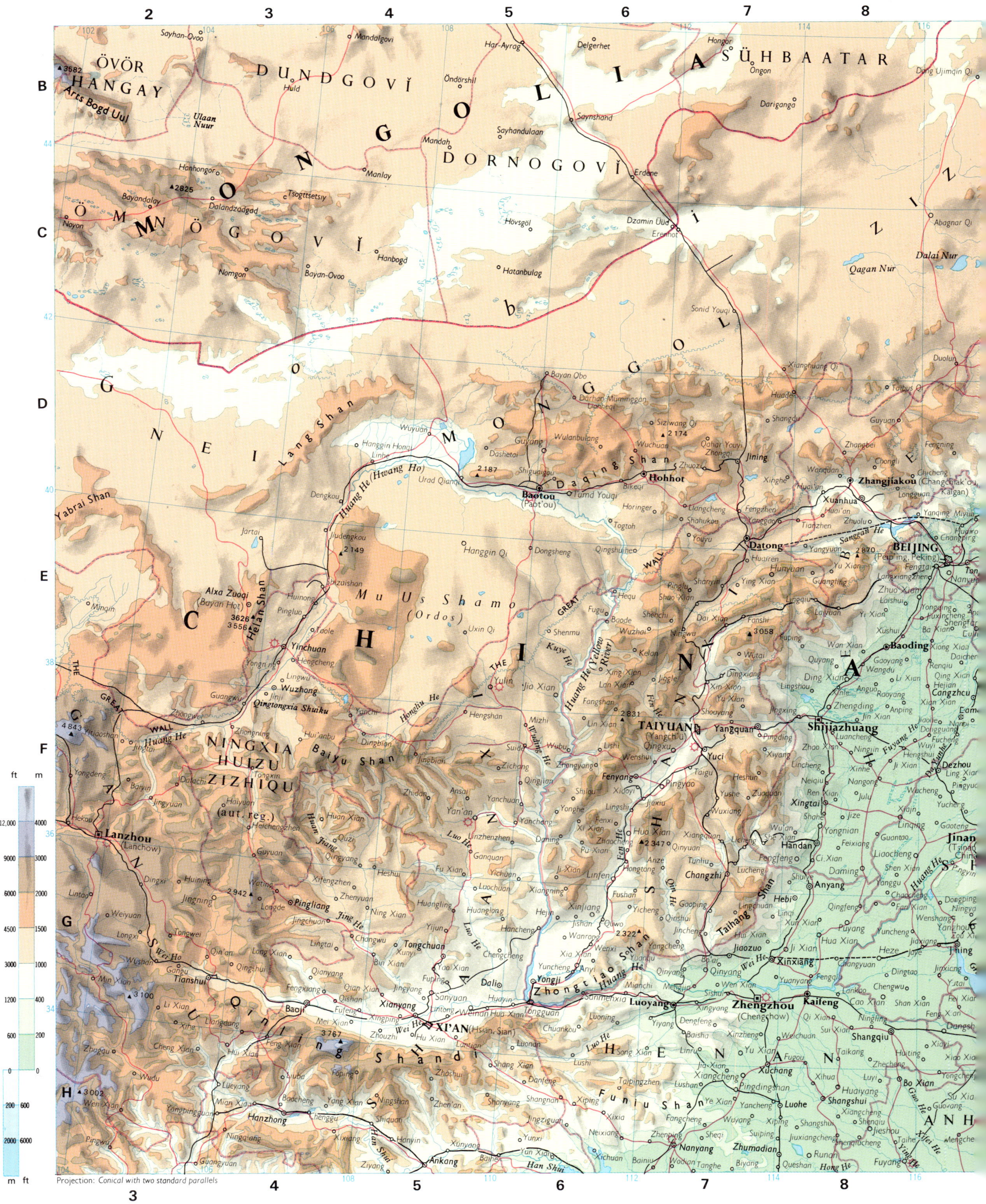

1:6 000 000
miles
km
HEILONGJIANG
JILIN
LIAONING
NEI MONGOL (cut off at the map edge; "H I Q U" visible)
SHANDONG (cut off at the map edge; "A N D O N G" visible)
JIANGSU
RUSSIA
NORTH KOREA
SOUTH KOREA
JAPAN
SEA OF JAPAN
Korea Bay
Liaodong Wan
Bo Hai
(Gulf of Chihli)
HUANG HAI
(Yellow Sea)
Laizhou Wan
Shandong Banda
Liaodong Bandao
Tongjosŏn Man
Korea Strait
Tsushima-kaikyō
Cease Fire Line
Changbai Shan
Zhangguangcai Ling
Dongbei (Manchuria)
HARBIN
(Haerbin)
Changchun
Jilin
(Kirin)
Shuangliao
Siping
Fushun
SHENYANG
(Mukden)
Anshan
Benxi
Jinzhou
Yingkou
Dandong
DALIAN
(Lüda)
Lüshun
Qinhuangdao
Tangshan
TIANJIN
(Tientsin)
Tanggu
Chifeng
Tongliao
Mudanjiang
Vladivostok
Ussuriysk
(Voroshilov)
Chongjin
Kimchaek
(Songjin)
Hamhung
Hŭngnam
Wŏnsan
P'YŎNGYANG
Sinŭiju
Kaesŏng
SOUL
(Seoul)
INCH'ŎN
Suwŏn
Ch'unch'ŏn
Kangnŭng
Taejŏn
Chŏnju
TAEGU
PUSAN
Kwangju
Mokpo
Ulsan
Pohang
Cheju
Cheju-do
Tsushima
Sasebo
Nagasaki
Ullung-do
Yantai
Weihai
QINGDAO
(Ch'ingtao)
Weifang
Zibo
Lianyungang
(Hsinhailien)
Xuzhou
Bengbu
Huai'an
Qingjiang
Hongze Hu
Paektu-san
2541
2522
1950
1915
1638
1678
East from Greenwich
COPYRIGHT, GEORGE PHILIP & SON, LTD.

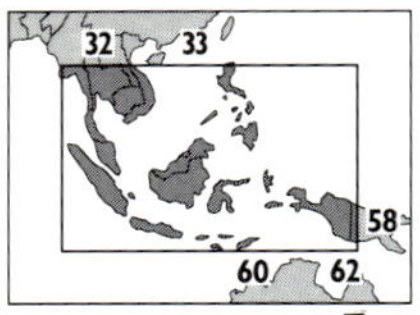
32
33
58
60
62

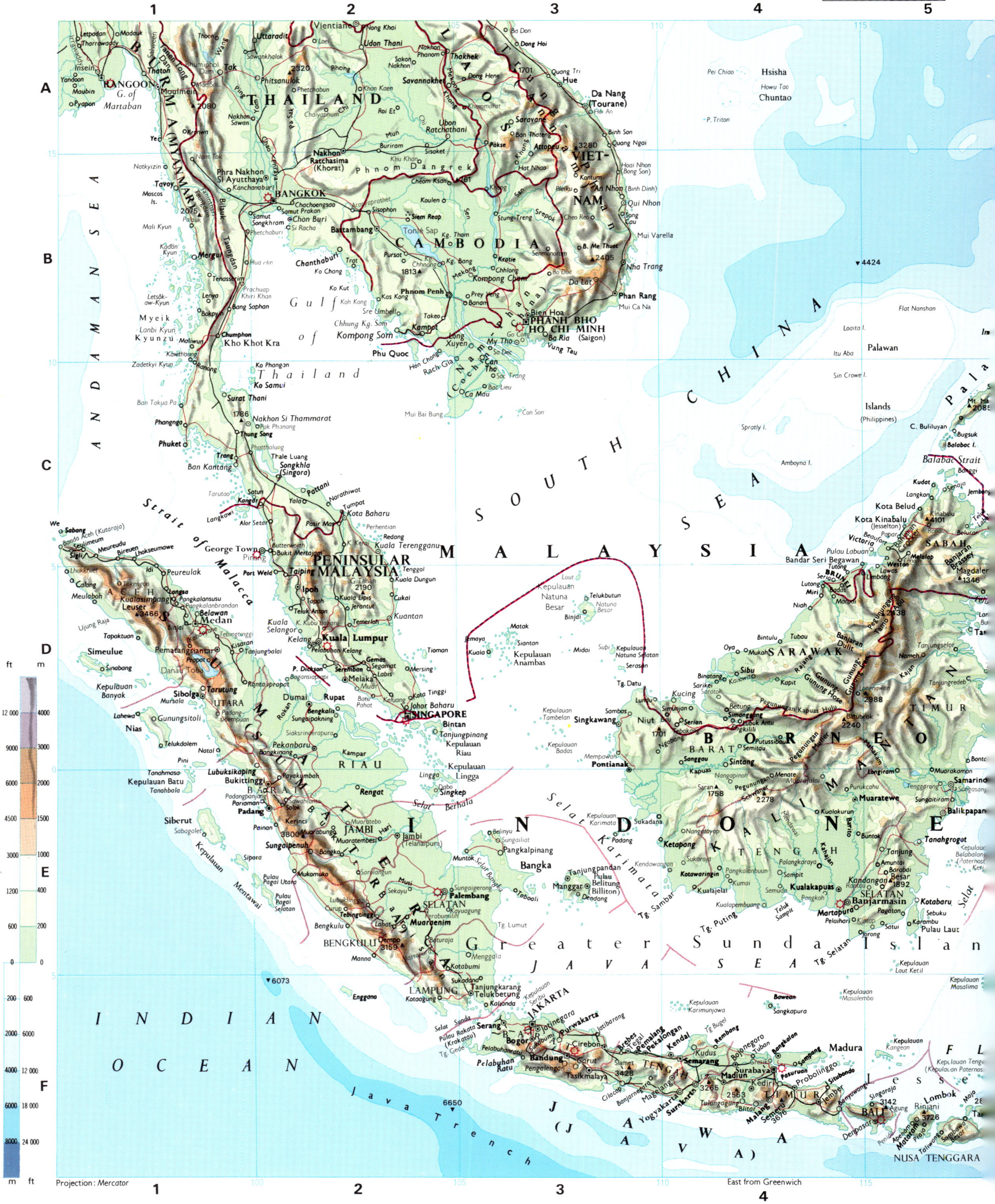
1
2
3
4
5
A
B
C
D
E
F
THAILAND
BURMA (MYANMAR)
LAOS
VIETNAM
CAMBODIA
RANGOON
G. of Martaban
BANGKOK
Vientiane
Hue
Da Nang (Tourane)
Phnom Penh
HO CHI MINH (Saigon)
Gulf of Thailand
ANDAMAN SEA
SOUTH CHINA SEA
MALAYSIA
PENINSULAR MALAYSIA
Kuala Lumpur
SINGAPORE
Strait of Malacca
Medan
Padang
Palembang
BENGKULU
SUMATERA
RIAU
JAMBI
Pontianak
BORNEO
SARAWAK
SABAH
BRUNEI
Bandar Seri Begawan
Kota Kinabalu
KALIMANTAN
Banjarmasin
INDONESIA
Bangka
JAKARTA
Bandung
Semarang
Surabaya
Madura
BALI
JAWA
JAVA SEA
Greater Sunda Islands
NUSA TENGGARA
INDIAN OCEAN
Java Trench
Palawan
Spratly I.
Hsisha
Natuna Besar
Kepulauan Anambas
Kepulauan Lingga
Siberut
Nias
Simeulue
Mentawai
Enggano
Projection: Mercator
East from Greenwich
ft
m

1:12 500 000
miles
km
JAVA AND MADURA
1:7 500 000
miles
km
Selat Sunda
JAKARTA
Bogor
Bandung
Cirebon
Semarang
Surakarta
Yogyakarta
Surabaya
Madura
Malang
Bali
Kepulauan Karimunjawa
Bawean
Nusa Barung
LUZON
Polillo Islands
MANILA
Mindoro
Samar
Leyte
Panay
Negros
Cebu
Bohol
Mindanao
Zamboanga
Davao
Sulu Arch.
SULU SEA
Palawan
SULAWESI SEA
Mindanao Trench
(Philippine Trench)
10 497
9540
PACIFIC OCEAN
BELAU
Babelthuap
FEDERATED STATES OF MICRONESIA
Yap Islands
Caroline Islands
Sonsorol Islands
Pulo Anna
Merir
Tobi
Helen Atoll
5798
Equator
Kepulauan Talaud
Kepulauan Sangihe
Manado
Halmahera
Morotai
Ternate
Tidore
MALUKU SEA
Kep. Bacan
Kepulauan Obi
Kepulauan Sula
Buru
Seram (Ceram)
Ambon
SULAWESI (CELEBES)
Teluk Tomini
Teluk Bone
Butung
Muna
Selayar
BANDA SEA
7440
FLORES SEA
Flores
Sumbawa
Sumba
Sawu Sea
Timor
Roti
Alor
NUSA TENGGARA TIMUR
Kepulauan Tanimbar
Yamdena
Kepulauan Kai
Kepulauan Aru
ARAFURA SEA
Misool
Waigeo
Jazirah Doberai (Vogelkop)
Manokwari
Teluk Cenderawasih
Yapen
Biak
IRIAN JAYA
Pegunungan Maoke
5029
Puncak Jaya
Jayapura
Merauke
PAPUA NEW GUINEA
COPYRIGHT. GEORGE PHILIP & SON. LTD.

Gulf of Tonkin
HANOI
Haiphong
Nam Dinh
Thanh Hoa
Vinh
Hue
Da Nang
Qui Nhon
Hainan
Haikou
Zhanjiang
Nanning
GUANGXI ZHUANGZU ZIZHIQU AUTONOMOUS REGION
YUNNAN
VIETNAM
LAOS
Vientiane
Luang Prabang
Tran Ninh
Savannakhet
Pakse
Udon Thani
Khon Kaen
Nakhon Ratchasima
Khorat
Ubon Ratchathani
Phnom Dangrek
CAMBODIA
Tonle Sap
Battambang
Siem Reap
THAILAND
BANGKOK
Thon Buri
Chiang Mai
Phitsanulok
Nakhon Sawan
Mekong
Salween
BURMA (MYANMAR)
SHAN STATE
Mandalay
Taunggyi
Toungoo
Rangoon
Pegu
Moulmein
Tavoy
Gulf of Martaban
Dawna Range
Central Highlands

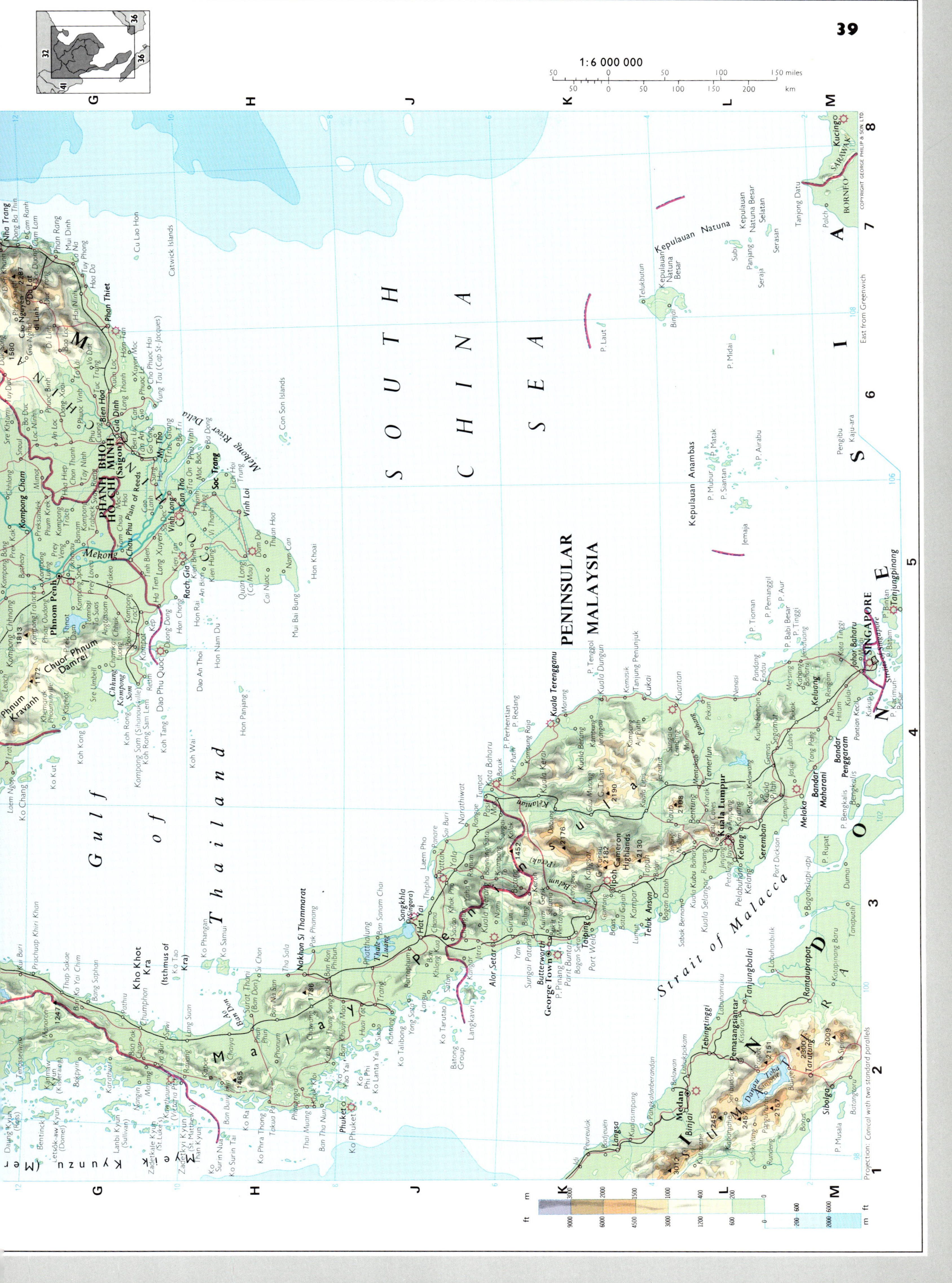
1:6 000 000
50 0 50 100 150 miles
50 0 50 100 150 200 km
SOUTH CHINA SEA
Gulf of Thailand
PENINSULAR MALAYSIA
Strait of Malacca
INDONESIA
VIETNAM
KAMPUCHEA
MALAYSIA
SINGAPORE
Kuala Lumpur
Phnom Penh
PHANH BHO HO CHI MINH (Saigon)
Mekong
Mekong River Delta
Kepulauan Natuna
Kepulauan Anambas
SARAWAK
BORNEO
Kuching
Medan
Danau Toba
Penang
George Town
Hat Yai
Songkhla
Phuket
Kuala Terengganu
Kuantan
Melaka
Tanjungpinang
East from Greenwich
Projection: Conical with two standard parallels
COPYRIGHT GEORGE PHILIP & SON, LTD.
m ft
3000 9000
2000 6000
1500 4500
1000 3000
400 1200
200 600
0 0
200 600
2000 6000

ARABIAN SEA
Gulf of Kachchh
Gulf of Khambhat
Gulf of Mannar (Manaar)
Palk Strait
Palk Bay
Rann of Kachchh
Mouths of the Indus
Kori Creek
Hindu Kush
Karakoram
Ladakh Range
Zaskar Mountains
Safid Kuh
Siahan Range
Central Makran Range
Makran Coast Range
Toba Kakar
Kirthar Range
Pab Hills
Thar or Great Indian Desert
Sind Sagar Doab
Bari Doab
Satpura Range
Ajanta Range
Balaghat Range
Western Ghats
Eastern Ghats
Nallamalai Hills
Malabar Coast
Coromandel Coast
Seistan
Dasht-e Khash
Dasht-e Margow
Registan
AFGHANISTAN
IRAN
PAKISTAN
NORTH WEST FRONTIER
JAMMU AND KASHMIR
HIMACHAL PRADESH
PUNJAB
HARYANA
RAJASTHAN
GUJARAT
MADHYA PRADESH
MAHARASHTRA
ANDHRA PRADESH
KARNATAKA
TAMIL NADU
SRI LANKA (CEYLON)
INDIA (BHARAT)
Kabul
Herat
Qandahar
Peshawar
Rawalpindi
Islamabad
Srinagar
Lahore
Amritsar
Multan
Quetta
Sukkur
Hyderabad
KARACHI
DELHI
Jaipur
Agra
Ahmadabad
Indore
Bhopal
BOMBAY
Pune (Poona)
Nagpur
Madras
Bangalore
Mysore
Madurai
Colombo
Galle
Kandy
Jaffna
Trincomalee
Cape Comorin
Dondra Head
Tropic of Cancer
Continuation Southwards on same scale
Projection: Conical with two standard parallels

1:10 000 000
miles
km
C H I N A
X I Z A N G
(T I B E T)
Q I N G H A I
S I C H U A N
Y U N N A N
Tanggula (Dangla) Shan
Bayan Har Shan
Nyainqêntanglha Shan
Nganglong Kangri
Lhasa
Xigazê
Gyangzê
Yarlung Zangbo Jiang (Brahmaputra)
Maquan He (Tsangpo)
Nam Co
Siling Co
Gyaring Co
NEPAL
Katmandu
Mt. Everest 8848
Kanchenjunga 8598
Dhaulagiri 8221
SIKKIM
BHUTAN
Thimphu
Punakha
ARUNACHAL PRADESH
ASSAM
NAGALAND
MANIPUR
MIZORAM
TRIPURA
MEGHALAYA
Shillong
Cherrapunji
BANGLADESH
Dhaka
Chittagong
Barisal
Khulna
Comilla
Sylhet
Mymensingh
Rajshahi
Rangpur
Dinajpur
Pabna
Jessore
Cox's Bazar
WEST BENGAL
CALCUTTA
Haora
Barddhaman
Durgapur
Asansol
Kharagpur
Siliguri
Darjiling
Jalpaiguri
BIHAR
Patna
Gaya
Ranchi
Jamshedpur
Dhanbad
Bhagalpur
Munger
Darbhanga
Muzaffarpur
Purnia
Chhapra
Hazaribag
Lucknow
Allahabad
Varanasi (Benares)
Gorakhpur
Faizabad
Jaunpur
Azamgarh
Mirzapur
Rewa
Bilaspur
Raipur
Durg
Jagdalpur
ORISSA
Cuttack
Bhubaneshwar
Puri
Chilka Lake
Raurkela
Sambalpur
Berhampur
Baleshwar
Vishakhapatnam
Vizianagaram
Kakinada (Cocanada)
Machilipatnam (Bandar)
Rajahmundry
Northern Circars
Eastern Ghats
Mouths of the Ganga
Sundarbans
BAY OF BENGAL
INDIAN OCEAN
BURMA
Mandalay
Rangoon
Bassein
Henzada
Prome
Pegu Yoma
Arakan Yoma
Arakan Coast
Akyab
Rambre Kyun
Manaung Kyun
Irrawaddy
Sittang Myit
Chindwin
Myitkyina
Bhamo
Lashio
Kalemyo
Sagaing
Meiktila
Pyinmana
Toungoo
Maulamyaing (Moulmein)
Gulf of Martaban
Tavoy
KACHIN
CHIN
SHAN
KAYAH
KAWTHOOLEI
THAILAND
Chiengmai
Lampang
Tak (Rahaeng)
Tanen Tong Dan
Tropic of Cancer
Preparis North Channel
Preparis South Channel
Coco Kyunzu (Burma)
Pariparit Kyun (Burma)
Heinze Is.
Moscos Islands
Lauinglon Bok Is.
East from Greenwich
COPYRIGHT. GEORGE PHILIP & SON. LTD

AFGHANISTAN
PAKISTAN
BALUCHISTAN
N.W. FRONTIER PROVINCE
PUNJAB
SIND
RAJASTHAN
HARYANA
JAMMU AND KASHMIR
HIMACHAL PRADESH
MADHYA PRADESH
ARABIAN SEA
Gulf of Kachchh
Rann of Kachchh
Mouths of the Indus
THAR DESERT (Great Indian Desert)
THAL DESERT
Salt Range
Kabul
Peshawar
Rawalpindi
Islamabad
Srinagar
Lahore
Amritsar
Multan
Quetta
Qandahar
Sukkur
Hyderabad
KARACHI
Bahawalpur
Delhi
Jaipur
Agra
Jodhpur
Bikaner
Ajmer
Udaipur
AHMADABAD
Vadodara
Rajkot
Jamnagar
Bhuj
Porbandar
Indore
Ujjain
Bhopal
Gwalior
Kota
Chandigarh
Ludhiana
Simla
Jammu
Sialkot
Faisalabad
Sargodha
Mardan
Bannu
Kohat
Meerut
Tropic of Cancer
Projection: Conical with two standard parallels
ft m
18,000 6000
12,000 4000
9000 3000
6000 2000
4500 1500
3000 1000
1200 400
600 200
0 0
200 600
2000 6000
m ft

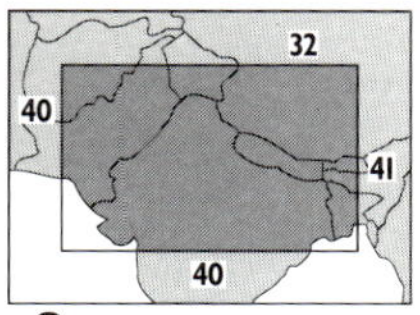

1:6 000 000

50 0 50 100 miles

50 0 50 100 150 km

1
2
3
4
5
B
C
D
E
F
TURKEY
ARMENIA
AZERB
CYPRUS
MEDITERRANEAN SEA
LEBANON
ISRAEL
SYRIA
JORDAN
IRAQ
EGYPT
SAUDI ARABIA
KUWAIT
RED SEA
AN NAFŪD
Konya
Kayseri
Sivas
Erzurum
Yerevan
Malatya
Elazığ
Diyarbakır
Kahramanmaraş
Gaziantep
Adana
Mersin
Tarsus
Iskenderun
Antakya
Şanliurfa
Mardin
Van Gölü
Tabrīz
Orūmīyeh
Nicosia
Famagusta
Limassol
Larnaca
Halab (Aleppo)
Al Lādhiqīyah (Latakia)
Ḥamāh
Ḥimṣ (Homs)
Tarābulus (Tripoli)
Bayrūt (Beirut)
Ṣaydā (Sidon)
DIMASHQ (Damascus)
Ḥefa (Haifa)
TEL AVIV-YAFO
Jerusalem
'Ammān
Az Zarqā'
Be'er Sheva
Al 'Aqabah
Ar Raqqah
Dayr az Zawr
Tudmur (Palmyra)
Al Qāmishlī
Al Ḥasakah
Al Mawṣil (Mosul)
Arbīl
Kirkūk
As Sulaymānīyah
Tikrīt
Sāmarrā'
BAGHDĀD
Karbalā
An Najaf
Al Ḥillah
Al Kūt
An Nāṣirīyah
Al Baṣrah
Ar Ruṭbah
Bakhtārān
Ḥā'il
Buraydah
'Unayzah
Al Madīnah (Medina)
Ar Riyāḍ (Riyadh)
Tabūk
Al Jawf
Hafar al Bāṭin
Gebel el Tīh (SINAI)
Khalīj al 'Aqabah
Khalīg el Suweis
ft m
18 000 6000
12 000 4000
9000 3000
6000 2000
4500 1500
3000 1000
1200 400
600 200
0 0
200 600
2000 6000
m ft
Projection: Conical with two standard parallels

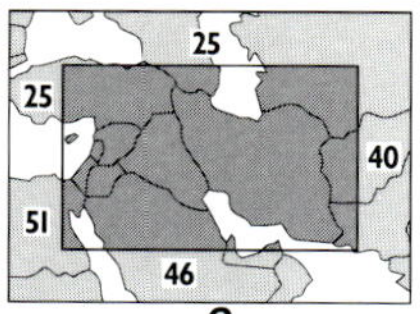

1:7 000 000

50 0 50 100 150 200 miles

50 0 50 100 150 200 250 300 km

ARABIA AND THE HORN OF AFRICA

1:15 000 000

Projection: Sanson-Flamsteed's Sinusoidal

East from Greenwich

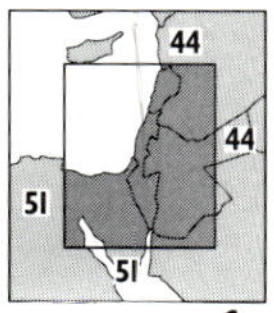

1:2 500 000

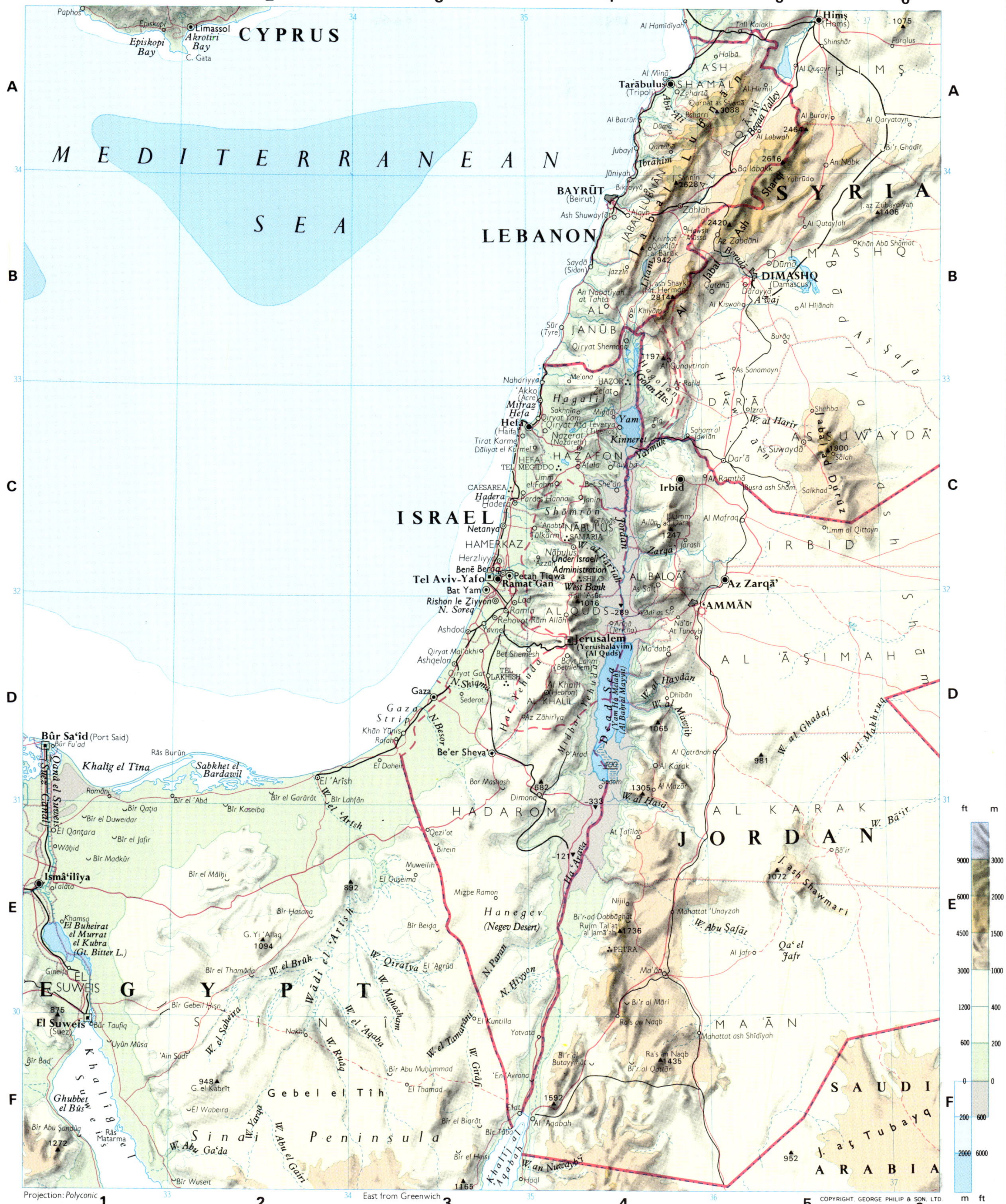

Projection: Polyconic
East from Greenwich
1949 Armistice Line, 1967 and 1974 Cease Fire Lines

1:40 000 000
200 0 200 400 600 800 1000 miles
200 0 200 400 600 800 1000 1200 1400 1600 km
British Isles
ATLANTIC OCEAN
Bay of Biscay
Carpathians
Aral Sea
Caspian Sea
Mt. Blanc 4807
Alps
Dinaric Alps
Adriatic Sea
Apennines
Black Sea
Elbrus 5633
Caucasus
Pyrenees
Iberian Peninsula
Corsica
Sardinia
Anatolia
Mediterranean Sea
C. Bon
Sicily
Malta
5121
Crete
Cyprus
Levant
Mesopotamia
Tigris
Euphrates
6576
Madeira
Str. of Gibraltar
High Plateaus
Saharan Atlas
Middle Atlas
High Atlas
Anti Atlas
Toubkal 4165
Dra
G. of Gabes
Chott Djerid
Tripolitania
G. of Sidra
Cyrenaica
Syrian Desert
Canary Is.
3718
Tenerife
Igidi
Siwa
Sinai 2642
Arabian Desert
Nile
Hejaz
Arabia
The Gulf
Bahrain I.
Tuat
Tasili Plateau
Fezzan
Kufra
Libyan Desert
Egypt
El Kharga
Red Sea
Tropic of Cancer
Hoggar
Sahara
El Djouf
Ras Nouadhibou
Nubian Desert
Nubia
Tibesti 3415
Air
Adrar
Bilma
Rub' al Khali
Cape Verde Is.
C. Vert
Senegal
Senegambia
Gambia
Niger (Joliba)
Niger
Volta
Atbara
Ras Dashan 4620
Tana
Perim I.
Gulf of Aden
Str. of Bab el Mandeb
Ras Asir
Socotra
Fouta Djalon
Sudan
L. Chad
Wadai
Darfur
Kordofan
White Nile
Blue Nile
Ethiopian Highlands
Chari
Bahr el Ghazal
Bahr el Jebel
Somali Peninsula
Guinea
Benue
Adamawa Highlands
Dar Banda
Shaballe
Gold Coast
Slave Coast
Bight of Benin
Grain Coast
Ivory Coast
C. Palmas
Cameroon Peak 4070
Uele
Turkana
6363
Bioko
Bight of Bonny
Gulf of Guinea
Principe
São Tomé
Annobón
C. Lopez
Ogoue
Congo
Zaire (Congo)
Oubangi
L. Mobutu Sese Seko
Chutes Boyoma
Ruwenzori 5109
L. Edward
Elgon 4321
Kenya 5199
Juba
Shibeli
Equator
L. Victoria
Tana
Basin
Lualaba
L. Kivu
Kilimanjaro 5895
INDIAN OCEAN
Kasai
Sankuru
Pool Malebo
Pemba
Zanzibar
L. Tanganyika
Ascension
Cuango
Lukuga
Cuanza
L. Mweru
Rungwe 2961
L. Nyasa
Aldabra Is.
Shaba
Bangweulu
Luapula
Ruvuma
C. Delgado
Malawi
Comoros Is.
Bié Plateau
Cuando
Zambezi
Mozambique Channel
ATLANTIC OCEAN
Cunene
Cubango
Mulanje 3000
Shire
Madagascar
St. Helena
C. Fria
Victoria Falls
2643
Namib Desert
Limpopo
Walvis Bay
Tropic of Capricorn
Mauritius
Réunion
Kalahari
Delagoa Bay
High Veld
Vaal
Orange
3482
Drakensberg
Compass B. 2505
Nuweveldberge
Gr. Karoo
Swartberg
C. of Good Hope
C. Agulhas
Agulhas Bank
Algoa Bay
Projection: Zenithal Equidistant.
West from Greenwich
East from Greenwich
COPYRIGHT. GEORGE PHILIP & SON LTD

1:40 000 000
200 0 200 400 600 800 1000 miles
200 0 200 400 600 800 1000 1200 1400 1600 km
ATLANTIC OCEAN
Bay of Biscay
UNITED KINGDOM
London
NETH.
BELG.
GERMANY
POLAND
Warsaw
Paris
FRANCE
SWITZ.
Prague
CZECHOSLOVAKIA
Vienna
AUSTRIA
HUNGARY
Kiev
UKRAINE
RUSSIA
Volgograd
KAZAKHSTAN
Aral Sea
Caspian Sea
Odessa
ROMANIA
Black Sea
YUGOSLAVIA
BULGARIA
Istanbul
ITALY
Adriatic Sea
Corsica
Rome
Sardinia
ALB.
GREECE
Athens
Madrid
SPAIN
PORTUGAL
Lisbon
Ankara
TURKEY
Baku
Tehran
Mediterranean Sea
Algiers
Annaba
Constantine
Oran
Tunis
MALTA
Sicily
Crete
CYPRUS
Aleppo
Mosul
SYRIA
LEB.
Damascus
Baghdad
Esfahan
IRAN
Tetouan
Gibraltar (Br.)
Casablanca
Rabat
Fès
MOROCCO
Marrakesh
Madeira (Port.)
Canary Is. (Sp.)
ALGERIA
TUNISIA
Sfax
Tripoli
Misratah
Benghazi
Alexandria
Port Said
Tel Aviv-Jaffa
ISRAEL
Jerusalem
JORDAN
Syrian Desert
IRAQ
Euphrates
Tigris
Basra
KUWAIT
The Gulf
Ghadames
LIBYA
CAIRO
Suez
El Faiyum
Asyut
Nile
EGYPT
Red Sea
Bahrain
QATAR
SAUDI ARABIA
Riyadh
Medina
Tropic of Cancer
Mecca
Jedda
El Aaiun
WESTERN SAHARA
Dakhla
F'Dérik
In Salah
Marzuq
Al Jawf
Aswan
Wadi-Halfa
Sahara
Ras Nouadhibou (Cap Blanc)
MAURITANIA
Nouakchott
Tombouctou (Timbuktu)
Agades
NIGER
CHAD
Pt. Sudan
Atbara
SUDAN
Omdurman
Khartoum
Kassala
Asmera
Mesewa
Eritrea
YEMEN
St. Louis
Dakar
SENEGAL
Senegal
MALI
GAMBIA
Banjul
GUINEA-BISSAU
Bissau
GUINEA
Conakry
Freetown
SIERRA LEONE
Monrovia
LIBERIA
Bamako
BURKINA FASO
Ouagadougou
Bobo-Dioulasso
Niger
Niamey
Kano
Maiduguri
L. Chad
Abéché
Ndjamena (Ft. Lamy)
El Fasher
El Obeid
Wad Medani
White Nile
Blue Nile
L. Tana
DJIBOUTI
Djibouti
G. of Aden
Socotra (Yemen)
Ras Asir (C. Guardafui)
Berbera
IVORY COAST
Bouake
Yamoussoukro
Abidjan
GHANA
Kumasi
Sekondi-Takoradi
TOGO
Lome
Accra
BENIN
Porto-Novo
Kaduna
NIGERIA
Abuja
Ibadan
Lagos
Benue
Enugu
Port Harcourt
Bight of Benin
Chari
CENTRAL AFRICAN REPUBLIC
Malakal
Addis Ababa
Harer
ETHIOPIA
Wau
Bahr el Jebel
Shabelle
SOMALI REP.
CAMEROON
Yaoundé
Bangui
Ubangi
Douala
Bioko
EQUATORIAL GUINEA
Rio Muni
Gulf of Guinea
SAO TOMÉ & PRINCIPE
Libreville
GABON
C. Lopez
Annobon
CONGO
Zaïre (Congo)
Mbandaka
Kisangani
L. Mobutu Sese Seko
UGANDA
Kampala
L. Edward
L. Victoria
Turkana
KENYA
Kisumu
Nairobi
Tana
Juba
Mogadishu (Mogadiscio)
Equator
Kismayu
INDIAN OCEAN
ZAÏRE
Lualaba
L. Kivu
Kigali
RWANDA
Bujumbura
BURUNDI
Mwanza
Kasai
Brazzaville
Kinshasa
Pointe Noire
CABINDA
Matadi
Kwango
Kananga
TANZANIA
L. Tanganyika
Dodoma
Zanzibar
Dar-es-Salaam
Mombasa
Ascension (Br.)
Luanda
Aldabra Is.
L. Mweru
Likasi
L. Nyasa (L. Malawi)
Ruvuma
C. Delgado
COMOROS
Antsiranana
ANGOLA
Lobito
Huambo
Lubumbashi
Ndola
ZAMBIA
Lilongwe
MALAWI
Lusaka
Zambezi
Blantyre
MOZAMBIQUE
Mozambique
Mahajanga
Mozambique Channel
Namibe
ATLANTIC
St. Helena (Br.)
Cunene
Cubango
C. Fria
Livingstone
Harare
ZIMBABWE
Bulawayo
Beira
Toamasina
Antananarivo
MADAGASCAR
MAURITIUS
Réunion (Fr.)
Fianarantsoa
NAMIBIA
Windhoek
BOTSWANA
OCEAN
Walvis Bay (South Africa)
Limpopo
Tropic of Capricorn
Gaborone
TRANSVAAL
Pretoria
Mbabane
SWAZILAND
Johannesburg
Maputo
Vaal
ORANGE FREE STATE
Orange
Kimberley
Bloemfontein
Maseru
LESOTHO
NATAL
Durban
SOUTH AFRICA
CAPE PROVINCE
East London
Port Elizabeth
Cape Town
C. of Good Hope
C. Agulhas
Nairobi Capital Cities
Projection: Zenithal Equidistant.
West from Greenwich
East from Greenwich
COPYRIGHT GEORGE PHILIP & SON LTD

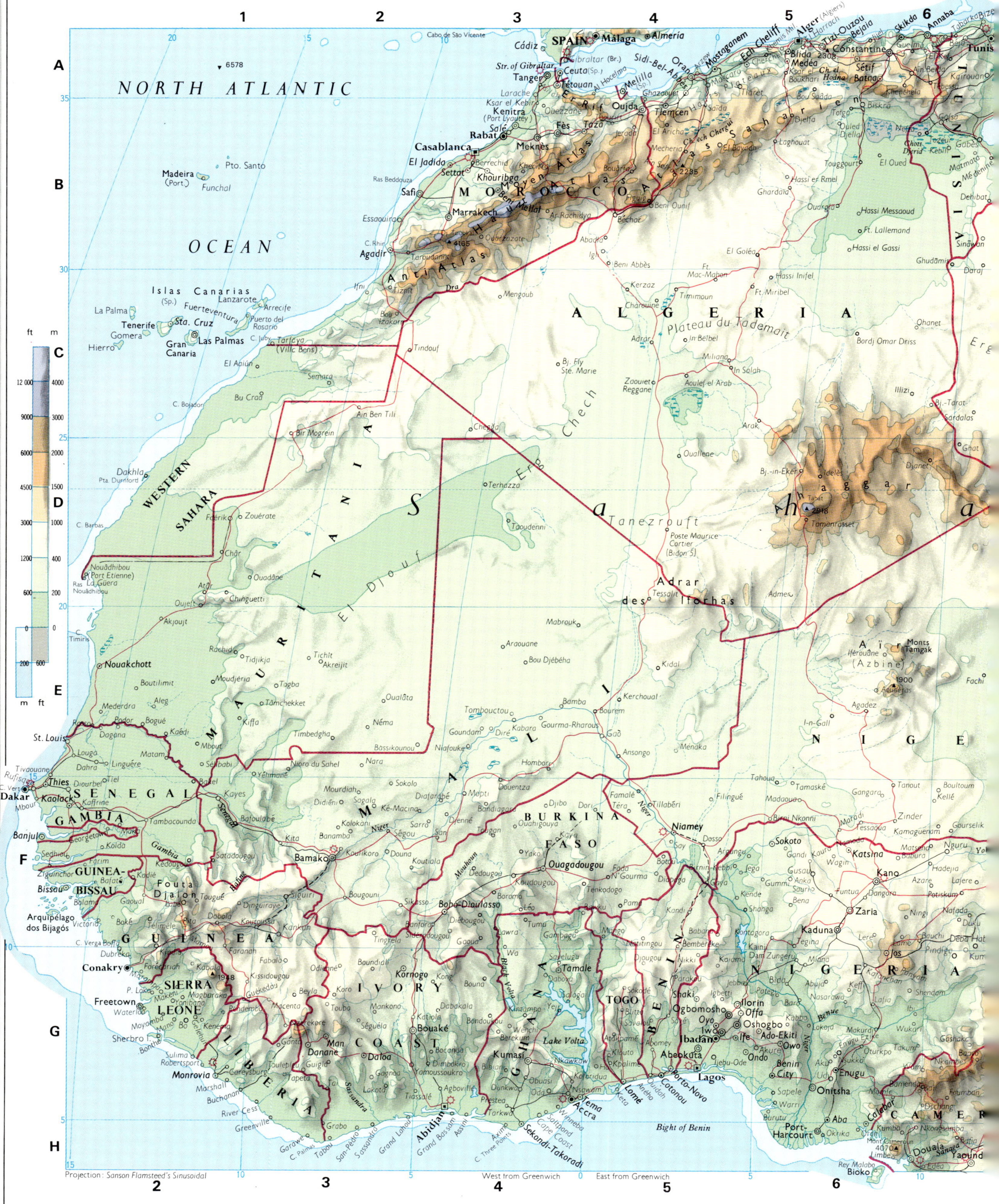
NORTH ATLANTIC
OCEAN
Madeira (Port.)
Funchal
Pto. Santo
Islas Canarias (Sp.)
Lanzarote
Fuerteventura
La Palma
Tenerife
Gomera
Hierro
Gran Canaria
Las Palmas
Sta. Cruz
SPAIN
Málaga
Almeria
Cádiz
Str. of Gibraltar
Gibraltar (Br.)
Ceuta (Sp.)
Tanger
Tetouan
Melilla
Oujda
MOROCCO
Casablanca
Rabat
Kenitra (Port Lyautey)
Fès
Meknès
Taza
El Jadida
Safi
Essaouira
Marrakech
Agadir
Anti Atlas
Tindouf
Oran
Alger (Algiers)
Constantine
Annaba
Tunis
TUNISIA
ALGERIA
Plateau du Tademait
Ahaggar
Tamanrasset
Tanezrouft
Adrar des Iforhas
Ghardaïa
Ouargla
In Salah
WESTERN SAHARA
Dakhla
MAURITANIA
Nouadhibou (Port Etienne)
Nouakchott
Atar
El Djouf
Erg Chech
MALI
Tombouctou
Gao
Bamako
Mopti
SENEGAL
Dakar
St. Louis
Thies
Kaolack
GAMBIA
Banjul
GUINEA-BISSAU
Bissau
Arquipélago dos Bijagós
GUINEA
Fouta Djalon
Conakry
SIERRA LEONE
Freetown
LIBERIA
Monrovia
IVORY COAST
Abidjan
Bouaké
BURKINA FASO
Ouagadougou
Bobo-Dioulasso
GHANA
Lake Volta
Kumasi
Accra
Tema
Sekondi-Takoradi
TOGO
Lomé
BENIN
Porto-Novo
Cotonou
Bight of Benin
NIGER
Niamey
Aïr (Azbine)
NIGERIA
Lagos
Ibadan
Kano
Kaduna
Zaria
Jos
Port-Harcourt
Enugu
Sokoto
Katsina
Bioko
Douala
Yaoundé
Projection: Sanson Flamsteed's Sinusoidal
West from Greenwich
East from Greenwich

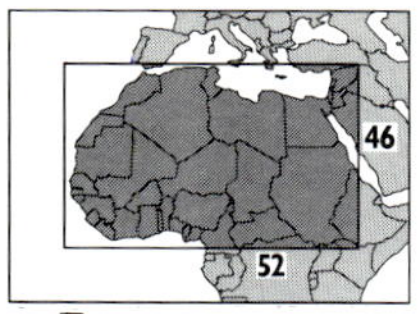

1:15 000 000

100 0 100 200 300 400 miles

100 0 100 200 300 400 500 600 km

ETHIOPIA
Addis Abeba
CENTRAL AFRICAN REPUBLIC
Kinshasa
Nairobi
Victoria
Kampala
Kisangani
Mombasa
Zanzibar
Dar-es-Salaam
Luanda
Libreville
Douala
Yaoundé
Ndjamena
Omdurman
El Khartûm
Kassala
El Obeid
Kigali
Bujumbura
Mbuji-Mayi
Kananga
Mbandaka
Pointe Noire
CABINDA
RWANDA
BURUNDI
EQUATORIAL GUINEA
GABON
NIGER
NIGERIA
Lac Tchad
Tanganyika
Kano
Maiduguri
Bangui
Juba
Bukavu
Mwanza
Tabora
Tanga
Tana
Lamu
Kismu
Entebbe

1:15 000 000
miles
km
MADAGASCAR
On same scale as General Map
ATLANTIC OCEAN
INDIAN OCEAN
Tropic of Capricorn
BOTSWANA
NAMIBIA
SOUTH AFRICA
ZIMBABWE
LESOTHO
Kalahari
Windhoek
Gaborone
Pretoria
Johannesburg
Bloemfontein
Kimberley
Cape Town
Durban
Port Elizabeth
East London
Pietermaritzburg
Bulawayo
Harare
Lusaka
Maputo (Lourenço Marques)
Beira
Lobito
Benguela
Antananarivo (Tananarive)
Projection: Sanson Flamsteed's Sinusoidal
East from Greenwich

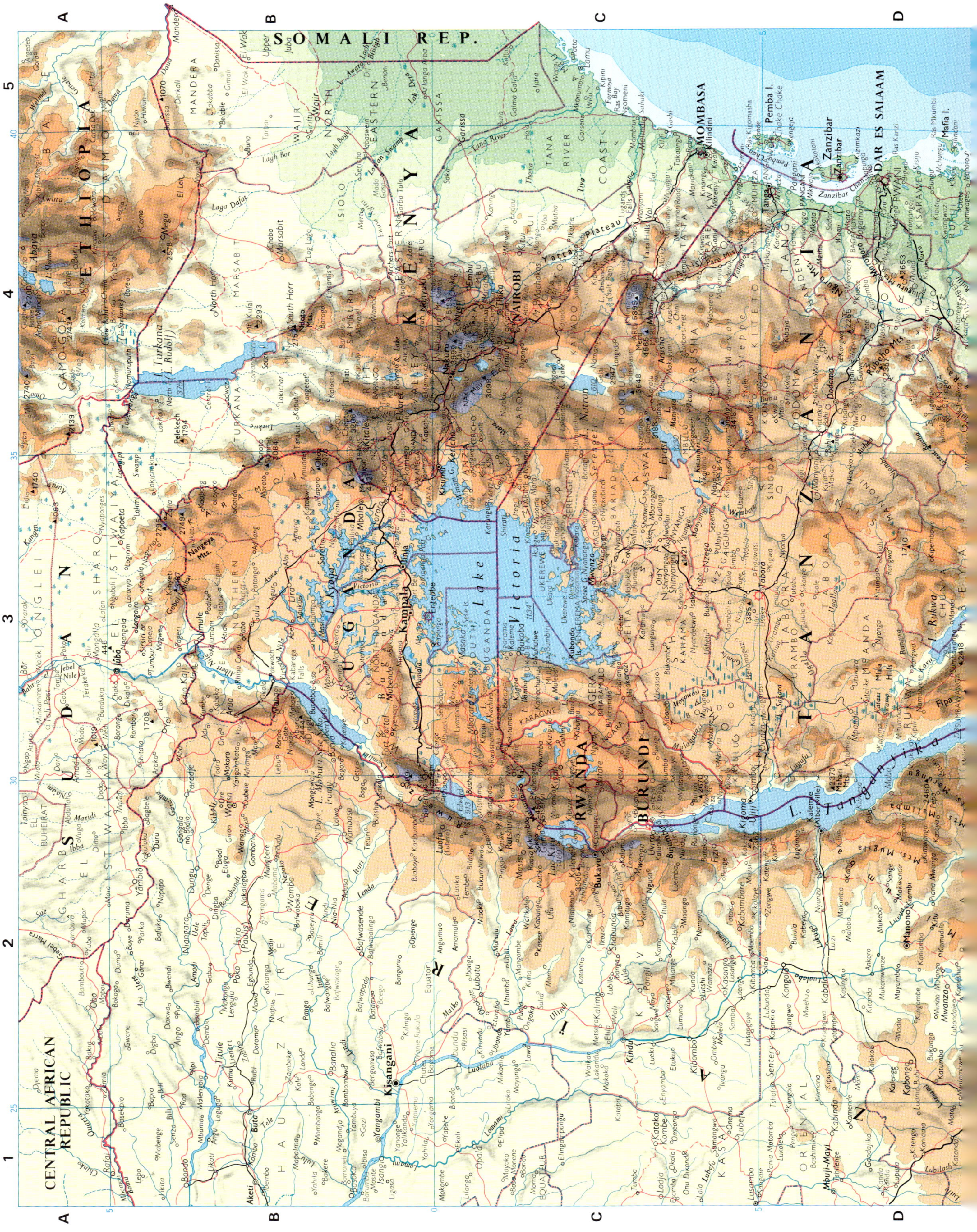
SOMALI REP.
ETHIOPIA
KENYA
UGANDA
TANZANIA
RWANDA
BURUNDI
SUDAN
CENTRAL AFRICAN REPUBLIC
ZAIRE
NAIROBI
MOMBASA
DAR ES SALAAM
Zanzibar
Pemba I.
Mafia I.
Lake Victoria
L. Turkana (L. Rudolf)
L. Tanganyika
Kampala
Kisangani
Juba
Kigoma
Tabora
Dodoma
Arusha
Bukavu
Entebbe
Mwanza

1:8 000 000

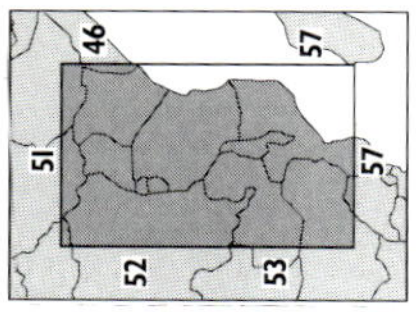

INDIAN OCEAN
ZAMBIA
MALAWI
ZIMBABWE
MOÇAMBIQUE
BOTSWANA
SOUTH AFRICA
ANGOLA
Lusaka
Harare
Bulawayo
Lilongwe
Blantyre
Beira
Livingstone
Kitwe
Ndola
Lubumbashi
Lake Malawi
Lake Kariba
Zambezi
East from Greenwich
Projection: Lambert's Equivalent Azimuthal

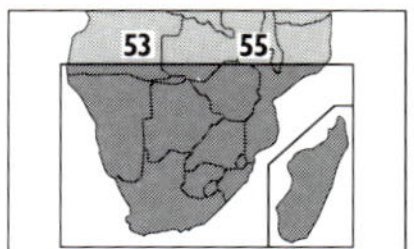

Projection: Lambert's Equivalent Azimuthal

1:8 000 000
50 0 50 100 150 200 miles
50 0 100 200 300 km
MALAWI
ZAMBÉZIA
TETE
MOZAMBIQUE CHANNEL
ZIMBABWE
MASHONALAND
MASVINGO
MANICALAND
MATABELELAND SOUTH
MOZAMBIQUE
INHAMBANE
GAZA
TRANSVAAL
VENDA
SWAZILAND
NATAL
LESOTHO
INDIAN OCEAN
HARARE (Salisbury)
Chitungwiza
Bulawayo
Gweru
Masvingo
Mutare
Beira
Maputo (Lourenço Marques)
PRETORIA
JOHANNESBURG
Benoni
Springs
Soweto
Germiston
Vereeniging
Pietermaritzburg
DURBAN
Umlazi
KwaMashu
Mpumalanga
East London
Umtata
Quelimane
Chinde
Angoche
I. do Bazaruto
I. Benguérua
Ile de Juan de Nova (Réunion)
Iles Glorieuses (Réunion)
MADAGASCAR
ANTANANARIVO
Antsiranana
Mahajanga
Toamasina
Fianarantsoa
Toliara
Antsirabe
Morondava
Taolanaro
Tropic of Capricorn
MADAGASCAR
On same scale as General Map
East from Greenwich

1:40 000 000

ft m
18 000 6000
12 000 4000
6000 2000
3000 1000
1200 400
600 200
0 0
200 600
2000 6000
4000 12 000
6000 18 000
8000 24 000
m ft
Admiralty Is.
New Ireland
Bismarck Archipelago
Bougainville
Solomon Is.
New Britain
9103
G. of Sarera
Maoke Mts.
5029
Sepik
New Guinea
Fly
Owen Stanley Ra.
D'Entrecasteaux Arch.
Louisiade Arch.
Guadalcanal
Malaita
S. Cristobal
Sta. Cruz Is.
Ellice Is.
Celebes
Sula Is.
Ceram
Buru
Ambon
7440
Banda Sea
Aru Is.
Tanimbar Is.
Arafura Sea
Torres Str.
Thursday I.
C. York
G. of Papua
Flores Sea
Sumbawa
Flores
Timor
Sumba
Timor Sea
Melville I.
C. Arnhem
Arnhem L.
Gulf of Carpentaria
C. York Pen.
Coral Sea
Great Barrier Reef
INDIAN OCEAN
King Sound
Victoria
L. Woods
Tanami Desert
Barkly Tableland
Flinders
Fitzroy
L. Mackay
L. Disappointment
Macdonnell Ra.
L. Amadeus
Musgrave Ra.
N.W. Cape
Mt. Bruce 1227
Ashburton
Gascoyne
Shark Bay
AUSTRALIA
Great Dividing Ra.
Hervey B.
Sandy C.
Gt. Sandy I.
Darling Downs
Warrego
Cooper Cr.
L. Eyre
Flinders Ras.
L. Torrens
L. Frome
Darling
New England Ra.
C. Byron
L. Barlee
Nullarbor Plain
Gairdner
Eyre Pen.
Lachlan
Murray
Botany B.
Darling Ra.
Great Australian Bight
Spencer Gulf
Kangaroo I.
Encounter B.
Australian Alps
Mt. Kosciusko 2230
C. Howe
Geographe B.
C. Naturaliste
C. Leeuwin
P. Phillip
King I.
Bass Strait
Flinders I.
TASMANIA
South C.
Chesterfield Is.
Espiritu Santo I.
Mallikolo I.
New Hebrides
7570
Loyalty Is.
New Caledonia
PACIFIC OCEAN
Rotuma
Vanua Levu
Fiji Is.
Viti Levu
Samoa Is.
Savaii
Upolu
Tongatabu I.
Tonga Is. (Friendly)
10 822
Tropic of Capricorn
Norfolk I.
Lord Howe I.
Kermadec Is.
Three Kings Is.
10 047
Tasman Sea
North C.
NORTH I.
B. of Plenty
East C.
Mt. Egmont
Taupo
Ruapehu
Hawke B.
Cook Strait
SOUTH I.
Mt. Cook 3764
Southern Alps
NEW ZEALAND
Canterbury Bight
Chatham I.
Stewart I.

PAPUA NEW GUINEA
New Ireland
Rabaul
Madang
New Guinea
Fly
Lae
New Britain
Papua
Port Moresby
Bougainville
IRIAN JAYA
Sula Is
Ceram
Celebes
Buru
Aru Is.
Ujung Pandang
INDONESIA
Banda Sea
Tanimbar Is.
Flores Sea
Sumbawa
Flores
Timor
Kupang
Sumba
Timor Sea
Arafura Sea
Torres Str.
Choiseul
Ysabel
SOLOMON IS.
Malaita
Honiara
Guadalcanal
S. Cristobal
Sta. Cruz Is.
KIRIBATI
Funafuti
TUVALU
Tokelau Is. (N.Z.)
Darwin
Katherine
Gulf of Carpentaria
Cooktown
Coral Sea Islands Territory
Cairns
Townsville
Espiritu Santo
Vila
VANUATU
Rotuma
Wallis and Futuna (Fr.)
WESTERN SAMOA
Savaii
Upolu
Apia
AMER. SAMOA
Vanua Levu
FIJI
Viti Levu
Suva
Chesterfield Is. (Fr.)
New Caledonia (Fr.)
Loyalty Is. (Fr.)
Nouméa
Wyndham
NORTHERN TERRITORY
QUEENSLAND
Charters Towers
Mt. Isa
Broome
Rockhampton
AUSTRALIA
Longreach
Alice Springs
Dampier
WESTERN AUSTRALIA
Onslow
Charleville
Toowoomba
Brisbane
Quilpie
Cunnamulla
Warwick
TONGA (Friendly)
Nuku'alofa
Tropic of Capricorn
PACIFIC OCEAN
International Date Line
Wiluna
Oodnadatta
L. Eyre
SOUTH AUSTRALIA
Laverton
Bourke
Darling
NEW SOUTH WALES
Norfolk I. (Aust.)
Lord Howe I. (Aust.)
Kermadec Is. (N.Z.)
Geraldton
Kalgoorlie-Boulder
Broken Hill
Newcastle
Sydney
P. Pirie
Hay
Goulburn
Canberra
Mildura
Murray
Adelaide
Bendigo
VICTORIA
Melbourne
Perth
Esperance
Great Australian Bight
Fremantle
Ballarat
Geelong
Albany
King I.
Bass Strait
Launceston
TASMANIA
Hobart
Tasman Sea
NORTH I.
Auckland
Hamilton
New Plymouth
Wellington
Napier
SOUTH I.
Greymouth
Nelson
NEW ZEALAND
Christchurch
Chatham I.
Invercargill
Dunedin
Vila Capital Cities
Projection: Bonne
East from Greenwich
West from Greenwich

1:6 000 000
miles
km
NEW ZEALAND & S.W. PACIFIC
1:60 000 000
SAMOA ISLANDS
1:12 000 000
FIJI AND TONGA ISLANDS
1:12 000 000
NORTH ISLAND
SOUTH ISLAND
TASMAN SEA
PACIFIC OCEAN
SOUTHERN OCEAN
Auckland
Wellington
Christchurch
Dunedin
Hamilton
Napier
Hastings
Gisborne
New Plymouth
Wanganui
Palmerston N.
Nelson
Blenheim
Westport
Greymouth
Hokitika
Timaru
Invercargill
Southern Alps
Mt. Cook 3764
Cook Strait
Foveaux Str.
Stewart I.
WESTERN SAMOA
AMERICAN SAMOA
Apia
Pago Pago
FIJI
Suva
Viti Levu
Vanua Levu
TONGA (Friendly Is.)
Nuku'alofa
Wallis & Futuna (Fr.)
KIRIBATI
TUVALU (Ellice Is.)
Tokelau Is. (N.Z.)
Cook Is. (N.Z.)
FRENCH POLYNESIA
Kermadec Is. (N.Z.)
Chatham Is.
Projection: Conical with two standard parallels
COPYRIGHT, GEORGE PHILIP & SON, LTD.

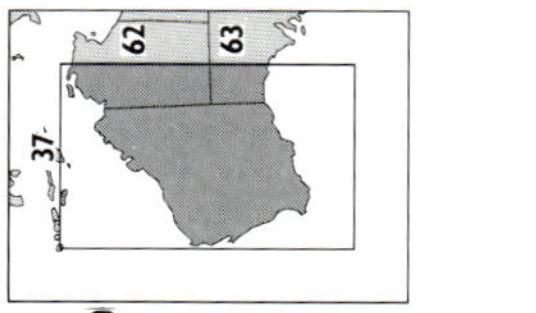
62
63
37

TIMOR SEA
INDONESIA
INDIAN OCEAN
NORTHERN TERRITORY
Tanami Desert
Great Sandy Desert
Gibson Desert
Joseph Bonaparte Gulf
Bonaparte Archipelago
King Leopold Ranges
Hamersley Range
Darwin
Melville I.
Bathurst I.
Port Hedland
Broome
Karratha
Newman
Timor
Sumba
Sumbawa
Lombok
Roti
Sawa
Eighty Mile Beach
Dampier Archipelago
Lake Mackay
Lake Disappointment
Macdonnell Ranges
Tropic of Capricorn

1:8 000 000

50 0 50 100 150 200 miles

50 0 100 200 300 km

Projection: Bonne

East from Greenwich

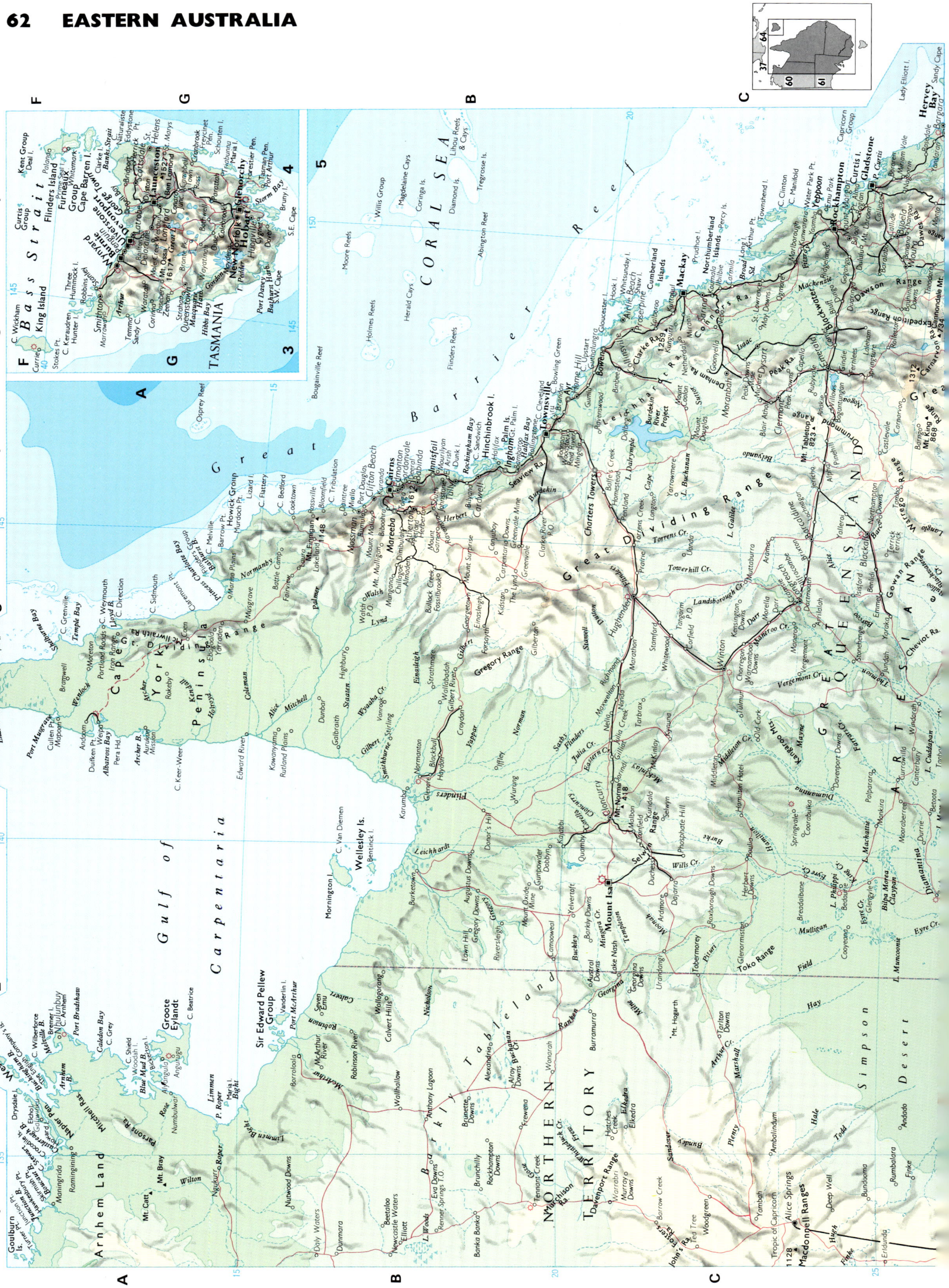
37
64
60
61
CORAL SEA
Great Barrier Reef
Gulf of Carpentaria
Cape York Peninsula
Arnhem Land
NORTHERN TERRITORY
QUEENSLAND
GREAT ARTESIAN BASIN
Great Dividing Range
Barkly Tableland
Simpson Desert
Bass Strait
TASMANIA
King Island
Flinders Island
Groote Eylandt
Wellesley Is.
Mornington I.
Sir Edward Pellew Group
Wessel Is.
Hinchinbrook I.
Cairns
Townsville
Mackay
Rockhampton
Gladstone
Mount Isa
Cloncurry
Charters Towers
Longreach
Winton
Hughenden
Alice Springs
Macdonnell Ranges
Tennant Creek
Launceston
Hobart
Devonport
Burnie
Hervey Bay
Tropic of Capricorn

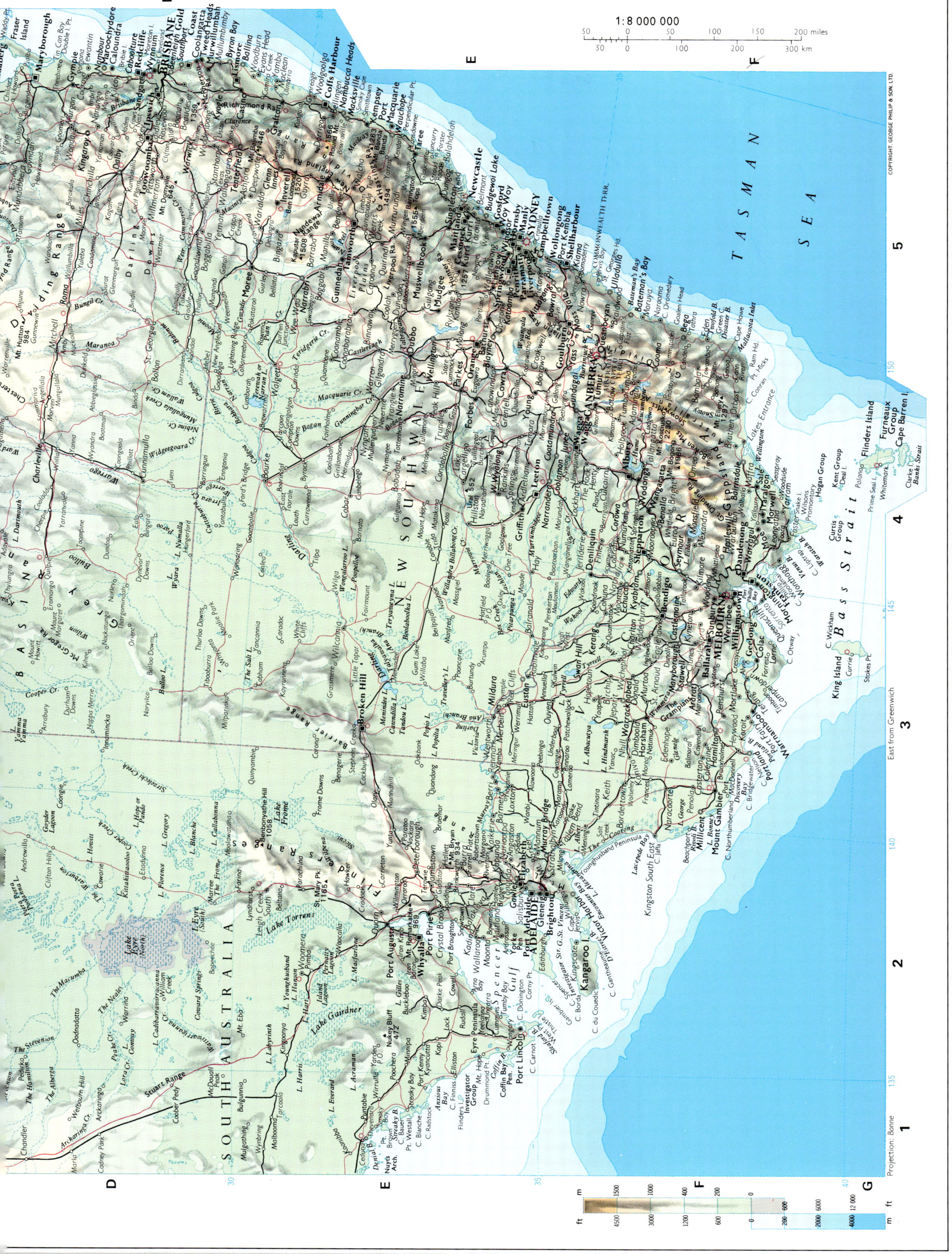
1:8 000 000
TASMAN SEA
NEW SOUTH WALES
VICTORIA
SOUTH AUSTRALIA
Bass Strait
BRISBANE
SYDNEY
CANBERRA
MELBOURNE
ADELAIDE
Projection: Bonne
East from Greenwich
COPYRIGHT GEORGE PHILIP & SON, LTD.

EUROPE
RUSSIA
St. Peterburg
Moskva
Yekaterinburg
Novosibirsk
Tomsk
Irkutsk
Ozero Baykal
Chita
KAZAKHSTAN
Semipalatinsk
Ozero Balkhash
Aralskoye More
Alma Ata
Tashkent
Urumqi
MONGOLIA
Ulaanbaatar
ASIA
Altai
Manchuria
Harbin
Changchun
Shenyang
Beijing
Tianjin
Dalian
KOREA
SŎUL
Taiyuan
Lanzhou
Xian
Qingdao
Nanjing
Wuhan
SHANGHAI
Chongqing
Changsha
Fuzhou
Kunming
Guangzhou
Taibei
Taiwan
MACAU (Port.)
HONG KONG (U.K.)
Hanoi
Hainan
CHINA
TIBET
Kunlun
Himalaya
Mt. Everest 8848
Lhasa
NEPAL
AFGHANISTAN
Kabul
Srinagar
Lahore
PAKISTAN
Delhi
Kanpur
Ganga
Brahmaputra
INDIA
Calcutta
BANGLADESH
Dhaka
Mandalay
BURMA
Hyderabad
Bay of Bengal
Rangoon
THAILAND
Bangkok
CAMBODIA
VIETNAM
Phnom Penh
Gulf of Thailand
Phanh Bho Ho Chi Minh
Madras
Andaman Is.
Nicobar Is.
SRI LANKA
Colombo
Kuala Lumpur
MALAYSIA
SINGAPORE
BRUNEI
SABAH
SARAWAK
Borneo
Sumatra
Palembang
Jakarta
Java Sea
Java
Surabaya
Sunda Strait
Bali
Sumbawa
Flores
Sumba
Timor
Java Trench
7450
Christmas I. (Austral.)
Cocos (Keeling) Is. (Austral.)
INDONESIA
Sunda Islands
South China Sea
Palawan
Mindoro
Manila
PHILIPPINES
C. Engano
Samar
Mindanao
Mindanao Trench
10,497
Sulu Sea
Celebes Sea
Celebes
Ujung Pandang
Flores Sea
Banda Sea
Moluccas
Halmahera
Buru
Ceram
7440
Irian Jaya
5029
New Guinea
PAPUA NEW GUINEA
Port Moresby
Arafura Sea
Torres Strait
C. York
Admiralty Is.
Bismarck Arch.
New Ireland
New Britain
Rabaul
9103
SOLOMON IS.
Guadalcanal
Honiara
Sta. Cruz I.
9165
Vladivostok
Sea of Japan
JAPAN
Hakodate
Sendai
TŌKYŌ
Yokohama
8412
Fuji-san 3776
Nagoya
Kyōto
Ōsaka
Kitakyūshū
Shikoku
Kyūshū
Yellow Sea
East China Sea
Ryūkyū-retto
Japan Trench
10,554
South Honshū Ridge
Ogasawara Gunto (Bonin Is.)
Kazan Retto (Volcano Is.)
Minami-Tori-S. (Marcus I.)
Marcus Necker Ridge
Wake I. (U.S.)
Blagoveshchensk
Amur
Khabarovsk
Sakhalin
G. of Sakhalin
Sea of Okhotsk
Okhotsk
La Pérouse Strait
Kuril'skiye Ostrova
Kuril Is.
10,542
Kuril Trench
Petropavlovsk
P-ov. Kamchatka
Komandorskiye O. (Russia)
7822
Aleutian Is.
Aleutian Trench
Andreanov Is.
Bering Sea
Emperor Seamount Chain
7168
6603
Midway Is.
Hawaiian
Lisianski I.
NORTHERN MARIANAS (U.S.)
Saipan
GUAM (U.S.)
11,022
Mariana Trench
Micronesia
Yap
BELAU (U.S.)
FEDERATED STATES OF MICRONESIA
Truk
Pohnpei
Caroline Islands
Melanesia
MARSHALL IS.
Bikini Atoll
Enewetak Atoll
Jaluit
Butaritari
Gilbert Is.
NAURU
Banaba
Baker I. (U.S.)
Abariringa
International Date Line
TUVALU
Tokelau
PACIFIC OCEAN
Rotuma
Wallis & Futuna (Fr.)
FIJI
Vanua Levu
Viti Levu
Suva
Tonga Trench
TONGA
10,822
VANUATU
7570
New Caledonia (Fr.)
Is. Loyauté
Nouméa
Louisiade Arch. (Austral.)
Coral Sea
Is. Chesterfield
Darwin
C. Arnhem
G. of Carpentaria
NORTHERN TERRITORY
Mt. Isa
Cairns
Townsville
AUSTRALIA
Great Dividing Range
Rockhampton
QUEENSLAND
Alice Springs
WESTERN AUSTRALIA
N.W. Cape
L. Eyre
SOUTH AUSTRALIA
Darling
Brisbane
NEW SOUTH WALES
Sydney
Perth
Great Australian Bight
Adelaide
Murray
Canberra
VICTORIA
Mt. Kosciusko 2230
Melbourne
Bass Strait
TASMANIA
Hobart
Lord Howe Rise
Norfolk I. (Aust.)
Lord Howe I. (Aust.)
Tasman Sea
Kermadec Is. (N.Z.)
Kermadec Trench
10,047
Auckland
NEW ZEALAND
Cook Strait
Wellington
Mt. Cook 3764
Christchurch
Dunedin
Invercargill
Chatham Is (N.Z.)
Bounty Is. (N.Z.)
Antipodes Is. (N.Z.)
Campbell I. (N.Z.)
Auckland Is. (N.Z.)
Macquarie Is. (Austral.)
INDIAN OCEAN
Nouvelle Amsterdam (Fr.)
Is. St. Paul (Fr.)
Mid-Indian Ridge
Is. Crozet (Fr.)
Kerguelen (Fr.)
Heard Is. (Aust.)
ft
m
18,000
12 000
6000
3000
600
0
200
2000
4000
6000
8000
600
6000
12 000
18,000
24,000
J
K
L
M
N
Projection: Mollweide's Homolographic
East from Greenwich
1 2 3 4 5 6 7 8 9 10
A B C D E F G H

1:54 000 000

ALASKA (U.S.)
Gulf of Alaska
Bristol Bay
Prince of Wales I.
Prince Rupert
Kitimat
Queen Charlotte Is.
Juneau
6050
CANADA
NORTH AMERICA
Edmonton
Calgary
Regina
Winnipeg
L. Winnipeg
Hudson Bay
GREENLAND
C. Farewell
Labrador
Newfoundland
St. Lawrence
Quebec
Montreal
Ottawa
Toronto
L. Superior
L. Huron
L. Ontario
L. Erie
Michigan
Pr. Edward I.
Saint John
Boston
C. Sable
Vancouver
Vancouver I.
Victoria
Seattle
Portland
Rocky Mountains
Boise
Snake
Salt Lake City
Colorado
Denver
Missouri
Minneapolis
CHICAGO
Detroit
Buffalo
Pittsburgh
Cincinnati
NEW YORK
Philadelphia
Baltimore
Washington
Appalachian Mts.
Kansas City
St. Louis
UNITED STATES
C. Mendocino
San Francisco
4418
Los Angeles
San Diego
Oklahoma
Memphis
Mississippi
Atlanta
Dallas
C. Hatteras
Jacksonville
Ciudad Juarez
Houston
New Orleans
San Antonio
MEXICO
Sierra Madre
Gulf of California
Monterrey
Gulf of Mexico
Miami
Florida Strait
BAHAMAS
La Habana
CUBA
Yucatan Channel
Mérida
México
Puebla
5700
Acapulco
Guadalajara
Is. Revilla Gigedo (Mexico)
BELIZE
HONDURAS
GUATEMALA
Guatemala
San Salvador
EL SALVADOR
NICARAGUA
Managua
CENTRAL AMERICA
COSTA RICA
San José
Colón
Panama Canal
PANAMA
7680
JAMAICA
Kingston
HAITI
DOM. REP.
Hispaniola
West Indies
9200
PUERTO RICO (U.S.)
Leeward Is.
Windward Is.
BARBADOS
TRINIDAD & TOBAGO
Caribbean Sea
Barranquilla
Maracaibo
Caracas
Orinoco
VENEZUELA
Medellín
Bogota
Cali
COLOMBIA
Quito
ECUADOR
Guayaquil
C. Pariñas
Iquitos
Manaus
Amazonas
BRAZIL
SOUTH AMERICA
Trujillo
PERU
Lima
Cuzco
Arequipa
L. Titicaca
Illampu & Ancohuma 6550
La Paz
BOLIVIA
6866
Peru-Chile Trench
Iquique
8050
Antofagasta
Tucumán
PARAGUAY
Asunción
Pto. Alegre
6960
Córdoba
Rosario
Valparaiso
Santiago
Buenos Aires
URUGUAY
Montevideo
Rio de la Plata
ARGENTINA
Concepcion
Andes
Patagonia
Punta Arenas
Str. of Magellan
Tierra del Fuego
C. Horn
Falkland Is. (U.K.)
South Georgia
6212
SOUTH ATLANTIC OCEAN
NORTH ATLANTIC OCEAN
Bermuda (U.K.)
U.K.
I. Clipperton (Fr.)
I. del Coco (Costa Rica)
Galápagos (Ecuador)
6369
San Félix (Chile)
San Ambrosio (Chile)
Arch. de Juan Fernández (Chile)
Sala-y-Gomez (Chile)
I. de Pascua (Easter I.) (Chile)
Chile Rise
East Pacific Ridge
Pacific-Antarctic Ridge
Tropic of Capricorn
Tropic of Cancer
Equator
6741
6225
Laysan I.
Hawaiian Is. (U.S.)
Oahu
Honolulu
Hawaii
Johnston I. (U.S.)
PACIFIC OCEAN
Christmas Island Ridge
Palmyra Is. (U.S.)
Teraina
Tabuaeran
Kiritimati
Jarvis I. (U.S.)
Phoenix Is.
Malden I.
Starbuck I.
Tongareva
Penrhyn Is.
Manihiki
Pukapuka
Suwarrow Is.
Vostok I.
Flint I.
Caroline I.
Îs. Marquises
Cook Islands (N.Z.)
Niue (N.Z.)
Manuae
Rarotonga
Îs. de la Société
Tahiti
FRENCH POLYNESIA
Îs. Tuamotu
Tuamotu Ridge
Austral Seamount Chain
Îs. Tubuai (Îs. Australes)
Rapa
Pitcairn I. (U.K.)
Ducie I (U.K.)
West from Greenwich
COPYRIGHT. GEORGE PHILIP & SON. LTD.

1:35 000 000

ARCTIC OCEAN
Beaufort Sea
Greenland
Iceland
Denmark Strait
Baffin Bay
Baffin Island
Davis Strait
Queen Elizabeth Islands
Ellesmere I.
Axel Heiberg Land
Sverdrup Is.
Parry Is.
Melville I.
Devon I.
Banks I.
Victoria I.
Prince of Wales I.
Lancaster Sound
Gulf of Boothia
Boothia Pen.
Melville Pen.
Foxe Basin
Southampton I.
Hudson Strait
Hudson Bay
James Bay
Ungava Peninsula
Labrador
Newfoundland
Gulf of St. Lawrence
Nova Scotia
Asia
Bering Strait
Bering Sea
Alaska
Alaska Range
Brook's Range
Alaska Pen.
Gulf of Alaska
Mt. McKinley 6194
Mt. St. Elias 5489
Mt. Logan 6050
Yukon
Mackenzie Mts.
Mackenzie
Great Bear L.
Great Slave L.
Arctic Circle
Athabasca L.
Reindeer L.
Lake Winnipeg
Alexander Archipelago
Queen Charlotte Islands
Queen Charlotte Sound
Vancouver I.
Juan de Fuca Strait
Coast Mountains
Rocky Mountains
Mt. Robson 3954
Mt. Waddington 3994
Edmonton
Calgary
Regina
Winnipeg
Great Plains
Laurentian Plateau
Mendocino Seascarp
Murray Seascarp
PACIFIC OCEAN
Seattle
Portland
Mt. Rainier 4392
Cascade Range
Coast Range
Mt. Shasta 4317
San Francisco
Sierra Nevada
Mt. Whitney 4418
Los Angeles
Great Basin
Great Salt Lake
Wasatch Mountains
Colorado Plateau
Grand Canyon
Mt. Elbert 4399
Denver
Llano Estacado
Snake
Colorado
Gila
Missouri
Mississippi
Arkansas
Red
Ohio
L. Superior
L. Michigan
L. Huron
L. Erie
L. Ontario
Minneapolis
Chicago
Detroit
Toronto
Ottawa
Montreal
Quebec
Kansas City
St. Louis
Memphis
Dallas
Houston
New Orleans
Atlanta
Washington
Philadelphia
New York
Appalachian Mts.
Allegheny Mts.
Blue Ridge
Cumberland Plateau
Ozark Plateau
Chesapeake Bay
Bermuda
ATLANTIC OCEAN
6399
Florida
Florida Strait
Bahama Islands
Gulf of Mexico
Mississippi Delta
Cuba
Havana
Hispaniola
Puerto Rico
Milwaukee Deep 9200
Jamaica
Greater Antilles
Cayman Trough
Caribbean Sea
Colombian Basin
Venezuelan Basin
Yucatán
Yucatán Peninsula
Gulf of Campeche
Gulf of Honduras
Gulf of California
Lower California
Western Sierra Madre
Eastern Sierra Madre
Mexican Plateau
Monterrey
Guadalajara
México
Popocatepetl 5452
Citlaltepetl 5700
Isthmus of Tehuantepec
G. of Tehuantepec
Guatemala
Guatemala Trench 6662
L. Nicaragua
Panama Canal
G. of Panama
G. of Darien
Andes
Maracaibo
Revilla Gigedo Is.
Clarion Fracture Zone
Tropic of Cancer
6225
Projection: Bonne
West from Greenwich
COPYRIGHT. GEORGE PHILIP & SON. LTD.

1:35 000 000

200 0 200 400 600 800 miles

400 0 400 800 1200 km

PACIFIC OCEAN
ALASKA
YUKON TERRITORY
NORTH WEST TERRITORIES
INUVIK
KITIKMEOT
BRITISH COLUMBIA
ALBERTA
SASKATCHEWAN
MANITOBA
MONTANA
NORTH DAKOTA
SOUTH DAKOTA
NEBRASKA
MINNESOTA
WYOMING
UNITED STATES
Mackenzie Mountains
Rocky Mountains
Cassiar Mountains
Coast Mountains
Great Slave L.
Gt. Bear Lake
Lake Athabasca
Lake Winnipeg
Victoria Island
Banks Island
Amundsen Gulf
Coronation Gulf
Queen Maud Gulf
Queen Charlotte Is.
Vancouver I.
Whitehorse
Yellowknife
Edmonton
Calgary
Vancouver
Seattle
Saskatoon
Regina
Winnipeg
Minneapolis
Anchorage
Fairbanks
Projection: Bonne
ALASKA
1:30 000 000
Brooks Range
BERING SEA
GULF OF ALASKA
West from Greenwich
ft m

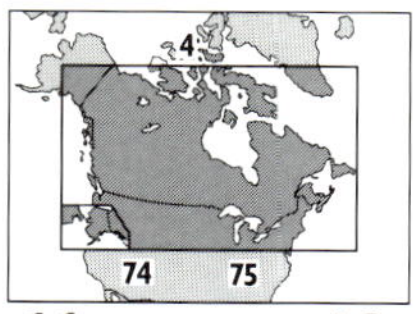

1:15 000 000

100 0 100 200 300 400 miles

100 0 100 200 300 400 500 600 km

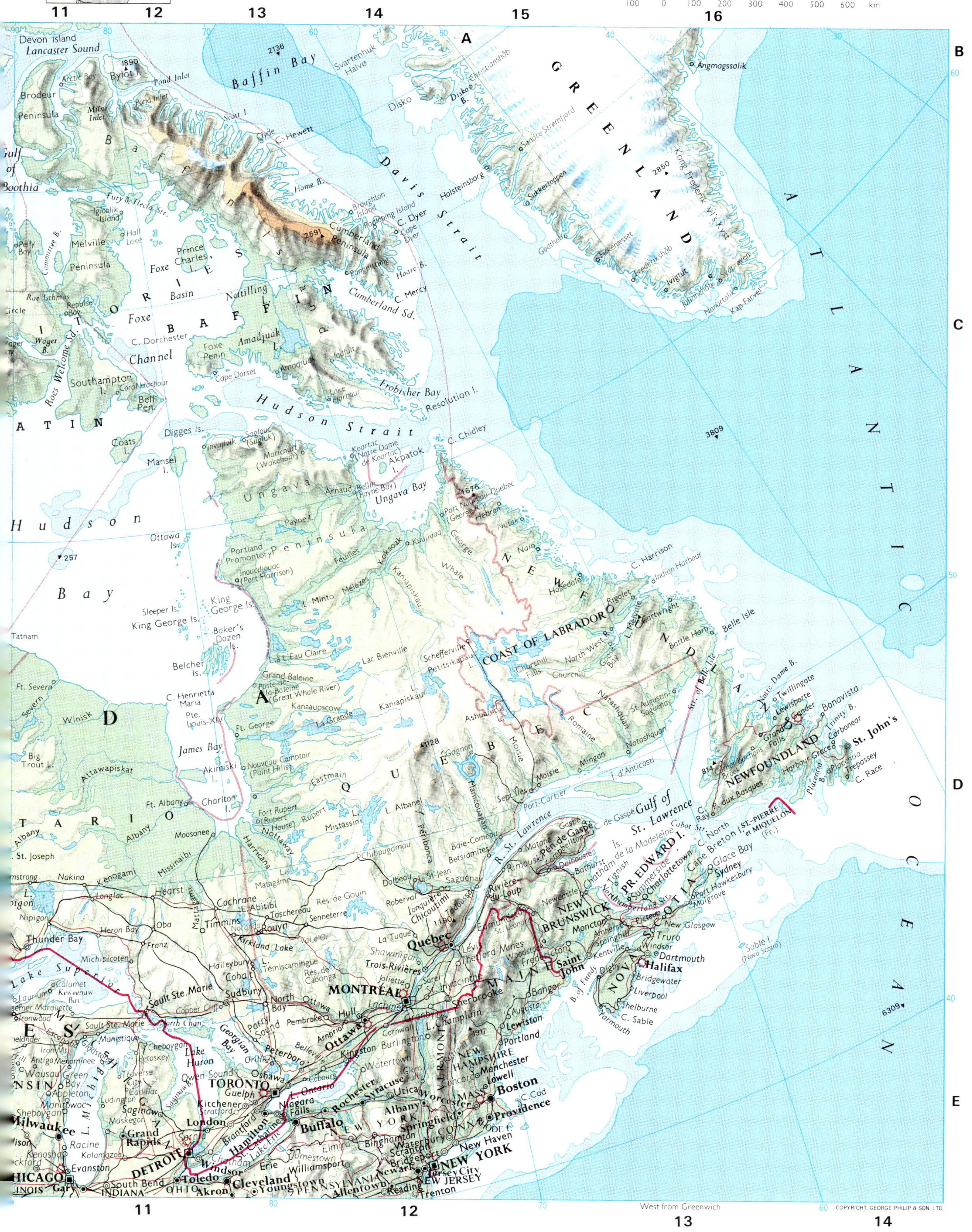

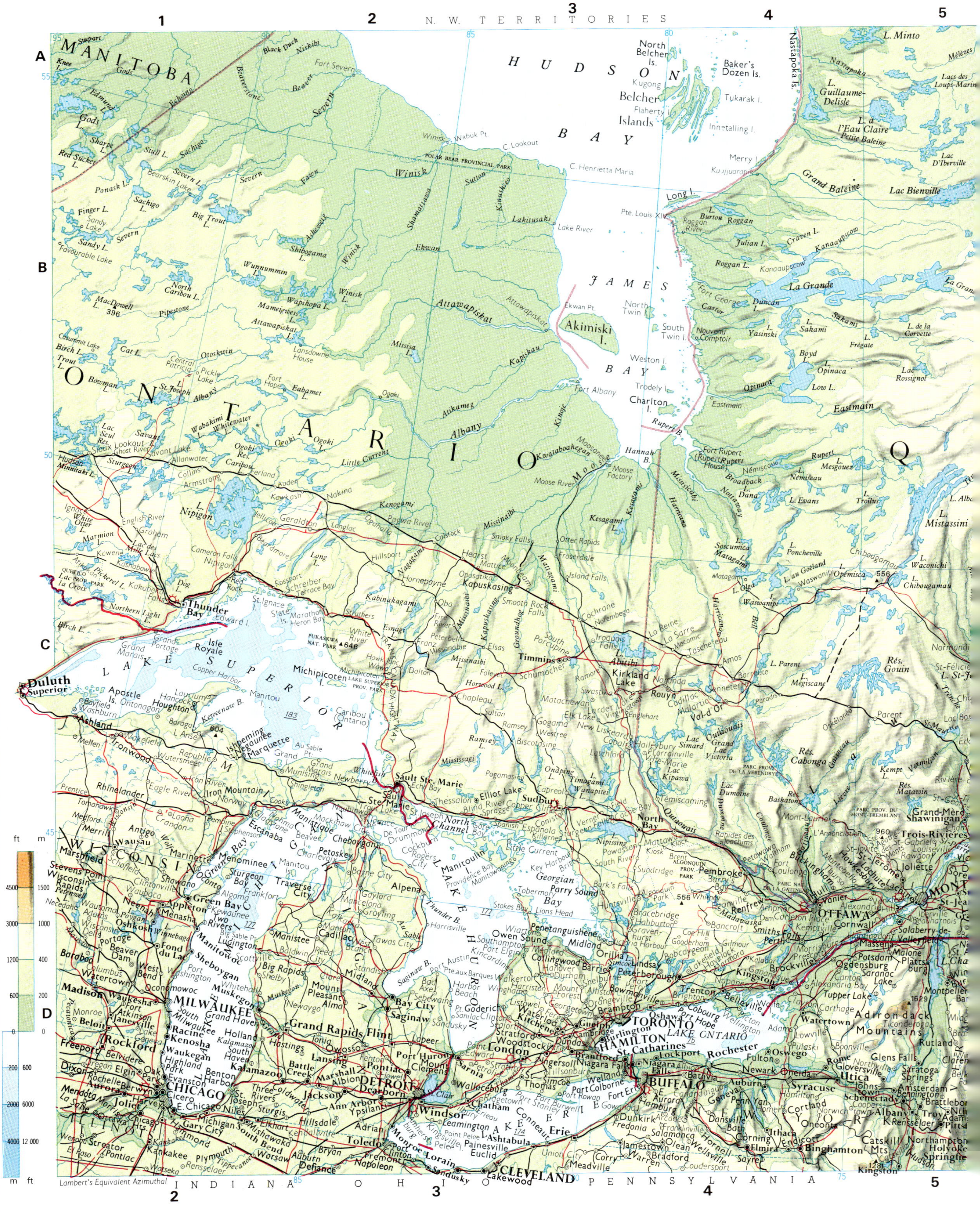

1
2
3
4
5
A
B
C
D
N. W. TERRITORIES
MANITOBA
HUDSON BAY
JAMES BAY
ONTARIO
Q
North Belcher Is.
Baker's Dozen Is.
Belcher Islands
Akimiski I.
Charlton I.
POLAR BEAR PROVINCIAL PARK
C. Henrietta Maria
Winisk
Attawapiskat
Albany
Moose Factory
Moosonee
Kapuskasing
Timmins
Kirkland Lake
Rouyn
Val-d'Or
La Grande
Fort George
Eastmain
Fort Rupert
Mistassini
Chibougamau
Rés. Gouin
Rés. Cabonga
Thunder Bay
Nipigon
Duluth
Superior
LAKE SUPERIOR
Isle Royale
Michipicoten I.
Marquette
Sault Ste. Marie
Elliot Lake
Sudbury
North Bay
Manitoulin I.
LAKE HURON
Georgian Bay
Owen Sound
Barrie
Pembroke
OTTAWA
Kingston
TORONTO
HAMILTON
St. Catharines
LAKE ONTARIO
Rochester
BUFFALO
Lake Erie
CLEVELAND
DETROIT
Windsor
London
Toledo
Saginaw
Flint
Lansing
Grand Rapids
MILWAUKEE
CHICAGO
Green Bay
Madison
Rockford
LAKE MICHIGAN
WISCONSIN
Syracuse
Utica
Schenectady
Albany
Adirondack Mountains
Trois-Rivières
Shawinigan
Joliette
Cornwall
INDIANA
OHIO
PENNSYLVANIA
Lambert's Equivalent Azimuthal
ft
m
4500
3000
1200
600
0
200
2000
4000
1500
1000
400
200
600
6000
12 000

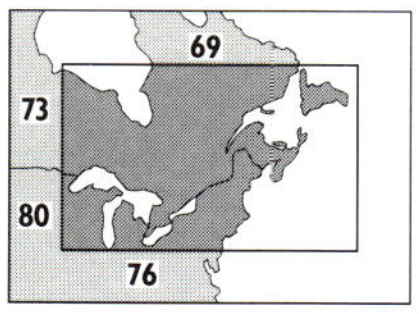

1:7 000 000

50 0 50 100 150 200 miles
50 0 50 100 150 200 250 300 km

1
2
3
4
5
6
A
B
C
D
YUKON TERRITORY
NORTH WEST TERRITORIES
FORT SMITH
ALASKA
BRITISH COLUMBIA
ALBERTA
WASHINGTON
IDAHO
PACIFIC OCEAN
QUEEN CHARLOTTE ISLANDS
VANCOUVER ISLAND
GREAT SLAVE LAKE
Whitehorse
Yellowknife
Juneau
Prince Rupert
Prince George
Kamloops
VANCOUVER
Victoria
SEATTLE
EDMONTON
Calgary
Red Deer
Lethbridge
Kelowna
Penticton
Nelson
Cranbrook
Dawson Creek
Grande Prairie
Fort St. John
Fort Nelson
Peace River
Hay River
Fort Simpson
Fort Providence
Fort Resolution
Jasper
Banff
Bellingham
New Westminster
Nanaimo
Port Alberni
Kitimat
Terrace
Stewart
Ketchikan
Sitka
Coast Mountains
Skeena Mountains
Cariboo Mountains
Selkirk Mts.
Rocky Mountains
Caribou Mts.
Birch Mountains
Buffalo Head Hills
WOOD BUFFALO NATIONAL PARK
St. Elias Mts.
Strait of Georgia
Juan de Fuca Str.
Hecate Strait
Queen Charlotte Sd.
Dixon Entrance
Chichagof I.
Baranof I.
Admiralty I.
Kupreanof I.
Prince of Wales I.
Revillagigedo I.
Moresby I.
Graham I.
Nootka I.
Mt. Robson 3954
Mt. Waddington 3994
ft
m
12 000
9000
6000
4500
3000
1200
600
0
200
2000
4000
3000
2000
1500
1000
400
200
0
600
6000
Projection: Lambert's Equivalent Azimuthal
West from Greenwich
130
125
120
115
55
50

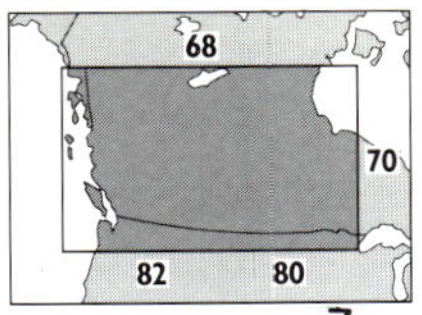
68
70
82
80

1:7 000 000

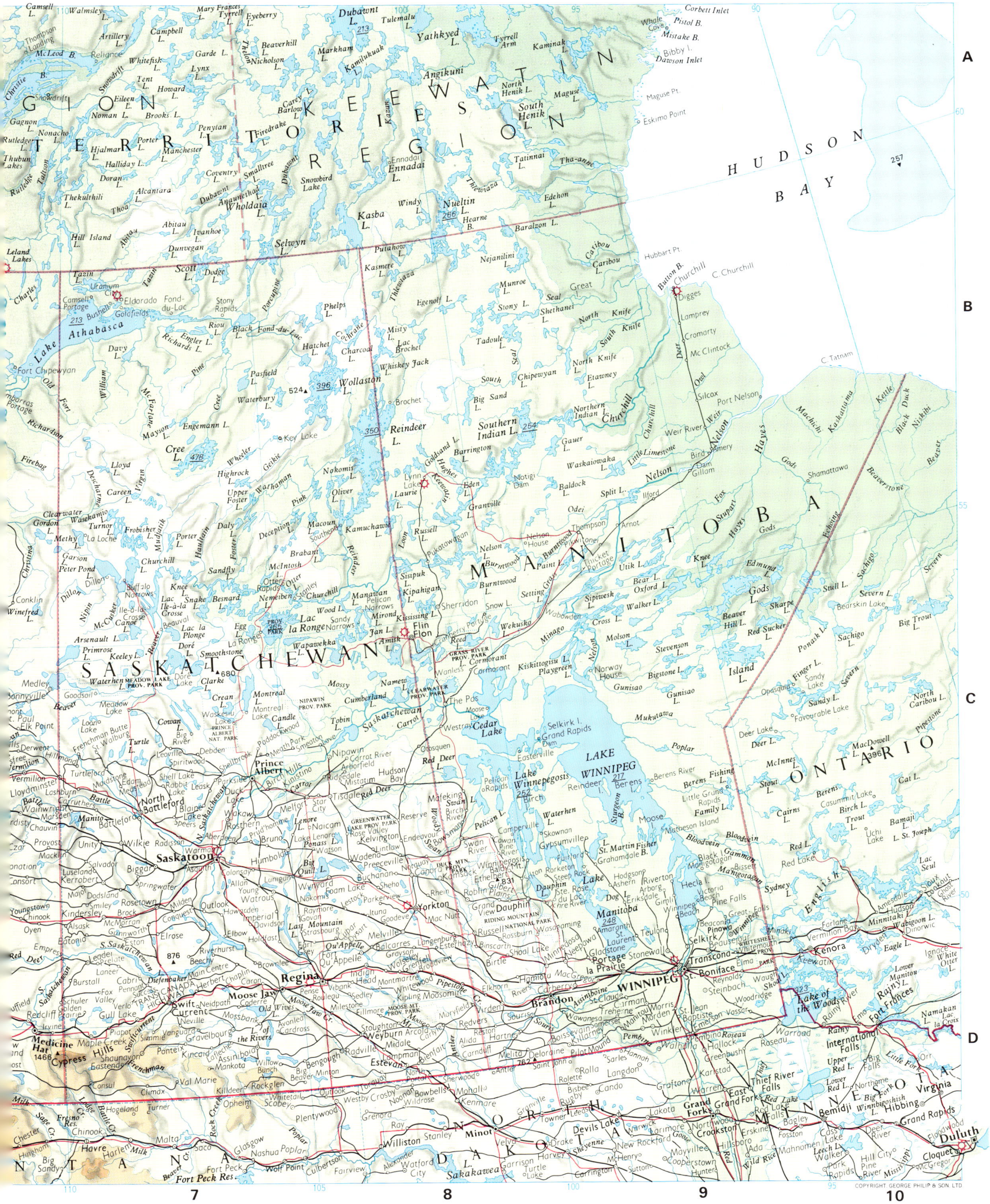
7
8
9
10
11
A
B
C
D
miles
km
HUDSON
BAY
KEEWATIN
REGION
TERRITORIES
MANITOBA
SASKATCHEWAN
ONTARIO
MINNESOTA
NORTH DAKOTA
LAKE WINNIPEG
Lake Winnipegosis
Lake Manitoba
Lake Athabasca
Reindeer L.
Wollaston L.
Southern Indian L.
Cedar Lake
Lake of the Woods
Churchill
Flin Flon
Prince Albert
North Battleford
Saskatoon
Regina
Moose Jaw
Swift Current
Medicine Hat
Yorkton
Brandon
WINNIPEG
Kenora
Fort Frances
International Falls
Grand Forks
Devils Lake
Minot
Williston
Bemidji
Duluth
COPYRIGHT GEORGE PHILIP & SON LTD.

PACIFIC OCEAN
CANADA
ALBERTA
SASKATCHEWAN
MANITOBA
BRITISH COLUMBIA
NORTH DAKOTA
SOUTH DAKOTA
NEBRASKA
KANSAS
OKLAHOMA
TEXAS
NEW MEXICO
ARIZONA
COLORADO
UTAH
NEVADA
CALIFORNIA
OREGON
WASHINGTON
IDAHO
MONTANA
WYOMING
MEXICO
SONORA
CHIHUAHUA
COAHUILA
DURANGO
BAJA CALIFORNIA NORTE
BAJA CALIFORNIA SUR
Golfo de California
ROCKY MOUNTAINS
Vancouver
Victoria
Seattle
Tacoma
Spokane
Portland
Calgary
Lethbridge
Regina
Saskatoon
Great Falls
Billings
Boise
Salt Lake City
Ogden
Great Salt Lake
Reno
Sacramento
San Francisco
Oakland
San Jose
Stockton
Fresno
Bakersfield
Santa Barbara
LOS ANGELES
Long Beach
San Bernardino
San Diego
Tijuana
Mexicali
Las Vegas
Phoenix
Tucson
Albuquerque
Santa Fe
El Paso
Ciudad Juárez
Denver
Colorado Springs
Pueblo
Cheyenne
Amarillo
Lubbock
Midland
Odessa
San Angelo
Abilene
Wichita Falls
Fort Worth
Austin
San Antonio
Laredo
Nuevo Laredo
Monterrey
Torreón
Chihuahua
Hermosillo
Corpus Christi
Matamoros
HAWAII
1:10 000 000
Kauai
Niihau
Oahu
Honolulu
Molokai
Lanai
Maui
Kahoolawe
Hawaii
Hilo
PACIFIC OCEAN
Hawaiian Islands
Projection: Albers Equal Area
West from Greenwich

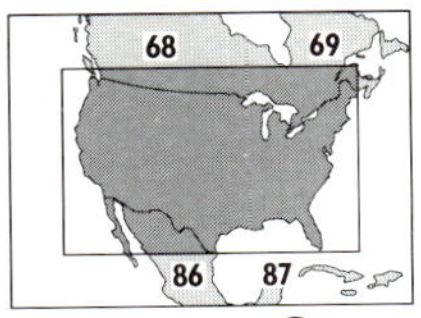
68
69
86
87

1:12 000 000

8
9
10
11
12
13
A
B
C
D
E
F
0 50 100 150 200 250 300 miles
0 50 100 150 200 250 300 350 400 450 km
Lake Winnipeg
Winnipeg
Lake of the Woods
Thunder Bay
Lake Superior
Lake Nipigon
Duluth
MINNESOTA
Minneapolis
St. Paul
WISCONSIN
Lake Michigan
Lake Huron
Georgian Bay
Lake Erie
Lake Ontario
TORONTO
MONTREAL
Ottawa
Québec
Hamilton
Buffalo
Rochester
Syracuse
NEW YORK
Boston
Providence
Hartford
New Haven
PHILADELPHIA
Baltimore
Washington
Pittsburgh
Cleveland
DETROIT
Toledo
CHICAGO
Milwaukee
Madison
Des Moines
Omaha
Lincoln
Kansas City
St. Louis
MISSOURI
Indianapolis
INDIANA
ILLINOIS
Cincinnati
Columbus
Dayton
Louisville
KENTUCKY
WEST VIRGINIA
Richmond
Norfolk
Virginia Beach
Nashville
Knoxville
Memphis
Charlotte
Greensboro
Raleigh
NORTH CAROLINA
SOUTH CAROLINA
Columbia
Charleston
Atlanta
Birmingham
Montgomery
ALABAMA
GEORGIA
Savannah
Jacksonville
MISSISSIPPI
Jackson
LOUISIANA
Baton Rouge
New Orleans
Shreveport
Dallas
Houston
Galveston
Oklahoma City
Tulsa
Little Rock
Tampa
St. Petersburg
Orlando
Miami
Key West
BAHAMAS
Andros I.
Eleuthera I.
GULF OF MEXICO
ATLANTIC OCEAN
Delta of the Mississippi
Florida Bay
Cape Hatteras
Chesapeake Bay
Delaware Bay
Maine
Bangor
Portland
Penobscot Bay
NEW BRUNSWICK
Sault Ste. Marie
Green Bay
Grand Rapids
Lansing
Flint
Saginaw
Fort Wayne
Evansville
Lexington
Chattanooga
Huntsville
Mobile
Pensacola
Tallahassee
Macon
Augusta
COPYRIGHT. GEORGE PHILIP & SON. LTD.

LAKE SUPERIOR
LAKE HURON
Georgian Bay
LAKE ONTARIO
LAKE ERIE
ONTARIO
QUEBEC
NEW YORK
PENNSYLVANIA
OHIO
INDIANA
KENTUCKY
VIRGINIA
WEST VIRGINIA
MARYLAND
NEW JERSEY
DELAWARE
MONTREAL
OTTAWA
TORONTO
CHICAGO
DETROIT
CLEVELAND
PITTSBURGH
PHILADELPHIA
BALTIMORE
WASHINGTON
BOSTON
NEW YORK
MILWAUKEE
BUFFALO
COLUMBUS
INDIANAPOLIS
CINCINNATI
Chesapeake Bay

1:6 000 000
50 0 50 100 150 miles
50 0 50 100 150 200 km
ATLANTIC OCEAN
GULF OF MEXICO
BAHAMAS
NORTH CAROLINA
SOUTH CAROLINA
GEORGIA
ALABAMA
TENNESSEE
MAINE
NEW HAMPSHIRE
CANADA
ATLANTA
JACKSONVILLE
Continuation Eastwards On same scale.
Projection: Alber's Equal Area with two standard parallels
West from Greenwich
COPYRIGHT GEORGE PHILIP & SON, LTD

Projection: Bonne

1:2 500 000
10 0 10 20 30 40 50 miles
10 0 10 20 30 40 50 60 70 80 km
8 9 10 11 12 13 14
A B C D E F G
MONTREAL
Ottawa
Hull
Sherbrooke
Q U É B E C
L. Memphremagog
L. St-François
Cornwall
Kingston
Watertown
Oswego
Syracuse
Utica
Rome
Auburn
Ithaca
Binghamton
Scranton
Wilkes-Barre
Allentown
Bethlehem
Reading
Lancaster
PHILADELPHIA
Camden
Trenton
Y O R K
NEW JERSEY
Newark
Elizabeth
Paterson
Jersey City
NEW YORK
Yonkers
Long Island
Long Beach
Long Island Sound
Block Island Sound
Bridgeport
Stamford
New Haven
Waterbury
Hartford
New Britain
Middletown
New London
C O N N E C T I C U T
RHODE ISLAND
Providence
Pawtucket
Cranston
Warwick
Newport
Fall River
New Bedford
Taunton
Brockton
BOSTON
Cambridge
Quincy
Lynn
Salem
Worcester
Springfield
Pittsfield
Holyoke
Chicopee
Lowell
Lawrence
Fitchburg
M A S S A C H U S E T T S
Albany
Schenectady
Troy
Amsterdam
Gloversville
Kingston
Poughkeepsie
Newburgh
Glens Falls
Adirondack Mountains
Catskill Mts.
Lake Champlain
Plattsburgh
Burlington
V E R M O N T
Green Mountains
Rutland
Lake George
NEW HAMPSHIRE
White Mountains
Mt. Washington 1917
Concord
Manchester
Nashua
Portsmouth
Lake Winnipesaukee
MAINE
ATLANTIC OCEAN
Martha's Vineyard
Buzzards Bay
Vest from Greenwich
COPYRIGHT GEORGE PHILIP & SON, LTD

1:6 000 000
miles
km
CANADA
LAKE SUPERIOR
MICHIGAN
WISCONSIN
MINNESOTA
NORTH DAKOTA
SOUTH DAKOTA
IOWA
NEBRASKA
ILLINOIS
MISSOURI
KANSAS
COLORADO
WYOMING
MONTANA
CHICAGO
MILWAUKEE
MINNEAPOLIS
ST. LOUIS
DENVER
Duluth
Des Moines
Omaha
Lincoln
Kansas City
Topeka
Bismarck
Pierre
Madison
Sioux Falls
Sand Hills
Laramie Mountains

NEW MEXICO
TEXAS
OKLAHOMA
ARKANSAS
LOUISIANA
MISSISSIPPI
TENNESSEE
MEXICO
CHIHUAHUA
COAHUILA
GULF OF MEXICO
Llano Estacado
Edwards Plateau
Stockton Plateau
Sangre de Cristo Mts.
Boston Mts.
Oklahoma City
Tulsa
Wichita
Amarillo
Lubbock
Dallas
Fort Worth
Arlington
Houston
San Antonio
Austin
Corpus Christi
Shreveport
Little Rock
Memphis
Jackson
New Orleans
Baton Rouge
Galveston
Laredo
Nuevo Laredo
Brownsville
Continuation Southwards on same scale
Projection: Albers' Equal Area with two standard parallels
West from Greenwich
COPYRIGHT. GEORGE PHILIP & SON. LTD.

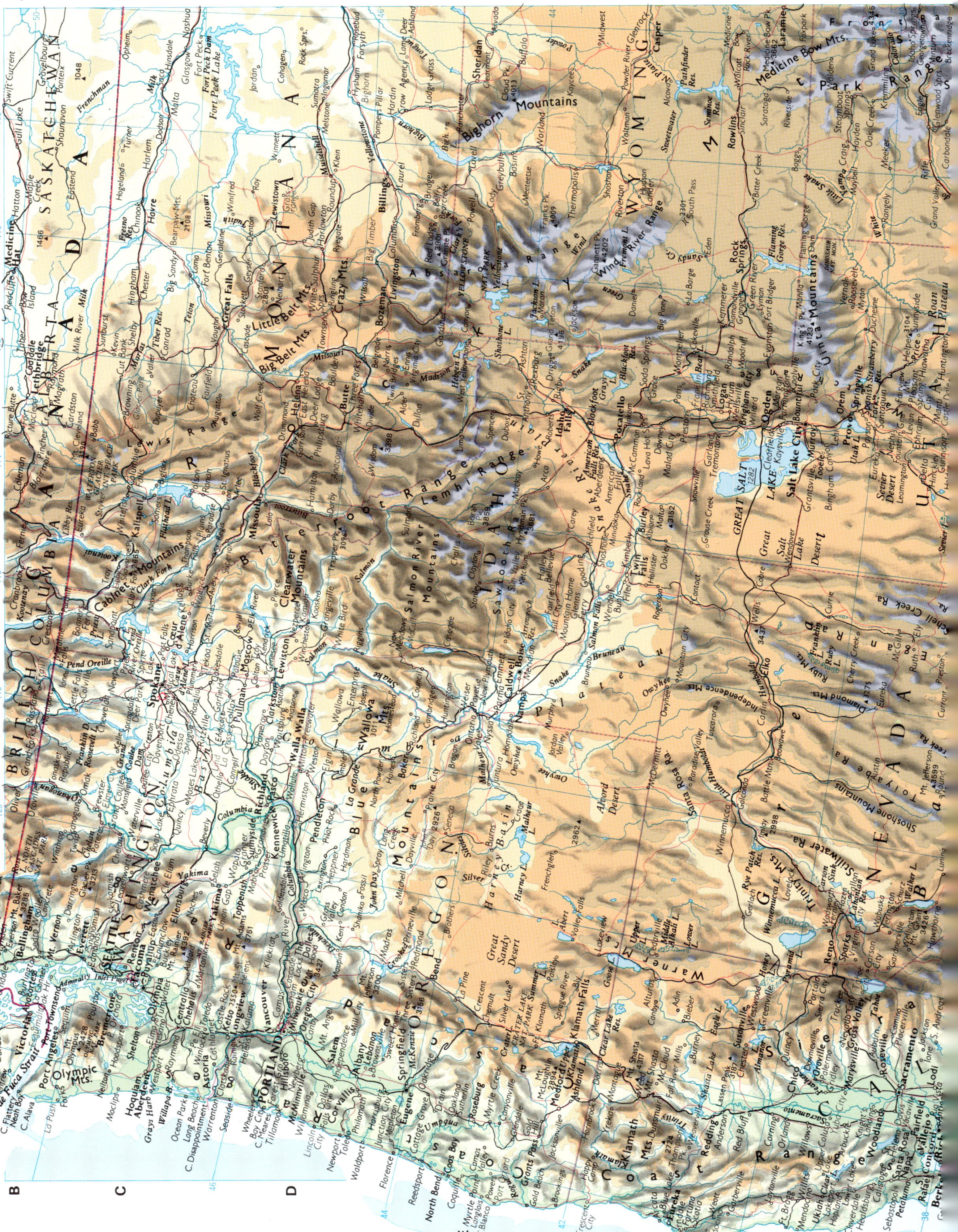

BRITISH COLUMBIA
ALBERTA
SASKATCHEWAN
CANADA
WASHINGTON
OREGON
IDAHO
MONTANA
WYOMING
NEVADA
UTAH
CALIFORNIA
SEATTLE
PORTLAND
Spokane
Salt Lake City
Sacramento
Vancouver
Victoria
Tacoma
Boise
Helena
Butte
Great Falls
Billings
Casper
Reno
Ogden
Provo
Eugene
Salem
Olympia
Yakima
Olympic Mts.
Cascade Range
Blue Mountains
Bitterroot Range
Clearwater Mountains
Salmon River Mountains
Sawtooth Mts.
Snake River Plain
Bighorn Mountains
Wind River Range
Uinta Mountains
Medicine Bow Mts.
Great Salt Lake
Great Salt Lake Desert
Great Sandy Desert
Harney Basin
Klamath Mts.
Columbia
Snake
Missouri
Yellowstone

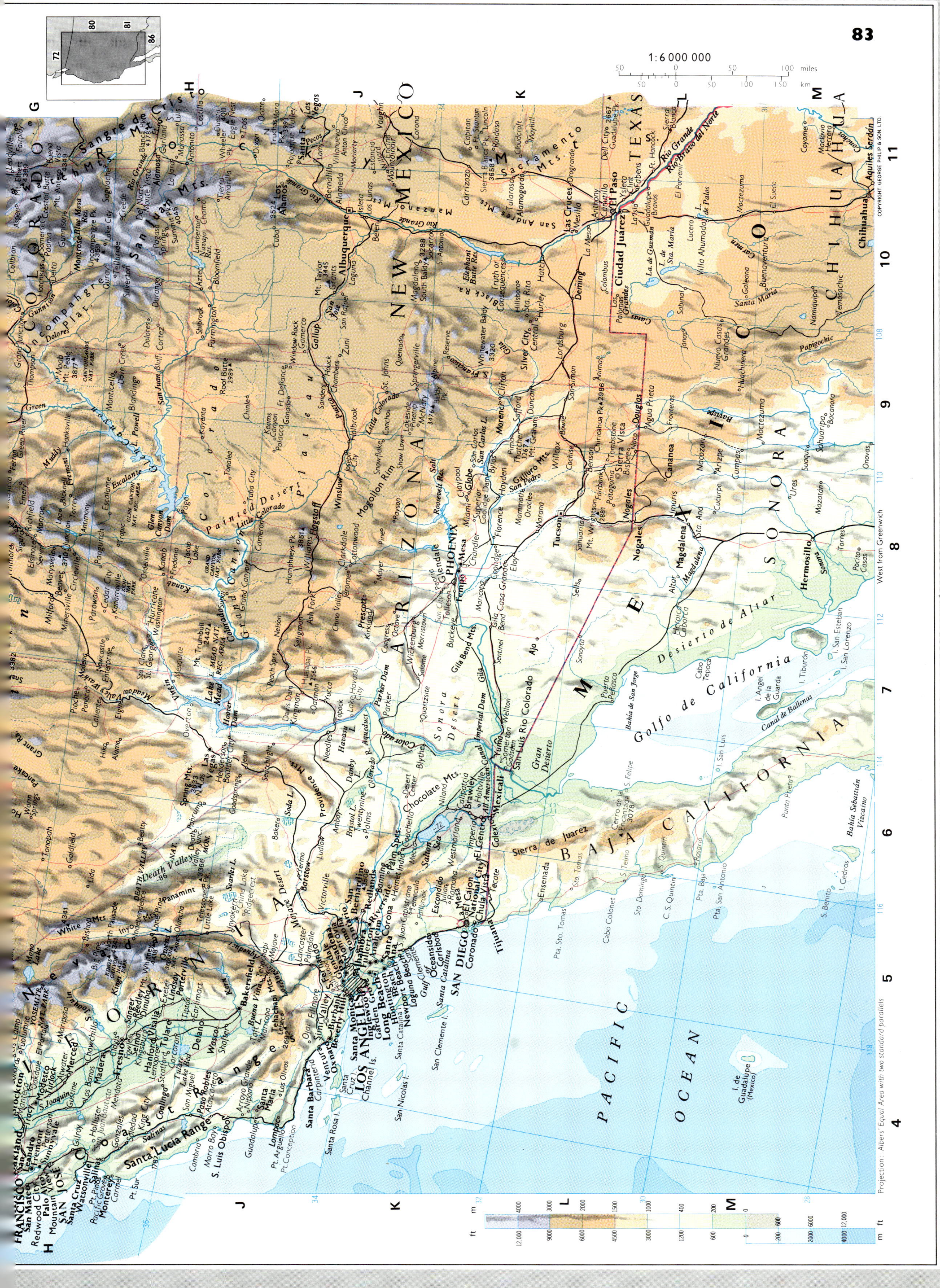
1:6 000 000
miles
km
PACIFIC
OCEAN
CALIFORNIA
NEVADA
ARIZONA
NEW MEXICO
COLORADO
TEXAS
MEXICO
SONORA
CHIHUAHUA
BAJA CALIFORNIA
Golfo de California
Colorado Plateau
Painted Desert
Sonora Desert
Gran Desierto
Desierto de Altar
Mojave Desert
Santa Lucia Range
Sierra de Juarez
San Juan Mts.
Sangre de Cristo Mts.
Sacramento Mts.
San Andres Mts.
LOS ANGELES
SAN DIEGO
SAN JOSE
PHOENIX
Tucson
Albuquerque
Santa Fe
El Paso
Ciudad Juárez
Chihuahua
Hermosillo
Tijuana
Mexicali
Las Vegas
Bakersfield
Fresno
Santa Barbara
Flagstaff
Yuma
Nogales
Las Cruces
Projection: Albers' Equal Area with two standard parallels
West from Greenwich
COPYRIGHT GEORGE PHILIP & SON, LTD.

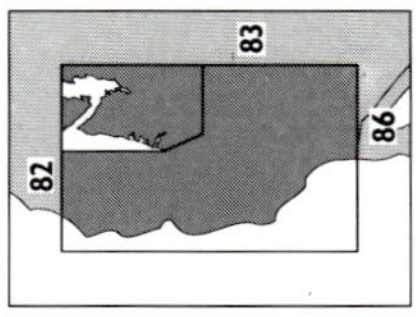
82
83
86

SEATTLE-PORTLAND REGION
On same scale
PACIFIC OCEAN
CANADA
VANCOUVER
Vancouver Island
Strait of Georgia
Juan de Fuca Strait
Victoria
Olympic Mountains
WASHINGTON
SEATTLE
Tacoma
Olympia
PORTLAND
OREGON
Pahute Mesa
White Mts.
Mono L.
L. Tahoe
Reno
Sacramento
Stockton
Modesto
Merced
Fresno
SAN FRANCISCO
Oakland
SAN JOSE
Monterey Bay
Salinas
Santa Lucia Range

1:2 500 000

10 0 10 20 30 40 50 miles

10 0 10 20 30 40 50 60 70 80 km

PACIFIC
OCEAN
Golfo de California
BAJA CALIFORNIA NORTE
BAJA CALIFORNIA SUR
SONORA
CHIHUAHUA
COAHUILA
DURANGO
NAYARIT
JALISCO
COLIMA
MICHOACAN
ZACATECAS
ARIZONA
NEW MEXICO
TIJUANA
MEXICALI
Ensenada
Yuma
San Luis Rio Colorado
TUCSON
Nogales
Hermosillo
Guaymas
Ciudad Obregón
Navojoa
Los Mochis
Culiacán
Mazatlán
La Paz
San José del Cabo
C. San Lucas
Santa Rosalía
CIUDAD JUÁREZ
EL PASO
Las Cruces
Roswell
Carlsbad
Hobbs
Lubbock
Big Spring
Sweetwater
San Angelo
Del Río
Piedras Negras
Acuña
Nueva Rosita
Monclova
MONTERREY
Saltillo
TORREÓN
Gómez Palacio
Lerdo
Hidalgo del Parral
Delicias
Victoria de Durango
Fresnillo
Zacatecas
Aguascalientes
Tepic
GUADALAJARA
Tlaquepaque
LEÓN
Guanajuato
Irapuato
Celaya
Morelia
Uruapan
Colima
Manzanillo
Puerto Vallarta
Ciudad Guzmán
Islas Tres Marías
Is. de Revillagigedo (Mexico)
Socorro
San Benedicto
Roca Partida
I. Cedros
I. Tiburón
I. Ángel de la Guarda
I. Santa Magdalena
I. Santa Margarita
Tropic of Cancer
ft m
12 000 4000
9000 3000
6000 2000
4500 1500
3000 1000
1200 400
600 200
0 0
200 600
2000 6000
4000 12 000
m ft
REFERENCE TO NUMBERS
1 Federal District
2 Aguascalientes
3 Guanajuato
4 Hidalgo
5 México
6 Morelos
7 Querétaro
8 Tlaxcala
Projection: Bi-polar oblique Conical Orthomorphic
West from Greenwich

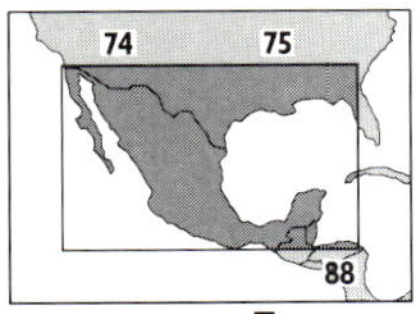

1:8 000 000

50 0 50 100 150 200 miles
50 0 100 200 300 km

GULF OF MEXICO
U. S. A.
West Palm Beach
Fort Myers
Boca Raton
Fort Lauderdale
Hialeah
MIAMI
Naples
C. Romano
Everglades
C. Sable
Florida Bay
Key West
Florida Keys
Dry Tortugas
Straits of Florida
Grand Bahama I.
Great Abaco I.
Northwest Providence Channel
Northeast Providence Channel
Bimini Is.
Berry Is.
Nassau
New Providence I.
Eleuthera I.
Andros Island
Exuma Sound
Great Exuma I.
GREAT BAHAMA BANK
Canal Viejo de Bahama
Cay Sal Bank
Santaren Channel
Canal Nicolas
(Havana) LA HABANA
MARIANAO
Guanabacoa
San Antonio de los Baños
Matanzas
Cárdenas
Colón
Sagua la Grande
Santa Clara
Caibarién
Pinar del Rio
San Luis
Güines
Batabanó
Jagüey Grande
Jovellanos
Placetas
Cienfuegos
Trinidad
Sancti-Spiritus
Isla de la Juventud
Nueva Gerona
Archipiélago de los Canarreos
Morón
Ciego de Avila
Florida
Camagüey
Nuevitas
Puerto Padre
Gibara
Holguín
Victoria de las Tunas
Bayamo
Manzanillo
Palma Soriano
Sierra Maestra
SANTIAGO DE CUBA
C. San Antonio
C. Corrientes
C. Catoche
GREATER
CUBA
Cayman Islands (Br.)
Cayman Brac
Little Cayman
Georgetown
Grand Cayman
7680
Montego Bay
Falmouth
St. Ann's Bay
Lucea
Savanna la Mar
Mandeville
May Pen
Spanish Town
KINGSTON
Port Antonio
JAMAICA
Pedro Cays (Jamaica)
Morant Cays (Jamaica)
Bajo Nuevo (Colombia)
Canal de Yucatán
Progreso
Mérida
Motul
Izamal
Tizimín
Valladolid
Cancun
Pto. Juárez
Isla Cozumel
Campeche
Champotón
Ciudad del Carmen
Laguna de Términos
CAMPECHE
YUCATÁN
QUINTANA ROO
Chetumal
B. de la Ascensión
B. del Espíritu Santo
Banco Chinchorro
Ambergris Cay
Belize City
Belmopan
Turneffe Is.
BELIZE
Dangriga
Swan Islands (U.S.A. & Honduras)
Golfo de Honduras
Islas de la Bahía
Roatán
Puerto Barrios
Puerto Cortés
Tela
La Ceiba
San Pedro Sula
HONDURAS
Tegucigalpa
Laguna Caratasca
C. Gracias á Dios
Cayos Miskitos (Nicaragua)
Mosquitia
GUATEMALA
Cobán
Huehuetenango
San Marcos
Totonicapán
Quezaltenango
Antigua
Jalapa
Zacapa
Chiquimula
Escuintla
Flores
L. Petén Itza
Santa Ana
Ahuachapán
SAN SALVADOR
EL SALVADOR
Cojutepeque
Zacatecoluca
Usulután
San Miguel
Golfo de Fonseca
Chinandega
León
MANAGUA
Masaya
Granada
Diriamba
NICARAGUA
Matagalpa
Boaco
Juigalpa
Estelí
Bluefields
Lago de Nicaragua
Isla de Ometepe
San Juan del Norte
Islas del Maiz (Nicaragua, U.S.A.)
I. de Providencia (Colombia)
I. de San Andrés (Colombia)
Cayos Roncador (U.S.A. & Colombia)
COSTA RICA
Liberia
Puntarenas
Alajuela
San José
Cartago
Limón
Golfo de Papagayo
Pen. de Nicoya
Golfo de Nicoya
Golfo Dulce
Pen. de Osa
Puerto Armuelles
David
Golfo de Chiriquí
Laguna de Chiriquí
Golfo de los Mosquitos
Colón
PANAMÁ
PANAMA
Gatun L.
Arch. de las Perlas
Golfo de Panamá
Archipiélago de las Mulatas
Golfo del Darién
CARTAGENA
Is. de San Bernardo
Montería
C A R I B
Projection: Bi-polar oblique Conical Orthomorphic

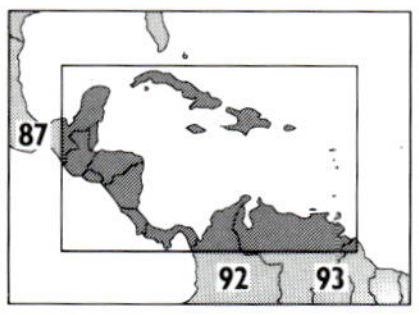
87
92
93

1:8 000 000
50 0 50 100 150 200 miles
50 0 100 200 300 km
5
6
7
8
A
B
C
D
E
AMAS
ATLANTIC
OCEAN
Tropic of Cancer
Arthur's Town
The Bight
Cat I.
San Salvador (Watling I., Guanahani)
Conception I.
Rum Cay
Long I.
Clarence Town
Atwood or Samana Cay
Sandy Cay
Crooked I. Passage
Crooked I.
Plana Cays
Acklins I.
Mayaguana I.
Cay Verde
Mira por vos Cay
Hogsty Reef
Caicos Passage
Caicos Islands (Br.)
Turks I. Passage
Turks Islands (Br.)
Little Inagua I.
Great Inagua I.
Lake Rose
Matthew Town
Banes
Antillo
Moa
Mayarí
Baracoa
Guantánamo
Paso de los Vientos (Windward Passage)
Cap-Haïtien
Port-de-Paix
Fort-Liberté
Monte Cristi
Puerto Plata
Santiago de los Caballeros
Gonaïves
Hinche
HAITI
DOMINICAN REP.
San Francisco de Macorís
Puerto Rico Trench
Milwaukee Deep 9200
Jérémie
PORT-AU-PRINCE
San Juan
Les Cayes
Jacmel
Barahona
SANTO DOMINGO
San Pedro de Macorís
Higüey
La Romana
Navassa I. (U.S.A.)
HISPANIOLA
ANTILLES
Aguadilla
Arecibo
Bayamón
SAN JUAN
Carolina
Fajardo
Mayagüez
Ponce
Caguas
Guayama
PUERTO RICO (U.S.A.)
Isla Mona (U.S.A.)
Charlotte Amalie
Christiansted
Virgin Is. (Br.)
Virgin Is. (U.S.A.)
St. Croix
Anegada
Road Town
Sombrero (Anguilla)
Anguilla (Br.)
St.-Martin (Guad.)
St. Maarten (Neth.)
St.-Barthélemy (Fr.)
Saba (Neth.)
Barbuda
St. Eustatius (Neth.)
Basseterre
ST. CHRISTOPHER-NEVIS
ANTIGUA & BARBUDA
St. Johns
Antigua
Redonda
Montserrat
Guadeloupe Passage
LEEWARD ISLANDS
LESSER ANTILLES
GUADELOUPE (Fr.)
Basse-Terre
Pointe-à-Pitre
Marie-Galante (Fr.)
Dominica Passage
I. de Aves (Bird I.) (Venezuela)
Roseau
DOMINICA
Martinique Passage
Fort-de-France
MARTINIQUE
St. Lucia Channel
Castries
ST. LUCIA
WINDWARD ISLANDS
St. Vincent Passage
Kingstown
ST. VINCENT & THE GRENADINES
Bridgetown
BARBADOS
GRENADINES
St. George's
GRENADA
BEAN
SEA
LESSER ANTILLES
Aruba (Neth.)
Curaçao
Bonaire
Willemstad
NETH. ANTILLES
Pta. Gallinas
Punto Fijo
Coro
FALCÓN
Riohacha
GUAJIRA
Golfo de Venezuela
MARACAIBO
Santa Marta
Ciénaga
Valledupar
Cabimas
Barquisimeto
Puerto Cabello
Valencia
Maracay
CARACAS
Los Teques
I. La Tortuga
I. Margarita
Porlamar
Cumaná
Barcelona
Carúpano
SUCRE
Maturín
MONAGAS
Port of Spain
TRINIDAD & TOBAGO
Tobago
San Fernando
Arima
Ciudad Guayana
Ciudad Bolívar
Upata
Tucupita
DELTA AMACURO
ANZOÁTEGUI
GUÁRICO
Calabozo
Valle de la Pascua
El Tigre
BARINAS
Barinas
Mérida
Trujillo
ZULIA
TÁCHIRA
Cúcuta
San Fernando de Apure
VENEZUELA
West from Greenwich
COPYRIGHT, GEORGE PHILIP & SON, LTD.

1:30 000 000
100 0 100 200 300 400 500 miles
100 0 200 400 600 800 km
ATLANTIC OCEAN
PACIFIC OCEAN
SOUTH ATLANTIC OCEAN
Equator
Tropic of Capricorn
Sa. Nevada de Santa Marta
Barranquilla
5800
Maracaibo
L. Maracaibo
G. of Darien
Panama Canal
Gulf of Panama
Caracas
Margarita
Tobago I.
Trinidad
Cord. de Mérida
Medellín
Bogotá
Cali
Cordillera Occidental
Cordillera Central
Cordillera Oriental
Magdalena
Llanos
Orinoco
Guiana Highlands
Georgetown
2810
Roraima
Sierra Pacaraima
Serra de Tumucumaque
C. Orange
C. de San Francisco
Quito
Cotopaxi
5897
Chimborazo
6267
Guayaquil
G. of Guayaquil
Pta. Pariñas
Pta. Aguja
Lobos Is.
Caquetá
Putumayo
Japurá
Napo
Negro
Manaus
Amazon
Amazonas
Marajó I.
Pará
Belém
Fortaleza
C. São Roque
C. Branco
Plateau of Borborema
Recife
Marañón
Ucayali
Juruá
Purus
Madeira
Tapajós
Xingu
Tocantins
Araguaia
Parnaíba
São Francisco
Huascarán
6768
Lima
Chincha Is.
Madre de Dios
Guaporé
Mamoré
Plateau of Mato Grosso
Brasília
Salvador
Brazilian Highlands
L. Titicaca
Ancohuma & Illampu
6550
La Paz
L. Poopó
Bolivian Plateau
Abrolhos Bank
Belo Horizonte
2890
Pico da Bandeira
Serra da Mantiqueira
Rio de Janeiro
C. Frio
São Paulo
Gran Chaco
Paraguay
Pilcomayo
Asunción
Paraná
Iguaçu Falls
Uruguay
Serra do Mar
Pôrto Alegre
Lagoa dos Patos
Atacama Desert
Peru Chile Trench
8050
S. Félix
S. Ambrosio
Ojos del Salado
6863
Tucumán
Salado
Salinas Grandes
Córdoba
Sierra de Córdoba
L. Mar Chiquita
Entre Ríos
Aconcagua
6960
Uspallata Pass
Valparaíso
Santiago
Arch. de Juan Fernández
Rosario
Buenos Aires
La Plata
Montevideo
Río de la Plata
Pampas
Pta. Mogotes
Colorado
Negro
Bahía Blanca
G. of San Matías
Valdés Peninsula
Chile Rise
Chiloé I.
Chonos Archipelago
Taitao Peninsula
G. of Peñas
Chubut
Patagonia
4058
S. Valentín
G. of San Jorge
Argentine Basin
6212
5994
Wellington
Madre de Dios I.
Magellan's Strait
Falkland Islands
West Falkland
East Falkland
Tierra del Fuego
Staten I.
Santa Inés
Cockburn Chan.
Beagle Chan.
C. Horn
Andes
ft m
18 000 6000
12 000 4000
9000 3000
6000 2000
3000 1000
1200 400
600 200
0 0
200 600
2000 6000
4000 12 000
6000 18 000
8000 24 000
m ft
Projection: Lambert's Equivalent Azimuthal
West from Greenwich
COPYRIGHT, GEORGE PHILIP & SON, LTD

1:30 000 000
100 0 100 200 300 400 500 miles
100 0 200 400 600 800 km
COSTA RICA
San José
PANAMA
Panamá
Colón
Golfo de Panamá
Golfo de Darién
Barranquilla
Cartagena
Maracaibo
Barquisimeto
Valencia
Caracas
Port of Spain
TRINIDAD AND TOBAGO
Cúcuta
San Cristóbal
Bucaramanga
Medellín
Magdalena
Meta
Bogotá
Cali
COLOMBIA
VENEZUELA
Orinoco
Ciudad Guayana
Georgetown
Paramaribo
Cayenne
GUYANA
SURINAM
FRENCH GUIANA
Essequibo
Corantijn
Maroni
C. Orange
C. de San Francisco
Quito
ECUADOR
Guayaquil
G. de Guayaquil
Caquetá
Putumayo
Napo
Iquitos
Marañón
Pta. Aguja
Chiclayo
Trujillo
Chimbote
Ucayali
PERU
Callao
Lima
Cuzco
Arequipa
Branco
Negro
Japurá
Manaus
Amazonas
(Amazon)
Santarem
Ilha de Marajó
Belém
São Luís
Tocantins
Fortaleza (Ceara)
Teresina
C. de São Roque
Natal
João Pessoa
Recife (Pernambuco)
Maceió
Aracaju
Salvador
Parnaíba
São Francisco
Juruá
Purus
Madeira
Tapajós
Xingu
Aripuanã
Araguaia
Pôrto Velho
Madre de Dios
Guaporé
Mamoré
BRAZIL
L. Titicaca
La Paz
BOLIVIA
Cochabamba
Santa Cruz
Sucre
Cuiabá
Brasília
Goiânia
Belo Horizonte
Campo Grande
Ribeirão Prêto
Vitória
Juiz de Fora
Campos
Paraná
Londrina
Campinas
Niterói
Santos
SÃO PAULO
RIO DE JANEIRO
Iquique
PARAGUAY
Paraguay
Pilcomayo
Asunción
Antofagasta
Tropic of Capricorn
Curitiba
Salta
San Miguel de Tucumán
Resistencia
Corrientes
Uruguay
Isla San Felix (Chile)
Isla San Ambrosio (Chile)
Salado
Pôrto Alegre
Lagoa dos Patos
Pelotas
ARGENTINA
Córdoba
San Juan
Santa Fe
Paraná
Rosario
Mendoza
URUGUAY
Viña del Mar
Valparaíso
Santiago
Arch. de Juan Fernández (Chile)
BUENOS AIRES
La Plata
Montevideo
Rio de la Plata
Talca
Concepción
Mar del Plata
Bahía Blanca
Colorado
Negro
Viedma
Valdivia
Puerto Montt
Chubut
Golfo San Jorge
Comodoro Rivadavia
G. de Penas
CHILE
FALKLAND ISLANDS
(U.K.)
West Falkland
Stanley
East Falkland
Strait of Magellan
Punta Arenas
Tierra del Fuego
Cape Horn
NORTH ATLANTIC OCEAN
Equator
SOUTH ATLANTIC OCEAN
PACIFIC OCEAN
Projection: Lambert's Equivalent Azimuthal
West from Greenwich
COPYRIGHT, GEORGE PHILIP & SON, LTD.

1 2 3 4 5 6 7
A B C D E F G H
NICARAGUA
COSTA RICA
PANAMA
COLOMBIA
VENEZUELA
GUYANA
ECUADOR
PERU
BOLIVIA
ARGENTINA
PARAGUA
TRINIDAD & TOBAGO
GRENADA
RORAIMA
AMAZONAS
ACRE
RONDÔNIA
PACIFIC OCEAN
Cocos Ridge
Milne Edwards Trench
Peru Chile Trench
Krümmel Trench
Equator
Sierra Pacaraima
Managua
Bluefields
San José
Panama
Colón
Barranquilla
Cartagena
Maracaibo
Caracas
Valencia
Barquisimeto
Port of Spain
Medellín
Bucaramanga
Cúcuta
San Cristóbal
Bogotá
Cali
Manizales
Pereira
Ciudad Bolívar
Ciudad Guayana
Georgetown
Quito
Guayaquil
Cuenca
Iquitos
Manaus
Chiclayo
Trujillo
Chimbote
Callao
LIMA
Huancayo
Cuzco
Arequipa
Lago Titicaca
La Paz
Cochabamba
Sucre
Potosí
Santa Cruz
Oruro
Arica
Iquique
Antofagasta
Porto Velho
Rio Branco
Amazonas
Negro
Madeira
Orinoco
Ucayali
Marañón
Solimões (Amazonas)
ft m
18,000 6000
12,000 4000
9000 3000
6000 2000
4500 1500
3000 1000
1200 400
600 200
0 0
200 600
2000 6000
4000 12,000
6000 18,000
8000 24,000
m ft
Projection : Sanson-Flamsteed's Sinusoidal
West from

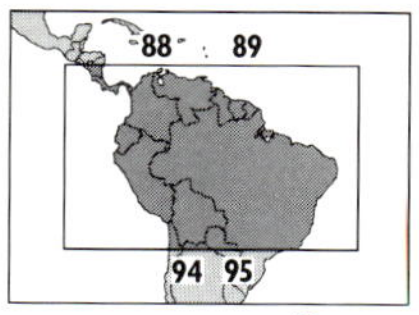

1:16 000 000

COPYRIGHT. GEORGE PHILIP & SON, LTD.

PACIFIC OCEAN
BOLIVIA
POTOSI
TARIJA
NUEVA ASUNCIÓN
ALTO PARAGUAY
BOQUERÓN
PARAGUAY
PRESIDENTE HAYES
Gran Chaco
JUJUY
ANTOFAGASTA
SALTA
FORMOSA
CHACO
CATAMARCA
TUCUMÁN
SANTIAGO DEL ESTERO
ATACAMA
CORRIENTES
LA RIOJA
SANTA FE
COQUIMBO
SAN JUAN
CÓRDOBA
ENTRE RIOS
URU
CHILE
ARGENTINA
ANDES
Cordillera Domeyko
Cordillera de los Andes
Pampa
MENDOZA
SAN LUIS
BUENOS AIRES
LA PAMPA
NEUQUÉN
MAULE
BIO BIO
SANTIAGO
O'HIGGINS
VALPARAÍSO
Iquique
Tocopilla
Calama
Antofagasta
Taltal
Chañaral
Copiapó
Vallenar
La Serena
Coquimbo
Ovalle
Viña del Mar
Valparaíso
Santiago
Rancagua
Talca
Chillán
Concepción
Talcahuano
Los Angeles
Tarija
Tupiza
Villazón
La Quiaca
Tartagal
San Ramón de la Nueva Orán
S. Salvador de Jujuy
Salta
San Miguel de Tucumán
Catamarca
La Rioja
Santiago del Estero
San Juan
Mendoza
San Rafael
San Luis
Rio Cuarto
Córdoba
Rosario
Santa Fe
Paraná
Resistencia
Corrientes
Formosa
Asunción
Concepción
Posadas
Buenos Aires
La Plata
Mar del Plata
Bahía Blanca
Santa Rosa
Tandil
Olavarría
Junín
Pergamino
Venado Tuerto
Villa María
Rafaela
Reconquista
Goya
Concordia
Paysandú
Salto
Gualeguaychú
Mercedes
Aconcagua 6960
Ojos del Salado 6863
Projection: Lambert's Equivalent Azimuthal
ft
m
18 000
6000
12 000
4000
9000
3000
6000
2000
4500
1500
3000
1000
1200
400
600
200
0
0
200
600
2000
6000
4000
12 000
6000
18 000
A
B
C
D
1
2
3
4

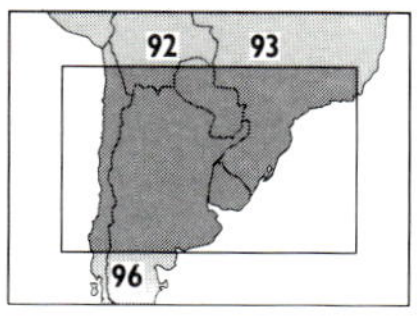

1: 8 000 000

50 0 50 100 150 200 miles

50 0 100 200 300 km

SOUTH AMERICA — SOUTH

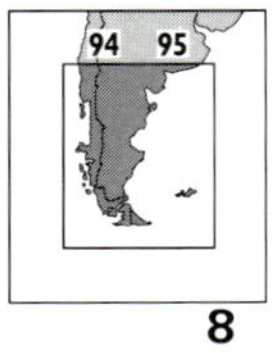

1 : 16 000 000

100 50 0 100 200 300 miles

100 0 100 200 300 400 km

Projection: Sanson-Flamsteed's Sinusoidal

INDEX

The index contains the names of all the principal places and features shown on the World Maps. Each name is followed by an additional entry in italics giving the country or region within which it is located. The alphabetical order of names composed of two or more words is governed primarily by the first word and then by the second. This is an example of the rule:

Mīr Kūh, *Iran*	**45**	**E8**
Mīr Shahdād, *Iran*	**45**	**E8**
Miraj, *India*	**40**	**L9**
Miram Shah, *Pakistan* ..	**42**	**C4**
Miramar, *Argentina*	**94**	**D4**

Physical features composed of a proper name (Erie) and a description (Lake) are positioned alphabetically by the proper name. The description is positioned after the proper name and is usually abbreviated:

Erie, L., *N. Amer.*	**78**	**D4**

Where a description forms part of a settlement or administrative name however, it is always written in full and put in its true alphabetic position:

Mount Morris, *U.S.A.* ...	**78**	**D7**

Names beginning with M' and Mc are indexed as if they were spelled Mac. Names beginning St. are alphabetised under Saint, but Sankt, Sint, Sant', Santa and San are all spelt in full and are alphabetised accordingly. If the same place name occurs two or more times in the index and all are in the same country, each is followed by the name of the administrative subdivision in which it is located. The names are placed in the alphabetical order of the subdivisions. For example:

Jackson, *Ky., U.S.A.*	**76**	**G4**
Jackson, *Mich., U.S.A.* ..	**76**	**D3**
Jackson, *Minn., U.S.A.* ..	**80**	**D7**

The number in bold type which follows each name in the index refers to the number of the map page where that feature or place will be found. This is usually the largest scale at which the place or feature appears. The letter and figure which are in bold type immediately after the page number give the grid square on the map page, within which the feature is situated. The letter represents the latitude and the figure the longitude.

In some cases the feature itself may fall within the specified square, while the name is outside. This is usually the case only with features which are larger than a grid square. Rivers are indexed to their mouths or confluences, and carry the symbol → after their names. A solid square ■ follows the name of a country while, an open square □ refers to a first order administrative area.

Abbreviations used in the index

A.C.T. – Australian Capital Territory
Afghan. – Afghanistan
Ala. – Alabama
Alta. – Alberta
Amer. – America(n)
Arch. – Archipelago
Ariz. – Arizona
Ark. – Arkansas
Atl. Oc. – Atlantic Ocean
B. – Baie, Bahía, Bay, Bucht, Bugt
B.C. – British Columbia
Bangla. – Bangladesh
Barr. – Barrage
Bos. & H. – Bosnia and Herzegovina
C. – Cabo, Cap, Cape, Coast
C.A.R. – Central African Republic
C. Prov. – Cape Province
Calif. – California
Cent. – Central
Chan. – Channel
Colo. – Colorado
Conn. – Connecticut
Cord. – Cordillera
Cr. – Creek
Czech. – Czechoslovakia
D.C. – District of Columbia
Del. – Delaware
Dep. – Dependency
Des. – Desert
Dist. – District
Dj. – Djebel
Domin. – Dominica
Dom. Rep. – Dominican Republic
E. – East
El Salv. – El Salvador
Eq. Guin. – Equatorial Guinea
Fla. – Florida
Falk. Is. – Falkland Is.
G. – Golfe, Golfo, Gulf, Guba, Gebel
Ga. – Georgia
Gt. – Great, Greater
Guinea-Biss. – Guinea-Bissau
H.K. – Hong Kong
H.P. – Himachal Pradesh
Hants. – Hampshire
Harb. – Harbor, Harbour
Hd. – Head
Hts. – Heights
I.(s). – Île, Ilha, Insel, Isla, Island, Isle
Ill. – Illinois
Ind. – Indiana
Ind. Oc. – Indian Ocean
Ivory C. – Ivory Coast
J. – Jabal, Jebel, Jazira
Junc. – Junction
K. – Kap, Kapp
Kans. – Kansas
Kep. – Kepulauan
Ky. – Kentucky
L. – Lac, Lacul, Lago, Lagoa, Lake, Limni, Loch, Lough
La. – Louisiana
Liech. – Liechtenstein
Lux. – Luxembourg
Mad. P. – Madhya Pradesh
Madag. – Madagascar
Man. – Manitoba
Mass. – Massachusetts
Md. – Maryland
Me. – Maine
Medit. S. – Mediterranean Sea
Mich. – Michigan
Minn. – Minnesota
Miss. – Mississippi
Mo. – Missouri
Mont. – Montana
Mozam. – Mozambique
Mt.(e). – Mont, Monte, Monti, Montaña, Mountain
N. – Nord, Norte, North, Northern, Nouveau
N.B. – New Brunswick
N.C. – North Carolina
N. Cal. – New Caledonia
N. Dak. – North Dakota
N.H. – New Hampshire
N.I. – North Island
N.J. – New Jersey
N. Mex. – New Mexico
N.S. – Nova Scotia
N.S.W. – New South Wales
N.W.T. – North West Territory
N.Y. – New York
N.Z. – New Zealand
Nebr. – Nebraska
Neths. – Netherlands
Nev. – Nevada
Nfld. – Newfoundland
Nic. – Nicaragua
O. – Oued, Ouadi
Occ. – Occidentale
O.F.S. – Orange Free State
Okla. – Oklahoma
Ont. – Ontario
Or. – Orientale
Oreg. – Oregon
Os. – Ostrov
Oz. – Ozero
P. – Pass, Passo, Pasul, Pulau
P.E.I. – Prince Edward Island
Pa. – Pennsylvania
Pac. Oc. – Pacific Ocean
Papua N.G. – Papua New Guinea
Pass. – Passage
Pen. – Peninsula, Péninsule
Phil. – Philippines
Pk. – Park, Peak
Plat. – Plateau
P-ov. – Poluostrov
Prov. – Province, Provincial
Pt. – Point
Pta. – Ponta, Punta
Pte. – Pointe
Qué. – Québec
Queens. – Queensland
R. – Rio, River
R.I. – Rhode Island
Ra.(s). – Range(s)
Raj. – Rajasthan
Reg. – Region
Rep. – Republic
Res. – Reserve, Reservoir
S. – San, South, Sea
Si. Arabia – Saudi Arabia
S.C. – South Carolina
S. Dak. – South Dakota
S.I. – South Island
S. Leone – Sierra Leone
Sa. – Serra, Sierra
Sask. – Saskatchewan
Scot. – Scotland
Sd. – Sound
Sev. – Severnaya
Sib. – Siberia
Sprs. – Springs
St. – Saint, Sankt, Sint
Sta. – Santa, Station
Ste. – Sainte
Sto. – Santo
Str. – Strait, Stretto
Switz. – Switzerland
Tas. – Tasmania
Tenn. – Tennessee
Tex. – Texas
Tg. – Tanjung
Trin. & Tob. – Trinidad & Tobago
U.A.E. – United Arab Emirates
U.K. – United Kingdom
U.S.A. – United States of America
Ut. P. – Uttar Pradesh
Va. – Virginia
Vdkhr. – Vodokhranilishche
Vf. – Vîrful
Vic. – Victoria
Vol. – Volcano
Vt. – Vermont
W. – Wadi, West
W. Va. – West Virginia
Wash. – Washington
Wis. – Wisconsin
Wlkp. – Wielkopolski
Wyo. – Wyoming
Yorks. – Yorkshire

A

Aachen, *Germany* 16 C3
Aalborg = Ålborg, *Denmark* 9 H10
A'âli en Nîl □, *Sudan* 51 G11
Aalsmeer, *Neths.* 15 B4
Aalst, *Belgium* 15 D4
Aalten, *Neths.* 15 C6
Aarau, *Switz.* 16 E4
Aare →, *Switz.* 16 E4
Aarhus = Århus, *Denmark* 9 H11
Aarschot, *Belgium* 15 D4
Aba, *Nigeria* 50 G6
Aba, *Zaïre* 54 B3
Âbâdân, *Iran* 45 D6
Âbâdeh, *Iran* 45 D7
Abadla, *Algeria* 50 B4
Abaetetuba, *Brazil* 93 D9
Abagnar Qi, *China* 34 C9
Abai, *Paraguay* 95 B4
Abakan, *Russia* 27 D10
Abariringa, *Kiribati* 64 H10
Abarqū, *Iran* 45 D7
Abashiri, *Japan* 30 B12
Abashiri-Wan, *Japan* 30 B12
Abay, *Kazakhstan* 26 E8
Abaya, L., *Ethiopia* 51 G12
Abaza, *Russia* 26 D10
'Abbāsābād, *Iran* 45 C8
Abbay = Nîl el Azraq →, *Sudan* 51 E11
Abbaye, Pt., *U.S.A.* 76 B1
Abbeville, *France* 18 A4
Abbeville, *La., U.S.A.* 81 K8
Abbeville, *S.C., U.S.A.* 77 H4
Abbieglassie, *Australia* 63 D4
Abbot Ice Shelf, *Antarctica* 5 D16
Abbotsford, *Canada* 72 D4
Abbotsford, *U.S.A.* 80 C9
Abbottabad, *Pakistan* 42 B5
Abd al Kūrī, *Ind. Oc.* 46 E5
Âbdar, *Iran* 45 D7
'Abdolābād, *Iran* 45 C8
Abéché, *Chad* 51 F9
Åbenrå, *Denmark* 9 J10
Abeokuta, *Nigeria* 50 G5
Aber, *Uganda* 54 B3
Aberaeron, *U.K.* 11 E3
Aberayron = Aberaeron, *U.K.* 11 E3
Abercorn = Mbala, *Zambia* 55 D3
Abercorn, *Australia* 63 D5
Aberdare, *U.K.* 11 F4
Aberdare Ra., *Kenya* 54 C4
Aberdeen, *Australia* 63 E5
Aberdeen, *Canada* 73 C7
Aberdeen, *S. Africa* 56 E3
Aberdeen, *U.K.* 12 D6
Aberdeen, *Ala., U.S.A.* 77 J1
Aberdeen, *Idaho, U.S.A.* 82 E7
Aberdeen, *S. Dak., U.S.A.* 80 C5
Aberdeen, *Wash., U.S.A.* 84 D3
Aberdovey = Aberdyfi, *U.K.* 11 E3
Aberdyfi, *U.K.* 11 E3
Aberfeldy, *U.K.* 12 E5
Abergavenny, *U.K.* 11 F4
Abernathy, *U.S.A.* 81 J4
Abert, L., *U.S.A.* 82 E3
Aberystwyth, *U.K.* 11 E3
Abhar, *Iran* 45 B6
Abhayapuri, *India* 43 F14
Abidjan, *Ivory C.* 50 G4
Abilene, *Kans., U.S.A.* 80 F6
Abilene, *Tex., U.S.A.* 81 J5
Abingdon, *U.K.* 11 F6
Abingdon, *Ill., U.S.A.* 80 E9
Abingdon, *Va., U.S.A.* 77 G5
Abington Reef, *Australia* 62 B4
Abitau →, *Canada* 73 B7
Abitau L., *Canada* 73 A7
Abitibi L., *Canada* 70 C4
Abkhaz Republic □, *Georgia* 25 F7
Abkit, *Russia* 27 C16
Abminga, *Australia* 63 D1
Abohar, *India* 42 D6
Abomey, *Benin* 50 G5
Abong-Mbang, *Cameroon* 52 D2
Abou-Deïa, *Chad* 51 F8
Aboyne, *U.K.* 12 D6
Abra Pampa, *Argentina* 94 A2
Abrantes, *Portugal* 19 C1
Abreojos, Pta., *Mexico* 86 B2
Abri, *Sudan* 51 D11
Abrolhos, Banka, *Brazil* 93 G11
Abrud, *Romania* 17 E11
Abruzzi □, *Italy* 20 C6
Absaroka Ra., *U.S.A.* 82 D9
Abū al Khaṣīb, *Iraq* 45 D6
Abū 'Alī, *Si. Arabia* 45 E6
Abū 'Alī →, *Lebanon* 47 A4
Abu 'Arīsh, *Si. Arabia* 46 D3
Abu Dhabi = Abū Ẓāby, *U.A.E.* 45 E7
Abū Dis, *Sudan* 51 E11
Abū Du'ān, *Syria* 44 B3
Abu el Gairi, W. →, *Egypt* 47 F2
Abu Ga'da, W. →, *Egypt* 47 F1
Abū Ḥadrīyah, *Si. Arabia* 45 E6
Abu Hamed, *Sudan* 51 E11
Abū Kamāl, *Syria* 44 C4
Abū Madd, Ra's, *Si. Arabia* 44 E3
Abu Matariq, *Sudan* 51 F10
Abu Ṣafāt, W. →, *Jordan* 47 E5
Abu Ṣukhayr, *Iraq* 44 D5
Abu Tig, *Egypt* 51 C11
Abû Zabad, *Sudan* 51 F10
Abū Ẓāby, *U.A.E.* 45 E7
Abū Zeydābād, *Iran* 45 C6
Abuja, *Nigeria* 50 G6
Abukuma-Gawa →, *Japan* 30 E10
Abukuma-Sammyaku, *Japan* 30 F10
Abunã, *Brazil* 92 E5
Abunã →, *Brazil* 92 E5
Aburo, *Zaïre* 54 B3
Abut Hd., *N.Z.* 59 K3
Abwong, *Sudan* 51 G11
Acajutla, *El Salv.* 88 D2
Acámbaro, *Mexico* 86 C4
Acaponeta, *Mexico* 86 C3
Acapulco, *Mexico* 87 D5
Acarigua, *Venezuela* 92 B5
Acatlán, *Mexico* 87 D5
Acayucan, *Mexico* 87 D6
Accomac, *U.S.A.* 76 G8
Accra, *Ghana* 50 G4
Accrington, *U.K.* 10 D5
Acebal, *Argentina* 94 C3
Aceh □, *Indonesia* 36 D1
Achalpur, *India* 40 J10
Acheng, *China* 35 B14
Acher, *India* 42 H5
Achill, *Ireland* 13 C2
Achill Hd., *Ireland* 13 C1
Achill I., *Ireland* 13 C1
Achill Sd., *Ireland* 13 C2
Achinsk, *Russia* 27 D10
Ackerman, *U.S.A.* 81 J10
Acklins I., *Bahamas* 89 B5
Acme, *Canada* 72 C6
Aconcagua □, *Chile* 94 C1
Aconcagua, Cerro, *Argentina* 94 C2
Aconquija, Mt., *Argentina* 94 B2
Açores, Is. dos = Azores, *Atl. Oc.* 2 C8
Acraman, L., *Australia* 63 E2
Acre = 'Akko, *Israel* 47 C4
Acre □, *Brazil* 92 E4
Acre →, *Brazil* 92 E5
Acton, *Canada* 78 C4
Ad Dammām, *Si. Arabia* 45 E6
Ad Dawhah, *Qatar* 45 E6
Ad Dawr, *Iraq* 44 C4
Ad Dir'īyah, *Si. Arabia* 44 E5
Ad Dīwānīyah, *Iraq* 44 D5
Ad Dujayl, *Iraq* 44 C5
Ad Durūz, J., *Jordan* 47 C5
Ada, *Minn., U.S.A.* 80 B6
Ada, *Okla., U.S.A.* 81 H6
Adaja →, *Spain* 19 B3
Adamaoua, Massif de l', *Cameroon* 51 G7
Adamawa Highlands = Adamaoua, Massif de l', *Cameroon* 51 G7
Adamello, Mt., *Italy* 20 A4
Adaminaby, *Australia* 63 F4
Adams, *Mass., U.S.A.* 79 D11
Adams, *N.Y., U.S.A.* 79 C8
Adams, *Wis., U.S.A.* 80 D10
Adams, Mt., *U.S.A.* 84 D5
Adam's Bridge, *Sri Lanka* 40 Q11
Adams L., *Canada* 72 C5
Adam's Peak, *Sri Lanka* 40 R12
Adana, *Turkey* 25 G6
Adapazarı, *Turkey* 25 F5
Adarama, *Sudan* 51 E11
Adare, C., *Antarctica* 5 D11
Adaut, *Indonesia* 37 F8
Adavale, *Australia* 63 D3
Adda →, *Italy* 20 B3
Addis Ababa = Addis Abeba, *Ethiopia* 51 G12
Addis Abeba, *Ethiopia* 51 G12
Addis Alem, *Ethiopia* 51 G12
Addison, *U.S.A.* 78 D7
Addo, *S. Africa* 56 E4
Ādeh, *Iran* 44 B5
Adel, *U.S.A.* 77 K4
Adelaide, *Australia* 63 E2
Adelaide, *Bahamas* 88 A4
Adelaide, *S. Africa* 56 E4
Adelaide I., *Antarctica* 5 C17
Adelaide Pen., *Canada* 68 B10
Adelaide River, *Australia* 60 B5
Adelanto, *U.S.A.* 85 L9
Adele I., *Australia* 60 C3
Adélie, Terre, *Antarctica* 5 C10
Aden = Al 'Adan, *Yemen* 46 E4
Aden, G. of, *Asia* 46 E4
Adendorp, *S. Africa* 56 E3
Adh Dhayd, *U.A.E.* 45 E7
Adhoi, *India* 42 H4
Adi, *Indonesia* 37 E8
Adi Ugri, *Ethiopia* 51 F12
Adieu, C., *Australia* 61 F5
Adieu Pt., *Australia* 60 C3
Adige →, *Italy* 20 B5
Adilabad, *India* 40 K11
Adin, *U.S.A.* 82 F3
Adin Khel, *Afghan.* 40 C6
Adirondack Mts., *U.S.A.* 79 C10
Adjumani, *Uganda* 54 B3
Adlavik Is., *Canada* 71 B8
Admer, *Algeria* 50 D6
Admiralty G., *Australia* 60 B4
Admiralty I., *U.S.A.* 68 C6
Admiralty Inlet, *U.S.A.* 82 C2
Admiralty Is., *Papua N. G.* 64 H6
Ado Ekiti, *Nigeria* 50 G6
Adonara, *Indonesia* 37 F6
Adoni, *India* 40 M10
Adour →, *France* 18 E3
Adra, *India* 43 H12
Adra, *Spain* 19 D4
Adrano, *Italy* 20 F6
Adrar, *Algeria* 50 C4
Adré, *Chad* 51 F9
Adrī, *Libya* 51 C7
Adrian, *Mich., U.S.A.* 76 E3
Adrian, *Tex., U.S.A.* 81 H3
Adriatic Sea, *Europe* 20 C6
Adua, *Indonesia* 37 E7
Adwa, *Ethiopia* 51 F12
Adzhar Republic □, *Georgia* 25 F7
Ægean Sea, *Europe* 21 E11
Æolian Is. = Eólie, Is., *Italy* 20 E6
Aerhtai Shan, *Mongolia* 32 B4
'Afak, *Iraq* 44 C5
Afándou, *Greece* 23 C10
Afars & Issas, Terr. of = Djibouti ■, *Africa* 46 E3
Afghanistan ■, *Asia* 40 C4
Afgoi, *Somali Rep.* 46 G3
Afognak I., *U.S.A.* 68 C4
Africa 48 E6
'Afrīn, *Syria* 44 B3
Afton, *U.S.A.* 79 D9
Afuá, *Brazil* 93 D8
Afula, *Israel* 47 C4
Afyonkarahisar, *Turkey* 25 G5
Agadès = Agadez, *Niger* 50 E6
Agadez, *Niger* 50 E6
Agadir, *Morocco* 50 B3
Agaete, *Canary Is.* 22 F4
Agapa, *Russia* 27 B9
Agar, *India* 42 H7
Agartala, *India* 41 H17
Agassiz, *Canada* 72 D4
Agats, *Indonesia* 37 F9
Agboville, *Ivory C.* 50 G4
Agde, *France* 18 E5
Agen, *France* 18 D4
Āgh Kand, *Iran* 45 B6
Aginskoye, *Russia* 27 D12
Agra, *India* 42 F7
Agri →, *Italy* 20 D7
Ağrı Dağı, *Turkey* 25 G7
Ağrı Karakose, *Turkey* 25 G7
Agrigento, *Italy* 20 F5
Agrinion, *Greece* 21 E9
Agua Caliente, *Baja Calif. N., Mexico* 85 N10
Agua Caliente, *Sinaloa, Mexico* 86 B3
Agua Caliente Springs, *U.S.A.* 85 N10
Água Clara, *Brazil* 93 H8
Agua Hechicero, *Mexico* 85 N10
Agua Prieta, *Mexico* 86 A3
Aguadas, *Colombia* 92 B3
Aguadilla, *Puerto Rico* 89 C6
Aguadulce, *Panama* 88 E3
Aguanga, *U.S.A.* 85 M10
Aguanish, *Canada* 71 B7
Aguanus →, *Canada* 71 B7
Aguapey →, *Argentina* 94 B4
Aguaray Guazú →, *Paraguay* 94 A4
Aguarico →, *Ecuador* 92 D3
Aguas Blancas, *Chile* 94 A2
Aguas Calientes, Sierra de, *Argentina* 94 B2
Aguascalientes, *Mexico* 86 C4
Aguascalientes □, *Mexico* 86 C4
Aguilares, *Argentina* 94 B2
Aguilas, *Spain* 19 D5
Agüimes, *Canary Is.* 22 G4
Agulhas, C., *S. Africa* 56 E3
Agulo, *Canary Is.* 22 F2
Agung, *Indonesia* 36 F5
Agur, *Uganda* 54 B3
Agusan →, *Phil.* 37 C7
Aha Mts., *Botswana* 56 B3
Ahaggar, *Algeria* 50 D6
Ahar, *Iran* 44 B5
Ahipara B., *N.Z.* 59 F4
Ahiri, *India* 40 K12
Ahmad Wal, *Pakistan* 42 E1
Ahmadabad, *India* 42 H5
Aḥmadābād, *Khorāsān, Iran* 45 C9
Aḥmadābād, *Khorāsān, Iran* 45 C8
Aḥmadī, *Iran* 45 E8
Ahmadnagar, *India* 40 K9
Ahmadpur, *Pakistan* 42 E4
Ahmedabad = Ahmadabad, *India* 42 H5
Ahmednagar = Ahmadnagar, *India* 40 K9
Ahome, *Mexico* 86 B3
Ahram, *Iran* 45 D6
Ahrax Pt., *Malta* 23 D1
Āhū, *Iran* 45 C6
Ahuachapán, *El Salv.* 88 D2
Ahvāz, *Iran* 45 D6
Ahvenanmaa = Åland, *Finland* 9 F16
Aḥwar, *Yemen* 46 E4
Aichi □, *Japan* 31 G8
Aigua, *Uruguay* 95 C5
Aigues-Mortes, *France* 18 E6
Aihui, *China* 33 A7
Aija, *Peru* 92 E3
Aikawa, *Japan* 30 E9
Aiken, *U.S.A.* 77 J5
Aillik, *Canada* 71 A8
Ailsa Craig, *U.K.* 12 F3
'Ailūn, *Jordan* 47 C4
Aim, *Russia* 27 D14
Aimere, *Indonesia* 37 F6
Aimogasta, *Argentina* 94 B2
Aimorés, *Brazil* 93 G10
Ain □, *France* 18 C6
Aïn Beïda, *Algeria* 50 A6
Aïn Ben Tili, *Mauritania* 50 C3
Aïn-Sefra, *Algeria* 50 B4
'Ain Sudr, *Egypt* 47 F2
Ainabo, *Somali Rep.* 46 F4
Ainsworth, *U.S.A.* 80 D5
Aïr, *Niger* 50 E6
Air Hitam, *Malaysia* 39 M4
Airdrie, *U.K.* 12 F5
Aire →, *U.K.* 10 D7
Aire, I. del, *Spain* 22 B11
Airlie Beach, *Australia* 62 C4
Aisne □, *France* 18 B5
Aisne →, *France* 18 B5
Aitkin, *U.S.A.* 80 B8
Aiud, *Romania* 17 E11
Aix-en-Provence, *France* 18 E6
Aix-la-Chapelle = Aachen, *Germany* 16 C3
Aiyansh, *Canada* 72 B3
Áíyina, *Greece* 21 F10
Aiyion, *Greece* 21 E10
Aizawl, *India* 41 H18
Aizuwakamatsu, *Japan* 30 F9
Ajaccio, *France* 18 F8
Ajalpan, *Mexico* 87 D5
Ajanta Ra., *India* 40 J9
Ajax, *Canada* 78 C5
Ajdâbiyah, *Libya* 51 B9
Ajmer, *India* 42 F6
Ajo, *U.S.A.* 83 K7
Akabira, *Japan* 30 C11
Akamas □, *Cyprus* 23 D11
Akanthou, *Cyprus* 23 D12
Akaroa, *N.Z.* 59 K4
Akashi, *Japan* 31 G7
Akelamo, *Indonesia* 37 D7
Akershus fylke □, *Norway* 9 G11
Aketi, *Zaïre* 52 D4
Akhelóös →, *Greece* 21 E9
Akhmîm, *Egypt* 51 C11
Akhnur, *India* 43 C6
Aki, *Japan* 31 H6
Akimiski I., *Canada* 70 B3
Akita, *Japan* 30 E10
Akita □, *Japan* 30 E10
Akjoujt, *Mauritania* 50 E2
Akkeshi, *Japan* 30 C12
'Akko, *Israel* 47 C4
Akkol, *Kazakhstan* 26 E8
Aklavik, *Canada* 68 B6
Akmolinsk = Tselinograd, *Kazakhstan* 26 D8
Akō, *Japan* 31 G7
Akobo →, *Ethiopia* 51 G11
Akola, *India* 40 J10
Akordat, *Ethiopia* 51 E12
Akpatok I., *Canada* 69 B13
Akranes, *Iceland* 8 D3
Akreïjit, *Mauritania* 50 E3
Akron, *Colo., U.S.A.* 80 E3
Akron, *Ohio, U.S.A.* 78 E3
Akrotiri, *Cyprus* 23 E11
Akrotiri Bay, *Cyprus* 23 E12
Aksai Chih, *India* 43 B8
Aksarka, *Russia* 26 C7
Aksay, *Kazakhstan* 24 D9
Aksenovo Zilovskoye, *Russia* 27 D12
Aksu, *China* 32 B3
Aksum, *Ethiopia* 51 F12
Aktogay, *Kazakhstan* 26 E8
Aktyubinsk, *Kazakhstan* 25 D10
Aku, *Nigeria* 50 G6
Akure, *Nigeria* 50 G6
Akureyri, *Iceland* 8 D4
Akuseki-Shima, *Japan* 31 K4
Akyab = Sittwe, *Burma* 41 J18
Al 'Adan, *Yemen* 46 E4
Al Aḥsā, *Si. Arabia* 45 E6
Al Ajfar, *Si. Arabia* 44 E4
Al Amādīyah, *Iraq* 44 B4
Al Amārah, *Iraq* 44 D5
Al 'Aqabah, *Jordan* 47 F4
Al Arak, *Syria* 44 C3
Al 'Aramah, *Si. Arabia* 44 E5
Al Arṭāwīyah, *Si. Arabia* 44 E5
Al 'Āṣimah □, *Jordan* 47 D5
Al' Assāfīyah, *Si. Arabia* 44 D3
Al 'Ayn, *Oman* 45 E7
Al 'Ayn, *Si. Arabia* 44 E3
Al A'ẓamīyah, *Iraq* 44 C5
Al 'Azīzīyah, *Iraq* 44 C5
Al Bāb, *Syria* 44 B3
Al Bad', *Si. Arabia* 44 D2
Al Bādī, *Iraq* 44 C4
Al Baḥrah, *Kuwait* 44 D5
Al Balqā' □, *Jordan* 47 C4
Al Bārūk, J., *Lebanon* 47 B4
Al Baṣrah, *Iraq* 44 D5
Al Baṭḥā, *Iraq* 44 D5
Al Batrūn, *Lebanon* 47 A4
Al Bi'r, *Si. Arabia* 44 D3
Al Bu'ayrāt, *Libya* 51 B8
Al Burayj, *Syria* 47 A5
Al Fallūjah, *Iraq* 44 C4
Al Fāw, *Iraq* 45 D6
Al Fujayrah, *U.A.E.* 45 E8
Al Ghadaf, W. →, *Jordan* 47 D5
Al Ghammās, *Iraq* 44 D5
Al Hābah, *Si. Arabia* 44 E5
Al Ḥadīthah, *Iraq* 44 C4
Al Ḥadīthah, *Si. Arabia* 44 D3
Al Ḥājānah, *Syria* 47 B5
Al Ḥāmad, *Si. Arabia* 44 D3
Al Hamdānīyah, *Syria* 44 C3
Al Ḥamīdīyah, *Syria* 47 A4
Al Ḥammār, *Iraq* 44 D5
Al Ḥarīr, W. →, *Syria* 47 C4
Al Ḥasā, W. →, *Jordan* 47 D4
Al Ḥasakah, *Syria* 44 B4
Al Ḥawrah, *Yemen* 46 E4
Al Ḥaydān, W. →, *Jordan* 47 D4
Al Ḥayy, *Iraq* 44 C5
Al Ḥijāz, *Si. Arabia* 46 B2
Al Ḥillah, *Iraq* 44 C5
Al Ḥillah, *Si. Arabia* 46 C4
Al Hirmil, *Lebanon* 47 A5
Al Hoceïma, *Morocco* 50 A4
Al Ḥudaydah, *Yemen* 46 E3
Al Hufūf, *Si. Arabia* 45 E6
Al Ḥumayḍah, *Si. Arabia* 44 D2
Al Ḥunayy, *Si. Arabia* 45 E6
Al Irq, *Libya* 51 C9
Al Īsāwīyah, *Si. Arabia* 44 D3
Al Ittihad = Madīnat ash Sha'b, *Yemen* 46 E3
Al Jafr, *Jordan* 47 E5
Al Jaghbūb, *Libya* 51 C9
Al Jahrah, *Kuwait* 44 D5
Al Jalāmīd, *Si. Arabia* 44 D3
Al Jamalīyah, *Qatar* 45 E6
Al Janūb □, *Lebanon* 47 B4
Al Jawf, *Libya* 51 D9
Al Jawf, *Si. Arabia* 44 D3
Al Jazirah, *Iraq* 44 C5
Al Jazirah, *Libya* 51 C9
Al Jithāmīyah, *Si. Arabia* 44 E4
Al Jubayl, *Si. Arabia* 45 E6
Al Jubaylah, *Si. Arabia* 44 E5
Al Jubb, *Si. Arabia* 44 E4
Al Junaynah, *Sudan* 51 F9
Al Kabā'ish, *Iraq* 44 D5
Al Karak, *Jordan* 47 D4
Al Karak □, *Jordan* 47 E5
Al Kāẓim Tyah, *Iraq* 44 C5
Al Khalīl, *Jordan* 47 D4
Al Khalīl □, *Jordan* 47 D4
Al Khawr, *Qatar* 45 E6
Al Khiḍr, *Iraq* 44 D5
Al Khiyām, *Lebanon* 47 B4
Al Kiswah, *Syria* 47 B5
Al Kufrah, *Libya* 51 D9
Al Kuhayfīyah, *Si. Arabia* 44 E4
Al Kūt, *Iraq* 44 C5
Al Kuwayt, *Kuwait* 44 D5
Al Labwah, *Lebanon* 47 A5
Al Lādhiqīyah, *Syria* 44 C2
Al Liwā', *Oman* 45 E8
Al Luḥayyah, *Yemen* 46 D3
Al Madīnah, *Iraq* 44 D5
Al Madīnah, *Si. Arabia* 46 C2
Al-Mafraq, *Jordan* 47 C5
Al Maḥmūdīyah, *Iraq* 44 C5
Al Majma'ah, *Si. Arabia* 44 E5
Al Makhruq, W. →, *Jordan* 47 D6
Al Makḥūl, *Si. Arabia* 44 E4
Al Manāmah, *Bahrain* 45 E6
Al Maqwa', *Kuwait* 44 D5
Al Marj, *Libya* 51 B9
Al Maṭlā, *Kuwait* 44 D5
Al Mawjib, W. →, *Jordan* 47 D4
Al Mawṣil, *Iraq* 44 B4
Al Mayādin, *Syria* 44 C4
Al Mazār, *Jordan* 47 D4
Al Midhnab, *Si. Arabia* 44 E5
Al Minā', *Lebanon* 47 A4
Al Miqdādīyah, *Iraq* 44 C5
Al Mubarraz, *Si. Arabia* 45 E6
Al Mughayrā', *U.A.E.* 45 E7
Al Muḥarraq, *Bahrain* 45 E6
Al Mukallā, *Yemen* 46 E4
Al Mukhā, *Yemen* 46 E3
Al Musayjīd, *Si. Arabia* 44 E3
Al Musayyib, *Iraq* 44 C5
Al Muwayliḥ, *Si. Arabia* 44 E2
Al Qā'im, *Iraq* 44 C4
Al Qalībah, *Si. Arabia* 44 D3
Al Qaryatayn, *Syria* 47 A6
Al Qaṣabāt, *Libya* 51 B7
Al Qaṭ'ā, *Syria* 44 C4
Al Qaṭīf, *Si. Arabia* 45 E6
Al Qatrānah, *Jordan* 47 D5
Al Qaṭrūn, *Libya* 51 D8
Al Qayṣūmah, *Si. Arabia* 44 D5
Al Quds = Jerusalem, *Israel* 47 D4
Al Quds □, *Jordan* 47 D4
Al Qunaytirah, *Syria* 47 C4
Al Qurnah, *Iraq* 44 D5
Al Quṣayr, *Iraq* 44 D5
Al Quṣayr, *Syria* 47 A5
Al Qutayfah, *Syria* 47 B5
Al' Uḍaylīyah, *Si. Arabia* 45 E6
Al 'Ulā, *Si. Arabia* 44 E3
Al Uqaylah ash Sharqīgah, *Libya* 51 B8
Al Uqayr, *Si. Arabia* 45 E6
Al 'Uwaynid, *Si. Arabia* 44 E5
Al' 'Uwayqīlah, *Si. Arabia* 44 D4
Al 'Uyūn, *Si. Arabia* 44 E4
Al 'Uyūn, *Si. Arabia* 44 E3
Al Wajh, *Si. Arabia* 44 E3
Al Wakrah, *Qatar* 45 E6
Al Wannān, *Si. Arabia* 45 E6

Al Waqbah, *Si. Arabia* 44 D5
Al Wari'āh, *Si. Arabia* 44 E5
Al Wusayl, *Qatar* 45 E6
Ala Tau Shankou = Dzhungarskiye Vorota, *Kazakhstan* 32 B3
Alabama □, *U.S.A.* 77 J2
Alabama →, *U.S.A.* 77 K2
Alaérma, *Greece* 23 C9
Alagoa Grande, *Brazil* 93 E11
Alagoas □, *Brazil* 93 E11
Alagoinhas, *Brazil* 93 F11
Alajero, *Canary Is.* 22 F2
Alajuela, *Costa Rica* 88 D3
Alakamisy, *Madag.* 57 C8
Alakurtti, *Russia* 24 A5
Alameda, *Calif., U.S.A.* 84 H4
Alameda, *N. Mex., U.S.A.* 83 J10
Alamo, *U.S.A.* 85 J11
Alamo Crossing, *U.S.A.* 85 L13
Alamogordo, *U.S.A.* 83 K11
Alamos, *Mexico* 86 B3
Alamosa, *U.S.A.* 83 H11
Åland, *Finland* 9 F16
Ålands hav, *Sweden* 9 G15
Alandur, *India* 40 N12
Alanya, *Turkey* 25 G5
Alaotra, Farihin', *Madag.* 57 B8
Alapayevsk, *Russia* 26 D7
Alaşehir, *Turkey* 25 G4
Alaska □, *U.S.A.* 68 B5
Alaska, G. of, *Pac. Oc.* 68 C5
Alaska Highway, *Canada* 72 B3
Alaska Pen., *U.S.A.* 68 C4
Alaska Range, *U.S.A.* 68 B4
Alatyr, *Russia* 24 D8
Alausi, *Ecuador* 92 D3
Alava, C., *U.S.A.* 82 B1
Alawoona, *Australia* 63 E3
'Alayh, *Lebanon* 47 B4
Alayor, *Spain* 22 B11
Alba, *Italy* 20 B3
Alba Iulia, *Romania* 17 E11
Albacete, *Spain* 19 C5
Albacutya, L., *Australia* 63 F3
Albania ■, *Europe* 21 D9
Albany, *Australia* 61 G2
Albany, *Ga., U.S.A.* 77 K3
Albany, *Minn., U.S.A.* 80 C7
Albany, *N.Y., U.S.A.* 79 D11
Albany, *Oreg., U.S.A.* 82 D2
Albany, *Tex., U.S.A.* 81 J5
Albany →, *Canada* 70 B3
Albardón, *Argentina* 94 C2
Albarracín, Sierra de, *Spain* 19 B5
Albatross B., *Australia* 62 A3
Albemarle, *U.S.A.* 77 H5
Albemarle Sd., *U.S.A.* 77 H7
Alberche →, *Spain* 19 C3
Alberdi, *Paraguay* 94 B4
Albert, L. = Mobutu Sese Seko, L., *Africa* 54 B3
Albert, L., *Australia* 63 F2
Albert Canyon, *Canada* 72 C5
Albert Edward Ra., *Australia* 60 C4
Albert Lea, *U.S.A.* 80 D8
Albert Nile →, *Uganda* 54 B3
Albert Town, *Bahamas* 89 B5
Alberta □, *Canada* 72 C6
Alberti, *Argentina* 94 D3
Albertinia, *S. Africa* 56 E3
Alberton, *Canada* 71 C7
Albertville = Kalemie, *Zaïre* 54 D2
Albi, *France* 18 E5
Albia, *U.S.A.* 80 E8
Albina, *Surinam* 93 B8
Albina, Ponta, *Angola* 56 B1
Albion, *Idaho, U.S.A.* 82 E7
Albion, *Mich., U.S.A.* 76 D3
Albion, *Nebr., U.S.A.* 80 E5
Albion, *Pa., U.S.A.* 78 E4
Ålborg, *Denmark* 9 H10
Alborz, Reshteh-ye Kūhhā-ye, *Iran* 45 C7
Albreda, *Canada* 72 C5
Albuquerque, *U.S.A.* 83 J10
Albuquerque, Cayos de, *Caribbean* 88 D3
Alburg, *U.S.A.* 79 B11
Alburquerque, *Spain* 19 C2
Albury, *Australia* 63 F4
Alcalá de Henares, *Spain* 19 B4
Alcalá la Real, *Spain* 19 D4
Alcamo, *Italy* 20 F5
Alcaniz, *Spain* 19 B5
Alcântara, *Brazil* 93 D10
Alcántara, *Spain* 19 C2
Alcantara L., *Canada* 73 A7
Alcaraz, Sierra de, *Spain* 19 C4
Alcaudete, *Spain* 19 D3
Alcázar de San Juan, *Spain* 19 C4
Alcira, *Spain* 19 C5
Alcoa, *U.S.A.* 77 H4
Alcobaça, *Portugal* 19 C1
Alcova, *U.S.A.* 82 E10
Alcoy, *Spain* 19 C5
Alcudia, *Spain* 22 B10
Alcudia, B. de, *Spain* 22 B10
Aldabra Is., *Seychelles* 3 E12
Aldama, *Mexico* 87 C5
Aldan, *Russia* 27 D13
Aldan →, *Russia* 27 C13
Aldea, Pta. de la, *Canary Is.* 22 G4
Aldeburgh, *U.K.* 11 E9
Alder, *U.S.A.* 82 D7
Alder Pk., *U.S.A.* 84 K5
Alderney, *Chan. Is.* 11 H5
Aldershot, *U.K.* 11 F7
Aledo, *U.S.A.* 80 E9
Aleg, *Mauritania* 50 E2
Alegranza, *Canary Is.* 22 E6
Alegranza, I., *Canary Is.* 22 E6
Alegre, *Brazil* 95 A7
Alegrete, *Brazil* 95 B4
Aleisk, *Russia* 26 D9
Aleksandrovsk-Sakhalinskiy, *Russia* 27 D15
Aleksandrovskiy Zavod, *Russia* 27 D12
Aleksandrovskoye, *Russia* 26 C8
Além Paraíba, *Brazil* 95 A7
Alemania, *Argentina* 94 B2
Alemania, *Chile* 94 B2
Alençon, *France* 18 B4
Alenuihaha Chan., *U.S.A.* 74 H17
Aleppo = Ḥalab, *Syria* 44 B3
Aléria, *France* 20 C3
Alert Bay, *Canada* 72 C3
Alès, *France* 18 D6
Alessándria, *Italy* 20 B3
Ålesund, *Norway* 8 E9
Aleutian Is., *Pac. Oc.* 68 C2
Aleutian Trench, *Pac. Oc.* 64 B10
Alexander, *U.S.A.* 80 B3
Alexander, Mt., *Australia* 61 E3
Alexander Arch., *U.S.A.* 72 B2
Alexander B., *S. Africa* 56 D2
Alexander Bay, *S. Africa* 56 D2
Alexander City, *U.S.A.* 77 J3
Alexander I., *Antarctica* 5 C17
Alexandra, *Australia* 63 F4
Alexandra, *N.Z.* 59 L2
Alexandra Falls, *Canada* 72 A5
Alexandretta = İskenderun, *Turkey* 25 G6
Alexandria = El Iskandarîya, *Egypt* 51 B10
Alexandria, *Australia* 62 B2
Alexandria, *B.C., Canada* 72 C4
Alexandria, *Ont., Canada* 70 C5
Alexandria, *S. Africa* 56 E4
Alexandria, *Ind., U.S.A.* 76 E3
Alexandria, *La., U.S.A.* 81 K8
Alexandria, *Minn., U.S.A.* 80 C7
Alexandria, *S. Dak., U.S.A.* 80 D6
Alexandria, *Va., U.S.A.* 76 F7
Alexandria Bay, *U.S.A.* 79 B9
Alexandrina, L., *Australia* 63 F2
Alexandroúpolis, *Greece* 21 D11
Alexis →, *Canada* 71 B8
Alexis Creek, *Canada* 72 C4
Alfabia, *Spain* 22 B9
Alfenas, *Brazil* 95 A6
Alford, *U.K.* 12 D6
Alfred, *Maine, U.S.A.* 79 C14
Alfred, *N.Y., U.S.A.* 78 D7
Alfreton, *U.K.* 10 D6
Alga, *Kazakhstan* 25 E10
Algaida, *Spain* 22 B9
Algarve, *Portugal* 19 D1
Algeciras, *Spain* 19 D3
Algemesí, *Spain* 19 C5
Alger, *Algeria* 50 A5
Algeria ■, *Africa* 50 C5
Alghero, *Italy* 20 D3
Algiers = Alger, *Algeria* 50 A5
Algoa B., *S. Africa* 56 E4
Algoma, *U.S.A.* 76 C2
Algona, *U.S.A.* 80 D7
Algonac, *U.S.A.* 78 D2
Alhama de Murcia, *Spain* 19 D5
Alhambra, *U.S.A.* 85 L8
Alhucemas = Al Hoceïma, *Morocco* 50 A4
'Alī al Gharbī, *Iraq* 44 C5
'Alī ash Sharqī, *Iraq* 44 C5
'Alī Khēl, *Afghan.* 42 C3
Alī Shāh, *Iran* 44 B5
'Alīābād, *Khorāsān, Iran* 45 C8
'Alīābād, *Kordestān, Iran* 44 C5
'Alīābād, *Yazd, Iran* 45 D7
Aliákmon →, *Greece* 21 D10
Alibo, *Ethiopia* 51 G12
Alicante, *Spain* 19 C5
Alice, *S. Africa* 56 E4
Alice, *U.S.A.* 81 M5
Alice →, *Queens., Australia* 62 C3
Alice →, *Queens., Australia* 62 B3
Alice Arm, *Canada* 72 B3
Alice Downs, *Australia* 60 C4
Alice Springs, *Australia* 62 C1
Alicedale, *S. Africa* 56 E4
Aliceville, *U.S.A.* 77 J1
Alick Cr. →, *Australia* 62 C3
Alida, *Canada* 73 D8
Aligarh, *Raj., India* 42 G7
Aligarh, *Ut. P., India* 42 F8
Alīgūdarz, *Iran* 45 C6
Alimnía, *Greece* 23 C9
Alingsås, *Sweden* 9 H12
Alipur, *Pakistan* 42 E4
Alipur Duar, *India* 41 F16
Aliquippa, *U.S.A.* 78 F4
Aliwal North, *S. Africa* 56 E4
Alix, *Canada* 72 C6
Aljustrel, *Portugal* 19 D1
Alkmaar, *Neths.* 15 B4
All American Canal, *U.S.A.* 83 K6
Allah Dad, *Pakistan* 42 G2
Allahabad, *India* 43 G9
Allakh-Yun, *Russia* 27 C14
Allan, *Canada* 73 C7
Allanmyo, *Burma* 41 K19
Allanridge, *S. Africa* 56 D4
Allanwater, *Canada* 70 B1
Allegan, *U.S.A.* 76 D3
Allegany, *U.S.A.* 78 D6
Allegheny →, *U.S.A.* 78 F5
Allegheny Plateau, *U.S.A.* 76 G6
Allegheny Res., *U.S.A.* 78 E6
Allen, Bog of, *Ireland* 13 C4
Allen, L., *Ireland* 13 B3
Allende, *Mexico* 86 B4
Allentown, *U.S.A.* 79 F9
Alleppey, *India* 40 Q10
Alliance, *Nebr., U.S.A.* 80 D3
Alliance, *Ohio, U.S.A.* 78 F3
Allier □, *France* 18 C5
Allier →, *France* 18 C5
Alliston, *Canada* 70 D4
Alloa, *U.K.* 12 E5
Allora, *Australia* 63 D5
Alluitsup Paa = Sydprøven, *Greenland* 4 C5
Alma, *Canada* 71 C5
Alma, *Ga., U.S.A.* 77 K4
Alma, *Kans., U.S.A.* 80 F6
Alma, *Mich., U.S.A.* 76 D3
Alma, *Nebr., U.S.A.* 80 E5
Alma, *Wis., U.S.A.* 80 C9
Alma Ata, *Kazakhstan* 26 E8
Almada, *Portugal* 19 C1
Almaden, *Australia* 62 B3
Almadén, *Spain* 19 C3
Almanor, L., *U.S.A.* 82 F3
Almansa, *Spain* 19 C5
Almanzor, Pico de, *Spain* 19 B3
Almanzora →, *Spain* 19 D5
Almazán, *Spain* 19 B4
Almeirim, *Brazil* 93 D8
Almelo, *Neths.* 15 B6
Almendralejo, *Spain* 19 C2
Almería, *Spain* 19 D4
Almirante, *Panama* 88 E3
Almiroú, Kólpos, *Greece* 23 D6
Almont, *U.S.A.* 78 D1
Almonte, *Canada* 79 A8
Almora, *India* 43 E8
Alnwick, *U.K.* 10 B6
Aloi, *Uganda* 54 B3
Alon, *Burma* 41 H19
Alor, *Indonesia* 37 F6
Alor Setar, *Malaysia* 39 J3
Aloysius, Mt., *Australia* 61 E4
Alpaugh, *U.S.A.* 84 K7
Alpena, *U.S.A.* 76 C4
Alpes-de-Haute-Provence □, *France* 18 D7
Alpes-Maritimes □, *France* 18 E7
Alpha, *Australia* 62 C4
Alpine, *Ariz., U.S.A.* 83 K9
Alpine, *Calif., U.S.A.* 85 N10
Alpine, *Tex., U.S.A.* 81 K3
Alps, *Europe* 16 E4
Alroy Downs, *Australia* 62 B2
Alsace, *France* 18 B7
Alsask, *Canada* 73 C7
Alsásua, *Spain* 19 A4
Alsten, *Norway* 8 D12
Alta, *Norway* 8 B17
Alta Gracia, *Argentina* 94 C3
Alta Lake, *Canada* 72 C4
Alta Sierra, *U.S.A.* 85 K8
Altaelva →, *Norway* 8 B17
Altafjorden, *Norway* 8 A17
Altagracia, *Venezuela* 92 A4
Altai = Aerhtai Shan, *Mongolia* 32 B4
Altamaha →, *U.S.A.* 77 K5
Altamira, *Brazil* 93 D8
Altamira, *Chile* 94 B2
Altamira, *Mexico* 87 C5
Altamont, *U.S.A.* 79 D10
Altanbulag, *Mongolia* 32 A5
Altar, *Mexico* 86 A2
Altata, *Mexico* 86 C3
Altavista, *U.S.A.* 76 G6
Altay, *China* 32 B3
Alto Adige = Trentino-Alto Adige □, *Italy* 20 A4
Alto-Alentejo, *Portugal* 19 C2
Alto Araguaia, *Brazil* 93 G8
Alto Cuchumatanes = Cuchumatanes, Sierra de los, *Guatemala* 88 C1
Alto del Inca, *Chile* 94 A2
Alto Ligonha, *Mozam.* 55 F4
Alto Molocue, *Mozam.* 55 F4
Alto Paraguay □, *Paraguay* 94 A4
Alto Paraná □, *Paraguay* 95 B5
Alton, *Canada* 78 C4
Alton, *U.S.A.* 80 F9
Alton Downs, *Australia* 63 D2
Altoona, *U.S.A.* 78 F6
Altūn Kūprī, *Iraq* 44 C5
Altun Shan, *China* 32 C3
Alturas, *U.S.A.* 82 F3
Altus, *U.S.A.* 81 H5
Alùla, *Somali Rep.* 46 E5
Alunite, *U.S.A.* 85 K12
Alusi, *Indonesia* 37 F8
Al'Uzayr, *Iraq* 44 D5
Alva, *U.S.A.* 81 G5
Alvarado, *Mexico* 87 D5
Alvarado, *U.S.A.* 81 J6
Alvaro Obregón, Presa, *Mexico* 86 B3
Alvear, *Argentina* 94 B4
Alvesta, *Sweden* 9 H13
Alvie, *Australia* 63 F3
Alvin, *U.S.A.* 81 L7
Alvinston, *Canada* 78 D3
Älvkarleby, *Sweden* 9 F14
Älvsborgs län □, *Sweden* 9 G12
Älvsbyn, *Sweden* 8 D16
Alwar, *India* 42 F7
Alxa Zuoqi, *China* 34 E3
Alyaskitovyy, *Russia* 27 C15
Alyata, *Azerbaijan* 25 G8
Alyth, *U.K.* 12 E5
Alzada, *U.S.A.* 80 C2
Am Dam, *Chad* 51 F9
Am-Timan, *Chad* 51 F9
Amadeus, L., *Australia* 61 D5
Amâdi, *Sudan* 51 G11
Amadi, *Zaïre* 54 B2
Amadjuak, *Canada* 69 B12
Amadjuak L., *Canada* 69 B12
Amagasaki, *Japan* 31 G7
Amakusa-Shotō, *Japan* 31 H5
Amalner, *India* 40 J9
Amambaí, *Brazil* 95 A4
Amambaí →, *Brazil* 95 A5
Amambay □, *Paraguay* 95 A4
Amambay, Cordillera de, *S. Amer.* 95 A4
Amami-Guntō, *Japan* 31 L4
Amami-Ō-Shima, *Japan* 31 L4
Amanda Park, *U.S.A.* 84 C3
Amangeldy, *Kazakhstan* 26 D7
Amapá, *Brazil* 93 C8
Amapá □, *Brazil* 93 C8
Amarante, *Brazil* 93 E10
Amaranth, *Canada* 73 C9
Amargosa, *Brazil* 93 F11
Amargosa →, *U.S.A.* 85 J10
Amargosa Ra., *U.S.A.* 85 J10
Amári, *Greece* 23 D6
Amarillo, *U.S.A.* 81 H4
Amaro, Mt., *Italy* 20 C6
Amarpur, *India* 43 G12
Amatikulu, *S. Africa* 57 D5
Amatitlán, *Guatemala* 88 D1
Amazon = Amazonas →, *S. Amer.* 93 C9
Amazonas □, *Brazil* 92 E6
Amazonas →, *S. Amer.* 93 C9
Ambahakily, *Madag.* 57 C7
Ambala, *India* 42 D7
Ambalavao, *Madag.* 57 C8
Ambalindum, *Australia* 62 C2
Ambam, *Cameroon* 52 D2
Ambanja, *Madag.* 57 A8
Ambarchik, *Russia* 27 C17
Ambarijeby, *Madag.* 57 A8
Ambaro, Helodranon', *Madag.* 57 A8
Ambartsevo, *Russia* 26 D9
Ambato, *Ecuador* 92 D3
Ambato, Sierra de, *Argentina* 94 B2
Ambato Boeny, *Madag.* 57 B8
Ambatofinandrahana, *Madag.* 57 C8
Ambatolampy, *Madag.* 57 B8
Ambatondrazaka, *Madag.* 57 B8
Ambatosoratra, *Madag.* 57 B8
Ambenja, *Madag.* 57 B8
Amberg, *Germany* 16 D5
Ambergris Cay, *Belize* 87 D7
Amberley, *N.Z.* 59 K4
Ambikapur, *India* 43 H10
Ambilobé, *Madag.* 57 A8
Ambinanindrano, *Madag.* 57 C8
Ambleside, *U.K.* 10 C5
Ambo, *Peru* 92 F3
Ambodifototra, *Madag.* 57 B8
Ambodilazana, *Madag.* 57 B8
Ambohimahasoa, *Madag.* 57 C8
Ambohimanga, *Madag.* 57 C8
Ambohitra, *Madag.* 57 A8
Ambon, *Indonesia* 37 E7
Amboseli L., *Kenya* 54 C4
Ambositra, *Madag.* 57 C8
Ambovombé, *Madag.* 57 D8
Amboy, *U.S.A.* 85 L11
Amboyna I., *S. China Sea* 36 C4
Ambridge, *U.S.A.* 78 F4
Ambriz, *Angola* 52 F2
Amby, *Australia* 63 D4
Amchitka I., *U.S.A.* 68 C1
Amderma, *Russia* 26 C7
Ameca, *Mexico* 86 C4
Ameca →, *Mexico* 86 C3
Amecameca, *Mexico* 87 D5
Ameland, *Neths.* 15 A5
Amen, *Russia* 27 C18
American Falls, *U.S.A.* 82 E7
American Falls Res., *U.S.A.* 82 E7
American Highland, *Antarctica* 5 D6
American Samoa ■, *Pac. Oc.* 59 B13
Americana, *Brazil* 95 A6
Americus, *U.S.A.* 77 J3
Amersfoort, *Neths.* 15 B5
Amersfoort, *S. Africa* 57 D4
Amery, *Australia* 61 F2
Amery, *Canada* 73 B10
Amery Ice Shelf, *Antarctica* 5 C6
Ames, *U.S.A.* 80 E8
Amesbury, *U.S.A.* 79 D14
Amga, *Russia* 27 C14
Amga →, *Russia* 27 C14
Amgu, *Russia* 27 E14
Amgun →, *Russia* 27 D14
Amherst, *Burma* 41 L20
Amherst, *Canada* 71 C7
Amherst, *Mass., U.S.A.* 79 D12
Amherst, *N.Y., U.S.A.* 78 D6
Amherst, *Ohio, U.S.A.* 78 E2
Amherst, *Tex., U.S.A.* 81 H3
Amherst I., *Canada* 79 B8
Amherstburg, *Canada* 70 D3
Amiata, Mte., *Italy* 20 C4
Amiens, *France* 18 B5
Amīrābād, *Iran* 44 C5
Amirante Is., *Seychelles* 3 E12
Amisk L., *Canada* 73 C8
Amistad, Presa de la, *Mexico* 86 B4
Amite, *U.S.A.* 81 K9
Amlwch, *U.K.* 10 D3
'Ammān, *Jordan* 47 D4
Ammanford, *U.K.* 11 F3
Ammassalik = Angmagssalik, *Greenland* 4 C6
Amnat Charoen, *Thailand* 38 E5
Āmol, *Iran* 45 B7
Amorgós, *Greece* 21 F11
Amory, *U.S.A.* 77 J1
Amos, *Canada* 70 C4
Amoy = Xiamen, *China* 33 D6
Ampang, *Malaysia* 39 L3
Ampanihy, *Madag.* 57 C7
Ampasindava, Helodranon', *Madag.* 57 A8
Ampasindava, Saikanosy, *Madag.* 57 A8
Ampenan, *Indonesia* 36 F5
Ampotaka, *Madag.* 57 D7
Ampoza, *Madag.* 57 C7
Amqui, *Canada* 71 C6
Amravati, *India* 40 J10
Amreli, *India* 42 J4
Amritsar, *India* 42 D6
Amroha, *India* 43 E8
Amsterdam, *Neths.* 15 B4
Amsterdam, *U.S.A.* 79 D10
Amsterdam, I., *Ind. Oc.* 3 F13
Amudarya →, *Uzbekistan* 26 E6
Amundsen Gulf, *Canada* 68 A7
Amundsen Sea, *Antarctica* 5 D15
Amuntai, *Indonesia* 36 E5
Amur →, *Russia* 27 D15
Amurang, *Indonesia* 37 D6
Amuri Pass, *N.Z.* 59 K4
Amursk, *Russia* 27 D14
Amurzet, *Russia* 27 E14
An Bien, *Vietnam* 39 H5
An Hoa, *Vietnam* 38 E7
An Khe, *Vietnam* 38 F7
An Nabatīyah at Tahta, *Lebanon* 47 B4
An Nabk, *Si. Arabia* 44 D3
An Nabk, *Syria* 47 A5
An Nabk Abū Qaşr, *Si. Arabia* 44 D3
An Nafūd, *Si. Arabia* 44 D4
An Najaf, *Iraq* 44 C5
An Nāşirīyah, *Iraq* 44 D5
An Nhon, *Vietnam* 38 F7
An Nîl □, *Sudan* 51 E11
An Nîl el Abyad □, *Sudan* 51 F11
An Nîl el Azraq □, *Sudan* 51 F11
An Nu'ayrīyah, *Si. Arabia* 45 E6
An Nuwayb'ī, W. →, *Si. Arabia* 47 F3
An Thoi, Dao, *Vietnam* 39 H4
An Uaimh, *Ireland* 13 C5
Anabar →, *Russia* 27 B12
Anaconda, *U.S.A.* 82 C7
Anacortes, *U.S.A.* 84 B4
Anadarko, *U.S.A.* 81 H5
Anadolu, *Turkey* 25 G5
Anadyr, *Russia* 27 C18
Anadyr →, *Russia* 27 C18
Anadyrskiy Zaliv, *Russia* 27 C19
Anaga, Pta. de, *Canary Is.* 22 F3
'Ānah, *Iraq* 44 C4
Anaheim, *U.S.A.* 85 M9
Anahim Lake, *Canada* 72 C3
Anáhuac, *Mexico* 86 B4
Anakapalle, *India* 41 L13
Anakie, *Australia* 62 C4
Analalava, *Madag.* 57 A8
Análipsis, *Greece* 23 A3
Anambar →, *Pakistan* 42 D3
Anambas, Kepulauan, *Indonesia* 36 D3
Anambas Is. = Anambas, Kepulauan, *Indonesia* 36 D3
Anamoose, *U.S.A.* 80 B4
Anamosa, *U.S.A.* 80 D9
Anamur, *Turkey* 25 G5
Anan, *Japan* 31 H7
Anand, *India* 42 H5
Anantnag, *India* 43 C6
Anapodháris →, *Greece* 23 E7
Anápolis, *Brazil* 93 G9
Anār, *Iran* 45 D7
Anārak, *Iran* 45 C7
Anatolia = Anadolu, *Turkey* 25 G5
Anatone, *U.S.A.* 82 C5
Anatsogno, *Madag.* 57 C7
Añatuya, *Argentina* 94 B3
Anaunethad L., *Canada* 73 A8
Anaye, *Niger* 51 E7

Anbyŏn, *N. Korea* 35 E14
Anchor Bay, *U.S.A.* 84 G3
Anchorage, *U.S.A.* 68 B5
Anci, *China* 34 E9
Ancohuma, Nevada, *Bolivia* 92 G5
Ancón, *Peru* 92 F3
Ancona, *Italy* 20 C5
Ancud, *Chile* 96 E2
Ancud, G. de, *Chile* 96 E2
Anda, *China* 33 B7
Andacollo, *Argentina* 94 D1
Andacollo, *Chile* 94 C1
Andado, *Australia* 62 D2
Andalgalá, *Argentina* 94 B2
Åndalsnes, *Norway* 8 E9
Andalucia □, *Spain* 19 D3
Andalusia, *U.S.A.* 77 K2
Andalusia □ = Andalucia □, *Spain* 19 D3
Andaman Is., *Ind. Oc.* 28 H13
Andaman Sea, *Ind. Oc.* 36 B1
Andara, *Namibia* 56 B3
Andenne, *Belgium* 15 D5
Anderson, *Calif., U.S.A.* 82 F2
Anderson, *Ind., U.S.A.* 76 E3
Anderson, *Mo., U.S.A.* 81 G7
Anderson, *S.C., U.S.A.* 77 H4
Anderson →, *Canada* 68 B7
Anderson, Mt., *S. Africa* 57 D5
Andes, *S. Amer.* 92 F3
Andes, Cord. de los, *S. Amer.* 92 F4
Andfjorden, *Norway* 8 B14
Andhra Pradesh □, *India* 40 L11
Andikíthira, *Greece* 21 G10
Andīmeshk, *Iran* 45 C6
Andizhan, *Uzbekistan* 26 E8
Andoany, *Madag.* 57 A8
Andong, *S. Korea* 35 F15
Andongwei, *China* 35 G10
Andorra ■, *Europe* 19 A6
Andorra La Vella, *Andorra* 19 A6
Andover, *U.K.* 11 F6
Andover, *Mass., U.S.A.* 79 D13
Andover, *N.Y., U.S.A.* 78 D7
Andover, *Ohio, U.S.A.* 78 E4
Andrahary, Mt., *Madag.* 57 A8
Andraitx, *Spain* 22 B9
Andramasina, *Madag.* 57 B8
Andranopasy, *Madag.* 57 C7
Andreanof Is., *U.S.A.* 68 C2
Andrewilla, *Australia* 63 D2
Andrews, *S.C., U.S.A.* 77 J6
Andrews, *Tex., U.S.A.* 81 J3
Ándria, *Italy* 20 D7
Andriba, *Madag.* 57 B8
Androka, *Madag.* 57 C7
Andropov = Rybinsk, *Russia* 24 C6
Ándros, *Greece* 21 F11
Andros I., *Bahamas* 88 B4
Andros Town, *Bahamas* 88 B4
Andújar, *Spain* 19 C3
Andulo, *Angola* 52 G3
Anegada I., *Virgin Is.* 89 C7
Anegada Passage, *W. Indies* 89 C7
Anécho, *Togo* 50 G5
Aneto, Pico de, *Spain* 19 A6
Ang Thong, *Thailand* 38 E3
Angamos, Punta, *Chile* 94 A1
Angara →, *Russia* 27 D10
Angarsk, *Russia* 27 D11
Angas Downs, *Australia* 61 E5
Angas Hills, *Australia* 60 D4
Angaston, *Australia* 63 E2
Ånge, *Sweden* 8 E13
Ángel de la Guarda, I., *Mexico* 86 B2
Angeles, *Phil.* 37 A6
Ängelholm, *Sweden* 9 H12
Angellala, *Australia* 63 D4
Angels Camp, *U.S.A.* 83 G3
Ångermanälven →, *Sweden* 8 E14
Angers, *Canada* 79 A9
Angers, *France* 18 C3
Ängesån →, *Sweden* 8 C17
Angikuni L., *Canada* 73 A9
Angkor, *Cambodia* 38 F4
Anglesey, *U.K.* 10 D3
Angleton, *U.S.A.* 81 L7
Anglisidhes, *Cyprus* 23 E12
Angmagssalik, *Greenland* 4 C6
Ango, *Zaïre* 54 B2
Angoche, *Mozam.* 55 F4
Angoche, I., *Mozam.* 55 F4
Angol, *Chile* 94 D1
Angola, *Ind., U.S.A.* 76 E3
Angola, *N.Y., U.S.A.* 78 D5
Angola ■, *Africa* 53 G3
Angoon, *U.S.A.* 72 B2
Angoulême, *France* 18 D4
Angoumois, *France* 18 D4
Angra dos Reis, *Brazil* 95 A7
Angren, *Uzbekistan* 26 E8
Angtassom, *Cambodia* 39 G5
Angu, *Zaïre* 54 B1
Anguang, *China* 35 B12
Anguilla, *W. Indies* 89 C7
Anguo, *China* 34 E8
Angurugu, *Australia* 62 A2
Angus, Braes of, *U.K.* 12 E5
Anhandui →, *Brazil* 95 A5
Anholt, *Denmark* 9 H11
Anhui □, *China* 33 C6
Anhwei □ = Anhui □, *China* 33 C6
Anichab, *Namibia* 56 C1
Animas, *U.S.A.* 83 L9
Anivorano, *Madag.* 57 B8
Anjar, *India* 42 H4
Anjidiv I., *India* 40 M9
Anjou, *France* 18 C3
Anjozorobe, *Madag.* 57 B8
Anju, *N. Korea* 35 E13
Anka, *Nigeria* 50 F6
Ankaboa, Tanjona, *Madag.* 57 C7
Ankang, *China* 34 H5
Ankara, *Turkey* 25 G5
Ankaramena, *Madag.* 57 C8
Ankazoabo, *Madag.* 57 C7
Ankazobe, *Madag.* 57 B8
Ankisabe, *Madag.* 57 B8
Ankoro, *Zaïre* 54 D2
Anmyŏn-do, *S. Korea* 35 F14
Ann, C., *U.S.A.* 79 D14
Ann Arbor, *U.S.A.* 76 D4
Anna, *U.S.A.* 81 G10
Anna Plains, *Australia* 60 C3
Annaba, *Algeria* 50 A6
Annalee →, *Ireland* 13 B4
Annam = Trung-Phan, *Vietnam* 38 E7
Annamitique, Chaîne, *Asia* 38 D6
Annan, *U.K.* 12 G5
Annan →, *U.K.* 12 G5
Annapolis, *U.S.A.* 76 F7
Annapolis Royal, *Canada* 71 D6
Annapurna, *Nepal* 43 E10
Annean, L., *Australia* 61 E2
Annecy, *France* 18 D7
Anning, *China* 32 D5
Anningie, *Australia* 60 D5
Anniston, *U.S.A.* 77 J3
Annobón, *Atl. Oc.* 49 G4
Annotto Bay, *Jamaica* 88 C4
Annuello, *Australia* 63 E3
Annville, *U.S.A.* 79 F8
Áno Viánnos, *Greece* 23 D7
Anoka, *U.S.A.* 80 C8
Anorotsangana, *Madag.* 57 A8
Anóyia, *Greece* 23 D6
Anping, *Hebei, China* 34 E8
Anping, *Liaoning, China* 35 D12
Anqing, *China* 33 C6
Anqiu, *China* 35 F10
Ansai, *China* 34 F5
Ansbach, *Germany* 16 D5
Anshan, *China* 33 B7
Anshan, *Liaoning, China* 35 D12
Anshun, *China* 32 D5
Ansirabe, *Madag.* 57 B8
Ansley, *U.S.A.* 80 E5
Anson, *U.S.A.* 81 J5
Anson B., *Australia* 60 B5
Ansongo, *Mali* 50 E5
Ansonia, *U.S.A.* 79 E11
Anstruther, *U.K.* 12 E6
Ansudu, *Indonesia* 37 E9
Antabamba, *Peru* 92 F4
Antakya, *Turkey* 25 G6
Antalaha, *Madag.* 57 A9
Antalya, *Turkey* 25 G5
Antalya Körfezi, *Turkey* 25 G5
Antananarivo, *Madag.* 57 B8
Antananarivo □, *Madag.* 57 B8
Antanimbaribe, *Madag.* 57 C7
Antarctic Pen., *Antarctica* 5 C18
Antarctica 5 E3
Antelope, *Zimbabwe* 55 G2
Antequera, *Paraguay* 94 A4
Antequera, *Spain* 19 D3
Antero, Mt., *U.S.A.* 83 G10
Anthony, *Kans., U.S.A.* 81 G5
Anthony, *N. Mex., U.S.A.* 83 K10
Anthony Lagoon, *Australia* 62 B2
Anti Atlas, *Morocco* 50 C3
Anti-Lebanon = Ash Sharqi, Al Jabal, *Lebanon* 47 B5
Anticosti, I. d', *Canada* 71 C7
Antigo, *U.S.A.* 80 C10
Antigonish, *Canada* 71 C7
Antigua, *Canary Is.* 22 F5
Antigua, *Guatemala* 88 D1
Antigua, *W. Indies* 89 C7
Antigua & Barbuda ■, *W. Indies* 89 C7
Antilla, *Cuba* 88 B4
Antimony, *U.S.A.* 83 G8
Antioch, *U.S.A.* 84 G5
Antioquia, *Colombia* 92 B3
Antipodes Is., *Pac. Oc.* 64 M9
Antler, *U.S.A.* 80 A4
Antler →, *Canada* 73 D8
Antlers, *U.S.A.* 81 H7
Antofagasta, *Chile* 94 A1
Antofagasta □, *Chile* 94 A2
Antofagasta de la Sierra, *Argentina* 94 B2
Antofalla, *Argentina* 94 B2
Antofalla, Salar de, *Argentina* 94 B2
Anton, *U.S.A.* 81 J3
Anton Chico, *U.S.A.* 83 J11
Antongila, Helodrano, *Madag.* 57 B8
Antonibé, *Madag.* 57 B8
Antonibé, Presqu'île d', *Madag.* 57 A8
Antonina, *Brazil* 95 B6
Antonito, *U.S.A.* 83 H10
Antrim, *U.K.* 13 B5
Antrim □, *U.K.* 13 B5
Antrim, Mts. of, *U.K.* 13 B5
Antrim Plateau, *Australia* 60 C4
Antsalova, *Madag.* 57 B7
Antsiranana, *Madag.* 57 A8
Antsohihy, *Madag.* 57 A8
Antsohimbondrona Seranana, *Madag.* 57 A8
Antu, *China* 35 C15
Antwerp = Antwerpen, *Belgium* 15 C4
Antwerp, *U.S.A.* 79 B9
Antwerpen, *Belgium* 15 C4
Antwerpen □, *Belgium* 15 C4
Anupgarh, *India* 42 E5
Anuradhapura, *Sri Lanka* 40 Q12
Anveh, *Iran* 45 E7
Anvers = Antwerpen, *Belgium* 15 C4
Anvers I., *Antarctica* 5 C17
Anxi, *China* 32 B4
Anxious B., *Australia* 63 E1
Anyang, *China* 34 F8
Anyi, *China* 34 G6
Anza, *U.S.A.* 85 M10
Anze, *China* 34 F7
Anzhero-Sudzhensk, *Russia* 26 D9
Ánzio, *Italy* 20 D5
Aoga-Shima, *Japan* 31 H9
Aomori, *Japan* 30 D10
Aomori □, *Japan* 30 D10
Aonla, *India* 43 E8
Aosta, *Italy* 20 B2
Aoudéras, *Niger* 50 E6
Aoulef el Arab, *Algeria* 50 C5
Apa →, *S. Amer.* 94 A4
Apache, *U.S.A.* 81 H5
Apalachee B., *U.S.A.* 77 L3
Apalachicola, *U.S.A.* 77 L3
Apalachicola →, *U.S.A.* 77 L3
Apaporis →, *Colombia* 92 D5
Aparri, *Phil.* 37 A6
Apàtity, *Russia* 24 A5
Apatzingán, *Mexico* 86 D4
Apeldoorn, *Neths.* 15 B5
Apennines = Appennini, *Italy* 20 C4
Apia, *W. Samoa* 59 A13
Apiacás, Serra dos, *Brazil* 92 E7
Apizaco, *Mexico* 87 D5
Aplao, *Peru* 92 G4
Apo, Mt., *Phil.* 37 C7
Apolakkiá, *Greece* 23 C9
Apolakkiá, Órmos, *Greece* 23 C9
Apollonia = Marsá Susah, *Libya* 51 B9
Apolo, *Bolivia* 92 F5
Apostle Is., *U.S.A.* 80 B9
Apóstoles, *Argentina* 95 B4
Apostolos Andreas, C., *Cyprus* 23 D13
Apoteri, *Guyana* 92 C7
Appalachian Mts., *U.S.A.* 76 G6
Appennini, *Italy* 20 C4
Apple Hill, *Canada* 79 A10
Apple Valley, *U.S.A.* 85 L9
Appleby, *U.K.* 10 C5
Appleton, *U.S.A.* 76 C1
Approuague, *Fr. Guiana* 93 C8
Apucarana, *Brazil* 95 A5
Apulia = Púglia □, *Italy* 20 D7
Apure →, *Venezuela* 92 B5
Apurimac →, *Peru* 92 F4
Aqabah = Al 'Aqabah, *Jordan* 47 F4
'Aqabah, Khalīj al, *Red Sea* 44 D2
'Aqdā, *Iran* 45 C7
Aqīq, *Sudan* 51 E12
Aqrah, *Iraq* 44 B4
Aquidauana, *Brazil* 93 H7
Aquiles Serdán, *Mexico* 86 B3
Aquin, *Haiti* 89 C5
Ar Rachidiya, *Morocco* 50 B4
Ar Rafid, *Syria* 47 C4
Ar Raḥḥālīyah, *Iraq* 44 C4
Ar Ramādī, *Iraq* 44 C4
Ar Ramthā, *Jordan* 47 C5
Ar Raqqah, *Syria* 44 C3
Ar Rass, *Si. Arabia* 44 E4
Ar Rifā'ī, *Si. Arabia* 44 D5
Ar Riyāḍ, *Si. Arabia* 46 C4
Ar Ru'ays, *Qatar* 45 E6
Ar Rukhaymīyah, *Iraq* 44 D5
Ar Ruqayyidah, *Si. Arabia* 45 E6
Ar Ruṣāfah, *Syria* 44 C3
Ar Ruṭbah, *Iraq* 44 C4
Ara, *India* 43 G11
'Arab, Bahr el →, *Sudan* 51 G10
'Arabābād, *Iran* 45 C8
Arabia, *Asia* 46 C4
Arabian Desert = Es Sahrâ' Esh Sharqîya, *Egypt* 51 C11
Arabian Gulf = Gulf, The, *Asia* 45 E6
Arabian Sea, *Ind. Oc.* 29 H10
Aracaju, *Brazil* 93 F11
Aracataca, *Colombia* 92 A4
Aracati, *Brazil* 93 D11
Araçatuba, *Brazil* 95 A5
Aracena, *Spain* 19 D2
Araçuai, *Brazil* 93 G10
'Arad, *Israel* 47 D4
Arad, *Romania* 17 E10
Arada, *Chad* 51 F9
Aradhippou, *Cyprus* 23 E12
Arafura Sea, *E. Indies* 37 F8
Aragón □, *Spain* 19 B5
Aragón →, *Spain* 19 A5
Araguacema, *Brazil* 93 E9
Araguaia →, *Brazil* 93 E9
Araguari, *Brazil* 93 G9
Araguari →, *Brazil* 93 C9
Arak, *Algeria* 50 C5
Arāk, *Iran* 45 C6
Arakan Coast, *Burma* 41 K19
Arakan Yoma, *Burma* 41 K19
Araks = Aras, Rūd-e →, *Iran* 44 B5
Aral Sea = Aralskoye More, *Asia* 26 E7
Aralsk, *Kazakhstan* 26 E7
Aralskoye More, *Asia* 26 E7
Aramac, *Australia* 62 C4
Arambag, *India* 43 H12
Aran I., *Ireland* 13 B3
Aran Is., *Ireland* 13 C2
Arandān, *Iran* 44 C5
Aranjuez, *Spain* 19 B4
Aranos, *Namibia* 56 C2
Aransas Pass, *U.S.A.* 81 M6
Araouane, *Mali* 50 E4
Arapahoe, *U.S.A.* 80 E5
Arapey Grande →, *Uruguay* 94 C4
Arapiraca, *Brazil* 93 E11
Arapongas, *Brazil* 95 A5
Ar'ar, *Si. Arabia* 44 D4
Araranguá, *Brazil* 95 B6
Araraquara, *Brazil* 93 H9
Ararás, Serra das, *Brazil* 95 B5
Ararat, *Australia* 63 F3
Ararat, Mt. = Ağrı Dağı, *Turkey* 25 G7
Araria, *India* 43 F12
Araripe, Chapada do, *Brazil* 93 E11
Araruama, L. de, *Brazil* 95 A7
Aras, Rūd-e →, *Iran* 44 B5
Arauca, *Colombia* 92 B4
Arauca →, *Venezuela* 92 B5
Arauco, *Chile* 94 D1
Arauco □, *Chile* 94 D1
Araxá, *Brazil* 93 G9
Araya, Pen. de, *Venezuela* 92 A6
Arbat, *Iraq* 44 C5
Arbatax, *Italy* 20 E3
Arbaza, *Russia* 27 D10
Arbīl, *Iraq* 44 B5
Arborfield, *Canada* 73 C8
Arborg, *Canada* 73 C9
Arbroath, *U.K.* 12 E6
Arbuckle, *U.S.A.* 84 F4
Arcachon, *France* 18 D3
Arcade, *U.S.A.* 78 D6
Arcadia, *Fla., U.S.A.* 77 M5
Arcadia, *La., U.S.A.* 81 J8
Arcadia, *Nebr., U.S.A.* 80 E5
Arcadia, *Pa., U.S.A.* 78 F6
Arcadia, *Wis., U.S.A.* 80 C9
Arcata, *U.S.A.* 82 F1
Archangel = Arkhangelsk, *Russia* 24 B7
Archbald, *U.S.A.* 79 E9
Archer →, *Australia* 62 A3
Archer B., *Australia* 62 A3
Archers Post, *Kenya* 54 B4
Arcila = Asilah, *Morocco* 50 A3
Arckaringa, *Australia* 63 D1
Arckaringa Cr. →, *Australia* 63 D2
Arco, *U.S.A.* 82 E7
Arcola, *Canada* 73 D8
Arcos, *Spain* 19 B4
Arcot, *India* 40 N11
Arcoverde, *Brazil* 93 E11
Arctic Bay, *Canada* 69 A11
Arctic Ocean, *Arctic* 4 B18
Arctic Red River, *Canada* 68 B6
Arda →, *Bulgaria* 21 D12
Ardabīl, *Iran* 45 B6
Ardakān = Sepīdān, *Iran* 45 D7
Ardèche □, *France* 18 D6
Ardee, *Ireland* 13 C5
Arden, *Canada* 78 B8
Arden, *Calif., U.S.A.* 84 G5
Arden, *Nev., U.S.A.* 85 J11
Ardenne, *Belgium* 15 E5
Ardennes □, *France* 18 B6
Ardestān, *Iran* 45 C7
Ardgour, *U.K.* 12 E3
Ardlethan, *Australia* 63 E4
Ardmore, *Australia* 62 C2
Ardmore, *Okla., U.S.A.* 81 H6
Ardmore, *Pa., U.S.A.* 79 G9
Ardmore, *S. Dak., U.S.A.* 80 D3
Ardnacrusha, *Ireland* 13 D3
Ardnamurchan, Pt. of, *U.K.* 12 E2
Ardrossan, *Australia* 63 E2
Ardrossan, *U.K.* 12 F4
Ards □, *U.K.* 13 B6
Ards Pen., *U.K.* 13 B6
Arecibo, *Puerto Rico* 89 C6
Areia Branca, *Brazil* 93 D11
Arena, Pt., *U.S.A.* 84 G3
Arendal, *Norway* 9 G10
Arequipa, *Peru* 92 G4
Arero, *Ethiopia* 51 H12
Arévalo, *Spain* 19 B3
Arezzo, *Italy* 20 C4
Argamakmur, *Indonesia* 36 E2
Argentário, Mte., *Italy* 20 C4
Argentia, *Canada* 71 C9
Argentina ■, *S. Amer.* 96 D3
Argentino Is., *Antarctica* 5 C17
Argentino, L., *Argentina* 96 G2
Argeş →, *Romania* 17 F13
Arghandab →, *Afghan.* 42 D1
Argo, *Sudan* 51 E11
Argolikós Kólpos, *Greece* 21 F10
Argonne, *France* 18 B6
Árgos, *Greece* 21 F10
Argostólion, *Greece* 21 E9
Arguello, Pt., *U.S.A.* 85 L6
Arguineguín, *Canary Is.* 22 G4
Argun →, *Russia* 27 D13
Argungu, *Nigeria* 50 F5
Argus Pk., *U.S.A.* 85 K9
Argyle, *U.S.A.* 80 A6
Argyle, L., *Australia* 60 C4
Århus, *Denmark* 9 H11
Ariadnoye, *Russia* 30 B7
Ariamsvlei, *Namibia* 56 D2
Arica, *Chile* 92 G4
Arica, *Colombia* 92 D4
Arico, *Canary Is.* 22 F3
Arid, C., *Australia* 61 F3
Arida, *Japan* 31 G7
Ariège □, *France* 18 E4
Arīḥā, *Syria* 44 C3
Arilla, Ákra, *Greece* 23 A3
Arima, *Trin. & Tob.* 89 D7
Arinos →, *Brazil* 92 F7
Ario de Rosales, *Mexico* 86 D4
Aripuanã, *Brazil* 92 E6
Aripuanã →, *Brazil* 92 E6
Ariquemes, *Brazil* 92 E6
Arisaig, *U.K.* 12 E3
Aristazabal I., *Canada* 72 C3
Arivaca, *U.S.A.* 83 L8
Arivonimamo, *Madag.* 57 B8
Arizaro, Salar de, *Argentina* 94 A2
Arizona, *Argentina* 94 D2
Arizona □, *U.S.A.* 83 J8
Arizpe, *Mexico* 86 A2
Arjeplog, *Sweden* 8 C15
Arjona, *Colombia* 92 A3
Arjuno, *Indonesia* 37 G15
Arka, *Russia* 27 C15
Arkadelphia, *U.S.A.* 81 H8
Arkaig, L., *U.K.* 12 E3
Arkalyk, *Kazakhstan* 26 D7
Arkansas □, *U.S.A.* 81 H8
Arkansas →, *U.S.A.* 81 J9
Arkansas City, *U.S.A.* 81 G6
Arkhángelos, *Greece* 23 C10
Arkhangelsk, *Russia* 24 B7
Arklow, *Ireland* 13 D5
Arkticheskiy, Mys, *Russia* 27 A10
Arlanzón →, *Spain* 19 A3
Arlberg Pass, *Austria* 16 E5
Arlee, *U.S.A.* 82 C6
Arles, *France* 18 E6
Arlington, *S. Africa* 57 D4
Arlington, *Oreg., U.S.A.* 82 D3
Arlington, *S. Dak., U.S.A.* 80 C6
Arlington, *Va., U.S.A.* 76 F7
Arlington, *Wash., U.S.A.* 84 B4
Arlon, *Belgium* 15 E5
Armagh, *U.K.* 13 B5
Armagh □, *U.K.* 13 B5
Armagnac, *France* 18 E4
Armavir, *Russia* 25 E7
Armenia, *Colombia* 92 C3
Armenia ■, *Asia* 25 F7
Armenistís, Ákra, *Greece* 23 C9
Armidale, *Australia* 63 E5
Armour, *U.S.A.* 80 D5
Armstrong, *B.C., Canada* 72 C5
Armstrong, *Ont., Canada* 70 B2
Armstrong, *U.S.A.* 81 M6
Armstrong →, *Australia* 60 C5
Arnarfjörður, *Iceland* 8 D2
Arnaud →, *Canada* 69 B12
Arnauti, C., *Cyprus* 23 D11
Årnes, *Iceland* 8 C3
Arnett, *U.S.A.* 81 G5
Arnhem, *Neths.* 15 C5
Arnhem, C., *Australia* 62 A2
Arnhem B., *Australia* 62 A2
Arnhem Land, *Australia* 62 A1
Arno →, *Italy* 20 C4
Arno Bay, *Australia* 63 E2
Arnold, *Calif., U.S.A.* 84 G6
Arnold, *Nebr., U.S.A.* 80 E4
Arnot, *Canada* 73 B9
Arnøy, *Norway* 8 A16
Arnprior, *Canada* 70 C4
Aroab, *Namibia* 56 D2
Arrabury, *Australia* 63 D3
Arran, *U.K.* 12 F3
Arrandale, *Canada* 72 C3
Arras, *France* 18 A5
Arrecife, *Canary Is.* 22 F6
Arrecifes, *Argentina* 94 C3
Arrée, Mts. d', *France* 18 B2
Arriaga, *Chiapas, Mexico* 87 D6
Arriaga, *San Luis Potosí, Mexico* 86 C4
Arrilalah P.O., *Australia* 62 C3
Arrino, *Australia* 61 E2
Arrow, L., *Ireland* 13 B3
Arrow Rock Res., *U.S.A.* 82 E6
Arrowhead, *Canada* 72 C5
Arrowhead, L., *U.S.A.* 85 L9
Arrowtown, *N.Z.* 59 L2
Arroyo Grande, *U.S.A.* 85 K6
Ars, *Iran* 44 B5
Arsenault L., *Canada* 73 B7
Arsenev, *Russia* 30 B6
Árta, *Greece* 21 E9

Artá, Spain 22 B10
Arteaga, Mexico 86 D4
Artem, Russia 30 C6
Artemovsk, Russia 27 D10
Artesia = Mosomane, Botswana 56 C4
Artesia, U.S.A. 81 J2
Artesia Wells, U.S.A. 81 L5
Artesian, U.S.A. 80 C6
Arthur →, Australia 62 G3
Arthur Cr. →, Australia 62 C2
Arthur Pt., Australia 62 C5
Arthur's Pass, N.Z. 59 K3
Arthur's Town, Bahamas 89 B4
Artigas, Uruguay 94 C4
Artillery L., Canada 73 A7
Artois, France 18 A5
Artvin, Turkey 25 F7
Aru, Kepulauan, Indonesia 37 F8
Aru Is. = Aru, Kepulauan, Indonesia 37 F8
Aru Meru □, Tanzania 54 C4
Arua, Uganda 54 B3
Aruanã, Brazil 93 F8
Aruba, Neth. Ant. 89 D6
Arucas, Canary Is. 22 F4
Arumpo, Australia 63 E3
Arun →, Nepal 43 F12
Arunachal Pradesh □, India 41 E19
Arusha, Tanzania 54 C4
Arusha □, Tanzania 54 C4
Arusha Chini, Tanzania 54 C4
Aruwimi →, Zaïre 54 B1
Arvada, U.S.A. 82 D10
Árvi, Greece 23 E7
Arvida, Canada 71 C5
Arvidsjaur, Sweden 8 D15
Arvika, Sweden 9 G12
Arvin, U.S.A. 85 K8
Arxan, China 33 B6
Aryirádhes, Greece 23 B3
Aryiroúpolis, Greece 23 D6
Arys, Kazakhstan 26 E7
Arzamas, Russia 24 C7
Arzew, Algeria 50 A4
Aş Şadr, U.A.E. 45 E7
Aş Şafā, Syria 47 B6
'As Saffānīyah, Si. Arabia 45 D6
As Safirah, Syria 44 B3
Aş Şahm, Oman 45 E8
As Sājir, Si. Arabia 44 E5
As Salamīyah, Syria 44 C3
As Salt, Jordan 47 C4
As Sal'w'a, Qatar 45 E6
As Samāwah, Iraq 44 D5
As Sanamayn, Syria 47 B5
As Sukhnah, Syria 44 C3
As Sulaymānīyah, Iraq 44 C5
As Sulaymī, Si. Arabia 44 E4
As Summān, Si. Arabia 44 E5
As Suwaydā', Syria 47 C5
As Suwaydā' □, Syria 47 C5
As Şuwayrah, Iraq 44 C5
Asab, Namibia 56 D2
Asahi-Gawa →, Japan 31 G6
Asahigawa, Japan 30 C11
Asansol, India 43 H12
Asbesberge, S. Africa 56 D3
Asbestos, Canada 71 C5
Asbury Park, U.S.A. 79 F10
Ascensión, Mexico 86 A3
Ascensión, B. de la, Mexico 87 D7
Ascension I., Atl. Oc. 2 E9
Aschaffenburg, Germany 16 D4
Áscoli Piceno, Italy 20 C5
Ascope, Peru 92 E3
Ascotán, Chile 94 A2
Aseb, Ethiopia 46 E3
Asela, Ethiopia 51 G12
Asgata, Cyprus 23 E12
Ash Fork, U.S.A. 83 J7
Ash Grove, U.S.A. 81 G8
Ash Shamāl □, Lebanon 47 A5
Ash Shāmīyah, Iraq 44 D5
Ash Shāriqah, U.A.E. 45 E7
Ash Sharmah, Si. Arabia 44 D2
Ash Sharqāt, Iraq 44 C4
Ash Sharqi, Al Jabal, Lebanon 47 B5
Ash Shaţrah, Iraq 44 D5
Ash Shawbak, Jordan 44 D2
Ash Shawmari, J., Jordan 47 E5
Ash Shaykh, J., Lebanon 47 B4
Ash Shināfīyah, Iraq 44 D5
Ash Shu'aybah, Si. Arabia 44 E5
Ash Shumlūl, Si. Arabia 44 E5
Ash Shūr'a, Iraq 44 C4
Ash Shurayf, Si. Arabia 44 E3
Ash Shuwayfāt, Lebanon 47 B4
Asha, Russia 24 D10
Ashau, Vietnam 38 D6
Ashburn, U.S.A. 77 K4
Ashburton, N.Z. 59 K3
Ashburton →, Australia 60 D1
Ashburton Downs, Australia 60 D2
Ashby de la Zouch, U.K. 10 E6
Ashcroft, Canada 72 C4
Ashdod, Israel 47 D3
Asheboro, U.S.A. 77 H6
Asherton, U.S.A. 81 L5
Asheville, U.S.A. 77 H4
Asheweig →, Canada 70 B2
Ashford, Australia 63 D5
Ashford, U.K. 11 F8
Ashford, U.S.A. 82 C2
Ashibetsu, Japan 30 C11
Ashikaga, Japan 31 F9
Ashizuri-Zaki, Japan 31 H6
Ashkarkot, Afghan. 42 C2
Ashkhabad, Turkmenistan 26 F6
Ashland, Kans., U.S.A. 81 G5
Ashland, Ky., U.S.A. 76 F4
Ashland, Maine, U.S.A. 71 C6
Ashland, Mont., U.S.A. 82 D10
Ashland, Nebr., U.S.A. 80 E6
Ashland, Ohio, U.S.A. 78 F2
Ashland, Oreg., U.S.A. 82 E2
Ashland, Pa., U.S.A. 79 F8
Ashland, Va., U.S.A. 76 G7
Ashland, Wis., U.S.A. 80 B9
Ashley, N. Dak., U.S.A. 80 B5
Ashley, Pa., U.S.A. 79 E9
Ashmont, Canada 72 C6
Ashmore Reef, Australia 60 B3
Ashq'elon, Israel 47 D3
Ashtabula, U.S.A. 78 E4
Ashton, S. Africa 56 E3
Ashton, U.S.A. 82 D8
Ashton under Lyne, U.K. 10 D5
Ashuanipi, L., Canada 71 B6
Asia 28 E11
Asia, Kepulauan, Indonesia 37 D8
Āsīā Bak, Iran 45 C6
Asifabad, India 40 K11
Asike, Indonesia 37 F10
Asilah, Morocco 50 A3
Asinara, Italy 20 D3
Asinara, G. dell', Italy 20 D3
Asino, Russia 26 D9
'Asīr □, Si. Arabia 46 D3
Asir, Ras, Somali Rep. 46 E5
Askersund, Sweden 9 G13
Askham, S. Africa 56 D3
Askja, Iceland 8 D5
Asmara = Asmera, Ethiopia 51 E12
Asmera, Ethiopia 51 E12
Asotin, U.S.A. 82 C5
Aspen, U.S.A. 83 G10
Aspermont, U.S.A. 81 J4
Aspiring, Mt., N.Z. 59 L2
Asprókavos, Ákra, Greece 23 B4
Aspur, India 42 H6
Asquith, Canada 73 C7
Assam □, India 41 F18
Asse, Belgium 15 D4
Assen, Neths. 15 B6
Assini, Ivory C. 50 G4
Assiniboia, Canada 73 D7
Assiniboine →, Canada 73 D9
Assis, Brazil 95 A5
Assisi, Italy 20 C5
Assynt, L., U.K. 12 C3
Astara, Azerbaijan 25 G8
Asteroúsia, Greece 23 E7
Asti, Italy 20 B3
Astipálaia, Greece 21 F12
Astorga, Spain 19 A2
Astoria, U.S.A. 84 D3
Astrakhan, Russia 25 E8
Astrakhan-Bazàr, Azerbaijan 25 G8
Asturias, Spain 19 A2
Asunción, Paraguay 94 B4
Asunción Nochixtlán, Mexico 87 D5
Aswa →, Uganda 54 B3
Aswân, Egypt 51 D11
Aswân High Dam = Sadd el Aali, Egypt 51 D11
Asyût, Egypt 51 C11
At Ţafilah, Jordan 47 E4
At Tā'if, Si. Arabia 46 C3
Aţ Ţirāq, Si. Arabia 44 E5
Atacama □, Chile 94 B2
Atacama, Desierto de, Chile 94 A2
Atacama, Salar de, Chile 94 A2
Atakpamé, Togo 50 G5
Atalaya, Peru 92 F4
Atalaya de Femes, Canary Is. 22 F6
Atami, Japan 31 G9
Atapupu, Indonesia 37 F6
Atâr, Mauritania 50 D2
Atara, Russia 27 C13
Atascadero, U.S.A. 83 J3
Atascadero, Calif., U.S.A. 84 K6
Atasu, Kazakhstan 26 E8
Atauro, Indonesia 37 F7
Atbara, Sudan 51 E11
'Atbara →, Sudan 51 E11
Atbasar, Kazakhstan 26 D7
Atchafalaya B., U.S.A. 81 L9
Atchison, U.S.A. 80 F7
Ath, Belgium 15 D3
Athabasca, Canada 72 C6
Athabasca →, Canada 73 B6
Athabasca, L., Canada 73 B7
Athboy, Ireland 13 C5
Athenry, Ireland 13 C3
Athens = Athínai, Greece 21 F10
Athens, Ala., U.S.A. 77 H2
Athens, Ga., U.S.A. 77 J4
Athens, N.Y., U.S.A. 79 D11
Athens, Ohio, U.S.A. 76 F4
Athens, Pa., U.S.A. 79 E8
Athens, Tenn., U.S.A. 77 H3
Athens, Tex., U.S.A. 81 J7
Atherley, Canada 78 B5
Atherton, Australia 62 B4
Athienou, Cyprus 23 D12
Athínai, Greece 21 F10
Athlone, Ireland 13 C4
Athna, Cyprus 23 D12
Atholl, Forest of, U.K. 12 E5
Atholville, Canada 71 C6
Áthos, Greece 21 D11
Athy, Ireland 13 D5
Ati, Chad 51 F8
Atiak, Uganda 54 B3
Atico, Peru 92 G4
Atikokan, Canada 70 C1
Atikonak L., Canada 71 B7
Atka, Russia 27 C16
Atkinson, U.S.A. 80 D5
Atlanta, Ga., U.S.A. 77 J3
Atlanta, Tex., U.S.A. 81 J7
Atlantic, U.S.A. 80 E7
Atlantic City, U.S.A. 76 F8
Atlantic Ocean 2 E9
Atlas Mts. = Haut Atlas, Morocco 50 B3
Atlin, Canada 72 B2
Atlin, L., Canada 72 B2
Atmore, U.S.A. 77 K2
Atoka, U.S.A. 81 H6
Atolia, U.S.A. 85 K9
Atoyac →, Mexico 87 D5
Atrak →, Iran 45 B8
Atrauli, India 42 E8
Atsuta, Japan 30 C10
Attalla, U.S.A. 77 H2
Attáviros, Greece 23 C9
Attawapiskat, Canada 70 B3
Attawapiskat →, Canada 70 B3
Attawapiskat, L., Canada 70 B2
Attica, U.S.A. 76 E2
Attikamagen L., Canada 71 A6
Attleboro, U.S.A. 79 E13
Attock, Pakistan 42 C5
Attopeu, Laos 38 E6
Attur, India 40 P11
Atuel →, Argentina 94 D2
Åtvidaberg, Sweden 9 G14
Atwater, U.S.A. 83 H3
Atwood, Canada 78 C3
Atwood, U.S.A. 80 F4
Au Sable →, U.S.A. 76 C4
Au Sable Pt., U.S.A. 70 C2
Aubarca, C., Spain 22 B7
Aube □, France 18 B6
Aube →, France 18 B5
Auberry, U.S.A. 84 H7
Auburn, Ala., U.S.A. 77 J3
Auburn, Calif., U.S.A. 84 G5
Auburn, Ind., U.S.A. 76 E3
Auburn, N.Y., U.S.A. 79 D8
Auburn, Nebr., U.S.A. 80 E7
Auburn, Wash., U.S.A. 84 C4
Auburn Ra., Australia 63 D5
Auburndale, U.S.A. 77 L5
Aubusson, France 18 D5
Auch, France 18 E4
Auckland, N.Z. 59 G5
Auckland Is., Pac. Oc. 64 N8
Aude □, France 18 E5
Aude →, France 18 E5
Auden, Canada 70 B2
Audubon, U.S.A. 80 E7
Augathella, Australia 63 D4
Augrabies Falls, S. Africa 56 D3
Augsburg, Germany 16 D5
Augusta, Italy 20 F6
Augusta, Ark., U.S.A. 81 H9
Augusta, Ga., U.S.A. 77 J5
Augusta, Kans., U.S.A. 81 G6
Augusta, Maine, U.S.A. 71 D6
Augusta, Mont., U.S.A. 82 C7
Augusta, Wis., U.S.A. 80 C9
Augustów, Poland 17 B11
Augustus, Mt., Australia 60 D2
Augustus Downs, Australia 62 B2
Augustus I., Australia 60 C3
Aukum, U.S.A. 84 G6
Auld, L., Australia 60 D3
Ault, U.S.A. 80 E2
Aunis, France 18 C3
Auponhia, Indonesia 37 E7
Aur, P., Malaysia 39 L5
Auraiya, India 43 F8
Aurangabad, Bihar, India 43 G11
Aurangabad, Maharashtra, India 40 K9
Aurillac, France 18 D5
Aurora, Canada 78 C5
Aurora, S. Africa 56 E2
Aurora, Colo., U.S.A. 80 F2
Aurora, Ill., U.S.A. 76 E1
Aurora, Mo., U.S.A. 81 G8
Aurora, Nebr., U.S.A. 80 E6
Aurora, Ohio, U.S.A. 78 E3
Aurukun Mission, Australia 62 A3
Aus, Namibia 56 D2
Aust-Agder fylke □, Norway 9 G9
Austerlitz = Slavkov, Czech. 16 D8
Austin, Minn., U.S.A. 80 D8
Austin, Nev., U.S.A. 82 G5
Austin, Pa., U.S.A. 78 E6
Austin, Tex., U.S.A. 81 K6
Austin, L., Australia 61 E2
Austral Downs, Australia 62 C2
Austral Is. = Tubuai Is., Pac. Oc. 65 K12
Austral Seamount Chain, Pac. Oc. 65 K13
Australia ■, Oceania 58 C3
Australian Alps, Australia 63 F4
Australian Capital Territory □, Australia 63 F4
Austria ■, Europe 16 E6
Austvågøy, Norway 8 B13
Autlán, Mexico 86 D4
Autun, France 18 C6
Auvergne, Australia 60 C5
Auvergne, France 18 D5
Auxerre, France 18 C5
Avallon, France 18 C5
Avalon, U.S.A. 85 M8
Avalon Pen., Canada 71 C9
Avaré, Brazil 95 A6
Avawatz Mts., U.S.A. 85 K10
Aveiro, Brazil 93 D7
Aveiro, Portugal 19 B1
Āvej, Iran 45 C6
Avellaneda, Argentina 94 C4
Avellino, Italy 20 D6
Avenal, U.S.A. 84 K6
Aversa, Italy 20 D6
Avery, U.S.A. 82 C6
Aves, I. de, W. Indies 89 C7
Aves, Is. de, Venezuela 89 D6
Avesta, Sweden 9 F14
Aveyron □, France 18 D5
Aviá Terai, Argentina 94 B3
Avignon, France 18 E6
Ávila, Spain 19 B3
Avila Beach, U.S.A. 85 K6
Avilés, Spain 19 A3
Avoca, Ireland 13 D5
Avoca, U.S.A. 78 D7
Avoca →, Australia 63 F3
Avola, Canada 72 C5
Avon, N.Y., U.S.A. 78 D7
Avon, S. Dak., U.S.A. 80 D5
Avon □, U.K. 11 F5
Avon →, Australia 61 F2
Avon →, Avon, U.K. 11 F5
Avon →, Hants., U.K. 11 G6
Avon →, Warks., U.K. 11 F5
Avondale, Zimbabwe 55 F3
Avonlea, Canada 73 D7
Avonmore, Canada 79 A10
Avonmouth, U.K. 11 F5
Avranches, France 18 B3
A'waj →, Syria 47 B5
Awaji-Shima, Japan 31 G7
'Awālī, Bahrain 45 E6
Awantipur, India 43 C6
Awash, Ethiopia 46 F3
Awatere →, N.Z. 59 J5
Awbārī, Libya 51 C7
Awe, L., U.K. 12 E3
Awjilah, Libya 51 C9
Axarfjörður, Iceland 8 C5
Axel Heiberg I., Canada 4 B3
Axim, Ghana 50 H4
Axminster, U.K. 11 G4
Ayabaca, Peru 92 D3
Ayabe, Japan 31 G7
Ayacucho, Argentina 94 D4
Ayacucho, Peru 92 F4
Ayaguz, Kazakhstan 26 E9
Ayamonte, Spain 19 D2
Ayan, Russia 27 D14
Ayaviri, Peru 92 F4
Ayer's Cliff, Canada 79 A12
Ayers Rock, Australia 61 E5
Ayia Aikateríni, Ákra, Greece 23 A3
Ayia Dhéka, Greece 23 D6
Ayia Gálini, Greece 23 D6
Ayia Napa, Cyprus 23 E13
Áyia Phyla, Cyprus 23 E12
Ayia Varvára, Greece 23 D7
Áyios Amvrósios, Cyprus 23 D12
Áyios Evstrátios, Greece 21 E11
Áyios Ioánnis, Ákra, Greece 23 D7
Áyios Isidhoros, Greece 23 C9
Áyios Matthaíos, Greece 23 B3
Áyios Nikólaos, Greece 23 D7
Áyios Seryios, Cyprus 23 D12
Ayios Theodhoros, Cyprus 23 D13
Aykin, Russia 24 B8
Aylesbury, U.K. 11 F7
Aylmer, Canada 78 D4
Aylmer, L., Canada 68 B8
Ayolas, Paraguay 94 B4
Ayon, Ostrov, Russia 27 C17
Ayr, Australia 62 B4
Ayr, U.K. 12 F4
Ayr →, U.K. 12 F4
Ayre, Pt. of, U.K. 10 C3
Aytos, Bulgaria 21 C12
Ayu, Kepulauan, Indonesia 37 D8
Ayutla, Guatemala 88 D1
Ayutla, Mexico 87 D5
Ayvalık, Turkey 25 G4
Az Zabdānī, Syria 47 B5
Az Zāhirīyah, Jordan 47 D3
Az Zahrān, Si. Arabia 45 E6
Az Zarqā, Jordan 47 C5
Az Zībār, Iraq 44 B5
Az-Zilfī, Si. Arabia 44 E5
Az Zubayr, Iraq 44 D5
Azamgarh, India 43 F10
Āzār Shahr, Iran 44 B5
Āzarbāyjān-e Gharbī □, Iran 44 B5
Āzarbāyjān-e Sharqī □, Iran 44 B5
Azare, Nigeria 50 F7
A'zāz, Syria 44 B3
Azbine = Aïr, Niger 50 E6
Azerbaijan ■, Asia 25 F8
Azimganj, India 43 G13
Azogues, Ecuador 92 D3
Azores, Atl. Oc. 2 C8
Azov, Russia 25 E6
Azov Sea = Azovskoye More, Europe 25 E6
Azovskoye More, Europe 25 E6
Azovy, Russia 26 C7
Aztec, U.S.A. 83 H10
Azúa, Dom. Rep. 89 C5
Azuaga, Spain 19 C3
Azuero, Pen. de, Panama 88 E3
Azul, Argentina 94 D4
Azusa, U.S.A. 85 L9
'Azzūn, Jordan 47 C4

B

Ba Don, Vietnam 38 D6
Ba Dong, Vietnam 39 H6
Ba Ngoi = Cam Lam, Vietnam 39 G7
Ba Ria, Vietnam 39 G6
Ba Tri, Vietnam 39 G6
Ba Xian, China 34 E9
Baa, Indonesia 37 F6
Baarle Nassau, Belgium 15 C4
Baarn, Neths. 15 B5
Bab el Mandeb, Red Sea 46 E3
Bābā Kalū, Iran 45 D6
Babahoyo, Ecuador 92 D3
Babakin, Australia 61 F2
Babana, Nigeria 50 F5
Babar, Indonesia 37 F7
Babar, Pakistan 42 D3
Babarkach, Pakistan 42 E2
Babb, U.S.A. 82 B7
Babi Besar, P., Malaysia 39 L4
Babinda, Australia 62 B4
Babine, Canada 72 B3
Babine →, Canada 72 B3
Babine L., Canada 72 C3
Babo, Indonesia 37 E8
Bābol, Iran 45 B7
Bābol Sar, Iran 45 B7
Baboua, C.A.R. 52 C2
Babura, Nigeria 50 F6
Babusar Pass, Pakistan 43 B5
Babuyan Chan., Phil. 37 A6
Babylon, Iraq 44 C5
Bac Can, Vietnam 38 A5
Bac Giang, Vietnam 38 B6
Bac Ninh, Vietnam 38 B6
Bac Phan, Vietnam 38 B5
Bac Quang, Vietnam 38 A5
Bacabal, Brazil 93 D10
Bacalar, Mexico 87 D7
Bacan, Indonesia 37 F7
Bacan, Kepulauan, Indonesia 37 E7
Bacan, Pulau, Indonesia 37 E7
Bacarra, Phil. 37 A6
Bacău, Romania 17 E13
Bacerac, Mexico 86 A3
Bach Long Vi, Dao, Vietnam 38 B6
Bachelina, Russia 26 D7
Back →, Canada 68 B9
Backstairs Passage, Australia 63 F2
Bacolod, Phil. 37 B6
Bacuk, Malaysia 39 J4
Bād, Iran 45 C7
Bad →, U.S.A. 80 C4
Bad Axe, U.S.A. 78 C2
Bad Ischl, Austria 16 E6
Bad Lands, U.S.A. 80 D3
Badagara, India 40 P9
Badajoz, Spain 19 C2
Badalona, Spain 19 B7
Badalzai, Afghan. 42 E1
Badampahar, India 41 H15
Badanah, Si. Arabia 44 D4
Badarinath, India 43 D8
Badas, Brunei 36 D4
Badas, Kepulauan, Indonesia 36 D3
Baddo →, Pakistan 40 F4
Bade, Indonesia 37 F9
Baden, Austria 16 D8
Baden-Baden, Germany 16 D4
Baden-Württemberg □, Germany 16 D4
Badenoch, U.K. 12 E4
Badgastein, Austria 16 E6
Badger, Canada 71 C8
Badger, U.S.A. 84 J7
Bādghīsāt □, Afghan. 40 B3
Badgom, India 43 B6
Badin, Pakistan 42 G3
Baduen, Somali Rep. 46 F4
Badulla, Sri Lanka 40 R12
Baeza, Spain 19 D4
Bafatá, Guinea-Biss. 50 F2
Baffin B., Canada 4 B4
Baffin I., Canada 69 B12
Bafia, Cameroon 50 H7
Bafing →, Mali 50 F2
Bafliyūn, Syria 44 B3
Bafoulabé, Mali 50 F2
Bāfq, Iran 45 D7
Bāft, Iran 45 D8
Bafwasende, Zaïre 54 B2
Bagamoyo, Tanzania 54 D4
Bagamoyo □, Tanzania 54 D4
Bagan Datoh, Malaysia 39 L3
Bagan Serai, Malaysia 39 K3
Baganga, Phil. 37 C7
Bagani, Namibia 56 B3

Bagansiapiapi, *Indonesia* 36 D2
Bagasra, *India* 42 J4
Bagdad, *U.S.A.* 85 L11
Bagdarin, *Russia* 27 D12
Bagé, *Brazil* 95 C5
Bagenalstown = Muine Bheag, *Ireland* 13 D5
Baggs, *U.S.A.* 82 F10
Bagh, *Pakistan* 43 C5
Baghdād, *Iraq* 44 C5
Baghlān, *Afghan.* 40 A6
Bagley, *U.S.A.* 80 B7
Bagotville, *Canada* 71 C5
Baguio, *Phil.* 37 A6
Bahadurgarh, *India* 42 E7
Bahama, Canal Viejo de, *W. Indies* 88 B4
Bahamas ■, *N. Amer.* 89 B5
Baharampur, *India* 43 G13
Bahau, *Malaysia* 39 L4
Bahawalnagar, *Pakistan* 42 D5
Bahawalpur, *Pakistan* 42 E4
Baheri, *India* 43 E8
Bahi, *Tanzania* 54 D4
Bahi Swamp, *Tanzania* 54 D4
Bahia = Salvador, *Brazil* 93 F11
Bahia □, *Brazil* 93 F10
Bahía, Is. de la, *Honduras* 88 C2
Bahía Blanca, *Argentina* 94 D3
Bahía de Caráquez, *Ecuador* 92 D2
Bahía Honda, *Cuba* 88 B3
Bahía Laura, *Argentina* 96 F3
Bahía Negra, *Paraguay* 92 H7
Bahmanzād, *Iran* 45 D6
Bahr Aouk →, *C.A.R.* 52 C3
Bahr el Ahmar □, *Sudan* 51 E12
Bahr el Ghazâl □, *Sudan* 51 G10
Bahr Salamat →, *Chad* 51 G8
Bahraich, *India* 43 F9
Bahrain ■, *Asia* 45 E6
Bahret Assad, *Syria* 44 C3
Bahror, *India* 42 F7
Bāhū Kalāt, *Iran* 45 E9
Bai Bung, Mui, *Vietnam* 39 H5
Bai Duc, *Vietnam* 38 C5
Bai Thuong, *Vietnam* 38 C5
Baia Mare, *Romania* 17 E11
Baïbokoum, *Chad* 51 G8
Baicheng, *China* 35 B12
Baidoa, *Somali Rep.* 46 G3
Baie Comeau, *Canada* 71 C6
Baie-St-Paul, *Canada* 71 C5
Baie Trinité, *Canada* 71 C6
Baie Verte, *Canada* 71 C8
Baihe, *China* 34 H6
Ba'ījī, *Iraq* 44 C4
Baikal, L. = Baykal, Oz., *Russia* 27 D11
Baile Atha Cliath = Dublin, *Ireland* 13 C5
Bailundo, *Angola* 53 G3
Bainbridge, *Ga., U.S.A.* 77 K3
Bainbridge, *N.Y., U.S.A.* 79 D9
Baing, *Indonesia* 37 F6
Bainiu, *China* 34 H7
Bainville, *U.S.A.* 80 A2
Bā'ir, *Jordan* 47 E5
Baird, *U.S.A.* 81 J5
Baird Mts., *U.S.A.* 68 B3
Bairin Youqi, *China* 35 C10
Bairin Zuoqi, *China* 35 C10
Bairnsdale, *Australia* 63 F4
Baisha, *China* 34 G7
Baitadi, *Nepal* 43 E9
Baixo-Alentejo, *Portugal* 19 D1
Baiyin, *China* 34 F3
Baiyu Shan, *China* 34 F4
Baj Baj, *India* 43 H13
Baja, *Hungary* 17 E9
Baja, Pta., *Mexico* 86 B1
Baja California, *Mexico* 86 A1
Bajamar, *Canary Is.* 22 F3
Bajana, *India* 42 H4
Bājgīrān, *Iran* 45 B8
Bajimba, Mt., *Australia* 63 D5
Bajo Nuevo, *Caribbean* 88 C4
Bajool, *Australia* 62 C5
Bakala, *C.A.R.* 51 G9
Bakchar, *Russia* 26 D9
Bakel, *Senegal* 50 F2
Baker, *Calif., U.S.A.* 85 K10
Baker, *Mont., U.S.A.* 80 B2
Baker, *Oreg., U.S.A.* 82 D5
Baker, L., *Canada* 68 B10
Baker I., *Pac. Oc.* 64 G10
Baker L., *Australia* 61 E4
Baker Lake, *Canada* 68 B10
Baker Mt., *U.S.A.* 82 B3
Bakers Creek, *Australia* 62 C4
Baker's Dozen Is., *Canada* 70 A4
Bakersfield, *Calif., U.S.A.* 85 K7
Bakersfield, *Vt., U.S.A.* 79 B12
Bākhtarān, *Iran* 44 C5
Bākhtarān □, *Iran* 44 C5
Bakkafjörður, *Iceland* 8 C6
Bakkagerði, *Iceland* 8 D7
Bakony Forest = Bakony Hegyseg, *Hungary* 17 E8
Bakony Hegyseg, *Hungary* 17 E8
Bakouma, *C.A.R.* 51 G9
Baku, *Azerbaijan* 25 F8
Bakutis Coast, *Antarctica* 5 D15
Bala, *Canada* 78 A5
Bala, L., *U.K.* 10 E4
Balabac I., *Phil.* 36 C5
Balabac Str., *E. Indies* 36 C5
Balabagh, *Afghan.* 42 B4
Balabakk, *Lebanon* 47 A5
Balabalangan, Kepulauan, *Indonesia* 36 E5
Balad, *Iraq* 44 C5
Balad Rūz, *Iraq* 44 C5
Bālādeh, *Fārs, Iran* 45 D6
Bāladeh, *Māzandaran, Iran* 45 B6
Balaghat, *India* 40 J12
Balaghat Ra., *India* 40 K10
Balaguer, *Spain* 19 B6
Balaklava, *Australia* 63 E2
Balaklava, *Ukraine* 25 F5
Balakovo, *Russia* 24 D8
Balancán, *Mexico* 87 D6
Balashov, *Russia* 24 D7
Balasinor, *India* 42 H5
Balasore = Baleshwar, *India* 41 J15
Balaton, *Hungary* 17 E8
Balboa, *Panama* 88 E4
Balbriggan, *Ireland* 13 C5
Balcarce, *Argentina* 94 D4
Balcarres, *Canada* 73 C8
Balchik, *Bulgaria* 21 C13
Balclutha, *N.Z.* 59 M2
Bald Hd., *Australia* 61 G2
Bald I., *Australia* 61 F2
Bald Knob, *U.S.A.* 81 H9
Baldock L., *Canada* 73 B9
Baldwin, *Fla., U.S.A.* 77 K4
Baldwin, *Mich., U.S.A.* 76 D3
Baldwinsville, *U.S.A.* 79 C8
Baldy Peak, *U.S.A.* 83 K9
Baleares, Is., *Spain* 22 B10
Balearic Is. = Baleares, Is., *Spain* 22 B10
Baler, *Phil.* 37 A6
Baleshwar, *India* 41 J15
Balfate, *Honduras* 88 C2
Balfe's Creek, *Australia* 62 C4
Balfour, *S. Africa* 57 D4
Bali, *Cameroon* 50 G7
Bali, *Greece* 23 D6
Bali, *Indonesia* 36 F5
Bali □, *Indonesia* 36 F5
Bali, Selat, *Indonesia* 37 H16
Balikeşir, *Turkey* 25 G4
Balikpapan, *Indonesia* 36 E5
Balimbing, *Phil.* 37 C5
Baling, *Malaysia* 39 K3
Balipara, *India* 41 F18
Baliza, *Brazil* 93 G8
Balkan Mts. = Stara Planina, *Bulgaria* 21 C10
Balkhash, *Kazakhstan* 26 E8
Balkhash, Ozero, *Kazakhstan* 26 E8
Balla, *Bangla.* 41 G17
Ballachulish, *U.K.* 12 E3
Balladonia, *Australia* 61 F3
Ballarat, *Australia* 63 F3
Ballard, L., *Australia* 61 E3
Ballater, *U.K.* 12 D5
Ballenas, Canal de, *Mexico* 86 B2
Balleny Is., *Antarctica* 5 C11
Ballia, *India* 43 G11
Ballidu, *Australia* 61 F2
Ballina, *Australia* 63 D5
Ballina, *Mayo, Ireland* 13 B2
Ballina, *Tipp., Ireland* 13 D3
Ballinasloe, *Ireland* 13 C3
Ballinger, *U.S.A.* 81 K5
Ballinrobe, *Ireland* 13 C2
Ballinskelligs B., *Ireland* 13 E1
Ballycastle, *U.K.* 13 A5
Ballymena, *U.K.* 13 B5
Ballymena □, *U.K.* 13 B5
Ballymoney, *U.K.* 13 A5
Ballymoney □, *U.K.* 13 A5
Ballyshannon, *Ireland* 13 B3
Balmaceda, *Chile* 96 F2
Balmoral, *Australia* 63 F3
Balmoral, *U.K.* 12 D5
Balmorhea, *U.S.A.* 81 K3
Balonne →, *Australia* 63 D4
Balrampur, *India* 43 F10
Balranald, *Australia* 63 E3
Balsas, *Mexico* 87 D5
Balsas →, *Mexico* 86 D4
Balston Spa, *U.S.A.* 79 D11
Balta, *Ukraine* 25 E4
Balta, *U.S.A.* 80 A4
Baltic Sea, *Europe* 9 H15
Baltimore, *Ireland* 13 E2
Baltimore, *U.S.A.* 76 F7
Baltit, *Pakistan* 43 A6
Baluchistan □, *Pakistan* 40 F4
Balurghat, *India* 43 G13
Balygychan, *Russia* 27 C16
Bam, *Iran* 45 D8
Bama, *Nigeria* 51 F7
Bamako, *Mali* 50 F3
Bamba, *Mali* 50 E4
Bambari, *C.A.R.* 51 G9
Bambaroo, *Australia* 62 B4
Bamberg, *Germany* 16 D5
Bamberg, *U.S.A.* 77 J5
Bambili, *Zaïre* 54 B2
Bamenda, *Cameroon* 50 G7
Bamfield, *Canada* 72 D3
Bāmīān □, *Afghan.* 40 B5
Bamiancheng, *China* 35 C13
Bampūr, *Iran* 45 E9
Ban Aranyaprathet, *Thailand* 38 F4
Ban Ban, *Laos* 38 C4
Ban Bang Hin, *Thailand* 39 H2
Ban Chiang Klang, *Thailand* 38 C3
Ban Chik, *Laos* 38 D4
Ban Choho, *Thailand* 38 E4
Ban Dan Lan Hoi, *Thailand* 38 D2
Ban Don = Surat Thani, *Thailand* 39 H2
Ban Don, *Vietnam* 38 F6
Ban Don, Ao, *Thailand* 39 H2
Ban Dong, *Thailand* 38 C3
Ban Hong, *Thailand* 38 C2
Ban Kaeng, *Thailand* 38 D3
Ban Keun, *Laos* 38 C4
Ban Khai, *Thailand* 38 F3
Ban Kheun, *Laos* 38 B3
Ban Khlong Kua, *Thailand* 39 J3
Ban Khuan Mao, *Thailand* 39 J2
Ban Khun Yuam, *Thailand* 38 C1
Ban Ko Yai Chim, *Thailand* 39 G2
Ban Kok, *Thailand* 38 D4
Ban Laem, *Thailand* 38 F2
Ban Lao Ngam, *Laos* 38 E6
Ban Le Kathe, *Thailand* 38 E2
Ban Mae Chedi, *Thailand* 38 C2
Ban Mae Laeng, *Thailand* 38 B2
Ban Mae Sariang, *Thailand* 38 C1
Ban Mê Thuôt = Buon Me Thuot, *Vietnam* 38 F7
Ban Mi, *Thailand* 38 E3
Ban Muong Mo, *Laos* 38 C4
Ban Na Mo, *Laos* 38 D5
Ban Na San, *Thailand* 39 H2
Ban Na Tong, *Laos* 38 B3
Ban Nam Bac, *Laos* 38 B4
Ban Nam Ma, *Laos* 38 A3
Ban Ngang, *Laos* 38 E6
Ban Nong Bok, *Laos* 38 D5
Ban Nong Boua, *Laos* 38 E6
Ban Nong Pling, *Thailand* 38 E3
Ban Pak Chan, *Thailand* 39 G2
Ban Phai, *Thailand* 38 D4
Ban Pong, *Thailand* 38 F2
Ban Ron Phibun, *Thailand* 39 H2
Ban Sanam Chai, *Thailand* 39 J3
Ban Sangkha, *Thailand* 38 E4
Ban Tak, *Thailand* 38 D2
Ban Tako, *Thailand* 38 E4
Ban Tha Dua, *Thailand* 38 D2
Ban Tha Li, *Thailand* 38 D3
Ban Tha Nun, *Thailand* 39 H2
Ban Thahine, *Laos* 38 E5
Ban Xien Kok, *Laos* 38 B3
Ban Yen Nhan, *Vietnam* 38 B6
Banaba, *Kiribati* 64 H8
Bañalbufar, *Spain* 22 B9
Banalia, *Zaïre* 54 B2
Banam, *Cambodia* 39 G5
Banamba, *Mali* 50 F3
Banana, *Australia* 62 C5
Bananal, I. do, *Brazil* 93 F8
Banaras = Varanasi, *India* 43 G10
Banas →, *Gujarat, India* 42 H4
Banas →, *Mad. P., India* 43 G9
Banbān, *Si. Arabia* 44 E5
Banbridge, *U.K.* 13 B5
Banbridge □, *U.K.* 13 B5
Banbury, *U.K.* 11 E6
Banchory, *U.K.* 12 D6
Bancroft, *Canada* 70 C4
Band Bonī, *Iran* 45 E8
Band Qīr, *Iran* 45 D6
Banda, *India* 43 G9
Banda, Kepulauan, *Indonesia* 37 E7
Banda Aceh, *Indonesia* 36 C1
Banda Banda, Mt., *Australia* 63 E5
Banda Elat, *Indonesia* 37 F8
Banda Is. = Banda, Kepulauan, *Indonesia* 37 E7
Banda Sea, *Indonesia* 37 F7
Bandai-San, *Japan* 30 F10
Bandān, *Iran* 45 D9
Bandanaira, *Indonesia* 37 E7
Bandanwara, *India* 42 F6
Bandar = Machilipatnam, *India* 41 L12
Bandār 'Abbās, *Iran* 45 E8
Bandar-e Anzalī, *Iran* 45 B6
Bandar-e Chārak, *Iran* 45 E7
Bandar-e Deylam, *Iran* 45 D6
Bandar-e Khomeynī, *Iran* 45 D6
Bandar-e Lengeh, *Iran* 45 E7
Bandar-e Maqām, *Iran* 45 E7
Bandar-e Ma'shur, *Iran* 45 D6
Bandar-e Nakhīlū, *Iran* 45 E7
Bandar-e Rīg, *Iran* 45 D6
Bandar-e Torkeman, *Iran* 45 B7
Bandar Maharani = Muar, *Malaysia* 39 L4
Bandar Penggaram = Batu Pahat, *Malaysia* 39 M4
Bandar Seri Begawan, *Brunei* 36 C4
Bandawe, *Malawi* 55 E3
Bandeira, Pico da, *Brazil* 95 A7
Bandera, *Argentina* 94 B3
Bandera, *U.S.A.* 81 L5
Banderas, B. de, *Mexico* 86 C3
Bandiagara, *Mali* 50 F4
Bandırma, *Turkey* 25 F4
Bandon, *Ireland* 13 E3
Bandon →, *Ireland* 13 E3
Bandula, *Mozam.* 55 F3
Bandundu, *Zaïre* 52 E3
Bandung, *Indonesia* 37 G12
Bandya, *Australia* 61 E3
Bāneh, *Iran* 44 C5
Banes, *Cuba* 89 B4
Banff, *Canada* 72 C5
Banff, *U.K.* 12 D6
Banff Nat. Park, *Canada* 72 C5
Banfora, *Burkina Faso* 50 F4
Bang Fai →, *Laos* 38 D5
Bang Hieng →, *Laos* 38 D5
Bang Krathum, *Thailand* 38 D3
Bang Lamung, *Thailand* 38 F3
Bang Mun Nak, *Thailand* 38 D3
Bang Pa In, *Thailand* 38 E3
Bang Rakam, *Thailand* 38 D3
Bang Saphan, *Thailand* 39 G2
Bangala Dam, *Zimbabwe* 55 G3
Bangalore, *India* 40 N10
Bangaon, *India* 43 H13
Bangassou, *C.A.R.* 52 D4
Banggai, Kepulauan, *Indonesia* 37 E6
Banggi, P., *Malaysia* 36 C5
Banghāzī, *Libya* 51 B9
Bangil, *Indonesia* 37 G15
Bangka, P., *Sulawesi, Indonesia* 37 D7
Bangka, P., *Sumatera, Indonesia* 36 E3
Bangka, Selat, *Indonesia* 36 E3
Bangkalan, *Indonesia* 37 G15
Bangkinang, *Indonesia* 36 D2
Bangko, *Indonesia* 36 E2
Bangkok, *Thailand* 38 F3
Bangladesh ■, *Asia* 41 H17
Bangong Co, *India* 43 B8
Bangor, *Down, U.K.* 13 B6
Bangor, *Gwynedd, U.K.* 10 D3
Bangor, *Maine, U.S.A.* 71 D6
Bangor, *Pa., U.S.A.* 79 F9
Bangued, *Phil.* 37 A6
Bangui, *C.A.R.* 52 D3
Banguru, *Zaïre* 54 B2
Bangweulu, L., *Zambia* 55 E3
Bangweulu Swamp, *Zambia* 55 E3
Bani, *Dom. Rep.* 89 C5
Banī Sa'd, *Iraq* 44 C5
Banī Walīd, *Libya* 51 B7
Banihal Pass, *India* 43 C6
Banīnah, *Libya* 51 B9
Bāniyās, *Syria* 44 C3
Banja Luka, *Bos. & H., Yug.* 20 B7
Banjar, *Indonesia* 37 G13
Banjarmasin, *Indonesia* 36 E4
Banjarnegara, *Indonesia* 37 G13
Banjul, *Gambia* 50 F1
Banka Banka, *Australia* 62 B1
Banket, *Zimbabwe* 55 F3
Bankipore, *India* 43 G11
Banks I., *B.C., Canada* 72 C3
Banks I., *N.W.T., Canada* 68 A7
Banks Pen., *N.Z.* 59 K4
Banks Str., *Australia* 62 G4
Bankura, *India* 43 H12
Bann →, *Down, U.K.* 13 B5
Bann →, *L'derry., U.K.* 13 A5
Bannang Sata, *Thailand* 39 J3
Banning, *U.S.A.* 85 M10
Banningville = Bandundu, *Zaïre* 52 E3
Bannockburn, *Canada* 78 B7
Bannockburn, *U.K.* 12 E5
Bannockburn, *Zimbabwe* 55 G2
Bannu, *Pakistan* 40 C7
Banská Bystrica, *Czech.* 17 D9
Banská Štiavnica, *Czech.* 17 D9
Banswara, *India* 42 H6
Banten, *Indonesia* 37 G12
Bantry, *Ireland* 13 E2
Bantry B., *Ireland* 13 E2
Bantul, *Indonesia* 37 G14
Bantva, *India* 42 J4
Banu, *Afghan.* 40 B6
Banyak, Kepulauan, *Indonesia* 36 D1
Banyo, *Cameroon* 50 G7
Banyumas, *Indonesia* 37 G13
Banyuwangi, *Indonesia* 37 H16
Banzare Coast, *Antarctica* 5 C9
Banzyville = Mobayi, *Zaïre* 52 D4
Bao Ha, *Vietnam* 38 A5
Bao Lac, *Vietnam* 38 A5
Bao Loc, *Vietnam* 39 G6
Baocheng, *China* 34 H4
Baode, *China* 34 E6
Baodi, *China* 35 E9
Baoding, *China* 34 E8
Baoji, *China* 34 G4
Baoshan, *China* 32 D4
Baotou, *China* 34 D6
Baoying, *China* 35 H10
Bap, *India* 42 F5
Bapatla, *India* 41 M12
Bāqerābād, *Iran* 45 C6
Ba'qūbah, *Iraq* 44 C5
Baquedano, *Chile* 94 A2
Bar, *Montenegro, Yug.* 21 C8
Bar Bigha, *India* 43 G11
Bar Harbor, *U.S.A.* 71 D6
Bar-le-Duc, *France* 18 B6
Barabai, *Indonesia* 36 E5
Barabinsk, *Russia* 26 D8
Baraboo, *U.S.A.* 80 D10
Baracaldo, *Spain* 19 A4
Baracoa, *Cuba* 89 B5
Baradero, *Argentina* 94 C4
Baraga, *U.S.A.* 80 B10
Barahona, *Dom. Rep.* 89 C5
Barail Range, *India* 41 G18
Barakhola, *India* 41 G18
Barakot, *India* 43 J11
Barakpur, *India* 43 H13
Barakula, *Australia* 63 D5
Baralaba, *Australia* 62 C4
Baralzon L., *Canada* 73 B9
Baramula, *India* 43 B6
Baran, *India* 42 G7
Baranof I., *U.S.A.* 72 B1
Baranovichi, *Belorussia* 24 D4
Barão de Melgaço, *Brazil* 92 F6
Barapasi, *Indonesia* 37 E9
Barasat, *India* 43 H13
Barat Daya, Kepulauan, *Indonesia* 37 F7
Barataria B., *U.S.A.* 81 L10
Baraut, *India* 42 E7
Barbacena, *Brazil* 95 A7
Barbacoas, *Colombia* 92 C3
Barbados ■, *W. Indies* 89 D8
Barberton, *S. Africa* 57 D5
Barberton, *U.S.A.* 78 E3
Barbourville, *U.S.A.* 77 G4
Barbuda, *W. Indies* 89 C7
Barcaldine, *Australia* 62 C4
Barcelona, *Spain* 19 B7
Barcelona, *Venezuela* 92 A6
Barcelos, *Brazil* 92 D6
Barcoo →, *Australia* 62 D3
Bardas Blancas, *Argentina* 94 D2
Barddhaman, *India* 43 H12
Bardera, *Somali Rep.* 46 G3
Bardia, *Libya* 51 B9
Bardsey I., *U.K.* 10 E3
Bardstown, *U.S.A.* 76 G3
Bareilly, *India* 43 E8
Barents Sea, *Arctic* 4 B9
Barentu, *Ethiopia* 51 E12
Bargal, *Somali Rep.* 46 E5
Bargara, *Australia* 62 C5
Barguzin, *Russia* 27 D11
Barh, *India* 43 G11
Barhaj, *India* 43 F10
Barhi, *India* 43 G11
Bari, *India* 42 F7
Bari, *Italy* 20 D7
Bari Doab, *Pakistan* 42 D5
Bariadi □, *Tanzania* 54 C3
Barīm, *Yemen* 46 E3
Barinas, *Venezuela* 92 B4
Baring, C., *Canada* 68 B8
Baringo, *Kenya* 54 B4
Baringo □, *Kenya* 54 B4
Baringo, L., *Kenya* 54 B4
Bârîs, *Egypt* 51 D11
Barisal, *Bangla.* 41 H17
Barisan, Bukit, *Indonesia* 36 E2
Barito →, *Indonesia* 36 E4
Bark L., *Canada* 78 A7
Barker, *U.S.A.* 78 C6
Barkley Sound, *Canada* 72 D3
Barkly Downs, *Australia* 62 C2
Barkly East, *S. Africa* 56 E4
Barkly Tableland, *Australia* 62 B2
Barkly West, *S. Africa* 56 D3
Barkol, *China* 32 B4
Barksdale, *U.S.A.* 81 L4
Barlee, L., *Australia* 61 E2
Barlee, Mt., *Australia* 61 D4
Barletta, *Italy* 20 D7
Barlovento, *Canary Is.* 22 F2
Barlow L., *Canada* 73 A8
Barmedman, *Australia* 63 E4
Barmer, *India* 42 G4
Barmera, *Australia* 63 E3
Barmouth, *U.K.* 10 E3
Barnagar, *India* 42 H6
Barnard Castle, *U.K.* 10 C6
Barnato, *Australia* 63 E3
Barnaul, *Russia* 26 D9
Barnesville, *U.S.A.* 77 J3
Barnet, *U.K.* 11 F7
Barneveld, *Neths.* 15 B5
Barneveld, *U.S.A.* 79 C9
Barngo, *Australia* 62 D4
Barnhart, *U.S.A.* 81 K4
Barnsley, *U.K.* 10 D6
Barnstaple, *U.K.* 11 F3
Barnsville, *U.S.A.* 80 B6
Baro, *Nigeria* 50 G6
Baroda = Vadodara, *India* 42 H5
Baroda, *India* 42 G7
Baroe, *S. Africa* 56 E3
Baron Ra., *Australia* 60 D4
Barpeta, *India* 41 F17
Barques, Pte. aux, *U.S.A.* 76 C4
Barquísimeto, *Venezuela* 92 A5
Barra, *Brazil* 93 F10
Barra, *U.K.* 12 E1
Barra, Sd. of, *U.K.* 12 D1
Barra de Navidad, *Mexico* 86 D4
Barra do Corda, *Brazil* 93 E9
Barra do Piraí, *Brazil* 95 A7
Barra Falsa, Pta. da, *Mozam.* 57 C6
Barra Hd., *U.K.* 12 E1
Barra Mansa, *Brazil* 95 A7
Barraba, *Australia* 63 E5
Barrackpur = Barakpur, *India* 43 H13
Barranca, *Lima, Peru* 92 F3
Barranca, *Loreto, Peru* 92 D3
Barrancabermeja, *Colombia* 92 B4
Barrancas, *Venezuela* 92 B6
Barrancos, *Portugal* 19 C2
Barranqueras, *Argentina* 94 B4

Barranquilla, *Colombia* 92 A4
Barras, *Brazil* 93 D10
Barraute, *Canada* 70 C4
Barre, *Mass., U.S.A.* 75 B12
Barre, *Vt., U.S.A.* 79 B12
Barreal, *Argentina* 94 C2
Barreiras, *Brazil* 93 F10
Barreirinhas, *Brazil* 93 D10
Barreiro, *Portugal* 19 C1
Barreiros, *Brazil* 93 E11
Barren, Nosy, *Madag.* 57 B7
Barretos, *Brazil* 93 H9
Barrhead, *Canada* 72 C6
Barrie, *Canada* 70 D4
Barrier Ra., *Australia* 63 E3
Barrière, *Canada* 72 C4
Barrington, *U.S.A.* 79 E13
Barrington L., *Canada* 73 B8
Barrington Tops, *Australia* 63 E5
Barringun, *Australia* 63 D4
Barrow, *U.S.A.* 68 A4
Barrow —►, *Ireland* 13 D4
Barrow, C., *U.S.A.* 66 B4
Barrow Creek, *Australia* 62 C1
Barrow I., *Australia* 60 D2
Barrow-in-Furness, *U.K.* 10 C4
Barrow Pt., *Australia* 62 A3
Barrow Ra., *Australia* 61 E4
Barrow Str., *Canada* 4 B3
Barry, *U.K.* 11 F4
Barry's Bay, *Canada* 70 C4
Barsat, *Pakistan* 43 A5
Barsham, *Syria* 44 C4
Barsi, *India* 40 K9
Barsoi, *India* 41 G15
Barstow, *Calif., U.S.A.* 85 L9
Barstow, *Tex., U.S.A.* 81 K3
Barthélemy, Col, *Vietnam* 38 C5
Bartica, *Guyana* 92 B7
Bartlesville, *U.S.A.* 81 G7
Bartlett, *Calif., U.S.A.* 84 J8
Bartlett, *Tex., U.S.A.* 81 K6
Bartlett, L., *Canada* 72 A5
Bartolomeu Dias, *Mozam.* 55 G4
Barton, *Australia* 61 F5
Barton upon Humber, *U.K.* 10 D7
Bartow, *U.S.A.* 77 M5
Barú, Volcan, *Panama* 88 E3
Barumba, *Zaïre* 54 B1
Barwani, *India* 42 H6
Barzān, *Iraq* 44 B5
Bas-Rhin □, *France* 18 B7
Bāsa'idū, *Iran* 45 E7
Basal, *Pakistan* 42 C5
Basankusa, *Zaïre* 52 D3
Basawa, *Afghan.* 42 B4
Bascuñán, C., *Chile* 94 B1
Basel, *Switz.* 16 E3
Bāshī, *Iran* 45 D6
Bashkir Republic □, *Russia* 24 D10
Basilan, *Phil.* 37 C6
Basilan Str., *Phil.* 37 C6
Basildon, *U.K.* 11 F8
Basilicata □, *Italy* 20 D7
Basim = Washim, *India* 40 J10
Basin, *U.S.A.* 82 D9
Basingstoke, *U.K.* 11 F6
Baskatong, Rés., *Canada* 70 C4
Basle = Basel, *Switz.* 16 E3
Basoda, *India* 42 H7
Basoka, *Zaïre* 54 B1
Basongo, *Zaïre* 52 E4
Basque Provinces = País Vasco □, *Spain* 19 A4
Basra = Al Başrah, *Iraq* 44 D5
Bass Rock, *U.K.* 12 E6
Bass Str., *Australia* 62 F4
Bassano, *Canada* 72 C6
Bassano del Grappa, *Italy* 20 B4
Bassas da India, *Ind. Oc.* 53 J7
Basse-Terre, *Guadeloupe* 89 C7
Bassein, *Burma* 41 L19
Basseterre, *St. Christopher-Nevis* 89 C7
Bassett, *Nebr., U.S.A.* 80 D5
Bassett, *Va., U.S.A.* 77 G6
Bassi, *India* 42 D7
Bassigny, *France* 18 C6
Bassikounou, *Mauritania* 50 E3
Bastak, *Iran* 45 E7
Baştām, *Iran* 45 B7
Bastar, *India* 41 K12
Basti, *India* 43 F10
Bastia, *France* 18 E9
Bastogne, *Belgium* 15 D5
Bastrop, *U.S.A.* 81 K6
Bat Yam, *Israel* 47 C3
Bata, *Eq. Guin.* 52 D1
Bataan, *Phil.* 37 B6
Batabanó, *Cuba* 88 B3
Batabanó, G. de, *Cuba* 88 B3
Batac, *Phil.* 37 A6
Batagoy, *Russia* 27 C14
Batalha, *Portugal* 19 C1
Batama, *Zaïre* 54 B2
Batamay, *Russia* 27 C13
Batang, *Indonesia* 37 G13
Batangafo, *C.A.R.* 51 G8
Batangas, *Phil.* 37 B6
Batanta, *Indonesia* 37 E8
Batatais, *Brazil* 95 A6
Batavia, *U.S.A.* 78 D6
Batchelor, *Australia* 60 B5
Bateman's B., *Australia* 63 F5
Batemans Bay, *Australia* 63 F5
Bates Ra., *Australia* 61 E3
Batesburg, *U.S.A.* 77 J5
Batesville, *Ark., U.S.A.* 81 H9
Batesville, *Miss., U.S.A.* 81 H10
Batesville, *Tex., U.S.A.* 81 L5
Bath, *U.K.* 11 F5
Bath, *Maine, U.S.A.* 71 D6
Bath, *N.Y., U.S.A.* 78 D7
Batheay, *Cambodia* 39 G5
Bathgate, *U.K.* 12 F5
Bathurst = Banjul, *Gambia* 50 F1
Bathurst, *Australia* 63 E4
Bathurst, *Canada* 71 C6
Bathurst, *S. Africa* 56 E4
Bathurst, C., *Canada* 68 A7
Bathurst B., *Australia* 62 A3
Bathurst Harb., *Australia* 62 G4
Bathurst I., *Australia* 60 B5
Bathurst I., *Canada* 4 B2
Bathurst Inlet, *Canada* 68 B9
Batlow, *Australia* 63 F4
Batna, *Algeria* 50 A6
Batoka, *Zambia* 55 F2
Baton Rouge, *U.S.A.* 81 K9
Batong, Ko, *Thailand* 39 J2
Batopilas, *Mexico* 86 B3
Batouri, *Cameroon* 52 D2
Battambang, *Cambodia* 38 F4
Batticaloa, *Sri Lanka* 40 R12
Battle, *U.K.* 11 G8
Battle —►, *Canada* 73 C7
Battle Camp, *Australia* 62 B3
Battle Creek, *U.S.A.* 76 D3
Battle Ground, *U.S.A.* 84 E4
Battle Harbour, *Canada* 71 B8
Battle Lake, *U.S.A.* 80 B7
Battle Mountain, *U.S.A.* 82 F5
Battlefields, *Zimbabwe* 55 F2
Battleford, *Canada* 73 C7
Batu, *Ethiopia* 46 F2
Batu, Kepulauan, *Indonesia* 36 E1
Batu Caves, *Malaysia* 39 L3
Batu Gajah, *Malaysia* 39 K3
Batu Is. = Batu, Kepulauan, *Indonesia* 36 E1
Batu Pahat, *Malaysia* 39 M4
Batuata, *Indonesia* 37 F6
Batumi, *Georgia* 25 F7
Baturaja, *Indonesia* 36 E2
Baturité, *Brazil* 93 D11
Bau, *Malaysia* 36 D4
Baubau, *Indonesia* 37 F6
Bauchi, *Nigeria* 50 F6
Baudette, *U.S.A.* 80 A7
Bauer, C., *Australia* 63 E1
Bauhinia Downs, *Australia* 62 C4
Bauru, *Brazil* 95 A6
Baús, *Brazil* 93 G8
Bautzen, *Germany* 16 C7
Bavānāt, *Iran* 45 D7
Bavaria = Bayern □, *Germany* 16 D5
Bavi Sadri, *India* 42 G6
Bavispe —►, *Mexico* 86 B3
Bawdwin, *Burma* 41 H20
Bawean, *Indonesia* 36 F4
Bawku, *Ghana* 50 F4
Bawlake, *Burma* 41 K20
Baxley, *U.S.A.* 77 K4
Baxter Springs, *U.S.A.* 81 G7
Bay, L. de, *Phil.* 37 B6
Bay Bulls, *Canada* 71 C9
Bay City, *Mich., U.S.A.* 76 D4
Bay City, *Oreg., U.S.A.* 82 D2
Bay City, *Tex., U.S.A.* 81 L7
Bay de Verde, *Canada* 71 C9
Bay Minette, *U.S.A.* 77 K2
Bay St. Louis, *U.S.A.* 81 K10
Bay Springs, *U.S.A.* 81 K10
Bay View, *N.Z.* 59 H6
Baya, *Zaïre* 55 E2
Bayamo, *Cuba* 88 B4
Bayamón, *Puerto Rico* 89 C6
Bayan Har Shan, *China* 32 C4
Bayan Hot = Alxa Zuoqi, *China* 34 E3
Bayan Obo, *China* 34 D5
Bayan-Ovoo, *Mongolia* 34 C4
Bayana, *India* 42 F7
Bayanaul, *Kazakhstan* 26 D8
Bayandalay, *Mongolia* 34 C2
Bayanhongor, *Mongolia* 32 B5
Bayard, *U.S.A.* 80 E3
Baybay, *Phil.* 37 B6
Bayern □, *Germany* 16 D5
Bayeux, *France* 18 B3
Bayfield, *Canada* 78 C3
Bayfield, *U.S.A.* 80 B9
Baykal, Oz., *Russia* 27 D11
Baykit, *Russia* 27 C10
Baykonur, *Kazakhstan* 26 E7
Baymak, *Russia* 24 D10
Baynes Mts., *Namibia* 56 B1
Bayombong, *Phil.* 37 A6
Bayonne, *France* 18 E3
Bayonne, *U.S.A.* 79 F10
Bayovar, *Peru* 92 E2
Bayram-Ali, *Turkmenistan* 26 F7
Bayreuth, *Germany* 16 D5
Bayrūt, *Lebanon* 47 B4
Bayt Lahm, *Jordan* 47 D4
Baytown, *U.S.A.* 81 L7
Baza, *Spain* 19 D4
Bazaruto, I. do, *Mozam.* 57 C6
Bazmān, Kūh-e, *Iran* 45 D9
Beach, *U.S.A.* 80 B3
Beach City, *U.S.A.* 78 F3
Beachport, *Australia* 63 F2
Beachy Hd., *U.K.* 11 G8
Beacon, *Australia* 61 F2
Beacon, *U.S.A.* 79 E11
Beaconia, *Canada* 73 C9
Beagle, Canal, *S. Amer.* 96 G3
Beagle Bay, *Australia* 60 C3
Bealanana, *Madag.* 57 A8
Beamsville, *Canada* 78 C5
Bear —►, *U.S.A.* 84 G5
Bear I., *Ireland* 13 E2
Bear L., *B.C., Canada* 72 B3
Bear L., *Man., Canada* 73 B9
Bear L., *U.S.A.* 82 E8
Bearcreek, *U.S.A.* 82 D9
Beardmore, *Canada* 70 C2
Beardmore Glacier, *Antarctica* 5 E11
Beardstown, *U.S.A.* 80 F9
Béarn, *France* 18 E3
Bearpaw Mts., *U.S.A.* 82 B9
Bearskin Lake, *Canada* 70 B1
Beata, C., *Dom. Rep.* 89 C5
Beata, I., *Dom. Rep.* 89 C5
Beatrice, *U.S.A.* 80 E6
Beatrice, *Zimbabwe* 55 F3
Beatrice, C., *Australia* 62 A2
Beatton —►, *Canada* 72 B4
Beatton River, *Canada* 72 B4
Beatty, *U.S.A.* 83 H5
Beauce, Plaine de la, *France* 18 B4
Beauceville, *Canada* 71 C5
Beaudesert, *Australia* 63 D5
Beaufort, *Malaysia* 36 C5
Beaufort, *N.C., U.S.A.* 77 H7
Beaufort, *S.C., U.S.A.* 77 J5
Beaufort Sea, *Arctic* 4 B1
Beaufort West, *S. Africa* 56 E3
Beauharnois, *Canada* 70 C5
Beaulieu —►, *Canada* 72 A6
Beauly, *U.K.* 12 D4
Beauly —►, *U.K.* 12 D4
Beaumaris, *U.K.* 10 D3
Beaumont, *Calif., U.S.A.* 85 M10
Beaumont, *Tex., U.S.A.* 81 K7
Beaune, *France* 18 C6
Beauséjour, *Canada* 73 C9
Beauvais, *France* 18 B5
Beauval, *Canada* 73 B7
Beaver, *Alaska, U.S.A.* 68 B5
Beaver, *Okla., U.S.A.* 81 G4
Beaver, *Pa., U.S.A.* 78 F4
Beaver, *Utah, U.S.A.* 83 G7
Beaver —►, *B.C., Canada* 72 B4
Beaver —►, *Ont., Canada* 70 A2
Beaver —►, *Sask., Canada* 73 B7
Beaver City, *U.S.A.* 80 E5
Beaver Dam, *U.S.A.* 80 D10
Beaver Falls, *U.S.A.* 78 F4
Beaver Hill L., *Canada* 73 C10
Beaver I., *U.S.A.* 76 C3
Beaverhill L., *Alta., Canada* 72 C6
Beaverhill L., *N.W.T., Canada* 73 A8
Beaverlodge, *Canada* 72 B5
Beavermouth, *Canada* 72 C5
Beaverstone —►, *Canada* 70 B2
Beaverton, *Canada* 78 B5
Beaverton, *U.S.A.* 84 E4
Beawar, *India* 42 F6
Bebedouro, *Brazil* 95 A6
Beboa, *Madag.* 57 B7
Beccles, *U.K.* 11 E9
Bečej, *Serbia, Yug.* 21 B9
Béchar, *Algeria* 50 B4
Beckley, *U.S.A.* 76 G5
Bedford, *Canada* 70 C5
Bedford, *S. Africa* 56 E4
Bedford, *U.K.* 11 E7
Bedford, *Ind., U.S.A.* 76 F2
Bedford, *Iowa, U.S.A.* 80 E7
Bedford, *Ohio, U.S.A.* 78 E3
Bedford, *Pa., U.S.A.* 78 F6
Bedford, *Va., U.S.A.* 76 G6
Bedford, C., *Australia* 62 B4
Bedford Downs, *Australia* 60 C4
Bedfordshire □, *U.K.* 11 E7
Bedourie, *Australia* 62 C2
Beech Grove, *U.S.A.* 76 F2
Beechy, *Canada* 73 C7
Beenleigh, *Australia* 63 D5
Be'er Menuḥa, *Israel* 44 D2
Be'er Sheva', *Israel* 47 D3
Beersheba = Be'er Sheva', *Israel* 47 D3
Beeston, *U.K.* 10 E6
Beetaloo, *Australia* 62 B1
Beeville, *U.S.A.* 81 L6
Befale, *Zaïre* 52 D4
Befandriana, *Madag.* 57 C7
Befotaka, *Madag.* 57 C8
Bega, *Australia* 63 F4
Begusarai, *India* 43 G12
Behābād, *Iran* 45 C8
Behara, *Madag.* 57 C8
Behbehān, *Iran* 45 D6
Behshahr, *Iran* 45 B7
Bei Jiang —►, *China* 33 D6
Bei'an, *China* 33 B7
Beihai, *China* 33 D5
Beijing, *China* 34 E9
Beijing □, *China* 34 E9
Beilen, *Neths.* 15 B6
Beilpajah, *Australia* 63 E3
Beipiao, *China* 35 D11
Beira, *Mozam.* 55 F3
Beira-Alta, *Portugal* 19 B2
Beira-Baixa, *Portugal* 19 B2
Beira-Litoral, *Portugal* 19 B1
Beirut = Bayrūt, *Lebanon* 47 B4
Beitaolaizhao, *China* 35 B13
Beitbridge, *Zimbabwe* 55 G3
Beizhen, *Liaoning, China* 35 D11
Beizhen, *Shandong, China* 35 F10
Beizhengzhen, *China* 35 B12
Beja, *Portugal* 19 C2
Béja, *Tunisia* 50 A6
Bejaia, *Algeria* 50 A6
Bejestān, *Iran* 45 C8
Bekasi, *Indonesia* 37 G12
Békéscsaba, *Hungary* 17 E10
Bekily, *Madag.* 57 C8
Bekok, *Malaysia* 39 L4
Bela, *India* 43 G9
Bela, *Pakistan* 42 F2
Bela Crkva, *Serbia, Yug.* 21 B9
Bela Vista, *Brazil* 94 A4
Bela Vista, *Mozam.* 57 D5
Belarus = Belorussia ■, *Europe* 24 D4
Belau I., *Pac. Oc.* 64 G5
Belavenona, *Madag.* 57 C8
Belawan, *Indonesia* 36 D1
Belaya —►, *Russia* 24 C9
Belaya Tserkov, *Ukraine* 25 E5
Belcher Is., *Canada* 69 C12
Belden, *U.S.A.* 84 E5
Belebey, *Russia* 24 D9
Belém, *Brazil* 93 D9
Belén, *Argentina* 94 B2
Belén, *Paraguay* 94 A4
Belen, *U.S.A.* 83 J10
Belet Uen, *Somali Rep.* 46 G4
Belev, *Russia* 24 D6
Belfair, *U.S.A.* 84 C4
Belfast, *S. Africa* 57 D5
Belfast, *U.K.* 13 B6
Belfast, *Maine, U.S.A.* 71 D6
Belfast, *N.Y., U.S.A.* 78 D6
Belfast □, *U.K.* 13 B6
Belfast L., *U.K.* 13 B6
Belfield, *U.S.A.* 80 B3
Belfort, *France* 18 C7
Belfort, Territoire de □, *France* 18 C7
Belfry, *U.S.A.* 82 D9
Belgaum, *India* 40 M9
Belgium ■, *Europe* 15 D5
Belgorod, *Russia* 25 D6
Belgorod-Dnestrovskiy, *Ukraine* 25 E5
Belgrade = Beograd, *Serbia, Yug.* 21 B9
Belgrade, *U.S.A.* 82 D8
Belhaven, *U.S.A.* 77 H7
Beli Drim —►, *Europe* 21 C9
Belinga, *Gabon* 52 D2
Belinyu, *Indonesia* 36 E3
Belitung, *Indonesia* 36 E3
Belize ■, *Cent. Amer.* 87 D7
Belize City, *Belize* 87 D7
Belkovskiy, Ostrov, *Russia* 27 B14
Bell —►, *Canada* 70 C4
Bell Bay, *Australia* 62 G4
Bell I., *Canada* 71 B8
Bell-Irving —►, *Canada* 72 B3
Bell Peninsula, *Canada* 69 B11
Bell Ville, *Argentina* 94 C3
Bella Bella, *Canada* 72 C3
Bella Coola, *Canada* 72 C3
Bella Unión, *Uruguay* 94 C4
Bella Vista, *Corrientes, Argentina* 94 B4
Bella Vista, *Tucuman, Argentina* 94 B2
Bellaire, *U.S.A.* 78 F4
Bellary, *India* 40 M10
Bellata, *Australia* 63 D4
Belle Fourche, *U.S.A.* 80 C3
Belle Fourche —►, *U.S.A.* 80 C3
Belle Glade, *U.S.A.* 77 M5
Belle-Ile, *France* 18 C2
Belle Isle, *Canada* 71 B8
Belle Isle, Str. of, *Canada* 71 B8
Belle Plaine, *Iowa, U.S.A.* 80 E8
Belle Plaine, *Minn., U.S.A.* 80 C8
Belledune, *Canada* 71 C6
Bellefontaine, *U.S.A.* 76 E4
Bellefonte, *U.S.A.* 78 F7
Belleoram, *Canada* 71 C8
Belleville, *Canada* 70 D4
Belleville, *Ill., U.S.A.* 80 F10
Belleville, *Kans., U.S.A.* 80 F6
Belleville, *N.Y., U.S.A.* 79 C8
Bellevue, *Canada* 72 D6
Bellevue, *Idaho, U.S.A.* 82 E6
Bellevue, *Ohio, U.S.A.* 78 E2
Bellevue, *Wash., U.S.A.* 84 C4
Bellin, *Canada* 69 B13
Bellingen, *Australia* 63 E5
Bellingham, *U.S.A.* 84 B4
Bellingshausen Sea, *Antarctica* 5 C17
Bellinzona, *Switz.* 16 E4
Bellows Falls, *U.S.A.* 79 C12
Bellpat, *Pakistan* 42 E3
Belluno, *Italy* 20 A5
Bellville, *U.S.A.* 81 L6
Bellwood, *U.S.A.* 78 F6
Bélmez, *Spain* 19 C3
Belmont, *Australia* 63 E5
Belmont, *Canada* 78 D3
Belmont, *S. Africa* 56 D3
Belmont, *U.S.A.* 78 D6
Belmonte, *Brazil* 93 G11
Belmopan, *Belize* 87 D7
Belmullet, *Ireland* 13 B2
Belo Horizonte, *Brazil* 93 G10
Belo-sur-Mer, *Madag.* 57 C7
Belo-Tsiribihina, *Madag.* 57 B7
Belogorsk, *Russia* 27 D13
Beloha, *Madag.* 57 D8
Beloit, *Kans., U.S.A.* 80 F5
Beloit, *Wis., U.S.A.* 80 D10
Belomorsk, *Russia* 24 B5
Belonia, *India* 41 H17
Beloretsk, *Russia* 24 D10
Belorussia ■, *Europe* 24 D4
Belovo, *Russia* 26 D9
Beloye, Oz., *Russia* 24 B6
Beloye More, *Russia* 24 A6
Belozersk, *Russia* 24 B6
Beltana, *Australia* 63 E2
Belterra, *Brazil* 93 D8
Belton, *S.C., U.S.A.* 77 H4
Belton, *Tex., U.S.A.* 81 K6
Belton Res., *U.S.A.* 81 K6
Beltsy, *Moldavia* 25 E4
Belturbet, *Ireland* 13 B4
Belukha, *Russia* 26 E9
Beluran, *Malaysia* 36 C5
Belvidere, *Ill., U.S.A.* 80 D10
Belvidere, *N.J., U.S.A.* 79 F9
Belyando —►, *Australia* 62 C4
Belyy, Ostrov, *Russia* 26 B8
Belyy Yar, *Russia* 26 D9
Belzoni, *U.S.A.* 81 J9
Bemaraha, Lembalemban' i, *Madag.* 57 B7
Bemarivo, *Madag.* 57 C7
Bemarivo —►, *Madag.* 57 B8
Bemavo, *Madag.* 57 C8
Bembéréke, *Benin* 50 F5
Bembesi, *Zimbabwe* 55 F2
Bembesi —►, *Zimbabwe* 55 F2
Bemidji, *U.S.A.* 80 B7
Ben, *Iran* 45 C6
Ben Cruachan, *U.K.* 12 E3
Ben Dearg, *U.K.* 12 D4
Ben Gardane, *Tunisia* 51 B7
Ben Hope, *U.K.* 12 C4
Ben Lawers, *U.K.* 12 E4
Ben Lomond, *N.S.W., Australia* 63 E5
Ben Lomond, *Tas., Australia* 62 G4
Ben Lomond, *U.K.* 12 E4
Ben Luc, *Vietnam* 39 G6
Ben Macdhui, *U.K.* 12 D5
Ben Mhor, *U.K.* 12 D1
Ben More, *Central, U.K.* 12 E4
Ben More, *Strath., U.K.* 12 E2
Ben More Assynt, *U.K.* 12 C4
Ben Nevis, *U.K.* 12 E4
Ben Quang, *Vietnam* 38 D6
Ben Tre, *Vietnam* 39 G6
Ben Vorlich, *U.K.* 12 E4
Ben Wyvis, *U.K.* 12 D4
Bena, *Nigeria* 50 F6
Bena Dibele, *Zaïre* 52 E4
Benagerie, *Australia* 63 E3
Benalla, *Australia* 63 F4
Benambra, Mt., *Australia* 63 F4
Benares = Varanasi, *India* 43 G10
Benavides, *U.S.A.* 81 M5
Benbecula, *U.K.* 12 D1
Benbonyathe, *Australia* 63 E2
Bencubbin, *Australia* 61 F2
Bend, *U.S.A.* 82 D3
Bender Beila, *Somali Rep.* 46 F5
Bendering, *Australia* 61 F2
Bendery, *Moldavia* 25 E4
Bendigo, *Australia* 63 F3
Benē Beraq, *Israel* 47 C3
Benenitra, *Madag.* 57 C8
Benevento, *Italy* 20 D6
Benga, *Mozam.* 55 F3
Bengal, Bay of, *Ind. Oc.* 41 K16
Bengbu, *China* 35 H9
Benghazi = Banghāzī, *Libya* 51 B9
Bengkalis, *Indonesia* 36 D2
Bengkulu, *Indonesia* 36 E2
Bengkulu □, *Indonesia* 36 E2
Bengough, *Canada* 73 D7
Benguela, *Angola* 53 G2
Benguérua, I., *Mozam.* 57 C6
Beni, *Zaïre* 54 B2
Beni —►, *Bolivia* 92 F5
Beni Abbès, *Algeria* 50 B4
Beni Mazâr, *Egypt* 51 C11
Beni Mellal, *Morocco* 50 B3
Beni Ounif, *Algeria* 50 B4
Beni Suef, *Egypt* 51 C11
Beniah L., *Canada* 72 A6
Benicia, *U.S.A.* 84 G4
Benidorm, *Spain* 19 C5
Benin ■, *Africa* 50 G5
Benin, Bight of, *W. Afr.* 50 H5
Benin City, *Nigeria* 50 G6
Benitses, *Greece* 23 A3
Benjamin Aceval, *Paraguay* 94 A4
Benjamin Constant, *Brazil* 92 D4
Benjamin Hill, *Mexico* 86 A2
Benkelman, *U.S.A.* 80 E4
Benlidi, *Australia* 62 C3

Bennett, *Canada* 72 B2
Bennett, L., *Australia* 60 D5
Bennett, Ostrov, *Russia* 27 B15
Bennettsville, *U.S.A.* 77 H6
Bennington, *U.S.A.* 79 D11
Benoni, *S. Africa* 57 D4
Benque Viejo, *Belize* 87 D7
Benson, *U.S.A.* 83 L8
Bent, *Iran* 45 E8
Benteng, *Indonesia* 37 F6
Bentinck I., *Australia* 62 B2
Bento Gonçalves, *Brazil* 95 B5
Benton, *Ark., U.S.A.* 81 H8
Benton, *Calif., U.S.A.* 84 H8
Benton, *Ill., U.S.A.* 80 F10
Benton Harbor, *U.S.A.* 76 D2
Bentung, *Malaysia* 39 L3
Benue —►, *Nigeria* 50 G6
Benxi, *China* 35 D12
Beo, *Indonesia* 37 D7
Beograd, *Serbia, Yug.* 21 B9
Beowawe, *U.S.A.* 82 F5
Beppu, *Japan* 31 H5
Berau, Teluk, *Indonesia* 37 E8
Berber, *Sudan* 51 E11
Berbera, *Somali Rep.* 46 E4
Berbérati, *C.A.R.* 52 D3
Berberia, C. del, *Spain* 22 C7
Berbice —►, *Guyana* 92 B7
Berdichev, *Ukraine* 25 E4
Berdsk, *Russia* 26 D9
Berdyansk, *Ukraine* 25 E6
Berea, *U.S.A.* 76 G3
Berebere, *Indonesia* 37 D7
Bereda, *Somali Rep.* 46 E5
Berekum, *Ghana* 50 G4
Berens —►, *Canada* 73 C9
Berens I., *Canada* 73 C9
Berens River, *Canada* 73 C9
Berevo, *Mahajanga, Madag.* 57 B7
Berevo, *Toliara, Madag.* 57 B7
Berezina —►, *Belorussia* 24 D5
Berezniki, *Russia* 26 D6
Berezovo, *Russia* 24 B11
Bérgamo, *Italy* 20 B3
Bergen, *Neths.* 15 B4
Bergen, *Norway* 9 F8
Bergen, *U.S.A.* 78 C7
Bergen-op-Zoom, *Neths.* 15 C4
Bergerac, *France* 18 D4
Bergum, *Neths.* 15 A5
Bergville, *S. Africa* 57 D4
Berhala, Selat, *Indonesia* 36 E2
Berhampore = Baharampur, *India* 43 G13
Berhampur, *India* 41 K14
Bering Sea, *Pac. Oc.* 68 C1
Bering Str., *U.S.A.* 68 B3
Beringen, *Belgium* 15 C5
Beringovskiy, *Russia* 27 C18
Berisso, *Argentina* 94 C4
Berja, *Spain* 19 D4
Berkeley, *U.K.* 11 F5
Berkeley, *U.S.A.* 84 H4
Berkeley Springs, *U.S.A.* 76 F6
Berkner I., *Antarctica* 5 D18
Berkshire □, *U.K.* 11 F6
Berland —►, *Canada* 72 C5
Berlin, *Germany* 16 B6
Berlin, *Md., U.S.A.* 76 F8
Berlin, *N.H., U.S.A.* 79 B13
Berlin, *Wis., U.S.A.* 76 D1
Bermejo —►, *Formosa, Argentina* 94 B4
Bermejo —►, *San Juan, Argentina* 94 C2
Bermuda ■, *Atl. Oc.* 2 C6
Bern, *Switz.* 16 E3
Bernado, *U.S.A.* 83 J10
Bernalillo, *U.S.A.* 83 J10
Bernardo de Irigoyen, *Argentina* 95 B5
Bernardo O'Higgins □, *Chile* 94 C1
Bernasconi, *Argentina* 94 D3
Bernburg, *Germany* 16 C5
Berne = Bern, *Switz.* 16 E3
Bernier I., *Australia* 61 D1
Beroroha, *Madag.* 57 C8
Beroun, *Czech.* 16 D7
Berrechid, *Morocco* 50 B3
Berri, *Australia* 63 E3
Berry, *Australia* 63 E5
Berry, *France* 18 C5
Berry Is., *Bahamas* 88 A4
Berryessa, L., *U.S.A.* 84 G4
Berryville, *U.S.A.* 81 G8
Berthold, *U.S.A.* 80 A4
Berthoud, *U.S.A.* 80 E2
Bertoua, *Cameroon* 52 D2
Bertrand, *U.S.A.* 80 E5
Berufjörður, *Iceland* 8 D6
Berwick, *U.S.A.* 79 E8
Berwick-upon-Tweed, *U.K.* 10 B5
Berwyn Mts., *U.K.* 10 E4
Besal, *Pakistan* 43 B5
Besalampy, *Madag.* 57 B7
Besançon, *France* 18 C7
Besar, *Indonesia* 36 E5
Besnard L., *Canada* 73 B7
Besor, N. —►, *Egypt* 47 D3
Bessarabiya, *Moldavia* 17 E14
Bessemer, *Ala., U.S.A.* 77 J2
Bessemer, *Mich., U.S.A.* 80 B9
Bet She'an, *Israel* 47 C4
Bet Shemesh, *Israel* 47 D3
Betafo, *Madag.* 57 B8
Betancuria, *Canary Is.* 22 F5
Bétaré Oya, *Cameroon* 52 C2
Bethal, *S. Africa* 57 D4
Bethanien, *Namibia* 56 D2
Bethany, *S. Africa* 56 D4
Bethany, *U.S.A.* 80 E7
Bethel, *Alaska, U.S.A.* 68 B3
Bethel, *Vt., U.S.A.* 79 C12
Bethel Park, *U.S.A.* 78 F4
Bethlehem = Bayt Lahm, *Jordan* 47 D4
Bethlehem, *S. Africa* 57 D4
Bethlehem, *U.S.A.* 79 F9
Bethulie, *S. Africa* 56 E4
Béthune, *France* 18 A5
Bethungra, *Australia* 63 E4
Betioky, *Madag.* 57 C7
Betong, *Thailand* 39 K3
Betoota, *Australia* 62 D3
Betroka, *Madag.* 57 C8
Betsiamites, *Canada* 71 C6
Betsiamites —►, *Canada* 71 C6
Betsiboka —►, *Madag.* 57 B8
Betsjoeanaland, *S. Africa* 56 D3
Bettiah, *India* 43 F11
Betul, *India* 40 J10
Betung, *Malaysia* 36 D4
Beulah, *U.S.A.* 80 B4
Beverley, *Australia* 61 F2
Beverley, *U.K.* 10 D7
Beverly, *Mass., U.S.A.* 79 D14
Beverly, *Wash., U.S.A.* 82 C4
Beverly Hills, *U.S.A.* 85 L8
Beverwijk, *Neths.* 15 B4
Beyānlū, *Iran* 44 C5
Beyla, *Guinea* 50 G3
Beyneu, *Kazakhstan* 25 E10
Beypazarı, *Turkey* 25 F5
Beyşehir Gölü, *Turkey* 25 G5
Bezhitsa, *Russia* 24 D5
Béziers, *France* 18 E5
Bezwada = Vijayawada, *India* 41 L12
Bhachau, *India* 40 H7
Bhadarwah, *India* 43 C6
Bhadrakh, *India* 41 J15
Bhadravati, *India* 40 N9
Bhagalpur, *India* 43 G12
Bhakkar, *Pakistan* 42 D4
Bhakra Dam, *India* 42 D7
Bhamo, *Burma* 41 G20
Bhandara, *India* 40 J11
Bhanrer Ra., *India* 42 H8
Bharat = India ■, *Asia* 40 K11
Bharatpur, *India* 42 F7
Bhatinda, *India* 42 D6
Bhatpara, *India* 43 H13
Bhaun, *Pakistan* 42 C5
Bhaunagar = Bhavnagar, *India* 42 J5
Bhavnagar, *India* 42 J5
Bhawanipatna, *India* 41 K12
Bhera, *Pakistan* 42 C5
Bhilsa = Vidisha, *India* 42 H7
Bhilwara, *India* 42 G6
Bhima —►, *India* 40 L10
Bhimavaram, *India* 41 L12
Bhimbar, *Pakistan* 43 C6
Bhind, *India* 43 F8
Bhiwandi, *India* 40 K8
Bhiwani, *India* 42 E7
Bhola, *Bangla.* 41 H17
Bhopal, *India* 42 H7
Bhubaneshwar, *India* 41 J14
Bhuj, *India* 42 H3
Bhumiphol Dam = Phumiphon, Khuan, *Thailand* 38 D2
Bhusaval, *India* 40 J9
Bhutan ■, *Asia* 41 F17
Biafra, B. of = Bonny, Bight of, *Africa* 52 D1
Biak, *Indonesia* 37 E9
Biała Podlaska, *Poland* 17 B11
Białystok, *Poland* 17 B11
Biārjmand, *Iran* 45 B7
Biaro, *Indonesia* 37 D7
Biarritz, *France* 18 E3
Bibai, *Japan* 30 C10
Bibala, *Angola* 53 G2
Bibby I., *Canada* 73 A10
Biberach, *Germany* 16 D4
Bibiani, *Ghana* 50 G4
Biboohra, *Australia* 62 B4
Bibungwa, *Zaire* 54 C2
Bic, *Canada* 71 C6
Bickerton I., *Australia* 62 A2
Bicknell, *Ind., U.S.A.* 76 F2
Bicknell, *Utah, U.S.A.* 83 G8
Bida, *Nigeria* 50 G6
Bidar, *India* 40 L10
Biddeford, *U.S.A.* 71 D5
Bideford, *U.K.* 11 F3
Bidon 5 = Poste Maurice Cortier, *Algeria* 50 D5
Bidor, *Malaysia* 39 K3
Bié, Planalto de, *Angola* 53 G3
Bieber, *U.S.A.* 82 F3
Biel, *Switz.* 16 E3
Bielé Karpaty, *Czech.* 17 D8
Bielefeld, *Germany* 16 B4
Biella, *Italy* 20 B3
Bielsko-Biała, *Poland* 17 D9
Bien Hoa, *Vietnam* 39 G6
Bienfait, *Canada* 73 D8
Bienne = Biel, *Switz.* 16 E3
Bienville, L., *Canada* 70 A5
Biesiesfontein, *S. Africa* 56 E2
Big —►, *Canada* 71 B8
Big B., *Canada* 71 A7
Big Bear City, *U.S.A.* 85 L10
Big Bear L., *U.S.A.* 85 L10
Big Beaver, *Canada* 73 D7
Big Belt Mts., *U.S.A.* 82 C8
Big Bend, *Swaziland* 57 D5
Big Bend Nat. Park, *U.S.A.* 81 L3
Big Black —►, *U.S.A.* 81 J9
Big Blue —►, *U.S.A.* 80 F6
Big Cr. —►, *Canada* 72 C4
Big Creek, *U.S.A.* 84 H7
Big Cypress Swamp, *U.S.A.* 77 M5
Big Falls, *U.S.A.* 80 A8
Big Fork —►, *U.S.A.* 80 A8
Big Horn Mts. = Bighorn Mts., *U.S.A.* 82 D10
Big Lake, *U.S.A.* 81 K4
Big Moose, *U.S.A.* 79 C10
Big Muddy —►, *U.S.A.* 80 A2
Big Pine, *U.S.A.* 83 H4
Big Piney, *U.S.A.* 82 E8
Big Quill L., *Canada* 73 C8
Big Rapids, *U.S.A.* 76 D3
Big River, *Canada* 73 C7
Big Run, *U.S.A.* 78 F6
Big Sable Pt., *U.S.A.* 76 C2
Big Sand L., *Canada* 73 B9
Big Sandy, *U.S.A.* 82 B8
Big Sandy Cr. —►, *U.S.A.* 80 F3
Big Sioux —►, *U.S.A.* 80 D6
Big Spring, *U.S.A.* 81 J4
Big Springs, *U.S.A.* 80 E3
Big Stone City, *U.S.A.* 80 C6
Big Stone Gap, *U.S.A.* 77 G4
Big Stone L., *U.S.A.* 80 C6
Big Sur, *U.S.A.* 84 J5
Big Timber, *U.S.A.* 82 D9
Big Trout L., *Canada* 70 B1
Bigfork, *U.S.A.* 82 B6
Biggar, *Canada* 73 C7
Biggar, *U.K.* 12 F5
Bigge I., *Australia* 60 B4
Biggenden, *Australia* 63 D5
Biggs, *U.S.A.* 84 F5
Bighorn, *U.S.A.* 82 C10
Bighorn —►, *U.S.A.* 82 C10
Bighorn Mts., *U.S.A.* 82 D10
Bigorre, *France* 18 E4
Bigstone L., *Canada* 73 C9
Bigwa, *Tanzania* 54 D4
Bihać, *Bos. & H., Yug.* 20 B6
Bihar, *India* 43 G11
Bihar □, *India* 43 G11
Biharamulo, *Tanzania* 54 C3
Biharamulo □, *Tanzania* 54 C3
Bijagós, Arquipélago dos, *Guinea-Biss.* 50 F1
Bijaipur, *India* 42 F7
Bijapur, *Karnataka, India* 40 L9
Bijapur, *Mad. P., India* 41 K12
Bījār, *Iran* 44 C5
Bijeljina, *Bos. & H., Yug.* 21 B8
Bijnor, *India* 42 E8
Bikaner, *India* 42 E5
Bikapur, *India* 43 F10
Bikeqi, *China* 34 D6
Bikfayyā, *Lebanon* 47 B4
Bikin, *Russia* 27 E14
Bikin —►, *Russia* 30 A7
Bikini Atoll, *Pac. Oc.* 64 F8
Bilara, *India* 42 F5
Bilaspur, *Mad. P., India* 43 H10
Bilaspur, *Punjab, India* 42 D7
Bilauk Taungdan, *Thailand* 38 F2
Bilbao, *Spain* 19 A4
Bildudalur, *Iceland* 8 D2
Bilecik, *Turkey* 25 F5
Bilibino, *Russia* 27 C17
Bilibiza, *Mozam.* 55 E5
Bilir, *Russia* 27 C14
Bill, *U.S.A.* 80 D2
Billabalong, *Australia* 61 E2
Billiluna, *Australia* 60 C4
Billingham, *U.K.* 10 C6
Billings, *U.S.A.* 82 D9
Billiton Is. = Belitung, *Indonesia* 36 E3
Bilma, *Niger* 51 E7
Biloela, *Australia* 62 C5
Biloxi, *U.S.A.* 81 K10
Bilpa Morea Claypan, *Australia* 62 D2
Biltine, *Chad* 51 F9
Bilyana, *Australia* 62 B4
Bima, *Indonesia* 37 F5
Bimbo, *C.A.R.* 52 D3
Bimini Is., *Bahamas* 88 A4
Bin Xian, *Heilongjiang, China* 35 B14
Bin Xian, *Shaanxi, China* 34 G5
Bina-Etawah, *India* 42 G8
Bināb, *Iran* 45 B6
Binalbagan, *Phil.* 37 B6
Binalong, *Australia* 63 E4
Binālūd, Kūh-e, *Iran* 45 B8
Binatang, *Malaysia* 36 D4
Binbee, *Australia* 62 C4
Binche, *Belgium* 15 D4
Binda, *Australia* 63 D4
Bindle, *Australia* 63 D4
Bindura, *Zimbabwe* 55 F3
Bingara, *N.S.W., Australia* 63 D5
Bingara, *Queens., Australia* 63 D3
Bingham, *U.S.A.* 71 C6
Bingham Canyon, *U.S.A.* 82 F7
Binghamton, *U.S.A.* 79 D9
Binh Dinh = An Nhon, *Vietnam* 38 F7
Binh Khe, *Vietnam* 38 F7
Binh Son, *Vietnam* 38 E7
Binhai, *China* 35 G10
Binisatua, *Spain* 22 B11
Binjai, *Indonesia* 36 D1
Binnaway, *Australia* 63 E4
Binongko, *Indonesia* 37 F6
Binscarth, *Canada* 73 C8
Bintan, *Indonesia* 36 D2
Bintulu, *Malaysia* 36 D4
Bintuni, *Indonesia* 37 E8
Binzert = Bizerte, *Tunisia* 50 A6
Bío Bío □, *Chile* 94 D1
Bioko, *Eq. Guin.* 50 H6
Bir, *India* 40 K9
Bîr Abu Muḩammad, *Egypt* 47 F3
Bi'r ad Dabbāghāt, *Jordan* 47 E4
Bi'r al Butayyihāt, *Jordan* 47 F4
Bi'r al Mārī, *Jordan* 47 E4
Bi'r al Qattār, *Jordan* 47 F4
Bir Autrun, *Sudan* 51 E10
Bîr Beiḍa, *Egypt* 47 E3
Bîr el 'Abd, *Egypt* 47 D2
Bîr el Biarât, *Egypt* 47 F3
Bîr el Duweidar, *Egypt* 47 E1
Bîr el Garârât, *Egypt* 47 D2
Bîr el Heisi, *Egypt* 47 F3
Bîr el Jafir, *Egypt* 47 E1
Bîr el Mâlḩi, *Egypt* 47 E2
Bîr el Thamâda, *Egypt* 47 E2
Bîr Gebeil Ḩiṣn, *Egypt* 47 E2
Bi'r Ghadīr, *Syria* 47 A6
Bîr Ḩasana, *Egypt* 47 E2
Bi'r Jadīd, *Iraq* 44 C4
Bîr Kaseiba, *Egypt* 47 E2
Bîr Lahfân, *Egypt* 47 D2
Bîr Madkûr, *Egypt* 47 E1
Bîr Mogrein, *Mauritania* 50 C2
Bi'r Muṭribah, *Kuwait* 44 D5
Bîr Qaṭia, *Egypt* 47 E1
Bîr Ungât, *Egypt* 51 D11
Bira, *Indonesia* 37 E8
Birao, *C.A.R.* 51 F9
Birawa, *Zaire* 54 C2
Birch Hills, *Canada* 73 C7
Birch I., *Canada* 73 C9
Birch L., *N.W.T., Canada* 72 A5
Birch L., *Ont., Canada* 70 B1
Birch L., *U.S.A.* 70 C1
Birch Mts., *Canada* 72 B6
Birch River, *Canada* 73 C8
Birchip, *Australia* 63 F3
Bird, *Canada* 73 B10
Bird City, *U.S.A.* 80 F4
Bird I. = Aves, I. de, *W. Indies* 89 C7
Bird I., *S. Africa* 56 E2
Birdlip, *U.K.* 11 F5
Birdsville, *Australia* 62 D2
Birdum, *Australia* 60 C5
Birein, *Israel* 47 E3
Bireuen, *Indonesia* 36 C1
Birigui, *Brazil* 95 A5
Birkenhead, *U.K.* 10 D4
Bîrlad, *Romania* 17 E13
Birmingham, *U.K.* 11 E6
Birmingham, *U.S.A.* 77 J2
Birmitrapur, *India* 41 H14
Birni Nkonni, *Niger* 50 F6
Birnin Kebbi, *Nigeria* 50 F5
Birobidzhan, *Russia* 27 E14
Birr, *Ireland* 13 C4
Birrie —►, *Australia* 63 D4
Birsilpur, *India* 42 E5
Birsk, *Russia* 24 C10
Birtle, *Canada* 73 C8
Birur, *India* 40 N9
Birzebugga, *Malta* 23 D2
Bisa, *Indonesia* 37 E7
Bisalpur, *India* 43 E8
Bisbee, *U.S.A.* 83 L9
Biscay, B. of, *Atl. Oc.* 18 F4
Biscayne B., *U.S.A.* 77 N5
Biscoe Bay, *Antarctica* 5 D13
Biscoe Is., *Antarctica* 5 C17
Biscostasing, *Canada* 70 C3
Bishkek, *Kirghizia* 26 E8
Bishnupur, *India* 43 H12
Bisho, *S. Africa* 57 E4
Bishop, *Calif., U.S.A.* 83 H4
Bishop, *Tex., U.S.A.* 81 M6
Bishop Auckland, *U.K.* 10 C6
Bishop's Falls, *Canada* 71 C8
Bishop's Stortford, *U.K.* 11 F8
Bisina, L., *Uganda* 54 B3
Biskra, *Algeria* 50 B6
Bislig, *Phil.* 37 C7
Bismarck, *U.S.A.* 80 B4
Bismarck Arch., *Papua N. G.* 64 H6
Biso, *Uganda* 54 B3
Bison, *U.S.A.* 80 C3
Bīsotūn, *Iran* 44 C5
Bispfors, *Sweden* 8 E14
Bissagos = Bijagós, Arquipélago dos, *Guinea-Biss.* 50 F1
Bissau, *Guinea-Biss.* 50 F1
Bissett, *Canada* 73 C9
Bistcho L., *Canada* 72 B5
Bistriţa, *Romania* 17 E12
Bistriţa —►, *Romania* 17 E13
Biswan, *India* 43 F9
Bitam, *Gabon* 52 D2
Bitkine, *Chad* 51 F8
Bitlis, *Turkey* 25 G7
Bitola, *Macedonia, Yug.* 21 D9
Bitolj = Bitola, *Macedonia, Yug.* 21 D9
Bitter Creek, *U.S.A.* 82 F9
Bitter L. = Buheirat-Murrat-el-Kubra, *Egypt* 51 B11
Bitterfontein, *S. Africa* 56 E2
Bitterroot —►, *U.S.A.* 82 C6
Bitterroot Range, *U.S.A.* 82 D6
Bitterwater, *U.S.A.* 84 J6
Biu, *Nigeria* 51 F7
Biwa-Ko, *Japan* 31 G8
Biwabik, *U.S.A.* 80 B8
Biyang, *China* 34 H7
Biysk, *Russia* 26 D9
Bizana, *S. Africa* 57 E4
Bizen, *Japan* 31 G7
Bizerte, *Tunisia* 50 A6
Bjargtangar, *Iceland* 8 D1
Bjelovar, *Croatia* 20 B7
Bjørnøya, *Arctic* 4 B8
Black = Da —►, *Vietnam* 38 B5
Black —►, *Canada* 78 B5
Black —►, *Ark., U.S.A.* 81 H9
Black —►, *N.Y., U.S.A.* 79 C8
Black —►, *Wis., U.S.A.* 80 D9
Black Diamond, *Canada* 72 C6
Black Forest = Schwarzwald, *Germany* 16 E4
Black Hills, *U.S.A.* 80 C3
Black I., *Canada* 73 C9
Black L., *Canada* 73 B7
Black L., *U.S.A.* 76 C3
Black Mesa, *U.S.A.* 81 G3
Black Mt. = Mynydd Du, *U.K.* 11 F4
Black Mts., *U.K.* 11 F4
Black Range, *U.S.A.* 83 K10
Black River, *Jamaica* 88 C4
Black River Falls, *U.S.A.* 80 C9
Black Sea, *Europe* 25 F6
Black Volta —►, *Africa* 50 G4
Black Warrior —►, *U.S.A.* 77 J2
Blackall, *Australia* 62 C4
Blackball, *N.Z.* 59 K3
Blackbull, *Australia* 62 B3
Blackburn, *U.K.* 10 D5
Blackduck, *U.S.A.* 80 B7
Blackfoot, *U.S.A.* 82 E7
Blackfoot —►, *U.S.A.* 82 C7
Blackfoot Res., *U.S.A.* 82 E8
Blackie, *Canada* 72 C6
Blackpool, *U.K.* 10 D4
Blackriver, *U.S.A.* 78 B1
Blacks Harbour, *Canada* 71 C6
Blacksburg, *U.S.A.* 76 G5
Blacksod B., *Ireland* 13 B2
Blackstone, *U.S.A.* 76 G6
Blackstone —►, *Canada* 72 A4
Blackstone Ra., *Australia* 61 E4
Blackville, *Canada* 71 C6
Blackwater, *Australia* 62 C4
Blackwater —►, *Ireland* 13 E4
Blackwater —►, *U.K.* 13 B5
Blackwater Cr. —►, *Australia* 63 D3
Blackwell, *U.S.A.* 81 G6
Blackwells Corner, *U.S.A.* 85 K7
Blaenau Ffestiniog, *U.K.* 10 E4
Blagodarnoye, *Russia* 25 E7
Blagoveshchensk, *Russia* 27 D13
Blaine, *U.S.A.* 84 B4
Blaine Lake, *Canada* 73 C7
Blair, *U.S.A.* 80 E6
Blair Athol, *Australia* 62 C4
Blair Atholl, *U.K.* 12 E5
Blairgowrie, *U.K.* 12 E5
Blairmore, *Canada* 72 D6
Blairsden, *U.S.A.* 84 F6
Blairsville, *U.S.A.* 78 F5
Blake Pt., *U.S.A.* 80 A10
Blakely, *U.S.A.* 77 K3
Blanc, Mont, *Alps* 18 D7
Blanca, B., *Argentina* 96 D4
Blanca Peak, *U.S.A.* 83 H11
Blanchard, *U.S.A.* 81 H6
Blanche, C., *Australia* 63 E1
Blanche, L., *S. Austral., Australia* 63 D2
Blanche, L., *W. Austral., Australia* 60 D3
Blanco, *S. Africa* 56 E3
Blanco, *U.S.A.* 81 K5
Blanco —►, *Argentina* 94 C2
Blanco, C., *Costa Rica* 88 E2
Blanco, C., *Spain* 22 B9
Blanco, C., *U.S.A.* 82 E1
Blanda —►, *Iceland* 8 D4
Blandford Forum, *U.K.* 11 G5
Blanding, *U.S.A.* 83 H9
Blankenberge, *Belgium* 15 C3
Blanquillo, *Uruguay* 95 C4
Blantyre, *Malawi* 55 F4
Blarney, *Ireland* 13 E3
Blåvands Huk, *Denmark* 9 J10
Blaydon, *U.K.* 10 C6
Blayney, *Australia* 63 E4
Blaze, Pt., *Australia* 60 B5
Blednaya, Gora, *Russia* 26 B7
Bleiburg, *Austria* 16 E7

Blekinge län □, Sweden 9 H13
Blenheim, Canada 78 D2
Blenheim, N.Z. 59 J4
Bletchley, U.K. 11 F7
Blida, Algeria 50 A5
Bligh Sound, N.Z. 59 L1
Blind River, Canada 70 C3
Blitar, Indonesia 37 H15
Blitta, Togo 50 G5
Block I., U.S.A. 79 E13
Block Island Sd., U.S.A. 79 E13
Blodgett Iceberg Tongue, Antarctica 5 C9
Bloemfontein, S. Africa 56 D4
Bloemhof, S. Africa 56 D4
Blois, France 18 C4
Blönduós, Iceland 8 D3
Bloodvein →, Canada 73 C9
Bloody Foreland, Ireland 13 A3
Bloomer, U.S.A. 80 C9
Bloomfield, Australia 62 B4
Bloomfield, Canada 78 C7
Bloomfield, Iowa, U.S.A. 80 E8
Bloomfield, N. Mex., U.S.A. 83 H10
Bloomfield, Nebr., U.S.A. 80 D6
Bloomington, Ill., U.S.A. 80 E10
Bloomington, Ind., U.S.A. 76 F2
Bloomsburg, U.S.A. 79 F8
Blora, Indonesia 37 G14
Blossburg, U.S.A. 78 E7
Blouberg, S. Africa 57 C4
Blountstown, U.S.A. 77 K3
Blue Island, U.S.A. 76 E2
Blue Lake, U.S.A. 82 F2
Blue Mesa Res., U.S.A. 83 G10
Blue Mts., Oreg., U.S.A. 82 D4
Blue Mts., Pa., U.S.A. 79 F8
Blue Mud B., Australia 62 A2
Blue Nile = An Nîl el Azraq □, Sudan 51 F11
Blue Nile = Nîl el Azraq →, Sudan 51 E11
Blue Rapids, U.S.A. 80 F6
Blue Ridge Mts., U.S.A. 77 G5
Blue Stack Mts., Ireland 13 B3
Blueberry →, Canada 72 B4
Bluefield, U.S.A. 76 G5
Bluefields, Nic. 88 D3
Bluff, Australia 62 C4
Bluff, N.Z. 59 M2
Bluff, U.S.A. 83 H9
Bluff Knoll, Australia 61 F2
Bluff Pt., Australia 61 E1
Bluffton, U.S.A. 76 E3
Blumenau, Brazil 95 B6
Blunt, U.S.A. 80 C4
Bly, U.S.A. 82 E3
Blyth, Canada 78 C3
Blyth, U.K. 10 B6
Blyth Bridge, U.K. 10 E5
Blythe, U.S.A. 85 M12
Bo, S. Leone 50 G2
Bo Duc, Vietnam 39 G6
Bo Hai, China 35 E10
Bo Xian, China 34 H8
Boa Vista, Brazil 92 C6
Boaco, Nic. 88 D2
Bo'ai, China 34 G7
Boardman, U.S.A. 78 E4
Boatman, Australia 63 D4
Bobadah, Australia 63 E4
Bobbili, India 41 K13
Bobcaygeon, Canada 70 D4
Bobo-Dioulasso, Burkina Faso 50 F4
Bóbr →, Poland 16 B7
Bobraomby, Tanjon' i, Madag. 57 A8
Bobruysk, Belorussia 24 D4
Bôca do Acre, Brazil 92 E5
Boca Raton, U.S.A. 77 M5
Bocaiúva, Brazil 93 G10
Bocanda, Ivory C. 50 G4
Bocaranga, C.A.R. 51 G8
Bocas del Toro, Panama 88 E3
Bocholt, Germany 16 C3
Bochum, Germany 16 C3
Bocoyna, Mexico 86 B3
Boda, C.A.R. 52 D3
Bodaybo, Russia 27 D12
Boddington, Australia 61 F2
Bodega Bay, U.S.A. 84 G3
Boden, Sweden 8 D16
Bodensee, Europe 16 E4
Bodhan, India 40 K10
Bodmin, U.K. 11 G3
Bodmin Moor, U.K. 11 G3
Bodrog →, Hungary 17 D10
Boegoebergdam, S. Africa 56 D3
Boende, Zaïre 52 E4
Boerne, U.S.A. 81 L5
Boffa, Guinea 50 F2
Bogalusa, U.S.A. 81 K10
Bogan Gate, Australia 63 E4
Bogantungan, Australia 62 C4
Bogata, U.S.A. 81 J7
Boggabilla, Australia 63 D5
Boggabri, Australia 63 E5
Boggeragh Mts., Ireland 13 D3
Bognor Regis, U.K. 11 G7
Bogo, Phil. 37 B6
Bogong, Mt., Australia 63 F4
Bogor, Indonesia 37 G12
Bogorodskoye, Russia 27 D15
Bogotá, Colombia 92 C4
Bogotol, Russia 26 D9
Bogra, Bangla. 41 G16
Boguchany, Russia 27 D10
Bogué, Mauritania 50 E2
Bohemia Downs, Australia 60 C4
Bohemian Forest = Böhmerwald, Germany 16 D6
Bohena Cr. →, Australia 63 E4
Böhmerwald, Germany 16 D6
Bohol, Phil. 37 C6
Bohol Sea, Phil. 37 C6
Bohotleh, Somali Rep. 46 F4
Boi, Pta. de, Brazil 95 A6
Boileau, C., Australia 60 C3
Boise, U.S.A. 82 E5
Boise City, U.S.A. 81 G3
Boissevain, Canada 73 D8
Bojador C., W. Sahara 50 C2
Bojana →, Albania 21 D8
Bojnūrd, Iran 45 B8
Bojonegoro, Indonesia 37 G14
Boké, Guinea 50 F2
Bokhara →, Australia 63 D4
Boknafjorden, Norway 9 G8
Bokoro, Chad 51 F8
Bokote, Zaïre 52 E4
Bokungu, Zaïre 52 E4
Bol, Chad 51 F7
Bolama, Guinea-Biss. 50 F1
Bolan Pass, Pakistan 40 E5
Bolaños →, Mexico 86 C4
Bolbec, France 18 B4
Boldāji, Iran 45 D6
Bole, China 32 B3
Bolesławiec, Poland 16 C7
Bolinao C., Phil. 37 A5
Bolívar, Argentina 94 D3
Bolívar, Colombia 92 C3
Bolivar, Mo., U.S.A. 81 G8
Bolivar, Tenn., U.S.A. 81 H10
Bolivia ■, S. Amer. 92 G6
Bolivian Plateau, S. Amer. 90 D3
Bollnäs, Sweden 9 F14
Bollon, Australia 63 D4
Bolobo, Zaïre 52 E3
Bologna, Italy 20 B4
Bologoye, Russia 24 C5
Bolomba, Zaïre 52 D3
Bolonchenticul, Mexico 87 D7
Bolong, Phil. 37 C6
Boloven, Cao Nguyen, Laos 38 E6
Bolpur, India 43 H12
Bolsena, L. di, Italy 20 C4
Bolshereche, Russia 26 D8
Bolshevik, Ostrov, Russia 27 B11
Bolshezemelskaya Tundra, Russia 24 A10
Bolshoi Kavkas, Asia 25 F7
Bolshoy Anyuy →, Russia 27 C17
Bolshoy Atlym, Russia 26 C7
Bolshoy Begichev, Ostrov, Russia 27 B12
Bolshoy Lyakhovskiy, Ostrov, Russia 27 B15
Bolsward, Neths. 15 A5
Bolton, Canada 78 C5
Bolton, U.K. 10 D5
Bolu, Turkey 25 F5
Bolvadin, Turkey 25 G5
Bolzano, Italy 20 A4
Bom Despacho, Brazil 93 G9
Bom Jesus da Lapa, Brazil 93 F10
Boma, Zaïre 52 F2
Bomaderry, Australia 63 E5
Bombala, Australia 63 F4
Bombay, India 40 K8
Bomboma, Zaïre 52 D3
Bombombwa, Zaïre 54 B2
Bomili, Zaïre 54 B2
Bomokandi →, Zaïre 54 B2
Bomongo, Zaïre 52 D3
Bomu →, C.A.R. 52 D4
Bon, C., Tunisia 51 A7
Bon Sar Pa, Vietnam 38 F6
Bonaire, Neth. Ant. 89 D6
Bonang, Australia 63 F4
Bonanza, Nic. 88 D3
Bonaparte Arch., Australia 60 B3
Bonaventure, Canada 71 C6
Bonavista, Canada 71 C9
Bonavista, C., Canada 71 C9
Bondo, Zaïre 54 B1
Bondoukou, Ivory C. 50 G4
Bondowoso, Indonesia 37 G15
Bone, Teluk, Indonesia 37 E6
Bone Rate, Indonesia 37 F6
Bone Rate, Kepulauan, Indonesia 37 F6
Bo'ness, U.K. 12 E5
Bong Son = Hoai Nhon, Vietnam 38 E7
Bongandanga, Zaïre 52 D4
Bongor, Chad 51 F8
Bonham, U.S.A. 81 J6
Bonifacio, France 18 F9
Bonifacio, Bouches de, Medit. S. 20 D3
Bonin Is. = Ogasawara Gunto, Pac. Oc. 64 E6
Bonn, Germany 16 C3
Bonne Terre, U.S.A. 81 G9
Bonners Ferry, U.S.A. 82 B5
Bonney, L., Australia 63 F3
Bonnie Downs, Australia 62 C3
Bonnie Rock, Australia 61 F2
Bonny, Bight of, Africa 52 D1
Bonnyville, Canada 73 C6
Bonoi, Indonesia 37 E9
Bonsall, U.S.A. 85 M9
Bontang, Indonesia 36 D5
Bonthain, Indonesia 37 F5
Bonthe, S. Leone 50 G2
Bontoc, Phil. 37 A6
Bonython Ra., Australia 60 D4
Bookabie, Australia 61 F5
Booker, U.S.A. 81 G4
Boolaboolka L., Australia 63 E3
Booligal, Australia 63 E3
Boom, Belgium 15 C4
Boonah, Australia 63 D5
Boone, Iowa, U.S.A. 80 D8
Boone, N.C., U.S.A. 77 G5
Booneville, Ark., U.S.A. 81 H8
Booneville, Miss., U.S.A. 77 H1
Boonville, Calif., U.S.A. 84 F3
Boonville, Ind., U.S.A. 76 F2
Boonville, Mo., U.S.A. 80 F8
Boonville, N.Y., U.S.A. 79 C9
Boorindal, Australia 63 E4
Boorowa, Australia 63 E4
Boothia, Gulf of, Canada 69 A11
Boothia Pen., Canada 68 A10
Bootle, Cumb., U.K. 10 C4
Bootle, Mersey., U.K. 10 D4
Booué, Gabon 52 E2
Bophuthatswana □, S. Africa 56 D4
Boquete, Panama 88 E3
Boquilla, Presa de la, Mexico 86 B3
Boquillas del Carmen, Mexico 86 B4
Bor, Serbia, Yug. 21 B10
Bôr, Sudan 51 G11
Bor Mashash, Israel 47 D3
Boradā →, Syria 47 B5
Borah Pk., U.S.A. 82 D7
Borama, Somali Rep. 46 F3
Borås, Sweden 9 H12
Borāzjān, Iran 45 D6
Borba, Brazil 92 D7
Bord Khūn-e Now, Iran 45 D6
Borda, C., Australia 63 F2
Bordeaux, France 18 D3
Borden, Australia 61 F2
Borden, Canada 71 C7
Borden I., Canada 4 B2
Borders □, U.K. 12 F6
Bordertown, Australia 63 F3
Borðeyri, Iceland 8 D3
Bordj Fly Ste. Marie, Algeria 50 C4
Bordj-in-Eker, Algeria 50 D6
Bordj Omar Driss, Algeria 50 C6
Bordj-Tarat, Algeria 50 C6
Borgå, Finland 9 F18
Borgarnes, Iceland 8 D3
Børgefjellet, Norway 8 D12
Borger, Neths. 15 B6
Borger, U.S.A. 81 H4
Borgholm, Sweden 9 H14
Borikhane, Laos 38 C4
Borisoglebsk, Russia 25 D7
Borisov, Belorussia 24 D4
Borja, Peru 92 D3
Borkou, Chad 51 E8
Borkum, Germany 16 B3
Borlänge, Sweden 9 F13
Borley, C., Antarctica 5 C5
Borneo, E. Indies 36 D5
Bornholm, Denmark 9 J13
Borobudur, Indonesia 37 G14
Borogontsy, Russia 27 C14
Boromo, Burkina Faso 50 F4
Boron, U.S.A. 85 L9
Borongan, Phil. 37 B7
Bororen, Australia 62 C5
Borovichi, Russia 24 C5
Borrego Springs, U.S.A. 85 M10
Borroloola, Australia 62 B2
Borth, U.K. 11 E3
Borujerd, Iran 45 C6
Borzya, Russia 27 D12
Bosa, Italy 20 D3
Bosanska Gradiška, Bos. & H., Yug. 20 B7
Bosaso, Somali Rep. 46 E4
Boscastle, U.K. 11 G3
Boshan, China 35 F9
Boshoek, S. Africa 56 D4
Boshof, S. Africa 56 D4
Boshrūyeh, Iran 45 C8
Bosna →, Bos. & H., Yug. 21 B8
Bosna i Hercegovina = Bosnia and Hercegovina □, Europe 20 B7
Bosnia and Hercegovina □, Europe 20 B7
Bosnik, Indonesia 37 E9
Bosobolo, Zaïre 52 D3
Bosporus = Karadeniz Boğazı, Turkey 21 D13
Bossangoa, C.A.R. 51 G8
Bossekop, Norway 8 B17
Bossembélé, C.A.R. 51 G8
Bossier City, U.S.A. 81 J8
Bosso, Niger 51 F7
Bostānābād, Iran 44 B5
Bosten Hu, China 32 B3
Boston, U.K. 10 E7
Boston, U.S.A. 79 D13
Boston Bar, Canada 72 D4
Boswell, Canada 72 D5
Boswell, Okla., U.S.A. 81 H7
Boswell, Pa., U.S.A. 78 F5
Botad, India 42 H4
Botany B., Australia 63 E5
Botene, Laos 38 D3
Bothaville, S. Africa 56 D4
Bothnia, G. of, Europe 8 E16
Bothwell, Australia 62 G4
Bothwell, Canada 78 D3
Botletle →, Botswana 56 C3
Botoşani, Romania 17 E13
Botswana ■, Africa 56 C3
Bottineau, U.S.A. 80 A4
Bottrop, Germany 15 C6
Botucatu, Brazil 95 A6
Botwood, Canada 71 C8
Bou Djébéha, Mali 50 E4
Bou Izakarn, Morocco 50 C3
Bouaké, Ivory C. 50 G3
Bouar, C.A.R. 52 C3
Bouârfa, Morocco 50 B4
Bouca, C.A.R. 51 G8
Boucaut B., Australia 62 A1
Bouches-du-Rhône □, France 18 E6
Bougainville, C., Australia 60 B4
Bougainville Reef, Australia 62 B4
Bougie = Bejaia, Algeria 50 A6
Bougouni, Mali 50 F3
Bouillon, Belgium 15 E5
Boulder, Colo., U.S.A. 80 E2
Boulder, Mont., U.S.A. 82 C7
Boulder City, U.S.A. 85 K12
Boulder Creek, U.S.A. 84 H4
Boulder Dam = Hoover Dam, U.S.A. 85 K12
Boulia, Australia 62 C2
Boulogne-sur-Mer, France 18 A4
Boultoum, Niger 50 F7
Boun Neua, Laos 38 B3
Boun Tai, Laos 38 B3
Bouna, Ivory C. 50 G4
Boundary Pk., U.S.A. 84 H8
Boundiali, Ivory C. 50 G3
Bountiful, U.S.A. 82 F8
Bounty Is., Pac. Oc. 64 M9
Bourbonnais, France 18 C5
Bourem, Mali 50 E4
Bourg-en-Bresse, France 18 C6
Bourges, France 18 C5
Bourget, Canada 79 A9
Bourgogne, France 18 C6
Bourke, Australia 63 E4
Bournemouth, U.K. 11 G6
Bouse, U.S.A. 85 M13
Bousso, Chad 51 F8
Boutilimit, Mauritania 50 E2
Bouvet I. = Bouvetøya, Antarctica 3 G10
Bouvetøya, Antarctica 3 G10
Bovigny, Belgium 15 D5
Bovill, U.S.A. 82 C5
Bow Island, Canada 72 D6
Bowbells, U.S.A. 80 A3
Bowdle, U.S.A. 80 C5
Bowelling, Australia 61 F2
Bowen, Australia 62 C4
Bowen Mts., Australia 63 F4
Bowie, Ariz., U.S.A. 83 K9
Bowie, Tex., U.S.A. 81 J6
Bowkān, Iran 44 B5
Bowland, Forest of, U.K. 10 D5
Bowling Green, Ky., U.S.A. 76 G2
Bowling Green, Ohio, U.S.A. 76 E4
Bowling Green, C., Australia 62 B4
Bowman, U.S.A. 80 B3
Bowman I., Antarctica 5 C8
Bowmans, Australia 63 E2
Bowmanville, Canada 70 D4
Bowmore, U.K. 12 F2
Bowral, Australia 63 E5
Bowraville, Australia 63 E5
Bowron →, Canada 72 C4
Bowser L., Canada 72 B3
Bowsman, Canada 73 C8
Bowwood, Zambia 55 F2
Boxtel, Neths. 15 C5
Boyce, U.S.A. 81 K8
Boyer →, Canada 72 B5
Boyle, Ireland 13 C3
Boyne →, Ireland 13 C5
Boyne City, U.S.A. 76 C3
Boynton Beach, U.S.A. 77 M5
Boyoma, Chutes, Zaïre 54 B2
Boyup Brook, Australia 61 F2
Bozeman, U.S.A. 82 D8
Bozen = Bolzano, Italy 20 A4
Bozoum, C.A.R. 51 G8
Brabant □, Belgium 15 D4
Brabant L., Canada 73 B8
Brač, Croatia 20 C7
Bracadale, L., U.K. 12 D2
Bracciano, L. di, Italy 20 C5
Bracebridge, Canada 70 C4
Brach, Libya 51 C7
Bräcke, Sweden 8 E13
Brackettville, U.S.A. 81 L4
Brad, Romania 17 E11
Bradenton, U.S.A. 77 M4
Bradford, Canada 78 B5
Bradford, U.K. 10 D6
Bradford, Pa., U.S.A. 78 E6
Bradford, Vt., U.S.A. 79 C12
Bradley, Ark., U.S.A. 81 J8
Bradley, Calif., U.S.A. 84 K6
Bradley, S. Dak., U.S.A. 80 C6
Bradley Institute, Zimbabwe 55 F3
Bradore Bay, Canada 71 B8
Bradshaw, Australia 60 C5
Brady, U.S.A. 81 K5
Braemar, Australia 63 E2
Braeside, Canada 79 A8
Braga, Portugal 19 B1
Bragado, Argentina 94 D3
Bragança, Brazil 93 D9
Bragança, Portugal 19 B2
Bragança Paulista, Brazil 95 A6
Brahmanbaria, Bangla. 41 H17
Brahmani →, India 41 J15
Brahmaputra →, India 43 G13
Braich-y-pwll, U.K. 10 E3
Braidwood, Australia 63 F4
Brăila, Romania 17 F13
Brainerd, U.S.A. 80 B7
Braintree, U.K. 11 F8
Braintree, U.S.A. 79 D14
Brak →, S. Africa 56 D3
Brakwater, Namibia 56 C2
Bralorne, Canada 72 C4
Brampton, Canada 70 D4
Bramwell, Australia 62 A3
Branco →, Brazil 92 D6
Brandenburg, Germany 16 B6
Brandfort, S. Africa 56 D4
Brandon, Canada 73 D9
Brandon, U.S.A. 79 C11
Brandon B., Ireland 13 D1
Brandon Mt., Ireland 13 D1
Brandsen, Argentina 94 D4
Brandvlei, S. Africa 56 E3
Branford, U.S.A. 79 E12
Braniewo, Poland 17 A9
Bransfield Str., Antarctica 5 C18
Brańsk, Poland 17 B11
Branson, Colo., U.S.A. 81 G3
Branson, Mo., U.S.A. 81 G8
Brantford, Canada 70 D3
Branxholme, Australia 63 F3
Bras d'Or, L., Canada 71 C7
Brasil, Planalto, Brazil 93 G9
Brasiléia, Brazil 92 F5
Brasília, Brazil 93 G9
Braşov, Romania 17 F12
Brasschaat, Belgium 15 C4
Brassey, Banjaran, Malaysia 36 D5
Brassey Ra., Australia 61 E3
Brasstown Bald, U.S.A. 77 H4
Bratislava, Czech. 16 D8
Bratsk, Russia 27 D11
Brattleboro, U.S.A. 79 D12
Braunschweig, Germany 16 B5
Braunton, U.K. 11 F3
Brava, Somali Rep. 46 G3
Bravo del Norte →, Mexico 86 B5
Brawley, U.S.A. 85 N11
Bray, Ireland 13 C5
Bray, Mt., Australia 62 A1
Bray-sur-Seine, France 18 B5
Brazeau →, Canada 72 C5
Brazil, U.S.A. 76 F2
Brazil ■, S. Amer. 93 F9
Brazilian Highlands = Brasil, Planalto, Brazil 93 G9
Brazo Sur →, S. Amer. 94 B4
Brazos →, U.S.A. 81 L7
Brazzaville, Congo 52 E3
Brčko, Bos. & H., Yug. 21 B8
Breadalbane, Australia 62 C2
Breadalbane, U.K. 12 E4
Breaden, L., Australia 61 E4
Breaksea Sd., N.Z. 59 L1
Bream B., N.Z. 59 F5
Bream Hd., N.Z. 59 F5
Breas, Chile 94 B1
Brebes, Indonesia 37 G13
Brechin, Canada 78 B5
Brechin, U.K. 12 E6
Breckenridge, Colo., U.S.A. 82 G10
Breckenridge, Minn., U.S.A. 80 B6
Breckenridge, Tex., U.S.A. 81 J5
Brecon, U.K. 11 F4
Brecon Beacons, U.K. 11 F4
Breda, Neths. 15 C4
Bredasdorp, S. Africa 56 E3
Bredbo, Australia 63 F4
Bregenz, Austria 16 E4
Breiðafjörður, Iceland 8 D2
Brejo, Brazil 93 D10
Bremen, Germany 16 B4
Bremer I., Australia 62 A2
Bremerhaven, Germany 16 B4
Bremerton, U.S.A. 84 C4
Brenham, U.S.A. 81 K6
Brenner Pass, Austria 16 E5
Brent, Canada 70 C4
Brent, U.K. 11 F7
Brentwood, U.K. 11 F8
Brentwood, U.S.A. 79 F11
Bréscia, Italy 20 B4
Breskens, Neths. 15 C3
Breslau = Wrocław, Poland 16 C8
Bressanone, Italy 20 A4
Bressay, U.K. 12 A7
Bresse, France 18 C6
Brest, Belorussia 24 D3
Brest, France 18 B1
Brest-Litovsk = Brest, Belorussia 24 D3
Bretagne, France 18 B2
Bretçu, Romania 17 E13
Breton, Canada 72 C6

Breton Sd., U.S.A. 81 L10
Brett, C., N.Z. 59 F5
Brevard, U.S.A. 77 H4
Brewarrina, Australia 63 D4
Brewer, U.S.A. 71 D6
Brewer, Mt., U.S.A. 84 J8
Brewster, N.Y., U.S.A. 79 E11
Brewster, Wash., U.S.A. 82 B4
Brewster, Kap, Greenland 4 B6
Brewton, U.S.A. 77 K2
Breyten, S. Africa 57 D4
Brezhnev = Naberezhnyye Chelny, Russia 26 D6
Bria, C.A.R. 51 G9
Briançon, France 18 D7
Bribie I., Australia 63 D5
Bridgehampton, U.S.A. 79 F12
Bridgend, U.K. 11 F4
Bridgeport, Calif., U.S.A. 83 G4
Bridgeport, Conn., U.S.A. 79 E11
Bridgeport, Nebr., U.S.A. 80 E3
Bridgeport, Tex., U.S.A. 81 J6
Bridger, U.S.A. 82 D9
Bridgeton, U.S.A. 76 F8
Bridgetown, Australia 61 F2
Bridgetown, Barbados 89 D8
Bridgetown, Canada 71 D6
Bridgewater, Canada 71 D7
Bridgewater, Mass., U.S.A. 79 E14
Bridgewater, S. Dak., U.S.A. 80 D6
Bridgewater, C., Australia 63 F3
Bridgnorth, U.K. 11 E5
Bridgton, U.S.A. 79 B14
Bridgwater, U.K. 11 F4
Bridlington, U.K. 10 C7
Bridport, Australia 62 G4
Bridport, U.K. 11 G5
Brie, Plaine de la, France 18 B5
Brig, Switz. 16 E3
Brigg, U.K. 10 D7
Briggsdale, U.S.A. 80 E2
Brigham City, U.S.A. 82 F7
Bright, Australia 63 F4
Brighton, Australia 63 F2
Brighton, Canada 70 D4
Brighton, U.K. 11 G7
Brighton, U.S.A. 80 F2
Brilliant, Canada 72 D5
Brilliant, U.S.A. 78 F4
Brindisi, Italy 21 D7
Brinkley, U.S.A. 81 H9
Brinkworth, Australia 63 E2
Brinnon, U.S.A. 84 C4
Brion, I., Canada 71 C7
Brisbane, Australia 63 D5
Brisbane →, Australia 63 D5
Bristol, U.K. 11 F5
Bristol, Conn., U.S.A. 79 E12
Bristol, Pa., U.S.A. 79 F10
Bristol, R.I., U.S.A. 79 E13
Bristol, S. Dak., U.S.A. 80 C6
Bristol, Tenn., U.S.A. 77 G4
Bristol B., U.S.A. 68 C4
Bristol Channel, U.K. 11 F3
Bristol I., Antarctica 5 B1
Bristol L., U.S.A. 83 J5
Bristow, U.S.A. 81 H6
British Columbia □, Canada 72 C3
British Guiana = Guyana ■, S. Amer. 92 C7
British Honduras = Belize ■, Cent. Amer. 87 D7
British Isles, Europe 6 E5
Brits, S. Africa 57 D4
Britstown, S. Africa 56 E3
Britt, Canada 70 C3
Brittany = Bretagne, France 18 B2
Britton, U.S.A. 80 C6
Brixton, Australia 62 C3
Brlik, Kazakhstan 26 E8
Brno, Czech. 16 D8
Broad →, U.S.A. 77 J5
Broad Arrow, Australia 61 F3
Broad B., U.K. 12 C2
Broad Haven, Ireland 13 B2
Broad Law, U.K. 12 F5
Broad Sd., Australia 62 C4
Broadhurst Ra., Australia 60 D3
Broads, The, U.K. 10 E9
Broadus, U.S.A. 80 C2
Broadview, Canada 73 C8
Brochet, Canada 73 B8
Brochet, L., Canada 73 B8
Brock, Canada 73 C7
Brocken, Germany 16 C5
Brockport, U.S.A. 78 C7
Brockton, U.S.A. 79 D13
Brockville, Canada 70 D4
Brockway, Mont., U.S.A. 80 B2
Brockway, Pa., U.S.A. 78 E6
Brocton, U.S.A. 78 D5
Brodeur Pen., Canada 69 A11
Brodick, U.K. 12 F3
Brogan, U.S.A. 82 D5
Broken Bow, Nebr., U.S.A. 80 E5
Broken Bow, Okla., U.S.A. 81 H7
Broken Hill = Kabwe, Zambia 55 E2
Broken Hill, Australia 63 E3
Bromfield, U.K. 11 E5
Bromley, U.K. 11 F8
Brønderslev, Denmark 9 H10
Bronkhorstspruit, S. Africa 57 D4
Bronte, U.S.A. 81 K4
Bronte Park, Australia 62 G4
Brook Park, U.S.A. 78 E4
Brookfield, U.S.A. 80 F8
Brookhaven, U.S.A. 81 K9
Brookings, Oreg., U.S.A. 82 E1
Brookings, S. Dak., U.S.A. 80 C6
Brooklin, Canada 78 C6
Brookmere, Canada 72 D4
Brooks, Canada 72 C6
Brooks B., Canada 72 C3
Brooks L., Canada 73 A7
Brooks Ra., U.S.A. 68 B5
Brooksville, U.S.A. 77 L4
Brookville, U.S.A. 76 F3
Brooloo, Australia 63 D5
Broom, L., U.K. 12 D3
Broome, Australia 60 C3
Broomehill, Australia 61 F2
Brora, U.K. 12 C5
Brora →, U.K. 12 C5
Brosna →, Ireland 13 C4
Brothers, U.S.A. 82 E3
Broughton Island, Canada 69 B13
Broughty Ferry, U.K. 12 E6
Brouwershaven, Neths. 15 C3
Browerville, U.S.A. 80 B7
Brown, Pt., Australia 63 E1
Brown Willy, U.K. 11 G3
Brownfield, U.S.A. 81 J3
Browning, U.S.A. 82 B7
Brownlee, Canada 73 C7
Brownsville, Oreg., U.S.A. 82 D2
Brownsville, Tenn., U.S.A. 81 H10
Brownsville, Tex., U.S.A. 81 N6
Brownwood, U.S.A. 81 K5
Brownwood, L., U.S.A. 81 K5
Browse I., Australia 60 B3
Bruas, Malaysia 39 K3
Bruay-en-Artois, France 18 A5
Bruce, Mt., Australia 60 D2
Bruce Pen., Canada 78 A3
Bruce Rock, Australia 61 F2
Bruck an der Leitha, Austria 16 D8
Brue →, U.K. 11 F5
Bruges = Brugge, Belgium 15 C3
Brugge, Belgium 15 C3
Brûlé, Canada 72 C5
Brumado, Brazil 93 F10
Brunchilly, Australia 62 B1
Brundidge, U.S.A. 77 K3
Bruneau, U.S.A. 82 E6
Bruneau →, U.S.A. 82 E6
Brunei = Bandar Seri Begawan, Brunei 36 C4
Brunei ■, Asia 36 D4
Brunette Downs, Australia 62 B2
Brunner, L., N.Z. 59 K3
Bruno, Canada 73 C7
Brunsbüttel, Germany 16 B4
Brunswick = Braunschweig, Germany 16 B5
Brunswick, Ga., U.S.A. 77 K5
Brunswick, Maine, U.S.A. 71 D6
Brunswick, Md., U.S.A. 76 F7
Brunswick, Mo., U.S.A. 80 F8
Brunswick, Ohio, U.S.A. 78 E3
Brunswick, Pen. de, Chile 96 G2
Brunswick B., Australia 60 C3
Brunswick Junction, Australia 61 F2
Bruny I., Australia 62 G4
Brus Laguna, Honduras 88 C3
Brush, U.S.A. 80 E3
Brushton, U.S.A. 79 B10
Brusque, Brazil 95 B6
Brussel, Belgium 15 D4
Brussels = Brussel, Belgium 15 D4
Brussels, Canada 78 C3
Bruthen, Australia 63 F4
Bruxelles = Brussel, Belgium 15 D4
Bryan, Ohio, U.S.A. 76 E3
Bryan, Tex., U.S.A. 81 K6
Bryan, Mt., Australia 63 E2
Bryansk, Russia 24 D5
Bryant, U.S.A. 80 C6
Bryne, Norway 9 G8
Bryson City, U.S.A. 77 H4
Bsharri, Lebanon 47 A5
Bû Baqarah, U.A.E. 45 E8
Bu Craa, W. Sahara 50 C2
Bû Ḥasā, U.A.E. 45 F7
Bua Yai, Thailand 38 E4
Buapinang, Indonesia 37 E6
Buayan, Phil. 37 C7
Bubanza, Burundi 54 C2
Būbiyān, Kuwait 45 D6
Bucaramanga, Colombia 92 B4
Buccaneer Arch., Australia 60 C3
Buchan, U.K. 12 D6
Buchan Ness, U.K. 12 D7
Buchanan, Canada 73 C8
Buchanan, Liberia 50 G2
Buchanan, L., Queens., Australia 62 C4
Buchanan, L., W. Austral., Australia 61 E3
Buchanan, L., U.S.A. 81 K5
Buchanan Cr. →, Australia 62 B2
Buchans, Canada 71 C8
Bucharest = Bucureşti, Romania 17 F13
Buchon, Pt., U.S.A. 84 K6
Buckeye, U.S.A. 83 K7
Buckhannon, U.S.A. 76 F5
Buckhaven, U.K. 12 E5
Buckie, U.K. 12 D6
Buckingham, Canada 70 C4
Buckingham, U.K. 11 F7
Buckingham B., Australia 62 A2
Buckinghamshire □, U.K. 11 F7
Buckle Hd., Australia 60 B4
Buckleboo, Australia 63 E2
Buckley, U.S.A. 82 C2
Buckley →, Australia 62 C2
Bucklin, U.S.A. 81 G5
Bucks L., U.S.A. 84 F5
Buctouche, Canada 71 C7
Bucureşti, Romania 17 F13
Bucyrus, U.S.A. 76 E4
Budalin, Burma 41 H19
Budapest, Hungary 17 E9
Budaun, India 43 E8
Budd Coast, Antarctica 5 C8
Bude, U.K. 11 G3
Budennovsk, Russia 25 F7
Budge Budge = Baj Baj, India 43 H13
Budgewoi, Australia 63 E5
Búðareyri, Iceland 8 D6
Búðir, Iceland 8 D2
Budjala, Zaïre 52 D3
Buellton, U.S.A. 85 L6
Buena Vista, Colo., U.S.A. 83 G10
Buena Vista, Va., U.S.A. 76 G6
Buena Vista L., U.S.A. 85 K7
Buenaventura, Colombia 92 C3
Buenaventura, Mexico 86 B3
Buenos Aires, Argentina 94 C4
Buenos Aires, Costa Rica 88 E3
Buenos Aires □, Argentina 94 D4
Buenos Aires, L., Chile 96 F2
Buffalo, Mo., U.S.A. 81 G8
Buffalo, N.Y., U.S.A. 78 D6
Buffalo, Okla., U.S.A. 81 G5
Buffalo, S. Dak., U.S.A. 80 C3
Buffalo, Wyo., U.S.A. 82 D10
Buffalo →, Canada 72 A5
Buffalo Head Hills, Canada 72 B5
Buffalo L., Canada 72 C6
Buffalo Narrows, Canada 73 B7
Buffels →, S. Africa 56 D2
Buford, U.S.A. 77 H4
Bug →, Poland 17 B10
Bug →, Ukraine 25 E5
Buga, Colombia 92 C3
Buganda, Uganda 54 C3
Buganga, Uganda 54 C3
Bugel, Tanjung, Indonesia 36 F4
Bugibba, Malta 23 D1
Bugsuk, Phil. 36 C5
Bugulma, Russia 24 D9
Bugun Shara, Mongolia 32 B5
Bugun Shara, Mongolia 32 B5
Buguruslan, Russia 24 D9
Buheirat-Murrat-el-Kubra, Egypt 51 B11
Buhl, Idaho, U.S.A. 82 E6
Buhl, Minn., U.S.A. 80 B8
Buick, U.S.A. 81 G9
Builth Wells, U.K. 11 E4
Buir Nur, Mongolia 33 B6
Bujumbura, Burundi 54 C2
Bukachacha, Russia 27 D12
Bukama, Zaïre 55 D2
Bukavu, Zaïre 54 C2
Bukene, Tanzania 54 C3
Bukhara, Uzbekistan 26 F7
Bukima, Tanzania 54 C3
Bukit Mertajam, Malaysia 39 K3
Bukittinggi, Indonesia 36 E2
Bukoba, Tanzania 54 C3
Bukoba □, Tanzania 54 C3
Bukuya, Uganda 54 B3
Bula, Indonesia 37 E8
Bulahdelah, Australia 63 E5
Bulan, Phil. 37 B6
Bulandshahr, India 42 E7
Bulawayo, Zimbabwe 55 G2
Bulgaria ■, Europe 21 C11
Bulgroo, Australia 63 D3
Bulgunnia, Australia 63 E1
Bulhar, Somali Rep. 46 E3
Buli, Teluk, Indonesia 37 D7
Buliluyan, C., Phil. 36 C5
Bulkley →, Canada 72 B3
Bull Shoals L., U.S.A. 81 G8
Bullara, Australia 60 D1
Bullaring, Australia 61 F2
Bulli, Australia 63 E5
Bullock Creek, Australia 62 B3
Bulloo →, Australia 63 D3
Bulloo Downs, Queens., Australia 63 D3
Bulloo Downs, W. Austral., Australia 60 D2
Bulloo L., Australia 63 D3
Bulls, N.Z. 59 J5
Bulnes, Chile 94 D1
Bulo Burti, Somali Rep. 46 G4
Bulsar = Valsad, India 40 J8
Bultfontein, S. Africa 56 D4
Bulu Karakelong, Indonesia 37 D7
Bulukumba, Indonesia 37 F6
Bulun, Russia 27 B13
Bumba, Zaïre 52 D4
Bumbiri I., Tanzania 54 C3
Bumhpa Bum, Burma 41 F20
Bumi →, Zimbabwe 55 F2
Buna, Kenya 54 B4
Bunazi, Tanzania 54 C3
Bunbah, Khalij, Libya 51 B9
Bunbury, Australia 61 F2
Buncrana, Ireland 13 A4
Bundaberg, Australia 63 C5
Bundey →, Australia 62 C2
Bundi, India 42 G6
Bundooma, Australia 62 C1
Bundoran, Ireland 13 B3
Bung Kan, Thailand 38 C4
Bungatakada, Japan 31 H5
Bungil Cr. →, Australia 62 D4
Bungo-Suidō, Japan 31 H6
Bungoma, Kenya 54 B3
Bungu, Tanzania 54 D4
Bunia, Zaïre 54 B3
Bunji, Pakistan 43 B6
Bunkie, U.S.A. 81 K8
Bunnell, U.S.A. 77 L5
Buntok, Indonesia 36 E4
Bunyu, Indonesia 36 D5
Buol, Indonesia 37 D6
Buon Brieng, Vietnam 38 F7
Buon Me Thuot, Vietnam 38 F7
Buong Long, Cambodia 38 F6
Buorkhaya, Mys, Russia 27 B14
Buqayq, Si. Arabia 45 E6
Bur Acaba, Somali Rep. 46 G3
Bûr Safâga, Egypt 51 C11
Bûr Sa'îd, Egypt 51 B11
Bûr Sûdân, Sudan 51 E12
Bura, Kenya 54 C4
Burao, Somali Rep. 46 F4
Burâq, Syria 47 B5
Buras, U.S.A. 81 L10
Buraydah, Si. Arabia 44 E5
Burbank, U.S.A. 85 L8
Burcher, Australia 63 E4
Burdekin →, Australia 62 B4
Burdett, Canada 72 D6
Burdur, Turkey 25 G5
Burdwan = Barddhaman, India 43 H12
Bure →, U.K. 10 E9
Bureya →, Russia 27 E13
Burford, Canada 78 C4
Burgas, Bulgaria 21 C12
Burgenland □, Austria 16 E8
Burgeo, Canada 71 C8
Burgersdorp, S. Africa 56 E4
Burges, Mt., Australia 61 F3
Burgos, Spain 19 A4
Burgsvik, Sweden 9 H15
Burgundy = Bourgogne, France 18 C6
Burias, Phil. 37 B6
Burica, Pta., Costa Rica 88 E3
Burigi, L., Tanzania 54 C3
Burin, Canada 71 C8
Buriram, Thailand 38 E4
Burj Sāfitā, Syria 44 C3
Burji, Ethiopia 51 G12
Burkburnett, U.S.A. 81 H5
Burke, U.S.A. 82 C6
Burke →, Australia 62 C2
Burketown, Australia 62 B2
Burkina Faso ■, Africa 50 F4
Burk's Falls, Canada 70 C4
Burley, U.S.A. 82 E7
Burlingame, U.S.A. 84 H4
Burlington, Canada 78 C5
Burlington, Colo., U.S.A. 80 F3
Burlington, Iowa, U.S.A. 80 E9
Burlington, Kans., U.S.A. 80 F7
Burlington, N.C., U.S.A. 77 G6
Burlington, N.J., U.S.A. 79 F10
Burlington, Vt., U.S.A. 79 B11
Burlington, Wash., U.S.A. 84 B4
Burlington, Wis., U.S.A. 76 D1
Burlyu-Tyube, Kazakhstan 26 E8
Burma ■, Asia 41 J20
Burnaby I., Canada 72 C2
Burnet, U.S.A. 81 K5
Burney, U.S.A. 82 F3
Burngup, Australia 61 F2
Burnham, U.S.A. 78 F7
Burnie, Australia 62 G4
Burnley, U.K. 10 D5
Burns, Oreg., U.S.A. 82 E4
Burns, Wyo., U.S.A. 80 E2
Burns Lake, Canada 72 C3
Burnside →, Canada 68 B9
Burnside, L., Australia 61 E3
Burnt River, Canada 78 B6
Burntwood →, Canada 73 B9
Burntwood L., Canada 73 B8
Burqān, Kuwait 44 D5
Burra, Australia 63 E2
Burramurra, Australia 62 C2
Burren Junction, Australia 63 E4
Burrendong Dam, Australia 63 E4
Burrinjuck Res., Australia 63 F4
Burro, Serranías del, Mexico 86 B4
Burruyacú, Argentina 94 B3
Burry Port, U.K. 11 F3
Bursa, Turkey 25 F4
Burstall, Canada 73 C7
Burton L., Canada 70 B4
Burton upon Trent, U.K. 10 E6
Burtundy, Australia 63 E3
Buru, Indonesia 37 E7
Burûn, Râs, Egypt 47 D2
Burundi ■, Africa 54 C3
Bururi, Burundi 54 C2
Burutu, Nigeria 50 G6
Burwell, U.S.A. 80 E5
Bury, U.K. 10 D5
Bury St. Edmunds, U.K. 11 E8
Buryat Republic □, Russia 27 D11
Busango Swamp, Zambia 55 E2
Buşayrah, Syria 44 C4
Buşayyah, Iraq 44 D5
Būshehr, Iran 45 D6
Būshehr □, Iran 45 D6
Bushell, Canada 73 B7
Bushenyi, Uganda 54 C3
Bushire = Būshehr, Iran 45 D6
Bushnell, Ill., U.S.A. 80 E9
Bushnell, Nebr., U.S.A. 80 E3
Busia □, Kenya 54 B3
Businga, Zaïre 52 D4
Buskerud fylke □, Norway 9 F10
Busoga □, Uganda 54 B3
Busra ash Shām, Syria 47 C5
Busselton, Australia 61 F2
Bussum, Neths. 15 B5
Busto Arsizio, Italy 20 B3
Busu-Djanoa, Zaïre 52 D4
Busuanga, Phil. 37 B5
Buta, Zaïre 54 B1
Butare, Rwanda 54 C2
Butaritari, Kiribati 64 G9
Bute, U.K. 12 F3
Bute Inlet, Canada 72 C4
Butemba, Uganda 54 B3
Butembo, Zaïre 54 B2
Butha Qi, China 33 B7
Butiaba, Uganda 54 B3
Butler, Mo., U.S.A. 80 F7
Butler, Pa., U.S.A. 78 F5
Butte, Mont., U.S.A. 82 C7
Butte, Nebr., U.S.A. 80 D5
Butte Creek →, U.S.A. 84 F5
Butterworth = Gcuwa, S. Africa 57 E4
Butterworth, Malaysia 39 K3
Buttfield, Mt., Australia 61 D4
Button B., Canada 73 B10
Buttonwillow, U.S.A. 85 K7
Butty Hd., Australia 61 F3
Butuan, Phil. 37 C7
Butung, Indonesia 37 E6
Buturlinovka, Russia 25 D7
Buxar, India 43 G10
Buxton, S. Africa 56 D3
Buxton, U.K. 10 D6
Buy, Russia 24 C7
Buyaga, Russia 27 D13
Buzău, Romania 17 F13
Buzău →, Romania 17 F13
Buzen, Japan 31 H5
Buzi →, Mozam. 55 F3
Buzuluk, Russia 24 D9
Buzzards Bay, U.S.A. 79 E14
Bwana Mkubwe, Zaïre 55 E2
Bydgoszcz, Poland 17 B8
Byelorussia = Belorussia ■, Europe 24 D4
Byers, U.S.A. 80 F2
Byesville, U.S.A. 78 G3
Byhalia, U.S.A. 81 H10
Bylas, U.S.A. 83 K8
Bylot I., Canada 69 A12
Byrd, C., Antarctica 5 C17
Byro, Australia 61 E2
Byrock, Australia 63 E4
Byron Bay, Australia 63 D5
Byrranga, Gory, Russia 27 B11
Byske, Sweden 8 D16
Byske älv →, Sweden 8 D16
Bytom, Poland 17 C9
Byumba, Rwanda 54 C3

C

C.I.S. = Commonwealth of Independent States ■, Eurasia 27 D11
Ca →, Vietnam 38 C5
Ca Mau = Quan Long, Vietnam 39 H5
Ca Mau, Mui = Bai Bung, Mui, Vietnam 39 H5
Ca Na, Vietnam 39 G7
Caacupé, Paraguay 94 B4
Caála, Angola 53 G3
Caamano Sd., Canada 72 C3
Caazapá, Paraguay 94 B4
Caazapá □, Paraguay 95 B4
Caballeria, C. de, Spain 22 A11
Cabanatuan, Phil. 37 A6
Cabano, Canada 71 C6
Cabazon, U.S.A. 85 M10
Cabedelo, Brazil 93 E12
Cabildo, Chile 94 C1
Cabimas, Venezuela 92 A4
Cabinda, Angola 52 F2
Cabinda □, Angola 52 F2
Cabinet Mts., U.S.A. 82 C6
Cabo Blanco, Argentina 96 F3
Cabo Frio, Brazil 95 A7
Cabo Pantoja, Peru 92 D3
Cabonga, Réservoir, Canada 70 C4
Cabool, U.S.A. 81 G8
Caboolture, Australia 63 D5
Cabora Bassa Dam = Cahora Bassa Dam, Mozam. 55 F3
Caborca, Mexico 86 A2
Cabot, Mt., U.S.A. 79 B13
Cabot Str., Canada 71 C8
Cabrera, I., Spain 22 B9
Cabri, Canada 73 C7

Cabriel →, *Spain* 19 C5
Čačak, *Serbia, Yug.* 21 C9
Cáceres, *Brazil* 92 G7
Cáceres, *Spain* 19 C2
Cache Bay, *Canada* 70 C4
Cache Cr. →, *U.S.A.* 84 G5
Cachi, *Argentina* 94 B2
Cachimbo, Serra do, *Brazil* 93 E7
Cachoeira, *Brazil* 93 F11
Cachoeira de Itapemirim, *Brazil* 95 A7
Cachoeira do Sul, *Brazil* 95 C5
Cacólo, *Angola* 52 G3
Caconda, *Angola* 53 G3
Cacongo, *Angola* 52 F2
Caddo, *U.S.A.* 81 H6
Cadell Cr. →, *Australia* 62 C3
Cader Idris, *U.K.* 10 E4
Cadibarrawirracanna, L., *Australia* 63 D2
Cadillac, *Canada* 70 C4
Cadillac, *U.S.A.* 76 C3
Cadiz, *Phil.* 37 B6
Cádiz, *Spain* 19 D2
Cadiz, *U.S.A.* 78 F4
Cádiz, G. de, *Spain* 19 D2
Cadney Park, *Australia* 63 D1
Cadomin, *Canada* 72 C5
Cadotte →, *Canada* 72 B5
Cadoux, *Australia* 61 F2
Caen, *France* 18 B3
Caernarfon, *U.K.* 10 D3
Caernarfon B., *U.K.* 10 D3
Caernarvon = Caernarfon, *U.K.* 10 D3
Caerphilly, *U.K.* 11 F4
Caesarea, *Israel* 47 C3
Caeté, *Brazil* 93 G10
Caetité, *Brazil* 93 F10
Cafayate, *Argentina* 94 B2
Cafu, *Angola* 56 B2
Cagayan →, *Phil.* 37 A6
Cagayan de Oro, *Phil.* 37 C6
Cágliari, *Italy* 20 E3
Cágliari, G. di, *Italy* 20 E3
Caguas, *Puerto Rico* 89 C6
Caha Mts., *Ireland* 13 E2
Cahama, *Angola* 56 B1
Caher, *Ireland* 13 D4
Cahersiveen, *Ireland* 13 E1
Cahora Bassa Dam, *Mozam.* 55 F3
Cahore Pt., *Ireland* 13 D5
Cahors, *France* 18 D4
Cahuapanas, *Peru* 92 E3
Cai Bau, Dao, *Vietnam* 38 B6
Cai Nuoc, *Vietnam* 39 H5
Caia, *Mozam.* 55 F4
Caianda, *Angola* 55 E1
Caibarién, *Cuba* 88 B4
Caicara, *Venezuela* 92 B5
Caicó, *Brazil* 93 E11
Caicos Is., *W. Indies* 89 B5
Caicos Passage, *W. Indies* 89 B5
Caird Coast, *Antarctica* 5 D1
Cairn Gorm, *U.K.* 12 D5
Cairn Toul, *U.K.* 12 D5
Cairngorm Mts., *U.K.* 12 D5
Cairns, *Australia* 62 B4
Cairo = El Qâhira, *Egypt* 51 B11
Cairo, *Ga., U.S.A.* 77 K3
Cairo, *Ill., U.S.A.* 81 G10
Caithness, Ord of, *U.K.* 12 C5
Caiundo, *Angola* 53 H3
Caiza, *Bolivia* 92 H5
Cajamarca, *Peru* 92 E3
Cajàzeiras, *Brazil* 93 E11
Cala d'Or, *Spain* 22 B10
Cala Figuera, C., *Spain* 22 B9
Cala Forcat, *Spain* 22 A10
Cala Mayor, *Spain* 22 B9
Cala Mezquida, *Spain* 22 B11
Cala Millor, *Spain* 22 B10
Cala Ratjada, *Spain* 22 B10
Calabar, *Nigeria* 50 H6
Calábria □, *Italy* 20 E7
Calafate, *Argentina* 96 G2
Calahorra, *Spain* 19 A5
Calais, *France* 18 A4
Calais, *U.S.A.* 71 C6
Calalaste, Cord. de, *Argentina* 94 B2
Calama, *Brazil* 92 E6
Calama, *Chile* 94 A2
Calamar, *Bolívar, Colombia* 92 A4
Calamar, *Vaupés, Colombia* 92 C4
Calamian Group, *Phil.* 37 B5
Calamocha, *Spain* 19 B5
Calán Porter, *Spain* 22 B11
Calang, *Indonesia* 36 D1
Calapan, *Phil.* 37 B6
Calatayud, *Spain* 19 B5
Calauag, *Phil.* 37 B6
Calavite, C., *Phil.* 37 B6
Calbayog, *Phil.* 37 B6
Calca, *Peru* 92 F4
Calcasieu L., *U.S.A.* 81 L8
Calcutta, *India* 43 H13
Calder →, *U.K.* 10 D6
Caldera, *Chile* 94 B1
Caldwell, *Idaho, U.S.A.* 82 E5
Caldwell, *Kans., U.S.A.* 81 G6
Caldwell, *Tex., U.S.A.* 81 K6
Caledon, *S. Africa* 56 E2
Caledon →, *S. Africa* 56 E4
Caledon B., *Australia* 62 A2
Caledonia, *Canada* 78 C5
Caledonia, *U.S.A.* 78 D7
Calella, *Spain* 19 B7
Calemba, *Angola* 56 B2
Calexico, *U.S.A.* 85 N11
Calf of Man, *U.K.* 10 C3
Calgary, *Canada* 72 C6
Calheta, *Madeira* 22 D2
Calhoun, *U.S.A.* 77 H3
Cali, *Colombia* 92 C3
Calicut, *India* 40 P9
Caliente, *U.S.A.* 83 H6
California, *Mo., U.S.A.* 80 F8
California, *Pa., U.S.A.* 78 F5
California □, *U.S.A.* 83 H4
California, Baja, *Mexico* 86 A1
California, Baja, T.N. □, *Mexico* 86 B2
California, Baja, T.S. □, *Mexico* 86 B2
California, G. de, *Mexico* 86 B2
California City, *U.S.A.* 85 K9
California Hot Springs, *U.S.A.* 85 K8
Calingasta, *Argentina* 94 C2
Calipatria, *U.S.A.* 85 M11
Calistoga, *U.S.A.* 84 G4
Calitzdorp, *S. Africa* 56 E3
Callabonna, L., *Australia* 63 D3
Callan, *Ireland* 13 D4
Callander, *U.K.* 12 E4
Callao, *Peru* 92 F3
Callaway, *U.S.A.* 80 E5
Calles, *Mexico* 87 C5
Callide, *Australia* 62 C5
Calling Lake, *Canada* 72 B6
Calliope, *Australia* 62 C5
Calola, *Angola* 56 B2
Caloundra, *Australia* 63 D5
Calpella, *U.S.A.* 84 F3
Calpine, *U.S.A.* 84 F6
Calstock, *Canada* 70 C3
Caltagirone, *Italy* 20 F6
Caltanissetta, *Italy* 20 F6
Calulo, *Angola* 52 G2
Calumet, *U.S.A.* 76 B1
Calunda, *Angola* 53 G4
Calvados □, *France* 18 B3
Calvert, *U.S.A.* 81 K6
Calvert →, *Australia* 62 B2
Calvert Hills, *Australia* 62 B2
Calvert I., *Canada* 72 C3
Calvert Ra., *Australia* 60 D3
Calvi, *France* 18 E8
Calvillo, *Mexico* 86 C4
Calvinia, *S. Africa* 56 E2
Calwa, *U.S.A.* 84 J7
Cam →, *U.K.* 11 E8
Cam Lam, *Vietnam* 39 G7
Cam Pha, *Vietnam* 38 B6
Cam Ranh, *Vietnam* 39 G7
Cam Xuyen, *Vietnam* 38 C6
Camabatela, *Angola* 52 F3
Camacha, *Madeira* 22 D3
Camacho, *Mexico* 86 C4
Camacupa, *Angola* 53 G3
Camagüey, *Cuba* 88 B4
Camaná, *Peru* 92 G4
Camanche Res., *U.S.A.* 84 G6
Camaquã →, *Brazil* 95 C5
Câmara de Lobos, *Madeira* 22 D3
Camaret, *France* 18 B1
Camargo, *Bolivia* 92 H5
Camarillo, *U.S.A.* 85 L7
Camarón, C., *Honduras* 88 C2
Camarones, *Argentina* 96 E3
Camas, *U.S.A.* 84 E4
Camas Valley, *U.S.A.* 82 E2
Cambará, *Brazil* 95 A5
Cambay = Khambhat, *India* 42 H5
Cambodia ■, *Asia* 38 F5
Camborne, *U.K.* 11 G2
Cambrai, *France* 18 A5
Cambria, *U.S.A.* 83 J3
Cambrian Mts., *U.K.* 11 E4
Cambridge, *Canada* 70 D3
Cambridge, *Jamaica* 88 C4
Cambridge, *N.Z.* 59 G5
Cambridge, *U.K.* 11 E8
Cambridge, *Idaho, U.S.A.* 82 D5
Cambridge, *Mass., U.S.A.* 79 D13
Cambridge, *Md., U.S.A.* 76 F7
Cambridge, *Minn., U.S.A.* 80 C8
Cambridge, *N.Y., U.S.A.* 79 C11
Cambridge, *Nebr., U.S.A.* 80 E4
Cambridge, *Ohio, U.S.A.* 78 F3
Cambridge Bay, *Canada* 68 B9
Cambridge G., *Australia* 60 B4
Cambridge Springs, *U.S.A.* 78 E4
Cambridgeshire □, *U.K.* 11 E8
Cambuci, *Brazil* 95 A7
Cambundi-Catembo, *Angola* 52 G3
Camden, *Ala., U.S.A.* 77 K2
Camden, *Ark., U.S.A.* 81 J8
Camden, *Maine, U.S.A.* 71 D6
Camden, *N.J., U.S.A.* 79 G9
Camden, *S.C., U.S.A.* 77 H5
Camden Sd., *Australia* 60 C3
Camdenton, *U.S.A.* 81 F8
Cameron, *Ariz., U.S.A.* 83 J8
Cameron, *La., U.S.A.* 81 L8
Cameron, *Mo., U.S.A.* 80 F7
Cameron, *Tex., U.S.A.* 81 K6
Cameron Falls, *Canada* 70 C2
Cameron Highlands, *Malaysia* 39 K3
Cameron Hills, *Canada* 72 B5
Cameroon ■, *Africa* 51 G7
Cameroun, Mt., *Cameroon* 50 H6
Cametá, *Brazil* 93 D9
Caminha, *Portugal* 19 B1
Camino, *U.S.A.* 84 G6
Camira Creek, *Australia* 63 D5
Camissombo, *Angola* 52 F4
Cammal, *U.S.A.* 78 E7
Camocim, *Brazil* 93 D10
Camooweal, *Australia* 62 B2
Camopi →, *Fr. Guiana* 93 C8
Camp Crook, *U.S.A.* 80 C3
Camp Nelson, *U.S.A.* 85 J8
Camp Wood, *U.S.A.* 81 L4
Campana, *Argentina* 94 C4
Campana, I., *Chile* 96 F1
Campanário, *Madeira* 22 D2
Campania □, *Italy* 20 D6
Campbell, *S. Africa* 56 D3
Campbell, *Calif., U.S.A.* 84 H5
Campbell, *Ohio, U.S.A.* 78 E4
Campbell I., *Pac. Oc.* 64 N8
Campbell L., *Canada* 73 A7
Campbell River, *Canada* 72 C3
Campbell Town, *Australia* 62 G4
Campbellford, *Canada* 78 B7
Campbellpur, *Pakistan* 42 C5
Campbellsville, *U.S.A.* 76 G3
Campbellton, *Canada* 71 C6
Campbelltown, *Australia* 63 E5
Campbeltown, *U.K.* 12 F3
Campeche, *Mexico* 87 D6
Campeche □, *Mexico* 87 D6
Campeche, B. de, *Mexico* 87 D6
Camperdown, *Australia* 63 F3
Camperville, *Canada* 73 C8
Campina Grande, *Brazil* 93 E11
Campinas, *Brazil* 95 A6
Campo, *Cameroon* 52 D1
Campo Belo, *Brazil* 93 H9
Campo Formoso, *Brazil* 93 F10
Campo Grande, *Brazil* 93 H8
Campo Maíor, *Brazil* 93 D10
Campo Mourão, *Brazil* 95 A5
Campoalegre, *Colombia* 92 C3
Campobasso, *Italy* 20 D6
Campos, *Brazil* 95 A7
Campos Belos, *Brazil* 93 F9
Campos del Puerto, *Spain* 22 B10
Campos Novos, *Brazil* 95 B5
Camptonville, *U.S.A.* 84 F5
Campuya →, *Peru* 92 D4
Camrose, *Canada* 72 C6
Camsell Portage, *Canada* 73 B7
Can Clavo, *Spain* 22 C7
Can Creu, *Spain* 22 C7
Can Gio, *Vietnam* 39 G6
Can Tho, *Vietnam* 39 G5
Canaan, *U.S.A.* 79 D11
Canada ■, *N. Amer.* 68 C10
Cañada de Gómez, *Argentina* 94 C3
Canadian, *U.S.A.* 81 H4
Canadian →, *U.S.A.* 81 H7
Çanakkale, *Turkey* 25 F4
Çanakkale Boğazı, *Turkey* 21 D12
Canal Flats, *Canada* 72 C5
Canalejas, *Argentina* 94 D2
Canals, *Argentina* 94 C3
Canandaigua, *U.S.A.* 78 D7
Cananea, *Mexico* 86 A2
Canarias, Is., *Atl. Oc.* 22 F4
Canarreos, Arch. de los, *Cuba* 88 B3
Canary Is. = Canarias, Is., *Atl. Oc.* 22 F4
Canatlán, *Mexico* 86 C4
Canaveral, C., *U.S.A.* 77 L5
Canavieiras, *Brazil* 93 G11
Canbelego, *Australia* 63 E4
Canberra, *Australia* 63 F4
Canby, *Calif., U.S.A.* 82 F3
Canby, *Minn., U.S.A.* 80 C6
Canby, *Oreg., U.S.A.* 84 E4
Cancún, *Mexico* 87 C7
Candala, *Somali Rep.* 46 E4
Candelaria, *Argentina* 95 B4
Candelaria, *Canary Is.* 22 F3
Candelo, *Australia* 63 F4
Candia = Iráklion, *Greece* 23 D7
Candle L., *Canada* 73 C7
Candlemas I., *Antarctica* 5 B1
Cando, *U.S.A.* 80 A5
Canea = Khaniá, *Greece* 23 D6
Canelones, *Uruguay* 95 C4
Cañete, *Chile* 94 D1
Cañete, *Peru* 92 F3
Cangas, *Spain* 19 A1
Canguaretama, *Brazil* 93 E11
Canguçu, *Brazil* 95 C5
Cangzhou, *China* 34 E9
Canim Lake, *Canada* 72 C4
Canindeyu □, *Paraguay* 95 A4
Canipaan, *Phil.* 36 C5
Canisteo, *U.S.A.* 78 D7
Canisteo →, *U.S.A.* 78 D7
Cañitas, *Mexico* 86 C4
Çankırı, *Turkey* 25 F5
Cankuzo, *Burundi* 54 C3
Canmore, *Canada* 72 C5
Cann River, *Australia* 63 F4
Canna, *U.K.* 12 D2
Cannanore, *India* 40 P9
Cannes, *France* 18 E7
Canning Town = Port Canning, *India* 43 H13
Cannington, *Canada* 78 B5
Cannock, *U.K.* 10 E5
Cannon Ball →, *U.S.A.* 80 B4
Cannondale Mt., *Australia* 62 D4
Canoas, *Brazil* 95 B5
Canoe L., *Canada* 73 B7
Canon City, *U.S.A.* 80 F2
Canora, *Canada* 73 C8
Canowindra, *Australia* 63 E4
Canso, *Canada* 71 C7
Cantabria □, *Spain* 19 A4
Cantabrian Mts. = Cantábrica, Cordillera, *Spain* 19 A3
Cantábrica, Cordillera, *Spain* 19 A3
Cantal □, *France* 18 D5
Canterbury, *Australia* 62 D3
Canterbury, *U.K.* 11 F9
Canterbury □, *N.Z.* 59 K3
Canterbury Bight, *N.Z.* 59 L3
Canterbury Plains, *N.Z.* 59 K3
Cantil, *U.S.A.* 85 K9
Canton = Guangzhou, *China* 33 D6
Canton, *Ga., U.S.A.* 77 H3
Canton, *Ill., U.S.A.* 80 E9
Canton, *Miss., U.S.A.* 81 J9
Canton, *Mo., U.S.A.* 80 E9
Canton, *N.Y., U.S.A.* 79 B9
Canton, *Ohio, U.S.A.* 78 F3
Canton, *Okla., U.S.A.* 81 G5
Canton, *S. Dak., U.S.A.* 80 D6
Canton L., *U.S.A.* 81 G5
Canudos, *Brazil* 92 E7
Canutama, *Brazil* 92 E6
Canutillo, *U.S.A.* 83 L10
Canyon, *Tex., U.S.A.* 81 H4
Canyon, *Wyo., U.S.A.* 82 D8
Canyonlands Nat. Park, *U.S.A.* 83 G9
Canyonville, *U.S.A.* 82 E2
Cao Bang, *Vietnam* 38 A6
Cao He →, *China* 35 D13
Cao Lanh, *Vietnam* 39 G5
Cao Xian, *China* 34 G8
Cap-aux-Meules, *Canada* 71 C7
Cap-Chat, *Canada* 71 C6
Cap-de-la-Madeleine, *Canada* 70 C5
Cap-Haïtien, *Haiti* 89 C5
Cap St.-Jacques = Vung Tau, *Vietnam* 39 G6
Capa, *Vietnam* 38 A4
Capaia, *Angola* 52 F4
Capanaparo →, *Venezuela* 92 B5
Cape →, *Australia* 62 C4
Cape Barren I., *Australia* 62 G4
Cape Breton Highlands Nat. Park, *Canada* 71 C7
Cape Breton I., *Canada* 71 C7
Cape Charles, *U.S.A.* 76 G8
Cape Coast, *Ghana* 50 G4
Cape Dorset, *Canada* 69 B12
Cape Dyer, *Canada* 69 B13
Cape Fear →, *U.S.A.* 77 H6
Cape Girardeau, *U.S.A.* 81 G10
Cape Jervis, *Australia* 63 F2
Cape May, *U.S.A.* 76 F8
Cape May Pt., *U.S.A.* 75 C12
Cape Province □, *S. Africa* 56 E3
Cape Tormentine, *Canada* 71 C7
Cape Town, *S. Africa* 56 E2
Cape Verde Is. ■, *Atl. Oc.* 2 D8
Cape Vincent, *U.S.A.* 79 B8
Cape York Peninsula, *Australia* 62 A3
Capela, *Brazil* 93 F11
Capella, *Australia* 62 C4
Capim →, *Brazil* 93 D9
Capitan, *U.S.A.* 83 K11
Capitola, *U.S.A.* 84 J5
Capoche →, *Mozam.* 55 F3
Capraia, *Italy* 20 C3
Capreol, *Canada* 70 C3
Caprera, *Italy* 20 D3
Capri, *Italy* 20 D6
Capricorn Group, *Australia* 62 C5
Capricorn Ra., *Australia* 60 D2
Caprivi Strip, *Namibia* 56 B3
Captainganj, *India* 43 F10
Captain's Flat, *Australia* 63 F4
Caquetá →, *Colombia* 92 D5
Caracal, *Romania* 17 F12
Caracas, *Venezuela* 92 A5
Caracol, *Brazil* 93 E10
Caradoc, *Australia* 63 E3
Carajás, Serra dos, *Brazil* 93 E8
Carangola, *Brazil* 95 A7
Carani, *Australia* 61 F2
Caransebeş, *Romania* 17 F11
Caratasca, L., *Honduras* 88 C3
Caratinga, *Brazil* 93 G10
Caraúbas, *Brazil* 93 E11
Caravaca, *Spain* 19 C5
Caravelas, *Brazil* 93 G11
Caraveli, *Peru* 92 G4
Caràzinho, *Brazil* 95 B5
Carballo, *Spain* 19 A1
Carberry, *Canada* 73 D9
Carbó, *Mexico* 86 B2
Carbon, *Canada* 72 C6
Carbonara, C., *Italy* 20 E3
Carbondale, *Colo., U.S.A.* 82 G10
Carbondale, *Ill., U.S.A.* 81 G10
Carbondale, *Pa., U.S.A.* 79 E9
Carbonear, *Canada* 71 C9
Carbonia, *Italy* 20 E3
Carcajou, *Canada* 72 B5
Carcasse, C., *Haiti* 89 C5
Carcassonne, *France* 18 E5
Carcross, *Canada* 68 B6
Cardabia, *Australia* 60 D1
Cardamon Hills, *India* 40 Q10
Cárdenas, *Cuba* 88 B3
Cárdenas, *San Luis Potosí, Mexico* 87 C5
Cárdenas, *Tabasco, Mexico* 87 D6
Cardiff, *U.K.* 11 F4
Cardiff-by-the-Sea, *U.S.A.* 85 M9
Cardigan, *U.K.* 11 E3
Cardigan B., *U.K.* 11 E3
Cardinal, *Canada* 79 B9
Cardona, *Spain* 19 B6
Cardona, *Uruguay* 94 C4
Cardross, *Canada* 73 D7
Cardston, *Canada* 72 D6
Cardwell, *Australia* 62 B4
Careen L., *Canada* 73 B7
Carei, *Romania* 17 E11
Careme, *Indonesia* 37 G13
Carey, *Idaho, U.S.A.* 82 E7
Carey, *Ohio, U.S.A.* 76 E4
Carey, L., *Australia* 61 E3
Carey L., *Canada* 73 A8
Careysburg, *Liberia* 50 G2
Carhué, *Argentina* 94 D3
Cariacica, *Brazil* 93 H10
Caribbean Sea, *W. Indies* 89 C5
Cariboo Mts., *Canada* 72 C4
Caribou, *U.S.A.* 71 C6
Caribou →, *Man., Canada* 73 B10
Caribou →, *N.W.T., Canada* 72 A3
Caribou I., *Canada* 70 C2
Caribou Is., *Canada* 72 A6
Caribou L., *Man., Canada* 73 B9
Caribou L., *Ont., Canada* 70 B2
Caribou Mts., *Canada* 72 B5
Carichic, *Mexico* 86 B3
Carillo, *Mexico* 86 B4
Carinda, *Australia* 63 E4
Carinhanha, *Brazil* 93 F10
Carinthia □ = Kärnten □, *Austria* 16 E6
Caripito, *Venezuela* 92 A6
Caritianas, *Brazil* 92 E6
Carleton Place, *Canada* 70 C4
Carletonville, *S. Africa* 56 D4
Carlin, *U.S.A.* 82 F5
Carlingford, L., *Ireland* 13 B5
Carlinville, *U.S.A.* 80 F10
Carlisle, *U.K.* 10 C5
Carlisle, *U.S.A.* 78 F7
Carlos Casares, *Argentina* 94 D3
Carlos Tejedor, *Argentina* 94 D3
Carlow, *Ireland* 13 D5
Carlow □, *Ireland* 13 D5
Carlsbad, *Calif., U.S.A.* 85 M9
Carlsbad, *N. Mex., U.S.A.* 81 J2
Carlyle, *Canada* 73 D8
Carlyle, *U.S.A.* 80 F10
Carmacks, *Canada* 68 B6
Carman, *Canada* 73 D9
Carmangay, *Canada* 72 C6
Carmanville, *Canada* 71 C9
Carmarthen, *U.K.* 11 F3
Carmarthen B., *U.K.* 11 F3
Carmel, *U.S.A.* 79 E11
Carmel-by-the-Sea, *U.S.A.* 83 H3
Carmel Valley, *U.S.A.* 84 J5
Carmelo, *Uruguay* 94 C4
Carmen, *Colombia* 92 B3
Carmen, *Paraguay* 95 B4
Carmen →, *Mexico* 86 A3
Carmen, I., *Mexico* 86 B2
Carmen de Patagones, *Argentina* 96 E4
Carmensa, *Argentina* 94 D2
Carmi, *U.S.A.* 76 F1
Carmichael, *U.S.A.* 84 G5
Carmila, *Australia* 62 C4
Carmona, *Spain* 19 D3
Carnarvon, *Queens., Australia* 62 C4
Carnarvon, *W. Austral., Australia* 61 D1
Carnarvon, *S. Africa* 56 E3
Carnarvon Ra., *Queens., Australia* 62 D4
Carnarvon Ra., *W. Austral., Australia* 61 E3
Carnation, *U.S.A.* 84 C5
Carndonagh, *Ireland* 13 A4
Carnduff, *Canada* 73 D8
Carnegie, *U.S.A.* 78 F4
Carnegie, L., *Australia* 61 E3
Carnic Alps = Karnische Alpen, *Europe* 16 E6
Carniche Alpi = Karnische Alpen, *Europe* 16 E6
Carnot, *C.A.R.* 52 D3
Carnot, C., *Australia* 63 E2
Carnot B., *Australia* 60 C3
Carnsore Pt., *Ireland* 13 D5
Caro, *U.S.A.* 76 D4
Carol City, *U.S.A.* 77 N5
Carolina, *Brazil* 93 E9
Carolina, *Puerto Rico* 89 C6
Carolina, *S. Africa* 57 D5
Caroline I., *Kiribati* 65 H12
Caroline Is., *Pac. Oc.* 64 G6
Caron, *Canada* 73 C7
Caroni →, *Venezuela* 92 B6

Caroona, Australia 63 E5
Carpathians, Europe 17 D10
Carpaţii Meridionali, Romania 17 F12
Carpentaria, G. of, Australia 62 A2
Carpentaria Downs, Australia 62 B3
Carpinteria, U.S.A. 85 L7
Carpolac = Morea, Australia 63 F3
Carr Boyd Ra., Australia 60 C4
Carrabelle, U.S.A. 77 L3
Carranya, Australia 60 C4
Carrara, Italy 20 B4
Carrauntoohill, Ireland 13 E2
Carrick-on-Shannon, Ireland 13 C3
Carrick-on-Suir, Ireland 13 D4
Carrickfergus, U.K. 13 B6
Carrickfergus □, U.K. 13 B6
Carrickmacross, Ireland 13 C5
Carrieton, Australia 63 E2
Carrington, U.S.A. 80 B5
Carrizal Bajo, Chile 94 B1
Carrizalillo, Chile 94 B1
Carrizo Cr. →, U.S.A. 81 G3
Carrizo Springs, U.S.A. 81 L5
Carrizozo, U.S.A. 83 K11
Carroll, U.S.A. 80 D7
Carrollton, Ga., U.S.A. 77 J3
Carrollton, Ill., U.S.A. 80 F9
Carrollton, Ky., U.S.A. 76 F3
Carrollton, Mo., U.S.A. 80 F8
Carrollton, Ohio, U.S.A. 78 F3
Carron →, U.K. 12 D3
Carron, L., U.K. 12 D3
Carrot →, Canada 73 C8
Carrot River, Canada 73 C8
Carruthers, Canada 73 C7
Carse of Gowrie, U.K. 12 E5
Carson, Calif., U.S.A. 85 M8
Carson, N. Dak., U.S.A. 80 B4
Carson →, U.S.A. 84 F8
Carson City, U.S.A. 84 F7
Carson Sink, U.S.A. 82 G4
Carstairs, U.K. 12 F5
Cartagena, Colombia 92 A3
Cartagena, Spain 19 D5
Cartago, Colombia 92 C3
Cartago, Costa Rica 88 E3
Cartersville, U.S.A. 77 H3
Carterton, N.Z. 59 J5
Carthage, Ark., U.S.A. 81 H8
Carthage, Ill., U.S.A. 80 E9
Carthage, Mo., U.S.A. 81 G7
Carthage, S. Dak., U.S.A. 80 C6
Carthage, Tex., U.S.A. 81 J7
Cartier I., Australia 60 B3
Cartwright, Canada 71 B8
Caruaru, Brazil 93 E11
Carúpano, Venezuela 92 A6
Caruthersville, U.S.A. 81 G10
Carvoeiro, Brazil 92 D6
Casa Grande, U.S.A. 83 K8
Casablanca, Chile 94 C1
Casablanca, Morocco 50 B3
Casale Monferrato, Italy 20 B3
Casas Grandes, Mexico 86 A3
Cascade, Idaho, U.S.A. 82 D5
Cascade, Mont., U.S.A. 82 C8
Cascade Locks, U.S.A. 84 E5
Cascade Ra., U.S.A. 84 D5
Cascavel, Brazil 95 A5
Caserta, Italy 20 D6
Cashel, Ireland 13 D4
Cashmere, U.S.A. 82 C3
Cashmere Downs, Australia 61 E2
Casiguran, Phil. 37 A6
Casilda, Argentina 94 C3
Casino, Australia 63 D5
Casiquiare →, Venezuela 92 C5
Caslan, Canada 72 C6
Casma, Peru 92 E3
Casmalia, U.S.A. 85 L6
Caspe, Spain 19 B5
Casper, U.S.A. 82 E10
Caspian Sea, Asia 25 F9
Cass City, U.S.A. 76 D4
Cass Lake, U.S.A. 80 B7
Casselman, Canada 79 A9
Casselton, U.S.A. 80 B6
Cassiar, Canada 72 B3
Cassiar Mts., Canada 72 B2
Cassinga, Angola 53 H3
Cassville, U.S.A. 81 G8
Castaic, U.S.A. 85 L8
Castellammare del Golfo, Italy 20 E5
Castellammare di Stábia, Italy 20 D6
Castelli, Argentina 94 D4
Castellón de la Plana, Spain 19 C5
Castelo, Brazil 95 A7
Castelo Branco, Portugal 19 C2
Castelvetrano, Italy 20 F5
Casterton, Australia 63 F3
Castilla La Mancha □, Spain 19 C4
Castilla La Nueva = Castilla La Mancha □, Spain 19 C4
Castilla La Vieja = Castilla y Leon □, Spain 19 B3
Castilla y Leon □, Spain 19 B3
Castillos, Uruguay 95 C5
Castle Dale, U.S.A. 82 G8
Castle Douglas, U.K. 12 G5
Castle Rock, Colo., U.S.A. 80 F2
Castle Rock, Wash., U.S.A. 84 D4
Castlebar, Ireland 13 C2
Castleblaney, Ireland 13 B5
Castlegar, Canada 72 D5
Castlemaine, Australia 63 F3
Castlereagh, Ireland 13 C3
Castlereagh □, U.K. 13 B6
Castlereagh →, Australia 63 E4
Castlereagh B., Australia 62 A2
Castletown, I. of Man 10 C3
Castletown Bearhaven, Ireland 13 E2
Castlevale, Australia 62 C4
Castor, Canada 72 C6
Castres, France 18 E5
Castries, St. Lucia 89 D7
Castro, Brazil 95 A5
Castro, Chile 96 E2
Castro Alves, Brazil 93 F11
Castro del Río, Spain 19 D3
Castroville, Calif., U.S.A. 84 J5
Castroville, Tex., U.S.A. 81 L5
Casummit Lake, Canada 70 B1
Cat Ba, Dao, Vietnam 38 B6
Cat I., Bahamas 89 B4
Cat I., U.S.A. 81 K10
Cat L., Canada 70 B1
Catacamas, Honduras 88 D2
Catacáos, Peru 92 E2
Cataguases, Brazil 95 A7
Catahoula L., U.S.A. 81 K8
Catalão, Brazil 93 G9
Catalina, Canada 71 C9
Catalonia = Cataluña □, Spain 19 B6
Cataluña □, Spain 19 B6
Catamarca, Argentina 94 B2
Catamarca □, Argentina 94 B2
Catanduanes, Phil. 37 B6
Catanduva, Brazil 95 A6
Catánia, Italy 20 F6
Catanzaro, Italy 20 E7
Catarman, Phil. 37 B6
Cateel, Phil. 37 C7
Cathcart, S. Africa 56 E4
Cathlamet, U.S.A. 84 D3
Catlettsburg, U.S.A. 76 F4
Catoche, C., Mexico 87 C7
Catrimani, Brazil 92 C6
Catskill, U.S.A. 79 D11
Catskill Mts., U.S.A. 79 D10
Catt, Mt., Australia 62 A1
Cattaraugus, U.S.A. 78 D6
Catuala, Angola 56 B2
Catur, Mozam. 55 E4
Catwick Is., Vietnam 39 G7
Cauca →, Colombia 92 B4
Caucaia, Brazil 93 D11
Caucasus = Bolshoi Kavkas, Asia 25 F7
Caúngula, Angola 52 F3
Cauquenes, Chile 94 D1
Caura →, Venezuela 92 B6
Cauresi →, Mozam. 55 F3
Causapscal, Canada 71 C6
Cauvery →, India 40 P11
Caux, Pays de, France 18 B4
Cavalier, U.S.A. 80 A6
Cavan, Ireland 13 C4
Cavan □, Ireland 13 C4
Cave City, U.S.A. 76 G3
Cavenagh Ra., Australia 61 E4
Cavendish, Australia 63 F3
Caviana, I., Brazil 93 C8
Cavite, Phil. 37 B6
Cawndilla L., Australia 63 E3
Cawnpore = Kanpur, India 43 F9
Caxias, Brazil 93 D10
Caxias do Sul, Brazil 95 B5
Caxito, Angola 52 F2
Cay Sal Bank, Bahamas 88 B3
Cayambe, Ecuador 92 C3
Cayenne, Fr. Guiana 93 B8
Cayman Brac, Cayman Is. 88 C4
Cayman Is., W. Indies 88 C3
Cayo Romano, Cuba 89 B4
Cayuga, Canada 78 D5
Cayuga, U.S.A. 79 D8
Cayuga L., U.S.A. 79 D8
Cazombo, Angola 53 G4
Ceanannus Mor, Ireland 13 C5
Ceará = Fortaleza, Brazil 93 D11
Ceará □, Brazil 93 E11
Ceará Mirim, Brazil 93 E11
Cebaco, I. de, Panama 88 E3
Cebollar, Argentina 94 B2
Cebu, Phil. 37 B6
Cecil Plains, Australia 63 D5
Cedar →, U.S.A. 80 E9
Cedar City, U.S.A. 83 H7
Cedar Creek Res., U.S.A. 81 J6
Cedar Falls, Iowa, U.S.A. 80 D8
Cedar Falls, Wash., U.S.A. 84 C5
Cedar Key, U.S.A. 77 L4
Cedar L., Canada 73 C8
Cedar Rapids, U.S.A. 80 E9
Cedartown, U.S.A. 77 H3
Cedarvale, Canada 72 B3
Cedarville, S. Africa 57 E4
Cedarville, U.S.A. 82 F3
Cedral, Mexico 86 C4
Cedro, Brazil 93 E11
Cedros, I. de, Mexico 86 B1
Ceduna, Australia 63 E1
Cefalù, Italy 20 E6
Cegléd, Hungary 17 E9
Cehegín, Spain 19 C5
Celaya, Mexico 86 C4
Celbridge, Ireland 13 C5
Celebes = Sulawesi □, Indonesia 37 E6
Celebes Sea, Indonesia 37 D6
Celina, U.S.A. 76 E3
Celje, Slovenia 20 A6
Celle, Germany 16 B5
Cement, U.S.A. 81 H5
Center, N. Dak., U.S.A. 80 B4
Center, Tex., U.S.A. 81 K7
Centerfield, U.S.A. 83 G8
Centerville, Calif., U.S.A. 84 J7
Centerville, Iowa, U.S.A. 80 E8
Centerville, Pa., U.S.A. 78 F5
Centerville, S. Dak., U.S.A. 80 D6
Centerville, Tenn., U.S.A. 77 H2
Centerville, Tex., U.S.A. 81 K7
Central, U.S.A. 83 K9
Central □, Kenya 54 C4
Central □, Malawi 55 E3
Central □, U.K. 12 E4
Central □, Zambia 55 E2
Central, Cordillera, Colombia 92 C4
Central, Cordillera, Costa Rica 88 D3
Central, Cordillera, Dom. Rep. 89 C5
Central African Republic ■, Africa 51 G9
Central City, Ky., U.S.A. 76 G2
Central City, Nebr., U.S.A. 80 E5
Central I., Kenya 54 B4
Central Makran Range, Pakistan 40 F4
Central Patricia, Canada 70 B1
Central Russian Uplands, Europe 6 E13
Central Siberian Plateau, Russia 28 C14
Centralia, Ill., U.S.A. 80 F10
Centralia, Mo., U.S.A. 80 F8
Centralia, Wash., U.S.A. 84 D4
Centreville, Ala., U.S.A. 77 J2
Centreville, Miss., U.S.A. 81 K9
Cephalonia = Kefallinia, Greece 21 E9
Cepu, Indonesia 37 G14
Ceram = Seram, Indonesia 37 E7
Ceram Sea = Seram Sea, Indonesia 37 E7
Ceres, Argentina 94 B3
Ceres, S. Africa 56 E2
Ceres, U.S.A. 84 H6
Cerignola, Italy 20 D6
Cerigo = Kíthira, Greece 21 F11
Cerknica, Slovenia 20 B6
Cernavodă, Romania 17 F14
Cerralvo, I., Mexico 86 C3
Cerritos, Mexico 86 C4
Cervera, Spain 19 B6
Cervera del Río Alhama, Spain 19 A5
Cesena, Italy 20 B5
České Budějovice, Czech. 16 D7
Ceskomoravská Vrchovina, Czech. 16 D7
Český Těšin, Czech. 17 D9
Cessnock, Australia 63 E5
Cetinje, Montenegro, Yug. 21 C8
Ceuta, Morocco 50 A3
Cévennes, France 18 D5
Ceyhan →, Turkey 25 G6
Ceylon = Sri Lanka ■, Asia 40 R12
Cha-am, Thailand 38 F2
Chablais, France 18 C7
Chacabuco, Argentina 94 C3
Chachapoyas, Peru 92 E3
Chachoengsao, Thailand 38 F3
Chachran, Pakistan 40 E7
Chachro, Pakistan 42 G4
Chaco □, Argentina 94 B3
Chaco □, Paraguay 94 B3
Chad ■, Africa 51 E8
Chad, L. = Tchad, L., Chad 51 F7
Chadan, Russia 27 D10
Chadileuvú →, Argentina 94 D2
Chadiza, Zambia 55 E3
Chadron, U.S.A. 80 D3
Chae Hom, Thailand 38 C2
Chaem →, Thailand 38 C2
Chaeryŏng, N. Korea 35 E13
Chagai Hills, Afghan. 40 E3
Chagda, Russia 27 D14
Chagos Arch., Ind. Oc. 28 K11
Chāh Ākhvor, Iran 45 C8
Chāh Bahār, Iran 45 E9
Chāh-e-Malek, Iran 45 D8
Chāh Kavir, Iran 45 D7
Chahar Burjak, Afghan. 40 D3
Chaibasa, India 41 H14
Chainat, Thailand 38 E3
Chaiya, Thailand 39 H2
Chaj Doab, Pakistan 42 C5
Chajari, Argentina 94 C4
Chake Chake, Tanzania 54 D4
Chakhānsūr, Afghan. 40 D3
Chakonipau, L., Canada 71 A6
Chakradharpur, India 43 H11
Chakwal, Pakistan 42 C5
Chala, Peru 92 G4
Chalchihuites, Mexico 86 C4
Chalcis = Khalkis, Greece 21 E10
Chaleur B., Canada 71 C6
Chalfant, U.S.A. 84 H8
Chalhuanca, Peru 92 F4
Chalisgaon, India 40 J9
Chalky Inlet, N.Z. 59 M1
Challapata, Bolivia 92 G5
Challis, U.S.A. 82 D6
Chalna, India 43 H13
Châlons-sur-Marne, France 18 B6
Chalyaphum, Thailand 38 E4
Cham, Cu Lao, Vietnam 38 E7
Chama, U.S.A. 83 H10
Chaman, Pakistan 40 D5
Chamba, India 42 C7
Chamba, Tanzania 55 E4
Chambal →, India 43 F8
Chamberlain, U.S.A. 80 D5
Chamberlain →, Australia 60 C4
Chambers, U.S.A. 83 J9
Chambersburg, U.S.A. 76 F7
Chambéry, France 18 D6
Chambly, Canada 79 A11
Chambord, Canada 71 C5
Chamchamal, Iraq 44 C5
Chamela, Mexico 86 D3
Chamical, Argentina 94 C2
Chamkar Luong, Cambodia 39 G4
Chamonix-Mont-Blanc, France 18 D7
Champa, India 43 H10
Champagne, Canada 72 A1
Champagne, Plaine de, France 18 B6
Champaign, U.S.A. 76 E1
Champassak, Laos 38 E5
Champlain, Canada 76 B9
Champlain, U.S.A. 79 B11
Champlain, L., U.S.A. 79 B11
Champotón, Mexico 87 D6
Chana, Thailand 39 J3
Chañaral, Chile 94 B1
Chanārān, Iran 45 B8
Chanasma, India 42 H5
Chandannagar, India 43 H13
Chandausi, India 43 E8
Chandeleur Is., U.S.A. 81 L10
Chandeleur Sd., U.S.A. 81 L10
Chandigarh, India 42 D7
Chandler, Australia 63 D1
Chandler, Canada 71 C7
Chandler, Ariz., U.S.A. 83 K8
Chandler, Okla., U.S.A. 81 H6
Chandpur, Bangla. 41 H17
Chandpur, India 42 E8
Chandrapur, India 40 K11
Chānf, Iran 45 E9
Chang, Pakistan 42 F3
Chang, Ko, Thailand 39 F4
Chang Jiang →, China 33 C7
Changa, India 43 C7
Changanacheri, India 40 Q10
Changane →, Mozam. 57 C5
Changbai, China 35 D15
Changbai Shan, China 35 C15
Changchiak'ou = Zhangjiakou, China 34 D8
Ch'angchou = Changzhou, China 33 C6
Changchun, China 35 C13
Changchunling, China 35 B13
Changde, China 33 D6
Changdo-ri, N. Korea 35 E14
Changhai = Shanghai, China 33 C7
Changhŭng, S. Korea 35 G14
Changhŭngni, N. Korea 35 D15
Changjiang, China 38 C7
Changjin, N. Korea 35 D14
Changjin-chŏsuji, N. Korea 35 D14
Changli, China 35 E10
Changling, China 35 B12
Changlun, Malaysia 39 J3
Changping, China 34 D9
Changsha, China 33 D6
Changwu, China 34 G4
Changyi, China 35 F10
Changyŏn, N. Korea 35 E13
Changyuan, China 34 G8
Changzhi, China 34 F7
Changzhou, China 33 C6
Chanhanga, Angola 56 B1
Channapatna, India 40 N10
Channel Is., U.K. 11 H5
Channel Is., U.S.A. 85 M7
Channel-Port aux Basques, Canada 71 C8
Channing, Mich., U.S.A. 76 B1
Channing, Tex., U.S.A. 81 H3
Chantada, Spain 19 A2
Chanthaburi, Thailand 38 F4
Chantrey Inlet, Canada 68 B10
Chanute, U.S.A. 81 G7
Chao Phraya →, Thailand 38 F3
Chao Phraya Lowlands, Thailand 38 E3
Chao'an, China 33 D6
Chaocheng, China 34 F8
Chaoyang, China 35 D11
Chapala, Mozam. 55 F4
Chapala, L. de, Mexico 86 C4
Chapayevo, Kazakhstan 25 D9
Chapayevsk, Russia 24 D8
Chapecó, Brazil 95 B5
Chapel Hill, U.S.A. 77 H6
Chapleau, Canada 70 C3
Chaplin, Canada 73 C7
Châr, Mauritania 50 D2
Chara, Russia 27 D12
Charadai, Argentina 94 B4
Charagua, Bolivia 92 G6
Charaña, Bolivia 92 G5
Charata, Argentina 94 B3
Charcas, Mexico 86 C4
Charcoal L., Canada 73 B8
Chard, U.K. 11 G5
Chardara, Kazakhstan 26 E7
Chardon, U.S.A. 78 E3
Chardzhou, Turkmenistan 26 F7
Charente □, France 18 D4
Charente-Maritime □, France 18 D3
Chari →, Chad 51 F7
Chārīkār, Afghan. 40 B6
Chariton →, U.S.A. 80 F8
Charkhari, India 43 G8
Charkhi Dadri, India 42 E7
Charleroi, Belgium 15 D4
Charleroi, U.S.A. 78 F5
Charles, C., U.S.A. 76 G8
Charles City, U.S.A. 80 D8
Charles L., Canada 73 B6
Charles Town, U.S.A. 76 F7
Charleston, Ill., U.S.A. 76 F1
Charleston, Miss., U.S.A. 81 H9
Charleston, Mo., U.S.A. 81 G10
Charleston, S.C., U.S.A. 77 J6
Charleston, W. Va., U.S.A. 76 F5
Charleston Pk., U.S.A. 85 J11
Charlestown, S. Africa 57 D4
Charlestown, U.S.A. 76 F3
Charlesville, Zaïre 52 F4
Charleville = Rath Luirc, Ireland 13 D3
Charleville, Australia 63 D4
Charleville-Mézières, France 18 B6
Charlevoix, U.S.A. 76 C3
Charlotte, Mich., U.S.A. 76 D3
Charlotte, N.C., U.S.A. 77 H5
Charlotte Amalie, Virgin Is. 89 C7
Charlotte Harbor, U.S.A. 77 M4
Charlottesville, U.S.A. 76 F6
Charlottetown, Canada 71 C7
Charlton, Australia 63 F3
Charlton, U.S.A. 80 E8
Charlton I., Canada 70 B4
Charny, Canada 71 C5
Charolles, France 18 C6
Charouine, Algeria 50 C4
Charre, Mozam. 55 F4
Charsadda, Pakistan 42 B4
Charters Towers, Australia 62 C4
Chartres, France 18 B4
Chascomús, Argentina 94 D4
Chasefu, Zambia 55 E3
Chasovnya-Uchurskaya, Russia 27 D14
Chāt, Iran 45 B7
Château-Salins, France 18 B7
Châteaubriant, France 18 C3
Châteauroux, France 18 C4
Châtellerault, France 18 C4
Chatfield, U.S.A. 80 D9
Chatham, N.B., Canada 71 C6
Chatham, Ont., Canada 70 D3
Chatham, U.K. 11 F8
Chatham, La., U.S.A. 81 J8
Chatham, N.Y., U.S.A. 79 D11
Chatham Is., Pac. Oc. 64 M10
Chatham Str., U.S.A. 72 B2
Chatmohar, Bangla. 43 G13
Chatra, India 43 G11
Chatrapur, India 41 K14
Chats, L. des, Canada 79 A8
Chatsworth, Canada 78 B4
Chatsworth, Zimbabwe 55 F3
Chattahoochee →, U.S.A. 77 K3
Chattanooga, U.S.A. 77 H3
Chaturat, Thailand 38 E3
Chau Doc, Vietnam 39 G5
Chauk, Burma 41 J19
Chaukan La, Burma 41 F20
Chaumont, France 18 B6
Chaumont, U.S.A. 79 B8
Chautauqua L., U.S.A. 78 D5
Chauvin, Canada 73 C6
Chaves, Brazil 93 D9
Chaves, Portugal 19 B2
Chavuma, Zambia 53 G4
Chawang, Thailand 39 H2
Chaykovskiy, Russia 24 C9
Chazy, U.S.A. 79 B11
Cheb, Czech. 16 C6
Cheboksary, Russia 24 C8
Cheboygan, U.S.A. 76 C3
Chech, Erg, Africa 50 D4
Checheno-Ingush Republic □, Russia 25 F8
Chechon, S. Korea 35 F15
Checleset B., Canada 72 C3
Checotah, U.S.A. 81 H7
Chedabucto B., Canada 71 C7
Cheduba I., Burma 41 K18
Cheepie, Australia 63 D4
Chegdomyn, Russia 27 D14
Chegga, Mauritania 50 C3
Chegutu, Zimbabwe 55 F3
Chehalis, U.S.A. 84 D4
Cheju Do, S. Korea 35 H14
Chekiang = Zhejiang □, China 33 D7
Chela, Sa. da, Angola 56 B1
Chelan, U.S.A. 82 C4
Chelan, L., U.S.A. 82 C3
Cheleken, Turkmenistan 25 G9

Chelforó, *Argentina* 96 D3
Chelkar, *Kazakhstan* 26 E6
Chelkar Tengiz, Solonchak, *Kazakhstan* 26 E7
Chełm, *Poland* 17 C11
Chełmno, *Poland* 17 B9
Chelmsford, *U.K.* 11 F8
Chelmsford Dam, *S. Africa* 57 D4
Chełmża, *Poland* 17 B9
Chelsea, *Okla., U.S.A.* 81 G7
Chelsea, *Vt., U.S.A.* 79 C12
Cheltenham, *U.K.* 11 F5
Chelyabinsk, *Russia* 26 D7
Chelyuskin, C., *Russia* 28 B14
Chemainus, *Canada* 72 D4
Chemnitz, *Germany* 16 C6
Chemult, *U.S.A.* 82 E3
Chen, Gora, *Russia* 27 C15
Chenab →, *Pakistan* 42 D4
Chenango Forks, *U.S.A.* 79 D9
Chencha, *Ethiopia* 51 G12
Cheney, *U.S.A.* 82 C5
Cheng Xian, *China* 34 H3
Chengcheng, *China* 34 G5
Chengchou = Zhengzhou, *China* 34 G7
Chengde, *China* 35 D9
Chengdu, *China* 32 C5
Chenggu, *China* 34 H4
Chengjiang, *China* 32 D5
Ch'engtu = Chengdu, *China* 32 C5
Chengwu, *China* 34 G8
Chengyang, *China* 35 F11
Chenjiagang, *China* 35 G10
Chenkán, *Mexico* 87 D6
Cheo Reo, *Vietnam* 38 F7
Cheom Ksan, *Cambodia* 38 E5
Chepén, *Peru* 92 E3
Chepes, *Argentina* 94 C2
Chepo, *Panama* 88 E4
Cheptulil, Mt., *Kenya* 54 B4
Chequamegon B., *U.S.A.* 80 B9
Cher □, *France* 18 C5
Cher →, *France* 18 C4
Cheraw, *U.S.A.* 77 H6
Cherbourg, *France* 18 B3
Cherchell, *Algeria* 50 A5
Cherdyn, *Russia* 24 B10
Cheremkhovo, *Russia* 27 D11
Cherepanovo, *Russia* 26 D9
Cherepovets, *Russia* 24 C6
Chergui, Chott ech, *Algeria* 50 B5
Cherkassy, *Ukraine* 25 E5
Cherlak, *Russia* 26 D8
Chernigov, *Ukraine* 24 D5
Chernikovsk, *Russia* 24 D10
Chernogorsk, *Russia* 27 D10
Chernovtsy, *Ukraine* 25 E4
Chernoye, *Russia* 27 B9
Chernyakhovsk, *Russia* 26 D3
Chernyshovskiy, *Russia* 27 C12
Cherokee, *Iowa, U.S.A.* 80 D7
Cherokee, *Okla., U.S.A.* 81 G5
Cherokees, L. O'The, *U.S.A.* 81 G7
Cherquenco, *Chile* 96 D2
Cherrapunji, *India* 41 G17
Cherry Creek, *U.S.A.* 82 G6
Cherry Valley, *U.S.A.* 85 M10
Cherryvale, *U.S.A.* 81 G7
Cherskiy, *Russia* 27 C17
Cherskogo Khrebet, *Russia* 27 C15
Cherwell →, *U.K.* 11 F6
Chesapeake, *U.S.A.* 76 G7
Chesapeake B., *U.S.A.* 76 F7
Cheshire □, *U.K.* 10 D5
Cheshskaya Guba, *Russia* 24 A8
Cheslatta L., *Canada* 72 C3
Chesley, *Canada* 78 B3
Chester, *U.K.* 10 D5
Chester, *Calif., U.S.A.* 82 F3
Chester, *Ill., U.S.A.* 81 G10
Chester, *Mont., U.S.A.* 82 B8
Chester, *Pa., U.S.A.* 76 F8
Chester, *S.C., U.S.A.* 77 H5
Chesterfield, *U.K.* 10 D6
Chesterfield, Is., *N. Cal.* 64 J7
Chesterfield Inlet, *Canada* 68 B10
Chesterton Ra., *Australia* 63 D4
Chesterville, *Canada* 79 A9
Chesuncook L., *U.S.A.* 71 C6
Chéticamp, *Canada* 71 C7
Chetumal, B. de, *Mexico* 87 D7
Chetwynd, *Canada* 72 B4
Cheviot, The, *U.K.* 10 B5
Cheviot Hills, *U.K.* 10 B5
Cheviot Ra., *Australia* 62 D3
Chew Bahir, *Ethiopia* 51 H12
Chewelah, *U.S.A.* 82 B5
Cheyenne, *Okla., U.S.A.* 81 H5
Cheyenne, *Wyo., U.S.A.* 80 E2
Cheyenne →, *U.S.A.* 80 C4
Cheyenne Wells, *U.S.A.* 80 F3
Cheyne B., *Australia* 61 F2
Chhabra, *India* 42 G7
Chhapra, *India* 43 G11
Chhata, *India* 42 F7
Chhatarpur, *India* 43 G8
Chhep, *Cambodia* 38 F5
Chhindwara, *India* 43 H8
Chhlong, *Cambodia* 39 F5
Chhuk, *Cambodia* 39 G5
Chi →, *Thailand* 38 E5
Chiamis, *Indonesia* 37 G13
Chiamussu = Jiamusi, *China* 33 B8
Chiang Dao, *Thailand* 38 C2
Chiang Kham, *Thailand* 38 C3
Chiang Khan, *Thailand* 38 D3
Chiang Khong, *Thailand* 38 B3
Chiang Mai, *Thailand* 38 C2
Chiang Saen, *Thailand* 38 B3
Chiange, *Angola* 53 H2
Chiapa →, *Mexico* 87 D6
Chiapa de Corzo, *Mexico* 87 D6
Chiapas □, *Mexico* 87 D6
Chiautla, *Mexico* 87 D5
Chiba, *Japan* 31 G10
Chibabava, *Mozam.* 57 C5
Chibatu, *Indonesia* 37 G12
Chibemba, *Cunene, Angola* 53 H2
Chibemba, *Huila, Angola* 56 B2
Chibia, *Angola* 53 H2
Chibougamau, *Canada* 70 C5
Chibougamau L., *Canada* 70 C5
Chibuk, *Nigeria* 51 F7
Chic-Chocs, Mts., *Canada* 71 C6
Chicacole = Srikakulam, *India* 41 K13
Chicago, *U.S.A.* 76 E2
Chicago Heights, *U.S.A.* 76 E2
Chichagof I., *U.S.A.* 72 B1
Chicheng, *China* 34 D8
Chichester, *U.K.* 11 G7
Chichibu, *Japan* 31 F9
Ch'ich'ihaerh = Qiqihar, *China* 33 B7
Chickasha, *U.S.A.* 81 H5
Chiclana de la Frontera, *Spain* 19 D2
Chiclayo, *Peru* 92 E3
Chico, *U.S.A.* 84 F5
Chico →, *Chubut, Argentina* 96 E3
Chico →, *Santa Cruz, Argentina* 96 G3
Chicomo, *Mozam.* 57 C5
Chicontepec, *Mexico* 87 C5
Chicopee, *U.S.A.* 79 D12
Chicoutimi, *Canada* 71 C5
Chicualacuala, *Mozam.* 57 C5
Chidambaram, *India* 40 P11
Chidenguele, *Mozam.* 57 C5
Chidley, C., *Canada* 69 B13
Chiede, *Angola* 56 B2
Chiefs Pt., *Canada* 78 B3
Chiem Hoa, *Vietnam* 38 A5
Chiengi, *Zambia* 55 D2
Chiengmai = Chiang Mai, *Thailand* 38 C2
Chiese →, *Italy* 20 B4
Chieti, *Italy* 20 C6
Chifeng, *China* 35 C10
Chignecto B., *Canada* 71 C7
Chiguana, *Bolivia* 94 A2
Chiha-ri, *N. Korea* 35 E14
Chihli, G. of = Bo Hai, *China* 35 E10
Chihuahua, *Mexico* 86 B3
Chihuahua □, *Mexico* 86 B3
Chiili, *Kazakhstan* 26 E7
Chik Bollapur, *India* 40 N10
Chikmagalur, *India* 40 N9
Chikwawa, *Malawi* 55 F3
Chilac, *Mexico* 87 D5
Chilako →, *Canada* 72 C4
Chilam Chavki, *Pakistan* 43 B6
Chilanga, *Zambia* 55 F2
Chilapa, *Mexico* 87 D5
Chilas, *Pakistan* 43 B6
Chilaw, *Sri Lanka* 40 R11
Chilcotin →, *Canada* 72 C4
Childers, *Australia* 63 D5
Childress, *U.S.A.* 81 H4
Chile ■, *S. Amer.* 96 D2
Chile Rise, *Pac. Oc.* 65 L18
Chilecito, *Argentina* 94 B2
Chilete, *Peru* 92 E3
Chililabombwe, *Zambia* 55 E2
Chilin = Jilin, *China* 35 C14
Chilka L., *India* 41 K14
Chilko →, *Canada* 72 C4
Chilko, L., *Canada* 72 C4
Chillagoe, *Australia* 62 B3
Chillán, *Chile* 94 D1
Chillicothe, *Ill., U.S.A.* 80 E10
Chillicothe, *Mo., U.S.A.* 80 F8
Chillicothe, *Ohio, U.S.A.* 76 F4
Chilliwack, *Canada* 72 D4
Chilo, *India* 42 F5
Chiloane, I., *Mozam.* 57 C5
Chiloé, I. de, *Chile* 96 E2
Chilpancingo, *Mexico* 87 D5
Chiltern Hills, *U.K.* 11 F7
Chilton, *U.S.A.* 76 C1
Chiluage, *Angola* 52 F4
Chilubi, *Zambia* 55 E2
Chilubula, *Zambia* 55 E3
Chilumba, *Malawi* 55 E3
Chilwa, L., *Malawi* 55 F4
Chimaltitán, *Mexico* 86 C4
Chimán, *Panama* 88 E4
Chimay, *Belgium* 15 D4
Chimbay, *Uzbekistan* 26 E6
Chimborazo, *Ecuador* 92 D3
Chimbote, *Peru* 92 E3
Chimkent, *Kazakhstan* 26 E7
Chimoio, *Mozam.* 55 F3
Chimpembe, *Zambia* 55 D2
Chin □, *Burma* 41 J18
Chin Ling Shan = Qinling Shandi, *China* 34 H5
China, *Mexico* 87 B5
China ■, *Asia* 33 D6
China Lake, *U.S.A.* 85 K9
Chinan = Jinan, *China* 34 F9
Chinandega, *Nic.* 88 D2
Chinati Pk., *U.S.A.* 81 K2
Chincha Alta, *Peru* 92 F3
Chinchilla, *Australia* 63 D5
Chinchón, *Spain* 19 B4
Chinchorro, Banco, *Mexico* 87 D7
Chinchou = Jinzhou, *China* 35 D11
Chincoteague, *U.S.A.* 76 G8
Chinde, *Mozam.* 55 F4
Chindo, *S. Korea* 35 G14
Chindwin →, *Burma* 41 J19
Chineni, *India* 43 C6
Chinga, *Mozam.* 55 F4
Chingola, *Zambia* 55 E2
Chingole, *Malawi* 55 E3
Ch'ingtao = Qingdao, *China* 35 F11
Chinguetti, *Mauritania* 50 D2
Chingune, *Mozam.* 57 C5
Chinhae, *S. Korea* 35 G15
Chinhanguanine, *Mozam.* 57 D5
Chinhoyi, *Zimbabwe* 55 F3
Chiniot, *Pakistan* 42 D5
Chinipas, *Mexico* 86 B3
Chinju, *S. Korea* 35 G15
Chinle, *U.S.A.* 83 H9
Chinnampo, *N. Korea* 35 E13
Chino, *Japan* 31 G9
Chino, *U.S.A.* 85 L9
Chino Valley, *U.S.A.* 83 J7
Chinon, *France* 18 C4
Chinook, *Canada* 73 C6
Chinook, *U.S.A.* 82 B9
Chinsali, *Zambia* 55 E3
Chióggia, *Italy* 20 B5
Chíos = Khíos, *Greece* 21 E12
Chipata, *Zambia* 55 E3
Chipewyan L., *Canada* 73 B9
Chipinge, *Zimbabwe* 55 G3
Chipley, *U.S.A.* 77 K3
Chipman, *Canada* 71 C6
Chipoka, *Malawi* 55 E3
Chippenham, *U.K.* 11 F5
Chippewa →, *U.S.A.* 80 C8
Chippewa Falls, *U.S.A.* 80 C9
Chiquián, *Peru* 92 F3
Chiquimula, *Guatemala* 88 D2
Chiquinquira, *Colombia* 92 B4
Chirala, *India* 40 M12
Chiramba, *Mozam.* 55 F3
Chirawa, *India* 42 E6
Chirchik, *Uzbekistan* 26 E7
Chiricahua Pk., *U.S.A.* 83 L9
Chiriquí, G. de, *Panama* 88 E3
Chiriquí, L. de, *Panama* 88 E3
Chirivira Falls, *Zimbabwe* 55 G3
Chirmiri, *India* 41 H13
Chiromo, *Malawi* 53 H7
Chirripó Grande, Cerro, *Costa Rica* 88 E3
Chisamba, *Zambia* 55 E2
Chisapani Garhi, *Nepal* 41 F14
Chisholm, *Canada* 72 C6
Chishtian Mandi, *Pakistan* 42 E5
Chisimba Falls, *Zambia* 55 E3
Chisos Mts., *U.S.A.* 81 L3
Chistopol, *Russia* 24 C9
Chita, *Russia* 27 D12
Chitado, *Angola* 53 H2
Chitembo, *Angola* 53 G3
Chitipa, *Malawi* 55 D3
Chitose, *Japan* 30 C10
Chitral, *Pakistan* 40 B7
Chitré, *Panama* 88 E3
Chittagong, *Bangla.* 41 H17
Chittagong □, *Bangla.* 41 G17
Chittaurgarh, *India* 42 G6
Chittoor, *India* 40 N11
Chitungwiza, *Zimbabwe* 55 F3
Chiusi, *Italy* 20 C4
Chivasso, *Italy* 20 B2
Chivhu, *Zimbabwe* 55 F3
Chivilcoy, *Argentina* 94 C4
Chiwanda, *Tanzania* 55 E3
Chizera, *Zambia* 55 E1
Chkalov = Orenburg, *Russia* 24 D10
Chloride, *U.S.A.* 85 K12
Cho Bo, *Vietnam* 38 B5
Cho-do, *N. Korea* 35 E13
Cho Phuoc Hai, *Vietnam* 39 G6
Choba, *Kenya* 54 B4
Chobe National Park, *Botswana* 56 B3
Chochiwŏn, *S. Korea* 35 F14
Choctawhatchee B., *U.S.A.* 75 D9
Choele Choel, *Argentina* 96 D3
Choix, *Mexico* 86 B3
Chojnice, *Poland* 17 B8
Chōkai-San, *Japan* 30 E10
Chokurdakh, *Russia* 27 B15
Cholame, *U.S.A.* 84 K6
Cholet, *France* 18 C3
Choluteca, *Honduras* 88 D2
Choluteca →, *Honduras* 88 D2
Chom Bung, *Thailand* 38 F2
Chom Thong, *Thailand* 38 C2
Choma, *Zambia* 55 F2
Chomun, *India* 42 F6
Chomutov, *Czech.* 16 C6
Chon Buri, *Thailand* 38 F3
Chon Thanh, *Vietnam* 39 G6
Chonan, *S. Korea* 35 F14
Chone, *Ecuador* 92 D2
Chong Kai, *Cambodia* 38 F4
Chong Mek, *Thailand* 38 E5
Chŏngdo, *S. Korea* 35 G15
Chŏngha, *S. Korea* 35 F15
Chongjin, *N. Korea* 35 D15
Chŏngju, *N. Korea* 35 E13
Chŏngju, *S. Korea* 35 F14
Chongli, *China* 34 D8
Chongqing, *China* 32 D5
Chŏngŭp, *S. Korea* 35 G14
Chŏnju, *S. Korea* 35 G14
Chonos, Arch. de los, *Chile* 96 F2
Chopim →, *Brazil* 95 B5
Chorbat La, *India* 43 B7
Chorley, *U.K.* 10 D5
Chorolque, Cerro, *Bolivia* 94 A2
Chorregon, *Australia* 62 C3
Chŏrwŏn, *S. Korea* 35 E14
Chorzów, *Poland* 17 C9
Chos-Malal, *Argentina* 94 D1
Chosan, *N. Korea* 35 D13
Choszczno, *Poland* 16 B7
Choteau, *U.S.A.* 82 C7
Chotila, *India* 42 H4
Chowchilla, *U.S.A.* 83 H3
Choybalsan, *Mongolia* 33 B6
Christchurch, *N.Z.* 59 K4
Christchurch, *U.K.* 11 G6
Christian I., *Canada* 78 B4
Christiana, *S. Africa* 56 D4
Christiansted, *Virgin Is.* 89 C7
Christie B., *Canada* 73 A6
Christina →, *Canada* 73 B6
Christmas Cr. →, *Australia* 60 C4
Christmas Creek, *Australia* 60 C4
Christmas I. = Kiritimati, *Kiribati* 65 G12
Christmas I., *Ind. Oc.* 64 J2
Christopher L., *Australia* 61 D4
Chtimba, *Malawi* 55 E3
Chu, *Kazakhstan* 26 E8
Chu →, *Vietnam* 38 C5
Chu Chua, *Canada* 72 C4
Chu Lai, *Vietnam* 38 E7
Ch'uanchou = Quanzhou, *China* 33 D6
Chuankou, *China* 34 G6
Chūbu □, *Japan* 31 F8
Chubut →, *Argentina* 96 E3
Chuchi L., *Canada* 72 B4
Chudskoye, Oz., *Estonia* 24 C4
Chūgoku □, *Japan* 31 G6
Chūgoku-Sanchi, *Japan* 31 G6
Chugwater, *U.S.A.* 80 E2
Chukotskiy Khrebet, *Russia* 27 C18
Chukotskoye More, *Russia* 27 C19
Chula Vista, *U.S.A.* 85 N9
Chulman, *Russia* 27 D13
Chulucanas, *Peru* 92 E2
Chulym →, *Russia* 26 D9
Chum Phae, *Thailand* 38 D4
Chum Saeng, *Thailand* 38 E3
Chumar, *India* 43 C8
Chumbicha, *Argentina* 94 B2
Chumikan, *Russia* 27 D14
Chumphon, *Thailand* 39 G2
Chumuare, *Mozam.* 55 E3
Chumunjin, *S. Korea* 35 F15
Chuna →, *Russia* 27 D10
Chunchŏn, *S. Korea* 35 F14
Chunchura, *India* 43 H13
Chunga, *Zambia* 55 F2
Chunggang-ŭp, *N. Korea* 35 D14
Chunghwa, *N. Korea* 35 E13
Chungju, *S. Korea* 35 F14
Chungking = Chongqing, *China* 32 D5
Chungmu, *S. Korea* 35 G15
Chungt'iaoshan = Zhongtiao Shan, *China* 34 G6
Chunian, *Pakistan* 42 D6
Chunya, *Tanzania* 55 D3
Chunya □, *Tanzania* 54 D3
Chunyang, *China* 35 C15
Chuquibamba, *Peru* 92 G4
Chuquicamata, *Chile* 94 A2
Chur, *Switz.* 16 E4
Churachandpur, *India* 41 G18
Churchill, *Canada* 73 B10
Churchill →, *Man., Canada* 73 B10
Churchill →, *Nfld., Canada* 71 B7
Churchill, C., *Canada* 73 B10
Churchill Falls, *Canada* 71 B7
Churchill L., *Canada* 73 B7
Churchill Pk., *Canada* 72 B3
Churu, *India* 42 E6
Chushal, *India* 43 C8
Chusovoy, *Russia* 24 C10
Chuuronjang, *N. Korea* 35 D15
Chuvash Republic□, *Russia* 24 C8
Chuwārtah, *Iraq* 44 C5
Ci Xian, *China* 34 F8
Cianjur, *Indonesia* 37 G12
Cibadok, *Indonesia* 37 G12
Cibatu, *Indonesia* 37 G12
Cibola, *U.S.A.* 85 M12
Cicero, *U.S.A.* 76 E2
Ciechanów, *Poland* 17 B10
Ciego de Avila, *Cuba* 88 B4
Ciénaga, *Colombia* 92 A4
Cienfuegos, *Cuba* 88 B3
Cieszyn, *Poland* 17 D9
Cieza, *Spain* 19 C5
Cihuatlán, *Mexico* 86 D4
Cijulang, *Indonesia* 37 G13
Cikajang, *Indonesia* 37 G12
Cikampek, *Indonesia* 37 G12
Cilacap, *Indonesia* 37 G13
Cima, *U.S.A.* 85 K11
Cimahi, *Indonesia* 37 G12
Cimarron, *Kans., U.S.A.* 81 G4
Cimarron, *N. Mex., U.S.A.* 81 G2
Cimarron →, *U.S.A.* 81 G6
Cimone, Mte., *Italy* 20 B4
Cîmpina, *Romania* 17 F12
Cîmpulung, *Romania* 17 F12
Cinca →, *Spain* 19 B6
Cincinnati, *U.S.A.* 76 F3
Ciney, *Belgium* 15 D5
Cinto, Mte., *France* 18 E8
Circle, *Alaska, U.S.A.* 68 B5
Circle, *Mont., U.S.A.* 80 B2
Circleville, *Ohio, U.S.A.* 76 F4
Circleville, *Utah, U.S.A.* 83 G7
Cirebon, *Indonesia* 37 G13
Cirencester, *U.K.* 11 F6
Cirium, *Cyprus* 23 E11
Cisco, *U.S.A.* 81 J5
Ciskei □, *S. Africa* 57 E4
Citlaltépetl, *Mexico* 87 D5
Citrus Heights, *U.S.A.* 84 G5
Citrusdal, *S. Africa* 56 E2
Ciudad Altamirano, *Mexico* 86 D4
Ciudad Bolívar, *Venezuela* 92 B6
Ciudad Camargo, *Mexico* 86 B3
Ciudad Chetumal, *Mexico* 87 D7
Ciudad de Valles, *Mexico* 87 C5
Ciudad del Carmen, *Mexico* 87 D6
Ciudad Delicias = Delicias, *Mexico* 86 B3
Ciudad Guayana, *Venezuela* 92 B6
Ciudad Guerrero, *Mexico* 86 B3
Ciudad Guzmán, *Mexico* 86 D4
Ciudad Juárez, *Mexico* 86 A3
Ciudad Madero, *Mexico* 87 C5
Ciudad Mante, *Mexico* 87 C5
Ciudad Obregón, *Mexico* 86 B3
Ciudad Real, *Spain* 19 C4
Ciudad Rodrigo, *Spain* 19 B2
Ciudad Trujillo = Santo Domingo, *Dom. Rep.* 89 C6
Ciudad Victoria, *Mexico* 87 C5
Ciudadela, *Spain* 22 B10
Civitanova Marche, *Italy* 20 C5
Civitavécchia, *Italy* 20 C4
Cizre, *Turkey* 25 G7
Clacton-on-Sea, *U.K.* 11 F9
Claire, L., *Canada* 72 B6
Clairemont, *U.S.A.* 81 J4
Clairton, *U.S.A.* 78 F5
Clallam Bay, *U.S.A.* 84 B2
Clanton, *U.S.A.* 77 J2
Clanwilliam, *S. Africa* 56 E2
Clara, *Ireland* 13 C4
Clara →, *Australia* 62 B3
Claraville, *U.S.A.* 85 K8
Clare, *Australia* 63 E2
Clare, *U.S.A.* 76 D3
Clare □, *Ireland* 13 D3
Clare →, *Ireland* 13 C2
Clare I., *Ireland* 13 C2
Claremont, *Calif., U.S.A.* 85 L9
Claremont, *N.H., U.S.A.* 79 C12
Claremont Pt., *Australia* 62 A3
Claremore, *U.S.A.* 81 G7
Claremorris, *Ireland* 13 C3
Clarence →, *Australia* 63 D5
Clarence →, *N.Z.* 59 K4
Clarence, I., *Chile* 96 G2
Clarence I., *Antarctica* 5 C18
Clarence Str., *Australia* 60 B5
Clarence Str., *U.S.A.* 72 B2
Clarence Town, *Bahamas* 89 B5
Clarendon, *Ark., U.S.A.* 81 H9
Clarendon, *Tex., U.S.A.* 81 H4
Clarenville, *Canada* 71 C9
Claresholm, *Canada* 72 C6
Clarie Coast, *Antarctica* 5 C9
Clarinda, *U.S.A.* 80 E7
Clarion, *Iowa, U.S.A.* 80 D8
Clarion, *Pa., U.S.A.* 78 E5
Clarion →, *U.S.A.* 78 E5
Clark, *U.S.A.* 80 C6
Clark, Pt., *Canada* 78 B3
Clark Fork, *U.S.A.* 82 B5
Clark Fork →, *U.S.A.* 82 B5
Clark Hill Res., *U.S.A.* 77 J4
Clarkdale, *U.S.A.* 83 J7
Clarke City, *Canada* 71 B6
Clarke I., *Australia* 62 G4
Clarke L., *Canada* 73 C7
Clarke Ra., *Australia* 62 C4
Clark's Fork →, *U.S.A.* 82 D9
Clark's Harbour, *Canada* 71 D6
Clarks Summit, *U.S.A.* 79 E9
Clarksburg, *U.S.A.* 76 F5
Clarksdale, *U.S.A.* 81 H9
Clarkston, *U.S.A.* 82 C5
Clarksville, *Ark., U.S.A.* 81 H8
Clarksville, *Tenn., U.S.A.* 77 G2
Clarksville, *Tex., U.S.A.* 81 J7
Clatskanie, *U.S.A.* 84 D3
Claude, *U.S.A.* 81 H4
Claveria, *Phil.* 37 A6
Clay, *U.S.A.* 84 G5
Clay Center, *U.S.A.* 80 F6
Claypool, *U.S.A.* 83 K8
Claysville, *U.S.A.* 78 F4
Clayton, *Idaho, U.S.A.* 82 D6
Clayton, *N. Mex., U.S.A.* 81 G3
Cle Elum, *U.S.A.* 82 C3

Clear, C., Ireland 13 E2
Clear I., Ireland 13 E2
Clear L., U.S.A. 84 F4
Clear Lake, S. Dak., U.S.A. 80 C6
Clear Lake, Wash., U.S.A. 82 B2
Clear Lake Res., U.S.A. 82 F3
Clearfield, Pa., U.S.A. 76 E6
Clearfield, Utah, U.S.A. 82 F7
Clearlake Highlands, U.S.A. 84 G4
Clearmont, U.S.A. 82 D10
Clearwater, Canada 72 C4
Clearwater, U.S.A. 77 M4
Clearwater →, Alta., Canada 72 C6
Clearwater →, Alta., Canada 73 B6
Clearwater Cr. →, Canada 72 A3
Clearwater Mts., U.S.A. 82 C6
Clearwater Prov. Park, Canada 73 C8
Cleburne, U.S.A. 81 J6
Cleethorpes, U.K. 10 D7
Cleeve Hill, U.K. 11 F6
Clerke Reef, Australia 60 C2
Clermont, Australia 62 C4
Clermont-Ferrand, France 18 D5
Clervaux, Lux. 15 D6
Cleveland, Australia 63 D5
Cleveland, Miss., U.S.A. 81 J9
Cleveland, Ohio, U.S.A. 78 E3
Cleveland, Okla., U.S.A. 81 G6
Cleveland, Tenn., U.S.A. 77 H3
Cleveland, Tex., U.S.A. 81 K7
Cleveland □, U.K. 10 C9
Cleveland, C., Australia 62 B4
Cleveland Heights, U.S.A. 78 E3
Clevelândia, Brazil 95 B5
Clew B., Ireland 13 C2
Clewiston, U.S.A. 77 M5
Clifden, Ireland 13 C1
Clifden, N.Z. 59 M1
Cliffdell, U.S.A. 84 D5
Clifton, Australia 63 D5
Clifton, Ariz., U.S.A. 83 K9
Clifton, Tex., U.S.A. 81 K6
Clifton Beach, Australia 62 B4
Clifton Forge, U.S.A. 76 G6
Clifton Hills, Australia 63 D2
Climax, Canada 73 D7
Clinch →, U.S.A. 77 H3
Clingmans Dome, U.S.A. 77 H4
Clint, U.S.A. 83 L10
Clinton, B.C., Canada 72 C4
Clinton, Ont., Canada 70 D3
Clinton, N.Z. 59 M2
Clinton, Ark., U.S.A. 81 H8
Clinton, Ill., U.S.A. 80 E10
Clinton, Ind., U.S.A. 76 F2
Clinton, Iowa, U.S.A. 80 E9
Clinton, Mass., U.S.A. 79 D13
Clinton, Mo., U.S.A. 80 F8
Clinton, N.C., U.S.A. 77 H6
Clinton, Okla., U.S.A. 81 H5
Clinton, S.C., U.S.A. 77 H5
Clinton, Tenn., U.S.A. 77 G3
Clinton, Wash., U.S.A. 84 C4
Clinton C., Australia 62 C5
Clinton Colden L., Canada 68 B9
Clintonville, U.S.A. 80 C10
Clipperton, I., Pac. Oc. 65 F17
Clive L., Canada 72 A5
Cloates, Pt., Australia 60 D1
Clocolan, S. Africa 57 D4
Clodomira, Argentina 94 B3
Clonakilty, Ireland 13 E3
Clonakilty B., Ireland 13 E3
Cloncurry, Australia 62 C3
Cloncurry →, Australia 62 B3
Clones, Ireland 13 B4
Clonmel, Ireland 13 D4
Cloquet, U.S.A. 80 B8
Clorinda, Argentina 94 B4
Cloud Peak, U.S.A. 82 D10
Cloudcroft, U.S.A. 83 K11
Cloverdale, U.S.A. 84 G4
Clovis, Calif., U.S.A. 83 H4
Clovis, N. Mex., U.S.A. 81 H3
Cluj-Napoca, Romania 17 E11
Clunes, Australia 63 F3
Cluny, France 18 C6
Clutha →, N.Z. 59 M2
Clwyd □, U.K. 10 D4
Clwyd →, U.K. 10 D4
Clyde, N.Z. 59 L2
Clyde, U.S.A. 78 C8
Clyde →, U.K. 12 F4
Clyde, Firth of, U.K. 12 F4
Clyde River, Canada 69 A13
Clydebank, U.K. 12 F4
Clymer, U.S.A. 78 D5
Coachella, U.S.A. 85 M10
Coachella Canal, U.S.A. 85 N12
Coahoma, U.S.A. 81 J4
Coahuayana →, Mexico 86 D4
Coahuayutla, Mexico 86 D4
Coahuila □, Mexico 86 B4
Coal →, Canada 72 B3
Coalane, Mozam. 55 F4
Coalcomán, Mexico 86 D4
Coaldale, Canada 72 D6
Coalgate, U.S.A. 81 H6
Coalinga, U.S.A. 83 H3
Coalville, U.K. 10 E6
Coalville, U.S.A. 82 F8
Coari, Brazil 92 D6
Coast □, Kenya 54 C4
Coast Mts., Canada 72 C3
Coast Ranges, U.S.A. 84 E4
Coatbridge, U.K. 12 F4
Coatepec, Mexico 87 D5
Coatepeque, Guatemala 88 D1
Coatesville, U.S.A. 76 F8
Coaticook, Canada 71 C5
Coats I., Canada 69 B11
Coats Land, Antarctica 5 D1
Coatzacoalcos, Mexico 87 D6
Cobalt, Canada 70 C4
Cobán, Guatemala 88 C1
Cobar, Australia 63 E4
Cóbh, Ireland 13 E3
Cobham, Australia 63 E3
Cobija, Bolivia 92 F5
Cobleskill, U.S.A. 79 D10
Coboconk, Canada 78 B6
Cobourg, Canada 70 D4
Cobourg Pen., Australia 60 B5
Cobram, Australia 63 F4
Cobre, U.S.A. 82 F6
Cóbué, Mozam. 55 E3
Coburg, Germany 16 C5
Cocanada = Kakinada, India 41 L13
Cochabamba, Bolivia 92 G5
Cochemane, Mozam. 55 F3
Cochin, India 40 Q10
Cochin China = Nam-Phan, Vietnam 39 G6
Cochise, U.S.A. 83 K9
Cochran, U.S.A. 77 J4
Cochrane, Alta., Canada 72 C6
Cochrane, Ont., Canada 70 C3
Cochrane →, Canada 73 B8
Cochrane, L., Chile 96 F2
Cockburn, Australia 63 E3
Cockburn, Canal, Chile 96 G2
Cockburn I., Canada 70 C3
Cockburn Ra., Australia 60 C4
Cocklebiddy Motel, Australia 61 F4
Coco →, Cent. Amer. 88 D3
Cocoa, U.S.A. 77 L5
Cocobeach, Gabon 52 D1
Cocos, I. del, Pac. Oc. 65 G19
Cocos Is., Ind. Oc. 64 J1
Cod, C., U.S.A. 75 B13
Codajás, Brazil 92 D6
Coderre, Canada 73 C7
Codó, Brazil 93 D10
Cody, U.S.A. 82 D9
Coe Hill, Canada 70 D4
Coelemu, Chile 94 D1
Coen, Australia 62 A3
Cœur d'Alene, U.S.A. 82 C5
Cœur d'Alene L., U.S.A. 82 C5
Coevorden, Neths. 15 B6
Cofete, Canary Is. 22 F5
Coffeyville, U.S.A. 81 G7
Coffin B., Australia 63 E2
Coffin Bay Peninsula, Australia 63 E2
Coffs Harbour, Australia 63 E5
Coghinas →, Italy 20 D3
Cognac, France 18 D3
Cohagen, U.S.A. 82 C10
Cohoes, U.S.A. 79 D11
Cohuna, Australia 63 F3
Coiba, I., Panama 88 E3
Coig →, Argentina 96 G3
Coihaique, Chile 96 F2
Coimbatore, India 40 P10
Coimbra, Brazil 92 G7
Coimbra, Portugal 19 B1
Coín, Spain 19 D3
Cojimies, Ecuador 92 C2
Cojutepequé, El Salv. 88 D2
Cokeville, U.S.A. 82 E8
Colac, Australia 63 F3
Colatina, Brazil 93 G10
Colbeck, C., Antarctica 5 D13
Colbinabbin, Australia 63 F3
Colborne, Canada 78 B7
Colby, U.S.A. 80 F4
Colchagua □, Chile 94 C1
Colchester, U.K. 11 F8
Coldstream, U.K. 12 F6
Coldwater, Canada 78 B5
Coldwater, U.S.A. 81 G5
Colebrook, Australia 62 G4
Colebrook, U.S.A. 79 B13
Coleman, Canada 72 D6
Coleman, U.S.A. 81 K5
Coleman →, Australia 62 B3
Colenso, S. Africa 57 D4
Coleraine, Australia 63 F3
Coleraine, U.K. 13 A5
Coleraine □, U.K. 13 A5
Coleridge, L., N.Z. 59 K3
Colesberg, S. Africa 56 E4
Coleville, U.S.A. 84 G7
Colfax, Calif., U.S.A. 84 F6
Colfax, La., U.S.A. 81 K8
Colfax, Wash., U.S.A. 82 C5
Colhué Huapi, L., Argentina 96 F3
Coligny, S. Africa 57 D4
Colima, Mexico 86 D4
Colima □, Mexico 86 D4
Colima, Nevado de, Mexico 86 D4
Colina, Chile 94 C1
Colinas, Brazil 93 E10
Coll, U.K. 12 E2
Collaguasi, Chile 94 A2
Collarenebri, Australia 63 D4
Collbran, U.S.A. 83 G10
Colleen Bawn, Zimbabwe 55 G2
College Park, U.S.A. 77 J3
Collette, Canada 71 C6
Collie, Australia 61 F2
Collier B., Australia 60 C3
Collier Ra., Australia 60 D2
Collingwood, Canada 78 B4
Collingwood, N.Z. 59 J4
Collins, Canada 70 B2
Collinsville, Australia 62 C4
Collipulli, Chile 94 D1
Collooney, Ireland 13 B3
Colmar, France 18 B7
Colne, U.K. 10 D5
Colo →, Australia 63 E5
Cologne = Köln, Germany 16 C3
Colom, I., Spain 22 B11
Coloma, U.S.A. 84 G6
Colomb-Béchar = Béchar, Algeria 50 B4
Colômbia, Brazil 93 H9
Colombia ■, S. Amer. 92 C4
Colombo, Sri Lanka 40 R11
Colome, U.S.A. 80 D5
Colón, Argentina 94 C4
Colón, Cuba 88 B3
Colón, Panama 88 E4
Colona, Australia 61 F5
Colonia, Uruguay 94 C4
Colonia de San Jordi, Spain 22 B9
Colonia Dora, Argentina 94 B3
Colonial Heights, U.S.A. 76 G7
Colonsay, Canada 73 C7
Colonsay, U.K. 12 E2
Colorado □, U.S.A. 74 C5
Colorado →, Argentina 96 D4
Colorado →, N. Amer. 83 L6
Colorado →, U.S.A. 81 L7
Colorado City, U.S.A. 81 J4
Colorado Desert, U.S.A. 74 D3
Colorado Plateau, U.S.A. 83 H8
Colorado River Aqueduct, U.S.A. 85 L12
Colorado Springs, U.S.A. 80 F2
Colotlán, Mexico 86 C4
Colton, Calif., U.S.A. 85 L9
Colton, N.Y., U.S.A. 79 B10
Colton, Wash., U.S.A. 82 C5
Columbia, La., U.S.A. 81 J8
Columbia, Miss., U.S.A. 81 K10
Columbia, Mo., U.S.A. 80 F8
Columbia, Pa., U.S.A. 79 F8
Columbia, S.C., U.S.A. 77 H5
Columbia, Tenn., U.S.A. 77 H2
Columbia →, N. Amer. 82 C1
Columbia, C., Canada 4 A4
Columbia, District of □, U.S.A. 76 F7
Columbia, Mt., Canada 72 C5
Columbia Basin, U.S.A. 82 C4
Columbia Falls, U.S.A. 82 B6
Columbia Heights, U.S.A. 80 C8
Columbiana, U.S.A. 78 F4
Columbretes, Is., Spain 19 C6
Columbus, Ga., U.S.A. 77 J3
Columbus, Ind., U.S.A. 76 F3
Columbus, Kans., U.S.A. 81 G7
Columbus, Miss., U.S.A. 77 J1
Columbus, Mont., U.S.A. 82 D9
Columbus, N. Dak., U.S.A. 80 A3
Columbus, N. Mex., U.S.A. 83 L10
Columbus, Nebr., U.S.A. 80 E6
Columbus, Ohio, U.S.A. 76 F4
Columbus, Tex., U.S.A. 81 L6
Columbus, Wis., U.S.A. 80 D10
Colusa, U.S.A. 84 F4
Colville, U.S.A. 82 B5
Colville →, U.S.A. 68 A4
Colville, C., N.Z. 59 G5
Colwyn Bay, U.K. 10 D4
Comácchio, Italy 20 B5
Comalcalco, Mexico 87 D6
Comallo, Argentina 96 E2
Comanche, Okla., U.S.A. 81 H6
Comanche, Tex., U.S.A. 81 K5
Comayagua, Honduras 88 D2
Combahee →, U.S.A. 77 J5
Comber, Canada 78 D2
Comblain-au-Pont, Belgium 15 D5
Comeragh Mts., Ireland 13 D4
Comet, Australia 62 C4
Comilla, Bangla. 41 H17
Comino, Malta 23 C1
Comitán, Mexico 87 D6
Commerce, Ga., U.S.A. 77 H4
Commerce, Tex., U.S.A. 81 J7
Committee B., Canada 69 B11
Commonwealth B., Antarctica 5 C10
Commonwealth of Independent States ■, Eurasia 27 D11
Commoron Cr. →, Australia 63 D5
Communism Pk. = Kommunizma, Pik, Tajikistan 26 F8
Como, Italy 20 B3
Como, L. di, Italy 20 A3
Comodoro Rivadavia, Argentina 96 F3
Comorin, C., India 40 Q10
Comoro Is. ■, Ind. Oc. 49 H8
Comox, Canada 72 D4
Compiègne, France 18 B5
Compostela, Mexico 86 C4
Comprida, I., Brazil 95 A6
Compton, U.S.A. 85 M8
Compton Downs, Australia 63 E4
Con Cuong, Vietnam 38 C5
Con Son, Is., Vietnam 39 H6
Conakry, Guinea 50 G2
Conara Junction, Australia 62 G4
Concarneau, France 18 C2
Conceição, Mozam. 55 F4
Conceição da Barra, Brazil 93 G11
Conceição do Araguaia, Brazil 93 E9
Concepción, Argentina 94 B2
Concepción, Bolivia 92 G6
Concepción, Chile 94 D1
Concepción, Mexico 87 D6
Concepción, Paraguay 94 A4
Concepción □, Chile 94 D1
Concepción →, Mexico 86 A2
Concepción, L., Bolivia 92 G6
Concepción, Punta, Mexico 86 B2
Concepción del Oro, Mexico 86 C4
Concepción del Uruguay, Argentina 94 C4
Conception, Pt., U.S.A. 85 L6
Conception B., Namibia 56 C1
Conception I., Bahamas 89 B4
Concession, Zimbabwe 55 F3
Conchas Dam, U.S.A. 81 H2
Conche, Canada 71 B8
Concho, U.S.A. 83 J9
Concho →, U.S.A. 81 K5
Conchos →, Chihuahua, Mexico 86 B4
Conchos →, Tamaulipas, Mexico 87 B5
Concord, Calif., U.S.A. 84 H4
Concord, N.C., U.S.A. 77 H5
Concord, N.H., U.S.A. 79 C13
Concordia, Argentina 94 C4
Concórdia, Brazil 92 D5
Concordia, Mexico 86 C3
Concordia, U.S.A. 80 F6
Concrete, U.S.A. 82 B3
Condamine, Australia 63 D5
Conde, U.S.A. 80 C5
Condeúba, Brazil 93 F10
Condobolin, Australia 63 E4
Condon, U.S.A. 82 D3
Conejera, I., Spain 22 B9
Conejos, Mexico 86 B4
Confuso →, Paraguay 94 B4
Congleton, U.K. 10 D5
Congo = Zaïre →, Africa 52 F2
Congo (Kinshasa) = Zaïre ■, Africa 52 E4
Congo ■, Africa 52 E3
Congo Basin, Africa 48 G6
Congonhas, Brazil 95 A7
Congress, U.S.A. 83 J7
Coniston, Canada 70 C3
Conjeeveram = Kanchipuram, India 40 N11
Conjuboy, Australia 62 B3
Conklin, Canada 73 B6
Conlea, Australia 63 E3
Conn, L., Ireland 13 B2
Connacht, Ireland 13 C3
Conneaut, U.S.A. 78 E4
Connecticut □, U.S.A. 79 E12
Connecticut →, U.S.A. 79 E12
Connell, U.S.A. 82 C4
Connellsville, U.S.A. 78 F5
Connemara, Ireland 13 C2
Connemaugh →, U.S.A. 78 F5
Connersville, U.S.A. 76 F3
Connors Ra., Australia 62 C4
Conoble, Australia 63 E3
Cononaco →, Ecuador 92 D3
Cononbridge, U.K. 12 D4
Conquest, Canada 73 C7
Conrad, U.S.A. 82 B8
Conran, C., Australia 63 F4
Conroe, U.S.A. 81 K7
Conselheiro Lafaiete, Brazil 95 A7
Consort, Canada 73 C6
Constance = Konstanz, Germany 16 E4
Constance, L. = Bodensee, Europe 16 E4
Constanța, Romania 17 F14
Constantina, Spain 19 D3
Constantine, Algeria 50 A6
Constitución, Chile 94 D1
Constitución, Uruguay 94 C4
Consul, Canada 73 D7
Contact, U.S.A. 82 F6
Contai, India 43 J12
Contamana, Peru 92 E4
Contas →, Brazil 93 F11
Contoocook, U.S.A. 79 C13
Contra Costa, Mozam. 57 D5
Conway = Conwy, U.K. 10 D4
Conway = Conwy →, U.K. 10 D4
Conway, Ark., U.S.A. 81 H8
Conway, N.H., U.S.A. 79 C13
Conway, S.C., U.S.A. 77 J6
Conway, L., Australia 63 D2
Conwy, U.K. 10 D4
Conwy →, U.K. 10 D4
Coober Pedy, Australia 63 D1
Cooch Behar = Koch Bihar, India 41 F16
Coodardy, Australia 61 E2
Cook, Australia 61 F5
Cook, U.S.A. 80 B8
Cook, B., Chile 96 H3
Cook, Mt., N.Z. 59 K3
Cook Inlet, U.S.A. 68 C4
Cook Is., Pac. Oc. 65 J11
Cook Strait, N.Z. 59 J5
Cookeville, U.S.A. 77 G3
Cookhouse, S. Africa 56 E4
Cookshire, Canada 79 A13
Cookstown, U.K. 13 B5
Cookstown □, U.K. 13 B5
Cooksville, Canada 78 C5
Cooktown, Australia 62 B4
Coolabah, Australia 63 E4
Cooladdi, Australia 63 D4
Coolah, Australia 63 E4
Coolamon, Australia 63 E4
Coolangatta, Australia 63 D5
Coolgardie, Australia 61 F3
Coolibah, Australia 60 C5
Coolidge, U.S.A. 83 K8
Coolidge Dam, U.S.A. 83 K8
Cooma, Australia 63 F4
Coonabarabran, Australia 63 E4
Coonamble, Australia 63 E4
Coonana, Australia 61 F3
Coondapoor, India 40 N9
Coongie, Australia 63 D3
Coongoola, Australia 63 D4
Cooninie, L., Australia 63 D2
Cooper, U.S.A. 81 J7
Cooper →, U.S.A. 77 J6
Cooper Cr. →, Australia 63 D2
Cooperstown, N. Dak., U.S.A. 80 B5
Cooperstown, N.Y., U.S.A. 79 D10
Coorabie, Australia 61 F5
Coorabulka, Australia 62 C3
Coorow, Australia 61 E2
Cooroy, Australia 63 D5
Coos Bay, U.S.A. 82 E1
Cootamundra, Australia 63 E4
Cootehill, Ireland 13 B4
Cooyar, Australia 63 D5
Cooyeana, Australia 62 C2
Copahue Paso, Argentina 94 D1
Copainalá, Mexico 87 D6
Copán, Honduras 88 D2
Cope, U.S.A. 80 F3
Copenhagen = København, Denmark 9 J12
Copiapó, Chile 94 B1
Copiapó →, Chile 94 B1
Copley, Australia 63 E2
Copp L., Canada 72 A6
Copper Center, U.S.A. 68 B5
Copper Cliff, Canada 70 C3
Copper Harbor, U.S.A. 76 B2
Copper Queen, Zimbabwe 55 F2
Copperbelt □, Zambia 55 E2
Coppermine, Canada 68 B8
Coppermine →, Canada 68 B8
Copperopolis, U.S.A. 84 H6
Coquet →, U.K. 10 B6
Coquilhatville = Mbandaka, Zaïre 52 D3
Coquille, U.S.A. 82 E1
Coquimbo, Chile 94 B1
Coquimbo □, Chile 94 C1
Corabia, Romania 17 G12
Coracora, Peru 92 G4
Coral Gables, U.S.A. 77 N5
Coral Harbour, Canada 69 B11
Coral Sea, Pac. Oc. 64 J7
Coraopolis, U.S.A. 78 F4
Corato, Italy 20 D7
Corbin, U.S.A. 76 G3
Corby Glen, U.K. 11 E7
Corcoran, U.S.A. 83 H4
Corcubión, Spain 19 A1
Cordele, U.S.A. 77 K4
Cordell, U.S.A. 81 H5
Córdoba, Argentina 94 C3
Córdoba, Mexico 87 D5
Córdoba, Spain 19 D3
Córdoba □, Argentina 94 C3
Córdoba, Sierra de, Argentina 94 C3
Cordon, Phil. 37 A6
Cordova, Ala., U.S.A. 77 J2
Cordova, Alaska, U.S.A. 68 B5
Corella →, Australia 62 B3
Corfield, Australia 62 C3
Corfu = Kérkira, Greece 23 A3
Corfu, Str of, Greece 23 A4
Corigliano Cálabro, Italy 20 E7
Coringa Is., Australia 62 B4
Corinna, Australia 62 G4
Corinth = Kórinthos, Greece 21 F10
Corinth, Miss., U.S.A. 77 H1
Corinth, N.Y., U.S.A. 79 C11
Corinth, G. of = Korinthiakós Kólpos, Greece 21 E10
Corinto, Brazil 93 G10
Corinto, Nic. 88 D2
Cork, Ireland 13 E3
Cork □, Ireland 13 E3
Cork Harbour, Ireland 13 E3
Cormack L., Canada 72 A4
Cormorant, Canada 73 C8
Cormorant L., Canada 73 C8
Corn Is. = Maiz, Is. del, Nic. 88 D3
Cornélio Procópio, Brazil 95 A5
Cornell, U.S.A. 80 C9
Corner Brook, Canada 71 C8
Corning, Ark., U.S.A. 81 G9
Corning, Calif., U.S.A. 82 G2
Corning, Iowa, U.S.A. 80 E7
Corning, N.Y., U.S.A. 78 D7
Cornwall, Canada 70 C5

Cornwall □, *U.K.* 11 G3
Corny Pt., *Australia* 63 E2
Coro, *Venezuela* 92 A5
Coroatá, *Brazil* 93 D10
Corocoro, *Bolivia* 92 G5
Coroico, *Bolivia* 92 G5
Coromandel, *N.Z.* 59 G5
Coromandel Coast, *India* 40 N12
Corona, *Australia* 63 E3
Corona, *Calif., U.S.A.* 85 M9
Corona, *N. Mex., U.S.A.* 83 J11
Coronada, *U.S.A.* 85 N9
Coronado, B. de, *Costa Rica* 88 E3
Coronados, Is. los, *U.S.A.* 85 N9
Coronation, *Canada* 72 C6
Coronation Gulf, *Canada* 68 B8
Coronation I., *Antarctica* 5 C18
Coronation I., *U.S.A.* 72 B2
Coronation Is., *Australia* 60 B3
Coronda, *Argentina* 94 C3
Coronel, *Chile* 94 D1
Coronel Bogado, *Paraguay* 94 B4
Coronel Dorrego, *Argentina* 94 D3
Coronel Oviedo, *Paraguay* 94 B4
Coronel Pringles, *Argentina* 94 D3
Coronel Suárez, *Argentina* 94 D3
Coronel Vidal, *Argentina* 94 D4
Corowa, *Australia* 63 F4
Corozal, *Belize* 87 D7
Corpus, *Argentina* 95 B4
Corpus Christi, *U.S.A.* 81 M6
Corpus Christi, L., *U.S.A.* 81 L6
Corque, *Bolivia* 92 G5
Corralejo, *Canary Is.* 22 F6
Correntes, C. das, *Mozam.* 57 C6
Corrèze □, *France* 18 D4
Corrib, L., *Ireland* 13 C2
Corrientes, *Argentina* 94 B4
Corrientes □, *Argentina* 94 B4
Corrientes →, *Argentina* 94 C4
Corrientes →, *Peru* 92 D4
Corrientes, C., *Colombia* 92 B3
Corrientes, C., *Cuba* 88 B3
Corrientes, C., *Mexico* 86 C3
Corrigan, *U.S.A.* 81 K7
Corrigin, *Australia* 61 F2
Corry, *U.S.A.* 78 E5
Corse, *France* 18 F9
Corse, C., *France* 20 C3
Corse-du-Sud □, *France* 18 F9
Corsica = Corse, *France* 18 F9
Corsicana, *U.S.A.* 81 J6
Cortez, *U.S.A.* 83 H9
Cortland, *U.S.A.* 79 D8
Cortona, *Italy* 20 C4
Çorum, *Turkey* 25 F5
Corumbá, *Brazil* 92 G7
Corumbá de Goiás, *Brazil* 93 G9
Corunna = La Coruña, *Spain* 19 A1
Corvallis, *U.S.A.* 82 D2
Corvette, L. de la, *Canada* 70 B5
Corydon, *U.S.A.* 80 E8
Cosalá, *Mexico* 86 C3
Cosamaloapan, *Mexico* 87 D5
Cosenza, *Italy* 20 E7
Coshocton, *U.S.A.* 78 F3
Cosmo Newberry, *Australia* 61 E3
Coso Junction, *U.S.A.* 85 J9
Coso Pk., *U.S.A.* 85 J9
Cosquín, *Argentina* 94 C3
Costa Blanca, *Spain* 19 C5
Costa Brava, *Spain* 19 B7
Costa del Sol, *Spain* 19 D3
Costa Dorada, *Spain* 19 B6
Costa Mesa, *U.S.A.* 85 M9
Costa Rica ■, *Cent. Amer.* 88 D3
Costilla, *U.S.A.* 83 H11
Cosumnes →, *U.S.A.* 84 G5
Cotabato, *Phil.* 37 C6
Cotagaita, *Bolivia* 94 A2
Côte-d'Ivoire ■ = Ivory Coast ■, *Africa* 50 G3
Côte-d'Or □, *France* 18 C6
Coteau des Prairies, *U.S.A.* 80 C6
Coteau du Missouri, *U.S.A.* 80 B4
Coteau Landing, *Canada* 79 A10
Cotentin, *France* 18 B3
Côtes-d'Armor □, *France* 18 B2
Côtes-du-Nord = Côtes-d'Armor □, *France* 18 B2
Cotillo, *Canary Is.* 22 F5
Cotonou, *Benin* 50 G5
Cotopaxi, *Ecuador* 92 D3
Cotswold Hills, *U.K.* 11 F5
Cottage Grove, *U.S.A.* 82 E2
Cottbus, *Germany* 16 C7
Cottonwood, *U.S.A.* 83 J7
Cotulla, *U.S.A.* 81 L5
Coudersport, *U.S.A.* 78 E6
Couedic, C. du, *Australia* 63 F2
Coulee City, *U.S.A.* 82 C4
Coulman I., *Antarctica* 5 D11
Coulonge →, *Canada* 70 C4
Coulterville, *U.S.A.* 84 H6
Council, *Alaska, U.S.A.* 68 B3
Council, *Idaho, U.S.A.* 82 D5
Council Bluffs, *U.S.A.* 80 E7
Council Grove, *U.S.A.* 80 F6
Coupeville, *U.S.A.* 84 B4
Courantyne →, *S. Amer.* 92 B7
Courtenay, *Canada* 72 D3
Courtland, *U.S.A.* 84 G5
Courtrai = Kortrijk, *Belgium* 15 D3
Courtright, *Canada* 78 D2
Coushatta, *U.S.A.* 81 J8
Coutts, *Canada* 72 D6
Coventry, *U.K.* 11 E6
Coventry L., *Canada* 73 A7
Covilhã, *Portugal* 19 B2
Covington, *Ga., U.S.A.* 77 J4
Covington, *Ky., U.S.A.* 76 F3
Covington, *Okla., U.S.A.* 81 G6
Covington, *Tenn., U.S.A.* 81 H10
Cowal, L., *Australia* 63 E4
Cowan, *Canada* 73 C8
Cowan, L., *Australia* 61 F3
Cowan L., *Canada* 73 C7
Cowangie, *Australia* 63 F3
Cowansville, *Canada* 79 A12
Cowarie, *Australia* 63 D2
Cowcowing Lakes, *Australia* 61 F2
Cowdenbeath, *U.K.* 12 E5
Cowell, *Australia* 63 E2
Cowes, *U.K.* 11 G6
Cowlitz →, *U.S.A.* 84 D4
Cowra, *Australia* 63 E4
Coxilha Grande, *Brazil* 95 B5
Coxim, *Brazil* 93 G8
Cox's Bazar, *Bangla.* 41 J17
Cox's Cove, *Canada* 71 C8
Coyame, *Mexico* 86 B3
Coyote Wells, *U.S.A.* 85 N11
Coyuca de Benítez, *Mexico* 87 D4
Coyuca de Catalan, *Mexico* 86 D4
Cozad, *U.S.A.* 80 E5
Cozumel, *Mexico* 87 C7
Cozumel, I. de, *Mexico* 87 C7
Craboon, *Australia* 63 E4
Cracow = Kraków, *Poland* 17 C9
Cracow, *Australia* 63 D5
Cradock, *S. Africa* 56 E4
Craig, *Alaska, U.S.A.* 72 B2
Craig, *Colo., U.S.A.* 82 F10
Craigavon = Lurgan, *U.K.* 13 B5
Craigmore, *Zimbabwe* 55 G3
Craiova, *Romania* 17 F11
Cramsie, *Australia* 62 C3
Cranberry Portage, *Canada* 73 C8
Cranbrook, *Tas., Australia* 62 G4
Cranbrook, *W. Austral., Australia* 61 F2
Cranbrook, *Canada* 72 D5
Crandon, *U.S.A.* 80 C10
Crane, *Oreg., U.S.A.* 82 E4
Crane, *Tex., U.S.A.* 81 K3
Cranston, *U.S.A.* 79 E13
Crater, L., *U.S.A.* 82 E2
Crateús, *Brazil* 93 E10
Crato, *Brazil* 93 E11
Crawford, *U.S.A.* 80 D3
Crawfordsville, *U.S.A.* 76 E2
Crawley, *U.K.* 11 F7
Crazy Mts., *U.S.A.* 82 C8
Crean L., *Canada* 73 C7
Crécy-en-Ponthieu, *France* 18 A4
Crediton, *Canada* 78 C3
Credo, *Australia* 61 F3
Cree →, *Canada* 73 B7
Cree →, *U.K.* 12 G4
Cree L., *Canada* 73 B7
Creede, *U.S.A.* 83 H10
Creel, *Mexico* 86 B3
Creighton, *U.S.A.* 80 D6
Cremona, *Italy* 20 B4
Cres, *Croatia* 20 B6
Cresbard, *U.S.A.* 80 C5
Crescent, *Okla., U.S.A.* 81 H6
Crescent, *Oreg., U.S.A.* 82 E3
Crescent City, *U.S.A.* 82 F1
Crespo, *Argentina* 94 C3
Cressy, *Australia* 63 F3
Crested Butte, *U.S.A.* 83 G10
Crestline, *Calif., U.S.A.* 85 L9
Crestline, *Ohio, U.S.A.* 78 F2
Creston, *Canada* 72 D5
Creston, *Calif., U.S.A.* 84 K6
Creston, *Iowa, U.S.A.* 80 E7
Creston, *Wash., U.S.A.* 82 C4
Crestview, *Calif., U.S.A.* 84 H8
Crestview, *Fla., U.S.A.* 77 K2
Crete = Kriti, *Greece* 23 D7
Crete, *U.S.A.* 80 E6
Creus, C., *Spain* 19 A7
Creuse □, *France* 18 C5
Creuse →, *France* 18 C4
Crewe, *U.K.* 10 D5
Criciúma, *Brazil* 95 B6
Crieff, *U.K.* 12 E5
Crimea = Krymskiy Poluostrov, *Ukraine* 25 E5
Crişul Alb →, *Romania* 17 E10
Crişul Negru →, *Romania* 17 E10
Crna Gora = Montenegro □, *Europe* 21 C8
Crna Gora, *Serbia, Yug.* 21 C9
Crna Reka →, *Macedonia, Yug.* 21 D9
Croaghpatrick, *Ireland* 13 C2
Croatia ■, *Europe* 20 B7
Crocker, Banjaran, *Malaysia* 36 C5
Crockett, *U.S.A.* 81 K7
Crocodile = Krokodil →, *Mozam.* 57 D5
Crocodile Is., *Australia* 62 A1
Croix, L. La, *Canada* 70 C1
Croker, C., *Australia* 60 B5
Croker I., *Australia* 60 B5
Cromarty, *Canada* 73 B10
Cromarty, *U.K.* 12 D4
Cromer, *U.K.* 10 E9
Cromwell, *N.Z.* 59 L2
Cronulla, *Australia* 63 E5
Crooked →, *Canada* 72 C4
Crooked →, *U.S.A.* 82 D3
Crooked I., *Bahamas* 89 B5
Crooked Island Passage, *Bahamas* 89 B5
Crookston, *Minn., U.S.A.* 80 B6
Crookston, *Nebr., U.S.A.* 80 D4
Crooksville, *U.S.A.* 76 F4
Crookwell, *Australia* 63 E4
Crosby, *Minn., U.S.A.* 80 B8
Crosby, *N. Dak., U.S.A.* 73 D8
Crosby, *Pa., U.S.A.* 78 E6
Crosbyton, *U.S.A.* 81 J4
Cross City, *U.S.A.* 77 L4
Cross Fell, *U.K.* 10 C5
Cross L., *Canada* 73 C9
Cross Plains, *U.S.A.* 81 J5
Cross Sound, *U.S.A.* 68 C6
Crossett, *U.S.A.* 81 J9
Crossfield, *Canada* 72 C6
Crosshaven, *Ireland* 13 E3
Croton-on-Hudson, *U.S.A.* 79 E11
Crotone, *Italy* 20 E7
Crow →, *Canada* 72 B4
Crow Agency, *U.S.A.* 82 D10
Crow Hd., *Ireland* 13 E1
Crowell, *U.S.A.* 81 J5
Crowley, *U.S.A.* 81 K8
Crowley, L., *U.S.A.* 84 H8
Crown Point, *U.S.A.* 76 E2
Crows Landing, *U.S.A.* 84 H5
Crows Nest, *Australia* 63 D5
Crowsnest Pass, *Canada* 72 D6
Croydon, *Australia* 62 B3
Croydon, *U.K.* 11 F7
Crozet Is., *Ind. Oc.* 3 G12
Cruz, C., *Cuba* 88 C4
Cruz Alta, *Brazil* 95 B5
Cruz del Eje, *Argentina* 94 C3
Cruzeiro, *Brazil* 95 A7
Cruzeiro do Oeste, *Brazil* 95 A5
Cruzeiro do Sul, *Brazil* 92 E4
Cry L., *Canada* 72 B3
Crystal Bay, *U.S.A.* 84 F7
Crystal Brook, *Australia* 63 E2
Crystal City, *Mo., U.S.A.* 80 F9
Crystal City, *Tex., U.S.A.* 81 L5
Crystal Falls, *U.S.A.* 76 B1
Crystal River, *U.S.A.* 77 L4
Crystal Springs, *U.S.A.* 81 K9
Csongrád, *Hungary* 17 E10
Cu Lao Hon, *Vietnam* 39 G7
Cua Rao, *Vietnam* 38 C5
Cuácua →, *Mozam.* 55 F4
Cuamato, *Angola* 56 B2
Cuamba, *Mozam.* 55 E4
Cuando →, *Angola* 53 H4
Cuando Cubango □, *Angola* 56 B3
Cuangar, *Angola* 56 B2
Cuanza →, *Angola* 48 G5
Cuarto →, *Argentina* 94 C3
Cuatrociénegas, *Mexico* 86 B4
Cuauhtémoc, *Mexico* 86 B3
Cuba, *N. Mex., U.S.A.* 83 J10
Cuba, *N.Y., U.S.A.* 78 D6
Cuba ■, *W. Indies* 88 B4
Cuballing, *Australia* 61 F2
Cubango →, *Africa* 56 B3
Cucamonga, *U.S.A.* 85 L9
Cuchi, *Angola* 53 G3
Cuchumatanes, Sierra de los, *Guatemala* 88 C1
Cucurpe, *Mexico* 86 A2
Cúcuta, *Colombia* 92 B4
Cudahy, *U.S.A.* 76 D2
Cuddalore, *India* 40 P11
Cuddapah, *India* 40 M11
Cuddapan, L., *Australia* 62 D3
Cudgewa, *Australia* 63 F4
Cue, *Australia* 61 E2
Cuenca, *Ecuador* 92 D3
Cuenca, *Spain* 19 B4
Cuenca, Serranía de, *Spain* 19 C5
Cuernavaca, *Mexico* 87 D5
Cuero, *U.S.A.* 81 L6
Cuervo, *U.S.A.* 81 H2
Cuevas del Almanzora, *Spain* 19 D5
Cuevo, *Bolivia* 92 H6
Cuiabá, *Brazil* 93 G7
Cuiabá →, *Brazil* 93 G7
Cuilco, *Guatemala* 88 C1
Cuillin Hills, *U.K.* 12 D2
Cuillin Sd., *U.K.* 12 D2
Cuima, *Angola* 53 G3
Cuito →, *Angola* 56 B3
Cuitzeo, L. de, *Mexico* 86 D4
Cukai, *Malaysia* 39 K4
Culbertson, *U.S.A.* 80 A2
Culcairn, *Australia* 63 F4
Culebra, Sierra de la, *Spain* 19 B2
Culgoa →, *Australia* 63 D4
Culiacán, *Mexico* 86 C3
Culiacán →, *Mexico* 86 C3
Culion, *Phil.* 37 B6
Cullarin Ra., *Australia* 63 E4
Cullen, *U.K.* 12 D6
Cullen Pt., *Australia* 62 A3
Cullera, *Spain* 19 C5
Cullman, *U.S.A.* 77 H2
Culloden Moor, *U.K.* 12 D4
Culpeper, *U.S.A.* 76 F7
Culuene →, *Brazil* 93 F8
Culver, Pt., *Australia* 61 F3
Culverden, *N.Z.* 59 K4
Cumaná, *Venezuela* 92 A6
Cumberland, *Canada* 72 D3
Cumberland, *Md., U.S.A.* 76 F6
Cumberland, *Wis., U.S.A.* 80 C8
Cumberland →, *U.S.A.* 77 G2
Cumberland I., *U.S.A.* 77 K5
Cumberland Is., *Australia* 62 C4
Cumberland L., *Canada* 73 C8
Cumberland Pen., *Canada* 69 B13
Cumberland Plateau, *U.S.A.* 77 H3
Cumberland Sd., *Canada* 69 B13
Cumborah, *Australia* 63 D4
Cumbria □, *U.K.* 10 C5
Cumbrian Mts., *U.K.* 10 C4
Cumbum, *India* 40 M11
Cummings Mt., *U.S.A.* 85 K8
Cummins, *Australia* 63 E2
Cumnock, *Australia* 63 E4
Cumnock, *U.K.* 12 F4
Cumpas, *Mexico* 86 A3
Cumplida, Pta., *Canary Is.* 22 F2
Cuncumén, *Chile* 94 C1
Cundeelee, *Australia* 61 F3
Cunderdin, *Australia* 61 F2
Cunene →, *Angola* 56 B1
Cúneo, *Italy* 20 B2
Cunillera, I., *Spain* 22 C7
Cunnamulla, *Australia* 63 D4
Cupar, *Canada* 73 C8
Cupar, *U.K.* 12 E5
Cupica, G. de, *Colombia* 92 B3
Curaçao, *Neth. Ant.* 89 D6
Curanilahue, *Chile* 94 D1
Curaray →, *Peru* 92 D4
Curepto, *Chile* 94 D1
Curiapo, *Venezuela* 92 B6
Curicó, *Chile* 94 C1
Curicó □, *Chile* 94 C1
Curitiba, *Brazil* 95 B6
Currabubula, *Australia* 63 E5
Currais Novos, *Brazil* 93 E11
Curralinho, *Brazil* 93 D9
Currant, *U.S.A.* 82 G6
Curraweena, *Australia* 63 E4
Currawilla, *Australia* 62 D3
Current →, *U.S.A.* 81 G9
Currie, *Australia* 62 F3
Currie, *U.S.A.* 82 F6
Currie, Mt., *S. Africa* 57 E4
Currituck Sd., *U.S.A.* 77 G8
Curtis, *U.S.A.* 80 E4
Curtis Group, *Australia* 62 F4
Curtis I., *Australia* 62 C5
Curuápanema →, *Brazil* 93 D7
Curuçá, *Brazil* 93 D9
Curuguaty, *Paraguay* 95 A4
Çürüksu Çayi →, *Turkey* 25 G4
Curup, *Indonesia* 36 E2
Cururupu, *Brazil* 93 D10
Curuzú Cuatiá, *Argentina* 94 B4
Cushing, *U.S.A.* 81 H6
Cushing, Mt., *Canada* 72 B3
Cusihuiriáchic, *Mexico* 86 B3
Custer, *U.S.A.* 80 D3
Cut Bank, *U.S.A.* 82 B7
Cuthbert, *U.S.A.* 77 K3
Cutler, *U.S.A.* 84 J7
Cuttaburra →, *Australia* 63 D3
Cuttack, *India* 41 J14
Cuvier, C., *Australia* 61 D1
Cuvier I., *N.Z.* 59 G5
Cuxhaven, *Germany* 16 B4
Cuyahoga Falls, *U.S.A.* 78 E3
Cuyo, *Phil.* 37 B6
Cuzco, *Bolivia* 92 H5
Cuzco, *Peru* 92 F4
Cwmbran, *U.K.* 11 F4
Cyangugu, *Rwanda* 54 C2
Cyclades = Kikládhes, *Greece* 21 F11
Cygnet, *Australia* 62 G4
Cynthiana, *U.S.A.* 76 F3
Cypress Hills, *Canada* 73 D7
Cyprus ■, *Medit. S.* 23 E12
Cyrenaica, *Libya* 51 C9
Cyrene = Shaḥḥāt, *Libya* 51 B9
Czar, *Canada* 73 C6
Czechoslovakia ■, *Europe* 16 D8
Czeremcha, *Poland* 17 B11
Częstochowa, *Poland* 17 C9

D

Da →, *Vietnam* 38 B5
Da Hinggan Ling, *China* 33 B7
Da Lat, *Vietnam* 39 G7
Da Nang, *Vietnam* 38 D7
Da Qaidam, *China* 32 C4
Da Yunhe →, *China* 35 G11
Da'an, *China* 35 B13
Daba Shan, *China* 33 C5
Dabakala, *Ivory C.* 50 G4
Dabhoi, *India* 42 H5
Dąbie, *Poland* 16 B7
Dabo, *Indonesia* 36 E2
Dabola, *Guinea* 50 F2
Daboya, *Ghana* 50 G4
Dabrowa Tarnówska, *Poland* 17 C10
Dabung, *Malaysia* 39 K4
Dacca = Dhaka, *Bangla.* 43 H14
Dacca = Dhaka □, *Bangla.* 43 G14
Dadanawa, *Guyana* 92 C7
Dade City, *U.S.A.* 77 L4
Dadra and Nagar Haveli □, *India* 40 J8
Dadri = Charkhi Dadri, *India* 42 E7
Dadu, *Pakistan* 42 F2
Daet, *Phil.* 37 B6
Dagana, *Senegal* 50 E1
Daggett, *U.S.A.* 85 L10
Daghestan Republic □, *Russia* 25 F8
Dagö = Hiiumaa, *Estonia* 24 C3
Dagu, *China* 35 E9
Dagupan, *Phil.* 37 A6
Dahlak Kebir, *Ethiopia* 46 D3
Dahlonega, *U.S.A.* 77 H4
Dahod, *India* 42 H6
Dahomey = Benin ■, *Africa* 50 G5
Dahra, *Senegal* 50 E1
Dai Hao, *Vietnam* 38 C6
Dai-Sen, *Japan* 31 G6
Dai Xian, *China* 34 E7
Daicheng, *China* 34 E9
Daingean, *Ireland* 13 C4
Daintree, *Australia* 62 B4
Daiō-Misaki, *Japan* 31 G8
Dairût, *Egypt* 51 C11
Daisetsu-Zan, *Japan* 30 C11
Dajarra, *Australia* 62 C2
Dak Dam, *Cambodia* 38 F6
Dak Nhe, *Vietnam* 38 E6
Dak Pek, *Vietnam* 38 E6
Dak Song, *Vietnam* 39 F6
Dak Sui, *Vietnam* 38 E6
Dakar, *Senegal* 50 F1
Dakhla, *Mauritania* 50 D1
Dakhla, El Wâhât el-, *Egypt* 51 C10
Dakhovskaya, *Russia* 25 F7
Dakor, *India* 42 H5
Dakota City, *U.S.A.* 80 D6
Đakovica, *Serbia, Yug.* 21 C9
Dalachi, *China* 34 F3
Dalai Nur, *China* 34 C9
Dālakī, *Iran* 45 D6
Dalälven, *Sweden* 9 F14
Dalandzadgad, *Mongolia* 34 C3
Dalarö, *Sweden* 9 G15
Dālbandīn, *Pakistan* 40 E4
Dalbeattie, *U.K.* 12 G5
Dalby, *Australia* 63 D5
Dalgān, *Iran* 45 E8
Dalhart, *U.S.A.* 81 G3
Dalhousie, *Canada* 71 C6
Dalhousie, *India* 42 C6
Dali, *Shaanxi, China* 34 G5
Dali, *Yunnan, China* 32 D5
Dalian, *China* 35 E11
Daliang Shan, *China* 32 D5
Daling He →, *China* 35 D11
Dāliyat el Karmel, *Israel* 47 C4
Dalkeith, *U.K.* 12 F5
Dall I., *U.S.A.* 72 C2
Dallarnil, *Australia* 63 D5
Dallas, *Oreg., U.S.A.* 82 D2
Dallas, *Tex., U.S.A.* 81 J6
Dalmacija = Dalmatia □, *Croatia* 20 C7
Dalmatia □, *Croatia* 20 C7
Dalmellington, *U.K.* 12 F4
Dalnegorsk, *Russia* 27 E14
Dalnerechensk, *Russia* 27 E14
Daloa, *Ivory C.* 50 G3
Daltenganj, *India* 43 G11
Dalton, *Canada* 70 C3
Dalton, *Ga., U.S.A.* 77 H3
Dalton, *Mass., U.S.A.* 79 D11
Dalton, *Nebr., U.S.A.* 80 E3
Dalton Iceberg Tongue, *Antarctica* 5 C9
Dalvik, *Iceland* 8 D4
Daly →, *Australia* 60 B5
Daly City, *U.S.A.* 84 H4
Daly L., *Canada* 73 B7
Daly Waters, *Australia* 62 B1
Dam Doi, *Vietnam* 39 H5
Dam Ha, *Vietnam* 38 B6
Daman, *India* 40 J8
Dāmaneh, *Iran* 45 C6
Damanhûr, *Egypt* 51 B11
Damanzhuang, *China* 34 E9
Damar, *Indonesia* 37 F7
Damaraland, *Namibia* 56 C2
Damascus = Dimashq, *Syria* 47 B5
Damāvand, *Iran* 45 C7
Damāvand, Qolleh-ye, *Iran* 45 C7
Damba, *Angola* 52 F3
Dame Marie, *Haiti* 89 C5
Dāmghān, *Iran* 45 B7
Damietta = Dumyât, *Egypt* 51 B11
Daming, *China* 34 F8
Damīr Qābū, *Syria* 44 B4
Damodar →, *India* 43 H12
Damoh, *India* 43 H8
Dampier, *Australia* 60 D2
Dampier, Selat, *Indonesia* 37 E8
Dampier Arch., *Australia* 60 D2
Damrei, Chuor Phnum, *Cambodia* 39 G4
Dana, *Indonesia* 37 F6
Dana, L., *Canada* 70 B4
Dana, Mt., *U.S.A.* 84 H7
Danbury, *U.S.A.* 79 E11
Danby L., *U.S.A.* 83 J6
Dand, *Afghan.* 42 D1
Dandaragan, *Australia* 61 F2

Dandeldhura, *Nepal* 43 E9
Dandeli, *India* 40 M9
Dandenong, *Australia* 63 F4
Dandong, *China* 35 D13
Danfeng, *China* 34 H6
Danforth, *U.S.A.* 71 C6
Danger Is. = Pukapuka, *Cook Is.* 65 J11
Danger Pt., *S. Africa* 56 E2
Dangora, *Nigeria* 50 F6
Dangrek, Phnom, *Thailand* 38 E5
Dangriga, *Belize* 87 D7
Dangshan, *China* 34 G9
Daniel, *U.S.A.* 82 E8
Daniel's Harbour, *Canada* 71 B8
Danielskuil, *S. Africa* 56 D3
Danielson, *U.S.A.* 79 E13
Danilov, *Russia* 24 C7
Daning, *China* 34 F6
Danissa, *Kenya* 54 B5
Dankhar Gompa, *India* 40 C11
Danlí, *Honduras* 88 D2
Dannemora, *Sweden* 9 F14
Dannemora, *U.S.A.* 79 B11
Dannevirke, *N.Z.* 59 J6
Dannhauser, *S. Africa* 57 D5
Dansville, *U.S.A.* 78 D7
Dantan, *India* 43 J12
Dante, *Somali Rep.* 46 E5
Danube →, *Europe* 17 F14
Danvers, *U.S.A.* 79 D14
Danville, *Ill., U.S.A.* 76 E2
Danville, *Ky., U.S.A.* 76 G3
Danville, *Va., U.S.A.* 77 G6
Danzig = Gdańsk, *Poland* 17 A9
Dao, *Phil.* 37 B6
Daoud = Aïn Beïda, *Algeria* 50 A6
Daqing Shan, *China* 34 D6
Dar es Salaam, *Tanzania* 54 D4
Dar Mazār, *Iran* 45 D8
Dar'ā, *Syria* 47 C5
Dar'ā □, *Syria* 47 C5
Dārāb, *Iran* 45 D7
Daraj, *Libya* 50 B7
Dārān, *Iran* 45 C6
Dārayyā, *Syria* 47 B5
Darband, *Pakistan* 42 B5
Darband, Kūh-e, *Iran* 45 D8
Darbhanga, *India* 43 F11
Darby, *U.S.A.* 82 C6
Dardanelle, *Ark., U.S.A.* 81 H8
Dardanelle, *Calif., U.S.A.* 84 G7
Dardanelles = Çanakkale Boğazı, *Turkey* 21 D12
Dārestān, *Iran* 45 D8
Dârfûr, *Sudan* 51 F9
Dargai, *Pakistan* 42 B4
Dargan Ata, *Uzbekistan* 26 E7
Dargaville, *N.Z.* 59 F4
Darhan Muminggan Lianheqi, *China* 34 D6
Darién, G. del, *Colombia* 92 B3
Dariganga, *Mongolia* 34 B7
Darjeeling = Darjiling, *India* 43 F13
Darjiling, *India* 43 F13
Dark Cove, *Canada* 71 C9
Darkan, *Australia* 61 F2
Darkhazineh, *Iran* 45 D6
Darkot Pass, *Pakistan* 43 A5
Darling →, *Australia* 63 E3
Darling Downs, *Australia* 63 D5
Darling Ra., *Australia* 61 F2
Darlington, *U.K.* 10 C6
Darlington, *S.C., U.S.A.* 77 H6
Darlington, *Wis., U.S.A.* 80 D9
Darlot, L., *Australia* 61 E3
Darłowo, *Poland* 16 A8
Darmstadt, *Germany* 16 D4
Darnah, *Libya* 51 B9
Darnall, *S. Africa* 57 D5
Darnley, C., *Antarctica* 5 C6
Darnley B., *Canada* 68 B7
Darr, *Australia* 62 C3
Darr →, *Australia* 62 C3
Darrington, *U.S.A.* 82 B3
Dart →, *U.K.* 11 G4
Dart, C., *Antarctica* 5 D14
Dartmoor, *U.K.* 11 G4
Dartmouth, *Australia* 62 C3
Dartmouth, *Canada* 71 D7
Dartmouth, *U.K.* 11 G4
Dartmouth, L., *Australia* 63 D4
Dartuch, C., *Spain* 22 B10
Darvaza, *Turkmenistan* 26 E6
Darvel, Teluk, *Malaysia* 37 D5
Darwha, *India* 40 J10
Darwin, *Australia* 60 B5
Darwin, *U.S.A.* 85 J9
Darwin River, *Australia* 60 B5
Dās, *U.A.E.* 45 E7
Dashetai, *China* 34 D5
Dasht, *Iran* 45 B8
Dasht →, *Pakistan* 40 G2
Dasht-e Mārgow, *Afghan.* 40 D3
Dasht-i-Nawar, *Afghan.* 42 C3
Daska, *Pakistan* 42 C6
Dasseneiland, *S. Africa* 56 E2
Datia, *India* 43 G8
Datong, *China* 34 D7
Datu, Tanjung, *Indonesia* 36 D3
Datu Piang, *Phil.* 37 C6
Daugava →, *Latvia* 24 C3
Daugavpils, *Latvia* 24 C4
Daulpur, *India* 42 F7
Dauphin, *Canada* 73 C8
Dauphin I., *U.S.A.* 77 K1
Dauphin L., *Canada* 73 C9
Dauphiné, *France* 18 D6
Dausa, *India* 42 F7
Davangere, *India* 40 M9
Davao, *Phil.* 37 C7
Davao, G. of, *Phil.* 37 C7
Dāvar Panāh, *Iran* 45 E9
Davenport, *Calif., U.S.A.* 84 H4
Davenport, *Iowa, U.S.A.* 80 E9
Davenport, *Wash., U.S.A.* 82 C4
Davenport Downs, *Australia* 62 C3
Davenport Ra., *Australia* 62 C1
David, *Panama* 88 E3
David City, *U.S.A.* 80 E6
Davidson, *Canada* 73 C7
Davis, *U.S.A.* 84 G5
Davis Dam, *U.S.A.* 85 K12
Davis Inlet, *Canada* 71 A7
Davis Mts., *U.S.A.* 81 K2
Davis Sea, *Antarctica* 5 C7
Davis Str., *N. Amer.* 69 B14
Davos, *Switz.* 16 E4
Davy L., *Canada* 73 B7
Dawes Ra., *Australia* 62 C5
Dawson, *Canada* 68 B6
Dawson, *Ga., U.S.A.* 77 K3
Dawson, *N. Dak., U.S.A.* 80 B5
Dawson, I., *Chile* 96 G2
Dawson Creek, *Canada* 72 B4
Dawson Inlet, *Canada* 73 A10
Dawson Ra., *Australia* 62 C4
Daxian, *China* 32 C5
Daxindian, *China* 35 F11
Daxinggou, *China* 35 C15
Daxue Shan, *China* 32 C5
Daylesford, *Australia* 63 F3
Dayr az Zawr, *Syria* 44 C4
Daysland, *Canada* 72 C6
Dayton, *Nev., U.S.A.* 84 F7
Dayton, *Ohio, U.S.A.* 76 F3
Dayton, *Pa., U.S.A.* 78 F5
Dayton, *Tenn., U.S.A.* 77 H3
Dayton, *Wash., U.S.A.* 82 C4
Daytona Beach, *U.S.A.* 77 L5
Dayville, *U.S.A.* 82 D4
De Aar, *S. Africa* 56 E3
De Funiak Springs, *U.S.A.* 77 K2
De Grey, *Australia* 60 D2
De Grey →, *Australia* 60 D2
De Kalb, *U.S.A.* 80 E10
De Land, *U.S.A.* 77 L5
De Leon, *U.S.A.* 81 J5
De Pere, *U.S.A.* 76 C1
De Queen, *U.S.A.* 81 H7
De Quincy, *U.S.A.* 81 K8
De Ridder, *U.S.A.* 81 K8
De Smet, *U.S.A.* 80 C6
De Soto, *U.S.A.* 80 F9
De Tour, *U.S.A.* 76 C4
De Witt, *U.S.A.* 81 H9
Dead Sea, *Asia* 47 D4
Deadwood, *U.S.A.* 80 C3
Deadwood L., *Canada* 72 B3
Deakin, *Australia* 61 F4
Deal, *U.K.* 11 F9
Deal I., *Australia* 62 F4
Dealesville, *S. Africa* 56 D4
Dean, Forest of, *U.K.* 11 F5
Deán Funes, *Argentina* 94 C3
Dearborn, *U.S.A.* 70 D3
Dease →, *Canada* 72 B3
Dease L., *Canada* 72 B2
Dease Lake, *Canada* 72 B2
Death Valley, *U.S.A.* 85 J10
Death Valley Junction, *U.S.A.* 85 J10
Death Valley Nat. Monument, *U.S.A.* 85 J10
Deba Habe, *Nigeria* 50 F7
Debar, *Macedonia, Yug.* 21 D9
Debden, *Canada* 73 C7
Debolt, *Canada* 72 B5
Deborah East, L., *Australia* 61 F2
Deborah West, L., *Australia* 61 F2
Debre Markos, *Ethiopia* 51 F12
Debre Tabor, *Ethiopia* 51 F12
Debrecen, *Hungary* 17 E10
Decatur, *Ala., U.S.A.* 77 H2
Decatur, *Ga., U.S.A.* 77 J3
Decatur, *Ill., U.S.A.* 80 F10
Decatur, *Ind., U.S.A.* 76 E3
Decatur, *Tex., U.S.A.* 81 J6
Deccan, *India* 40 M10
Deception L., *Canada* 73 B8
Deckerville, *U.S.A.* 78 C2
Decorah, *U.S.A.* 80 D9
Dedéagach = Alexandroúpolis, *Greece* 21 D11
Dedham, *U.S.A.* 79 D13
Dédougou, *Burkina Faso* 50 F4
Dedza, *Malawi* 55 E3
Dee →, *Clwyd, U.K.* 10 D4
Dee →, *Gramp., U.K.* 12 D6
Deep B., *Canada* 72 A5
Deep Well, *Australia* 62 C1
Deepwater, *Australia* 63 D5
Deer →, *Canada* 73 B10
Deer Lake, *Nfld., Canada* 71 C8
Deer Lake, *Ont., Canada* 73 C10
Deer Lodge, *U.S.A.* 82 C7
Deer Park, *U.S.A.* 82 C5
Deer River, *U.S.A.* 80 B8
Deeral, *Australia* 62 B4
Deerdepoort, *S. Africa* 56 C4
Deferiet, *U.S.A.* 79 B9
Defiance, *U.S.A.* 76 E3
Degeh Bur, *Ethiopia* 46 F3
Deggendorf, *Germany* 16 D6
Deh Bīd, *Iran* 45 D7
Deh-e Shīr, *Iran* 45 D7
Dehaj, *Iran* 45 D7
Dehdez, *Iran* 45 D6
Dehestān, *Iran* 45 D7
Dehgolān, *Iran* 44 C5
Dehi Titan, *Afghan.* 40 C3
Dehibat, *Tunisia* 50 B7
Dehlorān, *Iran* 44 C5
Dehnow-e Kūhestān, *Iran* 45 E8
Dehra Dun, *India* 42 D8
Dehri, *India* 43 G11
Dehui, *China* 35 B13
Deinze, *Belgium* 15 D3
Dej, *Romania* 17 E11
Dekese, *Zaïre* 52 E4
Del Mar, *U.S.A.* 85 N9
Del Norte, *U.S.A.* 83 H10
Del Rio, *U.S.A.* 81 L4
Delano, *U.S.A.* 85 K7
Delareyville, *S. Africa* 56 D4
Delavan, *U.S.A.* 80 D10
Delaware, *U.S.A.* 76 E4
Delaware □, *U.S.A.* 76 F8
Delaware →, *U.S.A.* 76 F8
Delaware B., *U.S.A.* 75 C12
Delegate, *Australia* 63 F4
Delft, *Neths.* 15 B4
Delfzijl, *Neths.* 15 A6
Delgado, C., *Mozam.* 55 E5
Delgerhet, *Mongolia* 34 B6
Delgo, *Sudan* 51 D11
Delhi, *Canada* 78 D4
Delhi, *India* 42 E7
Delhi, *U.S.A.* 79 D10
Delia, *Canada* 72 C6
Delice →, *Turkey* 25 G5
Delicias, *Mexico* 86 B3
Delījān, *Iran* 45 C6
Dell City, *U.S.A.* 83 L11
Dell Rapids, *U.S.A.* 80 D6
Delmar, *U.S.A.* 79 D11
Delmiro Gouveia, *Brazil* 93 E11
Delong, Ostrova, *Russia* 27 B15
Deloraine, *Australia* 62 G4
Deloraine, *Canada* 73 D8
Delphi, *U.S.A.* 76 E2
Delphos, *U.S.A.* 76 E3
Delportshoop, *S. Africa* 56 D3
Delray Beach, *U.S.A.* 77 M5
Delta, *Colo., U.S.A.* 83 G9
Delta, *Utah, U.S.A.* 82 G7
Delungra, *Australia* 63 D5
Demanda, Sierra de la, *Spain* 19 A4
Demba, *Zaïre* 52 F4
Dembecha, *Ethiopia* 51 F12
Dembia, *Zaïre* 54 B2
Dembidolo, *Ethiopia* 51 G11
Demer →, *Belgium* 15 D4
Deming, *N. Mex., U.S.A.* 83 K10
Deming, *Wash., U.S.A.* 84 B4
Demini →, *Brazil* 92 D6
Demopolis, *U.S.A.* 77 J2
Dempo, *Indonesia* 36 E2
Den Burg, *Neths.* 15 A4
Den Chai, *Thailand* 38 D3
Den Haag = 's-Gravenhage, *Neths.* 15 B4
Den Helder, *Neths.* 15 B4
Den Oever, *Neths.* 15 B5
Denain, *France* 18 A5
Denair, *U.S.A.* 84 H6
Denau, *Uzbekistan* 26 F7
Denbigh, *U.K.* 10 D4
Dendang, *Indonesia* 36 E3
Dendermonde, *Belgium* 15 C4
Dengfeng, *China* 34 G7
Dengkou, *China* 34 D4
Denham, *Australia* 61 E1
Denham Ra., *Australia* 62 C4
Denham Sd., *Australia* 61 E1
Denia, *Spain* 19 C6
Denial B., *Australia* 63 E1
Deniliquin, *Australia* 63 F3
Denison, *Iowa, U.S.A.* 80 D7
Denison, *Tex., U.S.A.* 81 J6
Denison Plains, *Australia* 60 C4
Denizli, *Turkey* 25 G4
Denman Glacier, *Antarctica* 5 C7
Denmark, *Australia* 61 F2
Denmark ■, *Europe* 9 J10
Denmark Str., *Atl. Oc.* 4 C6
Dennison, *U.S.A.* 78 F3
Denpasar, *Indonesia* 36 F5
Denton, *Mont., U.S.A.* 82 C9
Denton, *Tex., U.S.A.* 81 J6
D'Entrecasteaux, Pt., *Australia* 61 F2
Denver, *U.S.A.* 80 F2
Denver City, *U.S.A.* 81 J3
Deoband, *India* 42 E7
Deoghar, *India* 43 G12
Deolali, *India* 40 K8
Deoli = Devli, *India* 42 G6
Deoria, *India* 43 F10
Deosai Mts., *Pakistan* 43 B6
Deping, *China* 35 F9
Deposit, *U.S.A.* 79 D9
Depot Springs, *Australia* 61 E3
Deputatskiy, *Russia* 27 C14
Dera Ghazi Khan, *Pakistan* 42 D4
Dera Ismail Khan, *Pakistan* 42 D4
Derbent, *Russia* 25 F8
Derby, *Australia* 60 C3
Derby, *U.K.* 10 E6
Derby, *Conn., U.S.A.* 79 E11
Derby, *N.Y., U.S.A.* 78 D6
Derbyshire □, *U.K.* 10 E6
Derg →, *U.K.* 13 B4
Derg, L., *Ireland* 13 D3
Dergaon, *India* 41 F19
Dernieres Isles, *U.S.A.* 81 L9
Derry = Londonderry, *U.K.* 13 B4
Derryveagh Mts., *Ireland* 13 B3
Derudub, *Sudan* 51 E12
Derwent, *Canada* 73 C6
Derwent →, *Derby, U.K.* 10 E6
Derwent →, *N. Yorks., U.K.* 10 D7
Derwent Water, *U.K.* 10 C4
Des Moines, *Iowa, U.S.A.* 80 E8
Des Moines, *N. Mex., U.S.A.* 81 G3
Des Moines →, *U.S.A.* 80 E9
Desaguadero →, *Argentina* 94 C2
Desaguadero →, *Bolivia* 92 G5
Descanso, Pta., *Mexico* 85 N9
Deschaillons, *Canada* 71 C5
Descharme →, *Canada* 73 B7
Deschutes →, *U.S.A.* 82 D3
Dese, *Ethiopia* 46 E2
Desert Center, *U.S.A.* 85 M11
Desert Hot Springs, *U.S.A.* 85 M10
Désirade, I., *Guadeloupe* 89 C7
Deskenatlata L., *Canada* 72 A6
Desna →, *Ukraine* 24 D5
Desolación, I., *Chile* 96 G2
Despeñaperros, Paso, *Spain* 19 C4
Dessau, *Germany* 16 C6
Dessye = Dese, *Ethiopia* 46 E2
D'Estrees B., *Australia* 63 F2
Desuri, *India* 42 G5
Det Udom, *Thailand* 38 E5
Dete, *Zimbabwe* 55 F2
Detmold, *Germany* 16 C4
Detour Pt., *U.S.A.* 76 C2
Detroit, *Mich., U.S.A.* 75 B10
Detroit, *Tex., U.S.A.* 81 J7
Detroit Lakes, *U.S.A.* 80 B7
Deurne, *Belgium* 15 C4
Deurne, *Neths.* 15 C5
Deutsche Bucht, *Germany* 16 A4
Deux-Sèvres □, *France* 18 C3
Deva, *Romania* 17 F11
Devakottai, *India* 40 Q11
Devaprayag, *India* 43 D8
Deventer, *Neths.* 15 B6
Deveron →, *U.K.* 12 D6
Devgadh Bariya, *India* 42 H5
Devils Den, *U.S.A.* 84 K7
Devils Lake, *U.S.A.* 80 A5
Devils Paw, *Canada* 72 B2
Devizes, *U.K.* 11 F6
Devli, *India* 42 G6
Devon, *Canada* 72 C6
Devon □, *U.K.* 11 G4
Devon I., *Canada* 4 B3
Devonport, *Australia* 62 G4
Devonport, *N.Z.* 59 G5
Devonport, *U.K.* 11 G3
Dewas, *India* 42 H7
Dewetsdorp, *S. Africa* 56 D4
Dewsbury, *U.K.* 10 D6
Dexter, *Mo., U.S.A.* 81 G9
Dexter, *N. Mex., U.S.A.* 81 J2
Dey-Dey, L., *Australia* 61 E5
Deyhūk, *Iran* 45 C8
Deyyer, *Iran* 45 E6
Dezadeash L., *Canada* 72 A1
Dezfūl, *Iran* 45 C6
Dezhneva, Mys, *Russia* 27 C19
Dezhou, *China* 34 F9
Dháfni, *Greece* 23 D7
Dhahiriya = Az̧ Z̧āhirīyah, *Jordan* 47 D3
Dhahran = Az̧ Z̧ahrān, *Si. Arabia* 45 E6
Dhaka, *Bangla.* 43 H14
Dhaka □, *Bangla.* 43 G14
Dhali, *Cyprus* 23 D12
Dhamar, *Yemen* 46 E3
Dhampur, *India* 43 E8
Dhamtari, *India* 41 J12
Dhanbad, *India* 43 H12
Dhangarhi, *Nepal* 41 E12
Dhankuta, *Nepal* 43 F12
Dhar, *India* 42 H6
Dharampur, *India* 42 H6
Dharamsala = Dharmsala, *India* 42 C7
Dharmapuri, *India* 40 N11
Dharmsala, *India* 42 C7
Dharwad, *India* 40 M9
Dharwar, *India* 40 M9
Dhaulagiri, *Nepal* 43 E10
Dhebar, L., *India* 42 G6
Dheftera, *Cyprus* 23 D12
Dhenkanal, *India* 41 J14
Dherinia, *Cyprus* 23 D12
Dhiarrizos →, *Cyprus* 23 E11
Dhībān, *Jordan* 47 D4
Dhidhimótikhon, *Greece* 21 D12
Dhíkti Óros, *Greece* 23 D7
Dhírfis, *Greece* 21 E10
Dhodhekánisos, *Greece* 21 F12
Dholka, *India* 42 H5
Dhoraji, *India* 42 J4
Dhráhstis, Ákra, *Greece* 23 A3
Dhrangadhra, *India* 42 H4
Dhrápanon, Ákra, *Greece* 23 D6
Dhrol, *India* 42 H4
Dhuburi, *India* 41 F16
Dhule, *India* 40 J9
Dhut →, *Somali Rep.* 46 E5
Di Linh, *Vietnam* 39 G7
Di Linh, Cao Nguyen, *Vietnam* 39 G7
Día, *Greece* 23 D7
Diablo, Mt., *U.S.A.* 84 H5
Diablo Range, *U.S.A.* 84 J5
Diafarabé, *Mali* 50 F4
Diamante, *Argentina* 94 C3
Diamante →, *Argentina* 94 C2
Diamantina, *Brazil* 93 G10
Diamantina →, *Australia* 63 D2
Diamantino, *Brazil* 93 F7
Diamond Harbour, *India* 43 H13
Diamond Is., *Australia* 62 B5
Diamond Mts., *U.S.A.* 82 G6
Diamond Springs, *U.S.A.* 84 G6
Diamondville, *U.S.A.* 82 F8
Diapaga, *Burkina Faso* 50 F5
Dibā, *Oman* 45 E8
Dibaya, *Zaïre* 52 F4
Dibaya-Lubue, *Zaïre* 52 E3
Dibbi, *Ethiopia* 46 G3
Dibete, *Botswana* 56 C4
Dibrugarh, *India* 41 F19
Dickinson, *U.S.A.* 80 B3
Dickson, *U.S.A.* 77 G2
Dickson City, *U.S.A.* 79 E9
Didiéni, *Mali* 50 F3
Didsbury, *Canada* 72 C6
Didwana, *India* 42 F6
Diébougou, *Burkina Faso* 50 F4
Diefenbaker L., *Canada* 73 C7
Diego Garcia, *Ind. Oc.* 3 E13
Diekirch, *Lux.* 15 E6
Dien Ban, *Vietnam* 38 E7
Dien Bien, *Vietnam* 38 B4
Dien Khanh, *Vietnam* 39 F7
Dieppe, *France* 18 B4
Dieren, *Neths.* 15 B6
Dierks, *U.S.A.* 81 H7
Diest, *Belgium* 15 D5
Differdange, *Lux.* 15 E5
Dig, *India* 42 F7
Digba, *Zaïre* 54 B2
Digby, *Canada* 71 D6
Digges, *Canada* 73 B10
Digges Is., *Canada* 69 B12
Dighinala, *Bangla.* 41 H18
Dighton, *U.S.A.* 80 F4
Digne, *France* 18 D7
Digos, *Phil.* 37 C7
Digranes, *Iceland* 8 C6
Digul →, *Indonesia* 37 F9
Dihang →, *India* 41 F19
Dīhōk, *Iraq* 44 B3
Dijlah, Nahr →, *Asia* 44 D5
Dijon, *France* 18 C6
Dikomu di Kai, *Botswana* 56 C3
Diksmuide, *Belgium* 15 C2
Dikson, *Russia* 26 B9
Dikwa, *Nigeria* 51 F7
Dili, *Indonesia* 37 F7
Dilley, *U.S.A.* 81 L5
Dilling, *Sudan* 51 F10
Dillingham, *U.S.A.* 68 C4
Dillon, *Canada* 73 B7
Dillon, *Mont., U.S.A.* 82 D7
Dillon, *S.C., U.S.A.* 77 H6
Dillon →, *Canada* 73 B7
Dilolo, *Zaïre* 52 G4
Dilston, *Australia* 62 G4
Dimas, *Mexico* 86 C3
Dimashq, *Syria* 47 B5
Dimashq □, *Syria* 47 B5
Dimbaza, *S. Africa* 57 E4
Dimbokro, *Ivory C.* 50 G4
Dimboola, *Australia* 63 F3
Dîmbovița →, *Romania* 17 F13
Dimbulah, *Australia* 62 B4
Dimitrovgrad, *Bulgaria* 21 C11
Dimitrovgrad, *Russia* 24 D8
Dimmitt, *U.S.A.* 81 H3
Dimona, *Israel* 47 D4
Dinagat, *Phil.* 37 B7
Dinajpur, *Bangla.* 41 G16
Dinan, *France* 18 B2
Dīnān Āb, *Iran* 45 C8
Dinant, *Belgium* 15 D4
Dinapur, *India* 43 G11
Dinara Planina, *Croatia* 20 C7
Dinard, *France* 18 B2
Dinaric Alps = Dinara Planina, *Croatia* 20 C7
Dindigul, *India* 40 P11
Ding Xian, *China* 34 E8
Dingbian, *China* 34 F4
Dingle, *Ireland* 13 D1
Dingle B., *Ireland* 13 D1
Dingmans Ferry, *U.S.A.* 79 E10
Dingo, *Australia* 62 C4
Dingtao, *China* 34 G8
Dinguiraye, *Guinea* 50 F2
Dingwall, *U.K.* 12 D4
Dingxi, *China* 34 G3
Dingxiang, *China* 34 E7
Dinh, Mui, *Vietnam* 39 G7
Dinh Lap, *Vietnam* 38 B6
Dinokwe, *Botswana* 56 C4
Dinosaur National Monument, *U.S.A.* 82 F9
Dinuba, *U.S.A.* 83 H4
Diourbel, *Senegal* 50 F1
Diplo, *Pakistan* 42 G3
Dipolog, *Phil.* 37 C6
Dir, *Pakistan* 40 B7

Diré, *Mali* 50 E4
Dire Dawa, *Ethiopia* 46 F3
Diriamba, *Nic.* 88 D2
Dirico, *Angola* 53 H4
Dirk Hartog I., *Australia* 61 E1
Dirranbandi, *Australia* 63 D4
Disa, *India* 42 G5
Disappointment, C., *U.S.A.* 82 C1
Disappointment, L., *Australia* 60 D3
Disaster B., *Australia* 63 F4
Discovery B., *Australia* 63 F3
Disko, *Greenland* 4 C5
Disko Bugt, *Greenland* 4 C5
Disteghil Sar, *Pakistan* 43 A6
Distrito Federal □, *Brazil* 93 G9
Diu, *India* 42 J4
Dīvāndarreh, *Iran* 44 C5
Divide, *U.S.A.* 82 D7
Dividing Ra., *Australia* 61 E2
Divinópolis, *Brazil* 93 H10
Divnoye, *Russia* 25 E7
Dīwāl Kol, *Afghan.* 42 B2
Dixie Mt., *U.S.A.* 84 F6
Dixon, *Calif., U.S.A.* 84 G5
Dixon, *Ill., U.S.A.* 80 E10
Dixon, *Mont., U.S.A.* 82 C6
Dixon, *N. Mex., U.S.A.* 83 H11
Dixon Entrance, *U.S.A.* 72 C2
Dixonville, *Canada* 72 B5
Diyarbakır, *Turkey* 25 G7
Djado, *Niger* 51 D7
Djakarta = Jakarta, *Indonesia* 37 G12
Djamba, *Angola* 56 B1
Djambala, *Congo* 52 E2
Djanet, *Algeria* 50 D6
Djawa = Jawa, *Indonesia* 37 G14
Djelfa, *Algeria* 50 B5
Djema, *C.A.R.* 54 A2
Djenné, *Mali* 50 F4
Djerba, I. de, *Tunisia* 51 B7
Djerid, Chott, *Tunisia* 50 B6
Djibo, *Burkina Faso* 50 F4
Djibouti, *Djibouti* 46 E3
Djibouti ■, *Africa* 46 E3
Djolu, *Zaïre* 52 D4
Djougou, *Benin* 50 G5
Djoum, *Cameroon* 52 D2
Djourab, *Chad* 51 E8
Djugu, *Zaïre* 54 B3
Djúpivogur, *Iceland* 8 D6
Dmitriya Lapteva, Proliv, *Russia* 27 B15
Dnepr →, *Ukraine* 25 E5
Dneprodzerzhinsk, *Ukraine* 25 E5
Dnepropetrovsk, *Ukraine* 25 E5
Dnestr →, *Europe* 25 E5
Dnestrovski = Belgorod, *Russia* 25 D6
Dnieper = Dnepr →, *Ukraine* 25 E5
Dniester = Dnestr →, *Europe* 25 E5
Doan Hung, *Vietnam* 38 B5
Doba, *Chad* 51 G8
Dobbyn, *Australia* 62 B3
Doberai, Jazirah, *Indonesia* 37 E8
Doblas, *Argentina* 94 D3
Dobo, *Indonesia* 37 F8
Dobreta-Turnu-Severin, *Romania* 17 F11
Dobruja, *Romania* 17 F14
Doc, Mui, *Vietnam* 38 D6
Doda, *India* 43 C6
Dodecanese = Dhodhekánisos, *Greece* 21 F12
Dodge Center, *U.S.A.* 80 C8
Dodge City, *U.S.A.* 81 G5
Dodge L., *Canada* 73 B7
Dodgeville, *U.S.A.* 80 D9
Dodoma, *Tanzania* 54 D4
Dodoma □, *Tanzania* 54 D4
Dodsland, *Canada* 73 C7
Dodson, *U.S.A.* 82 B9
Doetinchem, *Neths.* 15 C6
Dog Creek, *Canada* 72 C4
Dog L., *Man., Canada* 73 C9
Dog L., *Ont., Canada* 70 C2
Dogger Bank, *N. Sea* 6 E6
Dogi, *Afghan.* 40 C3
Dogran, *Pakistan* 42 D5
Dohazari, *Bangla.* 41 H18
Doi, *Indonesia* 37 D7
Doi Luang, *Thailand* 38 C3
Doi Saket, *Thailand* 38 C2
Doig →, *Canada* 72 B4
Dois Irmãos, Sa., *Brazil* 93 E10
Dokka, *Norway* 9 F11
Dokkum, *Neths.* 15 A5
Dokri, *Pakistan* 42 F3
Doland, *U.S.A.* 80 C5
Dolbeau, *Canada* 71 C5
Dole, *France* 18 C6
Dolgellau, *U.K.* 10 E4
Dolgelley = Dolgellau, *U.K.* 10 E4
Dollart, *Neths.* 15 A7
Dolomites = Dolomiti, *Italy* 20 A4
Dolomiti, *Italy* 20 A4
Dolores, *Argentina* 94 D4
Dolores, *Uruguay* 94 C4
Dolores, *U.S.A.* 83 H9
Dolores →, *U.S.A.* 83 G9
Dolphin, C., *Falk. Is.* 96 G5
Dolphin and Union Str., *Canada* 68 B8
Dom Pedrito, *Brazil* 95 C5
Domasi, *Malawi* 55 F4
Dombarovskiy, *Russia* 26 D6
Dombås, *Norway* 9 E10
Dombes, *France* 18 D6
Domburg, *Neths.* 15 C3
Domeyko, *Chile* 94 B1
Domeyko, Cordillera, *Chile* 94 A2
Dominador, *Chile* 94 A2
Dominica ■, *W. Indies* 89 C7
Dominica Passage, *W. Indies* 89 C7
Dominican Rep. ■, *W. Indies* 89 C5
Domo, *Ethiopia* 46 F4
Domodóssola, *Italy* 20 A3
Domville, Mt., *Australia* 63 D5
Don →, *Russia* 25 E6
Don →, *Gramp., U.K.* 12 D6
Don →, *S. Yorks., U.K.* 10 D7
Don, C., *Australia* 60 B5
Don Benito, *Spain* 19 C3
Don Duong, *Vietnam* 39 G7
Don Martín, Presa de, *Mexico* 86 B4
Dona Ana = Nhamaabué, *Mozam.* 55 F4
Donaghadee, *U.K.* 13 B6
Donald, *Australia* 63 F3
Donalda, *Canada* 72 C6
Donaldsonville, *U.S.A.* 81 K9
Donalsonville, *U.S.A.* 77 K3
Donau →, *Austria* 16 D8
Donauwörth, *Germany* 16 D5
Doncaster, *U.K.* 10 D6
Dondo, *Angola* 52 F2
Dondo, *Mozam.* 55 F3
Dondo, Teluk, *Indonesia* 37 D6
Dondra Head, *Sri Lanka* 40 S12
Donegal, *Ireland* 13 B3
Donegal □, *Ireland* 13 B4
Donegal B., *Ireland* 13 B3
Donets →, *Russia* 25 E7
Donetsk, *Ukraine* 25 E6
Dong Ba Thin, *Vietnam* 39 F7
Dong Dang, *Vietnam* 38 B6
Dong Giam, *Vietnam* 38 C5
Dong Ha, *Vietnam* 38 D6
Dong Hene, *Laos* 38 D5
Dong Hoi, *Vietnam* 38 D6
Dong Khe, *Vietnam* 38 A6
Dong Ujimqin Qi, *China* 34 B9
Dong Van, *Vietnam* 38 A5
Dong Xoai, *Vietnam* 39 G6
Dongara, *Australia* 61 E1
Dongbei, *China* 35 D13
Dongchuan, *China* 32 D5
Dongfang, *China* 38 C7
Dongfeng, *China* 35 C13
Donggala, *Indonesia* 37 E5
Donggou, *China* 35 E13
Dongguang, *China* 34 F9
Dongjingcheng, *China* 35 B15
Dongning, *China* 35 B16
Dongola, *Sudan* 51 E11
Dongou, *Congo* 52 D3
Dongping, *China* 34 G9
Dongsheng, *China* 34 E6
Dongtai, *China* 35 H11
Dongting Hu, *China* 33 D6
Donington, C., *Australia* 63 E2
Doniphan, *U.S.A.* 81 G9
Dønna, *Norway* 8 C12
Donna, *U.S.A.* 81 M5
Donnaconna, *Canada* 71 C5
Donnelly's Crossing, *N.Z.* 59 F4
Donnybrook, *Australia* 61 F2
Donnybrook, *S. Africa* 57 D4
Donora, *U.S.A.* 78 F5
Donor's Hill, *Australia* 62 B3
Donostia = San Sebastián, *Spain* 19 A5
Doon →, *U.K.* 12 F4
Dora, L., *Australia* 60 D3
Dora Báltea →, *Italy* 20 B3
Doran L., *Canada* 73 A7
Dorchester, *U.K.* 11 G5
Dorchester, C., *Canada* 69 B12
Dordogne □, *France* 18 D4
Dordogne →, *France* 18 D3
Dordrecht, *Neths.* 15 C4
Dordrecht, *S. Africa* 56 E4
Dore, Mts., *France* 18 D5
Doré L., *Canada* 73 C7
Doré Lake, *Canada* 73 C7
Dori, *Burkina Faso* 50 F4
Doring →, *S. Africa* 56 E2
Doringbos, *S. Africa* 56 E2
Dorion, *Canada* 70 C5
Dornoch, *U.K.* 12 D4
Dornoch Firth, *U.K.* 12 D4
Dornogovĭ □, *Mongolia* 34 B6
Dorohoi, *Romania* 17 E13
Döröö Nuur, *Mongolia* 32 B4
Dorr, *Iran* 45 C6
Dorre I., *Australia* 61 E1
Dorrigo, *Australia* 63 E5
Dorris, *U.S.A.* 82 F3
Dorset, *Canada* 78 A6
Dorset, *U.S.A.* 78 E4
Dorset □, *U.K.* 11 G5
Dortmund, *Germany* 16 C3
Doruma, *Zaïre* 54 B2
Dorūneh, *Iran* 45 C8
Dos Bahías, C., *Argentina* 96 E3
Dos Palos, *U.S.A.* 84 J6
Dosso, *Niger* 50 F5
Dothan, *U.S.A.* 77 K3
Doty, *U.S.A.* 84 D3
Douai, *France* 18 A5
Douala, *Cameroon* 50 H6
Douarnenez, *France* 18 B1
Double Island Pt., *Australia* 63 D5
Doubs □, *France* 18 C7
Doubs →, *France* 18 C6
Doubtful Sd., *N.Z.* 59 L1
Doubtless B., *N.Z.* 59 F4
Douentza, *Mali* 50 F4
Douglas, *S. Africa* 56 D3
Douglas, *U.K.* 10 C3
Douglas, *Alaska, U.S.A.* 72 B2
Douglas, *Ariz., U.S.A.* 83 L9
Douglas, *Ga., U.S.A.* 77 K4
Douglas, *Wyo., U.S.A.* 80 D2
Douglastown, *Canada* 71 C7
Douglasville, *U.S.A.* 77 J3
Doumé, *Cameroon* 52 D2
Dounreay, *U.K.* 12 C5
Dourados, *Brazil* 95 A5
Dourados →, *Brazil* 95 A5
Douro →, *Europe* 19 B1
Douro Litoral, *Portugal* 19 B1
Dove →, *U.K.* 10 E6
Dove Creek, *U.S.A.* 83 H9
Dover, *Australia* 62 G4
Dover, *U.K.* 11 F9
Dover, *Del., U.S.A.* 76 F8
Dover, *N.H., U.S.A.* 79 C14
Dover, *N.J., U.S.A.* 79 F10
Dover, *Ohio, U.S.A.* 78 F3
Dover, Pt., *Australia* 61 F4
Dover, Str. of, *Europe* 18 A4
Dover-Foxcroft, *U.S.A.* 71 C6
Dover Plains, *U.S.A.* 79 E11
Dovey = Dyfi →, *U.K.* 11 E4
Dovrefjell, *Norway* 8 E10
Dow Rūd, *Iran* 45 C6
Dowa, *Malawi* 55 E3
Dowagiac, *U.S.A.* 76 E2
Dowgha'i, *Iran* 45 B8
Dowlatābād, *Iran* 45 D8
Down □, *U.K.* 13 B6
Downey, *Calif., U.S.A.* 85 M8
Downey, *Utah, U.S.A.* 82 E7
Downham Market, *U.K.* 11 E8
Downieville, *U.S.A.* 84 F6
Downpatrick, *U.K.* 13 B6
Downpatrick Hd., *Ireland* 13 B2
Dowsārī, *Iran* 45 D8
Doyle, *U.S.A.* 84 E6
Doylestown, *U.S.A.* 79 F9
Draa, Oued →, *Morocco* 50 C2
Drachten, *Neths.* 15 A6
Dragoman, Prokhod, *Bulgaria* 21 C10
Dragonera, I., *Spain* 22 B9
Draguignan, *France* 18 E7
Drain, *U.S.A.* 82 E2
Drake, *Australia* 63 D5
Drake, *U.S.A.* 80 B4
Drake Passage, *S. Ocean* 5 B17
Drakensberg, *S. Africa* 57 E4
Dráma, *Greece* 21 D11
Drammen, *Norway* 9 G11
Drangajökull, *Iceland* 8 C2
Dras, *India* 43 B6
Drau = Drava →, *Croatia* 21 B8
Drava →, *Croatia* 21 B8
Drayton Valley, *Canada* 72 C6
Drenthe □, *Neths.* 15 B6
Drepanum, C., *Cyprus* 23 E11
Dresden, *Canada* 78 D2
Dresden, *Germany* 16 C6
Dreux, *France* 18 B4
Driffield = Great Driffield, *U.K.* 10 C7
Driftwood, *U.S.A.* 78 E6
Driggs, *U.S.A.* 82 E8
Drina →, *Bos. & H., Yug.* 21 B8
Drøbak, *Norway* 9 G11
Drogheda, *Ireland* 13 C5
Drogobych, *Ukraine* 25 E3
Droichead Nua, *Ireland* 13 C5
Droitwich, *U.K.* 11 E5
Drôme □, *France* 18 D6
Dromedary, C., *Australia* 63 F5
Dronfield, *Australia* 62 C3
Drumbo, *Canada* 78 C4
Drumheller, *Canada* 72 C6
Drummond, *U.S.A.* 82 C7
Drummond I., *U.S.A.* 70 C3
Drummond Pt., *Australia* 63 E2
Drummond Ra., *Australia* 62 C4
Drummondville, *Canada* 70 C5
Drumright, *U.S.A.* 81 H6
Druzhina, *Russia* 27 C15
Dry Tortugas, *U.S.A.* 88 B3
Dryden, *Canada* 73 D10
Dryden, *U.S.A.* 81 K3
Drygalski I., *Antarctica* 5 C7
Drysdale →, *Australia* 60 B4
Drysdale I., *Australia* 62 A2
Dschang, *Cameroon* 50 G7
Du Bois, *U.S.A.* 78 E6
Du Quoin, *U.S.A.* 80 G10
Duanesburg, *U.S.A.* 79 D10
Duaringa, *Australia* 62 C4
Ḑubā, *Si. Arabia* 44 E2
Dubai = Dubayy, *U.A.E.* 45 E7
Dubawnt →, *Canada* 73 A8
Dubawnt, L., *Canada* 73 A8
Dubayy, *U.A.E.* 45 E7
Dubbo, *Australia* 63 E4
Dubele, *Zaïre* 54 B2
Dublin, *Ireland* 13 C5
Dublin, *Ga., U.S.A.* 77 J4
Dublin, *Tex., U.S.A.* 81 J5
Dublin □, *Ireland* 13 C5
Dublin B., *Ireland* 13 C5
Dubois, *U.S.A.* 82 D7
Dubovka, *Russia* 25 E7
Dubrajpur, *India* 43 H12
Dubréka, *Guinea* 50 G2
Dubrovnik, *Croatia* 21 C8
Dubrovskoye, *Russia* 27 D12
Dubuque, *U.S.A.* 80 D9
Duchesne, *U.S.A.* 82 F8
Duchess, *Australia* 62 C2
Ducie I., *Pac. Oc.* 65 K15
Duck Cr. →, *Australia* 60 D2
Duck Lake, *Canada* 73 C7
Duck Mountain Prov. Park, *Canada* 73 C8
Duckwall, Mt., *U.S.A.* 84 H6
Dudhi, *India* 41 G13
Dudinka, *Russia* 27 C9
Dudley, *U.K.* 11 E5
Duero = Douro →, *Europe* 19 B1
Dufftown, *U.K.* 12 D5
Dugi Otok, *Croatia* 20 B6
Duifken Pt., *Australia* 62 A3
Duisburg, *Germany* 16 C3
Duiwelskloof, *S. Africa* 57 C5
Dūkdamīn, *Iran* 45 C8
Duke I., *U.S.A.* 72 C2
Dukhān, *Qatar* 45 E6
Duki, *Pakistan* 40 D6
Duku, *Nigeria* 50 F7
Dulce →, *Argentina* 94 C3
Dulce, G., *Costa Rica* 88 E3
Dulf, *Iraq* 44 C5
Dulit, Banjaran, *Malaysia* 36 D4
Duliu, *China* 34 E9
Dullewala, *Pakistan* 42 D4
Dulq Maghār, *Syria* 44 B3
Dululu, *Australia* 62 C5
Duluth, *U.S.A.* 80 B8
Dum Dum, *India* 43 H13
Dum Duma, *India* 41 F19
Dum Hadjer, *Chad* 51 F8
Dūmā, *Lebanon* 47 A4
Dūmā, *Syria* 47 B5
Dumaguete, *Phil.* 37 C6
Dumai, *Indonesia* 36 D2
Dumaran, *Phil.* 37 B5
Dumas, *Ark., U.S.A.* 81 J9
Dumas, *Tex., U.S.A.* 81 H4
Dumbarton, *U.K.* 12 F4
Dumbleyung, *Australia* 61 F2
Dumfries, *U.K.* 12 F5
Dumfries & Galloway □, *U.K.* 12 F5
Dumka, *India* 43 G12
Dumoine →, *Canada* 70 C4
Dumoine L., *Canada* 70 C4
Dumraon, *India* 43 G11
Dumyât, *Egypt* 51 B11
Dun Laoghaire, *Ireland* 13 C5
Dunaföldvár, *Hungary* 17 E9
Dunărea →, *Romania* 17 F14
Dunay, *Russia* 30 C6
Dunback, *N.Z.* 59 L3
Dunbar, *Australia* 62 B3
Dunbar, *U.K.* 12 E6
Dunblane, *U.K.* 12 E5
Duncan, *Canada* 72 D4
Duncan, *Ariz., U.S.A.* 83 K9
Duncan, *Okla., U.S.A.* 81 H6
Duncan, L., *Canada* 70 B4
Duncan L., *Canada* 72 A6
Duncan Town, *Bahamas* 88 B4
Duncannon, *U.S.A.* 78 F7
Dundalk, *Canada* 78 B4
Dundalk, *Ireland* 13 B5
Dundalk Bay, *Ireland* 13 C5
Dundas, *Canada* 70 D4
Dundas, L., *Australia* 61 F3
Dundas I., *Canada* 72 C2
Dundas Str., *Australia* 60 B5
Dundee, *S. Africa* 57 D5
Dundee, *U.K.* 12 E6
Dundgovĭ □, *Mongolia* 34 B4
Dundoo, *Australia* 63 D3
Dundrum, *U.K.* 13 B6
Dundrum B., *U.K.* 13 B6
Dundwara, *India* 43 F8
Dunedin, *N.Z.* 59 L3
Dunedin, *U.S.A.* 77 L4
Dunedin →, *Canada* 72 B4
Dunfermline, *U.K.* 12 E5
Dungannon, *Canada* 78 C3
Dungannon, *U.K.* 13 B5
Dungannon □, *U.K.* 13 B5
Dungarpur, *India* 42 H5
Dungarvan, *Ireland* 13 D4
Dungarvan Bay, *Ireland* 13 D4
Dungeness, *U.K.* 11 G8
Dungo, L. do, *Angola* 56 B2
Dungog, *Australia* 63 E5
Dungu, *Zaïre* 54 B2
Dunhua, *China* 35 C15
Dunhuang, *China* 32 B4
Dunk I., *Australia* 62 B4
Dunkeld, *U.K.* 12 E5
Dunkerque, *France* 18 A5
Dunkery Beacon, *U.K.* 11 F4
Dunkirk = Dunkerque, *France* 18 A5
Dunkirk, *U.S.A.* 78 D5
Dunkwa, *Ghana* 50 G4
Dunlap, *U.S.A.* 80 E7
Dúnleary = Dun Laoghaire, *Ireland* 13 C5
Dunmanus B., *Ireland* 13 E2
Dunmara, *Australia* 62 B1
Dunmore, *U.S.A.* 79 E9
Dunmore Hd., *Ireland* 13 D1
Dunmore Town, *Bahamas* 88 A4
Dunn, *U.S.A.* 77 H6
Dunnellon, *U.S.A.* 77 L4
Dunnet Hd., *U.K.* 12 C5
Dunning, *U.S.A.* 80 E4
Dunnville, *Canada* 78 D5
Dunolly, *Australia* 63 F3
Dunoon, *U.K.* 12 F4
Dunqul, *Egypt* 51 D11
Duns, *U.K.* 12 F6
Dunseith, *U.S.A.* 80 A4
Dunsmuir, *U.S.A.* 82 F2
Dunstable, *U.K.* 11 F7
Dunstan Mts., *N.Z.* 59 L2
Dunster, *Canada* 72 C5
Dunvegan L., *Canada* 73 A7
Duolun, *China* 34 C9
Duong Dong, *Vietnam* 39 G4
Dupree, *U.S.A.* 80 C4
Dupuyer, *U.S.A.* 82 B7
Duque de Caxias, *Brazil* 95 A7
Durack →, *Australia* 60 C4
Durack Ra., *Australia* 60 C4
Durance →, *France* 18 E6
Durand, *U.S.A.* 76 D4
Durango = Victoria de Durango, *Mexico* 86 C4
Durango, *Spain* 19 A4
Durango, *U.S.A.* 83 H10
Durango □, *Mexico* 86 C4
Duranillin, *Australia* 61 F2
Durant, *U.S.A.* 81 J6
Durazno, *Uruguay* 94 C4
Durazzo = Durrësi, *Albania* 21 D8
Durban, *S. Africa* 57 D5
Durg, *India* 41 J12
Durgapur, *India* 43 H12
Durham, *Canada* 78 B4
Durham, *U.K.* 10 C6
Durham, *Calif., U.S.A.* 84 F5
Durham, *N.C., U.S.A.* 77 G6
Durham □, *U.K.* 10 C6
Durham Downs, *Australia* 63 D4
Durmitor, *Montenegro, Yug.* 21 C8
Durness, *U.K.* 12 C4
Durrësi, *Albania* 21 D8
Durrie, *Australia* 62 D3
Duru, *Zaïre* 54 B2
D'Urville, Tanjung, *Indonesia* 37 E9
D'Urville I., *N.Z.* 59 J4
Duryea, *U.S.A.* 79 E9
Dusa Mareb, *Somali Rep.* 46 F4
Dushak, *Turkmenistan* 26 F7
Dushanbe, *Tajikistan* 26 F7
Dusky Sd., *N.Z.* 59 L1
Dussejour, C., *Australia* 60 B4
Düsseldorf, *Germany* 16 C3
Dutch Harbor, *U.S.A.* 68 C3
Dutlwe, *Botswana* 56 C3
Dutton, *Canada* 78 D3
Dutton →, *Australia* 62 C3
Duyun, *China* 32 D5
Duzdab = Zāhedān, *Iran* 45 D9
Dvina, Sev. →, *Russia* 24 B7
Dvinsk = Daugavpils, *Latvia* 24 C4
Dvinskaya Guba, *Russia* 24 B6
Dwarka, *India* 42 H3
Dwellingup, *Australia* 61 F2
Dwight, *Canada* 78 A5
Dwight, *U.S.A.* 76 E1
Dyer, C., *Canada* 69 B13
Dyer Plateau, *Antarctica* 5 D17
Dyersburg, *U.S.A.* 81 G10
Dyfed □, *U.K.* 11 E3
Dyfi →, *U.K.* 11 E4
Dynevor Downs, *Australia* 63 D3
Dysart, *Canada* 73 C8
Dzamin Üüd, *Mongolia* 34 C6
Dzerzhinsk, *Belorussia* 24 D4
Dzerzhinsk, *Russia* 24 C7
Dzhalinda, *Russia* 27 D13
Dzhambul, *Kazakhstan* 26 E8
Dzhankoi, *Ukraine* 25 E5
Dzhardzhan, *Russia* 27 C13
Dzhelinde, *Russia* 27 C12
Dzhetygara, *Kazakhstan* 26 D7
Dzhezkazgan, *Kazakhstan* 26 E7
Dzhikimde, *Russia* 27 D13
Dzhizak, *Uzbekistan* 26 E7
Dzhugdzur, Khrebet, *Russia* 27 D14
Dzhungarskiye Vorota, *Kazakhstan* 32 B3
Dzilam de Bravo, *Mexico* 87 C7
Dzungaria = Junggar Pendi, *China* 32 B3
Dzungarian Gates = Dzhungarskiye Vorota, *Kazakhstan* 32 B3
Dzuumod, *Mongolia* 32 B5

E

Eabamet, L., *Canada* 70 B2
Eads, *U.S.A.* 80 F3
Eagle, *U.S.A.* 82 G10
Eagle →, *Canada* 71 B8
Eagle Butt, *U.S.A.* 80 C4
Eagle Grove, *U.S.A.* 80 D8
Eagle L., *Calif., U.S.A.* 82 F3
Eagle L., *Maine, U.S.A.* 71 C6

Eagle Lake, U.S.A. 81 L6
Eagle Mountain, U.S.A. 85 M11
Eagle Nest, U.S.A. 83 H11
Eagle Pass, U.S.A. 81 L4
Eagle Pk., U.S.A. 84 G7
Eagle Pt., Australia 60 C3
Eagle River, U.S.A. 80 C10
Ealing, U.K. 11 F7
Earaheedy, Australia 61 E3
Earl Grey, Canada 73 C8
Earle, U.S.A. 81 H9
Earlimart, U.S.A. 85 K7
Earn →, U.K. 12 E5
Earn, L., U.K. 12 E4
Earnslaw, Mt., N.Z. 59 L2
Earth, U.S.A. 81 H3
Easley, U.S.A. 77 H4
East Angus, Canada 71 C5
East Aurora, U.S.A. 78 D6
East B., U.S.A. 81 L10
East Bengal, Bangla. 41 G17
East Beskids = Vychodné Beskydy, Europe 17 D10
East Brady, U.S.A. 78 F5
East C., N.Z. 59 G7
East Chicago, U.S.A. 76 E2
East China Sea, Asia 33 C7
East Coulee, Canada 72 C6
East Falkland, Falk. Is. 96 G5
East Grand Forks, U.S.A. 80 B6
East Greenwich, U.S.A. 79 E13
East Hartford, U.S.A. 79 E12
East Helena, U.S.A. 82 C8
East Indies, Asia 37 E6
East Jordan, U.S.A. 76 C3
East Lansing, U.S.A. 76 D3
East Liverpool, U.S.A. 78 F4
East London, S. Africa 57 E4
East Main = Eastmain, Canada 70 B4
East Orange, U.S.A. 79 F10
East Pacific Ridge, Pac. Oc. 65 J17
East Pakistan = Bangladesh ■, Asia 41 H17
East Palestine, U.S.A. 78 F4
East Pine, Canada 72 B4
East Pt., Canada 71 C7
East Point, U.S.A. 77 J3
East Providence, U.S.A. 79 E13
East Retford, U.K. 10 D7
East St. Louis, U.S.A. 80 F9
East Schelde → = Oosterschelde, Neths. 15 C4
East Siberian Sea, Russia 27 B17
East Stroudsburg, U.S.A. 79 E9
East Sussex □, U.K. 11 G8
East Tawas, U.S.A. 76 C4
East Toorale, Australia 63 E4
East Walker →, U.S.A. 84 G7
Eastbourne, N.Z. 59 J5
Eastbourne, U.K. 11 G8
Eastend, Canada 73 D7
Easter Islands = Pascua, I. de, Pac. Oc. 65 K17
Eastern □, Kenya 54 B4
Eastern □, Uganda 54 B3
Eastern Cr. →, Australia 62 C3
Eastern Ghats, India 40 N11
Eastern Group = Lau Group, Fiji 59 C9
Eastern Group, Australia 61 F3
Easterville, Canada 73 C9
Easthampton, U.S.A. 79 D12
Eastland, U.S.A. 81 J5
Eastleigh, U.K. 11 G6
Eastmain, Canada 70 B4
Eastmain →, Canada 70 B4
Eastman, Canada 79 A12
Eastman, U.S.A. 77 J4
Easton, Md., U.S.A. 76 F7
Easton, Pa., U.S.A. 79 F9
Easton, Wash., U.S.A. 84 C5
Eastport, U.S.A. 71 D6
Eastsound, U.S.A. 84 B4
Eaton, U.S.A. 80 E2
Eatonia, Canada 73 C7
Eatonton, U.S.A. 77 J4
Eatontown, U.S.A. 79 F10
Eatonville, U.S.A. 84 D4
Eau Claire, U.S.A. 80 C9
Ebagoola, Australia 62 A3
Ebbw Vale, U.K. 11 F4
Ebeltoft, Denmark 9 H11
Ebensburg, U.S.A. 78 F6
Eberswalde, Germany 16 B6
Ebetsu, Japan 30 C10
Eboli, Italy 20 D6
Ebolowa, Cameroon 52 D2
Ebro →, Spain 19 B6
Ech Cheliff, Algeria 50 A5
Echigo-Sammyaku, Japan 31 F9
Echizen-Misaki, Japan 31 G7
Echo Bay, N.W.T., Canada 68 B8
Echo Bay, Ont., Canada 70 C3
Echoing →, Canada 73 B10
Echternach, Lux. 15 E6
Echuca, Australia 63 F3
Ecija, Spain 19 D3
Eclipse Is., Australia 60 B4
Ecuador ■, S. Amer. 92 D3
Ed Dâmer, Sudan 51 E11
Ed Debba, Sudan 51 E11
Ed Dueim, Sudan 51 F11
Edah, Australia 61 E2
Edam, Canada 73 C7
Edam, Neths. 15 B5
Eday, U.K. 12 B6
Edd, Ethiopia 46 E3
Eddrachillis B., U.K. 12 C3
Eddystone, U.K. 11 G3
Eddystone Pt., Australia 62 G4
Ede, Neths. 15 B5
Édea, Cameroon 50 H7
Edehon L., Canada 73 A9
Eden, Australia 63 F4
Eden, N.C., U.S.A. 77 G6
Eden, N.Y., U.S.A. 78 D6
Eden, Tex., U.S.A. 81 K5
Eden, Wyo., U.S.A. 82 E9
Eden →, U.K. 10 C4
Eden L., Canada 73 B8
Edenburg, S. Africa 56 D4
Edendale, S. Africa 57 D5
Edenderry, Ireland 13 C4
Edenton, U.S.A. 77 G7
Edenville, S. Africa 57 D4
Edgar, U.S.A. 80 E5
Edgartown, U.S.A. 79 E14
Edge Hill, U.K. 11 E6
Edgefield, U.S.A. 77 J5
Edgeley, U.S.A. 80 B5
Edgemont, U.S.A. 80 D3
Edgeøya, Svalbard 4 B9
Édhessa, Greece 21 D10
Edievale, N.Z. 59 L2
Edina, U.S.A. 80 E8
Edinburg, U.S.A. 81 M5
Edinburgh, U.K. 12 F5
Edirne, Turkey 21 D12
Edison, U.S.A. 84 B4
Edithburgh, Australia 63 F2
Edjudina, Australia 61 E3
Edmeston, U.S.A. 79 D9
Edmond, U.S.A. 81 H6
Edmonds, U.S.A. 84 C4
Edmonton, Australia 62 B4
Edmonton, Canada 72 C6
Edmund L., Canada 73 C10
Edmundston, Canada 71 C6
Edna, U.S.A. 81 L6
Edna Bay, U.S.A. 72 B2
Edson, Canada 72 C5
Eduardo Castex, Argentina 94 D3
Edward →, Australia 63 F3
Edward, L., Africa 54 C2
Edward I., Canada 70 C2
Edward River, Australia 62 A3
Edward VII Land, Antarctica 5 E13
Edwards, U.S.A. 85 L9
Edwards Plateau, U.S.A. 81 K4
Edwardsville, U.S.A. 79 E9
Edzo, Canada 72 A5
Eekloo, Belgium 15 C3
Effingham, U.S.A. 76 F1
Égadi, Ísole, Italy 20 F5
Eganville, Canada 70 C4
Egeland, U.S.A. 80 A5
Egenolf L., Canada 73 B9
Eger = Cheb, Czech. 16 C6
Eger, Hungary 17 E10
Egersund, Norway 9 G9
Egg L., Canada 73 B7
Eginbah, Australia 60 D2
Egmont, C., N.Z. 59 H4
Egmont, Mt., N.Z. 59 H5
Eğridir, Turkey 25 G5
Eğridir Gölü, Turkey 25 G5
Egvekinot, Russia 27 C19
Egypt ■, Africa 51 C11
Ehime □, Japan 31 H6
Ehrenberg, U.S.A. 85 M12
Eidsvold, Australia 63 D5
Eidsvoll, Norway 9 F11
Eifel, Germany 16 C3
Eiffel Flats, Zimbabwe 55 F3
Eigg, U.K. 12 E2
Eighty Mile Beach, Australia 60 C3
Eil, Somali Rep. 46 F4
Eil, L., U.K. 12 E3
Eildon, L., Australia 63 F4
Eileen L., Canada 73 A7
Einasleigh, Australia 62 B3
Einasleigh →, Australia 62 B3
Eindhoven, Neths. 15 C5
Eire ■, Europe 13 D4
Eiriksjökull, Iceland 8 D3
Eirunepé, Brazil 92 E5
Eisenach, Germany 16 C5
Eisenerz, Austria 16 E7
Ejutla, Mexico 87 D5
Ekalaka, U.S.A. 80 C2
Eketahuna, N.Z. 59 J5
Ekibastuz, Kazakhstan 26 D8
Ekimchan, Russia 27 D14
Ekoli, Zaïre 54 C1
Ekwan →, Canada 70 B3
Ekwan Pt., Canada 70 B3
El Aaiún, W. Sahara 50 C2
El 'Agrûd, Egypt 47 E3
El Alamein, Egypt 51 B10
El 'Aqaba, W. →, Egypt 47 E2
El Arenal, Spain 22 B9
El Aricha, Algeria 50 B4
El Arīhā, Jordan 47 D4
El Arish, Australia 62 B4
El 'Arîsh, Egypt 47 D2
El 'Arîsh, W. →, Egypt 47 D2
El Asnam = Ech Cheliff, Algeria 50 A5
El Bawiti, Egypt 51 C10
El Bayadh, Algeria 50 B5
El Bluff, Nic. 88 D3
El Brûk, W. →, Egypt 47 E2
El Buheirat □, Sudan 51 G10
El Cajon, U.S.A. 85 N10
El Callao, Venezuela 92 B6
El Campo, U.S.A. 81 L6
El Centro, U.S.A. 85 N11
El Cerro, Bolivia 92 G6
El Compadre, Mexico 85 N10
El Cuy, Argentina 96 D3
El Cuyo, Mexico 87 C7
El Daheir, Egypt 47 D3
El Dere, Somali Rep. 46 G4
El Descanso, Mexico 85 N10
El Desemboque, Mexico 86 A2
El Diviso, Colombia 92 C3
El Djouf, Mauritania 50 E3
El Dorado, Ark., U.S.A. 81 J8
El Dorado, Kans., U.S.A. 81 G6
El Dorado, Venezuela 92 B6
El Escorial, Spain 19 B3
El Faiyûm, Egypt 51 C11
El Fâsher, Sudan 51 F10
El Ferrol, Spain 19 A1
El Fuerte, Mexico 86 B3
El Gal, Somali Rep. 46 E5
El Geteina, Sudan 51 F11
El Gezira □, Sudan 51 F11
El Gîza, Egypt 51 C11
El Goléa, Algeria 50 B5
El Harrach, Algeria 50 A5
El Iskandarîya, Egypt 51 B10
El Jadida, Morocco 50 B3
El Jebelein, Sudan 51 F11
El Kab, Sudan 51 E11
El Kabrît, G., Egypt 47 F2
El Kala, Algeria 50 A6
El Kamlin, Sudan 51 E11
El Kef, Tunisia 50 A6
El Khandaq, Sudan 51 E11
El Khârga, Egypt 51 C11
El Khartûm, Sudan 51 E11
El Khartûm Bahrî, Sudan 51 E11
El Kuntilla, Egypt 47 E3
El Laqâwa, Sudan 51 F10
El Mafâza, Sudan 51 F11
El Mahalla el Kubra, Egypt 51 B11
El Mansûra, Egypt 51 B11
El Medano, Canary Is. 22 F3
El Milagro, Argentina 94 C2
El Minyâ, Egypt 51 C11
El Obeid, Sudan 51 F11
El Odaiya, Sudan 51 F10
El Oro, Mexico 87 D4
El Oued, Algeria 50 B6
El Palmito, Presa, Mexico 86 B3
El Paso, U.S.A. 83 L10
El Paso Robles, U.S.A. 84 K6
El Portal, U.S.A. 83 H4
El Porvenir, Mexico 86 A3
El Progreso, Honduras 88 C2
El Pueblito, Mexico 86 B3
El Pueblo, Canary Is. 22 F2
El Qâhira, Egypt 51 B11
El Qantara, Egypt 47 E1
El Qasr, Egypt 51 C10
El Quseima, Egypt 47 E3
El Reno, U.S.A. 81 H6
El Rio, U.S.A. 85 L7
El Roque, Pta., Canary Is. 22 F4
El Rosarito, Mexico 86 B2
El Saheira, W. →, Egypt 47 E2
El Salto, Mexico 86 C3
El Salvador ■, Cent. Amer. 88 D2
El Sauce, Nic. 88 D2
El Shallal, Egypt 51 D11
El Suweis, Egypt 51 C11
El Tamarâni, W. →, Egypt 47 E3
El Thamad, Egypt 47 F3
El Tigre, Venezuela 92 B6
El Tîh, G., Egypt 47 F2
El Tîna, Khalîg, Egypt 47 D1
El Tocuyo, Venezuela 92 B5
El Tofo, Chile 94 B1
El Tránsito, Chile 94 B1
El Turbio, Argentina 96 G2
El Uqsur, Egypt 51 C11
El Venado, Mexico 86 C4
El Vigía, Venezuela 92 B4
El Wabeira, Egypt 47 F2
El Wak, Kenya 54 B5
El Wuz, Sudan 51 E11
Elandsvlei, S. Africa 56 E2
Elat, Israel 47 F3
Elâzığ, Turkey 25 G6
Elba, Italy 20 C4
Elba, U.S.A. 77 K2
Elbasani, Albania 21 D9
Elbe, U.S.A. 84 D4
Elbe →, Europe 16 B4
Elbert, Mt., U.S.A. 83 G10
Elberta, U.S.A. 76 C2
Elberton, U.S.A. 77 H4
Elbeuf, France 18 B4
Elbing = Elbląg, Poland 17 A9
Elbląg, Poland 17 A9
Elbow, Canada 73 C7
Elbrus, Asia 25 F7
Elburg, Neths. 15 B5
Elburz Mts. = Alborz, Reshteh-ye Kūhhā-ye, Iran 45 C7
Elche, Spain 19 C5
Elcho I., Australia 62 A2
Eldon, Mo., U.S.A. 80 F8
Eldon, Wash., U.S.A. 84 C3
Eldora, U.S.A. 80 D8
Eldorado, Argentina 95 B5
Eldorado, Canada 73 B7
Eldorado, Mexico 86 C3
Eldorado, Ill., U.S.A. 76 G1
Eldorado, Tex., U.S.A. 81 K4
Eldorado Springs, U.S.A. 81 G8
Eldoret, Kenya 54 B4
Eldred, U.S.A. 78 E6
Elea, C., Cyprus 23 D13
Electra, U.S.A. 81 H5
Elefantes →, Mozam. 57 C5
Elektrostal, Russia 24 C6
Elephant Butte Res., U.S.A. 83 K10
Elephant I., Antarctica 5 C18
Eleuthera, Bahamas 88 A4
Elgeyo-Marakwet □, Kenya 54 B4
Elgin, N.B., Canada 71 C6
Elgin, Ont., Canada 79 B8
Elgin, U.K. 12 D5
Elgin, Ill., U.S.A. 76 D1
Elgin, N. Dak., U.S.A. 80 B4
Elgin, Nebr., U.S.A. 80 E5
Elgin, Nev., U.S.A. 83 H6
Elgin, Oreg., U.S.A. 82 D5
Elgin, Tex., U.S.A. 81 K6
Elgon, Mt., Africa 54 B3
Eliase, Indonesia 37 F8
Elida, U.S.A. 81 J3
Elim, S. Africa 56 E2
Elisabethville = Lubumbashi, Zaïre 55 E2
Elista, Russia 25 E7
Elizabeth, Australia 63 E2
Elizabeth, U.S.A. 79 F10
Elizabeth City, U.S.A. 77 G7
Elizabethton, U.S.A. 77 G4
Elizabethtown, Ky., U.S.A. 76 G3
Elizabethtown, N.Y., U.S.A. 79 B11
Elizabethtown, Pa., U.S.A. 79 F8
Elk City, U.S.A. 81 H5
Elk Creek, U.S.A. 84 F4
Elk Grove, U.S.A. 84 G5
Elk Island Nat. Park, Canada 72 C6
Elk Lake, Canada 70 C3
Elk Point, Canada 73 C6
Elk River, Idaho, U.S.A. 82 C5
Elk River, Minn., U.S.A. 80 C8
Elkedra, Australia 62 C2
Elkedra →, Australia 62 C2
Elkhart, Ind., U.S.A. 76 E3
Elkhart, Kans., U.S.A. 81 G4
Elkhorn, Canada 73 D8
Elkhorn →, U.S.A. 80 E6
Elkhovo, Bulgaria 21 C12
Elkin, U.S.A. 77 G5
Elkins, U.S.A. 76 F6
Elko, Canada 72 D5
Elko, U.S.A. 82 F6
Ell, L., Australia 61 E4
Ellef Ringnes I., Canada 4 B2
Ellendale, Australia 60 C3
Ellendale, U.S.A. 80 B5
Ellensburg, U.S.A. 82 C3
Ellenville, U.S.A. 79 E10
Ellery, Mt., Australia 63 F4
Ellesmere, L., N.Z. 59 M4
Ellesmere I., Canada 4 B4
Ellesmere Port, U.K. 10 D5
Ellice Is. = Tuvalu ■, Pac. Oc. 64 H9
Ellinwood, U.S.A. 80 F5
Elliot, Australia 62 B1
Elliot, S. Africa 57 E4
Elliot Lake, Canada 70 C3
Elliotdale = Xhora, S. Africa 57 E4
Ellis, U.S.A. 80 F5
Elliston, Australia 63 E1
Ellisville, U.S.A. 81 K10
Ellon, U.K. 12 D6
Ellore = Eluru, India 41 L12
Ells →, Canada 72 B6
Ellsworth, U.S.A. 80 F5
Ellsworth Land, Antarctica 5 D16
Ellsworth Mts., Antarctica 5 D16
Ellwood City, U.S.A. 78 F4
Elma, Canada 73 D9
Elma, U.S.A. 84 D3
Elmalı, Turkey 25 G4
Elmhurst, U.S.A. 76 E2
Elmira, Canada 78 C4
Elmira, U.S.A. 78 D8
Elmore, Australia 63 F3
Elmore, U.S.A. 85 M11
Elmvale, Canada 78 B5
Elora, Canada 78 C4
Eloúnda, Greece 23 D7
Eloy, U.S.A. 83 K8
Elrose, Canada 73 C7
Elsas, Canada 70 C3
Elsie, U.S.A. 84 E3
Elsinore = Helsingør, Denmark 9 H12
Elsinore, U.S.A. 83 G7
Eltham, N.Z. 59 H5
Eluru, India 41 L12
Elvas, Portugal 19 C2
Elverum, Norway 9 F11
Elvire →, Australia 60 C4
Elwood, Ind., U.S.A. 76 E3
Elwood, Nebr., U.S.A. 80 E5
Ely, U.K. 11 E8
Ely, Minn., U.S.A. 80 B9
Ely, Nev., U.S.A. 82 G6
Elyria, U.S.A. 78 E2
Emāmrūd, Iran 45 B7
Emba, Kazakhstan 26 E6
Emba →, Kazakhstan 25 E9
Embarcación, Argentina 94 A3
Embarras Portage, Canada 73 B6
Embetsu, Japan 30 B10
Embóna, Greece 23 C9
Embrun, France 18 D7
Embu, Kenya 54 C4
Embu □, Kenya 54 C4
Emden, Germany 16 B3
Emerald, Australia 62 C4
Emerson, Canada 73 D9
Emery, U.S.A. 83 G8
Emilia-Romagna □, Italy 20 B4
Eminabad, Pakistan 42 C6
Emlenton, U.S.A. 78 E5
Emmeloord, Neths. 15 B5
Emmen, Neths. 15 B6
Emmet, Australia 62 C3
Emmetsburg, U.S.A. 80 D7
Emmett, U.S.A. 82 E5
Empalme, Mexico 86 B2
Empangeni, S. Africa 57 D5
Empedrado, Argentina 94 B4
Emperor Seamount Chain, Pac. Oc. 64 D9
Emporia, Kans., U.S.A. 80 F6
Emporia, Va., U.S.A. 77 G7
Emporium, U.S.A. 78 E6
Empress, Canada 73 C6
Empty Quarter = Rub' al Khali, Si. Arabia 46 D4
Ems →, Germany 16 B3
Emsdale, Canada 78 A5
Emu, China 35 C15
Emu Park, Australia 62 C5
'En 'Avrona, Israel 47 F3
En Nahud, Sudan 51 F10
Ena, Japan 31 G8
Enana, Namibia 56 B2
Enaratoli, Indonesia 37 E9
Enard B., U.K. 12 C3
Enare = Inarijärvi, Finland 8 B19
Encantadas, Serra, Brazil 95 C5
Encanto, C., Phil. 37 A6
Encarnación, Paraguay 95 B4
Encarnación de Diaz, Mexico 86 C4
Encinal, U.S.A. 81 L5
Encinitas, U.S.A. 85 M9
Encino, U.S.A. 83 J11
Encounter B., Australia 63 F2
Ende, Indonesia 37 F6
Endeavour, Canada 73 C8
Endeavour Str., Australia 62 A3
Enderbury I., Kiribati 64 H10
Enderby, Canada 72 C5
Enderby I., Australia 60 D2
Enderby Land, Antarctica 5 C5
Enderlin, U.S.A. 80 B6
Endicott, N.Y., U.S.A. 79 D8
Endicott, Wash., U.S.A. 82 C5
Endyalgout I., Australia 60 B5
Enewetak Atoll, Pac. Oc. 64 F8
Enez, Turkey 21 D12
Enfield, U.K. 11 F7
Engadin, Switz. 16 E5
Engaño, C., Dom. Rep. 89 C6
Engaño, C., Phil. 37 A6
Engcobo, S. Africa 57 E4
Engels = Pokrovsk, Russia 24 D8
Engemann L., Canada 73 B7
Enggano, Indonesia 36 F2
Enghien, Belgium 15 D4
Engkilili, Malaysia 36 D4
England, U.S.A. 81 H9
England □, U.K. 7 E5
Englee, Canada 71 B8
Englehart, Canada 70 C4
Engler L., Canada 73 B7
Englewood, Colo., U.S.A. 80 F2
Englewood, Kans., U.S.A. 81 G5
English →, Canada 73 C10
English Bazar = Ingraj Bazar, India 43 G13
English Channel, Europe 11 G6
English River, Canada 70 C1
Enid, U.S.A. 81 G6
Enkhuizen, Neths. 15 B5
Enna, Italy 20 F6
Ennadai, Canada 73 A8
Ennadai L., Canada 73 A8
Ennedi, Chad 51 E9
Enngonia, Australia 63 D4
Ennis, Ireland 13 D3
Ennis, Mont., U.S.A. 82 D8
Ennis, Tex., U.S.A. 81 J6
Enniscorthy, Ireland 13 D5
Enniskillen, U.K. 13 B4
Ennistimon, Ireland 13 D2
Enns →, Austria 16 D7
Enontekiö, Finland 8 B17
Enriquillo, L., Dom. Rep. 89 C5
Enschede, Neths. 15 B6
Ensenada, Argentina 94 C4
Ensenada, Mexico 86 A1
Ensiola, Pta., Spain 22 B9
Entebbe, Uganda 54 B3
Enterprise, Canada 72 A5
Enterprise, Oreg., U.S.A. 82 D5
Enterprise, Utah, U.S.A. 83 H7
Entre Rios, Bolivia 94 A3
Entre Rios □, Argentina 94 C4
Enugu, Nigeria 50 G6
Enugu Ezike, Nigeria 50 G6

Enumclaw, U.S.A. 84 C5
Eólie, Is., Italy 20 E6
Epe, Neths. 15 B5
Épernay, France 18 B5
Ephraim, U.S.A. 82 G8
Ephrata, U.S.A. 82 C4
Épinal, France 18 B7
Episkopi, Cyprus 23 E11
Episkopí, Greece 23 D6
Episkopi Bay, Cyprus 23 E11
Epping, U.K. 11 F8
Epukiro, Namibia 56 C2
Equatorial Guinea ■, Africa 52 D1
Er Rahad, Sudan 51 F11
Er Rif, Morocco 50 A4
Er Roseires, Sudan 51 F11
Erāwadī Myit = Irrawaddy →, Burma 41 M19
Ercha, Russia 27 C15
Erciyaş Dağı, Turkey 25 G6
Erdao Jiang →, China 35 C14
Erdene, Mongolia 34 B6
Erebus, Mt., Antarctica 5 D11
Erechim, Brazil 95 B5
Ereğli, Konya, Turkey 25 G5
Ereğli, Zonguldak, Turkey 25 F5
Erenhot, China 34 C7
Eresma →, Spain 19 B3
Erewadi Myitwanya, Burma 41 M19
Erfenisdam, S. Africa 56 D4
Erfurt, Germany 16 C5
Erğene →, Turkey 21 D12
Ergeni Vozvyshennost, Russia 25 E7
Eriboll, L., U.K. 12 C4
Érice, Italy 20 E5
Erie, U.S.A. 78 D4
Erie, L., N. Amer. 78 D3
Erie Canal, U.S.A. 78 C6
Erieau, Canada 78 D3
Erigavo, Somali Rep. 46 E4
Erikoúsa, Greece 23 A3
Eriksdale, Canada 73 C9
Erímanthos, Greece 21 F9
Erimo-misaki, Japan 30 D11
Eritrea □, Ethiopia 51 F12
Erlangen, Germany 16 D5
Erldunda, Australia 62 D1
Ermelo, Neths. 15 B5
Ermelo, S. Africa 57 D4
Ermones, Greece 23 A3
Ermoúpolis = Síros, Greece 21 F11
Ernakulam = Cochin, India 40 Q10
Erne →, Ireland 13 B3
Erne, Lower L., U.K. 13 B4
Erne, Upper L., U.K. 13 B4
Ernest Giles Ra., Australia 61 E3
Erode, India 40 P10
Eromanga, Australia 63 D3
Erongo, Namibia 56 C2
Errabiddy, Australia 61 E2
Erramala Hills, India 40 M11
Errigal, Ireland 13 A3
Erris Hd., Ireland 13 B1
Erskine, U.S.A. 80 B7
Erwin, U.S.A. 77 G4
Erzgebirge, Germany 16 C6
Erzin, Russia 27 D10
Erzincan, Turkey 25 G6
Erzurum, Turkey 25 G7
Es Caló, Spain 22 C8
Es Caná, Spain 22 B8
Es Sahrâ' Esh Sharqîya, Egypt 51 C11
Es Sînâ', Egypt 51 C11
Esambo, Zaïre 54 C1
Esan-Misaki, Japan 30 D10
Esashi, Hokkaidō, Japan 30 B11
Esashi, Hokkaidō, Japan 30 D10
Esbjerg, Denmark 9 J10
Escalante, U.S.A. 83 H8
Escalante →, U.S.A. 83 H8
Escalón, Mexico 86 B4
Escambia →, U.S.A. 77 K2
Escanaba, U.S.A. 76 C2
Esch-sur-Alzette, Lux. 15 E6
Escondido, U.S.A. 85 M9
Escuinapa, Mexico 86 C3
Escuintla, Guatemala 88 D1
Eşfahān, Iran 45 C6
Esfideh, Iran 45 C8
Esh Sham = Dimashq, Syria 47 B5
Esh Shamâlîya □, Sudan 51 E10
Eshowe, S. Africa 57 D5
Esk →, Dumf. & Gall., U.K. 12 G5
Esk →, N. Yorks., U.K. 10 C7
Eskifjörður, Iceland 8 D7
Eskilstuna, Sweden 9 G14
Eskimo Pt., Canada 73 A10
Eskişehir, Turkey 25 G5
Esla →, Spain 19 B2
Eslāmābād-e Gharb, Iran 44 C5
Esmeraldas, Ecuador 92 C3
Espalmador, I., Spain 22 C7
Espanola, Canada 70 C3
Espardell, I. del, Spain 22 C7
Esparta, Costa Rica 88 E3
Esperance, Australia 61 F3
Esperance B., Australia 61 F3
Esperanza, Argentina 94 C3
Espichel, C., Portugal 19 C1
Espigão, Serra do, Brazil 95 B5
Espinal, Colombia 92 C4
Espinazo, Sierra del = Espinhaço, Serra do, Brazil 93 G10
Espinhaço, Serra do, Brazil 93 G10
Espinilho, Serra do, Brazil 95 B5
Espírito Santo □, Brazil 93 G10
Espíritu Santo, B. del, Mexico 87 D7
Espíritu Santo, I., Mexico 86 C2
Espita, Mexico 87 C7
Espungabera, Mozam. 57 C5
Esquel, Argentina 96 E2
Esquina, Argentina 94 B4
Essaouira, Morocco 50 B3
Essebie, Zaïre 54 B3
Essen, Belgium 15 C4
Essen, Germany 16 C3
Essendon, Mt., Australia 61 E3
Essequibo →, Guyana 92 B7
Essex, Canada 78 D2
Essex, Calif., U.S.A. 85 L11
Essex, N.Y., U.S.A. 79 B11
Essex □, U.K. 11 F8
Esslingen, Germany 16 D4
Essonne □, France 18 B5
Estados, I. de Los, Argentina 96 G4
Eşţahbānāt, Iran 45 D7
Estallenchs, Spain 22 B9
Estância, Brazil 93 F11
Estancia, U.S.A. 83 J10
Estārm, Iran 45 D8
Estcourt, S. Africa 57 D4
Estelí, Nic. 88 D2
Estelline, S. Dak., U.S.A. 80 C6
Estelline, Tex., U.S.A. 81 H4
Esterhazy, Canada 73 C8
Estevan, Canada 73 D8
Estevan Group, Canada 72 C3
Estherville, U.S.A. 80 D7
Eston, Canada 73 C7
Estonia ■, Europe 24 C4
Estoril, Portugal 19 C1
Estrêla, Serra da, Portugal 19 B2
Estremadura, Portugal 19 C1
Estrondo, Serra do, Brazil 93 E9
Esztergom, Hungary 17 E9
Etadunna, Australia 63 D2
Etah, India 43 F8
Etamamu, Canada 71 B8
Etanga, Namibia 56 B1
Etawah, India 43 F8
Etawah →, U.S.A. 77 H3
Etawney L., Canada 73 B9
Ethel, U.S.A. 84 D4
Ethel Creek, Australia 60 D3
Ethelbert, Canada 73 C8
Ethiopia ■, Africa 46 F3
Ethiopian Highlands, Ethiopia 48 E7
Etive, L., U.K. 12 E3
Etna, Italy 20 F6
Etoile, Zaïre 55 E2
Etolin I., U.S.A. 72 B2
Etosha Pan, Namibia 56 B2
Etowah, U.S.A. 77 H3
Ettrick Water →, U.K. 12 F6
Etuku, Zaïre 54 C2
Etzatlán, Mexico 86 C4
Euboea = Évvoia, Greece 21 E11
Eucla Motel, Australia 61 F4
Euclid, U.S.A. 78 E3
Eucumbene, L., Australia 63 F4
Eudora, U.S.A. 81 J9
Eufaula, Ala., U.S.A. 77 K3
Eufaula, Okla., U.S.A. 81 H7
Eufaula, L., U.S.A. 81 H7
Eugene, U.S.A. 82 E2
Eugowra, Australia 63 E4
Eulo, Australia 63 D4
Eunice, La., U.S.A. 81 K8
Eunice, N. Mex., U.S.A. 81 J3
Eupen, Belgium 15 D6
Euphrates = Furāt, Nahr al →, Asia 44 D5
Eure □, France 18 B4
Eure-et-Loir □, France 18 B4
Eureka, Canada 4 B3
Eureka, Calif., U.S.A. 82 F1
Eureka, Kans., U.S.A. 81 G6
Eureka, Mont., U.S.A. 82 B6
Eureka, Nev., U.S.A. 82 G5
Eureka, S. Dak., U.S.A. 80 C5
Eureka, Utah, U.S.A. 82 G7
Eureka, Mt., Australia 61 E3
Euroa, Australia 63 F4
Europa, Î., Ind. Oc. 53 J8
Europa, Picos de, Spain 19 A3
Europa, Pta. de, Gib. 19 D3
Europa Pt. = Europa, Pta. de, Gib. 19 D3
Europe 6 F10
Europoort, Neths. 15 C4
Eustis, U.S.A. 77 L5
Eutsuk L., Canada 72 C3
Eva Downs, Australia 62 B1
Evale, Angola 56 B2
Evans, U.S.A. 80 E2
Evans Head, Australia 63 D5
Evans L., Canada 70 B4
Evans Mills, U.S.A. 79 B9
Evanston, Ill., U.S.A. 76 D2
Evanston, Wyo., U.S.A. 82 F8
Evansville, Ind., U.S.A. 76 F2
Evansville, Wis., U.S.A. 80 D10
Evaz, Iran 45 E7
Eveleth, U.S.A. 80 B8
Evensk, Russia 27 C16
Everard, L., Australia 63 E1
Everard Park, Australia 61 E5
Everard Ras., Australia 61 E5
Everest, Mt., Nepal 43 E12
Everett, Pa., U.S.A. 78 F6
Everett, Wash., U.S.A. 84 C4
Everglades, U.S.A. 77 N5
Everglades City, U.S.A. 77 N5
Everglades Nat. Park., U.S.A. 77 N5
Evergreen, U.S.A. 77 K2
Everson, U.S.A. 82 B2
Evesham, U.K. 11 E6
Evinayong, Eq. Guin. 52 D2
Évora, Portugal 19 C2
Evowghlī, Iran 44 B5
Évreux, France 18 B4
Évvoia, Greece 21 E11
Ewe, L., U.K. 12 D3
Ewing, U.S.A. 80 D5
Ewo, Congo 52 E2
Exaltación, Bolivia 92 F5
Excelsior Springs, U.S.A. 80 F7
Exe →, U.K. 11 G4
Exeter, Canada 78 C3
Exeter, U.K. 11 G4
Exeter, Calif., U.S.A. 83 H4
Exeter, N.H., U.S.A. 79 D14
Exeter, Nebr., U.S.A. 80 E6
Exmoor, U.K. 11 F4
Exmouth, Australia 60 D1
Exmouth, U.K. 11 G4
Exmouth G., Australia 60 D1
Expedition Ra., Australia 62 C4
Extremadura □, Spain 19 C2
Exuma Sound, Bahamas 88 B4
Eyasi, L., Tanzania 54 C4
Eyeberry L., Canada 73 A8
Eyemouth, U.K. 12 F6
Eyjafjörður, Iceland 8 C4
Eyrarbakki, Iceland 8 E3
Eyre, Australia 61 F4
Eyre (North), L., Australia 63 D2
Eyre (South), L., Australia 63 D2
Eyre Cr. →, Australia 63 D2
Eyre Mts., N.Z. 59 L2
Eyre Pen., Australia 63 E2
Eyvānkī, Iran 45 C6
Ezouza →, Cyprus 23 E11

F

Fabens, U.S.A. 83 L10
Fabriano, Italy 20 C5
Facatativá, Colombia 92 C4
Fachi, Niger 50 E7
Fada, Chad 51 E9
Fada-n-Gourma, Burkina Faso 50 F5
Faddeyevskiy, Ostrov, Russia 27 B15
Fadghāmī, Syria 44 C4
Faenza, Italy 20 B4
Făgăras, Romania 17 F12
Fagernes, Norway 9 F10
Fagersta, Sweden 9 F13
Fagnano, L., Argentina 96 G3
Fahliān, Iran 45 D6
Fahraj, Kermān, Iran 45 D8
Fahraj, Yazd, Iran 45 D7
Faial, Madeira 22 D3
Fair Hd., U.K. 13 A5
Fair Oaks, U.S.A. 84 G5
Fairbank, U.S.A. 83 L8
Fairbanks, U.S.A. 68 B5
Fairbury, U.S.A. 80 E6
Fairfax, U.S.A. 81 G6
Fairfield, Ala., U.S.A. 77 J2
Fairfield, Calif., U.S.A. 84 G4
Fairfield, Conn., U.S.A. 79 E11
Fairfield, Idaho, U.S.A. 82 E6
Fairfield, Ill., U.S.A. 76 F1
Fairfield, Iowa, U.S.A. 80 E9
Fairfield, Mont., U.S.A. 82 C8
Fairfield, Tex., U.S.A. 81 K7
Fairford, Canada 73 C9
Fairhope, U.S.A. 77 K2
Fairlie, N.Z. 59 L3
Fairmead, U.S.A. 84 H6
Fairmont, Minn., U.S.A. 80 D7
Fairmont, W. Va., U.S.A. 76 F5
Fairmount, U.S.A. 85 L8
Fairplay, U.S.A. 83 G11
Fairport, N.Y., U.S.A. 78 C7
Fairport, Ohio, U.S.A. 78 E3
Fairview, Australia 62 B3
Fairview, Canada 72 B5
Fairview, N. Dak., U.S.A. 80 B2
Fairview, Okla., U.S.A. 81 G5
Fairview, Utah, U.S.A. 82 G8
Fairweather, Mt., U.S.A. 68 C6
Faisalabad, Pakistan 42 D5
Faith, U.S.A. 80 C3
Faizabad, India 43 F10
Fajardo, Puerto Rico 89 C6
Fakfak, Indonesia 37 E8
Faku, China 35 C12
Falaise, France 18 B3
Falaise, Mui, Vietnam 38 C5
Falam, Burma 41 H18
Falcón, C., Spain 22 C7
Falcon Dam, U.S.A. 81 M5
Falconer, U.S.A. 78 D5
Falfurrias, U.S.A. 81 M5
Falher, Canada 72 B5
Falirakí, Greece 23 C10
Falkenberg, Sweden 9 H12
Falkirk, U.K. 12 F5
Falkland Is., Atl. Oc. 96 G5
Falkland Is. Dependency □, Atl. Oc. 5 B1
Falkland Sd., Falk. Is. 96 G5
Falköping, Sweden 9 G12
Fall River, U.S.A. 79 E13
Fall River Mills, U.S.A. 82 F3
Fallbrook, U.S.A. 83 K5
Fallbrook, U.S.A. 85 M9
Fallon, Mont., U.S.A. 80 B2
Fallon, Nev., U.S.A. 82 G4
Falls City, Nebr., U.S.A. 80 E7
Falls City, Oreg., U.S.A. 82 D2
Falls Creek, U.S.A. 78 E6
Falmouth, Jamaica 88 C4
Falmouth, U.K. 11 G2
Falmouth, U.S.A. 76 F3
False B., S. Africa 56 E2
Falso, C., Honduras 88 C3
Falster, Denmark 9 J11
Falsterbo, Sweden 9 J12
Falun, Sweden 9 F13
Famagusta, Cyprus 23 D12
Famagusta Bay, Cyprus 23 D13
Famatina, Sierra de, Argentina 94 B2
Family L., Canada 73 C9
Famoso, U.S.A. 85 K7
Fan Xian, China 34 G8
Fandriana, Madag. 57 C8
Fang, Thailand 38 C2
Fangcheng, China 34 H7
Fangshan, China 34 E6
Fangzi, China 35 F10
Fanjiatun, China 35 C13
Fannich, L., U.K. 12 D4
Fannūj, Iran 45 E8
Fanny Bay, Canada 72 D4
Fano, Italy 20 C5
Fanshaw, U.S.A. 72 B2
Fanshi, China 34 E7
Fao = Al Fāw, Iraq 45 D6
Faqirwali, Pakistan 42 E5
Faradje, Zaïre 54 B2
Farafangana, Madag. 57 C8
Farāh, Afghan. 40 C3
Farāh □, Afghan. 40 C3
Farahalana, Madag. 57 A9
Faranah, Guinea 50 F2
Farasān, Jazā'ir, Si. Arabia 46 D3
Farasan Is. = Farasān, Jazā'ir, Si. Arabia 46 D3
Faratsiho, Madag. 57 B8
Fareham, U.K. 11 G6
Farewell, C., N.Z. 59 J4
Farewell C. = Farvel, Kap, Greenland 4 D5
Fargo, U.S.A. 80 B6
Fari'a →, Jordan 47 C4
Faribault, U.S.A. 80 C8
Faridkot, India 42 D6
Faridpur, Bangla. 43 H13
Farim, Guinea-Biss. 50 F1
Farīmān, Iran 45 C8
Farina, Australia 63 E2
Fariones, Pta., Canary Is. 22 E6
Farmerville, U.S.A. 81 J8
Farmington, Calif., U.S.A. 84 H6
Farmington, N.H., U.S.A. 79 C13
Farmington, N. Mex., U.S.A. 83 H9
Farmington, Utah, U.S.A. 82 F8
Farmington →, U.S.A. 79 E12
Farmville, U.S.A. 76 G6
Farnborough, U.K. 11 F7
Farne Is., U.K. 10 B6
Farnham, Canada 79 A12
Faro, Brazil 93 D7
Faro, Portugal 19 D2
Fårö, Sweden 9 H15
Faroe Is. = Føroyar, Atl. Oc. 7 C4
Farquhar, C., Australia 61 D1
Farrars Cr. →, Australia 62 D3
Farrāshband, Iran 45 D7
Farrell, U.S.A. 78 E4
Farrell Flat, Australia 63 E2
Farrokhī, Iran 45 C8
Farruch, C., Spain 22 B10
Farrukhabad-cum-Fatehgarh, India 43 F8
Fārs □, Iran 45 D7
Fársala, Greece 21 E10
Farsund, Norway 9 G9
Fartak, Râs, Si. Arabia 44 D2
Fartura, Serra da, Brazil 95 B5
Fārūj, Iran 45 B8
Farvel, Kap, Greenland 4 D5
Farwell, U.S.A. 81 H3
Fasā, Iran 45 D7
Fastnet Rock, Ireland 13 E2
Fatagar, Tanjung, Indonesia 37 E8
Fatehgarh, India 43 F8
Fatehpur, Raj., India 42 F6
Fatehpur, Ut. P., India 43 G9
Fatima, Canada 71 C7
Faulkton, U.S.A. 80 C5
Faure I., Australia 61 E1
Fauresmith, S. Africa 56 D4
Fauske, Norway 8 C13
Favara, Italy 20 F5
Favaritx, C., Spain 22 A11
Favignana, Italy 20 F5
Favourable Lake, Canada 70 B1
Fawn →, Canada 70 A2
Fawnskin, U.S.A. 85 L10
Faxaflói, Iceland 8 D2
Faya-Largeau, Chad 51 E8
Fayd, Si. Arabia 44 E4
Fayette, Ala., U.S.A. 77 J2
Fayette, Mo., U.S.A. 80 F8
Fayetteville, Ark., U.S.A. 81 G7
Fayetteville, N.C., U.S.A. 77 H6
Fayetteville, Tenn., U.S.A. 77 H2
Fazilka, India 42 D6
Fazilpur, Pakistan 42 E4
Fdérik, Mauritania 50 D2
Feale →, Ireland 13 D2
Fear, C., U.S.A. 77 J7
Feather →, U.S.A. 82 G3
Feather Falls, U.S.A. 84 F5
Featherston, N.Z. 59 J5
Featherstone, Zimbabwe 55 F3
Fécamp, France 18 B4
Federación, Argentina 94 C4
Fedeshkūh, Iran 45 D7
Fehmarn, Germany 16 A5
Fehmarn Bælt, Denmark 16 A5
Fei Xian, China 35 G9
Feilding, N.Z. 59 J5
Feira de Santana, Brazil 93 F11
Feixiang, China 34 F8
Felanitx, Spain 22 B10
Feldkirch, Austria 16 E4
Felipe Carrillo Puerto, Mexico 87 D7
Felixstowe, U.K. 11 F9
Felton, U.K. 10 B6
Felton, U.S.A. 84 H4
Femunden, Norway 8 E11
Fen He →, China 34 G6
Fenelon Falls, Canada 78 B6
Feng Xian, Jiangsu, China 34 G9
Feng Xian, Shaanxi, China 34 H4
Fengcheng, China 35 D13
Fengfeng, China 34 F8
Fengjie, China 33 C5
Fengning, China 34 D9
Fengqiu, China 34 G8
Fengrun, China 35 E10
Fengtai, China 34 E9
Fengxiang, China 34 G4
Fengyang, China 35 H9
Fengzhen, China 34 D7
Fenit, Ireland 13 D2
Fennimore, U.S.A. 80 D9
Fenoarivo Afovoany, Madag. 57 B8
Fenoarivo Atsinanana, Madag. 57 B8
Fens, The, U.K. 10 E8
Fenton, U.S.A. 76 D4
Fenxi, China 34 F6
Fenyang, China 33 C6
Fenyang, Shanxi, China 34 F6
Feodosiya, Ukraine 25 E6
Ferdows, Iran 45 C8
Ferfer, Somali Rep. 46 F4
Fergana, Uzbekistan 26 E8
Fergus, Canada 70 D3
Fergus Falls, U.S.A. 80 B6
Ferland, Canada 70 B2
Fermanagh □, U.K. 13 B4
Fermoy, Ireland 13 D3
Fernández, Argentina 94 B3
Fernandina Beach, U.S.A. 77 K5
Fernando de Noronha, Brazil 93 D12
Fernando Póo = Bioko, Eq. Guin. 50 H6
Ferndale, Calif., U.S.A. 82 F1
Ferndale, Wash., U.S.A. 84 B4
Fernie, Canada 72 D5
Fernlees, Australia 62 C4
Fernley, U.S.A. 82 G4
Ferozepore = Firozpur, India 42 D6
Ferrara, Italy 20 B4
Ferreñafe, Peru 92 E3
Ferrerias, Spain 22 B11
Ferriday, U.S.A. 81 K9
Ferron, U.S.A. 83 G8
Ferryland, Canada 71 C9
Fertile, U.S.A. 80 B6
Fès, Morocco 50 B4
Feshi, Zaïre 52 F3
Fessenden, U.S.A. 80 B5
Fetlar, U.K. 12 A8
Feuilles →, Canada 69 C12
Fezzan, Libya 51 C8
Ffestiniog, U.K. 10 E4
Fiambalá, Argentina 94 B2
Fianarantsoa, Madag. 57 C8
Fianarantsoa □, Madag. 57 B8
Fianga, Cameroon 51 G8
Fichtelgebirge, Germany 16 C6
Ficksburg, S. Africa 57 D4
Field, Canada 70 C3
Field →, Australia 62 C2
Field I., Australia 60 B5
Fife □, U.K. 12 E5
Fife Ness, U.K. 12 E6
Figeac, France 18 D5
Figtree, Zimbabwe 55 G2
Figueira da Foz, Portugal 19 B1
Figueras, Spain 19 A7
Figuig, Morocco 50 B4
Fihaonana, Madag. 57 B8
Fiherenana, Madag. 57 B8
Fiherenana →, Madag. 57 C7
Fiji ■, Pac. Oc. 59 C8
Filer, U.S.A. 82 E6

Filey, *U.K.* 10 C7
Filfla, *Malta* 23 D1
Filiatrá, *Greece* 21 F9
Filipstad, *Sweden* 9 G13
Fillmore, *Canada* 73 D8
Fillmore, *Calif., U.S.A.* 85 L8
Fillmore, *Utah, U.S.A.* 83 G7
Finch, *Canada* 79 A9
Findhorn →, *U.K.* 12 D5
Findlay, *U.S.A.* 76 E4
Finger L., *Canada* 73 C10
Fingõe, *Mozam.* 55 E3
Finistère □, *France* 18 B2
Finisterre, C., *Spain* 19 A1
Finke, *Australia* 62 D1
Finke →, *Australia* 63 D2
Finland ■, *Europe* 9 E19
Finland, G. of, *Europe* 9 G19
Finlay →, *Canada* 72 B3
Finley, *Australia* 63 F4
Finley, *U.S.A.* 80 B6
Finn →, *Ireland* 13 B4
Finnigan, Mt., *Australia* 62 B4
Finniss, C., *Australia* 63 E1
Finnmark fylke □, *Norway* 8 B18
Fiora →, *Italy* 20 C4
Fīq, *Syria* 47 C4
Firat = Furāt, Nahr al →, *Asia* 44 D5
Fire River, *Canada* 70 C3
Firebag →, *Canada* 73 B6
Firebaugh, *U.S.A.* 84 J6
Firedrake L., *Canada* 73 A8
Firenze, *Italy* 20 C4
Firk →, *Iraq* 44 D5
Firozabad, *India* 43 F8
Firozpur, *India* 42 D6
Fīrūzābād, *Iran* 45 D7
Fīrūzkūh, *Iran* 45 C7
Firvale, *Canada* 72 C3
Fish →, *Namibia* 56 D2
Fish →, *S. Africa* 56 E3
Fisher, *Australia* 61 F5
Fisher B., *Canada* 73 C9
Fishguard, *U.K.* 11 F3
Fishing L., *Canada* 73 C9
Fitchburg, *U.S.A.* 79 D13
Fitri, L., *Chad* 51 F8
Fitz Roy, *Argentina* 96 F3
Fitzgerald, *Canada* 72 B6
Fitzgerald, *U.S.A.* 77 K4
Fitzmaurice →, *Australia* 60 B5
Fitzroy →, *Queens., Australia* 62 C5
Fitzroy →, *W. Austral., Australia* 60 C3
Fitzroy Crossing, *Australia* 60 C4
Fitzwilliam I., *Canada* 78 A3
Fiume = Rijeka, *Croatia* 20 B6
Five Points, *U.S.A.* 84 J6
Fizi, *Zaïre* 54 C2
Flagler, *U.S.A.* 80 F3
Flagstaff, *U.S.A.* 83 J8
Flaherty I., *Canada* 70 A4
Flåm, *Norway* 9 F9
Flambeau →, *U.S.A.* 80 C9
Flamborough Hd., *U.K.* 10 C7
Flaming Gorge Dam, *U.S.A.* 82 F9
Flaming Gorge Res., *U.S.A.* 82 F9
Flamingo, Teluk, *Indonesia* 37 F9
Flanders = West-Vlaanderen □, *Belgium* 15 D3
Flandre Occidentale = West-Vlaanderen □, *Belgium* 15 D3
Flandre Orientale = Oost-Vlaanderen □, *Belgium* 15 C3
Flandreau, *U.S.A.* 80 C6
Flanigan, *U.S.A.* 84 E7
Flannan Is., *U.K.* 12 C1
Flåsjön, *Sweden* 8 D13
Flat →, *Canada* 72 A3
Flat River, *U.S.A.* 81 G9
Flatey, *Barðastrandarsýsla, Iceland* 8 C5
Flatey, *Suður-þingeyjarsýsla, Iceland* 8 D2
Flathead L., *U.S.A.* 82 C6
Flattery, C., *Australia* 62 A4
Flattery, C., *U.S.A.* 84 B2
Flaxton, *U.S.A.* 80 A3
Fleetwood, *U.K.* 10 D4
Flekkefjord, *Norway* 9 G9
Flemington, *U.S.A.* 78 E7
Flensburg, *Germany* 16 A4
Flesherton, *Canada* 78 B4
Flesko, Tanjung, *Indonesia* 37 D6
Flevoland □, *Neths.* 15 B5
Flin Flon, *Canada* 73 C8
Flinders, *Australia* 63 E2
Flinders →, *Australia* 62 B3
Flinders B., *Australia* 61 F2
Flinders Group, *Australia* 62 A3
Flinders I., *Australia* 62 F4
Flinders Reefs, *Australia* 62 B4
Flint, *U.K.* 10 D4
Flint, *U.S.A.* 76 D4
Flint →, *U.S.A.* 77 K3
Flint I., *Kiribati* 65 J12
Flinton, *Australia* 63 D4
Flodden, *U.K.* 10 B5
Floodwood, *U.S.A.* 80 B8
Flora, *U.S.A.* 76 F1
Florala, *U.S.A.* 77 K2
Florence = Firenze, *Italy* 20 C4
Florence, *Ala., U.S.A.* 77 H2
Florence, *Ariz., U.S.A.* 83 K8
Florence, *Colo., U.S.A.* 80 F2
Florence, *Oreg., U.S.A.* 82 E1
Florence, *S.C., U.S.A.* 77 H6
Florence, L., *Australia* 63 D2
Florennes, *Belgium* 15 D4
Florenville, *Belgium* 15 E5
Flores, *Guatemala* 88 C2
Flores, *Indonesia* 37 F6
Flores I., *Canada* 72 D3
Flores Sea, *Indonesia* 37 F6
Floresville, *U.S.A.* 81 L5
Floriano, *Brazil* 93 E10
Florianópolis, *Brazil* 95 B6
Florida, *Cuba* 88 B4
Florida, *Uruguay* 95 C4
Florida □, *U.S.A.* 77 L5
Florida, Straits of, *U.S.A.* 88 B3
Florida B., *U.S.A.* 88 A3
Florida Keys, *U.S.A.* 88 B3
Florø, *Norway* 9 F8
Flower Station, *Canada* 79 A8
Flower's Cove, *Canada* 71 B8
Floydada, *U.S.A.* 81 J4
Fluk, *Indonesia* 37 E7
Flushing = Vlissingen, *Neths.* 15 C3
Flying Fish, C., *Antarctica* 5 D15
Foam Lake, *Canada* 73 C8
Fóggia, *Italy* 20 D6
Fogo, *Canada* 71 C9
Fogo I., *Canada* 71 C9
Foix, *France* 18 E4
Folda, *Nord-Trøndelag, Norway* 8 D11
Folda, *Nordland, Norway* 8 C13
Foleyet, *Canada* 70 C3
Folgefonn, *Norway* 9 F9
Folkestone, *U.K.* 11 F9
Folkston, *U.S.A.* 77 K5
Follett, *U.S.A.* 81 G4
Folsom Res., *U.S.A.* 84 G5
Fond-du-Lac, *Canada* 73 B7
Fond du Lac, *U.S.A.* 80 D10
Fond-du-Lac →, *Canada* 73 B7
Fonda, *U.S.A.* 79 D10
Fonseca, G. de, *Cent. Amer.* 88 D2
Fontainebleau, *France* 18 B5
Fontas →, *Canada* 72 B4
Fonte Boa, *Brazil* 92 D5
Fontenay-le-Comte, *France* 18 C3
Fontur, *Iceland* 8 C6
Foochow = Fuzhou, *China* 33 D6
Foping, *China* 34 H4
Forbes, *Australia* 63 E4
Forbesganj, *India* 43 F12
Ford City, *Calif., U.S.A.* 85 K7
Ford City, *Pa., U.S.A.* 78 F5
Ford's Bridge, *Australia* 63 D4
Fordyce, *U.S.A.* 81 J8
Forécariah, *Guinea* 50 G2
Forel, Mt., *Greenland* 4 C6
Foremost, *Canada* 72 D6
Forest, *Canada* 78 C3
Forest, *U.S.A.* 81 J10
Forest City, *Iowa, U.S.A.* 80 D8
Forest City, *N.C., U.S.A.* 77 H5
Forest City, *Pa., U.S.A.* 79 E9
Forest Grove, *U.S.A.* 84 E3
Forestburg, *Canada* 72 C6
Foresthill, *U.S.A.* 84 F6
Forestier Pen., *Australia* 62 G4
Forestville, *Canada* 71 C6
Forestville, *Calif., U.S.A.* 84 G4
Forestville, *Wis., U.S.A.* 76 C2
Forez, Mts. du, *France* 18 D5
Forfar, *U.K.* 12 E6
Forks, *U.S.A.* 84 C2
Forlì, *Italy* 20 B5
Forman, *U.S.A.* 80 B6
Formby Pt., *U.K.* 10 D4
Formentera, *Spain* 22 C7
Formentor, C. de, *Spain* 22 B10
Formosa = Taiwan ■, *Asia* 33 D7
Formosa, *Argentina* 94 B4
Formosa □, *Argentina* 94 B3
Formosa, Serra, *Brazil* 93 F8
Formosa Bay, *Kenya* 54 C5
Fornells, *Spain* 22 A11
Føroyar, *Atl. Oc.* 7 C4
Forres, *U.K.* 12 D5
Forrest, *Vic., Australia* 63 F3
Forrest, *W. Austral., Australia* 61 F4
Forrest, Mt., *Australia* 61 D4
Forrest City, *U.S.A.* 81 H9
Forsayth, *Australia* 62 B3
Forster, *Australia* 63 E5
Forsyth, *Ga., U.S.A.* 77 J4
Forsyth, *Mont., U.S.A.* 82 C10
Fort Albany, *Canada* 70 B3
Fort Apache, *U.S.A.* 83 K9
Fort Assiniboine, *Canada* 72 C6
Fort Augustus, *U.K.* 12 D4
Fort Beaufort, *S. Africa* 56 E4
Fort Benton, *U.S.A.* 82 C8
Fort Bragg, *U.S.A.* 82 G2
Fort Bridger, *U.S.A.* 82 F8
Fort Chipewyan, *Canada* 73 B6
Fort Collins, *U.S.A.* 80 E2
Fort-Coulonge, *Canada* 70 C4
Fort Davis, *U.S.A.* 81 K3
Fort-de-France, *Martinique* 89 D7
Fort de Possel = Possel, *C.A.R.* 52 C3
Fort Defiance, *U.S.A.* 83 J9
Fort Dodge, *U.S.A.* 80 D7
Fort Edward, *U.S.A.* 79 C11
Fort Frances, *Canada* 73 D10
Fort Franklin, *Canada* 68 B7
Fort Garland, *U.S.A.* 83 H11
Fort George, *Canada* 70 B4
Fort Good-Hope, *Canada* 68 B7
Fort Hancock, *U.S.A.* 83 L11
Fort Hertz = Putao, *Burma* 41 F20
Fort Hope, *Canada* 70 B2
Fort Irwin, *U.S.A.* 85 K10
Fort Jameson = Chipata, *Zambia* 55 E3
Fort Kent, *U.S.A.* 71 C6
Fort Klamath, *U.S.A.* 82 E3
Fort Lallemand, *Algeria* 50 B6
Fort-Lamy = Ndjamena, *Chad* 51 F7
Fort Laramie, *U.S.A.* 80 D2
Fort Lauderdale, *U.S.A.* 77 M5
Fort Liard, *Canada* 72 A4
Fort Liberté, *Haiti* 89 C5
Fort Lupton, *U.S.A.* 80 E2
Fort Mackay, *Canada* 72 B6
Fort McKenzie, *Canada* 71 A6
Fort Macleod, *Canada* 72 D6
Fort MacMahon, *Algeria* 50 C5
Fort McMurray, *Canada* 72 B6
Fort McPherson, *Canada* 68 B6
Fort Madison, *U.S.A.* 80 E9
Fort Meade, *U.S.A.* 77 M5
Fort Miribel, *Algeria* 50 C5
Fort Morgan, *U.S.A.* 80 E3
Fort Myers, *U.S.A.* 77 M5
Fort Nelson, *Canada* 72 B4
Fort Nelson →, *Canada* 72 B4
Fort Norman, *Canada* 68 B7
Fort Payne, *U.S.A.* 77 H3
Fort Peck, *U.S.A.* 82 B10
Fort Peck Dam, *U.S.A.* 82 C10
Fort Peck L., *U.S.A.* 82 C10
Fort Pierce, *U.S.A.* 77 M5
Fort Pierre, *U.S.A.* 80 C4
Fort Plain, *U.S.A.* 79 D10
Fort Portal, *Uganda* 54 B3
Fort Providence, *Canada* 72 A5
Fort Qu'Appelle, *Canada* 73 C8
Fort Resolution, *Canada* 72 A6
Fort Rixon, *Zimbabwe* 55 G2
Fort Rosebery = Mansa, *Zambia* 55 E2
Fort Ross, *U.S.A.* 84 G3
Fort Rupert, *Canada* 70 B4
Fort St. James, *Canada* 72 C4
Fort St. John, *Canada* 72 B4
Fort Sandeman, *Pakistan* 42 D3
Fort Saskatchewan, *Canada* 72 C6
Fort Scott, *U.S.A.* 81 G7
Fort Severn, *Canada* 70 A2
Fort Shevchenko, *Kazakhstan* 25 F9
Fort-Sibut, *C.A.R.* 51 G8
Fort Simpson, *Canada* 72 A4
Fort Smith, *Canada* 72 B6
Fort Smith, *U.S.A.* 81 H7
Fort Stanton, *U.S.A.* 83 K11
Fort Stockton, *U.S.A.* 81 K3
Fort Sumner, *U.S.A.* 81 H2
Fort Trinquet = Bir Mogrein, *Mauritania* 50 C2
Fort Valley, *U.S.A.* 77 J4
Fort Vermilion, *Canada* 72 B5
Fort Walton Beach, *U.S.A.* 77 K2
Fort Wayne, *U.S.A.* 76 E3
Fort William, *U.K.* 12 E3
Fort Worth, *U.S.A.* 81 J6
Fort Yates, *U.S.A.* 80 B4
Fort Yukon, *U.S.A.* 68 B5
Fortaleza, *Brazil* 93 D11
Forteau, *Canada* 71 B8
Forth →, *U.K.* 12 E5
Forth, Firth of, *U.K.* 12 E6
Fortrose, *U.K.* 12 D4
Fortuna, *Calif., U.S.A.* 82 F1
Fortuna, *N. Dak., U.S.A.* 80 A3
Fortune B., *Canada* 71 C8
Foshan, *China* 33 D6
Fossil, *U.S.A.* 82 D3
Fossilbrook, *Australia* 62 B3
Fosston, *U.S.A.* 80 B7
Foster, *Canada* 79 A12
Foster →, *Canada* 73 B7
Fosters Ra., *Australia* 62 C1
Fostoria, *U.S.A.* 76 E4
Fougamou, *Gabon* 52 E2
Fougères, *France* 18 B3
Foul Pt., *Sri Lanka* 40 Q12
Foula, *U.K.* 12 A6
Foulness I., *U.K.* 11 F8
Foulpointe, *Madag.* 57 B8
Foumban, *Cameroon* 50 G7
Fountain, *Colo., U.S.A.* 80 F2
Fountain, *Utah, U.S.A.* 82 G8
Fountain Springs, *U.S.A.* 85 K8
Fourchu, *Canada* 71 C7
Fouriesburg, *S. Africa* 56 D4
Fouta Djalon, *Guinea* 50 F2
Foux, Cap-à-, *Haiti* 89 C5
Foveaux Str., *N.Z.* 59 M2
Fowey, *U.K.* 11 G3
Fowler, *Calif., U.S.A.* 83 H4
Fowler, *Colo., U.S.A.* 80 F2
Fowler, *Kans., U.S.A.* 81 G4
Fowlers B., *Australia* 61 F5
Fowlerton, *U.S.A.* 81 L5
Fox →, *Canada* 73 B10
Fox Valley, *Canada* 73 C7
Foxe Basin, *Canada* 69 B12
Foxe Chan., *Canada* 69 B11
Foxe Pen., *Canada* 69 B12
Foxpark, *U.S.A.* 82 F10
Foxton, *N.Z.* 59 J5
Foyle, Lough, *U.K.* 13 A4
Foynes, *Ireland* 13 D2
Fóz do Cunene, *Angola* 56 B1
Foz do Gregório, *Brazil* 92 E4
Foz do Iguaçu, *Brazil* 95 B5
Frackville, *U.S.A.* 79 F8
Framingham, *U.S.A.* 79 D13
Franca, *Brazil* 93 H9
Francavilla Fontana, *Italy* 21 D7
France ■, *Europe* 18 C5
Frances, *Australia* 63 F3
Frances →, *Canada* 72 A3
Frances L., *Canada* 72 A3
Francés Viejo, C., *Dom. Rep.* 89 C6
Franceville, *Gabon* 52 E2
Franche-Comté, *France* 18 C6
Francisco I. Madero, *Coahuila, Mexico* 86 B4
Francisco I. Madero, *Durango, Mexico* 86 C4
Francistown, *Botswana* 57 C4
François, *Canada* 71 C8
François L., *Canada* 72 C3
Franeker, *Neths.* 15 A5
Frankfort, *S. Africa* 57 D4
Frankfort, *Ind., U.S.A.* 76 E2
Frankfort, *Kans., U.S.A.* 80 F6
Frankfort, *Ky., U.S.A.* 76 F3
Frankfort, *Mich., U.S.A.* 76 C2
Frankfurt am Main, *Germany* 16 C4
Frankfurt an der Oder, *Germany* 16 B7
Fränkische Alb, *Germany* 16 D5
Frankland →, *Australia* 61 G2
Franklin, *Ky., U.S.A.* 77 G2
Franklin, *La., U.S.A.* 81 L9
Franklin, *Mass., U.S.A.* 79 D13
Franklin, *N.H., U.S.A.* 79 C13
Franklin, *Nebr., U.S.A.* 80 E5
Franklin, *Pa., U.S.A.* 78 E5
Franklin, *Tenn., U.S.A.* 77 H2
Franklin, *Va., U.S.A.* 77 G7
Franklin, *W. Va., U.S.A.* 76 F6
Franklin, L., *U.S.A.* 82 F6
Franklin B., *Canada* 68 B7
Franklin D. Roosevelt L., *U.S.A.* 82 B4
Franklin I., *Antarctica* 5 D11
Franklin Mts., *Canada* 68 B7
Franklin Str., *Canada* 68 A10
Franklinton, *U.S.A.* 81 K9
Franklinville, *U.S.A.* 78 D6
Franks Peak, *U.S.A.* 82 E9
Frankston, *Australia* 63 F4
Frantsa Iosifa, Zemlya, *Russia* 26 A6
Franz, *Canada* 70 C3
Franz Josef Land = Frantsa Iosifa, Zemlya, *Russia* 26 A6
Fraser →, *B.C., Canada* 72 D4
Fraser →, *Nfld., Canada* 71 A7
Fraser, Mt., *Australia* 61 E2
Fraser I., *Australia* 63 D5
Fraser Lake, *Canada* 72 C4
Fraserburg, *S. Africa* 56 E3
Fraserburgh, *U.K.* 12 D6
Fraserdale, *Canada* 70 C3
Fray Bentos, *Uruguay* 94 C4
Frazier Downs, *Australia* 60 C3
Fredericia, *Denmark* 9 J10
Frederick, *Md., U.S.A.* 76 F7
Frederick, *Okla., U.S.A.* 81 H5
Frederick, *S. Dak., U.S.A.* 80 C5
Frederick Sd., *U.S.A.* 72 B2
Fredericksburg, *Tex., U.S.A.* 81 K5
Fredericksburg, *Va., U.S.A.* 76 F7
Frederickstown, *U.S.A.* 81 G9
Frederico I. Madero, Presa, *Mexico* 86 B3
Fredericton, *Canada* 71 C6
Fredericton Junc., *Canada* 71 C6
Frederikshåb, *Greenland* 4 C5
Frederikshavn, *Denmark* 9 H11
Frederiksted, *Virgin Is.* 89 C7
Fredonia, *Ariz., U.S.A.* 83 H7
Fredonia, *Kans., U.S.A.* 81 G7
Fredonia, *N.Y., U.S.A.* 78 D5
Fredrikstad, *Norway* 9 G11
Freehold, *U.S.A.* 79 F10
Freel Pk., *U.S.A.* 84 G7
Freeland, *U.S.A.* 79 E9
Freels, C., *Canada* 71 C9
Freeman, *Calif., U.S.A.* 85 K9
Freeman, *S. Dak., U.S.A.* 80 D6
Freeport, *Bahamas* 88 A4
Freeport, *Canada* 71 D6
Freeport, *Ill., U.S.A.* 80 D10
Freeport, *N.Y., U.S.A.* 79 F11
Freeport, *Tex., U.S.A.* 81 L7
Freetown, *S. Leone* 50 G2
Frégate, L., *Canada* 70 B5
Freiburg, *Germany* 16 E3
Freire, *Chile* 96 D2
Freirina, *Chile* 94 B1
Freising, *Germany* 16 D5
Freistadt, *Austria* 16 D7
Fréjus, *France* 18 E7
Fremantle, *Australia* 61 F2
Fremont, *Calif., U.S.A.* 83 H2
Fremont, *Mich., U.S.A.* 76 D3
Fremont, *Nebr., U.S.A.* 80 E6
Fremont, *Ohio, U.S.A.* 76 E4
Fremont →, *U.S.A.* 83 G8
Fremont, L., *U.S.A.* 82 E9
French Camp, *U.S.A.* 84 H5
French Cr. →, *U.S.A.* 78 E5
French Guiana ■, *S. Amer.* 93 C8
French Pass, *N.Z.* 59 J4
French Polynesia □, *Pac. Oc.* 65 J13
French Terr. of Afars & Issas = Djibouti ■, *Africa* 46 E3
Frenchglen, *U.S.A.* 82 E4
Frenchman →, *N. Amer.* 82 B10
Frenchman Butte, *Canada* 73 C7
Frenchman Creek →, *U.S.A.* 80 E4
Fresco →, *Brazil* 93 E8
Freshfield, C., *Antarctica* 5 C10
Fresnillo, *Mexico* 86 C4
Fresno, *U.S.A.* 83 H4
Fresno Res., *U.S.A.* 82 B9
Frew →, *Australia* 62 C2
Frewena, *Australia* 62 B2
Freycinet Pen., *Australia* 62 G4
Fria, C., *Namibia* 56 B1
Friant, *U.S.A.* 84 J7
Frías, *Argentina* 94 B2
Friday Harbor, *U.S.A.* 84 B3
Friedrichshafen, *Germany* 16 E4
Friendly Is. = Tonga ■, *Pac. Oc.* 59 D11
Friesland □, *Neths.* 15 A5
Frio →, *U.S.A.* 81 L5
Friona, *U.S.A.* 81 H3
Fritch, *U.S.A.* 81 H4
Friuli-Venezia Giulia □, *Italy* 20 A5
Frobisher B., *Canada* 69 B13
Frobisher Bay = Iqaluit, *Canada* 69 B13
Frobisher L., *Canada* 73 B7
Frohavet, *Norway* 8 E10
Froid, *U.S.A.* 80 A2
Fromberg, *U.S.A.* 82 D9
Frome, *U.K.* 11 F5
Frome, L., *Australia* 63 E2
Frome Downs, *Australia* 63 E2
Front Range, *U.S.A.* 82 G11
Front Royal, *U.S.A.* 76 F6
Frontera, *Canary Is.* 22 G2
Frontera, *Mexico* 87 D6
Frosinone, *Italy* 20 D5
Frostburg, *U.S.A.* 76 F6
Frostisen, *Norway* 8 B14
Frøya, *Norway* 8 E10
Frunze = Bishkek, *Kirghizia* 26 E8
Frutal, *Brazil* 93 G9
Frýdek-Místek, *Czech.* 17 D9
Fu Xian, *Liaoning, China* 35 E11
Fu Xian, *Shaanxi, China* 34 F5
Fucheng, *China* 34 F9
Fuchou = Fuzhou, *China* 33 D6
Fuchū, *Japan* 31 G6
Fuencaliente, *Canary Is.* 22 F2
Fuencaliente, Pta., *Canary Is.* 22 F2
Fuente Ovejuna, *Spain* 19 C3
Fuentes de Oñoro, *Spain* 19 B2
Fuerte →, *Mexico* 86 B3
Fuerte Olimpo, *Paraguay* 94 A4
Fuerteventura, *Canary Is.* 22 F6
Fufeng, *China* 34 G4
Fugløysund, *Norway* 8 A16
Fugou, *China* 34 G8
Fugu, *China* 34 E6
Fuhai, *China* 32 B3
Fuḥaymī, *Iraq* 44 C4
Fuji, *Japan* 31 G9
Fuji-San, *Japan* 31 G9
Fuji-yoshida, *Japan* 31 G9
Fujian □, *China* 33 D6
Fujinomiya, *Japan* 31 G9
Fujisawa, *Japan* 31 G9
Fukien = Fujian □, *China* 33 D6
Fukuchiyama, *Japan* 31 G7
Fukue-Shima, *Japan* 31 H4
Fukui, *Japan* 31 F8
Fukui □, *Japan* 31 G8
Fukuoka, *Japan* 31 H5
Fukuoka □, *Japan* 31 H5
Fukushima, *Japan* 30 F10
Fukushima □, *Japan* 30 F10
Fukuyama, *Japan* 31 G6
Fulda, *Germany* 16 C4
Fulda →, *Germany* 16 C4
Fullerton, *Calif., U.S.A.* 85 M9
Fullerton, *Nebr., U.S.A.* 80 E5
Fulongquan, *China* 35 B13
Fulton, *Mo., U.S.A.* 80 F9
Fulton, *N.Y., U.S.A.* 79 C8
Fulton, *Tenn., U.S.A.* 77 G1
Funabashi, *Japan* 31 G10
Funchal, *Madeira* 22 D3
Fundación, *Colombia* 92 A4
Fundão, *Portugal* 19 B2
Fundy, B. of, *Canada* 71 D6
Funing, *Hebei, China* 35 E10
Funing, *Jiangsu, China* 35 H10
Funiu Shan, *China* 34 H7
Funtua, *Nigeria* 50 F6
Fuping, *Hebei, China* 34 E8
Fuping, *Shaanxi, China* 34 G5
Furano, *Japan* 30 C11
Furāt, Nahr al →, *Asia* 44 D5
Fūrg, *Iran* 45 D7
Furnás, *Spain* 22 B8
Furnas, Represa de, *Brazil* 95 A6

Furneaux Group, *Australia* 62 G4
Furness, *U.K.* 10 C4
Furqlus, *Syria* 47 A6
Fürth, *Germany* 16 D5
Furukawa, *Japan* 30 E10
Fury and Hecla Str., *Canada* 69 B11
Fusagasuga, *Colombia* 92 C4
Fushan, *Shandong, China* 35 F11
Fushan, *Shanxi, China* 34 G6
Fushun, *China* 35 D12
Fusong, *China* 35 C14
Futuna, *Wall. & F. Is.* 59 B8
Fuxin, *China* 35 C11
Fuyang, *China* 34 H8
Fuyang He →, *China* 34 E9
Fuyu, *China* 35 B13
Fuzhou, *China* 33 D6
Fylde, *U.K.* 10 D5
Fyn, *Denmark* 9 J11
Fyne, L., *U.K.* 12 F3

G

Gabela, *Angola* 52 G2
Gabès, *Tunisia* 50 B7
Gabès, G. de, *Tunisia* 51 B7
Gabon ■, *Africa* 52 E2
Gaborone, *Botswana* 56 C4
Gabriels, *U.S.A.* 79 B10
Gābrīk, *Iran* 45 E8
Gabrovo, *Bulgaria* 21 C11
Gāch Sār, *Iran* 45 B6
Gachsārān, *Iran* 45 D6
Gadag, *India* 40 M9
Gadap, *Pakistan* 42 G2
Gadarwara, *India* 43 H8
Gadhada, *India* 42 J4
Gadsden, *Ala., U.S.A.* 77 H2
Gadsden, *Ariz., U.S.A.* 83 K6
Gadwal, *India* 40 L10
Gaffney, *U.S.A.* 77 H5
Gafsa, *Tunisia* 50 B6
Gagetown, *Canada* 71 C6
Gagnoa, *Ivory C.* 50 G3
Gagnon, *Canada* 71 B6
Gagnon, L., *Canada* 73 A6
Gahini, *Rwanda* 54 C3
Gahmar, *India* 43 G10
Gai Xian, *China* 35 D12
Gaïdhouronísi, *Greece* 23 E7
Gail, *U.S.A.* 81 J4
Gaines, *U.S.A.* 78 E7
Gainesville, *Fla., U.S.A.* 77 L4
Gainesville, *Ga., U.S.A.* 77 H4
Gainesville, *Mo., U.S.A.* 81 G8
Gainesville, *Tex., U.S.A.* 81 J6
Gainsborough, *U.K.* 10 D7
Gairdner, L., *Australia* 63 E2
Gairloch, L., *U.K.* 12 D3
Gakuch, *Pakistan* 43 A5
Galán, Cerro, *Argentina* 94 B2
Galana →, *Kenya* 54 C5
Galangue, *Angola* 53 G3
Galápagos, *Pac. Oc.* 65 H18
Galashiels, *U.K.* 12 F6
Galaţi, *Romania* 17 F14
Galatina, *Italy* 21 D8
Galax, *U.S.A.* 77 G5
Galbraith, *Australia* 62 B3
Galcaio, *Somali Rep.* 46 F4
Galdhøpiggen, *Norway* 9 F10
Galeana, *Mexico* 86 C4
Galela, *Indonesia* 37 D7
Galera Point, *Trin. & Tob.* 89 D7
Galesburg, *U.S.A.* 80 E9
Galeton, *U.S.A.* 78 E7
Galich, *Russia* 24 C7
Galicia □, *Spain* 19 A2
Galilee = Hagalil, *Israel* 47 C4
Galilee, L., *Australia* 62 C4
Galilee, Sea of = Yam Kinneret, *Israel* 47 C4
Galinoporni, *Cyprus* 23 D13
Galion, *U.S.A.* 78 F2
Galiuro Mts., *U.S.A.* 83 K8
Gallabat, *Sudan* 51 F12
Gallatin, *U.S.A.* 77 G2
Galle, *Sri Lanka* 40 R12
Gállego →, *Spain* 19 B5
Gallegos →, *Argentina* 96 G3
Galley Hd., *Ireland* 13 E3
Gallinas, Pta., *Colombia* 92 A4
Gallipoli = Gelibolu, *Turkey* 21 D12
Gallípoli, *Italy* 21 D8
Gallipolis, *U.S.A.* 76 F4
Gällivare, *Sweden* 8 C16
Galloway, *U.K.* 12 G4
Galloway, Mull of, *U.K.* 12 G4
Gallup, *U.S.A.* 83 J9
Galong, *Australia* 63 E4
Galoya, *Sri Lanka* 40 Q12
Galt, *U.S.A.* 84 G5
Galty Mts., *Ireland* 13 D3
Galtymore, *Ireland* 13 D3
Galva, *U.S.A.* 80 E9
Galveston, *U.S.A.* 81 L7
Galveston B., *U.S.A.* 81 L7
Gálvez, *Argentina* 94 C3
Galway, *Ireland* 13 C2
Galway □, *Ireland* 13 C2
Galway B., *Ireland* 13 C2
Gam →, *Vietnam* 38 B5
Gamagori, *Japan* 31 G8
Gambaga, *Ghana* 50 F4
Gambat, *Pakistan* 42 F3
Gambela, *Ethiopia* 51 G11
Gambia ■, *W. Afr.* 50 F1
Gambia →, *W. Afr.* 50 F1
Gambier, C., *Australia* 60 B5
Gambier Is., *Australia* 63 F2
Gamboli, *Pakistan* 42 E3
Gamboma, *Congo* 52 E3
Gamerco, *U.S.A.* 83 J9
Gamlakarleby = Kokkola, *Finland* 8 E17
Gammon →, *Canada* 73 C9
Gan Jiang →, *China* 33 D6
Ganado, *Ariz., U.S.A.* 83 J9
Ganado, *Tex., U.S.A.* 81 L6
Gananoque, *Canada* 70 D4
Ganaveh, *Iran* 45 D6
Gand = Gent, *Belgium* 15 C3
Ganda, *Angola* 53 G2
Gandak →, *India* 43 G11
Gandava, *Pakistan* 42 E2
Gander, *Canada* 71 C9
Gander L., *Canada* 71 C9
Ganderowe Falls, *Zimbabwe* 55 F2
Gandhi Sagar, *India* 42 G6
Gandi, *Nigeria* 50 F6
Gando, Pta., *Canary Is.* 22 G4
Ganedidalem = Gani, *Indonesia* 37 E7
Ganga →, *India* 43 H14
Ganga, Mouths of the, *India* 43 J13
Ganganagar, *India* 42 E5
Gangapur, *India* 42 F7
Gangara, *Niger* 50 F6
Gangaw, *Burma* 41 H19
Gangdisê Shan, *China* 41 D12
Ganges = Ganga →, *India* 43 H14
Gangoh, *India* 42 E7
Gangtok, *India* 41 F16
Gangu, *China* 34 G3
Gangyao, *China* 35 B14
Gani, *Indonesia* 37 E7
Ganj, *India* 43 F8
Gannett Pk., *U.S.A.* 82 E9
Gannvalley, *U.S.A.* 80 C5
Ganquan, *China* 34 F5
Gansu □, *China* 34 G3
Ganta, *Liberia* 50 G3
Gantheaume, C., *Australia* 63 F2
Gantheaume B., *Australia* 61 E1
Ganyem, *Indonesia* 37 E10
Ganyu, *China* 35 G10
Ganzhou, *China* 33 D6
Gaomi, *China* 35 F10
Gaoping, *China* 34 G7
Gaotang, *China* 34 F9
Gaoua, *Burkina Faso* 50 F4
Gaoual, *Guinea* 50 F2
Gaoxiong, *Taiwan* 33 D7
Gaoyang, *China* 34 E8
Gaoyou Hu, *China* 35 H10
Gaoyuan, *China* 35 F9
Gap, *France* 18 D7
Gar, *China* 32 C2
Garachico, *Canary Is.* 22 F3
Garachiné, *Panama* 88 E4
Garafia, *Canary Is.* 22 F2
Garajonay, *Canary Is.* 22 F2
Garanhuns, *Brazil* 93 E11
Garawe, *Liberia* 50 H3
Garba Tula, *Kenya* 54 B4
Garber, *U.S.A.* 81 G6
Garberville, *U.S.A.* 82 F2
Gard, *Somali Rep.* 46 F4
Gard □, *France* 18 D6
Garda, L. di, *Italy* 20 B4
Garde L., *Canada* 73 A7
Garden City, *Kans., U.S.A.* 81 G4
Garden City, *Tex., U.S.A.* 81 K4
Garden Grove, *U.S.A.* 85 M9
Gardēz, *Afghan.* 42 C3
Gardiner, *U.S.A.* 82 D8
Gardiners I., *U.S.A.* 79 E12
Gardner, *U.S.A.* 79 D13
Gardner Canal, *Canada* 72 C3
Gardnerville, *U.S.A.* 84 G7
Garey, *U.S.A.* 85 L6
Garfield, *U.S.A.* 82 C5
Gargano, Mte., *Italy* 20 D6
Garhshankar, *India* 42 D7
Garibaldi Prov. Park, *Canada* 72 D4
Garies, *S. Africa* 56 E2
Garigliano →, *Italy* 20 D5
Garissa, *Kenya* 54 C4
Garissa □, *Kenya* 54 C5
Garland, *U.S.A.* 82 F7
Garm, *Tajikistan* 26 F8
Garmāb, *Iran* 45 C8
Garmsār, *Iran* 45 C7
Garner, *U.S.A.* 80 D8
Garnett, *U.S.A.* 80 F7
Garo Hills, *India* 43 G14
Garoe, *Somali Rep.* 46 F4
Garonne →, *France* 18 D3
Garoua, *Cameroon* 51 G7
Garrison, *Mont., U.S.A.* 82 C7
Garrison, *N. Dak., U.S.A.* 80 B4
Garrison, *Tex., U.S.A.* 81 K7
Garrison Res. = Sakakawea, L., *U.S.A.* 80 B3
Garry →, *U.K.* 12 E5
Garry, L., *Canada* 68 B9
Garsen, *Kenya* 54 C5
Garson L., *Canada* 73 B6
Garub, *Namibia* 56 D2
Garut, *Indonesia* 37 G12
Garvie Mts., *N.Z.* 59 L2
Garwa = Garoua, *Cameroon* 51 G7
Garwa, *India* 43 G10
Gary, *U.S.A.* 76 E2
Garzê, *China* 32 C5
Garzón, *Colombia* 92 C3
Gas-San, *Japan* 30 E10
Gasan Kuli, *Turkmenistan* 26 F6
Gascogne, *France* 18 E4
Gascogne, G. de, *Europe* 18 E3
Gascony = Gascogne, *France* 18 E4
Gascoyne →, *Australia* 61 D1
Gascoyne Junc. T.O., *Australia* 61 E2
Gashaka, *Nigeria* 50 G7
Gasherbrum, *Pakistan* 43 B7
Gaspé, *Canada* 71 C7
Gaspé, C. de, *Canada* 71 C7
Gaspé, Pén. de, *Canada* 71 C6
Gaspésie, Parc Prov. de la, *Canada* 71 C6
Gassaway, *U.S.A.* 76 F5
Gastonia, *U.S.A.* 77 H5
Gastre, *Argentina* 96 E3
Gata, C., *Cyprus* 23 E12
Gata, C. de, *Spain* 19 D4
Gata, Sierra de, *Spain* 19 B2
Gataga →, *Canada* 72 B3
Gates, *U.S.A.* 78 C7
Gateshead, *U.K.* 10 C6
Gatesville, *U.S.A.* 81 K6
Gaths, *Zimbabwe* 55 G3
Gatico, *Chile* 94 A1
Gâtinais, *France* 18 B5
Gatineau →, *Canada* 70 C4
Gatineau, Parc de la, *Canada* 70 C4
Gatun, L., *Panama* 88 E4
Gatyana, *S. Africa* 57 E4
Gau, *Fiji* 59 D8
Gauer L., *Canada* 73 B9
Gauhati, *India* 43 F14
Gaula →, *Norway* 8 E11
Gausta, *Norway* 9 G10
Gāv Koshī, *Iran* 45 D8
Gāvakān, *Iran* 45 D7
Gavāter, *Iran* 45 E9
Gāvbandī, *Iran* 45 E7
Gavdhopoúla, *Greece* 23 E6
Gávdhos, *Greece* 23 E6
Gaviota, *U.S.A.* 85 L6
Gävleborgs län □, *Sweden* 9 F14
Gawachab, *Namibia* 56 D2
Gawilgarh Hills, *India* 40 J10
Gawler, *Australia* 63 E2
Gaxun Nur, *China* 32 B5
Gay, *Russia* 24 D10
Gaya, *India* 43 G11
Gaya, *Niger* 50 F5
Gaylord, *U.S.A.* 76 C3
Gayndah, *Australia* 63 D5
Gaza, *Egypt* 47 D3
Gaza □, *Mozam.* 57 C5
Gaza Strip, *Egypt* 47 D3
Gāzbor, *Iran* 45 D8
Gazi, *Zaïre* 54 B1
Gaziantep, *Turkey* 25 G6
Gazli, *Uzbekistan* 26 E7
Gcuwa, *S. Africa* 57 E4
Gdańsk, *Poland* 17 A9
Gdańska, Zatoka, *Poland* 17 A9
Gdov, *Russia* 24 C4
Gdynia, *Poland* 17 A9
Gebe, *Indonesia* 37 D7
Gebeit Mine, *Sudan* 51 D12
Gedaref, *Sudan* 51 F12
Gede, Tanjung, *Indonesia* 36 F3
Gedser, *Denmark* 9 J11
Geegully Cr. →, *Australia* 60 C3
Geelong, *Australia* 63 F3
Geelvink Chan., *Australia* 61 E1
Geidam, *Nigeria* 51 F7
Geikie →, *Canada* 73 B8
Geili, *Sudan* 51 E11
Geita, *Tanzania* 54 C3
Geita □, *Tanzania* 54 C3
Gejiu, *China* 32 D5
Gela, *Italy* 20 F6
Geladi, *Ethiopia* 46 F4
Gelderland □, *Neths.* 15 B6
Geldermalsen, *Neths.* 15 C5
Geldrop, *Neths.* 15 C5
Geleen, *Neths.* 15 D5
Gelehun, *S. Leone* 50 G2
Gelibolu, *Turkey* 21 D12
Gelsenkirchen, *Germany* 16 C3
Gemas, *Malaysia* 39 L4
Gembloux, *Belgium* 15 D4
Gemena, *Zaïre* 52 D3
Gendringen, *Neths.* 15 C6
General Acha, *Argentina* 94 D3
General Alvear, *Buenos Aires, Argentina* 94 D3
General Alvear, *Mendoza, Argentina* 94 D2
General Artigas, *Paraguay* 94 B4
General Belgrano, *Argentina* 94 D4
General Cabrera, *Argentina* 94 C3
General Cepeda, *Mexico* 86 B4
General Guido, *Argentina* 94 D4
General Juan Madariaga, *Argentina* 94 D4
General La Madrid, *Argentina* 94 D3
General MacArthur, *Phil.* 37 B7
General Martin Miguel de Güemes, *Argentina* 94 A3
General Paz, *Argentina* 94 B4
General Pico, *Argentina* 94 D3
General Pinedo, *Argentina* 94 B3
General Pinto, *Argentina* 94 C3
General Santos, *Phil.* 37 C7
General Trevino, *Mexico* 87 B5
General Trías, *Mexico* 86 B3
General Viamonte, *Argentina* 94 D3
General Villegas, *Argentina* 94 D3
Genesee, *Idaho, U.S.A.* 82 C5
Genesee, *Pa., U.S.A.* 78 E7
Genesee →, *U.S.A.* 78 C7
Geneseo, *Ill., U.S.A.* 80 E9
Geneseo, *Kans., U.S.A.* 80 F5
Geneseo, *N.Y., U.S.A.* 78 D7
Geneva = Genève, *Switz.* 16 E3
Geneva, *Ala., U.S.A.* 77 K3
Geneva, *N.Y., U.S.A.* 78 D7
Geneva, *Nebr., U.S.A.* 80 E6
Geneva, *Ohio, U.S.A.* 78 E4
Geneva, L. = Léman, Lac, *Switz.* 16 E3
Geneva, L., *U.S.A.* 76 D1
Genève, *Switz.* 16 E3
Genil →, *Spain* 19 D3
Genk, *Belgium* 15 D5
Gennargentu, Mti. del, *Italy* 20 E3
Gennep, *Neths.* 15 C5
Genoa = Génova, *Italy* 20 B3
Genoa, *Australia* 63 F4
Genoa, *N.Y., U.S.A.* 79 D8
Genoa, *Nebr., U.S.A.* 80 E6
Genoa, *Nev., U.S.A.* 84 F7
Génova, *Italy* 20 B3
Génova, G. di, *Italy* 20 B3
Gent, *Belgium* 15 C3
Geographe B., *Australia* 61 F2
Geographe Chan., *Australia* 61 D1
Georga, Zemlya, *Russia* 26 A5
George, *S. Africa* 56 E3
George →, *Canada* 71 A6
George, L., *N.S.W., Australia* 63 F4
George, L., *S. Austral., Australia* 63 F3
George, L., *W. Austral., Australia* 60 D3
George, L., *Uganda* 54 B3
George, L., *Fla., U.S.A.* 77 L5
George, L., *N.Y., U.S.A.* 79 C11
George Gill Ra., *Australia* 60 D5
George River = Port Nouveau-Québec, *Canada* 69 C13
George Sound, *N.Z.* 59 L1
George Town, *Bahamas* 88 B4
George Town, *Malaysia* 39 K3
George V Land, *Antarctica* 5 C10
George VI Sound, *Antarctica* 5 D17
George West, *U.S.A.* 81 L5
Georgetown, *Australia* 62 B3
Georgetown, *Ont., Canada* 70 D4
Georgetown, *P.E.I., Canada* 71 C7
Georgetown, *Cayman Is.* 88 C3
Georgetown, *Gambia* 50 F2
Georgetown, *Guyana* 92 B7
Georgetown, *Calif., U.S.A.* 84 G6
Georgetown, *Colo., U.S.A.* 82 G11
Georgetown, *Ky., U.S.A.* 76 F3
Georgetown, *S.C., U.S.A.* 77 J6
Georgetown, *Tex., U.S.A.* 81 K6
Georgia □, *U.S.A.* 77 J4
Georgia ■, *Asia* 25 F7
Georgia, Str. of, *Canada* 72 D4
Georgian B., *Canada* 70 C3
Georgievsk, *Russia* 25 F7
Georgina →, *Australia* 62 C2
Georgina Downs, *Australia* 62 C2
Georgiu-Dezh = Liski, *Russia* 25 D6
Gera, *Germany* 16 C6
Geraardsbergen, *Belgium* 15 D3
Geral, Serra, *Brazil* 95 B6
Geral de Goiás, Serra, *Brazil* 93 F9
Geraldine, *U.S.A.* 82 C8
Geraldton, *Australia* 61 E1
Geraldton, *Canada* 70 C2
Gereshk, *Afghan.* 40 D4
Gerik, *Malaysia* 39 K3
Gering, *U.S.A.* 80 E3
Gerlach, *U.S.A.* 82 F4
Gerlogubi, *Ethiopia* 46 F4
Germansen Landing, *Canada* 72 B4
Germany ■, *Europe* 16 C5
Germiston, *S. Africa* 57 D4
Gero, *Japan* 31 G8
Gerona, *Spain* 19 B7
Gerrard, *Canada* 72 C5
Gers □, *France* 18 E4
Geser, *Indonesia* 37 E8
Gethsémani, *Canada* 71 B7
Gettysburg, *Pa., U.S.A.* 76 F7
Gettysburg, *S. Dak., U.S.A.* 80 C5
Getz Ice Shelf, *Antarctica* 5 D14
Gévaudan, *France* 18 D5
Geyser, *U.S.A.* 82 C8
Geyserville, *U.S.A.* 84 G4
Geysir, *Iceland* 8 D3
Ghaghara →, *India* 43 G11
Ghana ■, *W. Afr.* 50 G4
Ghansor, *India* 43 H9
Ghanzi, *Botswana* 56 C3
Ghanzi □, *Botswana* 56 C3
Gharb el Istiwa'iya □, *Sudan* 51 G10
Ghardaïa, *Algeria* 50 B5
Gharyān, *Libya* 51 B7
Ghat, *Libya* 50 D7
Ghatal, *India* 43 H12
Ghatampur, *India* 43 F9
Ghaţţī, *Si. Arabia* 44 D3
Ghawdex = Gozo, *Malta* 23 C1
Ghazal, Bahr el →, *Chad* 51 F8
Ghazâl, Bahr el →, *Sudan* 51 G11
Ghazaouet, *Algeria* 50 A4
Ghaziabad, *India* 42 E7
Ghazipur, *India* 43 G10
Ghaznī, *Afghan.* 42 C3
Ghaznī □, *Afghan.* 40 C6
Ghèlinsor, *Somali Rep.* 46 F4
Ghent = Gent, *Belgium* 15 C3
Ghizao, *Afghan.* 42 C1
Ghizar →, *Pakistan* 43 A5
Ghogha, *India* 42 J5
Ghotaru, *India* 42 F4
Ghotki, *Pakistan* 42 E3
Ghowr □, *Afghan.* 40 C4
Ghudaf, W. al →, *Iraq* 44 C4
Ghughri, *India* 43 H9
Ghugus, *India* 40 K11
Ghulam Mohammad Barrage, *Pakistan* 42 G3
Ghūrīān, *Afghan.* 40 B2
Gia Dinh, *Vietnam* 39 G6
Gia Lai = Pleiku, *Vietnam* 38 F7
Gia Nghia, *Vietnam* 39 G6
Gia Ngoc, *Vietnam* 38 E7
Gia Vuc, *Vietnam* 38 E7
Gian, *Phil.* 37 C7
Giant Forest, *U.S.A.* 84 J8
Giants Causeway, *U.K.* 13 A5
Giarabub = Al Jaghbūb, *Libya* 51 C9
Giarre, *Italy* 20 F6
Gibara, *Cuba* 88 B4
Gibb River, *Australia* 60 C4
Gibbon, *U.S.A.* 80 E5
Gibraltar, *Europe* 19 D3
Gibraltar, Str. of, *Medit. S.* 19 E3
Gibson Desert, *Australia* 60 D4
Gibsons, *Canada* 72 D4
Gibsonville, *U.S.A.* 84 F6
Giddings, *U.S.A.* 81 K6
Gidole, *Ethiopia* 51 G12
Giessen, *Germany* 16 C4
Gīfān, *Iran* 45 B8
Gifford Creek, *Australia* 60 D2
Gifu, *Japan* 31 G8
Gifu □, *Japan* 31 G8
Giganta, Sa. de la, *Mexico* 86 B2
Gigha, *U.K.* 12 F3
Gijón, *Spain* 19 A3
Gil I., *Canada* 72 C3
Gila →, *U.S.A.* 83 K6
Gila Bend, *U.S.A.* 83 K7
Gila Bend Mts., *U.S.A.* 83 K7
Gīlān □, *Iran* 45 B6
Gilbert →, *Australia* 62 B3
Gilbert Is., *Kiribati* 64 G9
Gilbert Plains, *Canada* 73 C8
Gilbert River, *Australia* 62 B3
Gilberton, *Australia* 62 B3
Gilford I., *Canada* 72 C3
Gilgandra, *Australia* 63 E4
Gilgil, *Kenya* 54 C4
Gilgit, *India* 43 B6
Gilgit →, *Pakistan* 43 B6
Gillam, *Canada* 73 B10
Gillen, L., *Australia* 61 E3
Gilles, L., *Australia* 63 E2
Gillette, *U.S.A.* 80 C2
Gilliat, *Australia* 62 C3
Gillingham, *U.K.* 11 F8
Gilmer, *U.S.A.* 81 J7
Gilmore, *Australia* 63 F4
Gilmore, L., *Australia* 61 F3
Gilmour, *Canada* 70 D4
Gilroy, *U.S.A.* 83 H3
Gimbi, *Ethiopia* 51 G12
Gimli, *Canada* 73 C9
Gin Gin, *Australia* 63 D5
Gindie, *Australia* 62 C4
Gingin, *Australia* 61 F2
Ginir, *Ethiopia* 46 F3
Giohar, *Somali Rep.* 46 G4
Gióna, Óros, *Greece* 21 E10
Gir Hills, *India* 42 J4
Girab, *India* 42 F4
Girâfi, W. →, *Egypt* 47 F3
Girard, *Kans., U.S.A.* 81 G7
Girard, *Ohio, U.S.A.* 78 E4
Girard, *Pa., U.S.A.* 78 D4
Girardot, *Colombia* 92 C4
Girdle Ness, *U.K.* 12 D6
Giresun, *Turkey* 25 F6
Girga, *Egypt* 51 C11
Giridih, *India* 43 G12
Girilambone, *Australia* 63 E4
Gironde □, *France* 18 D3
Gironde →, *France* 18 D3
Giru, *Australia* 62 B4
Girvan, *U.K.* 12 F4
Gisborne, *N.Z.* 59 H7
Gisenyi, *Rwanda* 54 C2
Gitega, *Burundi* 54 C2
Giuba →, *Somali Rep.* 46 G3
Giurgiu, *Romania* 17 G12
Giza = El Gîza, *Egypt* 51 C11
Gizhiga, *Russia* 27 C17

Gizhiginskaya Guba, *Russia* 27 C16
Giżycko, *Poland* 17 A10
Gjirokastra, *Albania* 21 D9
Gjoa Haven, *Canada* 68 B10
Gjøvik, *Norway* 9 F11
Glace Bay, *Canada* 71 C8
Glacier B., *U.S.A.* 72 B1
Glacier Nat. Park, *Canada* 72 C5
Glacier Park, *U.S.A.* 82 B7
Glacier Peak, *U.S.A.* 82 B3
Gladewater, *U.S.A.* 81 J7
Gladstone, *Queens., Australia* 62 C5
Gladstone, *S. Austral., Australia* 63 E2
Gladstone, *W. Austral., Australia* 61 E1
Gladstone, *Canada* 73 C9
Gladstone, *U.S.A.* 76 C2
Gladwin, *U.S.A.* 76 D3
Gladys L., *Canada* 72 B2
Gláma, *Iceland* 8 D2
Glåma →, *Norway* 9 G11
Glamis, *U.S.A.* 85 N11
Glasco, *Kans., U.S.A.* 80 F6
Glasco, *N.Y., U.S.A.* 79 D11
Glasgow, *U.K.* 12 F4
Glasgow, *Ky., U.S.A.* 76 G3
Glasgow, *Mont., U.S.A.* 82 B10
Glastonbury, *U.K.* 11 F5
Glastonbury, *U.S.A.* 79 E12
Glauchau, *Germany* 16 C6
Glazov, *Russia* 24 C9
Gleiwitz = Gliwice, *Poland* 17 C9
Glen, *U.S.A.* 79 B13
Glen Affric, *U.K.* 12 D4
Glen Canyon Dam, *U.S.A.* 83 H8
Glen Canyon Nat. Recreation Area, *U.S.A.* 83 H8
Glen Coe, *U.K.* 12 E4
Glen Cove, *U.S.A.* 79 F11
Glen Garry, *U.K.* 12 D3
Glen Innes, *Australia* 63 D5
Glen Lyon, *U.S.A.* 79 E8
Glen Mor, *U.K.* 12 D4
Glen Moriston, *U.K.* 12 D4
Glen Orchy, *U.K.* 12 E4
Glen Spean, *U.K.* 12 E4
Glen Ullin, *U.S.A.* 80 B4
Glenburgh, *Australia* 61 E2
Glencoe, *Canada* 78 D3
Glencoe, *S. Africa* 57 D5
Glencoe, *U.S.A.* 80 C7
Glendale, *Ariz., U.S.A.* 83 K7
Glendale, *Calif., U.S.A.* 85 L8
Glendale, *Oreg., U.S.A.* 82 E2
Glendale, *Zimbabwe* 55 F3
Glendive, *U.S.A.* 80 B2
Glendo, *U.S.A.* 80 D2
Glenelg, *Australia* 63 E2
Glenelg →, *Australia* 63 F3
Glenflorrie, *Australia* 60 D2
Glengarriff, *Ireland* 13 E2
Glengyle, *Australia* 62 C2
Glenmora, *U.S.A.* 81 K8
Glenmorgan, *Australia* 63 D4
Glenn, *U.S.A.* 84 F4
Glenns Ferry, *U.S.A.* 82 E6
Glenorchy, *Australia* 62 G4
Glenore, *Australia* 62 B3
Glenormiston, *Australia* 62 C2
Glenreagh, *Australia* 63 E5
Glenrock, *U.S.A.* 82 E11
Glenrothes, *U.K.* 12 E5
Glens Falls, *U.S.A.* 79 C11
Glenties, *Ireland* 13 B3
Glenville, *U.S.A.* 76 F5
Glenwood, *Alta., Canada* 72 D6
Glenwood, *Nfld., Canada* 71 C9
Glenwood, *Ark., U.S.A.* 81 H8
Glenwood, *Hawaii, U.S.A.* 74 J17
Glenwood, *Iowa, U.S.A.* 80 E7
Glenwood, *Minn., U.S.A.* 80 C7
Glenwood, *Wash., U.S.A.* 84 D5
Glenwood Springs, *U.S.A.* 82 G10
Gliwice, *Poland* 17 C9
Globe, *U.S.A.* 83 K8
Głogów, *Poland* 16 C8
Glorieuses, Is., *Ind. Oc.* 57 A8
Glossop, *U.K.* 10 D6
Gloucester, *Australia* 63 E5
Gloucester, *U.K.* 11 F5
Gloucester, *U.S.A.* 79 D14
Gloucester I., *Australia* 62 B4
Gloucestershire □, *U.K.* 11 F5
Gloversville, *U.S.A.* 79 C10
Glovertown, *Canada* 71 C9
Glückstadt, *Germany* 16 B4
Gmünd, *Austria* 16 D7
Gmunden, *Austria* 16 E6
Gniezno, *Poland* 17 B8
Gnowangerup, *Australia* 61 F2
Go Cong, *Vietnam* 39 G6
Gō-no-ura, *Japan* 31 H4
Go Quao, *Vietnam* 39 H5
Goa, *India* 40 M8
Goa □, *India* 40 M8
Goalen Hd., *Australia* 63 F5
Goalpara, *India* 41 F17
Goalundo Ghat, *Bangla.* 43 H13
Goat Fell, *U.K.* 12 F3
Goba, *Ethiopia* 46 F2
Goba, *Mozam.* 57 D5
Gobabis, *Namibia* 56 C2
Gobi, *Asia* 34 C5
Gobō, *Japan* 31 H7
Gochas, *Namibia* 56 C2
Godavari →, *India* 41 L13
Godavari Point, *India* 41 L13
Godbout, *Canada* 71 C6
Godda, *India* 43 G12
Goderich, *Canada* 70 D3
Godhavn, *Greenland* 4 C5
Godhra, *India* 42 H5
Godoy Cruz, *Argentina* 94 C2
Gods →, *Canada* 73 B10
Gods L., *Canada* 73 C10
Godthåb, *Greenland* 69 B14
Godwin Austen = K2, Mt., *Pakistan* 43 B7
Goeie Hoop, Kaap die = Good Hope, C. of, *S. Africa* 56 E2
Goéland, L. au, *Canada* 70 C4
Goeree, *Neths.* 15 C3
Goes, *Neths.* 15 C3
Gogama, *Canada* 70 C3
Gogango, *Australia* 62 C5
Gogebic, L., *U.S.A.* 80 B10
Gogra = Ghaghara →, *India* 43 G11
Goiânia, *Brazil* 93 G9
Goiás, *Brazil* 93 G8
Goiás □, *Brazil* 93 F9
Goio-Ere, *Brazil* 95 A5
Gojō, *Japan* 31 G7
Gojra, *Pakistan* 42 D5
Gokarannath, *India* 43 F9
Gokteik, *Burma* 41 H20
Gokurt, *Pakistan* 42 E2
Gola, *India* 43 E9
Golakganj, *India* 43 F13
Golan Heights = Hagolan, *Syria* 47 B4
Golāshkerd, *Iran* 45 E8
Golchikha, *Russia* 4 B12
Golconda, *U.S.A.* 82 F5
Gold Beach, *U.S.A.* 82 E1
Gold Coast, *Australia* 63 D5
Gold Coast, *W. Afr.* 48 F3
Gold Hill, *U.S.A.* 82 E2
Golden, *Canada* 72 C5
Golden, *U.S.A.* 80 F2
Golden B., *N.Z.* 59 J4
Golden Gate, *U.S.A.* 82 H2
Golden Hinde, *Canada* 72 D3
Golden Lake, *Canada* 78 A7
Golden Prairie, *Canada* 73 C7
Golden Vale, *Ireland* 13 D3
Goldendale, *U.S.A.* 82 D3
Goldfield, *U.S.A.* 83 H5
Goldfields, *Canada* 73 B7
Goldsand L., *Canada* 73 B8
Goldsboro, *U.S.A.* 77 H7
Goldsmith, *U.S.A.* 81 K3
Goldsworthy, *Australia* 60 D2
Goldthwaite, *U.S.A.* 81 K5
Goleniów, *Poland* 16 B7
Golestānak, *Iran* 45 D7
Goleta, *U.S.A.* 85 L7
Golfito, *Costa Rica* 88 E3
Goliad, *U.S.A.* 81 L6
Golpāyegān, *Iran* 45 C6
Golra, *Pakistan* 42 C5
Golspie, *U.K.* 12 D5
Goma, *Rwanda* 54 C2
Goma, *Zaïre* 54 C2
Gomati →, *India* 43 G10
Gombari, *Zaïre* 54 B2
Gombe →, *Tanzania* 54 C3
Gomel, *Belorussia* 24 D5
Gomera, *Canary Is.* 22 F2
Gómez Palacio, *Mexico* 86 B4
Gomīshān, *Iran* 45 B7
Gomogomo, *Indonesia* 37 F8
Gomoh, *India* 41 H15
Gompa = Ganta, *Liberia* 50 G3
Gonābād, *Iran* 45 C8
Gonaïves, *Haiti* 89 C5
Gonâve, G. de la, *Haiti* 89 C5
Gonâve, I. de la, *Haiti* 89 C5
Gonbab-e Kāvūs, *Iran* 45 B7
Gonda, *India* 43 F9
Gondal, *India* 42 J4
Gonder, *Ethiopia* 51 F12
Gondia, *India* 40 J12
Gondola, *Mozam.* 55 F3
Gonghe, *China* 32 C5
Gongolgon, *Australia* 63 E4
Goniri, *Nigeria* 51 F7
Gonzales, *Calif., U.S.A.* 83 H3
Gonzales, *Tex., U.S.A.* 81 L6
González Chaves, *Argentina* 94 D3
Good Hope, C. of, *S. Africa* 56 E2
Gooderham, *Canada* 70 D4
Goodeve, *Canada* 73 C8
Gooding, *U.S.A.* 82 E6
Goodland, *U.S.A.* 80 F4
Goodnight, *U.S.A.* 81 H4
Goodooga, *Australia* 63 D4
Goodsoil, *Canada* 73 C7
Goodsprings, *U.S.A.* 83 J6
Goole, *U.K.* 10 D7
Goolgowi, *Australia* 63 E4
Goomalling, *Australia* 61 F2
Goombalie, *Australia* 63 D4
Goonda, *Mozam.* 55 F3
Goondiwindi, *Australia* 63 D5
Goongarrie, L., *Australia* 61 F3
Goonyella, *Australia* 62 C4
Goor, *Neths.* 15 B6
Gooray, *Australia* 63 D5
Goose →, *Canada* 71 B7
Goose L., *U.S.A.* 82 F3
Gop, *India* 40 H6
Gopalganj, *India* 43 F11
Gorakhpur, *India* 43 F10
Gorda, *U.S.A.* 84 K5
Gorda, Pta., *Nic.* 88 D3
Gorda, Pta., *Canary Is.* 22 F2
Gordan B., *Australia* 60 B5
Gordon, *U.S.A.* 80 D3
Gordon →, *Australia* 62 G4
Gordon Downs, *Australia* 60 C4
Gordon L., *Alta., Canada* 73 B6
Gordon L., *N.W.T., Canada* 72 A6
Gordonia, *S. Africa* 56 D3
Gordonvale, *Australia* 62 B4
Gore, *Australia* 63 D5
Goré, *Chad* 51 G8
Gore, *Ethiopia* 51 G12
Gore, *N.Z.* 59 M2
Gore Bay, *Canada* 70 C3
Gorey, *Ireland* 13 D5
Gorg, *Iran* 45 D8
Gorgān, *Iran* 45 B7
Gorgona, I., *Colombia* 92 C3
Gorham, *U.S.A.* 79 B13
Gorinchem, *Neths.* 15 C4
Gorízia, *Italy* 20 B5
Gorki = Nizhniy Novgorod, *Russia* 24 C7
Gorkiy = Nizhniy Novgorod, *Russia* 24 C7
Gorkovskoye Vdkhr., *Russia* 24 C7
Görlitz, *Germany* 16 C7
Gorlovka, *Ukraine* 25 E6
Gorman, *Calif., U.S.A.* 85 L8
Gorman, *Tex., U.S.A.* 81 J5
Gorna Oryakhovitsa, *Bulgaria* 21 C11
Gorno-Altaysk, *Russia* 26 D9
Gorno Slinkino, *Russia* 26 C8
Gornyatski, *Russia* 24 A11
Gornyi, *Russia* 30 B6
Goromonzi, *Zimbabwe* 55 F3
Gorongose →, *Mozam.* 57 C5
Gorongoza, *Mozam.* 55 F3
Gorongoza, Sa. da, *Mozam.* 55 F3
Gorontalo, *Indonesia* 37 D6
Gort, *Ireland* 13 C3
Gortis, *Greece* 23 D6
Gorzów Wielkopolski, *Poland* 16 B7
Gosford, *Australia* 63 E5
Goshen, *Calif., U.S.A.* 84 J7
Goshen, *Ind., U.S.A.* 76 E3
Goshen, *N.Y., U.S.A.* 79 E10
Goshogawara, *Japan* 30 D10
Goslar, *Germany* 16 C5
Gospič, *Croatia* 20 B6
Gosport, *U.K.* 11 G6
Gosse →, *Australia* 62 B1
Göta kanal, *Sweden* 9 G12
Göteborg, *Sweden* 9 H11
Göteborgs och Bohus län □, *Sweden* 9 G11
Gotha, *Germany* 16 C5
Gothenburg, *U.S.A.* 80 E4
Gotland, *Sweden* 9 H15
Gotska Sandön, *Sweden* 9 G15
Gōtsu, *Japan* 31 G6
Göttingen, *Germany* 16 C4
Gottwaldov, *Czech.* 17 D8
Goubangzi, *China* 35 D11
Gouda, *Neths.* 15 B4
Goúdhoura, Ákra, *Greece* 23 E8
Gough I., *Atl. Oc.* 2 G9
Gouin, Rés., *Canada* 70 C5
Goulburn, *Australia* 63 E4
Goulburn Is., *Australia* 62 A1
Gounou-Gaya, *Chad* 51 G8
Gouri, *Chad* 51 E8
Gourits →, *S. Africa* 56 E3
Gourma Rharous, *Mali* 50 E4
Goúrnais, *Greece* 23 D7
Gourock Ra., *Australia* 63 F4
Gouverneur, *U.S.A.* 79 B9
Gouviá, *Greece* 23 A3
Govan, *Canada* 73 C8
Governador Valadares, *Brazil* 93 G10
Governor's Harbour, *Bahamas* 88 A4
Gowan Ra., *Australia* 62 C4
Gowanda, *U.S.A.* 78 D6
Gowd-e Zirreh, *Afghan.* 40 E3
Gower, *U.K.* 11 F3
Gowna, L., *Ireland* 13 C4
Goya, *Argentina* 94 B4
Goyder Lagoon, *Australia* 63 D2
Goyllarisquisga, *Peru* 92 F3
Goz Beïda, *Chad* 51 F9
Gozo, *Malta* 23 C1
Graaff-Reinet, *S. Africa* 56 E3
Gračac, *Croatia* 20 B6
Grace, *U.S.A.* 82 E8
Graceville, *U.S.A.* 80 C6
Gracias a Dios, C., *Honduras* 88 C3
Graciosa, I., *Canary Is.* 22 E6
Grado, *Spain* 19 A2
Gradule, *Australia* 63 D4
Grady, *U.S.A.* 81 H3
Graénalon, L., *Iceland* 8 D5
Grafton, *Australia* 63 D5
Grafton, *U.S.A.* 80 A6
Graham, *Canada* 70 C1
Graham, *N.C., U.S.A.* 77 G6
Graham, *Tex., U.S.A.* 81 J5
Graham →, *Canada* 72 B4
Graham Bell, Os., *Russia* 26 A7
Graham I., *Canada* 72 C2
Graham Land, *Antarctica* 5 C17
Graham Mt., *U.S.A.* 83 K9
Grahamdale, *Canada* 73 C9
Grahamstown, *S. Africa* 56 E4
Grain Coast, *W. Afr.* 48 F2
Grajaú, *Brazil* 93 E9
Grajaú →, *Brazil* 93 D10
Grampian □, *U.K.* 12 D6
Grampian Highlands = Grampian Mts., *U.K.* 12 E5
Grampian Mts., *U.K.* 12 E5
Gran Canaria, *Canary Is.* 22 F4
Gran Chaco, *S. Amer.* 94 B3
Gran Paradiso, *Italy* 20 B2
Gran Sasso d'Italia, *Italy* 20 C5
Granada, *Nic.* 88 D2
Granada, *Spain* 19 D4
Granada, *U.S.A.* 81 F3
Granadilla de Abona, *Canary Is.* 22 F3
Granard, *Ireland* 13 C4
Granbury, *U.S.A.* 81 J6
Granby, *Canada* 70 C5
Grand →, *Mo., U.S.A.* 80 F8
Grand →, *S. Dak., U.S.A.* 80 C4
Grand Bahama, *Bahamas* 88 A4
Grand Bank, *Canada* 71 C8
Grand Bassam, *Ivory C.* 50 G4
Grand-Bourg, *Guadeloupe* 89 C7
Grand Canal = Yun Ho →, *China* 35 E9
Grand Canyon, *U.S.A.* 83 H7
Grand Canyon National Park, *U.S.A.* 83 H7
Grand Cayman, *Cayman Is.* 88 C3
Grand Coulee, *U.S.A.* 82 C4
Grand Coulee Dam, *U.S.A.* 82 C4
Grand Falls, *Canada* 71 C8
Grand Forks, *Canada* 72 D5
Grand Forks, *U.S.A.* 80 B6
Grand Haven, *U.S.A.* 76 D2
Grand I., *U.S.A.* 76 B2
Grand Island, *U.S.A.* 80 E5
Grand Isle, *U.S.A.* 81 L10
Grand Junction, *U.S.A.* 83 G9
Grand Lac Victoria, *Canada* 70 C4
Grand Lahou, *Ivory C.* 50 G3
Grand L., *N.B., Canada* 71 C6
Grand L., *Nfld., Canada* 71 C8
Grand L., *Nfld., Canada* 71 B7
Grand Lake, *U.S.A.* 82 F11
Grand L., *U.S.A.* 81 L8
Grand Manan I., *Canada* 71 D6
Grand Marais, *Canada* 80 B9
Grand Marais, *U.S.A.* 76 B3
Grand-Mère, *Canada* 70 C5
Grand Portage, *U.S.A.* 70 C2
Grand Rapids, *Canada* 73 C9
Grand Rapids, *Mich., U.S.A.* 76 D2
Grand Rapids, *Minn., U.S.A.* 80 B8
Grand St-Bernard, Col du, *Switz.* 16 F3
Grand Teton, *U.S.A.* 82 E8
Grand Valley, *U.S.A.* 82 G9
Grand View, *Canada* 73 C8
Grande →, *Jujuy, Argentina* 94 A2
Grande →, *Mendoza, Argentina* 94 D2
Grande →, *Bolivia* 92 G6
Grande →, *Bahia, Brazil* 93 F10
Grande →, *Minas Gerais, Brazil* 93 H8
Grande →, *U.S.A.* 81 N6
Grande, B., *Argentina* 96 G3
Grande Baie, *Canada* 71 C5
Grande Baleine, R. de la →, *Canada* 70 A4
Grande Cache, *Canada* 72 C5
Grande de Santiago →, *Mexico* 86 C3
Grande-Entrée, *Canada* 71 C7
Grande Prairie, *Canada* 72 B5
Grande-Rivière, *Canada* 71 C7
Grande-Vallée, *Canada* 71 C6
Grandes-Bergeronnes, *Canada* 71 C6
Grandfalls, *U.S.A.* 81 K3
Grandoe Mines, *Canada* 72 B3
Grandview, *U.S.A.* 82 C4
Graneros, *Chile* 94 C1
Grangemouth, *U.K.* 12 E5
Granger, *Wash., U.S.A.* 82 C3
Granger, *Wyo., U.S.A.* 82 F9
Grangeville, *U.S.A.* 82 D5
Granite City, *U.S.A.* 80 F9
Granite Falls, *U.S.A.* 80 C7
Granite Mt., *U.S.A.* 85 M10
Granite Peak, *Australia* 61 E3
Granite Pk., *U.S.A.* 82 D9
Granity, *N.Z.* 59 J3
Granja, *Brazil* 93 D10
Granja de Torrehermosa, *Spain* 19 C3
Granollers, *Spain* 19 B7
Grant, *U.S.A.* 80 E4
Grant, Mt., *U.S.A.* 82 G4
Grant City, *U.S.A.* 80 E7
Grant I., *Australia* 60 B5
Grant Range Mts., *U.S.A.* 83 G6
Grantham, *U.K.* 10 E7
Grantown-on-Spey, *U.K.* 12 D5
Grants, *U.S.A.* 83 J10
Grants Pass, *U.S.A.* 82 E2
Grantsburg, *U.S.A.* 80 C8
Grantsville, *U.S.A.* 82 F7
Granville, *France* 18 B3
Granville, *N. Dak., U.S.A.* 80 A4
Granville, *N.Y., U.S.A.* 76 D9
Granville L., *Canada* 73 B8
Grapeland, *U.S.A.* 81 K7
Gras, L. de, *Canada* 68 B8
Graskop, *S. Africa* 57 C5
Grass →, *Canada* 73 B9
Grass Range, *U.S.A.* 82 C9
Grass River Prov. Park, *Canada* 73 C8
Grass Valley, *Calif., U.S.A.* 84 F6
Grass Valley, *Oreg., U.S.A.* 82 D3
Grasse, *France* 18 E7
Grassmere, *Australia* 63 E3
Gravelbourg, *Canada* 73 D7
's-Gravenhage, *Neths.* 15 B4
Gravenhurst, *Canada* 78 B5
Gravesend, *Australia* 63 D5
Gravesend, *U.K.* 11 F8
Gravois, Pointe-à-, *Haiti* 89 C5
Grayling, *U.S.A.* 76 C3
Grayling →, *Canada* 72 B3
Grays Harbor, *U.S.A.* 82 C1
Grays L., *U.S.A.* 82 E8
Grays River, *U.S.A.* 84 D3
Grayson, *Canada* 73 C8
Graz, *Austria* 16 E7
Greasy L., *Canada* 72 A4
Great Abaco I., *Bahamas* 88 A4
Great Artesian Basin, *Australia* 62 C3
Great Australian Bight, *Australia* 61 F5
Great Bahama Bank, *Bahamas* 88 B4
Great Barrier I., *N.Z.* 59 G5
Great Barrier Reef, *Australia* 62 B4
Great Barrington, *U.S.A.* 79 D11
Great Basin, *U.S.A.* 82 G5
Great Bear →, *Canada* 68 B7
Great Bear L., *Canada* 68 B8
Great Bena, *U.S.A.* 79 E9
Great Bend, *U.S.A.* 80 F5
Great Blasket I., *Ireland* 13 D1
Great Britain, *Europe* 6 E5
Great Central, *Canada* 72 D3
Great Dividing Ra., *Australia* 62 C4
Great Driffield, *U.K.* 10 C7
Great Exuma I., *Bahamas* 88 B4
Great Falls, *Canada* 73 C9
Great Falls, *U.S.A.* 82 C8
Great Fish = Groot Vis →, *S. Africa* 56 E4
Great Guana Cay, *Bahamas* 88 B4
Great Harbour Deep, *Canada* 71 B8
Great Inagua I., *Bahamas* 89 B5
Great Indian Desert = Thar Desert, *India* 42 F4
Great I., *Canada* 73 B9
Great Karoo, *S. Africa* 56 E3
Great Lake, *Australia* 62 G4
Great Ormes Head, *U.K.* 10 D4
Great Ouse →, *U.K.* 10 E8
Great Palm I., *Australia* 62 B4
Great Plains, *N. Amer.* 66 E9
Great Ruaha →, *Tanzania* 54 D4
Great Saint Bernard P. = Grand St-Bernard, Col du, *Switz.* 16 F3
Great Salt Lake, *U.S.A.* 82 F7
Great Salt Lake Desert, *U.S.A.* 82 F7
Great Salt Plains Res., *U.S.A.* 81 G5
Great Sandy Desert, *Australia* 60 D3
Great Slave L., *Canada* 72 A5
Great Smoky Mts. Nat. Park, *U.S.A.* 77 H4
Great Stour = Stour →, *U.K.* 11 F9
Great Victoria Desert, *Australia* 61 E4
Great Wall, *China* 34 E5
Great Whernside, *U.K.* 10 C6
Great Yarmouth, *U.K.* 10 E9
Greater Antilles, *W. Indies* 89 C5
Greater London □, *U.K.* 11 F7
Greater Manchester □, *U.K.* 10 D5
Greater Sunda Is., *Indonesia* 36 F4
Greco, C., *Cyprus* 23 E13
Gredos, Sierra de, *Spain* 19 B3
Greece, *U.S.A.* 78 C7
Greece ■, *Europe* 21 E10
Greeley, *Colo., U.S.A.* 80 E2
Greeley, *Nebr., U.S.A.* 80 E5
Green →, *Ky., U.S.A.* 76 G2
Green →, *Utah, U.S.A.* 83 G9
Green B., *U.S.A.* 76 C2
Green Bay, *U.S.A.* 76 C2
Green C., *Australia* 63 F5
Green Cove Springs, *U.S.A.* 77 L5
Green River, *U.S.A.* 83 G8
Greenbank, *U.S.A.* 84 B4
Greenbush, *Mich., U.S.A.* 78 B1
Greenbush, *Minn., U.S.A.* 80 A6
Greencastle, *U.S.A.* 76 F2
Greene, *U.S.A.* 79 D9
Greenfield, *Calif., U.S.A.* 84 J5
Greenfield, *Calif., U.S.A.* 85 K8
Greenfield, *Ind., U.S.A.* 76 F3
Greenfield, *Iowa, U.S.A.* 80 E7
Greenfield, *Mass., U.S.A.* 79 D12

Greenfield, Miss., U.S.A. 81 G8
Greenfield Park, Canada 79 A11
Greenland ■, N. Amer. 4 C5
Greenland Sea, Arctic 4 B7
Greenock, U.K. 12 F4
Greenore, Ireland 13 B5
Greenore Pt., Ireland 13 D5
Greenough →, Australia 61 E1
Greenport, U.S.A. 79 E12
Greensboro, Ga., U.S.A. 77 J4
Greensboro, N.C., U.S.A. 77 G6
Greensburg, Ind., U.S.A. 76 F3
Greensburg, Kans., U.S.A. 81 G5
Greensburg, Pa., U.S.A. 78 F5
Greenville, Liberia 50 G3
Greenville, Ala., U.S.A. 77 K2
Greenville, Calif., U.S.A. 84 E6
Greenville, Ill., U.S.A. 80 F10
Greenville, Maine, U.S.A. 71 C6
Greenville, Mich., U.S.A. 76 D3
Greenville, Miss., U.S.A. 81 J9
Greenville, N.C., U.S.A. 77 H7
Greenville, Ohio, U.S.A. 76 E3
Greenville, Pa., U.S.A. 78 E4
Greenville, S.C., U.S.A. 77 H4
Greenville, Tenn., U.S.A. 77 G4
Greenville, Tex., U.S.A. 81 J6
Greenwater Lake Prov. Park, Canada 73 C8
Greenwich, U.K. 11 F8
Greenwich, Conn., U.S.A. 79 E11
Greenwich, N.Y., U.S.A. 79 C11
Greenwich, Ohio, U.S.A. 78 E2
Greenwood, Canada 72 D5
Greenwood, Miss., U.S.A. 81 J9
Greenwood, S.C., U.S.A. 77 H4
Greenwood, Mt., Australia 60 B5
Gregory, U.S.A. 80 D5
Gregory →, Australia 62 B2
Gregory, L., S. Austral., Australia 63 D2
Gregory, L., W. Austral., Australia 61 E2
Gregory Downs, Australia 62 B2
Gregory L., Australia 60 D4
Gregory Ra., Queens., Australia 62 B3
Gregory Ra., W. Austral., Australia 60 D3
Greifswald, Germany 16 A6
Gremikha, Russia 24 A6
Grenada, U.S.A. 81 J10
Grenada ■, W. Indies 89 D7
Grenadines, W. Indies 89 D7
Grenen, Denmark 9 H11
Grenfell, Australia 63 E4
Grenfell, Canada 73 C8
Grenoble, France 18 D6
Grenora, U.S.A. 80 A3
Grenville, C., Australia 62 A3
Grenville Chan., Canada 72 C3
Gresham, U.S.A. 84 E4
Gresik, Indonesia 37 G15
Gretna Green, U.K. 12 F5
Grevenmacher, Lux. 15 E6
Grey →, N.Z. 59 K3
Grey, C., Australia 62 A2
Grey Ra., Australia 63 D3
Grey Res., Canada 71 C8
Greybull, U.S.A. 82 D9
Greymouth, N.Z. 59 K3
Greytown, N.Z. 59 J5
Greytown, S. Africa 57 D5
Gribbell I., Canada 72 C3
Gridley, U.S.A. 84 F5
Griekwastad, S. Africa 56 D3
Griffin, U.S.A. 77 J3
Griffith, Australia 63 E4
Grimari, C.A.R. 51 G9
Grimes, U.S.A. 84 F5
Grimsby, Canada 78 C5
Grimsby, U.K. 10 D7
Grimsey, Iceland 8 C5
Grimshaw, Canada 72 B5
Grimstad, Norway 9 G10
Grinnell, U.S.A. 80 E8
Gris-Nez, C., France 18 A4
Groais I., Canada 71 B8
Groblersdal, S. Africa 57 D4
Grodno, Belorussia 24 D3
Grodzisk Wielkopolski, Poland 16 B8
Groesbeck, U.S.A. 81 K6
Grójec, Poland 17 C10
Grong, Norway 8 D12
Groningen, Neths. 15 A6
Groningen □, Neths. 15 A6
Groom, U.S.A. 81 H4
Groot →, S. Africa 56 E3
Groot Berg →, S. Africa 56 E2
Groot-Brakrivier, S. Africa 56 E3
Groot-Kei →, S. Africa 57 E4
Groot Vis →, S. Africa 56 E4
Groote Eylandt, Australia 62 A2
Grootfontein, Namibia 56 B2
Grootlaagte →, Africa 56 C3
Grootvloer, S. Africa 56 E3
Gros C., Canada 72 A6
Grosa, Pta., Spain 22 B8
Gross Glockner, Austria 16 E6
Grossenhain, Germany 16 C6
Grosseto, Italy 20 C4
Groswater B., Canada 71 B8
Groton, Conn., U.S.A. 79 E12
Groton, S. Dak., U.S.A. 80 C5
Grouard Mission, Canada 72 B5
Groundhog →, Canada 70 C3
Grouse Creek, U.S.A. 82 F7
Grove City, U.S.A. 78 E4
Groveland, U.S.A. 84 H6
Grover City, U.S.A. 85 K6
Groveton, N.H., U.S.A. 79 B13
Groveton, Tex., U.S.A. 81 K7
Groznyy, Russia 25 F8
Grudziądz, Poland 17 B9
Grundy Center, U.S.A. 80 D8
Gruver, U.S.A. 81 G4
Gryazi, Russia 24 D6
Gryazovets, Russia 26 D5
Gua, India 41 H14
Gua Musang, Malaysia 39 K3
Guacanayabo, G. de, Cuba 88 B4
Guachípas →, Argentina 94 B2
Guadalajara, Mexico 86 C4
Guadalajara, Spain 19 B4
Guadalcanal, Solomon Is. 64 H8
Guadales, Argentina 94 C2
Guadalete →, Spain 19 D2
Guadalhorce →, Spain 19 D3
Guadalquivir →, Spain 19 D2
Guadalupe = Guadeloupe ■, W. Indies 89 C7
Guadalupe, Mexico 85 N10
Guadalupe, U.S.A. 85 L6
Guadalupe →, Mexico 85 N10
Guadalupe →, U.S.A. 81 L6
Guadalupe, Sierra de, Spain 19 C3
Guadalupe Bravos, Mexico 86 A3
Guadalupe Pk., U.S.A. 83 L11
Guadalupe y Calvo, Mexico 86 B3
Guadarrama, Sierra de, Spain 19 B4
Guadeloupe ■, W. Indies 89 C7
Guadeloupe Passage, W. Indies 89 C7
Guadiana →, Portugal 19 D2
Guadix, Spain 19 D4
Guafo, Boca del, Chile 96 E2
Guaíra, Brazil 95 A5
Guaitecas, Is., Chile 96 E2
Guajará-Mirim, Brazil 92 F5
Guajira, Pen. de la, Colombia 92 A4
Gualán, Guatemala 88 C2
Gualeguay, Argentina 94 C4
Gualeguaychú, Argentina 94 C4
Guam, Pac. Oc. 64 F6
Guaminí, Argentina 94 D3
Guamúchil, Mexico 86 B3
Guanabacoa, Cuba 88 B3
Guanacaste, Cordillera del, Costa Rica 88 D2
Guanaceví, Mexico 86 B3
Guanahani = San Salvador, Bahamas 89 B5
Guanajay, Cuba 88 B3
Guanajuato, Mexico 86 C4
Guanajuato □, Mexico 86 C4
Guandacol, Argentina 94 B2
Guane, Cuba 88 B3
Guangdong □, China 33 D6
Guangling, China 34 E8
Guangrao, China 35 F10
Guangwu, China 34 F3
Guangxi Zhuangzu Zizhiqu □, China 33 D5
Guangzhou, China 33 D6
Guanipa →, Venezuela 92 B6
Guannan, China 35 G10
Guantánamo, Cuba 89 B4
Guantao, China 34 F8
Guanyun, China 35 G10
Guápiles, Costa Rica 88 D3
Guaporé →, Brazil 92 F5
Guaqui, Bolivia 92 G5
Guarapari, Brazil 95 A7
Guarapuava, Brazil 95 B5
Guaratinguetá, Brazil 95 A6
Guaratuba, Brazil 95 B6
Guarda, Portugal 19 B2
Guardafui, C. = Asir, Ras, Somali Rep. 46 E5
Guaria □, Paraguay 94 B4
Guarujá, Brazil 95 A6
Guarus, Brazil 95 A7
Guasave, Mexico 86 B3
Guasdualito, Venezuela 92 B4
Guasipati, Venezuela 92 B6
Guatemala, Guatemala 88 D1
Guatemala ■, Cent. Amer. 88 C1
Guatire, Venezuela 92 A5
Guaviare □, Colombia 92 C4
Guaviare →, Colombia 92 C5
Guaxupé, Brazil 95 A6
Guayama, Puerto Rico 89 C6
Guayaquil, Ecuador 92 D3
Guayaquil, G. de, Ecuador 92 D2
Guaymas, Mexico 86 B2
Guba, Zaïre 55 E2
Gudbrandsdalen, Norway 9 F10
Guddu Barrage, Pakistan 40 E6
Gudivada, India 41 L12
Gudur, India 40 M11
Guecho, Spain 19 A4
Guékédou, Guinea 50 G2
Guelma, Algeria 50 A6
Guelph, Canada 70 D3
Guéréda, Chad 51 F9
Guéret, France 18 C4
Guerneville, U.S.A. 84 G4
Guernica, Spain 19 A4
Guernsey, U.K. 11 H5
Guernsey, U.S.A. 80 D2
Guerrero □, Mexico 87 D5
Gueydan, U.S.A. 81 K8
Gügher, Iran 45 D8
Guia, Canary Is. 22 F4
Guia de Isora, Canary Is. 22 F3
Guia Lopes da Laguna, Brazil 95 A4
Guiglo, Ivory C. 50 G3
Guijá, Mozam. 57 C5
Guildford, U.K. 11 F7
Guilford, U.S.A. 71 C6
Guilin, China 33 D6
Guilvinec, France 18 C1
Güimar, Canary Is. 22 F3
Guimarães, Brazil 93 D10
Guimaras, Phil. 37 B6
Guinda, U.S.A. 84 G4
Guinea ■, W. Afr. 50 F2
Guinea, Gulf of, Atl. Oc. 48 F3
Guinea-Bissau ■, Africa 50 F2
Güines, Cuba 88 B3
Guingamp, France 18 B2
Güiria, Venezuela 92 A6
Guiuan, Phil. 37 B7
Guiyang, China 32 D5
Guizhou □, China 32 D5
Gujarat □, India 42 H4
Gujranwala, Pakistan 42 C6
Gujrat, Pakistan 42 C6
Gulbarga, India 40 L10
Gulf, The, Asia 45 E6
Gulfport, U.S.A. 81 K10
Gulgong, Australia 63 E4
Gulistan, Pakistan 42 D2
Gull Lake, Canada 73 C7
Gulmarg, India 43 B6
Gulshad, Kazakhstan 26 E8
Gulu, Uganda 54 B3
Gulwe, Tanzania 54 D4
Gum Lake, Australia 63 E3
Gumal →, Pakistan 42 D4
Gumbaz, Pakistan 42 D3
Gumlu, Australia 62 B4
Gumma □, Japan 31 F9
Gummi, Nigeria 50 F6
Gumzai, Indonesia 37 F8
Guna, India 42 G7
Gundagai, Australia 63 F4
Gundih, Indonesia 37 G14
Gungu, Zaïre 52 F3
Gunisao →, Canada 73 C9
Gunisao L., Canada 73 C9
Gunnbjørn Fjeld, Greenland 4 C6
Gunnedah, Australia 63 E5
Gunningbar Cr. →, Australia 63 E4
Gunnison, Colo., U.S.A. 83 G10
Gunnison, Utah, U.S.A. 82 G8
Gunnison →, U.S.A. 83 G9
Gunpowder, Australia 62 B2
Guntakal, India 40 M10
Guntersville, U.S.A. 77 H2
Guntong, Malaysia 39 K3
Guntur, India 41 L12
Gunungapi, Indonesia 37 F7
Gunungsitoli, Indonesia 36 D1
Gunza, Angola 52 G2
Guo He →, China 35 H9
Guoyang, China 34 H9
Gupis, Pakistan 43 A5
Gurdaspur, India 42 C6
Gurdon, U.S.A. 81 J8
Gurgaon, India 42 E7
Gurha, India 42 G4
Gurkha, Nepal 43 E11
Gurley, Australia 63 D4
Gurué, Mozam. 55 F4
Gurun, Malaysia 39 K3
Gurupá, Brazil 93 D8
Gurupá, I. Grande de, Brazil 93 D8
Gurupi →, Brazil 93 D9
Guryev, Kazakhstan 25 E9
Gusau, Nigeria 50 F6
Gushan, China 35 E12
Gusinoozersk, Russia 27 D11
Gustine, U.S.A. 83 H3
Güstrow, Germany 16 B6
Gutha, Australia 61 E2
Guthalongra, Australia 62 B4
Guthrie, U.S.A. 81 H6
Guttenberg, U.S.A. 80 D9
Guyana ■, S. Amer. 92 C7
Guyang, China 34 D6
Guyenne, France 18 D4
Guymon, U.S.A. 81 G4
Guyra, Australia 63 E5
Guyuan, Hebei, China 34 D8
Guyuan, Ningxia Huizu, China 34 F4
Guzhen, China 35 H9
Guzmán, L. de, Mexico 86 A3
Gwa, Burma 41 L19
Gwaai, Zimbabwe 55 F2
Gwabegar, Australia 63 E4
Gwādar, Pakistan 40 G3
Gwalia, Australia 61 E3
Gwalior, India 42 F8
Gwanda, Zimbabwe 55 G2
Gwane, Zaïre 54 B2
Gweebarra B., Ireland 13 B3
Gweedore, Ireland 13 A3
Gwent □, U.K. 11 F5
Gweru, Zimbabwe 55 F2
Gwinn, U.S.A. 76 B2
Gwydir →, Australia 63 D4
Gwynedd □, U.K. 10 E4
Gyandzha, Azerbaijan 25 F8
Gyaring Hu, China 32 C4
Gydanskiy P-ov., Russia 26 C8
Gympie, Australia 63 D5
Gyöngyös, Hungary 17 E9
Györ, Hungary 17 E8
Gypsum Pt., Canada 72 A6
Gypsumville, Canada 73 C9

H

Ha 'Arava →, Israel 47 E4
Ha Coi, Vietnam 38 B6
Ha Dong, Vietnam 38 B5
Ha Giang, Vietnam 38 A5
Ha Tien, Vietnam 39 G5
Ha Tinh, Vietnam 38 C5
Ha Trung, Vietnam 38 C5
Haapamäki, Finland 8 E18
Haarlem, Neths. 15 B4
Haast →, N.Z. 59 K2
Haast Bluff, Australia 60 D5
Hab Nadi Chauki, Pakistan 42 G2
Habaswein, Kenya 54 B4
Habay, Canada 72 B5
Habbānīyah, Iraq 44 C4
Haboro, Japan 30 B10
Hachijō-Jima, Japan 31 H9
Hachinohe, Japan 30 D10
Hachiōji, Japan 31 G9
Hachŏn, N. Korea 35 D15
Hackensack, U.S.A. 79 F10
Hadali, Pakistan 42 C5
Hadarba, Ras, Sudan 51 D12
Hadarom □, Israel 47 E3
Haddington, U.K. 12 F6
Hadejia, Nigeria 50 F7
Haden, Australia 63 D5
Ḥadera, Israel 47 C3
Ḥadera, N. →, Israel 47 C3
Hadhramaut = Ḥaḍramawt, Yemen 46 D4
Hadong, S. Korea 35 G14
Ḥaḍramawt, Yemen 46 D4
Ḥadrānīyah, Iraq 44 C4
Hadrian's Wall, U.K. 10 C5
Haeju, N. Korea 35 E13
Haenam, S. Korea 35 G14
Haerhpin = Harbin, China 35 B14
Hafar al Bāṭin, Si. Arabia 44 D5
Ḥafīrat al 'Aydā, Si. Arabia 44 E3
Hafizabad, Pakistan 42 C5
Haflong, India 41 G18
Hafnarfjörður, Iceland 8 D3
Hafun, Ras, Somali Rep. 46 E5
Hagalil, Israel 47 C4
Hagen, Germany 16 C3
Hagerman, U.S.A. 81 J2
Hagerstown, U.S.A. 76 F7
Hagfors, Sweden 9 F12
Hagi, Iceland 8 D2
Hagi, Japan 31 G5
Hagolan, Syria 47 B4
Hagondange-Briey, France 18 B7
Hags Hd., Ireland 13 D2
Hague, C. de la, France 18 B3
Hague, The = 's-Gravenhage, Neths. 15 B4
Haguenau, France 18 B7
Hai □, Tanzania 54 C4
Hai Duong, Vietnam 38 B6
Haicheng, China 35 D12
Haidar Khel, Afghan. 42 C3
Haifa = Ḥefa, Israel 47 C3
Haig, Australia 61 F4
Haikou, China 33 D6
Ḥā'il, Si. Arabia 44 E4
Hailar, China 33 B6
Hailey, U.S.A. 82 E6
Haileybury, Canada 70 C4
Hailin, China 35 B15
Hailong, China 35 C13
Hailuoto, Finland 8 D18
Hainan □, China 33 E5
Hainaut □, Belgium 15 D4
Haines, U.S.A. 82 D5
Haines City, U.S.A. 77 L5
Haines Junction, Canada 72 A1
Haiphong, Vietnam 32 D5
Haiti ■, W. Indies 89 C5
Haiya Junction, Sudan 51 E12
Haiyang, China 35 F11
Haiyuan, China 34 F3
Haizhou, China 35 G10
Haizhou Wan, China 35 G10
Haja, Indonesia 37 E7
Hajar Bangar, Sudan 51 F9
Hajdúböszörmény, Hungary 17 E10
Hajipur, India 43 G11
Ḥājjī Muḥsin, Iraq 44 C5
Ḥājjīābād, Eṣfahan, Iran 45 C7
Ḥājjīābād, Hormozgān, Iran 45 D7
Hajnówka, Poland 17 B11
Hakansson, Mts., Zaïre 55 D2
Hakken-Zan, Japan 31 G7
Hakodate, Japan 30 D10
Haku-San, Japan 31 F8
Hakui, Japan 31 F8
Hala, Pakistan 40 G6
Ḥalab, Syria 44 B3
Ḥalabjah, Iraq 44 C5
Halaib, Sudan 51 D12
Hālat' Ammār, Si. Arabia 44 D3
Halbā, Lebanon 47 A5
Halberstadt, Germany 16 C5
Halcombe, N.Z. 59 J5
Halcon, Mt., Phil. 37 B6
Halden, Norway 9 G11
Haldia, India 41 H16
Haldwani, India 43 E8
Hale →, Australia 62 C2
Haleakala Crater, U.S.A. 74 H16
Haleyville, U.S.A. 77 H2
Halfway →, Canada 72 B4
Haliburton, Canada 70 C4
Halifax, Australia 62 B4
Halifax, Canada 71 D7
Halifax, U.K. 10 D6
Halifax B., Australia 62 B4
Halifax I., Namibia 56 D2
Halīl →, Iran 45 E8
Hall Beach, Canada 69 B11
Hall Pt., Australia 60 C3
Hallands län □, Sweden 9 H12
Halle, Belgium 15 D4
Halle, Germany 16 C5
Hällefors, Sweden 9 G13
Hallett, Australia 63 E2
Hallettsville, U.S.A. 81 L6
Halliday, U.S.A. 80 B3
Halliday L., Canada 73 A7
Hallim, S. Korea 35 H14
Hallingdal →, Norway 9 F10
Hällnäs, Sweden 8 D15
Hallock, U.S.A. 73 D9
Halls Creek, Australia 60 C4
Hallstead, U.S.A. 79 E9
Halmahera, Indonesia 37 D7
Halmstad, Sweden 9 H12
Halq el Oued, Tunisia 51 A7
Hals, Denmark 9 H11
Hälsingborg = Helsingborg, Sweden 9 H12
Halstad, U.S.A. 80 B6
Halul, Qatar 45 E7
Ḥalvān, Iran 45 C8
Ham Tan, Vietnam 39 G6
Ham Yen, Vietnam 38 A5
Hamab, Namibia 56 D2
Hamada, Japan 31 G6
Hamadān, Iran 45 C6
Hamadān □, Iran 45 C6
Ḥamāh, Syria 44 C3
Hamamatsu, Japan 31 G8
Hamar, Norway 9 F11
Hamarøy, Norway 8 B13
Hambantota, Sri Lanka 40 R12
Hamber Prov. Park, Canada 72 C5
Hamburg, Germany 16 B4
Hamburg, Ark., U.S.A. 81 J9
Hamburg, Iowa, U.S.A. 80 E7
Hamburg, N.Y., U.S.A. 78 D6
Hamburg, Pa., U.S.A. 79 F9
Ḥamḍ, W. al →, Si. Arabia 44 E3
Hamden, U.S.A. 79 E12
Hame □ = Hämeen lääni □, Finland 9 F18
Hämeen lääni □, Finland 9 F18
Hämeenlinna, Finland 9 F18
Hamelin Pool, Australia 61 E1
Hameln, Germany 16 B4
Hamerkaz □, Israel 47 C3
Hamersley Ra., Australia 60 D2
Hamhung, N. Korea 35 E14
Hami, China 32 B4
Hamilton, Australia 63 F3
Hamilton, Canada 70 D4
Hamilton, N.Z. 59 G5
Hamilton, U.K. 12 F4
Hamilton, Mo., U.S.A. 80 F8
Hamilton, Mont., U.S.A. 82 C6
Hamilton, N.Y., U.S.A. 79 D9
Hamilton, Ohio, U.S.A. 76 F3
Hamilton, Tex., U.S.A. 81 K5
Hamilton →, Australia 62 C2
Hamilton City, U.S.A. 84 F4
Hamilton Hotel, Australia 62 C3
Hamilton Inlet, Canada 71 B8
Hamiota, Canada 73 C8
Hamlet, U.S.A. 77 H6
Hamley Bridge, Australia 63 E2
Hamlin = Hameln, Germany 16 B4
Hamlin, N.Y., U.S.A. 78 C7
Hamlin, Tex., U.S.A. 81 J4
Hamm, Germany 16 C3
Hammerfest, Norway 8 A17
Hammond, Ind., U.S.A. 76 E2
Hammond, La., U.S.A. 81 K9
Hammonton, U.S.A. 76 F8
Hampden, N.Z. 59 L3
Hampshire □, U.K. 11 F6
Hampshire Downs, U.K. 11 F6
Hampton, Ark., U.S.A. 81 J8
Hampton, Iowa, U.S.A. 80 D8
Hampton, N.H., U.S.A. 79 D14
Hampton, S.C., U.S.A. 77 J5
Hampton, Va., U.S.A. 76 G7
Hampton Tableland, Australia 61 F4
Hamrat esh Sheykh, Sudan 51 F10
Hamyang, S. Korea 35 G14
Hana, U.S.A. 74 H17
Hanak, Si. Arabia 44 E3
Hanamaki, Japan 30 E10
Hanang, Tanzania 54 C4

Hanau, Germany 16 C4
Hanbogd, Mongolia 34 C4
Hancheng, China 34 G6
Hancock, Mich., U.S.A. 80 B10
Hancock, Minn., U.S.A. 80 C7
Hancock, Pa., U.S.A. 79 E9
Handa, Japan 31 G8
Handa, Somali Rep. 46 E5
Handan, China 34 F8
Handeni, Tanzania 54 D4
Handeni □, Tanzania 54 D4
Handwara, India 43 B6
Hanegev, Israel 47 E3
Haney, Canada 72 D4
Hanford, U.S.A. 83 H4
Hang Chat, Thailand 38 C2
Hang Dong, Thailand 38 C2
Hangang →, S. Korea 35 F14
Hangayn Nuruu, Mongolia 32 B4
Hangchou = Hangzhou, China 33 C7
Hanggin Houqi, China 34 D4
Hanggin Qi, China 34 E5
Hangö, Finland 9 G17
Hangu, China 35 E9
Hangzhou, China 33 C7
Hangzhou Wan, China 33 C7
Hanhongor, Mongolia 34 C3
Ḩanīdh, Si. Arabia 45 E6
Ḩanīsh, Yemen 46 E3
Hankinson, U.S.A. 80 B6
Hanko, Finland 9 G17
Hanksville, U.S.A. 83 G8
Hanle, India 43 C8
Hanmer Springs, N.Z. 59 K4
Hann →, Australia 60 C4
Hann, Mt., Australia 60 C4
Hanna, Canada 72 C6
Hannaford, U.S.A. 80 B5
Hannah, U.S.A. 80 A5
Hannah B., Canada 70 B4
Hannibal, U.S.A. 80 F9
Hannover, Germany 16 B4
Hanoi, Vietnam 32 D5
Hanover = Hannover, Germany 16 B4
Hanover, Canada 78 B3
Hanover, S. Africa 56 E3
Hanover, N.H., U.S.A. 79 C12
Hanover, Ohio, U.S.A. 78 F2
Hanover, Pa., U.S.A. 76 F7
Hanover, I., Chile 96 G2
Hansi, India 42 E6
Hanson, L., Australia 63 E2
Hanzhong, China 34 H4
Hanzhuang, China 35 G9
Haora, India 43 H13
Haparanda, Sweden 8 D18
Happy, U.S.A. 81 H4
Happy Camp, U.S.A. 82 F2
Happy Valley-Goose Bay, Canada 71 B7
Hapsu, N. Korea 35 D15
Hapur, India 42 E7
Ḩaql, Si. Arabia 47 F3
Har, Indonesia 37 F8
Har-Ayrag, Mongolia 34 B5
Har Hu, China 32 C4
Har Us Nuur, Mongolia 32 B4
Har Yehuda, Israel 47 D3
Ḩaraḑ, Si. Arabia 46 C4
Haranomachi, Japan 30 F10
Harardera, Somali Rep. 46 G4
Harare, Zimbabwe 55 F3
Harazé, Chad 51 F8
Harbin, China 35 B14
Harbor Beach, U.S.A. 76 D4
Harbor Springs, U.S.A. 76 C3
Harbour Breton, Canada 71 C8
Harbour Grace, Canada 71 C9
Harburg, Germany 16 B4
Harda, India 42 H7
Hardangerfjorden, Norway 9 F8
Hardap Dam, Namibia 56 C2
Hardenberg, Neths. 15 B6
Harderwijk, Neths. 15 B5
Hardey →, Australia 60 D2
Hardin, U.S.A. 82 D10
Harding, S. Africa 57 E4
Harding Ra., Australia 60 C3
Hardisty, Canada 72 C6
Hardman, U.S.A. 82 D4
Hardoi, India 43 F9
Hardwar = Haridwar, India 42 E8
Hardwick, U.S.A. 79 B12
Hardy, U.S.A. 81 G9
Hardy, Pen., Chile 96 H3
Hare B., Canada 71 B8
Harer, Ethiopia 46 F3
Hargeisa, Somali Rep. 46 F3
Hargshamn, Sweden 9 F15
Hari →, Indonesia 36 E2
Haria, Canary Is. 22 E6
Haridwar, India 42 E8
Haringhata →, Bangla. 41 J16
Harīrūd →, Asia 40 A2
Harlan, Iowa, U.S.A. 80 E7
Harlan, Tenn., U.S.A. 77 G4
Harlech, U.K. 10 E3
Harlem, U.S.A. 82 B9
Harlingen, Neths. 15 A5
Harlingen, U.S.A. 81 M6
Harlowton, U.S.A. 82 C9
Harney Basin, U.S.A. 82 E4
Harney L., U.S.A. 82 E4
Harney Pk., U.S.A. 80 D3
Härnösand, Sweden 8 E14
Harp L., Canada 71 A7
Harrand, Pakistan 42 E4
Harriman, U.S.A. 77 H3
Harrington Harbour, Canada 71 B8
Harris, U.K. 12 D2
Harris, Sd. of, U.K. 12 D1
Harris L., Australia 63 E2
Harrisburg, Ill., U.S.A. 81 G10
Harrisburg, Nebr., U.S.A. 80 E3
Harrisburg, Oreg., U.S.A. 82 D2
Harrisburg, Pa., U.S.A. 78 F8
Harrismith, S. Africa 57 D4
Harrison, Ark., U.S.A. 81 G8
Harrison, Idaho, U.S.A. 82 C5
Harrison, Nebr., U.S.A. 80 D3
Harrison, C., Canada 71 B8
Harrison B., U.S.A. 68 A4
Harrison L., Canada 72 D4
Harrisonburg, U.S.A. 76 F6
Harrisonville, U.S.A. 80 F7
Harriston, Canada 70 D3
Harrisville, U.S.A. 78 B1
Harrogate, U.K. 10 D6
Harrow, U.K. 11 F7
Harsīn, Iran 44 C5
Harstad, Norway 8 B14
Hart, U.S.A. 76 D2
Hart, L., Australia 63 E2
Hartbees →, S. Africa 56 D3
Hartford, Conn., U.S.A. 79 E12
Hartford, Ky., U.S.A. 76 G2
Hartford, S. Dak., U.S.A. 80 D6
Hartford, Wis., U.S.A. 80 D10
Hartford City, U.S.A. 76 E3
Hartland, Canada 71 C6
Hartland Pt., U.K. 11 F3
Hartlepool, U.K. 10 C6
Hartley Bay, Canada 72 C3
Hartmannberge, Namibia 56 B1
Hartney, Canada 73 D8
Harts →, S. Africa 56 D3
Hartselle, U.S.A. 77 H2
Hartshorne, U.S.A. 81 H7
Hartsville, U.S.A. 77 H5
Hartwell, U.S.A. 77 H4
Harunabad, Pakistan 42 E5
Harvand, Iran 45 D7
Harvey, Australia 61 F2
Harvey, Ill., U.S.A. 76 E2
Harvey, N. Dak., U.S.A. 80 B5
Harwich, U.K. 11 F9
Haryana □, India 42 E7
Harz, Germany 16 C5
Hasan Kiādeh, Iran 45 B6
Ḩasanābād, Iran 45 C7
Hasanpur, India 42 E8
Hashimoto, Japan 31 G7
Hashtjerd, Iran 45 C6
Haskell, Okla., U.S.A. 81 H7
Haskell, Tex., U.S.A. 81 J5
Hasselt, Belgium 15 D5
Hassi Inifel, Algeria 50 C5
Hassi Messaoud, Algeria 50 B6
Hastings, N.Z. 59 H6
Hastings, U.K. 11 G8
Hastings, Mich., U.S.A. 76 D3
Hastings, Minn., U.S.A. 80 C8
Hastings, Nebr., U.S.A. 80 E5
Hastings Ra., Australia 63 E5
Hat Yai, Thailand 39 J3
Hatanbulag, Mongolia 34 C5
Hatay = Antalya, Turkey 25 G5
Hatch, U.S.A. 83 K10
Hatches Creek, Australia 62 C2
Hatchet L., Canada 73 B8
Hateruma-Shima, Japan 31 M1
Hatfield P.O., Australia 63 E3
Hatgal, Mongolia 32 A5
Hathras, India 42 F8
Hatia, Bangla. 41 H17
Hato Mayor, Dom. Rep. 89 C6
Hattah, Australia 63 E3
Hatteras, C., U.S.A. 77 H8
Hattiesburg, U.S.A. 81 K10
Hatvan, Hungary 17 E9
Hau Bon = Cheo Reo, Vietnam 38 F7
Hau Duc, Vietnam 38 E7
Haugesund, Norway 9 G8
Haultain →, Canada 73 B7
Hauraki G., N.Z. 59 G5
Haut Atlas, Morocco 50 B3
Haut-Rhin □, France 18 C7
Haut Zaïre □, Zaïre 54 B2
Haute-Corse □, France 18 E9
Haute-Garonne □, France 18 E4
Haute-Loire □, France 18 D5
Haute-Marne □, France 18 B6
Haute-Saône □, France 18 C7
Haute-Savoie □, France 18 C7
Haute-Vienne □, France 18 D4
Hauterive, Canada 71 C6
Hautes-Alpes □, France 18 D7
Hautes Fagnes = Hohe Venn, Belgium 15 D6
Hautes-Pyrénées □, France 18 E4
Hauts-de-Seine □, France 18 B5
Hauts Plateaux, Algeria 50 A5
Havana = La Habana, Cuba 88 B3
Havana, U.S.A. 80 E9
Havant, U.K. 11 G7
Havasu, L., U.S.A. 85 L12
Havel →, Germany 16 B6
Havelange, Belgium 15 D5
Havelian, Pakistan 42 B5
Havelock, N.B., Canada 71 C6
Havelock, Ont., Canada 70 D4
Havelock, N.Z. 59 J4
Haverfordwest, U.K. 11 F3
Haverhill, U.S.A. 79 D13
Havering, U.K. 11 F8
Haverstraw, U.S.A. 79 E11
Havlíčkův Brod, Czech. 16 D7
Havre, U.S.A. 82 B9
Havre-Aubert, Canada 71 C7
Havre-St.-Pierre, Canada 71 B7
Haw →, U.S.A. 77 H6
Hawaii □, U.S.A. 74 H16
Hawaii I., Pac. Oc. 74 J17
Hawaiian Is., Pac. Oc. 74 H17
Hawaiian Ridge, Pac. Oc. 65 E11
Hawarden, Canada 73 C7
Hawarden, U.S.A. 80 D6
Hawea, L., N.Z. 59 L2
Hawera, N.Z. 59 H5
Hawick, U.K. 12 F6
Hawk Junction, Canada 70 C3
Hawke B., N.Z. 59 H6
Hawker, Australia 63 E2
Hawkesbury, Canada 70 C5
Hawkesbury I., Canada 72 C3
Hawkesbury Pt., Australia 62 A1
Hawkinsville, U.S.A. 77 J4
Hawkwood, Australia 63 D5
Hawley, U.S.A. 80 B6
Hawrān, Syria 47 C5
Hawsh Mūssá, Lebanon 47 B4
Hawthorne, U.S.A. 82 G4
Haxtun, U.S.A. 80 E3
Hay, Australia 63 E3
Hay →, Australia 62 C2
Hay →, Canada 72 A5
Hay, C., Australia 60 B4
Hay L., Canada 72 B5
Hay Lakes, Canada 72 C6
Hay-on-Wye, U.K. 11 E4
Hay River, Canada 72 A5
Hay Springs, U.S.A. 80 D3
Hayachine-San, Japan 30 E10
Hayden, Ariz., U.S.A. 83 K8
Hayden, Colo., U.S.A. 82 F10
Haydon, Australia 62 B3
Hayes, U.S.A. 80 C4
Hayes →, Canada 73 B10
Haynesville, U.S.A. 81 J8
Hays, Canada 72 C6
Hays, U.S.A. 80 F5
Hayward, Calif., U.S.A. 84 H4
Hayward, Wis., U.S.A. 80 B9
Haywards Heath, U.K. 11 F7
Hazafon □, Israel 47 C4
Hazarām, Kūh-e, Iran 45 D8
Hazard, U.S.A. 76 G4
Hazaribag, India 43 H11
Hazaribag Road, India 43 G11
Hazelton, Canada 72 B3
Hazelton, U.S.A. 80 B4
Hazen, N. Dak., U.S.A. 80 B4
Hazen, Nev., U.S.A. 82 G4
Hazlehurst, Ga., U.S.A. 77 K4
Hazlehurst, Miss., U.S.A. 81 K9
Hazleton, U.S.A. 79 F9
Hazlett, L., Australia 60 D4
Hazor, Israel 47 B4
Head of Bight, Australia 61 F5
Headlands, Zimbabwe 55 F3
Healdsburg, U.S.A. 84 G4
Healdton, U.S.A. 81 H6
Healesville, Australia 63 F4
Heanor, U.K. 10 D6
Heard I., Ind. Oc. 3 G13
Hearne, U.S.A. 81 K6
Hearne B., Canada 73 A9
Hearne L., Canada 72 A6
Hearst, Canada 70 C3
Heart →, U.S.A. 80 B4
Heart's Content, Canada 71 C9
Heath Pt., Canada 71 C7
Heath Steele, Canada 71 C6
Heavener, U.S.A. 81 H7
Hebbronville, U.S.A. 81 M5
Hebei □, China 34 E9
Hebel, Australia 63 D4
Heber, U.S.A. 85 N11
Heber Springs, U.S.A. 81 H9
Hebert, Canada 73 C7
Hebgen, L., U.S.A. 82 D8
Hebi, China 34 G8
Hebrides, U.K. 12 D1
Hebron = Al Khalīl, Jordan 47 D4
Hebron, Canada 69 C13
Hebron, N. Dak., U.S.A. 80 B3
Hebron, Nebr., U.S.A. 80 E6
Hecate Str., Canada 72 C2
Hechi, China 32 D5
Hechuan, China 32 C5
Hecla, U.S.A. 80 C5
Hecla I., Canada 73 C9
Hede, Sweden 8 E12
Hedemora, Sweden 9 F13
Hedley, U.S.A. 81 H4
Heemstede, Neths. 15 B4
Heerde, Neths. 15 B6
Heerenveen, Neths. 15 B5
Heerlen, Neths. 15 D5
Ḩefa, Israel 47 C3
Ḩefa □, Israel 47 C4
Hefei, China 33 C6
Hegang, China 33 B8
Heichengzhen, China 34 F4
Heidelberg, Germany 16 D4
Heidelberg, C. Prov., S. Africa 56 E3
Heidelberg, Trans., S. Africa 57 D4
Heilbron, S. Africa 57 D4
Heilbronn, Germany 16 D4
Heilongjiang □, China 35 B14
Heilunkiang = Heilongjiang □, China 35 B14
Heinola, Finland 9 F19
Heinze Is., Burma 41 M20
Heishan, China 35 D12
Heishui, China 35 C10
Hejaz = Al Ḩijāz, Si. Arabia 46 B2
Hejian, China 34 E9
Hejin, China 34 G6
Hekla, Iceland 8 E4
Hekou, Gansu, China 34 F2
Hekou, Yunnan, China 32 D5
Helan Shan, China 34 E3
Helena, Ark., U.S.A. 81 H9
Helena, Mont., U.S.A. 82 C7
Helendale, U.S.A. 85 L9
Helensburgh, U.K. 12 E4
Helensville, N.Z. 59 G5
Helgoland, Germany 16 A3
Heligoland = Helgoland, Germany 16 A3
Hellendoorn, Neths. 15 B6
Hellevoetsluis, Neths. 15 C4
Hellín, Spain 19 C5
Helmand □, Afghan. 40 D4
Helmand →, Afghan. 40 D2
Helmond, Neths. 15 C5
Helmsdale, U.K. 12 C5
Helong, China 35 C15
Helper, U.S.A. 82 G8
Helsingborg, Sweden 9 H12
Helsingfors, Finland 9 F18
Helsingør, Denmark 9 H12
Helsinki, Finland 9 F18
Helston, U.K. 11 G2
Helvellyn, U.K. 10 C4
Helwân, Egypt 51 C11
Hemet, U.S.A. 85 M10
Hemingford, U.S.A. 80 D3
Hemphill, U.S.A. 81 K8
Hempstead, U.S.A. 81 K6
Hemse, Sweden 9 H15
Henan □, China 34 G8
Henares →, Spain 19 B4
Henashi-Misaki, Japan 30 D9
Henderson, Argentina 94 D3
Henderson, Ky., U.S.A. 76 G2
Henderson, N.C., U.S.A. 77 G6
Henderson, Nev., U.S.A. 85 J12
Henderson, Pa., U.S.A. 77 H1
Henderson, Tex., U.S.A. 81 J7
Hendersonville, U.S.A. 77 H4
Hendījān, Iran 45 D6
Hendon, Australia 63 D5
Hengcheng, China 34 E4
Hengdaohezi, China 35 B15
Hengelo, Neths. 15 B6
Hengshan, China 34 F5
Hengshui, China 34 F8
Hengyang, China 33 D6
Henlopen, C., U.S.A. 76 F8
Hennenman, S. Africa 56 D4
Hennessey, U.S.A. 81 G6
Henrietta, U.S.A. 81 J5
Henrietta, Ostrov, Russia 27 B16
Henrietta Maria C., Canada 70 A3
Henry, U.S.A. 80 E10
Henryetta, U.S.A. 81 H6
Hensall, Canada 78 C3
Hentiyn Nuruu, Mongolia 33 B5
Henty, Australia 63 F4
Henzada, Burma 41 L19
Heppner, U.S.A. 82 D4
Hepworth, Canada 78 B3
Hequ, China 34 E6
Héraðsflói, Iceland 8 D6
Héraðsvötn →, Iceland 8 D4
Herald Cays, Australia 62 B4
Herāt, Afghan. 40 B3
Herāt □, Afghan. 40 B3
Hérault □, France 18 E5
Herbert →, Australia 62 B4
Herbert Downs, Australia 62 C2
Herberton, Australia 62 B4
Hercegnovi, Montenegro, Yug. 21 C8
Herðubreið, Iceland 8 D5
Hereford, U.K. 11 E5
Hereford, U.S.A. 81 H3
Hereford and Worcester □, U.K. 11 E5
Herentals, Belgium 15 C4
Herford, Germany 16 B4
Herington, U.S.A. 80 F6
Herjehogna, Norway 9 F12
Herkimer, U.S.A. 79 D10
Herlong, U.S.A. 84 E6
Herman, U.S.A. 80 C6
Hermann, U.S.A. 80 F9
Hermannsburg Mission, Australia 60 D5
Hermanus, S. Africa 56 E2
Hermidale, Australia 63 E4
Hermiston, U.S.A. 82 D4
Hermitage, N.Z. 59 K3
Hermite, I., Chile 96 H3
Hermon, Mt. = Ash Shaykh, J., Lebanon 47 B4
Hermosillo, Mexico 86 B2
Hernád →, Hungary 17 E10
Hernandarias, Paraguay 95 B5
Hernandez, U.S.A. 84 J6
Hernando, Argentina 94 C3
Hernando, U.S.A. 81 H10
Herne, Germany 15 C7
Herne Bay, U.K. 11 F9
Herning, Denmark 9 H10
Heroica = Caborca, Mexico 86 A2
Heroica Nogales = Nogales, Mexico 86 A2
Heron Bay, Canada 70 C2
Herradura, Pta. de la, Canary Is. 22 F5
Herreid, U.S.A. 80 C4
Herrera, Spain 19 D3
Herrick, Australia 62 G4
Herrin, U.S.A. 81 G10
Hersonissos, Greece 23 D7
Herstal, Belgium 15 D5
Hertford, U.K. 11 F7
Hertfordshire □, U.K. 11 F7
's-Hertogenbosch, Neths. 15 C5
Hertzogville, S. Africa 56 D4
Herzliyya, Israel 47 C3
Ḩeşār, Fārs, Iran 45 D6
Ḩeşār, Markazī, Iran 45 C6
Heshui, China 34 G5
Heshun, China 34 F7
Hesperia, U.S.A. 85 L9
Hesse = Hessen □, Germany 16 C4
Hessen □, Germany 16 C4
Hetch Hetchy Aqueduct, U.S.A. 84 H5
Hettinger, U.S.A. 80 C3
Hewett, C., Canada 69 A13
Hexham, U.K. 10 C5
Hexigten Qi, China 35 C9
Hexrivier, S. Africa 56 E2
Ḩeydarābād, Iran 45 D7
Heyfield, Australia 63 F4
Heysham, U.K. 10 C5
Heywood, Australia 63 F3
Heze, China 34 G8
Hi Vista, U.S.A. 85 L9
Hialeah, U.S.A. 77 N5
Hiawatha, Kans., U.S.A. 80 F7
Hiawatha, Utah, U.S.A. 82 G8
Hibbing, U.S.A. 80 B8
Hibbs B., Australia 62 G4
Hibernia Reef, Australia 60 B3
Hickory, U.S.A. 77 H5
Hicks, Pt., Australia 63 F4
Hicksville, U.S.A. 79 F11
Hida-Gawa →, Japan 31 G8
Hida-Sammyaku, Japan 31 F8
Hidaka-Sammyaku, Japan 30 C11
Hidalgo, Mexico 87 C5
Hidalgo □, Mexico 87 C5
Hidalgo, Presa M., Mexico 86 B3
Hidalgo, Pta. del, Canary Is. 22 F3
Hidalgo del Parral, Mexico 86 B3
Hierro, Canary Is. 22 G1
Higashiajima-San, Japan 30 F10
Higashiōsaka, Japan 31 G7
Higgins, U.S.A. 81 G4
Higgins Corner, U.S.A. 84 F5
Higginsville, Australia 61 F3
High Atlas = Haut Atlas, Morocco 50 B3
High I., Canada 71 A7
High Island, U.S.A. 81 L7
High Level, Canada 72 B5
High Point, U.S.A. 77 H6
High Prairie, Canada 72 B5
High River, Canada 72 C6
High Springs, U.S.A. 77 L4
High Wycombe, U.K. 11 F7
Highbury, Australia 62 B3
Highland □, U.K. 12 D4
Highland Park, U.S.A. 76 D2
Highmore, U.S.A. 80 C5
Highrock L., Canada 73 B7
Higüay, Dom. Rep. 89 C6
Hiiumaa, Estonia 24 C3
Ḩijāz □, Si. Arabia 46 C2
Hijo = Tagum, Phil. 37 C7
Hikari, Japan 31 H5
Hiko, U.S.A. 83 H6
Hikone, Japan 31 G8
Hikurangi, N.Z. 59 F5
Hikurangi, Mt., N.Z. 59 H6
Hildesheim, Germany 16 B4
Hill →, Australia 61 F2
Hill City, Idaho, U.S.A. 82 E6
Hill City, Kans., U.S.A. 80 F5
Hill City, Minn., U.S.A. 80 B8
Hill City, S. Dak., U.S.A. 80 D3
Hill Island L., Canada 73 A7
Hillcrest Center, U.S.A. 85 K8
Hillegom, Neths. 15 B4
Hillingdon, U.K. 11 F7
Hillman, U.S.A. 76 C4
Hillmond, Canada 73 C7
Hillsboro, Kans., U.S.A. 80 F6
Hillsboro, N. Dak., U.S.A. 80 B6
Hillsboro, N.H., U.S.A. 79 C13
Hillsboro, N. Mex., U.S.A. 83 K10
Hillsboro, Oreg., U.S.A. 84 E4
Hillsboro, Tex., U.S.A. 81 J6
Hillsborough, Grenada 89 D7
Hillsdale, Mich., U.S.A. 76 E3

Hillsdale, N.Y., U.S.A. 79 D11
Hillside, Australia 60 D2
Hillsport, Canada 70 C2
Hillston, Australia 63 E4
Hilo, U.S.A. 74 J17
Hilton, U.S.A. 78 C7
Hilversum, Neths. 15 B5
Himachal Pradesh □, India 42 D7
Himalaya, Asia 43 E11
Himatnagar, India 40 H8
Himeji, Japan 31 G7
Himi, Japan 31 F8
Ḥimṣ, Syria 47 A5
Ḥims □, Syria 47 A5
Hinche, Haiti 89 C5
Hinchinbrook I., Australia 62 B4
Hinckley, U.K. 11 E6
Hinckley, U.S.A. 82 G7
Hindaun, India 42 F7
Hindmarsh, L., Australia 63 F3
Hindu Bagh, Pakistan 42 D2
Hindu Kush, Asia 40 B7
Hindubagh, Pakistan 40 D5
Hindupur, India 40 N10
Hines Creek, Canada 72 B5
Hinganghat, India 40 J11
Hingham, U.S.A. 82 B8
Hingoli, India 40 K10
Hinna = Imi, Ethiopia 46 F3
Hinsdale, U.S.A. 82 B10
Hinton, Canada 72 C5
Hinton, U.S.A. 76 G5
Hippolytushoef, Neths. 15 B4
Hirado, Japan 31 H4
Hirakud Dam, India 41 J13
Hiratsuka, Japan 31 G9
Hiroo, Japan 30 C11
Hirosaki, Japan 30 D10
Hiroshima, Japan 31 G6
Hiroshima □, Japan 31 G6
Hisar, India 42 E6
Hisb —►, Iraq 44 D5
Ḥismá, Si. Arabia 44 D3
Hispaniola, W. Indies 89 C5
Hīt, Iraq 44 C4
Hita, Japan 31 H5
Hitachi, Japan 31 F10
Hitchin, U.K. 11 F7
Hitoyoshi, Japan 31 H5
Hitra, Norway 8 E10
Ḥiyyon, N. —►, Israel 47 E4
Hjalmar L., Canada 73 A7
Hjälmaren, Sweden 9 G13
Hjørring, Denmark 9 H10
Hluhluwe, S. Africa 57 D5
Ho, Ghana 50 G5
Ho Chi Minh City = Phanh Bho Ho Chi Minh, Vietnam 39 G6
Ho Thuong, Vietnam 38 C5
Hoa Binh, Vietnam 38 B5
Hoa Da, Vietnam 39 G7
Hoa Hiep, Vietnam 39 G5
Hoai Nhon, Vietnam 38 E7
Hoare B., Canada 69 B13
Hobart, Australia 62 G4
Hobart, U.S.A. 81 H5
Hobbs, U.S.A. 81 J3
Hobbs Coast, Antarctica 5 D14
Hoboken, Belgium 15 C4
Hoboken, U.S.A. 79 F10
Hobro, Denmark 9 H10
Hoburgen, Sweden 9 H15
Hodaka-Dake, Japan 31 F8
Hodgson, Canada 73 C9
Hódmezövásárhely, Hungary 17 E10
Hodna, Chott el, Algeria 50 A5
Hodonín, Czech. 16 D8
Hoeamdong, N. Korea 35 C16
Hoek van Holland, Neths. 15 C4
Hoengsŏng, S. Korea 35 F14
Hoeryong, N. Korea 35 C15
Hoeyang, N. Korea 35 E14
Hof, Germany 16 C5
Hof, Iceland 8 D6
Höfðakaupstaður, Iceland 8 D3
Hofmeyr, S. Africa 56 E4
Hofsjökull, Iceland 8 D4
Hofsós, Iceland 8 D4
Hōfu, Japan 31 G5
Hogan Group, Australia 62 F4
Hogansville, U.S.A. 77 J3
Hogeland, U.S.A. 82 B9
Hoggar = Ahaggar, Algeria 50 D6
Hogsty Reef, Bahamas 89 B5
Hoh —►, U.S.A. 84 C2
Hohe Rhön, Germany 16 C4
Hohe Venn, Belgium 15 D6
Hohenwald, U.S.A. 77 H2
Hohhot, China 34 D6
Hóhlakas, Greece 23 D9
Hoi An, Vietnam 38 E7
Hoi Xuan, Vietnam 38 B5
Hoisington, U.S.A. 80 F5
Hōjō, Japan 31 H6
Hokianga Harbour, N.Z. 59 F4
Hokitika, N.Z. 59 K3
Hokkaidō □, Japan 30 C11
Holbrook, Australia 63 F4
Holbrook, U.S.A. 83 J8
Holden, Canada 72 C6
Holden, U.S.A. 82 G7
Holdenville, U.S.A. 81 H6
Holderness, U.K. 10 D7
Holdfast, Canada 73 C7
Holdrege, U.S.A. 80 E5
Holguín, Cuba 88 B4
Hollams Bird I., Namibia 56 C1
Holland, U.S.A. 76 D2
Hollandia = Jayapura, Indonesia 37 E10
Hollidaysburg, U.S.A. 78 F6
Hollis, U.S.A. 81 H5
Hollister, Calif., U.S.A. 83 H3
Hollister, Idaho, U.S.A. 82 E6
Holly, U.S.A. 80 F3
Holly Hill, U.S.A. 77 L5
Holly Springs, U.S.A. 81 H10
Hollywood, Calif., U.S.A. 83 J4
Hollywood, Fla., U.S.A. 77 N5
Holman Island, Canada 68 A8
Hólmavík, Iceland 8 D3
Holmes Reefs, Australia 62 B4
Holmsund, Sweden 8 E16
Holroyd —►, Australia 62 A3
Holstebro, Denmark 9 H10
Holsworthy, U.K. 11 G3
Holt, Iceland 8 E4
Holton, Canada 71 B8
Holton, U.S.A. 80 F7
Holtville, U.S.A. 85 N11
Holwerd, Neths. 15 A5
Holy Cross, U.S.A. 68 B4
Holy I., Gwynedd, U.K. 10 D3
Holy I., Northumb., U.K. 10 B6
Holyhead, U.K. 10 D3
Holyoke, Colo., U.S.A. 80 E3
Holyoke, Mass., U.S.A. 79 D12
Holyrood, Canada 71 C9
Homa Bay, Kenya 54 C3
Homa Bay □, Kenya 54 C3
Homalin, Burma 41 G19
Homand, Iran 45 C8
Hombori, Mali 50 E4
Home B., Canada 69 B13
Home Hill, Australia 62 B4
Homedale, U.S.A. 82 E5
Homer, Alaska, U.S.A. 68 C4
Homer, La., U.S.A. 81 J8
Homestead, Australia 62 C4
Homestead, Fla., U.S.A. 77 N5
Homestead, Oreg., U.S.A. 82 D5
Homewood, U.S.A. 84 F6
Hominy, U.S.A. 81 G6
Homoine, Mozam. 57 C6
Homs = Ḥimṣ, Syria 47 A5
Hon Chong, Vietnam 39 G5
Hon Me, Vietnam 38 C5
Hon Quan, Vietnam 39 G6
Honan = Henan □, China 34 G8
Honbetsu, Japan 30 C11
Honcut, U.S.A. 84 F5
Honda, Colombia 92 B4
Hondeklipbaai, S. Africa 56 E2
Hondo, Japan 31 H5
Hondo, U.S.A. 81 L5
Hondo —►, Belize 87 D7
Honduras ■, Cent. Amer. 88 D2
Honduras, G. de, Caribbean 88 C2
Hønefoss, Norway 9 F11
Honesdale, U.S.A. 79 E9
Honey L., U.S.A. 84 E6
Honfleur, France 18 B4
Hong Gai, Vietnam 38 B6
Hong He —►, China 34 H8
Hong Kong ■, Asia 33 D6
Hongchŏn, S. Korea 35 F14
Hongjiang, China 33 D5
Hongliu He —►, China 34 F5
Hongor, Mongolia 34 B7
Hongsa, Laos 38 C3
Hongshui He —►, China 33 D5
Hongsŏng, S. Korea 35 F14
Hongtong, China 34 F6
Honguedo, Détroit d', Canada 71 C7
Hongwon, N. Korea 35 E14
Hongze Hu, China 35 H10
Honiara, Solomon Is. 64 H7
Honiton, U.K. 11 G4
Honjō, Japan 30 E10
Honolulu, U.S.A. 74 H16
Honshū, Japan 31 G9
Hood, Pt., Australia 61 F2
Hood Mt., U.S.A. 82 D3
Hood River, U.S.A. 82 D3
Hoodsport, U.S.A. 84 C3
Hoogeveen, Neths. 15 B6
Hoogezand, Neths. 15 A6
Hooghly = Hughli —►, India 43 J13
Hooghly-Chinsura = Chunchura, India 43 H13
Hook Hd., Ireland 13 D5
Hook I., Australia 62 C4
Hook of Holland = Hoek van Holland, Neths. 15 C4
Hooker, U.S.A. 81 G4
Hooker Creek, Australia 60 C5
Hoopeston, U.S.A. 76 E2
Hoopstad, S. Africa 56 D4
Hoorn, Neths. 15 B5
Hoover Dam, U.S.A. 85 K12
Hooversville, U.S.A. 78 F6
Hop Bottom, U.S.A. 79 E9
Hope, Canada 72 D4
Hope, Ariz., U.S.A. 85 M13
Hope, Ark., U.S.A. 81 J8
Hope, N. Dak., U.S.A. 80 B6
Hope, L., Australia 63 D2
Hope Pt., U.S.A. 68 B3
Hope Town, Bahamas 88 A4
Hopedale, Canada 71 A7
Hopefield, S. Africa 56 E2
Hopei = Hebei □, China 34 E9
Hopelchén, Mexico 87 D7
Hopetoun, Vic., Australia 63 F3
Hopetoun, W. Austral., Australia 61 F3
Hopetown, S. Africa 56 D3
Hopkins, U.S.A. 80 E7
Hopkins, L., Australia 60 D4
Hopkinsville, U.S.A. 77 G2
Hopland, U.S.A. 84 G3
Hoquiam, U.S.A. 84 D3
Hordaland fylke □, Norway 9 F9
Horden Hills, Australia 60 D5
Horinger, China 34 D6
Horlick Mts., Antarctica 5 E15
Hormoz, Iran 45 E7
Hormoz, Jaz. ye, Iran 45 E8
Hormuz Str., The Gulf 45 E8
Horn, Austria 16 D7
Horn, Ísafjarðarsýsla, Iceland 8 C2
Horn, Suður-Múlasýsla, Iceland 8 D7
Horn —►, Canada 72 A5
Horn, Cape = Hornos, C. de, Chile 96 H3
Horn Head, Ireland 13 A3
Horn I., Australia 62 A3
Horn I., U.S.A. 77 K1
Horn Mts., Canada 72 A5
Hornavan, Sweden 8 C14
Hornbeck, U.S.A. 81 K8
Hornbrook, U.S.A. 82 F2
Horncastle, U.K. 10 D7
Hornell, U.S.A. 78 D7
Hornell L., Canada 72 A5
Hornepayne, Canada 70 C3
Hornitos, U.S.A. 84 H6
Hornos, C. de, Chile 96 H3
Hornsby, Australia 63 E5
Hornsea, U.K. 10 D7
Horobetsu, Japan 30 C10
Horqin Youyi Qianqi, China 35 A12
Horqueta, Paraguay 94 A4
Horse Cr. —►, U.S.A. 80 E3
Horse Is., Canada 71 B8
Horsefly L., Canada 72 C4
Horsens, Denmark 9 J10
Horsham, Australia 63 F3
Horsham, U.K. 11 F7
Horten, Norway 9 G11
Horton, U.S.A. 80 F7
Horton —►, Canada 68 B7
Horwood, L., Canada 70 C3
Hose, Gunung-Gunung, Malaysia 36 D4
Ḥoseynābād, Khuzestān, Iran 45 C6
Ḥoseynābād, Kordestān, Iran 44 C5
Hoshangabad, India 42 H7
Hoshiarpur, India 42 D6
Hosmer, U.S.A. 80 C5
Hospet, India 40 M10
Hospitalet de Llobregat, Spain 19 B7
Hoste, I., Chile 96 H3
Hot, Thailand 38 C2
Hot Creek Ra., U.S.A. 82 G5
Hot Springs, Ark., U.S.A. 81 H8
Hot Springs, S. Dak., U.S.A. 80 D3
Hotagen, Sweden 8 E13
Hotan, China 32 C2
Hotazel, S. Africa 56 D3
Hotchkiss, U.S.A. 83 G10
Hotham, C., Australia 60 B5
Hoting, Sweden 8 D14
Hotte, Massif de la, Haiti 89 C5
Hottentotsbaai, Namibia 56 D1
Houck, U.S.A. 83 J9
Houei Sai, Laos 38 B3
Houffalize, Belgium 15 D5
Houghton, U.S.A. 80 B10
Houghton L., U.S.A. 76 C3
Houghton-le-Spring, U.K. 10 C6
Houhora, N.Z. 59 F4
Houlton, U.S.A. 71 C6
Houma, U.S.A. 81 L9
Houston, Canada 72 C3
Houston, Mo., U.S.A. 81 G9
Houston, Tex., U.S.A. 81 L7
Houtman Abrolhos, Australia 61 E1
Hovd, Mongolia 32 B4
Hove, U.K. 11 G7
Hoveyzeh, Iran 45 D6
Hövsgöl, Mongolia 34 C5
Hövsgöl Nuur, Mongolia 32 A5
Howard, Australia 63 D5
Howard, Kans., U.S.A. 81 G6
Howard, Pa., U.S.A. 78 E7
Howard, S. Dak., U.S.A. 80 C6
Howard I., Australia 62 A2
Howard L., Canada 73 A7
Howe, U.S.A. 82 E7
Howe, C., Australia 63 F5
Howell, U.S.A. 76 D4
Howick, Canada 79 A11
Howick, S. Africa 57 D5
Howick Group, Australia 62 A4
Howitt, L., Australia 63 D2
Howley, Canada 71 C8
Howrah = Haora, India 43 H13
Howth Hd., Ireland 13 C5
Hoy, U.K. 12 C5
Høyanger, Norway 9 F9
Hpungan Pass, Burma 41 F20
Hradec Králové, Czech. 16 C7
Hron —►, Czech. 17 E9
Hrvatska = Croatia ■, Europe 20 B7
Hsenwi, Burma 41 H20
Hsiamen = Xiamen, China 33 D6
Hsian = Xi'an, China 34 G5
Hsinhailien = Lianyungang, China 35 G10
Hsisha Chuntao, Pac. Oc. 36 A4
Hsüchou = Xuzhou, China 35 G9
Hu Xian, China 34 G5
Hua Hin, Thailand 38 F2
Hua Xian, Henan, China 34 G8
Hua Xian, Shaanxi, China 34 G5
Huachinera, Mexico 86 A3
Huacho, Peru 92 F3
Huachón, Peru 92 F3
Huade, China 34 D7
Huadian, China 35 C14
Huai He —►, China 33 C6
Huai Yot, Thailand 39 J2
Huai'an, Hebei, China 34 D8
Huai'an, Jiangsu, China 35 H10
Huaide, China 35 C13
Huaidezhen, China 35 C13
Huainan, China 33 C6
Huairen, China 34 E7
Huairou, China 34 D9
Huaiyang, China 34 H8
Huaiyuan, China 35 H9
Huajianzi, China 35 D13
Huajuapan de Leon, Mexico 87 D5
Hualapai Pk., U.S.A. 83 J7
Huallaga —►, Peru 92 E3
Huambo, Angola 53 G3
Huan Jiang —►, China 34 G5
Huan Xian, China 34 F4
Huancabamba, Peru 92 E3
Huancane, Peru 92 G5
Huancapi, Peru 92 F4
Huancavelica, Peru 92 F3
Huancayo, Peru 92 F3
Huang Hai = Yellow Sea, China 35 G12
Huang He —►, China 35 F10
Huang Xian, China 35 F11
Huangling, China 34 G5
Huanglong, China 34 G5
Huangshi, China 33 C6
Huangsongdian, China 35 C14
Huantai, China 35 F9
Huánuco, Peru 92 E3
Huaraz, Peru 92 E3
Huarmey, Peru 92 F3
Huascarán, Peru 92 E3
Huasco, Chile 94 B1
Huasco —►, Chile 94 B1
Huasna, U.S.A. 85 K6
Huatabampo, Mexico 86 B3
Huauchinango, Mexico 87 C5
Huautla de Jiménez, Mexico 87 D5
Huay Namota, Mexico 86 C4
Huayin, China 34 G6
Huayllay, Peru 92 F3
Hubbard, U.S.A. 81 K6
Hubbart Pt., Canada 73 B10
Hubei □, China 33 C6
Hubli-Dharwad = Dharwad, India 40 M9
Huchang, N. Korea 35 D14
Huddersfield, U.K. 10 D6
Hudiksvall, Sweden 9 F14
Hudson, Canada 73 C10
Hudson, Mass., U.S.A. 79 D13
Hudson, Mich., U.S.A. 76 E3
Hudson, N.Y., U.S.A. 79 D11
Hudson, Wis., U.S.A. 80 C8
Hudson, Wyo., U.S.A. 82 E9
Hudson —►, U.S.A. 79 F10
Hudson Bay, N.W.T., Canada 69 C11
Hudson Bay, Sask., Canada 73 C8
Hudson Falls, U.S.A. 79 C11
Hudson Mts., Antarctica 5 D16
Hudson Str., Canada 69 B13
Hudson's Hope, Canada 72 B4
Hue, Vietnam 38 D6
Huehuetenango, Guatemala 88 C1
Huejúcar, Mexico 86 C4
Huelva, Spain 19 D2
Huentelauquén, Chile 94 C1
Huerta, Sa. de la, Argentina 94 C2
Huesca, Spain 19 A5
Huetamo, Mexico 86 D4
Hugh —►, Australia 62 D1
Hughenden, Australia 62 C3
Hughes, Australia 61 F4
Hughli —►, India 43 J13
Hugo, U.S.A. 80 F3
Hugoton, U.S.A. 81 G4
Hui Xian, Gansu, China 34 H4
Hui Xian, Henan, China 34 G7
Hui'anbu, China 34 F4
Huichapán, Mexico 87 C5
Huifa He —►, China 35 C14
Huila, Nevado del, Colombia 92 C3
Huimin, China 35 F9
Huinan, China 35 C14
Huinca Renancó, Argentina 94 C3
Huining, China 34 G3
Huinong, China 34 E4
Huiting, China 34 G9
Huixtla, Mexico 87 D6
Huize, China 32 D5
Hukawng Valley, Burma 41 F20
Hukuntsi, Botswana 56 C3
Ḥulayfā', Si. Arabia 44 E4
Huld, Mongolia 34 B3
Hulin He —►, China 35 B12
Hull = Kingston upon Hull, U.K. 10 D7
Hull, Canada 70 C4
Hull —►, U.K. 10 D7
Hulst, Neths. 15 C4
Hulun Nur, China 33 B6
Humahuaca, Argentina 94 A2
Humaitá, Brazil 92 E6
Humaitá, Paraguay 94 B4
Humansdorp, S. Africa 56 E3
Humbe, Angola 56 B1
Humber —►, U.K. 10 D7
Humberside □, U.K. 10 D7
Humbert River, Australia 60 C5
Humble, U.S.A. 81 L8
Humboldt, Canada 73 C7
Humboldt, Iowa, U.S.A. 80 D7
Humboldt, Tenn., U.S.A. 81 H10
Humboldt —►, U.S.A. 82 F4
Humboldt Gletscher, Greenland 4 B4
Hume, U.S.A. 84 J8
Hume, L., Australia 63 F4
Humphreys, Mt., U.S.A. 84 H8
Humphreys Pk., U.S.A. 83 J8
Humptulips, U.S.A. 84 C3
Hūn, Libya 51 C8
Hun Jiang —►, China 35 D13
Húnaflói, Iceland 8 D3
Hunan □, China 33 D6
Hunchun, China 35 C16
Hundred Mile House, Canada 72 C4
Hunedoara, Romania 17 F11
Hung Yen, Vietnam 38 B6
Hungary ■, Europe 17 E9
Hungary, Plain of, Europe 6 F9
Hungerford, Australia 63 D3
Hŭngnam, N. Korea 35 E14
Hunsberge, Namibia 56 D2
Hunsrück, Germany 16 D3
Hunstanton, U.K. 10 E8
Hunter, N. Dak., U.S.A. 80 B6
Hunter, N.Y., U.S.A. 79 D10
Hunter I., Australia 62 G3
Hunter I., Canada 72 C3
Hunter Ra., Australia 63 E5
Hunters Road, Zimbabwe 55 F2
Hunterville, N.Z. 59 H5
Huntingburg, U.S.A. 76 F2
Huntingdon, Canada 70 C5
Huntingdon, U.K. 11 E7
Huntingdon, U.S.A. 78 F6
Huntington, Ind., U.S.A. 76 E3
Huntington, N.Y., U.S.A. 79 F11
Huntington, Oreg., U.S.A. 82 D5
Huntington, Utah, U.S.A. 82 G8
Huntington, W. Va., U.S.A. 76 F4
Huntington Beach, U.S.A. 85 M8
Huntington Park, U.S.A. 83 K4
Huntly, N.Z. 59 G5
Huntly, U.K. 12 D6
Huntsville, Canada 70 C4
Huntsville, Ala., U.S.A. 77 H2
Huntsville, Tex., U.S.A. 81 K7
Hunyani —►, Zimbabwe 55 F3
Hunyuan, China 34 E7
Hunza —►, India 43 B6
Huo Xian, China 34 F6
Huong Hoa, Vietnam 38 D6
Huong Khe, Vietnam 38 C5
Huonville, Australia 62 G4
Hupeh = Hubei □, China 33 C6
Hūr, Iran 45 D8
Hure Qi, China 35 C11
Hurley, N. Mex., U.S.A. 83 K9
Hurley, Wis., U.S.A. 80 B9
Huron, Calif., U.S.A. 84 J6
Huron, Ohio, U.S.A. 78 E2
Huron, S. Dak., U.S.A. 80 C5
Huron, L., N. Amer. 78 B2
Hurricane, U.S.A. 83 H7
Hurunui —►, N.Z. 59 K4
Húsavík, Iceland 8 C5
Huskvarna, Sweden 9 H13
Hussar, Canada 72 C6
Hutchinson, Kans., U.S.A. 81 F6
Hutchinson, Minn., U.S.A. 80 C7
Huttig, U.S.A. 81 J8
Hutton, Mt., Australia 63 D4
Huy, Belgium 15 D5
Hvammur, Iceland 8 D3
Hvar, Croatia 20 C7
Hvítá, Iceland 8 D3
Hvítá —►, Iceland 8 D3
Hvitárvatn, Iceland 8 D4
Hwachon-chosuji, S. Korea 35 E14
Hwang Ho = Huang He —►, China 35 F10
Hwange, Zimbabwe 55 F2
Hwange Nat. Park, Zimbabwe 56 B4
Hyannis, U.S.A. 80 E4
Hyargas Nuur, Mongolia 32 B4
Hyden, Australia 61 F2
Hyderabad, India 40 L11
Hyderabad, Pakistan 42 G3
Hyères, France 18 E7
Hyesan, N. Korea 35 D15
Hyland —►, Canada 72 B3
Hymia, India 43 C8
Hyndman Pk., U.S.A. 82 E6

Hyōgo □, *Japan* 31 G7
Hyrum, *U.S.A.* 82 F8
Hysham, *U.S.A.* 82 C10
Hythe, *U.K.* 11 F9
Hyūga, *Japan* 31 H5
Hyvinge = Hyvinkää, *Finland* 9 F18
Hyvinkää, *Finland* 9 F18

I

I-n-Gall, *Niger* 50 E6
Iaco —►, *Brazil* 92 E5
Iakora, *Madag.* 57 C8
Ialomiţa —►, *Romania* 17 F13
Iaşi, *Romania* 17 E13
Iba, *Phil.* 37 A6
Ibadan, *Nigeria* 50 G5
Ibagué, *Colombia* 92 C3
Ibar —►, *Serbia, Yug.* 21 C9
Ibaraki □, *Japan* 31 F10
Ibarra, *Ecuador* 92 C3
Ibembo, *Zaïre* 54 B1
Ibera, L., *Argentina* 94 B4
Iberian Peninsula, *Europe* 6 H5
Iberville, *Canada* 70 C5
Iberville, Lac d', *Canada* 70 A5
Ibi, *Nigeria* 50 G6
Ibiá, *Brazil* 93 G9
Ibicuy, *Argentina* 94 C4
Ibioapaba, Sa. da, *Brazil* 93 D10
Ibiza, *Spain* 22 C7
Ibo, *Mozam.* 55 E5
Ibonma, *Indonesia* 37 E8
Ibotirama, *Brazil* 93 F10
Ibrāhīm —►, *Lebanon* 47 A4
Ibu, *Indonesia* 37 D7
Ibusuki, *Japan* 31 J5
Icá, *Peru* 92 F3
Iça —►, *Brazil* 92 D5
Içana, *Brazil* 92 C5
Içel = Mersin, *Turkey* 25 G5
Iceland ■, *Atl. Oc.* 8 D4
Icha, *Russia* 27 D16
Ich'ang = Yichang, *China* 33 C6
Ichchapuram, *India* 41 K14
Ichihara, *Japan* 31 G10
Ichikawa, *Japan* 31 G9
Ichilo —►, *Bolivia* 92 G6
Ichinohe, *Japan* 30 D10
Ichinomiya, *Japan* 31 G8
Ichinoseki, *Japan* 30 E10
Ichŏn, *S. Korea* 35 F14
Icod, *Canary Is.* 22 F3
Icy Str., *U.S.A.* 72 B1
Ida Grove, *U.S.A.* 80 D7
Ida Valley, *Australia* 61 E3
Idabel, *U.S.A.* 81 J7
Idaho □, *U.S.A.* 82 D6
Idaho City, *U.S.A.* 82 E6
Idaho Falls, *U.S.A.* 82 E7
Idaho Springs, *U.S.A.* 82 G11
Idd el Ghanam, *Sudan* 51 F9
Iddan, *Somali Rep.* 46 F4
Idehan, *Libya* 51 C7
Idehan Marzūq, *Libya* 51 D7
Idelès, *Algeria* 50 D6
Idfû, *Egypt* 51 D11
Ídhi Óros, *Greece* 23 D6
Ídhra, *Greece* 21 F10
Idi, *Indonesia* 36 C1
Idiofa, *Zaïre* 52 E3
Idlib, *Syria* 44 C3
Idria, *U.S.A.* 84 J6
Idutywa, *S. Africa* 57 E4
Ieper, *Belgium* 15 D2
Ierápetra, *Greece* 23 E7
Ierzu, *Italy* 20 E3
'Ifāl, W. al —►, *Si. Arabia* 44 D2
Ifanadiana, *Madag.* 57 C8
Ife, *Nigeria* 50 G5
Iffley, *Australia* 62 B3
Ifni, *Morocco* 50 C2
Iforas, Adrar des, *Mali* 50 E5
Ifould, L., *Australia* 61 F5
Iganga, *Uganda* 54 B3
Igarapava, *Brazil* 93 H9
Igarapé Açu, *Brazil* 93 D9
Igarka, *Russia* 26 C9
Igatimi, *Paraguay* 95 A4
Igbetti, *Nigeria* 50 G5
Iggesund, *Sweden* 9 F14
Iglésias, *Italy* 20 E3
Igli, *Algeria* 50 B4
Igloolik, *Canada* 69 B11
Ignace, *Canada* 70 C1
Iguaçu —►, *Brazil* 95 B5
Iguaçu, Cat. del, *Brazil* 95 B5
Iguaçu Falls = Iguaçu, Cat. del, *Brazil* 95 B5
Iguala, *Mexico* 87 D5
Igualada, *Spain* 19 B6
Iguassu = Iguaçu —►, *Brazil* 95 B5
Iguatu, *Brazil* 93 E11
Iguéla, *Gabon* 52 E1
Igunga □, *Tanzania* 54 C3
Iheya-Shima, *Japan* 31 L3
Ihosy, *Madag.* 57 C8
Ihotry, L., *Madag.* 57 C7
Ii, *Finland* 8 D18
Ii-Shima, *Japan* 31 L3
Iida, *Japan* 31 G8
Iijoki —►, *Finland* 8 D18
Iisalmi, *Finland* 8 E19
Iiyama, *Japan* 31 F9
Iizuka, *Japan* 31 H5
Ijebu-Ode, *Nigeria* 50 G5
IJmuiden, *Neths.* 15 B4
IJssel —►, *Neths.* 15 B5
IJsselmeer, *Neths.* 15 B5
Ijuí —►, *Brazil* 95 B4
Ikaría, *Greece* 21 F12
Ikeda, *Japan* 31 G6
Ikela, *Zaïre* 52 E4
Iki, *Japan* 31 H4
Ikimba L., *Tanzania* 54 C3
Ikopa —►, *Madag.* 57 B8
Ikungu, *Tanzania* 54 C3
Ilagan, *Phil.* 37 A6
Īlām, *Iran* 44 C5
Ilam, *Nepal* 43 F12
Ilanskiy, *Russia* 27 D10
Ilbilbie, *Australia* 62 C4
Ile-à-la-Crosse, *Canada* 73 B7
Ile-à-la-Crosse, Lac, *Canada* 73 B7
Île-de-France, *France* 18 B5
Ilebo, *Zaïre* 52 E4
Ileje □, *Tanzania* 55 D3
Ilek, *Russia* 26 D6
Ilek —►, *Russia* 24 D9
Ilford, *Canada* 73 B9
Ilfracombe, *Australia* 62 C3
Ilfracombe, *U.K.* 11 F3
Ilhéus, *Brazil* 93 F11
Ili —►, *Kazakhstan* 26 E8
Ilich, *Kazakhstan* 26 E7
Iliff, *U.S.A.* 80 E3
Iligan, *Phil.* 37 C6
Iliodhrómia, *Greece* 21 E10
Ilion, *U.S.A.* 79 D9
Ilkeston, *U.K.* 10 E6
Illampu = Ancohuma, Nevada, *Bolivia* 92 G5
Illana B., *Phil.* 37 C6
Illapel, *Chile* 94 C1
Ille-et-Vilaine □, *France* 18 B3
Iller —►, *Germany* 16 D4
Illetas, *Spain* 22 B9
Illimani, *Bolivia* 92 G5
Illinois □, *U.S.A.* 75 C9
Illinois —►, *U.S.A.* 75 C8
Ilmen, Oz., *Russia* 24 C5
Ilo, *Peru* 92 G4
Iloilo, *Phil.* 37 B6
Ilorin, *Nigeria* 50 G5
Ilwaco, *U.S.A.* 84 D2
Ilwaki, *Indonesia* 37 F7
Imabari, *Japan* 31 G6
Imaloto —►, *Madag.* 57 C8
Imandra, Oz., *Russia* 24 A5
Imari, *Japan* 31 H4
Imbler, *U.S.A.* 82 D5
imeni 26 Bakinskikh Komissarov, *Azerbaijan* 25 G8
imeni 26 Bakinskikh Komissarov, *Turkmenistan* 25 G9
Imeni Poliny Osipenko, *Russia* 27 D14
Imeri, Serra, *Brazil* 92 C5
Imerimandroso, *Madag.* 57 B8
Imi, *Ethiopia* 46 F3
Imlay, *U.S.A.* 82 F4
Imlay City, *U.S.A.* 78 C1
Immingham, *U.K.* 10 D7
Immokalee, *U.S.A.* 77 M5
Imola, *Italy* 20 B4
Imperatriz, *Brazil* 93 E9
Impéria, *Italy* 20 C3
Imperial, *Canada* 73 C7
Imperial, *Calif., U.S.A.* 85 N11
Imperial, *Nebr., U.S.A.* 80 E4
Imperial Beach, *U.S.A.* 85 N9
Imperial Dam, *U.S.A.* 85 N12
Imperial Res., *U.S.A.* 85 N12
Imperial Valley, *U.S.A.* 85 N11
Imperieuse Reef, *Australia* 60 C2
Impfondo, *Congo* 52 D3
Imphal, *India* 41 G18
Imuruan B., *Phil.* 37 B5
In Belbel, *Algeria* 50 C5
In Salah, *Algeria* 50 C5
Ina, *Japan* 31 G8
Inangahua Junction, *N.Z.* 59 J3
Inanwatan, *Indonesia* 37 E8
Iñapari, *Peru* 92 F5
Inari, *Finland* 8 B19
Inarijärvi, *Finland* 8 B19
Inawashiro-Ko, *Japan* 30 F10
Inca, *Spain* 22 B9
Incaguasi, *Chile* 94 B1
İnce-Burnu, *Turkey* 25 F5
Inchon, *S. Korea* 35 F14
Incomáti —►, *Mozam.* 57 D5
Indalsälven —►, *Sweden* 8 E14
Indaw, *Burma* 41 G20
Independence, *Calif., U.S.A.* 83 H4
Independence, *Iowa, U.S.A.* 80 D9
Independence, *Kans., U.S.A.* 81 G7
Independence, *Mo., U.S.A.* 80 F7
Independence, *Oreg., U.S.A.* 82 D2
Independence Fjord, *Greenland* 4 A6
Independence Mts., *U.S.A.* 82 F5
Index, *U.S.A.* 84 C5
India ■, *Asia* 40 K11
Indian —►, *U.S.A.* 77 M5
Indian Cabins, *Canada* 72 B5
Indian Harbour, *Canada* 71 B8
Indian Head, *Canada* 73 C8
Indian Ocean 28 K11
Indian Springs, *U.S.A.* 85 J11
Indiana, *U.S.A.* 78 F5
Indiana □, *U.S.A.* 76 E3
Indianapolis, *U.S.A.* 76 F2
Indianola, *Iowa, U.S.A.* 80 E8
Indianola, *Miss., U.S.A.* 81 J9
Indiga, *Russia* 24 A8
Indigirka —►, *Russia* 27 B15
Indio, *U.S.A.* 85 M10
Indonesia ■, *Asia* 36 F5
Indore, *India* 42 H6
Indramayu, *Indonesia* 37 G13
Indravati —►, *India* 41 K12
Indre □, *France* 18 C4
Indre-et-Loire □, *France* 18 C4
Indus —►, *Pakistan* 42 G2
Indus, Mouth of the, *Pakistan* 42 H2
İnebolu, *Turkey* 25 F5
Infiernillo, Presa del, *Mexico* 86 D4
Ingende, *Zaïre* 52 E3
Ingenio, *Canary Is.* 22 G4
Ingenio Santa Ana, *Argentina* 94 B2
Ingersoll, *Canada* 78 C4
Ingham, *Australia* 62 B4
Ingleborough, *U.K.* 10 C5
Inglewood, *Queens., Australia* 63 D5
Inglewood, *Vic., Australia* 63 F3
Inglewood, *N.Z.* 59 H5
Inglewood, *U.S.A.* 85 M8
Ingólfshöfði, *Iceland* 8 E5
Ingolstadt, *Germany* 16 D5
Ingomar, *U.S.A.* 82 C10
Ingonish, *Canada* 71 C7
Ingraj Bazar, *India* 43 G13
Ingrid Christensen Coast, *Antarctica* 5 C6
Ingulec, *Ukraine* 25 E5
Ingwavuma, *S. Africa* 57 D5
Inhaca, I., *Mozam.* 57 D5
Inhafenga, *Mozam.* 57 C5
Inhambane, *Mozam.* 57 C6
Inhambane □, *Mozam.* 57 C5
Inhaminga, *Mozam.* 55 F4
Inharrime, *Mozam.* 57 C6
Inharrime —►, *Mozam.* 57 C6
Ining = Yining, *China* 32 B3
Inirida —►, *Colombia* 92 C5
Inishbofin, *Ireland* 13 C1
Inishmore, *Ireland* 13 C2
Inishowen, *Ireland* 13 A4
Injune, *Australia* 63 D4
Inklin, *Canada* 72 B2
Inklin —►, *Canada* 72 B2
Inkom, *U.S.A.* 82 E7
Inle L., *Burma* 41 J20
Inn —►, *Austria* 16 D6
Innamincka, *Australia* 63 D3
Inner Hebrides, *U.K.* 12 D2
Inner Mongolia = Nei Monggol Zizhiqu □, *China* 34 C6
Inner Sound, *U.K.* 12 D3
Innerkip, *Canada* 78 C4
Innetalling I., *Canada* 70 A4
Innisfail, *Australia* 62 B4
Innisfail, *Canada* 72 C6
In'no-shima, *Japan* 31 G6
Innsbruck, *Austria* 16 E5
Inny —►, *Ireland* 13 C4
Inongo, *Zaïre* 52 E3
Inoucdjouac, *Canada* 69 C12
Inowrocław, *Poland* 17 B9
Inpundong, *N. Korea* 35 D14
Inquisivi, *Bolivia* 92 G5
Inscription, C., *Australia* 61 E1
Insein, *Burma* 41 L20
Inta, *Russia* 24 A11
Intendente Alvear, *Argentina* 94 D3
Interior, *U.S.A.* 80 D4
Interlaken, *Switz.* 16 E3
International Falls, *U.S.A.* 80 A8
Intiyaco, *Argentina* 94 B3
Inútil, B., *Chile* 96 G2
Inuvik, *Canada* 68 B6
Inveraray, *U.K.* 12 E3
Inverbervie, *U.K.* 12 E6
Invercargill, *N.Z.* 59 M2
Inverell, *Australia* 63 D5
Invergordon, *U.K.* 12 D4
Invermere, *Canada* 72 C5
Inverness, *Canada* 71 C7
Inverness, *U.K.* 12 D4
Inverness, *U.S.A.* 77 L4
Inverurie, *U.K.* 12 D6
Inverway, *Australia* 60 C4
Investigator Group, *Australia* 63 E1
Investigator Str., *Australia* 63 F2
Inya, *Russia* 26 D9
Inyanga, *Zimbabwe* 55 F3
Inyangani, *Zimbabwe* 55 F3
Inyantue, *Zimbabwe* 55 F2
Inyo Mts., *U.S.A.* 83 H5
Inyokern, *U.S.A.* 85 K9
Inza, *Russia* 24 D8
Iō-Jima, *Japan* 31 J5
Iola, *U.S.A.* 81 G7
Iona, *U.K.* 12 E2
Ione, *Calif., U.S.A.* 84 G6
Ione, *Wash., U.S.A.* 82 B5
Ionia, *U.S.A.* 76 D3
Ionian Is. = Iónioi Nísoi, *Greece* 21 E9
Ionian Sea, *Europe* 21 E7
Iónioi Nísoi, *Greece* 21 E9
Íos, *Greece* 21 F11
Iowa □, *U.S.A.* 80 D8
Iowa City, *U.S.A.* 80 E9
Iowa Falls, *U.S.A.* 80 D8
Ipala, *Tanzania* 54 C3
Ipameri, *Brazil* 93 G9
Ipatinga, *Brazil* 93 G10
Ipiales, *Colombia* 92 C3
Ipin = Yibin, *China* 32 D5
Ípiros □, *Greece* 21 E9
Ipixuna, *Brazil* 92 E4
Ipoh, *Malaysia* 39 K3
Ippy, *C.A.R.* 51 G9
Ipswich, *Australia* 63 D5
Ipswich, *U.K.* 11 E9
Ipswich, *Mass., U.S.A.* 79 D14
Ipswich, *S. Dak., U.S.A.* 80 C5
Ipu, *Brazil* 93 D10
Iqaluit, *Canada* 69 B13
Iquique, *Chile* 92 H4
Iquitos, *Peru* 92 D4
Irabu-Jima, *Japan* 31 M2
Iracoubo, *Fr. Guiana* 93 B8
Īrafshān, *Iran* 45 E9
Iráklion, *Greece* 23 D7
Iráklion □, *Greece* 23 D7
Irala, *Paraguay* 95 B5
Iramba □, *Tanzania* 54 C3
Iran ■, *Asia* 45 C7
Iran, Gunung-Gunung, *Malaysia* 36 D4
Iran Ra. = Iran, Gunung-Gunung, *Malaysia* 36 D4
Īrānshahr, *Iran* 45 E9
Irapuato, *Mexico* 86 C4
Iraq ■, *Asia* 44 C5
Irati, *Brazil* 95 B5
Irbid, *Jordan* 47 C4
Irbid □, *Jordan* 47 C5
Irebu, *Zaïre* 52 E3
Ireland ■, *Europe* 13 D4
Ireland's Eye, *Ireland* 13 C5
Iret, *Russia* 27 C16
Irhyangdong, *N. Korea* 35 D15
Iri, *S. Korea* 35 G14
Irian Jaya □, *Indonesia* 37 E9
Iringa, *Tanzania* 54 D4
Iringa □, *Tanzania* 54 D4
Iriomote-Jima, *Japan* 31 M1
Iriona, *Honduras* 88 C2
Iriri —►, *Brazil* 93 D8
Irish Republic ■, *Europe* 13 D4
Irish Sea, *Europe* 10 D3
Irkineyeva, *Russia* 27 D10
Irkutsk, *Russia* 27 D11
Irma, *Canada* 73 C6
Irō-Zaki, *Japan* 31 G9
Iron Baron, *Australia* 63 E2
Iron Gate = Portile de Fier, *Europe* 17 F11
Iron Knob, *Australia* 63 E2
Iron Mountain, *U.S.A.* 76 C1
Iron Ra., *Australia* 62 A3
Iron River, *U.S.A.* 80 B10
Ironbridge, *U.K.* 11 E5
Irondequoit, *U.S.A.* 78 C7
Ironstone Kopje, *Botswana* 56 D3
Ironton, *Mo., U.S.A.* 81 G9
Ironton, *Ohio, U.S.A.* 76 F4
Ironwood, *U.S.A.* 80 B9
Iroquois Falls, *Canada* 70 C3
Irrara Cr. —►, *Australia* 63 D4
Irrawaddy □, *Burma* 41 L19
Irrawaddy —►, *Burma* 41 M19
Irtysh —►, *Russia* 26 C7
Irumu, *Zaïre* 54 B2
Irún, *Spain* 19 A5
Irvine, *Canada* 73 D6
Irvine, *U.K.* 12 F4
Irvine, *U.S.A.* 76 G4
Irvine, *Calif., U.S.A.* 85 M9
Irvinestown, *U.K.* 13 B4
Irvona, *U.S.A.* 78 F6
Irwin —►, *Australia* 61 E1
Irymple, *Australia* 63 E3
Isaac —►, *Australia* 62 C4
Isabel, *U.S.A.* 80 C4
Isabela, I., *Mexico* 86 C3
Isabela, *Phil.* 37 C6
Isabella, Cord., *Nic.* 88 D2
Isabella Ra., *Australia* 60 D3
Ísafjarðardjúp, *Iceland* 8 C2
Ísafjörður, *Iceland* 8 C2
Isagarh, *India* 42 G7
Isahaya, *Japan* 31 H5
Isaka, *Tanzania* 54 C3
Isangi, *Zaïre* 52 D4
Isar —►, *Germany* 16 D6
Íschia, *Italy* 20 D5
Isdell —►, *Australia* 60 C3
Ise, *Japan* 31 G8
Ise-Wan, *Japan* 31 G8
Iseramagazi, *Tanzania* 54 C3
Isère □, *France* 18 D6
Isère —►, *France* 18 D6
Ishigaki-Shima, *Japan* 31 M2
Ishikari-Gawa —►, *Japan* 30 C10
Ishikari-Sammyaku, *Japan* 30 C11
Ishikari-Wan, *Japan* 30 C10
Ishikawa □, *Japan* 31 F8
Ishim, *Russia* 26 D7
Ishim —►, *Russia* 26 D8
Ishinomaki, *Japan* 30 E10
Ishioka, *Japan* 31 F10
Ishkuman, *Pakistan* 43 A5
Ishpeming, *U.S.A.* 76 B2
Isil Kul, *Russia* 26 D8
Isiolo, *Kenya* 54 B4
Isiolo □, *Kenya* 54 B4
Isipingo Beach, *S. Africa* 57 E5
Isiro, *Zaïre* 54 B2
Isisford, *Australia* 62 C3
İskenderun, *Turkey* 25 G6
İskenderun Körfezi, *Turkey* 25 G6
Iskut —►, *Canada* 72 B2
Isla —►, *U.K.* 12 E5
Isla Vista, *U.S.A.* 85 L7
Islamabad, *Pakistan* 42 C5
Islamkot, *Pakistan* 42 G4
Island —►, *Canada* 72 A4
Island Falls, *Canada* 70 C3
Island Falls, *U.S.A.* 71 C6
Island L., *Canada* 73 C10
Island Lagoon, *Australia* 63 E2
Island Pond, *U.S.A.* 79 B13
Islands, B. of, *Canada* 71 C8
Islay, *U.K.* 12 F2
Isle aux Morts, *Canada* 71 C8
Isle of Wight □, *U.K.* 11 G6
Isle Royale, *U.S.A.* 80 A10
Isleta, *U.S.A.* 83 J10
Isleton, *U.S.A.* 84 G5
Ismail, *Ukraine* 25 E4
Ismâ'ilîya, *Egypt* 51 B11
Ismay, *U.S.A.* 80 B2
Isna, *Egypt* 51 C11
Isogstalo, *India* 43 B8
Isparta, *Turkey* 25 G5
Íspica, *Italy* 20 F6
Israel ■, *Asia* 47 D3
Issyk-Kul, Ozero, *Kirghizia* 26 E8
Istaihah, *U.A.E.* 45 F7
İstanbul, *Turkey* 21 D13
Istokpoga, L., *U.S.A.* 77 M5
Istra, *Croatia* 20 B5
Istria = Istra, *Croatia* 20 B5
Itá, *Paraguay* 94 B4
Itabaiana, *Brazil* 93 E11
Itaberaba, *Brazil* 93 F10
Itabira, *Brazil* 93 G10
Itabirito, *Brazil* 95 A7
Itabuna, *Brazil* 93 F11
Itaipu Dam, *Brazil* 95 B5
Itaituba, *Brazil* 93 D7
Itajaí, *Brazil* 95 B6
Itajubá, *Brazil* 95 A6
Itaka, *Tanzania* 55 D3
Italy ■, *Europe* 20 D5
Itampolo, *Madag.* 57 C7
Itapecuru-Mirim, *Brazil* 93 D10
Itaperuna, *Brazil* 95 A7
Itapetininga, *Brazil* 95 A6
Itapeva, *Brazil* 95 A6
Itapicuru —►, *Bahia, Brazil* 93 F11
Itapicuru —►, *Maranhão, Brazil* 93 D10
Itapipoca, *Brazil* 93 D11
Itapuá □, *Paraguay* 95 B4
Itaquari, *Brazil* 95 A7
Itaquatiara, *Brazil* 92 D7
Itaquí, *Brazil* 94 B4
Itararé, *Brazil* 95 A6
Itarsi, *India* 42 H7
Itati, *Argentina* 94 B4
Itatuba, *Brazil* 92 E6
Itchen —►, *U.K.* 11 G6
Itezhi Tezhi, L., *Zambia* 55 F2
Ithaca = Itháki, *Greece* 21 E9
Ithaca, *U.S.A.* 79 D8
Itháki, *Greece* 21 E9
Ito, *Japan* 31 G9
Itoigawa, *Japan* 31 F8
Itonamas —►, *Bolivia* 92 F6
Ittoqqortoormiit = Scoresbysund, *Greenland* 4 B6
Itu, *Brazil* 95 A6
Ituaçu, *Brazil* 93 F10
Ituiutaba, *Brazil* 93 G9
Itumbiara, *Brazil* 93 G9
Ituna, *Canada* 73 C8
Itunge Port, *Tanzania* 55 D3
Iturbe, *Argentina* 94 A2
Ituri —►, *Zaïre* 54 B2
Iturup, Ostrov, *Russia* 27 E15
Ituyuro —►, *Argentina* 94 A3
Ivaí —►, *Brazil* 95 A5
Ivalo, *Finland* 8 B19
Ivalojoki —►, *Finland* 8 B19
Ivanhoe, *N.S.W., Australia* 63 E3
Ivanhoe, *W. Austral., Australia* 60 C4
Ivanhoe, *U.S.A.* 84 J7
Ivanhoe L., *Canada* 73 A7
Ivano-Frankovsk, *Ukraine* 25 E3
Ivanovo, *Belorussia* 24 D3
Ivanovo, *Russia* 24 C7
Ivato, *Madag.* 57 C8
Ivdel, *Russia* 24 B11
Ivinheima —►, *Brazil* 95 A5
Iviza = Ibiza, *Spain* 22 C7
Ivohibe, *Madag.* 57 C8
Ivory Coast ■, *Africa* 50 G3
Ivrea, *Italy* 20 B2
Ivugivik, *Canada* 69 B12
Iwahig, *Phil.* 36 C5
Iwaizumi, *Japan* 30 E10
Iwaki, *Japan* 31 F10
Iwakuni, *Japan* 31 G6

Iwamizawa, *Japan* 30 C10
Iwanai, *Japan* 30 C10
Iwata, *Japan* 31 G8
Iwate □, *Japan* 30 E10
Iwate-San, *Japan* 30 E10
Iwo, *Nigeria* 50 G5
Ixiamas, *Bolivia* 92 F5
Ixopo, *S. Africa* 57 E5
Ixtepec, *Mexico* 87 D5
Ixtlán del Río, *Mexico* 86 C4
Iyo, *Japan* 31 H6
Izabal, L. de, *Guatemala* 88 C2
Izamal, *Mexico* 87 C7
Izegem, *Belgium* 15 D3
Izena-Shima, *Japan* 31 L3
Izhevsk, *Russia* 24 C9
İzmir, *Turkey* 25 G4
İzmit, *Turkey* 25 F4
Izra, *Syria* 47 C5
Izu-Shotō, *Japan* 31 G10
Izumi-sano, *Japan* 31 G7
Izumo, *Japan* 31 G6

J

Jabal Lubnân, *Lebanon* 47 B4
Jabalpur, *India* 43 H8
Jabbūl, *Syria* 44 B3
Jablah, *Syria* 44 C3
Jablonec, *Czech.* 16 C7
Jaboatão, *Brazil* 93 E11
Jaboticabal, *Brazil* 95 A6
Jaburu, *Brazil* 92 E6
Jaca, *Spain* 19 A5
Jacareí, *Brazil* 95 A6
Jacarèzinho, *Brazil* 95 A6
Jackman, *U.S.A.* 71 C5
Jacksboro, *U.S.A.* 81 J5
Jackson, *Australia* 63 D4
Jackson, *Ala., U.S.A.* 77 K2
Jackson, *Calif., U.S.A.* 84 G6
Jackson, *Ky., U.S.A.* 76 G4
Jackson, *Mich., U.S.A.* 76 D3
Jackson, *Minn., U.S.A.* 80 D7
Jackson, *Miss., U.S.A.* 81 J9
Jackson, *Mo., U.S.A.* 81 G10
Jackson, *Ohio, U.S.A.* 76 F4
Jackson, *Tenn., U.S.A.* 77 H1
Jackson, *Wyo., U.S.A.* 82 E8
Jackson, L., *U.S.A.* 82 E8
Jackson B., *N.Z.* 59 K2
Jacksons, *N.Z.* 59 K3
Jacksonville, *Ala., U.S.A.* 77 J3
Jacksonville, *Calif., U.S.A.* 84 H6
Jacksonville, *Fla., U.S.A.* 77 K5
Jacksonville, *Ill., U.S.A.* 80 F9
Jacksonville, *N.C., U.S.A.* 77 H7
Jacksonville, *Oreg., U.S.A.* 82 E2
Jacksonville, *Tex., U.S.A.* 81 K7
Jacksonville Beach, *U.S.A.* 77 K5
Jacmel, *Haiti* 89 C5
Jacob Lake, *U.S.A.* 83 H7
Jacobabad, *Pakistan* 42 E3
Jacobina, *Brazil* 93 F10
Jacques-Cartier, Mt., *Canada* 71 C6
Jacuí →, *Brazil* 95 C5
Jacumba, *U.S.A.* 85 N10
Jacundá →, *Brazil* 93 D8
Jadotville = Likasi, *Zaïre* 55 E2
Jādū, *Libya* 51 B7
Jaén, *Peru* 92 E3
Jaén, *Spain* 19 D4
Jaffa = Tel Aviv-Yafo, *Israel* 47 C3
Jaffa, C., *Australia* 63 F2
Jaffna, *Sri Lanka* 40 Q12
Jagadhri, *India* 42 D7
Jagadishpur, *India* 43 G11
Jagdalpur, *India* 41 K12
Jagersfontein, *S. Africa* 56 D4
Jagraon, *India* 40 D9
Jagtial, *India* 40 K11
Jaguariaíva, *Brazil* 95 A6
Jaguaribe →, *Brazil* 93 D11
Jagüey Grande, *Cuba* 88 B3
Jahangirabad, *India* 42 E8
Jahrom, *Iran* 45 D7
Jailolo, *Indonesia* 37 D7
Jailolo, Selat, *Indonesia* 37 D7
Jaipur, *India* 42 F6
Jājarm, *Iran* 45 B8
Jakarta, *Indonesia* 37 G12
Jakobstad, *Finland* 8 E17
Jal, *U.S.A.* 81 J3
Jalalabad, *Afghan.* 42 B4
Jalalabad, *India* 43 F8
Jalalpur Jattan, *Pakistan* 42 C6
Jalama, *U.S.A.* 85 L6
Jalapa, *Guatemala* 88 D2
Jalapa Enríquez, *Mexico* 87 D5
Jalaun, *India* 43 F8
Jaleswar, *Nepal* 43 F11
Jalgaon, *Maharashtra, India* 40 J10
Jalgaon, *Maharashtra, India* 40 J9
Jalibah, *Iraq* 44 D5
Jalisco □, *Mexico* 86 C4
Jalkot, *Pakistan* 43 B5
Jalna, *India* 40 K9
Jalón →, *Spain* 19 B5
Jalpa, *Mexico* 86 C4
Jalpaiguri, *India* 41 F16
Jaluit I., *Pac. Oc.* 64 G8
Jalūlā, *Iraq* 44 C5
Jamaica ■, *W. Indies* 88 C4
Jamalpur, *Bangla.* 41 G16
Jamalpur, *India* 43 G12
Jamalpurganj, *India* 43 H13
Jamanxim →, *Brazil* 93 D7
Jambe, *Indonesia* 37 E8
Jambi, *Indonesia* 36 E2
Jambi □, *Indonesia* 36 E2
Jambusar, *India* 42 H5
James →, *U.S.A.* 80 D6
James B., *Canada* 69 C11
James Ras., *Australia* 60 D5
James Ross I., *Antarctica* 5 C18
Jamestown, *Australia* 63 E2
Jamestown, *S. Africa* 56 E4
Jamestown, *Ky., U.S.A.* 76 G3
Jamestown, *N. Dak., U.S.A.* 80 B5
Jamestown, *N.Y., U.S.A.* 78 D5
Jamestown, *Pa., U.S.A.* 78 E4
Jamestown, *Tenn., U.S.A.* 77 G3
Jamilābād, *Iran* 45 C6
Jamiltepec, *Mexico* 87 D5
Jamkhandi, *India* 40 L9
Jammu, *India* 42 C6
Jammu & Kashmir □, *India* 43 B7
Jamnagar, *India* 42 H4
Jampur, *Pakistan* 42 E4
Jamrud, *Pakistan* 42 C4
Jamshedpur, *India* 43 H12
Jamtara, *India* 43 H12
Jämtlands län □, *Sweden* 8 E12
Jan Kempdorp, *S. Africa* 56 D3
Jan L., *Canada* 73 C8
Jan Mayen, *Arctic* 4 B7
Jand, *Pakistan* 42 C5
Jandaq, *Iran* 45 C7
Jandia, *Canary Is.* 22 F5
Jandia, Pta. de, *Canary Is.* 22 F5
Jandola, *Pakistan* 42 C4
Jandowae, *Australia* 63 D5
Janesville, *U.S.A.* 80 D10
Janin, *Jordan* 47 C4
Janos, *Mexico* 86 A3
Januária, *Brazil* 93 G10
Janub Dârfûr □, *Sudan* 51 F9
Janub Kordofân □, *Sudan* 51 F10
Janubio, *Canary Is.* 22 F6
Jaora, *India* 42 H6
Japan ■, *Asia* 31 G8
Japan, Sea of, *Asia* 30 E7
Japan Trench, *Pac. Oc.* 64 D6
Japen = Yapen, *Indonesia* 37 E9
Japurá →, *Brazil* 92 D5
Jaque, *Panama* 92 B3
Jarābulus, *Syria* 44 B3
Jarama →, *Spain* 19 B4
Jaranwala, *Pakistan* 42 D5
Jarash, *Jordan* 47 C4
Jardim, *Brazil* 94 A4
Jardines de la Reina, Is., *Cuba* 88 B4
Jargalang, *China* 35 C12
Jargalant = Hovd, *Mongolia* 32 B4
Jarir, W. al →, *Si. Arabia* 44 E4
Jarosław, *Poland* 17 C11
Jarrahdale, *Australia* 61 F2
Jarres, Plaine des, *Laos* 38 C4
Jarso, *Ethiopia* 51 G12
Jartai, *China* 34 E3
Jarud Qi, *China* 35 B11
Jarvis, *Canada* 78 D4
Jarvis I., *Pac. Oc.* 65 H12
Jarwa, *India* 43 F10
Jāsimīyah, *Iraq* 44 C5
Jasin, *Malaysia* 39 L4
Jāsk, *Iran* 45 E8
Jasło, *Poland* 17 D10
Jasper, *Alta., Canada* 72 C5
Jasper, *Ont., Canada* 79 B9
Jasper, *Ala., U.S.A.* 77 J2
Jasper, *Fla., U.S.A.* 77 K4
Jasper, *Minn., U.S.A.* 80 D6
Jasper, *Tex., U.S.A.* 81 K8
Jasper Nat. Park, *Canada* 72 C5
Jassy = Iaşi, *Romania* 17 E13
Jászberény, *Hungary* 17 E9
Jataí, *Brazil* 93 G8
Jati, *Pakistan* 42 G3
Jatibarang, *Indonesia* 37 G13
Jatinegara, *Indonesia* 37 G12
Játiva, *Spain* 19 C5
Jaú, *Brazil* 95 A6
Jauja, *Peru* 92 F3
Jaunpur, *India* 43 G10
Java = Jawa, *Indonesia* 37 G14
Java Sea, *Indonesia* 36 E3
Java Trench, *Ind. Oc.* 64 H2
Javhlant = Ulyasutay, *Mongolia* 32 B4
Jawa, *Indonesia* 37 G14
Jay, *U.S.A.* 81 G7
Jaya, Puncak, *Indonesia* 37 E9
Jayanti, *India* 41 F16
Jayapura, *Indonesia* 37 E10
Jayawijaya, Pegunungan, *Indonesia* 37 E9
Jaynagar, *India* 41 F15
Jayrūd, *Syria* 44 C3
Jayton, *U.S.A.* 81 J4
Jazireh-ye Shif, *Iran* 45 D6
Jazminal, *Mexico* 86 C4
Jazzīn, *Lebanon* 47 B4
Jean, *U.S.A.* 85 K11
Jean Marie River, *Canada* 72 A4
Jean Rabel, *Haiti* 89 C5
Jeanerette, *U.S.A.* 81 L9
Jeanette, Ostrov, *Russia* 27 B16
Jeannette, *U.S.A.* 78 F5
Jebba, *Nigeria* 50 G5
Jebel, Bahr el →, *Sudan* 51 G11
Jedburgh, *U.K.* 12 F6
Jedda = Jiddah, *Si. Arabia* 46 C2
Jędrzejów, *Poland* 17 C10
Jedway, *Canada* 72 C2
Jefferson, *Iowa, U.S.A.* 80 D7
Jefferson, *Ohio, U.S.A.* 78 E4
Jefferson, *Tex., U.S.A.* 81 J7
Jefferson, *Wis., U.S.A.* 80 D10
Jefferson, Mt., *Nev., U.S.A.* 82 G5
Jefferson, Mt., *Oreg., U.S.A.* 82 D3
Jefferson City, *Mo., U.S.A.* 80 F8
Jefferson City, *Tenn., U.S.A.* 77 G4
Jeffersonville, *U.S.A.* 76 F3
Jega, *Nigeria* 50 F5
Jelenia Góra, *Poland* 16 C7
Jelgava, *Latvia* 9 H17
Jellicoe, *Canada* 70 C2
Jemaja, *Indonesia* 36 D3
Jemaluang, *Malaysia* 39 L4
Jember, *Indonesia* 37 H15
Jembongan, *Malaysia* 36 C5
Jemeppe, *Belgium* 15 D5
Jena, *Germany* 16 C5
Jena, *U.S.A.* 81 K8
Jenkins, *U.S.A.* 76 G4
Jenner, *U.S.A.* 84 G3
Jennings, *U.S.A.* 81 K8
Jennings →, *Canada* 72 B2
Jeparit, *Australia* 63 F3
Jequié, *Brazil* 93 F10
Jequitinhonha, *Brazil* 93 G10
Jequitinhonha →, *Brazil* 93 G11
Jerada, *Morocco* 50 B4
Jerantut, *Malaysia* 39 L4
Jérémie, *Haiti* 89 C5
Jerez, Punta, *Mexico* 87 C5
Jerez de García Salinas, *Mexico* 86 C4
Jerez de la Frontera, *Spain* 19 D2
Jerez de los Caballeros, *Spain* 19 C2
Jericho = Arīḥā, *Syria* 44 C3
Jericho = El Arīhā, *Jordan* 47 D4
Jericho, *Australia* 62 C4
Jerilderie, *Australia* 63 F4
Jermyn, *U.S.A.* 79 E9
Jerome, *U.S.A.* 83 J8
Jersey, *Chan. Is.* 11 H5
Jersey City, *U.S.A.* 79 F10
Jersey Shore, *U.S.A.* 78 E7
Jerseyville, *U.S.A.* 80 F9
Jerusalem, *Israel* 47 D4
Jervis B., *Australia* 63 F5
Jesselton = Kota Kinabalu, *Malaysia* 36 C5
Jessore, *Bangla.* 41 H16
Jesup, *U.S.A.* 77 K5
Jesús Carranza, *Mexico* 87 D5
Jesús María, *Argentina* 94 C3
Jetmore, *U.S.A.* 81 F5
Jetpur, *India* 42 J4
Jewett, *Ohio, U.S.A.* 78 F3
Jewett, *Tex., U.S.A.* 81 K6
Jewett City, *U.S.A.* 79 E13
Jeyḥūnābād, *Iran* 45 C6
Jeypore, *India* 41 K13
Jhajjar, *India* 42 E7
Jhal Jhao, *Pakistan* 40 F4
Jhalawar, *India* 42 G7
Jhang Maghiana, *Pakistan* 42 D5
Jhansi, *India* 43 G8
Jharia, *India* 43 H12
Jharsaguda, *India* 41 J14
Jhelum, *Pakistan* 42 C5
Jhelum →, *Pakistan* 42 D5
Jhunjhunu, *India* 42 E6
Ji Xian, *Hebei, China* 34 F8
Ji Xian, *Henan, China* 34 G8
Ji Xian, *Shanxi, China* 34 F6
Jia Xian, *Henan, China* 34 H7
Jia Xian, *Shaanxi, China* 34 E6
Jiamusi, *China* 33 B8
Ji'an, *Jiangxi, China* 33 D6
Ji'an, *Jilin, China* 35 D14
Jianchang, *China* 35 D11
Jianchangying, *China* 35 D10
Jiangcheng, *China* 32 D5
Jiangmen, *China* 33 D6
Jiangsu □, *China* 35 H10
Jiangxi □, *China* 33 D6
Jiao Xian, *China* 35 F11
Jiaohe, *Hebei, China* 34 E9
Jiaohe, *Jilin, China* 35 C14
Jiaozhou Wan, *China* 35 F11
Jiaozuo, *China* 34 G7
Jiawang, *China* 35 G9
Jiaxiang, *China* 34 G9
Jiaxing, *China* 33 C7
Jiayi, *Taiwan* 33 D7
Jibuti = Djibouti ■, *Africa* 46 E3
Jicarón, I., *Panama* 88 E3
Jiddah, *Si. Arabia* 46 C2
Jido, *India* 41 E19
Jieshou, *China* 34 H8
Jiexiu, *China* 34 F6
Jiggalong, *Australia* 60 D3
Jihlava, *Czech.* 16 D7
Jihlava →, *Czech.* 16 D8
Jijel, *Algeria* 50 A6
Jijiga, *Ethiopia* 46 F3
Jilin, *China* 35 C14
Jilin □, *China* 35 C13
Jiloca →, *Spain* 19 B5
Jilong, *Taiwan* 33 D7
Jima, *Ethiopia* 51 G12
Jiménez, *Mexico* 86 B4
Jimo, *China* 35 F11
Jin Xian, *Hebei, China* 34 E8
Jin Xian, *Liaoning, China* 35 E11
Jinan, *China* 34 F9
Jincheng, *China* 34 G7
Jind, *India* 42 E7
Jindabyne, *Australia* 63 F4
Jing He →, *China* 34 G5
Jingbian, *China* 34 F5
Jingchuan, *China* 34 G4
Jingdezhen, *China* 33 D6
Jinggu, *China* 32 D5
Jinghai, *China* 34 E9
Jingle, *China* 34 E6
Jingning, *China* 34 G3
Jingpo Hu, *China* 35 C15
Jingtai, *China* 34 F3
Jingxing, *China* 34 E8
Jingyang, *China* 34 G5
Jingyu, *China* 35 C14
Jingyuan, *China* 34 F3
Jingziguan, *China* 34 H6
Jinhua, *China* 33 D6
Jining, *Nei Mongol Zizhiqu, China* 34 D7
Jining, *Shandong, China* 34 G9
Jinja, *Uganda* 54 B3
Jinjang, *Malaysia* 39 L3
Jinji, *China* 34 F4
Jinnah Barrage, *Pakistan* 40 C7
Jinotega, *Nic.* 88 D2
Jinotepe, *Nic.* 88 D2
Jinsha Jiang →, *China* 32 D5
Jinxi, *China* 35 D11
Jinxiang, *China* 34 G9
Jinzhou, *China* 35 D11
Jiparaná →, *Brazil* 92 E6
Jipijapa, *Ecuador* 92 D2
Jiquilpan, *Mexico* 86 D4
Jishan, *China* 34 G6
Jisr ash Shughūr, *Syria* 44 C3
Jitarning, *Australia* 61 F2
Jitra, *Malaysia* 39 J3
Jiu →, *Romania* 17 G11
Jiudengkou, *China* 34 E4
Jiujiang, *China* 33 D6
Jiutai, *China* 35 B13
Jiuxiangcheng, *China* 34 H8
Jiuxincheng, *China* 34 E8
Jixi, *China* 35 B16
Jiyang, *China* 35 F9
Jīzān, *Si. Arabia* 46 D3
Jize, *China* 34 F8
Jizō-Zaki, *Japan* 31 G6
Joaçaba, *Brazil* 95 B5
João Pessoa, *Brazil* 93 E12
Joaquín V. González, *Argentina* 94 B3
Jodhpur, *India* 42 F5
Joensuu, *Finland* 24 B4
Jofane, *Mozam.* 57 C5
Joggins, *Canada* 71 C7
Jogjakarta = Yogyakarta, *Indonesia* 37 G14
Johannesburg, *S. Africa* 57 D4
Johannesburg, *U.S.A.* 85 K9
John Day, *U.S.A.* 82 D4
John Day →, *U.S.A.* 82 D3
John H. Kerr Res., *U.S.A.* 77 G6
John o' Groats, *U.K.* 12 C5
Johnnie, *U.S.A.* 85 J10
John's Ra., *Australia* 62 C1
Johnson, *U.S.A.* 81 G4
Johnson City, *N.Y., U.S.A.* 79 D9
Johnson City, *Tenn., U.S.A.* 77 G4
Johnson City, *Tex., U.S.A.* 81 K5
Johnsonburg, *U.S.A.* 78 E6
Johnsondale, *U.S.A.* 85 K8
Johnson's Crossing, *Canada* 72 A2
Johnston, L., *Australia* 61 F3
Johnston Falls = Mambilima Falls, *Zambia* 55 E2
Johnston I., *Pac. Oc.* 65 F11
Johnstone Str., *Canada* 72 C3
Johnstown, *N.Y., U.S.A.* 79 C10
Johnstown, *Pa., U.S.A.* 78 F6
Johor Baharu, *Malaysia* 39 M4
Joinvile, *Brazil* 95 B6
Joinville I., *Antarctica* 5 C18
Jojutla, *Mexico* 87 D5
Jokkmokk, *Sweden* 8 C15
Jökulsá á Bru →, *Iceland* 8 D6
Jökulsá á Fjöllum →, *Iceland* 8 C5
Jolfā, *Āzarbājān-e Sharqī, Iran* 44 B5
Jolfā, *Eşfahan, Iran* 45 C6
Joliet, *U.S.A.* 76 E1
Joliette, *Canada* 70 C5
Jolo, *Phil.* 37 C6
Jolon, *U.S.A.* 84 K5
Jombang, *Indonesia* 37 G15
Jome, *Indonesia* 37 E7
Jones Sound, *Canada* 4 B3
Jonesboro, *Ark., U.S.A.* 81 H9
Jonesboro, *Ill., U.S.A.* 81 G10
Jonesboro, *La., U.S.A.* 81 J8
Jonesport, *U.S.A.* 71 D6
Jonglei □, *Sudan* 51 G11
Jönköping, *Sweden* 9 H13
Jönköpings län □, *Sweden* 9 H13
Jonquière, *Canada* 71 C5
Joplin, *U.S.A.* 81 G7
Jordan, *U.S.A.* 82 C10
Jordan ■, *Asia* 47 E5
Jordan →, *Asia* 47 D4
Jordan Valley, *U.S.A.* 82 E5
Jorhat, *India* 41 F19
Jörn, *Sweden* 8 D16
Jorong, *Indonesia* 36 E4
Jorquera →, *Chile* 94 B2
Jos, *Nigeria* 50 G6
José Batlle y Ordóñez, *Uruguay* 95 C4
Joseph, *U.S.A.* 82 D5
Joseph, L., *Nfld., Canada* 71 B6
Joseph, L., *Ont., Canada* 78 A5
Joseph Bonaparte G., *Australia* 60 B4
Joseph City, *U.S.A.* 83 J8
Joshua Tree, *U.S.A.* 85 L10
Joshua Tree Nat. Mon., *U.S.A.* 85 M10
Jostedal, *Norway* 9 F9
Jotunheimen, *Norway* 9 F10
Jourdanton, *U.S.A.* 81 L5
Joussard, *Canada* 72 B5
Jovellanos, *Cuba* 88 B3
Ju Xian, *China* 35 F10
Juan Aldama, *Mexico* 86 C4
Juan Bautista Alberdi, *Argentina* 94 C3
Juan de Fuca Str., *Canada* 84 B2
Juan de Nova, *Ind. Oc.* 57 B7
Juan Fernández, Arch. de, *Pac. Oc.* 65 L20
Juan José Castelli, *Argentina* 94 B3
Juan L. Lacaze, *Uruguay* 94 C4
Juárez, *Argentina* 94 D4
Juárez, *Mexico* 85 N11
Juárez, Sierra de, *Mexico* 86 A1
Juàzeiro, *Brazil* 93 E10
Juàzeiro do Norte, *Brazil* 93 E11
Jubayl, *Lebanon* 47 A4
Jubbah, *Si. Arabia* 44 D4
Jubbulpore = Jabalpur, *India* 43 H8
Jubilee L., *Australia* 61 E4
Juby, C., *Morocco* 50 C2
Júcar →, *Spain* 19 C5
Júcaro, *Cuba* 88 B4
Juchitán, *Mexico* 87 D5
Judaea = Har Yehuda, *Israel* 47 D3
Judith →, *U.S.A.* 82 C9
Judith Gap, *U.S.A.* 82 C9
Judith Pt., *U.S.A.* 79 E13
Jugoslavia = Yugoslavia ■, *Europe* 21 C8
Juigalpa, *Nic.* 88 D2
Juiz de Fora, *Brazil* 95 A7
Jujuy □, *Argentina* 94 A2
Julesburg, *U.S.A.* 80 E3
Juli, *Peru* 92 G5
Julia Cr. →, *Australia* 62 C3
Julia Creek, *Australia* 62 C3
Juliaca, *Peru* 92 G4
Julian, *U.S.A.* 85 M10
Julianehåb, *Greenland* 4 C5
Julimes, *Mexico* 86 B3
Jullundur, *India* 42 D6
Julu, *China* 34 F8
Jumbo, *Zimbabwe* 55 F3
Jumbo Pk., *U.S.A.* 85 J12
Jumentos Cays, *Bahamas* 89 B4
Jumet, *Belgium* 15 D4
Jumilla, *Spain* 19 C5
Jumla, *Nepal* 43 E10
Jumna = Yamuna →, *India* 43 G9
Junagadh, *India* 42 J4
Junction, *Tex., U.S.A.* 81 K5
Junction, *Utah, U.S.A.* 83 G7
Junction B., *Australia* 62 A1
Junction City, *Kans., U.S.A.* 80 F6
Junction City, *Oreg., U.S.A.* 82 D2
Junction Pt., *Australia* 62 A1
Jundah, *Australia* 62 C3
Jundiaí, *Brazil* 95 A6
Juneau, *U.S.A.* 68 C6
Junee, *Australia* 63 E4
Junggar Pendi, *China* 32 B3
Jungshahi, *Pakistan* 42 G2
Juniata →, *U.S.A.* 78 F7
Junín, *Argentina* 94 C3
Junín de los Andes, *Argentina* 96 D2
Jūniyah, *Lebanon* 47 B4
Juntura, *U.S.A.* 82 E4
Jupiter →, *Canada* 71 C7
Jur, Nahr el →, *Sudan* 51 G10
Jura, *U.K.* 12 F3
Jura □, *France* 18 C6
Jura, Mts. du, *Europe* 18 C7
Jura, Sd. of, *U.K.* 12 F3
Jurado, *Colombia* 92 B3
Juruá →, *Brazil* 92 D5
Juruèna →, *Brazil* 92 E7
Juruti, *Brazil* 93 D7
Justo Daract, *Argentina* 94 C2
Juticalpa, *Honduras* 88 D2
Jutland = Jylland, *Denmark* 9 H10
Juventud, I. de la, *Cuba* 88 B3
Juwain, *Afghan.* 40 D2
Jūy Zar, *Iran* 44 C5
Juye, *China* 34 G9
Jylland, *Denmark* 9 H10
Jyväskylä, *Finland* 8 E18

K

K2, Mt., Pakistan 43 B7
Kaap die Goeie Hoop, S. Africa 56 E2
Kaap Plateau, S. Africa 56 D3
Kaapkruis, Namibia 56 C1
Kaapstad = Cape Town, S. Africa 56 E2
Kabaena, Indonesia 37 F6
Kabala, S. Leone 50 G2
Kabale, Uganda 54 C3
Kabalo, Zaïre 54 D2
Kabambare, Zaïre 54 C2
Kabango, Zaïre 55 D2
Kabanjahe, Indonesia 36 D1
Kabara, Mali 50 E4
Kabardino-Balkar Republic □, Russia 25 F7
Kabare, Indonesia 37 E8
Kabarega Falls, Uganda 54 B3
Kabasalan, Phil. 37 C6
Kabba, Nigeria 50 G6
Kabin Buri, Thailand 38 F3
Kabinakagami L., Canada 70 C3
Kabīr, Zab al →, Iraq 44 C4
Kabkabīyah, Sudan 51 F9
Kabompo, Zambia 55 E1
Kabompo →, Zambia 53 G4
Kabondo, Zaïre 55 D2
Kabongo, Zaïre 54 D2
Kabra, Australia 62 C5
Kabūd Gonbad, Iran 45 B8
Kābul, Afghan. 42 B3
Kābul □, Afghan. 40 B6
Kabul →, Pakistan 42 C5
Kabunga, Zaïre 54 C2
Kaburuang, Indonesia 37 D7
Kabwe, Zambia 55 E2
Kachchh, Gulf of, India 42 H3
Kachchh, Rann of, India 42 G4
Kachebera, Zambia 55 E3
Kachin □, Burma 41 F20
Kachira, L., Uganda 54 C3
Kachiry, Kazakhstan 26 D8
Kachot, Cambodia 39 G4
Kackar, Turkey 25 F7
Kadan Kyun, Burma 36 B1
Kadanai →, Afghan. 42 D1
Kadi, India 42 H5
Kadina, Australia 63 E2
Kadiyevka, Ukraine 25 E6
Kadoka, U.S.A. 80 D4
Kadoma, Zimbabwe 55 F2
Kâdugli, Sudan 51 F10
Kaduna, Nigeria 50 F6
Kaédi, Mauritania 50 E2
Kaelé, Cameroon 51 F7
Kaeng Khoï, Thailand 38 E3
Kaesŏng, N. Korea 35 F14
Kāf, Si. Arabia 44 D3
Kafakumba, Zaïre 52 F4
Kafan, Armenia 25 G8
Kafanchan, Nigeria 50 G6
Kaffrine, Senegal 50 F1
Kafia Kingi, Sudan 51 G9
Kafinda, Zambia 55 E3
Kafirévs, Ákra, Greece 21 E11
Kafue, Zambia 55 F2
Kafue →, Zambia 53 H5
Kafue Flats, Zambia 55 F2
Kafue Nat. Park, Zambia 55 F2
Kafulwe, Zambia 55 D2
Kaga, Afghan. 42 B4
Kaga Bandoro, C.A.R. 51 G8
Kagan, Uzbekistan 26 F7
Kagawa □, Japan 31 G6
Kagera □, Tanzania 54 C3
Kagera →, Uganda 54 C3
Kagoshima, Japan 31 J5
Kagoshima □, Japan 31 J5
Kahak, Iran 45 B6
Kahama, Tanzania 54 C3
Kahama □, Tanzania 54 C3
Kahang, Malaysia 39 L4
Kahayan →, Indonesia 36 E4
Kahe, Tanzania 54 C4
Kahemba, Zaïre 52 F3
Kahniah →, Canada 72 B4
Kahnūj, Iran 45 E8
Kahoka, U.S.A. 80 E9
Kahoolawe, U.S.A. 74 H16
Kahramanmaraş, Turkey 25 G6
Kahuta, Pakistan 42 C5
Kai, Kepulauan, Indonesia 37 F8
Kai Besar, Indonesia 37 F8
Kai Is. = Kai, Kepulauan, Indonesia 37 F8
Kai-Ketil, Indonesia 37 F8
Kaiama, Nigeria 50 G5
Kaiapoi, N.Z. 59 K4
Kaieteur Falls, Guyana 92 B7
Kaifeng, China 34 G8
Kaikohe, N.Z. 59 F4
Kaikoura, N.Z. 59 K4
Kaikoura Ra., N.Z. 59 J4
Kailu, China 35 C11
Kailua, U.S.A. 74 J17
Kaimana, Indonesia 37 E8
Kaimanawa Mts., N.Z. 59 H5
Kaimganj, India 43 F8
Kaimur Hills, India 43 G9
Kaingaroa Forest, N.Z. 59 H6
Kainji Res., Nigeria 50 F5
Kaipara Harbour, N.Z. 59 G5
Kaipokok B., Canada 71 B8
Kairana, India 42 E7
Kaironi, Indonesia 37 E8
Kairouan, Tunisia 50 A7
Kaiserslautern, Germany 16 D3
Kaitaia, N.Z. 59 F4
Kaitangata, N.Z. 59 M2
Kaithal, India 42 E7
Kaitu →, Pakistan 42 C4
Kaiwi Channel, U.S.A. 74 H16
Kaiyuan, China 35 C13
Kajaani, Finland 8 D19
Kajabbi, Australia 62 B3
Kajana = Kajaani, Finland 8 D19
Kajang, Malaysia 39 L3
Kajiado, Kenya 54 C4
Kajiado □, Kenya 54 C4
Kajo Kaji, Sudan 51 H11
Kaka, Sudan 51 F11
Kakabeka Falls, Canada 70 C2
Kakamas, S. Africa 56 D3
Kakamega, Kenya 54 B3
Kakamega □, Kenya 54 B3
Kakanui Mts., N.Z. 59 L3
Kake, Japan 31 G6
Kakegawa, Japan 31 G9
Kakeroma-Jima, Japan 31 K4
Kakhovka, Ukraine 25 E5
Kakhovskoye Vdkhr., Ukraine 25 E5
Kakinada, India 41 L13
Kakisa →, Canada 72 A5
Kakisa L., Canada 72 A5
Kakogawa, Japan 31 G7
Kakwa →, Canada 72 C5
Kāl Gūsheh, Iran 45 D8
Kal Safīd, Iran 44 C5
Kalabagh, Pakistan 42 C4
Kalabahi, Indonesia 37 F6
Kalabáka, Greece 21 E9
Kalabo, Zambia 53 G4
Kalach, Russia 25 D7
Kaladan →, Burma 41 J18
Kaladar, Canada 78 B7
Kalahari, Africa 56 C3
Kalahari Gemsbok Nat. Park, S. Africa 56 D3
Kālak, Iran 45 E8
Kalakamati, Botswana 57 C4
Kalakan, Russia 27 D12
Kalakh, Syria 44 C3
K'alak'unlun Shank'ou, Pakistan 43 B7
Kalam, Pakistan 43 B5
Kalama, U.S.A. 84 E4
Kalama, Zaïre 54 C2
Kalamata, Greece 21 F10
Kalamazoo, U.S.A. 76 D3
Kalamazoo →, U.S.A. 76 D2
Kalambo Falls, Tanzania 55 D3
Kalannie, Australia 61 F2
Kalāntarī, Iran 45 C7
Kalao, Indonesia 37 F6
Kalaotoa, Indonesia 37 F6
Kalasin, Thailand 38 D4
Kalat, Pakistan 40 E5
Kalāteh, Iran 45 B7
Kalāteh-ye-Ganj, Iran 45 E8
Kalbarri, Australia 61 E1
Kalegauk Kyun, Burma 41 M20
Kalehe, Zaïre 54 C2
Kalema, Tanzania 54 C3
Kalemie, Zaïre 54 D2
Kalewa, Burma 41 H19
Kálfafellsstaður, Iceland 8 D6
Kalgan = Zhangjiakou, China 34 D8
Kalgoorlie-Boulder, Australia 61 F3
Kaliakra, Nos, Bulgaria 21 C13
Kalianda, Indonesia 36 F3
Kalibo, Phil. 37 B6
Kaliganj, Bangla. 43 H13
Kalima, Zaïre 54 C2
Kalimantan, Indonesia 36 E4
Kalimantan Barat □, Indonesia 36 E4
Kalimantan Selatan □, Indonesia 36 E5
Kalimantan Tengah □, Indonesia 36 E4
Kalimantan Timur □, Indonesia 36 D5
Kálimnos, Greece 21 F12
Kalimpong, India 43 F13
Kalinin = Tver, Russia 24 C6
Kaliningrad, Russia 24 C6
Kaliningrad, Russia 24 D3
Kaliro, Uganda 54 B3
Kalispell, U.S.A. 82 B6
Kalisz, Poland 17 C9
Kaliua, Tanzania 54 D3
Kalix →, Sweden 8 D17
Kalka, India 42 D7
Kalkaska, U.S.A. 76 C3
Kalkfeld, Namibia 56 C2
Kalkfontein, Botswana 56 C3
Kalkrand, Namibia 56 C2
Kallsjön, Sweden 8 E12
Kalmar, Sweden 9 H14
Kalmyk Republic □, Russia 25 E8
Kalmykovo, Kazakhstan 25 E9
Kalna, India 43 H13
Kalocsa, Hungary 17 E9
Kalokhorio, Cyprus 23 E12
Kaloko, Zaïre 54 D2
Kalol, Gujarat, India 42 H5
Kalol, Gujarat, India 42 H5
Kalomo, Zambia 55 F2
Kalpi, India 43 F8
Kalu, Pakistan 42 G2
Kaluga, Russia 24 D6
Kalulushi, Zambia 55 E2
Kalundborg, Denmark 9 J11
Kalutara, Sri Lanka 40 R11
Kalya, Russia 24 B10
Kama, Zaïre 54 C2
Kama →, Russia 24 C9
Kamachumu, Tanzania 54 C3
Kamaishi, Japan 30 E10
Kamalia, Pakistan 42 D5
Kamapanda, Zambia 55 E1
Kamaran, Yemen 46 D3
Kamativi, Zimbabwe 55 F2
Kambalda, Australia 61 F3
Kambar, Pakistan 42 F3
Kambarka, Russia 24 C9
Kambolé, Zambia 55 D3
Kambos, Cyprus 23 D11
Kambove, Zaïre 55 E2
Kamchatka, P-ov., Russia 27 D16
Kamen, Russia 26 D9
Kamen-Rybolov, Russia 30 B6
Kamenets-Podolskiy, Ukraine 25 E4
Kamenjak, Rt., Croatia 20 B5
Kamenka, Russia 24 A7
Kamensk Uralskiy, Russia 26 D7
Kamenskoye, Russia 27 C17
Kameoka, Japan 31 G7
Kamiah, U.S.A. 82 C5
Kamieskroon, S. Africa 56 E2
Kamilukuak, L., Canada 73 A8
Kamina, Zaïre 55 D1
Kaminak L., Canada 73 A9
Kaminoyama, Japan 30 E10
Kamiros, Greece 23 C9
Kamituga, Zaïre 54 C2
Kamloops, Canada 72 C4
Kamo, Japan 30 F9
Kamoke, Pakistan 42 C6
Kampala, Uganda 54 B3
Kampar, Malaysia 39 K3
Kampar →, Indonesia 36 D2
Kampen, Neths. 15 B5
Kamphaeng Phet, Thailand 38 D2
Kampolombo, L., Zambia 55 E2
Kampong To, Thailand 39 J3
Kampot, Cambodia 39 G5
Kampuchea = Cambodia ■, Asia 38 F5
Kampung →, Indonesia 37 F9
Kampung Air Putih, Malaysia 39 K4
Kampung Jerangau, Malaysia 39 K4
Kampung Raja, Malaysia 39 K4
Kampungbaru = Tolitoli, Indonesia 37 D6
Kamrau, Teluk, Indonesia 37 E8
Kamsack, Canada 73 C8
Kamskoye Vdkhr., Russia 24 C10
Kamuchawie L., Canada 73 B8
Kamui-Misaki, Japan 30 C10
Kāmyārān, Iran 44 C5
Kamyshin, Russia 25 D8
Kanaaupscow, Canada 70 B4
Kanab, U.S.A. 83 H7
Kanab Creek, U.S.A. 83 H7
Kanagi, Japan 30 D10
Kanairiktok →, Canada 71 A7
Kananga, Zaïre 52 F4
Kanarraville, U.S.A. 83 H7
Kanash, Russia 24 C8
Kanaskat, U.S.A. 84 C5
Kanawha →, U.S.A. 76 F4
Kanazawa, Japan 31 F8
Kanchanaburi, Thailand 38 E2
Kanchenjunga, Nepal 43 F13
Kanchipuram, India 40 N11
Kanda Kanda, Zaïre 52 F4
Kandahar = Qandahār, Afghan. 40 D4
Kandalaksha, Russia 24 A5
Kandalakshkiy Zaliv, Russia 24 A5
Kandalu, Afghan. 40 E3
Kandangan, Indonesia 36 E5
Kandanos, Greece 23 D5
Kandhkot, Pakistan 42 E3
Kandhla, India 42 E7
Kandi, Benin 50 F5
Kandi, India 43 H13
Kandla, India 42 H4
Kandos, Australia 63 E4
Kandy, Sri Lanka 40 R12
Kane, U.S.A. 78 E6
Kane Basin, Greenland 4 B4
Kangān, Fārs, Iran 45 E7
Kangān, Hormozgān, Iran 45 E8
Kangar, Malaysia 39 J3
Kangaroo I., Australia 63 F2
Kangavar, Iran 45 C6
Kāngdong, N. Korea 35 E14
Kangean, Kepulauan, Indonesia 36 F5
Kangean Is. = Kangean, Kepulauan, Indonesia 36 F5
Kanggye, N. Korea 35 D14
Kanggyŏng, S. Korea 35 F14
Kanghwa, S. Korea 35 F14
Kangnŭng, S. Korea 35 F15
Kango, Gabon 52 D2
Kangping, China 35 C12
Kangto, India 41 F18
Kaniama, Zaïre 54 D1
Kaniapiskau →, Canada 71 A6
Kaniapiskau L., Canada 71 B6
Kanin, P-ov., Russia 24 A8
Kanin Nos, Mys, Russia 24 A7
Kaniva, Australia 63 F3
Kanjut Sar, Pakistan 43 A6
Kankakee, U.S.A. 76 E2
Kankakee →, U.S.A. 76 E1
Kankan, Guinea 50 F3
Kanker, India 41 J12
Kankunskiy, Russia 27 D13
Kannapolis, U.S.A. 77 H5
Kannauj, India 43 F8
Kannod, India 40 H10
Kano, Nigeria 50 F6
Kan'onji, Japan 31 G6
Kanowit, Malaysia 36 D4
Kanowna, Australia 61 F3
Kanoya, Japan 31 J5
Kanpetlet, Burma 41 J18
Kanpur, India 43 F9
Kansas □, U.S.A. 80 F6
Kansas →, U.S.A. 80 F7
Kansas City, Kans., U.S.A. 80 F7
Kansas City, Mo., U.S.A. 80 F7
Kansenia, Zaïre 55 E2
Kansk, Russia 27 D10
Kansŏng, S. Korea 35 E15
Kansu = Gansu □, China 34 G3
Kantang, Thailand 39 J2
Kantharalak, Thailand 38 E5
Kantō □, Japan 31 F9
Kantō-Sanchi, Japan 31 G9
Kanturk, Ireland 13 D3
Kanuma, Japan 31 F9
Kanus, Namibia 56 D2
Kanye, Botswana 56 C4
Kanzenze, Zaïre 55 E2
Kanzi, Ras, Tanzania 54 D4
Kaohsiung = Gaoxiong, Taiwan 33 D7
Kaokoveld, Namibia 56 B1
Kaolack, Senegal 50 F1
Kaoshan, China 35 B13
Kapadvanj, India 42 H5
Kapanga, Zaïre 52 F4
Kapchagai, Kazakhstan 26 E8
Kapela, Croatia 20 B6
Kapema, Zaïre 55 E2
Kapfenberg, Austria 16 E7
Kapiri Mposhi, Zambia 55 E2
Kapiskau →, Canada 70 B3
Kapit, Malaysia 36 D4
Kapiti I., N.Z. 59 J5
Kapoe, Thailand 39 H2
Kapoeta, Sudan 51 H11
Kaposvár, Hungary 17 E8
Kapowsin, U.S.A. 84 D4
Kapps, Namibia 56 C2
Kapsan, N. Korea 35 D15
Kapuas →, Indonesia 36 E3
Kapuas Hulu, Pegunungan, Malaysia 36 D4
Kapuas Hulu Ra. = Kapuas Hulu, Pegunungan, Malaysia 36 D4
Kapulo, Zaïre 55 D2
Kapunda, Australia 63 E2
Kapuni, N.Z. 59 H5
Kapurthala, India 42 D6
Kapuskasing, Canada 70 C3
Kapuskasing →, Canada 70 C3
Kaputar, Australia 63 E5
Kaputir, Kenya 54 B4
Kara, Russia 26 C7
Kara Bogaz Gol, Zaliv, Turkmenistan 25 F9
Kara Kalpak Republic □, Uzbekistan 26 E6
Kara Kum = Karakum, Peski, Turkmenistan 26 F6
Kara Sea, Russia 26 B7
Karabutak, Kazakhstan 26 E7
Karachi, Pakistan 42 G2
Karad, India 40 L9
Karadeniz Boğazı, Turkey 21 D13
Karaganda, Kazakhstan 26 E8
Karagayly, Kazakhstan 26 E8
Karaginskiy, Ostrov, Russia 27 D17
Karagiye Depression, Kazakhstan 25 F9
Karagwe □, Tanzania 54 C3
Karaikal, India 40 P11
Karaikkudi, India 40 P11
Karaj, Iran 45 C6
Karak, Malaysia 39 L4
Karakas, Kazakhstan 26 E9
Karakitang, Indonesia 37 D7
Karaklis, Armenia 25 F7
Karakoram Pass, Pakistan 43 B7
Karakoram Ra., Pakistan 43 B7
Karakum, Peski, Turkmenistan 26 F6
Karalon, Russia 27 D12
Karaman, Turkey 25 G5
Karamay, China 32 B3
Karambu, Indonesia 36 E5
Karamea Bight, N.Z. 59 J3
Karamoja □, Uganda 54 B3
Karamsad, India 42 H5
Karand, Iran 44 C5
Karanganyar, Indonesia 37 G13
Karasburg, Namibia 56 D2
Karasino, Russia 26 C9
Karasjok, Norway 8 B18
Karasuk, Russia 26 D8
Karasuyama, Japan 31 F10
Karatau, Kazakhstan 26 E8
Karatau, Khrebet, Kazakhstan 26 E7
Karauli, India 42 F7
Karavostasi, Cyprus 23 D11
Karawang, Indonesia 37 G12
Karawanken, Europe 20 A6
Karazhal, Kazakhstan 26 E8
Karbalā, Iraq 44 C5
Karcag, Hungary 17 E10
Karcha →, Pakistan 43 B7
Karda, Russia 27 D11
Kardhítsa, Greece 21 E9
Kareeberge, S. Africa 56 E3
Karelian Republic □, Russia 24 A5
Kārevāndar, Iran 45 E9
Kargasok, Russia 26 D9
Kargat, Russia 26 D9
Kargil, India 43 B7
Kargopol, Russia 24 B6
Kariān, Iran 45 E8
Kariba, Zimbabwe 55 F2
Kariba, L., Zimbabwe 55 F2
Kariba Dam, Zimbabwe 55 F2
Kariba Gorge, Zambia 55 F2
Karibib, Namibia 56 C2
Karimata, Kepulauan, Indonesia 36 E3
Karimata, Selat, Indonesia 36 E3
Karimata I. = Karimata, Kepulauan, Indonesia 36 E3
Karimnagar, India 40 K11
Karimunjawa, Kepulauan, Indonesia 36 F4
Karin, Somali Rep. 46 E4
Karīt, Iran 45 C8
Kariya, Japan 31 G8
Karkaralinsk, Kazakhstan 26 E8
Karkinitskiy Zaliv, Ukraine 25 E5
Karl-Marx-Stadt = Chemnitz, Germany 16 C6
Karlovac, Croatia 20 B6
Karlovy Vary, Czech. 16 C6
Karlsbad = Karlovy Vary, Czech. 16 C6
Karlsborg, Sweden 9 G13
Karlshamn, Sweden 9 H13
Karlskoga, Sweden 9 G13
Karlskrona, Sweden 9 H13
Karlsruhe, Germany 16 D4
Karlstad, Sweden 9 G12
Karlstad, U.S.A. 80 A6
Karnal, India 42 E7
Karnali →, Nepal 43 E9
Karnaphuli Res., Bangla. 41 H18
Karnataka □, India 40 N10
Karnes City, U.S.A. 81 L6
Karnische Alpen, Europe 16 E6
Kärnten □, Austria 16 E6
Karoi, Zimbabwe 55 F2
Karonga, Malawi 55 D3
Karoonda, Australia 63 F2
Karora, Sudan 51 E12
Karpasia □, Cyprus 23 D13
Kárpathos, Greece 21 G12
Karpinsk, Russia 24 C11
Karpogory, Russia 24 B7
Kars, Turkey 25 F7
Karsakpay, Kazakhstan 26 E7
Karshi, Uzbekistan 26 F7
Karsiyang, India 43 F13
Karsun, Russia 24 D8
Kartaly, Russia 26 D7
Kartapur, India 42 D6
Karthaus, U.S.A. 78 E6
Karufa, Indonesia 37 E8
Karumba, Australia 62 B3
Karumo, Tanzania 54 C3
Karumwa, Tanzania 54 C3
Karungu, Kenya 54 C3
Karwar, India 40 M9
Karwi, India 43 G9
Kasache, Malawi 55 E3
Kasai →, Zaïre 52 E3
Kasai Oriental □, Zaïre 54 C1
Kasaji, Zaïre 55 E1
Kasama, Zambia 55 E3
Kasan-dong, N. Korea 35 D14
Kasane, Namibia 56 B3
Kasanga, Tanzania 55 D3
Kasangulu, Zaïre 52 E3
Kasaragod, India 40 N9
Kasba L., Canada 73 A8
Kāseh Garān, Iran 44 C5
Kasempa, Zambia 55 E2
Kasenga, Zaïre 55 E2
Kasese, Uganda 54 B3
Kasewa, Zambia 55 E2
Kasganj, India 43 F8
Kashabowie, Canada 70 C1
Kāshān, Iran 45 C6
Kashi, China 32 C2
Kashimbo, Zaïre 55 E2
Kashipur, India 43 E8
Kashiwazaki, Japan 31 F9
Kashk-e Kohneh, Afghan. 40 B3
Kāshmar, Iran 45 C8
Kashmir, Asia 43 C7
Kashmor, Pakistan 42 E3
Kashun Noerh = Gaxun Nur, China 32 B5
Kasimov, Russia 24 D7
Kasinge, Zaïre 54 D2
Kasiruta, Indonesia 37 E7
Kaskaskia →, U.S.A. 80 G10
Kaskattama →, Canada 73 B10
Kaskinen, Finland 8 E16

Kaskö, *Finland* 8 E16
Kaslo, *Canada* 72 D5
Kasmere L., *Canada* 73 B8
Kasongo, *Zaïre* 54 C2
Kasongo Lunda, *Zaïre* 52 F3
Kásos, *Greece* 21 G12
Kassala, *Sudan* 51 E12
Kassalâ □, *Sudan* 51 E12
Kassel, *Germany* 16 C4
Kassiópi, *Greece* 23 A3
Kassue, *Indonesia* 37 F9
Kastamonu, *Turkey* 25 F5
Kastélli, *Greece* 23 D5
Kastéllion, *Greece* 23 D7
Kastoría, *Greece* 21 D9
Kasulu, *Tanzania* 54 C3
Kasulu □, *Tanzania* 54 C3
Kasumi, *Japan* 31 G7
Kasungu, *Malawi* 55 E3
Kasur, *Pakistan* 42 D6
Kata, *Russia* 27 D11
Kataba, *Zambia* 55 F2
Katako Kombe, *Zaïre* 54 C1
Katale, *Tanzania* 54 C3
Katamatite, *Australia* 63 F4
Katanda, *Kivu, Zaïre* 54 C2
Katanda, *Shaba, Zaïre* 54 D1
Katangi, *India* 40 J11
Katangli, *Russia* 27 D15
Katavi Swamp, *Tanzania* 54 D3
Katha, *Burma* 41 G20
Katherine, *Australia* 60 B5
Kathiawar, *India* 42 H4
Kathikas, *Cyprus* 23 E11
Katihar, *India* 43 G12
Katima Mulilo, *Zambia* 56 B3
Katimbira, *Malawi* 55 E3
Katingan = Mendawai →, *Indonesia* 36 E4
Katiola, *Ivory C.* 50 G3
Katmandu, *Nepal* 43 F11
Káto Arkhánai, *Greece* 23 D7
Káto Khorió, *Greece* 23 D7
Kato Pyrgos, *Cyprus* 23 D11
Katompe, *Zaïre* 54 D2
Katonga →, *Uganda* 54 B3
Katoomba, *Australia* 63 E5
Katowice, *Poland* 17 C9
Katrine, L., *U.K.* 12 E4
Katrineholm, *Sweden* 9 G14
Katsepe, *Madag.* 57 B8
Katsina, *Nigeria* 50 F6
Katsumoto, *Japan* 31 H4
Katsuura, *Japan* 31 G10
Katsuyama, *Japan* 31 F8
Kattaviá, *Greece* 23 D9
Kattegatt, *Denmark* 9 H11
Katumba, *Zaïre* 54 D2
Katungu, *Kenya* 54 C5
Katwa, *India* 43 H13
Katwijk-aan-Zee, *Neths.* 15 B4
Kauai, *U.S.A.* 74 H15
Kauai Chan., *U.S.A.* 74 H15
Kaufman, *U.S.A.* 81 J6
Kaukauna, *U.S.A.* 76 C1
Kaukauveld, *Namibia* 56 C3
Kaukonen, *Finland* 8 C18
Kauliranta, *Finland* 8 C17
Kaunas, *Lithuania* 24 D3
Kaura Namoda, *Nigeria* 50 F6
Kautokeino, *Norway* 8 B17
Kavacha, *Russia* 27 C17
Kavalerovo, *Russia* 30 B7
Kavali, *India* 40 M12
Kavālla, *Greece* 21 D11
Kavār, *Iran* 45 D7
Kavos, *Greece* 23 B4
Kaw, *Fr. Guiana* 93 C8
Kawagama L., *Canada* 78 A6
Kawagoe, *Japan* 31 G9
Kawaguchi, *Japan* 31 G9
Kawaihae, *U.S.A.* 74 H17
Kawambwa, *Zambia* 55 D2
Kawanoe, *Japan* 31 G6
Kawardha, *India* 43 J9
Kawasaki, *Japan* 31 G9
Kawene, *Canada* 70 C1
Kawerau, *N.Z.* 59 H6
Kawhia Harbour, *N.Z.* 59 H5
Kawio, Kepulauan, *Indonesia* 37 D7
Kawnro, *Burma* 41 H21
Kawthoolei = Kawthule □, *Burma* 41 L20
Kawthule □, *Burma* 41 L20
Kaya, *Burkina Faso* 50 F4
Kayah □, *Burma* 41 K20
Kayan →, *Indonesia* 36 D5
Kaycee, *U.S.A.* 82 E10
Kayeli, *Indonesia* 37 E7
Kayenta, *U.S.A.* 83 H8
Kayes, *Mali* 50 F2
Kayoa, *Indonesia* 37 D7
Kayomba, *Zambia* 55 E1
Kayrunnera, *Australia* 63 E3
Kayseri, *Turkey* 25 G6
Kaysville, *U.S.A.* 82 F8
Kayuagung, *Indonesia* 36 E2
Kazachinskoye, *Russia* 27 D11
Kazachye, *Russia* 27 B14
Kazakhstan ■, *Asia* 26 E7
Kazan, *Russia* 24 C8
Kazan-Rettō, *Pac. Oc.* 64 E6
Kazanlŭk, *Bulgaria* 21 C11
Kāzerūn, *Iran* 45 D6
Kazumba, *Zaïre* 52 F4
Kazuno, *Japan* 30 D10
Kazym →, *Russia* 26 C7
Ké-Macina, *Mali* 50 F3
Kéa, *Greece* 21 F11
Keams Canyon, *U.S.A.* 83 J8
Kearney, *U.S.A.* 80 E5
Keban, *Turkey* 25 G6
Kebnekaise, *Sweden* 8 C15
Kebri Dehar, *Ethiopia* 46 F3
Kebumen, *Indonesia* 37 G13
Kechika →, *Canada* 72 B3
Kecskemét, *Hungary* 17 E9
Kedgwick, *Canada* 71 C6
Kédhros Óros, *Greece* 23 D6
Kedia Hill, *Botswana* 56 C3
Kediri, *Indonesia* 37 G15
Kédougou, *Senegal* 50 F2
Keeler, *U.S.A.* 84 J9
Keeley L., *Canada* 73 C7
Keeling Is. = Cocos Is., *Ind. Oc.* 64 J1
Keene, *Calif., U.S.A.* 85 K8
Keene, *N.H., U.S.A.* 79 D12
Keeper Hill, *Ireland* 13 D3
Keer-Weer, C., *Australia* 62 A3
Keeseville, *U.S.A.* 79 B11
Keetmanshoop, *Namibia* 56 D2
Keewatin, *U.S.A.* 80 B8
Keewatin □, *Canada* 73 A9
Keewatin →, *Canada* 73 B8
Kefallinia, *Greece* 21 E9
Kefamenanu, *Indonesia* 37 F6
Keffi, *Nigeria* 50 G6
Keflavík, *Iceland* 8 D2
Keg River, *Canada* 72 B5
Kegaska, *Canada* 71 B7
Keighley, *U.K.* 10 D6
Keimoes, *S. Africa* 56 D3
Keith, *Australia* 63 F3
Keith, *U.K.* 12 D6
Keith Arm, *Canada* 68 B7
Kejser Franz Joseph Fjord = Kong Franz Joseph Fd., *Greenland* 4 B6
Kekri, *India* 42 G6
Kël, *Russia* 27 C13
Kelan, *China* 34 E6
Kelang, *Malaysia* 39 L3
Kelantan →, *Malaysia* 39 J4
Kelibia, *Tunisia* 51 A7
Kellé, *Congo* 52 E2
Keller, *U.S.A.* 82 B4
Kellerberrin, *Australia* 61 F2
Kellett, C., *Canada* 4 B1
Kelleys I., *U.S.A.* 78 E2
Kellogg, *U.S.A.* 82 C5
Kelloselkä, *Finland* 8 C20
Kells = Ceanannus Mor, *Ireland* 13 C5
Kélo, *Chad* 51 G8
Kelokedhara, *Cyprus* 23 E11
Kelowna, *Canada* 72 D5
Kelsey Bay, *Canada* 72 C3
Kelseyville, *U.S.A.* 84 G4
Kelso, *N.Z.* 59 L2
Kelso, *U.K.* 12 F6
Kelso, *U.S.A.* 84 D4
Keluang, *Malaysia* 39 L4
Kelvington, *Canada* 73 C8
Kem, *Russia* 24 B5
Kem →, *Russia* 24 B5
Kema, *Indonesia* 37 D7
Kemano, *Canada* 72 C3
Kemasik, *Malaysia* 39 K4
Kemerovo, *Russia* 26 D9
Kemi, *Finland* 8 D18
Kemi älv = Kemijoki →, *Finland* 8 D18
Kemijärvi, *Finland* 8 C19
Kemijoki →, *Finland* 8 D18
Kemmerer, *U.S.A.* 82 F8
Kemmuna = Comino, *Malta* 23 C1
Kemp L., *U.S.A.* 81 J5
Kemp Land, *Antarctica* 5 C5
Kempsey, *Australia* 63 E5
Kempt, L., *Canada* 70 C5
Kempten, *Germany* 16 E5
Kemptville, *Canada* 70 C4
Kendal, *Indonesia* 36 F4
Kendal, *U.K.* 10 C5
Kendall, *Australia* 63 E5
Kendall →, *Australia* 62 A3
Kendallville, *U.S.A.* 76 E3
Kendari, *Indonesia* 37 E6
Kendawangan, *Indonesia* 36 E4
Kende, *Nigeria* 50 F5
Kendenup, *Australia* 61 F2
Kendrapara, *India* 41 J15
Kendrew, *S. Africa* 56 E3
Kendrick, *U.S.A.* 82 C5
Kene Thao, *Laos* 38 D3
Kenedy, *U.S.A.* 81 L6
Kenema, *S. Leone* 50 G2
Keng Kok, *Laos* 38 D5
Keng Tawng, *Burma* 41 J21
Keng Tung, *Burma* 41 J21
Kenge, *Zaïre* 52 E3
Kengeja, *Tanzania* 54 D4
Kenhardt, *S. Africa* 56 D3
Kenitra, *Morocco* 50 B3
Kenli, *China* 35 F10
Kenmare, *Ireland* 13 E2
Kenmare, *U.S.A.* 80 A3
Kenmare →, *Ireland* 13 E2
Kennebec, *U.S.A.* 80 D5
Kennedy, *Zimbabwe* 55 F2
Kennedy Ra., *Australia* 61 D2
Kennedy Taungdeik, *Burma* 41 H18
Kennet →, *U.K.* 11 F7
Kenneth Ra., *Australia* 60 D2
Kennett, *U.S.A.* 81 G9
Kennewick, *U.S.A.* 82 C4
Kénogami, *Canada* 71 C5
Kenogami →, *Canada* 70 B3
Kenora, *Canada* 73 D10
Kenosha, *U.S.A.* 76 D2
Kensington, *Canada* 71 C7
Kensington, *U.S.A.* 80 F5
Kensington Downs, *Australia* 62 C3
Kent, *Ohio, U.S.A.* 78 E3
Kent, *Oreg., U.S.A.* 82 D3
Kent, *Tex., U.S.A.* 81 K2
Kent, *Wash., U.S.A.* 84 C4
Kent □, *U.K.* 11 F8
Kent Group, *Australia* 62 F4
Kent Pen., *Canada* 68 B9
Kentau, *Kazakhstan* 26 E7
Kentland, *U.S.A.* 76 E2
Kenton, *U.S.A.* 76 E4
Kentucky □, *U.S.A.* 76 G3
Kentucky →, *U.S.A.* 76 F3
Kentucky L., *U.S.A.* 77 G2
Kentville, *Canada* 71 C7
Kentwood, *U.S.A.* 81 K9
Kentwood, *La., U.S.A.* 81 K9
Kenya ■, *Africa* 54 B4
Kenya, Mt., *Kenya* 54 C4
Keo Neua, Deo, *Vietnam* 38 C5
Keokuk, *U.S.A.* 80 E9
Kep, *Cambodia* 39 G5
Kep, *Vietnam* 38 B6
Kepi, *Indonesia* 37 F9
Kerala □, *India* 40 P10
Kerama-Rettō, *Japan* 31 L3
Keran, *Pakistan* 43 B5
Kerang, *Australia* 63 F3
Keraudren, C., *Australia* 60 C2
Kerch, *Ukraine* 25 E6
Kerchoual, *Mali* 50 E5
Keren, *Ethiopia* 51 E12
Kerguelen, *Ind. Oc.* 3 G13
Kericho, *Kenya* 54 C4
Kericho □, *Kenya* 54 C4
Kerinci, *Indonesia* 36 E2
Kerki, *Turkmenistan* 26 F7
Kérkira, *Greece* 23 A3
Kerkrade, *Neths.* 15 D6
Kermadec Is., *Pac. Oc.* 64 K10
Kermadec Trench, *Pac. Oc.* 64 L10
Kermān, *Iran* 45 D8
Kerman, *U.S.A.* 84 J6
Kermān □, *Iran* 45 D8
Kermānshāh = Bākhtarān, *Iran* 44 C5
Kermit, *U.S.A.* 81 K3
Kern →, *U.S.A.* 85 K7
Kernville, *U.S.A.* 85 K8
Keroh, *Malaysia* 39 K3
Kerrobert, *Canada* 73 C7
Kerrville, *U.S.A.* 81 K5
Kerry □, *Ireland* 13 D2
Kerry Hd., *Ireland* 13 D2
Kertosono, *Indonesia* 37 G15
Kerulen →, *Asia* 33 B6
Kerzaz, *Algeria* 50 C4
Kesagami →, *Canada* 70 B4
Kesagami L., *Canada* 70 B3
Kesennuma, *Japan* 30 E10
Keshit, *Iran* 45 D8
Keski-Suomen lääni □, *Finland* 8 E18
Kestell, *S. Africa* 57 D4
Kestenga, *Russia* 24 A5
Keswick, *U.K.* 10 C4
Ket →, *Russia* 26 D9
Keta, *Ghana* 50 G5
Ketapang, *Indonesia* 36 E4
Ketchikan, *U.S.A.* 68 C6
Ketchum, *U.S.A.* 82 E6
Keti Bandar, *Pakistan* 42 G2
Ketri, *India* 42 E6
Kettering, *U.K.* 11 E7
Kettle →, *Canada* 73 B11
Kettle Falls, *U.S.A.* 82 B4
Kettleman City, *U.S.A.* 84 J7
Kevin, *U.S.A.* 82 B8
Kewanee, *U.S.A.* 80 E10
Kewaunee, *U.S.A.* 76 C2
Keweenaw B., *U.S.A.* 76 B1
Keweenaw Pen., *U.S.A.* 76 B2
Keweenaw Pt., *U.S.A.* 76 B2
Key Harbour, *Canada* 70 C3
Key West, *U.S.A.* 75 F10
Keyser, *U.S.A.* 76 F6
Keystone, *U.S.A.* 80 D3
Kezhma, *Russia* 27 D11
Khabarovo, *Russia* 26 C7
Khabarovsk, *Russia* 27 E14
Khabr, *Iran* 45 D8
Khābūr →, *Syria* 44 C4
Khachrod, *India* 42 H6
Khadro, *Pakistan* 42 F3
Khadzhilyangar, *India* 43 B8
Khagaria, *India* 43 G12
Khaipur, *Bahawalpur, Pakistan* 42 E5
Khaipur, *Hyderabad, Pakistan* 42 F3
Khair, *India* 42 F7
Khairabad, *India* 43 F9
Khairagarh, *India* 43 J9
Khairpur, *Pakistan* 40 F6
Khakhea, *Botswana* 56 C3
Khalafābād, *Iran* 45 D6
Khalilabad, *India* 43 F10
Khalīlī, *Iran* 45 E7
Khalkhāl, *Iran* 45 B6
Khalkís, *Greece* 21 E10
Khalmer-Sede = Tazovskiy, *Russia* 26 C8
Khalmer Yu, *Russia* 24 A12
Khalturin, *Russia* 24 C8
Khalūf, *Oman* 46 C6
Kham Keut, *Laos* 38 C5
Khamas Country, *Botswana* 56 C4
Khambat, G. of, *India* 42 J5
Khambhaliya, *India* 42 H3
Khambhat, *India* 42 H5
Khamīr, *Iran* 45 E7
Khamir, *Yemen* 46 D3
Khamsa, *Egypt* 47 E1
Khān Abū Shāmat, *Syria* 47 B5
Khān Azād, *Iraq* 44 C5
Khān Mujiddah, *Iraq* 44 C4
Khān Shaykhūn, *Syria* 44 C3
Khān Yūnis, *Egypt* 47 D3
Khānaqīn, *Iraq* 44 C5
Khānbāghī, *Iran* 45 B7
Khandwa, *India* 40 J10
Khandyga, *Russia* 27 C14
Khāneh, *Iran* 44 B5
Khanewal, *Pakistan* 42 D4
Khanh Duong, *Vietnam* 38 F7
Khaniá, *Greece* 23 D6
Khaniá □, *Greece* 23 D6
Khanion, Kólpos, *Greece* 23 D5
Khanka, Ozero, *Asia* 27 E14
Khankendy, *Azerbaijan* 25 G8
Khanna, *India* 42 D7
Khanpur, *Pakistan* 42 E4
Khanty-Mansiysk, *Russia* 26 C7
Khapalu, *Pakistan* 43 B7
Khapcheranga, *Russia* 27 E12
Kharagpur, *India* 43 H12
Khárakas, *Greece* 23 D7
Kharan Kalat, *Pakistan* 40 E4
Kharānaq, *Iran* 45 C7
Kharda, *India* 40 K9
Khardung La, *India* 43 B7
Khârga, El Wâhât el, *Egypt* 51 C11
Khargon, *India* 40 J9
Khārk, Jazireh, *Iran* 45 D6
Kharkov, *Ukraine* 25 E6
Kharovsk, *Russia* 24 C7
Khartoum = El Khartûm, *Sudan* 51 E11
Khasan, *Russia* 30 C5
Khāsh, *Iran* 40 E2
Khashm el Girba, *Sudan* 51 F12
Khaskovo, *Bulgaria* 21 D11
Khatanga, *Russia* 27 B11
Khatanga →, *Russia* 27 B11
Khatauli, *India* 42 E7
Khātūnābād, *Iran* 45 C6
Khatyrka, *Russia* 27 C18
Khaybar, Harrat, *Si. Arabia* 44 E4
Khāzimiyah, *Iraq* 44 C4
Khe Bo, *Vietnam* 38 C5
Khe Long, *Vietnam* 38 B5
Khed Brahma, *India* 40 G8
Khekra, *India* 42 E7
Khemarak Phouminville, *Cambodia* 39 G4
Khemmarat, *Thailand* 38 D5
Khenāmān, *Iran* 45 D8
Khenchela, *Algeria* 50 A6
Khenifra, *Morocco* 50 B3
Kherson, *Ukraine* 25 E5
Khersónisos Akrotíri, *Greece* 23 D6
Kheta →, *Russia* 27 B11
Khilok, *Russia* 27 D12
Khíos, *Greece* 21 E12
Khirbat Qanāfār, *Lebanon* 47 B4
Khiuma = Hiiumaa, *Estonia* 24 C3
Khiva, *Uzbekistan* 26 E7
Khiyāv, *Iran* 44 B5
Khlong Khlung, *Thailand* 38 D2
Khmelnitskiy, *Ukraine* 25 E4
Khmer Rep. = Cambodia ■, *Asia* 38 F5
Khoai, Hon, *Vietnam* 39 H5
Khodzent, *Tajikistan* 26 E7
Khojak P., *Afghan.* 40 D5
Khok Kloi, *Thailand* 39 H2
Khok Pho, *Thailand* 39 J3
Kholm, *Russia* 24 C5
Kholmsk, *Russia* 27 E15
Khomas Hochland, *Namibia* 56 C2
Khomayn, *Iran* 45 C6
Khon Kaen, *Thailand* 38 D4
Khong, *Laos* 38 E5
Khong Sedone, *Laos* 38 E5
Khonu, *Russia* 27 C15
Khoper →, *Russia* 26 E5
Khóra Sfakion, *Greece* 23 D6
Khorāsān □, *Iran* 45 C8
Khorat = Nakhon Ratchasima, *Thailand* 38 E4
Khorat, Cao Nguyen, *Thailand* 38 E4
Khorixas, *Namibia* 56 C1
Khorog, *Tajikistan* 26 F8
Khorramābād, *Khorāsān, Iran* 45 C8
Khorramābād, *Lorestān, Iran* 45 C6
Khorrāmshahr, *Iran* 45 D6
Khosravī, *Iran* 45 D6
Khosrowābād, *Khuzestān, Iran* 45 D6
Khosrowābād, *Kordestān, Iran* 44 C5
Khosūyeh, *Iran* 45 D7
Khouribga, *Morocco* 50 B3
Khowai, *Bangla.* 41 G17
Khrysokhou B., *Cyprus* 23 D11
Khu Khan, *Thailand* 38 E5
Khuff, *Si. Arabia* 44 E5
Khūgīānī, *Afghan.* 42 D1
Khulna, *Bangla.* 41 H16
Khulna □, *Bangla.* 41 H16
Khumago, *Botswana* 56 C3
Khūnsorkh, *Iran* 45 E8
Khūr, *Iran* 45 C8
Khurai, *India* 42 G8
Khurayş, *Si. Arabia* 45 E6
Khūrīyā Mūrīyā, Jazā 'ir, *Oman* 46 D6
Khurja, *India* 42 E7
Khūsf, *Iran* 45 C8
Khush, *Afghan.* 40 C3
Khushab, *Pakistan* 42 C5
Khuzdar, *Pakistan* 42 F2
Khūzestān □, *Iran* 45 D6
Khvājeh, *Iran* 44 B5
Khvānsār, *Iran* 45 D7
Khvor, *Iran* 45 C7
Khvorgū, *Iran* 45 E8
Khvormūj, *Iran* 45 D6
Khvoy, *Iran* 44 B5
Khyber Pass, *Afghan.* 42 B4
Kiabukwa, *Zaïre* 55 D1
Kiama, *Australia* 63 E5
Kiamba, *Phil.* 37 C6
Kiambi, *Zaïre* 54 D2
Kiambu, *Kenya* 54 C4
Kiangsi = Jiangxi □, *China* 33 D6
Kiangsu = Jiangsu □, *China* 35 H10
Kibanga Port, *Uganda* 54 B3
Kibangou, *Congo* 52 E2
Kibara, *Tanzania* 54 C3
Kibare, Mts., *Zaïre* 54 D2
Kibombo, *Zaïre* 54 C2
Kibondo, *Tanzania* 54 C3
Kibondo □, *Tanzania* 54 C3
Kibumbu, *Burundi* 54 C2
Kibungu, *Rwanda* 54 C3
Kibuye, *Burundi* 54 C2
Kibuye, *Rwanda* 54 C2
Kibwesa, *Tanzania* 54 D2
Kibwezi, *Kenya* 54 C4
Kichiga, *Russia* 27 D17
Kicking Horse Pass, *Canada* 72 C5
Kidal, *Mali* 50 E5
Kidderminster, *U.K.* 11 E5
Kidete, *Tanzania* 54 D4
Kidnappers, C., *N.Z.* 59 H6
Kidston, *Australia* 62 B3
Kidugallo, *Tanzania* 54 D4
Kiel, *Germany* 16 A5
Kiel Kanal = Nord-Ostsee Kanal, *Germany* 16 A4
Kielce, *Poland* 17 C10
Kieler Bucht, *Germany* 16 A5
Kien Binh, *Vietnam* 39 H5
Kien Tan, *Vietnam* 39 G5
Kienge, *Zaïre* 55 E2
Kiev = Kiyev, *Ukraine* 25 D5
Kiffa, *Mauritania* 50 E2
Kifrī, *Iraq* 44 C5
Kigali, *Rwanda* 54 C3
Kigarama, *Tanzania* 54 C3
Kigoma □, *Tanzania* 54 D2
Kigoma-Ujiji, *Tanzania* 54 C2
Kigomasha, Ras, *Tanzania* 54 C4
Kihee, *Australia* 63 D3
Kii-Sanchi, *Japan* 31 G7
Kii-Suidō, *Japan* 31 H7
Kikaiga-Shima, *Japan* 31 K4
Kikinda, *Serbia, Yug.* 21 B9
Kikládhes, *Greece* 21 F11
Kikwit, *Zaïre* 52 E3
Kilauea Crater, *U.S.A.* 74 J17
Kilcoy, *Australia* 63 D5
Kildare, *Ireland* 13 C5
Kildare □, *Ireland* 13 C5
Kilgore, *U.S.A.* 81 J7
Kilifi, *Kenya* 54 C4
Kilifi □, *Kenya* 54 C4
Kilimanjaro, *Tanzania* 54 C4
Kilimanjaro □, *Tanzania* 54 C4
Kilindini, *Kenya* 54 C4
Kilju, *N. Korea* 35 D15
Kilkee, *Ireland* 13 D2
Kilkenny, *Ireland* 13 D4
Kilkenny □, *Ireland* 13 D4
Kilkieran B., *Ireland* 13 C2
Killala, *Ireland* 13 B2
Killala B., *Ireland* 13 B2
Killaloe, *Ireland* 13 D3
Killaloe Sta., *Canada* 78 A7
Killam, *Canada* 72 C6
Killarney, *Australia* 63 D5
Killarney, *Canada* 70 C3
Killarney, *Ireland* 13 D2
Killarney, Lakes of, *Ireland* 13 E2
Killary Harbour, *Ireland* 13 C2
Killdeer, *Canada* 73 D7
Killdeer, *U.S.A.* 80 B3
Killeen, *U.S.A.* 81 K6
Killiecrankie, Pass of, *U.K.* 12 E5
Killin, *U.K.* 12 E4
Killíni, *Greece* 21 F10
Killybegs, *Ireland* 13 B3
Kilmarnock, *U.K.* 12 F4
Kilmore, *Australia* 63 F3
Kilondo, *Tanzania* 55 D3
Kilosa, *Tanzania* 54 D4

Kilosa □, *Tanzania* 54 D4
Kilrush, *Ireland* 13 D2
Kilwa □, *Tanzania* 55 D4
Kilwa Kisiwani, *Tanzania* 55 D4
Kilwa Kivinje, *Tanzania* 55 D4
Kilwa Masoko, *Tanzania* 55 D4
Kim, *U.S.A.* 81 G3
Kimaam, *Indonesia* 37 F9
Kimamba, *Tanzania* 54 D4
Kimba, *Australia* 63 E2
Kimball, *Nebr., U.S.A.* 80 E3
Kimball, *S. Dak., U.S.A.* 80 D5
Kimberley, *Canada* 72 D5
Kimberley, *S. Africa* 56 D3
Kimberley Downs, *Australia* 60 C3
Kimberly, *U.S.A.* 82 E6
Kimchaek, *N. Korea* 35 D15
Kimchŏn, *S. Korea* 35 F15
Kimje, *S. Korea* 35 G14
Kimry, *Russia* 24 C6
Kimsquit, *Canada* 72 C3
Kinabalu, *Malaysia* 36 C5
Kinaskan L., *Canada* 72 B2
Kinbasket L., *Canada* 72 C5
Kincaid, *Canada* 73 D7
Kincardine, *Canada* 70 D3
Kinda, *Zaïre* 55 D2
Kinder Scout, *U.K.* 10 D6
Kindersley, *Canada* 73 C7
Kindia, *Guinea* 50 G2
Kindu, *Zaïre* 54 C2
Kineshma, *Russia* 24 C7
Kinesi, *Tanzania* 54 C3
King, L., *Australia* 61 F2
King, Mt., *Australia* 62 D4
King City, *U.S.A.* 83 H3
King Cr. —►, *Australia* 62 C2
King Edward —►, *Australia* 60 B4
King Frederick VI Land = Kong Frederik VI.s Kyst, *Greenland* 4 C5
King George B., *Falk. Is.* 96 G4
King George I., *Antarctica* 5 C18
King George Is., *Canada* 69 C11
King I. = Kadan Kyun, *Burma* 36 B1
King I., *Australia* 62 F3
King I., *Canada* 72 C3
King Leopold Ras., *Australia* 60 C4
King Sd., *Australia* 60 C3
King William I., *Canada* 68 B10
King William's Town, *S. Africa* 56 E4
Kingaroy, *Australia* 63 D5
Kingfisher, *U.S.A.* 81 H6
Kingirbān, *Iraq* 44 C5
Kingman, *Ariz., U.S.A.* 85 K12
Kingman, *Kans., U.S.A.* 81 G5
Kingoonya, *Australia* 63 E2
Kings —►, *U.S.A.* 83 H4
Kings Canyon National Park, *U.S.A.* 83 H4
King's Lynn, *U.K.* 10 E8
Kings Mountain, *U.S.A.* 77 H5
King's Peak, *U.S.A.* 82 F8
Kingsbridge, *U.K.* 11 G4
Kingsburg, *U.S.A.* 83 H4
Kingscote, *Australia* 63 F2
Kingscourt, *Ireland* 13 C5
Kingsley, *U.S.A.* 80 D7
Kingsport, *U.S.A.* 77 G4
Kingston, *Canada* 70 D4
Kingston, *Jamaica* 88 C4
Kingston, *N.Z.* 59 L2
Kingston, *N.Y., U.S.A.* 79 E10
Kingston, *Pa., U.S.A.* 79 E9
Kingston, *R.I., U.S.A.* 79 E13
Kingston Pk., *U.S.A.* 85 K11
Kingston South East, *Australia* 63 F2
Kingston upon Hull, *U.K.* 10 D7
Kingston-upon-Thames, *U.K.* 11 F7
Kingstown, *St. Vincent* 89 D7
Kingstree, *U.S.A.* 77 J6
Kingsville, *Canada* 70 D3
Kingsville, *U.S.A.* 81 M6
Kingussie, *U.K.* 12 D4
Kinistino, *Canada* 73 C7
Kinkala, *Congo* 52 E2
Kinki □, *Japan* 31 H8
Kinleith, *N.Z.* 59 H5
Kinmount, *Canada* 78 B6
Kinnaird, *Canada* 72 D5
Kinnairds Hd., *U.K.* 12 D7
Kinnarodden, *Norway* 6 A11
Kino, *Mexico* 86 B2
Kinoje —►, *Canada* 70 B3
Kinomoto, *Japan* 31 G8
Kinoni, *Uganda* 54 C3
Kinross, *U.K.* 12 E5
Kinsale, *Ireland* 13 E3
Kinsale, Old Hd. of, *Ireland* 13 E3
Kinshasa, *Zaïre* 52 E3
Kinsley, *U.S.A.* 81 G5
Kinston, *U.S.A.* 77 H7
Kintampo, *Ghana* 50 G4
Kintap, *Indonesia* 36 E5
Kintore Ra., *Australia* 60 D4
Kintyre, *U.K.* 12 F3
Kintyre, Mull of, *U.K.* 12 F3
Kinushseo —►, *Canada* 70 A3
Kinuso, *Canada* 72 B5
Kinyangiri, *Tanzania* 54 C3
Kinzua, *U.S.A.* 78 E6
Kinzua Dam, *U.S.A.* 78 E5
Kiosk, *Canada* 70 C4
Kiowa, *Kans., U.S.A.* 81 G5
Kiowa, *Okla., U.S.A.* 81 H7
Kipahigan L., *Canada* 73 B8
Kipanga, *Tanzania* 54 D4
Kiparissía, *Greece* 21 F9
Kiparissiakós Kólpos, *Greece* 21 F9
Kipembawe, *Tanzania* 54 D3
Kipengere Ra., *Tanzania* 55 D3
Kipili, *Tanzania* 54 D3
Kipini, *Kenya* 54 C5
Kipling, *Canada* 73 C8
Kippure, *Ireland* 13 C5
Kipushi, *Zaïre* 55 E2
Kiratpur, *India* 42 E8
Kirensk, *Russia* 27 D11
Kirgella Rocks, *Australia* 61 F3
Kirghizia ■, *Asia* 26 E8
Kirgizia = Kirghizia ■, *Asia* 26 E8
Kirgiziya Steppe, *Kazakhstan* 25 D10
Kiri, *Zaïre* 52 E3
Kiribati ■, *Pac. Oc.* 64 H9
Kırıkkale, *Turkey* 25 G5
Kirillov, *Russia* 24 C6
Kirin = Jilin, *China* 35 C14
Kirin = Jilin □, *China* 35 C13
Kiritimati, *Kiribati* 65 G12
Kirkcaldy, *U.K.* 12 E5
Kirkcudbright, *U.K.* 12 G4
Kirkee, *India* 40 K8
Kirkenes, *Norway* 8 B21
Kirkintilloch, *U.K.* 12 F4
Kirkjubæjarklaustur, *Iceland* 8 E4
Kirkland, *U.S.A.* 83 J7
Kirkland Lake, *Canada* 70 C3
Kırklareli, *Turkey* 21 D12
Kirksville, *U.S.A.* 80 E8
Kirkūk, *Iraq* 44 C5
Kirkwall, *U.K.* 12 C6
Kirkwood, *S. Africa* 56 E4
Kirov = Vyatka, *Russia* 26 D5
Kirovabad = Gyandzha, *Azerbaijan* 25 F8
Kirovakan = Karaklis, *Armenia* 25 F7
Kirovograd = Yelizavetgrad, *Ukraine* 25 E5
Kirovsk, *Russia* 24 A5
Kirovsk, *Turkmenistan* 26 F7
Kirovskiy, *Russia* 27 D16
Kirovskiy, *Russia* 30 B6
Kirriemuir, *U.K.* 12 E6
Kirsanov, *Russia* 24 D7
Kırşehir, *Turkey* 25 G5
Kirstonia, *S. Africa* 56 D3
Kirthar Range, *Pakistan* 42 F2
Kiruna, *Sweden* 8 C16
Kirundu, *Zaïre* 54 C2
Kirup, *Australia* 61 F2
Kiryū, *Japan* 31 F9
Kisaga, *Tanzania* 54 C3
Kisalaya, *Nic.* 88 D3
Kisámou, Kólpos, *Greece* 23 D5
Kisanga, *Zaïre* 54 B2
Kisangani, *Zaïre* 54 B2
Kisar, *Indonesia* 37 F7
Kisaran, *Indonesia* 36 D1
Kisarawe, *Tanzania* 54 D4
Kisarawe □, *Tanzania* 54 D4
Kisarazu, *Japan* 31 G9
Kiselevsk, *Russia* 26 D9
Kishanganga —►, *Pakistan* 43 B5
Kishanganj, *India* 43 F13
Kishangarh, *India* 42 F4
Kishinev, *Moldavia* 25 E4
Kishiwada, *Japan* 31 G7
Kishtwar, *India* 43 C6
Kisii, *Kenya* 54 C3
Kisii □, *Kenya* 54 C3
Kisiju, *Tanzania* 54 D4
Kisizi, *Uganda* 54 C2
Kiska I., *U.S.A.* 68 C1
Kiskatinaw —►, *Canada* 72 B4
Kiskittogisu L., *Canada* 73 C9
Kiskőrös, *Hungary* 17 E9
Kiskunfélegyháza, *Hungary* 17 E9
Kiskunhalas, *Hungary* 17 E9
Kislovodsk, *Russia* 25 F7
Kiso-Gawa —►, *Japan* 31 G8
Kiso-Sammyaku, *Japan* 31 G8
Kisofukushima, *Japan* 31 G8
Kisoro, *Uganda* 54 C2
Kissidougou, *Guinea* 50 G2
Kissimmee, *U.S.A.* 77 L5
Kissimmee —►, *U.S.A.* 77 M5
Kississing L., *Canada* 73 B8
Kissónerga, *Cyprus* 23 E11
Kisumu, *Kenya* 54 C3
Kiswani, *Tanzania* 54 C4
Kiswere, *Tanzania* 55 D4
Kit Carson, *U.S.A.* 80 F3
Kita, *Mali* 50 F3
Kitab, *Uzbekistan* 26 F7
Kitaibaraki, *Japan* 31 F10
Kitakami, *Japan* 30 E10
Kitakami-Gawa —►, *Japan* 30 E10
Kitakami-Sammyaku, *Japan* 30 E10
Kitakata, *Japan* 30 F9
Kitakyūshū, *Japan* 31 H5
Kitale, *Kenya* 54 B4
Kitami, *Japan* 30 C11
Kitami-Sammyaku, *Japan* 30 B11
Kitangiri, L., *Tanzania* 54 C3
Kitaya, *Tanzania* 55 E5
Kitchener, *Australia* 61 F3
Kitchener, *Canada* 70 D3
Kitega = Gitega, *Burundi* 54 C2
Kitengo, *Zaïre* 54 D1
Kiteto □, *Tanzania* 54 C4
Kitgum, *Uganda* 54 B3
Kíthira, *Greece* 21 F11
Kíthnos, *Greece* 21 F11
Kiti, *Cyprus* 23 E12
Kiti, C., *Cyprus* 23 E12
Kitikmeot □, *Canada* 68 B9
Kitimat, *Canada* 72 C3
Kitinen —►, *Finland* 8 C19
Kitsuki, *Japan* 31 H5
Kittakittaooloo, L., *Australia* 63 D2
Kittanning, *U.S.A.* 78 F5
Kittatinny Mts., *U.S.A.* 79 E10
Kittery, *U.S.A.* 77 D10
Kitui, *Kenya* 54 C4
Kitui □, *Kenya* 54 C4
Kitwe, *Zambia* 55 E2
Kivalo, *Finland* 8 C19
Kivarli, *India* 42 G5
Kividhes, *Cyprus* 23 E11
Kivu □, *Zaïre* 54 C2
Kivu, L., *Zaïre* 54 C2
Kiyev, *Ukraine* 25 D5
Kiyevskoye Vdkhr., *Ukraine* 25 D5
Kizel, *Russia* 24 C10
Kiziguru, *Rwanda* 54 C3
Kızıl Irmak —►, *Turkey* 25 F6
Kizil Jilga, *India* 43 B8
Kizimkazi, *Tanzania* 54 D4
Kizlyar, *Russia* 25 F8
Kizyl-Arvat, *Turkmenistan* 26 F6
Kladno, *Czech.* 16 C7
Klaeng, *Thailand* 38 F3
Klagenfurt, *Austria* 16 E7
Klaipeda, *Lithuania* 24 C3
Klamath —►, *U.S.A.* 82 F1
Klamath Falls, *U.S.A.* 82 E3
Klamath Mts., *U.S.A.* 82 F2
Klappan —►, *Canada* 72 B3
Klarälven —►, *Sweden* 9 G12
Klaten, *Indonesia* 37 G14
Klatovy, *Czech.* 16 D6
Klawak, *U.S.A.* 72 B2
Klawer, *S. Africa* 56 E2
Kleena Kleene, *Canada* 72 C4
Klein, *U.S.A.* 82 C9
Klein-Karas, *Namibia* 56 D2
Klerksdorp, *S. Africa* 56 D4
Kletskiy, *Russia* 25 E7
Klickitat, *U.S.A.* 82 D3
Klickitat —►, *U.S.A.* 84 E5
Klidhes, *Cyprus* 23 D13
Klin, *Russia* 26 D4
Klinaklini —►, *Canada* 72 C3
Klipdale, *S. Africa* 56 E2
Klipplaat, *S. Africa* 56 E3
Kłodzko, *Poland* 16 C8
Klondike, *Canada* 68 B6
Klouto, *Togo* 50 G5
Kluane L., *Canada* 68 B6
Klyuchevskaya, Gora, *Russia* 27 D17
Knaresborough, *U.K.* 10 C6
Knee L., *Man., Canada* 73 B10
Knee L., *Sask., Canada* 73 B7
Knight Inlet, *Canada* 72 C3
Knighton, *U.K.* 11 E4
Knights Ferry, *U.S.A.* 84 H6
Knight's Landing, *U.S.A.* 84 G5
Knob, C., *Australia* 61 F2
Knockmealdown Mts., *Ireland* 13 D4
Knokke, *Belgium* 15 C3
Knossós, *Greece* 23 D7
Knox, *U.S.A.* 76 E2
Knox, C., *Canada* 72 C2
Knox City, *U.S.A.* 81 J5
Knox Coast, *Antarctica* 5 C8
Knoxville, *Iowa, U.S.A.* 80 E8
Knoxville, *Tenn., U.S.A.* 77 H4
Knysna, *S. Africa* 56 E3
Ko Kha, *Thailand* 38 C2
Ko Tao, *Thailand* 39 G2
Koartac, *Canada* 69 B13
Koba, *Aru, Indonesia* 37 F8
Koba, *Bangka, Indonesia* 36 E3
Kobarid, *Slovenia* 20 A5
Kobayashi, *Japan* 31 J5
Kobdo = Hovd, *Mongolia* 32 B4
Kōbe, *Japan* 31 G7
København, *Denmark* 9 J12
Kōbi-Sho, *Japan* 31 M1
Koblenz, *Germany* 16 C3
Kobroor, Kepulauan, *Indonesia* 37 F8
Kocaeli = İzmit, *Turkey* 25 F4
Kočani, *Macedonia, Yug.* 21 D10
Kočevje, *Slovenia* 20 B6
Koch Bihar, *India* 41 F16
Kochang, *S. Korea* 35 G14
Kochas, *India* 43 G10
Kocheya, *Russia* 27 D13
Kōchi, *Japan* 31 H6
Kōchi □, *Japan* 31 H6
Kochiu = Gejiu, *China* 32 D5
Kodiak, *U.S.A.* 68 C4
Kodiak I., *U.S.A.* 68 C4
Kodinar, *India* 42 J4
Koes, *Namibia* 56 D2
Koffiefontein, *S. Africa* 56 D4
Kofiau, *Indonesia* 37 E7
Koforidua, *Ghana* 50 G4
Kōfu, *Japan* 31 G9
Koga, *Japan* 31 F9
Kogaluk —►, *Canada* 71 A7
Kogan, *Australia* 63 D5
Koh-i-Bābā, *Afghan.* 40 B5
Koh-i-Khurd, *Afghan.* 42 C1
Kohat, *Pakistan* 42 C4
Kohima, *India* 41 G19
Kohkīlūyeh va Būyer Aḥmadi □, *Iran* 45 D6
Kohler Ra., *Antarctica* 5 D15
Koin-dong, *N. Korea* 35 D14
Kojŏ, *N. Korea* 35 E14
Kojonup, *Australia* 61 F2
Kojūr, *Iran* 45 B6
Kokand, *Uzbekistan* 26 E8
Kokanee Glacier Prov. Park, *Canada* 72 D5
Kokas, *Indonesia* 37 E8
Kokchetav, *Kazakhstan* 26 D7
Kokemäenjoki, *Finland* 9 F16
Kokkola, *Finland* 8 E17
Koko Kyunzu, *Burma* 41 M18
Kokomo, *U.S.A.* 76 E2
Kokonau, *Indonesia* 37 E9
Koksan, *N. Korea* 35 E14
Koksoak —►, *Canada* 69 C13
Kokstad, *S. Africa* 57 E4
Kokubu, *Japan* 31 J5
Kokuora, *Russia* 27 B15
Kola, *Indonesia* 37 F8
Kola, *Russia* 24 A5
Kola Pen. = Kolskiy Poluostrov, *Russia* 24 A6
Kolahoi, *India* 43 B6
Kolaka, *Indonesia* 37 E6
Kolar, *India* 40 N11
Kolar Gold Fields, *India* 40 N11
Kolari, *Finland* 8 C17
Kolayat, *India* 40 F8
Kolchugino = Leninsk-Kuznetskiy, *Russia* 26 D9
Kolda, *Senegal* 50 F2
Kolding, *Denmark* 9 J10
Kole, *Zaïre* 52 E4
Kolepom = Yos Sudarso, Pulau, *Indonesia* 37 F9
Kolguyev, Ostrov, *Russia* 24 A8
Kolhapur, *India* 40 L9
Kolín, *Czech.* 16 C7
Kolmanskop, *Namibia* 56 D2
Köln, *Germany* 16 C3
Koło, *Poland* 17 B9
Kołobrzeg, *Poland* 16 A7
Kolokani, *Mali* 50 F3
Kolomna, *Russia* 24 C6
Kolomyya, *Ukraine* 25 E4
Kolonodale, *Indonesia* 37 E6
Kolosib, *India* 41 G18
Kolpashevo, *Russia* 26 D9
Kolpino, *Russia* 24 C5
Kolskiy Poluostrov, *Russia* 24 A6
Kolskiy Zaliv, *Russia* 24 A5
Kolwezi, *Zaïre* 55 E2
Kolyma —►, *Russia* 27 C17
Kolymskoye, Okhotsko, *Russia* 27 C16
Komandorskiye Ostrova, *Russia* 27 D17
Komárno, *Czech.* 17 E9
Komatipoort, *S. Africa* 57 D5
Komatou Yialou, *Cyprus* 23 D13
Komatsu, *Japan* 31 F8
Komatsujima, *Japan* 31 H7
Komi Republic □, *Russia* 24 B10
Kommunarsk, *Ukraine* 25 E6
Kommunizma, Pik, *Tajikistan* 26 F8
Komodo, *Indonesia* 37 F5
Komono, *Congo* 52 E2
Komoran, Pulau, *Indonesia* 37 F9
Komoro, *Japan* 31 F9
Komotini, *Greece* 21 D11
Kompasberg, *S. Africa* 56 E3
Kompong Bang, *Cambodia* 39 F5
Kompong Cham, *Cambodia* 39 F5
Kompong Chhnang, *Cambodia* 39 F5
Kompong Chikreng, *Cambodia* 38 F5
Kompong Kleang, *Cambodia* 38 F5
Kompong Luong, *Cambodia* 39 G5
Kompong Pranak, *Cambodia* 38 F5
Kompong Som, *Cambodia* 39 G4
Kompong Som, Chhung, *Cambodia* 39 G4
Kompong Speu, *Cambodia* 39 G5
Kompong Sralao, *Cambodia* 38 E5
Kompong Thom, *Cambodia* 38 F5
Kompong Trabeck, *Cambodia* 38 F5
Kompong Trabeck, *Cambodia* 39 G5
Kompong Trach, *Cambodia* 39 G5
Kompong Tralach, *Cambodia* 39 G5
Komsberg, *S. Africa* 56 E3
Komsomolets, Ostrov, *Russia* 27 A10
Komsomolsk, *Russia* 27 D14
Konarhá □, *Afghan.* 40 B7
Konārī, *Iran* 45 D6
Konawa, *U.S.A.* 81 H6
Konch, *India* 43 G8
Kondakovo, *Russia* 27 C16
Konde, *Tanzania* 54 C4
Kondinin, *Australia* 61 F2
Kondoa, *Tanzania* 54 C4
Kondoa □, *Tanzania* 54 D4
Kondókali, *Greece* 23 A3
Kondopaga, *Russia* 24 B5
Kondratyevo, *Russia* 27 D10
Konduga, *Nigeria* 51 F7
Konevo, *Russia* 24 B6
Kong, *Ivory C.* 50 G4
Kong —►, *Cambodia* 38 F5
Kong, Koh, *Cambodia* 39 G4
Kong Christian IX.s Land, *Greenland* 4 C6
Kong Christian X.s Land, *Greenland* 4 B6
Kong Franz Joseph Fd., *Greenland* 4 B6
Kong Frederik IX.s Land, *Greenland* 4 C5
Kong Frederik VI.s Kyst, *Greenland* 4 C5
Kong Frederik VIII.s Land, *Greenland* 4 B6
Kong Oscar Fjord, *Greenland* 4 B6
Kongju, *S. Korea* 35 F14
Konglu, *Burma* 41 F20
Kongolo, *Kasai Or., Zaïre* 54 D1
Kongolo, *Shaba, Zaïre* 54 D2
Kongor, *Sudan* 51 G11
Kongsberg, *Norway* 9 G10
Kongsvinger, *Norway* 9 F12
Kongwa, *Tanzania* 54 D4
Koni, *Zaïre* 55 E2
Koni, Mts., *Zaïre* 55 E2
Königsberg = Kaliningrad, *Russia* 24 D3
Konin, *Poland* 17 B9
Konjic, *Bos. & H., Yug.* 21 C7
Konkiep, *Namibia* 56 D2
Konosha, *Russia* 24 B7
Kōnosu, *Japan* 31 F9
Konotop, *Ukraine* 25 D5
Końskie, *Poland* 17 C10
Konstanz, *Germany* 16 E4
Kont, *Iran* 45 E9
Kontagora, *Nigeria* 50 F6
Kontum, *Vietnam* 38 E7
Kontum, Plateau du, *Vietnam* 38 E7
Konya, *Turkey* 25 G5
Konza, *Kenya* 54 C4
Kookynie, *Australia* 61 E3
Kooline, *Australia* 60 D2
Kooloonong, *Australia* 63 E3
Koolyanobbing, *Australia* 61 F2
Koondrook, *Australia* 63 F3
Koonibba, *Australia* 63 E1
Koorawatha, *Australia* 63 E4
Koorda, *Australia* 61 F2
Kooskia, *U.S.A.* 82 C6
Kootenai —►, *Canada* 82 B5
Kootenay L., *Canada* 72 D5
Kootenay Nat. Park, *Canada* 72 C5
Kootjieskolk, *S. Africa* 56 E3
Kopaonik, *Serbia, Yug.* 21 C9
Kópavogur, *Iceland* 8 D3
Koper, *Slovenia* 20 B5
Kopervik, *Norway* 9 G8
Kopeysk, *Russia* 26 D7
Kopi, *Australia* 63 E2
Köping, *Sweden* 9 G14
Kopparberg, *Sweden* 9 G13
Kopparbergs län □, *Sweden* 9 F13
Koppies, *S. Africa* 57 D4
Korab, *Macedonia, Yug.* 21 D9
Korakiána, *Greece* 23 A3
Korba, *India* 43 H10
Korbu, G., *Malaysia* 39 K3
Korça, *Albania* 21 D9
Korce = Korça, *Albania* 21 D9
Korčula, *Croatia* 20 C7
Kord Kūy, *Iran* 45 B7
Kord Sheykh, *Iran* 45 D7
Kordestān □, *Iran* 44 C5
Korea, North ■, *Asia* 35 E14
Korea, South ■, *Asia* 35 F15
Korea Bay, *Korea* 35 E13
Korea Strait, *Asia* 35 G15
Korhogo, *Ivory C.* 50 G3
Korim, *Indonesia* 37 E9
Korinthiakós Kólpos, *Greece* 21 E10
Kórinthos, *Greece* 21 F10
Korissa, Límni, *Greece* 23 B3
Kōriyama, *Japan* 30 F10
Korla, *China* 32 B3
Kormakiti, C., *Cyprus* 23 D11
Koro, *Fiji* 59 C8
Koro, *Ivory C.* 50 G3
Koro, *Mali* 50 F4
Koro Sea, *Fiji* 59 C9
Korogwe, *Tanzania* 54 D4
Korogwe □, *Tanzania* 54 D4
Koroit, *Australia* 63 F3
Koror, *Pac. Oc.* 37 C8
Körös —►, *Hungary* 17 E10
Korraraika, Helodranon' i, *Madag.* 57 B7
Korsakov, *Russia* 27 E15
Korshunovo, *Russia* 27 D12
Korsør, *Denmark* 9 J11
Korti, *Sudan* 51 E11
Kortrijk, *Belgium* 15 D3
Korwai, *India* 42 G8
Koryakskiy Khrebet, *Russia* 27 C18
Koryŏng, *S. Korea* 35 G15
Kos, *Greece* 21 F12
Koschagyl, *Kazakhstan* 25 E9
Kościan, *Poland* 16 B8
Kosciusko, *U.S.A.* 81 J10
Kosciusko, Mt., *Australia* 63 F4
Kosciusko I., *U.S.A.* 72 B2
Kosha, *Sudan* 51 D11
K'oshih = Kashi, *China* 32 C2
Koshiki-Rettō, *Japan* 31 J4

Kosi, *India* 42 F7
Kosi-meer, *S. Africa* 57 D5
Košice, *Czech.* 17 D10
Koskhinoú, *Greece* 23 C10
Koslan, *Russia* 24 B8
Kosŏng, *N. Korea* 35 E15
Kosovska-Mitrovica, *Serbia, Yug.* 21 C9
Kostamuksa, *Russia* 24 B5
Koster, *S. Africa* 56 D4
Kôstî, *Sudan* 51 F11
Kostroma, *Russia* 24 C7
Koszalin, *Poland* 16 A8
Kot Addu, *Pakistan* 42 D4
Kot Moman, *Pakistan* 42 C5
Kota, *India* 42 G6
Kota Baharu, *Malaysia* 39 J4
Kota Belud, *Malaysia* 36 C5
Kota Kinabalu, *Malaysia* 36 C5
Kota Tinggi, *Malaysia* 39 M4
Kotaagung, *Indonesia* 36 F2
Kotabaru, *Indonesia* 36 E5
Kotabumi, *Indonesia* 36 E2
Kotagede, *Indonesia* 37 G14
Kotamobagu, *Indonesia* 37 D6
Kotaneelee —►, *Canada* 72 A4
Kotawaringin, *Indonesia* 36 E4
Kotcho L., *Canada* 72 B4
Kotelnich, *Russia* 24 C8
Kotelnikovo, *Russia* 26 E5
Kotelnyy, Ostrov, *Russia* 27 B14
Kothi, *India* 43 G9
Kotiro, *Pakistan* 42 F2
Kotka, *Finland* 9 F19
Kotlas, *Russia* 24 B8
Kotli, *Pakistan* 42 C5
Kotmul, *Pakistan* 43 B6
Kotor, *Montenegro, Yug.* 21 C8
Kotputli, *India* 42 F7
Kotri, *Pakistan* 42 G3
Kottayam, *India* 40 Q10
Kotturu, *India* 40 M10
Kotuy —►, *Russia* 27 B11
Kotzebue, *U.S.A.* 68 B3
Kouango, *C.A.R.* 52 C4
Koudougou, *Burkina Faso* 50 F4
Koufonísi, *Greece* 23 E8
Kougaberge, *S. Africa* 56 E3
Kouilou —►, *Congo* 52 E2
Kouki, *C.A.R.* 52 C3
Koula Moutou, *Gabon* 52 E2
Koulen, *Cambodia* 38 F5
Koulikoro, *Mali* 50 F3
Kouloúra, *Greece* 23 A3
Koúm-bournoú, Ákra, *Greece* 23 C10
Koumala, *Australia* 62 C4
Koumra, *Chad* 51 G8
Kounradskiy, *Kazakhstan* 26 E8
Kountze, *U.S.A.* 81 K7
Kouris —►, *Cyprus* 23 E11
Kouroussa, *Guinea* 50 F3
Kousseri, *Cameroon* 51 F7
Koutiala, *Mali* 50 F3
Kovdor, *Russia* 24 A5
Kovel, *Ukraine* 24 D3
Kovrov, *Russia* 24 C7
Kowanyama, *Australia* 62 B3
Kowkash, *Canada* 70 B2
Kowŏn, *N. Korea* 35 E14
Koyabuti, *Indonesia* 37 E10
Koyuk, *U.S.A.* 68 B3
Koyukuk —►, *U.S.A.* 68 B4
Koza, *Japan* 31 L3
Kozáni, *Greece* 21 D9
Kozhikode = Calicut, *India* 40 P9
Kozhva, *Russia* 24 A10
Kpalimé, *Togo* 50 G5
Kra, Isthmus of = Kra, Kho Khot, *Thailand* 39 G2
Kra, Kho Khot, *Thailand* 39 G2
Kra Buri, *Thailand* 39 G2
Krabi, *Thailand* 39 H2
Kragan, *Indonesia* 37 G14
Kragerø, *Norway* 9 G10
Kragujevac, *Serbia, Yug.* 21 B9
Krakatau = Rakata, Pulau, *Indonesia* 36 F3
Krakor, *Cambodia* 38 F5
Kraków, *Poland* 17 C9
Kraksaan, *Indonesia* 37 G15
Kralanh, *Cambodia* 38 F4
Kraljevo, *Serbia, Yug.* 21 C9
Kramatorsk, *Ukraine* 25 E6
Kramfors, *Sweden* 8 E14
Krankskop, *S. Africa* 57 D5
Krasavino, *Russia* 24 B8
Kraskino, *Russia* 27 E14
Kraśnik, *Poland* 17 C11
Krasnoarmeysk, *Russia* 26 D5
Krasnodar, *Russia* 25 E6
Krasnokamsk, *Russia* 24 C10
Krasnoperekopsk, *Ukraine* 25 E5
Krasnorechenskiy, *Russia* 30 B7
Krasnoselkupsk, *Russia* 26 C9
Krasnoturinsk, *Russia* 24 C11
Krasnoufimsk, *Russia* 24 C10
Krasnouralsk, *Russia* 24 C11
Krasnovishersk, *Russia* 24 B10
Krasnovodsk, *Turkmenistan* 25 F9
Krasnoyarsk, *Russia* 27 D10
Krasnyy Luch, *Ukraine* 25 E6
Krasnyy Yar, *Russia* 25 E8
Kratie, *Cambodia* 38 F6
Krau, *Indonesia* 37 E10
Kravanh, Chuor Phnum, *Cambodia* 39 G4
Krefeld, *Germany* 16 C3
Kremenchug, *Ukraine* 25 E5
Kremenchugskoye Vdkhr., *Ukraine* 25 E5
Kremmling, *U.S.A.* 82 F10
Kremnica, *Czech.* 17 D9
Kribi, *Cameroon* 52 D1
Kriós, Ákra, *Greece* 23 D5
Krishna —►, *India* 41 M12
Krishnanagar, *India* 43 H13
Kristiansand, *Norway* 9 G10
Kristianstad, *Sweden* 9 H13
Kristianstads län □, *Sweden* 9 H13
Kristiansund, *Norway* 8 E9
Kristiinankaupunki, *Finland* 8 E16
Kristinehamn, *Sweden* 9 G13
Kristinestad, *Finland* 8 E16
Kríti, *Greece* 23 D7
Kritsá, *Greece* 23 D7
Krivoy Rog, *Ukraine* 25 E5
Krk, *Croatia* 20 B6
Krokodil —►, *Mozam.* 57 D5
Kronobergs län □, *Sweden* 9 H13
Kronprins Olav Kyst, *Antarctica* 5 C5
Kronshtadt, *Russia* 24 B4
Kroonstad, *S. Africa* 56 D4
Kropotkin, *Russia* 25 E7
Kropotkin, *Russia* 27 D12
Krosno, *Poland* 17 D10
Krotoszyn, *Poland* 17 C8
Kroussón, *Greece* 23 D6
Kruger Nat. Park, *S. Africa* 57 C5
Krugersdorp, *S. Africa* 57 D4
Kruisfontein, *S. Africa* 56 E3
Krung Thep = Bangkok, *Thailand* 38 F3
Kruševac, *Serbia, Yug.* 21 C9
Kruzof I., *U.S.A.* 72 B1
Krymskiy Poluostrov, *Ukraine* 25 E5
Ksar el Boukhari, *Algeria* 50 A5
Ksar el Kebir, *Morocco* 50 B3
Ksar es Souk = Ar Rachidiya, *Morocco* 50 B4
Kuala, *Indonesia* 36 D3
Kuala Berang, *Malaysia* 39 K4
Kuala Dungun, *Malaysia* 39 K4
Kuala Kangsar, *Malaysia* 39 K3
Kuala Kelawang, *Malaysia* 39 L4
Kuala Kerai, *Malaysia* 39 K4
Kuala Kubu Baharu, *Malaysia* 39 L3
Kuala Lipis, *Malaysia* 39 K4
Kuala Lumpur, *Malaysia* 39 L3
Kuala Nerang, *Malaysia* 39 J3
Kuala Pilah, *Malaysia* 39 L4
Kuala Rompin, *Malaysia* 39 L4
Kuala Selangor, *Malaysia* 39 L3
Kuala Terengganu, *Malaysia* 39 K4
Kualajelai, *Indonesia* 36 E4
Kualakapuas, *Indonesia* 36 E4
Kualakurun, *Indonesia* 36 E4
Kualapembuang, *Indonesia* 36 E4
Kualasimpang, *Indonesia* 36 D1
Kuancheng, *China* 35 D10
Kuandang, *Indonesia* 37 D6
Kuandian, *China* 35 D13
Kuangchou = Guangzhou, *China* 33 D6
Kuantan, *Malaysia* 39 L4
Kuba, *Azerbaijan* 25 F8
Kuban —►, *Russia* 25 E6
Kubokawa, *Japan* 31 H6
Kucha Gompa, *India* 43 B7
Kuchaman, *India* 42 F6
Kuchino-eruba-Jima, *Japan* 31 J5
Kuchino-Shima, *Japan* 31 K4
Kuchinotsu, *Japan* 31 H5
Kucing, *Malaysia* 36 D4
Kud —►, *Pakistan* 42 F2
Kuda, *India* 40 H7
Kudat, *Malaysia* 36 C5
Kudus, *Indonesia* 37 G14
Kudymkar, *Russia* 26 D6
Kueiyang = Guiyang, *China* 32 D5
Kufstein, *Austria* 16 E6
Kugong I., *Canada* 70 A4
Kūh-e Dīnār, *Iran* 45 D6
Kūh-e-Hazārām, *Iran* 45 D8
Kūhak, *Iran* 40 F3
Kūhbonān, *Iran* 45 D8
Kūhestak, *Iran* 45 E8
Kūhīn, *Iran* 45 C6
Kūhīrī, *Iran* 45 E9
Kūhpāyeh, *Eşfahan, Iran* 45 C7
Kūhpāyeh, *Kermān, Iran* 45 D8
Kui Buri, *Thailand* 39 F2
Kuito, *Angola* 53 G3
Kujang, *N. Korea* 35 E14
Kuji, *Japan* 30 D10
Kujū-San, *Japan* 31 H5
Kukawa, *Nigeria* 51 F7
Kukerin, *Australia* 61 F2
Kukup, *Malaysia* 39 M4
Kulai, *Malaysia* 39 M4
Kulal, Mt., *Kenya* 54 B4
Kulasekarappattinam, *India* 40 Q11
Kuldja = Yining, *China* 32 B3
Kulgam, *India* 43 C6
Kulim, *Malaysia* 39 K3
Kulin, *Australia* 61 F2
Kulja, *Australia* 61 F2
Kulm, *U.S.A.* 80 B5
Kulsary, *Kazakhstan* 25 E9
Kulti, *India* 43 H12
Kulumbura, *Australia* 60 B4
Kulunda, *Russia* 26 D8
Kulungar, *Afghan.* 42 C3
Kūlvand, *Iran* 45 D7
Kulwin, *Australia* 63 F3
Kulyab, *Tajikistan* 26 F7
Kum Tekei, *Kazakhstan* 26 E8
Kuma —►, *Russia* 25 F8
Kumagaya, *Japan* 31 F9
Kumai, *Indonesia* 36 E4
Kumamba, Kepulauan, *Indonesia* 37 E9
Kumamoto, *Japan* 31 H5
Kumamoto □, *Japan* 31 H5
Kumanovo, *Macedonia, Yug.* 21 C9
Kumara, *N.Z.* 59 K3
Kumarl, *Australia* 61 F3
Kumasi, *Ghana* 50 G4
Kumayri, *Armenia* 25 F7
Kumba, *Cameroon* 50 H6
Kumbakonam, *India* 40 P11
Kumbarilla, *Australia* 63 D5
Kŭmchŏn, *N. Korea* 35 E14
Kumdok, *India* 43 C8
Kume-Shima, *Japan* 31 L3
Kumertau, *Russia* 24 D10
Kŭmhwa, *S. Korea* 35 E14
Kumi, *Uganda* 54 B3
Kumla, *Sweden* 9 G13
Kumo, *Nigeria* 50 F7
Kumon Bum, *Burma* 41 F20
Kunama, *Australia* 63 F4
Kunashir, Ostrov, *Russia* 27 E15
Kundla, *India* 42 J4
Kungala, *Australia* 63 D5
Kunghit I., *Canada* 72 C2
Kungrad, *Uzbekistan* 26 E6
Kungsbacka, *Sweden* 9 H12
Kungur, *Russia* 24 C10
Kungurri, *Australia* 62 C4
Kunhar —►, *Pakistan* 43 B5
Kuningan, *Indonesia* 37 G13
Kunlong, *Burma* 41 H21
Kunlun Shan, *Asia* 32 C3
Kunming, *China* 32 D5
Kunsan, *S. Korea* 35 G14
Kununurra, *Australia* 60 C4
Kunwarara, *Australia* 62 C5
Kunya-Urgench, *Turkmenistan* 26 E6
Kuopio, *Finland* 8 E19
Kuopion lääni □, *Finland* 8 E19
Kupa —►, *Croatia* 20 B7
Kupang, *Indonesia* 37 F6
Kupyansk, *Ukraine* 26 E4
Kuqa, *China* 32 B3
Kura —►, *Azerbaijan* 25 G8
Kuranda, *Australia* 62 B4
Kurashiki, *Japan* 31 G6
Kurayoshi, *Japan* 31 G6
Kure, *Japan* 31 G6
Kurgaldzhino, *Kazakhstan* 26 D8
Kurgan, *Russia* 26 D7
Kuria Maria Is. = Khūrīyā Mūrīyā, Jazā 'ir, *Oman* 46 D6
Kuridala, *Australia* 62 C3
Kurigram, *Bangla.* 41 G16
Kuril Is. = Kurilskiye Ostrova, *Russia* 27 E15
Kuril Trench, *Pac. Oc.* 64 C7
Kurilsk, *Russia* 27 E15
Kurilskiye Ostrova, *Russia* 27 E15
Kurino, *Japan* 31 J5
Kurmuk, *Sudan* 51 F11
Kurnool, *India* 40 M10
Kuro-Shima, *Kagoshima, Japan* 31 J4
Kuro-Shima, *Okinawa, Japan* 31 M2
Kurow, *N.Z.* 59 L3
Kurrajong, *Australia* 63 E5
Kurram —►, *Pakistan* 42 C4
Kurri Kurri, *Australia* 63 E5
Kursk, *Russia* 24 D6
Kuršumlija, *Serbia, Yug.* 21 C9
Kuruktag, *China* 32 B3
Kuruman, *S. Africa* 56 D3
Kuruman —►, *S. Africa* 56 D3
Kurume, *Japan* 31 H5
Kurunegala, *Sri Lanka* 40 R12
Kurya, *Russia* 27 C11
Kusatsu, *Japan* 31 F9
Kusawa L., *Canada* 72 A1
Kushikino, *Japan* 31 J5
Kushima, *Japan* 31 J5
Kushimoto, *Japan* 31 H7
Kushiro, *Japan* 30 C12
Kushiro —►, *Japan* 30 C12
Kūshk, *Iran* 45 D8
Kushka, *Turkmenistan* 26 F7
Kūshkī, *Īlām, Iran* 44 C5
Kūshkī, *Khorāsān, Iran* 45 B8
Kūshkū, *Iran* 45 E7
Kushol, *India* 43 C7
Kushtia, *Bangla.* 41 H16
Kushva, *Russia* 24 C10
Kuskokwim —►, *U.S.A.* 68 B3
Kuskokwim Bay, *U.S.A.* 68 C3
Kussharo-Ko, *Japan* 30 C12
Kustanay, *Kazakhstan* 26 D7
Kut, Ko, *Thailand* 39 G4
Kütahya, *Turkey* 25 G5
Kutaisi, *Georgia* 25 F7
Kutaraja = Banda Aceh, *Indonesia* 36 C1
Kutch, Gulf of = Kachchh, Gulf of, *India* 42 H3
Kutch, Rann of = Kachchh, Rann of, *India* 42 G4
Kutiyana, *India* 42 J4
Kutno, *Poland* 17 B9
Kuttabul, *Australia* 62 C4
Kutu, *Zaïre* 52 E3
Kutum, *Sudan* 51 F9
Kuujjuaq, *Canada* 69 C13
Kuŭp-tong, *N. Korea* 35 D14
Kuwait = Al Kuwayt, *Kuwait* 44 D5
Kuwait ■, *Asia* 44 D5
Kuwana, *Japan* 31 G8
Kuybyshev = Samara, *Russia* 24 D9
Kuybyshev, *Russia* 26 D8
Kuybyshevskoye Vdkhr., *Russia* 24 C8
Kuye He —►, *China* 34 E6
Kūyeh, *Iran* 44 B5
Kūysanjaq, *Iraq* 44 B5
Kuyto, Oz., *Russia* 24 B5
Kuyumba, *Russia* 27 C10
Kuzey Anadolu Dağları, *Turkey* 25 F6
Kuznetsk, *Russia* 24 D8
Kuzomen, *Russia* 24 A6
Kvænangen, *Norway* 8 A16
Kvarner, *Croatia* 20 B6
Kvarnerič, *Croatia* 20 B6
Kwabhaca, *S. Africa* 57 E4
Kwadacha —►, *Canada* 72 B3
Kwakhanai, *Botswana* 56 C3
Kwakoegron, *Surinam* 93 B7
Kwale, *Kenya* 54 C4
Kwale □, *Kenya* 54 C4
KwaMashu, *S. Africa* 57 D5
Kwamouth, *Zaïre* 52 E3
Kwando —►, *Africa* 56 B3
Kwangdaeri, *N. Korea* 35 D14
Kwangju, *S. Korea* 35 G14
Kwangsi-Chuang = Guangxi Zhuangzu Zizhiqu □, *China* 33 D5
Kwangtung = Guangdong □, *China* 33 D6
Kwataboahegan —►, *Canada* 70 B3
Kwatisore, *Indonesia* 37 E8
Kweichow = Guizhou □, *China* 32 D5
Kwekwe, *Zimbabwe* 55 F2
Kwimba □, *Tanzania* 54 C3
Kwinana New Town, *Australia* 61 F2
Kwoka, *Indonesia* 37 E8
Kyabé, *Chad* 51 G8
Kyabra Cr. —►, *Australia* 63 D3
Kyabram, *Australia* 63 F4
Kyaikto, *Burma* 38 D1
Kyakhta, *Russia* 27 D11
Kyancutta, *Australia* 63 E2
Kyangin, *Burma* 41 K19
Kyaukpadaung, *Burma* 41 J19
Kyaukpyu, *Burma* 41 K18
Kyaukse, *Burma* 41 J20
Kyburz, *U.S.A.* 84 G6
Kycen, *Russia* 27 D11
Kyenjojo, *Uganda* 54 B3
Kyle Dam, *Zimbabwe* 55 G3
Kyle of Lochalsh, *U.K.* 12 D3
Kyneton, *Australia* 63 F3
Kynuna, *Australia* 62 C3
Kyō-ga-Saki, *Japan* 31 G7
Kyoga, L., *Uganda* 54 B3
Kyogle, *Australia* 63 D5
Kyongju, *S. Korea* 35 G15
Kyongpyaw, *Burma* 41 L19
Kyŏngsŏng, *N. Korea* 35 D15
Kyōto, *Japan* 31 G7
Kyōto □, *Japan* 31 G7
Kyparissovouno, *Cyprus* 23 D12
Kyperounda, *Cyprus* 23 E11
Kyrenia, *Cyprus* 23 D12
Kystatyam, *Russia* 27 C13
Kytal Ktakh, *Russia* 27 C13
Kythréa, *Cyprus* 23 D12
Kyulyunken, *Russia* 27 C14
Kyunhla, *Burma* 41 H19
Kyuquot, *Canada* 72 C3
Kyūshū, *Japan* 31 H5
Kyūshū □, *Japan* 31 H5
Kyūshū-Sanchi, *Japan* 31 H5
Kyustendil, *Bulgaria* 21 C10
Kyusyur, *Russia* 27 B13
Kywong, *Australia* 63 E4
Kyzyl, *Russia* 27 D10
Kyzyl-Kiya, *Kirghizia* 26 E8
Kyzylkum, Peski, *Uzbekistan* 26 E7
Kzyl-Orda, *Kazakhstan* 26 E7

L

La Asunción, *Venezuela* 92 A6
La Banda, *Argentina* 94 B3
La Barca, *Mexico* 86 C4
La Barge, *U.S.A.* 82 E8
La Belle, *U.S.A.* 77 M5
La Biche —►, *Canada* 72 B4
La Bomba, *Mexico* 86 A1
La Calera, *Chile* 94 C1
La Canal, *Spain* 22 C7
La Carlota, *Argentina* 94 C3
La Carolina, *Spain* 19 C4
La Ceiba, *Honduras* 88 C2
La Chaux de Fonds, *Switz.* 16 E3
La Cocha, *Argentina* 94 B2
La Concordia, *Mexico* 87 D6
La Conner, *U.S.A.* 82 B2
La Coruña, *Spain* 19 A1
La Crete, *Canada* 72 B5
La Crosse, *Kans., U.S.A.* 80 F5
La Crosse, *Wis., U.S.A.* 80 D9
La Cruz, *Costa Rica* 88 D2
La Cruz, *Mexico* 86 C3
La Dorada, *Colombia* 92 B4
La Escondida, *Mexico* 86 C5
La Esmeralda, *Paraguay* 94 A3
La Esperanza, *Cuba* 88 B3
La Esperanza, *Honduras* 88 D2
La Estrada, *Spain* 19 A1
La Fayette, *U.S.A.* 77 H3
La Fé, *Cuba* 88 B3
La Follette, *U.S.A.* 77 G3
La Grande, *U.S.A.* 82 D4
La Grange, *U.S.A.* 84 H6
La Grange, *Ga., U.S.A.* 77 J3
La Grange, *Ky., U.S.A.* 76 F3
La Grange, *Tex., U.S.A.* 81 L6
La Guaira, *Venezuela* 92 A5
La Güera, *Mauritania* 50 D1
La Habana, *Cuba* 88 B3
La Harpe, *U.S.A.* 80 E9
La Independencia, *Mexico* 87 D6
La Isabela, *Dom. Rep.* 89 C5
La Jara, *U.S.A.* 83 H11
La Junta, *U.S.A.* 81 F3
La Laguna, *Canary Is.* 22 F3
La Libertad, *Guatemala* 88 C1
La Libertad, *Mexico* 86 B2
La Ligua, *Chile* 94 C1
La Línea de la Concepción, *Spain* 19 D3
La Loche, *Canada* 73 B7
La Louvière, *Belgium* 15 D4
La Malbaie, *Canada* 71 C5
La Mancha, *Spain* 19 C4
La Mesa, *Calif., U.S.A.* 85 N9
La Mesa, *N. Mex., U.S.A.* 83 K10
La Misión, *Mexico* 86 A1
La Moure, *U.S.A.* 80 B5
La Negra, *Chile* 94 A1
La Oliva, *Canary Is.* 22 F6
La Orotava, *Canary Is.* 22 F3
La Palma, *Canary Is.* 22 F2
La Palma, *Panama* 88 E4
La Palma, *Spain* 19 D2
La Paloma, *Chile* 94 C1
La Pampa □, *Argentina* 94 D2
La Paragua, *Venezuela* 92 B6
La Paz, *Entre Ríos, Argentina* 94 C4
La Paz, *San Luis, Argentina* 94 C2
La Paz, *Bolivia* 92 G5
La Paz, *Honduras* 88 D2
La Paz, *Mexico* 86 C2
La Paz Centro, *Nic.* 88 D2
La Pedrera, *Colombia* 92 D5
La Perouse Str., *Asia* 30 B11
La Pesca, *Mexico* 87 C5
La Piedad, *Mexico* 86 C4
La Pine, *U.S.A.* 82 E3
La Plant, *U.S.A.* 80 C4
La Plata, *Argentina* 94 D4
La Porte, *U.S.A.* 76 E2
La Purísima, *Mexico* 86 B2
La Push, *U.S.A.* 84 C2
La Quiaca, *Argentina* 94 A2
La Reine, *Canada* 70 C4
La Restinga, *Canary Is.* 22 G2
La Rioja, *Argentina* 94 B2
La Rioja □, *Argentina* 94 B2
La Rioja □, *Spain* 19 A4
La Robla, *Spain* 19 A3
La Rochelle, *France* 18 C3
La Roda, *Spain* 19 C4
La Romana, *Dom. Rep.* 89 C6
La Ronge, *Canada* 73 B7
La Rumorosa, *Mexico* 85 N10
La Sabina, *Spain* 22 C7
La Sagra, *Spain* 19 D4
La Salle, *U.S.A.* 80 E10
La Santa, *Canary Is.* 22 E6
La Sarre, *Canada* 70 C4
La Scie, *Canada* 71 C8
La Selva Beach, *U.S.A.* 84 J5
La Serena, *Chile* 94 B1
La Spézia, *Italy* 20 B3
La Tortuga, *Venezuela* 89 D6
La Tuque, *Canada* 70 C5
La Unión, *Chile* 96 E2
La Unión, *El Salv.* 88 D2
La Unión, *Mexico* 86 D4
La Urbana, *Venezuela* 92 B5
La Vega, *Dom. Rep.* 89 C5
La Venta, *Mexico* 87 D6
La Ventura, *Mexico* 86 C4
Labe = Elbe —►, *Europe* 16 B4
Labé, *Guinea* 50 F2
Laberge, L., *Canada* 72 A1
Labis, *Malaysia* 39 L4
Laboulaye, *Argentina* 94 C3
Labrador, Coast of □, *Canada* 71 B7
Labrador City, *Canada* 71 B6
Lábrea, *Brazil* 92 E6
Labuan, Pulau, *Malaysia* 36 C5
Labuha, *Indonesia* 37 E7
Labuhan, *Indonesia* 37 G11
Labuhanbajo, *Indonesia* 37 F6
Labuk, Telok, *Malaysia* 36 C5
Labyrinth, L., *Australia* 63 E2
Labytnangi, *Russia* 24 A12

Lac Allard, Canada 71 B7
Lac Bouchette, Canada 71 C5
Lac du Flambeau, U.S.A. 80 B10
Lac Édouard, Canada 70 C5
Lac La Biche, Canada 72 C6
Lac la Martre, Canada 68 B8
Lac-Mégantic, Canada 71 C5
Lac Seul, Res., Canada 70 B1
Lac Thien, Vietnam 38 F7
Lacantúm →, Mexico 87 D6
Laccadive Is. = Lakshadweep Is., Ind. Oc. 28 J11
Lacepede B., Australia 63 F2
Lacepede Is., Australia 60 C3
Lacerdónia, Mozam. 55 F4
Lacey, U.S.A. 84 C4
Lachhmangarh, India 42 F6
Lachi, Pakistan 42 C4
Lachine, Canada 70 C5
Lachlan →, Australia 63 E3
Lachute, Canada 70 C5
Lackawanna, U.S.A. 78 D6
Lacolle, Canada 79 A11
Lacombe, Canada 72 C6
Lacona, U.S.A. 79 C8
Laconia, U.S.A. 79 C13
Lacrosse, U.S.A. 82 C5
Ladakh Ra., India 43 B8
Ladismith, S. Africa 56 E3
Lādīz, Iran 45 D9
Ladnun, India 42 F6
Ladoga, L. = Ladozhskoye Ozero, Russia 24 B5
Ladozhskoye Ozero, Russia 24 B5
Lady Grey, S. Africa 56 E4
Ladybrand, S. Africa 56 D4
Ladysmith, Canada 72 D4
Ladysmith, S. Africa 57 D4
Ladysmith, U.S.A. 80 C9
Lae, Papua N. G. 64 H6
Laem Ngop, Thailand 39 F4
Laem Pho, Thailand 39 J3
Læsø, Denmark 9 H11
Lafayette, Colo., U.S.A. 80 F2
Lafayette, Ind., U.S.A. 76 E2
Lafayette, La., U.S.A. 81 K9
Lafayette, Tenn., U.S.A. 77 G3
Laferte →, Canada 72 A5
Lafia, Nigeria 50 G6
Lafleche, Canada 73 D7
Lagan →, U.K. 13 B6
Lagarfljót →, Iceland 8 D6
Lågen →, Norway 9 F11
Laghouat, Algeria 50 B5
Lagonoy Gulf, Phil. 37 B6
Lagos, Nigeria 50 G5
Lagos, Portugal 19 D1
Lagos de Moreno, Mexico 86 C4
Lagrange, Australia 60 C3
Lagrange B., Australia 60 C3
Laguna, Brazil 95 B6
Laguna, U.S.A. 83 J10
Laguna Beach, U.S.A. 85 M9
Laguna Limpia, Argentina 94 B4
Laguna Madre, U.S.A. 87 B5
Lagunas, Chile 94 A2
Lagunas, Peru 92 E3
Lahad Datu, Malaysia 37 C5
Lahan Sai, Thailand 38 E4
Lahanam, Laos 38 D5
Laharpur, India 43 F9
Lahat, Indonesia 36 E2
Lahewa, Indonesia 36 D1
Lāhījān, Iran 45 B6
Lahn →, Germany 16 C3
Laholm, Sweden 9 H12
Lahontan Res., U.S.A. 82 G4
Lahore, Pakistan 42 D6
Lahti, Finland 9 F18
Lahtis = Lahti, Finland 9 F18
Laï, Chad 51 G8
Lai Chau, Vietnam 38 A4
Laidley, Australia 63 D5
Laikipia □, Kenya 54 B4
Laingsburg, S. Africa 56 E3
Lairg, U.K. 12 C4
Laishui, China 34 E8
Laiwu, China 35 F9
Laixi, China 35 F11
Laiyang, China 35 F11
Laiyuan, China 34 E8
Laizhou Wan, China 35 F10
Laja →, Mexico 86 C4
Lajere, Nigeria 50 F7
Lajes, Brazil 95 B5
Lak Sao, Laos 38 C5
Lakaband, Pakistan 42 D3
Lakar, Indonesia 37 F7
Lake Alpine, U.S.A. 84 G7
Lake Andes, U.S.A. 80 D5
Lake Anse, U.S.A. 76 B1
Lake Arthur, U.S.A. 81 K8
Lake Cargelligo, Australia 63 E4
Lake Charles, U.S.A. 81 K8
Lake City, Colo., U.S.A. 83 G10
Lake City, Fla., U.S.A. 77 K4
Lake City, Iowa, U.S.A. 80 D7
Lake City, Mich., U.S.A. 76 C3
Lake City, Minn., U.S.A. 80 C8
Lake City, Pa., U.S.A. 78 D4
Lake City, S.C., U.S.A. 77 J6
Lake George, U.S.A. 79 C11
Lake Grace, Australia 61 F2
Lake Harbour, Canada 69 B13
Lake Havasu City, U.S.A. 85 L12
Lake Hughes, U.S.A. 85 L8
Lake Isabella, U.S.A. 85 K8
Lake King, Australia 61 F2
Lake Lenore, Canada 73 C8
Lake Louise, Canada 72 C5
Lake Mead Nat. Rec. Area, U.S.A. 85 K12
Lake Mills, U.S.A. 80 D8
Lake Nash, Australia 62 C2
Lake Providence, U.S.A. 81 J9
Lake River, Canada 70 B3
Lake Superior Prov. Park, Canada 70 C3
Lake Village, U.S.A. 81 J9
Lake Wales, U.S.A. 77 M5
Lake Worth, U.S.A. 77 M5
Lakefield, Canada 70 D4
Lakeland, Australia 62 B3
Lakeland, U.S.A. 77 L5
Lakemba, Fiji 59 D9
Lakeport, U.S.A. 84 F4
Lakes Entrance, Australia 63 F4
Lakeside, Ariz., U.S.A. 83 J9
Lakeside, Calif., U.S.A. 85 N10
Lakeside, Nebr., U.S.A. 80 D3
Lakeview, U.S.A. 82 E3
Lakewood, Colo., U.S.A. 80 F2
Lakewood, N.J., U.S.A. 79 F10
Lakewood, Ohio, U.S.A. 78 E3
Lakewood Center, U.S.A. 84 C4
Lakhaniá, Greece 23 D9
Lakhonpheng, Laos 38 E5
Lakhpat, India 42 H3
Laki, Iceland 8 D4
Lakin, U.S.A. 81 G4
Lakitusaki →, Canada 70 B3
Lákkoi, Greece 23 D5
Lakonikós Kólpos, Greece 21 F10
Lakota, Ivory C. 50 G3
Lakota, U.S.A. 80 A5
Laksefjorden, Norway 8 A19
Lakselv, Norway 8 A18
Lakshadweep Is., Ind. Oc. 28 J11
Lakshmikantapur, India 43 H13
Lala Ghat, India 41 G18
Lala Musa, Pakistan 42 C5
Lalago, Tanzania 54 C3
Lalapanzi, Zimbabwe 55 F3
Lalganj, India 43 G11
Lalibela, Ethiopia 51 F12
Lalin, China 35 B14
Lalín, Spain 19 A1
Lalin He →, China 35 B13
Lalitapur = Patan, Nepal 41 F14
Lalitpur, India 43 G8
Lam, Vietnam 38 B6
Lam Pao Res., Thailand 38 D4
Lamaing, Burma 41 M20
Lamar, Colo., U.S.A. 80 F3
Lamar, Mo., U.S.A. 81 G7
Lamas, Peru 92 E3
Lambaréné, Gabon 52 E2
Lambasa, Fiji 59 C8
Lambay I., Ireland 13 C5
Lambert, U.S.A. 80 B2
Lambert Glacier, Antarctica 5 D6
Lamberts Bay, S. Africa 56 E2
Lame, Nigeria 50 F6
Lame Deer, U.S.A. 82 D10
Lamego, Portugal 19 B2
Lamèque, Canada 71 C7
Lameroo, Australia 63 F3
Lamesa, U.S.A. 81 J4
Lamia, Greece 21 E10
Lammermuir Hills, U.K. 12 F6
Lamon Bay, Phil. 37 B6
Lamont, Canada 72 C6
Lamont, U.S.A. 85 K8
Lampa, Peru 92 G4
Lampang, Thailand 38 C2
Lampasas, U.S.A. 81 K5
Lampazos de Naranjo, Mexico 86 B4
Lampedusa, Medit. S. 20 G5
Lampeter, U.K. 11 E3
Lampman, Canada 73 D8
Lamprey, Canada 73 B10
Lampung □, Indonesia 36 F2
Lamu, Kenya 54 C5
Lamu □, Kenya 54 C5
Lamy, U.S.A. 83 J11
Lan Xian, China 34 E6
Lanai I., U.S.A. 74 H16
Lanak La, India 43 B8
Lanak'o Shank'ou = Lanak La, India 43 B8
Lanao, L., Phil. 37 C6
Lanark, Canada 79 A8
Lanark, U.K. 12 F5
Lancang Jiang →, China 32 D5
Lancashire □, U.K. 10 D5
Lancaster, Canada 79 A10
Lancaster, U.K. 10 C5
Lancaster, Calif., U.S.A. 85 L8
Lancaster, Ky., U.S.A. 76 G3
Lancaster, N.H., U.S.A. 79 B13
Lancaster, N.Y., U.S.A. 78 D6
Lancaster, Pa., U.S.A. 79 F8
Lancaster, S.C., U.S.A. 77 H5
Lancaster, Wis., U.S.A. 80 D9
Lancaster Sd., Canada 69 A11
Lancer, Canada 73 C7
Lanchow = Lanzhou, China 34 F2
Lanciano, Italy 20 C6
Lancun, China 35 F11
Landeck, Austria 16 E5
Landen, Belgium 15 D5
Lander, U.S.A. 82 E9
Lander →, Australia 60 D5
Landes, France 18 E3
Landes □, France 18 E3
Landi Kotal, Pakistan 42 B4
Landor, Australia 61 E2
Land's End, U.K. 11 G2
Landsborough Cr. →, Australia 62 C3
Landshut, Germany 16 D6
Landskrona, Sweden 9 J12
Lanesboro, U.S.A. 79 E9
Lanett, U.S.A. 77 J3
Lang Bay, Canada 72 D4
Lang Qua, Vietnam 38 A5
Lang Shan, China 34 D4
Lang Son, Vietnam 38 B6
Lang Suan, Thailand 39 H2
La'nga Co, China 41 D12
Langar, Iran 45 C9
Langara I., Canada 72 C2
Langdon, U.S.A. 80 A5
Langeberg, S. Africa 56 E3
Langeberge, S. Africa 56 D3
Langenburg, Canada 73 C8
Langholm, U.K. 12 F6
Langjökull, Iceland 8 D3
Langkawi, P., Malaysia 39 J2
Langklip, S. Africa 56 D3
Langkon, Malaysia 36 C5
Langlade, St- P. & M. 71 C8
Langlois, U.S.A. 82 E1
Langøya, Norway 8 B13
Langres, France 18 C6
Langres, Plateau de, France 18 C6
Langsa, Indonesia 36 D1
Langtry, U.S.A. 81 L4
Langu, Thailand 39 J2
Languedoc, France 18 E5
Langxiangzhen, China 34 E9
Lanigan, Canada 73 C7
Lankao, China 34 G8
L'Annonciation, Canada 70 C5
Lansdale, U.S.A. 79 F9
Lansdowne, Australia 63 E5
Lansdowne, Canada 79 B8
Lansdowne House, Canada 70 B2
L'Anse, U.S.A. 70 C2
L'Anse au Loup, Canada 71 B8
Lansford, U.S.A. 79 F9
Lansing, U.S.A. 76 D3
Lanta Yai, Ko, Thailand 39 J2
Lantian, China 34 G5
Lanus, Argentina 94 C4
Lanzarote, Canary Is. 22 E6
Lanzhou, China 34 F2
Lao Bao, Laos 38 D6
Lao Cai, Vietnam 38 A4
Laoag, Phil. 37 A6
Laoang, Phil. 37 B7
Laoha He →, China 35 C11
Laois □, Ireland 13 D4
Laon, France 18 B5
Laona, U.S.A. 76 C1
Laos ■, Asia 38 D5
Lapa, Brazil 95 B6
Laparan, Phil. 37 C6
Lapeer, U.S.A. 76 D4
Lapi □ = Lapin lääni □, Finland 8 C19
Lapin lääni □, Finland 8 C19
Lapithos, Cyprus 23 D12
Lapland = Lappland, Europe 8 B18
Laporte, U.S.A. 79 E8
Lappland, Europe 8 B18
Laprida, Argentina 94 D3
Laptev Sea, Russia 27 B13
L'Áquila, Italy 20 C5
Lār, Āzarbājān-e Sharqī, Iran 44 B5
Lār, Fārs, Iran 45 E7
Larache, Morocco 50 A3
Laramie, U.S.A. 80 E2
Laramie Mts., U.S.A. 80 E2
Laranjeiras do Sul, Brazil 95 B5
Larantuka, Indonesia 37 F6
Larap, Phil. 37 B6
Larat, Indonesia 37 F8
Larde, Mozam. 55 F4
Larder Lake, Canada 70 C4
Lardhos, Ákra, Greece 23 C10
Lardhos, Órmos, Greece 23 C10
Laredo, U.S.A. 81 M5
Laredo Sd., Canada 72 C3
Largs, U.K. 12 F4
Lariang, Indonesia 37 E5
Larimore, U.S.A. 80 B6
Lārīn, Iran 45 C7
Lárisa, Greece 21 E10
Larkana, Pakistan 42 F3
Larnaca, Cyprus 23 E12
Larnaca Bay, Cyprus 23 E12
Larne, U.K. 13 B6
Larned, U.S.A. 80 F5
Larrimah, Australia 60 C5
Larsen Ice Shelf, Antarctica 5 C17
Larvik, Norway 9 G11
Laryak, Russia 26 C8
Las Animas, U.S.A. 80 F3
Las Anod, Somali Rep. 46 F4
Las Brenãs, Argentina 94 B3
Las Chimeneas, Mexico 85 N10
Las Cruces, U.S.A. 83 K10
Las Flores, Argentina 94 D4
Las Heras, Argentina 94 C2
Las Khoreh, Somali Rep. 46 E4
Las Lajas, Argentina 96 D2
Las Lomitas, Argentina 94 A3
Las Palmas, Argentina 94 B4
Las Palmas, Canary Is. 22 F4
Las Palmas →, Mexico 85 N10
Las Piedras, Uruguay 95 C4
Las Pipinas, Argentina 94 D4
Las Plumas, Argentina 96 E3
Las Rosas, Argentina 94 C3
Las Tablas, Panama 88 E3
Las Termas, Argentina 94 B3
Las Truchas, Mexico 86 D4
Las Varillas, Argentina 94 C3
Las Vegas, N. Mex., U.S.A. 83 J11
Las Vegas, Nev., U.S.A. 85 J11
Lascano, Uruguay 95 C5
Lashburn, Canada 73 C7
Lashio, Burma 41 H20
Lashkar, India 42 F8
Lasithi, Greece 23 D7
Lasíthi □, Greece 23 D7
Lassen Pk., U.S.A. 82 F3
Last Mountain L., Canada 73 C7
Lastchance Cr. →, U.S.A. 84 E5
Lastoursville, Gabon 52 E2
Lastovo, Croatia 20 C7
Lat Yao, Thailand 38 E2
Latacunga, Ecuador 92 D3
Latakia = Al Lādhiqīyah, Syria 44 C2
Latchford, Canada 70 C4
Latham, Australia 61 E2
Lathrop Wells, U.S.A. 85 J10
Latina, Italy 20 D5
Latium = Lazio □, Italy 20 C5
Laton, U.S.A. 84 J7
Latouche Treville, C., Australia 60 C3
Latrobe, Australia 62 G4
Latrobe, U.S.A. 78 F5
Latvia ■, Europe 24 C3
Lau Group, Fiji 59 C9
Lauchhammer, Germany 16 C6
Lauenburg, Germany 16 B5
Laugarbakki, Iceland 8 D3
Launceston, Australia 62 G4
Launceston, U.K. 11 G3
Laune →, Ireland 13 D2
Laura, Australia 62 B3
Laurel, Miss., U.S.A. 81 K10
Laurel, Mont., U.S.A. 82 D9
Laurencekirk, U.K. 12 E6
Laurens, U.S.A. 77 H4
Laurentian Plateau, Canada 71 B6
Laurentides, Parc Prov. des, Canada 71 C5
Laurie L., Canada 73 B8
Laurinburg, U.S.A. 77 H6
Laurium, U.S.A. 76 B1
Lausanne, Switz. 16 E3
Laut, Indonesia 36 D3
Laut Ketil, Kepulauan, Indonesia 36 E5
Lautoka, Fiji 59 C7
Lauzon, Canada 71 C5
Lava Hot Springs, U.S.A. 82 E7
Laval, France 18 B3
Lavalle, Argentina 94 B2
Laverne, U.S.A. 81 G5
Laverton, Australia 61 E3
Lavras, Brazil 95 A7
Lavrentiya, Russia 27 C19
Lávrion, Greece 21 F11
Lávris, Greece 23 D6
Lavumisa, Swaziland 57 D5
Lawas, Malaysia 36 D5
Lawele, Indonesia 37 F6
Lawn Hill, Australia 62 B2
Lawng Pit, Burma 41 G20
Lawqar, Si. Arabia 44 D4
Lawrence, N.Z. 59 L2
Lawrence, Kans., U.S.A. 80 F7
Lawrence, Mass., U.S.A. 79 D13
Lawrenceburg, Ind., U.S.A. 76 F3
Lawrenceburg, Tenn., U.S.A. 77 H2
Lawrenceville, U.S.A. 77 J4
Laws, U.S.A. 84 H8
Lawton, U.S.A. 81 H5
Lawu, Indonesia 37 G14
Laxford, L., U.K. 12 C3
Laylān, Iraq 44 C5
Laysan I., Pac. Oc. 65 E11
Laytonville, U.S.A. 82 G2
Lazio □, Italy 20 C5
Lazo, Russia 30 C6
Le Creusot, France 18 C6
Le François, Martinique 89 D7
Le Havre, France 18 B4
Le Mans, France 18 C4
Le Marinel, Zaïre 55 E2
Le Mars, U.S.A. 80 D6
Le Mont-St.-Michel, France 18 B3
Le Moule, Guadeloupe 89 C7
Le Puy, France 18 D5
Le Roy, U.S.A. 81 F7
Le Sueur, U.S.A. 80 C8
Le Thuy, Vietnam 38 D6
Le Tréport, France 18 A4
Le Verdon-sur-Mer, France 18 D3
Lea →, U.K. 11 F7
Leach, Cambodia 39 F4
Lead, U.S.A. 80 C3
Leader, Canada 73 C7
Leadhills, U.K. 12 F5
Leadville, U.S.A. 83 G10
Leaf →, U.S.A. 81 K10
Leakey, U.S.A. 81 L5
Leamington, Canada 70 D3
Leamington, U.S.A. 82 G7
Leamington Spa = Royal Leamington Spa, U.K. 11 E6
Leandro Norte Alem, Argentina 95 B4
Learmonth, Australia 60 D1
Leask, Canada 73 C7
Leavenworth, Kans., U.S.A. 80 F7
Leavenworth, Wash., U.S.A. 82 C3
Lebak, Phil. 37 C6
Lebam, U.S.A. 84 D3
Lebanon, Ind., U.S.A. 76 E2
Lebanon, Kans., U.S.A. 80 F5
Lebanon, Ky., U.S.A. 76 G3
Lebanon, Mo., U.S.A. 81 G8
Lebanon, Oreg., U.S.A. 82 D2
Lebanon, Pa., U.S.A. 79 F8
Lebanon, Tenn., U.S.A. 77 G2
Lebanon ■, Asia 47 B4
Lebec, U.S.A. 85 L8
Lebomboberge, S. Africa 57 C5
Lebrija, Spain 19 D2
Lebu, Chile 94 D1
Lecce, Italy 21 D8
Lecco, Italy 20 B3
Łęczyca, Poland 17 B9
Ledbury, U.K. 11 E5
Ledong, China 38 C7
Leduc, Canada 72 C6
Lee, U.S.A. 79 D11
Lee →, Ireland 13 E3
Lee Vining, U.S.A. 84 H7
Leech L., U.S.A. 80 B7
Leedey, U.S.A. 81 H5
Leeds, U.K. 10 D6
Leeds, U.S.A. 77 J2
Leek, U.K. 10 D5
Leesburg, U.S.A. 77 L5
Leesville, U.S.A. 81 K8
Leeton, Australia 63 E4
Leetonia, U.S.A. 78 F4
Leeu Gamka, S. Africa 56 E3
Leeuwarden, Neths. 15 A5
Leeuwin, C., Australia 61 F2
Leeward Is., Atl. Oc. 89 C7
Lefka, Cyprus 23 D11
Lefkoniko, Cyprus 23 D12
Lefors, U.S.A. 81 H4
Lefroy, L., Australia 61 F3
Legal, Canada 72 C6
Leganés, Spain 19 B4
Legazpi, Phil. 37 B6
Legendre I., Australia 60 D2
Leghorn = Livorno, Italy 20 C4
Legnica, Poland 16 C8
Legume, Australia 63 D5
Leh, India 43 B7
Lehi, U.S.A. 82 F8
Lehighton, U.S.A. 79 F9
Lehututu, Botswana 56 C3
Leiah, Pakistan 42 D4
Leicester, U.K. 11 E6
Leicestershire □, U.K. 11 E6
Leichhardt →, Australia 62 B2
Leichhardt Ra., Australia 62 C4
Leiden, Neths. 15 B4
Leie →, Belgium 15 C3
Leine →, Germany 16 B4
Leinster, Australia 61 E3
Leinster □, Ireland 13 C4
Leinster, Mt., Ireland 13 D5
Leipzig, Germany 16 C6
Leiria, Portugal 19 C1
Leisler, Mt., Australia 60 D4
Leith, U.K. 12 F5
Leith Hill, U.K. 11 F7
Leitrim, Ireland 13 B3
Leitrim □, Ireland 13 B3
Leizhou Bandao, China 33 D6
Lek →, Neths. 15 C4
Leksula, Indonesia 37 E7
Leland, U.S.A. 81 J9
Leland Lakes, Canada 73 A6
Leleque, Argentina 96 E2
Lelystad, Neths. 15 B5
Léman, Lac, Switz. 16 E3
Lemera, Zaïre 54 C2
Lemhi Ra., U.S.A. 82 D7
Lemmer, Neths. 15 B5
Lemmon, U.S.A. 80 C3
Lemon Grove, U.S.A. 85 N9
Lemoore, U.S.A. 83 H4
Lemvig, Denmark 9 H10
Lena →, Russia 27 B13
Léndas, Greece 23 E6
Lendeh, Iran 45 D6
Lenggong, Malaysia 39 K3
Lengua de Vaca, Pta., Chile 94 C1
Leninabad = Khodzent, Tajikistan 26 E7
Leninakan = Kumayri, Armenia 25 F7
Leningrad = Sankt-Peterburg, Russia 24 C5
Leninogorsk = Ridder, Kazakhstan 26 D9
Leninsk, Russia 25 E8
Leninsk-Kuznetskiy, Russia 26 D9
Leninskoye, Russia 27 E14
Lenkoran, Azerbaijan 25 G8
Lenmalu, Indonesia 37 E8
Lennoxville, Canada 79 A13
Lenoir, U.S.A. 77 H5
Lenoir City, U.S.A. 77 H3
Lenora, U.S.A. 80 F4

Lenore L., *Canada* 73 C8
Lenox, *U.S.A.* 79 D11
Lens, *France* 18 A5
Lensk, *Russia* 27 C12
Lentini, *Italy* 20 F6
Lenwood, *U.S.A.* 85 L9
Leoben, *Austria* 16 E7
Leola, *U.S.A.* 80 C5
Leominster, *U.K.* 11 E5
Leominster, *U.S.A.* 79 D13
León, *Mexico* 86 C4
León, *Nic.* 88 D2
León, *Spain* 19 A3
Leon, *U.S.A.* 80 E8
León □, *Spain* 19 A3
León, Montañas de, *Spain* 19 A2
Leonardtown, *U.S.A.* 76 F7
Leongatha, *Australia* 63 F4
Leonora, *Australia* 61 E3
Léopold II, Lac = Mai-Ndombe, L., *Zaïre* 52 E3
Leopoldina, *Brazil* 95 A7
Leopoldsburg, *Belgium* 15 C5
Léopoldville = Kinshasa, *Zaïre* 52 E3
Leoti, *U.S.A.* 80 F4
Leoville, *Canada* 73 C7
Lépa, L. do, *Angola* 56 B2
Lepel, *Belorussia* 24 D4
Lepikha, *Russia* 27 C13
Lerdo, *Mexico* 86 B4
Léré, *Chad* 51 G7
Leribe, *Lesotho* 57 D4
Lérida, *Spain* 19 B6
Lerwick, *U.K.* 12 A7
Les Cayes, *Haiti* 89 C5
Les Étroits, *Canada* 71 C6
Les Sables-d'Olonne, *France* 18 C3
Lesbos = Lésvos, *Greece* 21 E12
Leshan, *China* 32 D5
Leshukonskoye, *Russia* 24 B8
Leskov I., *Antarctica* 5 B1
Leskovac, *Serbia, Yug.* 21 C9
Leslie, *U.S.A.* 81 H8
Lesopilnoye, *Russia* 30 A7
Lesotho ■, *Africa* 57 D4
Lesozavodsk, *Russia* 27 E14
Lesse →, *Belgium* 15 D4
Lesser Antilles, *W. Indies* 89 C7
Lesser Slave L., *Canada* 72 B5
Lesser Sunda Is., *Indonesia* 37 F6
Lessines, *Belgium* 15 D3
Lester, *U.S.A.* 84 C5
Lestock, *Canada* 73 C8
Lesuer I., *Australia* 60 B4
Lésvos, *Greece* 21 E12
Leszno, *Poland* 16 C8
Letchworth, *U.K.* 11 F7
Lethbridge, *Canada* 72 D6
Leti, Kepulauan, *Indonesia* 37 F7
Leti Is. = Leti, Kepulauan, *Indonesia* 37 F7
Letiahau →, *Botswana* 56 C3
Leticia, *Colombia* 92 D4
Leting, *China* 35 E10
Letjiesbos, *S. Africa* 56 E3
Letlhakeng, *Botswana* 56 C3
Letpadan, *Burma* 41 L19
Letpan, *Burma* 41 K19
Letterkenny, *Ireland* 13 B4
Leucadia, *U.S.A.* 85 M9
Leuser, G., *Indonesia* 36 D1
Leuven, *Belgium* 15 D4
Leuze, *Hainaut, Belgium* 15 D3
Leuze, *Namur, Belgium* 15 D4
Levan, *U.S.A.* 82 G8
Levanger, *Norway* 8 E11
Levelland, *U.S.A.* 81 J3
Leven, *U.K.* 12 E6
Leven, L., *U.K.* 12 E5
Leven, Toraka, *Madag.* 57 A8
Leveque C., *Australia* 60 C3
Leverkusen, *Germany* 16 C3
Levin, *N.Z.* 59 J5
Lévis, *Canada* 71 C5
Levis, L., *Canada* 72 A5
Levittown, *N.Y., U.S.A.* 79 F11
Levittown, *Pa., U.S.A.* 79 F10
Lévka Óri, *Greece* 23 D6
Levkás, *Greece* 21 E9
Levkímmi, *Greece* 23 B4
Levkímmi, Ákra, *Greece* 23 B4
Levkôsia = Nicosia, *Cyprus* 23 D12
Lewellen, *U.S.A.* 80 E3
Lewes, *U.K.* 11 G8
Lewes, *U.S.A.* 76 F8
Lewis, *U.K.* 12 C2
Lewis →, *U.S.A.* 84 E4
Lewis, Butt of, *U.K.* 12 C2
Lewis Ra., *Australia* 60 D4
Lewis Ra., *U.S.A.* 82 C7
Lewisburg, *Pa., U.S.A.* 78 F8
Lewisburg, *Tenn., U.S.A.* 77 H2
Lewisporte, *Canada* 71 C8
Lewiston, *Idaho, U.S.A.* 82 C5
Lewiston, *Maine, U.S.A.* 77 C11
Lewistown, *Mont., U.S.A.* 82 C9
Lewistown, *Pa., U.S.A.* 78 F7
Lexington, *Ill., U.S.A.* 80 E10
Lexington, *Ky., U.S.A.* 76 F3
Lexington, *Miss., U.S.A.* 81 J9
Lexington, *Mo., U.S.A.* 80 F8
Lexington, *N.C., U.S.A.* 77 H5
Lexington, *Nebr., U.S.A.* 80 E5
Lexington, *Ohio, U.S.A.* 78 F2
Lexington, *Oreg., U.S.A.* 82 D4
Lexington, *Tenn., U.S.A.* 77 H1
Lexington Park, *U.S.A.* 76 F7
Leyte, *Phil.* 37 B6
Lhasa, *China* 32 D4
Lhazê, *China* 32 D3
Lhokkruet, *Indonesia* 36 D1
Lhokseumawe, *Indonesia* 36 C1
Lhuntsi Dzong, *India* 41 F17
Li, *Thailand* 38 D2
Li Xian, *Gansu, China* 34 G3
Li Xian, *Hebei, China* 34 E8
Lianga, *Phil.* 37 C7
Liangcheng, *Nei Mongol Zizhiqu, China* 34 D7
Liangcheng, *Shandong, China* 35 G10
Liangdang, *China* 34 H4
Lianshanguan, *China* 35 D12
Lianshui, *China* 35 H10
Lianyungang, *China* 35 G10
Liao He →, *China* 35 D11
Liaocheng, *China* 34 F8
Liaodong Bandao, *China* 35 E12
Liaodong Wan, *China* 35 D11
Liaoning □, *China* 33 B7
Liaoning □, *Liaoning, China* 35 D12
Liaoyang, *China* 35 D12
Liaoyuan, *China* 35 C13
Liaozhong, *China* 35 D12
Liard →, *Canada* 72 A4
Liari, *Pakistan* 42 G2
Libau = Liepaja, *Latvia* 24 C3
Libby, *U.S.A.* 82 B6
Libenge, *Zaïre* 52 D3
Liberal, *Kans., U.S.A.* 81 G4
Liberal, *Mo., U.S.A.* 81 G7
Liberec, *Czech.* 16 C7
Liberia, *Costa Rica* 88 D2
Liberia ■, *W. Afr.* 50 G3
Liberty, *Mo., U.S.A.* 80 F7
Liberty, *Tex., U.S.A.* 81 K7
Lībīya, Sahrâ', *Africa* 51 C9
Libobo, Tanjung, *Indonesia* 37 E7
Libode, *S. Africa* 57 E4
Libonda, *Zambia* 53 G4
Libourne, *France* 18 D3
Libramont, *Belgium* 15 E5
Libreville, *Gabon* 52 D1
Libya ■, *N. Afr.* 51 C8
Libyan Desert = Lībīya, Sahrâ', *Africa* 51 C9
Licantén, *Chile* 94 D1
Licata, *Italy* 20 F5
Licheng, *China* 34 F7
Lichfield, *U.K.* 10 E6
Lichinga, *Mozam.* 55 E4
Lichtenburg, *S. Africa* 56 D4
Lida, *U.S.A.* 83 H5
Lidköping, *Sweden* 9 G12
Liebig, Mt., *Australia* 60 D5
Liechtenstein ■, *Europe* 16 E4
Liège, *Belgium* 15 D5
Liège □, *Belgium* 15 D5
Liegnitz = Legnica, *Poland* 16 C8
Lienart, *Zaïre* 54 B2
Lienyünchiangshih = Lianyungang, *China* 35 G10
Lienz, *Austria* 16 E6
Liepaja, *Latvia* 24 C3
Lier, *Belgium* 15 C4
Lièvre →, *Canada* 70 C4
Liffey →, *Ireland* 13 C5
Lifford, *Ireland* 13 B4
Lifudzin, *Russia* 30 B7
Lightning Ridge, *Australia* 63 D4
Liguria □, *Italy* 20 B3
Ligurian Sea, *Italy* 20 C3
Lihou Reefs and Cays, *Australia* 62 B5
Lihue, *U.S.A.* 74 H15
Lijiang, *China* 32 D5
Likasi, *Zaïre* 55 E2
Likati, *Zaïre* 52 D4
Likoma I., *Malawi* 55 E3
Likumburu, *Tanzania* 55 D4
Lille, *France* 18 A5
Lille Bælt, *Denmark* 9 J10
Lillehammer, *Norway* 9 F11
Lillesand, *Norway* 9 G10
Lilleshall, *U.K.* 11 E5
Lillestrøm, *Norway* 9 G11
Lillian Point, Mt., *Australia* 61 E4
Lillooet →, *Canada* 72 D4
Lilongwe, *Malawi* 55 E3
Liloy, *Phil.* 37 C6
Lima, *Indonesia* 37 E7
Lima, *Peru* 92 F3
Lima, *Mont., U.S.A.* 82 D7
Lima, *Ohio, U.S.A.* 76 E3
Limages, *Canada* 79 A9
Limassol, *Cyprus* 23 E12
Limavady, *U.K.* 13 A5
Limavady □, *U.K.* 13 B5
Limay →, *Argentina* 96 D3
Limay Mahuida, *Argentina* 94 D2
Limbang, *Brunei* 36 D5
Limbdi, *India* 42 H4
Limbe, *Cameroon* 50 H6
Limbri, *Australia* 63 E5
Limbunya, *Australia* 60 C4
Limburg □, *Belgium* 15 C5
Limburg □, *Neths.* 15 C5
Limeira, *Brazil* 95 A6
Limerick, *Ireland* 13 D3
Limerick □, *Ireland* 13 D3
Limestone, *U.S.A.* 78 D6
Limestone →, *Canada* 73 B10
Limfjorden, *Denmark* 9 H10
Limmen Bight, *Australia* 62 A2
Limmen Bight →, *Australia* 62 B2
Límnos, *Greece* 21 E11
Limoeiro do Norte, *Brazil* 93 E11
Limoges, *France* 18 D4
Limón, *Costa Rica* 88 D3
Limon, *U.S.A.* 80 F3
Limousin, *France* 18 D4
Limpopo →, *Africa* 57 D5
Limuru, *Kenya* 54 C4
Lin Xian, *China* 34 F6
Linares, *Chile* 94 D1
Linares, *Mexico* 87 C5
Linares, *Spain* 19 C4
Linares □, *Chile* 94 D1
Lincheng, *China* 34 F8
Lincoln, *Argentina* 94 C3
Lincoln, *N.Z.* 59 K4
Lincoln, *U.K.* 10 D7
Lincoln, *Calif., U.S.A.* 84 G5
Lincoln, *Ill., U.S.A.* 80 E10
Lincoln, *Kans., U.S.A.* 80 F5
Lincoln, *Maine, U.S.A.* 71 C6
Lincoln, *N.H., U.S.A.* 79 B13
Lincoln, *N. Mex., U.S.A.* 83 K11
Lincoln, *Nebr., U.S.A.* 80 E6
Lincoln Hav = Lincoln Sea, *Arctic* 4 A5
Lincoln Sea, *Arctic* 4 A5
Lincoln Wolds, *U.K.* 10 D7
Lincolnshire □, *U.K.* 10 D7
Lincolnton, *U.S.A.* 77 H5
Lind, *U.S.A.* 82 C4
Linda, *U.S.A.* 84 F5
Linden, *Guyana* 92 B7
Linden, *Calif., U.S.A.* 84 G5
Linden, *Tex., U.S.A.* 81 J7
Lindenhurst, *U.S.A.* 79 F11
Lindesnes, *Norway* 6 D7
Líndhos, *Greece* 23 C10
Lindi, *Tanzania* 55 D4
Lindi □, *Tanzania* 55 D4
Lindi →, *Zaïre* 54 B2
Lindsay, *Canada* 70 D4
Lindsay, *Calif., U.S.A.* 83 H4
Lindsay, *Okla., U.S.A.* 81 H6
Lindsborg, *U.S.A.* 80 F6
Linfen, *China* 34 F6
Ling Xian, *China* 34 F9
Lingao, *China* 38 C7
Lingayen, *Phil.* 37 A6
Lingayen G., *Phil.* 37 A6
Lingbi, *China* 35 H9
Lingchuan, *China* 34 G7
Lingen, *Germany* 16 B3
Lingga, *Indonesia* 36 E2
Lingga, Kepulauan, *Indonesia* 36 E2
Lingga Arch. = Lingga, Kepulauan, *Indonesia* 36 E2
Lingle, *U.S.A.* 80 D2
Lingqiu, *China* 34 E8
Lingshi, *China* 34 F6
Lingshou, *China* 34 E8
Lingshui, *China* 38 C8
Lingtai, *China* 34 G4
Linguéré, *Senegal* 50 E1
Lingwu, *China* 34 E4
Lingyuan, *China* 35 D10
Linh Cam, *Vietnam* 38 C5
Linhai, *China* 33 D7
Linhares, *Brazil* 93 G10
Linhe, *China* 34 D4
Linjiang, *China* 35 D14
Linköping, *Sweden* 9 G13
Linkou, *China* 35 B16
Linlithgow, *U.K.* 12 F5
Linnhe, L., *U.K.* 12 E3
Linqi, *China* 34 G7
Linqing, *China* 34 F8
Linqu, *China* 35 F10
Linru, *China* 34 G7
Lins, *Brazil* 95 A6
Lintao, *China* 34 G2
Lintlaw, *Canada* 73 C8
Linton, *Canada* 71 C5
Linton, *Ind., U.S.A.* 76 F2
Linton, *N. Dak., U.S.A.* 80 B4
Lintong, *China* 34 G5
Linville, *Australia* 63 D5
Linwood, *Canada* 78 C4
Linxi, *China* 35 C10
Linxia, *China* 32 C5
Linyanti →, *Africa* 56 B4
Linyi, *China* 35 G10
Linz, *Austria* 16 D7
Linzhenzhen, *China* 34 F5
Linzi, *China* 35 F10
Lion, G. du, *France* 18 E6
Lionárisso, *Cyprus* 23 D13
Lion's Den, *Zimbabwe* 55 F3
Lion's Head, *Canada* 70 D3
Lipa, *Phil.* 37 B6
Lipali, *Mozam.* 55 F4
Lípari, Is., *Italy* 20 E6
Lipetsk, *Russia* 24 D6
Lipovcy Manzovka, *Russia* 30 B6
Lippe →, *Germany* 16 C3
Lipscomb, *U.S.A.* 81 G4
Liptrap C., *Australia* 63 F4
Lira, *Uganda* 54 B3
Liria, *Spain* 19 C5
Lisala, *Zaïre* 52 D4
Lisboa, *Portugal* 19 C1
Lisbon = Lisboa, *Portugal* 19 C1
Lisbon, *N. Dak., U.S.A.* 80 B6
Lisbon, *N.H., U.S.A.* 79 B13
Lisbon, *Ohio, U.S.A.* 78 F4
Lisburn, *U.K.* 13 B5
Lisburne, C., *U.S.A.* 68 B3
Liscannor, B., *Ireland* 13 D2
Lishi, *China* 34 F6
Lishu, *China* 35 C13
Lisianski I., *Pac. Oc.* 64 E10
Lisichansk, *Ukraine* 25 E6
Lisieux, *France* 18 B4
Liski, *Russia* 25 D6
Lismore, *Australia* 63 D5
Lismore, *Ireland* 13 D4
Lisse, *Neths.* 15 B4
Lista, *Norway* 9 G9
Lista, *Sweden* 9 G14
Lister, Mt., *Antarctica* 5 D11
Liston, *Australia* 63 D5
Listowel, *Canada* 70 D3
Listowel, *Ireland* 13 D2
Litang, *Malaysia* 37 C5
Litani →, *Lebanon* 47 B4
Litchfield, *Calif., U.S.A.* 84 E6
Litchfield, *Conn., U.S.A.* 79 E11
Litchfield, *Ill., U.S.A.* 80 F10
Litchfield, *Minn., U.S.A.* 80 C7
Lithgow, *Australia* 63 E5
Líthinon, Ákra, *Greece* 23 E6
Lithuania ■, *Europe* 24 C3
Litoměřice, *Czech.* 16 C7
Little Abaco I., *Bahamas* 88 A4
Little Barrier I., *N.Z.* 59 G5
Little Belt Mts., *U.S.A.* 82 C8
Little Blue →, *U.S.A.* 80 F6
Little Bushman Land, *S. Africa* 56 D2
Little Cadotte →, *Canada* 72 B5
Little Cayman, I., *Cayman Is.* 88 C3
Little Churchill →, *Canada* 73 B9
Little Colorado →, *U.S.A.* 83 H8
Little Current, *Canada* 70 C3
Little Current →, *Canada* 70 B3
Little Falls, *Minn., U.S.A.* 80 C7
Little Falls, *N.Y., U.S.A.* 79 C10
Little Fork →, *U.S.A.* 80 A8
Little Grand Rapids, *Canada* 73 C9
Little Humboldt →, *U.S.A.* 82 F5
Little Inagua I., *Bahamas* 89 B5
Little Karoo, *S. Africa* 56 E3
Little Lake, *U.S.A.* 85 K9
Little Laut Is. = Laut Ketil, Kepulauan, *Indonesia* 36 E5
Little Minch, *U.K.* 12 D2
Little Missouri →, *U.S.A.* 80 B3
Little Namaqualand, *S. Africa* 56 D2
Little Ouse →, *U.K.* 11 E8
Little Rann, *India* 42 H4
Little Red →, *U.S.A.* 81 H9
Little River, *N.Z.* 59 K4
Little Rock, *U.S.A.* 81 H8
Little Ruaha →, *Tanzania* 54 D4
Little Sable Pt., *U.S.A.* 76 D2
Little Sioux →, *U.S.A.* 80 E6
Little Smoky →, *Canada* 72 C5
Little Snake →, *U.S.A.* 82 F9
Little Valley, *U.S.A.* 78 D6
Little Wabash →, *U.S.A.* 76 G1
Littlefield, *U.S.A.* 81 J3
Littlefork, *U.S.A.* 80 A8
Littlehampton, *U.K.* 11 G7
Littleton, *U.S.A.* 79 B13
Liu He →, *China* 35 D11
Liuba, *China* 34 H4
Liugou, *China* 35 D10
Liuhe, *China* 35 C13
Liukang Tenggaja, *Indonesia* 37 F5
Liuli, *Tanzania* 55 E3
Liuwa Plain, *Zambia* 53 G4
Liuzhou, *China* 33 D5
Liuzhuang, *China* 35 H11
Livadhia, *Cyprus* 23 E12
Live Oak, *Calif., U.S.A.* 84 F5
Live Oak, *Fla., U.S.A.* 77 K4
Liveras, *Cyprus* 23 D11
Liveringa, *Australia* 60 C3
Livermore, *U.S.A.* 84 H5
Livermore, Mt., *U.S.A.* 81 K2
Liverpool, *Australia* 63 E5
Liverpool, *Canada* 71 D7
Liverpool, *U.K.* 10 D5
Liverpool Plains, *Australia* 63 E5
Liverpool Ra., *Australia* 63 E5
Livingston, *Guatemala* 88 C2
Livingston, *Calif., U.S.A.* 84 H6
Livingston, *Mont., U.S.A.* 82 D8
Livingston, *Tex., U.S.A.* 81 K7
Livingstone, *Zambia* 55 F2
Livingstone Mts., *Tanzania* 55 D3
Livingstonia, *Malawi* 55 E3
Livny, *Russia* 24 D6
Livonia, *U.S.A.* 76 D4
Livorno, *Italy* 20 C4
Livramento, *Brazil* 95 C4
Liwale, *Tanzania* 55 D4
Liwale □, *Tanzania* 55 D4
Lizard I., *Australia* 62 A4
Lizard Pt., *U.K.* 11 H2
Ljubljana, *Slovenia* 20 A6
Ljungan →, *Sweden* 8 E14
Ljungby, *Sweden* 9 H12
Ljusdal, *Sweden* 9 F14
Ljusnan →, *Sweden* 9 F14
Ljusne, *Sweden* 9 F14
Llancanelo, Salina, *Argentina* 94 D2
Llandeilo, *U.K.* 11 F3
Llandovery, *U.K.* 11 F4
Llandrindod Wells, *U.K.* 11 E4
Llandudno, *U.K.* 10 D4
Llanelli, *U.K.* 11 F3
Llanes, *Spain* 19 A3
Llangollen, *U.K.* 10 E4
Llanidloes, *U.K.* 11 E4
Llano, *U.S.A.* 81 K5
Llano →, *U.S.A.* 81 K5
Llano Estacado, *U.S.A.* 81 J3
Llanos, *S. Amer.* 90 B2
Llebetx, C., *Spain* 22 B9
Llentrisca, C., *Spain* 22 C7
Llera, *Mexico* 87 C5
Llico, *Chile* 94 C1
Llobregat →, *Spain* 19 B7
Lloret de Mar, *Spain* 19 B7
Lloyd B., *Australia* 62 A3
Lloyd L., *Canada* 73 B7
Lloydminster, *Canada* 73 C6
Lluchmayor, *Spain* 22 B9
Llullaillaco, Volcán, *S. Amer.* 94 A2
Lo →, *Vietnam* 38 B5
Loa, *U.S.A.* 83 G8
Loa →, *Chile* 94 A1
Lobatse, *Botswana* 56 D4
Lobería, *Argentina* 94 D4
Lobito, *Angola* 53 G2
Lobos, *Argentina* 94 D4
Lobos, I., *Mexico* 86 B2
Lobos, Is., *Peru* 90 C1
Lobos, I. de, *Canary Is.* 22 F6
Loc Binh, *Vietnam* 38 B6
Loc Ninh, *Vietnam* 39 G6
Locarno, *Switz.* 16 E4
Lochaber, *U.K.* 12 E4
Lochcarron, *U.K.* 12 D3
Lochem, *Neths.* 15 B6
Loches, *France* 18 C4
Lochgelly, *U.K.* 12 E5
Lochgilphead, *U.K.* 12 E3
Lochinver, *U.K.* 12 C3
Lochnagar, *Australia* 62 C4
Lochnagar, *U.K.* 12 E5
Lochy →, *U.K.* 12 E3
Lock, *Australia* 63 E2
Lock Haven, *U.S.A.* 78 E7
Lockeford, *U.S.A.* 84 G5
Lockeport, *Canada* 71 D6
Lockerbie, *U.K.* 12 F5
Lockhart, *U.S.A.* 81 L6
Lockhart, L., *Australia* 61 F2
Lockney, *U.S.A.* 81 H4
Lockport, *U.S.A.* 78 C6
Lod, *Israel* 47 D3
Lodeinoye Pole, *Russia* 24 B5
Lodge Grass, *U.S.A.* 82 D10
Lodgepole, *U.S.A.* 80 E3
Lodgepole Cr. →, *U.S.A.* 80 E2
Lodhran, *Pakistan* 42 E4
Lodi, *U.S.A.* 84 G5
Lodja, *Zaïre* 54 C1
Lodwar, *Kenya* 54 B4
Łódź, *Poland* 17 C9
Loei, *Thailand* 38 D3
Loengo, *Zaïre* 54 C2
Loeriesfontein, *S. Africa* 56 E2
Lofoten, *Norway* 8 B13
Logan, *Kans., U.S.A.* 80 F5
Logan, *Ohio, U.S.A.* 76 F4
Logan, *Utah, U.S.A.* 82 F8
Logan, *W. Va., U.S.A.* 76 G5
Logan, Mt., *Canada* 68 B5
Logan Pass, *U.S.A.* 72 D6
Logandale, *U.S.A.* 85 J12
Logansport, *Ind., U.S.A.* 76 E2
Logansport, *La., U.S.A.* 81 K8
Logone →, *Chad* 51 F8
Logroño, *Spain* 19 A4
Lohardaga, *India* 43 H11
Loi-kaw, *Burma* 41 K20
Loimaa, *Finland* 9 F17
Loir →, *France* 18 C3
Loir-et-Cher □, *France* 18 C4
Loire □, *France* 18 D6
Loire →, *France* 18 C2
Loire-Atlantique □, *France* 18 C3
Loiret □, *France* 18 C5
Loja, *Ecuador* 92 D3
Loja, *Spain* 19 D3
Loji, *Indonesia* 37 E7
Lokandu, *Zaïre* 54 C2
Lokeren, *Belgium* 15 C3
Lokichokio, *Kenya* 54 B3
Lokitaung, *Kenya* 54 B4
Lokka, *Finland* 8 C19
Løkken Verk, *Norway* 8 E10
Lokoja, *Nigeria* 50 G6
Lokolama, *Zaïre* 52 E3
Lola, Mt., *U.S.A.* 84 F6
Loliondo, *Tanzania* 54 C4
Lolland, *Denmark* 9 J11
Lolo, *U.S.A.* 82 C6
Lom, *Bulgaria* 21 C10
Lom Kao, *Thailand* 38 D3
Lom Sak, *Thailand* 38 D3
Loma, *U.S.A.* 82 C8
Loma Linda, *U.S.A.* 85 L9
Lomami →, *Zaïre* 54 B1
Lomas de Zamóra, *Argentina* 94 C4
Lombadina, *Australia* 60 C3
Lombardia □, *Italy* 20 B3
Lombardy = Lombardia □, *Italy* 20 B3
Lomblen, *Indonesia* 37 F6

Lombok, *Indonesia* 36 F5
Lomé, *Togo* 50 G5
Lomela, *Zaïre* 52 E4
Lomela →, *Zaïre* 52 E4
Lometa, *U.S.A.* 81 K5
Lomié, *Cameroon* 52 D2
Lomond, *Canada* 72 C6
Lomond, L., *U.K.* 12 E4
Lomphat, *Cambodia* 38 F6
Lompobatang, *Indonesia* 37 F5
Lompoc, *U.S.A.* 85 L6
Łomza, *Poland* 17 B11
Loncoche, *Chile* 96 D2
Londa, *India* 40 M9
Londiani, *Kenya* 54 C4
London, *Canada* 70 D3
London, *U.K.* 11 F7
London, *Ky., U.S.A.* 76 G3
London, *Ohio, U.S.A.* 76 F4
London, Greater □, *U.K.* 11 F7
Londonderry, *U.K.* 13 B4
Londonderry □, *U.K.* 13 B4
Londonderry, C., *Australia* 60 B4
Londonderry, I., *Chile* 96 H2
Londrina, *Brazil* 95 A5
Lone Pine, *U.S.A.* 83 H4
Long Beach, *Calif., U.S.A.* 85 M8
Long Beach, *N.Y., U.S.A.* 79 F11
Long Beach, *Wash., U.S.A.* 84 D2
Long Branch, *U.S.A.* 79 F11
Long Creek, *U.S.A.* 82 D4
Long Eaton, *U.K.* 10 E6
Long I., *Australia* 62 C4
Long I., *Bahamas* 89 B4
Long I., *U.S.A.* 79 F11
Long Island Sd., *U.S.A.* 79 E12
Long L., *Canada* 70 C2
Long Lake, *U.S.A.* 79 C10
Long Pine, *U.S.A.* 80 D5
Long Pt., *Nfld., Canada* 71 C8
Long Pt., *Ont., Canada* 78 D4
Long Point B., *Canada* 78 D4
Long Range Mts., *Canada* 71 C8
Long Reef, *Australia* 60 B4
Long Str. = Longa, Proliv, *Russia* 4 C16
Long Thanh, *Vietnam* 39 G6
Long Xian, *China* 34 G4
Long Xuyen, *Vietnam* 39 G5
Longa, Proliv, *Russia* 4 C16
Longde, *China* 34 G4
Longford, *Australia* 62 G4
Longford, *Ireland* 13 C4
Longford □, *Ireland* 13 C4
Longguan, *China* 34 D8
Longhua, *China* 35 D9
Longido, *Tanzania* 54 C4
Longiram, *Indonesia* 36 E5
Longkou, *China* 35 F11
Longlac, *Canada* 70 C2
Longmont, *U.S.A.* 80 E2
Longnawan, *Indonesia* 36 D4
Longreach, *Australia* 62 C3
Longton, *Australia* 62 C4
Longtown, *U.K.* 11 F5
Longueuil, *Canada* 79 A11
Longview, *Canada* 72 C6
Longview, *Tex., U.S.A.* 81 J7
Longview, *Wash., U.S.A.* 84 D4
Longxi, *China* 34 G3
Lonoke, *U.S.A.* 81 H9
Lons-le-Saunier, *France* 18 C6
Lookout, C., *Canada* 70 A3
Lookout, C., *U.S.A.* 77 H7
Loolmalasin, *Tanzania* 54 C4
Loon →, *Alta., Canada* 72 B5
Loon →, *Man., Canada* 73 B8
Loon Lake, *Canada* 73 C7
Loongana, *Australia* 61 F4
Loop Hd., *Ireland* 13 D2
Lop Buri, *Thailand* 38 E3
Lop Nor = Lop Nur, *China* 32 B4
Lop Nur, *China* 32 B4
Lopatina, G., *Russia* 27 D15
Lopez, C., *Gabon* 52 E1
Lopphavet, *Norway* 8 A16
Lora →, *Afghan.* 40 D4
Lora, Hamun-i-, *Pakistan* 40 E4
Lora Cr. →, *Australia* 63 D2
Lorain, *U.S.A.* 78 E2
Loralai, *Pakistan* 42 D3
Lorca, *Spain* 19 D5
Lord Howe I., *Pac. Oc.* 64 L7
Lord Howe Ridge, *Pac. Oc.* 64 L8
Lordsburg, *U.S.A.* 83 K9
Loreto, *Brazil* 93 E9
Loreto, *Italy* 20 C5
Loreto, *Mexico* 86 B2
Lorient, *France* 18 C2
Lorn, *U.K.* 12 E3
Lorn, Firth of, *U.K.* 12 E3
Lorne, *Australia* 63 F3
Lorovouno, *Cyprus* 23 D11
Lorraine, *France* 18 B7
Lorrainville, *Canada* 70 C4
Los Alamos, *Calif., U.S.A.* 85 L6
Los Alamos, *N. Mex., U.S.A.* 83 J10
Los Altos, *U.S.A.* 84 H4
Los Andes, *Chile* 94 C1
Los Angeles, *Chile* 94 D1
Los Angeles, *U.S.A.* 85 L8
Los Angeles Aqueduct, *U.S.A.* 85 K9
Los Banos, *U.S.A.* 83 H3
Los Blancos, *Argentina* 94 A3
Los Cristianos, *Canary Is.* 22 F3
Los Gatos, *U.S.A.* 84 H5
Los Hermanos, *Venezuela* 89 D7
Los Islotes, *Canary Is.* 22 E6
Los Llanos de Aridane, *Canary Is.* 22 F2
Los Lunas, *U.S.A.* 83 J10
Los Mochis, *Mexico* 86 B3
Los Olivos, *U.S.A.* 85 L6
Los Palacios, *Cuba* 88 B3
Los Reyes, *Mexico* 86 D4
Los Roques, *Venezuela* 92 A5
Los Testigos, *Venezuela* 92 A6
Los Vilos, *Chile* 94 C1
Loshkalakh, *Russia* 27 C15
Lošinj, *Croatia* 20 B6
Lossiemouth, *U.K.* 12 D5
Lot □, *France* 18 D4
Lot →, *France* 18 D4
Lot-et-Garonne □, *France* 18 D4
Lota, *Chile* 94 D1
Loṭfābād, *Iran* 45 B8
Lothair, *S. Africa* 57 D5
Lothian □, *U.K.* 12 F5
Loubomo, *Congo* 52 E2
Loudon, *U.S.A.* 77 H3
Loudonville, *U.S.A.* 78 F2
Louga, *Senegal* 50 E1
Loughborough, *U.K.* 10 E6
Loughrea, *Ireland* 13 C3
Loughros More B., *Ireland* 13 B3
Louis Trichardt, *S. Africa* 57 C4
Louis XIV, Pte., *Canada* 70 B4
Louisa, *U.S.A.* 76 F4
Louisbourg, *Canada* 71 C8
Louise I., *Canada* 72 C2
Louiseville, *Canada* 70 C5
Louisiade Arch., *Papua N. G.* 64 J7
Louisiana, *U.S.A.* 80 F9
Louisiana □, *U.S.A.* 81 K9
Louisville, *Ky., U.S.A.* 76 F3
Louisville, *Miss., U.S.A.* 81 J10
Loulé, *Portugal* 19 D1
Loup City, *U.S.A.* 80 E5
Lourdes, *France* 18 E3
Lourdes-du-Blanc-Sablon, *Canada* 71 B8
Lourenço-Marques = Maputo, *Mozam.* 57 D5
Louth, *Australia* 63 E4
Louth, *Ireland* 13 C5
Louth, *U.K.* 10 D7
Louth □, *Ireland* 13 C5
Louvain = Leuven, *Belgium* 15 D4
Louwsburg, *S. Africa* 57 D5
Love, *Canada* 73 C8
Loveland, *U.S.A.* 80 E2
Lovell, *U.S.A.* 82 D9
Lovelock, *U.S.A.* 82 F4
Loviisa = Lovisa, *Finland* 9 F19
Loving, *U.S.A.* 81 J2
Lovington, *U.S.A.* 81 J3
Lovisa, *Finland* 9 F19
Low Pt., *Australia* 61 F4
Lowa, *Zaïre* 54 C2
Lowa →, *Zaïre* 54 C2
Lowell, *U.S.A.* 79 D13
Lower Arrow L., *Canada* 72 D5
Lower California = Baja California, *Mexico* 86 A1
Lower California = California, Baja, *Mexico* 86 A1
Lower Hutt, *N.Z.* 59 J5
Lower L., *U.S.A.* 82 F3
Lower Lake, *U.S.A.* 84 G4
Lower Post, *Canada* 72 B3
Lower Red L., *U.S.A.* 80 B7
Lower Tunguska = Tunguska, Nizhnyaya →, *Russia* 27 C9
Lowestoft, *U.K.* 11 E9
Łowicz, *Poland* 17 B9
Lowville, *U.S.A.* 79 C9
Loxton, *Australia* 63 E3
Loxton, *S. Africa* 56 E3
Loyalton, *U.S.A.* 84 F6
Loyalty Is. = Loyauté, Is., *N. Cal.* 64 K8
Loyang = Luoyang, *China* 34 G7
Loyauté, Is., *N. Cal.* 64 K8
Loyoro, *Uganda* 54 B3
Lozère □, *France* 18 D5
Luachimo, *Angola* 52 F4
Luacono, *Angola* 52 G4
Lualaba →, *Zaïre* 54 B5
Luampa, *Zambia* 55 F1
Luan Chau, *Vietnam* 38 B4
Luan He →, *China* 35 E10
Luan Xian, *China* 35 E10
Luancheng, *China* 34 F8
Luanda, *Angola* 52 F2
Luang Prabang, *Laos* 38 C4
Luang Thale, *Thailand* 39 J3
Luangwa, *Zambia* 55 F3
Luangwa →, *Zambia* 55 E3
Luangwa Valley, *Zambia* 55 E3
Luanne, *China* 35 D9
Luanping, *China* 35 D9
Luanshya, *Zambia* 55 E2
Luapula □, *Zambia* 55 E2
Luapula →, *Africa* 55 D2
Luarca, *Spain* 19 A2
Luashi, *Zaïre* 55 E1
Luau, *Angola* 52 G4
Lubalo, *Angola* 52 F3
Lubang Is., *Phil.* 37 B6
Lubbock, *U.S.A.* 81 J4
Lübeck, *Germany* 16 B5
Lubefu, *Zaïre* 54 C1
Lubefu →, *Zaïre* 54 C1
Lubero = Luofu, *Zaïre* 54 C2
Lubicon L., *Canada* 72 B5
Lublin, *Poland* 17 C11
Lubnān, J., *Lebanon* 47 B4
Lubny, *Ukraine* 26 D4
Lubongola, *Zaïre* 54 C2
Lubuagan, *Phil.* 37 A6
Lubudi →, *Zaïre* 55 D2
Lubuk Antu, *Malaysia* 36 D4
Lubuklinggau, *Indonesia* 36 E2
Lubuksikaping, *Indonesia* 36 D2
Lubumbashi, *Zaïre* 55 E2
Lubunda, *Zaïre* 54 D2
Lubungu, *Zambia* 55 E2
Lubutu, *Zaïre* 54 C2
Luc An Chau, *Vietnam* 38 A5
Lucan, *Canada* 78 C3
Lucca, *Italy* 20 C4
Luce Bay, *U.K.* 12 G4
Lucea, *Jamaica* 88 C4
Lucedale, *U.S.A.* 77 K1
Lucena, *Phil.* 37 B6
Lucena, *Spain* 19 D3
Lučenec, *Czech.* 17 D9
Lucerne = Luzern, *Switz.* 16 E4
Lucerne, *U.S.A.* 84 F4
Lucerne Valley, *U.S.A.* 85 L10
Lucero, *Mexico* 86 A3
Lucheng, *China* 34 F7
Lucheringo →, *Mozam.* 55 E4
Lucira, *Angola* 53 G2
Luckenwalde, *Germany* 16 B6
Lucknow, *India* 43 F9
Lüda = Dalian, *China* 35 E11
Lüderitz, *Namibia* 56 D2
Ludewe □, *Tanzania* 55 D3
Ludhiana, *India* 42 D6
Ludington, *U.S.A.* 76 D2
Ludlow, *U.K.* 11 E5
Ludlow, *Calif., U.S.A.* 85 L10
Ludlow, *Vt., U.S.A.* 79 C12
Ludvika, *Sweden* 9 F13
Ludwigsburg, *Germany* 16 D4
Ludwigshafen, *Germany* 16 D4
Luebo, *Zaïre* 52 F4
Lueki, *Zaïre* 54 C2
Luena, *Zaïre* 55 D2
Luena, *Zambia* 55 E3
Lüeyang, *China* 34 H4
Lufira →, *Zaïre* 55 D2
Lufkin, *U.S.A.* 81 K7
Lufupa, *Zaïre* 55 E1
Luga, *Russia* 24 C4
Lugano, *Switz.* 16 E4
Lugansk, *Ukraine* 25 E6
Lugard's Falls, *Kenya* 54 C4
Lugela, *Mozam.* 55 F4
Lugenda →, *Mozam.* 55 E4
Lugh Ganana, *Somali Rep.* 46 G3
Lugnaquilla, *Ireland* 13 D5
Lugo, *Spain* 19 A2
Lugoj, *Romania* 17 F10
Lugovoye, *Kazakhstan* 26 E8
Luiana, *Angola* 56 B3
Luis Correia, *Brazil* 93 D10
Luitpold Coast, *Antarctica* 5 D1
Luiza, *Zaïre* 52 F4
Luizi, *Zaïre* 54 D2
Luján, *Argentina* 94 C4
Lukanga Swamp, *Zambia* 55 E2
Lukenie →, *Zaïre* 52 E3
Lukhisaral, *India* 43 G12
Lukolela, *Equateur, Zaïre* 52 E3
Lukolela, *Kasai Or., Zaïre* 54 D1
Lukosi, *Zimbabwe* 55 F2
Łuków, *Poland* 17 C11
Lule älv →, *Sweden* 8 D17
Luleå, *Sweden* 8 D17
Luling, *U.S.A.* 81 L6
Lulong, *China* 35 E10
Lulonga →, *Zaïre* 52 D3
Lulua →, *Zaïre* 52 E4
Luluabourg = Kananga, *Zaïre* 52 F4
Lumai, *Angola* 53 G4
Lumajang, *Indonesia* 37 H15
Lumbala N'guimbo, *Angola* 53 G4
Lumberton, *Miss., U.S.A.* 81 K10
Lumberton, *N.C., U.S.A.* 77 H6
Lumberton, *N. Mex., U.S.A.* 83 H10
Lumbwa, *Kenya* 54 C4
Lumsden, *N.Z.* 59 L2
Lumut, *Malaysia* 39 K3
Lumut, Tg., *Indonesia* 36 E3
Lunavada, *India* 42 H5
Lund, *U.S.A.* 82 G6
Lundazi, *Zambia* 55 E3
Lundi →, *Zimbabwe* 55 G3
Lundu, *Malaysia* 36 D3
Lundy, *U.K.* 11 F3
Lune →, *U.K.* 10 C5
Lüneburg, *Germany* 16 B5
Lüneburg Heath = Lüneburger Heide, *Germany* 16 B5
Lüneburger Heide, *Germany* 16 B5
Lunenburg, *Canada* 71 D7
Lunéville, *France* 18 B7
Lunga →, *Zambia* 55 E2
Lunglei, *India* 41 H18
Luni, *India* 42 F5
Luni →, *India* 42 G4
Luning, *U.S.A.* 82 G4
Lunsemfwa →, *Zambia* 55 E3
Lunsemfwa Falls, *Zambia* 55 E2
Luo He →, *China* 34 G6
Luochuan, *China* 34 G5
Luofu, *Zaïre* 54 C2
Luohe, *China* 34 H8
Luonan, *China* 34 G6
Luoning, *China* 34 G6
Luoyang, *China* 34 G7
Luozi, *Zaïre* 52 E2
Luozigou, *China* 35 C16
Lupilichi, *Mozam.* 55 E4
Luqa, *Malta* 20 G6
Luque, *Paraguay* 94 B4
Luray, *U.S.A.* 76 F6
Luremo, *Angola* 52 F3
Lurgan, *U.K.* 13 B5
Lusaka, *Zambia* 55 F2
Lusambo, *Zaïre* 54 C1
Lusangaye, *Zaïre* 54 C2
Luseland, *Canada* 73 C7
Lushan, *China* 34 H7
Lushi, *China* 34 G6
Lushoto, *Tanzania* 54 C4
Lushoto □, *Tanzania* 54 C4
Lüshun, *China* 35 E11
Lusk, *U.S.A.* 80 D2
Luta = Dalian, *China* 35 E11
Luton, *U.K.* 11 F7
Lutong, *Malaysia* 36 D4
Lutsk, *Ukraine* 24 D4
Lützow Holmbukta, *Antarctica* 5 C4
Lutzputs, *S. Africa* 56 D3
Luverne, *U.S.A.* 80 D6
Luvua, *Zaïre* 55 D2
Luvua →, *Zaïre* 54 D2
Luwegu →, *Tanzania* 55 D4
Luwuk, *Indonesia* 37 E6
Luxembourg, *Lux.* 15 E6
Luxembourg □, *Belgium* 15 E5
Luxembourg ■, *Europe* 15 E6
Luxi, *China* 32 D4
Luxor = El Uqsur, *Egypt* 51 C11
Luyi, *China* 34 H8
Luza, *Russia* 24 B8
Luzern, *Switz.* 16 E4
Luzhou, *China* 32 D5
Luziânia, *Brazil* 93 G9
Luzon, *Phil.* 37 A6
Lvov, *Ukraine* 25 E3
Lyakhovskiye, Ostrova, *Russia* 27 B15
Lyallpur = Faisalabad, *Pakistan* 42 D5
Lycksele, *Sweden* 8 D15
Lydda = Lod, *Israel* 47 D3
Lydenburg, *S. Africa* 57 D5
Lyell, *N.Z.* 59 J4
Lyell I., *Canada* 72 C2
Lyell Ra., *N.Z.* 59 J4
Lyman, *U.S.A.* 82 F8
Lyme Regis, *U.K.* 11 G5
Lymington, *U.K.* 11 G6
Łyńa →, *Poland* 17 A10
Lynchburg, *U.S.A.* 76 G6
Lynd →, *Australia* 62 B3
Lynd Ra., *Australia* 63 D4
Lynden, *Canada* 78 C4
Lynden, *U.S.A.* 84 B4
Lyndhurst, *Queens., Australia* 62 B3
Lyndhurst, *S. Austral., Australia* 63 E2
Lyndon →, *Australia* 61 D1
Lyndonville, *N.Y., U.S.A.* 78 C6
Lyndonville, *Vt., U.S.A.* 79 B12
Lynher Reef, *Australia* 60 C3
Lynn, *U.S.A.* 79 D14
Lynn Canal, *U.S.A.* 72 B1
Lynn Lake, *Canada* 73 B8
Lynnwood, *U.S.A.* 84 C4
Lynton, *U.K.* 11 F4
Lynx L., *Canada* 73 A7
Lyon, *France* 18 D6
Lyonnais, *France* 18 D6
Lyons = Lyon, *France* 18 D6
Lyons, *Colo., U.S.A.* 80 E2
Lyons, *Ga., U.S.A.* 77 J4
Lyons, *Kans., U.S.A.* 80 F5
Lyons, *N.Y., U.S.A.* 78 C8
Lys = Leie →, *Belgium* 15 C3
Lysva, *Russia* 24 C10
Lytle, *U.S.A.* 81 L5
Lyttelton, *N.Z.* 59 K4
Lytton, *Canada* 72 C4
Lyubertsy, *Russia* 24 C6

M

Ma →, *Vietnam* 38 C5
Ma'adaba, *Jordan* 47 E4
Maamba, *Zambia* 56 B4
Ma'ân, *Jordan* 47 E4
Ma'ân □, *Jordan* 47 F5
Ma'anshan, *China* 33 C6
Maarianhamina, *Finland* 9 F15
Ma'arrat an Nu'mân, *Syria* 44 C3
Maas →, *Neths.* 15 C4
Maaseik, *Belgium* 15 C5
Maassluis, *Neths.* 15 C4
Maastricht, *Neths.* 15 D5
Maave, *Mozam.* 57 C5
Mabel L., *Canada* 72 C5
Mabenge, *Zaïre* 54 B1
Mablethorpe, *U.K.* 10 D8
Maboma, *Zaïre* 54 B2
Mabrouk, *Mali* 50 E4
Mabton, *U.S.A.* 82 C3
Mac Bac, *Vietnam* 39 H6
Macachín, *Argentina* 94 D3
Macaé, *Brazil* 95 A7
McAlester, *U.S.A.* 81 H7
McAllen, *U.S.A.* 81 M5
Macamic, *Canada* 70 C4
Macao = Macau ■, *China* 33 D6
Macapá, *Brazil* 93 C8
McArthur →, *Australia* 62 B2
McArthur, Port, *Australia* 62 B2
McArthur River, *Australia* 62 B2
Macau, *Brazil* 93 E11
Macau ■, *China* 33 D6
McBride, *Canada* 72 C4
McCall, *U.S.A.* 82 D5
McCamey, *U.S.A.* 81 K3
McCammon, *U.S.A.* 82 E7
McCauley I., *Canada* 72 C2
McCleary, *U.S.A.* 84 C3
Macclesfield, *U.K.* 10 D5
McClintock, *Canada* 73 B10
McClintock Ra., *Australia* 60 C4
McCloud, *U.S.A.* 82 F2
McCluer I., *Australia* 60 B5
McClure, *U.S.A.* 78 F7
McClure, L., *U.S.A.* 84 H6
M'Clure Str., *Canada* 4 B2
McClusky, *U.S.A.* 80 B4
McComb, *U.S.A.* 81 K9
McConaughy, L., *U.S.A.* 80 E4
McCook, *U.S.A.* 80 E4
McCullough Mt., *U.S.A.* 85 K11
McCusker →, *Canada* 73 B7
McDame, *Canada* 72 B3
McDermitt, *U.S.A.* 82 F5
Macdonald, L., *Australia* 60 D4
McDonald Is., *Ind. Oc.* 3 G13
Macdonnell Ras., *Australia* 60 D5
McDouall Peak, *Australia* 63 D1
Macdougall L., *Canada* 68 B10
MacDowell L., *Canada* 70 B1
Macduff, *U.K.* 12 D6
Macedonia = Makedhonia □, *Greece* 21 D10
Macedonia □, *Europe* 21 D9
Maceió, *Brazil* 93 E11
Macenta, *Guinea* 50 G3
Macerata, *Italy* 20 C5
McFarland, *U.S.A.* 85 K7
McFarlane →, *Canada* 73 B7
Macfarlane, L., *Australia* 63 E2
McGehee, *U.S.A.* 81 J9
McGill, *U.S.A.* 82 G6
Macgillycuddy's Reeks, *Ireland* 13 D2
MacGregor, *Canada* 73 D9
McGregor, *U.S.A.* 80 D9
McGregor →, *Canada* 72 B4
McGregor Ra., *Australia* 63 D3
Mach, *Pakistan* 40 E5
Māch Kowr, *Iran* 45 E9
Machado = Jiparaná →, *Brazil* 92 E6
Machagai, *Argentina* 94 B3
Machakos, *Kenya* 54 C4
Machakos □, *Kenya* 54 C4
Machala, *Ecuador* 92 D3
Machanga, *Mozam.* 57 C6
Machattie, L., *Australia* 62 C2
Machava, *Mozam.* 57 D5
Machece, *Mozam.* 55 F4
Machevna, *Russia* 27 C18
Machias, *U.S.A.* 71 D6
Machichi →, *Canada* 73 B10
Machico, *Madeira* 22 D3
Machilipatnam, *India* 41 L12
Machiques, *Venezuela* 92 A4
Machupicchu, *Peru* 92 F4
Machynlleth, *U.K.* 11 E4
McIlwraith Ra., *Australia* 62 A3
McIntosh, *U.S.A.* 80 C4
McIntosh L., *Canada* 73 B8
Macintosh Ra., *Australia* 61 E4
Macintyre →, *Australia* 63 D5
Mackay, *Australia* 62 C4
Mackay, *U.S.A.* 82 E7
MacKay →, *Canada* 72 B6
Mackay, L., *Australia* 60 D4
McKay Ra., *Australia* 60 D3
McKeesport, *U.S.A.* 78 F5
McKenna, *U.S.A.* 84 D4
Mackenzie, *Canada* 72 B4
McKenzie, *U.S.A.* 77 G1
Mackenzie →, *Australia* 62 C4
Mackenzie →, *Canada* 68 B6
McKenzie →, *U.S.A.* 82 D2
Mackenzie City = Linden, *Guyana* 92 B7
Mackenzie Highway, *Canada* 72 B5
Mackenzie Mts., *Canada* 68 B7
Mackinaw City, *U.S.A.* 76 C3
McKinlay, *Australia* 62 C3
McKinlay →, *Australia* 62 C3
McKinley, Mt., *U.S.A.* 68 B4
McKinley Sea, *Arctic* 4 A7
McKinney, *U.S.A.* 81 J6
Mackinnon Road, *Kenya* 54 C4
Macksville, *Australia* 63 E5
McLaughlin, *U.S.A.* 80 C4
Maclean, *Australia* 63 D5

McLean, *U.S.A.* 81 H4
McLeansboro, *U.S.A.* 80 F10
Maclear, *S. Africa* 57 E4
Macleay →, *Australia* 63 E5
McLennan, *Canada* 72 B5
MacLeod, B., *Canada* 73 A7
McLeod, L., *Australia* 61 D1
MacLeod Lake, *Canada* 72 C4
M'Clintock Chan., *Canada* 68 A9
McLoughlin, Mt., *U.S.A.* 82 E2
McLure, *Canada* 72 C4
McMechen, *U.S.A.* 78 G4
McMillan L., *U.S.A.* 81 J2
McMinnville, *Oreg., U.S.A.* 82 D2
McMinnville, *Tenn., U.S.A.* 77 H3
McMorran, *Canada* 73 C7
McMurdo Sd., *Antarctica* 5 D11
McMurray = Fort McMurray, *Canada* 72 B6
McMurray, *U.S.A.* 84 B4
McNary, *U.S.A.* 83 J9
MacNutt, *Canada* 73 C8
Macodoene, *Mozam.* 57 C6
Macomb, *U.S.A.* 80 E9
Mâcon, *France* 18 C6
Macon, *Ga., U.S.A.* 77 J4
Macon, *Miss., U.S.A.* 77 J1
Macon, *Mo., U.S.A.* 80 F8
Macondo, *Angola* 53 G4
Macossa, *Mozam.* 55 F3
Macoun L., *Canada* 73 B8
Macovane, *Mozam.* 57 C6
McPherson, *U.S.A.* 80 F6
McPherson Pk., *U.S.A.* 85 L7
McPherson Ra., *Australia* 63 D5
Macquarie Harbour, *Australia* 62 G4
Macquarie Is., *Pac. Oc.* 64 N7
MacRobertson Land, *Antarctica* 5 D6
Macroom, *Ireland* 13 E3
Macroy, *Australia* 60 D2
MacTier, *Canada* 78 A5
Macubela, *Mozam.* 55 F4
Macuiza, *Mozam.* 55 F3
Macuse, *Mozam.* 55 F4
Macuspana, *Mexico* 87 D6
Macusse, *Angola* 56 B3
McVille, *U.S.A.* 80 B5
Madadeni, *S. Africa* 57 D5
Madagali, *Nigeria* 51 F7
Madagascar ■, *Africa* 57 C8
Madā'in Sālih, *Si. Arabia* 44 E3
Madama, *Niger* 51 D7
Madame I., *Canada* 71 C7
Madaoua, *Niger* 50 F6
Madaripur, *Bangla.* 41 H17
Madauk, *Burma* 41 L20
Madawaska, *Canada* 78 A7
Madawaska →, *Canada* 78 A8
Madaya, *Burma* 41 H20
Madeira, *Atl. Oc.* 22 D3
Madeira →, *Brazil* 92 D7
Madeleine, Is. de la, *Canada* 71 C7
Madera, *U.S.A.* 83 H3
Madha, *India* 40 L9
Madhubani, *India* 43 F12
Madhya Pradesh □, *India* 42 J7
Madikeri, *India* 40 N9
Madill, *U.S.A.* 81 H6
Madimba, *Zaïre* 52 E3
Ma'din, *Syria* 44 C3
Madinat ash Sha'b, *Yemen* 46 E3
Madingou, *Congo* 52 E2
Madirovalo, *Madag.* 57 B8
Madison, *Calif., U.S.A.* 84 G5
Madison, *Fla., U.S.A.* 77 K4
Madison, *Ind., U.S.A.* 76 F3
Madison, *Nebr., U.S.A.* 80 E6
Madison, *Ohio, U.S.A.* 78 E3
Madison, *S. Dak., U.S.A.* 80 D6
Madison, *Wis., U.S.A.* 80 D10
Madison →, *U.S.A.* 82 D8
Madisonville, *Ky., U.S.A.* 76 G2
Madisonville, *Tex., U.S.A.* 81 K7
Madista, *Botswana* 56 C4
Madiun, *Indonesia* 37 G14
Madley, *U.K.* 11 E5
Madras = Tamil Nadu □, *India* 40 P10
Madras, *India* 40 N12
Madras, *U.S.A.* 82 D3
Madre, L., *Mexico* 87 B5
Madre, L., *U.S.A.* 81 M6
Madre, Sierra, *Phil.* 37 A6
Madre de Dios →, *Bolivia* 92 F5
Madre de Dios, I., *Chile* 96 G1
Madre del Sur, Sierra, *Mexico* 87 D5
Madre Occidental, Sierra, *Mexico* 86 B3
Madre Oriental, Sierra, *Mexico* 86 C4
Madri, *India* 42 G5
Madrid, *Spain* 19 B4
Madura, Selat, *Indonesia* 37 G15
Madura Motel, *Australia* 61 F4
Madurai, *India* 40 Q11
Madurantakam, *India* 40 N11
Mae Chan, *Thailand* 38 B2
Mae Hong Son, *Thailand* 38 C2
Mae Khlong →, *Thailand* 38 F3
Mae Phrik, *Thailand* 38 D2
Mae Ramat, *Thailand* 38 D2
Mae Rim, *Thailand* 38 C2
Mae Sot, *Thailand* 38 D2
Mae Suai, *Thailand* 38 C2
Mae Tha, *Thailand* 38 C2
Maebashi, *Japan* 31 F9
Maesteg, *U.K.* 11 F4
Maestra, Sierra, *Cuba* 88 B4
Maestrazgo, Mts. del, *Spain* 19 B5
Maevatanana, *Madag.* 57 B8
Mafeking = Mafikeng, *S. Africa* 56 D4
Mafeking, *Canada* 73 C8
Mafeteng, *Lesotho* 56 D4
Maffra, *Australia* 63 F4
Mafia I., *Tanzania* 54 D4
Mafikeng, *S. Africa* 56 D4
Mafra, *Brazil* 95 B6
Mafra, *Portugal* 19 C1
Mafungabusi Plateau, *Zimbabwe* 55 F2
Magadan, *Russia* 27 D16
Magadi, *Kenya* 54 C4
Magadi, L., *Kenya* 54 C4
Magaliesburg, *S. Africa* 57 D4
Magallanes, Estrecho de, *Chile* 96 G2
Magangué, *Colombia* 92 B4
Magburaka, *S. Leone* 50 G2
Magdalena, *Argentina* 94 D4
Magdalena, *Bolivia* 92 F6
Magdalena, *Malaysia* 36 D5
Magdalena, *Mexico* 86 A2
Magdalena, *U.S.A.* 83 J10
Magdalena →, *Colombia* 92 A4
Magdalena →, *Mexico* 86 A2
Magdalena, B., *Mexico* 86 C2
Magdalena, Llano de la, *Mexico* 86 C2
Magdeburg, *Germany* 16 B5
Magdelaine Cays, *Australia* 62 B5
Magee, *U.S.A.* 81 K10
Magee, I., *U.K.* 13 B6
Magelang, *Indonesia* 37 G14
Magellan's Str. = Magallanes, Estrecho de, *Chile* 96 G2
Magenta, L., *Australia* 61 F2
Maggiore, L., *Italy* 20 A3
Magherafelt, *U.K.* 13 B5
Magnetic Pole (North) = North Magnetic Pole, *Canada* 4 B2
Magnetic Pole (South) = South Magnetic Pole, *Antarctica* 5 C9
Magnitogorsk, *Russia* 24 D10
Magnolia, *Ark., U.S.A.* 81 J8
Magnolia, *Miss., U.S.A.* 81 K9
Magog, *Canada* 71 C5
Magoro, *Uganda* 54 B3
Magosa = Famagusta, *Cyprus* 23 D12
Magouládhes, *Greece* 23 A3
Magoye, *Zambia* 55 F2
Magpie L., *Canada* 71 B7
Magrath, *Canada* 72 D6
Magu □, *Tanzania* 54 C3
Maguarinho, C., *Brazil* 93 D9
Maguse L., *Canada* 73 A9
Maguse Pt., *Canada* 73 A10
Magwe, *Burma* 41 J19
Maha Sarakham, *Thailand* 38 D4
Mahābād, *Iran* 44 B5
Mahabharat Lekh, *Nepal* 43 E9
Mahabo, *Madag.* 57 C7
Mahadeo Hills, *India* 42 H8
Mahagi, *Zaïre* 54 B3
Mahajamba →, *Madag.* 57 B8
Mahajamba, Helodranon' i, *Madag.* 57 B8
Mahajan, *India* 42 E5
Mahajanga, *Madag.* 57 B8
Mahajanga □, *Madag.* 57 B8
Mahajilo →, *Madag.* 57 B8
Mahakam →, *Indonesia* 36 E5
Mahalapye, *Botswana* 56 C4
Maḥallāt, *Iran* 45 C6
Māhān, *Iran* 45 D8
Mahanadi →, *India* 41 J15
Mahanoro, *Madag.* 57 B8
Mahanoy City, *U.S.A.* 79 F8
Maharashtra □, *India* 40 J9
Mahari Mts., *Tanzania* 54 D2
Mahasham, W. →, *Egypt* 47 E3
Mahasolo, *Madag.* 57 B8
Mahattat ash Shīdīyah, *Jordan* 47 F4
Mahattat 'Unayzah, *Jordan* 47 E4
Mahaxay, *Laos* 38 D5
Mahbubnagar, *India* 40 L10
Maḥḍah, *Oman* 45 E7
Mahdia, *Tunisia* 51 A7
Mahe, *India* 43 C8
Mahenge, *Tanzania* 55 D4
Maheno, *N.Z.* 59 L3
Mahesana, *India* 42 H5
Mahia Pen., *N.Z.* 59 H6
Mahmud Kot, *Pakistan* 42 D4
Mahnomen, *U.S.A.* 80 B7
Mahoba, *India* 43 G8
Mahón, *Spain* 22 B11
Mahone Bay, *Canada* 71 D7
Mai-Ndombe, L., *Zaïre* 52 E3
Mai-Sai, *Thailand* 38 B2
Maicurú →, *Brazil* 93 D8
Maidan Khula, *Afghan.* 42 C3
Maidenhead, *U.K.* 11 F7
Maidstone, *Canada* 73 C7
Maidstone, *U.K.* 11 F8
Maiduguri, *Nigeria* 51 F7
Maijdi, *Bangla.* 41 H17
Maikala Ra., *India* 41 J12
Mailsi, *Pakistan* 42 E5
Main →, *Germany* 16 D4
Main →, *U.K.* 13 B5
Main Centre, *Canada* 73 C7
Maine, *France* 18 C3
Maine □, *U.S.A.* 71 C6
Maine →, *Ireland* 13 D2
Maine-et-Loire □, *France* 18 C3
Maingkwan, *Burma* 41 F20
Mainit, L., *Phil.* 37 C7
Mainland, *Orkney, U.K.* 12 C5
Mainland, *Shet., U.K.* 12 A7
Mainpuri, *India* 43 F8
Maintirano, *Madag.* 57 B7
Mainz, *Germany* 16 D4
Maipú, *Argentina* 94 D4
Maiquetía, *Venezuela* 92 A5
Mairabari, *India* 41 F18
Maisí, *Cuba* 89 B5
Maisi, Pta. de, *Cuba* 89 B5
Maitland, *N.S.W., Australia* 63 E5
Maitland, *S. Austral., Australia* 63 E2
Maitland →, *Canada* 78 C3
Maiz, Is. del, *Nic.* 88 D3
Maizuru, *Japan* 31 G7
Majalengka, *Indonesia* 37 G13
Majene, *Indonesia* 37 E5
Maji, *Ethiopia* 51 G12
Major, *Canada* 73 C7
Majorca = Mallorca, *Spain* 22 B10
Maka, *Senegal* 50 F2
Makale, *Indonesia* 37 E5
Makamba, *Burundi* 54 C2
Makari, *Cameroon* 52 B2
Makarikari = Makgadikgadi Salt Pans, *Botswana* 56 C4
Makarovo, *Russia* 27 D11
Makasar = Ujung Pandang, *Indonesia* 37 F5
Makasar, Selat, *Indonesia* 37 E5
Makasar, Str. of = Makasar, Selat, *Indonesia* 37 E5
Makat, *Kazakhstan* 25 E9
Makedhonía □, *Greece* 21 D10
Makedonija = Macedonia □, *Europe* 21 D9
Makena, *U.S.A.* 74 H16
Makeni, *S. Leone* 50 G2
Makeyevka, *Ukraine* 25 E6
Makgadikgadi Salt Pans, *Botswana* 56 C4
Makhachkala, *Russia* 25 F8
Makhmūr, *Iraq* 44 C4
Makian, *Indonesia* 37 D7
Makindu, *Kenya* 54 C4
Makinsk, *Kazakhstan* 26 D8
Makkah, *Si. Arabia* 46 C2
Makkovik, *Canada* 71 A8
Makó, *Hungary* 17 E10
Makokou, *Gabon* 52 D2
Makongo, *Zaïre* 54 B2
Makoro, *Zaïre* 54 B2
Makoua, *Congo* 52 E3
Makrai, *India* 40 H10
Makran Coast Range, *Pakistan* 40 G4
Makrana, *India* 42 F6
Makriyialos, *Greece* 23 D7
Maksimkin Yar, *Russia* 26 D9
Mākū, *Iran* 44 B5
Makumbi, *Zaïre* 52 F4
Makunda, *Botswana* 56 C3
Makurazaki, *Japan* 31 J5
Makurdi, *Nigeria* 50 G6
Makūyeh, *Iran* 45 D7
Makwassie, *S. Africa* 56 D4
Mal B., *Ireland* 13 D2
Mala, Pta., *Panama* 88 E3
Malabang, *Phil.* 37 C6
Malabar Coast, *India* 40 P9
Malabo = Rey Malabo, *Eq. Guin.* 50 H6
Malacca, Str. of, *Indonesia* 39 L3
Malad City, *U.S.A.* 82 E7
Málaga, *Spain* 19 D3
Malaga, *U.S.A.* 81 J2
Málaga □, *Spain* 19 D3
Malagarasi, *Tanzania* 54 D3
Malagarasi →, *Tanzania* 54 D2
Malaimbandy, *Madag.* 57 C8
Malakâl, *Sudan* 51 G11
Malakand, *Pakistan* 42 B4
Malakoff, *U.S.A.* 81 J7
Malamyzh, *Russia* 27 E14
Malang, *Indonesia* 37 G15
Malange, *Angola* 52 F3
Mälaren, *Sweden* 9 G14
Malargüe, *Argentina* 94 D2
Malartic, *Canada* 70 C4
Malatya, *Turkey* 25 G6
Malawi ■, *Africa* 55 E3
Malawi, L., *Africa* 55 E3
Malay Pen., *Asia* 39 J3
Malaybalay, *Phil.* 37 C7
Malāyer, *Iran* 45 C6
Malaysia ■, *Asia* 36 D4
Malazgirt, *Turkey* 25 G7
Malbon, *Australia* 62 C3
Malbooma, *Australia* 63 E1
Malbork, *Poland* 17 A9
Malcolm, *Australia* 61 E3
Malcolm, Pt., *Australia* 61 F3
Maldegem, *Belgium* 15 C3
Malden, *Mass., U.S.A.* 79 D13
Malden, *Mo., U.S.A.* 81 G10
Malden I., *Kiribati* 65 H12
Maldives ■, *Ind. Oc.* 29 J11
Maldonado, *Uruguay* 95 C5
Maldonado, Punta, *Mexico* 87 D5
Malé Karpaty, *Czech.* 16 D8
Maléa, Ákra, *Greece* 21 F10
Malebo, Pool, *Africa* 48 G5
Malegaon, *India* 40 J9
Malei, *Mozam.* 55 F4
Malek Kandī, *Iran* 44 B5
Malela, *Zaïre* 54 C2
Malema, *Mozam.* 55 E4
Máleme, *Greece* 23 D5
Malerkotla, *India* 42 D6
Máles, *Greece* 23 D7
Malgomaj, *Sweden* 8 D14
Malha, *Sudan* 51 E10
Malhão, Sa. do, *Portugal* 19 D1
Malheur →, *U.S.A.* 82 D5
Malheur L., *U.S.A.* 82 E4
Mali ■, *Africa* 50 E4
Mali →, *Burma* 41 G20
Malibu, *U.S.A.* 85 L8
Malik, *Indonesia* 37 E6
Malili, *Indonesia* 37 E6
Malimba, Mts., *Zaïre* 54 D2
Malin Hd., *Ireland* 13 A4
Malindi, *Kenya* 54 C5
Malines = Mechelen, *Belgium* 15 C4
Maling, *Indonesia* 37 D6
Malinyi, *Tanzania* 55 D4
Malita, *Phil.* 37 C7
Mallacoota, *Australia* 63 F4
Mallacoota Inlet, *Australia* 63 F4
Mallaig, *U.K.* 12 E3
Mallawan, *India* 43 F9
Mallawi, *Egypt* 51 C11
Mállia, *Greece* 23 D7
Mallión, Kólpos, *Greece* 23 D7
Mallorca, *Spain* 22 B10
Mallorytown, *Canada* 79 B9
Mallow, *Ireland* 13 D3
Malmberget, *Sweden* 8 C16
Malmédy, *Belgium* 15 D6
Malmesbury, *S. Africa* 56 E2
Malmö, *Sweden* 9 J12
Malmöhus län □, *Sweden* 9 J12
Malolos, *Phil.* 37 B6
Malombe L., *Malawi* 55 E4
Malone, *U.S.A.* 79 B10
Malozemelskaya Tundra, *Russia* 24 A9
Malpaso, *Canary Is.* 22 G1
Malpelo, *Colombia* 92 C2
Malta, *Idaho, U.S.A.* 82 E7
Malta, *Mont., U.S.A.* 82 B10
Malta ■, *Europe* 23 D1
Maltahöhe, *Namibia* 56 C2
Malton, *Canada* 78 C5
Malton, *U.K.* 10 C7
Maluku, *Indonesia* 37 E7
Maluku □, *Indonesia* 37 E7
Maluku Sea, *Indonesia* 37 E6
Malvan, *India* 40 L8
Malvern, *U.S.A.* 81 H8
Malvinas, Is. = Falkland Is., *Atl. Oc.* 96 G5
Malya, *Tanzania* 54 C3
Malyy Lyakhovskiy, Ostrov, *Russia* 27 B15
Mama, *Russia* 27 D12
Mamaia, *Romania* 17 F14
Mamanguape, *Brazil* 93 E11
Mamasa, *Indonesia* 37 E5
Mambasa, *Zaïre* 54 B2
Mamberamo →, *Indonesia* 37 E9
Mambilima Falls, *Zambia* 55 E2
Mambirima, *Zaïre* 55 E2
Mambo, *Tanzania* 54 C4
Mambrui, *Kenya* 54 C5
Mamburao, *Phil.* 37 B6
Mameigwess L., *Canada* 70 B2
Mamfe, *Cameroon* 50 G6
Mammoth, *U.S.A.* 83 K8
Mamoré →, *Bolivia* 92 F5
Mamou, *Guinea* 50 F2
Mamuju, *Indonesia* 37 E5
Man, *Ivory C.* 50 G3
Man, I. of, *U.K.* 10 C3
Man Na, *Burma* 41 H20
Mana, *Fr. Guiana* 93 B8
Manaar, G. of = Mannar, G. of, *Asia* 40 Q11
Manacapuru, *Brazil* 92 D6
Manacor, *Spain* 22 B10
Manado, *Indonesia* 37 D6
Managua, *Nic.* 88 D2
Managua, L., *Nic.* 88 D2
Manakara, *Madag.* 57 C8
Manambao →, *Madag.* 57 B7
Manambato, *Madag.* 57 A8
Manambolo →, *Madag.* 57 B7
Manambolosy, *Madag.* 57 B8
Mananara, *Madag.* 57 B8
Mananara →, *Madag.* 57 C8
Mananjary, *Madag.* 57 C8
Manantenina, *Madag.* 57 C8
Manaos = Manaus, *Brazil* 92 D7
Manapouri, *N.Z.* 59 L1
Manapouri, L., *N.Z.* 59 L1
Manas, *China* 32 B3
Manas →, *India* 41 F17
Manaslu, *Nepal* 43 E11
Manasquan, *U.S.A.* 79 F10
Manassa, *U.S.A.* 83 H11
Manaung, *Burma* 41 K18
Manaus, *Brazil* 92 D7
Manawan L., *Canada* 73 B8
Manay, *Phil.* 37 C7
Manbij, *Syria* 44 B3
Mancelona, *U.S.A.* 76 C3
Manche □, *France* 18 B3
Manchegorsk, *Russia* 24 A5
Manchester, *U.K.* 10 D5
Manchester, *Calif., U.S.A.* 84 G3
Manchester, *Conn., U.S.A.* 79 E12
Manchester, *Ga., U.S.A.* 77 J3
Manchester, *Iowa, U.S.A.* 80 D9
Manchester, *Ky., U.S.A.* 76 G4
Manchester, *N.H., U.S.A.* 79 D13
Manchester, *N.Y., U.S.A.* 78 D7
Manchester, *Vt., U.S.A.* 79 C11
Manchester L., *Canada* 73 A7
Manchuria = Dongbei, *China* 35 D13
Mand →, *Iran* 45 D7
Manda, *Chunya, Tanzania* 54 D3
Manda, *Ludewe, Tanzania* 55 E3
Mandabé, *Madag.* 57 C7
Mandaguari, *Brazil* 95 A5
Mandah, *Mongolia* 34 B5
Mandal, *Norway* 9 G9
Mandalay, *Burma* 41 J20
Mandale = Mandalay, *Burma* 41 J20
Mandalgovi, *Mongolia* 34 B4
Mandali, *Iraq* 44 C5
Mandan, *U.S.A.* 80 B4
Mandar, Teluk, *Indonesia* 37 E5
Mandasor = Mandsaur, *India* 42 G6
Mandaue, *Phil.* 37 B6
Mandera, *Kenya* 54 B5
Mandera □, *Kenya* 54 B5
Mandi, *India* 42 D7
Mandimba, *Mozam.* 55 E4
Mandioli, *Indonesia* 37 E7
Mandla, *India* 43 H9
Mandoto, *Madag.* 57 B8
Mandra, *Pakistan* 42 C5
Mandrare →, *Madag.* 57 D8
Mandritsara, *Madag.* 57 B8
Mandsaur, *India* 42 G6
Mandurah, *Australia* 61 F2
Mandvi, *India* 42 H3
Mandya, *India* 40 N10
Mandzai, *Pakistan* 42 D2
Maneh, *Iran* 45 B8
Maneroo, *Australia* 62 C3
Maneroo Cr. →, *Australia* 62 C3
Manfalût, *Egypt* 51 C11
Manfred, *Australia* 63 E3
Mangalia, *Romania* 17 G14
Mangalore, *India* 40 N9
Mangaweka, *N.Z.* 59 H5
Manggar, *Indonesia* 36 E3
Manggawitu, *Indonesia* 37 E8
Mangkalihat, Tanjung, *Indonesia* 37 D5
Mangla Dam, *Pakistan* 43 C5
Manglaur, *India* 42 E7
Mangnai, *China* 32 C4
Mango, *Togo* 50 F5
Mangoche, *Malawi* 55 E4
Mangoky →, *Madag.* 57 C7
Mangole, *Indonesia* 37 E7
Mangombe, *Zaïre* 54 C2
Mangonui, *N.Z.* 59 F4
Mangueigne, *Chad* 51 F9
Mangueira, L. da, *Brazil* 95 C5
Mangum, *U.S.A.* 81 H5
Mangyshlak Poluostrov, *Kazakhstan* 26 E6
Manhattan, *U.S.A.* 80 F6
Manhiça, *Mozam.* 57 D5
Manhuaçu, *Brazil* 93 H10
Mania →, *Madag.* 57 B8
Manica, *Mozam.* 57 B5
Manica e Sofala □, *Mozam.* 57 B5
Manicaland □, *Zimbabwe* 55 F3
Manicoré, *Brazil* 92 E6
Manicouagan →, *Canada* 71 C6
Manīfah, *Si. Arabia* 45 E6
Manifold, *Australia* 62 C5
Manifold, C., *Australia* 62 C5
Manigotagan, *Canada* 73 C9
Manihiki, *Cook Is.* 65 J11
Manika, Plateau de la, *Zaïre* 55 E2
Manila, *Phil.* 37 B6
Manila, *U.S.A.* 82 F9
Manila B., *Phil.* 37 B6
Manilla, *Australia* 63 E5
Maningrida, *Australia* 62 A1
Manipur □, *India* 41 G18
Manipur →, *Burma* 41 H19
Manisa, *Turkey* 25 G4
Manistee, *U.S.A.* 76 C2
Manistee →, *U.S.A.* 76 C2
Manistique, *U.S.A.* 76 C2
Manito L., *Canada* 73 C7
Manitoba □, *Canada* 73 B9
Manitoba, L., *Canada* 73 C9
Manitou, *Canada* 73 D9
Manitou I., *U.S.A.* 70 C2
Manitou Is., *U.S.A.* 76 C2
Manitou L., *Canada* 71 B6
Manitou Springs, *U.S.A.* 80 F2
Manitoulin I., *Canada* 70 C3
Manitowaning, *Canada* 70 C3
Manitowoc, *U.S.A.* 76 C2
Manizales, *Colombia* 92 B3

Manja, *Madag.* 57 C7
Manjacaze, *Mozam.* 57 C5
Manjakandriana, *Madag.* 57 B8
Manjhand, *Pakistan* 42 G3
Manjil, *Iran* 45 B6
Manjimup, *Australia* 61 F2
Manjra →, *India* 40 K10
Mankato, *Kans., U.S.A.* 80 F5
Mankato, *Minn., U.S.A.* 80 C8
Mankayane, *Swaziland* 57 D5
Mankono, *Ivory C.* 50 G3
Mankota, *Canada* 73 D7
Manlay, *Mongolia* 34 B4
Manly, *Australia* 63 E5
Manmad, *India* 40 J9
Mann Ras., *Australia* 61 E5
Manna, *Indonesia* 36 E2
Mannahill, *Australia* 63 E3
Mannar, *Sri Lanka* 40 Q11
Mannar, G. of, *Asia* 40 Q11
Mannar I., *Sri Lanka* 40 Q11
Mannheim, *Germany* 16 D4
Manning, *Canada* 72 B5
Manning, *Oreg., U.S.A.* 84 E3
Manning, *S.C., U.S.A.* 77 J5
Manning Prov. Park, *Canada* 72 D4
Mannington, *U.S.A.* 76 F5
Mannum, *Australia* 63 E2
Mano, *S. Leone* 50 G2
Manokwari, *Indonesia* 37 E8
Manombo, *Madag.* 57 C7
Manono, *Zaïre* 54 D2
Manouane, L., *Canada* 71 B5
Manpojin, *N. Korea* 35 D14
Manresa, *Spain* 19 B6
Mansa, *Gujarat, India* 42 H5
Mansa, *Punjab, India* 42 E6
Mansa, *Zambia* 55 E2
Mansehra, *Pakistan* 42 B5
Mansel I., *Canada* 69 B11
Mansfield, *Australia* 63 F4
Mansfield, *U.K.* 10 D6
Mansfield, *La., U.S.A.* 81 J8
Mansfield, *Mass., U.S.A.* 79 D13
Mansfield, *Ohio, U.S.A.* 78 F2
Mansfield, *Pa., U.S.A.* 78 E7
Mansfield, *Wash., U.S.A.* 82 C4
Manson Creek, *Canada* 72 B4
Manta, *Ecuador* 92 D2
Mantalingajan, Mt., *Phil.* 36 C5
Mantare, *Tanzania* 54 C3
Manteca, *U.S.A.* 83 H3
Manteo, *U.S.A.* 77 H8
Mantes-la-Jolie, *France* 18 B4
Manthani, *India* 40 K11
Manti, *U.S.A.* 82 G8
Mantiqueira, Serra da, *Brazil* 95 A7
Manton, *U.S.A.* 76 C3
Mántova, *Italy* 20 B4
Mänttä, *Finland* 8 E18
Mantua = Mántova, *Italy* 20 B4
Manu, *Peru* 92 F4
Manua Is., *Amer. Samoa* 59 B14
Manuae, *Cook Is.* 65 J12
Manuel Alves →, *Brazil* 93 F9
Manui, *Indonesia* 37 E6
Manville, *U.S.A.* 80 D2
Many, *U.S.A.* 81 K8
Manyara, L., *Tanzania* 54 C4
Manych-Gudilo, Oz., *Russia* 25 E7
Manyonga →, *Tanzania* 54 C3
Manyoni, *Tanzania* 54 D3
Manyoni □, *Tanzania* 54 D3
Manzai, *Pakistan* 42 C4
Manzanares, *Spain* 19 C4
Manzanillo, *Cuba* 88 B4
Manzanillo, *Mexico* 86 D4
Manzanillo, Pta., *Panama* 88 E4
Manzano Mts., *U.S.A.* 83 J10
Manzarīyeh, *Iran* 45 C6
Manzhouli, *China* 33 B6
Manzini, *Swaziland* 57 D5
Mao, *Chad* 51 F8
Maoke, Pegunungan, *Indonesia* 37 E9
Maolin, *China* 35 C12
Maoming, *China* 33 D6
Maoxing, *China* 35 B13
Mapam Yumco, *China* 32 C3
Mapastepec, *Mexico* 87 D6
Mapia, Kepulauan, *Indonesia* 37 D8
Mapimí, *Mexico* 86 B4
Mapimí, Bolsón de, *Mexico* 86 B4
Mapinga, *Tanzania* 54 D4
Mapinhane, *Mozam.* 57 C6
Maple Creek, *Canada* 73 D7
Maple Valley, *U.S.A.* 84 C4
Mapleton, *U.S.A.* 82 D2
Mapuera →, *Brazil* 92 D7
Maputo, *Mozam.* 57 D5
Maputo, B. de, *Mozam.* 57 D5
Maqiaohe, *China* 35 B16
Maqnā, *Si. Arabia* 44 D2
Maquela do Zombo, *Angola* 52 F3
Maquinchao, *Argentina* 96 E3
Maquoketa, *U.S.A.* 80 D9
Mar, Serra do, *Brazil* 95 B6
Mar Chiquita, L., *Argentina* 94 C3
Mar del Plata, *Argentina* 94 D4
Mara, *Tanzania* 54 C3
Mara □, *Tanzania* 54 C3
Maraã, *Brazil* 92 D5
Marabá, *Brazil* 93 E9
Maracá, I. de, *Brazil* 93 C8
Maracaibo, *Venezuela* 92 A4
Maracaibo, L. de, *Venezuela* 92 B4
Maracaju, *Brazil* 95 A4
Maracay, *Venezuela* 92 A5
Marādah, *Libya* 51 C8
Maradi, *Niger* 50 F6
Marāgheh, *Iran* 44 B5
Marāh, *Si. Arabia* 44 E5
Marajó, I. de, *Brazil* 93 D9
Marākand, *Iran* 44 B5
Maralal, *Kenya* 54 B4
Maralinga, *Australia* 61 F5
Marama, *Australia* 63 F3
Marampa, *S. Leone* 50 G2
Maran, *Malaysia* 39 L4
Marana, *U.S.A.* 83 K8
Maranboy, *Australia* 60 B5
Marand, *Iran* 44 B5
Marang, *Malaysia* 39 K4
Maranguape, *Brazil* 93 D11
Maranhão = São Luís, *Brazil* 93 D10
Maranhão □, *Brazil* 93 E9
Maranoa →, *Australia* 63 D4
Marañón →, *Peru* 92 D4
Marão, *Mozam.* 57 C5
Maraş = Kahramanmaraş, *Turkey* 25 G6
Marathasa □, *Cyprus* 23 E11
Marathon, *Australia* 62 C3
Marathon, *Canada* 70 C2
Marathón, *Greece* 21 E10
Marathon, *N.Y., U.S.A.* 79 D8
Marathon, *Tex., U.S.A.* 81 K3
Marathóvouno, *Cyprus* 23 D12
Maratua, *Indonesia* 37 D5
Maravatío, *Mexico* 86 D4
Marāwih, *U.A.E.* 45 E7
Marbella, *Spain* 19 D3
Marble Bar, *Australia* 60 D2
Marble Falls, *U.S.A.* 81 K5
Marblehead, *U.S.A.* 79 D14
Marburg, *Germany* 16 C4
March, *U.K.* 11 E8
Marche, *France* 18 C4
Marche □, *Italy* 20 C5
Marche-en-Famenne, *Belgium* 15 D5
Marches = Marche □, *Italy* 20 C5
Marcos Juárez, *Argentina* 94 C3
Marcus I. = Minami-Tori-Shima, *Pac. Oc.* 64 E7
Marcus Necker Ridge, *Pac. Oc.* 64 F9
Marcy Mt., *U.S.A.* 79 B11
Mardan, *Pakistan* 42 B5
Mardie, *Australia* 60 D2
Mardin, *Turkey* 25 G7
Maree L., *U.K.* 12 D3
Mareeba, *Australia* 62 B4
Marek = Stanke Dimitrov, *Bulgaria* 21 C10
Marek, *Indonesia* 37 E6
Maremma, *Italy* 20 C4
Marengo, *U.S.A.* 80 E8
Marenyi, *Kenya* 54 C4
Marerano, *Madag.* 57 C7
Marfa, *U.S.A.* 81 K2
Marfa Pt., *Malta* 23 D1
Margaret →, *Australia* 60 C4
Margaret Bay, *Canada* 72 C3
Margaret L., *Canada* 72 B5
Margaret River, *Australia* 60 C4
Margarita, I. de, *Venezuela* 92 A6
Margaritovo, *Russia* 30 C7
Margate, *S. Africa* 57 E5
Margate, *U.K.* 11 F9
Margelan, *Uzbekistan* 26 E8
Marguerite, *Canada* 72 C4
Mari Republic □, *Russia* 24 C8
María Elena, *Chile* 94 A2
María Grande, *Argentina* 94 C4
Maria I., *N. Terr., Australia* 62 A2
Maria I., *Tas., Australia* 62 G4
Maria van Diemen, C., *N.Z.* 59 F4
Mariakani, *Kenya* 54 C4
Marian L., *Canada* 72 A5
Mariana Trench, *Pac. Oc.* 64 F6
Marianao, *Cuba* 88 B3
Marianna, *Ark., U.S.A.* 81 H9
Marianna, *Fla., U.S.A.* 77 K3
Marias →, *U.S.A.* 82 C8
Mariato, Punta, *Panama* 88 E3
Ma'rib, *Yemen* 46 D4
Maribor, *Slovenia* 20 A6
Marico →, *Africa* 56 C4
Maricopa, *Ariz., U.S.A.* 83 K7
Maricopa, *Calif., U.S.A.* 85 K7
Marîdî, *Sudan* 51 H10
Marie Byrd Land, *Antarctica* 5 D14
Marie-Galante, *Guadeloupe* 89 C7
Mariecourt, *Canada* 69 B12
Mariehamn, *Finland* 9 F15
Marienberg, *Neths.* 15 B6
Marienbourg, *Belgium* 15 D4
Mariental, *Namibia* 56 C2
Marienville, *U.S.A.* 78 E5
Mariestad, *Sweden* 9 G12
Marietta, *Ga., U.S.A.* 77 J3
Marietta, *Ohio, U.S.A.* 76 F5
Marieville, *Canada* 79 A11
Mariinsk, *Russia* 26 D9
Marília, *Brazil* 95 A5
Marillana, *Australia* 60 D2
Marín, *Spain* 19 A1
Marina, *U.S.A.* 84 J5
Marina Plains, *Australia* 62 A3
Marinduque, *Phil.* 37 B6
Marine City, *U.S.A.* 76 D4
Marinette, *U.S.A.* 76 C2
Maringá, *Brazil* 95 A5
Marion, *Ala., U.S.A.* 77 J2
Marion, *Ill., U.S.A.* 81 G10
Marion, *Ind., U.S.A.* 76 E3
Marion, *Iowa, U.S.A.* 80 D9
Marion, *Kans., U.S.A.* 80 F6
Marion, *Mich., U.S.A.* 76 C3
Marion, *N.C., U.S.A.* 77 H4
Marion, *Ohio, U.S.A.* 76 E4
Marion, *S.C., U.S.A.* 77 H6
Marion, *Va., U.S.A.* 77 G5
Marion, L., *U.S.A.* 77 J5
Mariposa, *U.S.A.* 83 H4
Mariscal Estigarribia, *Paraguay* 94 A3
Maritime Alps = Maritimes, Alpes, *Europe* 20 B2
Maritimes, Alpes, *Europe* 20 B2
Maritsa, *Greece* 23 C10
Maritsa →, *Bulgaria* 21 D12
Mariupol, *Ukraine* 25 E6
Marīvān, *Iran* 44 C5
Markazī □, *Iran* 45 C6
Markdale, *Canada* 78 B4
Marked Tree, *U.S.A.* 81 H9
Marken, *Neths.* 15 B5
Market Drayton, *U.K.* 10 E5
Market Harborough, *U.K.* 11 E7
Markham, *Canada* 78 C5
Markham, Mt., *Antarctica* 5 E11
Markham L., *Canada* 73 A8
Markleeville, *U.S.A.* 84 G7
Markovo, *Russia* 27 C17
Marks, *Russia* 24 D8
Marksville, *U.S.A.* 81 K8
Marla, *Australia* 63 D1
Marlboro, *U.S.A.* 79 D13
Marlborough, *Australia* 62 C4
Marlborough □, *N.Z.* 59 J4
Marlborough Downs, *U.K.* 11 F6
Marlin, *U.S.A.* 81 K6
Marlow, *U.S.A.* 81 H6
Marmagao, *India* 40 M8
Marmara, *Turkey* 21 D12
Marmara, Sea of = Marmara Denizi, *Turkey* 21 D13
Marmara Denizi, *Turkey* 21 D13
Marmarth, *U.S.A.* 80 B3
Marmion, Mt., *Australia* 61 E2
Marmion L., *Canada* 70 C1
Marmolada, Mte., *Italy* 20 A4
Marmora, *Canada* 70 D4
Marne □, *France* 18 B6
Marne →, *France* 18 B5
Maroala, *Madag.* 57 B8
Maroantsetra, *Madag.* 57 B8
Maromandia, *Madag.* 57 A8
Marondera, *Zimbabwe* 55 F3
Maroni →, *Fr. Guiana* 93 B8
Maroochydore, *Australia* 63 D5
Maroona, *Australia* 63 F3
Marosakoa, *Madag.* 57 B8
Maroua, *Cameroon* 51 F7
Marovoay, *Madag.* 57 B8
Marquard, *S. Africa* 56 D4
Marquesas Is. = Marquises, Is., *Pac. Oc.* 65 H14
Marquette, *U.S.A.* 76 B2
Marquises, Is., *Pac. Oc.* 65 H14
Marracuene, *Mozam.* 57 D5
Marrakech, *Morocco* 50 B3
Marrawah, *Australia* 62 G3
Marree, *Australia* 63 D2
Marrilla, *Australia* 60 D1
Marrimane, *Mozam.* 57 C5
Marromeu, *Mozam.* 57 B6
Marrowie Cr. →, *Australia* 63 E4
Marrubane, *Mozam.* 55 F4
Marrupa, *Mozam.* 55 E4
Marsá Matrûh, *Egypt* 51 B10
Marsá Susah, *Libya* 51 B9
Marsabit, *Kenya* 54 B4
Marsabit □, *Kenya* 54 B4
Marsala, *Italy* 20 F5
Marsalforn, *Malta* 23 C1
Marsaxlokk, *Malta* 20 G6
Marsden, *Australia* 63 E4
Marseille, *France* 18 E6
Marseilles = Marseille, *France* 18 E6
Marsh I., *U.S.A.* 81 L9
Marsh L., *U.S.A.* 80 C6
Marshall, *Liberia* 50 G2
Marshall, *Ark., U.S.A.* 81 H8
Marshall, *Mich., U.S.A.* 76 D3
Marshall, *Minn., U.S.A.* 80 C7
Marshall, *Mo., U.S.A.* 80 F8
Marshall, *Tex., U.S.A.* 81 J7
Marshall →, *Australia* 62 C2
Marshall Is., *Pac. Oc.* 64 G9
Marshalltown, *U.S.A.* 80 D8
Marshfield, *Mo., U.S.A.* 81 G8
Marshfield, *Wis., U.S.A.* 80 C9
Marshūn, *Iran* 45 B6
Marstrand, *Sweden* 9 H11
Mart, *U.S.A.* 81 K6
Martaban, *Burma* 41 L20
Martaban, G. of, *Burma* 41 L20
Martapura, *Kalimantan, Indonesia* 36 E4
Martapura, *Sumatera, Indonesia* 36 E2
Marte, *Nigeria* 51 F7
Martelange, *Belgium* 15 E5
Martha's Vineyard, *U.S.A.* 79 E14
Martin, *S. Dak., U.S.A.* 80 D4
Martin, *Tenn., U.S.A.* 81 G10
Martin, L., *U.S.A.* 77 J3
Martinborough, *N.Z.* 59 J5
Martinez, *U.S.A.* 84 G4
Martinique ■, *W. Indies* 89 D7
Martinique Passage, *W. Indies* 89 C7
Martinópolis, *Brazil* 95 A5
Martins Ferry, *U.S.A.* 78 F4
Martinsburg, *Pa., U.S.A.* 78 F6
Martinsburg, *W. Va., U.S.A.* 76 F7
Martinsville, *Ind., U.S.A.* 76 F2
Martinsville, *Va., U.S.A.* 77 G6
Marton, *N.Z.* 59 J5
Martos, *Spain* 19 D4
Marudi, *Malaysia* 36 D4
Ma'ruf, *Afghan.* 40 D5
Marugame, *Japan* 31 G6
Marulan, *Australia* 63 E5
Marunga, *Angola* 56 B3
Marungu, Mts., *Zaïre* 54 D2
Marvast, *Iran* 45 D7
Marwar, *India* 42 G5
Mary, *Turkmenistan* 26 F7
Mary Frances L., *Canada* 73 A7
Mary Kathleen, *Australia* 62 C2
Maryborough = Port Laoise, *Ireland* 13 C4
Maryborough, *Queens., Australia* 63 D5
Maryborough, *Vic., Australia* 63 F3
Maryfield, *Canada* 73 D8
Maryland □, *U.S.A.* 76 F7
Maryland Junction, *Zimbabwe* 55 F3
Maryport, *U.K.* 10 C4
Mary's Harbour, *Canada* 71 B8
Marystown, *Canada* 71 C8
Marysvale, *U.S.A.* 83 G7
Marysville, *Canada* 72 D5
Marysville, *Calif., U.S.A.* 84 F5
Marysville, *Kans., U.S.A.* 80 F6
Marysville, *Mich., U.S.A.* 78 D2
Marysville, *Ohio, U.S.A.* 76 E4
Marysville, *Wash., U.S.A.* 84 B4
Maryvale, *Australia* 63 D5
Maryville, *U.S.A.* 77 H4
Marzūq, *Libya* 51 C7
Masahunga, *Tanzania* 54 C3
Masai, *Malaysia* 39 M4
Masai Steppe, *Tanzania* 54 C4
Masaka, *Uganda* 54 C3
Masalembo, Kepulauan, *Indonesia* 36 F4
Masalima, Kepulauan, *Indonesia* 36 F5
Masamba, *Indonesia* 37 E6
Masan, *S. Korea* 35 G15
Masasi, *Tanzania* 55 E4
Masasi □, *Tanzania* 55 E4
Masaya, *Nic.* 88 D2
Masbate, *Phil.* 37 B6
Mascara, *Algeria* 50 A5
Mascota, *Mexico* 86 C4
Masela, *Indonesia* 37 F7
Maseru, *Lesotho* 56 D4
Mashaba, *Zimbabwe* 55 G3
Mashābih, *Si. Arabia* 44 E3
Masherbrum, *Pakistan* 43 B7
Mashhad, *Iran* 45 B8
Mashīz, *Iran* 45 D8
Mashkel, Hamun-i-, *Pakistan* 40 E3
Mashki Chāh, *Pakistan* 40 E3
Mashonaland Central □, *Zimbabwe* 57 B5
Mashonaland East □, *Zimbabwe* 57 B5
Mashonaland West □, *Zimbabwe* 57 B4
Masi, *Norway* 8 B17
Masi Manimba, *Zaïre* 52 E3
Masindi, *Uganda* 54 B3
Masindi Port, *Uganda* 54 B3
Masisea, *Peru* 92 E4
Masisi, *Zaïre* 54 C2
Masjed Soleyman, *Iran* 45 D6
Mask, L., *Ireland* 13 C2
Masoala, Tanjon' i, *Madag.* 57 B9
Masoarivo, *Madag.* 57 B7
Masohi, *Indonesia* 37 E7
Masomeloka, *Madag.* 57 C8
Mason, *Nev., U.S.A.* 84 G7
Mason, *Tex., U.S.A.* 81 K5
Mason City, *U.S.A.* 80 D8
Maspalomas, *Canary Is.* 22 G4
Maspalomas, Pta., *Canary Is.* 22 G4
Masqat, *Oman* 46 C6
Massa, *Italy* 20 B4
Massachusetts □, *U.S.A.* 79 D12
Massachusetts B., *U.S.A.* 79 D14
Massaguet, *Chad* 51 F8
Massakory, *Chad* 51 F8
Massanella, *Spain* 22 B9
Massangena, *Mozam.* 57 C5
Massawa = Mitsiwa, *Ethiopia* 51 E12
Massena, *U.S.A.* 79 B10
Massénya, *Chad* 51 F8
Masset, *Canada* 72 C2
Massif Central, *France* 18 D5
Massillon, *U.S.A.* 78 F3
Massinga, *Mozam.* 57 C6
Masson, *Canada* 79 A9
Masson I., *Antarctica* 5 C7
Masterton, *N.Z.* 59 J5
Mastuj, *Pakistan* 43 A5
Mastung, *Pakistan* 40 E5
Masuda, *Japan* 31 G5
Masvingo, *Zimbabwe* 55 G3
Masvingo □, *Zimbabwe* 55 G3
Maswa □, *Tanzania* 54 C3
Maşyāf, *Syria* 44 C3
Matabeleland North □, *Zimbabwe* 55 F2
Matabeleland South □, *Zimbabwe* 55 G2
Mataboor, *Indonesia* 37 E9
Matachewan, *Canada* 70 C3
Matadi, *Zaïre* 52 F2
Matagalpa, *Nic.* 88 D2
Matagami, *Canada* 70 C4
Matagami, L., *Canada* 70 C4
Matagorda, *U.S.A.* 81 L7
Matagorda B., *U.S.A.* 81 L6
Matagorda I., *U.S.A.* 81 L6
Matak, P., *Indonesia* 39 L6
Matakana, *Australia* 63 E4
Mátala, *Greece* 23 E6
Matam, *Senegal* 50 E2
Matamoros, *Campeche, Mexico* 87 D6
Matamoros, *Coahuila, Mexico* 86 B4
Matamoros, *Puebla, Mexico* 87 D5
Matamoros, *Tamaulipas, Mexico* 87 B5
Ma'ṭan as Sarra, *Libya* 51 D9
Matandu →, *Tanzania* 55 D3
Matane, *Canada* 71 C6
Matanzas, *Cuba* 88 B3
Matapan, C. = Taínaron, Ákra, *Greece* 21 F10
Matapédia, *Canada* 71 C6
Matara, *Sri Lanka* 40 S12
Mataram, *Indonesia* 36 F5
Matarani, *Peru* 92 G4
Mataranka, *Australia* 60 B5
Matarma, Râs, *Egypt* 47 E1
Matatiele, *S. Africa* 57 E4
Mataura, *N.Z.* 59 M2
Matehuala, *Mexico* 86 C4
Mateke Hills, *Zimbabwe* 55 G3
Matera, *Italy* 20 D7
Matetsi, *Zimbabwe* 55 F2
Matheson Island, *Canada* 73 C9
Mathis, *U.S.A.* 81 L6
Mathura, *India* 42 F7
Mati, *Phil.* 37 C7
Matías Romero, *Mexico* 87 D5
Matibane, *Mozam.* 55 E5
Matima, *Botswana* 56 C3
Matlock, *U.K.* 10 D6
Matmata, *Tunisia* 50 B6
Mato Grosso □, *Brazil* 93 F8
Mato Grosso, Planalto do, *Brazil* 93 G8
Mato Grosso do Sul □, *Brazil* 93 G8
Matochkin Shar, *Russia* 26 B6
Matopo Hills, *Zimbabwe* 55 G2
Matopos, *Zimbabwe* 55 G2
Matosinhos, *Portugal* 19 B1
Matsue, *Japan* 31 G6
Matsumae, *Japan* 30 D10
Matsumoto, *Japan* 31 F9
Matsusaka, *Japan* 31 G8
Matsuura, *Japan* 31 H4
Matsuyama, *Japan* 31 H6
Mattagami →, *Canada* 70 B3
Mattancheri, *India* 40 Q10
Mattawa, *Canada* 70 C4
Mattawamkeag, *U.S.A.* 71 C6
Matterhorn, *Switz.* 16 F3
Matthew Town, *Bahamas* 89 B5
Matthew's Ridge, *Guyana* 92 B6
Mattice, *Canada* 70 C3
Mattituck, *U.S.A.* 79 F12
Matuba, *Mozam.* 57 C5
Matucana, *Peru* 92 F3
Matun, *Afghan.* 42 C3
Maturín, *Venezuela* 92 B6
Mau, *India* 43 G10
Mau Escarpment, *Kenya* 54 C4
Mau Ranipur, *India* 43 G8
Maud, Pt., *Australia* 60 D1
Maude, *Australia* 63 E3
Maudin Sun, *Burma* 41 M19
Maués, *Brazil* 92 D7
Mauganj, *India* 41 G12
Maui, *U.S.A.* 74 H16
Maulamyaing = Moulmein, *Burma* 41 L20
Maule □, *Chile* 94 D1
Maumee, *U.S.A.* 76 E4
Maumee →, *U.S.A.* 76 E4
Maumere, *Indonesia* 37 F6
Maun, *Botswana* 56 B3
Mauna Kea, *U.S.A.* 74 J17
Mauna Loa, *U.S.A.* 74 H16
Maungmagan Kyunzu, *Burma* 41 M20
Maupin, *U.S.A.* 82 D3
Maurepas L., *U.S.A.* 81 K9
Maures, *France* 18 E7
Maurice, L., *Australia* 61 E5
Mauritania ■, *Africa* 50 D3
Mauritius ■, *Ind. Oc.* 3 F12
Mauston, *U.S.A.* 80 D9
Mavinga, *Angola* 53 H4
Mavli, *India* 42 G5
Mavuradonha Mts., *Zimbabwe* 55 F3

Mawa, *Zaïre* 54 B2
Mawana, *India* 42 E7
Mawand, *Pakistan* 42 E3
Mawk Mai, *Burma* 41 J20
Mawlaik, *Burma* 41 H19
Mawquq, *Si. Arabia* 44 E4
Mawson Coast, *Antarctica* 5 C6
Max, *U.S.A.* 80 B4
Maxcanú, *Mexico* 87 C6
Maxesibeni, *S. Africa* 57 E4
Maxhamish L., *Canada* 72 B4
Maxixe, *Mozam.* 57 C6
Maxville, *Canada* 79 A10
Maxwell, *U.S.A.* 84 F4
Maxwelton, *Australia* 62 C3
May Downs, *Australia* 62 C4
May Pen, *Jamaica* 88 C4
Maya →, *Russia* 27 D14
Maya Mts., *Belize* 87 D7
Mayaguana, *Bahamas* 89 B5
Mayagüez, *Puerto Rico* 89 C6
Mayāmey, *Iran* 45 B7
Mayarí, *Cuba* 89 B4
Maybell, *U.S.A.* 82 F9
Maydān, *Iraq* 44 C5
Maydena, *Australia* 62 G4
Mayenne, *France* 18 B3
Mayenne □, *France* 18 B3
Mayer, *U.S.A.* 83 J7
Mayerthorpe, *Canada* 72 C5
Mayfield, *U.S.A.* 77 G1
Mayhill, *U.S.A.* 83 K11
Maykop, *Russia* 25 F7
Maymyo, *Burma* 38 A1
Maynard, *U.S.A.* 84 C4
Maynard Hills, *Australia* 61 E2
Mayne →, *Australia* 62 C3
Maynooth, *Ireland* 13 C5
Mayo, *Canada* 68 B6
Mayo □, *Ireland* 13 C2
Mayo L., *Canada* 68 B6
Mayon Volcano, *Phil.* 37 B6
Mayor I., *N.Z.* 59 G6
Mayson L., *Canada* 73 B7
Maysville, *U.S.A.* 76 F4
Mayu, *Indonesia* 37 D7
Mayville, *N. Dak., U.S.A.* 80 B6
Mayville, *N.Y., U.S.A.* 78 D5
Mayya, *Russia* 27 C14
Mazabuka, *Zambia* 55 F2
Mazagán = El Jadida, *Morocco* 50 B3
Mazagão, *Brazil* 93 D8
Mazán, *Peru* 92 D4
Māzandarān □, *Iran* 45 B7
Mazapil, *Mexico* 86 C4
Mazarredo, *Argentina* 96 F3
Mazarrón, *Spain* 19 D5
Mazaruni →, *Guyana* 92 B7
Mazatán, *Mexico* 86 B2
Mazatenango, *Guatemala* 88 D1
Mazatlán, *Mexico* 86 C3
Māzhān, *Iran* 45 C8
Mazīnān, *Iran* 45 B8
Mazoe, *Mozam.* 55 F3
Mazoe →, *Mozam.* 55 F3
Mazowe, *Zimbabwe* 55 F3
Mazurian Lakes = Mazurski, Pojezierze, *Poland* 17 B10
Mazurski, Pojezierze, *Poland* 17 B10
Mbabane, *Swaziland* 57 D5
Mbaïki, *C.A.R.* 52 D3
Mbala, *Zambia* 55 D3
Mbale, *Uganda* 54 B3
Mbalmayo, *Cameroon* 52 D2
Mbamba Bay, *Tanzania* 55 E3
Mbandaka, *Zaïre* 52 D3
Mbanza Congo, *Angola* 52 F2
Mbanza Ngungu, *Zaïre* 52 F2
Mbarara, *Uganda* 54 C3
Mbashe →, *S. Africa* 57 E4
Mbenkuru →, *Tanzania* 55 D4
Mberengwa, *Zimbabwe* 55 G2
Mberengwa, Mt., *Zimbabwe* 55 G2
Mbesuma, *Zambia* 55 D3
Mbeya, *Tanzania* 55 D3
Mbeya □, *Tanzania* 54 D3
Mbinga, *Tanzania* 55 E4
Mbinga □, *Tanzania* 55 E3
Mbini □, *Eq. Guin.* 52 D2
Mbour, *Senegal* 50 F1
Mbout, *Mauritania* 50 E2
Mbozi □, *Tanzania* 55 D3
Mbuji-Mayi, *Zaïre* 54 D1
Mbulu, *Tanzania* 54 C4
Mbulu □, *Tanzania* 54 C4
Mburucuyá, *Argentina* 94 B4
Mchinja, *Tanzania* 55 D4
Mchinji, *Malawi* 55 E3
Mdina, *Malta* 20 G6
Mead, L., *U.S.A.* 85 J12
Meade, *U.S.A.* 81 G4
Meadow, *Australia* 61 E1
Meadow Lake, *Canada* 73 C7
Meadow Lake Prov. Park, *Canada* 73 C7
Meadow Valley Wash →, *U.S.A.* 85 J12
Meadville, *U.S.A.* 78 E4
Meaford, *Canada* 70 D3
Mealy Mts., *Canada* 71 B8
Meander River, *Canada* 72 B5
Meares, C., *U.S.A.* 82 D2
Mearim →, *Brazil* 93 D10
Meath □, *Ireland* 13 C5
Meath Park, *Canada* 73 C7
Meaux, *France* 18 B5
Mebechi-Gawa →, *Japan* 30 D10
Mecanhelas, *Mozam.* 55 F4
Mecca = Makkah, *Si. Arabia* 46 C2
Mecca, *U.S.A.* 85 M10
Mechanicsburg, *U.S.A.* 78 F8
Mechanicville, *U.S.A.* 79 D11
Mechelen, *Belgium* 15 C4
Mecheria, *Algeria* 50 B4
Mecklenburger Bucht, *Germany* 16 A5
Meconta, *Mozam.* 55 E4
Meda, *Australia* 60 C3
Medan, *Indonesia* 36 D1
Medanosa, Pta., *Argentina* 96 F3
Medéa, *Algeria* 50 A5
Medellín, *Colombia* 92 B3
Medemblik, *Neths.* 15 B5
Mederdra, *Mauritania* 50 E1
Medford, *Mass., U.S.A.* 79 D13
Medford, *Oreg., U.S.A.* 82 E2
Medford, *Wis., U.S.A.* 80 C9
Media Agua, *Argentina* 94 C2
Media Luna, *Argentina* 94 C2
Mediaş, *Romania* 17 E12
Medical Lake, *U.S.A.* 82 C5
Medicine Bow, *U.S.A.* 82 F10
Medicine Bow Pk., *U.S.A.* 82 F10
Medicine Bow Ra., *U.S.A.* 82 F10
Medicine Hat, *Canada* 73 D6
Medicine Lake, *U.S.A.* 80 A2
Medicine Lodge, *U.S.A.* 81 G5
Medina = Al Madīnah, *Si. Arabia* 46 C2
Medina, *N. Dak., U.S.A.* 80 B5
Medina, *N.Y., U.S.A.* 78 C6
Medina, *Ohio, U.S.A.* 78 E3
Medina →, *U.S.A.* 81 L5
Medina del Campo, *Spain* 19 B3
Medina L., *U.S.A.* 81 L5
Medina-Sidonia, *Spain* 19 D3
Medinipur, *India* 43 H12
Mediterranean Sea, *Europe* 6 C5
Medley, *Canada* 73 C6
Médoc, *France* 18 D3
Medport = Marsaxlokk, *Malta* 20 G6
Medstead, *Canada* 73 C7
Medveditsa →, *Russia* 25 E7
Medvezhi, Ostrava, *Russia* 27 B17
Medvezhyegorsk, *Russia* 24 B5
Medway →, *U.K.* 11 F8
Meeberrie, *Australia* 61 E2
Meekatharra, *Australia* 61 E2
Meeker, *U.S.A.* 82 F10
Meerut, *India* 42 E7
Meeteetse, *U.S.A.* 82 D9
Mega, *Ethiopia* 51 H12
Mégara, *Greece* 21 F10
Meghalaya □, *India* 41 G17
Mégiscane, L., *Canada* 70 C4
Mehadia, *Romania* 17 F11
Mehndawal, *India* 43 F10
Mehr Jān, *Iran* 45 C7
Mehrābād, *Iran* 44 B5
Mehrān, *Iran* 44 C5
Mehrīz, *Iran* 45 D7
Mei Xian, *Guangdong, China* 33 D6
Mei Xian, *Shaanxi, China* 34 G4
Meiganga, *Cameroon* 52 C2
Meiktila, *Burma* 41 J19
Meissen, *Germany* 16 C6
Mejillones, *Chile* 94 A1
Meka, *Australia* 61 E2
Mékambo, *Gabon* 52 D2
Mekdela, *Ethiopia* 51 F12
Mekhtar, *Pakistan* 40 D6
Meknès, *Morocco* 50 B3
Mekong →, *Asia* 39 H6
Mekongga, *Indonesia* 37 E6
Melagiri Hills, *India* 40 N10
Melaka, *Malaysia* 39 L4
Melalap, *Malaysia* 36 C5
Mélambes, *Greece* 23 D6
Melanesia, *Pac. Oc.* 64 H7
Melbourne, *Australia* 63 F3
Melbourne, *U.S.A.* 77 L5
Melchor Múzquiz, *Mexico* 86 B4
Melchor Ocampo, *Mexico* 86 C4
Mélèzes →, *Canada* 69 C12
Melfi, *Chad* 51 F8
Melfort, *Canada* 73 C8
Melfort, *Zimbabwe* 55 F3
Melilla, *Morocco* 50 A4
Melipilla, *Chile* 94 C1
Mélissa, Ákra, *Greece* 23 D6
Melita, *Canada* 73 D8
Melitopol, *Ukraine* 25 E6
Melk, *Austria* 16 D7
Mellansel, *Sweden* 8 E15
Mellen, *U.S.A.* 80 B9
Mellerud, *Sweden* 9 G12
Mellette, *U.S.A.* 80 C5
Mellieha, *Malta* 23 D1
Melo, *Uruguay* 95 C5
Melolo, *Indonesia* 37 F6
Melouprey, *Cambodia* 38 F5
Melrose, *N.S.W., Australia* 63 E4
Melrose, *W. Austral., Australia* 61 E3
Melrose, *U.K.* 12 F6
Melrose, *U.S.A.* 81 H3
Melstone, *U.S.A.* 82 C10
Melton Mowbray, *U.K.* 10 E7
Melun, *France* 18 B5
Melut, *Sudan* 51 F11
Melville, *Canada* 73 C8
Melville, C., *Australia* 62 A3
Melville, L., *Canada* 71 B8
Melville B., *Australia* 62 A2
Melville I., *Australia* 60 B5
Melville I., *Canada* 4 B2
Melville Pen., *Canada* 69 B11
Melvin →, *Canada* 72 B5
Memba, *Mozam.* 55 E5
Memboro, *Indonesia* 37 F5
Memel = Klaipeda, *Lithuania* 24 C3
Memel, *S. Africa* 57 D4
Memmingen, *Germany* 16 E5
Mempawah, *Indonesia* 36 D3
Memphis, *Tenn., U.S.A.* 81 H10
Memphis, *Tex., U.S.A.* 81 H4
Mena, *U.S.A.* 81 H7
Menai Strait, *U.K.* 10 D3
Ménaka, *Mali* 50 E5
Menan = Chao Phraya →, *Thailand* 38 F3
Menarandra →, *Madag.* 57 D7
Menard, *U.S.A.* 81 K5
Menasha, *U.S.A.* 76 C1
Menate, *Indonesia* 36 E4
Mendawai →, *Indonesia* 36 E4
Mende, *France* 18 D5
Mendez, *Mexico* 87 B5
Mendhar, *India* 43 C6
Mendip Hills, *U.K.* 11 F5
Mendocino, *U.S.A.* 82 G2
Mendocino, C., *U.S.A.* 82 F1
Mendota, *Calif., U.S.A.* 83 H3
Mendota, *Ill., U.S.A.* 80 E10
Mendoza, *Argentina* 94 C2
Mendoza □, *Argentina* 94 C2
Mene Grande, *Venezuela* 92 B4
Menen, *Belgium* 15 D3
Menfi, *Italy* 20 F5
Menggala, *Indonesia* 36 E3
Mengjin, *China* 34 G7
Mengyin, *China* 35 G9
Mengzi, *China* 32 D5
Menihek L., *Canada* 71 B6
Menin = Menen, *Belgium* 15 D3
Menindee, *Australia* 63 E3
Menindee L., *Australia* 63 E3
Meningie, *Australia* 63 F2
Menlo Park, *U.S.A.* 84 H4
Menominee, *U.S.A.* 76 C2
Menominee →, *U.S.A.* 76 C2
Menomonie, *U.S.A.* 80 C9
Menongue, *Angola* 53 G3
Menorca, *Spain* 22 B11
Mentakab, *Malaysia* 39 L4
Mentawai, Kepulauan, *Indonesia* 36 E1
Menton, *France* 18 E7
Mentor, *U.S.A.* 78 E3
Mentz Dam, *S. Africa* 56 E4
Menzelinsk, *Russia* 24 C9
Menzies, *Australia* 61 E3
Me'ona, *Israel* 47 B4
Meoqui, *Mexico* 86 B3
Mepaco, *Mozam.* 55 F3
Meppel, *Neths.* 15 B6
Mer Rouge, *U.S.A.* 81 J9
Merabéllou, Kólpos, *Greece* 23 D7
Meramangye, L., *Australia* 61 E5
Meran = Merano, *Italy* 20 A4
Merano, *Italy* 20 A4
Merauke, *Indonesia* 37 F10
Merbabu, *Indonesia* 37 G14
Merbein, *Australia* 63 E3
Merca, *Somali Rep.* 46 G3
Mercadal, *Spain* 22 B11
Merced, *U.S.A.* 83 H3
Merced Pk., *U.S.A.* 84 H7
Mercedes, *Buenos Aires, Argentina* 94 C4
Mercedes, *Corrientes, Argentina* 94 B4
Mercedes, *San Luis, Argentina* 94 C2
Mercedes, *Uruguay* 94 C4
Merceditas, *Chile* 94 B1
Mercer, *N.Z.* 59 G5
Mercer, *U.S.A.* 78 E4
Mercury, *U.S.A.* 85 J11
Mercy C., *Canada* 69 B13
Meredith, C., *Falk. Is.* 96 G4
Meredith, L., *U.S.A.* 81 H4
Merga = Nukheila, *Sudan* 51 E10
Mergui Arch. = Myeik Kyunzu, *Burma* 39 G1
Mérida, *Mexico* 87 C7
Mérida, *Spain* 19 C2
Mérida, *Venezuela* 92 B4
Mérida, Cord. de, *Venezuela* 90 B2
Meriden, *U.S.A.* 79 E12
Meridian, *Calif., U.S.A.* 84 F5
Meridian, *Idaho, U.S.A.* 82 E5
Meridian, *Miss., U.S.A.* 77 J1
Meridian, *Tex., U.S.A.* 81 K6
Meriruma, *Brazil* 93 C8
Merkel, *U.S.A.* 81 J4
Merksem, *Belgium* 15 C4
Mermaid Reef, *Australia* 60 C2
Merowe, *Sudan* 51 E11
Merredin, *Australia* 61 F2
Merrick, *U.K.* 12 F4
Merrickville, *Canada* 79 B9
Merrill, *Oreg., U.S.A.* 82 E3
Merrill, *Wis., U.S.A.* 80 C10
Merriman, *U.S.A.* 80 D4
Merritt, *Canada* 72 C4
Merriwa, *Australia* 63 E5
Merriwagga, *Australia* 63 E4
Merry I., *Canada* 70 A4
Merrygoen, *Australia* 63 E4
Merryville, *U.S.A.* 81 K8
Mersa Fatma, *Ethiopia* 46 E3
Mersch, *Lux.* 15 E6
Merseburg, *Germany* 16 C5
Mersey →, *U.K.* 10 D5
Merseyside □, *U.K.* 10 D5
Mersin, *Turkey* 25 G5
Mersing, *Malaysia* 39 L4
Merta, *India* 42 F6
Merthyr Tydfil, *U.K.* 11 F4
Mertzon, *U.S.A.* 81 K4
Meru, *Kenya* 54 B4
Meru, *Tanzania* 54 C4
Meru □, *Kenya* 54 B4
Mesa, *U.S.A.* 83 K8
Mesanagrós, *Greece* 23 C9
Mesaoría □, *Cyprus* 23 D12
Mesarás, Kólpos, *Greece* 23 D6
Mesgouez, L., *Canada* 70 B4
Meshed = Mashhad, *Iran* 45 B8
Meshoppen, *U.S.A.* 79 E8
Meshra er Req, *Sudan* 51 G10
Mesick, *U.S.A.* 76 C3
Mesilinka →, *Canada* 72 B4
Mesilla, *U.S.A.* 83 K10
Mesolóngion, *Greece* 21 E9
Mesopotamia = Al Jazirah, *Iraq* 44 C5
Mesquite, *U.S.A.* 83 H6
Mess Cr. →, *Canada* 72 B2
Messalo →, *Mozam.* 55 E4
Messina, *Italy* 20 E6
Messina, *S. Africa* 57 C5
Messina, Str. di, *Italy* 20 E6
Messíni, *Greece* 21 F10
Messiniakós Kólpos, *Greece* 21 F10
Messonghi, *Greece* 23 B3
Mesta →, *Bulgaria* 21 D11
Meta →, *S. Amer.* 92 B5
Metairie, *U.S.A.* 81 L9
Metaline Falls, *U.S.A.* 82 B5
Metán, *Argentina* 94 B3
Metangula, *Mozam.* 55 E3
Metema, *Ethiopia* 51 F12
Metengobalame, *Mozam.* 55 E3
Methven, *N.Z.* 59 K3
Methy L., *Canada* 73 B7
Metil, *Mozam.* 55 F4
Metlakatla, *U.S.A.* 72 B2
Metropolis, *U.S.A.* 81 G10
Mettur Dam, *India* 40 P10
Metz, *France* 18 B7
Meulaboh, *Indonesia* 36 D1
Meureudu, *Indonesia* 36 C1
Meurthe-et-Moselle □, *France* 18 B7
Meuse □, *France* 18 B6
Meuse →, *Europe* 18 A6
Mexborough, *U.K.* 10 D6
Mexia, *U.S.A.* 81 K6
Mexiana, I., *Brazil* 93 C9
Mexicali, *Mexico* 86 A1
México, *Mexico* 87 D5
Mexico, *Maine, U.S.A.* 79 B14
Mexico, *Mo., U.S.A.* 80 F9
México □, *Mexico* 86 D5
Mexico ■, *Cent. Amer.* 86 C4
Mexico, G. of, *Cent. Amer.* 87 C7
Meymaneh, *Afghan.* 40 B4
Mezen, *Russia* 24 A7
Mezen →, *Russia* 24 A7
Mezőkövesd, *Hungary* 17 E10
Mezőtúr, *Hungary* 17 E10
Mezquital, *Mexico* 86 C4
Mgeta, *Tanzania* 55 D4
Mhlaba Hills, *Zimbabwe* 55 F3
Mhow, *India* 42 H6
Miahuatlán, *Mexico* 87 D5
Miallo, *Australia* 62 B4
Miami, *Ariz., U.S.A.* 83 K8
Miami, *Fla., U.S.A.* 77 N5
Miami, *Tex., U.S.A.* 81 H4
Miami →, *U.S.A.* 76 F3
Miami Beach, *U.S.A.* 77 N5
Miamisburg, *U.S.A.* 76 F3
Mian Xian, *China* 34 H4
Mianchi, *China* 34 G6
Mīāndowāb, *Iran* 44 B5
Miandrivazo, *Madag.* 57 B8
Mīāneh, *Iran* 44 B5
Mianwali, *Pakistan* 42 C4
Miarinarivo, *Madag.* 57 B8
Miass, *Russia* 24 D11
Michigan □, *U.S.A.* 75 B9
Michigan, L., *U.S.A.* 76 C2
Michigan City, *U.S.A.* 76 E2
Michikamau L., *Canada* 71 B7
Michipicoten, *Canada* 70 C3
Michipicoten I., *Canada* 70 C2
Michoacan □, *Mexico* 86 D4
Michurinsk, *Russia* 24 D7
Miclere, *Australia* 62 C4
Mico, Pta. , *Nic.* 88 D3
Micronesia, Federated States of ■, *Pac. Oc.* 64 G7
Mid Glamorgan □, *U.K.* 11 F4
Midai, P., *Indonesia* 39 L6
Midale, *Canada* 73 D8
Middelburg, *Neths.* 15 C3
Middelburg, *C. Prov., S. Africa* 56 E3
Middelburg, *Trans., S. Africa* 57 D4
Middelwit, *S. Africa* 56 C4
Middle Alkali L., *U.S.A.* 82 F3
Middle Fork Feather →, *U.S.A.* 84 F5
Middle I., *Australia* 61 F3
Middle Loup →, *U.S.A.* 80 E5
Middleboro, *U.S.A.* 79 E14
Middleburg, *N.Y., U.S.A.* 79 D10
Middleburg, *Pa., U.S.A.* 78 F7
Middlebury, *U.S.A.* 79 B11
Middleport, *U.S.A.* 76 F4
Middlesboro, *U.S.A.* 75 C10
Middlesboro, *U.S.A.* 77 G4
Middlesbrough, *U.K.* 10 C6
Middlesex, *Belize* 88 C2
Middlesex, *U.S.A.* 79 F10
Middleton, *Australia* 62 C3
Middleton, *Canada* 71 D6
Middletown, *Calif., U.S.A.* 84 G4
Middletown, *Conn., U.S.A.* 79 E12
Middletown, *N.Y., U.S.A.* 79 E10
Middletown, *Ohio, U.S.A.* 76 F3
Middletown, *Pa., U.S.A.* 79 F8
Midi, Canal du →, *France* 18 E4
Midland, *Canada* 70 D4
Midland, *Calif., U.S.A.* 85 M12
Midland, *Mich., U.S.A.* 76 D3
Midland, *Pa., U.S.A.* 78 F4
Midland, *Tex., U.S.A.* 81 K3
Midlands □, *Zimbabwe* 55 F2
Midleton, *Ireland* 13 E3
Midlothian, *U.S.A.* 81 J6
Midongy, Tangorombohitr' i, *Madag.* 57 C8
Midongy Atsimo, *Madag.* 57 C8
Midway Is., *Pac. Oc.* 64 E10
Midway Wells, *U.S.A.* 85 N11
Midwest, *U.S.A.* 82 E10
Mie □, *Japan* 31 G8
Międzychód, *Poland* 16 B7
Międzyrzec Podlaski, *Poland* 17 C11
Mienga, *Angola* 56 B2
Miercurea Ciuc, *Romania* 17 E12
Mieres, *Spain* 19 A3
Mifflintown, *U.S.A.* 78 F7
Mifraz Hefa, *Israel* 47 C4
Migdāl, *Israel* 47 C4
Miguel Alemán, Presa, *Mexico* 87 D5
Miguel Alves, *Brazil* 93 D10
Mihara, *Japan* 31 G6
Mikese, *Tanzania* 54 D4
Mikinai, *Greece* 21 F10
Mikkeli, *Finland* 9 F19
Mikkeli □ = Mikkelin lääni □, *Finland* 8 E19
Mikkelin lääni □, *Finland* 8 E19
Mikkwa →, *Canada* 72 B6
Míkonos, *Greece* 21 F11
Mikumi, *Tanzania* 54 D4
Mikun, *Russia* 24 B9
Milaca, *U.S.A.* 80 C8
Milagro, *Ecuador* 92 D3
Milan = Milano, *Italy* 20 B3
Milan, *Mo., U.S.A.* 80 E8
Milan, *Tenn., U.S.A.* 77 H1
Milang, *Australia* 63 E2
Milange, *Mozam.* 55 F4
Milano, *Italy* 20 B3
Milâs, *Turkey* 25 G4
Milatos, *Greece* 23 D7
Milazzo, *Italy* 20 E6
Milbank, *U.S.A.* 80 C6
Milden, *Canada* 73 C7
Mildmay, *Canada* 78 B3
Mildura, *Australia* 63 E3
Mileh Tharthār, *Iraq* 44 C4
Miles, *Australia* 63 D5
Miles, *U.S.A.* 81 K4
Miles City, *U.S.A.* 80 B2
Milestone, *Canada* 73 D8
Mileura, *Australia* 61 E2
Milford, *Calif., U.S.A.* 84 E6
Milford, *Conn., U.S.A.* 79 E11
Milford, *Del., U.S.A.* 76 F8
Milford, *Mass., U.S.A.* 79 D13
Milford, *Pa., U.S.A.* 79 E10
Milford, *Utah, U.S.A.* 83 G7
Milford Haven, *U.K.* 11 F2
Milford Sd., *N.Z.* 59 L1
Milgun, *Australia* 61 D2
Milh, Bahr al, *Iraq* 44 C4
Miliana, *Algeria* 50 C5
Miling, *Australia* 61 F2
Milk →, *N. Amer.* 82 B10
Milk River, *Canada* 72 D6
Mill City, *U.S.A.* 82 D2
Mill I., *Antarctica* 5 C8
Mill Valley, *U.S.A.* 84 H4
Millbridge, *Canada* 78 B7
Millbrook, *Canada* 78 B6
Mille Lacs, L., *U.S.A.* 80 B8
Mille Lacs, L. des, *Canada* 70 C1
Milledgeville, *U.S.A.* 77 J4
Millen, *U.S.A.* 77 J5
Miller, *U.S.A.* 80 C5
Millersburg, *Ohio, U.S.A.* 78 F3
Millersburg, *Pa., U.S.A.* 78 F8
Millerton, *U.S.A.* 79 E11
Millerton L., *U.S.A.* 84 J7
Millicent, *Australia* 63 F3
Millinocket, *U.S.A.* 71 C6
Millmerran, *Australia* 63 D5
Mills L., *Canada* 72 A5
Millsboro, *U.S.A.* 78 G4
Milltown Malbay, *Ireland* 13 D2

Millville, *U.S.A.* 76 F8
Millwood Res., *U.S.A.* 81 J8
Milne →, *Australia* 62 C2
Milne Inlet, *Canada* 69 A11
Milnor, *U.S.A.* 80 B6
Milo, *Canada* 72 C6
Milos, *Greece* 21 F11
Milparinka P.O., *Australia* 63 D3
Milton, *Canada* 78 C5
Milton, *N.Z.* 59 M2
Milton, *U.K.* 12 D4
Milton, *Calif., U.S.A.* 84 G6
Milton, *Fla., U.S.A.* 77 K2
Milton, *Pa., U.S.A.* 78 F8
Milton-Freewater, *U.S.A.* 82 D4
Milton Keynes, *U.K.* 11 E7
Miltou, *Chad* 51 F8
Milverton, *Canada* 78 C4
Milwaukee, *U.S.A.* 76 D2
Milwaukee Deep, *Atl. Oc.* 89 C6
Milwaukie, *U.S.A.* 84 E4
Min Chiang →, *China* 33 D6
Min Jiang →, *China* 32 D5
Min Xian, *China* 34 G3
Mina, *U.S.A.* 83 G4
Mina Pirquitas, *Argentina* 94 A2
Minā Su'ud, *Si. Arabia* 45 D6
Minā'al Aḥmadī, *Kuwait* 45 D6
Mīnāb, *Iran* 45 E8
Minago →, *Canada* 73 C9
Minaki, *Canada* 73 D10
Minamata, *Japan* 31 H5
Minami-Tori-Shima, *Pac. Oc.* 64 E7
Minas, *Uruguay* 95 C4
Minas, Sierra de las, *Guatemala* 88 C2
Minas Basin, *Canada* 71 C7
Minas de Rio Tinto, *Spain* 19 D2
Minas Gerais □, *Brazil* 93 G9
Minatitlán, *Mexico* 87 D6
Minbu, *Burma* 41 J19
Mindanao, *Phil.* 37 C6
Mindanao Sea = Bohol Sea, *Phil.* 37 C6
Mindanao Trench, *Pac. Oc.* 37 B7
Minden, *Canada* 78 B6
Minden, *Germany* 16 B4
Minden, *La., U.S.A.* 81 J8
Minden, *Nev., U.S.A.* 84 G7
Mindiptana, *Indonesia* 37 F10
Mindoro, *Phil.* 37 B6
Mindoro Str., *Phil.* 37 B6
Mindouli, *Congo* 52 E2
Mine, *Japan* 31 G5
Minehead, *U.K.* 11 F4
Mineola, *U.S.A.* 81 J7
Mineral King, *U.S.A.* 84 J8
Mineral Wells, *U.S.A.* 81 J5
Minersville, *Pa., U.S.A.* 79 F8
Minersville, *Utah, U.S.A.* 83 G7
Minerva, *U.S.A.* 78 F3
Minetto, *U.S.A.* 79 C8
Mingan, *Canada* 71 B7
Mingechaurskoye Vdkhr., *Azerbaijan* 25 F8
Mingela, *Australia* 62 B4
Mingenew, *Australia* 61 E2
Mingera Cr. →, *Australia* 62 C2
Mingin, *Burma* 41 H19
Mingt'iehkaitafan = Mintaka Pass, *Pakistan* 43 A6
Mingyuegue, *China* 35 C15
Minho, *Portugal* 19 B1
Minho →, *Spain* 19 B1
Minidoka, *U.S.A.* 82 E7
Minigwal, L., *Australia* 61 E3
Minilya, *Australia* 61 D1
Minilya →, *Australia* 61 D1
Minipi, L., *Canada* 71 B7
Mink L., *Canada* 72 A5
Minna, *Nigeria* 50 G6
Minneapolis, *Kans., U.S.A.* 80 F6
Minneapolis, *Minn., U.S.A.* 80 C8
Minnedosa, *Canada* 73 C9
Minnesota □, *U.S.A.* 80 B7
Minnie Creek, *Australia* 61 D2
Minnipa, *Australia* 63 E2
Minnitaki L., *Canada* 70 C1
Mino, *Japan* 31 G8
Miño →, *Spain* 19 B1
Minorca = Menorca, *Spain* 22 B11
Minore, *Australia* 63 E4
Minot, *U.S.A.* 80 A4
Minqin, *China* 34 E2
Minsk, *Belorussia* 24 D4
Mińsk Mazowiecki, *Poland* 17 B10
Mintaka Pass, *Pakistan* 43 A6
Minto, *U.S.A.* 68 B5
Minton, *Canada* 73 D8
Minturn, *U.S.A.* 82 G10
Minusinsk, *Russia* 27 D10
Minutang, *India* 41 E20
Minvoul, *Gabon* 52 D2
Mir, *Niger* 51 F7
Mīr Kūh, *Iran* 45 E8
Mīr Shahdād, *Iran* 45 E8
Mira por vos Cay, *Bahamas* 89 B5
Miraj, *India* 40 L9
Miram Shah, *Pakistan* 42 C4
Miramar, *Argentina* 94 D4
Miramar, *Mozam.* 57 C6
Miramichi B., *Canada* 71 C7
Miranda, *Brazil* 93 H7
Miranda de Ebro, *Spain* 19 A4
Mirando City, *U.S.A.* 81 M5
Mirandópolis, *Brazil* 95 A5
Mirango, *Malawi* 55 E3
Mirani, *Australia* 62 C4
Mirassol, *Brazil* 95 A6
Mirbāṭ, *Oman* 46 D5
Miri, *Malaysia* 36 D4
Miriam Vale, *Australia* 62 C5
Mirim, L., *S. Amer.* 95 C5
Mirnyy, *Russia* 27 C12
Mirond L., *Canada* 73 B8
Mirpur, *Pakistan* 43 C5
Mirpur Bibiwari, *Pakistan* 42 E2
Mirpur Khas, *Pakistan* 42 G3
Mirpur Sakro, *Pakistan* 42 G2
Mirror, *Canada* 72 C6
Miryang, *S. Korea* 35 G15
Mirzapur, *India* 43 G10
Mirzapur-cum-Vindhyachal = Mirzapur, *India* 43 G10
Misantla, *Mexico* 87 D5
Misawa, *Japan* 30 D10
Miscou I., *Canada* 71 C7
Mish'āb, Ra'as al, *Si. Arabia* 45 D6
Mishan, *China* 33 B8
Mishawaka, *U.S.A.* 76 E2
Mishima, *Japan* 31 G9
Misión, *Mexico* 85 N10
Misiones □, *Argentina* 95 B5
Misiones □, *Paraguay* 94 B4
Miskah, *Si. Arabia* 44 E4
Miskitos, Cayos, *Nic.* 88 D3
Miskolc, *Hungary* 17 D10
Misoke, *Zaïre* 54 C2
Misool, *Indonesia* 37 E8
Misrātah, *Libya* 51 B8
Missanabie, *Canada* 70 C3
Missinaibi →, *Canada* 70 B3
Missinaibi L., *Canada* 70 C3
Mission, *S. Dak., U.S.A.* 80 D4
Mission, *Tex., U.S.A.* 81 M5
Mission City, *Canada* 72 D4
Mission Viejo, *U.S.A.* 85 M9
Missisa L., *Canada* 70 B2
Missisagi →, *Canada* 70 C3
Mississippi □, *U.S.A.* 75 D9
Mississippi →, *U.S.A.* 81 L10
Mississippi, Delta of the, *U.S.A.* 81 L9
Mississippi L., *Canada* 79 A8
Mississippi Sd., *U.S.A.* 81 K10
Missoula, *U.S.A.* 82 C6
Missouri □, *U.S.A.* 80 F8
Missouri →, *U.S.A.* 80 F9
Missouri Valley, *U.S.A.* 80 E7
Mist, *U.S.A.* 84 E3
Mistake B., *Canada* 73 A10
Mistassini →, *Canada* 71 C5
Mistassini L., *Canada* 70 B5
Mistastin L., *Canada* 71 A7
Mistatim, *Canada* 73 C8
Mistretta, *Italy* 20 F6
Misty L., *Canada* 73 B8
Mitchell, *Australia* 63 D4
Mitchell, *Canada* 78 C3
Mitchell, *Ind., U.S.A.* 76 F2
Mitchell, *Nebr., U.S.A.* 80 E3
Mitchell, *Oreg., U.S.A.* 82 D3
Mitchell, *S. Dak., U.S.A.* 80 D5
Mitchell →, *Australia* 62 B3
Mitchell, Mt., *U.S.A.* 77 H4
Mitchell Ras., *Australia* 62 A2
Mitchelstown, *Ireland* 13 D3
Mitha Tiwana, *Pakistan* 42 C5
Mito, *Japan* 31 F10
Mitsinjo, *Madag.* 57 B8
Mitsiwa, *Ethiopia* 51 E12
Mitsukaidō, *Japan* 31 F9
Mittagong, *Australia* 63 E5
Mitú, *Colombia* 92 C4
Mitumba, *Tanzania* 54 D3
Mitumba, Chaîne des, *Zaïre* 54 D2
Mitwaba, *Zaïre* 55 D2
Mityana, *Uganda* 54 B3
Mitzic, *Gabon* 52 D2
Mixteco →, *Mexico* 87 D5
Miyagi □, *Japan* 30 E10
Miyah, W. el →, *Syria* 44 C3
Miyake-Jima, *Japan* 31 G9
Miyako, *Japan* 30 E10
Miyako-Jima, *Japan* 31 M2
Miyako-Rettō, *Japan* 31 M2
Miyakonojō, *Japan* 31 J5
Miyanoura-Dake, *Japan* 31 J5
Miyazaki, *Japan* 31 J5
Miyazaki □, *Japan* 31 H5
Miyazu, *Japan* 31 G7
Miyet, Bahr el = Dead Sea, *Asia* 47 D4
Miyoshi, *Japan* 31 G6
Miyun, *China* 34 D9
Miyun Shuiku, *China* 35 D9
Mizamis = Ozamis, *Phil.* 37 C6
Mizdah, *Libya* 51 B7
Mizen Hd., *Cork, Ireland* 13 E2
Mizen Hd., *Wick., Ireland* 13 D5
Mizhi, *China* 34 F6
Mizoram □, *India* 41 H18
Mizpe Ramon, *Israel* 47 E3
Mizusawa, *Japan* 30 E10
Mjölby, *Sweden* 9 G13
Mjøsa, *Norway* 9 F11
Mkata, *Tanzania* 54 D4
Mkokotoni, *Tanzania* 54 D4
Mkomazi, *Tanzania* 54 C4
Mkomazi →, *S. Africa* 57 E5
Mkulwe, *Tanzania* 55 D3
Mkumbi, Ras, *Tanzania* 54 D4
Mkushi, *Zambia* 55 E2
Mkushi River, *Zambia* 55 E2
Mkuze, *S. Africa* 57 D5
Mkuze →, *S. Africa* 57 D5
Mladá Boleslav, *Czech.* 16 C7
Mlala Hills, *Tanzania* 54 D3
Mlange, *Malawi* 55 F4
Mława, *Poland* 17 B10
Mmabatho, *S. Africa* 56 D4
Mo i Rana, *Norway* 8 C13
Moa, *Indonesia* 37 F7
Moab, *U.S.A.* 83 G9
Moabi, *Gabon* 52 E2
Moala, *Fiji* 59 D8
Moalie Park, *Australia* 63 D3
Moba, *Zaïre* 54 D2
Mobārakābād, *Iran* 45 D7
Mobārakīyeh, *Iran* 45 C6
Mobaye, *C.A.R.* 52 D4
Mobayi, *Zaïre* 52 D4
Moberly, *U.S.A.* 80 F8
Moberly →, *Canada* 72 B4
Mobile, *U.S.A.* 77 K1
Mobile B., *U.S.A.* 77 K2
Mobridge, *U.S.A.* 80 C4
Mobutu Sese Seko, L., *Africa* 54 B3
Moc Chau, *Vietnam* 38 B5
Moc Hoa, *Vietnam* 39 G5
Mocabe Kasari, *Zaïre* 55 D2
Moçambique, *Mozam.* 55 F5
Moçâmedes = Namibe, *Angola* 53 H2
Mochudi, *Botswana* 56 C4
Mocimboa da Praia, *Mozam.* 55 E5
Moclips, *U.S.A.* 84 C2
Mocoa, *Colombia* 92 C3
Mococa, *Brazil* 95 A6
Mocorito, *Mexico* 86 B3
Moctezuma, *Mexico* 86 B3
Moctezuma →, *Mexico* 87 C5
Mocuba, *Mozam.* 55 F4
Mocúzari, Presa, *Mexico* 86 B3
Modane, *France* 18 D7
Modasa, *India* 42 H5
Modder →, *S. Africa* 56 D3
Modderrivier, *S. Africa* 56 D3
Módena, *Italy* 20 B4
Modena, *U.S.A.* 83 H7
Modesto, *U.S.A.* 83 H3
Módica, *Italy* 20 F6
Moe, *Australia* 63 F4
Moebase, *Mozam.* 55 F4
Moengo, *Surinam* 93 B8
Moffat, *U.K.* 12 F5
Moga, *India* 42 D6
Mogadishu = Muqdisho, *Somali Rep.* 46 G4
Mogador = Essaouira, *Morocco* 50 B3
Mogalakwena →, *S. Africa* 57 C4
Mogami →, *Japan* 30 E10
Mogán, *Canary Is.* 22 G4
Mogaung, *Burma* 41 G20
Mogi das Cruzes, *Brazil* 95 A6
Mogi-Guaçu →, *Brazil* 95 A6
Mogi-Mirim, *Brazil* 95 A6
Mogilev, *Belorussia* 24 D5
Mogilev-Podolskiy, *Moldavia* 25 E4
Mogincual, *Mozam.* 55 F5
Mogocha, *Russia* 27 D12
Mogoi, *Indonesia* 37 E8
Mogok, *Burma* 41 H20
Mogumber, *Australia* 61 F2
Mohács, *Hungary* 17 F9
Mohales Hoek, *Lesotho* 56 E4
Mohall, *U.S.A.* 80 A4
Moḥammadābād, *Iran* 45 B8
Mohave, L., *U.S.A.* 85 K12
Mohawk →, *U.S.A.* 79 D11
Mohoro, *Tanzania* 54 D4
Moidart, L., *U.K.* 12 E3
Mointy, *Kazakhstan* 26 E8
Moíres, *Greece* 23 D6
Moisie, *Canada* 71 B6
Moisie →, *Canada* 71 B6
Moïssala, *Chad* 51 G8
Mojave, *U.S.A.* 85 K8
Mojave Desert, *U.S.A.* 85 L10
Mojo, *Bolivia* 94 A2
Mojokerto, *Indonesia* 37 G15
Mokai, *N.Z.* 59 H5
Mokambo, *Zaïre* 55 E2
Mokameh, *India* 43 G11
Mokelumne →, *U.S.A.* 84 G5
Mokelumne Hill, *U.S.A.* 84 G6
Mokhós, *Greece* 23 D7
Mokhotlong, *Lesotho* 57 D4
Mokokchung, *India* 41 F19
Mol, *Belgium* 15 C5
Molchanovo, *Russia* 26 D9
Mold, *U.K.* 10 D4
Moldavia ■, *Europe* 25 E4
Molde, *Norway* 8 E9
Molepolole, *Botswana* 56 C4
Molfetta, *Italy* 20 D7
Moline, *U.S.A.* 80 E9
Molinos, *Argentina* 94 B2
Moliro, *Zaïre* 54 D3
Molise □, *Italy* 20 D6
Mollahat, *Bangla.* 43 H13
Mollendo, *Peru* 92 G4
Mollerin, L., *Australia* 61 F2
Mölndal, *Sweden* 9 H12
Molokai, *U.S.A.* 74 H16
Molong, *Australia* 63 E4
Molopo →, *Africa* 56 D3
Molotov = Perm, *Russia* 24 C10
Moloundou, *Cameroon* 52 D3
Molson L., *Canada* 73 C9
Molteno, *S. Africa* 56 E4
Molu, *Indonesia* 37 F8
Molucca Sea = Maluku Sea, *Indonesia* 37 E6
Moluccas = Maluku, *Indonesia* 37 E7
Moma, *Mozam.* 55 F4
Moma, *Zaïre* 54 C1
Mombasa, *Kenya* 54 C4
Mombetsu, *Japan* 30 B11
Momi, *Zaïre* 54 C2
Mompós, *Colombia* 92 B4
Møn, *Denmark* 9 J12
Mon →, *Burma* 41 J19
Mona, Canal de la, *W. Indies* 89 C6
Mona, I., *Puerto Rico* 89 C6
Mona, Pta., *Costa Rica* 88 E3
Monach Is., *U.K.* 12 D1
Monaco ■, *Europe* 18 E7
Monadhliath Mts., *U.K.* 12 D4
Monaghan, *Ireland* 13 B5
Monaghan □, *Ireland* 13 B5
Monahans, *U.S.A.* 81 K3
Monapo, *Mozam.* 55 E5
Monarch Mt., *Canada* 72 C3
Monastir = Bitola, *Macedonia, Yug.* 21 D9
Monastir, *Tunisia* 51 A7
Moncayo, Sierra del, *Spain* 19 B5
Mönchengladbach, *Germany* 16 C3
Monchique, *Portugal* 19 D1
Monchique, Sa. de, *Portugal* 19 D1
Monclova, *Mexico* 86 B4
Moncton, *Canada* 71 C7
Mondego →, *Portugal* 19 B1
Mondeodo, *Indonesia* 37 E6
Mondovi, *Italy* 20 B2
Mondovi, *U.S.A.* 80 C9
Mondrain I., *Australia* 61 F3
Monduli □, *Tanzania* 54 C4
Monessen, *U.S.A.* 78 F5
Monett, *U.S.A.* 81 G8
Monforte, *Portugal* 19 C2
Mong Hsu, *Burma* 41 J21
Mong Kung, *Burma* 41 J20
Mong Nai, *Burma* 41 J20
Mong Pawk, *Burma* 41 H21
Mong Ton, *Burma* 41 J21
Mong Wa, *Burma* 41 J22
Mong Yai, *Burma* 41 H21
Mongalla, *Sudan* 51 G11
Mongers, L., *Australia* 61 E2
Monghyr = Munger, *India* 43 G12
Mongo, *Chad* 51 F8
Mongolia ■, *Asia* 32 B5
Mongororo, *Chad* 51 F9
Mongu, *Zambia* 53 H4
Môngua, *Angola* 56 B2
Monkey Bay, *Malawi* 55 E4
Monkey River, *Belize* 87 D7
Monkira, *Australia* 62 C3
Monkoto, *Zaïre* 52 E4
Monmouth, *U.K.* 11 F5
Monmouth, *U.S.A.* 80 E9
Mono, L., *U.S.A.* 83 H4
Monolith, *U.S.A.* 85 K8
Monólithos, *Greece* 23 C9
Monongahela, *U.S.A.* 78 F5
Monópoli, *Italy* 20 D7
Monqoumba, *C.A.R.* 52 D3
Monroe, *Ga., U.S.A.* 77 J4
Monroe, *La., U.S.A.* 81 J8
Monroe, *Mich., U.S.A.* 76 E4
Monroe, *N.C., U.S.A.* 77 H5
Monroe, *N.Y., U.S.A.* 79 E10
Monroe, *Utah, U.S.A.* 83 G7
Monroe, *Wash., U.S.A.* 84 C5
Monroe, *Wis., U.S.A.* 80 D10
Monroe City, *U.S.A.* 80 F9
Monroeville, *Ala., U.S.A.* 77 K2
Monroeville, *Pa., U.S.A.* 78 F5
Monrovia, *Liberia* 50 G2
Monrovia, *U.S.A.* 83 J4
Mons, *Belgium* 15 D3
Monse, *Indonesia* 37 E6
Mont-de-Marsan, *France* 18 E3
Mont-Joli, *Canada* 71 C6
Mont-Laurier, *Canada* 70 C4
Mont-St.-Michel, Le = Le Mont-St.-Michel, *France* 18 B3
Mont Tremblant Prov. Park, *Canada* 70 C5
Montagu, *S. Africa* 56 E3
Montagu I., *Antarctica* 5 B1
Montague, *Canada* 71 C7
Montague, *U.S.A.* 82 F2
Montague, I., *Mexico* 86 A2
Montague Ra., *Australia* 61 E2
Montague Sd., *Australia* 60 B4
Montalbán, *Spain* 19 B5
Montalvo, *U.S.A.* 85 L7
Montaña, *Peru* 92 E4
Montana □, *U.S.A.* 74 A5
Montaña Clara, I., *Canary Is.* 22 E6
Montargis, *France* 18 C5
Montauban, *France* 18 D4
Montauk, *U.S.A.* 79 E13
Montauk Pt., *U.S.A.* 79 E13
Montbéliard, *France* 18 C7
Montclair, *U.S.A.* 79 F10
Monte Albán, *Mexico* 87 D5
Monte Alegre, *Brazil* 93 D8
Monte Azul, *Brazil* 93 G10
Monte Bello Is., *Australia* 60 D2
Monte-Carlo, *Monaco* 18 E7
Monte Caseros, *Argentina* 94 C4
Monte Comán, *Argentina* 94 C2
Monte Cristi, *Dom. Rep.* 89 C5
Monte Lindo →, *Paraguay* 94 A4
Monte Quemado, *Argentina* 94 B3
Monte Rio, *U.S.A.* 84 G4
Monte Sant' Ángelo, *Italy* 20 D6
Monte Santu, C. di, *Italy* 20 D3
Monte Vista, *U.S.A.* 83 H10
Monteagudo, *Argentina* 95 B5
Montebello, *Canada* 70 C5
Montecito, *U.S.A.* 85 L7
Montecristi, *Ecuador* 92 D2
Montego Bay, *Jamaica* 88 C4
Montejinnie, *Australia* 60 C5
Montélimar, *France* 18 D6
Montello, *U.S.A.* 80 D10
Montemorelos, *Mexico* 87 B5
Montenegro, *Brazil* 95 B5
Montenegro □, *Europe* 21 C8
Montepuez, *Mozam.* 55 E4
Montepuez →, *Mozam.* 55 E5
Monterey, *U.S.A.* 83 H3
Monterey B., *U.S.A.* 84 J5
Montería, *Colombia* 92 B3
Monteros, *Argentina* 94 B2
Monterrey, *Mexico* 86 B4
Montes Claros, *Brazil* 93 G10
Montesano, *U.S.A.* 84 D3
Montevideo, *Uruguay* 95 C4
Montevideo, *U.S.A.* 80 C7
Montezuma, *U.S.A.* 80 E8
Montgomery = Sahiwal, *Pakistan* 42 D5
Montgomery, *U.K.* 11 E4
Montgomery, *Ala., U.S.A.* 77 J2
Montgomery, *W. Va., U.S.A.* 76 F5
Monticello, *Ark., U.S.A.* 81 J9
Monticello, *Fla., U.S.A.* 77 K4
Monticello, *Ind., U.S.A.* 76 E2
Monticello, *Iowa, U.S.A.* 80 D9
Monticello, *Ky., U.S.A.* 77 G3
Monticello, *Minn., U.S.A.* 80 C8
Monticello, *Miss., U.S.A.* 81 K9
Monticello, *N.Y., U.S.A.* 79 E10
Monticello, *Utah, U.S.A.* 83 H9
Montijo, *Spain* 19 C2
Montilla, *Spain* 19 D3
Montluçon, *France* 18 C5
Montmagny, *Canada* 71 C5
Montmartre, *Canada* 73 C8
Montmorency, *Canada* 71 C5
Monto, *Australia* 62 C5
Montoro, *Spain* 19 C3
Montour Falls, *U.S.A.* 78 D8
Montpelier, *Idaho, U.S.A.* 82 E8
Montpelier, *Ohio, U.S.A.* 76 E3
Montpelier, *Vt., U.S.A.* 79 B12
Montpellier, *France* 18 E5
Montréal, *Canada* 70 C5
Montreal L., *Canada* 73 C7
Montreal Lake, *Canada* 73 C7
Montreuil, *France* 18 A4
Montreux, *Switz.* 16 E3
Montrose, *U.K.* 12 E6
Montrose, *Colo., U.S.A.* 83 G10
Montrose, *Pa., U.S.A.* 79 E9
Monts, Pte. des, *Canada* 71 C6
Montserrat, *W. Indies* 89 C7
Montuiri, *Spain* 22 B9
Monveda, *Zaïre* 52 D4
Monywa, *Burma* 41 H19
Monza, *Italy* 20 B3
Monze, *Zambia* 55 F2
Monze, C., *Pakistan* 42 G2
Monzón, *Spain* 19 B6
Mooi River, *S. Africa* 57 D4
Moolawatana, *Australia* 63 D2
Mooliabeenee, *Australia* 61 F2
Mooloogool, *Australia* 61 E2
Moomin Cr. →, *Australia* 63 D4
Moonah →, *Australia* 62 C2
Moonbeam, *Canada* 70 C3
Moonda, L., *Australia* 62 D3
Moonie, *Australia* 63 D5
Moonie →, *Australia* 63 D4
Moonta, *Australia* 63 E2
Moora, *Australia* 61 F2
Mooraberree, *Australia* 62 D3
Moorarie, *Australia* 61 E2
Moorcroft, *U.S.A.* 80 C2
Moore →, *Australia* 61 F2
Moore, L., *Australia* 61 E2
Moore Reefs, *Australia* 62 B4
Moorefield, *U.S.A.* 76 F6
Moores Res., *U.S.A.* 79 B13
Mooresville, *U.S.A.* 77 H5
Moorfoot Hills, *U.K.* 12 F5
Moorhead, *U.S.A.* 80 B6
Mooroopna, *Australia* 63 F4
Moorpark, *U.S.A.* 85 L8
Moorreesburg, *S. Africa* 56 E2
Moose →, *Canada* 70 B3
Moose Factory, *Canada* 70 B3
Moose I., *Canada* 73 C9
Moose Jaw, *Canada* 73 C7
Moose Jaw →, *Canada* 73 C7
Moose Lake, *Canada* 73 C8
Moose Lake, *U.S.A.* 80 B8
Moose Mountain Cr. →, *Canada* 73 D8
Moose Mountain Prov. Park, *Canada* 73 D8
Moose River, *Canada* 70 B3

Moosehead L., U.S.A. 71 C6
Moosomin, Canada 73 C8
Moosonee, Canada 70 B3
Moosup, U.S.A. 79 E13
Mopeia Velha, Mozam. 55 F4
Mopipi, Botswana 56 C3
Mopoi, C.A.R. 54 A2
Mopti, Mali 50 F4
Moquegua, Peru 92 G4
Mora, Sweden 9 F13
Mora, Minn., U.S.A. 80 C8
Mora, N. Mex., U.S.A. 83 J11
Moradabad, India 43 E8
Morafenobe, Madag. 57 B7
Moramanga, Madag. 57 B8
Moran, Kans., U.S.A. 81 G7
Moran, Wyo., U.S.A. 82 E8
Moranbah, Australia 62 C4
Morant Cays, Jamaica 88 C4
Morant Pt., Jamaica 88 C4
Morar, L., U.K. 12 E3
Moratuwa, Sri Lanka 40 R11
Morava →, Czech. 16 D8
Moravia, U.S.A. 80 E8
Moravian Hts. = Ceskomoravská Vrchovina, Czech. 16 D7
Morawa, Australia 61 E2
Morawhanna, Guyana 92 B7
Moray Firth, U.K. 12 D5
Morbi, India 42 H4
Morbihan □, France 18 C2
Morden, Canada 73 D9
Mordovian Republic □, Russia 24 D7
Møre og Romsdal fylke □, Norway 8 E9
Morea, Australia 63 F3
Morea, Greece 6 H10
Moreau →, U.S.A. 80 C4
Morecambe, U.K. 10 C5
Morecambe B., U.K. 10 C5
Moree, Australia 63 D4
Morehead, U.S.A. 76 F4
Morehead City, U.S.A. 77 H7
Morelia, Mexico 86 D4
Morella, Australia 62 C3
Morella, Spain 19 B5
Morelos, Mexico 86 B3
Morelos □, Mexico 87 D5
Morena, Sierra, Spain 19 C3
Morenci, U.S.A. 83 K9
Moresby I., Canada 72 C2
Moreton, Australia 62 A3
Moreton I., Australia 63 D5
Morey, Spain 22 B10
Morgan, Australia 63 E2
Morgan, U.S.A. 82 F8
Morgan City, U.S.A. 81 L9
Morgan Hill, U.S.A. 84 H5
Morganfield, U.S.A. 76 G2
Morganton, U.S.A. 77 H5
Morgantown, U.S.A. 76 F6
Morgenzon, S. Africa 57 D4
Morghak, Iran 45 D8
Morice L., Canada 72 C3
Morinville, Canada 72 C6
Morioka, Japan 30 E10
Moris, Mexico 86 B3
Morlaix, France 18 B2
Mornington, Vic., Australia 63 F4
Mornington, W. Austral., Australia 60 C4
Mornington, I., Chile 96 F1
Mornington I., Australia 62 B2
Moro G., Phil. 37 C6
Morocco ■, N. Afr. 50 B3
Morococha, Peru 92 F3
Morogoro, Tanzania 54 D4
Morogoro □, Tanzania 54 D4
Moroleón, Mexico 86 C4
Morombe, Madag. 57 C7
Moron, Argentina 94 C4
Morón, Cuba 88 B4
Morón de la Frontera, Spain 19 D3
Morondava, Madag. 57 C7
Morongo Valley, U.S.A. 85 L10
Morotai, Indonesia 37 D7
Moroto, Uganda 54 B3
Moroto Summit, Kenya 54 B3
Morpeth, U.K. 10 B6
Morphou, Cyprus 23 D11
Morphou Bay, Cyprus 23 D11
Morrilton, U.S.A. 81 H8
Morrinhos, Brazil 93 G9
Morrinsville, N.Z. 59 G5
Morris, Canada 73 D9
Morris, Ill., U.S.A. 76 E1
Morris, Minn., U.S.A. 80 C7
Morris, Mt., Australia 61 E5
Morrisburg, Canada 70 D4
Morrison, U.S.A. 80 E10
Morristown, Ariz., U.S.A. 83 K7
Morristown, N.J., U.S.A. 79 F10
Morristown, S. Dak., U.S.A. 80 C4
Morristown, Tenn., U.S.A. 77 G4
Morro, Pta., Chile 94 B1
Morro Bay, U.S.A. 83 J3
Morro del Jable, Canary Is. 22 F5
Morro Jable, Pta. de, Canary Is. 22 F5
Morrosquillo, G. de, Colombia 88 E4
Morrumbene, Mozam. 57 C6
Morshansk, Russia 24 D7
Morteros, Argentina 94 C3
Mortes, R. das →, Brazil 93 F8
Mortlake, Australia 63 F3
Morton, Tex., U.S.A. 81 J3
Morton, Wash., U.S.A. 84 D4
Morundah, Australia 63 E4
Moruya, Australia 63 F5
Morvan, France 18 C6
Morven, Australia 63 D4
Morvern, U.K. 12 E3
Morwell, Australia 63 F4
Morzhovets, Ostrov, Russia 24 A7
Moscos Is., Burma 38 E1
Moscow = Moskva, Russia 24 C6
Moscow, U.S.A. 82 C5
Mosel →, Europe 18 A7
Moselle = Mosel →, Europe 18 A7
Moselle □, France 18 B7
Moses Lake, U.S.A. 82 C4
Mosgiel, N.Z. 59 L3
Moshi, Tanzania 54 C4
Moshi □, Tanzania 54 C4
Moshupa, Botswana 56 C4
Mosjøen, Norway 8 D12
Moskenesøya, Norway 8 C12
Moskenstraumen, Norway 8 C12
Moskva, Russia 24 C6
Moskva →, Russia 24 C6
Mosomane, Botswana 56 C4
Mosquera, Colombia 92 C3
Mosquero, U.S.A. 81 H3
Mosquitia, Honduras 88 C3
Mosquitos, G. de los, Panama 88 E3
Moss, Norway 9 G11
Moss Vale, Australia 63 E5
Mossaka, Congo 52 E3
Mossbank, Canada 73 D7
Mossburn, N.Z. 59 L2
Mosselbaai, S. Africa 56 E3
Mossendjo, Congo 52 E2
Mossgiel, Australia 63 E3
Mossman, Australia 62 B4
Mossoró, Brazil 93 E11
Mossuril, Mozam. 55 E5
Mossy →, Canada 73 C8
Most, Czech. 16 C6
Mosta, Malta 23 D1
Moşţafáābād, Iran 45 C7
Mostaganem, Algeria 50 A5
Mostar, Bos. & H., Yug. 21 C7
Mostardas, Brazil 95 C5
Mosul = Al Mawşil, Iraq 44 B4
Mosulpo, S. Korea 35 H14
Motagua →, Guatemala 88 C2
Motala, Sweden 9 G13
Motherwell, U.K. 12 F5
Motihari, India 43 F11
Motozintla de Mendoza, Mexico 87 D6
Mott, U.S.A. 80 B3
Motueka, N.Z. 59 J4
Motueka →, N.Z. 59 J4
Motul, Mexico 87 C7
Mouanda, Gabon 52 E2
Mouchalagane →, Canada 71 B6
Moúdhros, Greece 21 E11
Moudjeria, Mauritania 50 E2
Mouila, Gabon 52 E2
Moulamein, Australia 63 F3
Moulianá, Greece 23 D7
Moulins, France 18 C5
Moulmein, Burma 41 L20
Moulton, U.S.A. 81 L6
Moultrie, U.S.A. 77 K4
Moultrie, L., U.S.A. 77 J5
Mound City, Mo., U.S.A. 80 E7
Mound City, S. Dak., U.S.A. 80 C4
Moundou, Chad 51 G8
Moundsville, U.S.A. 78 G4
Moung, Cambodia 38 F4
Mount Airy, U.S.A. 77 G5
Mount Albert, Canada 78 B5
Mount Amherst, Australia 60 C4
Mount Angel, U.S.A. 82 D2
Mount Augustus, Australia 60 D2
Mount Barker, S. Austral., Australia 63 F2
Mount Barker, W. Austral., Australia 61 F2
Mount Carmel, U.S.A. 76 F2
Mount Clemens, U.S.A. 78 D2
Mount Coolon, Australia 62 C4
Mount Darwin, Zimbabwe 55 F3
Mount Desert I., U.S.A. 71 D6
Mount Dora, U.S.A. 77 L5
Mount Douglas, Australia 62 C4
Mount Eba, Australia 63 E2
Mount Edgecumbe, U.S.A. 72 B1
Mount Elizabeth, Australia 60 C4
Mount Fletcher, S. Africa 57 E4
Mount Forest, Canada 70 D3
Mount Gambier, Australia 63 F3
Mount Garnet, Australia 62 B4
Mount Hope, N.S.W., Australia 63 E4
Mount Hope, S. Austral., Australia 63 E2
Mount Hope, U.S.A. 76 G5
Mount Horeb, U.S.A. 80 D10
Mount Howitt, Australia 63 D3
Mount Isa, Australia 62 C2
Mount Keith, Australia 61 E3
Mount Laguna, U.S.A. 85 N10
Mount Larcom, Australia 62 C5
Mount Lofty Ra., Australia 63 E2
Mount McKinley Nat. Park, U.S.A. 68 B5
Mount Magnet, Australia 61 E2
Mount Margaret, Australia 63 D3
Mount Maunganui, N.Z. 59 G6
Mount Molloy, Australia 62 B4
Mount Monger, Australia 61 F3
Mount Morgan, Australia 62 C5
Mount Morris, U.S.A. 78 D7
Mount Mulligan, Australia 62 B3
Mount Narryer, Australia 61 E2
Mount Oxide Mine, Australia 62 B2
Mount Pearl, Canada 71 C9
Mount Perry, Australia 63 D5
Mount Phillips, Australia 60 D2
Mount Pleasant, Iowa, U.S.A. 80 E9
Mount Pleasant, Mich., U.S.A. 76 D3
Mount Pleasant, Pa., U.S.A. 78 F5
Mount Pleasant, S.C., U.S.A. 77 J6
Mount Pleasant, Tenn., U.S.A. 77 H2
Mount Pleasant, Tex., U.S.A. 81 J7
Mount Pleasant, Utah, U.S.A. 82 G8
Mount Pocono, U.S.A. 79 E9
Mount Rainier Nat. Park, U.S.A. 84 D5
Mount Revelstoke Nat. Park, Canada 72 C5
Mount Robson Prov. Park, Canada 72 C5
Mount Sandiman, Australia 61 D2
Mount Shasta, U.S.A. 82 F2
Mount Signal, U.S.A. 85 N11
Mount Sterling, Ill., U.S.A. 80 F9
Mount Sterling, Ky., U.S.A. 76 F4
Mount Surprise, Australia 62 B3
Mount Union, U.S.A. 78 F7
Mount Vernon, Australia 60 D2
Mount Vernon, Ind., U.S.A. 80 F10
Mount Vernon, N.Y., U.S.A. 79 F11
Mount Vernon, Ohio, U.S.A. 78 F2
Mount Vernon, Wash., U.S.A. 84 B4
Mountain Center, U.S.A. 85 M10
Mountain City, Nev., U.S.A. 82 F6
Mountain City, Tenn., U.S.A. 77 G5
Mountain Grove, U.S.A. 81 G8
Mountain Home, Ark., U.S.A. 81 G8
Mountain Home, Idaho, U.S.A. 82 E6
Mountain Iron, U.S.A. 80 B8
Mountain Park, Canada 72 C5
Mountain Pass, U.S.A. 85 K11
Mountain View, Ark., U.S.A. 81 H8
Mountain View, Calif., U.S.A. 83 H2
Mountainair, U.S.A. 83 J10
Mountmellick, Ireland 13 C4
Moura, Australia 62 C4
Moura, Brazil 92 D6
Mourdi, Dépression du, Chad 51 E9
Mourdiah, Mali 50 F3
Mourilyan, Australia 62 B4
Mourne →, U.K. 13 B4
Mourne Mts., U.K. 13 B5
Mournies, Greece 23 D6
Mouscron, Belgium 15 D3
Moussoro, Chad 51 F8
Moutohara, N.Z. 59 H6
Moutong, Indonesia 37 D6
Movas, Mexico 86 B3
Moville, Ireland 13 A4
Moy →, Ireland 13 B3
Moyale, Kenya 46 G2
Moyamba, S. Leone 50 G2
Moyen Atlas, Morocco 50 B3
Moyle □, U.K. 13 A5
Moyo, Indonesia 36 F5
Moyobamba, Peru 92 E3
Moyyero →, Russia 27 C11
Mozambique = Moçambique, Mozam. 55 F5
Mozambique ■, Africa 55 F4
Mozambique Chan., Africa 57 B7
Mozdok, Russia 25 F7
Mozdūrān, Iran 45 B9
Mozhnābād, Iran 45 C9
Mozyr, Belorussia 24 D4
Mpanda, Tanzania 54 D3
Mpanda □, Tanzania 54 D3
Mpika, Zambia 55 E3
Mpulungu, Zambia 55 D3
Mpumalanga, S. Africa 57 D5
Mpwapwa, Tanzania 54 D4
Mpwapwa □, Tanzania 54 D4
Msaken, Tunisia 51 A7
Msambansovu, Zimbabwe 55 F3
Msoro, Zambia 55 E3
Mtama, Tanzania 55 E4
Mtilikwe →, Zimbabwe 55 G3
Mtubatuba, S. Africa 57 D5
Mtwara-Mikindani, Tanzania 55 E5
Mu Gia, Deo, Vietnam 38 D5
Mu Us Shamo, China 34 E5
Muaná, Brazil 93 D9
Muang Chiang Rai, Thailand 38 C2
Muang Lamphun, Thailand 38 C2
Muang Pak Beng, Laos 38 C3
Muar, Malaysia 39 L4
Muarabungo, Indonesia 36 E2
Muaraenim, Indonesia 36 E2
Muarajuloi, Indonesia 36 E4
Muarakaman, Indonesia 36 E5
Muaratebo, Indonesia 36 E2
Muaratembesi, Indonesia 36 E2
Muaratewe, Indonesia 36 E4
Mubarakpur, India 43 F10
Mubarraz = Al Mubarraz, Si. Arabia 45 E6
Mubende, Uganda 54 B3
Mubi, Nigeria 51 F7
Mubur, P., Indonesia 39 L6
Muchachos, Roque de los, Canary Is. 22 F2
Muchinga Mts., Zambia 55 E3
Muck, U.K. 12 E2
Muckadilla, Australia 63 D4
Muconda, Angola 52 G4
Mucuri, Brazil 93 G11
Mucusso, Angola 56 B3
Muda, Canary Is. 22 F6
Mudan Jiang →, China 35 A15
Mudanjiang, China 35 B15
Muddy →, U.S.A. 83 H8
Mudgee, Australia 63 E4
Mudjatik →, Canada 73 B7
Muecate, Mozam. 55 E4
Muêda, Mozam. 55 E4
Mueller Ra., Australia 60 C4
Muende, Mozam. 55 E3
Muerto, Mar, Mexico 87 D6
Mufindi □, Tanzania 55 D4
Mufulira, Zambia 55 E2
Mufumbiro Range, Africa 54 C2
Mughayrā', Si. Arabia 44 D3
Mugi, Japan 31 H7
Mugila, Mts., Zaïre 54 D2
Muğla, Turkey 25 G4
Mugu, Nepal 43 E10
Muhammad Qol, Sudan 51 D12
Muhammadabad, India 43 F10
Muhesi →, Tanzania 54 D4
Muheza □, Tanzania 54 C4
Mühlig Hofmann fjella, Antarctica 5 D3
Muhutwe, Tanzania 54 C3
Muikamachi, Japan 31 F9
Muine Bheag, Ireland 13 D5
Muir, L., Australia 61 F2
Mukah, Malaysia 36 D4
Mukdahan, Thailand 38 D5
Mukden = Shenyang, China 35 D12
Mukhtuya = Lensk, Russia 27 C12
Mukinbudin, Australia 61 F2
Mukishi, Zaïre 55 D1
Mukomuko, Indonesia 36 E2
Mukomwenze, Zaïre 54 D2
Muktsar, India 42 D6
Mukur, Afghan. 42 C2
Mukutawa →, Canada 73 C9
Mukwela, Zambia 55 F2
Mulange, Zaïre 54 C2
Mulchén, Chile 94 D1
Mulde →, Germany 16 C6
Mule Creek, U.S.A. 80 D2
Muleba, Tanzania 54 C3
Muleba □, Tanzania 54 C3
Muleshoe, U.S.A. 81 H3
Mulgathing, Australia 63 E1
Mulgrave, Canada 71 C7
Mulhacén, Spain 19 D4
Mülheim, Germany 16 C3
Mulhouse, France 18 C7
Muling, China 35 B16
Mull, U.K. 12 E3
Mullaittivu, Sri Lanka 40 Q12
Mullen, U.S.A. 80 D4
Mullengudgery, Australia 63 E4
Mullens, U.S.A. 76 G5
Muller, Pegunungan, Indonesia 36 D4
Mullet Pen., Ireland 13 B1
Mullewa, Australia 61 E2
Mulligan →, Australia 62 C2
Mullin, U.S.A. 81 K5
Mullingar, Ireland 13 C4
Mullins, U.S.A. 77 H6
Mullumbimby, Australia 63 D5
Mulobezi, Zambia 55 F2
Multan, Pakistan 42 D4
Mulumbe, Mts., Zaïre 55 D2
Mulungushi Dam, Zambia 55 E2
Mulvane, U.S.A. 81 G6
Mulwala, Australia 63 F4
Mumbwa, Zambia 55 E2
Mun →, Thailand 38 E5
Muna, Indonesia 37 F6
München, Germany 16 D5
Munchen-Gladbach = Mönchengladbach, Germany 16 C3
Muncho Lake, Canada 72 B3
Munchŏn, N. Korea 35 E14
Muncie, U.S.A. 76 E3
Muncoonie, L., Australia 62 D2
Mundala, Indonesia 37 E10
Mundare, Canada 72 C6
Munday, U.S.A. 81 J5
Münden, Germany 16 C4
Mundiwindi, Australia 60 D3
Mundo Novo, Brazil 93 F10
Mundra, India 42 H3
Mundrabilla, Australia 61 F4
Mungallala, Australia 63 D4
Mungallala Cr. →, Australia 63 D4
Mungana, Australia 62 B3
Mungaoli, India 42 G8
Mungari, Mozam. 55 F3
Mungbere, Zaïre 54 B2
Munger, India 43 G12
Mungindi, Australia 63 D4
Munhango, Angola 53 G3
Munich = München, Germany 16 D5
Munising, U.S.A. 76 B2
Munku-Sardyk, Russia 27 D11
Muñoz Gamero, Pen., Chile 96 G2
Munroe L., Canada 73 B9
Munsan, S. Korea 35 F14
Münster, Germany 16 C3
Munster □, Ireland 13 D3
Muntadgin, Australia 61 F2
Muntok, Indonesia 36 E3
Munyak, Uzbekistan 26 E6
Munyama, Zambia 55 F2
Muong Beng, Laos 38 B3
Muong Boum, Vietnam 38 A4
Muong Et, Laos 38 B5
Muong Hai, Laos 38 B3
Muong Hiem, Laos 38 B4
Muong Houn, Laos 38 B3
Muong Hung, Vietnam 38 B4
Muong Kau, Laos 38 E5
Muong Khao, Laos 38 C4
Muong Khoua, Laos 38 B4
Muong Liep, Laos 38 C3
Muong May, Laos 38 E6
Muong Ngeun, Laos 38 B3
Muong Ngoi, Laos 38 B4
Muong Nhie, Vietnam 38 A4
Muong Nong, Laos 38 D6
Muong Ou Tay, Laos 38 A3
Muong Oua, Laos 38 C3
Muong Peun, Laos 38 B4
Muong Phalane, Laos 38 D5
Muong Phieng, Laos 38 C3
Muong Phine, Laos 38 D6
Muong Sai, Laos 38 B3
Muong Saiapoun, Laos 38 C3
Muong Sen, Vietnam 38 C5
Muong Sing, Laos 38 B3
Muong Son, Laos 38 B4
Muong Soui, Laos 38 C4
Muong Va, Laos 38 B4
Muong Xia, Vietnam 38 B5
Muonio, Finland 8 C17
Mupa, Angola 53 H3
Muping, China 35 F11
Muqdisho, Somali Rep. 46 G4
Mur →, Austria 16 E8
Murakami, Japan 30 E9
Murallón, Cuerro, Chile 96 F2
Muranda, Rwanda 54 C2
Murang'a, Kenya 54 C4
Murashi, Russia 24 C8
Murayama, Japan 30 E10
Murban, U.A.E. 45 F7
Murchison →, Australia 61 E1
Murchison, Mt., Antarctica 5 D11
Murchison Falls = Kabarega Falls, Uganda 54 B3
Murchison House, Australia 61 E1
Murchison Ra., Australia 62 C1
Murchison Rapids, Malawi 55 F3
Murcia, Spain 19 C5
Murcia □, Spain 19 D5
Murdo, U.S.A. 80 D4
Murdoch Pt., Australia 62 A3
Mureş →, Romania 17 E10
Mureşul = Mureş →, Romania 17 E10
Murfreesboro, U.S.A. 77 H2
Murgab, Tajikistan 26 F8
Murgon, Australia 63 D5
Murgoo, Australia 61 E2
Muria, Indonesia 37 G14
Muriaé, Brazil 95 A7
Muriel Mine, Zimbabwe 55 F3
Müritz See, Germany 16 B6
Murka, Kenya 54 C4
Murmansk, Russia 24 A5
Muro, Spain 22 B10
Murom, Russia 24 C7
Muroran, Japan 30 C10
Muroto, Japan 31 H7
Muroto-Misaki, Japan 31 H7
Murphy, U.S.A. 82 E5
Murphys, U.S.A. 84 G6
Murphysboro, U.S.A. 81 G10
Murray, Ky., U.S.A. 77 G1
Murray, Utah, U.S.A. 82 F8
Murray →, Australia 63 F2
Murray →, Canada 72 B4
Murray, L., U.S.A. 77 H5
Murray Bridge, Australia 63 F2
Murray Downs, Australia 62 C1
Murray Harbour, Canada 71 C7
Murraysburg, S. Africa 56 E3
Murree, Pakistan 42 C5
Murrieta, U.S.A. 85 M9
Murrin Murrin, Australia 61 E3
Murrumbidgee →, Australia 63 E3
Murrumburrah, Australia 63 E4
Murrurundi, Australia 63 E5
Mursala, Indonesia 36 D1
Murshidabad, India 43 G13
Murtle L., Canada 72 C5
Murtoa, Australia 63 F3
Murungu, Tanzania 54 C3
Murwara, India 43 H9
Murwillumbah, Australia 63 D5
Mürzzuschlag, Austria 16 E7
Muş, Turkey 25 G7
Musa Khel, Pakistan 42 D3
Mūsá Qal'eh, Afghan. 40 C4
Musaffargarh, Pakistan 40 D7
Musala, Bulgaria 21 C10
Musan, N. Korea 35 C15

Musangu, *Zaïre* 55 E1
Musasa, *Tanzania* 54 C3
Musay'id, *Qatar* 45 E6
Muscat = Masqat, *Oman* 46 C6
Muscat & Oman = Oman ■, *Asia* 46 C6
Muscatine, *U.S.A.* 80 E9
Musgrave, *Australia* 62 A3
Musgrave Ras., *Australia* 61 E5
Mushie, *Zaïre* 52 E3
Musi →, *Indonesia* 36 E2
Muskeg →, *Canada* 72 A4
Muskegon, *U.S.A.* 76 D2
Muskegon →, *U.S.A.* 76 D2
Muskegon Heights, *U.S.A.* 76 D2
Muskogee, *U.S.A.* 81 H7
Muskwa →, *Canada* 72 B4
Muslimiyah, *Syria* 44 B3
Musmar, *Sudan* 51 E12
Musofu, *Zambia* 55 E2
Musoma, *Tanzania* 54 C3
Musoma □, *Tanzania* 54 C3
Musquaro, L., *Canada* 71 B7
Musquodoboit Harbour, *Canada* 71 D7
Musselburgh, *U.K.* 12 F5
Musselshell →, *U.S.A.* 82 C10
Mussoorie, *India* 42 D8
Mussuco, *Angola* 56 B2
Mustang, *Nepal* 43 E10
Musters, L., *Argentina* 96 F3
Musudan, *N. Korea* 35 D15
Muswellbrook, *Australia* 63 E5
Mût, *Egypt* 51 C10
Mutanda, *Mozam.* 57 C5
Mutanda, *Zambia* 55 E2
Mutaray, *Russia* 27 C11
Mutare, *Zimbabwe* 55 F3
Muting, *Indonesia* 37 F10
Mutshatsha, *Zaïre* 55 E1
Mutsu, *Japan* 30 D10
Mutsu-Wan, *Japan* 30 D10
Muttaburra, *Australia* 62 C3
Mutuáli, *Mozam.* 55 E4
Muweilih, *Egypt* 47 E3
Muxima, *Angola* 52 F2
Muy Muy, *Nic.* 88 D2
Muya, *Russia* 27 D12
Muyinga, *Burundi* 54 C3
Muzaffarabad, *Pakistan* 43 B5
Muzaffargarh, *Pakistan* 42 D4
Muzaffarnagar, *India* 42 E7
Muzaffarpur, *India* 43 F11
Muzhi, *Russia* 26 C7
Muzon C., *U.S.A.* 72 C2
Mvuma, *Zimbabwe* 55 F3
Mvurwi, *Zimbabwe* 55 F3
Mwadui, *Tanzania* 54 C3
Mwambo, *Tanzania* 55 E5
Mwandi, *Zambia* 55 F1
Mwanza, *Tanzania* 54 C3
Mwanza, *Zaïre* 54 D2
Mwanza, *Zambia* 55 F1
Mwanza □, *Tanzania* 54 C3
Mwaya, *Tanzania* 55 D3
Mweelrea, *Ireland* 13 C2
Mweka, *Zaïre* 52 E4
Mwenezi, *Zimbabwe* 55 G3
Mwenezi →, *Mozam.* 55 G3
Mwenga, *Zaïre* 54 C2
Mweru, L., *Zambia* 55 D2
Mweza Range, *Zimbabwe* 55 G3
Mwilambwe, *Zaïre* 54 D5
Mwimbi, *Tanzania* 55 D3
Mwinilunga, *Zambia* 55 E1
My Tho, *Vietnam* 39 G6
Myajlar, *India* 42 F4
Myanaung, *Burma* 41 K19
Myanmar = Burma ■, *Asia* 41 J20
Myaungmya, *Burma* 41 L19
Mycenae = Mikínai, *Greece* 21 F10
Myeik Kyunzu, *Burma* 39 G1
Myerstown, *U.S.A.* 79 F8
Myingyan, *Burma* 41 J19
Myitkyina, *Burma* 41 G20
Mymensingh, *Bangla.* 41 G17
Mynydd Du, *U.K.* 11 F4
Mýrdalsjökull, *Iceland* 8 E4
Myroodah, *Australia* 60 C3
Myrtle Beach, *U.S.A.* 77 J6
Myrtle Creek, *U.S.A.* 82 E2
Myrtle Point, *U.S.A.* 82 E1
Myrtou, *Cyprus* 23 D12
Mysore = Karnataka □, *India* 40 N10
Mysore, *India* 40 N10
Mystic, *U.S.A.* 79 E13
Myton, *U.S.A.* 82 F8
Mývatn, *Iceland* 8 D5
Mzimba, *Malawi* 55 E3
Mzimkulu →, *S. Africa* 57 E5
Mzimvubu →, *S. Africa* 57 E4
Mzuzu, *Malawi* 55 E3

N

Na Noi, *Thailand* 38 C3
Na Phao, *Laos* 38 D5
Na Sam, *Vietnam* 38 A6
Na San, *Vietnam* 38 B5
Naab →, *Germany* 16 D6
Naantali, *Finland* 9 F17
Naas, *Ireland* 13 C5
Nababiep, *S. Africa* 56 D2
Nabadwip = Navadwip, *India* 43 H13
Nabari, *Japan* 31 G8
Nabawa, *Australia* 61 E1
Nabberu, L., *Australia* 61 E3
Naberezhnyye Chelny, *Russia* 26 D6
Nabeul, *Tunisia* 51 A7
Nabha, *India* 42 D7
Nabīd, *Iran* 45 D8
Nabire, *Indonesia* 37 E9
Nabisar, *Pakistan* 42 G3
Nabisipi →, *Canada* 71 B7
Nabiswera, *Uganda* 54 B3
Nablus = Nābulus, *Jordan* 47 C4
Naboomspruit, *S. Africa* 57 C4
Nābulus, *Jordan* 47 C4
Nābulus □, *Jordan* 47 C4
Nacala, *Mozam.* 55 E5
Nacala-Velha, *Mozam.* 55 E5
Nacaome, *Honduras* 88 D2
Nacaroa, *Mozam.* 55 E4
Naches, *U.S.A.* 82 C3
Naches →, *U.S.A.* 84 D6
Nachingwea, *Tanzania* 55 E4
Nachingwea □, *Tanzania* 55 E4
Nachna, *India* 42 F4
Nacimiento Res., *U.S.A.* 84 K6
Nackara, *Australia* 63 E2
Naco, *Mexico* 86 A3
Naco, *U.S.A.* 83 L9
Nacogdoches, *U.S.A.* 81 K7
Nácori Chico, *Mexico* 86 B3
Nacozari, *Mexico* 86 A3
Nadiad, *India* 42 H5
Nadur, *Malta* 23 C1
Nadūshan, *Iran* 45 C7
Nadvoitsy, *Russia* 24 B5
Nadym, *Russia* 26 C8
Nadym →, *Russia* 26 C8
Nafada, *Nigeria* 50 F7
Naftshahr, *Iran* 44 C5
Naga, *Phil.* 37 B6
Nagagami →, *Canada* 70 C3
Nagahama, *Japan* 31 G8
Nagai, *Japan* 30 E10
Nagaland □, *India* 41 F19
Nagano, *Japan* 31 F9
Nagano □, *Japan* 31 F9
Nagaoka, *Japan* 31 F9
Nagappattinam, *India* 40 P11
Nagar Parkar, *Pakistan* 42 G4
Nagasaki, *Japan* 31 H4
Nagasaki □, *Japan* 31 H4
Nagato, *Japan* 31 G5
Nagaur, *India* 42 F5
Nagercoil, *India* 40 Q10
Nagina, *India* 43 E8
Nagīneh, *Iran* 45 C8
Nagir, *Pakistan* 43 A6
Nagoorin, *Australia* 62 C5
Nagornyy, *Russia* 27 D13
Nagoya, *Japan* 31 G8
Nagpur, *India* 40 J11
Nagua, *Dom. Rep.* 89 C6
Nagykanizsa, *Hungary* 16 E8
Nagykörös, *Hungary* 17 E9
Naha, *Japan* 31 L3
Nahanni Butte, *Canada* 72 A4
Nahanni Nat. Park, *Canada* 72 A3
Nahariyya, *Israel* 44 C2
Nahāvand, *Iran* 45 C6
Nahlin, *Canada* 72 B2
Naicá, *Mexico* 86 B3
Naicam, *Canada* 73 C8
Nā'ifah, *Si. Arabia* 46 D5
Nain, *Canada* 71 A7
Nā'īn, *Iran* 45 C7
Naini Tal, *India* 43 E8
Nainpur, *India* 40 H12
Naira, *Indonesia* 37 E7
Nairn, *U.K.* 12 D5
Nairobi, *Kenya* 54 C4
Naivasha, *Kenya* 54 C4
Naivasha, L., *Kenya* 54 C4
Najafābād, *Iran* 45 C6
Najibabad, *India* 42 E8
Najin, *N. Korea* 35 C16
Najmah, *Si. Arabia* 45 E6
Naju, *S. Korea* 35 G14
Nakadōri-Shima, *Japan* 31 H4
Nakalagba, *Zaïre* 54 B2
Nakaminato, *Japan* 31 F10
Nakamura, *Japan* 31 H6
Nakano, *Japan* 31 F9
Nakano-Shima, *Japan* 31 K4
Nakashibetsu, *Japan* 30 C12
Nakfa, *Ethiopia* 51 E12
Nakhichevan, *Azerbaijan* 25 G8
Nakhichevan Republic □, *Azerbaijan* 25 G8
Nakhl, *Egypt* 47 F2
Nakhl-e Taqī, *Iran* 45 E7
Nakhodka, *Russia* 27 E14
Nakhon Nayok, *Thailand* 38 E3
Nakhon Pathom, *Thailand* 38 F3
Nakhon Phanom, *Thailand* 38 D5
Nakhon Ratchasima, *Thailand* 38 E4
Nakhon Sawan, *Thailand* 38 E3
Nakhon Si Thammarat, *Thailand* 39 H3
Nakhon Thai, *Thailand* 38 D3
Nakina, *B.C., Canada* 72 B2
Nakina, *Ont., Canada* 70 B2
Nakodar, *India* 42 D6
Nakskov, *Denmark* 9 J11
Naktong →, *S. Korea* 35 G15
Nakuru, *Kenya* 54 C4
Nakuru □, *Kenya* 54 C4
Nakuru, L., *Kenya* 54 C4
Nakusp, *Canada* 72 C5
Nal →, *Pakistan* 42 G1
Nalchik, *Russia* 25 F7
Nalgonda, *India* 40 L11
Nalhati, *India* 43 G12
Nallamalai Hills, *India* 40 M11
Nalón →, *Spain* 19 A2
Nālūt, *Libya* 51 B7
Nam Can, *Vietnam* 39 H5
Nam Co, *China* 32 C4
Nam Dinh, *Vietnam* 38 B6
Nam Du, Hon, *Vietnam* 39 H5
Nam Ngum Dam, *Laos* 38 C4
Nam-Phan, *Vietnam* 39 G6
Nam Phong, *Thailand* 38 D4
Nam Tha, *Laos* 38 B3
Nam Tok, *Thailand* 38 E2
Namacunde, *Angola* 56 B2
Namacurra, *Mozam.* 57 B6
Namak, Daryācheh-ye, *Iran* 45 C7
Namak, Kavir-e, *Iran* 45 C8
Namaland, *Namibia* 56 C2
Namangan, *Uzbekistan* 26 E8
Namapa, *Mozam.* 55 E4
Namaqualand, *S. Africa* 56 D2
Namasagali, *Uganda* 54 B3
Namber, *Indonesia* 37 E8
Nambour, *Australia* 63 D5
Nambucca Heads, *Australia* 63 E5
Namcha Barwa, *China* 32 D4
Namche Bazar, *Nepal* 43 F12
Namchonjŏm, *N. Korea* 35 E14
Namecunda, *Mozam.* 55 E4
Nameh, *Indonesia* 36 D5
Nameponda, *Mozam.* 55 F4
Nametil, *Mozam.* 55 F4
Namew L., *Canada* 73 C8
Namib Desert = Namibwoestyn, *Namibia* 56 C2
Namibe, *Angola* 53 H2
Namibe □, *Angola* 56 B1
Namibia ■, *Africa* 56 C2
Namibwoestyn, *Namibia* 56 C2
Namlea, *Indonesia* 37 E7
Namoi →, *Australia* 63 E4
Nampa, *U.S.A.* 82 E5
Nampō-Shotō, *Japan* 31 J10
Nampula, *Mozam.* 55 F4
Namrole, *Indonesia* 37 E7
Namse Shankou, *China* 41 E13
Namsen →, *Norway* 8 D11
Namsos, *Norway* 8 D11
Namtay, *Russia* 27 C13
Namtu, *Burma* 41 H20
Namtumbo, *Tanzania* 55 E4
Namu, *Canada* 72 C3
Namur, *Belgium* 15 D4
Namur □, *Belgium* 15 D4
Namutoni, *Namibia* 56 B2
Namwala, *Zambia* 55 F2
Namwŏn, *S. Korea* 35 G14
Nan, *Thailand* 38 C3
Nan →, *Thailand* 38 E3
Nanaimo, *Canada* 72 D4
Nanam, *N. Korea* 35 D15
Nanango, *Australia* 63 D5
Nanao, *Japan* 31 F8
Nanchang, *China* 33 D6
Nanching = Nanjing, *China* 33 C6
Nanchong, *China* 32 C5
Nancy, *France* 18 B7
Nanda Devi, *India* 43 D8
Nandan, *Japan* 31 G7
Nanded, *India* 40 K10
Nandewar Ra., *Australia* 63 E5
Nandi, *Fiji* 59 C7
Nandi □, *Kenya* 54 B4
Nandurbar, *India* 40 J9
Nandyal, *India* 40 M11
Nanga, *Australia* 61 E1
Nanga-Eboko, *Cameroon* 52 D2
Nanga Parbat, *Pakistan* 43 B6
Nangade, *Mozam.* 55 E4
Nangapinoh, *Indonesia* 36 E4
Nangarhár □, *Afghan.* 40 B7
Nangatayap, *Indonesia* 36 E4
Nangeya Mts., *Uganda* 54 B3
Nangong, *China* 34 F8
Nanhuang, *China* 35 F11
Nanjeko, *Zambia* 55 F1
Nanjing, *China* 33 C6
Nanjirinji, *Tanzania* 55 D4
Nankana Sahib, *Pakistan* 42 D5
Nanking = Nanjing, *China* 33 C6
Nankoku, *Japan* 31 H6
Nanning, *China* 32 D5
Nannup, *Australia* 61 F2
Nanpara, *India* 43 F9
Nanpi, *China* 34 E9
Nanping, *China* 33 D6
Nanripe, *Mozam.* 55 E4
Nansei-Shotō = Ryūkyū-rettō, *Japan* 31 M2
Nansen Sd., *Canada* 4 A3
Nansio, *Tanzania* 54 C3
Nantes, *France* 18 C3
Nanticoke, *U.S.A.* 79 E8
Nanton, *Canada* 72 C6
Nantong, *China* 33 C7
Nantucket I., *U.S.A.* 66 E12
Nanuque, *Brazil* 93 G10
Nanutarra, *Australia* 60 D2
Nanyang, *China* 34 H7
Nanyuan, *China* 34 E9
Nanyuki, *Kenya* 54 B4
Nào, C. de la, *Spain* 19 C6
Naococane L., *Canada* 71 B5
Naoetsu, *Japan* 31 F9
Napa, *U.S.A.* 84 G4
Napa →, *U.S.A.* 84 G4
Napanee, *Canada* 70 D4
Napanoch, *U.S.A.* 79 E10
Nape, *Laos* 38 C5
Nape Pass = Keo Neua, Deo, *Vietnam* 38 C5
Napier, *N.Z.* 59 H6
Napier Broome B., *Australia* 60 B4
Napier Downs, *Australia* 60 C3
Napier Pen., *Australia* 62 A2
Naples = Nápoli, *Italy* 20 D6
Naples, *U.S.A.* 77 M5
Napo →, *Peru* 92 D4
Napoleon, *N. Dak., U.S.A.* 80 B5
Napoleon, *Ohio, U.S.A.* 76 E3
Nápoli, *Italy* 20 D6
Napopo, *Zaïre* 54 B2
Nappa Merrie, *Australia* 63 D3
Naqqāsh, *Iran* 45 C6
Nara, *Japan* 31 G7
Nara, *Mali* 50 E3
Nara □, *Japan* 31 G8
Nara Canal, *Pakistan* 42 G3
Nara Visa, *U.S.A.* 81 H3
Naracoorte, *Australia* 63 F3
Naradhan, *Australia* 63 E4
Narasapur, *India* 41 L12
Narathiwat, *Thailand* 39 J3
Narayanganj, *Bangla.* 41 H17
Narayanpet, *India* 40 L10
Narbonne, *France* 18 E5
Nardīn, *Iran* 45 B7
Nardò, *Italy* 21 D8
Narembeen, *Australia* 61 F2
Nares Str., *Arctic* 66 B13
Naretha, *Australia* 61 F3
Nari →, *Pakistan* 42 E2
Narin, *Afghan.* 40 A6
Narindra, Helodranon' i, *Madag.* 57 A8
Narita, *Japan* 31 G10
Narmada →, *India* 42 J5
Narnaul, *India* 42 E7
Narodnaya, *Russia* 24 A10
Narok, *Kenya* 54 C4
Narok □, *Kenya* 54 C4
Narooma, *Australia* 63 F5
Narowal, *Pakistan* 42 C6
Narrabri, *Australia* 63 E4
Narran →, *Australia* 63 D4
Narrandera, *Australia* 63 E4
Narraway →, *Canada* 72 B5
Narrogin, *Australia* 61 F2
Narromine, *Australia* 63 E4
Narsimhapur, *India* 43 H8
Naruto, *Japan* 31 G7
Narva, *Estonia* 24 C4
Narvik, *Norway* 8 B14
Narwana, *India* 42 E7
Naryan-Mar, *Russia* 24 A9
Naryilco, *Australia* 63 D3
Narym, *Russia* 26 D9
Narymskoye, *Kazakhstan* 26 E9
Naryn, *Kirghizia* 26 E8
Nasa, *Norway* 8 C13
Nasarawa, *Nigeria* 50 G6
Naseby, *N.Z.* 59 L3
Naselle, *U.S.A.* 84 D3
Naser, Buheirat en, *Egypt* 51 D11
Nashua, *Iowa, U.S.A.* 80 D8
Nashua, *Mont., U.S.A.* 82 B10
Nashua, *N.H., U.S.A.* 79 D13
Nashville, *Ark., U.S.A.* 81 J8
Nashville, *Ga., U.S.A.* 77 K4
Nashville, *Tenn., U.S.A.* 77 G2
Nasik, *India* 40 K8
Nasirabad, *India* 42 F6
Naskaupi →, *Canada* 71 B7
Naṣrīān-e Pā'īn, *Iran* 44 C5
Nass →, *Canada* 72 B3
Nassau, *Bahamas* 88 A4
Nassau, *U.S.A.* 79 D11
Nassau, B., *Chile* 96 H3
Nasser, L. = Naser, Buheirat en, *Egypt* 51 D11
Nässjö, *Sweden* 9 H13
Nat Kyizin, *Burma* 41 M20
Nata, *Botswana* 56 C4
Natagaima, *Colombia* 92 C3
Natal, *Brazil* 93 E11
Natal, *Canada* 72 D6
Natal, *Indonesia* 36 D1
Natal □, *S. Africa* 57 D5
Naṭanz, *Iran* 45 C6
Natashquan, *Canada* 71 B7
Natashquan →, *Canada* 71 B7
Natchez, *U.S.A.* 81 K9
Natchitoches, *U.S.A.* 81 K8
Nathalia, *Australia* 63 F4
Nathdwara, *India* 42 G5
Nati, Pta., *Spain* 22 A10
Natimuk, *Australia* 63 F3
Nation →, *Canada* 72 B4
National City, *U.S.A.* 85 N9
Natitingou, *Benin* 50 F5
Natividad, I., *Mexico* 86 B1
Natoma, *U.S.A.* 80 F5
Natron, L., *Tanzania* 54 C4
Natrona Heights, *U.S.A.* 78 F5
Natuna Besar, Kepulauan, *Indonesia* 39 L7
Natuna Is. = Natuna Besar, Kepulauan, *Indonesia* 39 L7
Natuna Selatan, Kepulauan, *Indonesia* 39 L7
Natural Bridge, *U.S.A.* 79 B9
Naturaliste, C., *Australia* 62 G4
Nau Qala, *Afghan.* 42 B3
Naubinway, *U.S.A.* 70 C2
Naugatuck, *U.S.A.* 79 E11
Naumburg, *Germany* 16 C5
Nā'ūr at Tunayb, *Jordan* 47 D4
Nauru ■, *Pac. Oc.* 64 H8
Naushahra = Nowshera, *Pakistan* 40 B8
Nauta, *Peru* 92 D4
Nautanwa, *India* 41 F13
Nautla, *Mexico* 87 C5
Nava, *Mexico* 86 B4
Navadwip, *India* 43 H13
Navajo Res., *U.S.A.* 83 H10
Navalcarnero, *Spain* 19 B3
Navan = An Uaimh, *Ireland* 13 C5
Navarino, I., *Chile* 96 H3
Navarra □, *Spain* 19 A5
Navarre, *U.S.A.* 78 F3
Navarro, *U.S.A.* 84 F3
Navasota, *U.S.A.* 81 K6
Navassa, *W. Indies* 89 C4
Naver →, *U.K.* 12 C4
Navidad, *Chile* 94 C1
Navoi, *Uzbekistan* 26 E7
Navojoa, *Mexico* 86 B3
Navolato, *Mexico* 86 C3
Navolok, *Russia* 24 B6
Návpaktos, *Greece* 21 E9
Návplion, *Greece* 21 F10
Navsari, *India* 40 J8
Nawa Kot, *Pakistan* 42 E4
Nawabganj, *Ut. P., India* 43 F9
Nawabganj, *Ut. P., India* 43 E8
Nawabshah, *Pakistan* 42 F3
Nawada, *India* 43 G11
Nawakot, *Nepal* 43 F11
Nawalgarh, *India* 42 F6
Nawanshahr, *India* 43 C6
Náxos, *Greece* 21 F11
Nāy Band, *Iran* 45 E7
Nayakhan, *Russia* 27 C16
Nayarit □, *Mexico* 86 C4
Nayoro, *Japan* 30 B11
Nayyāl, W. →, *Si. Arabia* 44 D3
Nazareth = Naẓerat, *Israel* 47 C4
Nazas, *Mexico* 86 B4
Nazas →, *Mexico* 86 B4
Naze, The, *U.K.* 11 F9
Naẓerat, *Israel* 47 C4
Nāzik, *Iran* 44 B5
Nazir Hat, *Bangla.* 41 H17
Nazko, *Canada* 72 C4
Nazko →, *Canada* 72 C4
Nchanga, *Zambia* 55 E2
Ncheu, *Malawi* 55 E3
Ndala, *Tanzania* 54 C3
Ndalatando, *Angola* 52 F2
Ndareda, *Tanzania* 54 C4
Ndélé, *C.A.R.* 51 G9
Ndendé, *Gabon* 52 E2
Ndjamena, *Chad* 51 F7
Ndjolé, *Gabon* 52 E2
Ndola, *Zambia* 55 E2
Ndoto Mts., *Kenya* 54 B4
Nduguti, *Tanzania* 54 C3
Neagh, Lough, *U.K.* 13 B5
Neah Bay, *U.S.A.* 84 B2
Neale, L., *Australia* 60 D5
Neápolis, *Greece* 23 D7
Near Is., *U.S.A.* 68 C1
Neath, *U.K.* 11 F4
Nebine Cr. →, *Australia* 63 D4
Nebit Dag, *Turkmenistan* 25 G9
Nebraska □, *U.S.A.* 80 E5
Nebraska City, *U.S.A.* 80 E7
Nébrodi, Monti, *Italy* 20 F6
Necedah, *U.S.A.* 80 C9
Nechako →, *Canada* 72 C4
Neches →, *U.S.A.* 81 L8
Neckar →, *Germany* 16 D4
Necochea, *Argentina* 94 D4
Needles, *U.S.A.* 85 L12
Needles, The, *U.K.* 11 G6
Ñeembucú □, *Paraguay* 94 B4
Neemuch = Nimach, *India* 42 G6
Neenah, *U.S.A.* 76 C1
Neepawa, *Canada* 73 C9
Neft-chala = imeni 26 Bakinskikh Komissarov, *Azerbaijan* 25 G8
Nefta, *Tunisia* 50 B6
Neftyannyye Kamni, *Azerbaijan* 25 F9
Negapatam = Nagappattinam, *India* 40 P11
Negaunee, *U.S.A.* 76 B2
Negele, *Ethiopia* 46 F2
Negev Desert = Hanegev, *Israel* 47 E3
Negoiul, Vf., *Romania* 17 F12
Negombo, *Sri Lanka* 40 R11
Negotin, *Serbia, Yug.* 21 B10
Negra Pt., *Phil.* 37 A6
Negro →, *Argentina* 96 E4
Negro →, *Brazil* 92 D6
Negro →, *Uruguay* 95 C4

Negros, *Phil.* 37 C6
Nehalem →, *U.S.A.* 84 E3
Nehāvand, *Iran* 45 C6
Nehbandān, *Iran* 45 D9
Nei Monggol Zizhiqu □, *China* 34 C6
Neidpath, *Canada* 73 C7
Neihart, *U.S.A.* 82 C8
Neijiang, *China* 32 D5
Neilton, *U.S.A.* 82 C2
Neiqiu, *China* 34 F8
Neisse →, *Europe* 16 B7
Neiva, *Colombia* 92 C3
Neixiang, *China* 34 H6
Nejanilini L., *Canada* 73 B9
Nekā, *Iran* 45 B7
Nekemte, *Ethiopia* 51 G12
Neksø, *Denmark* 9 J13
Nelia, *Australia* 62 C3
Neligh, *U.S.A.* 80 D5
Nelkan, *Russia* 27 D14
Nellore, *India* 40 M11
Nelma, *Russia* 27 E14
Nelson, *Canada* 72 D5
Nelson, *N.Z.* 59 J4
Nelson, *U.K.* 10 D5
Nelson, *U.S.A.* 83 J7
Nelson →, *Canada* 73 C9
Nelson, C., *Australia* 63 F3
Nelson, Estrecho, *Chile* 96 G2
Nelson Forks, *Canada* 72 B4
Nelson House, *Canada* 73 B9
Nelson L., *Canada* 73 B8
Nelspoort, *S. Africa* 56 E3
Nelspruit, *S. Africa* 57 D5
Néma, *Mauritania* 50 E3
Neman →, *Lithuania* 24 C3
Nemeiben L., *Canada* 73 B7
Nemunas = Neman →, *Lithuania* 24 C3
Nemuro, *Japan* 30 C12
Nemuro-Kaikyō, *Japan* 30 C12
Nemuy, *Russia* 27 D14
Nen Jiang →, *China* 35 B13
Nenagh, *Ireland* 13 D3
Nenana, *U.S.A.* 68 B5
Nenasi, *Malaysia* 39 L4
Nene →, *U.K.* 10 E8
Nenjiang, *China* 33 B7
Neno, *Malawi* 55 F3
Nenusa, Kepulauan, *Indonesia* 37 D7
Neodesha, *U.S.A.* 81 G7
Neosho, *U.S.A.* 81 G7
Neosho →, *U.S.A.* 81 H7
Nepal ■, *Asia* 43 F11
Nepalganj, *Nepal* 43 E9
Nephi, *U.S.A.* 82 G8
Nephin, *Ireland* 13 B2
Neptune City, *U.S.A.* 79 F10
Nerchinsk, *Russia* 27 D12
Nerchinskiy Zavod, *Russia* 27 D12
Néret L., *Canada* 71 B5
Neretva →, *Croatia* 21 C7
Nerva, *Spain* 19 D2
Nes, *Iceland* 8 D5
Neskaupstaður, *Iceland* 8 D7
Ness, L., *U.K.* 12 D4
Nesttun, *Norway* 9 F8
Netanya, *Israel* 47 C3
Nète →, *Belgium* 15 C4
Netherdale, *Australia* 62 C4
Netherlands ■, *Europe* 15 C5
Netherlands Antilles ■, *S. Amer.* 92 A5
Netherlands Guiana = Surinam ■, *S. Amer.* 93 C7
Nettilling L., *Canada* 69 B12
Netzahualcoyotl, Presa, *Mexico* 87 D6
Neubrandenburg, *Germany* 16 B6
Neuchâtel, *Switz.* 16 E3
Neuchâtel, Lac de, *Switz.* 16 E3
Neufchâteau, *Belgium* 15 E5
Neumünster, *Germany* 16 A4
Neunkirchen, *Germany* 16 D3
Neuquén, *Argentina* 96 D3
Neuquén □, *Argentina* 94 D2
Neuruppin, *Germany* 16 B6
Neuse →, *U.S.A.* 77 H7
Neusiedler See, *Austria* 16 E8
Neuss, *Germany* 15 C6
Neustrelitz, *Germany* 16 B6
Neva →, *Russia* 24 C5
Nevada, *U.S.A.* 81 G7
Nevada □, *U.S.A.* 82 G5
Nevada, Sierra, *Spain* 19 D4
Nevada, Sierra, *U.S.A.* 82 G3
Nevada City, *U.S.A.* 84 F6
Nevado, Cerro, *Argentina* 94 D2
Nevanka, *Russia* 27 D10
Nevers, *France* 18 C5
Nevertire, *Australia* 63 E4
Neville, *Canada* 73 D7
Nevinnomyssk, *Russia* 25 F7
Nevis, *W. Indies* 89 C7
Nevyansk, *Russia* 24 C11
New Albany, *Ind., U.S.A.* 76 F3
New Albany, *Miss., U.S.A.* 81 H10
New Albany, *Pa., U.S.A.* 79 E8
New Amsterdam, *Guyana* 92 B7
New Angledool, *Australia* 63 D4
New Bedford, *U.S.A.* 79 E14
New Bern, *U.S.A.* 77 H7
New Bethlehem, *U.S.A.* 78 E5
New Bloomfield, *U.S.A.* 78 F7
New Boston, *U.S.A.* 81 J7
New Braunfels, *U.S.A.* 81 L5
New Brighton, *N.Z.* 59 K4
New Brighton, *U.S.A.* 78 F4
New Britain, *Papua N. G.* 64 H7
New Britain, *U.S.A.* 79 E12
New Brunswick, *U.S.A.* 79 F10
New Brunswick □, *Canada* 71 C6
New Caledonia, *Pac. Oc.* 64 K8
New Castile = Castilla La Mancha □, *Spain* 19 C4
New Castle, *Ind., U.S.A.* 76 F3
New Castle, *Pa., U.S.A.* 78 E4
New City, *U.S.A.* 79 E11
New Cumberland, *U.S.A.* 78 F4
New Cuyama, *U.S.A.* 85 L7
New Delhi, *India* 42 E7
New Denver, *Canada* 72 D5
New Don Pedro Res., *U.S.A.* 84 H6
New England, *U.S.A.* 80 B3
New England Ra., *Australia* 63 E5
New Forest, *U.K.* 11 G6
New Glasgow, *Canada* 71 C7
New Guinea, *Oceania* 64 H5
New Hamburg, *Canada* 78 C4
New Hampshire □, *U.S.A.* 79 C13
New Hampton, *U.S.A.* 80 D8
New Hanover, *S. Africa* 57 D5
New Haven, *Conn., U.S.A.* 79 E12
New Haven, *Mich., U.S.A.* 78 D2
New Hazelton, *Canada* 72 B3
New Hebrides = Vanuatu ■, *Pac. Oc.* 64 J8
New Iberia, *U.S.A.* 81 K9
New Ireland, *Papua N. G.* 64 H7
New Jersey □, *U.S.A.* 79 F10
New Kensington, *U.S.A.* 78 F5
New Lexington, *U.S.A.* 76 F4
New Liskeard, *Canada* 70 C4
New London, *Conn., U.S.A.* 79 E12
New London, *Minn., U.S.A.* 80 C7
New London, *Ohio, U.S.A.* 78 E2
New London, *Wis., U.S.A.* 80 C10
New Madrid, *U.S.A.* 81 G10
New Meadows, *U.S.A.* 82 D5
New Melones L., *U.S.A.* 84 H6
New Mexico □, *U.S.A.* 74 D5
New Milford, *Conn., U.S.A.* 79 E11
New Milford, *Pa., U.S.A.* 79 E9
New Norcia, *Australia* 61 F2
New Norfolk, *Australia* 62 G4
New Orleans, *U.S.A.* 81 K9
New Philadelphia, *U.S.A.* 78 F3
New Plymouth, *N.Z.* 59 H5
New Plymouth, *U.S.A.* 82 E5
New Providence, *Bahamas* 88 A4
New Radnor, *U.K.* 11 E4
New Richmond, *U.S.A.* 80 C8
New Roads, *U.S.A.* 81 K9
New Rochelle, *U.S.A.* 79 F11
New Rockford, *U.S.A.* 80 B5
New Ross, *Ireland* 13 D5
New Salem, *U.S.A.* 80 B4
New Scone, *U.K.* 12 E5
New Siberian Is. = Novosibirskiye Ostrova, *Russia* 27 B15
New Smyrna Beach, *U.S.A.* 77 L5
New South Wales □, *Australia* 63 E4
New Springs, *Australia* 61 E3
New Town, *U.S.A.* 80 A3
New Ulm, *U.S.A.* 80 C7
New Waterford, *Canada* 71 C7
New Westminster, *Canada* 72 D4
New York □, *U.S.A.* 79 D9
New York City, *U.S.A.* 79 F11
New Zealand ■, *Oceania* 59 J5
Newala, *Tanzania* 55 E4
Newala □, *Tanzania* 55 E4
Newark, *Del., U.S.A.* 76 F8
Newark, *N.J., U.S.A.* 79 F10
Newark, *N.Y., U.S.A.* 78 C7
Newark, *Ohio, U.S.A.* 78 F2
Newark-on-Trent, *U.K.* 10 D7
Newaygo, *U.S.A.* 76 D3
Newberg, *U.S.A.* 82 D2
Newberry, *Mich., U.S.A.* 76 B3
Newberry, *S.C., U.S.A.* 77 H5
Newberry Springs, *U.S.A.* 85 L10
Newbrook, *Canada* 72 C6
Newburgh, *U.S.A.* 79 E10
Newbury, *U.K.* 11 F6
Newbury, *U.S.A.* 79 B12
Newburyport, *U.S.A.* 79 D14
Newcastle, *Australia* 63 E5
Newcastle, *Canada* 71 C6
Newcastle, *S. Africa* 57 D4
Newcastle, *U.K.* 13 B6
Newcastle, *Calif., U.S.A.* 84 G5
Newcastle, *Wyo., U.S.A.* 80 D2
Newcastle Emlyn, *U.K.* 11 E3
Newcastle Ra., *Australia* 60 C5
Newcastle-under-Lyme, *U.K.* 10 D5
Newcastle-upon-Tyne, *U.K.* 10 C6
Newcastle Waters, *Australia* 62 B1
Newdegate, *Australia* 61 F2
Newell, *U.S.A.* 80 C3
Newfoundland □, *Canada* 71 B8
Newhalem, *U.S.A.* 72 D4
Newhall, *U.S.A.* 85 L8
Newham, *U.K.* 11 F8
Newhaven, *U.K.* 11 G8
Newkirk, *U.S.A.* 81 G6
Newman, *Australia* 60 D2
Newman, *U.S.A.* 84 H5
Newmarket, *Canada* 78 B5
Newmarket, *Ireland* 13 D3
Newmarket, *U.K.* 11 E8
Newmarket, *U.S.A.* 79 C14
Newnan, *U.S.A.* 77 J3
Newport, *Gwent, U.K.* 11 F5
Newport, *I. of W., U.K.* 11 G6
Newport, *Shrops., U.K.* 11 E5
Newport, *Ark., U.S.A.* 81 H9
Newport, *Ky., U.S.A.* 76 F3
Newport, *N.H., U.S.A.* 79 C12
Newport, *Oreg., U.S.A.* 82 D1
Newport, *Pa., U.S.A.* 78 F7
Newport, *R.I., U.S.A.* 79 E13
Newport, *Tenn., U.S.A.* 77 H4
Newport, *Vt., U.S.A.* 79 B12
Newport, *Wash., U.S.A.* 82 B5
Newport Beach, *U.S.A.* 85 M9
Newport News, *U.S.A.* 76 G7
Newquay, *U.K.* 11 G2
Newry, *U.K.* 13 B5
Newry & Mourne □, *U.K.* 13 B5
Newton, *Iowa, U.S.A.* 80 E8
Newton, *Mass., U.S.A.* 79 D13
Newton, *Miss., U.S.A.* 81 J10
Newton, *N.C., U.S.A.* 77 H5
Newton, *N.J., U.S.A.* 79 E10
Newton, *Tex., U.S.A.* 81 K8
Newton Abbot, *U.K.* 11 G4
Newton Boyd, *Australia* 63 D5
Newton Stewart, *U.K.* 12 G4
Newtonmore, *U.K.* 12 D4
Newtown, *U.K.* 11 E4
Newtownabbey □, *U.K.* 13 B6
Newtownards, *U.K.* 13 B6
Newville, *U.S.A.* 78 F7
Neya, *Russia* 24 C7
Neyrīz, *Iran* 45 D7
Neyshābūr, *Iran* 45 B8
Nezhin, *Ukraine* 25 D5
Nezperce, *U.S.A.* 82 C5
Ngabang, *Indonesia* 36 D3
Ngabordamlu, Tanjung, *Indonesia* 37 F8
Ngami Depression, *Botswana* 56 C3
Ngamo, *Zimbabwe* 55 F2
Nganglong Kangri, *China* 41 C12
Nganjuk, *Indonesia* 37 G14
Ngao, *Thailand* 38 C2
Ngaoundéré, *Cameroon* 52 C2
Ngapara, *N.Z.* 59 L3
Ngara, *Tanzania* 54 C3
Ngara □, *Tanzania* 54 C3
Ngawi, *Indonesia* 37 G14
Nghia Lo, *Vietnam* 38 B5
Ngoma, *Malawi* 55 E3
Ngomahura, *Zimbabwe* 55 G3
Ngomba, *Tanzania* 55 D3
Ngoring Hu, *China* 32 C4
Ngorongoro, *Tanzania* 54 C4
Ngozi, *Burundi* 54 C2
Ngudu, *Tanzania* 54 C3
Nguigmi, *Niger* 51 F7
Ngukurr, *Australia* 62 A1
Ngunga, *Tanzania* 54 C3
Nguru, *Nigeria* 50 F7
Nguru Mts., *Tanzania* 54 D4
Nguyen Binh, *Vietnam* 38 A5
Nha Trang, *Vietnam* 39 F7
Nhacoongo, *Mozam.* 57 C6
Nhamaabué, *Mozam.* 55 F4
Nhangutazi, L., *Mozam.* 57 C5
Nhill, *Australia* 63 F3
Nho Quan, *Vietnam* 38 B5
Nhulunbuy, *Australia* 62 A2
Nia-nia, *Zaïre* 54 B2
Niafounké, *Mali* 50 E4
Niagara, *U.S.A.* 76 C1
Niagara Falls, *Canada* 70 D4
Niagara Falls, *U.S.A.* 78 C6
Niagara-on-the-Lake, *Canada* 78 C5
Niah, *Malaysia* 36 D4
Niamey, *Niger* 50 F5
Niangara, *Zaïre* 54 B2
Nias, *Indonesia* 36 D1
Niassa □, *Mozam.* 55 E4
Nicaragua ■, *Cent. Amer.* 88 D2
Nicaragua, L. de, *Nic.* 88 D2
Nicastro, *Italy* 20 E7
Nice, *France* 18 E7
Niceville, *U.S.A.* 77 K2
Nichinan, *Japan* 31 J5
Nicholás, Canal, *W. Indies* 88 B3
Nicholasville, *U.S.A.* 76 G3
Nichols, *U.S.A.* 79 D8
Nicholson, *Australia* 60 C4
Nicholson, *U.S.A.* 79 E9
Nicholson →, *Australia* 62 B2
Nicholson Ra., *Australia* 61 E2
Nicobar Is., *Ind. Oc.* 28 J13
Nicola, *Canada* 72 C4
Nicolet, *Canada* 70 C5
Nicolls Town, *Bahamas* 88 A4
Nicosia, *Cyprus* 23 D12
Nicoya, *Costa Rica* 88 D2
Nicoya, G. de, *Costa Rica* 88 E3
Nicoya, Pen. de, *Costa Rica* 88 E2
Nidd →, *U.K.* 10 C6
Niekerkshoop, *S. Africa* 56 D3
Niemba, *Zaïre* 54 D2
Nienburg, *Germany* 16 B4
Nieu Bethesda, *S. Africa* 56 E3
Nieuw Amsterdam, *Surinam* 93 B7
Nieuw Nickerie, *Surinam* 93 B7
Nieuwoudtville, *S. Africa* 56 E2
Nieuwpoort, *Belgium* 15 C2
Nieves, Pico de las, *Canary Is.* 22 G4
Nièvre □, *France* 18 C5
Niğde, *Turkey* 25 G5
Nigel, *S. Africa* 57 D4
Niger ■, *W. Afr.* 50 E6
Niger →, *W. Afr.* 50 G6
Nigeria ■, *W. Afr.* 50 G6
Nightcaps, *N.Z.* 59 L2
Nihtaur, *India* 43 E8
Nii-Jima, *Japan* 31 G9
Niigata, *Japan* 30 F9
Niigata □, *Japan* 31 F9
Niihama, *Japan* 31 H6
Niihau, *U.S.A.* 74 H14
Niimi, *Japan* 31 G6
Niitsu, *Japan* 30 F9
Nijil, *Jordan* 47 E4
Nijkerk, *Neths.* 15 B5
Nijmegen, *Neths.* 15 C5
Nijverdal, *Neths.* 15 B6
Nīk Pey, *Iran* 45 B6
Nikel, *Russia* 8 B21
Nikiniki, *Indonesia* 37 F6
Nikki, *Benin* 50 G5
Nikkō, *Japan* 31 F9
Nikolayev, *Ukraine* 25 E5
Nikolayevsk, *Russia* 25 D8
Nikolayevsk-na-Amur, *Russia* 27 D15
Nikolskoye, *Russia* 27 D17
Nikopol, *Ukraine* 25 E5
Nīkshahr, *Iran* 45 E9
Nîl, Nahr en →, *Africa* 51 B11
Nîl el Abyad →, *Sudan* 51 E11
Nîl el Azraq →, *Sudan* 51 E11
Niland, *U.S.A.* 85 M11
Nile = Nîl, Nahr en →, *Africa* 51 B11
Nile □, *Uganda* 54 B3
Niles, *U.S.A.* 78 E4
Nimach, *India* 42 G6
Nimbahera, *India* 42 G6
Nîmes, *France* 18 E6
Nimmitabel, *Australia* 63 F4
Nimneryskiy, *Russia* 27 D13
Nimule, *Sudan* 52 D6
Ninawá, *Iraq* 44 B4
Nindigully, *Australia* 63 D4
Ninemile, *U.S.A.* 72 B2
Nineveh = Nīnawá, *Iraq* 44 B4
Ning Xian, *China* 34 G4
Ningaloo, *Australia* 60 D1
Ning'an, *China* 35 B15
Ningbo, *China* 33 D7
Ningcheng, *China* 35 D10
Ningjin, *China* 34 F8
Ningjing Shan, *China* 32 C4
Ningling, *China* 34 G8
Ningpo = Ningbo, *China* 33 D7
Ningqiang, *China* 34 H4
Ningshan, *China* 34 H5
Ningsia Hui A.R. = Ningxia Huizu Zizhiqu □, *China* 34 E3
Ningwu, *China* 34 E7
Ningxia Huizu Zizhiqu □, *China* 34 E3
Ningyang, *China* 34 G9
Ninh Binh, *Vietnam* 38 B5
Ninh Giang, *Vietnam* 38 B6
Ninh Hoa, *Vietnam* 38 F7
Ninh Ma, *Vietnam* 38 F7
Ninove, *Belgium* 15 D4
Nioaque, *Brazil* 95 A4
Niobrara, *U.S.A.* 80 D6
Niobrara →, *U.S.A.* 80 D6
Nioro du Sahel, *Mali* 50 E3
Niort, *France* 18 C3
Nipawin, *Canada* 73 C8
Nipawin Prov. Park, *Canada* 73 C8
Nipigon, *Canada* 70 C2
Nipigon, L., *Canada* 70 C2
Nipin →, *Canada* 73 B7
Nipishish L., *Canada* 71 B7
Nipissing L., *Canada* 70 C4
Nipomo, *U.S.A.* 85 K6
Nipton, *U.S.A.* 85 K11
Niquelândia, *Brazil* 93 F9
Nīr, *Iran* 44 B5
Nirasaki, *Japan* 31 G9
Nirmal, *India* 40 K11
Nirmali, *India* 43 F12
Niš, *Serbia, Yug.* 21 C9
Nişāb, *Yemen* 46 E4
Nishinomiya, *Japan* 31 G7
Nishin'omote, *Japan* 31 J5
Nishiwaki, *Japan* 31 G7
Niskibi →, *Canada* 70 A2
Nisqually →, *U.S.A.* 84 C4
Nissáki, *Greece* 23 A3
Nisutlin →, *Canada* 72 A2
Nitchequon, *Canada* 71 B5
Niterói, *Brazil* 95 A7
Nith →, *U.K.* 12 F5
Nitra, *Czech.* 17 D9
Nitra →, *Czech.* 17 E9
Niuafo'ou, *Tonga* 59 B11
Niue, *Cook Is.* 65 J11
Niut, *Indonesia* 36 D4
Niuzhuang, *China* 35 D12
Nivelles, *Belgium* 15 D4
Nivernais, *France* 18 C5
Nixon, *U.S.A.* 81 L6
Nizamabad, *India* 40 K11
Nizamghat, *India* 41 E19
Nizhne Kolymsk, *Russia* 27 C17
Nizhne-Vartovsk, *Russia* 26 C8
Nizhneangarsk, *Russia* 27 D11
Nizhnekamsk, *Russia* 24 C9
Nizhneudinsk, *Russia* 27 D10
Nizhneyansk, *Russia* 27 B14
Nizhniy Novgorod, *Russia* 24 C7
Nizhniy Tagil, *Russia* 24 C10
Nizké Tatry, *Czech.* 17 D9
Njakwa, *Malawi* 55 E3
Njanji, *Zambia* 55 E3
Njinjo, *Tanzania* 55 D4
Njombe, *Tanzania* 55 D3
Njombe □, *Tanzania* 55 D3
Njombe →, *Tanzania* 54 D4
Nkambe, *Cameroon* 50 G7
Nkana, *Zambia* 55 E2
Nkawkaw, *Ghana* 50 G4
Nkayi, *Zimbabwe* 55 F2
Nkhata Bay, *Malawi* 52 G6
Nkhota Kota, *Malawi* 55 E3
Nkongsamba, *Cameroon* 50 H6
Nkurenkuru, *Namibia* 56 B2
Nmai →, *Burma* 41 G20
Noakhali = Maijdi, *Bangla.* 41 H17
Noatak, *U.S.A.* 68 B3
Nobel, *Canada* 78 A4
Nobeoka, *Japan* 31 H5
Noblesville, *U.S.A.* 76 E3
Nocera Inferiore, *Italy* 20 D6
Nockatunga, *Australia* 63 D3
Nocona, *U.S.A.* 81 J6
Noda, *Japan* 31 G9
Noel, *U.S.A.* 81 G7
Nogales, *Mexico* 86 A2
Nogales, *U.S.A.* 83 L8
Nōgata, *Japan* 31 H5
Noggerup, *Australia* 61 F2
Noginsk, *Russia* 27 C10
Nogoa →, *Australia* 62 C4
Nogoyá, *Argentina* 94 C4
Nohar, *India* 42 E6
Noirmoutier, I. de, *France* 18 C2
Nojane, *Botswana* 56 C3
Nojima-Zaki, *Japan* 31 G9
Nok Kundi, *Pakistan* 40 E3
Nokaneng, *Botswana* 56 B3
Nokhtuysk, *Russia* 27 C12
Nokomis, *Canada* 73 C8
Nokomis L., *Canada* 73 B8
Nola, *C.A.R.* 52 D3
Noma Omuramba →, *Namibia* 56 B3
Noman L., *Canada* 73 A7
Nombre de Dios, *Panama* 88 E4
Nome, *U.S.A.* 68 B3
Nomo-Zaki, *Japan* 31 H4
Nonacho L., *Canada* 73 A7
Nonda, *Australia* 62 C3
Nong Chang, *Thailand* 38 E2
Nong Het, *Laos* 38 C4
Nong Khai, *Thailand* 38 D4
Nong'an, *China* 35 B13
Nongoma, *S. Africa* 57 D5
Nonoava, *Mexico* 86 B3
Nonthaburi, *Thailand* 38 F3
Noonamah, *Australia* 60 B5
Noonan, *U.S.A.* 80 A3
Noondoo, *Australia* 63 D4
Noonkanbah, *Australia* 60 C3
Noord Brabant □, *Neths.* 15 C5
Noord Holland □, *Neths.* 15 B4
Noordbeveland, *Neths.* 15 C3
Noordoostpolder, *Neths.* 15 B5
Noordwijk aan Zee, *Neths.* 15 B4
Nootka, *Canada* 72 D3
Nootka I., *Canada* 72 D3
Nóqui, *Angola* 52 F2
Noranda, *Canada* 70 C4
Norco, *U.S.A.* 85 M9
Nord □, *France* 18 A5
Nord-Ostsee Kanal, *Germany* 16 A4
Nord-Trøndelag fylke □, *Norway* 8 D12
Nordaustlandet, *Svalbard* 4 B9
Nordegg, *Canada* 72 C5
Nordhausen, *Germany* 16 C5
Nordkapp, *Norway* 8 A18
Nordkapp, *Svalbard* 4 A9
Nordkinn = Kinnarodden, *Norway* 6 A11
Nordland fylke □, *Norway* 8 D12
Nordrhein-Westfalen □, *Germany* 16 C3
Nordvik, *Russia* 27 B12
Norembega, *Canada* 70 C3
Norfolk, *Nebr., U.S.A.* 80 D6
Norfolk, *Va., U.S.A.* 76 G7
Norfolk □, *U.K.* 10 E9
Norfolk Broads, *U.K.* 10 E9
Norfolk I., *Pac. Oc.* 64 K8
Norfork Res., *U.S.A.* 81 G8
Norilsk, *Russia* 27 C9
Norley, *Australia* 63 D3
Norma, Mt., *Australia* 62 C3
Normal, *U.S.A.* 80 E10
Norman, *U.S.A.* 81 H6
Norman →, *Australia* 62 B3
Norman Wells, *Canada* 68 B7
Normanby →, *Australia* 62 A3
Normandie, *France* 18 B4
Normandin, *Canada* 70 C5

Normandy = Normandie, France 18 B4
Normanhurst, Mt., Australia 61 E3
Normanton, Australia 62 B3
Norquay, Canada 73 C8
Norquinco, Argentina 96 E2
Norrbotten □, Sweden 8 C17
Norrby, Sweden 8 D15
Nørresundby, Denmark 9 H10
Norris, U.S.A. 82 D8
Norristown, U.S.A. 79 F9
Norrköping, Sweden 9 G14
Norrland, Sweden 8 E13
Norrtälje, Sweden 9 G15
Norseman, Australia 61 F3
Norsk, Russia 27 D14
Norte, Pta. del, Canary Is. 22 G2
North Adams, U.S.A. 79 D11
North America 66 F10
North Battleford, Canada 73 C7
North Bay, Canada 70 C4
North Belcher Is., Canada 70 A4
North Bend, Canada 72 D4
North Bend, Oreg., U.S.A. 82 E1
North Bend, Pa., U.S.A. 78 E7
North Bend, Wash., U.S.A. 84 C5
North Berwick, U.K. 12 E6
North Berwick, U.S.A. 79 C14
North Buganda □, Uganda 54 B3
North Canadian →, U.S.A. 81 H7
North C., Canada 71 C7
North C., N.Z. 59 F4
North Caribou L., Canada 70 B1
North Carolina □, U.S.A. 77 H5
North Channel, Canada 70 C3
North Channel, U.K. 12 G3
North Chicago, U.S.A. 76 D2
North Dakota □, U.S.A. 80 B5
North Dandalup, Australia 61 F2
North Down □, U.K. 13 B6
North Downs, U.K. 11 F8
North East, U.S.A. 78 D5
North East Frontier Agency = Arunachal Pradesh □, India 41 E19
North East Providence Chan., W. Indies 88 A4
North Eastern □, Kenya 54 B5
North Esk →, U.K. 12 E6
North European Plain, Europe 6 D11
North Foreland, U.K. 11 F9
North Fork, U.S.A. 84 H7
North Fork American →, U.S.A. 84 G5
North Fork Feather →, U.S.A. 84 F5
North Henik L., Canada 73 A9
North Highlands, U.S.A. 84 G5
North Horr, Kenya 54 B4
North I., Kenya 54 B4
North I., N.Z. 59 H5
North Kingsville, U.S.A. 78 E4
North Knife →, Canada 73 B10
North Koel →, India 43 G10
North Korea ■, Asia 35 E14
North Lakhimpur, India 41 F19
North Las Vegas, U.S.A. 85 J11
North Loup →, U.S.A. 80 E5
North Magnetic Pole, Canada 4 B2
North Minch, U.K. 12 C3
North Nahanni →, Canada 72 A4
North Olmsted, U.S.A. 78 E3
North Ossetian Republic □, Russia 25 F7
North Pagai, I. = Pagai Utara, Indonesia 36 E2
North Palisade, U.S.A. 83 H4
North Platte, U.S.A. 80 E4
North Platte →, U.S.A. 80 E4
North Pt., Canada 71 C7
North Pole, Arctic 4 A
North Portal, Canada 73 D8
North Powder, U.S.A. 82 D5
North Ronaldsay, U.K. 12 B6
North Saskatchewan →, Canada 73 C7
North Sea, Europe 6 D6
North Sporades = Voríai Sporádhes, Greece 21 E10
North Sydney, Canada 71 C7
North Taranaki Bight, N.Z. 59 H5
North Thompson →, Canada 72 C4
North Tonawanda, U.S.A. 78 C6
North Troy, U.S.A. 79 B12
North Truchas Pk., U.S.A. 83 J11
North Twin I., Canada 70 B3
North Tyne →, U.K. 10 C5
North Uist, U.K. 12 D1
North Vancouver, Canada 72 D4
North Vernon, U.S.A. 76 F3
North Wabasca L., Canada 72 B6
North Walsham, U.K. 10 E9
North West C., Australia 60 D1
North West Christmas I. Ridge, Pac. Oc. 65 G11
North West Frontier □, Pakistan 42 C4
North West Highlands, U.K. 12 D3
North West Providence Channel, W. Indies 88 A4
North West River, Canada 71 B7
North West Territories □, Canada 68 B9
North Western □, Zambia 55 E2
North York Moors, U.K. 10 C7
North Yorkshire □, U.K. 10 C6
Northallerton, U.K. 10 C6
Northam, S. Africa 56 C4
Northampton, Australia 61 E1
Northampton, U.K. 11 E7
Northampton, Mass., U.S.A. 79 D12
Northampton, Pa., U.S.A. 79 F9
Northampton Downs, Australia 62 C4
Northamptonshire □, U.K. 11 E7
Northbridge, U.S.A. 79 D13
Northcliffe, Australia 61 F2
Northern □, Malawi 55 E3
Northern □, Uganda 54 B3
Northern □, Zambia 55 E3
Northern Circars, India 41 L13
Northern Indian L., Canada 73 B9
Northern Ireland □, U.K. 13 B5
Northern Light, L., Canada 70 C1
Northern Marianas □, Pac. Oc. 64 F6
Northern Territory □, Australia 60 D5
Northfield, U.S.A. 80 C8
Northland □, N.Z. 59 F4
Northome, U.S.A. 80 B7
Northport, Ala., U.S.A. 77 J2
Northport, Mich., U.S.A. 76 C3
Northport, Wash., U.S.A. 82 B5
Northumberland □, U.K. 10 B5
Northumberland, C., Australia 63 F3
Northumberland Is., Australia 62 C4
Northumberland Str., Canada 71 C7
Northwich, U.K. 10 D5
Northwood, Iowa, U.S.A. 80 D8
Northwood, N. Dak., U.S.A. 80 B6
Norton, U.S.A. 80 F5
Norton, Zimbabwe 55 F3
Norton Sd., U.S.A. 68 B3
Norwalk, Calif., U.S.A. 85 M8
Norwalk, Conn., U.S.A. 79 E11
Norwalk, Ohio, U.S.A. 78 E2
Norway, U.S.A. 76 C2
Norway ■, Europe 8 E11
Norway House, Canada 73 C9
Norwegian Sea, Atl. Oc. 4 C8
Norwich, Canada 78 D4
Norwich, U.K. 10 E9
Norwich, Conn., U.S.A. 79 E12
Norwich, N.Y., U.S.A. 79 D9
Norwood, Canada 78 B7
Noshiro, Japan 30 D10
Nosok, Russia 26 B9
Noss Hd., U.K. 12 C5
Nossob →, S. Africa 56 D3
Nosy Bé, Madag. 53 G9
Nosy Boraha, Madag. 57 B8
Nosy Mitsio, Madag. 53 G9
Nosy Varika, Madag. 57 C8
Notigi Dam, Canada 73 B9
Notikewin →, Canada 72 B5
Noto, Italy 20 F6
Notre-Dame, Canada 71 C7
Notre Dame B., Canada 71 C8
Notre Dame de Koartac = Koartac, Canada 69 B13
Notre Dame d'Ivugivic = Ivugivik, Canada 69 B12
Nottaway →, Canada 70 B4
Nottingham, U.K. 10 E6
Nottinghamshire □, U.K. 10 D7
Nottoway →, U.S.A. 76 G7
Notwane →, Botswana 56 C4
Nouâdhibou, Mauritania 50 D1
Nouâdhibou, Ras, Mauritania 50 D1
Nouakchott, Mauritania 50 E1
Nouméa, N. Cal. 64 K8
Noupoort, S. Africa 56 E3
Nouveau Comptoir, Canada 70 B4
Nouvelle-Calédonie = New Caledonia, Pac. Oc. 64 K8
Nova Casa Nova, Brazil 93 E10
Nova Cruz, Brazil 93 E11
Nova Esperança, Brazil 95 A5
Nova Friburgo, Brazil 95 A7
Nova Gaia = Cambundi-Catembo, Angola 52 G3
Nova Iguaçu, Brazil 95 A7
Nova Iorque, Brazil 93 E10
Nova Lima, Brazil 95 A7
Nova Lisboa = Huambo, Angola 53 G3
Nova Lusitânia, Mozam. 55 F3
Nova Mambone, Mozam. 57 C6
Nova Scotia □, Canada 71 C7
Nova Sofala, Mozam. 57 C5
Nova Venécia, Brazil 93 G10
Novara, Italy 20 B3
Novata, U.S.A. 84 G4
Novaya Ladoga, Russia 24 B5
Novaya Lyalya, Russia 26 D7
Novaya Sibir, Ostrov, Russia 27 B16
Novaya Zemlya, Russia 26 B6
Nové Zámky, Czech. 17 D9
Novgorod, Russia 24 C5
Novgorod-Severskiy, Ukraine 24 D5
Novi Sad, Serbia, Yug. 21 B8
Nôvo Hamburgo, Brazil 95 B5
Novo Remanso, Brazil 93 E10
Novoataysk, Russia 26 D9
Novocherkassk, Russia 25 E7
Novokachalinsk, Russia 30 B6
Novokazalinsk, Kazakhstan 26 E7
Novokuybyshevsk, Russia 24 D8
Novokuznetsk, Russia 26 D9
Novomoskovsk, Russia 24 D6
Novorossiysk, Russia 25 F6
Novorybnoye, Russia 27 B11
Novoshakhtinsk, Russia 25 E6
Novosibirsk, Russia 26 D9
Novosibirskiye Ostrova, Russia 27 B15
Novotroitsk, Russia 26 D6
Novouzensk, Russia 25 D8
Novska, Croatia 20 B7
Novvy Port, Russia 26 C8
Now Shahr, Iran 45 B6
Nowbarān, Iran 45 C6
Nowghāb, Iran 45 C8
Nowgong, India 41 F18
Nowra, Australia 63 E5
Nowshera, Pakistan 40 B8
Nowy Sącz, Poland 17 D10
Nowy Tomyśl, Poland 16 B8
Noxen, U.S.A. 79 E8
Noxon, U.S.A. 82 C6
Noyes I., U.S.A. 72 B2
Noyon, Mongolia 34 C2
Nsanje, Malawi 55 F4
Nsawam, Ghana 50 G4
Nsomba, Zambia 55 E2
Nsukka, Nigeria 50 G6
Nu Jiang →, China 32 D4
Nu Shan, China 32 D4
Nubian Desert = Nûbîya, Es Sahrâ En, Sudan 51 D11
Nûbîya, Es Sahrâ En, Sudan 51 D11
Ñuble □, Chile 94 D1
Nuboai, Indonesia 37 E9
Nubra →, India 43 B7
Nueces →, U.S.A. 81 M6
Nueltin L., Canada 73 A9
Nueva Asunción □, Paraguay 94 A3
Nueva Gerona, Cuba 88 B3
Nueva Imperial, Chile 96 D2
Nueva Palmira, Uruguay 94 C4
Nueva Rosita, Mexico 86 B4
Nueva San Salvador, El Salv. 88 D2
Nuéve de Julio, Argentina 94 D3
Nuevitas, Cuba 88 B4
Nuevo, G., Argentina 96 E4
Nuevo Guerrero, Mexico 87 B5
Nuevo Laredo, Mexico 87 B5
Nuevo León □, Mexico 86 C4
Nugget Pt., N.Z. 59 M2
Nuhaka, N.Z. 59 H6
Nukey Bluff, Australia 63 E2
Nukheila, Sudan 51 E10
Nuku'alofa, Tonga 59 E11
Nukus, Uzbekistan 26 E6
Nulato, U.S.A. 68 B4
Nullagine →, Australia 60 D3
Nullarbor, Australia 61 F5
Nullarbor Plain, Australia 61 F4
Numalla, L., Australia 63 D3
Numan, Nigeria 51 G7
Numata, Japan 31 F9
Numazu, Japan 31 G9
Numbulwar, Australia 62 A2
Numfoor, Indonesia 37 E8
Numurkah, Australia 63 F4
Nunaksaluk I., Canada 71 A7
Nuneaton, U.K. 11 E6
Nungo, Mozam. 55 E4
Nungwe, Tanzania 54 C3
Nunivak, U.S.A. 68 B3
Nunkun, India 43 C7
Nunspeet, Neths. 15 B5
Nūrābād, Iran 45 E8
Nuremburg = Nürnberg, Germany 16 D5
Nuri, Mexico 86 B3
Nurina, Australia 61 F4
Nuriootpa, Australia 63 E2
Nürnberg, Germany 16 D5
Nurran, L. = Terewah, L., Australia 63 D4
Nurrari Lakes, Australia 61 E5
Nusa Barung, Indonesia 37 H15
Nusa Kambangan, Indonesia 37 G13
Nusa Tenggara Barat □, Indonesia 36 F5
Nusa Tenggara Timur □, Indonesia 37 F6
Nusaybin, Turkey 25 G7
Nushki, Pakistan 42 E2
Nutak, Canada 69 C13
Nutwood Downs, Australia 62 B1
Nuuk = Godthåb, Greenland 69 B14
Nuwakot, Nepal 43 E10
Nuweveldberge, S. Africa 56 E3
Nuyts, C., Australia 61 F5
Nuyts Arch., Australia 63 E1
Nxau-Nxau, Botswana 56 B3
Nyack, U.S.A. 79 E11
Nyah West, Australia 63 F3
Nyahanga, Tanzania 54 C3
Nyahua, Tanzania 54 D3
Nyahururu, Kenya 54 B4
Nyainqentanglha Shan, China 32 D3
Nyakanazi, Tanzania 54 C3
Nyâlâ, Sudan 51 F9
Nyamandhlovu, Zimbabwe 55 F2
Nyambiti, Tanzania 54 C3
Nyamwaga, Tanzania 54 C3
Nyandekwa, Tanzania 54 C3
Nyandoma, Russia 24 B7
Nyangana, Namibia 56 B3
Nyanguge, Tanzania 54 C3
Nyanza, Burundi 54 C2
Nyanza, Rwanda 54 C2
Nyanza □, Kenya 54 C3
Nyarling →, Canada 72 A6
Nyasa, L. = Malawi, L., Africa 55 E3
Nyazepetrovsk, Russia 24 C10
Nyazura, Zimbabwe 55 F3
Nyazwidzi →, Zimbabwe 55 F3
Nybro, Sweden 9 H13
Nyda, Russia 26 C8
Nyeri, Kenya 54 C4
Nyíregyháza, Hungary 17 E10
Nykarleby, Finland 8 E17
Nykøbing, Denmark 9 J11
Nyköping, Sweden 9 G14
Nylstroom, S. Africa 57 C4
Nymagee, Australia 63 E4
Nynäshamn, Sweden 9 G14
Nyngan, Australia 63 E4
Nysa, Poland 17 C8
Nysa →, Europe 16 B7
Nyssa, U.S.A. 82 E5
Nyunzu, Zaïre 54 D2
Nyurba, Russia 27 C12
Nzega, Tanzania 54 C3
Nzega □, Tanzania 54 C3
N'Zérékoré, Guinea 50 G3
Nzeto, Angola 52 F2
Nzilo, Chutes de, Zaïre 55 E2
Nzubuka, Tanzania 54 C3

O

Ō-Shima, Nagasaki, Japan 31 G4
Ō-Shima, Shizuoka, Japan 31 G9
Oacoma, U.S.A. 80 D5
Oahe Dam, U.S.A. 80 C4
Oahe L., U.S.A. 80 C4
Oahu, U.S.A. 74 H16
Oak Creek, U.S.A. 82 F10
Oak Harbour, U.S.A. 84 B4
Oak Hill, U.S.A. 76 G5
Oak Park, U.S.A. 76 E2
Oak Ridge, U.S.A. 77 G3
Oak View, U.S.A. 85 L7
Oakan-Dake, Japan 30 C12
Oakbank, Australia 63 E3
Oakdale, Calif., U.S.A. 83 H3
Oakdale, La., U.S.A. 81 K8
Oakengates, U.K. 10 E5
Oakes, U.S.A. 80 B5
Oakesdale, U.S.A. 82 C5
Oakey, Australia 63 D5
Oakham, U.K. 10 E7
Oakhurst, U.S.A. 84 H7
Oakland, Calif., U.S.A. 83 H2
Oakland, Oreg., U.S.A. 82 E2
Oakland City, U.S.A. 76 F2
Oakley, Idaho, U.S.A. 82 E7
Oakley, Kans., U.S.A. 80 F4
Oakover →, Australia 60 D3
Oakridge, U.S.A. 82 E2
Oakville, U.S.A. 84 D3
Oamaru, N.Z. 59 L3
Oasis, Calif., U.S.A. 85 M10
Oasis, Nev., U.S.A. 84 H9
Oates Land, Antarctica 5 C11
Oatman, U.S.A. 85 K12
Oaxaca, Mexico 87 D5
Oaxaca □, Mexico 87 D5
Ob →, Russia 26 C7
Oba, Canada 70 C3
Obama, Japan 31 G7
Oban, U.K. 12 E3
Obbia, Somali Rep. 46 F4
Obed, Canada 72 C5
Obera, Argentina 95 B4
Oberhausen, Germany 16 C3
Oberlin, Kans., U.S.A. 80 F4
Oberlin, La., U.S.A. 81 K8
Oberlin, Ohio, U.S.A. 78 E2
Oberon, Australia 63 E4
Obi, Kepulauan, Indonesia 37 E7
Obi Is. = Obi, Kepulauan, Indonesia 37 E7
Óbidos, Brazil 93 D7
Obihiro, Japan 30 C11
Obilatu, Indonesia 37 E7
Obluchye, Russia 27 E14
Obo, C.A.R. 54 A2
Oboa, Mt., Uganda 54 B3
Oboyan, Russia 26 D4
Obozerskaya, Russia 26 C5
Observatory Inlet, Canada 72 B3
Obshchi Syrt, Kazakhstan 6 E16
Obskaya Guba, Russia 26 C8
Obuasi, Ghana 50 G4
Ocala, U.S.A. 77 L4
Ocampo, Mexico 86 B3
Ocaña, Spain 19 C4
Ocanomowoc, U.S.A. 80 D10
Ocate, U.S.A. 81 G2
Occidental, Cordillera, Colombia 92 C3
Ocean City, N.J., U.S.A. 76 F8
Ocean City, Wash., U.S.A. 84 C2
Ocean I. = Banaba, Kiribati 64 H8
Ocean Park, U.S.A. 84 D2
Oceano, U.S.A. 85 K6
Oceanport, U.S.A. 79 F10
Oceanside, U.S.A. 85 M9
Ochil Hills, U.K. 12 E5
Ochre River, Canada 73 C9
Ocilla, U.S.A. 77 K4
Ocmulgee →, U.S.A. 77 K4
Oconee →, U.S.A. 77 K4
Oconto, U.S.A. 76 C2
Oconto Falls, U.S.A. 76 C1
Ocosingo, Mexico 87 D6
Ocotal, Nic. 88 D2
Ocotlán, Mexico 86 C4
Octave, U.S.A. 83 J7
Ocumare del Tuy, Venezuela 92 A5
Ōda, Japan 31 G6
Ódáðahraun, Iceland 8 D5
Odate, Japan 30 D10
Odawara, Japan 31 G9
Odda, Norway 9 F9
Oddur, Somali Rep. 46 G3
Odei →, Canada 73 B9
Odendaalsrus, S. Africa 56 D4
Odense, Denmark 9 J11
Oder →, Germany 16 B7
Odessa, Canada 79 B8
Odessa, Ukraine 25 E5
Odessa, Tex., U.S.A. 81 K3
Odessa, Wash., U.S.A. 82 C4
Odiakwe, Botswana 56 C4
Odienné, Ivory C. 50 G3
Odintsovo, Russia 24 C6
O'Donnell, U.S.A. 81 J4
Odorheiu Secuiesc, Romania 17 E12
Odra →, Poland 16 B7
Odžak, Bos. & H., Yug. 21 B8
Odzi, Zimbabwe 57 B5
Oeiras, Brazil 93 E10
Oelrichs, U.S.A. 80 D3
Oelwein, U.S.A. 80 D9
Oenpelli, Australia 60 B5
Ofanto →, Italy 20 D7
Offa, Nigeria 50 G5
Offenbach, Germany 16 C4
Ofotfjorden, Norway 8 B14
Ōfunato, Japan 30 E10
Oga, Japan 30 E9
Oga-Hantō, Japan 30 E9
Ogahalla, Canada 70 B2
Ōgaki, Japan 31 G8
Ogallala, U.S.A. 80 E4
Ogasawara Gunto, Pac. Oc. 64 E6
Ogbomosho, Nigeria 50 G5
Ogden, Iowa, U.S.A. 80 D8
Ogden, Utah, U.S.A. 82 F7
Ogdensburg, U.S.A. 79 B9
Ogeechee →, U.S.A. 77 K5
Ogilby, U.S.A. 85 N12
Oglio →, Italy 20 B4
Ogmore, Australia 62 C4
Ogoki →, Canada 70 B2
Ogoki L., Canada 70 B2
Ogoki Res., Canada 70 B2
Ogooué →, Gabon 52 E1
Ogowe = Ogooué →, Gabon 52 E1
Ohai, N.Z. 59 L2
Ohakune, N.Z. 59 H5
Ohanet, Algeria 50 C6
Ohata, Japan 30 D10
Ohau, L., N.Z. 59 L2
Ohey, Belgium 15 D5
Ohio □, U.S.A. 76 E3
Ohio →, U.S.A. 76 G1
Ohre →, Czech. 16 C7
Ohridsko, Jezero, Macedonia, Yug. 21 D9
Ohrigstad, S. Africa 57 C5
Oikou, China 35 E9
Oil City, U.S.A. 78 E5
Oildale, U.S.A. 85 K7
Oise □, France 18 B5
Ōita, Japan 31 H5
Ōita □, Japan 31 H5
Oiticica, Brazil 93 E10
Ojai, U.S.A. 85 L7
Ojinaga, Mexico 86 B4
Ojiya, Japan 31 F9
Ojos del Salado, Cerro, Argentina 94 B2
Oka →, Russia 26 D5
Okaba, Indonesia 37 F9
Okahandja, Namibia 56 C2
Okahukura, N.Z. 59 H5
Okanagan L., Canada 72 C5
Okandja, Gabon 52 E2
Okanogan, U.S.A. 82 B4
Okanogan →, U.S.A. 82 B4
Okaputa, Namibia 56 C2
Okara, Pakistan 42 D5
Okarito, N.Z. 59 K3
Okaukuejo, Namibia 56 B2
Okavango Swamps, Botswana 56 B3
Okaya, Japan 31 F9
Okayama, Japan 31 G6
Okayama □, Japan 31 G6
Okazaki, Japan 31 G8
Okeechobee, U.S.A. 77 M5
Okeechobee, L., U.S.A. 77 M5
Okefenokee Swamp, U.S.A. 77 K4
Okehampton, U.K. 11 G3
Okha, Russia 27 D15
Okhotsk, Russia 27 D15

Okhotsk, Sea of, Asia 27 D15
Okhotskiy Perevoz, Russia 27 C14
Okhotsko Kolymskoye, Russia 27 C16
Oki-Shotō, Japan 31 F6
Okiep, S. Africa 56 D2
Okinawa □, Japan 31 L3
Okinawa-Guntō, Japan 31 L3
Okinawa-Jima, Japan 31 L4
Okino-erabu-Shima, Japan 31 L4
Oklahoma □, U.S.A. 81 H6
Oklahoma City, U.S.A. 81 H6
Okmulgee, U.S.A. 81 H7
Okolo, Uganda 54 B3
Okolona, U.S.A. 81 H10
Okrika, Nigeria 50 H6
Oktabrsk, Kazakhstan 25 E10
Oktyabrskiy, Russia 24 D9
Oktyabrskoy Revolyutsii, Os., Russia 27 B10
Oktyabrskoye, Russia 26 C7
Okuru, N.Z. 59 K2
Okushiri-Tō, Japan 30 C9
Okwa →, Botswana 56 C3
Ola, U.S.A. 81 H8
Ólafsfjörður, Iceland 8 C4
Ólafsvík, Iceland 8 D2
Olancha, U.S.A. 85 J8
Olancha Pk., U.S.A. 85 J8
Olanchito, Honduras 88 C2
Öland, Sweden 9 H14
Olary, Australia 63 E3
Olascoaga, Argentina 94 D3
Olathe, U.S.A. 80 F7
Olavarría, Argentina 94 D3
Ólbia, Italy 20 D3
Old Bahama Chan. = Bahama, Canal Viejo de, W. Indies 88 B4
Old Baldy Pk. = San Antonio, Mt., U.S.A. 85 L9
Old Castile = Castilla y Leon □, Spain 19 B3
Old Castle, Ireland 13 C4
Old Cork, Australia 62 C3
Old Crow, Canada 68 B6
Old Dale, U.S.A. 85 L11
Old Fletton, U.K. 11 E7
Old Forge, N.Y., U.S.A. 79 C10
Old Forge, Pa., U.S.A. 79 E9
Old Fort →, Canada 73 B6
Old Shinyanga, Tanzania 54 C3
Old Speck, Mt., U.S.A. 79 B14
Old Town, U.S.A. 71 D6
Old Wives L., Canada 73 C7
Oldbury, U.K. 11 F5
Oldeani, Tanzania 54 C4
Oldenburg, Germany 16 B4
Oldenzaal, Neths. 15 B6
Oldham, U.K. 10 D5
Oldman →, Canada 72 D6
Olds, Canada 72 C6
Olean, U.S.A. 78 D6
Olekma →, Russia 27 C13
Olekminsk, Russia 27 C13
Olema, U.S.A. 84 G4
Olenegorsk, Russia 24 A5
Olenek, Russia 27 C12
Olenek →, Russia 27 B13
Oléron, I. d', France 18 D3
Oleśnica, Poland 17 C8
Olga, Russia 27 E14
Olga, L., Canada 70 C4
Olga, Mt., Australia 61 E5
Olifants →, Africa 57 C5
Olifantshoek, S. Africa 56 D3
Ólimbos, Óros, Greece 21 D10
Olímpia, Brazil 95 A6
Olinda, Brazil 93 E12
Oliva, Argentina 94 C3
Olivehurst, U.S.A. 84 F5
Oliveira, Brazil 93 H10
Olivenza, Spain 19 C2
Oliver, Canada 72 D5
Oliver L., Canada 73 B8
Ollagüe, Chile 94 A2
Olney, Ill., U.S.A. 76 F1
Olney, Tex., U.S.A. 81 J5
Olomane →, Canada 71 B7
Olomouc, Czech. 16 D8
Olonets, Russia 24 B5
Olongapo, Phil. 37 B6
Olovo, Bos. & H., Yug. 21 B8
Olovo, Yugoslavia 21 B8
Olovyannaya, Russia 27 D12
Oloy →, Russia 27 C16
Olsztyn, Poland 17 B10
Olt →, Romania 17 G12
Olteniţa, Romania 17 F13
Olton, U.S.A. 81 H3
Olymbos, Cyprus 23 D12
Olympia, Greece 21 F9
Olympia, U.S.A. 84 D4
Olympic Mts., U.S.A. 84 C3
Olympic Nat. Park, U.S.A. 84 C3
Olympus, Cyprus 23 E11
Olympus, Mt. = Ólimbos, Óros, Greece 21 D10
Olympus, Mt., U.S.A. 84 C3
Olyphant, U.S.A. 79 E9
Om →, Russia 26 D8
Om Koi, Thailand 38 D2
Ōma, Japan 30 D10
Ōmachi, Japan 31 F8
Omae-Zaki, Japan 31 G9
Ōmagari, Japan 30 E10
Omagh, U.K. 13 B4
Omagh □, U.K. 13 B4
Omaha, U.S.A. 80 E7
Omak, U.S.A. 82 B4
Omalos, Greece 23 D5
Oman ■, Asia 46 C6
Oman, G. of, Asia 45 E8
Omaruru, Namibia 56 C2
Omaruru →, Namibia 56 C1
Omate, Peru 92 G4
Ombai, Selat, Indonesia 37 F6
Omboué, Gabon 52 E1
Ombrone →, Italy 20 C4
Omdurmân, Sudan 51 E11
Omeonga, Zaïre 54 C1
Ometepe, I. de, Nic. 88 D2
Ometepec, Mexico 87 D5
Ominato, Japan 30 D10
Omineca →, Canada 72 B4
Omitara, Namibia 56 C2
Ōmiya, Japan 31 G9
Ommen, Neths. 15 B6
Ömnögovĭ □, Mongolia 34 C3
Omo →, Ethiopia 51 G12
Omodhos, Cyprus 23 E11
Omolon →, Russia 27 C16
Omono-Gawa →, Japan 30 E10
Omsk, Russia 26 D8
Omsukchan, Russia 27 C16
Ōmu, Japan 30 B11
Omul, Vf., Romania 17 F12
Ōmura, Japan 31 H4
Omuramba Omatako →, Namibia 53 H4
Ōmuta, Japan 31 H5
Onaga, U.S.A. 80 F6
Onalaska, U.S.A. 80 D9
Onamia, U.S.A. 80 B8
Onancock, U.S.A. 76 G8
Onang, Indonesia 37 E5
Onaping L., Canada 70 C3
Onavas, Mexico 86 B3
Onawa, U.S.A. 80 D6
Onaway, U.S.A. 76 C3
Oncócua, Angola 56 B1
Onda, Spain 19 C5
Ondaejin, N. Korea 35 D15
Ondangua, Namibia 56 B2
Ondjiva, Angola 56 B2
Ondo, Nigeria 50 G5
Öndörshil, Mongolia 34 B5
Öndverðarnes, Iceland 8 D1
Onega, Russia 24 B6
Onega →, Russia 24 B6
Onega, G. of = Onezhskaya Guba, Russia 24 B6
Onega, L. = Onezhskoye Ozero, Russia 24 B6
Onehunga, N.Z. 59 G5
Oneida, U.S.A. 79 C9
Oneida L., U.S.A. 79 C9
O'Neill, U.S.A. 80 D5
Onekotan, Ostrov, Russia 27 E16
Onema, Zaïre 54 C1
Oneonta, Ala., U.S.A. 77 J2
Oneonta, N.Y., U.S.A. 79 D9
Onezhskaya Guba, Russia 24 B6
Onezhskoye Ozero, Russia 24 B6
Ongarue, N.Z. 59 H5
Ongerup, Australia 61 F2
Ongjin, N. Korea 35 F13
Ongkharak, Thailand 38 E3
Ongniud Qi, China 35 C10
Ongoka, Zaïre 54 C2
Ongole, India 40 M12
Ongon, Mongolia 34 B7
Onguren, Russia 27 D11
Onida, U.S.A. 80 C4
Onilahy →, Madag. 57 C7
Onitsha, Nigeria 50 G6
Onoda, Japan 31 G5
Onpyŏng-ni, S. Korea 35 H14
Onslow, Australia 60 D2
Onslow B., U.S.A. 77 H7
Onstwedde, Neths. 15 A7
Ontake-San, Japan 31 G8
Ontario, Calif., U.S.A. 85 L9
Ontario, Oreg., U.S.A. 82 D5
Ontario □, Canada 70 B2
Ontario, L., N. Amer. 70 D4
Ontonagon, U.S.A. 80 B10
Onyx, U.S.A. 85 K8
Oodnadatta, Australia 63 D2
Ooldea, Australia 61 F5
Oombulgurri, Australia 60 C4
Oona River, Canada 72 C2
Oorindi, Australia 62 C3
Oost-Vlaanderen □, Belgium 15 C3
Oostende, Belgium 15 C2
Oosterhout, Neths. 15 C4
Oosterschelde, Neths. 15 C4
Ootacamund, India 40 P10
Ootsa L., Canada 72 C3
Opala, Russia 27 D16
Opala, Zaïre 54 C1
Opanake, Sri Lanka 40 R12
Opasatika, Canada 70 C3
Opasquia, Canada 73 C10
Opava, Czech. 17 D8
Opelousas, U.S.A. 81 K8
Opémisca, L., Canada 70 C5
Opheim, U.S.A. 82 B10
Ophthalmia Ra., Australia 60 D2
Opinaca →, Canada 70 B4
Opinaca L., Canada 70 B4
Opiskotish, L., Canada 71 B6
Opole, Poland 17 C8
Oporto = Porto, Portugal 19 B1
Opotiki, N.Z. 59 H6
Opp, U.S.A. 77 K2
Oppland fylke □, Norway 9 F10
Opua, N.Z. 59 F5
Opunake, N.Z. 59 H4
Ora, Cyprus 23 E12
Ora Banda, Australia 61 F3
Oracle, U.S.A. 83 K8
Oradea, Romania 17 E10
Öræfajökull, Iceland 8 D5
Orai, India 43 G8
Oran, Algeria 50 A4
Oran, Argentina 94 A3
Orange = Oranje →, S. Africa 56 D2
Orange, Australia 63 E4
Orange, France 18 D6
Orange, Calif., U.S.A. 85 M9
Orange, Mass., U.S.A. 79 D12
Orange, Tex., U.S.A. 81 K8
Orange, Va., U.S.A. 76 F6
Orange, C., Brazil 93 C8
Orange Cove, U.S.A. 84 J7
Orange Free State □, S. Africa 56 D4
Orange Grove, U.S.A. 81 M6
Orange Walk, Belize 87 D7
Orangeburg, U.S.A. 77 J5
Orangeville, Canada 70 D3
Oranienburg, Germany 16 B6
Oranje →, S. Africa 56 D2
Oranje Vrystaat = Orange Free State □, S. Africa 56 D4
Oranjemund, Namibia 56 D2
Oranjerivier, S. Africa 56 D3
Oras, Phil. 37 B7
Oraşul Stalin = Braşov, Romania 17 F12
Orbetello, Italy 20 C4
Orbost, Australia 63 F4
Orchila, I., Venezuela 92 A5
Orcutt, U.S.A. 85 L6
Ord →, Australia 60 C4
Ord, Mt., Australia 60 C4
Orderville, U.S.A. 83 H7
Ordos = Mu Us Shamo, China 34 E5
Ordway, U.S.A. 80 F3
Ordzhonikidze = Vladikavkaz, Russia 25 F7
Ore, Zaïre 54 B2
Ore Mts. = Erzgebirge, Germany 16 C6
Örebro, Sweden 9 G13
Örebro län □, Sweden 9 G13
Oregon, U.S.A. 80 D10
Oregon □, U.S.A. 82 E3
Oregon City, U.S.A. 84 E4
Orekhovo-Zuyevo, Russia 24 C6
Orel, Russia 24 D6
Orem, U.S.A. 82 F8
Orenburg, Russia 24 D10
Orense, Spain 19 A2
Orepuki, N.Z. 59 M1
Øresund, Europe 9 H12
Orford Ness, U.K. 11 E9
Organos, Pta. de los, Canary Is. 22 F2
Orhon Gol →, Mongolia 32 A5
Orient, Australia 63 D3
Oriental, Cordillera, Colombia 92 B4
Oriente, Argentina 94 D3
Orihuela, Spain 19 C5
Orinoco →, Venezuela 92 B6
Orissa □, India 41 K14
Oristano, Italy 20 E3
Oristano, G. di, Italy 20 E3
Orizaba, Mexico 87 D5
Orkanger, Norway 8 E10
Orkla →, Norway 8 E10
Orkney, S. Africa 56 D4
Orkney □, U.K. 12 C6
Orkney Is., U.K. 12 C6
Orland, U.S.A. 84 F4
Orlando, U.S.A. 77 L5
Orléanais, France 18 C4
Orléans, France 18 C4
Orleans, U.S.A. 79 B12
Orléans, I. d', Canada 71 C5
Ormara, Pakistan 40 G4
Ormoc, Phil. 37 B6
Ormond, N.Z. 59 H6
Ormond Beach, U.S.A. 77 L5
Ormstown, Canada 79 A11
Orne □, France 18 B4
Örnsköldsvik, Sweden 8 E15
Oro, N. Korea 35 D14
Oro →, Mexico 86 B3
Oro Grande, U.S.A. 85 L9
Orocué, Colombia 92 C4
Orogrande, U.S.A. 83 K10
Oromocto, Canada 71 C6
Orono, Canada 78 C6
Oroqen Zizhiqi, China 33 A7
Oroquieta, Phil. 37 C6
Orós, Brazil 93 E11
Orotukan, Russia 27 C16
Oroville, Calif., U.S.A. 84 F5
Oroville, Wash., U.S.A. 82 B4
Oroville Res., U.S.A. 84 F5
Orroroo, Australia 63 E2
Orrville, U.S.A. 78 F3
Orsha, Belorussia 24 D5
Orsk, Russia 24 D10
Orşova, Romania 17 F11
Ortegal, C., Spain 19 A2
Orthez, France 18 E3
Ortigueira, Spain 19 A2
Orting, U.S.A. 84 C4
Ortles, Italy 20 A4
Ortón →, Bolivia 92 F5
Ortona, Italy 20 C6
Orūmīyeh, Iran 44 B5
Orūmīyeh, Daryācheh-ye, Iran 44 B5
Oruro, Bolivia 92 G5
Oruzgān □, Afghan. 40 C5
Orvieto, Italy 20 C5
Orwell, U.S.A. 78 E4
Orwell →, U.K. 11 E9
Oryakhovo, Bulgaria 21 C10
Osa, Russia 24 C10
Osa, Pen. de, Costa Rica 88 E3
Osage, Iowa, U.S.A. 80 D8
Osage, Wyo., U.S.A. 80 D2
Osage →, U.S.A. 80 F9
Osage City, U.S.A. 80 F7
Ōsaka, Japan 31 G7
Osan, S. Korea 35 F14
Osawatomie, U.S.A. 80 F7
Osborne, U.S.A. 80 F5
Osceola, Ark., U.S.A. 81 H10
Osceola, Iowa, U.S.A. 80 E8
Oscoda, U.S.A. 78 B1
Ösel = Saaremaa, Estonia 24 C3
Osh, Kirghizia 26 E8
Oshawa, Canada 70 D4
Oshkosh, Nebr., U.S.A. 80 E3
Oshkosh, Wis., U.S.A. 80 C10
Oshnovīyeh, Iran 44 B5
Oshogbo, Nigeria 50 G5
Oshtorīnān, Iran 45 C6
Oshwe, Zaïre 52 E3
Osijek, Croatia 21 B8
Osipenko = Berdyansk, Ukraine 25 E6
Osizweni, S. Africa 57 D5
Oskaloosa, U.S.A. 80 E8
Oskarshamn, Sweden 9 H14
Oskélanéo, Canada 70 C4
Oslo, Norway 9 G11
Oslob, Phil. 37 C6
Oslofjorden, Norway 9 G11
Osmanabad, India 40 K10
Osmaniye, Turkey 25 G6
Osnabrück, Germany 16 B4
Osorio, Brazil 95 B5
Osorno, Chile 96 E2
Osoyoos, Canada 72 D5
Ospika →, Canada 72 B4
Osprey Reef, Australia 62 A4
Oss, Neths. 15 C5
Ossa, Mt., Australia 62 G4
Óssa, Oros, Greece 21 E10
Ossabaw I., U.S.A. 77 K5
Ossining, U.S.A. 79 E11
Ossipee, U.S.A. 79 C13
Ossokmanuan L., Canada 71 B7
Ossora, Russia 27 D17
Ostend = Oostende, Belgium 15 C2
Österdalälven →, Sweden 9 F12
Östergötlands län □, Sweden 9 G13
Östersund, Sweden 8 E13
Østfold fylke □, Norway 9 G11
Ostfriesische Inseln, Germany 16 B3
Ostrava, Czech. 17 D9
Ostróda, Poland 17 B9
Ostrołęka, Poland 17 B10
Ostrów Mazowiecka, Poland 17 B10
Ostrów Wielkopolski, Poland 17 C8
Ostrowiec-Świętokrzyski, Poland 17 C10
Ōsumi-Kaikyō, Japan 31 J5
Ōsumi-Shotō, Japan 31 J5
Osuna, Spain 19 D3
Oswego, U.S.A. 79 C8
Oswestry, U.K. 10 E4
Otago □, N.Z. 59 L2
Otago Harbour, N.Z. 59 L3
Ōtake, Japan 31 G6
Otaki, N.Z. 59 J5
Otaru, Japan 30 C10
Otaru-Wan = Ishikari-Wan, Japan 30 C10
Otavalo, Ecuador 92 C3
Otavi, Namibia 56 B2
Otchinjau, Angola 56 B1
Othello, U.S.A. 82 C4
Otira Gorge, N.Z. 59 K3
Otis, U.S.A. 80 E3
Otjiwarongo, Namibia 56 C2
Otoineppu, Japan 30 B11
Otorohanga, N.Z. 59 H5
Otoskwin →, Canada 70 B2
Otosquen, Canada 73 C8
Otranto, Italy 21 D8
Otranto, C. d', Italy 21 D8
Otranto, Str. of, Italy 21 D8
Otse, S. Africa 56 D4
Ōtsu, Japan 31 G7
Ōtsuki, Japan 31 G9
Ottawa = Outaouais →, Canada 70 C5
Ottawa, Canada 70 C4
Ottawa, Ill., U.S.A. 80 E10
Ottawa, Kans., U.S.A. 80 F7
Ottawa Is., Canada 69 C11
Otter L., Canada 73 B8
Otter Rapids, Ont., Canada 70 B3
Otter Rapids, Sask., Canada 73 B8
Otterville, Canada 78 D4
Otto Beit Bridge, Zimbabwe 55 F2
Ottosdal, S. Africa 56 D4
Ottoshoop, S. Africa 56 D4
Ottumwa, U.S.A. 80 E8
Oturkpo, Nigeria 50 G6
Otway, B., Chile 96 G2
Otway, C., Australia 63 F3
Otwock, Poland 17 B10
Ou →, Laos 38 B4
Ou Neua, Laos 38 A3
Ou-Sammyaku, Japan 30 E10
Ouachita →, U.S.A. 81 K9
Ouachita, L., U.S.A. 81 H8
Ouachita Mts., U.S.A. 81 H7
Ouadâne, Mauritania 50 D2
Ouadda, C.A.R. 51 G9
Ouagadougou, Burkina Faso 50 F4
Ouahran = Oran, Algeria 50 A4
Ouallene, Algeria 50 D5
Ouanda Djallé, C.A.R. 51 G9
Ouango, C.A.R. 52 D4
Ouargla, Algeria 50 B6
Ouarzazate, Morocco 50 B3
Oubangi →, Zaïre 52 E3
Ouddorp, Neths. 15 C3
Oude Rijn →, Neths. 15 B4
Oudenaarde, Belgium 15 D3
Oudtshoorn, S. Africa 56 E3
Ouessant, I. d', France 18 B1
Ouesso, Congo 52 D3
Ouest, Pte., Canada 71 C7
Ouezzane, Morocco 50 B3
Ouidah, Benin 50 G5
Oujda, Morocco 50 B4
Oujeft, Mauritania 50 D2
Ouled Djellal, Algeria 50 B6
Oulu, Finland 8 D18
Oulu □ = Oulun lääni □, Finland 8 D19
Oulujärvi, Finland 8 D19
Oulujoki →, Finland 8 D18
Oulun lääni □, Finland 8 D19
Oum Chalouba, Chad 51 E9
Ounguati, Namibia 56 C2
Ounianga-Kébir, Chad 51 E9
Ounianga Sérir, Chad 51 E9
Our →, Lux. 15 E6
Ouray, U.S.A. 83 G10
Ouricuri, Brazil 93 E10
Ourinhos, Brazil 95 A6
Ouro Fino, Brazil 95 A6
Ouro Prêto, Brazil 95 A7
Ourthe →, Belgium 15 D5
Ouse, Australia 62 G4
Ouse →, E. Susx., U.K. 11 G8
Ouse →, N. Yorks., U.K. 10 C8
Outaouais →, Canada 70 C5
Outardes →, Canada 71 C6
Outer Hebrides, U.K. 12 D1
Outer I., Canada 71 B8
Outjo, Namibia 56 C2
Outlook, Canada 73 C7
Outlook, U.S.A. 80 A2
Ouyen, Australia 63 F3
Ovalau, Fiji 59 C8
Ovalle, Chile 94 C1
Ovar, Portugal 19 B1
Overflakkee, Neths. 15 C4
Overijssel □, Neths. 15 B6
Overpelt, Belgium 15 C5
Overton, U.S.A. 85 J12
Övertorneå, Sweden 8 C17
Ovid, U.S.A. 80 E3
Oviedo, Spain 19 A3
Övör Hangay □, Mongolia 34 B2
Ovruch, Ukraine 26 D3
Owaka, N.Z. 59 M2
Owase, Japan 31 G8
Owatonna, U.S.A. 80 C8
Owbeh, Afghan. 40 B3
Owego, U.S.A. 79 D8
Owen Falls, Uganda 54 B3
Owen Sound, Canada 70 D3
Owendo, Gabon 52 D1
Owens →, U.S.A. 84 J9
Owens L., U.S.A. 85 J9
Owensboro, U.S.A. 76 G2
Owensville, U.S.A. 80 F9
Owl →, Canada 73 B10
Owo, Nigeria 50 G6
Owosso, U.S.A. 76 D3
Owyhee, U.S.A. 82 F5
Owyhee →, U.S.A. 82 E5
Owyhee, L., U.S.A. 82 E5
Ox Mts., Ireland 13 B3
Oxelösund, Sweden 9 G14
Oxford, N.Z. 59 K4
Oxford, U.K. 11 F6
Oxford, Miss., U.S.A. 81 H10
Oxford, N.C., U.S.A. 77 G6
Oxford, Ohio, U.S.A. 76 F3
Oxford L., Canada 73 C9
Oxfordshire □, U.K. 11 F6
Oxley, Australia 63 E3
Oxnard, U.S.A. 85 L7
Oxus = Amudarya →, Uzbekistan 26 E6
Oya, Malaysia 36 D4

Oyama, *Japan* 31 F9
Oyem, *Gabon* 52 D2
Oyen, *Canada* 73 C6
Oykel →, *U.K.* 12 D4
Oymyakon, *Russia* 27 C15
Oyo, *Nigeria* 50 G5
Oyster Bay, *U.S.A.* 79 F11
Ōyūbari, *Japan* 30 C11
Ozamis, *Phil.* 37 C6
Ozark, *Ala., U.S.A.* 77 K3
Ozark, *Ark., U.S.A.* 81 H8
Ozark, *Mo., U.S.A.* 81 G8
Ozark Plateau, *U.S.A.* 81 G9
Ozarks, L. of the, *U.S.A.* 80 F8
Ozette, L., *U.S.A.* 84 B2
Ozona, *U.S.A.* 81 K4
Ozuluama, *Mexico* 87 C5

P

P.K. le Roux Dam, *S. Africa* 56 E3
Pa-an, *Burma* 41 L20
Pa Mong Dam, *Thailand* 38 D4
Paamiut = Frederikshåb, *Greenland* 4 C5
Paarl, *S. Africa* 56 E2
Paatsi →, *Russia* 8 B20
Paauilo, *U.S.A.* 74 H17
Pab Hills, *Pakistan* 42 F2
Pabna, *Bangla.* 41 G16
Pabo, *Uganda* 54 B3
Pacaja →, *Brazil* 93 D8
Pacaraima, Sierra, *Venezuela* 92 C6
Pacasmayo, *Peru* 92 E3
Pachhar, *India* 42 G7
Pachpadra, *India* 40 G8
Pachuca, *Mexico* 87 C5
Pacific, *Canada* 72 C3
Pacific-Antarctic Ridge, *Pac. Oc.* 65 M16
Pacific Grove, *U.S.A.* 83 H3
Pacific Ocean, *Pac. Oc.* 65 G14
Pacifica, *U.S.A.* 84 H4
Pacitan, *Indonesia* 37 H14
Packwood, *U.S.A.* 84 D5
Padaido, Kepulauan, *Indonesia* 37 E9
Padang, *Indonesia* 36 E2
Padangpanjang, *Indonesia* 36 E2
Padangsidempuan, *Indonesia* 36 D1
Paddockwood, *Canada* 73 C7
Paderborn, *Germany* 16 C4
Padloping Island, *Canada* 69 B13
Pádova, *Italy* 20 B4
Padra, *India* 42 H5
Padrauna, *India* 43 F10
Padre I., *U.S.A.* 81 M6
Padstow, *U.K.* 11 G3
Padua = Pádova, *Italy* 20 B4
Paducah, *Ky., U.S.A.* 76 G1
Paducah, *Tex., U.S.A.* 81 H4
Paengnyong-do, *S. Korea* 35 F13
Paeroa, *N.Z.* 59 G5
Pafúri, *Mozam.* 57 C5
Pag, *Croatia* 20 B6
Pagadian, *Phil.* 37 C6
Pagai Selatan, P., *Indonesia* 36 E2
Pagai Utara, *Indonesia* 36 E2
Pagalu = Annobón, *Atl. Oc.* 49 G4
Pagastikós Kólpos, *Greece* 21 E10
Pagatan, *Indonesia* 36 E5
Page, *Ariz., U.S.A.* 83 H8
Page, *N. Dak., U.S.A.* 80 B6
Pago Pago, *Amer. Samoa* 59 B13
Pagosa Springs, *U.S.A.* 83 H10
Pagwa River, *Canada* 70 B2
Pahala, *U.S.A.* 74 J17
Pahang →, *Malaysia* 39 L4
Pahiatua, *N.Z.* 59 J5
Pahokee, *U.S.A.* 77 M5
Pahrump, *U.S.A.* 85 J11
Pahute Mesa, *U.S.A.* 84 H10
Pai, *Thailand* 38 C2
Paia, *U.S.A.* 74 H16
Paicines, *U.S.A.* 84 J5
Paignton, *U.K.* 11 G4
Päijänne, *Finland* 9 F18
Painan, *Indonesia* 36 E2
Painesville, *U.S.A.* 78 E3
Paint Hills = Nouveau Comptoir, *Canada* 70 B4
Paint L., *Canada* 73 B9
Paint Rock, *U.S.A.* 81 K5
Painted Desert, *U.S.A.* 83 J8
Paintsville, *U.S.A.* 76 G4
País Vasco □, *Spain* 19 A4
Paisley, *Canada* 78 B3
Paisley, *U.K.* 12 F4
Paisley, *U.S.A.* 82 E3
Paita, *Peru* 92 E2
Pak Lay, *Laos* 38 C3
Pak Phanang, *Thailand* 39 H3
Pak Sane, *Laos* 38 C4
Pak Song, *Laos* 38 E6
Pak Suong, *Laos* 38 C4
Pakaraima Mts., *Guyana* 92 B6
Pákhnes, *Greece* 23 D6
Pakistan ■, *Asia* 42 E3
Pakistan, East = Bangladesh ■, *Asia* 41 H17
Pakkading, *Laos* 38 C4
Pakokku, *Burma* 41 J19
Pakpattan, *Pakistan* 42 D5
Pakse, *Laos* 38 E5
Paktīā □, *Afghan.* 40 C6
Pakwach, *Uganda* 54 B3
Pala, *Chad* 51 G8
Pala, *U.S.A.* 85 M9
Pala, *Zaïre* 54 D2
Palabek, *Uganda* 54 B3
Palacios, *U.S.A.* 81 L6
Palagruža, *Croatia* 20 C7
Palaiókastron, *Greece* 23 D8
Palaiokhóra, *Greece* 23 D5
Palam, *India* 40 K10
Palamós, *Spain* 19 B7
Palampur, *India* 42 C7
Palana, *Australia* 62 F4
Palana, *Russia* 27 D16
Palanan, *Phil.* 37 A6
Palanan Pt., *Phil.* 37 A6
Palandri, *Pakistan* 43 C5
Palangkaraya, *Indonesia* 36 E4
Palani Hills, *India* 40 P10
Palanpur, *India* 42 G5
Palapye, *Botswana* 56 C4
Palas, *Pakistan* 43 B5
Palatka, *Russia* 27 C16
Palatka, *U.S.A.* 77 L5
Palawan, *Phil.* 36 C5
Palayankottai, *India* 40 Q10
Paleleh, *Indonesia* 37 D6
Palembang, *Indonesia* 36 E2
Palencia, *Spain* 19 A3
Paleokastrítsa, *Greece* 23 A3
Paleometokho, *Cyprus* 23 D12
Palermo, *Italy* 20 E5
Palermo, *U.S.A.* 82 G3
Palestine, *Asia* 47 D4
Palestine, *U.S.A.* 81 K7
Paletwa, *Burma* 41 J18
Palghat, *India* 40 P10
Palgrave, Mt., *Australia* 60 D2
Pali, *India* 42 G5
Palisade, *U.S.A.* 80 E4
Palitana, *India* 42 J4
Palizada, *Mexico* 87 D6
Palk Bay, *Asia* 40 Q11
Palk Strait, *Asia* 40 Q11
Palkānah, *Iraq* 44 C5
Palla Road = Dinokwe, *Botswana* 56 C4
Pallisa, *Uganda* 54 B3
Pallu, *India* 42 E6
Palm Beach, *U.S.A.* 77 M6
Palm Desert, *U.S.A.* 85 M10
Palm Is., *Australia* 62 B4
Palm Springs, *U.S.A.* 85 M10
Palma, *Mozam.* 55 E5
Palma →, *Brazil* 93 F9
Palma, B. de, *Spain* 22 B9
Palma de Mallorca, *Spain* 22 B9
Palma Soriano, *Cuba* 88 B4
Palmares, *Brazil* 93 E11
Palmas, *Brazil* 95 B5
Palmas, C., *Liberia* 50 H3
Pálmas, G. di, *Italy* 20 E3
Palmdale, *U.S.A.* 85 L8
Palmeira dos Índios, *Brazil* 93 E11
Palmeirinhas, Pta. das, *Angola* 52 F2
Palmer, *U.S.A.* 68 B5
Palmer →, *Australia* 62 B3
Palmer Arch., *Antarctica* 5 C17
Palmer Lake, *U.S.A.* 80 F2
Palmer Land, *Antarctica* 5 D18
Palmerston, *Canada* 78 C4
Palmerston, *N.Z.* 59 L3
Palmerston North, *N.Z.* 59 J5
Palmerton, *U.S.A.* 79 F9
Palmetto, *U.S.A.* 77 M4
Palmi, *Italy* 20 E6
Palmira, *Argentina* 94 C2
Palmira, *Colombia* 92 C3
Palmyra = Tudmur, *Syria* 44 C3
Palmyra, *Mo., U.S.A.* 80 F9
Palmyra, *N.Y., U.S.A.* 78 C7
Palmyra Is., *Pac. Oc.* 65 G11
Palo Alto, *U.S.A.* 83 H2
Palo Verde, *U.S.A.* 85 M12
Palopo, *Indonesia* 37 E6
Palos, C. de, *Spain* 19 D5
Palos Verdes, *U.S.A.* 85 M8
Palos Verdes, Pt., *U.S.A.* 85 M8
Palouse, *U.S.A.* 82 C5
Palparara, *Australia* 62 C3
Palu, *Indonesia* 37 E5
Palu, *Turkey* 25 G7
Paluan, *Phil.* 37 B6
Palwal, *India* 42 E7
Pama, *Burkina Faso* 50 F5
Pamanukan, *Indonesia* 37 G12
Pamekasan, *Indonesia* 37 G15
Pamirs, *Tajikistan* 26 F8
Pamlico →, *U.S.A.* 77 H7
Pamlico Sd., *U.S.A.* 77 H8
Pampa, *U.S.A.* 81 H4
Pampa de las Salinas, *Argentina* 94 C2
Pampanua, *Indonesia* 37 E6
Pampas, *Argentina* 94 D3
Pampas, *Peru* 92 F4
Pamplona, *Colombia* 92 B4
Pamplona, *Spain* 19 A5
Pampoenpoort, *S. Africa* 56 E3
Pana, *U.S.A.* 80 F10
Panaca, *U.S.A.* 83 H6
Panaitan, *Indonesia* 37 G11
Panaji, *India* 40 M8
Panamá, *Panama* 88 E4
Panama ■, *Cent. Amer.* 88 E4
Panamá, G. de, *Panama* 88 E4
Panama Canal, *Panama* 88 E4
Panama City, *U.S.A.* 77 K3
Panamint Ra., *U.S.A.* 85 J9
Panamint Springs, *U.S.A.* 85 J9
Panão, *Peru* 92 E3
Panare, *Thailand* 39 J3
Panarukan, *Indonesia* 37 G15
Panay, *Phil.* 37 B6
Panay, G., *Phil.* 37 B6
Pancake Ra., *U.S.A.* 83 G6
Pančevo, *Serbia, Yug.* 21 B9
Pancorbo, Paso, *Spain* 19 A4
Pandan, *Phil.* 37 B6
Pandegelang, *Indonesia* 37 G12
Pandharpur, *India* 40 L9
Pando, *Uruguay* 95 C4
Pando, L. = Hope, L., *Australia* 63 D2
Pandokrátor, *Greece* 23 A3
Pandora, *Costa Rica* 88 E3
Panevezys, *Lithuania* 24 C3
Panfilov, *Kazakhstan* 26 E8
Pang-Long, *Burma* 41 H21
Pang-Yang, *Burma* 41 H21
Panga, *Zaïre* 54 B2
Pangalanes, Canal des, *Madag.* 57 C8
Pangani, *Tanzania* 54 D4
Pangani □, *Tanzania* 54 D4
Pangani →, *Tanzania* 54 D4
Pangfou = Bengbu, *China* 35 H9
Pangil, *Zaïre* 54 C2
Pangkah, Tanjung, *Indonesia* 37 G15
Pangkajene, *Indonesia* 37 E5
Pangkalanbrandan, *Indonesia* 36 D1
Pangkalanbuun, *Indonesia* 36 E4
Pangkalansusu, *Indonesia* 36 D1
Pangkalpinang, *Indonesia* 36 E3
Pangkoh, *Indonesia* 36 E4
Pangnirtung, *Canada* 69 B13
Pangrango, *Indonesia* 37 G12
Panguitch, *U.S.A.* 83 H7
Pangutaran Group, *Phil.* 37 C6
Panhandle, *U.S.A.* 81 H4
Pani Mines, *India* 42 H5
Pania-Mutombo, *Zaïre* 54 D1
Panipat, *India* 42 E7
Panjal Range, *India* 42 C7
Panjgur, *Pakistan* 40 F4
Panjim = Panaji, *India* 40 M8
Panjinad Barrage, *Pakistan* 40 E7
Panjwai, *Afghan.* 42 D1
Panmunjŏm, *N. Korea* 35 F14
Panna, *India* 43 G9
Panna Hills, *India* 43 G9
Pano Lefkara, *Cyprus* 23 E12
Pano Panayia, *Cyprus* 23 E11
Panorama, *Brazil* 95 A5
Pánormon, *Greece* 23 D6
Panshan, *China* 35 D12
Panshi, *China* 35 C14
Pantar, *Indonesia* 37 F6
Pantelleria, *Italy* 20 F5
Pánuco, *Mexico* 87 C5
Panyam, *Nigeria* 50 G6
Paola, *Malta* 23 D2
Paola, *U.S.A.* 80 F7
Paonia, *U.S.A.* 83 G10
Paoting = Baoding, *China* 34 E8
Paot'ou = Baotou, *China* 34 D6
Paoua, *C.A.R.* 51 G8
Pápa, *Hungary* 17 E8
Papagayo →, *Mexico* 87 D5
Papagayo, G. de, *Costa Rica* 88 D2
Papakura, *N.Z.* 59 G5
Papantla, *Mexico* 87 C5
Papar, *Malaysia* 36 C5
Paphos, *Cyprus* 23 E11
Papien Chiang = Da →, *Vietnam* 38 B5
Papigochic →, *Mexico* 86 B3
Paposo, *Chile* 94 B1
Papoutsa, *Cyprus* 23 E12
Papua New Guinea ■, *Oceania* 64 H6
Papudo, *Chile* 94 C1
Papun, *Burma* 41 K20
Papunya, *Australia* 60 D5
Pará = Belém, *Brazil* 93 D9
Pará □, *Brazil* 93 D8
Paraburdoo, *Australia* 60 D2
Paracatu, *Brazil* 93 G9
Paracel Is. = Hsisha Chuntao, *Pac. Oc.* 36 A4
Parachilna, *Australia* 63 E2
Parachinar, *Pakistan* 42 C4
Paradhisi, *Greece* 23 C10
Paradip, *India* 41 J15
Paradise, *Calif., U.S.A.* 84 F5
Paradise, *Mont., U.S.A.* 82 C6
Paradise, *Nev., U.S.A.* 85 J11
Paradise →, *Canada* 71 B8
Paradise Valley, *U.S.A.* 82 F5
Parado, *Indonesia* 37 F5
Paragould, *U.S.A.* 81 G9
Paragua →, *Venezuela* 92 B6
Paraguaçu →, *Brazil* 93 F11
Paraguaçu Paulista, *Brazil* 95 A5
Paraguaná, Pen. de, *Venezuela* 92 A4
Paraguarí, *Paraguay* 94 B4
Paraguarí □, *Paraguay* 94 B4
Paraguay ■, *S. Amer.* 94 A4
Paraguay →, *Paraguay* 94 B4
Paraíba = João Pessoa, *Brazil* 93 E12
Paraíba □, *Brazil* 93 E11
Paraíba do Sul →, *Brazil* 95 A7
Parainen, *Finland* 9 F17
Paraiso, *Mexico* 87 D6
Parak, *Iran* 45 E7
Parakou, *Benin* 50 G5
Paralimni, *Cyprus* 23 D12
Paramaribo, *Surinam* 93 B7
Paramushir, Ostrov, *Russia* 27 D16
Paran →, *Israel* 47 E4
Paraná, *Argentina* 94 C3
Paranã, *Brazil* 93 F9
Paraná □, *Brazil* 95 A5
Paraná →, *Argentina* 94 C4
Paranaguá, *Brazil* 95 B6
Paranaíba →, *Brazil* 93 H8
Paranapanema →, *Brazil* 95 A5
Paranapiacaba, Serra do, *Brazil* 95 A6
Paranavaí, *Brazil* 95 A5
Parang, *Jolo, Phil.* 37 C6
Parang, *Mindanao, Phil.* 37 C6
Paratinga, *Brazil* 93 F10
Paratoo, *Australia* 63 E2
Parattah, *Australia* 62 G4
Parbati →, *India* 42 G7
Parbhani, *India* 40 K10
Parchim, *Germany* 16 B5
Pardes Hanna, *Israel* 47 C3
Pardo →, *Bahia, Brazil* 93 G11
Pardo →, *Mato Grosso, Brazil* 95 A5
Pardo →, *São Paulo, Brazil* 93 H9
Pardubice, *Czech.* 16 C7
Pare, *Indonesia* 37 G15
Pare □, *Tanzania* 54 C4
Pare Mts., *Tanzania* 54 C4
Parecis, Serra dos, *Brazil* 92 F7
Pareh, *Iran* 44 B5
Paren, *Russia* 27 C17
Parent, *Canada* 70 C5
Parent, L., *Canada* 70 C4
Parepare, *Indonesia* 37 E5
Pargo, Pta. do, *Madeira* 22 D2
Parguba, *Russia* 24 B5
Pariaguán, *Venezuela* 92 B6
Pariaman, *Indonesia* 36 E2
Paricutín, Cerro, *Mexico* 86 D4
Parigi, *Java, Indonesia* 37 G13
Parigi, *Sulawesi, Indonesia* 37 E6
Parika, *Guyana* 92 B7
Parima, Serra, *Brazil* 92 C6
Parinari, *Peru* 92 D4
Paring, *Romania* 17 F11
Parintins, *Brazil* 93 D7
Pariparit Kyun, *Burma* 41 M18
Paris, *Canada* 70 D3
Paris, *France* 18 B5
Paris, *Idaho, U.S.A.* 82 E8
Paris, *Ky., U.S.A.* 76 F3
Paris, *Tenn., U.S.A.* 77 G1
Paris, *Tex., U.S.A.* 81 J7
Paris, Ville de □, *France* 18 B5
Parish, *U.S.A.* 79 C8
Pariti, *Indonesia* 37 F6
Park, *U.S.A.* 84 B4
Park City, *U.S.A.* 82 F8
Park Falls, *U.S.A.* 80 C9
Park Range, *U.S.A.* 82 G10
Park Rapids, *U.S.A.* 80 B7
Park River, *U.S.A.* 80 A6
Park Rynie, *S. Africa* 57 E5
Parkā Bandar, *Iran* 45 E8
Parker, *Ariz., U.S.A.* 85 L12
Parker, *S. Dak., U.S.A.* 80 D6
Parker Dam, *U.S.A.* 85 L12
Parkersburg, *U.S.A.* 76 F5
Parkerview, *Canada* 73 C8
Parkes, *Australia* 63 E4
Parkfield, *U.S.A.* 84 K6
Parkland, *U.S.A.* 84 C4
Parkside, *Canada* 73 C7
Parkston, *U.S.A.* 80 D5
Parksville, *Canada* 72 D4
Parma, *Italy* 20 B4
Parma, *Idaho, U.S.A.* 82 E5
Parma, *Ohio, U.S.A.* 78 E3
Parnaguá, *Brazil* 93 F10
Parnaíba, *Piauí, Brazil* 93 D10
Parnaíba, *São Paulo, Brazil* 93 G8
Parnaíba →, *Brazil* 93 D10
Parnassós, *Greece* 21 E10
Pärnu, *Estonia* 24 C3
Paroo →, *Australia* 63 E3
Páros, *Greece* 21 F11
Parowan, *U.S.A.* 83 H7
Parral, *Chile* 94 D1
Parramatta, *Australia* 63 E5
Parras, *Mexico* 86 B4
Parrett →, *U.K.* 11 F5
Parris I., *U.S.A.* 77 J5
Parrsboro, *Canada* 71 C7
Parry Is., *Canada* 4 B2
Parry Sound, *Canada* 70 C3
Parshall, *U.S.A.* 80 B3
Parsnip →, *Canada* 72 B4
Parsons, *U.S.A.* 81 G7
Parsons Ra., *Australia* 62 A2
Paru →, *Brazil* 93 D8
Paruro, *Peru* 92 F4
Parvān □, *Afghan.* 40 B6
Parvatipuram, *India* 41 K13
Parys, *S. Africa* 56 D4
Pas-de-Calais □, *France* 18 A5
Pasadena, *Calif., U.S.A.* 85 L8
Pasadena, *Tex., U.S.A.* 81 L7
Pasaje, *Ecuador* 92 D3
Pasaje →, *Argentina* 94 B3
Pascagoula, *U.S.A.* 81 K10
Pascagoula →, *U.S.A.* 81 K10
Pasco, *U.S.A.* 82 C4
Pasco, Cerro de, *Peru* 92 F3
Pascua, I. de, *Pac. Oc.* 65 K17
Pasfield L., *Canada* 73 B7
Pashiwari, *Pakistan* 43 B6
Pashmakli = Smolyan, *Bulgaria* 21 D11
Pasirian, *Indonesia* 37 H15
Paskūh, *Iran* 45 E9
Pasley, C., *Australia* 61 F3
Pasni, *Pakistan* 40 G3
Paso Cantinela, *Mexico* 85 N11
Paso de Indios, *Argentina* 96 E3
Paso de los Libres, *Argentina* 94 B4
Paso de los Toros, *Uruguay* 94 C4
Paso Robles, *U.S.A.* 83 J3
Paspébiac, *Canada* 71 C6
Pasrur, *Pakistan* 42 C6
Passage West, *Ireland* 13 E3
Passaic, *U.S.A.* 79 F10
Passau, *Germany* 16 D6
Passero, C., *Italy* 20 F6
Passo Fundo, *Brazil* 95 B5
Passos, *Brazil* 93 H9
Pastaza →, *Peru* 92 D3
Pasto, *Colombia* 92 C3
Pasuruan, *Indonesia* 37 G15
Patagonia, *Argentina* 96 F3
Patagonia, *U.S.A.* 83 L8
Patambar, *Iran* 45 D9
Patan, *India* 40 H8
Patan, *Maharashtra, India* 42 H5
Patan, *Nepal* 41 F14
Patani, *Indonesia* 37 D7
Pataudi, *India* 42 E7
Patchewollock, *Australia* 63 F3
Patchogue, *U.S.A.* 79 F11
Patea, *N.Z.* 59 H5
Pategi, *Nigeria* 50 G6
Patensie, *S. Africa* 56 E3
Paternò, *Italy* 20 F6
Pateros, *U.S.A.* 82 B4
Paterson, *U.S.A.* 79 F10
Paterson Ra., *Australia* 60 D3
Pathankot, *India* 42 C6
Pathfinder Res., *U.S.A.* 82 E10
Pathiu, *Thailand* 39 G2
Pathum Thani, *Thailand* 38 E3
Pati, *Indonesia* 37 G14
Patiala, *India* 42 D7
Patkai Bum, *India* 41 F19
Pátmos, *Greece* 21 F12
Patna, *India* 43 G11
Patonga, *Uganda* 54 B3
Patos, L. dos, *Brazil* 95 C5
Patos de Minas, *Brazil* 93 G9
Patquía, *Argentina* 94 C2
Pátrai, *Greece* 21 E9
Pátraikós Kólpos, *Greece* 21 E9
Patrocínio, *Brazil* 93 G9
Patta, *Kenya* 54 C5
Pattani, *Thailand* 39 J3
Patten, *U.S.A.* 71 C6
Patterson, *Calif., U.S.A.* 83 H3
Patterson, *La., U.S.A.* 81 L9
Patterson, Mt., *U.S.A.* 84 G7
Patti, *India* 42 D6
Patti, *Italy* 20 E6
Pattoki, *Pakistan* 42 D5
Patton, *U.S.A.* 78 F6
Patuakhali, *Bangla.* 41 H17
Patuca →, *Honduras* 88 C3
Patuca, Punta, *Honduras* 88 C3
Pátzcuaro, *Mexico* 86 D4
Pau, *France* 18 E3
Pauillac, *France* 18 D3
Pauini →, *Brazil* 92 D6
Pauk, *Burma* 41 J19
Paul I., *Canada* 71 A7
Paulis = Isiro, *Zaïre* 54 B2
Paulistana, *Brazil* 93 E10
Paullina, *U.S.A.* 80 D7
Paulo Afonso, *Brazil* 93 E11
Paulpietersburg, *S. Africa* 57 D5
Pauls Valley, *U.S.A.* 81 H6
Pauma Valley, *U.S.A.* 85 M10
Pāveh, *Iran* 44 C5
Pavia, *Italy* 20 B3
Pavlodar, *Kazakhstan* 26 D8
Pavlograd, *Ukraine* 25 E6
Pavlovo, *Russia* 24 C7
Pavlovo, *Russia* 27 C12
Pavlovsk, *Russia* 25 D7
Pawhuska, *U.S.A.* 81 G6
Pawling, *U.S.A.* 79 E11
Pawnee, *U.S.A.* 81 G6
Pawnee City, *U.S.A.* 80 E6
Pawtucket, *U.S.A.* 79 E13
Paximádhia, *Greece* 23 D6
Paxton, *Ill., U.S.A.* 76 E1
Paxton, *Nebr., U.S.A.* 80 E4
Payakumbuh, *Indonesia* 36 E2
Payette, *U.S.A.* 82 D5
Payne Bay = Bellin, *Canada* 69 B13

Payne L., *Canada* 69 C12
Paynes Find, *Australia* 61 E2
Paynesville, *U.S.A.* 80 C7
Paysandú, *Uruguay* 94 C4
Payson, *Ariz., U.S.A.* 83 J8
Payson, *Utah, U.S.A.* 82 F8
Paz →, *Guatemala* 88 D1
Paz, B. la, *Mexico* 86 C2
Pāzanān, *Iran* 45 D6
Pazardzhik, *Bulgaria* 21 C11
Pe Ell, *U.S.A.* 84 D3
Peabody, *U.S.A.* 79 D14
Peace →, *Canada* 72 B6
Peace Point, *Canada* 72 B6
Peace River, *Canada* 72 B5
Peach Springs, *U.S.A.* 83 J7
Peak Downs, *Australia* 62 C4
Peak Downs Mine, *Australia* 62 C4
Peak Hill, *N.S.W., Australia* 63 E4
Peak Hill, *W. Austral., Australia* 61 E2
Peak Ra., *Australia* 62 C4
Peake, *Australia* 63 F2
Peake Cr. →, *Australia* 63 D2
Peale Mt., *U.S.A.* 83 G9
Pearblossom, *U.S.A.* 85 L9
Pearl →, *U.S.A.* 81 K10
Pearl City, *U.S.A.* 74 H16
Pearsall, *U.S.A.* 81 L5
Pearse I., *Canada* 72 C2
Peary Land, *Greenland* 4 A6
Pease →, *U.S.A.* 81 H5
Pebane, *Mozam.* 55 F4
Pebas, *Peru* 92 D4
Pebble Beach, *U.S.A.* 84 J5
Peč, *Serbia, Yug.* 21 C9
Pechenga, *Russia* 24 A5
Pechiguera, Pta., *Canary Is.* 22 F6
Pechora →, *Russia* 24 A9
Pechorskaya Guba, *Russia* 24 A9
Pecos, *U.S.A.* 81 K3
Pecos →, *U.S.A.* 81 L3
Pécs, *Hungary* 17 E9
Pedder, L., *Australia* 62 G4
Peddie, *S. Africa* 57 E4
Pédernales, *Dom. Rep.* 89 C5
Pedieos →, *Cyprus* 23 D12
Pedirka, *Australia* 63 D2
Pedra Azul, *Brazil* 93 G10
Pedreiras, *Brazil* 93 D10
Pedro Afonso, *Brazil* 93 E9
Pedro Cays, *Jamaica* 88 C4
Pedro de Valdivia, *Chile* 94 A2
Pedro Juan Caballero, *Paraguay* 95 A4
Peebinga, *Australia* 63 E3
Peebles, *U.K.* 12 F5
Peekskill, *U.S.A.* 79 E11
Peel, *U.K.* 10 C3
Peel →, *Australia* 63 E5
Peel →, *Canada* 68 B6
Peera Peera Poolanna L., *Australia* 63 D2
Peers, *Canada* 72 C5
Pegasus Bay, *N.Z.* 59 K4
Pegu, *Burma* 41 L20
Pegu Yoma, *Burma* 41 K19
Pehuajó, *Argentina* 94 D3
Pei Xian, *China* 34 G9
Peine, *Chile* 94 A2
Peip'ing = Beijing, *China* 34 E9
Peixe, *Brazil* 93 F9
Pekalongan, *Indonesia* 37 G13
Pekan, *Malaysia* 39 L4
Pekanbaru, *Indonesia* 36 D2
Pekin, *U.S.A.* 80 E10
Peking = Beijing, *China* 34 E9
Pelabuhan Kelang, *Malaysia* 39 L3
Pelabuhan Ratu, Teluk, *Indonesia* 37 G12
Pelabuhanratu, *Indonesia* 37 G12
Pelaihari, *Indonesia* 36 E4
Peleaga, *Romania* 17 F11
Pelée, Mt., *Martinique* 89 D7
Pelee, Pt., *Canada* 70 D3
Pelee I., *Canada* 70 D3
Pelekech, *Kenya* 54 B4
Peleng, *Indonesia* 37 E6
Pelham, *U.S.A.* 77 K3
Pelican L., *Canada* 73 C8
Pelican Narrows, *Canada* 73 B8
Pelican Rapids, *Canada* 73 C8
Pelkosenniemi, *Finland* 8 C19
Pella, *S. Africa* 56 D2
Pella, *U.S.A.* 80 E8
Pelly →, *Canada* 68 B6
Pelly Bay, *Canada* 69 B11
Pelly L., *Canada* 68 B9
Peloponnese = Pelopónnisos □, *Greece* 21 F10
Pelopónnisos □, *Greece* 21 F10
Peloro, C., *Italy* 20 E6
Pelorus Sd., *N.Z.* 59 J4
Pelotas, *Brazil* 95 C5
Pelvoux, Massif de, *France* 18 D7
Pemalang, *Indonesia* 37 G13
Pematangsiantar, *Indonesia* 36 D1
Pemba, *Mozam.* 55 E5
Pemba, *Zambia* 55 F2
Pemba Channel, *Tanzania* 54 D4
Pemba I., *Tanzania* 54 D4
Pemberton, *Australia* 61 F2
Pemberton, *Canada* 72 C4
Pembina, *U.S.A.* 73 D9
Pembina →, *U.S.A.* 73 D9
Pembine, *U.S.A.* 76 C2
Pembino, *U.S.A.* 80 A6
Pembroke, *Canada* 70 C4
Pembroke, *U.K.* 11 F3
Pembroke, *U.S.A.* 77 J5
Pen-y-Ghent, *U.K.* 10 C5
Peña de Francia, Sierra de, *Spain* 19 B2
Peñalara, Pico, *Spain* 19 B4
Penang = Pinang, *Malaysia* 39 K3
Penápolis, *Brazil* 95 A6
Peñarroya-Pueblonuevo, *Spain* 19 C3
Peñas, C. de, *Spain* 19 A3
Penas, G. de, *Chile* 96 F2
Peñas del Chache, *Canary Is.* 22 E6
Pench'i = Benxi, *China* 35 D12
Pend Oreille →, *U.S.A.* 82 B5
Pend Oreille, L., *U.S.A.* 82 C5
Pendembu, *S. Leone* 50 G2
Pender B., *Australia* 60 C3
Pendleton, *Calif., U.S.A.* 85 M9
Pendleton, *Oreg., U.S.A.* 82 D4
Penedo, *Brazil* 93 F11
Penetanguishene, *Canada* 70 D4
Pengalengan, *Indonesia* 37 G12
Penge, *Kasai Or., Zaïre* 54 D1
Penge, *Kivu, Zaïre* 54 C2
Penglai, *China* 35 F11
Penguin, *Australia* 62 G4
Penhalonga, *Zimbabwe* 55 F3
Peniche, *Portugal* 19 C1
Penicuik, *U.K.* 12 F5
Penida, *Indonesia* 36 F5
Peninsular Malaysia □, *Malaysia* 39 L4
Penmarch, Pte. de, *France* 18 C1
Penn Hills, *U.S.A.* 78 F5
Penn Yan, *U.S.A.* 78 D7
Pennant, *Canada* 73 C7
Penner →, *India* 40 M12
Pennines, *U.K.* 10 C5
Pennington, *U.S.A.* 84 F5
Pennsylvania □, *U.S.A.* 76 E6
Penny, *Canada* 72 C4
Penola, *Australia* 63 F3
Penong, *Australia* 61 F5
Penonomé, *Panama* 88 E3
Penrith, *Australia* 63 E5
Penrith, *U.K.* 10 C5
Pensacola, *U.S.A.* 77 K2
Pensacola Mts., *Antarctica* 5 E1
Pense, *Canada* 73 C8
Penshurst, *Australia* 63 F3
Penticton, *Canada* 72 D5
Pentland, *Australia* 62 C4
Pentland Firth, *U.K.* 12 C5
Pentland Hills, *U.K.* 12 F5
Penylan L., *Canada* 73 A7
Penza, *Russia* 24 D8
Penzance, *U.K.* 11 G2
Penzhino, *Russia* 27 C17
Penzhinskaya Guba, *Russia* 27 C17
Peoria, *Ariz., U.S.A.* 83 K7
Peoria, *Ill., U.S.A.* 80 E10
Pera Hd., *Australia* 62 A3
Perabumulih, *Indonesia* 36 E2
Pérama, *Kérkira, Greece* 23 A3
Pérama, *Kríti, Greece* 23 D6
Percé, *Canada* 71 C7
Perche, *France* 18 B4
Percival Lakes, *Australia* 60 D4
Percy Is., *Australia* 62 C5
Perdido, Mte., *Spain* 19 A6
Perdu, Mt. = Perdido, Mte., *Spain* 19 A6
Pereira, *Colombia* 92 C3
Perekerten, *Australia* 63 E3
Perenjori, *Australia* 61 E2
Pereyaslav Khmelnitskiy, *Ukraine* 25 D5
Pérez, I., *Mexico* 87 C7
Pergamino, *Argentina* 94 C3
Perham, *U.S.A.* 80 B7
Perhentian, Kepulauan, *Malaysia* 39 K4
Péribonca →, *Canada* 71 C5
Péribonca, L., *Canada* 71 B5
Perico, *Argentina* 94 A2
Pericos, *Mexico* 86 B3
Périgord, *France* 18 D4
Périgueux, *France* 18 D4
Perijá, Sierra de, *Colombia* 92 B4
Peristerona →, *Cyprus* 23 D12
Perlas, Arch. de las, *Panama* 88 E4
Perlas, Punta de, *Nic.* 88 D3
Perm, *Russia* 24 C10
Pernambuco = Recife, *Brazil* 93 E12
Pernambuco □, *Brazil* 93 E11
Pernatty Lagoon, *Australia* 63 E2
Peron, C., *Australia* 61 E1
Peron Is., *Australia* 60 B5
Peron Pen., *Australia* 61 E1
Perow, *Canada* 72 C3
Perpendicular Pt., *Australia* 63 E5
Perpignan, *France* 18 E5
Perris, *U.S.A.* 85 M9
Perry, *Fla., U.S.A.* 77 K4
Perry, *Ga., U.S.A.* 77 J4
Perry, *Iowa, U.S.A.* 80 E7
Perry, *Maine, U.S.A.* 77 C12
Perry, *Okla., U.S.A.* 81 G6
Perryton, *U.S.A.* 81 G4
Perryville, *U.S.A.* 81 G10
Persia = Iran ■, *Asia* 45 C7
Persian Gulf = Gulf, The, *Asia* 45 E6
Perth, *Australia* 61 F2
Perth, *Canada* 70 D4
Perth, *U.K.* 12 E5
Perth Amboy, *U.S.A.* 79 F10
Peru, *Ill., U.S.A.* 80 E10
Peru, *Ind., U.S.A.* 76 E2
Peru ■, *S. Amer.* 92 E3
Peru-Chile Trench, *Pac. Oc.* 65 K20
Perúgia, *Italy* 20 C5
Pervomaysk, *Ukraine* 25 E5
Pervouralsk, *Russia* 24 C10
Pes, Pta. del, *Spain* 22 C7
Pésaro, *Italy* 20 C5
Pescara, *Italy* 20 C6
Peshawar, *Pakistan* 42 B4
Peshtigo, *U.S.A.* 76 C2
Pesqueira, *Brazil* 93 E11
Petah Tiqwa, *Israel* 47 C3
Petaling Jaya, *Malaysia* 39 L3
Petaloudhes, *Greece* 23 C10
Petaluma, *U.S.A.* 84 G4
Petange, *Lux.* 15 E5
Petatlán, *Mexico* 86 D4
Petauke, *Zambia* 55 E3
Petawawa, *Canada* 70 C4
Petén Itzá, L., *Guatemala* 88 C2
Peter I.s Øy, *Antarctica* 5 C16
Peter Pond L., *Canada* 73 B7
Peterbell, *Canada* 70 C3
Peterborough, *Australia* 63 E2
Peterborough, *Canada* 78 B6
Peterborough, *U.K.* 11 E7
Peterborough, *U.S.A.* 79 D13
Peterhead, *U.K.* 12 D7
Petermann Bjerg, *Greenland* 66 B17
Petersburg, *Alaska, U.S.A.* 72 B2
Petersburg, *Ind., U.S.A.* 76 F2
Petersburg, *Va., U.S.A.* 76 G7
Petersburg, *W. Va., U.S.A.* 76 F6
Petford, *Australia* 62 B3
Petit Bois I., *U.S.A.* 77 K1
Petit-Cap, *Canada* 71 C7
Petit Goâve, *Haiti* 89 C5
Petit Lac Manicouagan, *Canada* 71 B6
Petitcodiac, *Canada* 71 C6
Petite Baleine →, *Canada* 70 A4
Petite Saguenay, *Canada* 71 C5
Petitsikapau, L., *Canada* 71 B6
Petlad, *India* 42 H5
Peto, *Mexico* 87 C7
Petone, *N.Z.* 59 J5
Petoskey, *U.S.A.* 76 C3
Petra, *Jordan* 47 E4
Petra, *Spain* 22 B10
Petra, Ostrova, *Russia* 4 B13
Petra Velikogo, Zaliv, *Russia* 30 C5
Petrich, *Bulgaria* 21 D10
Petrograd = Sankt-Peterburg, *Russia* 24 C5
Petrolândia, *Brazil* 93 E11
Petrolia, *Canada* 70 D3
Petrolina, *Brazil* 93 E10
Petropavlovsk, *Kazakhstan* 26 D7
Petropavlovsk-Kamchatskiy, *Russia* 27 D16
Petrópolis, *Brazil* 95 A7
Petroşeni, *Romania* 17 F11
Petrovaradin, *Serbia, Yug.* 21 B8
Petrovsk, *Russia* 24 D8
Petrovsk-Zabaykalskiy, *Russia* 27 D11
Petrozavodsk, *Russia* 24 B5
Petrus Steyn, *S. Africa* 57 D4
Petrusburg, *S. Africa* 56 D4
Peumo, *Chile* 94 C1
Peureulak, *Indonesia* 36 D1
Pevek, *Russia* 27 C18
Pforzheim, *Germany* 16 D4
Phagwara, *India* 40 D9
Phaistós, *Greece* 23 D6
Phala, *Botswana* 56 C4
Phalera = Phulera, *India* 42 F6
Phalodi, *India* 42 F5
Phan, *Thailand* 38 C2
Phan Rang, *Vietnam* 39 G7
Phan Ri = Hoa Da, *Vietnam* 39 G7
Phan Thiet, *Vietnam* 39 G7
Phanat Nikhom, *Thailand* 38 F3
Phangan, Ko, *Thailand* 39 H3
Phangnga, *Thailand* 39 H2
Phanh Bho Ho Chi Minh, *Vietnam* 39 G6
Phanom Sarakham, *Thailand* 38 F3
Pharenda, *India* 43 F10
Phatthalung, *Thailand* 39 J3
Phayao, *Thailand* 38 C2
Phelps, *N.Y., U.S.A.* 78 D7
Phelps, *Wis., U.S.A.* 80 B10
Phelps L., *Canada* 73 B8
Phenix City, *U.S.A.* 77 J3
Phet Buri, *Thailand* 38 F2
Phetchabun, *Thailand* 38 D3
Phetchabun, Thiu Khao, *Thailand* 38 E3
Phetchaburi = Phet Buri, *Thailand* 38 F2
Phi Phi, Ko, *Thailand* 39 J2
Phiafay, *Laos* 38 E6
Phibun Mangsahan, *Thailand* 38 E5
Phichai, *Thailand* 38 D3
Phichit, *Thailand* 38 D3
Philadelphia, *Miss., U.S.A.* 81 J10
Philadelphia, *N.Y., U.S.A.* 79 B9
Philadelphia, *Pa., U.S.A.* 79 F9
Philip, *U.S.A.* 80 C4
Philippeville, *Belgium* 15 D4
Philippi L., *Australia* 62 C2
Philippines ■, *Asia* 37 B6
Philippolis, *S. Africa* 56 E4
Philippopolis = Plovdiv, *Bulgaria* 21 C11
Philipsburg, *Mont., U.S.A.* 82 C7
Philipsburg, *Pa., U.S.A.* 78 F6
Philipstown, *S. Africa* 56 E3
Phillip I., *Australia* 63 F4
Phillips, *Tex., U.S.A.* 81 H4
Phillips, *Wis., U.S.A.* 80 C9
Phillipsburg, *Kans., U.S.A.* 80 F5
Phillipsburg, *Pa., U.S.A.* 79 F9
Phillott, *Australia* 63 D4
Philmont, *U.S.A.* 79 D11
Philomath, *U.S.A.* 82 D2
Phimai, *Thailand* 38 E4
Phitsanulok, *Thailand* 38 D3
Phnom Dangrek, *Thailand* 38 E5
Phnom Penh, *Cambodia* 39 G5
Phoenix, *Ariz., U.S.A.* 83 K7
Phoenix, *N.Y., U.S.A.* 79 C8
Phoenix Is., *Kiribati* 64 H10
Phoenixville, *U.S.A.* 79 F9
Phon, *Thailand* 38 E4
Phon Tiou, *Laos* 38 D5
Phong →, *Thailand* 38 D4
Phong Saly, *Laos* 38 B4
Phong Tho, *Vietnam* 38 A4
Phonhong, *Laos* 38 C4
Phonum, *Thailand* 39 H2
Phosphate Hill, *Australia* 62 C2
Photharam, *Thailand* 38 F2
Phra Chedi Sam Ong, *Thailand* 38 E2
Phra Nakhon Si Ayutthaya, *Thailand* 38 E3
Phra Thong, Ko, *Thailand* 39 H2
Phrae, *Thailand* 38 C3
Phrom Phiram, *Thailand* 38 D3
Phu Dien, *Vietnam* 38 C5
Phu Loi, *Laos* 38 B4
Phu Ly, *Vietnam* 38 B5
Phu Tho, *Vietnam* 38 B5
Phuc Yen, *Vietnam* 38 B5
Phuket, *Thailand* 39 J2
Phuket, Ko, *Thailand* 39 J2
Phulera, *India* 42 F6
Phumiphon, Khuan, *Thailand* 38 D2
Phun Phin, *Thailand* 39 H2
Piacenza, *Italy* 20 B3
Pialba, *Australia* 63 D5
Pian Cr. →, *Australia* 63 E4
Piapot, *Canada* 73 D7
Piatra Neamţ, *Romania* 17 E13
Piauí □, *Brazil* 93 E10
Piave →, *Italy* 20 B5
Piazza Ármerina, *Italy* 20 F6
Pibor Post, *Sudan* 51 G11
Pica, *Chile* 92 H5
Picardie, *France* 18 B5
Picardy = Picardie, *France* 18 B5
Picayune, *U.S.A.* 81 K10
Pichilemu, *Chile* 94 C1
Pickerel L., *Canada* 70 C1
Pickle Lake, *Canada* 70 B1
Pico Truncado, *Argentina* 96 F3
Picton, *Australia* 63 E5
Picton, *Canada* 70 D4
Picton, *N.Z.* 59 J5
Pictou, *Canada* 71 C7
Picture Butte, *Canada* 72 D6
Picún Leufú, *Argentina* 96 D3
Pidurutalagala, *Sri Lanka* 40 R12
Piedmont = Piemonte □, *Italy* 20 B2
Piedmont, *U.S.A.* 77 J3
Piedmont Plateau, *U.S.A.* 77 J5
Piedras, R. de las →, *Peru* 92 F5
Piedras Negras, *Mexico* 86 B4
Piemonte □, *Italy* 20 B2
Pierce, *U.S.A.* 82 C6
Piercefield, *U.S.A.* 79 B10
Pierre, *U.S.A.* 80 C4
Piet Retief, *S. Africa* 57 D5
Pietarsaari = Jakobstad, *Finland* 8 E17
Pietermaritzburg, *S. Africa* 57 D5
Pietersburg, *S. Africa* 57 C4
Pietrosul, *Romania* 17 E12
Pigeon, *U.S.A.* 76 D4
Piggott, *U.S.A.* 81 G9
Pigüe, *Argentina* 94 D3
Pihani, *India* 43 F9
Pikes Peak, *U.S.A.* 80 F2
Piketberg, *S. Africa* 56 E2
Pikeville, *U.S.A.* 76 G4
Pikou, *China* 35 E12
Pikwitonei, *Canada* 73 B9
Pilani, *India* 42 E6
Pilar, *Brazil* 93 E11
Pilar, *Paraguay* 94 B4
Pilas Group, *Phil.* 37 C6
Pilcomayo →, *Paraguay* 94 B4
Pilibhit, *India* 43 E8
Pilica →, *Poland* 17 C10
Pilkhawa, *India* 42 E7
Pilos, *Greece* 21 F9
Pilot Mound, *Canada* 73 D9
Pilot Point, *U.S.A.* 81 J6
Pilot Rock, *U.S.A.* 82 D4
Pilsen = Plzeň, *Czech.* 16 D6
Pima, *U.S.A.* 83 K9
Pimba, *Australia* 63 E2
Pimenta Bueno, *Brazil* 92 F6
Pimentel, *Peru* 92 E3
Pinang, *Malaysia* 39 K3
Pinar, C. del, *Spain* 22 B10
Pinar del Río, *Cuba* 88 B3
Pincher Creek, *Canada* 72 D6
Pinchi L., *Canada* 72 C4
Pinckneyville, *U.S.A.* 80 F10
Pińczów, *Poland* 17 C10
Pind Dadan Khan, *Pakistan* 42 C5
Pindar, *Australia* 61 E2
Pindi Gheb, *Pakistan* 42 C5
Pindiga, *Nigeria* 50 G7
Pindos Óros, *Greece* 21 E9
Pindus Mts. = Pindos Óros, *Greece* 21 E9
Pine, *U.S.A.* 83 J8
Pine →, *Canada* 73 B7
Pine, C., *Canada* 71 C9
Pine Bluff, *U.S.A.* 81 H8
Pine City, *U.S.A.* 80 C8
Pine Falls, *Canada* 73 C9
Pine Flat Res., *U.S.A.* 84 J7
Pine Pass, *Canada* 72 B4
Pine Point, *Canada* 72 A6
Pine Ridge, *U.S.A.* 80 D3
Pine River, *Canada* 73 C8
Pine River, *U.S.A.* 80 B7
Pine Valley, *U.S.A.* 85 N10
Pinecrest, *U.S.A.* 84 G6
Pinedale, *U.S.A.* 84 J7
Pinega →, *Russia* 24 B8
Pinehill, *Australia* 62 C4
Pinerolo, *Italy* 20 B2
Pinetop, *U.S.A.* 83 J9
Pinetown, *S. Africa* 57 D5
Pinetree, *U.S.A.* 82 E11
Pineville, *Ky., U.S.A.* 77 G4
Pineville, *La., U.S.A.* 81 K8
Ping →, *Thailand* 38 E3
Pingaring, *Australia* 61 F2
Pingding, *China* 34 F7
Pingdingshan, *China* 34 H7
Pingdong, *Taiwan* 33 D7
Pingdu, *China* 35 F10
Pingelly, *Australia* 61 F2
Pingliang, *China* 34 G4
Pinglu, *China* 34 E7
Pingluo, *China* 34 E4
Pingquan, *China* 35 D10
Pingrup, *Australia* 61 F2
Pingwu, *China* 34 H3
Pingxiang, *China* 32 D5
Pingyao, *China* 34 F7
Pingyi, *China* 35 G9
Pingyin, *China* 34 F9
Pingyuan, *China* 34 F9
Pinhal, *Brazil* 95 A6
Pinhel, *Portugal* 19 B2
Pini, *Indonesia* 36 D1
Piniós →, *Greece* 21 E10
Pinjarra, *Australia* 61 F2
Pink →, *Canada* 73 B8
Pinnacles, *Australia* 61 E3
Pinnacles, *U.S.A.* 84 J5
Pinnaroo, *Australia* 63 F3
Pinon Hills, *U.S.A.* 85 L9
Pinos, *Mexico* 86 C4
Pinos, Mt., *U.S.A.* 85 L7
Pinos Pt., *U.S.A.* 83 H3
Pinotepa Nacional, *Mexico* 87 D5
Pinrang, *Indonesia* 37 E5
Pinsk, *Belorussia* 24 D4
Pintados, *Chile* 92 H5
Pintumba, *Australia* 61 F5
Pinyug, *Russia* 24 B8
Pioche, *U.S.A.* 83 H6
Piombino, *Italy* 20 C4
Pioner, Os., *Russia* 27 B10
Piorini, L., *Brazil* 92 D6
Piotrków Trybunalski, *Poland* 17 C9
Pip, *Iran* 45 E9
Pipar, *India* 42 F5
Piparia, *India* 42 H8
Pipestone, *U.S.A.* 80 D6
Pipestone →, *Canada* 70 B2
Pipestone Cr. →, *Canada* 73 D8
Pipmuacan, Rés., *Canada* 71 C5
Pippingarra, *Australia* 60 D2
Piqua, *U.S.A.* 76 E3
Piquiri →, *Brazil* 95 A5
Pīr Sohrāb, *Iran* 45 E9
Piracicaba, *Brazil* 95 A6
Piracuruca, *Brazil* 93 D10
Piræus = Piraiévs, *Greece* 21 F10
Piraiévs, *Greece* 21 F10
Pirajuí, *Brazil* 95 A6
Pirané, *Argentina* 94 B4
Pirapora, *Brazil* 93 G10
Pírgos, *Greece* 21 F9
Piribebuy, *Paraguay* 94 B4
Pirin Planina, *Bulgaria* 21 D10
Pirineos, *Spain* 19 A6
Piripiri, *Brazil* 93 D10
Pirot, *Serbia, Yug.* 21 C10
Piru, *Indonesia* 37 E7
Piru, *U.S.A.* 85 L8
Pisa, *Italy* 20 C4
Pisagua, *Chile* 92 G4
Pisco, *Peru* 92 F3
Písek, *Czech.* 16 D7
Pishan, *China* 32 C2

Pishin Lora →, *Pakistan* . . . 42 E1
Pising, *Indonesia* 37 F6
Pismo Beach, *U.S.A.* 85 K6
Pissouri, *Cyprus* 23 E11
Pistóia, *Italy* 20 C4
Pistol B., *Canada* 73 A10
Pisuerga →, *Spain* 19 B3
Pitarpunga, L., *Australia* . . . 63 E3
Pitcairn I., *Pac. Oc.* 65 K14
Pite älv →, *Sweden* 8 D16
Piteå, *Sweden* 8 D16
Piteşti, *Romania* 17 F12
Pithapuram, *India* 41 L13
Pithara, *Australia* 61 F2
Pitlochry, *U.K.* 12 E5
Pitsilia □, *Cyprus* 23 E12
Pitt I., *Canada* 72 C3
Pittsburg, *Kans., U.S.A.* 81 G7
Pittsburg, *Tex., U.S.A.* 81 J7
Pittsburgh, *U.S.A.* 78 F5
Pittsfield, *Ill., U.S.A.* 80 F9
Pittsfield, *Mass., U.S.A.* 79 D11
Pittsfield, *N.H., U.S.A.* 79 C13
Pittston, *U.S.A.* 79 E9
Pittsworth, *Australia* 63 D5
Pituri →, *Australia* 62 C2
Piura, *Peru* 92 E2
Pixley, *U.S.A.* 84 K7
Pizzo, *Italy* 20 E7
Placentia, *Canada* 71 C9
Placentia B., *Canada* 71 C9
Placerville, *U.S.A.* 84 G6
Placetas, *Cuba* 88 B4
Plain Dealing, *U.S.A.* 81 J8
Plainfield, *U.S.A.* 79 F10
Plains, *Kans., U.S.A.* 81 G4
Plains, *Mont., U.S.A.* 82 C6
Plains, *Tex., U.S.A.* 81 J3
Plainview, *Nebr., U.S.A.* 80 D6
Plainview, *Tex., U.S.A.* 81 H4
Plainville, *U.S.A.* 80 F5
Plainwell, *U.S.A.* 76 D3
Pláka, Ákra, *Greece* 23 D8
Plakhino, *Russia* 26 C9
Plana Cays, *Bahamas* 89 B5
Planada, *U.S.A.* 84 H6
Plankinton, *U.S.A.* 80 D5
Plano, *U.S.A.* 81 J6
Plant City, *U.S.A.* 77 L4
Plaquemine, *U.S.A.* 81 K9
Plasencia, *Spain* 19 B2
Plaster City, *U.S.A.* 85 N11
Plaster Rock, *Canada* 71 C6
Plastun, *Russia* 30 B8
Plata, Río de la, *S. Amer.* . . . 94 C4
Platani →, *Italy* 20 F5
Plátanos, *Greece* 23 D5
Plateau du Coteau du
Missouri, *U.S.A.* 80 B4
Plati, Ákra, *Greece* 21 D11
Plato, *Colombia* 92 B4
Platte, *U.S.A.* 80 D5
Platte →, *U.S.A.* 80 F7
Platteville, *U.S.A.* 80 E2
Plattsburg, *U.S.A.* 79 B11
Plattsmouth, *U.S.A.* 80 E7
Plauen, *Germany* 16 C6
Playa Blanca, *Canary Is.* . . . 22 F6
Playa Blanca Sur, *Canary Is.* 22 F6
Playa de las Americas,
Canary Is. 22 F3
Playa de Mogán, *Canary Is.* 22 G4
Playa del Inglés, *Canary Is.* . 22 G4
Playa Esmerelda, *Canary Is.* 22 F5
Playgreen L., *Canada* 73 C9
Pleasant Bay, *Canada* 71 C7
Pleasant Hill, *Calif., U.S.A.* . 84 H4
Pleasant Hill, *Mo., U.S.A.* . . 80 F7
Pleasanton, *U.S.A.* 81 L5
Pleasantville, *U.S.A.* 76 F8
Pleiku, *Vietnam* 38 F7
Plenty →, *Australia* 62 C2
Plenty, B. of, *N.Z.* 59 G6
Plentywood, *U.S.A.* 80 A2
Plesetsk, *Russia* 24 B7
Plessisville, *Canada* 71 C5
Pletipi L., *Canada* 71 B5
Pleven, *Bulgaria* 21 C11
Plevlja, *Montenegro, Yug.* . . 21 C8
Płock, *Poland* 17 B9
Ploieşti, *Romania* 17 F13
Plonge, Lac la, *Canada* 73 B7
Plovdiv, *Bulgaria* 21 C11
Plum, *U.S.A.* 78 F5
Plum I., *U.S.A.* 79 E12
Plumas, *U.S.A.* 84 F7
Plummer, *U.S.A.* 82 C5
Plumtree, *Zimbabwe* 55 G2
Plymouth, *U.K.* 11 G3
Plymouth, *Calif., U.S.A.* 84 G6
Plymouth, *Ind., U.S.A.* 76 E2
Plymouth, *Mass., U.S.A.* . . . 79 E14
Plymouth, *N.C., U.S.A.* 77 H7
Plymouth, *N.H., U.S.A.* 79 C13
Plymouth, *Pa., U.S.A.* 79 E9
Plymouth, *Wis., U.S.A.* 76 D2
Plynlimon = Pumlumon
Fawr, *U.K.* 11 E4
Plzeň, *Czech.* 16 D6
Po →, *Italy* 20 B5
Po Hai = Bo Hai, *China* 35 E10
Pobeda, *Russia* 27 C15
Pobedino, *Russia* 27 E15
Pobedy Pik, *Kirghizia* 26 E8
Pocahontas, *Ark., U.S.A.* . . . 81 G9
Pocahontas, *Iowa, U.S.A.* . . 80 D7
Pocatello, *U.S.A.* 82 E7
Pochutla, *Mexico* 87 D5
Pocito Casas, *Mexico* 86 B2
Pocomoke City, *U.S.A.* 76 F8
Poços de Caldas, *Brazil* 95 A6
Podgorica = Titograd,
Montenegro, Yug. 21 C8
Podkamennaya
Tunguska →, *Russia* 27 C10
Podolsk, *Russia* 24 C6
Podor, *Senegal* 50 E1
Podporozhy, *Russia* 24 B5
Pofadder, *S. Africa* 56 D2
Pogamasing, *Canada* 70 C3
Pogranitšnyi, *Russia* 30 B5
Poh, *Indonesia* 37 E6
Pohang, *S. Korea* 35 F15
Pohnpei, *Pac. Oc.* 64 G7
Poinsett, C., *Antarctica* 5 C8
Point Edward, *Canada* 70 D3
Point Pedro, *Sri Lanka* 40 Q12
Point Pleasant, *N.J., U.S.A.* . 79 F10
Point Pleasant, *W. Va.,*
U.S.A. 76 F4
Pointe-à-la Hache, *U.S.A.* . . 81 L10
Pointe-à-Pitre, *Guadeloupe* . 89 C7
Pointe Noire, *Congo* 52 E2
Poisonbush Ra., *Australia* . . 60 D3
Poitiers, *France* 18 C4
Pojoaque Valley, *U.S.A.* 83 J11
Pokaran, *India* 40 F7
Pokataroo, *Australia* 63 D4
Poko, *Zaïre* 54 B2
Pokrovsk, *Russia* 24 D8
Pokrovsk, *Russia* 27 C13
Polacca, *U.S.A.* 83 J8
Polan, *Iran* 45 E9
Poland ■, *Europe* 17 C10
Polcura, *Chile* 94 D1
Polden Hills, *U.K.* 11 F5
Polesye, *Belorussia* 24 D4
Polevskoy, *Russia* 24 C11
Polewali, *Indonesia* 37 E5
Pŏlgyo-ri, *S. Korea* 35 G14
Poli, *Cameroon* 52 C2
Polillo Is., *Phil.* 37 B6
Polis, *Cyprus* 23 D11
Políyiros, *Greece* 21 D10
Polk, *U.S.A.* 78 E5
Pollachi, *India* 40 P10
Pollensa, *Spain* 22 B10
Pollensa, B. de, *Spain* 22 B10
Pollock, *U.S.A.* 80 C4
Polnovat, *Russia* 26 C7
Polo, *U.S.A.* 80 E10
Polotsk, *Belorussia* 24 C4
Polson, *U.S.A.* 82 C6
Poltava, *Ukraine* 25 E5
Polunochnoye, *Russia* 24 B11
Polyarny, *Russia* 24 A5
Polynesia, *Pac. Oc.* 65 H11
Pomaro, *Mexico* 86 D4
Pombal, *Brazil* 93 E11
Pombal, *Portugal* 19 C1
Pómbia, *Greece* 23 D6
Pomeroy, *Ohio, U.S.A.* 76 F4
Pomeroy, *Wash., U.S.A.* 82 C5
Pomona, *U.S.A.* 85 L9
Pomos, *Cyprus* 23 D11
Pomos, C., *Cyprus* 23 D11
Pompano Beach, *U.S.A.* 77 M5
Pompeys Pillar, *U.S.A.* 82 D10
Ponape = Pohnpei, *Pac. Oc.* 64 G7
Ponask, L., *Canada* 70 B1
Ponass L., *Canada* 73 C8
Ponca, *U.S.A.* 80 D6
Ponca City, *U.S.A.* 81 G6
Ponce, *Puerto Rico* 89 C6
Ponchatoula, *U.S.A.* 81 K9
Poncheville, L., *Canada* 70 B4
Pond, *U.S.A.* 85 K7
Pond Inlet, *Canada* 69 A12
Pondicherry, *India* 40 P11
Ponds, I. of, *Canada* 71 B8
Ponferrada, *Spain* 19 A2
Ponnani, *India* 40 P9
Ponnyadaung, *Burma* 41 J19
Ponoi, *Russia* 24 A7
Ponoi →, *Russia* 24 A7
Ponoka, *Canada* 72 C6
Ponorogo, *Indonesia* 37 G14
Ponta do Sol, *Madeira* 22 D2
Ponta Grossa, *Brazil* 95 B5
Ponta Pora, *Brazil* 95 A4
Pontarlier, *France* 18 C7
Pontchartrain, L., *U.S.A.* . . . 81 K9
Ponte do Pungué, *Mozam.* . . 55 F3
Ponte Macassar, *Indonesia* . 37 F6
Ponte Nova, *Brazil* 95 A7
Pontedera, *Italy* 20 C4
Pontefract, *U.K.* 10 D6
Ponteix, *Canada* 73 D7
Pontevedra, *Spain* 19 A1
Pontiac, *Ill., U.S.A.* 80 E10
Pontiac, *Mich., U.S.A.* 76 D4
Pontian Kecil, *Malaysia* 39 M4
Pontianak, *Indonesia* 36 E3
Pontic Mts. = Kuzey Anadolu
Dağları, *Turkey* 25 F6
Pontine Is. = Ponziane, Isole,
Italy 20 D5
Pontine Mts. = Kuzey
Anadolu Dağları, *Turkey* . . 25 F6
Ponton →, *Canada* 72 B5
Pontypool, *Canada* 78 B6
Pontypool, *U.K.* 11 F4
Pontypridd, *U.K.* 11 F4
Ponziane, Isole, *Italy* 20 D5
Poochera, *Australia* 63 E1
Poole, *U.K.* 11 G6
Pooley I., *Canada* 72 C3
Poona = Pune, *India* 40 K8
Pooncarie, *Australia* 63 E3
Poopelloe L., *Australia* 63 E3
Poopó, L. de, *Bolivia* 92 G5
Popanyinning, *Australia* 61 F2
Popayán, *Colombia* 92 C3
Poperinge, *Belgium* 15 D2
Popigay, *Russia* 27 B12
Popilta, L., *Australia* 63 E3
Popio L., *Australia* 63 E3
Poplar, *U.S.A.* 80 A2
Poplar →, *Man., Canada* . . . 73 C9
Poplar →, *N.W.T., Canada* . . 72 A4
Poplar Bluff, *U.S.A.* 81 G9
Poplarville, *U.S.A.* 81 K10
Popocatepetl, *Mexico* 87 D5
Popokabaka, *Zaïre* 52 F3
Porali →, *Pakistan* 42 G2
Porbandar, *India* 42 J3
Porcher I., *Canada* 72 C2
Porcupine →, *Canada* 73 B8
Porcupine →, *U.S.A.* 68 B5
Pori, *Finland* 9 F16
Porjus, *Sweden* 8 C15
Porkkala, *Finland* 9 G18
Porlamar, *Venezuela* 92 A6
Poronaysk, *Russia* 27 E15
Poroshiri-Dake, *Japan* 30 C11
Poroto Mts., *Tanzania* 55 D3
Porpoise B., *Antarctica* 5 C9
Porreras, *Spain* 22 B10
Porretta, Passo di, *Italy* 20 B4
Porsangen, *Norway* 8 A18
Port Adelaide, *Australia* 63 E2
Port Alberni, *Canada* 72 D4
Port Alfred, *Canada* 71 C5
Port Alfred, *S. Africa* 56 E4
Port Alice, *Canada* 72 C3
Port Allegany, *U.S.A.* 78 E6
Port Allen, *U.S.A.* 81 K9
Port Alma, *Australia* 62 C5
Port Angeles, *U.S.A.* 84 B3
Port Antonio, *Jamaica* 88 C4
Port Aransas, *U.S.A.* 81 M6
Port Arthur = Lüshun, *China* 35 E11
Port Arthur, *Australia* 62 G4
Port Arthur, *U.S.A.* 81 L8
Port au Port B., *Canada* 71 C8
Port-au-Prince, *Haiti* 89 C5
Port Augusta, *Australia* 63 E2
Port Augusta West, *Australia* 63 E2
Port Austin, *U.S.A.* 78 B2
Port Bell, *Uganda* 54 B3
Port Bergé Vaovao, *Madag.* . 57 B8
Port Blandford, *Canada* 71 C9
Port Bradshaw, *Australia* . . . 62 A2
Port Broughton, *Australia* . . . 63 E2
Port Burwell, *Canada* 70 D3
Port Canning, *India* 43 H13
Port-Cartier, *Canada* 71 B6
Port Chalmers, *N.Z.* 59 L3
Port Chester, *U.S.A.* 79 F11
Port Clements, *Canada* 72 C2
Port Clinton, *U.S.A.* 76 E4
Port Colborne, *Canada* 70 D4
Port Coquitlam, *Canada* 72 D4
Port Credit, *Canada* 78 C5
Port Curtis, *Australia* 62 C5
Port Dalhousie, *Canada* 78 C5
Port Darwin, *Australia* 60 B5
Port Darwin, *Falk. Is.* 96 G5
Port Davey, *Australia* 62 G4
Port-de-Paix, *Haiti* 89 C5
Port Dickson, *Malaysia* 39 L3
Port Douglas, *Australia* 62 B4
Port Dover, *Canada* 78 D4
Port Edward, *Canada* 72 C2
Port Elgin, *Canada* 70 D3
Port Elizabeth, *S. Africa* 56 E4
Port Ellen, *U.K.* 12 F2
Port-en-Bessin, *France* 18 B3
Port Erin, *I. of Man* 10 C3
Port Essington, *Australia* . . . 60 B5
Port Etienne = Nouâdhibou,
Mauritania 50 D1
Port Fairy, *Australia* 63 F3
Port Gamble, *U.S.A.* 84 C4
Port-Gentil, *Gabon* 52 E1
Port Gibson, *U.S.A.* 81 K9
Port Glasgow, *U.K.* 12 F4
Port Harcourt, *Nigeria* 50 H6
Port Hardy, *Canada* 72 C3
Port Harrison = Inoucdjouac,
Canada 69 C12
Port Hawkesbury, *Canada* . . 71 C7
Port Hedland, *Australia* 60 D2
Port Henry, *U.S.A.* 79 B11
Port Hood, *Canada* 71 C7
Port Hope, *Canada* 70 D4
Port Hueneme, *U.S.A.* 85 L7
Port Huron, *U.S.A.* 76 D4
Port Isabel, *U.S.A.* 81 M6
Port Jefferson, *U.S.A.* 79 F11
Port Jervis, *U.S.A.* 79 E10
Port Kembla, *Australia* 63 E5
Port Kenny, *Australia* 63 E1
Port-la-Nouvelle, *France* 18 E5
Port Laoise, *Ireland* 13 C4
Port Lavaca, *U.S.A.* 81 L6
Port Lincoln, *Australia* 63 E2
Port Loko, *S. Leone* 50 G2
Port Lyautey = Kenitra,
Morocco 50 B3
Port MacDonnell, *Australia* . . 63 F3
Port Macquarie, *Australia* . . . 63 E5
Port Maria, *Jamaica* 88 C4
Port Mellon, *Canada* 72 D4
Port-Menier, *Canada* 71 C7
Port Morant, *Jamaica* 88 C4
Port Moresby, *Papua N. G.* . . 64 H6
Port Mouton, *Canada* 71 D7
Port Musgrave, *Australia* 62 A3
Port Nelson, *Canada* 73 B10
Port Nolloth, *S. Africa* 56 D2
Port Nouveau-Québec,
Canada 69 C13
Port O'Connor, *U.S.A.* 81 L6
Port of Spain, *Trin. & Tob.* . . 89 D7
Port Orchard, *U.S.A.* 84 C4
Port Orford, *U.S.A.* 82 E1
Port Pegasus, *N.Z.* 59 M1
Port Perry, *Canada* 70 D4
Port Phillip B., *Australia* 63 F3
Port Pirie, *Australia* 63 E2
Port Radium = Echo Bay,
Canada 68 B8
Port Renfrew, *Canada* 72 D4
Port Roper, *Australia* 62 A2
Port Rowan, *Canada* 78 D4
Port Safaga = Bûr Safâga,
Egypt 51 C11
Port Said = Bûr Sa'îd, *Egypt* 51 B11
Port St. Joe, *U.S.A.* 77 L3
Port St. Johns, *S. Africa* 57 E4
Port-St.-Louis-du-Rhône,
France 18 E6
Port Sanilac, *U.S.A.* 78 C2
Port Saunders, *Canada* 71 B8
Port Severn, *Canada* 78 B5
Port Shepstone, *S. Africa* . . . 57 E5
Port Simpson, *Canada* 72 C2
Port Stanley = Stanley,
Falk. Is. 96 G5
Port Stanley, *Canada* 70 D3
Port Sudan = Bûr Sûdân,
Sudan 51 E12
Port Talbot, *U.K.* 11 F4
Port Townsend, *U.S.A.* 84 B4
Port-Vendres, *France* 18 E5
Port Vladimir, *Russia* 24 A5
Port Wakefield, *Australia* 63 E2
Port Washington, *U.S.A.* 76 D2
Port Weld, *Malaysia* 39 K3
Portachuelo, *Bolivia* 92 G6
Portadown, *U.K.* 13 B5
Portage, *U.S.A.* 80 D10
Portage La Prairie, *Canada* . . 73 D9
Portageville, *U.S.A.* 81 G10
Portalegre, *Portugal* 19 C2
Portales, *U.S.A.* 81 H3
Portarlington, *Ireland* 13 C4
Porter L., *N.W.T., Canada* . . . 73 A7
Porter L., *Sask., Canada* 73 B7
Porterville, *S. Africa* 56 E2
Porterville, *U.S.A.* 83 H4
Porthcawl, *U.K.* 11 F4
Porthill, *U.S.A.* 82 B5
Portile de Fier, *Europe* 17 F11
Portimão, *Portugal* 19 D1
Portland, *N.S.W., Australia* . . 63 E4
Portland, *Vic., Australia* 63 F3
Portland, *Canada* 79 B8
Portland, *Conn., U.S.A.* 79 E12
Portland, *Maine, U.S.A.* 71 D5
Portland, *Mich., U.S.A.* 76 D3
Portland, *Oreg., U.S.A.* 84 E4
Portland, I. of, *U.K.* 11 G5
Portland B., *Australia* 63 F3
Portland Bill, *U.K.* 11 G5
Portland Prom., *Canada* 69 C12
Portlands Roads, *Australia* . . 62 A3
Portneuf, *Canada* 71 C5
Porto, *Portugal* 19 B1
Pôrto Alegre, *Brazil* 95 C5
Porto Amboim = Gunza,
Angola 52 G2
Porto Cristo, *Spain* 22 B10
Pôrto de Móz, *Brazil* 93 D8
Porto Empédocle, *Italy* 20 F5
Pôrto Esperança, *Brazil* 92 G7
Pôrto Franco, *Brazil* 93 E9
Pôrto Mendes, *Brazil* 95 A5
Porto Moniz, *Madeira* 22 D2
Pôrto Murtinho, *Brazil* 92 H7
Pôrto Nacional, *Brazil* 93 F9
Porto Novo, *Benin* 50 G5
Porto Petro, *Spain* 22 B10
Porto Santo, *Madeira* 50 B1
Pôrto São José, *Brazil* 95 A5
Pôrto Seguro, *Brazil* 93 G11
Porto Tórres, *Italy* 20 D3
Pôrto União, *Brazil* 95 B5
Pôrto Válter, *Brazil* 92 E4
Porto-Vecchio, *France* 18 F9
Pôrto Velho, *Brazil* 92 E6
Portobelo, *Panama* 88 E4
Portoferráio, *Italy* 20 C4
Portola, *U.S.A.* 84 F6
Portoscuso, *Italy* 20 E3
Portoviejo, *Ecuador* 92 D2
Portpatrick, *U.K.* 12 G3
Portree, *U.K.* 12 D2
Portrush, *U.K.* 13 A5
Portsmouth, *Domin.* 89 C7
Portsmouth, *U.K.* 11 G6
Portsmouth, *N.H., U.S.A.* . . . 79 C14
Portsmouth, *Ohio, U.S.A.* . . . 76 F4
Portsmouth, *R.I., U.S.A.* 79 E13
Portsmouth, *Va., U.S.A.* 76 G7
Portsoy, *U.K.* 12 D6
Porttipahta, *Finland* 8 B19
Portugal ■, *Europe* 19 C2
Portuguese-Guinea =
Guinea-Bissau ■, *Africa* . . 50 F2
Portuguese Timor ■ =
Timor, *Indonesia* 37 F7
Portumna, *Ireland* 13 C3
Portville, *U.S.A.* 78 D6
Porvenir, *Chile* 96 G2
Porvoo = Borgå, *Finland* 9 F18
Posadas, *Argentina* 95 B4
Poshan = Boshan, *China* 35 F9
Posht-e-Badam, *Iran* 45 C7
Poso, *Indonesia* 37 E6
Posong, *S. Korea* 35 G14
Posse, *Brazil* 93 F9
Possel, *C.A.R.* 52 C3
Possession I., *Antarctica* 5 D11
Post, *U.S.A.* 81 J4
Post Falls, *U.S.A.* 82 C5
Poste Maurice Cortier,
Algeria 50 D5
Postmasburg, *S. Africa* 56 D3
Postojna, *Slovenia* 20 B6
Poston, *U.S.A.* 85 M12
Potchefstroom, *S. Africa* 56 D4
Poteau, *U.S.A.* 81 H7
Poteet, *U.S.A.* 81 L5
Potenza, *Italy* 20 D6
Poteriteri, L., *N.Z.* 59 M1
Potgietersrus, *S. Africa* 57 C4
Poti, *Georgia* 25 F7
Potiskum, *Nigeria* 50 F7
Potomac →, *U.S.A.* 76 F7
Potosí, *Bolivia* 92 G5
Potosi Mt., *U.S.A.* 85 K11
Pototan, *Phil.* 37 B6
Potrerillos, *Chile* 94 B2
Potsdam, *Germany* 16 B6
Potsdam, *U.S.A.* 79 B10
Potter, *U.S.A.* 80 E3
Pottstown, *U.S.A.* 79 F9
Pottsville, *U.S.A.* 79 F8
Pottuvil, *Sri Lanka* 40 R12
Pouce Coupé, *Canada* 72 B4
Poughkeepsie, *U.S.A.* 79 E11
Poulaphouca Res., *Ireland* . . 13 C5
Poulsbo, *U.S.A.* 84 C4
Pouso Alegre, *Mato Grosso,*
Brazil 93 F7
Pouso Alegre, *Minas Gerais,*
Brazil 95 A6
Povenets, *Russia* 24 B5
Poverty B., *N.Z.* 59 H7
Póvoa de Varzim, *Portugal* . . 19 B1
Powassan, *Canada* 70 C4
Poway, *U.S.A.* 85 N9
Powder →, *U.S.A.* 80 B2
Powder River, *U.S.A.* 82 E10
Powell, *U.S.A.* 82 D9
Powell, L., *U.S.A.* 83 H8
Powell River, *Canada* 72 D4
Powers, *Mich., U.S.A.* 76 C2
Powers, *Oreg., U.S.A.* 82 E1
Powers Lake, *U.S.A.* 80 A3
Powys □, *U.K.* 11 E4
Poyang Hu, *China* 33 D6
Poyarkovo, *Russia* 27 E13
Poza Rica, *Mexico* 87 C5
Požarevac, *Serbia, Yug.* 21 B9
Poznań, *Poland* 16 B8
Pozo, *U.S.A.* 85 K6
Pozo Almonte, *Chile* 92 H5
Pozo Colorado, *Paraguay* . . . 94 A4
Pozo del Dátil, *Mexico* 86 B2
Pozoblanco, *Spain* 19 C3
Prachin Buri, *Thailand* 38 E3
Prachuap Khiri Khan,
Thailand 39 G2
Prado, *Brazil* 93 G11
Prague = Praha, *Czech.* 16 C7
Praha, *Czech.* 16 C7
Praid, *Romania* 17 E12
Prainha, *Amazonas, Brazil* . . 92 E6
Prainha, *Pará, Brazil* 93 D8
Prairie, *Australia* 62 C3
Prairie →, *U.S.A.* 81 H5
Prairie City, *U.S.A.* 82 D4
Prairie du Chien, *U.S.A.* 80 D9
Pran Buri, *Thailand* 38 F2
Prapat, *Indonesia* 36 D1
Prasonísi, Ákra, *Greece* 23 D9
Prata, *Brazil* 93 G9
Pratapgarh, *India* 42 G6
Prato, *Italy* 20 C4
Pratt, *U.S.A.* 81 G5
Prattville, *U.S.A.* 77 J2
Pravia, *Spain* 19 A2
Praya, *Indonesia* 36 F5
Precordillera, *Argentina* 94 C2
Preeceville, *Canada* 73 C8
Prelate, *Canada* 73 C7
Premier, *Canada* 72 B3
Premont, *U.S.A.* 81 M5
Prentice, *U.S.A.* 80 C9
Prenzlau, *Germany* 16 B6
Preobrazheniye, *Russia* 30 C6
Prepansko Jezero,
Macedonia, Yug. 21 D9

Preparis North Channel, *Ind. Oc.* 41 M18
Preparis South Channel, *Ind. Oc.* 41 M18
Přerov, *Czech.* 17 D8
Prescott, *Canada* 70 D4
Prescott, *Ariz., U.S.A.* 83 J7
Prescott, *Ark., U.S.A.* 81 J8
Preservation Inlet, *N.Z.* 59 M1
Presho, *U.S.A.* 80 D4
Presidencia de la Plaza, *Argentina* 94 B4
Presidencia Roque Saenz Peña, *Argentina* 94 B3
Presidente Epitácio, *Brazil* 93 H8
Presidente Hayes □, *Paraguay* 94 A4
Presidente Hermes, *Brazil* 92 F6
Presidente Prudente, *Brazil* 95 A5
Presidio, *Mexico* 86 B4
Presidio, *U.S.A.* 81 L2
Prespa, L. = Prepansko Jezero, *Macedonia, Yug.* 21 D9
Presque Isle, *U.S.A.* 71 C6
Prestbury, *U.K.* 11 F5
Presteigne, *U.K.* 11 E5
Preston, *Canada* 78 C4
Preston, *U.K.* 10 D5
Preston, *Idaho, U.S.A.* 82 E8
Preston, *Minn., U.S.A.* 80 D8
Preston, *Nev., U.S.A.* 82 G6
Preston, C., *Australia* 60 D2
Prestonpans, *U.K.* 12 F6
Prestwick, *U.K.* 12 F4
Pretoria, *S. Africa* 57 D4
Préveza, *Greece* 21 E9
Pribilof Is., *Bering S.* 4 D17
Příbram, *Czech.* 16 D7
Price, *U.S.A.* 82 G8
Price I., *Canada* 72 C3
Prichard, *U.S.A.* 77 K1
Prieska, *S. Africa* 56 D3
Priest L., *U.S.A.* 82 B5
Priest River, *U.S.A.* 82 B5
Priest Valley, *U.S.A.* 84 J6
Priestly, *Canada* 72 C3
Prikaspiyskaya Nizmennost, *Asia* 25 E8
Prilep, *Macedonia, Yug.* 21 D9
Priluki, *Ukraine* 25 D5
Prime Seal I., *Australia* 62 G4
Primrose L., *Canada* 73 C7
Prince Albert, *Canada* 73 C7
Prince Albert, *S. Africa* 56 E3
Prince Albert Mts., *Antarctica* 5 D11
Prince Albert Nat. Park, *Canada* 73 C7
Prince Albert Pen., *Canada* 68 A8
Prince Albert Sd., *Canada* 68 A8
Prince Alfred, C., *Canada* 4 B1
Prince Charles I., *Canada* 69 B12
Prince Charles Mts., *Antarctica* 5 D6
Prince Edward I. □, *Canada* 71 C7
Prince Edward Is., *Ind. Oc.* 3 G11
Prince George, *Canada* 72 C4
Prince of Wales, C., *U.S.A.* 66 C3
Prince of Wales I., *Australia* 62 A3
Prince of Wales I., *Canada* 68 A10
Prince of Wales I., *U.S.A.* 72 B2
Prince Patrick I., *Canada* 4 B2
Prince Regent Inlet, *Canada* 4 B3
Prince Rupert, *Canada* 72 C2
Princess Charlotte B., *Australia* 62 A3
Princess May Ras., *Australia* 60 C4
Princess Royal I., *Canada* 72 C3
Princeton, *Canada* 72 D4
Princeton, *Calif., U.S.A.* 84 F4
Princeton, *Ill., U.S.A.* 80 E10
Princeton, *Ind., U.S.A.* 76 F2
Princeton, *Ky., U.S.A.* 76 G2
Princeton, *Mo., U.S.A.* 80 E8
Princeton, *N.J., U.S.A.* 79 F10
Princeton, *W. Va., U.S.A.* 76 G5
Principe, I. de, *Atl. Oc.* 48 F4
Principe Chan., *Canada* 72 C2
Principe da Beira, *Brazil* 92 F6
Prineville, *U.S.A.* 82 D3
Prins Harald Kyst, *Antarctica* 5 D4
Prinsesse Astrid Kyst, *Antarctica* 5 D3
Prinsesse Ragnhild Kyst, *Antarctica* 5 D4
Prinzapolca, *Nic.* 88 D3
Priozersk, *Russia* 24 B5
Pripet = Pripyat →, *Europe* 24 D5
Pripet Marshes = Polesye, *Belorussia* 24 D4
Pripyat →, *Europe* 24 D5
Pripyat Marshes = Polesye, *Belorussia* 24 D4
Priština, *Serbia, Yug.* 21 C9
Privas, *France* 18 D6
Privolzhskaya Vozvyshennost, *Russia* 25 D8
Prizren, *Serbia, Yug.* 21 C9
Probolinggo, *Indonesia* 37 G15
Proddatur, *India* 40 M11
Prodhromos, *Cyprus* 23 E11
Profitis Ilias, *Greece* 23 C9
Progreso, *Mexico* 87 C7
Prokopyevsk, *Russia* 26 D9
Prome = Pyè, *Burma* 41 K19
Prophet →, *Canada* 72 B4
Propriá, *Brazil* 93 F11
Proserpine, *Australia* 62 C4
Prosser, *U.S.A.* 82 C4
Prostějov, *Czech.* 16 D8
Proston, *Australia* 63 D5
Protection, *U.S.A.* 81 G5
Provence, *France* 18 E6
Providence, *Ky., U.S.A.* 76 G2
Providence, *R.I., U.S.A.* 79 E13
Providence Bay, *Canada* 70 C3
Providence Mts., *U.S.A.* 83 J6
Providencia, I. de, *Colombia* 88 D3
Provideniya, *Russia* 27 C19
Provins, *France* 18 B5
Provo, *U.S.A.* 82 F8
Provost, *Canada* 73 C6
Prud'homme, *Canada* 73 C7
Pruszków, *Poland* 17 B10
Prut →, *Romania* 17 F14
Prydz B., *Antarctica* 5 C6
Pryor, *U.S.A.* 81 G7
Przemysl, *Poland* 17 D11
Przeworsk, *Poland* 17 C11
Przhevalsk, *Kirghizia* 26 E8
Psíra, *Greece* 23 D7
Pskov, *Russia* 24 C4
Pu Xian, *China* 34 F6
Pua, *Thailand* 38 C3
Puán, *Argentina* 94 D3
Puan, *S. Korea* 35 G14
Pucallpa, *Peru* 92 E4
Pudozh, *Russia* 24 B6
Pudukkottai, *India* 40 P11
Puebla, *Mexico* 87 D5
Puebla □, *Mexico* 87 D5
Pueblo, *U.S.A.* 80 F2
Pueblo Hundido, *Chile* 94 B1
Puelches, *Argentina* 94 D2
Puelén, *Argentina* 94 D2
Puente Alto, *Chile* 94 C1
Puente-Genil, *Spain* 19 D3
Puerco →, *U.S.A.* 83 J10
Puerto, *Canary Is.* 22 F2
Puerto Aisén, *Chile* 96 F2
Puerto Ángel, *Mexico* 87 D5
Puerto Arista, *Mexico* 87 D6
Puerto Armuelles, *Panama* 88 E3
Puerto Ayacucho, *Venezuela* 92 B5
Puerto Barrios, *Guatemala* 88 C2
Puerto Bermejo, *Argentina* 94 B4
Puerto Bermúdez, *Peru* 92 F4
Puerto Bolívar, *Ecuador* 92 D3
Puerto Cabello, *Venezuela* 92 A5
Puerto Cabezas, *Nic.* 88 D3
Puerto Cabo Gracias á Dios, *Nic.* 88 D3
Puerto Carreño, *Colombia* 92 B5
Puerto Castilla, *Honduras* 88 C2
Puerto Chicama, *Peru* 92 E3
Puerto Coig, *Argentina* 96 G3
Puerto Cortes, *Costa Rica* 88 E3
Puerto Cortés, *Honduras* 88 C2
Puerto Cumarebo, *Venezuela* 92 A5
Puerto de Alcudia, *Spain* 22 B10
Puerto de Andraitx, *Spain* 22 B9
Puerto de Cabrera, *Spain* 22 B9
Puerto de Gran Tarajal, *Canary Is.* 22 F5
Puerto de la Cruz, *Canary Is.* 22 F3
Puerto de Pozo Negro, *Canary Is.* 22 F6
Puerto de Santa María, *Spain* 19 D2
Puerto de Sóller, *Spain* 22 B9
Pto. del Carmen, *Canary Is.* 22 F6
Puerto del Rosario, *Canary Is.* 22 F6
Puerto Deseado, *Argentina* 96 F3
Puerto Heath, *Bolivia* 92 F5
Puerto Juárez, *Mexico* 87 C7
Puerto La Cruz, *Venezuela* 92 A6
Puerto Leguízamo, *Colombia* 92 D4
Puerto Lobos, *Argentina* 96 E3
Puerto Madryn, *Argentina* 96 E3
Puerto Maldonado, *Peru* 92 F5
Puerto Manotí, *Cuba* 88 B4
Puerto Montt, *Chile* 96 E2
Puerto Morelos, *Mexico* 87 C7
Puerto Natales, *Chile* 96 G2
Puerto Padre, *Cuba* 88 B4
Puerto Páez, *Venezuela* 92 B5
Puerto Peñasco, *Mexico* 86 A2
Puerto Pinasco, *Paraguay* 94 A4
Puerto Pirámides, *Argentina* 96 E4
Puerto Plata, *Dom. Rep.* 89 C5
Puerto Pollensa, *Spain* 22 B10
Puerto Princesa, *Phil.* 37 C5
Puerto Quellón, *Chile* 96 E2
Puerto Quepos, *Costa Rica* 88 E3
Puerto Rico, *Canary Is.* 22 G4
Puerto Rico ■, *W. Indies* 89 C6
Puerto Rico Trench, *Atl. Oc.* 89 C6
Puerto Sastre, *Paraguay* 94 A4
Puerto Suárez, *Bolivia* 92 G7
Puerto Vallarta, *Mexico* 86 C3
Puerto Wilches, *Colombia* 92 B4
Puertollano, *Spain* 19 C3
Pueyrredón, L., *Argentina* 96 F2
Pugachev, *Kazakhstan* 24 D8
Puge, *Tanzania* 54 C3
Puget Sd., *U.S.A.* 82 C2
Púglia □, *Italy* 20 D7
Pugŏdong, *N. Korea* 35 C16
Pugu, *Tanzania* 54 D4
Pūgūnzi, *Iran* 45 E8
Puig Mayor, *Spain* 22 B9
Puigcerdá, *Spain* 19 A6
Puigpuñent, *Spain* 22 B9
Pujon-chosuji, *N. Korea* 35 D14
Pukaki L., *N.Z.* 59 L3
Pukapuka, *Cook Is.* 65 J11
Pukatawagan, *Canada* 73 B8
Pukchin, *N. Korea* 35 D13
Pukchŏng, *N. Korea* 35 D15
Pukekohe, *N.Z.* 59 G5
Pulaski, *N.Y., U.S.A.* 79 C8
Pulaski, *Tenn., U.S.A.* 77 H2
Pulaski, *Va., U.S.A.* 76 G5
Pulga, *U.S.A.* 84 F5
Pulicat, L., *India* 40 N12
Pullman, *U.S.A.* 82 C5
Pulog, *Phil.* 37 A6
Pumlumon Fawr, *U.K.* 11 E4
Puna, *Bolivia* 92 G5
Puná, I., *Ecuador* 92 D2
Punakha, *Bhutan* 41 F16
Punasar, *India* 42 F5
Punata, *Bolivia* 92 G5
Punch, *India* 43 C6
Pune, *India* 40 K8
Pungsan, *N. Korea* 35 D15
Pungue, Ponte de, *Mozam.* 55 F3
Punjab □, *India* 42 D6
Punjab □, *Pakistan* 42 E6
Puno, *Peru* 92 G4
Punta Alta, *Argentina* 96 D4
Punta Arenas, *Chile* 96 G2
Punta de Díaz, *Chile* 94 B1
Punta Gorda, *Belize* 87 D7
Punta Gorda, *U.S.A.* 77 M5
Punta Prieta, *Mexico* 86 B2
Punta Prima, *Spain* 22 B11
Puntabie, *Australia* 63 E1
Puntarenas, *Costa Rica* 88 E3
Punto Fijo, *Venezuela* 92 A4
Punxsutawney, *U.S.A.* 78 F5
Puquio, *Peru* 92 F4
Pur →, *Russia* 26 C8
Purace, Vol., *Colombia* 92 C3
Purbeck, Isle of, *U.K.* 11 G5
Purcell, *U.S.A.* 81 H6
Puri, *India* 41 K14
Purmerend, *Neths.* 15 B4
Purnia, *India* 43 G12
Purukcahu, *Indonesia* 36 E4
Puruliya, *India* 43 H12
Purus →, *Brazil* 92 D6
Purwakarta, *Indonesia* 37 G12
Purwodadi, *Jawa, Indonesia* 37 G14
Purwodadi, *Jawa, Indonesia* 37 G13
Purwokerto, *Indonesia* 37 G13
Purworejo, *Indonesia* 37 G14
Puryŏng, *N. Korea* 35 C15
Pusan, *S. Korea* 35 G15
Pushchino, *Russia* 27 D16
Pushkino, *Russia* 25 D8
Putahow L., *Canada* 73 B8
Putao, *Burma* 41 F20
Putaruru, *N.Z.* 59 H5
Puthein Myit →, *Burma* 41 M19
Putignano, *Italy* 20 D7
Puting, Tanjung, *Indonesia* 36 E4
Putnam, *U.S.A.* 79 E13
Putorana, Gory, *Russia* 27 C10
Puttalam, *Sri Lanka* 40 Q11
Putten, *Neths.* 15 B5
Puttgarden, *Germany* 16 A5
Putumayo →, *S. Amer.* 92 D5
Putussibau, *Indonesia* 36 D4
Puy-de-Dôme, *France* 18 D5
Puy-de-Dôme □, *France* 18 D5
Puyallup, *U.S.A.* 84 C4
Puyang, *China* 34 G8
Pūzeh Rīg, *Iran* 45 E8
Pwani □, *Tanzania* 54 D4
Pweto, *Zaïre* 55 D2
Pwllheli, *U.K.* 10 E3
Pya-ozero, *Russia* 24 A5
Pyapon, *Burma* 41 L19
Pyasina →, *Russia* 27 B9
Pyatigorsk, *Russia* 25 F7
Pyè, *Burma* 41 K19
Pyinmana, *Burma* 41 K20
Pyla, C., *Cyprus* 23 E12
Pyŏktong, *N. Korea* 35 D13
Pyŏnggang, *N. Korea* 35 E14
Pyŏngtaek, *S. Korea* 35 F14
P'yŏngyang, *N. Korea* 35 E13
Pyote, *U.S.A.* 81 K3
Pyramid L., *U.S.A.* 82 G4
Pyramid Pk., *U.S.A.* 85 J10
Pyrénées, *Europe* 18 E4
Pyrénées-Atlantiques □, *France* 18 E3
Pyrénées-Orientales □, *France* 18 E5
Pyu, *Burma* 41 K20

Q

Qaanaaq = Thule, *Greenland* 4 B4
Qachasnek, *S. Africa* 57 E4
Qādib, *Yemen* 46 E5
Qa'el Jafr, *Jordan* 47 E5
Qa'emābād, *Iran* 45 D9
Qā'emshahr, *Iran* 45 B7
Qagan Nur, *China* 34 C8
Qahar Youyi Zhongqi, *China* 34 D7
Qahremānshahr = Bākhtarān, *Iran* 44 C5
Qaidam Pendi, *China* 32 C4
Qajarīyeh, *Iran* 45 D6
Qala, Ras il, *Malta* 23 C1
Qala-i-Jadid, *Afghan.* 42 D2
Qala Yangi, *Afghan.* 42 B2
Qal'at al Akhḍar, *Si. Arabia* 44 E3
Qal'at Sukkar, *Iraq* 44 D5
Qal'eh Darreh, *Iran* 44 B5
Qal'eh Shaharak, *Afghan.* 40 B4
Qamar, Ghubbat al, *Yemen* 46 D5
Qamdo, *China* 32 C4
Qamruddin Karez, *Pakistan* 42 D3
Qandahār, *Afghan.* 40 D4
Qandahār □, *Afghan.* 40 D4
Qapān, *Iran* 45 B7
Qaqortoq = Julianehåb, *Greenland* 4 C5
Qâra, *Egypt* 51 C10
Qara Qash →, *India* 43 B8
Qārah, *Si. Arabia* 44 D4
Qareh →, *Iran* 44 B5
Qareh Tekān, *Iran* 45 B6
Qarqan He →, *China* 32 C3
Qartabā, *Lebanon* 47 A4
Qaryat al Gharab, *Iraq* 44 D5
Qaryat al 'Ulyā, *Si. Arabia* 44 E5
Qasr 'Amra, *Jordan* 44 D3
Qaṣr-e Qand, *Iran* 45 E9
Qasr Farâfra, *Egypt* 51 C10
Qatanā, *Syria* 47 B5
Qatar ■, *Asia* 45 E6
Qatlīsh, *Iran* 45 B8
Qattâra, Munkhafed el, *Egypt* 51 C10
Qattâra Depression = Qattâra, Munkhafed el, *Egypt* 51 C10
Qawām al Ḥamzah, *Iraq* 44 D5
Qāyen, *Iran* 45 C8
Qazvin, *Iran* 45 B6
Qena, *Egypt* 51 C11
Qeqertarsuaq = Disko, *Greenland* 4 C5
Qeqertarsuaq = Godhavn, *Greenland* 4 C5
Qeshlāq, *Iran* 44 C5
Qeshm, *Iran* 45 E8
Qezi'ot, *Israel* 47 E3
Qi Xian, *China* 34 G8
Qian Gorlos, *China* 35 B13
Qian Xian, *China* 34 G5
Qianyang, *China* 34 G4
Qibā', *Si. Arabia* 44 E5
Qila Safed, *Pakistan* 40 E2
Qila Saifullāh, *Pakistan* 42 D3
Qilian Shan, *China* 32 C4
Qin He →, *China* 34 G7
Qin Ling = Qinling Shandi, *China* 34 H5
Qin'an, *China* 34 G3
Qing Xian, *China* 34 E9
Qingcheng, *China* 35 F9
Qingdao, *China* 35 F11
Qingfeng, *China* 34 G8
Qinghai □, *China* 32 C4
Qinghai Hu, *China* 32 C5
Qinghecheng, *China* 35 D13
Qinghemen, *China* 35 D11
Qingjian, *China* 34 F6
Qingjiang, *China* 35 H10
Qingshui, *China* 34 G4
Qingshuihe, *China* 34 E6
Qingtongxia Shuiku, *China* 34 F3
Qingxu, *China* 34 F7
Qingyang, *China* 34 F4
Qingyuan, *China* 35 C13
Qingyun, *China* 35 F9
Qinhuangdao, *China* 35 E10
Qinling Shandi, *China* 34 H5
Qinshui, *China* 34 G7
Qinyang, *China* 34 G7
Qinyuan, *China* 34 F7
Qinzhou, *China* 32 D5
Qionghai, *China* 38 C8
Qiongshan, *China* 38 C8
Qiongzhou Haixia, *China* 38 B8
Qiqihar, *China* 33 B7
Qiraîya, W. →, *Egypt* 47 E3
Qiryat Ata, *Israel* 47 C4
Qiryat Gat, *Israel* 47 D3
Qiryat Mal'akhi, *Israel* 47 D3
Qiryat Shemona, *Israel* 47 B4
Qiryat Yam, *Israel* 47 C4
Qishan, *China* 34 G4
Qitai, *China* 32 B3
Qixia, *China* 35 F11
Qojūr, *Iran* 44 B5
Qom, *Iran* 45 C6
Qomsheh, *Iran* 45 D6
Qu Xian, *China* 33 D6
Quairading, *Australia* 61 F2
Quakertown, *U.S.A.* 79 F9
Qualeup, *Australia* 61 F2
Quambatook, *Australia* 63 F3
Quambone, *Australia* 63 E4
Quamby, *Australia* 62 C3
Quan Long, *Vietnam* 39 H5
Quanah, *U.S.A.* 81 H5
Quandialla, *Australia* 63 E4
Quang Ngai, *Vietnam* 38 E7
Quang Yen, *Vietnam* 38 B6
Quantock Hills, *U.K.* 11 F4
Quanzhou, *China* 33 D6
Quaraí, *Brazil* 94 C4
Quartzsite, *U.S.A.* 85 M12
Quatsino, *Canada* 72 C3
Quatsino Sd., *Canada* 72 C3
Qūchān, *Iran* 45 B8
Queanbeyan, *Australia* 63 F4
Québec, *Canada* 71 C5
Québec □, *Canada* 71 B6
Queen Alexandra Ra., *Antarctica* 5 E11
Queen Charlotte, *Canada* 72 C2
Queen Charlotte Is., *Canada* 72 C2
Queen Charlotte Str., *Canada* 72 C3
Queen Elizabeth Is., *Canada* 66 B10
Queen Elizabeth Nat. Park, *Uganda* 54 C3
Queen Mary Land, *Antarctica* 5 D7
Queen Maud G., *Canada* 68 B9
Queen Maud Land, *Antarctica* 5 D3
Queen Maud Mts., *Antarctica* 5 E13
Queens Chan., *Australia* 60 C4
Queenscliff, *Australia* 63 F3
Queensland □, *Australia* 62 C3
Queenstown, *Australia* 62 G4
Queenstown, *N.Z.* 59 L2
Queenstown, *S. Africa* 56 E4
Queets, *U.S.A.* 84 C2
Queguay Grande →, *Uruguay* 94 C4
Queimadas, *Brazil* 93 F11
Quela, *Angola* 52 F3
Quelimane, *Mozam.* 55 F4
Quelpart = Cheju Do, *S. Korea* 35 H14
Quemado, *N. Mex., U.S.A.* 83 J9
Quemado, *Tex., U.S.A.* 81 L4
Quemú-Quemú, *Argentina* 94 D3
Quequén, *Argentina* 94 D4
Querétaro, *Mexico* 86 C4
Querétaro □, *Mexico* 86 C5
Queshan, *China* 34 H8
Quesnel, *Canada* 72 C4
Quesnel →, *Canada* 72 C4
Quesnel L., *Canada* 72 C4
Questa, *U.S.A.* 83 H11
Quetico Prov. Park, *Canada* 70 C1
Quetta, *Pakistan* 42 D2
Quezaltenango, *Guatemala* 88 D1
Quezon City, *Phil.* 37 B6
Qufār, *Si. Arabia* 44 E4
Qui Nhon, *Vietnam* 38 F7
Quibaxe, *Angola* 52 F2
Quibdo, *Colombia* 92 B3
Quiberon, *France* 18 C2
Quick, *Canada* 72 C3
Quiet L., *Canada* 72 A2
Quiindy, *Paraguay* 94 B4
Quila, *Mexico* 86 C3
Quilán, C., *Chile* 96 E2
Quilcene, *U.S.A.* 84 C4
Quilengues, *Angola* 53 G2
Quilimarí, *Chile* 94 C1
Quilino, *Argentina* 94 C3
Quillabamba, *Peru* 92 F4
Quillagua, *Chile* 94 A2
Quillaicillo, *Chile* 94 C1
Quillota, *Chile* 94 C1
Quilmes, *Argentina* 94 C4
Quilon, *India* 40 Q10
Quilpie, *Australia* 63 D3
Quilpué, *Chile* 94 C1
Quilua, *Mozam.* 55 F4
Quimilí, *Argentina* 94 B3
Quimper, *France* 18 B1
Quimperlé, *France* 18 C2
Quinault →, *U.S.A.* 84 C2
Quincy, *Calif., U.S.A.* 84 F6
Quincy, *Fla., U.S.A.* 77 K3
Quincy, *Ill., U.S.A.* 80 F9
Quincy, *Mass., U.S.A.* 79 D14
Quincy, *Wash., U.S.A.* 82 C4
Quines, *Argentina* 94 C2
Quinga, *Mozam.* 55 F5
Quintana Roo □, *Mexico* 87 D7
Quintanar de la Orden, *Spain* 19 C4
Quintanar de la Sierra, *Spain* 19 B4
Quintero, *Chile* 94 C1
Quinyambie, *Australia* 63 E3
Quipungo, *Angola* 53 G2
Quirihue, *Chile* 94 D1
Quirindi, *Australia* 63 E5
Quissanga, *Mozam.* 55 E5
Quitilipi, *Argentina* 94 B3
Quitman, *Ga., U.S.A.* 77 K4
Quitman, *Miss., U.S.A.* 77 J1
Quitman, *Tex., U.S.A.* 81 J7
Quito, *Ecuador* 92 D3
Quixadá, *Brazil* 93 D11
Quixaxe, *Mozam.* 55 F5
Qumbu, *S. Africa* 57 E4
Quneitra, *Syria* 47 B4
Quoin I., *Australia* 60 B4
Quoin Pt., *S. Africa* 56 E2
Quondong, *Australia* 63 E3
Quorn, *Australia* 63 E2
Qurnat as Sawdā', *Lebanon* 47 A5
Qûs, *Egypt* 51 C11
Qusaybah, *Iraq* 44 C4
Quseir, *Egypt* 51 C11
Qūshchī, *Iran* 44 B5
Quthing, *Lesotho* 57 E4
Qūṭīābād, *Iran* 45 C6
Quwo, *China* 34 G6
Quyang, *China* 34 E8
Quynh Nhai, *Vietnam* 38 B4
Quzi, *China* 34 F4

R

Ra, Ko, *Thailand* 39 H2
Raahe, *Finland* 8 D18
Raasay, *U.K.* 12 D2
Raasay, Sd. of, *U.K.* 12 D2
Raba, *Indonesia* 37 F5
Rabai, *Kenya* 54 C4
Rabat, *Malta* 23 D1
Rabat, *Morocco* 50 B3
Rabaul, *Papua N. G.* 64 H7
Rabbit →, *Canada* 72 B3
Rabbit Lake, *Canada* 73 C7
Rabbitskin →, *Canada* 72 A4
Rābor, *Iran* 45 D8
Race, C., *Canada* 71 C9
Rach Gia, *Vietnam* 39 G5
Racine, *U.S.A.* 76 D2
Rackerby, *U.S.A.* 84 F5
Radama, Nosy, *Madag.* 57 A8
Radama, Saikanosy, *Madag.* 57 A8
Rădăuţi, *Romania* 17 E12
Radford, *U.S.A.* 76 G5
Radhanpur, *India* 42 H4
Radisson, *Canada* 73 C7
Radium Hot Springs, *Canada* 72 C5
Radnor Forest, *U.K.* 11 E4
Radom, *Poland* 17 C10
Radomir, *Bulgaria* 21 C10
Radomsko, *Poland* 17 C9
Radstock, *U.K.* 11 F5
Radstock, C., *Australia* 63 E1
Radville, *Canada* 73 D8
Rae, *Canada* 72 A5
Rae Bareli, *India* 43 F9
Rae Isthmus, *Canada* 69 B11
Raeren, *Belgium* 15 D6
Raeside, L., *Australia* 61 E3
Raetihi, *N.Z.* 59 H5
Rafaela, *Argentina* 94 C3
Rafah, *Egypt* 47 D3
Rafai, *C.A.R.* 54 B1
Rafḩā, *Si. Arabia* 44 D4
Rafsanjān, *Iran* 45 D8
Raft Pt., *Australia* 60 C3
Ragama, *Sri Lanka* 40 R11
Ragged, Mt., *Australia* 61 F3
Raglan, *Australia* 62 C5
Raglan, *N.Z.* 59 G5
Ragusa, *Italy* 20 F6
Raha, *Indonesia* 37 E6
Rahad al Bardī, *Sudan* 51 F9
Rahaeng = Tak, *Thailand* 38 D2
Raḩīmah, *Si. Arabia* 45 E6
Rahimyar Khan, *Pakistan* 42 E4
Rāhjerd, *Iran* 45 C6
Raichur, *India* 40 L10
Raiganj, *India* 43 G13
Raigarh, *India* 41 J13
Raijua, *Indonesia* 37 F6
Railton, *Australia* 62 G4
Rainbow Lake, *Canada* 72 B5
Rainier, *U.S.A.* 84 D4
Rainier, Mt., *U.S.A.* 84 D5
Rainy L., *Canada* 73 D10
Rainy River, *Canada* 73 D10
Raipur, *India* 41 J12
Raj Nandgaon, *India* 41 J12
Raja, Ujung, *Indonesia* 36 D1
Raja Ampat, Kepulauan, *Indonesia* 37 E7
Rajahmundry, *India* 41 L12
Rajajooseppi, *Finland* 8 B20
Rajang →, *Malaysia* 36 D4
Rajapalaiyam, *India* 40 Q10
Rajasthan □, *India* 42 F5
Rajasthan Canal, *India* 42 E5
Rajauri, *India* 43 C6
Rajgarh, *Mad. P., India* 42 G7
Rajgarh, *Raj., India* 42 E6
Rajkot, *India* 42 H4
Rajmahal Hills, *India* 43 G12
Rajpipla, *India* 40 J8
Rajpura, *India* 42 D7
Rajshahi, *Bangla.* 41 G16
Rajshahi □, *Bangla.* 43 G13
Rakaia, *N.Z.* 59 K4
Rakaia →, *N.Z.* 59 K4
Rakan, Ra's, *Qatar* 45 E6
Rakaposhi, *Pakistan* 43 A6
Rakata, Pulau, *Indonesia* 36 F3
Rakhni, *Pakistan* 42 D3
Rakitnoye, *Russia* 30 B7
Rakops, *Botswana* 56 C3
Raleigh, *U.S.A.* 77 H6
Raleigh B., *U.S.A.* 77 H7
Ralls, *U.S.A.* 81 J4
Ram →, *Canada* 72 A4
Rām Allāh, *Jordan* 47 D4
Ram Hd., *Australia* 63 F4
Rama, *Nic.* 88 D3
Raman, *Thailand* 39 J3
Ramanathapuram, *India* 40 Q11
Ramanetaka, B. de, *Madag.* 57 A8
Ramat Gan, *Israel* 47 C3
Ramatlhabama, *S. Africa* 56 D4
Ramban, *India* 43 C6
Rambipuji, *Indonesia* 37 H15
Ramea, *Canada* 71 C8
Ramechhap, *Nepal* 43 F12
Ramelau, *Indonesia* 37 F7
Ramgarh, *Bihar, India* 43 H11
Ramgarh, *Raj., India* 42 F6
Ramgarh, *Raj., India* 42 F4
Rāmhormoz, *Iran* 45 D6
Ramiān, *Iran* 45 B7
Ramingining, *Australia* 62 A2
Ramla, *Israel* 47 D3
Ramnad = Ramanathapuram, *India* 40 Q11
Ramnagar, *India* 43 C6
Ramona, *U.S.A.* 85 M10
Ramore, *Canada* 70 C3
Ramotswa, *Botswana* 56 C4
Rampur, *H.P., India* 42 D7
Rampur, *Mad. P., India* 42 H5
Rampur, *Ut. P., India* 43 E8
Rampur Hat, *India* 43 G12
Rampura, *India* 42 G6
Ramree Kyun, *Burma* 41 K18
Rāmsar, *Iran* 45 B6
Ramsey, *Canada* 70 C3
Ramsey, *U.K.* 10 C3
Ramsgate, *U.K.* 11 F9
Ramtek, *India* 40 J11
Ranaghat, *India* 43 H13
Ranahu, *Pakistan* 42 G3
Ranau, *Malaysia* 36 C5
Rancagua, *Chile* 94 C1
Rancheria →, *Canada* 72 A3
Ranchester, *U.S.A.* 82 D10
Ranchi, *India* 43 H11
Randers, *Denmark* 9 H11
Randfontein, *S. Africa* 57 D4
Randle, *U.S.A.* 84 D5
Randolph, *Mass., U.S.A.* 79 D13
Randolph, *N.Y., U.S.A.* 78 D6
Randolph, *Utah, U.S.A.* 82 F8
Randolph, *Vt., U.S.A.* 79 C12
Råne älv →, *Sweden* 8 D17
Rangae, *Thailand* 39 J3
Rangaunu B., *N.Z.* 59 F4
Rangeley, *U.S.A.* 79 B14
Rangely, *U.S.A.* 82 F9
Ranger, *U.S.A.* 81 J5
Rangia, *India* 41 F17
Rangiora, *N.Z.* 59 K4
Rangitaiki →, *N.Z.* 59 G6
Rangitata →, *N.Z.* 59 K3
Rangkasbitung, *Indonesia* 37 G12
Rangon →, *Burma* 41 L20
Rangoon, *Burma* 41 L20
Rangpur, *Bangla.* 41 G16
Rangsit, *Thailand* 38 F3
Ranibennur, *India* 40 M9
Raniganj, *India* 43 H12
Raniwara, *India* 40 G8
Rāniyah, *Iraq* 44 B5
Ranken →, *Australia* 62 C2
Rankin, *U.S.A.* 81 K4
Rankin Inlet, *Canada* 68 B10
Rankins Springs, *Australia* 63 E4
Rannoch, L., *U.K.* 12 E4
Rannoch Moor, *U.K.* 12 E4
Ranobe, Helodranon' i, *Madag.* 57 C7
Ranohira, *Madag.* 57 C8
Ranomafana, *Toamasina, Madag.* 57 B8
Ranomafana, *Toliara, Madag.* 57 C8
Ranong, *Thailand* 39 H2
Rānsa, *Iran* 45 C6
Ransiki, *Indonesia* 37 E8
Rantau, *Indonesia* 36 E5
Rantauprapat, *Indonesia* 36 D1
Rantekombola, *Indonesia* 37 E5
Rantoul, *U.S.A.* 76 E1
Raoyang, *China* 34 E8
Rapa, *Pac. Oc.* 65 K13
Rāpch, *Iran* 45 E8
Rapid →, *Canada* 72 B3
Rapid City, *U.S.A.* 80 D3
Rapid River, *U.S.A.* 76 C2
Rapides des Joachims, *Canada* 70 C4
Rarotonga, *Cook Is.* 65 K12
Ra's al' Ayn, *Syria* 44 B4
Ra's al Khaymah, *U.A.E.* 45 E8
Ra's al-Unuf, *Libya* 51 B8
Ra's an Naqb, *Jordan* 47 F4
Ras Bânâs, *Egypt* 51 D12
Ras Dashen, *Ethiopia* 51 F12
Râs Timirist, *Mauritania* 50 E1
Rasa, Punta, *Argentina* 96 E4
Rasca, Pta. de la, *Canary Is.* 22 G3
Rashad, *Sudan* 51 F11
Rashîd, *Egypt* 51 B11
Rasht, *Iran* 45 B6
Rasi Salai, *Thailand* 38 E5
Rason L., *Australia* 61 E3
Rasra, *India* 43 G10
Rat Buri, *Thailand* 38 F2
Rat Is., *U.S.A.* 68 C1
Rat River, *Canada* 72 A6
Ratangarh, *India* 42 E6
Raţāwī, *Iraq* 44 D5
Rath, *India* 43 G8
Rath Luirc, *Ireland* 13 D3
Rathdrum, *Ireland* 13 D5
Rathenow, *Germany* 16 B6
Rathkeale, *Ireland* 13 D3
Rathlin, *U.K.* 13 A5
Rathlin O'Birne I., *Ireland* 13 B3
Ratlam, *India* 42 H6
Ratnagiri, *India* 40 L8
Raton, *U.S.A.* 81 G2
Rattaphum, *Thailand* 39 J3
Rattray Hd., *U.K.* 12 D7
Ratz, Mt., *Canada* 72 B2
Raub, *Malaysia* 39 L3
Rauch, *Argentina* 94 D4
Raufarhöfn, *Iceland* 8 C6
Raukumara Ra., *N.Z.* 59 H6
Rauma, *Finland* 9 F16
Raurkela, *India* 43 H11
Rausu-Dake, *Japan* 30 B12
Ravānsar, *Iran* 44 C5
Rāvar, *Iran* 45 D8
Ravena, *U.S.A.* 79 D11
Ravenna, *Italy* 20 B5
Ravenna, *Nebr., U.S.A.* 80 E5
Ravenna, *Ohio, U.S.A.* 78 E3
Ravensburg, *Germany* 16 E4
Ravenshoe, *Australia* 62 B4
Ravensthorpe, *Australia* 61 F3
Ravenswood, *Australia* 62 C4
Ravenswood, *U.S.A.* 76 F5
Ravi →, *Pakistan* 42 D4
Rawalpindi, *Pakistan* 42 C5
Rawāndūz, *Iraq* 44 B5
Rawang, *Malaysia* 39 L3
Rawdon, *Canada* 70 C5
Rawene, *N.Z.* 59 F4
Rawlinna, *Australia* 61 F4
Rawlins, *U.S.A.* 82 F10
Rawlinson Ra., *Australia* 61 D4
Rawson, *Argentina* 96 E3
Ray, *U.S.A.* 80 A3
Ray, C., *Canada* 71 C8
Rayadurg, *India* 40 M10
Rayagada, *India* 41 K13
Raychikhinsk, *Russia* 27 E13
Rāyen, *Iran* 45 D8
Raymond, *Canada* 72 D6
Raymond, *Calif., U.S.A.* 84 H7
Raymond, *Wash., U.S.A.* 84 D3
Raymondville, *U.S.A.* 81 M6
Raymore, *Canada* 73 C8
Rayne, *U.S.A.* 81 K8
Rayón, *Mexico* 86 B2
Rayong, *Thailand* 38 F3
Rayville, *U.S.A.* 81 J9
Raz, Pte. du, *France* 18 B1
Razan, *Iran* 45 C6
Razdolnoye, *Russia* 30 C5
Razeh, *Iran* 45 C6
Razgrad, *Bulgaria* 21 C12
Razmak, *Pakistan* 42 C3
Ré, I. de, *France* 18 C3
Reading, *U.K.* 11 F7
Reading, *U.S.A.* 79 F9
Realicó, *Argentina* 94 D3
Reata, *Mexico* 86 B4
Rebecca, L., *Australia* 61 F3
Rebi, *Indonesia* 37 F8
Rebiana, *Libya* 51 D9
Rebun-Tō, *Japan* 30 B10
Recherche, Arch. of the, *Australia* 61 F3
Recife, *Brazil* 93 E12
Recklinghausen, *Germany* 15 C7
Reconquista, *Argentina* 94 B4
Recreo, *Argentina* 94 B2
Red →, *N. Amer.* 80 A6
Red →, *U.S.A.* 81 K9
Red Bank, *U.S.A.* 79 F10
Red Bay, *Canada* 71 B8
Red Bluff, *U.S.A.* 82 F2
Red Bluff L., *U.S.A.* 81 K3
Red Cliffs, *Australia* 63 E3
Red Cloud, *U.S.A.* 80 E5
Red Deer, *Canada* 72 C6
Red Deer →, *Alta., Canada* 73 C6
Red Deer →, *Man., Canada* 73 C8
Red Deer L., *Canada* 73 C8
Red Indian L., *Canada* 71 C8
Red Lake, *Canada* 73 C10
Red Lake Falls, *U.S.A.* 80 B6
Red Lodge, *U.S.A.* 82 D9
Red Mountain, *U.S.A.* 85 K9
Red Oak, *U.S.A.* 80 E7
Red Rock, *Canada* 70 C2
Red Rock, L., *U.S.A.* 80 E8
Red Rocks Pt., *Australia* 61 F4
Red Sea, *Asia* 46 C2
Red Slate Mt., *U.S.A.* 84 H8
Red Sucker L., *Canada* 73 C10
Red Tower Pass = Turnu Rosu Pasul, *Romania* 17 F12
Red Wing, *U.S.A.* 80 C8
Redbridge, *U.K.* 11 F8
Redcar, *U.K.* 10 C6
Redcliff, *Canada* 73 C6
Redcliffe, *Australia* 63 D5
Redcliffe, Mt., *Australia* 61 E3
Reddersburg, *S. Africa* 56 D4
Redding, *U.S.A.* 82 F2
Redditch, *U.K.* 11 E6
Redfield, *U.S.A.* 80 C5
Redknife →, *Canada* 72 A5
Redlands, *U.S.A.* 85 M9
Redmond, *Australia* 61 F2
Redmond, *Oreg., U.S.A.* 82 D3
Redmond, *Wash., U.S.A.* 84 C4
Redonda, *Antigua* 89 C7
Redondela, *Spain* 19 A1
Redondo, *Portugal* 19 C2
Redondo Beach, *U.S.A.* 85 M8
Redrock Pt., *Canada* 72 A5
Redruth, *U.K.* 11 G2
Redvers, *Canada* 73 D8
Redwater, *Canada* 72 C6
Redwood, *U.S.A.* 79 B9
Redwood City, *U.S.A.* 83 H2
Redwood Falls, *U.S.A.* 80 C7
Ree, L., *Ireland* 13 C4
Reed, L., *Canada* 73 C8
Reed City, *U.S.A.* 76 D3
Reeder, *U.S.A.* 80 B3
Reedley, *U.S.A.* 83 H4
Reedsburg, *U.S.A.* 80 D9
Reedsport, *U.S.A.* 82 E1
Reefton, *N.Z.* 59 K3
Refugio, *U.S.A.* 81 L6
Regensburg, *Germany* 16 D6
Réggio di Calábria, *Italy* 20 E6
Réggio nell' Emilia, *Italy* 20 B4
Regina, *Canada* 73 C8
Registro, *Brazil* 95 A6
Rehar →, *India* 43 H10
Rehoboth, *Namibia* 56 C2
Rehovot, *Israel* 47 D3
Rei-Bouba, *Cameroon* 51 G7
Reichenbach, *Germany* 16 C6
Reid, *Australia* 61 F4
Reid River, *Australia* 62 B4
Reidsville, *U.S.A.* 77 G6
Reigate, *U.K.* 11 F7
Reims, *France* 18 B6
Reina Adelaida, Arch., *Chile* 96 G2
Reinbeck, *U.S.A.* 80 D8
Reindeer →, *Canada* 73 B8
Reindeer I., *Canada* 73 C9
Reindeer L., *Canada* 73 B8
Reinga, C., *N.Z.* 59 F4
Reitz, *S. Africa* 57 D4
Reivilo, *S. Africa* 56 D3
Rekinniki, *Russia* 27 C17
Reliance, *Canada* 73 A7
Remarkable, Mt., *Australia* 63 E2
Rembang, *Indonesia* 37 G14
Remedios, *Panama* 88 E3
Remeshk, *Iran* 45 E8
Remich, *Lux.* 15 E6
Remscheid, *Germany* 16 C3
Ren Xian, *China* 34 F8
Rendsburg, *Germany* 16 A4
Rene, *Russia* 27 C19
Renfrew, *Canada* 70 C4
Renfrew, *U.K.* 12 F4
Rengat, *Indonesia* 36 E2
Rengo, *Chile* 94 C1
Renk, *Sudan* 51 F11
Renkum, *Neths.* 15 C5
Renmark, *Australia* 63 E3
Rennell Sd., *Canada* 72 C2
Renner Springs T.O., *Australia* 62 B1
Rennes, *France* 18 B3
Reno, *U.S.A.* 84 F7
Reno →, *Italy* 20 B5
Renovo, *U.S.A.* 78 E7
Renqiu, *China* 34 E9
Rensselaer, *Ind., U.S.A.* 76 E2
Rensselaer, *N.Y., U.S.A.* 79 D11
Renton, *U.S.A.* 84 C4
Reotipur, *India* 43 G10
Republic, *Mich., U.S.A.* 76 B2
Republic, *Wash., U.S.A.* 82 B4
Republican →, *U.S.A.* 80 F6
Republican City, *U.S.A.* 80 E5
Repulse Bay, *Canada* 69 B11
Requena, *Peru* 92 E4
Requena, *Spain* 19 C5
Reserve, *Canada* 73 C8
Reserve, *U.S.A.* 83 K9
Resht = Rasht, *Iran* 45 B6
Resistencia, *Argentina* 94 B4
Reşiţa, *Romania* 17 F10
Resolution I., *Canada* 69 B13
Resolution I., *N.Z.* 59 L1
Ressano Garcia, *Mozam.* 57 D5
Reston, *Canada* 73 D8
Retalhuleu, *Guatemala* 88 D1
Retenue, L. de, *Zaïre* 55 E2
Réthímnon, *Greece* 23 D6
Réthímnon □, *Greece* 23 D6
Réunion ■, *Ind. Oc.* 3 F12
Reutlingen, *Germany* 16 D4
Reval = Tallinn, *Estonia* 24 C3
Revda, *Russia* 24 C10
Revelganj, *India* 43 G11
Revelstoke, *Canada* 72 C5
Revilla Gigedo, Is., *Pac. Oc.* 65 F16
Revillagigedo I., *U.S.A.* 72 B2
Revuè →, *Mozam.* 55 F3
Rewa, *India* 43 G9
Rewari, *India* 42 E7
Rexburg, *U.S.A.* 82 E8
Rey, *Iran* 45 C6
Rey Malabo, *Eq. Guin.* 50 H6
Reyes, Pt., *U.S.A.* 84 H3
Reykjahlíð, *Iceland* 8 D5
Reykjanes, *Iceland* 8 E2
Reykjavík, *Iceland* 8 D3
Reynolds, *Canada* 73 D9
Reynolds Ra., *Australia* 60 D5
Reynoldsville, *U.S.A.* 78 E6
Reynosa, *Mexico* 87 B5
Rezvān, *Iran* 45 E8
Rhayader, *U.K.* 11 E4
Rheden, *Neths.* 15 B6
Rhein, *Canada* 73 C8
Rhein →, *Europe* 15 C6
Rheine, *Germany* 16 B3
Rheinland-Pfalz □, *Germany* 16 C3
Rhin = Rhein →, *Europe* 15 C6
Rhine = Rhein →, *Europe* 15 C6
Rhineland-Palatinate □ = Rheinland-Pfalz □, *Germany* 16 C3
Rhinelander, *U.S.A.* 80 C10
Rhino Camp, *Uganda* 54 B3
Rhode Island □, *U.S.A.* 79 E13
Rhodes = Ródhos, *Greece* 23 C10
Rhodesia = Zimbabwe ■, *Africa* 55 F2
Rhodope Mts. = Rhodopi Planina, *Bulgaria* 21 D11
Rhodopi Planina, *Bulgaria* 21 D11
Rhondda, *U.K.* 11 F4
Rhône □, *France* 18 D6
Rhône →, *France* 18 E6
Rhum, *U.K.* 12 E2
Rhyl, *U.K.* 10 D4
Rhymney, *U.K.* 11 F4
Riachão, *Brazil* 93 E9
Riasi, *India* 43 C6
Riau □, *Indonesia* 36 D2
Riau, Kepulauan, *Indonesia* 36 D2
Riau Arch. = Riau, Kepulauan, *Indonesia* 36 D2
Ribadeo, *Spain* 19 A2
Ribatejo, *Portugal* 19 C1
Ribble →, *U.K.* 10 C5
Ribe, *Denmark* 9 J10
Ribeira Brava, *Madeira* 22 D2
Ribeirão Prêto, *Brazil* 95 A6
Riberalta, *Bolivia* 92 F5
Riccarton, *N.Z.* 59 K4
Rice, *U.S.A.* 85 L12
Rice L., *Canada* 78 B6
Rice Lake, *U.S.A.* 80 C9
Rich Hill, *U.S.A.* 81 F7
Richards Bay, *S. Africa* 57 D5
Richards L., *Canada* 73 B7
Richardson →, *Canada* 73 B6
Richardson Springs, *U.S.A.* 84 F5
Richardton, *U.S.A.* 80 B3
Riche, C., *Australia* 61 F2
Richey, *U.S.A.* 80 B2
Richfield, *Idaho, U.S.A.* 82 E6
Richfield, *Utah, U.S.A.* 83 G8
Richford, *U.S.A.* 79 B12
Richibucto, *Canada* 71 C7
Richland, *Ga., U.S.A.* 77 J3
Richland, *Oreg., U.S.A.* 82 D5
Richland, *Wash., U.S.A.* 82 C4
Richland Center, *U.S.A.* 80 D9
Richlands, *U.S.A.* 76 G5
Richmond, *N.S.W., Australia* 63 E5
Richmond, *Queens., Australia* 62 C3
Richmond, *N.Z.* 59 J4
Richmond, *S. Africa* 57 D5
Richmond, *U.K.* 10 C6
Richmond, *Calif., U.S.A.* 84 H4
Richmond, *Ind., U.S.A.* 76 F3
Richmond, *Ky., U.S.A.* 76 G3
Richmond, *Mich., U.S.A.* 78 D2
Richmond, *Mo., U.S.A.* 80 F8
Richmond, *Tex., U.S.A.* 81 L7
Richmond, *Utah, U.S.A.* 82 F8
Richmond, *Va., U.S.A.* 76 G7
Richmond Ra., *Australia* 63 D5
Richmond-upon-Thames, *U.K.* 11 F7
Richton, *U.S.A.* 77 K1
Richwood, *U.S.A.* 76 F5
Ridder, *Kazakhstan* 26 D9
Ridgecrest, *U.S.A.* 85 K9
Ridgedale, *Canada* 73 C8
Ridgefield, *U.S.A.* 84 E4
Ridgeland, *U.S.A.* 77 J5
Ridgelands, *Australia* 62 C5
Ridgetown, *Canada* 70 D3
Ridgewood, *U.S.A.* 79 F10
Ridgway, *U.S.A.* 78 E6
Riding Mountain Nat. Park, *Canada* 73 C8
Ridley, Mt., *Australia* 61 F3
Ried, *Austria* 16 D6
Riet →, *S. Africa* 56 D3
Rieti, *Italy* 20 C5
Riffe, L., *U.S.A.* 84 D4
Rifle, *U.S.A.* 82 G10
Rifstangi, *Iceland* 8 C5
Rift Valley □, *Kenya* 54 B4
Rig Rig, *Chad* 51 F7
Riga, *Latvia* 24 C3
Riga, G. of = Rīgas Jūras Līcis, *Latvia* 24 C3
Rīgān, *Iran* 45 D8
Rīgas Jūras Līcis, *Latvia* 24 C3
Rigaud, *Canada* 79 A10
Rigby, *U.S.A.* 82 E8
Rīgestān □, *Afghan.* 40 D4
Riggins, *U.S.A.* 82 D5
Rigolet, *Canada* 71 B8
Riihimäki, *Finland* 9 F18
Riiser-Larsen-halvøya, *Antarctica* 5 C4
Rijeka, *Croatia* 20 B6
Rijn →, *Neths.* 15 B4
Rijssen, *Neths.* 15 B6
Rijswijk, *Neths.* 15 B4
Rikuzentakada, *Japan* 30 E10
Riley, *U.S.A.* 82 E4
Rimah, Wadi ar →, *Si. Arabia* 44 E4
Rimbey, *Canada* 72 C6
Rimini, *Italy* 20 B5
Rîmnicu Sărat, *Romania* 17 F13
Rîmnicu Vîlcea, *Romania* 17 F12
Rimouski, *Canada* 71 C6
Rimrock, *U.S.A.* 84 D5

Rinca, *Indonesia* 37 F5
Rincón de Romos, *Mexico* 86 C4
Rinconada, *Argentina* 94 A2
Ringkøbing, *Denmark* 9 H10
Ringling, *U.S.A.* 82 C8
Ringvassøy, *Norway* 8 B15
Rinía, *Greece* 21 F11
Rinjani, *Indonesia* 36 F5
Rio Branco, *Brazil* 92 E5
Río Branco, *Uruguay* 95 C5
Rio Brilhante, *Brazil* 95 A5
Rio Claro, *Brazil* 95 A6
Rio Claro, *Trin. & Tob.* 89 D7
Río Colorado, *Argentina* 96 D4
Río Cuarto, *Argentina* 94 C3
Rio das Pedras, *Mozam.* 57 C6
Rio de Janeiro, *Brazil* 95 A7
Rio de Janeiro □, *Brazil* 95 A7
Rio do Sul, *Brazil* 95 B6
Río Gallegos, *Argentina* 96 G3
Río Grande, *Argentina* 96 G3
Rio Grande, *Brazil* 95 C5
Río Grande, *Mexico* 86 C4
Río Grande, *Nic.* 88 D3
Rio Grande →, *U.S.A.* 81 N6
Rio Grande City, *U.S.A.* 81 M5
Río Grande del Norte →, *N. Amer.* 75 E7
Rio Grande do Norte □, *Brazil* 93 E11
Rio Grande do Sul □, *Brazil* 95 C5
Río Hato, *Panama* 88 E3
Río Lagartos, *Mexico* 87 C7
Rio Largo, *Brazil* 93 E11
Río Mulatos, *Bolivia* 92 G5
Río Muni = Mbini □, *Eq. Guin.* 52 D2
Rio Negro, *Brazil* 95 B6
Rio Pardo, *Brazil* 95 C5
Río Segundo, *Argentina* 94 C3
Río Tercero, *Argentina* 94 C3
Rio Verde, *Brazil* 93 G8
Río Verde, *Mexico* 87 C5
Rio Vista, *U.S.A.* 84 G5
Riobamba, *Ecuador* 92 D3
Ríohacha, *Colombia* 92 A4
Riosucio, *Caldas, Colombia* 92 B3
Riosucio, *Choco, Colombia* 92 B3
Riou L., *Canada* 73 B7
Ripley, *Canada* 78 B3
Ripley, *Calif., U.S.A.* 85 M12
Ripley, *N.Y., U.S.A.* 78 D5
Ripley, *Tenn., U.S.A.* 81 H10
Ripon, *U.K.* 10 C6
Ripon, *Calif., U.S.A.* 84 H5
Ripon, *Wis., U.S.A.* 76 D1
Risalpur, *Pakistan* 42 B4
Rishā', W. ar →, *Si. Arabia* 44 E5
Rishiri-Tō, *Japan* 30 B10
Rishon le Ẓiyyon, *Israel* 47 D3
Rison, *U.S.A.* 81 J8
Risør, *Norway* 9 G10
Rittman, *U.S.A.* 78 F3
Ritzville, *U.S.A.* 82 C4
Rivadavia, *Buenos Aires, Argentina* 94 D3
Rivadavia, *Mendoza, Argentina* 94 C2
Rivadavia, *Salta, Argentina* 94 A3
Rivadavia, *Chile* 94 B1
Rivas, *Nic.* 88 D2
Rivera, *Uruguay* 95 C4
Riverdale, *U.S.A.* 84 J7
Riverdsale, *S. Africa* 56 E3
Riverhead, *U.S.A.* 79 F12
Riverhurst, *Canada* 73 C7
Riverina, *Australia* 61 E3
Rivers, *Canada* 73 C8
Rivers, L. of the, *Canada* 73 D7
Rivers Inlet, *Canada* 72 C3
Riverside, *Calif., U.S.A.* 85 M9
Riverside, *Wyo., U.S.A.* 82 F10
Riversleigh, *Australia* 62 B2
Riverton, *Australia* 63 E2
Riverton, *Canada* 73 C9
Riverton, *N.Z.* 59 M1
Riverton, *U.S.A.* 82 E9
Riverton Heights, *U.S.A.* 84 C4
Riviera, *Europe* 16 F4
Riviera di Levante, *Italy* 20 B3
Riviera di Ponente, *Italy* 20 C2
Rivière-à-Pierre, *Canada* 71 C5
Rivière-au-Renard, *Canada* 71 C7
Rivière-du-Loup, *Canada* 71 C6
Rivière-Pentecôte, *Canada* 71 C6
Rivière-Pilot, *Martinique* 89 D7
Rivoli B., *Australia* 63 F3
Riyadh = Ar Riyāḍ, *Si. Arabia* 46 C4
Rize, *Turkey* 25 F7
Rizhao, *China* 35 G10
Rizokarpaso, *Cyprus* 23 D13
Rizzuto, C., *Italy* 20 E7
Rjukan, *Norway* 9 G10
Road Town, *Virgin Is.* 89 C7
Roag, L., *U.K.* 12 C2
Roanne, *France* 18 C6
Roanoke, *Ala., U.S.A.* 77 J3
Roanoke, *Va., U.S.A.* 76 G6
Roanoke →, *U.S.A.* 77 H7
Roanoke I., *U.S.A.* 77 H8
Roanoke Rapids, *U.S.A.* 77 G7
Roatán, *Honduras* 88 C2
Robbins I., *Australia* 62 G4
Robe →, *Australia* 60 D2
Robe →, *Ireland* 13 C2
Robert Lee, *U.S.A.* 81 K4
Roberts, *U.S.A.* 82 E7
Robertsganj, *India* 43 G10
Robertson, *S. Africa* 56 E2
Robertson I., *Antarctica* 5 C18
Robertson Ra., *Australia* 60 D3
Robertsport, *Liberia* 50 G2
Robertstown, *Australia* 63 E2
Roberval, *Canada* 71 C5
Robeson Chan., *Greenland* 4 A4
Robinson →, *Australia* 62 B2
Robinson Ra., *Australia* 61 E2
Robinson River, *Australia* 62 B2
Robinvale, *Australia* 63 E3
Roblin, *Canada* 73 C8
Roboré, *Bolivia* 92 G7
Robson, Mt., *Canada* 72 C5
Robstown, *U.S.A.* 81 M6
Roca, C. da, *Portugal* 19 C1
Roca Partida, I., *Mexico* 86 D2
Rocas, I., *Brazil* 93 D12
Rocha, *Uruguay* 95 C5
Rochdale, *U.K.* 10 D5
Rochefort, *Belgium* 15 D5
Rochefort, *France* 18 D3
Rochelle, *U.S.A.* 80 E10
Rocher River, *Canada* 72 A6
Rochester, *Canada* 72 C6
Rochester, *U.K.* 11 F8
Rochester, *Ind., U.S.A.* 76 E2
Rochester, *Minn., U.S.A.* 80 C8
Rochester, *N.H., U.S.A.* 79 C14
Rochester, *N.Y., U.S.A.* 78 C7
Rock →, *Canada* 72 A3
Rock Hill, *U.S.A.* 77 H5
Rock Island, *U.S.A.* 80 E9
Rock Rapids, *U.S.A.* 80 D6
Rock River, *U.S.A.* 82 F11
Rock Sound, *Bahamas* 88 B4
Rock Springs, *Mont., U.S.A.* 82 C10
Rock Springs, *Wyo., U.S.A.* 82 F9
Rock Valley, *U.S.A.* 80 D6
Rockall, *Atl. Oc.* 6 D3
Rockdale, *Tex., U.S.A.* 81 K6
Rockdale, *Wash., U.S.A.* 84 C5
Rockefeller Plateau, *Antarctica* 5 E14
Rockford, *U.S.A.* 80 D10
Rockglen, *Canada* 73 D7
Rockhampton, *Australia* 62 C5
Rockhampton Downs, *Australia* 62 B2
Rockingham, *Australia* 61 F2
Rockingham B., *Australia* 62 B4
Rockingham Forest, *U.K.* 11 E7
Rocklake, *U.S.A.* 80 A5
Rockland, *Canada* 79 A9
Rockland, *Idaho, U.S.A.* 82 E7
Rockland, *Maine, U.S.A.* 71 D6
Rockland, *Mich., U.S.A.* 80 B10
Rocklin, *U.S.A.* 84 G5
Rockmart, *U.S.A.* 77 H3
Rockport, *Mo., U.S.A.* 80 E7
Rockport, *Tex., U.S.A.* 81 L6
Rocksprings, *U.S.A.* 81 K4
Rockville, *Conn., U.S.A.* 79 E12
Rockville, *Md., U.S.A.* 76 F7
Rockwall, *U.S.A.* 81 J6
Rockwell City, *U.S.A.* 80 D7
Rockwood, *U.S.A.* 77 H3
Rocky Ford, *U.S.A.* 80 F3
Rocky Gully, *Australia* 61 F2
Rocky Lane, *Canada* 72 B5
Rocky Mount, *U.S.A.* 77 H7
Rocky Mountain House, *Canada* 72 C6
Rocky Mts., *N. Amer.* 72 C4
Rockyford, *Canada* 72 C6
Rod, *Pakistan* 40 E3
Rødbyhavn, *Denmark* 9 J11
Roddickton, *Canada* 71 B8
Roderick I., *Canada* 72 C3
Rodez, *France* 18 D5
Rodhopoú, *Greece* 23 D5
Ródhos, *Greece* 23 C10
Rodney, *Canada* 78 D3
Rodney, C., *N.Z.* 59 G5
Rodriguez, *Ind. Oc.* 3 E13
Roe →, *U.K.* 13 A5
Roebling, *U.S.A.* 79 F10
Roebourne, *Australia* 60 D2
Roebuck B., *Australia* 60 C3
Roebuck Plains, *Australia* 60 C3
Roermond, *Neths.* 15 C5
Roes Welcome Sd., *Canada* 69 B11
Roeselare, *Belgium* 15 D3
Rogagua, L., *Bolivia* 92 F5
Rogaland fylke □, *Norway* 9 G9
Rogdhia, *Greece* 23 D7
Rogers, *U.S.A.* 81 G7
Rogers City, *U.S.A.* 76 C4
Rogerson, *U.S.A.* 82 E6
Rogersville, *U.S.A.* 77 G4
Roggan River, *Canada* 70 B4
Roggeveldberge, *S. Africa* 56 E3
Rogoaguado, L., *Bolivia* 92 F5
Rogue →, *U.S.A.* 82 E1
Róhda, *Greece* 23 A3
Rohnert Park, *U.S.A.* 84 G4
Rohri, *Pakistan* 42 F3
Rohri Canal, *Pakistan* 42 F3
Rohtak, *India* 42 E7
Roi Et, *Thailand* 38 D4
Rojas, *Argentina* 94 C3
Rojo, C., *Mexico* 87 C5
Rokan →, *Indonesia* 36 D2
Rokeby, *Australia* 62 A3
Rolândia, *Brazil* 95 A5
Rolette, *U.S.A.* 80 A5
Rolla, *Kans., U.S.A.* 81 G4
Rolla, *Mo., U.S.A.* 81 G9
Rolla, *N. Dak., U.S.A.* 80 A5
Rolleston, *Australia* 62 C4
Rollingstone, *Australia* 62 B4
Roma, *Australia* 63 D4
Roma, *Italy* 20 D5
Roma, *Sweden* 9 H15
Roman, *Romania* 17 E13
Roman, *Russia* 27 C12
Romang, *Indonesia* 37 F7
Românĭ, *Egypt* 47 E1
Romania ■, *Europe* 17 F12
Romano, Cayo, *Cuba* 88 B4
Romblon, *Phil.* 37 B6
Rombo □, *Tanzania* 54 C4
Rome = Roma, *Italy* 20 D5
Rome, *Ga., U.S.A.* 77 H3
Rome, *N.Y., U.S.A.* 79 C9
Romney, *U.S.A.* 76 F6
Romney Marsh, *U.K.* 11 F8
Romorantin-Lanthenay, *France* 18 C4
Romsdalen, *Norway* 8 E10
Ron, *Vietnam* 38 D6
Rona, *U.K.* 12 D3
Ronan, *U.S.A.* 82 C6
Roncador, Cayos, *Caribbean* 88 D3
Roncador, Serra do, *Brazil* 93 F8
Ronceverte, *U.S.A.* 76 G5
Ronda, *Spain* 19 D3
Rondane, *Norway* 9 F10
Rondônia □, *Brazil* 92 F6
Rondonópolis, *Brazil* 93 G8
Ronge, L. la, *Canada* 73 B7
Ronne Ice Shelf, *Antarctica* 5 D18
Ronsard, C., *Australia* 61 D1
Ronse, *Belgium* 15 D3
Roodepoort, *S. Africa* 57 D4
Roof Butte, *U.S.A.* 83 H9
Roorkee, *India* 42 E7
Roosendaal, *Neths.* 15 C4
Roosevelt, *Minn., U.S.A.* 80 A7
Roosevelt, *Utah, U.S.A.* 82 F8
Roosevelt →, *Brazil* 92 E6
Roosevelt, Mt., *Canada* 72 B3
Roosevelt I., *Antarctica* 5 D12
Roosevelt Res., *U.S.A.* 83 K8
Roper →, *Australia* 62 A2
Ropesville, *U.S.A.* 81 J3
Roque Pérez, *Argentina* 94 D4
Roraima □, *Brazil* 92 C6
Roraima, Mt., *Venezuela* 92 B6
Rorketon, *Canada* 73 C9
Røros, *Norway* 8 E11
Rosa, *Zambia* 55 D3
Rosa, Monte, *Europe* 16 F3
Rosalia, *U.S.A.* 82 C5
Rosamond, *U.S.A.* 85 L8
Rosario, *Argentina* 94 C3
Rosário, *Brazil* 93 D10
Rosario, *Baja Calif. N., Mexico* 86 A1
Rosario, *Sinaloa, Mexico* 86 C3
Rosario, *Paraguay* 94 A4
Rosario de la Frontera, *Argentina* 94 B3
Rosario de Lerma, *Argentina* 94 A2
Rosario del Tala, *Argentina* 94 C4
Rosário do Sul, *Brazil* 95 C5
Rosarito, *U.S.A.* 85 N9
Rosas, *Spain* 19 A7
Rosas, G. de, *Spain* 19 A7
Roscoe, *U.S.A.* 80 C5
Roscommon, *Ireland* 13 C3
Roscommon, *U.S.A.* 76 C3
Roscommon □, *Ireland* 13 C3
Roscrea, *Ireland* 13 D4
Rose →, *Australia* 62 A2
Rose Blanche, *Canada* 71 C8
Rose Harbour, *Canada* 72 C2
Rose Pt., *Canada* 72 C2
Rose Valley, *Canada* 73 C8
Roseau, *Domin.* 89 C7
Roseau, *U.S.A.* 80 A7
Rosebery, *Australia* 62 G4
Rosebud, *U.S.A.* 81 K6
Roseburg, *U.S.A.* 82 E2
Rosedale, *Australia* 62 C5
Rosedale, *U.S.A.* 81 J9
Roseland, *U.S.A.* 84 G4
Rosemary, *Canada* 72 C6
Rosenberg, *U.S.A.* 81 L7
Rosenheim, *Germany* 16 E6
Rosetown, *Canada* 73 C7
Rosetta = Rashîd, *Egypt* 51 B11
Roseville, *U.S.A.* 84 G5
Rosewood, *N. Terr., Australia* 60 C4
Rosewood, *Queens., Australia* 63 D5
Roshkhvār, *Iran* 45 C8
Rosignol, *Guyana* 92 B7
Roskilde, *Denmark* 9 J12
Roslavl, *Russia* 24 D5
Roslyn, *Australia* 63 E4
Rosmead, *S. Africa* 56 E4
Ross, *Australia* 62 G4
Ross, *N.Z.* 59 K3
Ross I., *Antarctica* 5 D11
Ross Ice Shelf, *Antarctica* 5 E12
Ross L., *U.S.A.* 82 B3
Ross-on-Wye, *U.K.* 11 F5
Ross Sea, *Antarctica* 5 D11
Rossan Pt., *Ireland* 13 B3
Rossburn, *Canada* 73 C8
Rosseau, *Canada* 78 A5
Rossignol, L., *Canada* 70 B5
Rossignol Res., *Canada* 71 D6
Rossland, *Canada* 72 D5
Rosslare, *Ireland* 13 D5
Rosso, *Mauritania* 50 E1
Rossosh, *Russia* 25 D6
Rossport, *Canada* 70 C2
Røssvatnet, *Norway* 8 D13
Rossville, *Australia* 62 B4
Rosthern, *Canada* 73 C7
Rostock, *Germany* 16 A6
Rostov, *Russia* 24 C6
Rostov, *Russia* 25 E6
Roswell, *U.S.A.* 81 J2
Rosyth, *U.K.* 12 E5
Rotan, *U.S.A.* 81 J4
Rothaargebirge, *Germany* 16 C4
Rother →, *U.K.* 11 G8
Rotherham, *U.K.* 10 D6
Rothes, *U.K.* 12 D5
Rothesay, *Canada* 71 C6
Rothesay, *U.K.* 12 F3
Roti, *Indonesia* 37 F6
Roto, *Australia* 63 E4
Rotoroa, L., *N.Z.* 59 J4
Rotorua, *N.Z.* 59 H6
Rotorua, L., *N.Z.* 59 H6
Rotterdam, *Neths.* 15 C4
Rottnest I., *Australia* 61 F2
Rottumeroog, *Neths.* 15 A6
Rottweil, *Germany* 16 D4
Rotuma, *Fiji* 64 J9
Roubaix, *France* 18 A5
Rouen, *France* 18 B4
Rouleau, *Canada* 73 C8
Round Mt., *Australia* 63 E5
Round Mountain, *U.S.A.* 82 G5
Roundup, *U.S.A.* 82 C9
Rousay, *U.K.* 12 B5
Rouses Point, *U.S.A.* 79 B11
Roussillon, *France* 18 E5
Rouxville, *S. Africa* 56 E4
Rouyn, *Canada* 70 C4
Rovaniemi, *Finland* 8 C18
Rovereto, *Italy* 20 B4
Rovigo, *Italy* 20 B4
Rovinj, *Croatia* 20 B5
Rovno, *Ukraine* 25 D4
Rovuma →, *Tanzania* 55 E5
Row'ān, *Iran* 45 C6
Rowena, *Australia* 63 D4
Rowley Shoals, *Australia* 60 C2
Roxas, *Phil.* 37 B6
Roxboro, *U.S.A.* 77 G6
Roxborough Downs, *Australia* 62 C2
Roxburgh, *N.Z.* 59 L2
Roy, *Mont., U.S.A.* 82 C9
Roy, *N. Mex., U.S.A.* 81 H2
Roy Hill, *Australia* 60 D2
Royal Leamington Spa, *U.K.* 11 E6
Royan, *France* 18 D3
Rtishchevo, *Russia* 24 C7
Ruacaná, *Angola* 56 B1
Ruahine Ra., *N.Z.* 59 H6
Ruapehu, *N.Z.* 59 H5
Ruapuke I., *N.Z.* 59 M2
Ruâq, W. →, *Egypt* 47 F2
Rub' al Khali, *Si. Arabia* 46 D4
Rubeho Mts., *Tanzania* 54 D4
Rubh a' Mhail, *U.K.* 12 F2
Rubha Hunish, *U.K.* 12 D2
Rubicon →, *U.S.A.* 84 G5
Rubicone →, *Italy* 20 B5
Rubio, *Venezuela* 92 B4
Rubtsovsk, *Russia* 26 D9
Ruby L., *U.S.A.* 82 F6
Ruby Mts., *U.S.A.* 82 F6
Rūd Sar, *Iran* 45 B6
Rudall, *Australia* 63 E2
Rudall →, *Australia* 60 D3
Rudewa, *Tanzania* 55 E3
Rudnichnyy, *Russia* 24 C9
Rudnogorsk, *Russia* 27 D11
Rudnyy, *Kazakhstan* 26 D7
Rudolf, Ostrov, *Russia* 26 A6
Rudyard, *U.S.A.* 76 B3
Rufa'a, *Sudan* 51 F11
Rufiji □, *Tanzania* 54 D4
Rufiji →, *Tanzania* 54 D4
Rufino, *Argentina* 94 C3
Rufisque, *Senegal* 50 F1
Rufunsa, *Zambia* 55 F2
Rugby, *U.K.* 11 E6
Rugby, *U.S.A.* 80 A5
Rügen, *Germany* 16 A6
Ruhengeri, *Rwanda* 54 C2
Ruhr →, *Germany* 16 C3
Ruhuhu →, *Tanzania* 55 E3
Ruidosa, *U.S.A.* 81 L2
Ruidoso, *U.S.A.* 83 K11
Ruivo, Pico, *Madeira* 22 D3
Rujm Tal'at al Jamā'ah, *Jordan* 47 E4
Ruk, *Pakistan* 42 F3
Rukwa □, *Tanzania* 54 D3
Rukwa L., *Tanzania* 54 D3
Rulhieres, C., *Australia* 60 B4
Rum Cay, *Bahamas* 89 B5
Rum Jungle, *Australia* 60 B5
Rumāḥ, *Si. Arabia* 44 E5
Rumania = Romania ■, *Europe* 17 F12
Rumaylah, *Iraq* 44 D5
Rumbalara, *Australia* 62 D1
Rumbêk, *Sudan* 51 G10
Rumford, *U.S.A.* 79 B14
Rumoi, *Japan* 30 C10
Rumonge, *Burundi* 54 C2
Rumsey, *Canada* 72 C6
Rumula, *Australia* 62 B4
Rumuruti, *Kenya* 54 B4
Runan, *China* 34 H8
Runanga, *N.Z.* 59 K3
Runaway, C., *N.Z.* 59 G6
Runcorn, *U.K.* 10 D5
Rungwa, *Tanzania* 54 D3
Rungwa →, *Tanzania* 54 D3
Rungwe, *Tanzania* 55 D3
Rungwe □, *Tanzania* 55 D3
Runton Ra., *Australia* 60 D3
Ruoqiang, *China* 32 C3
Rupa, *India* 41 F18
Rupar, *India* 42 D7
Rupat, *Indonesia* 36 D2
Rupert →, *Canada* 70 B4
Rupert House = Fort Rupert, *Canada* 70 B4
Rurrenabaque, *Bolivia* 92 F5
Rusambo, *Zimbabwe* 55 F3
Rusape, *Zimbabwe* 55 F3
Ruschuk = Ruse, *Bulgaria* 21 C11
Ruse, *Bulgaria* 21 C11
Rushan, *China* 35 F11
Rushden, *U.K.* 11 E7
Rushford, *U.S.A.* 80 D9
Rushville, *Ill., U.S.A.* 80 E9
Rushville, *Ind., U.S.A.* 76 F3
Rushville, *Nebr., U.S.A.* 80 D3
Rushworth, *Australia* 63 F4
Russas, *Brazil* 93 D11
Russell, *Canada* 73 C8
Russell, *U.S.A.* 80 F5
Russell L., *Man., Canada* 73 B8
Russell L., *N.W.T., Canada* 72 A5
Russellkonda, *India* 41 K14
Russellville, *Ala., U.S.A.* 77 H2
Russellville, *Ark., U.S.A.* 81 H8
Russellville, *Ky., U.S.A.* 77 G2
Russian →, *U.S.A.* 84 G3
Russian Federation ■, *Eurasia* 27 C11
Russkaya Polyana, *Kazakhstan* 26 D8
Russkoye Ustie, *Russia* 4 B15
Rustam, *Pakistan* 42 B5
Rustam Shahr, *Pakistan* 42 F2
Rustavi, *Georgia* 25 F8
Rustenburg, *S. Africa* 56 D4
Ruston, *U.S.A.* 81 J8
Rutana, *Burundi* 54 C2
Ruteng, *Indonesia* 37 F6
Ruth, *Mich., U.S.A.* 78 C2
Ruth, *Nev., U.S.A.* 82 G6
Rutherford, *U.S.A.* 84 G4
Rutherglen, *U.K.* 12 F4
Rutland Plains, *Australia* 62 B3
Rutledge →, *Canada* 73 A6
Rutledge L., *Canada* 73 A6
Rutshuru, *Zaïre* 54 C2
Ruurlo, *Neths.* 15 B6
Ruvu, *Tanzania* 54 D4
Ruvu →, *Tanzania* 54 D4
Ruvuma □, *Tanzania* 55 E4
Ruwais, *U.A.E.* 45 E7
Ruwenzori, *Africa* 54 B2
Ruyigi, *Burundi* 54 C3
Ružomberok, *Czech.* 17 D9
Rwanda ■, *Africa* 54 C3
Ryan, L., *U.K.* 12 G3
Ryazan, *Russia* 24 D6
Ryazhsk, *Russia* 24 D7
Rybache, *Kazakhstan* 26 E9
Rybachiy Poluostrov, *Russia* 24 A5
Rybinsk, *Russia* 24 C6
Rybinskoye Vdkhr., *Russia* 24 C6
Ryde, *U.K.* 11 G6
Ryderwood, *U.S.A.* 84 D3
Rye, *U.K.* 11 G8
Rye →, *U.K.* 10 C7
Rye Patch Res., *U.S.A.* 82 F4
Ryegate, *U.S.A.* 82 C9
Rylstone, *Australia* 63 E4
Ryōthu, *Japan* 30 E9
Rypin, *Poland* 17 B9
Ryūgasaki, *Japan* 31 G10
Ryūkyū Is. = Ryūkyū-rettō, *Japan* 31 M2
Ryūkyū-rettō, *Japan* 31 M2
Rzeszów, *Poland* 17 C10
Rzhev, *Russia* 24 C5

S

Sa, *Thailand* 38 C3
Sa Dec, *Vietnam* 39 G5
Sa'ādatābād, *Fārs, Iran* 45 D7
Sa'ādatābād, *Kermān, Iran* 45 D7
Saale →, *Germany* 16 C5
Saar →, *Europe* 16 D3
Saarbrücken, *Germany* 16 D3

Saaremaa, *Estonia* 24 C3
Saariselkä, *Finland* 8 B20
Saarland □, *Germany* 15 E7
Sab 'Bi'ār, *Syria* 44 C3
Saba, *W. Indies* 89 C7
Sabadell, *Spain* 19 B7
Sabah □, *Malaysia* 36 C5
Sabak Bernam, *Malaysia* 39 L3
Sábana de la Mar, *Dom. Rep.* 89 C6
Sábanalarga, *Colombia* 92 A4
Sabang, *Indonesia* 36 C1
Sabará, *Brazil* 93 G10
Sabarania, *Indonesia* 37 E9
Sabattis, *U.S.A.* 79 B10
Sabáudia, *Italy* 20 D5
Sabhah, *Libya* 51 C7
Sabie, *S. Africa* 57 D5
Sabinal, *Mexico* 86 A3
Sabinal, *U.S.A.* 81 L5
Sabinas, *Mexico* 86 B4
Sabinas →, *Mexico* 86 B4
Sabinas Hidalgo, *Mexico* 86 B4
Sabine →, *U.S.A.* 81 L8
Sabine L., *U.S.A.* 81 L8
Sabine Pass, *U.S.A.* 81 L8
Sabkhet el Bardawîl, *Egypt* 47 D2
Sablayan, *Phil.* 37 B6
Sable, C., *Canada* 71 D6
Sable, C., *U.S.A.* 75 E10
Sable I., *Canada* 71 D8
Sabolev, *Russia* 27 D16
Sabrina Coast, *Antarctica* 5 C9
Sabulubek, *Indonesia* 36 E1
Sabzevār, *Iran* 45 B8
Sabzvārān, *Iran* 45 D8
Sac City, *U.S.A.* 80 D7
Sachigo →, *Canada* 70 A2
Sachigo, L., *Canada* 70 B1
Sackets Harbor, *U.S.A.* 79 C8
Saco, *Maine, U.S.A.* 77 D10
Saco, *Mont., U.S.A.* 82 B10
Sacramento, *U.S.A.* 84 G5
Sacramento →, *U.S.A.* 84 G5
Sacramento Mts., *U.S.A.* 83 K11
Sacramento Valley, *U.S.A.* 84 G5
Sádaba, *Spain* 19 A5
Sadani, *Tanzania* 54 D4
Sadao, *Thailand* 39 J3
Sadd el Aali, *Egypt* 51 D11
Saddle Mt., *U.S.A.* 84 E3
Sadimi, *Zaïre* 55 D1
Sado, *Japan* 30 E9
Sadon, *Burma* 41 G20
Saegerstown, *U.S.A.* 78 E4
Şafājah, *Si. Arabia* 44 E3
Säffle, *Sweden* 9 G12
Safford, *U.S.A.* 83 K9
Saffron Walden, *U.K.* 11 E8
Safi, *Morocco* 50 B3
Şafīābād, *Iran* 45 B8
Safīd Dasht, *Iran* 45 C6
Safīd Kūh, *Afghan.* 40 B3
Safwān, *Iraq* 44 D5
Sag Harbor, *U.S.A.* 79 F12
Saga, *Indonesia* 37 E8
Saga, *Japan* 31 H5
Saga □, *Japan* 31 H5
Sagae, *Japan* 30 E10
Sagala, *Mali* 50 F3
Sagar, *India* 40 M9
Sagara, L., *Tanzania* 54 D3
Saginaw, *U.S.A.* 76 D4
Saginaw B., *U.S.A.* 76 D4
Sagîr, Zab as →, *Iraq* 44 C4
Saglouc, *Canada* 69 B12
Sagō-ri, *S. Korea* 35 G14
Sagres, *Portugal* 19 D1
Sagua la Grande, *Cuba* 88 B3
Saguache, *U.S.A.* 83 G10
Saguenay →, *Canada* 71 C5
Sagunto, *Spain* 19 C5
Sahagún, *Spain* 19 A3
Saḩam al Jawlān, *Syria* 47 C4
Sahand, Kūh-e, *Iran* 44 B5
Sahara, *Africa* 50 D5
Saharan Atlas = Saharien, Atlas, *Algeria* 50 B5
Saharanpur, *India* 42 E7
Saharien, Atlas, *Algeria* 50 B5
Sahasinaka, *Madag.* 57 C8
Sahaswan, *India* 43 E8
Sahibganj, *India* 43 G12
Sahiwal, *Pakistan* 42 D5
Şahneh, *Iran* 44 C5
Sahtaneh →, *Canada* 72 B4
Sahuaripa, *Mexico* 86 B3
Sahuarita, *U.S.A.* 83 L8
Sahuayo, *Mexico* 86 C4
Sai Buri, *Thailand* 39 J3
Sa'id Bundas, *Sudan* 51 G9
Saïda, *Algeria* 50 B5
Saïdābād, *Kermān, Iran* 45 D7
Sa'īdābād, *Semnān, Iran* 45 B7
Sa'īdīyeh, *Iran* 45 B6
Saidpur, *Bangla.* 41 G16
Saidu, *Pakistan* 43 B5
Saigon = Phanh Bho Ho Chi Minh, *Vietnam* 39 G6
Saijō, *Japan* 31 H6
Saikhoa Ghat, *India* 41 F19
Saiki, *Japan* 31 H5
Sailolof, *Indonesia* 37 E8
Şa'in Dezh, *Iran* 44 B5
St. Abb's Head, *U.K.* 12 F6
St. Alban's, *Canada* 71 C8
St. Albans, *U.K.* 11 F7
St. Albans, *Vt., U.S.A.* 79 B11
St. Albans, *W. Va., U.S.A.* 76 F5
St. Alban's Head, *U.K.* 11 G5
St. Albert, *Canada* 72 C6
St. Andrew's, *Canada* 71 C8
St. Andrews, *U.K.* 12 E6
St-Anicet, *Canada* 79 A10
St. Ann B., *Canada* 71 C7
St. Ann's Bay, *Jamaica* 88 C4
St. Anthony, *Canada* 71 B8
St. Anthony, *U.S.A.* 82 E8
St. Arnaud, *Australia* 63 F3
St. Arthur, *Canada* 71 C6
St. Asaph, *U.K.* 10 D4
St-Augustin-Saguenay, *Canada* 71 B8
St. Augustine, *U.S.A.* 77 L5
St. Austell, *U.K.* 11 G3
St.-Barthélemy, I., *W. Indies* 89 C7
St. Bee's Hd., *U.K.* 10 C4
St. Boniface, *Canada* 73 D9
St. Bride's, *Canada* 71 C9
St. Brides B., *U.K.* 11 F2
St.-Brieuc, *France* 18 B2
St. Catharines, *Canada* 70 D4
St. Catherines I., *U.S.A.* 77 K5
St. Catherine's Pt., *U.K.* 11 G6
St. Charles, *Ill., U.S.A.* 76 E1
St. Charles, *Mo., U.S.A.* 80 F9
St. Christopher, *W. Indies* 89 C7
St. Christopher-Nevis ■, *W. Indies* 89 C7
St. Clair, *Mich., U.S.A.* 78 D2
St. Clair, *Pa., U.S.A.* 79 F8
St. Clair, L., *Canada* 70 D3
St. Clairsville, *U.S.A.* 78 F4
St. Claude, *Canada* 73 D9
St. Cloud, *Fla., U.S.A.* 77 L5
St. Cloud, *Minn., U.S.A.* 80 C7
St-Coeur de Marie, *Canada* 71 C5
St. Cricq, C., *Australia* 61 E1
St. Croix, *Virgin Is.* 89 C7
St. Croix →, *U.S.A.* 80 C8
St. Croix Falls, *U.S.A.* 80 C8
St. David's, *Canada* 71 C8
St. David's, *U.K.* 11 F2
St. David's Head, *U.K.* 11 F2
St.-Denis, *France* 18 B5
St. Elias, Mt., *U.S.A.* 68 B5
St. Elias Mts., *Canada* 72 A1
St.-Étienne, *France* 18 D6
St. Eugène, *Canada* 79 A10
St. Eustatius, *W. Indies* 89 C7
St-Félicien, *Canada* 70 C5
St.-Flour, *France* 18 D5
St. Francis, *U.S.A.* 80 F4
St. Francis →, *U.S.A.* 81 H9
St. Francis, C., *S. Africa* 56 E3
St. Francisville, *U.S.A.* 81 K9
St-François, L., *Canada* 79 A10
St-Gabriel-de-Brandon, *Canada* 70 C5
St. George, *Australia* 63 D4
St. George, *Canada* 71 C6
St. George, *S.C., U.S.A.* 77 J5
St. George, *Utah, U.S.A.* 83 H7
St. George, C., *Canada* 71 C8
St. George, C., *U.S.A.* 77 L3
St. George Ra., *Australia* 60 C4
St-Georges, *Belgium* 15 D5
St. George's, *Canada* 71 C8
St-Georges, *Canada* 71 C5
St.-Georges, *Fr. Guiana* 93 C8
St. George's, *Grenada* 89 D7
St. George's B., *Canada* 71 C8
St. Georges Basin, *Australia* 60 C4
St. George's Channel, *U.K.* 13 E6
St. Georges Hd., *Australia* 63 F5
St. Gotthard P. = San Gottardo, Paso del, *Switz.* 16 E4
St. Helena, *Atl. Oc.* 2 E9
St. Helena, *U.S.A.* 82 G2
St. Helena, Mt., *U.S.A.* 84 G4
St. Helena B., *S. Africa* 56 E2
St. Helens, *Australia* 62 G4
St. Helens, *U.K.* 10 D5
St. Helens, *U.S.A.* 84 E4
St. Helens, Mt., *U.S.A.* 84 D4
St. Helier, *U.K.* 11 H5
St-Hubert, *Belgium* 15 D5
St-Hyacinthe, *Canada* 70 C5
St. Ignace, *U.S.A.* 76 C3
St. Ignace I., *Canada* 70 C2
St. Ignatius, *U.S.A.* 82 C6
St. Ives, *Cambs., U.K.* 11 E7
St. Ives, *Corn., U.K.* 11 G2
St. James, *U.S.A.* 80 D7
St-Jean, *Canada* 70 C5
St-Jean →, *Canada* 71 B7
St-Jean, L., *Canada* 71 C5
St. Jean Baptiste, *Canada* 73 D9
St-Jean-Port-Joli, *Canada* 71 C5
St-Jérôme, *Qué., Canada* 70 C5
St-Jérôme, *Qué., Canada* 71 C5
St. John, *Canada* 71 C6
St. John, *Kans., U.S.A.* 81 G5
St. John, *N. Dak., U.S.A.* 80 A5
St. John →, *N. Amer.* 71 C6
St. John, C., *Canada* 71 B8
St. John's, *Antigua* 89 C7
St. John's, *Canada* 71 C9
St. Johns, *Ariz., U.S.A.* 83 J9
St. Johns, *Mich., U.S.A.* 76 D3
St. John's →, *U.S.A.* 77 K5
St. Johnsbury, *U.S.A.* 79 B12
St. Johnsville, *U.S.A.* 79 C10
St. Joseph, *La., U.S.A.* 81 K9
St. Joseph, *Mich., U.S.A.* 76 D2
St. Joseph, *Mo., U.S.A.* 80 F7
St. Joseph →, *U.S.A.* 76 D2
St. Joseph, I., *Canada* 70 C3
St. Joseph, L., *Canada* 70 B1
St-Jovite, *Canada* 70 C5
St. Kilda, *N.Z.* 59 L3
St. Kitts = St. Christopher, *W. Indies* 89 C7
St. Laurent, *Canada* 73 C9
St.-Laurent, *Fr. Guiana* 93 B8
St. Lawrence, *Australia* 62 C4
St. Lawrence, *Canada* 71 C8
St. Lawrence →, *Canada* 71 C6
St. Lawrence, Gulf of, *Canada* 71 C7
St. Lawrence I., *U.S.A.* 68 B3
St. Leonard, *Canada* 71 C6
St. Lewis →, *Canada* 71 B8
St.-Lô, *France* 18 B3
St-Louis, *Senegal* 50 E1
St. Louis, *Mich., U.S.A.* 76 D3
St. Louis, *Mo., U.S.A.* 80 F9
St. Louis →, *U.S.A.* 80 B8
St. Lucia ■, *W. Indies* 89 D7
St. Lucia, L., *S. Africa* 57 D5
St. Lucia Channel, *W. Indies* 89 D7
St. Lunaire-Griquet, *Canada* 71 B8
St. Maarten, *W. Indies* 89 C7
St.-Malo, *France* 18 B2
St-Marc, *Haiti* 89 C5
St. Maries, *U.S.A.* 82 C5
St-Martin, *W. Indies* 89 C7
St. Martin, L., *Canada* 73 C9
St. Martins, *Canada* 71 C6
St. Martinsville, *U.S.A.* 81 K9
St. Mary Pk., *Australia* 63 E2
St. Marys, *Australia* 62 G4
St. Marys, *Canada* 78 C3
St. Mary's, *U.K.* 11 H1
St. Marys, *U.S.A.* 78 E6
St. Mary's, C., *Canada* 71 C9
St. Mary's B., *Canada* 71 C9
St. Marys Bay, *Canada* 71 D6
St.-Mathieu, Pte., *France* 18 B1
St. Matthews, I. = Zadetkyi Kyun, *Burma* 39 H2
St-Maurice →, *Canada* 70 C5
St. Michael's Mount, *U.K.* 11 G2
St.-Nazaire, *France* 18 C2
St. Neots, *U.K.* 11 E7
St.-Omer, *France* 18 A5
St-Pacome, *Canada* 71 C6
St-Pamphile, *Canada* 71 C6
St. Pascal, *Canada* 71 C6
St. Paul, *Canada* 72 C6
St. Paul, *Minn., U.S.A.* 80 C8
St. Paul, *Nebr., U.S.A.* 80 E5
St. Paul, I., *Ind. Oc.* 3 F13
St. Paul I., *Canada* 71 C7
St. Peter, *U.S.A.* 80 C8
St. Peter Port, *Chan. Is.* 11 H5
St. Peters, *N.S., Canada* 71 C7
St. Peters, *P.E.I., Canada* 71 C7
St. Petersburg = Sankt-Peterburg, *Russia* 24 C5
St. Petersburg, *U.S.A.* 77 M4
St.-Pierre, *St- P. & M.* 71 C8
St-Pierre, L., *Canada* 70 C5
St.-Pierre et Miquelon □, *St- P. & M.* 71 C8
St.-Quentin, *France* 18 B5
St. Regis, *U.S.A.* 82 C6
St. Sebastien, Tanjon' i, *Madag.* 57 A8
St-Siméon, *Canada* 71 C6
St. Stephen, *Canada* 71 C6
St. Thomas, *Canada* 70 D3
St. Thomas, *Virgin Is.* 89 C7
St-Tite, *Canada* 70 C5
St.-Tropez, *France* 18 E7
St. Troud = Sint Truiden, *Belgium* 15 D5
St.-Valéry-sur-Somme, *France* 18 A4
St. Vincent, *W. Indies* 89 D7
St. Vincent, G., *Australia* 63 F2
St. Vincent and the Grenadines ■, *W. Indies* 89 D7
St. Vincent Passage, *W. Indies* 89 D7
St-Vith, *Belgium* 15 D6
Ste-Agathe-des-Monts, *Canada* 70 C5
Ste-Anne de Beaupré, *Canada* 71 C5
Ste-Anne-des-Monts, *Canada* 71 C6
Ste. Genevieve, *U.S.A.* 80 G9
Ste-Marguerite →, *Canada* 71 B6
Ste.-Marie, *Martinique* 89 D7
Ste-Marie de la Madeleine, *Canada* 71 C5
Ste.-Rose, *Guadeloupe* 89 C7
Ste. Rose du Lac, *Canada* 73 C9
Saintes, *France* 18 D3
Saintes, I. des, *Guadeloupe* 89 C7
Saintonge, *France* 18 D3
Saipan, *Pac. Oc.* 64 F6
Sairang, *India* 41 H18
Sairecábur, Cerro, *Bolivia* 94 A2
Saitama □, *Japan* 31 F9
Sajama, *Bolivia* 92 G5
Sajum, *India* 43 C8
Sak →, *S. Africa* 56 E3
Sakai, *Japan* 31 G7
Sakaide, *Japan* 31 G6
Sakaiminato, *Japan* 31 G6
Sakākah, *Si. Arabia* 44 D4
Sakakawea, L., *U.S.A.* 80 B3
Sakami, L., *Canada* 70 B4
Sakania, *Zaïre* 55 E2
Sakarya = Adapazarı, *Turkey* 25 F5
Sakarya →, *Turkey* 25 F5
Sakashima-Guntō, *Japan* 31 M2
Sakata, *Japan* 30 E9
Sakchu, *N. Korea* 35 D13
Sakeny →, *Madag.* 57 C8
Sakhalin, *Russia* 27 D15
Sakhalinskiy Zaliv, *Russia* 27 D15
Sakon Nakhon, *Thailand* 38 D5
Sakrand, *Pakistan* 42 F3
Sakrivier, *S. Africa* 56 E3
Sakuma, *Japan* 31 G8
Sakurai, *Japan* 31 G7
Sala, *Sweden* 9 G14
Sala-y-Gómez, *Pac. Oc.* 65 K17
Salaberry-de-Valleyfield, *Canada* 70 C5
Saladas, *Argentina* 94 B4
Saladillo, *Argentina* 94 D4
Salado →, *Buenos Aires, Argentina* 94 D4
Salado →, *La Pampa, Argentina* 96 D3
Salado →, *Santa Fe, Argentina* 94 C3
Salado →, *Mexico* 86 B5
Salaga, *Ghana* 50 G4
Sālah, *Syria* 47 C5
Sálakhos, *Greece* 23 C9
Salālah, *Oman* 46 D5
Salamanca, *Chile* 94 C1
Salamanca, *Spain* 19 B3
Salamanca, *U.S.A.* 78 D6
Salāmatābād, *Iran* 44 C5
Salamis, *Cyprus* 23 D12
Salamis, *Greece* 21 F10
Salar de Atacama, *Chile* 94 A2
Salar de Uyuni, *Bolivia* 92 H5
Salatiga, *Indonesia* 37 G14
Salavat, *Russia* 24 D10
Salaverry, *Peru* 92 E3
Salawati, *Indonesia* 37 E8
Salayar, *Indonesia* 37 F6
Salcombe, *U.K.* 11 G4
Saldaña, *Spain* 19 A3
Saldanha, *S. Africa* 56 E2
Saldanha B., *S. Africa* 56 E2
Sale, *Australia* 63 F4
Salé, *Morocco* 50 B3
Sale, *U.K.* 10 D5
Salekhard, *Russia* 24 A12
Salem, *India* 40 P11
Salem, *Ind., U.S.A.* 76 F2
Salem, *Mass., U.S.A.* 79 D14
Salem, *Mo., U.S.A.* 81 G9
Salem, *N.J., U.S.A.* 76 F8
Salem, *Ohio, U.S.A.* 78 F4
Salem, *Oreg., U.S.A.* 82 D2
Salem, *S. Dak., U.S.A.* 80 D6
Salem, *Va., U.S.A.* 76 G5
Salerno, *Italy* 20 D6
Salford, *U.K.* 10 D5
Salida, *U.S.A.* 74 C5
Salima, *Malawi* 53 G6
Salina, *Italy* 20 E6
Salina, *U.S.A.* 80 F6
Salina Cruz, *Mexico* 87 D5
Salinas, *Brazil* 93 G10
Salinas, *Chile* 94 A2
Salinas, *Ecuador* 92 D2
Salinas, *U.S.A.* 83 H3
Salinas →, *Guatemala* 87 D6
Salinas →, *U.S.A.* 83 H3
Salinas, B. de, *Nic.* 88 D2
Salinas, C. de, *Spain* 22 B10
Salinas, Pampa de las, *Argentina* 94 C2
Salinas Ambargasta, *Argentina* 94 B3
Salinas de Hidalgo, *Mexico* 86 C4
Salinas Grandes, *Argentina* 94 B2
Saline →, *Ark., U.S.A.* 81 J8
Saline →, *Kans., U.S.A.* 80 F6
Salines, *Spain* 22 B10
Salinópolis, *Brazil* 93 D9
Salisbury = Harare, *Zimbabwe* 55 F3
Salisbury, *Australia* 63 E2
Salisbury, *U.K.* 11 F6
Salisbury, *Md., U.S.A.* 76 F8
Salisbury, *N.C., U.S.A.* 77 H5
Salisbury Plain, *U.K.* 11 F6
Salkhad, *Jordan* 47 C5
Sallisaw, *U.S.A.* 81 H7
Salmās, *Iran* 44 B5
Salmo, *Canada* 72 D5
Salmon, *U.S.A.* 82 D7
Salmon →, *Canada* 72 C4
Salmon →, *U.S.A.* 82 D5
Salmon Arm, *Canada* 72 C5
Salmon Falls, *U.S.A.* 82 E6
Salmon Gums, *Australia* 61 F3
Salmon Res., *Canada* 71 C8
Salmon River Mts., *U.S.A.* 82 D6
Salo, *Finland* 9 F17
Salome, *U.S.A.* 85 M13
Salonica = Thessaloníki, *Greece* 21 D10
Salonta, *Romania* 17 E10
Salsacate, *Argentina* 94 C2
Salsk, *Russia* 25 E7
Salso →, *Italy* 20 F5
Salt →, *Canada* 72 B6
Salt →, *U.S.A.* 83 K7
Salt Creek, *Australia* 63 F2
Salt Fork →, *U.S.A.* 81 G6
Salt Lake City, *U.S.A.* 82 F8
Salt Range, *Pakistan* 42 C5
Salta, *Argentina* 94 A2
Salta □, *Argentina* 94 A2
Saltcoats, *U.K.* 12 F4
Saltee Is., *Ireland* 13 D5
Saltfjorden, *Norway* 8 C13
Salthólmavík, *Iceland* 8 D3
Saltillo, *Mexico* 86 B4
Salto, *Argentina* 94 C3
Salto, *Uruguay* 94 C4
Salton City, *U.S.A.* 85 M11
Salton Sea, *U.S.A.* 85 M11
Saltpond, *Ghana* 50 G4
Saltville, *U.S.A.* 76 G5
Saluda →, *U.S.A.* 77 H5
Salûm, *Egypt* 51 B10
Salûm, Khâlig el, *Egypt* 51 B10
Salur, *India* 41 K13
Saluzzo, *Italy* 20 B2
Salvador, *Brazil* 93 F11
Salvador, *Canada* 73 C7
Salvador, L., *U.S.A.* 81 L9
Salween →, *Burma* 41 L20
Salyany, *Azerbaijan* 25 G8
Salyersville, *U.S.A.* 76 G4
Salzburg, *Austria* 16 E6
Salzburg □, *Austria* 16 E6
Salzgitter, *Germany* 16 B5
Sam Neua, *Laos* 38 B5
Sam Ngao, *Thailand* 38 D2
Sam Rayburn Res., *U.S.A.* 81 K7
Sam Son, *Vietnam* 38 C5
Sam Teu, *Laos* 38 C5
Sama, *Russia* 26 C7
Sama de Langreo, *Spain* 19 A3
Samagaltai, *Russia* 27 D10
Samales Group, *Phil.* 37 C6
Samana, *India* 42 D7
Samana Cay, *Bahamas* 89 B5
Samanga, *Tanzania* 55 D4
Samangwa, *Zaïre* 54 C1
Samani, *Japan* 30 C11
Samar, *Phil.* 37 B7
Samara, *Russia* 24 D9
Samaria = Shōmrōn, *Jordan* 47 C4
Samariá, *Greece* 23 D5
Samarinda, *Indonesia* 36 E5
Samarkand, *Uzbekistan* 26 F7
Sāmarrā, *Iraq* 44 C4
Samastipur, *India* 43 G11
Samba, *India* 43 C6
Samba, *Zaïre* 54 C2
Sambalpur, *India* 41 J14
Sambar, Tanjung, *Indonesia* 36 E4
Sambas, *Indonesia* 36 D3
Sambava, *Madag.* 57 A9
Sambawizi, *Zimbabwe* 55 F2
Sambhal, *India* 43 E8
Sambhar, *India* 42 F6
Sambor, *Cambodia* 38 F6
Sambre →, *Europe* 15 D4
Samburu □, *Kenya* 54 B4
Samchŏk, *S. Korea* 35 F15
Samchonpo, *S. Korea* 35 G15
Same, *Tanzania* 54 C4
Samfya, *Zambia* 55 E2
Samnah, *Si. Arabia* 44 E3
Samo Alto, *Chile* 94 C1
Samoorombón, B., *Argentina* 94 D4
Sámos, *Greece* 21 F12
Samothráki, *Évros, Greece* 21 D11
Samothráki, *Kérkira, Greece* 23 A3
Sampacho, *Argentina* 94 C3
Sampang, *Indonesia* 37 G15
Sampit, *Indonesia* 36 E4
Sampit, Teluk, *Indonesia* 36 E4
Samrong, *Cambodia* 38 E4
Samrong, *Thailand* 38 E3
Samsun, *Turkey* 25 F6
Samui, Ko, *Thailand* 39 H3
Samusole, *Zaïre* 55 E1
Samut Prakan, *Thailand* 38 F3
Samut Sakhon, *Thailand* 38 F3
Samut Songkhram →, *Thailand* 38 F3
Samwari, *Pakistan* 42 E2
San, *Mali* 50 F4
San →, *Cambodia* 38 F5
San →, *Poland* 17 C10
San Agustin, C., *Phil.* 37 C7
San Agustín de Valle Fértil, *Argentina* 94 C2
San Ambrosio, *Pac. Oc.* 65 K20
San Andreas, *U.S.A.* 84 G6
San Andrés, I. de, *Caribbean* 88 D3
San Andres Mts., *U.S.A.* 83 K10
San Andrés Tuxtla, *Mexico* 87 D5
San Angelo, *U.S.A.* 81 K4
San Anselmo, *U.S.A.* 84 H4
San Antonio, *Belize* 87 D7
San Antonio, *Chile* 94 C1
San Antonio, *N. Mex., U.S.A.* 83 K10
San Antonio, *Tex., U.S.A.* 81 L5
San Antonio →, *U.S.A.* 81 L6

San Antonio, C., Argentina 94 D4
San Antonio, C., Cuba 88 B3
San Antonio, Mt., U.S.A. 85 L9
San Antonio Abad, Spain 22 C7
San Antonio de los Baños, Cuba 88 B3
San Antonio de los Cobres, Argentina 94 A2
San Antonio Oeste, Argentina 96 E4
San Ardo, U.S.A. 84 J6
San Augustín, Canary Is. 22 G4
San Augustine, U.S.A. 81 K7
San Bartolomé, Canary Is. 22 F6
San Bartolomé de Tirajana, Canary Is. 22 G4
San Benedicto, I., Mexico 86 D2
San Benito, U.S.A. 81 M6
San Benito →, U.S.A. 84 J5
San Benito Mt., U.S.A. 84 J6
San Bernardino, U.S.A. 85 L9
San Bernardino Mts., U.S.A. 85 L10
San Bernardino Str., Phil. 37 B6
San Bernardo, Chile 94 C1
San Bernardo, I. de, Colombia 92 B3
San Blas, Mexico 86 B3
San Blas, Arch. de, Panama 88 E4
San Blas, C., U.S.A. 77 L3
San Borja, Bolivia 92 F5
San Buenaventura, Mexico 86 B4
San Carlos, Argentina 94 C2
San Carlos, Chile 94 D1
San Carlos, Mexico 86 B4
San Carlos, Nic. 88 D3
San Carlos, Phil. 37 B6
San Carlos, Spain 22 B8
San Carlos, Uruguay 95 C5
San Carlos, U.S.A. 83 K8
San Carlos, Amazonas, Venezuela 92 C5
San Carlos, Cojedes, Venezuela 92 B5
San Carlos de Bariloche, Argentina 96 E2
San Carlos del Zulia, Venezuela 92 B4
San Carlos L., U.S.A. 83 K8
San Clemente, Chile 94 D1
San Clemente, U.S.A. 85 M9
San Clemente I., U.S.A. 85 N8
San Cristóbal, Argentina 94 C3
San Cristóbal, Dom. Rep. 89 C5
San Cristóbal, Mexico 87 D6
San Cristóbal, Spain 22 B11
San Cristóbal, Venezuela 92 B4
San Diego, Calif., U.S.A. 85 N9
San Diego, Tex., U.S.A. 81 M5
San Diego, C., Argentina 96 G3
San Diego de la Unión, Mexico 86 C4
San Dimitri, Ras, Malta 23 C1
San Estanislao, Paraguay 94 A4
San Felipe, Chile 94 C1
San Felipe, Mexico 86 A2
San Felipe, Venezuela 92 A5
San Felipe →, U.S.A. 85 M11
San Feliu de Guixols, Spain 19 B7
San Félix, Pac. Oc. 65 K20
San Fernando, Chile 94 C1
San Fernando, Mexico 86 B1
San Fernando, La Union, Phil. 37 A6
San Fernando, Pampanga, Phil. 37 A6
San Fernando, Baleares, Spain 22 C7
San Fernando, Cádiz, Spain 19 D2
San Fernando, Trin. & Tob. 89 D7
San Fernando, U.S.A. 85 L8
San Fernando →, Mexico 86 C5
San Fernando de Apure, Venezuela 92 B5
San Fernando de Atabapo, Venezuela 92 C5
San Francisco, Argentina 94 C3
San Francisco, U.S.A. 83 H2
San Francisco →, U.S.A. 83 K9
San Francisco, Paso de, S. Amer. 94 B2
San Francisco de Macorís, Dom. Rep. 89 C5
San Francisco del Monte de Oro, Argentina 94 C2
San Francisco del Oro, Mexico 86 B3
San Francisco Javier, Spain 22 C7
San Gil, Colombia 92 B4
San Gorgonio Mt., U.S.A. 85 L10
San Gottardo, Paso del, Switz. 16 E4
San Gregorio, Uruguay 95 C4
San Gregorio, U.S.A. 84 H4
San Ignacio, Belize 87 D7
San Ignacio, Bolivia 92 G6
San Ignacio, Mexico 86 B2
San Ignacio, Paraguay 94 B4
San Ignacio, L., Mexico 86 B2
San Ildefonso, C., Phil. 37 A6
San Isidro, Argentina 94 C4
San Jacinto, U.S.A. 85 M10
San Jaime, Spain 22 B11
San Javier, Misiones, Argentina 95 B4
San Javier, Santa Fe, Argentina 94 C4
San Javier, Bolivia 92 G6
San Javier, Chile 94 D1
San Jeronimo Taviche, Mexico 87 D5
San Joaquin, U.S.A. 84 J6
San Joaquin →, U.S.A. 83 G3
San Joaquin Valley, U.S.A. 84 J6
San Jordi, Spain 22 B9
San Jorge, Argentina 94 C3
San Jorge, Spain 22 C7
San Jorge, B. de, Mexico 86 A2
San Jorge, G., Argentina 96 F3
San Jorge, G. de, Spain 19 B5
San José, Bolivia 92 G6
San José, Costa Rica 88 E3
San José, Guatemala 88 D1
San José, Mexico 86 C2
San Jose, Phil. 37 A6
San José, Spain 22 C7
San Jose, U.S.A. 83 H3
San Jose →, U.S.A. 83 J10
San Jose de Buenovista, Phil. 37 B6
San José de Feliciano, Argentina 94 C4
San José de Jáchal, Argentina 94 C2
San José de Mayo, Uruguay 94 C4
San José de Ocune, Colombia 92 C4
San José del Cabo, Mexico 86 C3
San José del Guaviare, Colombia 92 C4
San Juan, Argentina 94 C2
San Juan, Mexico 86 C4
San Juan, Phil. 37 C7
San Juan, Puerto Rico 89 C6
San Juan □, Argentina 94 C2
San Juan →, Argentina 94 C2
San Juan →, Nic. 88 D3
San Juan →, Calif., U.S.A. 84 J5
San Juan →, Utah, U.S.A. 83 H8
San Juan, C., Eq. Guin. 52 D1
San Juan Bautista, Paraguay 94 B4
San Juan Bautista, Spain 22 B8
San Juan Bautista, U.S.A. 83 H3
San Juan Bautista Valle Nacional, Mexico 87 D5
San Juan Capistrano, U.S.A. 85 M9
San Juan de Guadalupe, Mexico 86 C4
San Juan de los Morros, Venezuela 92 B5
San Juan del Norte, Nic. 88 D3
San Juan del Norte, B. de, Nic. 88 D3
San Juan del Río, Mexico 87 C5
San Juan del Sur, Nic. 88 D2
San Juan I., U.S.A. 84 B3
San Juan Mts., U.S.A. 83 H10
San Julián, Argentina 96 F3
San Justo, Argentina 94 C3
San Kamphaeng, Thailand 38 C2
San Lázaro, C., Mexico 86 C2
San Lázaro, Sa., Mexico 86 C3
San Leandro, U.S.A. 83 H2
San Lorenzo, Argentina 94 C3
San Lorenzo, Ecuador 92 C3
San Lorenzo, Paraguay 94 B4
San Lorenzo, Spain 22 B10
San Lorenzo →, Mexico 86 C3
San Lorenzo, I., Mexico 86 B2
San Lorenzo, I., Peru 92 F3
San Lorenzo, Mt., Argentina 96 F2
San Lucas, Bolivia 92 H5
San Lucas, Baja Calif. S., Mexico 86 C3
San Lucas, Baja Calif. S., Mexico 86 B2
San Lucas, U.S.A. 84 J5
San Lucas, C., Mexico 86 C3
San Luis, Argentina 94 C2
San Luis, Cuba 88 B3
San Luis, Guatemala 88 C2
San Luis, U.S.A. 83 H11
San Luis □, Argentina 94 C2
San Luis, I., Mexico 86 B2
San Luis, Sierra de, Argentina 94 C2
San Luis de la Paz, Mexico 86 C4
San Luis Obispo, U.S.A. 85 K6
San Luis Potosí, Mexico 86 C4
San Luis Potosí □, Mexico 86 C4
San Luis Res., U.S.A. 84 H5
San Luis Río Colorado, Mexico 86 A2
San Marcos, Guatemala 88 D1
San Marcos, Mexico 86 B2
San Marcos, U.S.A. 81 L6
San Marino ■, Europe 20 C5
San Martín, Argentina 94 C2
San Martín, L., Argentina 96 F2
San Mateo, Spain 22 B7
San Mateo, U.S.A. 83 H2
San Matías, Bolivia 92 G7
San Matías, G., Argentina 96 E4
San Miguel, El Salv. 88 D2
San Miguel, Panama 88 E4
San Miguel, Spain 22 B7
San Miguel, U.S.A. 83 J3
San Miguel →, Bolivia 92 F6
San Miguel de Tucumán, Argentina 94 B2
San Miguel del Monte, Argentina 94 D4
San Miguel I., U.S.A. 85 L6
San Narciso, Phil. 37 A6
San Nicolás, Canary Is. 22 G4
San Nicolás de los Arroyas, Argentina 94 C3
San Nicolas I., U.S.A. 85 M7
San Onofre, U.S.A. 85 M9
San Pablo, Bolivia 94 A2
San Pedro, Buenos Aires, Argentina 95 B5
San Pedro, Jujuy, Argentina 94 A3
San-Pédro, Ivory C. 50 H3
San Pedro, Mexico 86 C2
San Pedro □, Paraguay 94 A4
San Pedro →, Chihuahua, Mexico 86 B3
San Pedro →, Michoacan, Mexico 86 D4
San Pedro →, Nayarit, Mexico 86 C3
San Pedro →, U.S.A. 83 K8
San Pedro, Pta., Chile 94 B1
San Pedro Channel, U.S.A. 85 M8
San Pedro de Atacama, Chile 94 A2
San Pedro de Jujuy, Argentina 94 A3
San Pedro de las Colonias, Mexico 86 B4
San Pedro de Lloc, Peru 92 E3
San Pedro de Macorís, Dom. Rep. 89 C6
San Pedro del Norte, Nic. 88 D3
San Pedro del Paraná, Paraguay 94 B4
San Pedro Mártir, Sierra, Mexico 86 A1
San Pedro Mixtepec, Mexico 87 D5
San Pedro Ocampo = Melchor Ocampo, Mexico 86 C4
San Pedro Sula, Honduras 88 C2
San Quintín, Mexico 86 A1
San Rafael, Argentina 94 C2
San Rafael, Calif., U.S.A. 84 H4
San Rafael, N. Mex., U.S.A. 83 J10
San Rafael Mt., U.S.A. 85 L7
San Rafael Mts., U.S.A. 85 L7
San Ramón de la Nueva Orán, Argentina 94 A3
San Remo, Italy 20 C2
San Roque, Argentina 94 B4
San Rosendo, Chile 94 D1
San Saba, U.S.A. 81 K5
San Salvador, Bahamas 89 B5
San Salvador, El Salv. 88 D2
San Salvador, Spain 22 B10
San Salvador de Jujuy, Argentina 94 A3
San Salvador I., Bahamas 89 B5
San Sebastián, Argentina 96 G3
San Sebastián, Spain 19 A5
San Sebastian de la Gomera, Canary Is. 22 F2
San Serra, Spain 22 B10
San Simeon, U.S.A. 84 K5
San Simon, U.S.A. 83 K9
San Telmo, Mexico 86 A1
San Telmo, Spain 22 B9
San Tiburcio, Mexico 86 C4
San Valentin, Mte., Chile 96 F2
San Vicente de la Barquera, Spain 19 A3
San Ygnacio, U.S.A. 81 M5
Sana', Yemen 46 D3
Sana →, Bos. & H., Yug. 20 B7
Sanaga →, Cameroon 50 H6
Sanaloa, Presa, Mexico 86 C3
Sanana, Indonesia 37 E7
Sanand, India 42 H5
Sanandaj, Iran 44 C5
Sanandita, Bolivia 94 A3
Sanawad, India 42 H7
Sancellas, Spain 22 B9
Sanchahe, China 35 B14
Sánchez, Dom. Rep. 89 C6
Sanchor, India 42 G4
Sanco Pt., Phil. 37 C7
Sancti-Spíritus, Cuba 88 B4
Sand →, S. Africa 57 C5
Sand Springs, U.S.A. 81 G6
Sanda, Japan 31 G7
Sandakan, Malaysia 36 C5
Sandan = Sambor, Cambodia 38 F6
Sanday, U.K. 12 B6
Sanders, U.S.A. 83 J9
Sanderson, U.S.A. 81 K3
Sandfly L., Canada 73 B7
Sandgate, Australia 63 D5
Sandía, Peru 92 F5
Sandnes, Norway 9 G8
Sandness, U.K. 12 A7
Sandoa, Zaïre 52 F4
Sandomierz, Poland 17 C10
Sandover →, Australia 62 C2
Sandoway, Burma 41 K19
Sandpoint, U.S.A. 82 B5
Sandringham, U.K. 10 E8
Sandspit, Canada 72 C2
Sandstone, Australia 61 E2
Sandusky, Mich., U.S.A. 78 C2
Sandusky, Ohio, U.S.A. 78 E2
Sandviken, Sweden 9 F14
Sandwich, C., Australia 62 B4
Sandwich B., Canada 71 B8
Sandwich B., Namibia 56 C1
Sandwip Chan., Bangla. 41 H17
Sandy, Nev., U.S.A. 85 K11
Sandy, Oreg., U.S.A. 84 E4
Sandy Bight, Australia 61 F3
Sandy C., Queens., Australia 62 C5
Sandy C., Tas., Australia 62 G3
Sandy Cay, Bahamas 89 B4
Sandy Cr. →, U.S.A. 82 F9
Sandy L., Canada 70 B1
Sandy Lake, Canada 70 B1
Sandy Narrows, Canada 73 B8
Sanford, Fla., U.S.A. 77 L5
Sanford, Maine, U.S.A. 79 C14
Sanford, N.C., U.S.A. 77 H6
Sanford →, Australia 61 E2
Sanford Mt., U.S.A. 68 B5
Sang-i-Masha, Afghan. 42 C2
Sanga, Mozam. 55 E4
Sanga →, Congo 52 E3
Sanga-Tolon, Russia 27 C15
Sangamner, India 40 K9
Sangar, Afghan. 42 C1
Sangar, Russia 27 C13
Sangar Sarai, Afghan. 42 B4
Sangasangadalam, Indonesia 36 E5
Sange, Zaïre 54 D2
Sangeang, Indonesia 37 F5
Sanger, U.S.A. 83 H4
Sanggan He →, China 34 E9
Sanggau, Indonesia 36 D4
Sangihe, Kepulauan, Indonesia 37 D7
Sangihe, P., Indonesia 37 D7
Sangju, S. Korea 35 F15
Sangkapura, Indonesia 36 F4
Sangkhla, Thailand 38 E2
Sangli, India 40 L9
Sangmélina, Cameroon 52 D2
Sangonera →, Spain 19 D5
Sangre de Cristo Mts., U.S.A. 81 G2
Sangudo, Canada 72 C6
Sāniyah, Iraq 44 C4
Sanje, Uganda 54 C3
Sanjo, Japan 30 F9
Sankt Gallen, Switz. 16 E4
Sankt Moritz, Switz. 16 E4
Sankt-Peterburg, Russia 24 C5
Sankuru →, Zaïre 52 E4
Sanlúcar de Barrameda, Spain 19 D2
Sanmenxia, China 34 G6
Sanming, China 33 D6
Sannaspos, S. Africa 56 D4
Sannicandro Gargánico, Italy 20 D6
Sannieshof, S. Africa 56 D4
Sannin, J., Lebanon 47 B4
Sanok, Poland 17 D11
Sanquhar, U.K. 12 F5
Santa Ana, Bolivia 92 F5
Santa Ana, Ecuador 92 D2
Santa Ana, El Salv. 88 D2
Santa Ana, Mexico 86 A2
Santa Ana, U.S.A. 85 M9
Santa Bárbara, Honduras 88 D2
Santa Bárbara, Mexico 86 B3
Santa Barbara, U.S.A. 85 L7
Santa Barbara Channel, U.S.A. 85 L7
Santa Barbara I., U.S.A. 85 M7
Santa Catalina, Mexico 86 B2
Santa Catalina, G. of, U.S.A. 85 N9
Santa Catalina I., U.S.A. 85 M8
Santa Catarina □, Brazil 95 B6
Santa Catarina, I. de, Brazil 95 B6
Santa Cecília, Brazil 95 B5
Santa Clara, Cuba 88 B4
Santa Clara, Calif., U.S.A. 83 H3
Santa Clara, Utah, U.S.A. 83 H7
Santa Clara de Olimar, Uruguay 95 C5
Santa Clotilde, Peru 92 D4
Santa Coloma de Gramanet, Spain 19 B7
Santa Cruz, Argentina 96 G3
Santa Cruz, Bolivia 92 G6
Santa Cruz, Chile 94 C1
Santa Cruz, Costa Rica 88 D2
Santa Cruz, Madeira 22 D3
Santa Cruz, Phil. 37 B6
Santa Cruz, U.S.A. 83 H2
Santa Cruz →, Argentina 96 G3
Santa Cruz de la Palma, Canary Is. 22 F2
Santa Cruz de Tenerife, Canary Is. 22 F3
Santa Cruz del Norte, Cuba 88 B3
Santa Cruz del Sur, Cuba 88 B4
Santa Cruz do Rio Pardo, Brazil 95 A6
Santa Cruz do Sul, Brazil 95 B5
Santa Cruz I., Solomon Is. 64 J8
Santa Cruz I., U.S.A. 85 M7
Santa Domingo, Cay, Bahamas 88 B4
Santa Elena, Argentina 94 C4
Santa Elena, Ecuador 92 D2
Santa Elena, C., Costa Rica 88 D2
Santa Eugenia, Pta., Mexico 86 B1
Santa Eulalia, Spain 22 C8
Santa Fe, Argentina 94 C3
Santa Fe, U.S.A. 83 J11
Santa Fé □, Argentina 94 C3
Santa Filomena, Brazil 93 E9
Santa Galdana, Spain 22 B10
Santa Gertrudis, Spain 22 B7
Santa Inés, Spain 22 B7
Santa Inés, I., Chile 96 G2
Santa Isabel = Rey Malabo, Eq. Guin. 50 H6
Santa Isabel, Argentina 94 D2
Santa Isabel, Brazil 93 F8
Santa Lucía, Corrientes, Argentina 94 B4
Santa Lucía, San Juan, Argentina 94 C2
Santa Lucia, Uruguay 94 C4
Santa Lucia Range, U.S.A. 83 J3
Santa Magdalena, I., Mexico 86 C2
Santa Margarita, Argentina 94 D3
Santa Margarita, Mexico 86 C2
Santa Margarita, Spain 22 B10
Santa Margarita, U.S.A. 84 K6
Santa Margarita →, U.S.A. 85 M9
Santa María, Argentina 94 B2
Santa Maria, Brazil 95 B5
Santa María, Spain 22 B9
Santa Maria, U.S.A. 85 L6
Santa María →, Mexico 86 A3
Santa María, B. de, Mexico 86 B3
Santa Maria da Vitória, Brazil 93 F10
Santa Maria di Leuca, C., Italy 21 E8
Santa Marta, Colombia 92 A4
Santa Marta, Sierra Nevada de, Colombia 92 A4
Santa Marta Grande, C., Brazil 95 B6
Santa Maura = Levkás, Greece 21 E9
Santa Monica, U.S.A. 85 M8
Santa Ponsa, Spain 22 B9
Santa Rita, U.S.A. 83 K10
Santa Rosa, La Pampa, Argentina 94 D3
Santa Rosa, San Luis, Argentina 94 C2
Santa Rosa, Bolivia 92 F5
Santa Rosa, Brazil 95 B5
Santa Rosa, Calif., U.S.A. 84 G4
Santa Rosa, N. Mex., U.S.A. 81 H2
Santa Rosa de Copán, Honduras 88 D2
Santa Rosa de Río Primero, Argentina 94 C3
Santa Rosa I., Calif., U.S.A. 85 M6
Santa Rosa I., Fla., U.S.A. 77 K2
Santa Rosa Ra., U.S.A. 82 F5
Santa Rosalía, Mexico 86 B2
Santa Sylvina, Argentina 94 B3
Santa Tecla = Nueva San Salvador, El Salv. 88 D2
Santa Teresa, Argentina 94 C3
Santa Teresa, Mexico 87 B5
Santa Vitória do Palmar, Brazil 95 C5
Santa Ynez, U.S.A. 85 L6
Santa Ynez →, U.S.A. 85 L6
Santa Ysabel, U.S.A. 85 M10
Santai, China 32 C5
Santana, Madeira 22 D3
Santana, Coxilha de, Brazil 95 C4
Santana do Livramento, Brazil 95 C4
Santanayi, Spain 22 B10
Santander, Spain 19 A4
Santander Jiménez, Mexico 87 C5
Santaquin, U.S.A. 82 G8
Santarém, Brazil 93 D8
Santarém, Portugal 19 C1
Santaren Channel, W. Indies 88 B4
Santee, U.S.A. 85 N10
Santiago, Brazil 95 B5
Santiago, Chile 94 C1
Santiago, Panama 88 E3
Santiago □, Chile 94 C1
Santiago →, Peru 92 D3
Santiago de Compostela, Spain 19 A1
Santiago de Cuba, Cuba 88 C4
Santiago de los Cabelleros, Dom. Rep. 89 C5
Santiago del Estero, Argentina 94 B3
Santiago del Estero □, Argentina 94 B3
Santiago del Teide, Canary Is. 22 F3
Santiago Ixcuintla, Mexico 86 C3
Santiago Papasquiaro, Mexico 86 B3
Santiaguillo, L. de, Mexico 86 C4
Santo Amaro, Brazil 93 F11
Santo Anastácio, Brazil 95 A5
Santo André, Brazil 95 A6
Santo Ângelo, Brazil 95 B5
Santo Antonio, Brazil 93 G7
Santo Corazón, Bolivia 92 G7
Santo Domingo, Dom. Rep. 89 C6
Santo Domingo, Baja Calif. N., Mexico 86 A1
Santo Domingo, Baja Calif. S., Mexico 86 B2
Santo Domingo, Nic. 88 D3
Santo Tomás, Mexico 86 A1
Santo Tomás, Peru 92 F4
Santo Tomé, Argentina 95 B4
Santo Tomé de Guayana = Ciudad Guayana, Venezuela 92 B6
Santoña, Spain 19 A4

Santos, Brazil 95 A6
Santos Dumont, Brazil 95 A7
Sanyuan, China 34 G5
Sanza Pombo, Angola 52 F3
São Anastácio, Brazil 95 A5
São Bernado de Campo, Brazil 95 A6
São Borja, Brazil 95 B4
São Carlos, Brazil 95 A6
São Cristóvão, Brazil 93 F11
São Domingos, Brazil 93 F9
São Francisco, Brazil 93 G10
São Francisco →, Brazil 93 F11
São Francisco do Sul, Brazil 95 B6
São Gabriel, Brazil 95 C5
São Gonçalo, Brazil 95 A7
Sao Hill, Tanzania 55 D4
São João da Boa Vista, Brazil 95 A6
São João del Rei, Brazil 95 A7
São João do Araguaia, Brazil 93 E9
São João do Piauí, Brazil 93 E10
São Jorge, Pta. de, Madeira 22 D3
São José do Rio Prêto, Brazil 95 A6
São José dos Campos, Brazil 95 A6
São Leopoldo, Brazil 95 B5
São Lourenço, Brazil 95 A6
São Lourenço →, Brazil 93 G7
São Lourenço, Pta. de, Madeira 22 D3
São Luís, Brazil 93 D10
São Luís Gonzaga, Brazil 95 B5
São Marcos →, Brazil 93 G9
São Marcos, B. de, Brazil 93 D10
São Mateus, Brazil 93 G11
São Paulo, Brazil 95 A6
São Paulo □, Brazil 95 A6
São Paulo, I., Atl. Oc. 2 D8
São Roque, Madeira 22 D3
São Roque, C. de, Brazil 93 E11
São Sebastião, I. de, Brazil 95 A6
São Sebastião do Paraíso, Brazil 95 A6
São Tomé, Atl. Oc. 48 F4
São Tomé, C. de, Brazil 95 A7
São Tomé & Principe ■, Africa 49 F4
São Vicente, Brazil 95 A6
São Vicente, Madeira 22 D2
São Vicente, C. de, Portugal 19 D1
Saona, I., Dom. Rep. 89 C6
Saône →, France 18 D6
Saône-et-Loire □, France 18 C6
Saonek, Indonesia 37 E8
Saparua, Indonesia 37 E7
Sapele, Nigeria 50 G6
Sapelo I., U.S.A. 77 K5
Saposoa, Peru 92 E3
Sappho, U.S.A. 84 B2
Sapporo, Japan 30 C10
Sapudi, Indonesia 37 G16
Sapulpa, U.S.A. 81 G7
Saqqez, Iran 44 B5
Sar Dasht, Iran 45 C6
Sar Gachīneh, Iran 45 D6
Sar Planina, Macedonia, Yug. 21 C9
Sara Buri, Thailand 38 E3
Sarāb, Iran 44 B5
Sarabadi, Iraq 44 C5
Sarada →, India 41 F12
Saragossa = Zaragoza, Spain 19 B5
Saraguro, Ecuador 92 D3
Sarajevo, Bos. & H., Yug. 21 C8
Saran, G., Indonesia 36 E4
Saranac Lake, U.S.A. 79 B10
Saranda, Tanzania 54 D3
Sarandí del Yi, Uruguay 95 C4
Sarandí Grande, Uruguay 94 C4
Sarangani B., Phil. 37 C7
Sarangani Is., Phil. 37 C7
Sarangarh, India 41 J13
Saransk, Russia 24 D8
Sarapul, Russia 24 C9
Sarasota, U.S.A. 77 M4
Saratoga, Calif., U.S.A. 84 H4
Saratoga, Wyo., U.S.A. 82 F10
Saratoga Springs, U.S.A. 79 C11
Saratov, Russia 24 D8
Saravane, Laos 38 E6
Sarawak □, Malaysia 36 D4
Sarbāz, Iran 45 E9
Sarbīsheh, Iran 45 C8
Sardalas, Libya 50 C7
Sardarshahr, India 42 E6
Sardegna, Italy 20 E3
Sardhana, India 42 E7
Sardina, Pta., Canary Is. 22 F4
Sardinia = Sardegna, Italy 20 E3
Sārdūīyeh = Dar Mazār, Iran 45 D8
Sargent, U.S.A. 80 E5
Sargodha, Pakistan 42 C5
Sarh, Chad 51 G8
Sārī, Iran 45 B7
Sarikei, Malaysia 36 D4
Sarina, Australia 62 C4
Sarita, U.S.A. 81 M6
Sariwŏn, N. Korea 35 E13
Sark, Chan. Is. 11 H5
Sarlat-la-Canéda, France 18 D4
Sarles, U.S.A. 80 A5
Sarmi, Indonesia 37 E9
Sarmiento, Argentina 96 F3
Sarnia, Canada 70 D3
Sarny, Ukraine 24 D4
Sarolangun, Indonesia 36 E2
Saronikós Kólpos, Greece 21 F10
Saros Körfezi, Turkey 21 D12
Sarpsborg, Norway 9 G11
Sarre = Saar →, Europe 16 D3
Sarro, Mali 50 F3
Sartène, France 20 D3
Sarthe □, France 18 C4
Sarthe →, France 18 C3
Sartynya, Russia 26 C7
Sarvestān, Iran 45 D7
Sary-Tash, Kirghizia 26 F8
Saryshagan, Kazakhstan 26 E8
Sasabeneh, Ethiopia 46 F3
Sasaram, India 43 G11
Sasebo, Japan 31 H4
Saser, India 43 B7
Saskatchewan □, Canada 73 C7
Saskatchewan →, Canada 73 C8
Saskatoon, Canada 73 C7
Saskylakh, Russia 27 B12
Sasolburg, S. Africa 57 D4
Sasovo, Russia 24 D7
Sassandra, Ivory C. 50 H3
Sassandra →, Ivory C. 50 H3
Sássari, Italy 20 D3
Sassnitz, Germany 16 A6
Sasumua Dam, Kenya 54 C4
Sata-Misaki, Japan 31 J5
Satadougou, Mali 50 F2
Satanta, U.S.A. 81 G4
Satara, India 40 L8
Satilla →, U.S.A. 77 K5
Satka, Russia 24 C10
Satmala Hills, India 40 J9
Satna, India 43 G9
Sátoraljaújhely, Hungary 17 D10
Satpura Ra., India 42 J7
Satsuna-Shotō, Japan 31 K5
Sattahip, Thailand 38 F3
Satu Mare, Romania 17 E11
Satui, Indonesia 36 E5
Satun, Thailand 39 J3
Saturnina →, Brazil 92 F7
Sauce, Argentina 94 C4
Sauceda, Mexico 86 B4
Saucillo, Mexico 86 B3
Sauda, Norway 9 G9
Sauðarkrókur, Iceland 8 D4
Saudi Arabia ■, Asia 46 B3
Sauer →, Germany 15 E6
Saugeen →, Canada 78 B3
Saugerties, U.S.A. 79 D11
Sauk Centre, U.S.A. 80 C7
Sauk Rapids, U.S.A. 80 C7
Sault Ste. Marie, Canada 70 C3
Sault Ste. Marie, U.S.A. 76 B3
Saumlaki, Indonesia 37 F8
Saumur, France 18 C3
Saunders C., N.Z. 59 L3
Saunders I., Antarctica 5 B1
Saunders Point, Australia 61 E4
Saurbær, Borgarfjarðarsýsla, Iceland 8 D3
Saurbær, Eyjafjarðarsýsla, Iceland 8 D4
Sauri, Nigeria 50 F6
Saurimo, Angola 52 F4
Sausalito, U.S.A. 84 H4
Savá, Honduras 88 C2
Sava →, Serbia, Yug. 21 B9
Savage, U.S.A. 80 B2
Savage I. = Niue, Cook Is. 65 J11
Savai'i, W. Samoa 59 A12
Savalou, Benin 50 G5
Savane, Mozam. 55 F4
Savanna, U.S.A. 80 D9
Savanna la Mar, Jamaica 88 C4
Savannah, Ga., U.S.A. 77 J5
Savannah, Mo., U.S.A. 80 F7
Savannah, Tenn., U.S.A. 77 H1
Savannah →, U.S.A. 77 J5
Savannakhet, Laos 38 D5
Savant L., Canada 70 B1
Savant Lake, Canada 70 B1
Savanur, India 40 M9
Savé, Benin 50 G5
Save →, Mozam. 57 C5
Sāveh, Iran 45 C6
Savelugu, Ghana 50 G4
Savoie □, France 18 D7
Savona, Italy 20 B3
Savonlinna, Finland 24 B4
Sawahlunto, Indonesia 36 E2
Sawai, Indonesia 37 E7
Sawai Madhopur, India 42 F7
Sawang Daen Din, Thailand 38 D4
Sawankhalok, Thailand 38 D2
Sawara, Japan 31 G10
Sawatch Mts., U.S.A. 83 G10
Sawel, U.K. 13 B4
Sawi, Thailand 39 G2
Sawmills, Zimbabwe 55 F2
Sawu, Indonesia 37 F6
Sawu Sea, Indonesia 37 F6
Saxby →, Australia 62 B3
Saxton, U.S.A. 78 F6
Say, Niger 50 F5
Sayabec, Canada 71 C6
Sayaboury, Laos 38 C3
Sayán, Peru 92 F3
Sayan, Vostochnyy, Russia 27 D10
Sayan, Zapadnyy, Russia 27 D10
Saydā, Lebanon 47 B4
Sayhan-Ovoo, Mongolia 34 B2
Sayhandulaan, Mongolia 34 B5
Sayḩut, Yemen 46 D5
Saynshand, Mongolia 34 B6
Sayre, Okla., U.S.A. 81 H5
Sayre, Pa., U.S.A. 79 E8
Sayula, Mexico 86 D4
Sazan, Albania 21 D8
Sázava →, Czech. 16 D7
Sazin, Pakistan 43 B5
Scafell Pikes, U.K. 10 C4
Scalpay, U.K. 12 D2
Scandia, Canada 72 C6
Scandinavia, Europe 8 E12
Scapa Flow, U.K. 12 C5
Scappoose, U.S.A. 84 E4
Scarborough, Trin. & Tob. 89 D7
Scarborough, U.K. 10 C7
Scebeli, Wabi →, Somali Rep. 46 G3
Scenic, U.S.A. 80 D3
Schaffhausen, Switz. 16 E4
Schagen, Neths. 15 B4
Schefferville, Canada 71 B6
Schelde →, Belgium 15 C4
Schell Creek Ra., U.S.A. 82 G6
Schenectady, U.S.A. 79 D11
Scheveningen, Neths. 15 B4
Schiedam, Neths. 15 C4
Schiermonnikoog, Neths. 15 A6
Schio, Italy 20 B4
Schleswig, Germany 16 A4
Schleswig-Holstein □, Germany 16 A4
Schofield, U.S.A. 80 C10
Scholls, U.S.A. 84 E4
Schouten I., Australia 62 G4
Schouten Is. = Supriori, Kepulauan, Indonesia 37 E9
Schouwen, Neths. 15 C3
Schreiber, Canada 70 C2
Schuler, Canada 73 C6
Schumacher, Canada 70 C3
Schurz, U.S.A. 82 G4
Schuyler, U.S.A. 80 E6
Schuylkill Haven, U.S.A. 79 F8
Schwäbische Alb, Germany 16 D4
Schwaner, Pegunungan, Indonesia 36 E4
Schwarzwald, Germany 16 E4
Schweinfurt, Germany 16 C5
Schweizer-Reneke, S. Africa 56 D4
Schwerin, Germany 16 B5
Schwyz, Switz. 16 E4
Sciacca, Italy 20 F5
Scilla, Italy 20 E6
Scilly, Isles of, U.K. 11 H1
Scioto →, U.S.A. 76 F4
Scobey, U.S.A. 80 A2
Scone, Australia 63 E5
Scoresbysund, Greenland 4 B6
Scotia, Calif., U.S.A. 82 F1
Scotia, N.Y., U.S.A. 79 D11
Scotia Sea, Antarctica 5 B18
Scotland, U.S.A. 80 D6
Scotland □, U.K. 12 E5
Scotland Neck, U.S.A. 77 G7
Scott, C., Australia 60 B4
Scott City, U.S.A. 80 F4
Scott Glacier, Antarctica 5 C8
Scott I., Antarctica 5 C11
Scott Inlet, Canada 69 A12
Scott Is., Canada 72 C3
Scott L., Canada 73 B7
Scott Reef, Australia 60 B3
Scottburgh, S. Africa 57 E5
Scottdale, U.S.A. 78 F5
Scottsbluff, U.S.A. 80 E3
Scottsboro, U.S.A. 77 H2
Scottsburg, U.S.A. 76 F3
Scottsdale, Australia 62 G4
Scottsville, Ky., U.S.A. 77 G2
Scottsville, N.Y., U.S.A. 78 C7
Scottville, U.S.A. 76 D2
Scranton, U.S.A. 79 E9
Scugog, L., Canada 78 B6
Scunthorpe, U.K. 10 D7
Scusciuban, Somali Rep. 46 E5
Scutari = Üsküdar, Turkey 21 D13
Seabrook, L., Australia 61 F2
Seaford, U.S.A. 76 F8
Seaforth, Canada 70 D3
Seagraves, U.S.A. 81 J3
Seal →, Canada 73 B10
Seal Cove, Canada 71 C8
Seal L., Canada 71 B7
Sealy, U.S.A. 81 L6
Searchlight, U.S.A. 85 K12
Searcy, U.S.A. 81 H9
Searles L., U.S.A. 85 K9
Seaside, Calif., U.S.A. 84 J5
Seaside, Oreg., U.S.A. 84 E3
Seaspray, Australia 63 F4
Seattle, U.S.A. 84 C4
Seaview Ra., Australia 62 B4
Sebastián Vizcaino, B., Mexico 86 B2
Sebastopol = Sevastopol, Ukraine 25 F5
Sebastopol, U.S.A. 84 G4
Sebewaing, U.S.A. 76 D4
Sebring, Fla., U.S.A. 77 M5
Sebring, Ohio, U.S.A. 78 F3
Sebringville, Canada 78 C3
Sebta = Ceuta, Morocco 50 A3
Sebuku, Indonesia 36 E5
Sebuku, Teluk, Malaysia 36 D5
Sechelt, Canada 72 D4
Sechura, Desierto de, Peru 92 E2
Secretary I., N.Z. 59 L1
Secunderabad, India 40 L11
Sedalia, U.S.A. 80 F8
Sedan, Australia 63 E2
Sedan, France 18 B6
Sedan, U.S.A. 81 G6
Seddon, N.Z. 59 J5
Seddonville, N.Z. 59 J4
Sedeh, Fārs, Iran 45 D7
Sedeh, Khorāsān, Iran 45 C8
Sederot, Israel 47 D3
Sedgewick, Canada 72 C6
Sedhiou, Senegal 50 F1
Sedley, Canada 73 C8
Sedova, Pik, Russia 26 B6
Sedro Woolley, U.S.A. 84 B4
Seeheim, Namibia 56 D2
Seekoei →, S. Africa 56 E4
Seg-ozero, Russia 24 B5
Segamat, Malaysia 39 L4
Seget, Indonesia 37 E8
Segezha, Russia 24 B5
Ségou, Mali 50 F3
Segovia = Coco →, Cent. Amer. 88 D3
Segovia, Spain 19 B3
Segre →, Spain 19 B6
Séguéla, Ivory C. 50 G3
Seguin, U.S.A. 81 L6
Segundo →, Argentina 94 C3
Segura →, Spain 19 C5
Seh Qal'eh, Iran 45 C8
Sehitwa, Botswana 56 C3
Sehore, India 42 H7
Sehwan, Pakistan 42 F2
Seiland, Norway 8 A17
Seiling, U.S.A. 81 G5
Seinäjoki →, Finland 8 E17
Seine →, France 18 B4
Seine-et-Marne □, France 18 B5
Seine-Maritime □, France 18 B4
Seine-St.-Denis □, France 18 B5
Seistan, Iran 45 D9
Sekayu, Indonesia 36 E2
Seke, Tanzania 54 C3
Sekenke, Tanzania 54 C3
Sekondi-Takoradi, Ghana 50 H4
Sekuma, Botswana 56 C3
Selah, U.S.A. 82 C3
Selama, Malaysia 39 K3
Selaru, Indonesia 37 F8
Selby, U.K. 10 D6
Selby, U.S.A. 80 C4
Selden, U.S.A. 80 F4
Sele →, Italy 20 D6
Selemdzha →, Russia 27 D13
Selenga = Selenge Mörön →, Asia 32 A5
Selenge Mörön →, Asia 32 A5
Seletan, Tg., Indonesia 36 E4
Selfridge, U.S.A. 80 B4
Sélibabi, Mauritania 50 E2
Seligman, U.S.A. 83 J7
Selîma, El Wâhât el, Sudan 51 D10
Selinda Spillway, Botswana 56 B3
Selkirk, Canada 73 C9
Selkirk, U.K. 12 F6
Selkirk I., Canada 73 C9
Selkirk Mts., Canada 72 C5
Selliá, Greece 23 D6
Sells, U.S.A. 83 L8
Selma, Ala., U.S.A. 77 J2
Selma, Calif., U.S.A. 83 H4
Selma, N.C., U.S.A. 77 H6
Selmer, U.S.A. 77 H1
Selowandoma Falls, Zimbabwe 55 G3
Selpele, Indonesia 37 E8
Selsey Bill, U.K. 11 G7
Selu, Indonesia 37 F8
Selva, Argentina 94 B3
Selvas, Brazil 92 E5
Selwyn, Australia 62 C3
Selwyn L., Canada 73 A8
Selwyn Ra., Australia 62 C3
Seman →, Albania 21 D8
Semarang, Indonesia 37 G14
Semau, Indonesia 37 F6
Sembabule, Uganda 54 C3
Semeru, Indonesia 37 H15
Seminoe Res., U.S.A. 82 E10
Seminole, Okla., U.S.A. 81 H6
Seminole, Tex., U.S.A. 81 J3
Semiozernoye, Kazakhstan 26 D7
Semipalatinsk, Kazakhstan 26 D9
Semirara Is., Phil. 37 B6
Semisopochnoi, U.S.A. 68 C2
Semitau, Indonesia 36 D4
Semiyarskoye, Kazakhstan 26 D8
Semmering Pass, Austria 16 E7
Semnān, Iran 45 C7
Semnān □, Iran 45 C7
Semois →, Europe 15 E4
Semporna, Malaysia 37 D5
Semuda, Indonesia 36 E4
Senā, Iran 45 D6
Sena, Mozam. 55 F3
Sena Madureira, Brazil 92 E5
Senador Pompeu, Brazil 93 E11
Senaja, Malaysia 36 C5
Senanga, Zambia 56 B3
Senatobia, U.S.A. 81 H10
Sendai, Kagoshima, Japan 31 J5
Sendai, Miyagi, Japan 30 E10
Sendai-Wan, Japan 30 E10
Seneca, Oreg., U.S.A. 82 D4
Seneca, S.C., U.S.A. 77 H4
Seneca Falls, U.S.A. 79 D8
Seneca L., U.S.A. 78 D8
Senegal ■, W. Afr. 50 F2
Senegal →, W. Afr. 50 E1
Senegambia, Africa 48 E2
Senekal, S. Africa 57 D4
Senga Hill, Zambia 55 D3
Senge Khambab = Indus →, Pakistan 42 G2
Sengerema □, Tanzania 54 C3
Sengkang, Indonesia 37 E6
Sengua →, Zimbabwe 55 F2
Senhor-do-Bonfim, Brazil 93 F10
Senigállia, Italy 20 C5
Senj, Croatia 20 B6
Senja, Norway 8 B14
Senlis, France 18 B5
Senmonorom, Cambodia 38 F6
Sennâr, Sudan 51 F11
Senneterre, Canada 70 C4
Seno, Laos 38 D5
Sens, France 18 B5
Senta, Serbia, Yug. 21 B9
Sentery, Zaïre 54 D2
Sentinel, U.S.A. 83 K7
Sentolo, Indonesia 37 G14
Seo de Urgel, Spain 19 A6
Seohara, India 43 E8
Seoni, India 43 H8
Seoul = Sŏul, S. Korea 35 F14
Separation Point, Canada 71 B8
Sepīdān, Iran 45 D7
Sepo-ri, N. Korea 35 E14
Sepone, Laos 38 D6
Sept-Îles, Canada 71 B6
Sequim, U.S.A. 84 B3
Sequoia Nat. Park, U.S.A. 83 H4
Seraing, Belgium 15 D5
Seraja, Indonesia 39 L7
Serakhis →, Cyprus 23 D11
Seram, Indonesia 37 E7
Seram Laut, Kepulauan, Indonesia 37 E8
Seram Sea, Indonesia 37 E7
Serang, Indonesia 37 G12
Serasan, Indonesia 39 L7
Serbia □, Europe 21 C9
Serdobsk, Russia 24 D7
Seremban, Malaysia 39 L3
Serengeti □, Tanzania 54 C3
Serengeti Plain, Tanzania 54 C3
Serenje, Zambia 55 E3
Sereth = Siret →, Romania 17 F14
Sergino, Russia 26 C7
Sergipe □, Brazil 93 F11
Sergiyev Posad, Russia 24 C6
Seria, Brunei 36 D4
Serian, Malaysia 36 D4
Seribu, Kepulauan, Indonesia 36 F3
Seringapatam Reef, Australia 60 B3
Sermata, Indonesia 37 F7
Serny Zavod, Turkmenistan 26 F6
Serov, Russia 24 C11
Serowe, Botswana 56 C4
Serpentine, Australia 61 F2
Serpentine Lakes, Australia 61 E4
Serpukhov, Russia 24 D6
Sérrai, Greece 21 D10
Serrezuela, Argentina 94 C2
Serrinha, Brazil 93 F11
Sertânia, Brazil 93 E11
Sertanópolis, Brazil 95 A5
Serua, Indonesia 37 F8
Serui, Indonesia 37 E9
Serule, Botswana 56 C4
Sese Is., Uganda 54 C3
Sesepe, Indonesia 37 E7
Sesfontein, Namibia 56 B1
Sesheke, Zambia 56 B3
S'estañol, Spain 22 B9
Setana, Japan 30 C9
Sète, France 18 E5
Sete Lagôas, Brazil 93 G10
Sétif, Algeria 50 A6
Seto, Japan 31 G8
Setonaikai, Japan 31 G6
Settat, Morocco 50 B3
Setté-Cama, Gabon 52 E1
Setting L., Canada 73 B9
Settle, U.K. 10 C5
Settlement Pt., Bahamas 77 M6
Setúbal, Portugal 19 C1
Setúbal, B. de, Portugal 19 C1
Seulimeum, Indonesia 36 C1
Sevan, Ozero, Armenia 25 F8
Sevastopol, Ukraine 25 F5
Seven Emu, Australia 62 B2
Seven Sisters, Canada 72 C3
Severn →, Canada 70 A2
Severn →, U.K. 11 F5
Severn L., Canada 70 B1
Severnaya Zemlya, Russia 27 B10
Severnyye Uvaly, Russia 24 C8
Severo-Kurilsk, Russia 27 D16
Severo-Yeniseyskiy, Russia 27 C10
Severodvinsk, Russia 24 B6
Severomorsk, Russia 24 A5
Severouralsk, Russia 24 B10
Sevier, U.S.A. 83 G7
Sevier →, U.S.A. 83 G7
Sevier L., U.S.A. 82 G7

Sevilla, *Spain* 19 D3
Seville = Sevilla, *Spain* 19 D3
Seward, *Alaska, U.S.A.* 68 B5
Seward, *Nebr., U.S.A.* 80 E6
Seward Pen., *U.S.A.* 68 B3
Sewell, *Chile* 94 C1
Sewer, *Indonesia* 37 F8
Sewickley, *U.S.A.* 78 F4
Sexsmith, *Canada* 72 B5
Seychelles ■, *Ind. Oc.* 29 K9
Seyðisfjörður, *Iceland* 8 D7
Seydvān, *Iran* 44 B5
Seymchan, *Russia* 27 C16
Seymour, *Australia* 63 F4
Seymour, *S. Africa* 57 E4
Seymour, *Conn., U.S.A.* 79 E11
Seymour, *Ind., U.S.A.* 76 F3
Seymour, *Tex., U.S.A.* 81 J5
Seymour, *Wis., U.S.A.* 76 C1
Sfax, *Tunisia* 51 B7
Sfîntu Gheorghe, *Romania* 17 F12
Shaanxi □, *China* 34 G5
Shaba □, *Zaïre* 54 D2
Shabunda, *Zaïre* 54 C2
Shache, *China* 32 C2
Shackleton Ice Shelf, *Antarctica* 5 C8
Shackleton Inlet, *Antarctica* 5 E11
Shādegān, *Iran* 45 D6
Shadi, *India* 43 C7
Shadrinsk, *Russia* 26 D7
Shafter, *Calif., U.S.A.* 85 K7
Shafter, *Tex., U.S.A.* 81 L2
Shaftesbury, *U.K.* 11 F5
Shagram, *Pakistan* 43 A5
Shah Bunder, *Pakistan* 42 G2
Shahabad, *Punjab, India* 42 D7
Shahabad, *Raj., India* 42 G7
Shahabad, *Ut. P., India* 43 F8
Shahadpur, *Pakistan* 42 G3
Shahba, *Syria* 47 C5
Shahdād, *Iran* 45 D8
Shahdadkot, *Pakistan* 42 F2
Shahe, *China* 34 F8
Shahganj, *India* 43 F10
Shahgarh, *India* 40 F6
Shaḩḩāt, *Libya* 51 B9
Shahjahanpur, *India* 43 F8
Shahpur, *India* 42 H7
Shahpur, *Pakistan* 42 E3
Shahpura, *India* 43 H9
Shahr Kord, *Iran* 45 C6
Shāhrakht, *Iran* 45 C9
Shahrig, *Pakistan* 42 D2
Shahukou, *China* 34 D7
Shaikhabad, *Afghan.* 42 B3
Shajapur, *India* 42 H7
Shakargarh, *Pakistan* 42 C6
Shakawe, *Botswana* 56 B3
Shaker Heights, *U.S.A.* 78 E3
Shakhty, *Russia* 25 E7
Shakhunya, *Russia* 24 C8
Shaki, *Nigeria* 50 G5
Shakopee, *U.S.A.* 80 C8
Shala, L., *Ethiopia* 51 G12
Shallow Lake, *Canada* 78 B3
Shaluli Shan, *China* 32 C4
Shām, *Iran* 45 E8
Shamâl Dârfûr □, *Sudan* 51 E10
Shamâl Kordofân □, *Sudan* 51 F10
Shamattawa, *Canada* 73 B10
Shamattawa →, *Canada* 70 A2
Shamil, *Iran* 45 E8
Shāmkūh, *Iran* 45 C8
Shamli, *India* 42 E7
Shamo = Gobi, *Asia* 34 C5
Shamo, L., *Ethiopia* 51 G12
Shamokin, *U.S.A.* 79 F8
Shamrock, *U.S.A.* 81 H4
Shamva, *Zimbabwe* 55 F3
Shan □, *Burma* 41 J21
Shan Xian, *China* 34 G9
Shanchengzhen, *China* 35 C13
Shāndak, *Iran* 45 D9
Shandon, *U.S.A.* 84 K6
Shandong □, *China* 35 F10
Shandong Bandao, *China* 35 F11
Shang Xian, *China* 34 H5
Shangalowe, *Zaïre* 55 E2
Shangani →, *Zimbabwe* 55 F2
Shangbancheng, *China* 35 D10
Shangdu, *China* 34 D7
Shanghai, *China* 33 C7
Shanghe, *China* 35 F9
Shangnan, *China* 34 H6
Shangqiu, *China* 34 G8
Shangrao, *China* 33 D6
Shangshui, *China* 34 H8
Shangzhi, *China* 35 B14
Shanhetun, *China* 35 B14
Shaniko, *U.S.A.* 82 D3
Shannon, *Greenland* 4 B7
Shannon, *N.Z.* 59 J5
Shannon →, *Ireland* 13 D2
Shansi = Shanxi □, *China* 34 F7
Shantar, Ostrov Bolshoy, *Russia* 27 D14
Shantipur, *India* 43 H13
Shantou, *China* 33 D6
Shantung = Shandong □, *China* 35 F10
Shanxi □, *China* 34 F7
Shanyang, *China* 34 H5
Shanyin, *China* 34 E7
Shaoguan, *China* 33 D6
Shaoxing, *China* 33 C7
Shaoyang, *China* 33 D6
Shapinsay, *U.K.* 12 B6
Shaqra', *Si. Arabia* 44 E5
Shaqrā', *Yemen* 46 E4
Sharbot Lake, *Canada* 79 B8
Shari, *Japan* 30 C12
Sharjah = Ash Shāriqah, *U.A.E.* 45 E7
Shark B., *Australia* 61 E1
Sharon, *Mass., U.S.A.* 79 D13
Sharon, *Pa., U.S.A.* 78 E4
Sharon Springs, *U.S.A.* 80 F4
Sharp Pt., *Australia* 62 A3
Sharpe L., *Canada* 73 C10
Sharpsville, *U.S.A.* 78 E4
Sharq el Istiwa'iya □, *Sudan* 51 G11
Sharya, *Russia* 24 C8
Shashi, *Botswana* 57 C4
Shashi, *China* 33 C6
Shashi →, *Africa* 55 G2
Shasta, Mt., *U.S.A.* 82 F2
Shasta L., *U.S.A.* 82 F2
Shatt al'Arab →, *Iraq* 45 D6
Shattuck, *U.S.A.* 81 G5
Shaunavon, *Canada* 73 D7
Shaver Lake, *U.S.A.* 84 H7
Shaw →, *Australia* 60 D2
Shaw I., *Australia* 62 C4
Shawanaga, *Canada* 78 A4
Shawano, *U.S.A.* 76 C1
Shawinigan, *Canada* 70 C5
Shawnee, *U.S.A.* 81 H6
Shaybārā, *Si. Arabia* 44 E3
Shaykh Sa'īd, *Iraq* 44 C5
Shcherbakov = Rybinsk, *Russia* 24 C6
Shchuchiosk, *Kazakhstan* 26 D8
She Xian, *China* 34 F7
Shebele = Scebeli, Wabi →, *Somali Rep.* 46 G3
Sheboygan, *U.S.A.* 76 D2
Shediac, *Canada* 71 C7
Sheelin, L., *Ireland* 13 C4
Sheep Haven, *Ireland* 13 A4
Sheerness, *U.K.* 11 F8
Sheet Harbour, *Canada* 71 D7
Sheffield, *U.K.* 10 D6
Sheffield, *Ala., U.S.A.* 77 H2
Sheffield, *Mass., U.S.A.* 79 D11
Sheffield, *Pa., U.S.A.* 78 E5
Sheffield, *Tex., U.S.A.* 81 K4
Sheho, *Canada* 73 C8
Sheikhpura, *India* 43 G11
Shekhupura, *Pakistan* 42 D5
Shelburne, *N.S., Canada* 71 D6
Shelburne, *Ont., Canada* 70 D3
Shelburne, *U.S.A.* 79 B11
Shelburne B., *Australia* 62 A3
Shelburne Falls, *U.S.A.* 79 D12
Shelby, *Mich., U.S.A.* 76 D2
Shelby, *Mont., U.S.A.* 82 B8
Shelby, *N.C., U.S.A.* 77 H5
Shelby, *Ohio, U.S.A.* 78 F2
Shelbyville, *Ill., U.S.A.* 80 F10
Shelbyville, *Ind., U.S.A.* 76 F3
Shelbyville, *Tenn., U.S.A.* 77 H2
Sheldon, *U.S.A.* 80 D7
Sheldrake, *Canada* 71 B7
Shelikhova, Zaliv, *Russia* 27 D16
Shell Lake, *Canada* 73 C7
Shell Lakes, *Australia* 61 E4
Shellbrook, *Canada* 73 C7
Shellharbour, *Australia* 63 E5
Shelling Rocks, *Ireland* 13 E1
Shelton, *Conn., U.S.A.* 79 E11
Shelton, *Wash., U.S.A.* 84 C3
Shen Xian, *China* 34 F8
Shenandoah, *Iowa, U.S.A.* 80 E7
Shenandoah, *Pa., U.S.A.* 79 F8
Shenandoah, *Va., U.S.A.* 76 F6
Shenandoah →, *U.S.A.* 76 F7
Shenchi, *China* 34 E7
Shendam, *Nigeria* 50 G6
Shendî, *Sudan* 51 E11
Shengfang, *China* 34 E9
Shenjingzi, *China* 35 B13
Shenmu, *China* 34 E6
Shenqiu, *China* 34 H8
Shenqiucheng, *China* 34 H8
Shensi = Shaanxi □, *China* 34 G5
Shenyang, *China* 35 D12
Sheopur Kalan, *India* 40 G10
Shepparton, *Australia* 63 F4
Sheqi, *China* 34 H7
Sher Qila, *Pakistan* 43 A6
Sherborne, *U.K.* 11 G5
Sherbro I., *S. Leone* 50 G2
Sherbrooke, *Canada* 71 C5
Sheridan, *Ark., U.S.A.* 81 H8
Sheridan, *Wyo., U.S.A.* 82 D10
Sherkot, *India* 43 E8
Sherman, *U.S.A.* 81 J6
Sherridon, *Canada* 73 B8
Sherwood, *N. Dak., U.S.A.* 80 A4
Sherwood, *Tex., U.S.A.* 81 K4
Sherwood Forest, *U.K.* 10 D6
Sheslay, *Canada* 72 B2
Sheslay →, *Canada* 72 B2
Shethanei L., *Canada* 73 B9
Shetland □, *U.K.* 12 A7
Shetland Is., *U.K.* 12 A7
Sheyenne, *U.S.A.* 80 B5
Sheyenne →, *U.S.A.* 80 B6
Shibām, *Yemen* 46 D4
Shibata, *Japan* 30 F9
Shibecha, *Japan* 30 C12
Shibetsu, *Japan* 30 B11
Shibogama L., *Canada* 70 B2
Shibushi, *Japan* 31 J5
Shidao, *China* 35 F12
Shido, *Japan* 31 G7
Shiel, L., *U.K.* 12 E3
Shield, C., *Australia* 62 A2
Shiga □, *Japan* 31 G8
Shigaib, *Sudan* 51 E9
Shiguaigou, *China* 34 D6
Shihchiachuangi = Shijiazhuang, *China* 34 E8
Shijiazhuang, *China* 34 E8
Shikarpur, *India* 42 E8
Shikarpur, *Pakistan* 42 F3
Shikoku □, *Japan* 31 H6
Shikoku-Sanchi, *Japan* 31 H6
Shilabo, *Ethiopia* 46 F3
Shiliguri, *India* 41 F16
Shilka, *Russia* 27 D12
Shilka →, *Russia* 27 D13
Shillelagh, *Ireland* 13 D5
Shillong, *India* 41 G17
Shilo, *Jordan* 47 C4
Shilou, *China* 34 F6
Shimabara, *Japan* 31 H5
Shimada, *Japan* 31 G9
Shimane □, *Japan* 31 G6
Shimanovsk, *Russia* 27 D13
Shimizu, *Japan* 31 G9
Shimodate, *Japan* 31 F9
Shimoga, *India* 40 N9
Shimoni, *Kenya* 54 C4
Shimonoseki, *Japan* 31 H5
Shimpuru Rapids, *Angola* 56 B2
Shin, L., *U.K.* 12 C4
Shin-Tone →, *Japan* 31 G10
Shinano →, *Japan* 31 F9
Shindand, *Afghan.* 40 C3
Shingleton, *U.S.A.* 70 C2
Shingū, *Japan* 31 H7
Shinjō, *Japan* 30 E10
Shinshār, *Syria* 47 A5
Shinyanga, *Tanzania* 54 C3
Shinyanga □, *Tanzania* 54 C3
Shiogama, *Japan* 30 E10
Shiojiri, *Japan* 31 F8
Ship I., *U.S.A.* 81 K10
Shiping, *China* 32 D5
Shipki La, *India* 40 D11
Shippegan, *Canada* 71 C7
Shippensburg, *U.S.A.* 78 F7
Shiprock, *U.S.A.* 83 H9
Shiqma, N. →, *Israel* 47 D3
Shiquan, *China* 34 H5
Shīr Kūh, *Iran* 45 D7
Shiragami-Misaki, *Japan* 30 D10
Shirakawa, *Fukushima, Japan* 31 F10
Shirakawa, *Gifu, Japan* 31 F8
Shirane-San, *Gumma, Japan* 31 F9
Shirane-San, *Yamanashi, Japan* 31 G9
Shiraoi, *Japan* 30 C10
Shīrāz, *Iran* 45 D7
Shire →, *Africa* 55 F4
Shiretoko-Misaki, *Japan* 30 B12
Shirinab →, *Pakistan* 42 D2
Shiriya-Zaki, *Japan* 30 D10
Shiroishi, *Japan* 30 E10
Shīrvān, *Iran* 45 B8
Shirwa, L. = Chilwa, L., *Malawi* 55 F4
Shivpuri, *India* 42 G7
Shixian, *China* 35 C15
Shizuishan, *China* 34 E4
Shizuoka, *Japan* 31 G9
Shizuoka □, *Japan* 31 G9
Shkoder = Shkodra, *Albania* 21 C8
Shkodra, *Albania* 21 C8
Shkumbini →, *Albania* 21 D8
Shmidta, O., *Russia* 27 A10
Shō-Gawa →, *Japan* 31 F8
Shoal Lake, *Canada* 73 C8
Shōdo-Shima, *Japan* 31 G7
Shoeburyness, *U.K.* 11 F8
Sholapur = Solapur, *India* 40 L9
Shologontsy, *Russia* 27 C12
Shōmrōn, *Jordan* 47 C4
Shoshone, *Calif., U.S.A.* 85 K10
Shoshone, *Idaho, U.S.A.* 82 E6
Shoshone L., *U.S.A.* 82 D8
Shoshone Mts., *U.S.A.* 82 G5
Shoshong, *Botswana* 56 C4
Shoshoni, *U.S.A.* 82 E9
Shouguang, *China* 35 F10
Shouyang, *China* 34 F7
Show Low, *U.S.A.* 83 J9
Shreveport, *U.S.A.* 81 J8
Shrewsbury, *U.K.* 10 E5
Shrirampur, *India* 43 H13
Shropshire □, *U.K.* 11 E5
Shuangcheng, *China* 35 B14
Shuanggou, *China* 35 G9
Shuangliao, *China* 35 C12
Shuangshanzi, *China* 35 D10
Shuangyang, *China* 35 C13
Shuangyashan, *China* 33 B8
Shuguri Falls, *Tanzania* 55 D4
Shuicheng, *China* 32 D5
Shuiye, *China* 34 F8
Shujalpur, *India* 42 H7
Shukpa Kunzang, *India* 43 B8
Shulan, *China* 35 B14
Shule, *China* 32 C2
Shumagin Is., *U.S.A.* 68 C4
Shumikha, *Russia* 26 D7
Shungnak, *U.S.A.* 68 B4
Shuo Xian, *China* 34 E7
Shūr →, *Iran* 45 D7
Shūr Āb, *Iran* 45 C6
Shūr Gaz, *Iran* 45 D8
Shūrāb, *Iran* 45 C8
Shūrjestān, *Iran* 45 D7
Shurugwi, *Zimbabwe* 55 F3
Shūsf, *Iran* 45 D9
Shūshtar, *Iran* 45 D6
Shuswap L., *Canada* 72 C5
Shuyang, *China* 35 G10
Shūzū, *Iran* 45 D7
Shwebo, *Burma* 41 H19
Shwegu, *Burma* 41 G20
Shweli →, *Burma* 41 H20
Shyok, *India* 43 B8
Shyok →, *Pakistan* 43 B6
Si Chon, *Thailand* 39 H2
Si Kiang = Xi Jiang →, *China* 33 D6
Si Prachan, *Thailand* 38 E3
Si Racha, *Thailand* 38 F3
Si Xian, *China* 35 H9
Siahan Range, *Pakistan* 40 F4
Siaksrindrapura, *Indonesia* 36 D2
Sialkot, *Pakistan* 42 C6
Siam = Thailand ■, *Asia* 38 E4
Sian = Xi'an, *China* 34 G5
Siantan, P., *Indonesia* 39 L6
Siāreh, *Iran* 45 D9
Siargao, *Phil.* 37 C7
Siari, *Pakistan* 43 B7
Siasi, *Phil.* 37 C6
Siau, *Indonesia* 37 D7
Šiauliai, *Lithuania* 24 C3
Siaya □, *Kenya* 54 B3
Sibasa, *S. Africa* 57 C5
Sibay, *Russia* 24 D10
Sibayi, L., *S. Africa* 57 D5
Šibenik, *Croatia* 20 C6
Siberia, *Russia* 4 D13
Siberut, *Indonesia* 36 E1
Sibi, *Pakistan* 42 E2
Sibil, *Indonesia* 37 E10
Sibiti, *Congo* 52 E2
Sibiu, *Romania* 17 F12
Sibley, *Iowa, U.S.A.* 80 D7
Sibley, *La., U.S.A.* 81 J8
Sibolga, *Indonesia* 36 D1
Sibsagar, *India* 41 F19
Sibu, *Malaysia* 36 D4
Sibuco, *Phil.* 37 C6
Sibuguey B., *Phil.* 37 C6
Sibutu, *Phil.* 37 D5
Sibutu Passage, *E. Indies* 37 D5
Sibuyan, *Phil.* 37 B6
Sibuyan Sea, *Phil.* 37 B6
Sicamous, *Canada* 72 C5
Sichuan □, *China* 32 C5
Sicilia, *Italy* 20 F6
Sicilia □, *Italy* 20 F6
Sicily = Sicilia, *Italy* 20 F6
Sicuani, *Peru* 92 F4
Sidári, *Greece* 23 A3
Siddhapur, *India* 42 H5
Siddipet, *India* 40 K11
Sidéradougou, *Burkina Faso* 50 F4
Sidheros, Ákra, *Greece* 23 D8
Sîdi Barrâni, *Egypt* 51 B10
Sidi-bel-Abbès, *Algeria* 50 A4
Sidlaw Hills, *U.K.* 12 E5
Sidley, Mt., *Antarctica* 5 D14
Sidmouth, *U.K.* 11 G4
Sidmouth, C., *Australia* 62 A3
Sidney, *Canada* 72 D4
Sidney, *Mont., U.S.A.* 80 B2
Sidney, *N.Y., U.S.A.* 79 D9
Sidney, *Nebr., U.S.A.* 80 E3
Sidney, *Ohio, U.S.A.* 76 E3
Sidoarjo, *Indonesia* 37 G15
Sidon = Saydā, *Lebanon* 47 B4
Sidra, G. of = Surt, Khalīj, *Libya* 51 B8
Siedlce, *Poland* 17 B11
Siegen, *Germany* 16 C4
Siem Pang, *Cambodia* 38 E6
Siem Reap, *Cambodia* 38 F4
Siena, *Italy* 20 C4
Sierra Blanca, *U.S.A.* 83 L11
Sierra Blanca Pk., *U.S.A.* 83 K11
Sierra City, *U.S.A.* 84 F6
Sierra Colorada, *Argentina* 96 E3
Sierra Gorda, *Chile* 94 A2
Sierra Leone ■, *W. Afr.* 50 G2
Sierra Madre, *Mexico* 87 D6
Sierra Mojada, *Mexico* 86 B4
Sierraville, *U.S.A.* 84 F6
Sifnos, *Greece* 21 F11
Sifton, *Canada* 73 C8
Sifton Pass, *Canada* 72 B3
Sighetu-Marmatiei, *Romania* 17 E11
Sighişoara, *Romania* 17 E12
Sigli, *Indonesia* 36 C1
Siglufjörður, *Iceland* 8 C4
Signal, *U.S.A.* 85 L13
Signal Pk., *U.S.A.* 85 M12
Sigsig, *Ecuador* 92 D3
Sigtuna, *Sweden* 9 G14
Sigüenza, *Spain* 19 B4
Siguiri, *Guinea* 50 F3
Sigurd, *U.S.A.* 83 G8
Sihanoukville = Kompong Som, *Cambodia* 39 G4
Sijarira Ra., *Zimbabwe* 55 F2
Sikao, *Thailand* 39 J2
Sikar, *India* 42 F6
Sikasso, *Mali* 50 F3
Sikeston, *U.S.A.* 81 G10
Sikhote Alin, Khrebet, *Russia* 27 E14
Sikinos, *Greece* 21 F11
Sikkani Chief →, *Canada* 72 B4
Sikkim □, *India* 41 F16
Sikotu-Ko, *Japan* 30 C10
Sil →, *Spain* 19 A2
Silacayoapan, *Mexico* 87 D5
Silchar, *India* 41 G18
Silcox, *Canada* 73 B10
Siler City, *U.S.A.* 77 H6
Silesia = Śląsk, *Poland* 16 C8
Silgarhi Doti, *Nepal* 43 E9
Silghat, *India* 41 F18
Silifke, *Turkey* 25 G5
Siling Co, *China* 32 C3
Silistra, *Bulgaria* 21 B12
Siljan, *Sweden* 9 F13
Silkeborg, *Denmark* 9 H10
Sillajhuay, Cordillera, *Chile* 92 G5
Siloam Springs, *U.S.A.* 81 G7
Silsbee, *U.S.A.* 81 K7
Silva Porto = Kuito, *Angola* 53 G3
Silver City, *N. Mex., U.S.A.* 83 K9
Silver City, *Nev., U.S.A.* 82 G4
Silver Cr. →, *U.S.A.* 82 E4
Silver Creek, *U.S.A.* 78 D5
Silver L., *U.S.A.* 84 G6
Silver Lake, *Calif., U.S.A.* 85 K10
Silver Lake, *Oreg., U.S.A.* 82 E3
Silver Streams, *S. Africa* 56 D3
Silverton, *Colo., U.S.A.* 83 H10
Silverton, *Tex., U.S.A.* 81 H4
Silvies →, *U.S.A.* 82 E4
Simanggang, *Malaysia* 36 D4
Simard, L., *Canada* 70 C4
Simba, *Tanzania* 54 C4
Simbirsk, *Russia* 24 D8
Simbo, *Tanzania* 54 C2
Simcoe, *Canada* 70 D3
Simcoe, L., *Canada* 70 D4
Simenga, *Russia* 27 C11
Simeulue, *Indonesia* 36 D1
Simferopol, *Ukraine* 25 F5
Simi Valley, *U.S.A.* 85 L8
Simikot, *Nepal* 43 E9
Simla, *India* 42 D7
Simmie, *Canada* 73 D7
Simmler, *U.S.A.* 85 K7
Simojärvi, *Finland* 8 C19
Simojoki →, *Finland* 8 D18
Simojovel, *Mexico* 87 D6
Simonette →, *Canada* 72 B5
Simonstown, *S. Africa* 56 E2
Simplon Pass = Simplonpass, *Switz.* 16 E4
Simplonpass, *Switz.* 16 E4
Simpson Desert, *Australia* 62 D2
Simpungdong, *N. Korea* 35 D15
Simunjan, *Malaysia* 36 D4
Simushir, Ostrov, *Russia* 27 E16
Sinabang, *Indonesia* 36 D1
Sinadogo, *Somali Rep.* 46 F4
Sinai = Es Sînâ', *Egypt* 51 C11
Sinai Peninsula, *Egypt* 47 F2
Sinaloa □, *Mexico* 86 C3
Sinaloa de Levya, *Mexico* 86 B3
Sinarádhes, *Greece* 23 A3
Sināwan, *Libya* 50 B7
Sincelejo, *Colombia* 92 B3
Sinchang, *N. Korea* 35 D15
Sinchang-ni, *N. Korea* 35 E14
Sinclair, *U.S.A.* 82 F10
Sinclair Mills, *Canada* 72 C4
Sincorá, Serra do, *Brazil* 93 F10
Sind, *Pakistan* 42 G3
Sind □, *Pakistan* 42 F3
Sind →, *India* 43 B6
Sind Sagar Doab, *Pakistan* 42 D4
Sindangan, *Phil.* 37 C6
Sindangbarang, *Indonesia* 37 G12
Sinde, *Zambia* 55 F2
Sines, *Portugal* 19 D1
Sineu, *Spain* 22 B10
Sing Buri, *Thailand* 38 E3
Singa, *Sudan* 51 F11
Singapore ■, *Asia* 39 M4
Singapore, Straits of, *Asia* 39 M5
Singaraja, *Indonesia* 36 F5
Singida, *Tanzania* 54 C3
Singida □, *Tanzania* 54 D3
Singitikós Kólpos, *Greece* 21 D10
Singkaling Hkamti, *Burma* 41 G19
Singkawang, *Indonesia* 36 D3
Singleton, *Australia* 63 E5
Singleton, Mt., *N. Terr., Australia* 60 D5
Singleton, Mt., *W. Austral., Australia* 61 E2
Singoli, *India* 42 G6
Singora = Songkhla, *Thailand* 39 J3
Singosan, *N. Korea* 35 E14
Sinhung, *N. Korea* 35 D14
Sînî □, *Egypt* 47 F2
Sinjai, *Indonesia* 37 F6
Sinjār, *Iraq* 44 B4
Sinkat, *Sudan* 51 E12

Sinkiang Uighur = Xinjiang Uygur Zizhiqu □, China 32 B3
Sinmak, N. Korea 35 E14
Sinni →, Italy 20 D7
Sinnuris, Egypt 51 C11
Sinop, Turkey 25 F6
Sinpo, N. Korea 35 E15
Sinskoye, Russia 27 C13
Sint Eustatius, I., Neth. Ant. 89 C7
Sint Maarten, I., W. Indies 89 C7
Sint Niklaas, Belgium 15 C4
Sint Truiden, Belgium 15 D5
Sintang, Indonesia 36 D4
Sinton, U.S.A. 81 L6
Sintra, Portugal 19 C1
Sinŭiju, N. Korea 35 D13
Siocon, Phil. 37 C6
Sioma, Zambia 56 B3
Sion, Switz. 16 E3
Sioux City, U.S.A. 80 D6
Sioux Falls, U.S.A. 80 D6
Sioux Lookout, Canada 70 B1
Sip Song Chau Thai, Vietnam 38 B4
Siping, China 35 C13
Sipiwesk L., Canada 73 B9
Sipora, Indonesia 36 E1
Siquia →, Nic. 88 D3
Siquijor, Phil. 37 C6
Siquirres, Costa Rica 88 D3
Sir Edward Pellew Group, Australia 62 B2
Sir Graham Moore Is., Australia 60 B4
Siracusa, Italy 20 F6
Sirajganj, Bangla. 43 G13
Sirdān, Iran 45 B6
Sirer, Spain 22 C7
Siret →, Romania 17 F14
Sirohi, India 42 G5
Sironj, India 42 G7
Siros, Greece 21 F11
Sirretta Pk., U.S.A. 85 K8
Sirsa, India 42 E6
Sisak, Croatia 20 B7
Sisaket, Thailand 38 E5
Sishen, S. Africa 56 D3
Sishui, Henan, China 34 G7
Sishui, Shandong, China 35 G9
Sisipuk L., Canada 73 B8
Sisophon, Cambodia 38 F4
Sisseton, U.S.A. 80 C6
Sīstān va Balūchestān □, Iran 45 E9
Sisters, U.S.A. 82 D3
Sitamarhi, India 43 F11
Sitapur, India 43 F9
Siteki, Swaziland 57 D5
Sitges, Spain 19 B6
Sitia, Greece 23 D8
Sitka, U.S.A. 68 C6
Sitoti, Botswana 56 C3
Sittang Myit →, Burma 41 L20
Sittard, Neths. 15 C5
Sittwe, Burma 41 J18
Siuna, Nic. 88 D3
Siuri, India 43 H12
Sivana, India 42 E8
Sivand, Iran 45 D7
Sivas, Turkey 25 G6
Sivomaskinskiy, Russia 24 A11
Sivrihisar, Turkey 25 G5
Siwa, Egypt 51 C10
Siwalik Range, Nepal 43 F10
Siwan, India 43 F11
Sizewell, U.K. 11 E9
Siziwang Qi, China 34 D6
Sjælland, Denmark 9 J11
Sjumen = Šumen, Bulgaria 21 C12
Skagafjörður, Iceland 8 D4
Skagastølstindane, Norway 9 F9
Skagerrak, Denmark 9 H10
Skagit →, U.S.A. 84 B4
Skagway, U.S.A. 72 B1
Skaidi, Norway 8 A18
Skara, Sweden 9 G12
Skaraborgs län □, Sweden 9 G12
Skardu, Pakistan 43 B6
Skeena →, Canada 72 C2
Skeena Mts., Canada 72 B3
Skegness, U.K. 10 D8
Skeldon, Guyana 92 B7
Skellefte älv →, Sweden 8 D16
Skellefteå, Sweden 8 D16
Skelleftehamn, Sweden 8 D16
Skerries, The, U.K. 10 D3
Skibbereen, Ireland 13 E2
Skiddaw, U.K. 10 C4
Skien, Norway 9 G10
Skierniewice, Poland 17 C10
Skikda, Algeria 50 A6
Skilloura, Cyprus 23 D12
Skipton, Australia 63 F3
Skipton, U.K. 10 D5
Skirmish Pt., Australia 62 A1
Skiros, Greece 21 E11
Skive, Denmark 9 H10
Skjálfandafljót →, Iceland 8 D5
Skjálfandi, Iceland 8 C5
Skoghall, Sweden 9 G12
Skopi, Greece 23 D8
Skopje, Macedonia, Yug. 21 C9
Skövde, Sweden 9 G12
Skovorodino, Russia 27 D13
Skowhegan, U.S.A. 71 D6
Skownan, Canada 73 C9
Skudeneshavn, Norway 9 G8
Skull, Ireland 13 E2
Skunk →, U.S.A. 80 E9
Skwierzyna, Poland 16 B7
Skye, U.K. 12 D2
Skykomish, U.S.A. 82 C3
Skyros = Skíros, Greece 21 E11
Slamet, Indonesia 36 F3
Slaney →, Ireland 13 D5
Śląsk, Poland 16 C8
Slate Is., Canada 70 C2
Slatina, Romania 17 F12
Slaton, U.S.A. 81 J4
Slave →, Canada 72 A6
Slave Coast, W. Afr. 48 F4
Slave Lake, Canada 72 B6
Slave Pt., Canada 72 A5
Slavgorod, Russia 26 D8
Slavkov, Czech. 16 D8
Slavyanka, Russia 30 C5
Slavyansk, Ukraine 25 E6
Sleaford, U.K. 10 E7
Sleaford B., Australia 63 E2
Sleat, Sd. of, U.K. 12 D3
Sleeper Is., Canada 69 C11
Sleepy Eye, U.S.A. 80 C7
Sleman, Indonesia 37 G14
Slemon L., Canada 72 A5
Slidell, U.S.A. 81 K10
Sliedrecht, Neths. 15 C4
Sliema, Malta 23 D2
Slieve Aughty, Ireland 13 C3
Slieve Bloom, Ireland 13 C4
Slieve Donard, U.K. 13 B6
Slieve Gullion, U.K. 13 B5
Slieve Mish, Ireland 13 D2
Slievenamon, Ireland 13 D4
Sligo, Ireland 13 B3
Sligo □, Ireland 13 B3
Sligo B., Ireland 13 B3
Slite, Sweden 9 H15
Sliven, Bulgaria 21 C12
Sloan, U.S.A. 85 K11
Sloansville, U.S.A. 79 D10
Slobodskoy, Russia 24 C9
Slocan, Canada 72 D5
Slochteren, Neths. 15 A6
Slough, U.K. 11 F7
Sloughhouse, U.S.A. 84 G5
Slovakian Ore Mts. = Slovenské Rudohorie, Czech. 17 D9
Slovenia ■, Europe 20 B6
Slovenija = Slovenia ■, Europe 20 B6
Slovenské Rudohorie, Czech. 17 D9
Sluis, Neths. 15 C3
Slurry, S. Africa 56 D4
Slyne Hd., Ireland 13 C1
Slyudyanka, Russia 27 D11
Smalltree L., Canada 73 A7
Smara, Morocco 50 B3
Smartt Syndicate Dam, S. Africa 56 E3
Smartville, U.S.A. 84 F5
Smeaton, Canada 73 C8
Smederevo, Serbia, Yug. 21 B9
Smethport, U.S.A. 78 E6
Smidovich, Russia 27 E14
Smiley, Canada 73 C7
Smith, Canada 72 B6
Smith →, Canada 72 B3
Smith Arm, Canada 68 B7
Smith Center, U.S.A. 80 F5
Smith Sund, Greenland 4 B4
Smithburne →, Australia 62 B3
Smithers, Canada 72 C3
Smithfield, S. Africa 57 E4
Smithfield, N.C., U.S.A. 77 H6
Smithfield, Utah, U.S.A. 82 F8
Smiths Falls, Canada 70 D4
Smithton, Australia 62 G4
Smithtown, Australia 63 E5
Smithville, Canada 78 C5
Smithville, U.S.A. 81 K6
Smoky →, Canada 72 B5
Smoky Bay, Australia 63 E1
Smoky Falls, Canada 70 B3
Smoky Hill →, U.S.A. 80 F6
Smoky Lake, Canada 72 C6
Smøla, Norway 8 E10
Smolensk, Russia 24 D5
Smolikas, Óros, Greece 21 D9
Smolyan, Bulgaria 21 D11
Smooth Rock Falls, Canada 70 C3
Smoothstone L., Canada 73 C7
Smyrna = İzmir, Turkey 25 G4
Snaefell, U.K. 10 C3
Snæfellsjökull, Iceland 8 D2
Snake →, U.S.A. 82 C4
Snake I., Australia 63 F4
Snake L., Canada 73 B7
Snake Ra., U.S.A. 82 G6
Snake River Plain, U.S.A. 82 E7
Sneek, Neths. 15 A5
Sneeuberge, S. Africa 56 E3
Snelling, U.S.A. 84 H6
Snizort, L., U.K. 12 D2
Snøhetta, Norway 8 E10
Snohomish, U.S.A. 84 C4
Snoul, Cambodia 39 F6
Snow Hill, U.S.A. 76 F8
Snow Lake, Canada 73 C8
Snow Mt., U.S.A. 84 F4
Snowbird L., Canada 73 A8
Snowdon, U.K. 10 D3
Snowdrift, Canada 73 A6
Snowdrift →, Canada 73 A6
Snowflake, U.S.A. 83 J8
Snowshoe Pk., U.S.A. 82 B6
Snowtown, Australia 63 E2
Snowville, U.S.A. 82 F7
Snowy →, Australia 63 F4
Snowy Mts., Australia 63 F4
Snug Corner, Bahamas 89 B5
Snyder, Okla., U.S.A. 81 H5
Snyder, Tex., U.S.A. 81 J4
Soahanina, Madag. 57 B7
Soalala, Madag. 57 B8
Soan →, Pakistan 42 C4
Soanierana-Ivongo, Madag. 57 B8
Soap Lake, U.S.A. 82 C4
Sobat, Nahr →, Sudan 51 G11
Sobhapur, India 42 H8
Sobral, Brazil 93 D10
Soc Giang, Vietnam 38 A6
Soc Trang, Vietnam 39 H5
Soch'e = Shache, China 32 C2
Sochi, Russia 25 F6
Société, Is. de la, Pac. Oc. 65 J12
Society Is. = Société, Is. de la, Pac. Oc. 65 J12
Socompa, Portezuelo de, Chile 94 A2
Socorro, Colombia 92 B4
Socorro, U.S.A. 83 J10
Socorro, I., Mexico 86 D2
Socotra, Ind. Oc. 46 E5
Soda L., U.S.A. 83 J5
Soda Plains, India 43 B8
Soda Springs, U.S.A. 82 E8
Söderhamn, Sweden 9 F14
Söderköping, Sweden 9 G14
Södermanlands län □, Sweden 9 G14
Södertälje, Sweden 9 G14
Sodiri, Sudan 51 F10
Sodo, Ethiopia 51 G12
Sodus, U.S.A. 78 C7
Soekmekaar, S. Africa 57 C4
Soest, Neths. 15 B5
Sofia = Sofiya, Bulgaria 21 C10
Sofia →, Madag. 57 B8
Sofiiski, Russia 27 D14
Sofiya, Bulgaria 21 C10
Sōfu-Gan, Japan 31 K10
Sogamoso, Colombia 92 B4
Sogār, Iran 45 E8
Sogn og Fjordane fylke □, Norway 9 F9
Sogndalsfjøra, Norway 9 F9
Sognefjorden, Norway 9 F8
Sŏgwi-po, S. Korea 35 H14
Soh, Iran 45 C6
Sohâg, Egypt 51 C11
Sŏhori, N. Korea 35 D15
Soignies, Belgium 15 D4
Soissons, France 18 B5
Sōja, Japan 31 G6
Sojat, India 42 G5
Sokelo, Zaïre 55 D1
Sokodé, Togo 50 G5
Sokol, Russia 24 C7
Sokółka, Poland 17 B11
Sokolo, Mali 50 F3
Sokoto, Nigeria 50 F6
Sol Iletsk, Russia 24 D10
Solai, Kenya 54 B4
Solano, Phil. 37 A6
Solapur, India 40 L9
Soléa □, Cyprus 23 D12
Soledad, U.S.A. 83 H3
Soledad, Venezuela 92 B6
Solent, The, U.K. 11 G6
Solfonn, Norway 9 F9
Soligalich, Russia 24 C7
Solikamsk, Russia 24 C10
Solila, Madag. 57 C8
Solimões = Amazonas →, S. Amer. 93 C9
Solingen, Germany 15 C7
Sollefteå, Sweden 8 E14
Sóller, Spain 22 B9
Sologne, France 18 C4
Solok, Indonesia 36 E2
Sololá, Guatemala 88 D1
Solomon, N. Fork →, U.S.A. 80 F5
Solomon, S. Fork →, U.S.A. 80 F5
Solomon Is. ■, Pac. Oc. 64 H7
Solon, China 33 B7
Solon Springs, U.S.A. 80 B9
Solor, Indonesia 37 F6
Solothurn, Switz. 16 E3
Solṭānābād, Khorāsān, Iran 45 C8
Solṭānābād, Khorāsān, Iran 45 B8
Solṭānābād, Markazī, Iran 45 C6
Solunska Glava, Macedonia, Yug. 21 D9
Solvang, U.S.A. 85 L6
Solvay, U.S.A. 79 C8
Solvychegodsk, Russia 24 B8
Solway Firth, U.K. 10 C4
Solwezi, Zambia 55 E2
Sōma, Japan 30 F10
Somali Rep. ■, Africa 46 F4
Sombor, Serbia, Yug. 21 B8
Sombra, Canada 78 D2
Sombrerete, Mexico 86 C4
Sombrero, Anguilla 89 C7
Somers, U.S.A. 82 B6
Somerset, Canada 73 D9
Somerset, Colo., U.S.A. 83 G10
Somerset, Ky., U.S.A. 76 G3
Somerset, Mass., U.S.A. 79 E13
Somerset, Pa., U.S.A. 78 F5
Somerset □, U.K. 11 F5
Somerset East, S. Africa 56 E4
Somerset I., Canada 68 A10
Somerset West, S. Africa 56 E2
Somerton, U.S.A. 83 K6
Somerville, U.S.A. 79 F10
Someş →, Romania 17 E11
Sommariva, Australia 63 D4
Somme □, France 18 B5
Somoto, Nic. 88 D2
Somport, Puerto de, Spain 19 A5
Son Ha, Vietnam 38 E7
Son Hoa, Vietnam 38 F7
Son La, Vietnam 38 B4
Son Tay, Vietnam 38 B5
Soná, Panama 88 E3
Sonamarg, India 43 B6
Sonamukhi, India 43 H12
Sŏnchŏn, N. Korea 35 E13
Sondags →, S. Africa 56 E4
Sondar, India 43 C6
Sønderborg, Denmark 9 J10
Sone, Mozam. 55 F3
Sonepur, India 41 J13
Song, Thailand 38 C3
Song Cau, Vietnam 38 F7
Song Xian, China 34 G7
Songchŏn, N. Korea 35 E14
Songea, Tanzania 55 E4
Songea □, Tanzania 55 E4
Songhua Hu, China 35 C14
Songhua Jiang →, China 33 B8
Songjin, N. Korea 35 D15
Songjŏng-ni, S. Korea 35 G14
Songkhla, Thailand 39 J3
Songnim, N. Korea 35 E13
Songpan, China 32 C5
Songwe, Zaïre 54 C2
Songwe →, Africa 55 D3
Sonid Youqi, China 34 C7
Sonipat, India 42 E7
Sonmiani, Pakistan 42 G2
Sono →, Brazil 93 E9
Sonora, Calif., U.S.A. 83 H3
Sonora, Tex., U.S.A. 81 K4
Sonora □, Mexico 86 B2
Sonora →, Mexico 86 B2
Sonora Desert, U.S.A. 85 M12
Sonoyta, Mexico 86 A2
Sŏnsan, S. Korea 35 F15
Sonsonate, El Salv. 88 D2
Soochow = Suzhou, China 33 C7
Sop Hao, Laos 38 B5
Sop Prap, Thailand 38 D2
Sopi, Indonesia 37 D7
Sopot, Poland 17 A9
Sop's Arm, Canada 71 C8
Sopur, India 43 B6
Sør-Rondane, Antarctica 5 D4
Sør-Trøndelag fylke □, Norway 8 E10
Sorah, Pakistan 42 F3
Sorata, Bolivia 92 G5
Sorel, Canada 70 C5
Soreq, N. →, Israel 47 D3
Soria, Spain 19 B4
Soriano, Uruguay 94 C4
Sorkh, Kuh-e, Iran 45 C8
Sorocaba, Brazil 95 A6
Sorochinsk, Russia 24 D9
Soron, India 43 F8
Sorong, Indonesia 37 E8
Soroní, Greece 23 C10
Soroti, Uganda 54 B3
Sørøya, Norway 8 A17
Sørøysundet, Norway 8 A17
Sorrento, Australia 63 F3
Sorrento, Italy 20 D6
Sorsele, Sweden 8 D14
Sorsogon, Phil. 37 B6
Sortavala, Russia 24 B5
Sŏsan, S. Korea 35 F14
Soscumica, L., Canada 70 B4
Sosnogorsk, Russia 24 B9
Sosnovka, Russia 27 D11
Sosnowiec, Poland 17 C9
Sŏsura, N. Korea 35 C16
Sosva, Russia 24 C11
Soto la Marina →, Mexico 87 C5
Sotuta, Mexico 87 C7
Souanké, Congo 52 D2
Soúdha, Greece 23 D6
Soúdhas, Kólpos, Greece 23 D6
Soukhouma, Laos 38 E5
Sŏul, S. Korea 35 F14
Sound, The = Øresund, Europe 9 H12
Sound, The, U.K. 11 G3
Sources, Mt. aux, Lesotho 57 D4
Soure, Brazil 93 D9
Souris, Man., Canada 73 D8
Souris, P.E.I., Canada 71 C7
Souris →, Canada 80 A5
Sousa, Brazil 93 E11
Sousel, Brazil 93 D8
Sousse, Tunisia 51 A7
South Africa ■, Africa 56 E3
South Aulatsivik I., Canada 71 A7
South Australia □, Australia 63 E2
South Baldy, U.S.A. 83 J10
South Bend, Ind., U.S.A. 76 E2
South Bend, Wash., U.S.A. 84 D3
South Boston, U.S.A. 77 G6
South Branch, Canada 71 C8
South Brook, Canada 71 C8
South Buganda □, Uganda 54 C3
South Carolina □, U.S.A. 77 J5
South Charleston, U.S.A. 76 F5
South China Sea, Asia 36 C4
South Dakota □, U.S.A. 80 C5
South Downs, U.K. 11 G7
South East C., Australia 62 G4
South East Is., Australia 61 F3
South Esk →, U.K. 12 E5
South Foreland, U.K. 11 F9
South Fork →, U.S.A. 82 C7
South Fork, American →, U.S.A. 84 G5
South Fork, Feather →, U.S.A. 84 F5
South Georgia, Antarctica 5 B1
South Glamorgan □, U.K. 11 F4
South Haven, U.S.A. 76 D2
South Henik, L., Canada 73 A9
South Honshu Ridge, Pac. Oc. 64 E6
South Horr, Kenya 54 B4
South I., Kenya 54 B4
South I., N.Z. 59 L3
South Invercargill, N.Z. 59 M2
South Knife →, Canada 73 B10
South Korea ■, Asia 35 F15
South Lake Tahoe, U.S.A. 84 G6
South Loup →, U.S.A. 80 E5
South Magnetic Pole, Antarctica 5 C9
South Milwaukee, U.S.A. 76 D2
South Molton, U.K. 11 F4
South Nahanni →, Canada 72 A4
South Negril Pt., Jamaica 88 C4
South Orkney Is., Antarctica 5 C18
South Pagai, I. = Pagai Selatan, P., Indonesia 36 E2
South Pass, U.S.A. 82 E9
South Pittsburg, U.S.A. 77 H3
South Platte →, U.S.A. 80 E4
South Pole, Antarctica 5 E
South Porcupine, Canada 70 C3
South River, Canada 70 C4
South River, U.S.A. 79 F10
South Ronaldsay, U.K. 12 C6
South Sandwich Is., Antarctica 5 B1
South Saskatchewan →, Canada 73 C7
South Seal →, Canada 73 B9
South Shetland Is., Antarctica 5 C18
South Shields, U.K. 10 C6
South Sioux City, U.S.A. 80 D6
South Taranaki Bight, N.Z. 59 H5
South Thompson →, Canada 72 C4
South Twin I., Canada 70 B4
South Tyne →, U.K. 10 C5
South Uist, U.K. 12 D1
South West Africa = Namibia ■, Africa 56 C2
South West C., Australia 62 G4
South Yorkshire □, U.K. 10 D6
Southampton, Canada 70 D3
Southampton, U.K. 11 G6
Southampton, U.S.A. 79 F12
Southampton I., Canada 69 B11
Southbridge, N.Z. 59 K4
Southbridge, U.S.A. 79 D12
Southend, Canada 73 B8
Southend-on-Sea, U.K. 11 F8
Southern □, Malawi 55 F4
Southern □, Zambia 55 F2
Southern Alps, N.Z. 59 K3
Southern Cross, Australia 61 F2
Southern Hills, Australia 61 F3
Southern Indian L., Canada 73 B9
Southern Ocean, Antarctica 5 C6
Southern Pines, U.S.A. 77 H6
Southern Uplands, U.K. 12 F5
Southington, U.S.A. 79 E12
Southold, U.S.A. 79 E12
Southport, Australia 63 D5
Southport, U.K. 10 D4
Southport, U.S.A. 77 J6
Southwest C., N.Z. 59 M1
Southwold, U.K. 11 E9
Soutpansberg, S. Africa 57 C4
Sovetsk, France 24 C3
Sovetsk, Russia 24 C8
Sovetskaya Gavan, Russia 27 E15
Soviet Union = Commonwealth of Independent States ■, Eurasia 27 D11
Soweto, S. Africa 57 D4
Sōya-Kaikyō = La Perouse Str., Asia 30 B11
Sōya-Misaki, Japan 30 B10
Soyo, Angola 52 F2
Sozh →, Belorussia 24 D5
Spa, Belgium 15 D5
Spain ■, Europe 19 C4
Spalding, Australia 63 E2
Spalding, U.K. 10 E7
Spalding, U.S.A. 80 E5
Spangler, U.S.A. 78 F6
Spaniard's Bay, Canada 71 C9

Spanish, Canada 70 C3
Spanish Fork, U.S.A. 82 F8
Spanish Town, Jamaica 88 C4
Sparks, U.S.A. 84 F7
Sparta = Spárti, Greece 21 F10
Sparta, Ga., U.S.A. 77 J4
Sparta, Wis., U.S.A. 80 D9
Spartanburg, U.S.A. 77 H4
Spartansburg, U.S.A. 78 E5
Spárti, Greece 21 F10
Spartivento, C., Calabria, Italy 20 F7
Spartivento, C., Sard., Italy 20 E3
Spassk-Dalniy, Russia 27 E14
Spátha, Ákra, Greece 23 D5
Spatsizi →, Canada 72 B3
Spearfish, U.S.A. 80 C3
Spearman, U.S.A. 81 G4
Speers, Canada 73 C7
Speightstown, Barbados 89 D8
Speke Gulf, Tanzania 54 C3
Spence Bay, Canada 68 B10
Spencer, Idaho, U.S.A. 82 D7
Spencer, Iowa, U.S.A. 80 D7
Spencer, N.Y., U.S.A. 79 D8
Spencer, Nebr., U.S.A. 80 D5
Spencer, W. Va., U.S.A. 76 F5
Spencer, C., Australia 63 F2
Spencer B., Namibia 56 D1
Spencer G., Australia 63 E2
Spencerville, Canada 79 B9
Spences Bridge, Canada 72 C4
Spenser Mts., N.Z. 59 K4
Sperrin Mts., U.K. 13 B5
Spessart, Germany 16 C4
Spey →, U.K. 12 D5
Speyer, Germany 16 D4
Spili, Greece 23 D6
Spin Baldak = Qala-i-Jadid, Afghan. 42 D2
Spinalónga, Greece 23 D7
Spinazzola, Italy 20 D7
Spirit Lake, Idaho, U.S.A. 82 C5
Spirit Lake, Wash., U.S.A. 84 D4
Spirit River, Canada 72 B5
Spiritwood, Canada 73 C7
Spithead, U.K. 11 G6
Spitzbergen = Svalbard, Arctic 4 B8
Split, Croatia 20 C7
Split L., Canada 73 B9
Splügenpass, Switz. 16 E4
Spofford, U.S.A. 81 L4
Spokane, U.S.A. 82 C5
Spoleto, Italy 20 C5
Spooner, U.S.A. 80 C9
Sporyy Navolok, Mys, Russia 26 B7
Spragge, Canada 70 C3
Sprague, U.S.A. 82 C5
Sprague River, U.S.A. 82 E3
Spratly I., S. China Sea 36 C4
Spray, U.S.A. 82 D4
Spree →, Germany 16 B6
Spremberg, Germany 16 C7
Spring City, U.S.A. 82 G8
Spring Garden, U.S.A. 84 F6
Spring Mts., U.S.A. 83 H6
Spring Valley, Calif., U.S.A. 85 N10
Spring Valley, Minn., U.S.A. 80 D8
Springbok, S. Africa 56 D2
Springdale, Canada 71 C8
Springdale, Ark., U.S.A. 81 G7
Springdale, Wash., U.S.A. 82 B5
Springer, U.S.A. 81 G2
Springerville, U.S.A. 83 J9
Springfield, Canada 78 D4
Springfield, N.Z. 59 K3
Springfield, Colo., U.S.A. 81 G3
Springfield, Ill., U.S.A. 80 F10
Springfield, Mass., U.S.A. 79 D12
Springfield, Mo., U.S.A. 81 G8
Springfield, Ohio, U.S.A. 76 F4
Springfield, Oreg., U.S.A. 82 D2
Springfield, Tenn., U.S.A. 77 G2
Springfield, Vt., U.S.A. 79 C12
Springfontein, S. Africa 56 E4
Springhill, Canada 71 C7
Springhouse, Canada 72 C4
Springhurst, Australia 63 F4
Springs, S. Africa 57 D4
Springsure, Australia 62 C4
Springvale, Queens., Australia 62 C3
Springvale, W. Austral., Australia 60 C4
Springvale, U.S.A. 79 C14
Springville, Calif., U.S.A. 84 J8
Springville, N.Y., U.S.A. 78 D6
Springville, Utah, U.S.A. 82 F8
Springwater, Canada 73 C7
Spruce-Creek, U.S.A. 78 F6
Spur, U.S.A. 81 J4
Spurn Hd., U.K. 10 D8
Spuzzum, Canada 72 D4
Squam L., U.S.A. 79 C13
Squamish, Canada 72 D4
Square Islands, Canada 71 B8
Squires, Mt., Australia 61 E4
Sragen, Indonesia 37 G14
Srbija = Serbia □, Europe 21 C9
Sre Khtum, Cambodia 39 F6
Sre Umbell, Cambodia 39 G4
Sredinnyy Khrebet, Russia 27 D16
Sredinnyy Ra. = Sredinnyy Khrebet, Russia 27 D16
Sredne Tambovskoye, Russia 27 D14
Srednekolymsk, Russia 27 C16
Srednevilyuysk, Russia 27 C13
Srepok →, Cambodia 38 F6
Sretensk, Russia 27 D12
Sri Lanka ■, Asia 40 R12
Srikakulam, India 41 K13
Srinagar, India 43 B6
Staaten →, Australia 62 B3
Staðarhólskirkja, Iceland 8 D3
Stadlandet, Norway 8 E8
Stadskanaal, Neths. 15 A6
Stafafell, Iceland 8 D6
Staffa, U.K. 12 E2
Stafford, U.K. 10 E5
Stafford, U.S.A. 81 G5
Stafford Springs, U.S.A. 79 E12
Staffordshire □, U.K. 10 E5
Staines, U.K. 11 F7
Stakhanov = Kadiyevka, Ukraine 25 E6
Stalingrad = Volgograd, Russia 25 E7
Staliniri = Tskhinvali, Georgia 25 F7
Stalino = Donetsk, Ukraine 25 E6
Stalinogorsk = Novomoskovsk, Russia 24 D6
Stalis, Greece 23 D7
Stalybridge, U.K. 10 D5
Stamford, Australia 62 C3
Stamford, U.K. 11 E7
Stamford, Conn., U.S.A. 79 E11
Stamford, Tex., U.S.A. 81 J5
Stamps, U.S.A. 81 J8
Stanberry, U.S.A. 80 E7
Standerton, S. Africa 57 D4
Standish, U.S.A. 76 D4
Stanford, U.S.A. 82 C8
Stanger, S. Africa 57 D5
Stanislaus →, U.S.A. 84 H5
Stanislav = Ivano-Frankovsk, Ukraine 25 E3
Stanke Dimitrov, Bulgaria 21 C10
Stanley, Australia 62 G4
Stanley, N.B., Canada 71 C6
Stanley, Sask., Canada 73 B8
Stanley, Falk. Is. 96 G5
Stanley, Idaho, U.S.A. 82 D6
Stanley, N. Dak., U.S.A. 80 A3
Stanley, N.Y., U.S.A. 78 D7
Stanley, Wis., U.S.A. 80 C9
Stanovoy Khrebet, Russia 27 D13
Stanovoy Ra. = Stanovoy Khrebet, Russia 27 D13
Stansmore Ra., Australia 60 D4
Stanthorpe, Australia 63 D5
Stanton, U.S.A. 81 J4
Stanwood, U.S.A. 84 B4
Staples, U.S.A. 80 B7
Stapleton, U.S.A. 80 E4
Star City, Canada 73 C8
Stara Planina, Bulgaria 21 C10
Stara Zagora, Bulgaria 21 C11
Staraya Russa, Russia 24 C5
Starbuck I., Kiribati 65 H12
Staritsa, Russia 24 C5
Starke, U.S.A. 77 K4
Starkville, Colo., U.S.A. 81 G2
Starkville, Miss., U.S.A. 77 J1
Starogard, Poland 17 B9
Start Pt., U.K. 11 G4
Staryy Kheydzhan, Russia 27 C15
Staryy Oskol, Russia 24 D6
State College, U.S.A. 78 F7
Stateline, U.S.A. 84 G7
Staten, I. = Estados, I. de Los, Argentina 96 G4
Staten I., U.S.A. 79 F10
Statesboro, U.S.A. 77 J5
Statesville, U.S.A. 77 H5
Stauffer, U.S.A. 85 L7
Staunton, Ill., U.S.A. 80 F10
Staunton, Va., U.S.A. 76 F6
Stavanger, Norway 9 G8
Staveley, N.Z. 59 K3
Stavelot, Belgium 15 D5
Staveren, Neths. 15 B5
Stavern, Norway 9 G11
Stavropol, Russia 25 E7
Stavros, Cyprus 23 D11
Stavrós, Greece 23 D6
Stavros, Ákra, Greece 23 D6
Stawell, Australia 63 F3
Stawell →, Australia 62 C3
Stayner, Canada 78 B4
Steamboat Springs, U.S.A. 82 F10
Steele, U.S.A. 80 B5
Steelton, U.S.A. 78 F8
Steelville, U.S.A. 81 G9
Steen River, Canada 72 B5
Steenkool = Bintuni, Indonesia 37 E8
Steenwijk, Neths. 15 B6
Steep Pt., Australia 61 E1
Steep Rock, Canada 73 C9
Stefanie L. = Chew Bahir, Ethiopia 51 H12
Stefansson Bay, Antarctica 5 C5
Steiermark □, Austria 16 E7
Steilacoom, U.S.A. 84 C4
Steinbach, Canada 73 D9
Steinfort, Lux. 15 E5
Steinkjer, Norway 8 E11
Steinkopf, S. Africa 56 D2
Stellarton, Canada 71 C7
Stellenbosch, S. Africa 56 E2
Stendal, Germany 16 B5
Stensele, Sweden 8 D14
Stepanakert = Khankendy, Azerbaijan 25 G8
Stephan, U.S.A. 80 A6
Stephens Creek, Australia 63 E3
Stephens I., Canada 72 C2
Stephenville, Canada 71 C8
Stephenville, U.S.A. 81 J5
Stepnoi = Elista, Russia 25 E7
Stepnyak, Kazakhstan 26 D8
Steppe, Asia 28 E9
Sterkstroom, S. Africa 56 E4
Sterling, Colo., U.S.A. 80 E3
Sterling, Ill., U.S.A. 80 E10
Sterling, Kans., U.S.A. 80 F5
Sterling City, U.S.A. 81 K4
Sterling Run, U.S.A. 78 E6
Sterlitamak, Russia 24 D10
Stérnes, Greece 23 D6
Stettin = Szczecin, Poland 16 B7
Stettler, Canada 72 C6
Steubenville, U.S.A. 78 F4
Stevens Point, U.S.A. 80 C10
Stevenson, U.S.A. 84 E5
Stevenson L., Canada 73 C9
Stewart, B.C., Canada 72 B3
Stewart, N.W.T., Canada 68 B6
Stewart, U.S.A. 84 F7
Stewart, C., Australia 62 A1
Stewart, I., Chile 96 G2
Stewart I., N.Z. 59 M1
Stewarts Point, U.S.A. 84 G3
Stewiacke, Canada 71 C7
Steynsburg, S. Africa 56 E4
Steyr, Austria 16 D7
Steytlerville, S. Africa 56 E3
Stigler, U.S.A. 81 H7
Stikine →, Canada 72 B2
Stilfontein, S. Africa 56 D4
Stillwater, N.Z. 59 K3
Stillwater, Minn., U.S.A. 80 C8
Stillwater, N.Y., U.S.A. 79 D11
Stillwater, Okla., U.S.A. 81 G6
Stillwater Ra., U.S.A. 82 G4
Stilwell, U.S.A. 81 H7
Štip, Macedonia, Yug. 21 D10
Stirling, Australia 62 B3
Stirling, Canada 72 D6
Stirling, U.K. 12 E5
Stirling Ra., Australia 61 F2
Stittsville, Canada 79 A9
Stockerau, Austria 16 D8
Stockett, U.S.A. 82 C8
Stockholm, Sweden 9 G15
Stockport, U.K. 10 D5
Stockton, Calif., U.S.A. 83 H3
Stockton, Kans., U.S.A. 80 F5
Stockton, Mo., U.S.A. 81 G8
Stockton-on-Tees, U.K. 10 C6
Stoke on Trent, U.K. 10 D5
Stokes Bay, Canada 70 C3
Stokes Pt., Australia 62 G3
Stokes Ra., Australia 60 C5
Stokkseyri, Iceland 8 E3
Stokksnes, Iceland 8 D6
Stolac, Bos. & H., Yug. 21 C7
Stolbovaya, Russia 27 C16
Stolbovoy, Ostrov, Russia 27 D17
Stomion, Greece 23 D5
Stonehaven, U.K. 12 E6
Stonehenge, Australia 62 C3
Stonewall, Canada 73 C9
Stony L., Man., Canada 73 B9
Stony L., Ont., Canada 78 B6
Stony Rapids, Canada 73 B7
Stony Tunguska = Podkamennaya Tunguska →, Russia 27 C10
Stonyford, U.S.A. 84 F4
Stora Lulevatten, Sweden 8 C15
Stora Sjöfallet, Sweden 8 C15
Storavan, Sweden 8 D15
Store Bælt, Denmark 9 J11
Store Creek, Australia 63 E4
Støren, Norway 8 E11
Storm B., Australia 62 G4
Storm Lake, U.S.A. 80 D7
Stormberge, S. Africa 56 E4
Stormsrivier, S. Africa 56 E3
Stornoway, U.K. 12 C2
Storsjön, Sweden 8 E12
Storuman, Sweden 8 D14
Stoughton, Canada 73 D8
Stour →, Dorset, U.K. 11 G5
Stour →, Here. & Worcs., U.K. 11 E5
Stour →, Kent, U.K. 11 F9
Stour →, Suffolk, U.K. 11 F9
Stourbridge, U.K. 11 E5
Stout, L., Canada 73 C10
Stove Pipe Wells Village, U.S.A. 85 J9
Stowmarket, U.K. 11 E9
Strabane, U.K. 13 B4
Strabane □, U.K. 13 B4
Strahan, Australia 62 G4
Stralsund, Germany 16 A6
Strand, S. Africa 56 E2
Strangford L., U.K. 13 B6
Strangsville, U.S.A. 78 E3
Stranraer, U.K. 12 G3
Strasbourg, Canada 73 C8
Strasbourg, France 18 B7
Strasburg, U.S.A. 80 B4
Stratford, Canada 70 D3
Stratford, N.Z. 59 H5
Stratford, Calif., U.S.A. 83 H4
Stratford, Conn., U.S.A. 79 E11
Stratford, Tex., U.S.A. 81 G3
Stratford-upon-Avon, U.K. 11 E6
Strath Spey, U.K. 12 D5
Strathalbyn, Australia 63 F2
Strathclyde □, U.K. 12 F4
Strathcona Prov. Park, Canada 72 D3
Strathmore, Australia 62 B3
Strathmore, Canada 72 C6
Strathmore, U.K. 12 E5
Strathmore, U.S.A. 84 J7
Strathnaver, Canada 72 C4
Strathpeffer, U.K. 12 D4
Strathroy, Canada 70 D3
Strathy Pt., U.K. 12 C4
Stratton, U.S.A. 80 F3
Straumnes, Iceland 8 C2
Strawberry Res., U.S.A. 82 F8
Strawn, U.S.A. 81 J5
Streaky B., Australia 63 E1
Streaky Bay, Australia 63 E1
Streator, U.S.A. 80 E10
Streeter, U.S.A. 80 B5
Streetsville, Canada 78 C5
Strelka, Russia 27 D10
Streng →, Cambodia 38 F4
Strezhevoy, Russia 26 C8
Strómboli, Italy 20 E6
Stromeferry, U.K. 12 D3
Stromness, U.K. 12 C5
Ströms vattudal, Sweden 8 D13
Strömstad, Sweden 9 G11
Strömsund, Sweden 8 E13
Stronsay, U.K. 12 B6
Stronsburg, U.S.A. 80 E6
Stroud, U.K. 11 F5
Stroud Road, Australia 63 E5
Stroudsberg, U.S.A. 79 F9
Stroumbi, Cyprus 23 E11
Struer, Denmark 9 H10
Strumica, Macedonia, Yug. 21 D10
Struthers, Canada 70 C2
Struthers, U.S.A. 78 E4
Stryker, U.S.A. 82 B6
Strzelecki Cr. →, Australia 63 D2
Stuart, Fla., U.S.A. 77 M5
Stuart, Nebr., U.S.A. 80 D5
Stuart →, Canada 72 C4
Stuart Bluff Ra., Australia 60 D5
Stuart L., Canada 72 C4
Stuart Ra., Australia 63 D1
Stull, L., Canada 70 B1
Stung Treng, Cambodia 38 F5
Stupart →, Canada 73 B10
Sturgeon B., Canada 73 C9
Sturgeon Bay, U.S.A. 76 C2
Sturgeon Falls, Canada 70 C4
Sturgeon L., Alta., Canada 72 B5
Sturgeon L., Ont., Canada 70 B1
Sturgeon L., Ont., Canada 78 B6
Sturgis, Mich., U.S.A. 76 E3
Sturgis, S. Dak., U.S.A. 80 C3
Sturt Cr. →, Australia 60 C4
Sturt Creek, Australia 60 C4
Stutterheim, S. Africa 56 E4
Stuttgart, Germany 16 D4
Stuttgart, U.S.A. 81 H9
Stuyvesant, U.S.A. 79 D11
Stykkishólmur, Iceland 8 D2
Styria = Steiermark □, Austria 16 E7
Su Xian, China 34 H9
Suakin, Sudan 51 E12
Suan, N. Korea 35 E14
Suaqui, Mexico 86 B3
Subang, Indonesia 37 G12
Subansiri →, India 41 F18
Subayhah, Si. Arabia 44 D3
Subi, Indonesia 39 L7
Subotica, Serbia, Yug. 21 A8
Success, Canada 73 C7
Suceava, Romania 17 E13
Suchan, Russia 30 C6
Suchitoto, El Salv. 88 D2
Suchou = Suzhou, China 33 C7
Süchow = Xuzhou, China 35 G9
Suck →, Ireland 13 C3
Sucre, Bolivia 92 G5
Sud, Pte., Canada 71 C7
Sud-Ouest, Pte. du, Canada 71 C7
Sudan, U.S.A. 81 H3
Sudan ■, Africa 51 E11
Sudbury, Canada 70 C3
Sudbury, U.K. 11 E8
Sûdd, Sudan 51 G11
Sudeten Mts. = Sudety, Europe 16 C8
Sudety, Europe 16 C8
Sudi, Tanzania 55 E4
Sudirman, Pegunungan, Indonesia 37 E9
Sueca, Spain 19 C5
Suez = El Suweis, Egypt 51 C11
Suez, G. of = Suweis, Khalîg el, Egypt 51 C11
Suffield, Canada 73 C6
Suffolk, U.S.A. 76 G7
Suffolk □, U.K. 11 E9
Sugar City, U.S.A. 80 F3
Sugluk = Saglouc, Canada 69 B12
Suhār, Oman 45 E8
Sühbaatar □, Mongolia 34 B8
Sui Xian, China 34 G8
Suide, China 34 F6
Suifenhe, China 35 B16
Suihua, China 33 B7
Suining, China 35 H9
Suiping, China 34 H7
Suir →, Ireland 13 D4
Suiyang, China 35 B16
Suizhong, China 35 D11
Sujangarh, India 42 F6
Sukabumi, Indonesia 37 G12
Sukadana, Kalimantan, Indonesia 36 E3
Sukadana, Sumatera, Indonesia 36 F3
Sukagawa, Japan 31 F10
Sukaraja, Indonesia 36 E4
Sukarnapura = Jayapura, Indonesia 37 E10
Sukchŏn, N. Korea 35 E13
Sukhona →, Russia 24 C6
Sukhothai, Thailand 38 D2
Sukhumi, Georgia 25 F7
Sukkur, Pakistan 42 F3
Sukkur Barrage, Pakistan 42 F3
Sukumo, Japan 31 H6
Sukunka →, Canada 72 B4
Sula, Kepulauan, Indonesia 37 E7
Sulaco →, Honduras 88 C2
Sulaiman Range, Pakistan 42 D3
Sūlār, Iran 45 D6
Sulawesi □, Indonesia 37 E6
Sulima, S. Leone 50 G2
Sulina, Romania 17 F14
Sulitälma, Sweden 8 C14
Sulitjelma, Norway 8 C14
Sullana, Peru 92 D2
Sullivan, Ill., U.S.A. 80 F10
Sullivan, Ind., U.S.A. 76 F2
Sullivan, Mo., U.S.A. 80 F9
Sullivan Bay, Canada 72 C3
Sulphur, La., U.S.A. 81 K8
Sulphur, Okla., U.S.A. 81 H6
Sulphur Pt., Canada 72 A6
Sulphur Springs, U.S.A. 81 J7
Sulphur Springs Draw →, U.S.A. 81 J4
Sultan, Canada 70 C3
Sultan, U.S.A. 84 C5
Sultanpur, India 43 F10
Sultsa, Russia 24 B8
Sulu Arch., Phil. 37 C6
Sulu Sea, E. Indies 37 C6
Suluq, Libya 51 B9
Sulzberger Ice Shelf, Antarctica 5 D10
Sumalata, Indonesia 37 D6
Sumampa, Argentina 94 B3
Sumatera □, Indonesia 36 D2
Sumatra = Sumatera □, Indonesia 36 D2
Sumatra, U.S.A. 82 C10
Sumba, Indonesia 37 F5
Sumba, Selat, Indonesia 37 F5
Sumbawa, Indonesia 36 F5
Sumbawa Besar, Indonesia 36 F5
Sumbawanga □, Tanzania 54 D3
Sumbe, Angola 52 G2
Sumburgh Hd., U.K. 12 B7
Sumdo, India 43 B8
Sumedang, Indonesia 37 G12
Šumen, Bulgaria 21 C12
Sumenep, Indonesia 37 G15
Sumgait, Azerbaijan 25 F8
Summer L., U.S.A. 82 E3
Summerland, Canada 72 D5
Summerside, Canada 71 C7
Summerville, Ga., U.S.A. 77 H3
Summerville, S.C., U.S.A. 77 J5
Summit Lake, Canada 72 C4
Summit Pk., U.S.A. 83 H10
Sumner, Iowa, U.S.A. 80 D8
Sumner, Wash., U.S.A. 84 C4
Sumoto, Japan 31 G7
Sumperk, Czech. 16 D8
Sumter, U.S.A. 77 J5
Sumy, Ukraine 25 D5
Sun City, Ariz., U.S.A. 83 K7
Sun City, Calif., U.S.A. 85 M9
Sunagawa, Japan 30 C10
Sunan, N. Korea 35 E13
Sunart, L., U.K. 12 E3
Sunburst, U.S.A. 82 B8
Sunbury, Australia 63 F3
Sunbury, U.S.A. 79 F8
Sunchales, Argentina 94 C3
Suncho Corral, Argentina 94 B3
Sunchon, S. Korea 35 G14
Suncook, U.S.A. 79 C13
Sunda, Selat, Indonesia 36 F3
Sunda Is., Indonesia 64 H2
Sunda Str. = Sunda, Selat, Indonesia 36 F3
Sundance, U.S.A. 80 C2
Sundarbans, The, Asia 41 J16
Sundargarh, India 41 H14
Sundays = Sondags →, S. Africa 56 E4
Sunderland, Canada 78 B5
Sunderland, U.K. 10 C6
Sundre, Canada 72 C6
Sundridge, Canada 70 C4

Sundsvall, Sweden 8 E14
Sung Hei, Vietnam 39 G6
Sungai Kolok, Thailand 39 J3
Sungai Lembing, Malaysia 39 L4
Sungai Patani, Malaysia 39 K3
Sungaigerong, Indonesia 36 E2
Sungailiat, Indonesia 36 E3
Sungaipakning, Indonesia 36 D2
Sungaipenuh, Indonesia 36 E2
Sungaitiram, Indonesia 36 E5
Sungari = Songhua Jiang →, China 33 B8
Sungguminasa, Indonesia 37 F5
Sunghua Chiang = Songhua Jiang →, China 33 B8
Sunnyside, Utah, U.S.A. 82 G8
Sunnyside, Wash., U.S.A. 82 C3
Sunnyvale, U.S.A. 83 H2
Sunray, U.S.A. 81 G4
Suntar, Russia 27 C12
Suoyarvi, Russia 24 B5
Supai, U.S.A. 83 H7
Supaul, India 43 F12
Superior, Ariz., U.S.A. 83 K8
Superior, Mont., U.S.A. 82 C6
Superior, Nebr., U.S.A. 80 E5
Superior, Wis., U.S.A. 80 B8
Superior, L., N. Amer. 70 C2
Suphan Buri, Thailand 38 E3
Supriori, Kepulauan, Indonesia 37 E9
Supung Sk., China 35 D13
Sūq Suwayq, Si. Arabia 44 E3
Suqian, China 35 H10
Sūr, Lebanon 47 B4
Sur, Pt., U.S.A. 83 H3
Sura →, Russia 24 C8
Surab, Pakistan 42 E2
Surabaja = Surabaya, Indonesia 37 G15
Surabaya, Indonesia 37 G15
Surakarta, Indonesia 37 G14
Surat, Australia 63 D4
Surat, India 40 J8
Surat Thani, Thailand 39 H2
Suratgarh, India 42 E5
Sûre = Sauer →, Germany 15 E6
Surendranagar, India 42 H4
Surf, U.S.A. 85 L6
Surgut, Russia 26 C8
Suriapet, India 40 L11
Surigao, Phil. 37 C7
Surin, Thailand 38 E4
Surin Nua, Ko, Thailand 39 H1
Surinam ■, S. Amer. 93 C7
Suriname →, Surinam 93 B7
Sūrmaq, Iran 45 D7
Surprise L., Canada 72 B2
Surrey □, U.K. 11 F7
Surt, Libya 51 B8
Surt, Khalīj, Libya 51 B8
Surtsey, Iceland 8 E3
Suruga-Wan, Japan 31 G9
Susa, Italy 20 B2
Susaki, Japan 31 H6
Süsangerd, Iran 45 D6
Susanino, Russia 27 D15
Susanville, U.S.A. 82 F3
Susquehanna →, U.S.A. 79 G8
Susquehanna Depot, U.S.A. 79 E9
Susques, Argentina 94 A2
Sussex, Canada 71 C6
Sussex, U.S.A. 79 E10
Sussex, E. □, U.K. 11 G8
Sussex, W. □, U.K. 11 G7
Sustut →, Canada 72 B3
Susuman, Russia 27 C15
Susunu, Indonesia 37 E8
Sutherland, S. Africa 56 E3
Sutherland, U.S.A. 80 E4
Sutherland Falls, N.Z. 59 L1
Sutherlin, U.S.A. 82 E2
Sutlej →, Pakistan 42 E4
Sutter, U.S.A. 84 F5
Sutter Creek, U.S.A. 84 G6
Sutton, Canada 79 A12
Sutton, U.S.A. 80 E6
Sutton →, Canada 70 A3
Sutton in Ashfield, U.K. 10 D6
Suttor →, Australia 62 C4
Suttsu, Japan 30 C10
Suva, Fiji 59 D8
Suva Planina, Serbia, Yug. 21 C10
Suvorov Is. = Suwarrow Is., Cook Is. 65 J11
Suwałki, Poland 17 A11
Suwannaphum, Thailand 38 E4
Suwannee →, U.S.A. 77 L4
Suwanose-Jima, Japan 31 K4
Suwarrow Is., Cook Is. 65 J11
Suwayq aş Şuqban, Iraq 44 D5
Suweis, Khalîg el, Egypt 51 C11
Suwŏn, S. Korea 35 F14
Suzdal, Russia 24 C7
Suzhou, China 33 C7
Suzu, Japan 31 F8
Suzu-Misaki, Japan 31 F8
Suzuka, Japan 31 G8
Svalbard, Arctic 4 B8
Svalbarð, Iceland 8 C6
Svanvik, Norway 8 B21
Svappavaara, Sweden 8 C16
Svartisen, Norway 8 C12
Svay Chek, Cambodia 38 F4
Svay Rieng, Cambodia 39 G5
Svealand □, Sweden 9 G13
Sveg, Sweden 9 E13
Svendborg, Denmark 9 J11
Sverdlovsk = Yekaterinburg, Russia 24 C11
Sverdrup Is., Canada 4 B3
Svetlaya, Russia 30 A9
Svir →, Russia 24 B5
Svishtov, Bulgaria 21 C11
Svobodnyy, Russia 27 D13
Svolvær, Norway 8 B13
Swabian Alps = Schwäbische Alb, Germany 16 D4
Swainsboro, U.S.A. 77 J4
Swakopmund, Namibia 56 C1
Swale →, U.K. 10 C6
Swan Hill, Australia 63 F3
Swan Hills, Canada 72 C5
Swan Is., W. Indies 88 C3
Swan L., Canada 73 C8
Swan River, Canada 73 C8
Swanage, U.K. 11 G6
Swansea, Australia 63 E5
Swansea, U.K. 11 F4
Swar →, Pakistan 43 B5
Swartberge, S. Africa 56 E3
Swartmodder, S. Africa 56 D3
Swartruggens, S. Africa 56 D4
Swastika, Canada 70 C3
Swatow = Shantou, China 33 D6
Swaziland ■, Africa 57 D5
Sweden ■, Europe 9 H13
Sweet Home, U.S.A. 82 D2
Sweetwater, Nev., U.S.A. 84 G7
Sweetwater, Tex., U.S.A. 81 J4
Sweetwater →, U.S.A. 82 E10
Swellendam, S. Africa 56 E3
Świdnica, Poland 16 C8
Świebodzin, Poland 16 B7
Swift Current, Canada 73 C7
Swiftcurrent →, Canada 73 C7
Swilly, L., Ireland 13 A4
Swindle, I., Canada 72 C3
Swindon, U.K. 11 F6
Swinemünde = Świnoujście, Poland 16 B7
Świnoujście, Poland 16 B7
Switzerland ■, Europe 16 E4
Swords, Ireland 13 C5
Sydney, Australia 63 E5
Sydney, Canada 71 C7
Sydney Mines, Canada 71 C7
Sydprøven, Greenland 4 C5
Sydra G. of = Surt, Khalīj, Libya 51 B8
Syktyvkar, Russia 24 B9
Sylacauga, U.S.A. 77 J2
Sylarna, Sweden 8 E12
Sylhet, Bangla. 41 G17
Sylvan Lake, Canada 72 C6
Sylvania, U.S.A. 77 J5
Sylvester, U.S.A. 77 K4
Sym, Russia 26 C9
Symón, Mexico 86 C4
Synnott Ra., Australia 60 C4
Syracuse, Kans., U.S.A. 81 F4
Syracuse, N.Y., U.S.A. 79 C8
Syrdarya →, Kazakhstan 26 E7
Syria ■, Asia 44 C3
Syul'dzhyukyor, Russia 27 C12
Syzran, Russia 24 D8
Szczecin, Poland 16 B7
Szczecinek, Poland 16 B8
Szechwan = Sichuan □, China 32 C5
Szeged, Hungary 17 E10
Székesfehérvár, Hungary 17 E9
Szekszárd, Hungary 17 E9
Szentes, Hungary 17 E10
Szolnok, Hungary 17 E10
Szombathely, Hungary 16 E8

T

Ta Khli Khok, Thailand 38 E3
Ta Lai, Vietnam 39 G6
Tabacal, Argentina 94 A3
Tabaco, Phil. 37 B6
Ţābah, Si. Arabia 44 E4
Tabarka, Tunisia 50 A6
Ţabas, Khorāsān, Iran 45 C9
Ţabas, Khorāsān, Iran 45 C8
Tabasará, Serranía de, Panama 88 E3
Tabasco □, Mexico 87 D6
Tabatinga, Serra da, Brazil 93 F10
Tabāzīn, Iran 45 D8
Taber, Canada 72 D6
Tablas, Phil. 37 B6
Table B. = Tafelbaai, S. Africa 56 E2
Table B., Canada 71 B8
Table Mt., S. Africa 56 E2
Tableland, Australia 60 C4
Tabletop, Mt., Australia 62 C4
Tábor, Czech. 16 D7
Tabora, Tanzania 54 D3
Tabora □, Tanzania 54 D3
Tabou, Ivory C. 50 H3
Tabrīz, Iran 44 B5
Tabuaeran, Pac. Oc. 65 G12
Tabūk, Si. Arabia 44 D3
Tacámbaro de Codallos, Mexico 86 D4
Tacheng, China 32 B3
Tach'ing Shan = Daqing Shan, China 34 D6
Tacloban, Phil. 37 B6
Tacna, Peru 92 G4
Tacoma, U.S.A. 84 C4
Tacuarembó, Uruguay 95 C4
Tademaït, Plateau du, Algeria 50 C5
Tadjoura, Djibouti 46 E3
Tadmor, N.Z. 59 J4
Tadoule, L., Canada 73 B9
Tadoussac, Canada 71 C6
Tadzhikistan = Tajikistan ■, Asia 26 F8
Taechŏn-ni, S. Korea 35 F14
Taegu, S. Korea 35 G15
Taegwan, N. Korea 35 D13
Taejŏn, S. Korea 35 F14
Tafalla, Spain 19 A5
Tafelbaai, S. Africa 56 E2
Tafermaar, Indonesia 37 F8
Tafí Viejo, Argentina 94 B2
Tafīhān, Iran 45 D7
Taft, Iran 45 D7
Taft, Phil. 37 B7
Taft, Calif., U.S.A. 85 K7
Taft, Tex., U.S.A. 81 M6
Taga Dzong, Bhutan 41 F16
Taganrog, Russia 25 E6
Tagbilaran, Phil. 37 C6
Tagish, Canada 72 A2
Tagish L., Canada 72 A2
Tagliamento →, Italy 20 B5
Tagomago, I. de, Spain 22 B8
Taguatinga, Brazil 93 F10
Tagum, Phil. 37 C7
Tagus = Tejo →, Europe 19 C1
Tahakopa, N.Z. 59 M2
Tahan, Gunong, Malaysia 39 K4
Tahat, Algeria 50 D6
Tāherī, Iran 45 E7
Tahiti, Pac. Oc. 65 J13
Tahoe, L., U.S.A. 84 G6
Tahoe City, U.S.A. 84 F6
Taholah, U.S.A. 84 C2
Tahoua, Niger 50 F6
Tahta, Egypt 51 C11
Tahulandang, Indonesia 37 D7
Tahuna, Indonesia 37 D7
Taï, Ivory C. 50 G3
Tai Shan, China 35 F9
Tai'an, China 35 F9
Taibei, Taiwan 33 D7
Taibique, Canary Is. 22 G2
Taibus Qi, China 34 D8
T'aichung = Taizhong, Taiwan 33 D7
Taieri →, N.Z. 59 M3
Taigu, China 34 F7
Taihang Shan, China 34 G7
Taihape, N.Z. 59 H5
Taihe, China 34 H8
Taikang, China 34 G8
Tailem Bend, Australia 63 F2
Taimyr Peninsula = Taymyr, Poluostrov, Russia 27 B11
Tain, U.K. 12 D4
Tainan, Taiwan 33 D7
Taínaron, Ákra, Greece 21 F10
T'aipei = Taibei, Taiwan 33 D7
Taiping, Malaysia 39 K3
Taipingzhen, China 34 H6
Taita □, Kenya 54 C4
Taita Hills, Kenya 54 C4
Taitao, Pen. de, Chile 96 F2
Taivalkoski, Finland 8 D20
Taiwan ■, Asia 33 D7
Taïyetos Óros, Greece 21 F10
Taiyiba, Israel 47 C4
Taiyuan, China 34 F7
Taizhong, Taiwan 33 D7
Ta'izz, Yemen 46 E3
Tājābād, Iran 45 D7
Tajikistan ■, Asia 26 F8
Tajima, Japan 31 F9
Tajo = Tejo →, Europe 19 C1
Tajrīsh, Iran 45 C6
Tājūrā, Libya 51 B7
Tak, Thailand 38 D2
Takāb, Iran 44 B5
Takachiho, Japan 31 H5
Takada, Japan 31 F9
Takahagi, Japan 31 F10
Takaka, N.Z. 59 J4
Takamatsu, Japan 31 G7
Takaoka, Japan 31 F8
Takapuna, N.Z. 59 G5
Takasaki, Japan 31 F9
Takatsuki, Japan 31 G7
Takaungu, Kenya 54 C4
Takayama, Japan 31 F8
Take-Shima, Japan 31 J5
Takefu, Japan 31 G8
Takengon, Indonesia 36 D1
Takeo, Cambodia 39 G5
Takeo, Japan 31 H5
Tākestān, Iran 45 C6
Taketa, Japan 31 H5
Takh, India 43 C7
Takhman, Cambodia 39 G5
Takikawa, Japan 30 C10
Takla L., Canada 72 B3
Takla Landing, Canada 72 B3
Takla Makan = Taklamakan Shamo, China 28 F12
Taklamakan Shamo, China 28 F12
Taku →, Canada 72 B2
Takum, Nigeria 50 G6
Tal Halāl, Iran 45 D7
Tala, Uruguay 95 C4
Talagante, Chile 94 C1
Talamanca, Cordillera de, Cent. Amer. 88 E3
Talara, Peru 92 D2
Talas, Kirghizia 26 E8
Talâta, Egypt 47 E1
Talaud, Kepulauan, Indonesia 37 D7
Talaud Is. = Talaud, Kepulauan, Indonesia 37 D7
Talavera de la Reina, Spain 19 C3
Talawana, Australia 60 D3
Talayan, Phil. 37 C6
Talbot, C., Australia 60 B4
Talbragar →, Australia 63 E4
Talca, Chile 94 D1
Talca □, Chile 94 D1
Talcahuano, Chile 94 D1
Talcher, India 41 J14
Taldy Kurgan, Kazakhstan 26 E8
Ţālesh, Iran 45 B6
Ţālesh, Kūhhā-ye, Iran 45 B6
Tali Post, Sudan 51 G11
Taliabu, Indonesia 37 E6
Talibon, Phil. 37 B6
Talibong, Ko, Thailand 39 J2
Talihina, U.S.A. 81 H7
Taliwang, Indonesia 36 F5
Tall 'Asūr, Jordan 47 D4
Tall Kalakh, Syria 47 A5
Talladega, U.S.A. 77 J2
Tallahassee, U.S.A. 77 K3
Tallangatta, Australia 63 F4
Tallarook, Australia 63 F4
Tallering Pk., Australia 61 E2
Tallinn, Estonia 24 C3
Tallulah, U.S.A. 81 J9
Talodi, Sudan 51 F11
Talpa de Allende, Mexico 86 C4
Taltal, Chile 94 B1
Taltson →, Canada 72 A6
Talwood, Australia 63 D4
Talyawalka Cr. →, Australia 63 E3
Tam Chau, Vietnam 39 G5
Tam Ky, Vietnam 38 E7
Tam Quan, Vietnam 38 E7
Tama, U.S.A. 80 E8
Tamala, Australia 61 E1
Tamale, Ghana 50 G4
Tamano, Japan 31 G6
Tamanrasset, Algeria 50 D6
Tamaqua, U.S.A. 79 F9
Tamar →, U.K. 11 G3
Tamarang, Australia 63 E5
Tamarinda, Spain 22 B10
Tamashima, Japan 31 G6
Tamaské, Niger 50 F6
Tamaulipas □, Mexico 87 C5
Tamaulipas, Sierra de, Mexico 87 C5
Tamazula, Mexico 86 C3
Tamazunchale, Mexico 87 C5
Tambacounda, Senegal 50 F2
Tambelan, Kepulauan, Indonesia 36 D3
Tambellup, Australia 61 F2
Tambo, Australia 62 C4
Tambo de Mora, Peru 92 F3
Tambohorano, Madag. 57 B7
Tambora, Indonesia 36 F5
Tambov, Russia 24 D7
Tambuku, Indonesia 37 G15
Tamburâ, Sudan 51 G10
Tâmchekket, Mauritania 50 E2
Tamega →, Portugal 19 B1
Tamenglong, India 41 G18
Tamgak, Mts., Niger 50 E6
Tamiahua, L. de, Mexico 87 C5
Tamil Nadu □, India 40 P10
Tamluk, India 43 H12
Tammerfors = Tampere, Finland 9 F17
Tammisaari, Finland 9 F17
Tamo Abu, Pegunungan, Malaysia 36 D5
Tampa, U.S.A. 77 M4
Tampa B., U.S.A. 77 M4
Tampere, Finland 9 F17
Tampico, Mexico 87 C5
Tampin, Malaysia 39 L4
Tamrida = Qādib, Yemen 46 E5
Tamu, Burma 41 G19
Tamworth, Australia 63 E5
Tamworth, U.K. 11 E6
Tamyang, S. Korea 35 G14
Tan An, Vietnam 39 G6
Tana, Norway 8 A20
Tana →, Kenya 54 C5
Tana →, Norway 8 A20
Tana, L., Ethiopia 51 F12
Tana River, Kenya 54 C4
Tanabe, Japan 31 H7
Tanafjorden, Norway 8 A20
Tanaga, Pta., Canary Is. 22 G1
Tanahbala, Indonesia 36 E1
Tanahgrogot, Indonesia 36 E5
Tanahjampea, Indonesia 37 F6
Tanahmasa, Indonesia 36 E1
Tanahmerah, Indonesia 37 F10
Tanakura, Japan 31 F10
Tanami, Australia 60 C4
Tanami Desert, Australia 60 C5
Tanana, U.S.A. 68 B4
Tanana →, U.S.A. 68 B4
Tananarive = Antananarivo, Madag. 57 B8
Tánaro →, Italy 20 B3
Tanbar, Australia 62 D3
Tancheng, China 35 G10
Tanchŏn, N. Korea 35 D15
Tanda, Ut. P., India 43 F10
Tanda, Ut. P., India 43 E8
Tandag, Phil. 37 C7
Tandaia, Tanzania 55 D3
Tandaué, Angola 56 B2
Tandil, Argentina 94 D4
Tandil, Sa. del, Argentina 94 D4
Tandlianwala, Pakistan 42 D5
Tando Adam, Pakistan 42 G3
Tandou L., Australia 63 E3
Tane-ga-Shima, Japan 31 J5
Taneatua, N.Z. 59 H6
Tanen Tong Dan, Burma 38 D2
Tanezrouft, Algeria 50 D5
Tang, Koh, Cambodia 39 G4
Tang Krasang, Cambodia 38 F5
Tanga, Tanzania 54 D4
Tanga □, Tanzania 54 D4
Tanganyika, L., Africa 54 D2
Tanger, Morocco 50 A3
Tangerang, Indonesia 37 G12
Tanggu, China 35 E9
Tanggula Shan, China 32 C4
Tanghe, China 34 H7
Tangier = Tanger, Morocco 50 A3
Tangorin P.O., Australia 62 C3
Tangshan, China 35 E10
Tangtou, China 35 G10
Tanimbar, Kepulauan, Indonesia 37 F8
Tanimbar Is. = Tanimbar, Kepulauan, Indonesia 37 F8
Tanjay, Phil. 37 C6
Tanjong Malim, Malaysia 39 L3
Tanjore = Thanjavur, India 40 P11
Tanjung, Indonesia 36 E5
Tanjungbalai, Indonesia 36 D1
Tanjungbatu, Indonesia 36 D5
Tanjungkarang Telukbetung, Indonesia 36 F3
Tanjungpandan, Indonesia 36 E3
Tanjungpinang, Indonesia 36 D2
Tanjungpriok, Indonesia 37 G12
Tanjungredeb, Indonesia 36 D5
Tanjungselor, Indonesia 36 D5
Tank, Pakistan 42 C4
Tannu-Ola, Russia 27 D10
Tanout, Niger 50 F6
Tanta, Egypt 51 B11
Tantoyuca, Mexico 87 C5
Tantung = Dandong, China 35 D13
Tanunda, Australia 63 E2
Tanzania ■, Africa 54 D3
Tanzilla →, Canada 72 B2
Tao Ko, Thailand 39 G2
Tao'an, China 35 B12
Tao'er He →, China 35 B13
Taolanaro, Madag. 57 D8
Taole, China 34 E4
Taos, U.S.A. 83 H11
Taoudenni, Mali 50 D4
Taourirt, Morocco 50 B4
Tapa Shan = Daba Shan, China 33 C5
Tapachula, Mexico 87 E6
Tapah, Malaysia 39 K3
Tapajós →, Brazil 93 D8
Tapaktuan, Indonesia 36 D1
Tapanui, N.Z. 59 L2
Tapauá →, Brazil 92 E6
Tapeta, Liberia 50 G3
Taphan Hin, Thailand 38 D3
Tapi →, India 40 J8
Tapirapecó, Serra, Venezuela 92 C6
Tappahannock, U.S.A. 76 G7
Tapuaenuku, Mt., N.Z. 59 J4
Tapul Group, Phil. 37 C6
Taqīābād, Iran 45 C8
Ţaqţaq, Iraq 44 C5
Taquara, Brazil 95 B5
Taquari →, Brazil 92 G7
Tara, Australia 63 D5
Tara, Canada 78 B3
Tara, Russia 26 D8
Tara, Zambia 55 F2
Tara →, Montenegro, Yug. 21 C8
Tara →, Russia 26 D8
Tarabagatay, Khrebet, Kazakhstan 26 E9
Tarābulus, Lebanon 47 A4
Tarābulus, Libya 51 B7
Tarajalejo, Canary Is. 22 F5
Tarakan, Indonesia 36 D5
Tarakit, Mt., Kenya 54 B4
Taralga, Australia 63 E4
Tarama-Jima, Japan 31 M2
Taranagar, India 42 E6
Taranaki □, N.Z. 59 H5
Taranga, India 42 H5
Taranga Hill, India 42 H5
Táranto, Italy 20 D7

Táranto, G. di, *Italy* 20 D7
Tarapacá, *Colombia* 92 D5
Tarapacá □, *Chile* 94 A2
Tararua Ra., *N.Z.* 59 J5
Tarauacá, *Brazil* 92 E4
Tarauacá →, *Brazil* 92 E5
Tarawera, *N.Z.* 59 H6
Tarawera L., *N.Z.* 59 H6
Tarbat Ness, *U.K.* 12 D5
Tarbela Dam, *Pakistan* 42 B5
Tarbert, *Strath., U.K.* 12 F3
Tarbert, *W. Isles, U.K.* 12 D2
Tarbes, *France* 18 E4
Tarboro, *U.S.A.* 77 H7
Tarbrax, *Australia* 62 C3
Tarcoola, *Australia* 63 E1
Tarcoon, *Australia* 63 E4
Taree, *Australia* 63 E5
Tarentaise, *France* 18 D7
Tarfaya, *Morocco* 50 C2
Tarifa, *Spain* 19 D3
Tarija, *Bolivia* 94 A3
Tarija □, *Bolivia* 94 A3
Tariku →, *Indonesia* 37 E9
Tarim Basin = Tarim Pendi, *China* 32 B3
Tarim He →, *China* 32 C3
Tarim Pendi, *China* 32 B3
Tarime □, *Tanzania* 54 C3
Taritatu →, *Indonesia* 37 E9
Tarka →, *S. Africa* 56 E4
Tarkastad, *S. Africa* 56 E4
Tarkhankut, Mys, *Ukraine* 25 E5
Tarko Sale, *Russia* 26 C8
Tarkwa, *Ghana* 50 G4
Tarlac, *Phil.* 37 A6
Tarlton Downs, *Australia* 62 C2
Tarma, *Peru* 92 F3
Tarn □, *France* 18 E5
Tarn →, *France* 18 D4
Tarn-et-Garonne □, *France* 18 D4
Tarnów, *Poland* 17 C10
Tarnowskie Góry, *Poland* 17 C9
Taroom, *Australia* 63 D4
Taroudannt, *Morocco* 50 B3
Tarpon Springs, *U.S.A.* 77 L4
Tarragona, *Spain* 19 B6
Tarrasa, *Spain* 19 B7
Tarrytown, *U.S.A.* 79 E11
Tarshiha = Me'ona, *Israel* 47 B4
Tarso Emissi, *Chad* 51 D8
Tarsus, *Turkey* 25 G5
Tartagal, *Argentina* 94 A3
Tartu, *Estonia* 24 C4
Tarṭūs, *Syria* 44 C2
Tarumizu, *Japan* 31 J5
Tarutao, Ko, *Thailand* 39 J2
Tarutung, *Indonesia* 36 D1
Tasāwah, *Libya* 51 C7
Taschereau, *Canada* 70 C4
Taseko →, *Canada* 72 C4
Tash-Kumyr, *Kirghizia* 26 E8
Tashauz, *Turkmenistan* 26 E6
Tashi Chho Dzong = Thimphu, *Bhutan* 41 F16
Tashkent, *Uzbekistan* 26 E7
Tashtagol, *Russia* 26 D9
Tasikmalaya, *Indonesia* 37 G13
Tåsjön, *Sweden* 8 D13
Taskan, *Russia* 27 C16
Tasman B., *N.Z.* 59 J4
Tasman Mts., *N.Z.* 59 J4
Tasman Pen., *Australia* 62 G4
Tasman Sea, *Pac. Oc.* 64 L8
Tasmania □, *Australia* 62 G4
Tasu Sd., *Canada* 72 C2
Tatar Republic □, *Russia* 24 C9
Tatarsk, *Russia* 26 D8
Tateyama, *Japan* 31 G9
Tathlina L., *Canada* 72 A5
Tathra, *Australia* 63 F4
Tatinnai L., *Canada* 73 A9
Tatnam, C., *Canada* 73 B10
Tatra = Tatry, *Czech.* 17 D10
Tatry, *Czech.* 17 D10
Tatsuno, *Japan* 31 G7
Tatta, *Pakistan* 42 G2
Tatuí, *Brazil* 95 A6
Tatum, *U.S.A.* 81 J3
Tat'ung = Datong, *China* 34 D7
Tatvan, *Turkey* 25 G7
Taubaté, *Brazil* 95 A6
Tauern, *Austria* 16 E6
Taumarunui, *N.Z.* 59 H5
Taumaturgo, *Brazil* 92 E4
Taung, *S. Africa* 56 D3
Taungdwingyi, *Burma* 41 J19
Taunggyi, *Burma* 41 J20
Taungup, *Burma* 41 K19
Taungup Pass, *Burma* 41 K19
Taungup Taunggya, *Burma* 41 K18
Taunsa Barrage, *Pakistan* 42 D4
Taunton, *U.K.* 11 F4
Taunton, *U.S.A.* 79 E13
Taunus, *Germany* 16 C4
Taupo, *N.Z.* 59 H6
Taupo, L., *N.Z.* 59 H5
Tauranga, *N.Z.* 59 G6
Tauranga Harb., *N.Z.* 59 G6
Taurianova, *Italy* 20 E7
Taurus Mts. = Toros Dağları, *Turkey* 25 G5
Tavda, *Russia* 26 D7
Tavda →, *Russia* 26 D7
Taveta, *Tanzania* 54 C4
Taveuni, *Fiji* 59 C9
Tavira, *Portugal* 19 D2
Tavistock, *Canada* 78 C4
Tavistock, *U.K.* 11 G3
Tavoy, *Burma* 38 E2
Taw →, *U.K.* 11 F3
Tawas City, *U.S.A.* 76 C4
Tawau, *Malaysia* 36 D5
Tawitawi, *Phil.* 37 B6
Taxila, *Pakistan* 42 C5
Tay →, *U.K.* 12 E5
Tay, Firth of, *U.K.* 12 E5
Tay, L., *Australia* 61 F3
Tay, L., *U.K.* 12 E4
Tay Ninh, *Vietnam* 39 G6
Tayabamba, *Peru* 92 E3
Taylakovy, *Russia* 26 D8
Taylor, *Canada* 72 B4
Taylor, *Nebr., U.S.A.* 80 E5
Taylor, *Pa., U.S.A.* 79 E9
Taylor, *Tex., U.S.A.* 81 K6
Taylor Mt., *U.S.A.* 83 J10
Taylorville, *U.S.A.* 80 F10
Taymā, *Si. Arabia* 44 E3
Taymyr, Oz., *Russia* 27 B11
Taymyr, Poluostrov, *Russia* 27 B11
Tayport, *U.K.* 12 E6
Tayshet, *Russia* 27 D10
Tayside □, *U.K.* 12 E5
Taytay, *Phil.* 37 B5
Taz →, *Russia* 26 C8
Taza, *Morocco* 50 B4
Tāzah Khurmātū, *Iraq* 44 C5
Tazawa-Ko, *Japan* 30 E10
Tazin L., *Canada* 73 B7
Tazovskiy, *Russia* 26 C8
Tbilisi, *Georgia* 25 F7
Tchad = Chad ■, *Africa* 51 E8
Tchad, L., *Chad* 51 F7
Tch'eng-tou = Chengdu, *China* 32 C5
Tchentlo L., *Canada* 72 B4
Tchibanga, *Gabon* 52 E2
Tch'ong-k'ing = Chongqing, *China* 32 D5
Te Anau, L., *N.Z.* 59 L1
Te Aroha, *N.Z.* 59 G5
Te Awamutu, *N.Z.* 59 H5
Te Kuiti, *N.Z.* 59 H5
Te Puke, *N.Z.* 59 G6
Te Waewae B., *N.Z.* 59 M1
Tea Tree, *Australia* 62 C1
Teague, *U.S.A.* 81 K6
Teapa, *Mexico* 87 D6
Tebakang, *Malaysia* 36 D4
Tébessa, *Algeria* 50 A6
Tebicuary →, *Paraguay* 94 B4
Tebingtinggi, *Indonesia* 36 D1
Tecate, *Mexico* 85 N10
Tecomán, *Mexico* 86 D4
Tecopa, *U.S.A.* 85 K10
Tecoripa, *Mexico* 86 B3
Tecuala, *Mexico* 86 C3
Tecuci, *Romania* 17 F13
Tecumseh, *U.S.A.* 76 D4
Tedzhen, *Turkmenistan* 26 F7
Tees →, *U.K.* 10 C6
Teesside, *U.K.* 10 C6
Teeswater, *Canada* 78 C3
Tefé, *Brazil* 92 D6
Tegal, *Indonesia* 37 G13
Tegelen, *Neths.* 15 C6
Teghra, *India* 43 G11
Tegid, L. = Bala, L., *U.K.* 10 E4
Tegina, *Nigeria* 50 F6
Tegucigalpa, *Honduras* 88 D2
Tehachapi, *U.S.A.* 85 K8
Tehachapi Mts., *U.S.A.* 85 L8
Tehrān, *Iran* 45 C6
Tehuacán, *Mexico* 87 D5
Tehuantepec, *Mexico* 87 D5
Tehuantepec, G. de, *Mexico* 87 D5
Tehuantepec, Istmo de, *Mexico* 87 D6
Teide, *Canary Is.* 22 F3
Teifi →, *U.K.* 11 E3
Teign →, *U.K.* 11 G4
Teignmouth, *U.K.* 11 G4
Tejo →, *Europe* 19 C1
Tejon Pass, *U.S.A.* 85 L8
Tekamah, *U.S.A.* 80 E6
Tekapo, L., *N.Z.* 59 K3
Tekax, *Mexico* 87 C7
Tekeli, *Kazakhstan* 26 E8
Tekirdağ, *Turkey* 21 D12
Tekkali, *India* 41 K14
Tekoa, *U.S.A.* 82 C5
Tel Aviv-Yafo, *Israel* 47 C3
Tel Lakhish, *Israel* 47 D3
Tel Megiddo, *Israel* 47 C4
Tela, *Honduras* 88 C2
Telanaipura = Jambi, *Indonesia* 36 E2
Telavi, *Georgia* 25 F8
Telde, *Canary Is.* 22 G4
Telegraph Creek, *Canada* 72 B2
Telemark fylke □, *Norway* 9 G10
Telén, *Argentina* 94 D2
Teleng, *Iran* 45 E9
Teles Pires →, *Brazil* 92 E7
Telescope Peak, *U.S.A.* 85 J9
Telford, *U.K.* 10 E5
Télimélé, *Guinea* 50 F2
Telkwa, *Canada* 72 C3
Tell City, *U.S.A.* 76 G2
Tellicherry, *India* 40 P9
Telluride, *U.S.A.* 83 H10
Teloloapán, *Mexico* 87 D5
Telpos Iz, *Russia* 24 B10
Telsen, *Argentina* 96 E3
Teluk Anson, *Malaysia* 39 K3
Teluk Betung = Tanjungkarang Telukbetung, *Indonesia* 36 F3
Teluk Intan = Teluk Anson, *Malaysia* 39 K3
Telukbutun, *Indonesia* 39 K7
Telukdalem, *Indonesia* 36 D1
Tema, *Ghana* 50 G5
Temanggung, *Indonesia* 37 G14
Temapache, *Mexico* 87 C5
Temax, *Mexico* 87 C7
Temba, *S. Africa* 57 D4
Tembe, *Zaïre* 54 C2
Temblor Ra., *U.S.A.* 85 K7
Teme →, *U.K.* 11 E5
Temecula, *U.S.A.* 85 M9
Temerloh, *Malaysia* 39 L4
Temir, *Kazakhstan* 26 E6
Temirtau, *Kazakhstan* 26 D8
Temirtau, *Russia* 26 D9
Témiscaming, *Canada* 70 C4
Temma, *Australia* 62 G3
Temora, *Australia* 63 E4
Temosachic, *Mexico* 86 B3
Tempe, *U.S.A.* 83 K8
Tempe Downs, *Australia* 60 D5
Tempiute, *U.S.A.* 84 H11
Temple, *U.S.A.* 81 K6
Temple B., *Australia* 62 A3
Templemore, *Ireland* 13 D4
Templeton, *U.S.A.* 84 K6
Templeton →, *Australia* 62 C2
Tempoal, *Mexico* 87 C5
Temuco, *Chile* 96 D2
Temuka, *N.Z.* 59 L3
Tenabo, *Mexico* 87 C6
Tenaha, *U.S.A.* 81 K7
Tenali, *India* 40 L12
Tenancingo, *Mexico* 87 D5
Tenango, *Mexico* 87 D5
Tenasserim, *Burma* 39 F2
Tenasserim □, *Burma* 38 F2
Tenby, *U.K.* 11 F3
Tendaho, *Ethiopia* 46 E3
Tenerife, *Canary Is.* 22 F3
Tenerife, Pico, *Canary Is.* 22 G1
Teng Xian, *China* 35 G9
Tengah □, *Indonesia* 37 E6
Tengah Kepulauan, *Indonesia* 36 F5
Tengchong, *China* 32 D4
Tengchowfu = Penglai, *China* 35 F11
Tenggara □, *Indonesia* 37 E6
Tenggarong, *Indonesia* 36 E5
Tenggol, P., *Malaysia* 39 K4
Tengiz, Ozero, *Kazakhstan* 26 D7
Tenino, *U.S.A.* 84 D4
Tenkasi, *India* 40 Q10
Tenke, *Shaba, Zaïre* 55 E2
Tenke, *Shaba, Zaïre* 55 E2
Tenkodogo, *Burkina Faso* 50 F4
Tennant Creek, *Australia* 62 B1
Tennessee □, *U.S.A.* 75 C9
Tennessee →, *U.S.A.* 76 G1
Tennille, *U.S.A.* 77 J4
Teno, Pta. de, *Canary Is.* 22 F3
Tenom, *Malaysia* 36 C5
Tenosique, *Mexico* 87 D6
Tenryū-Gawa →, *Japan* 31 G8
Tent L., *Canada* 73 A7
Tenterfield, *Australia* 63 D5
Teófilo Otoni, *Brazil* 93 G10
Teotihuacán, *Mexico* 87 D5
Tepa, *Indonesia* 37 F7
Tepalcatepec →, *Mexico* 86 D4
Tepehuanes, *Mexico* 86 B3
Tepetongo, *Mexico* 86 C4
Tepic, *Mexico* 86 C4
Teplice, *Czech.* 16 C6
Tepoca, C., *Mexico* 86 A2
Tequila, *Mexico* 86 C4
Ter →, *Spain* 19 A7
Ter Apel, *Neths.* 15 B7
Téra, *Niger* 50 F5
Teraina, *Kiribati* 65 G11
Téramo, *Italy* 20 C5
Terang, *Australia* 63 F3
Tercero →, *Argentina* 94 C3
Terek →, *Russia* 25 F8
Teresina, *Brazil* 93 E10
Terewah, L., *Australia* 63 D4
Terhazza, *Mali* 50 D3
Teridgerie Cr. →, *Australia* 63 E4
Termez, *Uzbekistan* 26 F7
Términos, L. de, *Mexico* 87 D6
Térmoli, *Italy* 20 D6
Ternate, *Indonesia* 37 D7
Terneuzen, *Neths.* 15 C3
Terney, *Russia* 27 E14
Terni, *Italy* 20 C5
Terowie, *N.S.W., Australia* 63 E4
Terowie, *S. Austral., Australia* 63 E2
Terra Bella, *U.S.A.* 85 K7
Terrace, *Canada* 72 C3
Terrace Bay, *Canada* 70 C2
Terracina, *Italy* 20 D5
Terralba, *Italy* 20 E3
Terranova = Ólbia, *Italy* 20 D3
Terre Haute, *U.S.A.* 76 F2
Terrebonne B., *U.S.A.* 81 L9
Terrell, *U.S.A.* 81 J6
Terrenceville, *Canada* 71 C9
Terrick Terrick, *Australia* 62 C4
Terry, *U.S.A.* 80 B2
Terschelling, *Neths.* 15 A5
Teruel, *Spain* 19 B5
Tervola, *Finland* 8 C18
Teryaweyna L., *Australia* 63 E3
Tešanj, *Bos. & H., Yug.* 21 B7
Teshio, *Japan* 30 B10
Teshio-Gawa →, *Japan* 30 B10
Tesiyn Gol →, *Mongolia* 32 A4
Teslin, *Canada* 72 A2
Teslin →, *Canada* 72 A2
Teslin L., *Canada* 72 A2
Tessalit, *Mali* 50 D5
Tessaoua, *Niger* 50 F6
Test →, *U.K.* 11 F6
Tetachuck L., *Canada* 72 C3
Tetas, Pta., *Chile* 94 A1
Tete, *Mozam.* 55 F3
Tete □, *Mozam.* 55 F3
Teteven, *Bulgaria* 21 C11
Tethul →, *Canada* 72 A6
Teton →, *U.S.A.* 82 C8
Tétouan, *Morocco* 50 A3
Tetovo, *Macedonia, Yug.* 21 C9
Tetuán = Tétouan, *Morocco* 50 A3
Tetyukhe Pristan, *Russia* 30 B7
Teuco →, *Argentina* 94 B3
Teulon, *Canada* 73 C9
Teun, *Indonesia* 37 F7
Teutoburger Wald, *Germany* 16 B4
Tevere →, *Italy* 20 D5
Teverya, *Israel* 47 C4
Teviot →, *U.K.* 12 F6
Tewantin, *Australia* 63 D5
Tewkesbury, *U.K.* 11 F5
Texada I., *Canada* 72 D4
Texarkana, *Ark., U.S.A.* 81 J8
Texarkana, *Tex., U.S.A.* 81 J7
Texas, *Australia* 63 D5
Texas □, *U.S.A.* 81 K5
Texas City, *U.S.A.* 81 L7
Texel, *Neths.* 15 A4
Texhoma, *U.S.A.* 81 G4
Texline, *U.S.A.* 81 G3
Texoma L., *U.S.A.* 81 J6
Tezin, *Afghan.* 42 B3
Teziutlán, *Mexico* 87 D5
Tezpur, *India* 41 F18
Tezzeron L., *Canada* 72 C4
Tha-anne →, *Canada* 73 A10
Tha Deua, *Laos* 38 D4
Tha Deua, *Laos* 38 C3
Tha Pla, *Thailand* 38 D3
Tha Rua, *Thailand* 38 E3
Tha Sala, *Thailand* 39 H2
Tha Song Yang, *Thailand* 38 D1
Thaba Nchu, *S. Africa* 56 D4
Thaba Putsoa, *Lesotho* 57 D4
Thabana Ntlenyana, *Lesotho* 57 D4
Thabazimbi, *S. Africa* 57 C4
Thai Binh, *Vietnam* 38 B6
Thai Hoa, *Vietnam* 38 C5
Thai Muang, *Thailand* 39 H2
Thai Nguyen, *Vietnam* 38 B5
Thailand ■, *Asia* 38 E4
Thailand, G. of, *Asia* 39 G3
Thakhek, *Laos* 38 D5
Thal, *Pakistan* 42 C4
Thal Desert, *Pakistan* 42 D4
Thala La, *Burma* 41 E20
Thalabarivat, *Cambodia* 38 F5
Thallon, *Australia* 63 D4
Thame →, *U.K.* 11 F6
Thames, *N.Z.* 59 G5
Thames →, *Canada* 70 D3
Thames →, *U.K.* 11 F8
Thames →, *U.S.A.* 79 E12
Thamesford, *Canada* 78 C3
Thamesville, *Canada* 78 D3
Than Uyen, *Vietnam* 38 B4
Thane, *India* 40 K8
Thanesar, *India* 42 D7
Thanet, I. of, *U.K.* 11 F9
Thangoo, *Australia* 60 C3
Thangool, *Australia* 62 C5
Thanh Hoa, *Vietnam* 38 C5
Thanh Hung, *Vietnam* 39 H5
Thanh Pho Ho Chi Minh = Phanh Bho Ho Chi Minh, *Vietnam* 39 G6
Thanh Thuy, *Vietnam* 38 A5
Thanjavur, *India* 40 P11
Thap Sakae, *Thailand* 39 G2
Thap Than, *Thailand* 38 E2
Thar Desert, *India* 42 F4
Tharad, *India* 42 G4
Thargomindah, *Australia* 63 D3
Tharrawaddy, *Burma* 41 L19
Tharthar, W. →, *Iraq* 44 C4
Thásos, *Greece* 21 D11
That Khe, *Vietnam* 38 A6
Thatcher, *Ariz., U.S.A.* 83 K9
Thatcher, *Colo., U.S.A.* 81 G2
Thaton, *Burma* 41 L20
Thaungdut, *Burma* 41 G19
Thayer, *U.S.A.* 81 G9
Thayetmyo, *Burma* 41 K19
Thazi, *Burma* 41 J20
The Alberga →, *Australia* 63 D2
The Bight, *Bahamas* 89 B4
The Coorong, *Australia* 63 F2
The Dalles, *U.S.A.* 82 D3
The English Company's Is., *Australia* 62 A2
The Frome →, *Australia* 63 D2
The Grampians, *Australia* 63 F3
The Great Divide = Great Dividing Ra., *Australia* 62 C4
The Hague = 's-Gravenhage, *Neths.* 15 B4
The Hamilton →, *Australia* 63 D2
The Macumba →, *Australia* 63 D2
The Neales →, *Australia* 63 D2
The Officer →, *Australia* 61 E5
The Pas, *Canada* 73 C8
The Range, *Zimbabwe* 55 F3
The Rock, *Australia* 63 F4
The Salt L., *Australia* 63 E3
The Stevenson →, *Australia* 63 D2
The Warburton →, *Australia* 63 D2
Thebes = Thívai, *Greece* 21 E10
Thedford, *Canada* 78 C3
Thedford, *U.S.A.* 80 E4
Theebine, *Australia* 63 D5
Thekulthili L., *Canada* 73 A7
Thelon →, *Canada* 73 A8
Theodore, *Australia* 62 C5
Thepha, *Thailand* 39 J3
Theresa, *U.S.A.* 79 B9
Thermaïkos Kólpos, *Greece* 21 D10
Thermopolis, *U.S.A.* 82 E9
Thermopylae P., *Greece* 21 E10
Thessalía □, *Greece* 21 E9
Thessalon, *Canada* 70 C3
Thessaloníki, *Greece* 21 D10
Thessaloníki, Gulf of = Thermaïkos Kólpos, *Greece* 21 D10
Thessaly = Thessalía □, *Greece* 21 E9
Thetford, *U.K.* 11 E8
Thetford Mines, *Canada* 71 C5
Theun →, *Laos* 38 C5
Theunissen, *S. Africa* 56 D4
Thevenard, *Australia* 63 E1
Thibodaux, *U.S.A.* 81 L9
Thicket Portage, *Canada* 73 B9
Thief River Falls, *U.S.A.* 80 A6
Thiel Mts., *Antarctica* 5 E16
Thiérache, *France* 18 B5
Thies, *Senegal* 50 F1
Thika, *Kenya* 54 C4
Thikombia, *Fiji* 59 B9
Thimphu, *Bhutan* 41 F16
þingvallavatn, *Iceland* 8 D3
Thionville, *France* 18 B7
Thíra, *Greece* 21 F11
Thirsk, *U.K.* 10 C6
Thisted, *Denmark* 9 H10
Thistle I., *Australia* 63 F2
Thívai, *Greece* 21 E10
þjórsá →, *Iceland* 8 E3
Thlewiaza →, *Man., Canada* 73 B8
Thlewiaza →, *N.W.T., Canada* 73 A10
Thmar Puok, *Cambodia* 38 F4
Tho Vinh, *Vietnam* 38 C5
Thoa →, *Canada* 73 A7
Thoen, *Thailand* 38 D2
Thoeng, *Thailand* 38 C3
Tholdi, *Pakistan* 43 B7
Thomas, *Okla., U.S.A.* 81 H5
Thomas, *W. Va., U.S.A.* 76 F6
Thomas, L., *Australia* 63 D2
Thomaston, *U.S.A.* 77 J3
Thomasville, *Ala., U.S.A.* 77 K2
Thomasville, *Ga., U.S.A.* 77 K3
Thomasville, *N.C., U.S.A.* 77 H5
Thompson, *Canada* 73 B9
Thompson, *U.S.A.* 83 G9
Thompson →, *Canada* 72 C4
Thompson →, *U.S.A.* 80 F8
Thompson Falls, *U.S.A.* 82 C6
Thompson Landing, *Canada* 73 A6
Thompson Pk., *U.S.A.* 82 F2
Thomson's Falls = Nyahururu, *Kenya* 54 B4
Thon Buri, *Thailand* 39 F3
þórisvatn, *Iceland* 8 D4
þorlákshöfn, *Iceland* 8 E3
Thornaby on Tees, *U.K.* 10 C6
Thornbury, *Canada* 78 B4
Thorold, *Canada* 78 C5
þórshöfn, *Iceland* 8 C6
Thouin, C., *Australia* 60 D2
Thousand Oaks, *U.S.A.* 85 L8
Thrace = Thráki □, *Greece* 21 D11
Thráki □, *Greece* 21 D11
Three Forks, *U.S.A.* 82 D8
Three Hills, *Canada* 72 C6
Three Hummock I., *Australia* 62 G3
Three Lakes, *U.S.A.* 80 C10
Three Points, C., *Ghana* 50 H4
Three Rivers, *Australia* 61 E2
Three Rivers, *Calif., U.S.A.* 84 J8
Three Rivers, *Tex., U.S.A.* 81 L5
Three Sisters, *U.S.A.* 82 D3
Throssell, L., *Australia* 61 E3
Throssell Ra., *Australia* 60 D3
Thuan Hoa, *Vietnam* 39 H5
Thubun Lakes, *Canada* 73 A6
Thuin, *Belgium* 15 D4
Thule, *Greenland* 4 B4
Thun, *Switz.* 16 E3

Thundelarra, *Australia* 61 E2
Thunder B., *U.S.A.* 78 B1
Thunder Bay, *Canada* 70 C2
Thung Song, *Thailand* 39 H2
Thunkar, *Bhutan* 41 F17
Thuong Tra, *Vietnam* 38 D6
Thüringer Wald, *Germany* 16 C5
Thurles, *Ireland* 13 D4
Thurloo Downs, *Australia* 63 D3
Thursday I., *Australia* 62 A3
Thurso, *Canada* 70 C4
Thurso, *U.K.* 12 C5
Thurston I., *Antarctica* 5 D16
Thutade L., *Canada* 72 B3
Thylungra, *Australia* 63 D3
Thyolo, *Malawi* 55 F4
Thysville = Mbanza Ngungu, *Zaïre* 52 F2
Tia, *Australia* 63 E5
Tian Shan, *China* 32 B3
Tianjin, *China* 35 E9
Tianshui, *China* 34 G3
Tianzhen, *China* 34 D8
Tianzhuangtai, *China* 35 D12
Tiaret, *Algeria* 50 A5
Tiassalé, *Ivory C.* 50 G4
Tibagi, *Brazil* 95 A5
Tibagi —►, *Brazil* 95 A5
Tibati, *Cameroon* 51 G7
Tiber = Tevere —►, *Italy* 20 D5
Tiber Res., *U.S.A.* 82 B8
Tiberias = Teverya, *Israel* 47 C4
Tiberias, L. = Yam Kinneret, *Israel* 47 C4
Tibesti, *Chad* 51 D8
Tibet = Xizang □, *China* 32 C3
Tibnī, *Syria* 44 C3
Tibooburra, *Australia* 63 D3
Tiburón, *Mexico* 86 B2
Tîchît, *Mauritania* 50 E3
Ticino —►, *Italy* 16 F4
Ticonderoga, *U.S.A.* 79 C11
Ticul, *Mexico* 87 C7
Tiddim, *Burma* 41 H18
Tidjikja, *Mauritania* 50 E2
Tidore, *Indonesia* 37 D7
Tiel, *Neths.* 15 C5
Tiel, *Senegal* 50 F1
Tieling, *China* 35 C12
Tielt, *Belgium* 15 D3
Tien Shan, *Asia* 28 E11
Tien-tsin = Tianjin, *China* 35 E9
Tien Yen, *Vietnam* 38 B6
T'ienching = Tianjin, *China* 35 E9
Tienen, *Belgium* 15 D4
Tientsin = Tianjin, *China* 35 E9
Tierra Amarilla, *Chile* 94 B1
Tierra Amarilla, *U.S.A.* 83 H10
Tierra Colorada, *Mexico* 87 D5
Tierra de Campos, *Spain* 19 A3
Tierra del Fuego, I. Gr. de, *Argentina* 96 G3
Tiétar —►, *Spain* 19 C2
Tieté —►, *Brazil* 95 A5
Tieyon, *Australia* 63 D1
Tiffin, *U.S.A.* 76 E4
Tiflis = Tbilisi, *Georgia* 25 F7
Tifton, *U.S.A.* 77 K4
Tifu, *Indonesia* 37 E7
Tigil, *Russia* 27 D16
Tignish, *Canada* 71 C7
Tigre —►, *Peru* 92 D4
Tigris = Dijlah, Nahr —►, *Asia* 44 D5
Tigyaing, *Burma* 41 H20
Tîh, Gebel el, *Egypt* 51 C11
Tijuana, *Mexico* 85 N9
Tikal, *Guatemala* 88 C2
Tikamgarh, *India* 43 G8
Tikhoretsk, *Russia* 25 E7
Tikrīt, *Iraq* 44 C4
Tiksi, *Russia* 27 B13
Tilamuta, *Indonesia* 37 D6
Tilburg, *Neths.* 15 C5
Tilbury, *Canada* 70 D3
Tilbury, *U.K.* 11 F8
Tilcara, *Argentina* 94 A2
Tilden, *Nebr., U.S.A.* 80 D6
Tilden, *Tex., U.S.A.* 81 L5
Tilhar, *India* 43 F8
Tilichiki, *Russia* 27 C17
Tilissos, *Greece* 23 D7
Till —►, *U.K.* 10 B5
Tillabéri, *Niger* 50 F5
Tillamook, *U.S.A.* 82 D2
Tillsonburg, *Canada* 70 D3
Tillyeria □, *Cyprus* 23 D11
Tilos, *Greece* 21 F12
Tilpa, *Australia* 63 E3
Tilsit = Sovetsk, *France* 24 C3
Tilt —►, *U.K.* 12 E5
Tilton, *U.S.A.* 79 C13
Timagami L., *Canada* 70 C3
Timanskiy Kryazh, *Russia* 24 A9
Timaru, *N.Z.* 59 L3
Timau, *Kenya* 54 B4
Timbákion, *Greece* 23 D6
Timbedgha, *Mauritania* 50 E3
Timber Lake, *U.S.A.* 80 C4
Timber Mt., *U.S.A.* 84 H10
Timboon, *Australia* 63 F3
Timbuktu = Tombouctou, *Mali* 50 E4
Timi, *Cyprus* 23 E11
Timimoun, *Algeria* 50 C5
Timişoara, *Romania* 17 F10
Timmins, *Canada* 70 C3
Timok —►, *Serbia, Yug.* 21 B10
Timon, *Brazil* 93 E10
Timor, *Indonesia* 37 F7
Timor □, *Indonesia* 37 F7
Timor Sea, *Ind. Oc.* 60 B4
Tin Mt., *U.S.A.* 84 J9
Tinaca Pt., *Phil.* 37 C7
Tinajo, *Canary Is.* 22 E6
Tindouf, *Algeria* 50 C3
Tinggi, Pulau, *Malaysia* 39 L5
Tingo Maria, *Peru* 92 E3
Tinh Bien, *Vietnam* 39 G5
Tinjoub, *Algeria* 50 C3
Tinkurrin, *Australia* 61 F2
Tinnevelly = Tirunelveli, *India* 40 Q10
Tinnoset, *Norway* 9 G10
Tinogasta, *Argentina* 94 B2
Tinos, *Greece* 21 F11
Tintina, *Argentina* 94 B3
Tintinara, *Australia* 63 F3
Tioga, *U.S.A.* 78 E7
Tioman, Pulau, *Malaysia* 39 L5
Tionesta, *U.S.A.* 78 E5
Tipongpani, *India* 41 F19
Tipperary, *Ireland* 13 D3
Tipperary □, *Ireland* 13 D4
Tipton, *U.K.* 11 E5
Tipton, *Calif., U.S.A.* 83 H4
Tipton, *Ind., U.S.A.* 76 E2
Tipton, *Iowa, U.S.A.* 80 E9
Tipton, Mt., *U.S.A.* 85 K12
Tiptonville, *U.S.A.* 81 G10
Tīrān, *Iran* 45 C6
Tirana, *Albania* 21 D8
Tiranë = Tirana, *Albania* 21 D8
Tiraspol, *Moldavia* 25 E4
Tirat Karmel, *Israel* 47 C3
Tirebolu, *Turkey* 25 F6
Tiree, *U.K.* 12 E2
Tîrgovişte, *Romania* 17 F12
Tîrgu-Jiu, *Romania* 17 F11
Tîrgu Mureş, *Romania* 17 E12
Tirich Mir, *Pakistan* 40 A7
Tirodi, *India* 40 J11
Tirol □, *Austria* 16 E5
Tirso —►, *Italy* 20 E3
Tiruchchirappalli, *India* 40 P11
Tirunelveli, *India* 40 Q10
Tirupati, *India* 40 N11
Tiruppur, *India* 40 P10
Tiruvannamalai, *India* 40 N11
Tisa —►, *Hungary* 17 E10
Tisa —►, *Serbia, Yug.* 17 F10
Tisdale, *Canada* 73 C8
Tishomingo, *U.S.A.* 81 H6
Tisza = Tisa —►, *Hungary* 17 E10
Tit-Ary, *Russia* 27 B13
Tithwal, *Pakistan* 43 B5
Titicaca, L., *S. Amer.* 92 G5
Titograd, *Montenegro, Yug.* 21 C8
Titov Veles, *Macedonia, Yug.* 21 D9
Titovo Užice, *Serbia, Yug.* 21 C8
Titule, *Zaïre* 54 B2
Titusville, *Fla., U.S.A.* 77 L5
Titusville, *Pa., U.S.A.* 78 E5
Tivaouane, *Senegal* 50 F1
Tiverton, *U.K.* 11 G4
Tívoli, *Italy* 20 D5
Tizi-Ouzou, *Algeria* 50 A5
Tizimín, *Mexico* 87 C7
Tiznit, *Morocco* 50 C3
Tjeggelvas, *Sweden* 8 C14
Tjirebon = Cirebon, *Indonesia* 37 G13
Tlacotalpan, *Mexico* 87 D5
Tlahualilo, *Mexico* 86 B4
Tlaquepaque, *Mexico* 86 C4
Tlaxcala, *Mexico* 87 D5
Tlaxcala □, *Mexico* 87 D5
Tlaxiaco, *Mexico* 87 D5
Tlell, *Canada* 72 C2
Tlemcen, *Algeria* 50 B4
Tmassah, *Libya* 51 C8
To Bong, *Vietnam* 38 F7
Toad —►, *Canada* 72 B4
Toamasina, *Madag.* 57 B8
Toamasina □, *Madag.* 57 B8
Toay, *Argentina* 94 D3
Toba, *Japan* 31 G8
Toba Kakar, *Pakistan* 42 D3
Toba Tek Singh, *Pakistan* 42 D5
Tobago, *W. Indies* 89 D7
Tobelo, *Indonesia* 37 D7
Tobermorey, *Australia* 62 C2
Tobermory, *Canada* 70 C3
Tobermory, *U.K.* 12 E2
Tobin, *U.S.A.* 84 F5
Tobin, L., *Australia* 60 D4
Tobin L., *Canada* 73 C8
Toboali, *Indonesia* 36 E3
Tobol, *Kazakhstan* 26 D7
Tobol —►, *Russia* 26 D7
Toboli, *Indonesia* 37 E6
Tobolsk, *Russia* 26 D7
Tobruk = Tubruq, *Libya* 51 B9
Tobyhanna, *U.S.A.* 79 E9
Tocantinópolis, *Brazil* 93 E9
Tocantins □, *Brazil* 93 F9
Tocantins —►, *Brazil* 93 D9
Toccoa, *U.S.A.* 77 H4
Tochigi, *Japan* 31 F9
Tochigi □, *Japan* 31 F9
Tocopilla, *Chile* 94 A1
Tocumwal, *Australia* 63 F4
Tocuyo —►, *Venezuela* 92 A5
Todd —►, *Australia* 62 C2
Todeli, *Indonesia* 37 E6
Todenyang, *Kenya* 54 B4
Todos os Santos, B. de, *Brazil* 93 F11
Todos Santos, *Mexico* 86 C2
Tofield, *Canada* 72 C6
Tofino, *Canada* 72 D3
Tofua, *Tonga* 59 D11
Tōgane, *Japan* 31 G10
Togba, *Mauritania* 50 E2
Togian, Kepulauan, *Indonesia* 37 E6
Togliatti, *Russia* 24 D8
Togo ■, *W. Afr.* 50 G5
Togtoh, *China* 34 D6
Tōhoku □, *Japan* 30 E10
Toinya, *Sudan* 51 G10
Tojo, *Indonesia* 37 E6
Tōjō, *Japan* 31 G6
Tokachi-Dake, *Japan* 30 C11
Tokachi-Gawa —►, *Japan* 30 C11
Tokaj, *Hungary* 17 D10
Tokala, *Indonesia* 37 E6
Tōkamachi, *Japan* 31 F9
Tokanui, *N.Z.* 59 M2
Tokar, *Sudan* 51 E12
Tokara-Rettō, *Japan* 31 K4
Tokarahi, *N.Z.* 59 L3
Tokashiki-Shima, *Japan* 31 L3
Tŏkchŏn, *N. Korea* 35 E14
Tokeland, *U.S.A.* 84 D3
Tokelau Is., *Pac. Oc.* 64 H10
Tokmak, *Kirghizia* 26 E8
Toko Ra., *Australia* 62 C2
Tokoro-Gawa —►, *Japan* 30 B12
Tokuno-Shima, *Japan* 31 L4
Tokushima, *Japan* 31 G7
Tokushima □, *Japan* 31 H7
Tokuyama, *Japan* 31 G5
Tōkyō, *Japan* 31 G9
Tolaga Bay, *N.Z.* 59 H7
Tolbukhin, *Bulgaria* 21 C12
Toledo, *Spain* 19 C3
Toledo, *Ohio, U.S.A.* 76 E4
Toledo, *Oreg., U.S.A.* 82 D2
Toledo, *Wash., U.S.A.* 82 C2
Toledo, Montes de, *Spain* 19 C3
Tolga, *Algeria* 50 B6
Toliara, *Madag.* 57 C7
Toliara □, *Madag.* 57 C8
Tolima, *Colombia* 92 C3
Tolitoli, *Indonesia* 37 D6
Tolleson, *U.S.A.* 83 K7
Tollhouse, *U.S.A.* 84 H7
Tolo, *Zaïre* 52 E3
Tolo, Teluk, *Indonesia* 37 E6
Tolosa, *Spain* 19 A4
Toluca, *Mexico* 87 D5
Tom Burke, *S. Africa* 57 C4
Tom Price, *Australia* 60 D2
Tomah, *U.S.A.* 80 D9
Tomahawk, *U.S.A.* 80 C10
Tomakomai, *Japan* 30 C10
Tomales, *U.S.A.* 84 G4
Tomales B., *U.S.A.* 84 G3
Tomar, *Portugal* 19 C1
Tomaszów Mazowiecki, *Poland* 17 C9
Tomatlán, *Mexico* 86 D3
Tombé, *Sudan* 51 G11
Tombigbee —►, *U.S.A.* 77 K2
Tombouctou, *Mali* 50 E4
Tombstone, *U.S.A.* 83 L8
Tombua, *Angola* 56 B1
Tomé, *Chile* 94 D1
Tomelloso, *Spain* 19 C4
Tomingley, *Australia* 63 E4
Tomini, *Indonesia* 37 D6
Tomini, Teluk, *Indonesia* 37 E6
Tomkinson Ras., *Australia* 61 E4
Tommot, *Russia* 27 D13
Tomnavoulin, *U.K.* 12 D5
Tomnop Ta Suos, *Cambodia* 39 G5
Toms Place, *U.S.A.* 84 H8
Toms River, *U.S.A.* 79 G10
Tomsk, *Russia* 26 D9
Tonalá, *Mexico* 87 D6
Tonalea, *U.S.A.* 83 H8
Tonantins, *Brazil* 92 D5
Tonasket, *U.S.A.* 82 B4
Tonawanda, *U.S.A.* 78 D6
Tonbridge, *U.K.* 11 F8
Tondano, *Indonesia* 37 D6
Tonekābon, *Iran* 45 B6
Tong Xian, *China* 34 E9
Tonga ■, *Pac. Oc.* 59 D11
Tonga Trench, *Pac. Oc.* 64 J10
Tongaat, *S. Africa* 57 D5
Tongareva, *Cook Is.* 65 H12
Tongatapu, *Tonga* 59 E11
Tongchŏn-ni, *N. Korea* 35 E14
Tongchuan, *China* 34 G5
Tongeren, *Belgium* 15 D5
Tongguan, *China* 34 G6
Tonghua, *China* 35 D13
Tongjosŏn Man, *N. Korea* 35 E14
Tongking, G. of = Tonkin, G. of, *Asia* 38 B7
Tongliao, *China* 35 C12
Tongnae, *S. Korea* 35 G15
Tongobory, *Madag.* 57 C7
Tongoy, *Chile* 94 C1
Tongres = Tongeren, *Belgium* 15 D5
Tongsa Dzong, *Bhutan* 41 F17
Tongue, *U.K.* 12 C4
Tongue —►, *U.S.A.* 80 B2
Tongwei, *China* 34 G3
Tongxin, *China* 34 F3
Tongyang, *N. Korea* 35 E14
Tongyu, *China* 35 B12
Tonk, *India* 42 F6
Tonkawa, *U.S.A.* 81 G6
Tonkin = Bac Phan, *Vietnam* 38 B5
Tonkin, G. of, *Asia* 38 B7
Tonlé Sap, *Cambodia* 38 F4
Tono, *Japan* 30 E10
Tonopah, *U.S.A.* 83 G5
Tonosí, *Panama* 88 E3
Tønsberg, *Norway* 9 G11
Tooele, *U.S.A.* 82 F7
Toompine, *Australia* 63 D3
Toonpan, *Australia* 62 B4
Toora, *Australia* 63 F4
Toora-Khem, *Russia* 27 D10
Toowoomba, *Australia* 63 D5
Top-ozero, *Russia* 24 A5
Topaz, *U.S.A.* 84 G7
Topeka, *U.S.A.* 80 F7
Topki, *Russia* 26 D9
Topley, *Canada* 72 C3
Topocalma, Pta., *Chile* 94 C1
Topock, *U.S.A.* 85 L12
Topolobampo, *Mexico* 86 B3
Toppenish, *U.S.A.* 82 C3
Toraka Vestale, *Madag.* 57 B7
Torata, *Peru* 92 G4
Torbay, *Canada* 71 C9
Torbay, *U.K.* 11 G4
Tordesillas, *Spain* 19 B3
Torfajökull, *Iceland* 8 E4
Torgau, *Germany* 16 C6
Torhout, *Belgium* 15 C3
Tori-Shima, *Japan* 31 J10
Torin, *Mexico* 86 B2
Torino, *Italy* 20 B2
Torit, *Sudan* 51 H11
Tormes —►, *Spain* 19 B2
Tornado Mt., *Canada* 72 D6
Torne älv —►, *Sweden* 8 D18
Torneå = Tornio, *Finland* 8 D18
Torneträsk, *Sweden* 8 B15
Tornio, *Finland* 8 D18
Tornionjoki —►, *Finland* 8 D18
Tornquist, *Argentina* 94 D3
Toro, *Spain* 22 B11
Toro, Cerro del, *Chile* 94 B2
Toro Pk., *U.S.A.* 85 M10
Toronîios Kólpos, *Greece* 21 D10
Toronto, *Australia* 63 E5
Toronto, *Canada* 70 D4
Toronto, *U.S.A.* 78 F4
Toropets, *Russia* 24 C5
Tororo, *Uganda* 54 B3
Toros Dağları, *Turkey* 25 G5
Torquay, *Canada* 73 D8
Torquay, *U.K.* 11 G4
Torrance, *U.S.A.* 85 M8
Tôrre de Moncorvo, *Portugal* 19 B2
Torre del Greco, *Italy* 20 D6
Torrelavega, *Spain* 19 A3
Torremolinos, *Spain* 19 D3
Torrens, L., *Australia* 63 E2
Torrens Cr. —►, *Australia* 62 C4
Torrens Creek, *Australia* 62 C4
Torréon, *Mexico* 86 B4
Torres, *Mexico* 86 B2
Torres Strait, *Australia* 64 H6
Torres Vedras, *Portugal* 19 C1
Torrevieja, *Spain* 19 D5
Torrey, *U.S.A.* 83 G8
Torridge —►, *U.K.* 11 G3
Torridon, L., *U.K.* 12 D3
Torrington, *Conn., U.S.A.* 79 E11
Torrington, *Wyo., U.S.A.* 80 D2
Tortola, *Virgin Is.* 89 C7
Tortosa, *Spain* 19 B6
Tortosa, C., *Spain* 19 B6
Tortue, I. de la, *Haiti* 89 B5
Ţorūd, *Iran* 45 C7
Toruń, *Poland* 17 B9
Tory I., *Ireland* 13 A3
Tosa, *Japan* 31 H6
Tosa-Shimizu, *Japan* 31 H6
Tosa-Wan, *Japan* 31 H6
Toscana, *Italy* 20 C4
Tostado, *Argentina* 94 B3
Tostón, Pta. de, *Canary Is.* 22 F5
Tosu, *Japan* 31 H5
Toteng, *Botswana* 56 C3
Totma, *Russia* 24 C7
Totnes, *U.K.* 11 G4
Totonicapán, *Guatemala* 88 D1
Totten Glacier, *Antarctica* 5 C8
Tottenham, *Australia* 63 E4
Tottenham, *Canada* 78 B5
Tottori, *Japan* 31 G7
Tottori □, *Japan* 31 G7
Touba, *Ivory C.* 50 G3
Toubkal, Djebel, *Morocco* 50 B3
Tougan, *Burkina Faso* 50 F4
Touggourt, *Algeria* 50 B6
Tougué, *Guinea* 50 F2
Toul, *France* 18 B6
Toulepleu, *Ivory C.* 50 G3
Toulon, *France* 18 E6
Toulouse, *France* 18 E4
Toummo, *Niger* 51 D7
Toungoo, *Burma* 41 K20
Touraine, *France* 18 C4
Tourane = Da Nang, *Vietnam* 38 D7
Tourcoing, *France* 18 A5
Tournai, *Belgium* 15 D3
Tournon, *France* 18 D6
Tours, *France* 18 C4
Touwsrivier, *S. Africa* 56 E3
Towada, *Japan* 30 D10
Towada-Ko, *Japan* 30 D10
Towamba, *Australia* 63 F4
Towanda, *U.S.A.* 79 E8
Towang, *India* 41 F17
Tower, *U.S.A.* 80 B8
Towerhill Cr. —►, *Australia* 62 C3
Towner, *U.S.A.* 80 A4
Townsend, *U.S.A.* 82 C8
Townshend I., *Australia* 62 C5
Townsville, *Australia* 62 B4
Towson, *U.S.A.* 76 F7
Toya-Ko, *Japan* 30 C10
Toyah, *U.S.A.* 81 K3
Toyahvale, *U.S.A.* 81 K3
Toyama, *Japan* 31 F8
Toyama □, *Japan* 31 F8
Toyama-Wan, *Japan* 31 F8
Toyohashi, *Japan* 31 G8
Toyokawa, *Japan* 31 G8
Toyonaka, *Japan* 31 G7
Toyooka, *Japan* 31 G7
Toyota, *Japan* 31 G8
Tozeur, *Tunisia* 50 B6
Tra On, *Vietnam* 39 H5
Trabzon, *Turkey* 25 F6
Tracadie, *Canada* 71 C7
Tracy, *Calif., U.S.A.* 83 H3
Tracy, *Minn., U.S.A.* 80 C7
Tradovoye, *Russia* 30 C6
Trafalgar, C., *Spain* 19 D2
Trail, *Canada* 72 D5
Trainor L., *Canada* 72 A4
Trákhonas, *Cyprus* 23 D12
Tralee, *Ireland* 13 D2
Tralee B., *Ireland* 13 D2
Tramore, *Ireland* 13 D4
Tran Ninh, Cao Nguyen, *Laos* 38 C4
Tranås, *Sweden* 9 G13
Trancas, *Argentina* 94 B2
Trang, *Thailand* 39 J2
Trangahy, *Madag.* 57 B7
Trangan, *Indonesia* 37 F8
Trangie, *Australia* 63 E4
Trani, *Italy* 20 D7
Tranoroa, *Madag.* 57 C8
Tranqueras, *Uruguay* 95 C4
Trans Nzoia □, *Kenya* 54 B3
Transantarctic Mts., *Antarctica* 5 E12
Transcaucasia = Zakavkazye, *Asia* 25 F7
Transcona, *Canada* 73 D9
Transilvania, *Romania* 17 F12
Transkei □, *S. Africa* 57 E4
Transvaal □, *S. Africa* 56 D4
Transylvania = Transilvania, *Romania* 17 F12
Transylvanian Alps, *Romania* 6 F10
Trápani, *Italy* 20 E5
Trapper Peak, *U.S.A.* 82 D6
Traralgon, *Australia* 63 F4
Tras os Montes e Alto Douro, *Portugal* 19 B2
Trasimeno, L., *Italy* 20 C5
Trat, *Thailand* 39 F4
Traveller's L., *Australia* 63 E3
Travers, Mt., *N.Z.* 59 K4
Traverse City, *U.S.A.* 76 C3
Travnik, *Bos. & H., Yug.* 21 B7
Trayning, *Australia* 61 F2
Trébbia —►, *Italy* 20 B3
Trebinje, *Bos. & H., Yug.* 21 C8
Třeboň, *Czech.* 16 D7
Tredegar, *U.K.* 11 F4
Tregaron, *U.K.* 11 E4
Tregrosse Is., *Australia* 62 B5
Tréguier, *France* 18 B2
Treherne, *Canada* 73 D9
Treinta y Tres, *Uruguay* 95 C5
Trekveld, *S. Africa* 56 E2
Trelew, *Argentina* 96 E3
Trelleborg, *Sweden* 9 J12
Tremonton, *U.S.A.* 82 F7
Tremp, *Spain* 19 A6
Trenche —►, *Canada* 70 C5
Trenggalek, *Indonesia* 37 H14
Trenque Lauquen, *Argentina* 94 D3
Trent —►, *U.K.* 10 D7
Trentino-Alto Adige □, *Italy* 20 A4
Trento, *Italy* 20 A4
Trenton, *Canada* 70 D4
Trenton, *Mo., U.S.A.* 80 E8
Trenton, *N.J., U.S.A.* 79 F10
Trenton, *Nebr., U.S.A.* 80 E4
Trenton, *Tenn., U.S.A.* 81 H10
Trepassey, *Canada* 71 C9
Tres Arroyos, *Argentina* 94 D3
Três Corações, *Brazil* 95 A6
Três Lagoas, *Brazil* 93 H8
Tres Marías, *Mexico* 86 C3
Tres Montes, C., *Chile* 96 F1
Tres Pinos, *U.S.A.* 84 J5

Três Pontas, Brazil 95 A6
Tres Puentes, Chile 94 B1
Tres Puntas, C., Argentina 96 F3
Três Rios, Brazil 95 A7
Tres Valles, Mexico 87 D5
Treungen, Norway 9 G10
Treviso, Italy 20 B5
Triabunna, Australia 62 G4
Triánda, Greece 23 C10
Triang, Malaysia 39 L4
Tribulation, C., Australia 62 B4
Tribune, U.S.A. 80 F4
Trichinopoly = Tiruchchirappalli, India 40 P11
Trichur, India 40 P10
Trida, Australia 63 E4
Trier, Germany 16 D3
Trieste, Italy 20 B5
Triglav, Slovenia 20 A5
Trikkala, Greece 21 E9
Trikomo, Cyprus 23 D12
Trikora, Puncak, Indonesia 37 E9
Trim, Ireland 13 C5
Trincomalee, Sri Lanka 40 Q12
Trindade, I., Atl. Oc. 2 F8
Trinidad, Bolivia 92 F6
Trinidad, Colombia 92 B4
Trinidad, Cuba 88 B3
Trinidad, Uruguay 94 C4
Trinidad, U.S.A. 81 G2
Trinidad, W. Indies 89 D7
Trinidad →, Mexico 87 D5
Trinidad, I., Argentina 96 D4
Trinidad & Tobago ■, W. Indies 89 D7
Trinity, Canada 71 C9
Trinity, U.S.A. 81 K7
Trinity →, Calif., U.S.A. 82 F2
Trinity →, Tex., U.S.A. 81 L7
Trinity B., Canada 71 C9
Trinity Mts., U.S.A. 82 F4
Trinkitat, Sudan 51 E12
Trion, U.S.A. 77 H3
Tripoli = Tarābulus, Lebanon 47 A4
Tripoli = Tarābulus, Libya 51 B7
Trípolis, Greece 21 F10
Tripp, U.S.A. 80 D6
Tripura □, India 41 H17
Tripylos, Cyprus 23 E11
Tristan da Cunha, Atl. Oc. 2 F9
Trivandrum, India 40 Q10
Trnava, Czech. 17 D8
Trochu, Canada 72 C6
Trodely I., Canada 70 B4
Troglav, Croatia 20 C7
Troilus, L., Canada 70 B5
Trois-Pistoles, Canada 71 C6
Trois-Rivières, Canada 70 C5
Troitsk, Russia 26 D7
Troitsko Pechorsk, Russia 24 B10
Trölladyngja, Iceland 8 D5
Trollhättan, Sweden 9 G12
Troms fylke □, Norway 8 B15
Tromsø, Norway 8 B15
Trona, U.S.A. 85 K9
Tronador, Argentina 96 E2
Trondheim, Norway 8 E11
Trondheimsfjorden, Norway 8 E11
Troodos, Cyprus 23 E11
Troon, U.K. 12 F4
Tropic, U.S.A. 83 H7
Trossachs, The, U.K. 12 E4
Trostan, U.K. 13 A5
Trotternish, U.K. 12 D2
Troup, U.S.A. 81 J7
Trout →, Canada 72 A5
Trout L., N.W.T., Canada 72 A4
Trout L., Ont., Canada 73 C10
Trout Lake, Mich., U.S.A. 70 C2
Trout Lake, Wash., U.S.A. 84 E5
Trout River, Canada 71 C8
Trouville-sur-Mer, France 18 B4
Trowbridge, U.K. 11 F5
Troy, Ala., U.S.A. 77 K3
Troy, Idaho, U.S.A. 82 C5
Troy, Kans., U.S.A. 80 F7
Troy, Mo., U.S.A. 80 F9
Troy, Mont., U.S.A. 82 B6
Troy, N.Y., U.S.A. 79 D11
Troy, Ohio, U.S.A. 76 E3
Troyes, France 18 B6
Trucial States = United Arab Emirates ■, Asia 45 F7
Truckee, U.S.A. 84 F6
Trujillo, Honduras 88 C2
Trujillo, Peru 92 E3
Trujillo, Spain 19 C3
Trujillo, U.S.A. 81 H2
Trujillo, Venezuela 92 B4
Truk, Pac. Oc. 64 G7
Trumann, U.S.A. 81 H9
Trumbull, Mt., U.S.A. 83 H7
Trundle, Australia 63 E4
Trung-Phan, Vietnam 38 E7
Truro, Canada 71 C7
Truro, U.K. 11 G2
Truslove, Australia 61 F3
Truth or Consequences, U.S.A. 83 K10
Trutnov, Czech. 16 C7
Tryon, U.S.A. 77 H4
Tryonville, U.S.A. 78 E5
Tsaratanana, Madag. 57 B8
Tsaratanana, Mt. de, Madag. 57 A8
Tsau, Botswana 56 C3
Tselinograd, Kazakhstan 26 D8
Tsetserleg, Mongolia 32 B5
Tshabong, Botswana 56 D3
Tshane, Botswana 56 C3
Tshela, Zaïre 52 E2
Tshesebe, Botswana 57 C4
Tshibeke, Zaïre 54 C2
Tshibinda, Zaïre 54 C2
Tshikapa, Zaïre 52 F4
Tshilenge, Zaïre 54 D1
Tshinsenda, Zaïre 55 E2
Tshofa, Zaïre 54 D2
Tshwane, Botswana 56 C3
Tsigara, Botswana 56 C4
Tsihombe, Madag. 57 D8
Tsimlyanskoye Vdkhr., Russia 25 E7
Tsinan = Jinan, China 34 F9
Tsineng, S. Africa 56 D3
Tsinghai = Qinghai □, China 32 C4
Tsingtao = Qingdao, China 35 F11
Tsinjomitondraka, Madag. 57 B8
Tsiroanomandidy, Madag. 57 B8
Tsivory, Madag. 57 C8
Tskhinvali, Georgia 25 F7
Tsna →, Russia 24 D7
Tso Moriri, L., India 43 C8
Tsodilo Hill, Botswana 56 B3
Tsogttsetsiy, Mongolia 34 C3
Tsolo, S. Africa 57 E4
Tsomo, S. Africa 57 E4
Tsu, Japan 31 G8
Tsu L., Canada 72 A6
Tsuchiura, Japan 31 F10
Tsugaru-Kaikyō, Japan 30 D10
Tsumeb, Namibia 56 B2
Tsumis, Namibia 56 C2
Tsuruga, Japan 31 G8
Tsurugi-San, Japan 31 H7
Tsuruoka, Japan 30 E9
Tsushima, Gifu, Japan 31 G8
Tsushima, Nagasaki, Japan 31 G4
Tual, Indonesia 37 F8
Tuam, Ireland 13 C3
Tuamotu Is., Pac. Oc. 65 J13
Tuamotu Ridge, Pac. Oc. 65 K14
Tuao, Phil. 37 A6
Tuapse, Russia 25 F6
Tuatapere, N.Z. 59 M1
Tuba City, U.S.A. 83 H8
Tuban, Indonesia 37 G15
Tubarão, Brazil 95 B6
Tūbās, Jordan 47 C4
Tubau, Malaysia 36 D4
Tübingen, Germany 16 D4
Tubruq, Libya 51 B9
Tubuai Is., Pac. Oc. 65 K12
Tuc Trung, Vietnam 39 G6
Tucacas, Venezuela 92 A5
Tuchodi →, Canada 72 B4
Tucson, U.S.A. 83 K8
Tucumán □, Argentina 94 B2
Tucumcari, U.S.A. 81 H3
Tucupita, Venezuela 92 B6
Tucuruí, Brazil 93 D9
Tudela, Spain 19 A5
Tudmur, Syria 44 C3
Tudor, L., Canada 71 A6
Tuen, Australia 63 D4
Tugela →, S. Africa 57 D5
Tuguegarao, Phil. 37 A6
Tugur, Russia 27 D14
Tuineje, Canary Is. 22 F5
Tukangbesi, Kepulauan, Indonesia 37 F6
Tukarak I., Canada 70 A4
Tukayyid, Iraq 44 D5
Tūkrah, Libya 51 B9
Tuktoyaktuk, Canada 68 B6
Tukuyu, Tanzania 55 D3
Tula, Hidalgo, Mexico 87 C5
Tula, Tamaulipas, Mexico 87 C5
Tula, Russia 24 D6
Tulancingo, Mexico 87 C5
Tulare, U.S.A. 83 H4
Tulare Lake Bed, U.S.A. 83 J4
Tularosa, U.S.A. 83 K10
Tulbagh, S. Africa 56 E2
Tulcán, Ecuador 92 C3
Tulcea, Romania 17 F14
Tūleh, Iran 45 C7
Tulemalu L., Canada 73 A9
Tuli, Indonesia 37 E6
Tuli, Zimbabwe 55 G2
Tulia, U.S.A. 81 H4
Ţulkarm, Jordan 47 C4
Tullahoma, U.S.A. 77 H2
Tullamore, Australia 63 E4
Tulle, France 18 D4
Tullibigeal, Australia 63 E4
Tullow, Ireland 13 D4
Tully, Australia 62 B4
Ţulmaythah, Libya 51 B9
Tulmur, Australia 62 C3
Tulsa, U.S.A. 81 G7
Tulsequah, Canada 72 B2
Tulua, Colombia 92 C3
Tulun, Russia 27 D11
Tulungagung, Indonesia 36 F4
Tum, Indonesia 37 E8
Tuma →, Nic. 88 D3
Tumaco, Colombia 92 C3
Tumatumari, Guyana 92 B7
Tumba, L., Zaïre 52 E3
Tumbarumba, Australia 63 F4
Tumbaya, Argentina 94 A2
Túmbes, Peru 92 D2
Tumbwe, Zaïre 55 E2
Tumby Bay, Australia 63 E2
Tumd Youqi, China 34 D6
Tumen, China 35 C15
Tumen Jiang →, China 35 C16
Tumeremo, Venezuela 92 B6
Tumkur, India 40 N10
Tummel, L., U.K. 12 E5
Tump, Pakistan 40 F3
Tumpat, Malaysia 39 J4
Tumu, Ghana 50 F4
Tumucumaque, Serra, Brazil 93 C8
Tumut, Australia 63 F4
Tumwater, U.S.A. 82 C2
Tunas de Zaza, Cuba 88 B4
Tunbridge Wells, U.K. 11 F8
Tuncurry, Australia 63 E5
Tunduru, Tanzania 55 E4
Tunduru □, Tanzania 55 E4
Tundzha →, Bulgaria 21 D12
Tunga Pass, India 41 E19
Tungabhadra →, India 40 M11
Tungaru, Sudan 51 F11
Tungla, Nic. 88 D3
Tungnafellsjökull, Iceland 8 D5
Tungsten, Canada 72 A3
Tunguska, Nizhnyaya →, Russia 27 C9
Tunica, U.S.A. 81 H9
Tunis, Tunisia 50 A7
Tunisia ■, Africa 50 B6
Tunja, Colombia 92 B4
Tunkhannock, U.S.A. 79 E9
Tunliu, China 34 F7
Tunnsjøen, Norway 8 D12
Tunungayualok I., Canada 71 A7
Tunuyán, Argentina 94 C2
Tunuyán →, Argentina 94 C2
Tunxi, China 33 D6
Tuolumne, U.S.A. 83 H3
Tuolumne →, U.S.A. 84 H5
Tuoy-Khaya, Russia 27 C12
Tūp Āghāj, Iran 44 B5
Tupã, Brazil 95 A5
Tupelo, U.S.A. 77 H1
Tupik, Russia 27 D12
Tupinambaranas, Brazil 92 D7
Tupiza, Bolivia 94 A2
Tupman, U.S.A. 85 K7
Tupper, Canada 72 B4
Tupper Lake, U.S.A. 79 B10
Tupungato, Cerro, S. Amer. 94 C2
Tuquan, China 35 B11
Túquerres, Colombia 92 C3
Tura, Russia 27 C11
Turabah, Si. Arabia 44 D4
Tūrān, Iran 45 C8
Turan, Russia 27 D10
Turayf, Si. Arabia 44 D3
Turda, Romania 17 E11
Turek, Poland 17 B9
Turfan = Turpan, China 32 B3
Turgutlu, Turkey 25 G4
Turia →, Spain 19 C5
Turiaçu, Brazil 93 D9
Turiaçu →, Brazil 93 D9
Turin = Torino, Italy 20 B2
Turin, Canada 72 D6
Turkana □, Kenya 54 B4
Turkana, L., Africa 54 B4
Turkestan, Kazakhstan 26 E7
Turkey ■, Eurasia 25 G6
Turkey Creek, Australia 60 C4
Turkmenistan ■, Asia 26 F6
Turks Is., W. Indies 89 B5
Turks Island Passage, W. Indies 89 B5
Turku, Finland 9 F17
Turkwe →, Kenya 54 B4
Turlock, U.S.A. 83 H3
Turnagain →, Canada 72 B3
Turnagain, C., N.Z. 59 J6
Turneffe Is., Belize 87 D7
Turner, Australia 60 C4
Turner, U.S.A. 82 B9
Turner Pt., Australia 62 A1
Turner Valley, Canada 72 C6
Turners Falls, U.S.A. 79 D12
Turnhout, Belgium 15 C4
Turnor L., Canada 73 B7
Tŭrnovo, Bulgaria 21 C11
Turnu Măgurele, Romania 17 G12
Turnu Rosu Pasul, Romania 17 F12
Turon, U.S.A. 81 G5
Turpan, China 32 B3
Turriff, U.K. 12 D6
Tursāq, Iraq 44 C5
Turtle Head I., Australia 62 A3
Turtle L., Canada 73 C7
Turtle Lake, N. Dak., U.S.A. 80 B4
Turtle Lake, Wis., U.S.A. 80 C8
Turtleford, Canada 73 C7
Turukhansk, Russia 27 C9
Turun ja Porin lääni □, Finland 9 F17
Tuscaloosa, U.S.A. 77 J2
Tuscany = Toscana, Italy 20 C4
Tuscola, Ill., U.S.A. 76 F1
Tuscola, Tex., U.S.A. 81 J5
Tuscumbia, U.S.A. 77 H2
Tuskar Rock, Ireland 13 D5
Tuskegee, U.S.A. 77 J3
Tuticorin, India 40 Q11
Tutóia, Brazil 93 D10
Tutong, Brunei 36 D4
Tutrakan, Bulgaria 21 B12
Tutshi L., Canada 72 B2
Tuttle, U.S.A. 80 B5
Tuttlingen, Germany 16 E4
Tutuala, Indonesia 37 F7
Tutuila, Amer. Samoa 59 B13
Tututepec, Mexico 87 D5
Tuva Republic □, Russia 27 D10
Tuvalu ■, Pac. Oc. 64 H9
Tuxpan, Mexico 87 C5
Tuxtla Gutiérrez, Mexico 87 D6
Tuy, Spain 19 A1
Tuy An, Vietnam 38 F7
Tuy Duc, Vietnam 39 F6
Tuy Hoa, Vietnam 38 F7
Tuy Phong, Vietnam 39 G7
Tuya L., Canada 72 B2
Tuyen Hoa, Vietnam 38 D6
Tuyen Quang, Vietnam 38 B5
Tūysarkān, Iran 45 C6
Tuz Gölü, Turkey 25 G5
Ţūz Khurmātū, Iraq 44 C5
Tuzla, Bos. & H., Yug. 21 B8
Tver, Russia 24 C6
Twain, U.S.A. 84 E5
Twain Harte, U.S.A. 84 G6
Tweed, Canada 78 B7
Tweed →, U.K. 12 F7
Tweed Heads, Australia 63 D5
Tweedsmuir Prov. Park, Canada 72 C3
Twentynine Palms, U.S.A. 85 L10
Twillingate, Canada 71 C9
Twin Bridges, U.S.A. 82 D7
Twin Falls, U.S.A. 82 E6
Twin Valley, U.S.A. 80 B6
Twisp, U.S.A. 82 B3
Two Harbors, U.S.A. 80 B9
Two Hills, Canada 72 C6
Two Rivers, U.S.A. 76 C2
Twofold B., Australia 63 F4
Tychy, Poland 17 C9
Tyler, U.S.A. 75 D7
Tyler, Minn., U.S.A. 80 C6
Tyler, Tex., U.S.A. 81 J7
Tynda, Russia 27 D13
Tyne →, U.K. 10 C6
Tyne & Wear □, U.K. 10 C6
Tynemouth, U.K. 10 B6
Tyre = Sūr, Lebanon 47 B4
Tyrifjorden, Norway 9 F11
Tyrol = Tirol □, Austria 16 E5
Tyrone, U.S.A. 78 F6
Tyrrell →, Australia 63 F3
Tyrrell, L., Australia 63 F3
Tyrrell Arm, Canada 73 A9
Tyrrell L., Canada 73 A7
Tyrrhenian Sea, Europe 20 E5
Tysfjorden, Norway 8 B14
Tyulgan, Russia 24 D10
Tyumen, Russia 26 D7
Tywi →, U.K. 11 F3
Tywyn, U.K. 11 E3
Tzaneen, S. Africa 57 C5
Tzermiádhes, Greece 23 D7
Tzukong = Zigong, China 32 D5

U

U Taphao, Thailand 38 F3
Uanda, Australia 62 C3
Uarsciek, Somali Rep. 46 G4
Uasin □, Kenya 54 B4
Uato-Udo, Indonesia 37 F7
Uatumã →, Brazil 92 D7
Uaupés, Brazil 92 D5
Uaupés →, Brazil 92 C5
Uaxactún, Guatemala 88 C2
Ubá, Brazil 95 A7
Ubaitaba, Brazil 93 F11
Ubangi = Oubangi →, Zaïre 52 E3
Ubauro, Pakistan 42 E3
Ube, Japan 31 H5
Ubeda, Spain 19 C4
Uberaba, Brazil 93 G9
Uberlândia, Brazil 93 G9
Ubolratna Res., Thailand 38 D4
Ubombo, S. Africa 57 D5
Ubon Ratchathani, Thailand 38 E5
Ubondo, Zaïre 54 C2
Ubundu, Zaïre 54 C2
Ucayali →, Peru 92 D4
Uchi Lake, Canada 73 C10
Uchiura-Wan, Japan 30 C10
Uchur →, Russia 27 D14
Ucluelet, Canada 72 D3
Uda →, Russia 27 D14
Udaipur, India 42 G5
Udaipur Garhi, Nepal 43 F12
Uddevalla, Sweden 9 G11
Uddjaur, Sweden 8 D16
Udgir, India 40 K10
Udhampur, India 43 C6
Udi, Nigeria 50 G6
Údine, Italy 20 A5
Udmurt Republic □, Russia 24 C9
Udon Thani, Thailand 38 D4
Udupi, India 40 N9
Udzungwa Range, Tanzania 55 D4
Ueda, Japan 31 F9
Uedineniya, Os., Russia 4 B12
Uele →, Zaïre 52 D4
Uelen, Russia 27 C19
Uelzen, Germany 16 B5
Ufa, Russia 24 D10
Ufa →, Russia 24 D10
Ugab →, Namibia 56 C1
Ugalla →, Tanzania 54 D3
Uganda ■, Africa 54 B3
Ugie, S. Africa 57 E4
Uglegorsk, Russia 27 E15
Ugolyak, Russia 27 C13
Ugûn Mûsa, Egypt 47 F1
Uhrichsville, U.S.A. 78 F3
Uige, Angola 52 F2
Uijŏngbu, S. Korea 35 F14
Ŭiju, N. Korea 35 D13
Uinta Mts., U.S.A. 82 F8
Uitenhage, S. Africa 56 E4
Uithuizen, Neths. 15 A6
Ujhani, India 43 F8
Uji-guntō, Japan 31 J4
Ujjain, India 42 H6
Újpest, Hungary 17 E9
Ujung Pandang, Indonesia 37 F5
Uka, Russia 27 D17
Ukara I., Tanzania 54 C3
Uke-Shima, Japan 31 K4
Ukerewe □, Tanzania 54 C3
Ukerewe I., Tanzania 54 C3
Ukhrul, India 41 G19
Ukhta, Russia 24 B9
Ukiah, U.S.A. 84 F3
Ukki Fort, India 43 C7
Ukraine ■, Europe 25 E5
Ukwi, Botswana 56 C3
Ulaanbaatar, Mongolia 32 B5
Ulaangom, Mongolia 32 A4
Ulamba, Zaïre 55 D1
Ulan Bator = Ulaanbaatar, Mongolia 32 B5
Ulan Ude, Russia 27 D11
Ulanga □, Tanzania 55 D4
Ulaya, Morogoro, Tanzania 54 D4
Ulaya, Tabora, Tanzania 54 C3
Ulcinj, Montenegro, Yug. 21 D8
Ulco, S. Africa 56 D3
Ulhasnagar, India 40 K8
Ulladulla, Australia 63 F5
Ullapool, U.K. 12 D3
Ullswater, U.K. 10 C5
Ullung-do, S. Korea 35 F16
Ulm, Germany 16 D4
Ulmarra, Australia 63 D5
Ulonguè, Mozam. 55 E3
Ulricehamn, Sweden 9 H12
Ulsan, S. Korea 35 G15
Ulster □, U.K. 13 B5
Ulubaria, India 43 H13
Uluguru Mts., Tanzania 54 D4
Ulungur He →, China 32 B3
Ulutau, Kazakhstan 26 E7
Ulverston, U.K. 10 C4
Ulverstone, Australia 62 G4
Ulya, Russia 27 D15
Ulyanovsk = Simbirsk, Russia 24 D8
Ulyasutay, Mongolia 32 B4
Ulysses, U.S.A. 81 G4
Umala, Bolivia 92 G5
Uman, Ukraine 25 E5
Umaria, India 41 H12
Umarkot, Pakistan 40 G6
Umatilla, U.S.A. 82 D4
Umba, Russia 24 A5
Umbrella Mts., N.Z. 59 L2
Umbria □, Italy 20 C5
Ume älv →, Sweden 8 E16
Umeå, Sweden 8 E16
Umera, Indonesia 37 E7
Umfuli →, Zimbabwe 55 F2
Umgusa, Zimbabwe 55 F2
Umkomaas, S. Africa 57 E5
Umm ad Daraj, J., Jordan 47 C4
Umm al Qaywayn, U.A.E. 45 E7
Umm al Qittayn, Jordan 47 C5
Umm Bāb, Qatar 45 E6
Umm Bel, Sudan 51 F10
Umm el Fahm, Israel 47 C4
Umm Lajj, Si. Arabia 44 E3
Umm Ruwaba, Sudan 51 F11
Umnak, U.S.A. 68 C3
Umniati →, Zimbabwe 55 F2
Umpqua →, U.S.A. 82 E1
Umreth, India 42 H5
Umtata, S. Africa 57 E4
Umuarama, Brazil 95 A5
Umvukwe Ra., Zimbabwe 55 F3
Umzimvubu = Port St. Johns, S. Africa 57 E4
Umzingwane →, Zimbabwe 55 G2
Umzinto, S. Africa 57 E5
Una, India 42 J4
Unac →, Bos. & H., Yug. 20 B7
Unadilla, U.S.A. 79 D9
Unalaska, U.S.A. 68 C3
Uncia, Bolivia 92 G5
Uncompahgre Pk., U.S.A. 83 G10
Underberg, S. Africa 57 D4
Underbool, Australia 63 F3
Ungarie, Australia 63 E4
Ungarra, Australia 63 E2
Ungava B., Canada 69 C13
Ungava Pen., Canada 69 C12
Unggi, N. Korea 35 C16

União da Vitória, Brazil 95 B5
Unimak, U.S.A. 68 C3
Union, Miss., U.S.A. 81 J10
Union, Mo., U.S.A. 80 F9
Union, S.C., U.S.A. 77 H5
Union, Mt., U.S.A. 83 J7
Union City, Calif., U.S.A. 84 H4
Union City, N.J., U.S.A. 79 F10
Union City, Pa., U.S.A. 78 E5
Union City, Tenn., U.S.A. 81 G10
Union Gap, U.S.A. 82 C3
Union of Soviet Socialist Republics = Commonwealth of Independent States ■, Eurasia 27 D11
Union Springs, U.S.A. 77 J3
Uniondale, S. Africa 56 E3
Uniontown, U.S.A. 76 F6
Unionville, U.S.A. 80 E8
United Arab Emirates ■, Asia 45 F7
United Kingdom ■, Europe 7 E5
United States of America ■, N. Amer. 74 C7
Unity, Canada 73 C7
Unjha, India 42 H5
Unnao, India 43 F9
Unst, U.K. 12 A8
Unuk →, Canada 72 B2
Uozu, Japan 31 F8
Upata, Venezuela 92 B6
Upemba, L., Zaïre 55 D2
Upernavik, Greenland 4 B5
Upington, S. Africa 56 D3
Upleta, India 42 J4
Upolu, W. Samoa 59 A13
Upper Alkali Lake, U.S.A. 82 F3
Upper Arrow L., Canada 72 C5
Upper Foster L., Canada 73 B7
Upper Hutt, N.Z. 59 J5
Upper Klamath L., U.S.A. 82 E3
Upper Lake, U.S.A. 84 F4
Upper Musquodoboit, Canada 71 C7
Upper Red L., U.S.A. 80 A7
Upper Sandusky, U.S.A. 76 E4
Upper Volta = Burkina Faso ■, Africa 50 F4
Uppsala, Sweden 9 G14
Uppsala län □, Sweden 9 G14
Upshi, India 43 C7
Upstart, C., Australia 62 B4
Upton, U.S.A. 80 C2
Ur, Iraq 44 D5
Uracara, Brazil 92 D7
Urad Qianqi, China 34 D5
Urakawa, Japan 30 C11
Ural, Australia 63 E4
Ural →, Kazakhstan 25 E9
Ural Mts. = Uralskie Gory, Russia 24 C10
Uralla, Australia 63 E5
Uralsk, Kazakhstan 24 D9
Uralskie Gory, Russia 24 C10
Urambo, Tanzania 54 D3
Urambo □, Tanzania 54 D3
Urandangi, Australia 62 C2
Uranium City, Canada 73 B7
Uranquinty, Australia 63 F4
Urawa, Japan 31 G9
Uray, Russia 26 C7
'Uray'irah, Si. Arabia 45 E6
Urbana, Ill., U.S.A. 76 E1
Urbana, Ohio, U.S.A. 76 E4
Urbino, Italy 20 C5
Urbión, Picos de, Spain 19 A4
Urcos, Peru 92 F4
Urda, Kazakhstan 25 E8
Urdinarrain, Argentina 94 C4
Urdzhar, Kazakhstan 26 E9
Ure →, U.K. 10 C6
Ures, Mexico 86 B2
Urfa, Turkey 25 G6
Urfahr, Austria 16 D7
Urgench, Uzbekistan 26 E7
Uri, India 43 B6
Uribia, Colombia 92 A4
Uriondo, Bolivia 94 A3
Urique, Mexico 86 B3
Urique →, Mexico 86 B3
Urk, Neths. 15 B5
Urmia = Orūmīyeh, Iran 44 B5
Urmia, L. = Orūmīyeh, Daryācheh-ye, Iran 44 B5
Uruana, Brazil 93 G9
Uruapan, Mexico 86 D4
Urubamba, Peru 92 F4
Urubamba →, Peru 92 F4
Uruçuí, Brazil 93 E10
Uruguai →, Brazil 95 B5
Uruguaiana, Brazil 94 B4
Uruguay ■, S. Amer. 94 C4
Uruguay →, S. Amer. 94 C4
Urumchi = Ürümqi, China 32 B3
Ürümqi, China 32 B3
Urup, Os., Russia 27 E16
Uryung-Khaya, Russia 27 B12
Usa →, Russia 24 A10
Uşak, Turkey 25 G4
Usakos, Namibia 56 C2
Usedom, Germany 16 B6
Ush-Tobe, Kazakhstan 26 E8
Ushakova, Os., Russia 4 A12
Ushant = Ouessant, I. d', France 18 B1
Ushashi, Tanzania 54 C3
Ushibuka, Japan 31 H5
Ushuaia, Argentina 96 G3
Ushumun, Russia 27 D13
Usk →, U.K. 11 F5
Üsküdar, Turkey 21 D13
Usman, Russia 24 D6
Usoke, Tanzania 54 D3
Usolye Sibirskoye, Russia 27 D11
Uspallata, P. de, Argentina 94 C2
Uspenskiy, Kazakhstan 26 E8
Ussuri →, Asia 30 A7
Ussuriysk, Russia 27 E14
Ussurka, Russia 30 B6
Ust-Aldan = Batamay, Russia 27 C13
Ust Amginskoye = Khandyga, Russia 27 C14
Ust-Bolsheretsk, Russia 27 D16
Ust Chaun, Russia 27 C18
Ust'-Ilga, Russia 27 D11
Ust Ilimpeya = Yukti, Russia 27 C11
Ust-Ilimsk, Russia 27 D11
Ust Ishim, Russia 26 D8
Ust-Kamchatsk, Russia 27 D17
Ust-Kamenogorsk, Kazakhstan 26 E9
Ust-Karenga, Russia 27 D12
Ust Khayryuzova, Russia 27 D16
Ust-Kut, Russia 27 D11
Ust Kuyga, Russia 27 B14
Ust Maya, Russia 27 C14
Ust-Mil, Russia 27 D14
Ust-Nera, Russia 27 C15
Ust-Nyukzha, Russia 27 D13
Ust Olenek, Russia 27 B12
Ust-Omchug, Russia 27 C15
Ust Port, Russia 26 C9
Ust Tsilma, Russia 24 A9
Ust-Tungir, Russia 27 D13
Ust Urt = Ustyurt, Plato, Kazakhstan 26 E6
Ust Usa, Russia 24 A10
Ust Vorkuta, Russia 26 C7
Ústí nad Labem, Czech. 16 C7
Ustica, Italy 20 E5
Ustinov = Izhevsk, Russia 24 C9
Ustye, Russia 27 D10
Ustyurt, Plato, Kazakhstan 26 E6
Usu, China 32 B3
Usuki, Japan 31 H5
Usulután, El Salv. 88 D2
Usumacinta →, Mexico 87 D6
Usumbura = Bujumbura, Burundi 54 C2
Usure, Tanzania 54 C3
Uta, Indonesia 37 E9
Utah □, U.S.A. 82 G8
Utah, L., U.S.A. 82 F8
Ute Cr. →, U.S.A. 81 H3
Utete, Tanzania 54 D4
Uthai Thani, Thailand 38 E3
Uthal, Pakistan 42 G2
Utiariti, Brazil 92 F7
Utica, N.Y., U.S.A. 79 C9
Utica, Ohio, U.S.A. 78 F2
Utik L., Canada 73 B9
Utikuma L., Canada 72 B5
Utrecht, Neths. 15 B5
Utrecht, S. Africa 57 D5
Utrecht □, Neths. 15 B5
Utrera, Spain 19 D3
Utsjoki, Finland 8 B19
Utsunomiya, Japan 31 F9
Uttar Pradesh □, India 43 F9
Uttaradit, Thailand 38 D3
Uttoxeter, U.K. 10 E6
Uudenmaan lääni □, Finland 9 F18
Uusikaarlepyy, Finland 8 E17
Uusikaupunki, Finland 9 F16
Uva, Russia 24 C9
Uvalde, U.S.A. 81 L5
Uvat, Russia 26 D7
Uvinza, Tanzania 54 D3
Uvira, Zaïre 54 C2
Uvs Nuur, Mongolia 32 A4
Uwajima, Japan 31 H6
Uxbridge, Canada 78 B5
Uxin Qi, China 34 E5
Uxmal, Mexico 87 C7
Uyandi, Russia 27 C15
Uyuni, Bolivia 92 H5
Uzbekistan ■, Asia 26 E7
Uzen, Kazakhstan 25 F9
Uzerche, France 18 D4

V

Vaal →, S. Africa 56 D3
Vaal Dam, S. Africa 57 D4
Vaalwater, S. Africa 57 C4
Vaasa, Finland 8 E16
Vaasan lääni □, Finland 8 E17
Vác, Hungary 17 E9
Vacaria, Brazil 95 B5
Vacaville, U.S.A. 84 G5
Vach →, Russia 26 C8
Vache, I.-à-, Haiti 89 C5
Vadnagar, India 42 H5
Vadodara, India 42 H5
Vadsø, Norway 8 A20
Værøy, Norway 8 C12
Váh →, Czech. 17 E9
Vahsel B., Antarctica 5 D1
Vaí, Greece 23 D8
Vaigach, Russia 26 B6
Val-de-Marne □, France 18 B5
Val-d'Oise □, France 18 B5
Val d'Or, Canada 70 C4
Val Marie, Canada 73 D7
Valahia, Romania 17 F12
Valcheta, Argentina 96 E3
Valdayskaya Vozvyshennost, Russia 24 C5
Valdepeñas, Spain 19 C4
Valdés, Pen., Argentina 96 E4
Valdez, U.S.A. 68 B5
Valdivia, Chile 96 D2
Valdosta, U.S.A. 77 K4
Vale, U.S.A. 82 E5
Valença, Brazil 93 F11
Valença do Piauí, Brazil 93 E10
Valence, France 18 D6
Valencia, Spain 19 C5
Valencia, Venezuela 92 A5
Valencia □, Spain 19 C5
Valencia, Albufera de, Spain 19 C5
Valencia, G. de, Spain 19 C6
Valencia de Alcántara, Spain 19 C2
Valenciennes, France 18 A5
Valentia Harbour, Ireland 13 E1
Valentia I., Ireland 13 E1
Valentim, Sa. do, Brazil 93 E10
Valentin, Russia 30 C7
Valentine, Nebr., U.S.A. 80 D4
Valentine, Tex., U.S.A. 81 K2
Valera, Venezuela 92 B4
Valier, U.S.A. 82 B7
Valjevo, Serbia, Yug. 21 B8
Valkeakoski, Finland 9 F18
Valkenswaard, Neths. 15 C5
Valladolid, Mexico 87 C7
Valladolid, Spain 19 B3
Valldemosa, Spain 22 B9
Valle d'Aosta □, Italy 20 B2
Valle de la Pascua, Venezuela 92 B5
Valle de las Palmas, Mexico 85 N10
Valle de Santiago, Mexico 86 C4
Valle de Suchil, Mexico 86 C4
Valle de Zaragoza, Mexico 86 B3
Valle Fértil, Sierra del, Argentina 94 C2
Valle Hermoso, Mexico 87 B5
Vallecas, Spain 19 B4
Valledupar, Colombia 92 A4
Vallehermoso, Canary Is. 22 F2
Vallejo, U.S.A. 84 G4
Vallenar, Chile 94 B1
Valletta, Malta 23 D2
Valley Center, U.S.A. 85 M9
Valley City, U.S.A. 80 B6
Valley Falls, U.S.A. 82 E3
Valley Springs, U.S.A. 84 G6
Valley Wells, U.S.A. 85 K11
Valleyview, Canada 72 B5
Vallimanca, Arroyo, Argentina 94 D4
Valls, Spain 19 B6
Valognes, France 18 B3
Valparaíso, Chile 94 C1
Valparaíso, Mexico 86 C4
Valparaiso, U.S.A. 76 E2
Valparaíso □, Chile 94 C1
Vals →, S. Africa 56 D4
Vals, Tanjung, Indonesia 37 F9
Valsad, India 40 J8
Valverde, Canary Is. 22 G2
Valverde del Camino, Spain 19 D2
Vámos, Greece 23 D6
Van, Turkey 25 G7
Van, L. = Van Gölü, Turkey 25 G7
Van Alstyne, U.S.A. 81 J6
Van Bruyssel, Canada 71 C5
Van Buren, Canada 71 C6
Van Buren, Ark., U.S.A. 81 H7
Van Buren, Maine, U.S.A. 77 B11
Van Buren, Mo., U.S.A. 81 G9
Van Canh, Vietnam 38 F7
Van Diemen, C., N. Terr., Australia 60 B5
Van Diemen, C., Queens., Australia 62 B2
Van Diemen G., Australia 60 B5
Van Gölü, Turkey 25 G7
Van Horn, U.S.A. 81 K2
Van Ninh, Vietnam 38 F7
Van Reenen P., S. Africa 57 D4
Van Rees, Pegunungan, Indonesia 37 E9
Van Tassell, U.S.A. 80 D2
Van Wert, U.S.A. 76 E3
Van Yen, Vietnam 38 B5
Vanavara, Russia 27 C11
Vancouver, Canada 72 D4
Vancouver, U.S.A. 84 E4
Vancouver, C., Australia 61 G2
Vancouver I., Canada 72 D3
Vandalia, Ill., U.S.A. 80 F10
Vandalia, Mo., U.S.A. 80 F9
Vandenburg, U.S.A. 85 L6
Vanderbijlpark, S. Africa 57 D4
Vandergrift, U.S.A. 78 F5
Vanderhoof, Canada 72 C4
Vanderlin I., Australia 62 B2
Vandyke, Australia 62 C4
Vänern, Sweden 9 G12
Vänersborg, Sweden 9 G12
Vang Vieng, Laos 38 C4
Vanga, Kenya 54 C4
Vangaindrano, Madag. 57 C8
Vanguard, Canada 73 D7
Vanier, Canada 70 C4
Vankarem, Russia 27 C18
Vankleek Hill, Canada 70 C5
Vanna, Norway 8 A15
Vännäs, Sweden 8 E15
Vannes, France 18 C2
Vanrhynsdorp, S. Africa 56 E2
Vanrook, Australia 62 B3
Vansbro, Sweden 9 F13
Vansittart B., Australia 60 B4
Vanthli, India 42 J4
Vanua Levu, Fiji 59 C8
Vanua Mbalavu, Fiji 59 C9
Vanuatu ■, Pac. Oc. 64 J8
Vanwyksvlei, S. Africa 56 E3
Vanzylsrus, S. Africa 56 D3
Var □, France 18 E7
Varanasi, India 43 G10
Varangerfjorden, Norway 8 A20
Varaždin, Croatia 20 A7
Varberg, Sweden 9 H12
Vardar →, Macedonia, Yug. 21 D10
Varella, Mui, Vietnam 38 F7
Varese, Italy 20 B3
Varginha, Brazil 95 A6
Variadero, U.S.A. 81 H2
Varillas, Chile 94 A1
Värmlands län □, Sweden 9 G12
Varna, Bulgaria 21 C12
Värnamo, Sweden 9 H13
Vars, Canada 79 A9
Varzaneh, Iran 45 C7
Vasa, Finland 8 E16
Vasa Barris →, Brazil 93 F11
Vascongadas = País Vasco □, Spain 19 A4
Vasht = Khāsh, Iran 40 E2
Vaslui, Romania 17 E13
Vassar, Canada 73 D9
Vassar, U.S.A. 76 D4
Västerås, Sweden 9 G14
Västerbottens län □, Sweden 8 D14
Västernorrlands län □, Sweden 8 E14
Västervik, Sweden 9 H14
Västmanlands län □, Sweden 9 G14
Vasto, Italy 20 C6
Vatili, Cyprus 23 D12
Vatnajökull, Iceland 8 D5
Vatneyri, Iceland 8 D2
Vatoa, Fiji 59 D9
Vatólakkos, Greece 23 D5
Vatoloha, Madag. 57 B8
Vatomandry, Madag. 57 B8
Vatra-Dornei, Romania 17 E12
Vättern, Sweden 9 G13
Vaucluse □, France 18 E6
Vaughn, Mont., U.S.A. 82 C8
Vaughn, N. Mex., U.S.A. 83 J11
Vaupés = Uaupés →, Brazil 92 C5
Vauxhall, Canada 72 C6
Vava'u, Tonga 59 D11
Växjö, Sweden 9 H13
Vaygach, Ostrov, Russia 26 C6
Váyia, Ákra, Greece 23 C10
Vechte →, Neths. 15 B6
Vedea →, Romania 17 G12
Vedia, Argentina 94 C3
Vedra, I. del, Spain 22 C7
Veendam, Neths. 15 A6
Veenendaal, Neths. 15 B5
Vefsna →, Norway 8 D12
Vega, Norway 8 D11
Vega, U.S.A. 81 H3
Vegafjorden, Norway 8 D12
Veghel, Neths. 15 C5
Vegreville, Canada 72 C6
Vejer de la Frontera, Spain 19 D3
Vejle, Denmark 9 J10
Velas, C., Costa Rica 88 D2
Velasco, Sierra de, Argentina 94 B2
Velay, Mts. du, France 18 D5
Velddrif, S. Africa 56 E2
Velebit Planina, Croatia 20 B6
Vélez, Colombia 92 B4
Vélez Málaga, Spain 19 D3
Vélez Rubio, Spain 19 D4
Velhas →, Brazil 93 G10
Velikaya →, Russia 24 C4
Velikaya Kema, Russia 30 B8
Veliki Ustyug, Russia 24 B8
Velikiye Luki, Russia 24 C5
Velikonda Range, India 40 M11
Velletri, Italy 20 D5
Vellore, India 40 N11
Velsen-Noord, Neths. 15 B4
Velsk, Russia 24 B7
Velva, U.S.A. 80 A4
Venado Tuerto, Argentina 94 C3
Venda □, S. Africa 57 C5
Vendée □, France 18 C3
Véneto □, Italy 20 B5
Venézia, Italy 20 B5
Venézia, G. di, Italy 20 B5
Venezuela ■, S. Amer. 92 B5
Venezuela, G. de, Venezuela 92 A4
Vengurla, India 40 M8
Venice = Venézia, Italy 20 B5
Venkatapuram, India 41 K12
Venlo, Neths. 15 C6
Venraij, Neths. 15 C5
Ventana, Punta de la, Mexico 86 C3
Ventana, Sa. de la, Argentina 94 D3
Ventersburg, S. Africa 56 D4
Venterstad, S. Africa 56 E4
Ventnor, U.K. 11 G6
Ventspils, Latvia 9 H16
Ventuarí →, Venezuela 92 C5
Ventucopa, U.S.A. 85 L7
Ventura, U.S.A. 85 L7
Venus B., Australia 63 F4
Vera, Argentina 94 B3
Vera, Spain 19 D5
Veracruz, Mexico 87 D5
Veracruz □, Mexico 87 D5
Veraval, India 42 J4
Vercelli, Italy 20 B3
Verdalsøra, Norway 8 E11
Verde →, Argentina 96 E3
Verde →, Chihuahua, Mexico 86 B3
Verde →, Oaxaca, Mexico 87 D5
Verde →, Veracruz, Mexico 86 C4
Verde →, Paraguay 94 A4
Verde, Cay, Bahamas 88 B4
Verden, Germany 16 B4
Verdi, U.S.A. 84 F7
Verdigre, U.S.A. 80 D5
Verdun, France 18 B6
Vereeniging, S. Africa 57 D4
Vérendrye, Parc Prov. de la, Canada 70 C4
Verga, C., Guinea 50 F2
Vergemont, Australia 62 C3
Vergemont Cr. →, Australia 62 C3
Vergennes, U.S.A. 79 B11
Verkhnevilyuysk, Russia 27 C13
Verkhneye Kalinino, Russia 27 D11
Verkhniy Baskunchak, Russia 25 E8
Verkhoyansk, Russia 27 C14
Verkhoyansk Ra. = Verkhoyanskiy Khrebet, Russia 27 C13
Verkhoyanskiy Khrebet, Russia 27 C13
Verlo, Canada 73 C7
Vermilion, Canada 73 C6
Vermilion →, Alta., Canada 73 C6
Vermilion →, Qué., Canada 70 C5
Vermilion, B., U.S.A. 81 L9
Vermilion Bay, Canada 73 D10
Vermilion Chutes, Canada 72 B6
Vermilion L., U.S.A. 80 B8
Vermillion, U.S.A. 80 D6
Vermont □, U.S.A. 79 C12
Vernal, U.S.A. 82 F9
Vernalis, U.S.A. 84 H5
Verner, Canada 70 C3
Verneukpan, S. Africa 56 D3
Vernon, Canada 72 C5
Vernon, U.S.A. 81 H5
Vernonia, U.S.A. 84 E3
Vero Beach, U.S.A. 77 M5
Véroia, Greece 21 D10
Verona, Italy 20 B4
Veropol, Russia 27 C17
Versailles, France 18 B5
Vert, C., Senegal 50 F1
Verulam, S. Africa 57 D5
Verviers, Belgium 15 D5
Veselovskoye Vdkhr., Russia 25 E7
Vesoul, France 18 C7
Vest-Agder fylke □, Norway 9 G9
Vesterålen, Norway 8 B13
Vestfjorden, Norway 8 C13
Vestfold fylke □, Norway 9 G11
Vestmannaeyjar, Iceland 8 E3
Vestspitsbergen, Svalbard 4 B8
Vestvågøy, Norway 8 B12
Vesuvio, Italy 20 D6
Vesuvius, Mt. = Vesuvio, Italy 20 D6
Veszprém, Hungary 17 E8
Vetlanda, Sweden 9 H13
Vetlugu →, Russia 26 D5
Veurne, Belgium 15 C2
Veys, Iran 45 D6
Vezhen, Bulgaria 21 C11
Vi Thanh, Vietnam 39 H5
Viacha, Bolivia 92 G5
Viamão, Brazil 95 C5
Viana, Brazil 93 D10
Viana, Portugal 19 C2
Viana do Castelo, Portugal 19 B1
Vianópolis, Brazil 93 G9
Vibank, Canada 73 C8
Viborg, Denmark 9 H10
Vicenza, Italy 20 B4
Vich, Spain 19 B7
Vichy, France 18 C5
Vicksburg, Ariz., U.S.A. 85 M13
Vicksburg, Mich., U.S.A. 76 D3
Vicksburg, Miss., U.S.A. 81 J9
Viçosa, Brazil 93 E11
Victor, India 42 J4
Victor, Colo., U.S.A. 80 F2
Victor, N.Y., U.S.A. 78 D7
Victor Harbor, Australia 63 F2
Victoria, Argentina 94 C3
Victoria, Canada 72 D4
Victoria, Chile 96 D2
Victoria, Guinea 50 F2
Victoria, Malaysia 36 C5
Victoria, Malta 23 C1
Victoria, Kans., U.S.A. 80 F5
Victoria, Tex., U.S.A. 81 L6

Victoria □, *Australia* 63 F3
Victoria →, *Australia* 60 C4
Victoria, Grand L., *Canada* 70 C4
Victoria, L., *Africa* 54 C3
Victoria, L., *Australia* 63 E3
Victoria Beach, *Canada* 73 C9
Victoria de Durango, *Mexico* 86 C4
Victoria de las Tunas, *Cuba* 88 B4
Victoria Falls, *Zimbabwe* 55 F2
Victoria Harbour, *Canada* 70 D4
Victoria I., *Canada* 68 A8
Victoria Ld., *Antarctica* 5 D11
Victoria Nile →, *Uganda* 54 B3
Victoria Res., *Canada* 71 C8
Victoria River Downs, *Australia* 60 C5
Victoria Taungdeik, *Burma* 41 J18
Victoria West, *S. Africa* 56 E3
Victoriaville, *Canada* 71 C5
Victorica, *Argentina* 94 D2
Victorville, *U.S.A.* 85 L9
Vicuña, *Chile* 94 C1
Vicuña Mackenna, *Argentina* 94 C3
Vidal, *U.S.A.* 85 L12
Vidal Junction, *U.S.A.* 85 L12
Vidalia, *U.S.A.* 77 J4
Vidho, *Greece* 23 A3
Vidin, *Bulgaria* 21 C10
Vidisha, *India* 42 H7
Viedma, *Argentina* 96 E4
Viedma, L., *Argentina* 96 F2
Vieng Pou Kha, *Laos* 38 B3
Vienna = Wien, *Austria* 16 D8
Vienna, *U.S.A.* 81 G10
Vienne, *France* 18 D6
Vienne □, *France* 18 C4
Vienne →, *France* 18 C4
Vientiane, *Laos* 38 D4
Vientos, Paso de los, *Caribbean* 89 C5
Vierzon, *France* 18 C5
Vietnam ■, *Asia* 38 C5
Vigan, *Phil.* 37 A6
Vigia, *Brazil* 93 D9
Vigía Chico, *Mexico* 87 D7
Víglas, Ákra, *Greece* 23 D9
Vigo, *Spain* 19 A1
Vijayawada, *India* 41 L12
Viking, *Canada* 72 C6
Vikna, *Norway* 8 D11
Vikulovo, *Russia* 26 D8
Vila da Maganja, *Mozam.* 55 F4
Vila de João Belo = Xai-Xai, *Mozam.* 57 D5
Vila do Chibuto, *Mozam.* 57 C5
Vila Franca de Xira, *Portugal* 19 C1
Vila Gamito, *Mozam.* 55 E3
Vila Gomes da Costa, *Mozam.* 57 C5
Vila Machado, *Mozam.* 55 F3
Vila Mouzinho, *Mozam.* 55 E3
Vila Real, *Portugal* 19 B2
Vila Real de Santo António, *Portugal* 19 D2
Vila Vasco da Gama, *Mozam.* 55 E3
Vila Velha, *Brazil* 95 A7
Vilaine →, *France* 18 C2
Vilanandro, Tanjona, *Madag.* 57 B7
Vilanculos, *Mozam.* 57 C6
Vilhelmina, *Sweden* 8 D14
Vilhena, *Brazil* 92 F6
Viliga, *Russia* 27 C16
Villa Abecia, *Bolivia* 94 A2
Villa Ahumada, *Mexico* 86 A3
Villa Ana, *Argentina* 94 B4
Villa Ángela, *Argentina* 94 B3
Villa Bella, *Bolivia* 92 F5
Villa Bens = Tarfaya, *Morocco* 50 C2
Villa Cañás, *Argentina* 94 C3
Villa Carlos, *Spain* 22 B11
Villa Cisneros = Dakhla, *Mauritania* 50 D1
Villa Colón, *Argentina* 94 C2
Villa Constitución, *Argentina* 94 C3
Villa de María, *Argentina* 94 B3
Villa Dolores, *Argentina* 94 C2
Villa Frontera, *Mexico* 86 B4
Villa Guillermina, *Argentina* 94 B4
Villa Hayes, *Paraguay* 94 B4
Villa Iris, *Argentina* 94 D3
Villa Juárez, *Mexico* 86 B4
Villa María, *Argentina* 94 C3
Villa Mazán, *Argentina* 94 B2
Villa Montes, *Bolivia* 94 A3
Villa Ocampo, *Argentina* 94 B4
Villa Ocampo, *Mexico* 86 B3
Villa Ojo de Agua, *Argentina* 94 B3
Villa San José, *Argentina* 94 C4
Villa San Martín, *Argentina* 94 B3
Villa Unión, *Mexico* 86 C3
Villach, *Austria* 16 E6
Villafranca de los Caballeros, *Spain* 22 B10
Villagarcía de Arosa, *Spain* 19 A1
Villagrán, *Mexico* 87 C5
Villaguay, *Argentina* 94 C4
Villahermosa, *Mexico* 87 D6
Villalba, *Spain* 19 A2
Villanueva, *U.S.A.* 83 J11
Villanueva de la Serena, *Spain* 19 C3
Villarreal, *Spain* 19 C5
Villarrica, *Chile* 96 D2
Villarrica, *Paraguay* 94 B4
Villarrobledo, *Spain* 19 C4
Villavicencio, *Argentina* 94 C2
Villavicencio, *Colombia* 92 C4
Villaviciosa, *Spain* 19 A3
Villazón, *Bolivia* 94 A2
Ville-Marie, *Canada* 70 C4
Ville Platte, *U.S.A.* 81 K8
Villena, *Spain* 19 C5
Villiers, *S. Africa* 57 D4
Villisca, *U.S.A.* 80 E7
Vilna, *Canada* 72 C6
Vilnius, *Lithuania* 24 D4
Vilskutskogo, Proliv, *Russia* 27 B11
Vilvoorde, *Belgium* 15 D4
Vilyuy →, *Russia* 27 C13
Vilyuysk, *Russia* 27 C13
Viña del Mar, *Chile* 94 C1
Vinaroz, *Spain* 19 B6
Vincennes, *U.S.A.* 76 F2
Vincent, *U.S.A.* 85 L8
Vinchina, *Argentina* 94 B2
Vindel älven →, *Sweden* 8 E15
Vindeln, *Sweden* 8 D15
Vindhya Ra., *India* 42 H7
Vineland, *U.S.A.* 76 F8
Vinh, *Vietnam* 38 C5
Vinh Linh, *Vietnam* 38 D6
Vinh Long, *Vietnam* 39 G5
Vinh Yen, *Vietnam* 38 B5
Vinita, *U.S.A.* 81 G7
Vinkovci, *Croatia* 21 B8
Vinnitsa, *Ukraine* 25 E4
Vinton, *Calif., U.S.A.* 84 F6
Vinton, *Iowa, U.S.A.* 80 D8
Vinton, *La., U.S.A.* 81 K8
Viqueque, *Indonesia* 37 F7
Virac, *Phil.* 37 B6
Virachei, *Cambodia* 38 F6
Virago Sd., *Canada* 72 C2
Viramgam, *India* 42 H5
Virden, *Canada* 73 D8
Vire, *France* 18 B3
Vírgenes, C., *Argentina* 96 G3
Virgin →, *Canada* 73 B7
Virgin →, *U.S.A.* 83 H6
Virgin Gorda, *Virgin Is.* 89 C7
Virgin Is., *W. Indies* 89 C7
Virginia, *S. Africa* 56 D4
Virginia, *U.S.A.* 80 B8
Virginia □, *U.S.A.* 76 G7
Virginia Beach, *U.S.A.* 76 G8
Virginia City, *Mont., U.S.A.* 82 D8
Virginia City, *Nev., U.S.A.* 84 F7
Virginia Falls, *Canada* 72 A3
Virginiatown, *Canada* 70 C4
Viroqua, *U.S.A.* 80 D9
Virton, *Belgium* 15 E5
Virudunagar, *India* 40 Q10
Vis, *Croatia* 20 C7
Visalia, *U.S.A.* 83 H4
Visayan Sea, *Phil.* 37 B6
Visby, *Sweden* 9 H15
Viscount Melville Sd., *Canada* 4 B2
Visé, *Belgium* 15 D5
Višegrad, *Bos. & H., Yug.* 21 C8
Viseu, *Brazil* 93 D9
Viseu, *Portugal* 19 B2
Vishakhapatnam, *India* 41 L13
Visnagar, *India* 42 H5
Viso, Mte., *Italy* 20 B2
Visokoi I., *Antarctica* 5 B1
Vista, *U.S.A.* 85 M9
Vistula = Wisła →, *Poland* 17 A9
Vitebsk, *Belorussia* 24 C5
Viterbo, *Italy* 20 C5
Viti Levu, *Fiji* 59 C7
Vitim, *Russia* 27 D12
Vitim →, *Russia* 27 D12
Vitória, *Brazil* 93 H10
Vitoria, *Spain* 19 A4
Vitória da Conquista, *Brazil* 93 F10
Vittória, *Italy* 20 F6
Vittório Véneto, *Italy* 20 B5
Vivero, *Spain* 19 A2
Vizcaíno, Desierto de, *Mexico* 86 B2
Vizcaíno, Sierra, *Mexico* 86 B2
Vizianagaram, *India* 41 K13
Vlaardingen, *Neths.* 15 C4
Vladikavkaz, *Russia* 25 F7
Vladimir, *Russia* 24 C7
Vladivostok, *Russia* 27 E14
Vlieland, *Neths.* 15 A4
Vlissingen, *Neths.* 15 C3
Vltava →, *Czech.* 16 C7
Vo Dat, *Vietnam* 39 G6
Vogelkop = Doberai, Jazirah, *Indonesia* 37 E8
Vogelsberg, *Germany* 16 C4
Vohibinany, *Madag.* 57 B8
Vohimarina, *Madag.* 57 A9
Vohimena, Tanjon' i, *Madag.* 57 D8
Vohipeno, *Madag.* 57 C8
Voi, *Kenya* 54 C4
Voisey B., *Canada* 71 A7
Vojmsjön, *Sweden* 8 D14
Volborg, *U.S.A.* 80 C2
Volcano Is. = Kazan-Rettō, *Pac. Oc.* 64 E6
Volchayevka, *Russia* 27 E14
Volda, *Norway* 8 E9
Volga →, *Russia* 25 E8
Volga Hts. = Privolzhskaya Vozvyshennost, *Russia* 25 D8
Volgodonsk, *Russia* 25 E7
Volgograd, *Russia* 25 E7
Volgogradskoye Vdkhr., *Russia* 25 D8
Volkhov →, *Russia* 24 B5
Volksrust, *S. Africa* 57 D4
Vollenhove, *Neths.* 15 B5
Volochanka, *Russia* 27 B10
Vologda, *Russia* 24 C6
Vólos, *Greece* 21 E10
Volsk, *Russia* 24 D8
Volta →, *Ghana* 50 F4
Volta, L., *Ghana* 50 G5
Volta Redonda, *Brazil* 95 A7
Voltaire, C., *Australia* 60 B4
Volterra, *Italy* 20 C4
Volturno →, *Italy* 20 D5
Volvo, *Australia* 63 E3
Volzhskiy, *Russia* 25 E7
Vondrozo, *Madag.* 57 C8
Voorburg, *Neths.* 15 B4
Vopnafjörður, *Iceland* 8 D6
Vorarlberg □, *Austria* 16 E5
Voríai Sporádhes, *Greece* 21 E10
Vorkuta, *Russia* 24 A11
Voronezh, *Russia* 24 D6
Voroshilovgrad = Lugansk, *Ukraine* 25 E6
Voroshilovsk = Kommunarsk, *Ukraine* 25 E6
Vorovskoye, *Russia* 27 D16
Vosges, *France* 18 B7
Vosges □, *France* 18 B7
Voss, *Norway* 9 F9
Vostok I., *Kiribati* 65 J12
Votkinsk, *Russia* 24 C9
Votkinskoye Vdkhr., *Russia* 24 C10
Vouga →, *Portugal* 19 B1
Voúxa, Ákra, *Greece* 23 D5
Vozhe Oz., *Russia* 24 B6
Voznesenka, *Russia* 27 D10
Voznesensk, *Ukraine* 25 E5
Voznesenye, *Russia* 24 B6
Vrangelya, Ostrov, *Russia* 27 B19
Vranje, *Serbia, Yug.* 21 C9
Vratsa, *Bulgaria* 21 C10
Vrbas →, *Bos. & H., Yug.* 21 B7
Vrede, *S. Africa* 57 D4
Vredefort, *S. Africa* 56 D4
Vredenburg, *S. Africa* 56 E2
Vredendal, *S. Africa* 56 E2
Vrindavan, *India* 42 F7
Vrises, *Greece* 23 D6
Vršac, *Serbia, Yug.* 21 B9
Vryburg, *S. Africa* 56 D3
Vryheid, *S. Africa* 57 D5
Vu Liet, *Vietnam* 38 C5
Vught, *Neths.* 15 C5
Vulcan, *Canada* 72 C6
Vulcan, *U.S.A.* 76 C2
Vulcano, *Italy* 20 E6
Vunduzi →, *Mozam.* 55 F3
Vung Tau, *Vietnam* 39 G6
Vyatka, *Russia* 26 D5
Vyatka →, *Russia* 24 C9
Vyatskiye Polyany, *Russia* 24 C9
Vyazemskiy, *Russia* 27 E14
Vyazma, *Russia* 24 C5
Vyborg, *Russia* 24 B4
Vychegda →, *Russia* 24 B8
Vychodné Beskydy, *Europe* 17 D10
Vyg-ozero, *Russia* 24 B5
Vyrnwy, L., *U.K.* 10 E4
Vyshniy Volochek, *Russia* 24 C5
Vyshzha = imeni 26 Bakinskikh Komissarov, *Turkmenistan* 25 G9
Vytegra, *Russia* 24 B6

W

W.A.C. Bennett Dam, *Canada* 72 B4
Wa, *Ghana* 50 F4
Waal →, *Neths.* 15 C5
Wabakimi L., *Canada* 70 B2
Wabana, *Canada* 71 C9
Wabasca, *Canada* 72 B6
Wabash, *U.S.A.* 76 E3
Wabash →, *U.S.A.* 76 G1
Wabeno, *U.S.A.* 76 C1
Wabigoon L., *Canada* 73 D10
Wabowden, *Canada* 73 C9
Wąbrzeźno, *Poland* 17 B9
Wabuk Pt., *Canada* 70 A2
Wabush, *Canada* 71 B6
Wabuska, *U.S.A.* 82 G4
Waco, *U.S.A.* 81 K6
Waconichi, L., *Canada* 70 B5
Wad Banda, *Sudan* 51 F10
Wad Hamid, *Sudan* 51 E11
Wâd Medanî, *Sudan* 51 F11
Wad Thana, *Pakistan* 42 F2
Wadayama, *Japan* 31 G7
Waddeneilanden, *Neths.* 15 A5
Waddenzee, *Neths.* 15 A5
Wadderin Hill, *Australia* 61 F2
Waddington, *U.S.A.* 79 B9
Waddington, Mt., *Canada* 72 C3
Waddy Pt., *Australia* 63 C5
Wadena, *Canada* 73 C8
Wadena, *U.S.A.* 80 B7
Wadesboro, *U.S.A.* 77 H5
Wadhams, *Canada* 72 C3
Wādī as Sīr, *Jordan* 47 D4
Wadi Halfa, *Sudan* 51 D11
Wadsworth, *U.S.A.* 82 G4
Waegwan, *S. Korea* 35 G15
Wafrah, *Si. Arabia* 44 D5
Wageningen, *Neths.* 15 C5
Wager B., *Canada* 69 B11
Wager Bay, *Canada* 69 B10
Wagga Wagga, *Australia* 63 F4
Waghete, *Indonesia* 37 E9
Wagin, *Australia* 61 F2
Wagon Mound, *U.S.A.* 81 G2
Wagoner, *U.S.A.* 81 G7
Wah, *Pakistan* 42 C5
Wahai, *Indonesia* 37 E7
Wahiawa, *U.S.A.* 74 H15
Wâhid, *Egypt* 47 E1
Wahnai, *Afghan.* 42 C1
Wahoo, *U.S.A.* 80 E6
Wahpeton, *U.S.A.* 80 B6
Wai, Koh, *Cambodia* 39 H4
Waiau →, *N.Z.* 59 K4
Waibeem, *Indonesia* 37 E8
Waigeo, *Indonesia* 37 E8
Waihi, *N.Z.* 59 G5
Waihou →, *N.Z.* 59 G5
Waika, *Zaïre* 54 C2
Waikabubak, *Indonesia* 37 F5
Waikari, *N.Z.* 59 K4
Waikato →, *N.Z.* 59 G5
Waikerie, *Australia* 63 E2
Waikokopu, *N.Z.* 59 H6
Waikouaiti, *N.Z.* 59 L3
Waimakariri →, *N.Z.* 59 K4
Waimate, *N.Z.* 59 L3
Wainganga →, *India* 40 K11
Waingapu, *Indonesia* 37 F6
Wainwright, *Canada* 73 C6
Wainwright, *U.S.A.* 68 A3
Waiouru, *N.Z.* 59 H5
Waipara, *N.Z.* 59 K4
Waipawa, *N.Z.* 59 H6
Waipiro, *N.Z.* 59 H7
Waipu, *N.Z.* 59 F5
Waipukurau, *N.Z.* 59 J6
Wairakei, *N.Z.* 59 H6
Wairarapa, L., *N.Z.* 59 J5
Wairoa, *N.Z.* 59 H6
Waitaki →, *N.Z.* 59 L3
Waitara, *N.Z.* 59 H5
Waitsburg, *U.S.A.* 82 C5
Waiuku, *N.Z.* 59 G5
Wajima, *Japan* 31 F8
Wajir, *Kenya* 54 B5
Wajir □, *Kenya* 54 B5
Wakasa, *Japan* 31 G7
Wakasa-Wan, *Japan* 31 G7
Wakatipu, L., *N.Z.* 59 L2
Wakaw, *Canada* 73 C7
Wakayama, *Japan* 31 G7
Wakayama-ken □, *Japan* 31 H7
Wake Forest, *U.S.A.* 77 H6
Wake I., *Pac. Oc.* 64 F8
Wakefield, *N.Z.* 59 J4
Wakefield, *U.K.* 10 D6
Wakefield, *Mass., U.S.A.* 79 D13
Wakefield, *Mich., U.S.A.* 80 B10
Wakema, *Burma* 41 L19
Wakkanai, *Japan* 30 B10
Wakkerstroom, *S. Africa* 57 D5
Wakool, *Australia* 63 F3
Wakool →, *Australia* 63 F3
Wakre, *Indonesia* 37 E8
Wakuach L., *Canada* 71 A6
Walamba, *Zambia* 55 E2
Wałbrzych, *Poland* 16 C8
Walbury Hill, *U.K.* 11 F6
Walcha, *Australia* 63 E5
Walcheren, *Neths.* 15 C3
Walcott, *U.S.A.* 82 F10
Waldburg Ra., *Australia* 60 D2
Walden, *Colo., U.S.A.* 82 F10
Walden, *N.Y., U.S.A.* 79 E10
Waldport, *U.S.A.* 82 D1
Waldron, *U.S.A.* 81 H7
Wales □, *U.K.* 11 E4
Walgett, *Australia* 63 E4
Walgreen Coast, *Antarctica* 5 D15
Walhalla, *Australia* 63 F4
Walhalla, *U.S.A.* 73 D9
Walker, *U.S.A.* 80 B7
Walker L., *Man., Canada* 73 C9
Walker L., *Qué., Canada* 71 B6
Walker L., *U.S.A.* 82 G4
Walkerston, *Australia* 62 C4
Walkerton, *Canada* 78 B3
Wall, *U.S.A.* 80 C3
Walla Walla, *U.S.A.* 82 C4
Wallabadah, *Australia* 62 B3
Wallace, *Idaho, U.S.A.* 82 C6
Wallace, *N.C., U.S.A.* 77 H7
Wallace, *Nebr., U.S.A.* 80 E4
Wallaceburg, *Canada* 70 D3
Wallachia = Valahia, *Romania* 17 F12
Wallal, *Australia* 63 D4
Wallal Downs, *Australia* 60 C3
Wallambin, L., *Australia* 61 F2
Wallaroo, *Australia* 63 E2
Wallasey, *U.K.* 10 D4
Wallerawang, *Australia* 63 E5
Wallhallow, *Australia* 62 B2
Wallingford, *U.S.A.* 79 E12
Wallis & Futuna, Is., *Pac. Oc.* 64 J10
Wallowa, *U.S.A.* 82 D5
Wallowa Mts., *U.S.A.* 82 D5
Wallsend, *Australia* 63 E5
Wallsend, *U.K.* 10 C6
Wallula, *U.S.A.* 82 C4
Wallumbilla, *Australia* 63 D4
Walmsley, L., *Canada* 73 A7
Walney, I. of, *U.K.* 10 C4
Walnut Creek, *U.S.A.* 84 H4
Walnut Ridge, *U.S.A.* 81 G9
Walsall, *U.K.* 11 E6
Walsenburg, *U.S.A.* 81 G2
Walsh, *U.S.A.* 81 G3
Walsh →, *Australia* 62 B3
Walsh P.O., *Australia* 62 B3
Walterboro, *U.S.A.* 77 J5
Walters, *U.S.A.* 81 H5
Waltham, *U.S.A.* 79 D13
Waltham Station, *Canada* 70 C4
Waltman, *U.S.A.* 82 E10
Walton, *U.S.A.* 79 D9
Walvisbaai, *S. Africa* 56 C1
Wamba, *Kenya* 54 B4
Wamba, *Zaïre* 54 B2
Wamego, *U.S.A.* 80 F6
Wamena, *Indonesia* 37 E9
Wamsasi, *Indonesia* 37 E7
Wan Xian, *China* 34 E8
Wana, *Pakistan* 42 C3
Wanaaring, *Australia* 63 D3
Wanaka, *N.Z.* 59 L2
Wanaka L., *N.Z.* 59 L2
Wanapiri, *Indonesia* 37 E9
Wanapitei L., *Canada* 70 C3
Wanbi, *Australia* 63 E3
Wandarrie, *Australia* 61 E2
Wanderer, *Zimbabwe* 55 F3
Wandoan, *Australia* 63 D4
Wanfu, *China* 35 D12
Wang →, *Thailand* 38 D2
Wang Noi, *Thailand* 38 E3
Wang Saphung, *Thailand* 38 D3
Wang Thong, *Thailand* 38 D3
Wanga, *Zaïre* 54 B2
Wangal, *Indonesia* 37 F8
Wanganella, *Australia* 63 F3
Wanganui, *N.Z.* 59 H5
Wangaratta, *Australia* 63 F4
Wangary, *Australia* 63 E2
Wangdu, *China* 34 E8
Wangerooge, *Germany* 16 B3
Wangi, *Kenya* 54 C5
Wangiwangi, *Indonesia* 37 F6
Wangqing, *China* 35 C15
Wankaner, *India* 42 H4
Wanless, *Canada* 73 C8
Wanon Niwat, *Thailand* 38 D4
Wanquan, *China* 34 D8
Wanrong, *China* 34 G6
Wanxian, *China* 33 C5
Wapakoneta, *U.S.A.* 76 E3
Wapato, *U.S.A.* 82 C3
Wapawekka L., *Canada* 73 C8
Wapikopa L., *Canada* 70 B2
Wappingers Falls, *U.S.A.* 79 E11
Wapsipinicon →, *U.S.A.* 80 E9
Warangal, *India* 40 L11
Waratah, *Australia* 62 G4
Waratah B., *Australia* 63 F4
Warburton, *Vic., Australia* 63 F4
Warburton, *W. Austral., Australia* 61 E4
Warburton Ra., *Australia* 61 E4
Ward, *N.Z.* 59 J5
Ward →, *Australia* 63 D4
Ward Cove, *U.S.A.* 72 B2
Ward Mt., *U.S.A.* 84 H8
Warden, *S. Africa* 57 D4
Wardha, *India* 40 J11
Wardha →, *India* 40 K11
Wardlow, *Canada* 72 C6
Ware, *Canada* 72 B3
Ware, *U.S.A.* 79 D12
Wareham, *U.S.A.* 79 E14
Warialda, *Australia* 63 D5
Wariap, *Indonesia* 37 E8
Warin Chamrap, *Thailand* 38 E5
Warkopi, *Indonesia* 37 E8
Warley, *U.K.* 11 E6
Warm Springs, *U.S.A.* 83 G5
Warman, *Canada* 73 C7
Warmbad, *Namibia* 56 D2
Warmbad, *S. Africa* 57 C4
Warnambool Downs, *Australia* 62 C3
Warnemünde, *Germany* 16 A6
Warner, *Canada* 72 D6
Warner Mts., *U.S.A.* 82 F3
Warner Robins, *U.S.A.* 77 J4
Waroona, *Australia* 61 F2
Warracknabeal, *Australia* 63 F3
Warragul, *Australia* 63 F4
Warrawagine, *Australia* 60 D3
Warrego →, *Australia* 63 E4
Warrego Ra., *Australia* 62 C4
Warren, *Australia* 63 E4
Warren, *Ark., U.S.A.* 81 J8
Warren, *Mich., U.S.A.* 76 D4
Warren, *Minn., U.S.A.* 80 A6
Warren, *Ohio, U.S.A.* 78 E4
Warren, *Pa., U.S.A.* 78 E5
Warrenpoint, *U.K.* 13 B5
Warrensburg, *U.S.A.* 80 F8
Warrenton, *S. Africa* 56 D3
Warrenton, *U.S.A.* 84 D3
Warrenville, *Australia* 63 D4

Warri, Nigeria 50 G6
Warrina, Australia 63 D2
Warrington, U.K. 10 D5
Warrington, U.S.A. 77 K2
Warrnambool, Australia 63 F3
Warroad, U.S.A. 80 A7
Warsa, Indonesia 37 E9
Warsaw = Warszawa, Poland 17 B10
Warsaw, Ind., U.S.A. 76 E3
Warsaw, N.Y., U.S.A. 78 D6
Warsaw, Ohio, U.S.A. 78 F2
Warszawa, Poland 17 B10
Warta →, Poland 16 B7
Warthe = Warta →, Poland 16 B7
Waru, Indonesia 37 E8
Warwick, Australia 63 D5
Warwick, U.K. 11 E6
Warwick, U.S.A. 79 E13
Warwickshire □, U.K. 11 E6
Wasaga Beach, Canada 78 B4
Wasatch Ra., U.S.A. 82 F8
Wasbank, S. Africa 57 D5
Wasco, Calif., U.S.A. 85 K7
Wasco, Oreg., U.S.A. 82 D3
Waseca, U.S.A. 80 C8
Wasekamio L., Canada 73 B7
Wash, The, U.K. 10 E8
Washago, Canada 78 B5
Washburn, N. Dak., U.S.A. 80 B4
Washburn, Wis., U.S.A. 80 B9
Washim, India 40 J10
Washington, D.C., U.S.A. 76 F7
Washington, Ga., U.S.A. 77 J4
Washington, Ind., U.S.A. 76 F2
Washington, Iowa, U.S.A. 80 E9
Washington, Mo., U.S.A. 80 F9
Washington, N.C., U.S.A. 77 H7
Washington, N.J., U.S.A. 79 F10
Washington, Pa., U.S.A. 78 F4
Washington, Utah, U.S.A. 83 H7
Washington □, U.S.A. 82 C3
Washington, Mt., U.S.A. 79 B13
Washington I., U.S.A. 76 C2
Washougal, U.S.A. 84 E4
Wasian, Indonesia 37 E8
Wasior, Indonesia 37 E8
Waskaiowaka, L., Canada 73 B9
Waskesiu Lake, Canada 73 C7
Wassenaar, Neths. 15 B4
Waswanipi, Canada 70 C4
Waswanipi, L., Canada 70 C4
Watangpone, Indonesia 37 E6
Water Park Pt., Australia 62 C5
Water Valley, U.S.A. 81 H10
Waterberge, S. Africa 57 C4
Waterbury, Conn., U.S.A. 79 E11
Waterbury, Vt., U.S.A. 79 B12
Waterbury L., Canada 73 B8
Waterdown, Canada 78 C5
Waterford, Canada 78 D4
Waterford, Ireland 13 D4
Waterford, U.S.A. 84 H6
Waterford □, Ireland 13 D4
Waterford Harbour, Ireland 13 D5
Waterhen L., Man., Canada 73 C9
Waterhen L., Sask., Canada 73 C7
Waterloo, Belgium 15 D4
Waterloo, Ont., Canada 70 D3
Waterloo, Qué., Canada 79 A12
Waterloo, S. Leone 50 G2
Waterloo, Ill., U.S.A. 80 F9
Waterloo, Iowa, U.S.A. 80 D8
Waterloo, N.Y., U.S.A. 78 D8
Watersmeet, U.S.A. 80 B10
Waterton-Glacier Int. Peace Park, U.S.A. 82 B7
Watertown, Conn., U.S.A. 79 E11
Watertown, N.Y., U.S.A. 79 C9
Watertown, S. Dak., U.S.A. 80 C6
Watertown, Wis., U.S.A. 80 D10
Waterval-Boven, S. Africa 57 D5
Waterville, Canada 79 A13
Waterville, Maine, U.S.A. 71 D6
Waterville, N.Y., U.S.A. 79 D9
Waterville, Pa., U.S.A. 78 E7
Waterville, Wash., U.S.A. 82 C3
Watervliet, U.S.A. 79 D11
Wates, Indonesia 37 G14
Watford, Canada 78 D3
Watford, U.K. 11 F7
Watford City, U.S.A. 80 B3
Wathaman →, Canada 73 B8
Watheroo, Australia 61 F2
Wating, China 34 G4
Watkins Glen, U.S.A. 78 D8
Watling I. = San Salvador, Bahamas 89 B5
Watonga, U.S.A. 81 H5
Watrous, Canada 73 C7
Watrous, U.S.A. 81 H2
Watsa, Zaïre 54 B2
Watseka, U.S.A. 76 E2
Watson, Australia 61 F5
Watson, Canada 73 C8
Watson Lake, Canada 72 A3
Watsonville, U.S.A. 83 H3
Wattiwarriganna Cr. →, Australia 63 D2
Watuata = Batuata, Indonesia 37 F6
Watubela, Kepulauan, Indonesia 37 E8
Watubella Is. = Watubela, Kepulauan, Indonesia 37 E8
Waubamik, Canada 78 A4
Waubay, U.S.A. 80 C6
Waubra, Australia 63 F3
Wauchope, Australia 63 E5
Wauchula, U.S.A. 77 M5
Waugh, Canada 73 D9
Waukarlycarly, L., Australia 60 D3
Waukegan, U.S.A. 76 D2
Waukesha, U.S.A. 76 D1
Waukon, U.S.A. 80 D9
Wauneta, U.S.A. 80 E4
Waupaca, U.S.A. 80 C10
Waupun, U.S.A. 80 D10
Waurika, U.S.A. 81 H6
Wausau, U.S.A. 80 C10
Wautoma, U.S.A. 80 C10
Wauwatosa, U.S.A. 76 D2
Wave Hill, Australia 60 C5
Waveney →, U.K. 11 E9
Waverley, N.Z. 59 H5
Waverly, Iowa, U.S.A. 80 D8
Waverly, N.Y., U.S.A. 79 D8
Wavre, Belgium 15 D4
Wâw, Sudan 51 G10
Wâw al Kabir, Libya 51 C8
Wawa, Canada 70 C3
Wawanesa, Canada 73 D9
Wawona, U.S.A. 84 H7
Waxahachie, U.S.A. 81 J6
Way, L., Australia 61 E3
Wayabula Rau, Indonesia 37 D7
Wayatinah, Australia 62 G4
Waycross, U.S.A. 77 K4
Wayne, Nebr., U.S.A. 80 D6
Wayne, W. Va., U.S.A. 76 F4
Waynesboro, Ga., U.S.A. 77 J4
Waynesboro, Miss., U.S.A. 77 K1
Waynesboro, Pa., U.S.A. 76 F7
Waynesboro, Va., U.S.A. 76 F6
Waynesburg, U.S.A. 76 F5
Waynesville, U.S.A. 77 H4
Waynoka, U.S.A. 81 G5
Wazirabad, Pakistan 42 C6
We, Indonesia 36 C1
Weald, The, U.K. 11 F8
Wear →, U.K. 10 C6
Weatherford, Okla., U.S.A. 81 H5
Weatherford, Tex., U.S.A. 81 J6
Weaverville, U.S.A. 82 F2
Webb City, U.S.A. 81 G7
Webster, Mass., U.S.A. 79 D13
Webster, N.Y., U.S.A. 78 C7
Webster, S. Dak., U.S.A. 80 C6
Webster, Wis., U.S.A. 80 C8
Webster City, U.S.A. 80 D8
Webster Green, U.S.A. 80 F9
Webster Springs, U.S.A. 76 F5
Weda, Indonesia 37 D7
Weda, Teluk, Indonesia 37 D7
Weddell I., Falk. Is. 96 G4
Weddell Sea, Antarctica 5 D1
Wedderburn, Australia 63 F3
Wedgeport, Canada 71 D6
Wedza, Zimbabwe 55 F3
Wee Waa, Australia 63 E4
Weed, U.S.A. 82 F2
Weed Heights, U.S.A. 84 G7
Weedsport, U.S.A. 79 C8
Weedville, U.S.A. 78 E6
Weemelah, Australia 63 D4
Weenen, S. Africa 57 D5
Weert, Neths. 15 C5
Wei He →, Hebei, China 34 F8
Wei He →, Shaanxi, China 34 G6
Weichang, China 35 D9
Weichuan, China 34 G7
Weifang, China 33 C6
Weifang, Shandong, China 35 F10
Weihai, China 35 F12
Weimar, Germany 16 C5
Weinan, China 34 G5
Weipa, Australia 62 A3
Weir →, Australia 63 D4
Weir →, Canada 73 B10
Weir River, Canada 73 B10
Weirton, U.S.A. 78 F4
Weiser, U.S.A. 82 D5
Weishan, China 35 G9
Weiyuan, China 34 G3
Wejherowo, Poland 17 A9
Wekusko L., Canada 73 C9
Welbourn Hill, Australia 63 D1
Welch, U.S.A. 76 G5
Welkom, S. Africa 56 D4
Welland, Canada 70 D4
Welland →, U.K. 10 E7
Wellesley Is., Australia 62 B2
Wellin, Belgium 15 D5
Wellingborough, U.K. 11 E7
Wellington, Australia 63 E4
Wellington, Canada 70 D4
Wellington, N.Z. 59 J5
Wellington, S. Africa 56 E2
Wellington, Shrops., U.K. 10 E5
Wellington, Somst., U.K. 11 G4
Wellington, Colo., U.S.A. 80 E2
Wellington, Kans., U.S.A. 81 G6
Wellington, Nev., U.S.A. 84 G7
Wellington, Ohio, U.S.A. 78 E2
Wellington, Tex., U.S.A. 81 H4
Wellington, I., Chile 96 F1
Wellington, L., Australia 63 F4
Wells, Norfolk, U.K. 10 E8
Wells, Somst., U.K. 11 F5
Wells, Maine, U.S.A. 79 C14
Wells, Minn., U.S.A. 80 D8
Wells, Nev., U.S.A. 82 F6
Wells, L., Australia 61 E3
Wells Gray Prov. Park, Canada 72 C4
Wells River, U.S.A. 79 B12
Wellsboro, U.S.A. 78 E7
Wellsburg, U.S.A. 78 F4
Wellsville, Mo., U.S.A. 80 F9
Wellsville, N.Y., U.S.A. 78 D7
Wellsville, Ohio, U.S.A. 78 F4
Wellsville, Utah, U.S.A. 82 F8
Wellton, U.S.A. 83 K6
Wels, Austria 16 D7
Welshpool, U.K. 11 E4
Wem, U.K. 10 E5
Wembere →, Tanzania 54 C3
Wen Xian, Gansu, China 34 H3
Wen Xian, Henan, China 34 G7
Wenatchee, U.S.A. 82 C3
Wenchang, China 38 C8
Wenchi, Ghana 50 G4
Wenchow = Wenzhou, China 33 D7
Wendell, U.S.A. 82 E6
Wendeng, China 35 F12
Wendesi, Indonesia 37 E8
Wendon, U.S.A. 85 M13
Wendover, U.S.A. 82 F6
Wenlock →, Australia 62 A3
Wenshan, China 32 D5
Wenshang, China 34 G9
Wenshui, China 34 F7
Wensu, China 32 B3
Wentworth, Australia 63 E3
Wenut, Indonesia 37 E8
Wenxi, China 34 G6
Wenzhou, China 33 D7
Weott, U.S.A. 82 F2
Wepener, S. Africa 56 D4
Werda, Botswana 56 D3
Werder, Ethiopia 46 F4
Weri, Indonesia 37 E8
Werribee, Australia 63 F3
Werrimull, Australia 63 E3
Werris Creek, Australia 63 E5
Wersar, Indonesia 37 E8
Weser →, Germany 16 B4
Wesiri, Indonesia 37 F7
Wesley Vale, U.S.A. 83 J10
Wesleyville, Canada 71 C9
Wesleyville, U.S.A. 78 D4
Wessel, C., Australia 62 A2
Wessel Is., Australia 62 A2
Wessington, U.S.A. 80 C5
Wessington Springs, U.S.A. 80 C5
West, U.S.A. 81 K6
West B., U.S.A. 81 L10
West Baines →, Australia 60 C4
West Bend, U.S.A. 76 D1
West Bengal □, India 43 H12
West Branch, U.S.A. 76 C3
West Bromwich, U.K. 11 E5
West Cape Howe, Australia 61 G2
West Chazy, U.S.A. 79 B11
West Chester, U.S.A. 76 F8
West Columbia, U.S.A. 81 L7
West Covina, U.S.A. 85 L9
West Des Moines, U.S.A. 80 E8
West End, Bahamas 88 A4
West Falkland, Falk. Is. 96 G4
West Frankfort, U.S.A. 80 G10
West Glamorgan □, U.K. 11 F4
West Hartford, U.S.A. 79 E12
West Haven, U.S.A. 79 E12
West Helena, U.S.A. 81 H9
West Ice Shelf, Antarctica 5 C7
West Indies, Cent. Amer. 89 C7
West Lorne, Canada 78 D3
West Lunga →, Zambia 55 E1
West Memphis, U.S.A. 81 H9
West Midlands □, U.K. 11 E6
West Mifflin, U.S.A. 78 F5
West Monroe, U.S.A. 81 J8
West Newton, U.S.A. 78 F5
West Nicholson, Zimbabwe 55 G2
West Palm Beach, U.S.A. 77 M5
West Plains, U.S.A. 81 G9
West Pt., Australia 63 F2
West Point, Ga., U.S.A. 77 J3
West Point, Miss., U.S.A. 77 J1
West Point, Nebr., U.S.A. 80 E6
West Point, Va., U.S.A. 76 G7
West Pokot □, Kenya 54 B4
West Road →, Canada 72 C4
West Rutland, U.S.A. 79 C11
West Schelde = Westerschelde →, Neths. 15 C3
West Seneca, U.S.A. 78 D6
West Siberian Plain, Russia 28 C11
West Sussex □, U.K. 11 G7
West-Terschelling, Neths. 15 A5
West Virginia □, U.S.A. 76 F5
West-Vlaanderen □, Belgium 15 D3
West Walker →, U.S.A. 84 G7
West Wyalong, Australia 63 E4
West Yellowstone, U.S.A. 82 D8
West Yorkshire □, U.K. 10 D6
Westall Pt., Australia 63 E1
Westbrook, Maine, U.S.A. 77 D10
Westbrook, Tex., U.S.A. 81 J4
Westbury, Australia 62 G4
Westby, U.S.A. 80 A2
Westend, U.S.A. 85 K9
Western □, Kenya 54 B3
Western □, Uganda 54 B3
Western □, Zambia 55 F1
Western Australia □, Australia 61 E2
Western Ghats, India 40 N9
Western Isles □, U.K. 12 D1
Western Sahara ■, Africa 50 D2
Western Samoa ■, Pac. Oc. 59 A13
Westernport, U.S.A. 76 F6
Westerschelde →, Neths. 15 C3
Westerwald, Germany 16 C3
Westfield, Mass., U.S.A. 79 D12
Westfield, N.Y., U.S.A. 78 D5
Westfield, Pa., U.S.A. 78 E7
Westhope, U.S.A. 80 A4
Westland □, N.Z. 59 K2
Westland Bight, N.Z. 59 K3
Westlock, Canada 72 C6
Westmeath □, Ireland 13 C4
Westminster, U.S.A. 76 F7
Westmorland, U.S.A. 83 K6
Weston, Malaysia 36 C5
Weston, Oreg., U.S.A. 82 D4
Weston, W. Va., U.S.A. 76 F5
Weston I., Canada 70 B4
Weston-super-Mare, U.K. 11 F5
Westport, Canada 79 B8
Westport, Ireland 13 C2
Westport, N.Z. 59 J3
Westport, Oreg., U.S.A. 84 D3
Westport, Wash., U.S.A. 82 C1
Westray, Canada 73 C8
Westray, U.K. 12 B6
Westree, Canada 70 C3
Westville, Calif., U.S.A. 84 F6
Westville, Ill., U.S.A. 76 E2
Westville, Okla., U.S.A. 81 G7
Westwood, U.S.A. 82 F3
Wetar, Indonesia 37 F7
Wetaskiwin, Canada 72 C6
Wethersfield, U.S.A. 79 E12
Wetteren, Belgium 15 D3
Wetzlar, Germany 16 C4
Wewaka, U.S.A. 81 H6
Wexford, Ireland 13 D5
Wexford □, Ireland 13 D5
Wexford Harbour, Ireland 13 D5
Weyburn, Canada 73 D8
Weyburn L., Canada 72 A5
Weymouth, Canada 71 D6
Weymouth, U.K. 11 G5
Weymouth, U.S.A. 79 D14
Weymouth, C., Australia 62 A3
Whakatane, N.Z. 59 G6
Whale →, Canada 71 A6
Whale Cove, Canada 73 A10
Whales, B. of, Antarctica 5 D12
Whalsay, U.K. 12 A7
Whangamomona, N.Z. 59 H5
Whangarei, N.Z. 59 F5
Whangarei Harb., N.Z. 59 F5
Wharfe →, U.K. 10 D6
Wharfedale, U.K. 10 C5
Wharton, N.J., U.S.A. 79 F10
Wharton, Pa., U.S.A. 78 E6
Wharton, Tex., U.S.A. 81 L6
Wheatland, Calif., U.S.A. 84 F5
Wheatland, Wyo., U.S.A. 80 D2
Wheatley, Canada 78 D2
Wheaton, U.S.A. 80 C6
Wheelbarrow Pk., U.S.A. 84 H10
Wheeler, Oreg., U.S.A. 82 D2
Wheeler, Tex., U.S.A. 81 H4
Wheeler →, Canada 73 B7
Wheeler Pk., N. Mex., U.S.A. 83 H11
Wheeler Pk., Nev., U.S.A. 83 G6
Wheeler Ridge, U.S.A. 85 L8
Wheeling, U.S.A. 78 F4
Whernside, U.K. 10 C5
Whidbey I., U.S.A. 72 D4
Whiskey Gap, Canada 72 D6
Whiskey Jack L., Canada 73 B8
Whistleduck Cr. →, Australia 62 C2
Whitby, Canada 78 C6
Whitby, U.K. 10 C7
White →, Ark., U.S.A. 81 J9
White →, Colo., U.S.A. 82 F9
White →, Ind., U.S.A. 76 F2
White →, S. Dak., U.S.A. 80 D5
White →, Wash., U.S.A. 84 C4
White, L., Australia 60 D4
White B., Canada 71 B8
White Bear Res., Canada 71 C8
White Bird, U.S.A. 82 D5
White Butte, U.S.A. 80 B3
White City, U.S.A. 80 F6
White Cliffs, Australia 63 E3
White Deer, U.S.A. 81 H4
White Hall, U.S.A. 80 F9
White Haven, U.S.A. 79 E9
White I., N.Z. 59 G6
White L., Canada 79 A8
White L., U.S.A. 81 L8
White Mts., Calif., U.S.A. 83 H4
White Mts., N.H., U.S.A. 75 B12
White Nile = Nîl el Abyad →, Sudan 51 E11
White Otter L., Canada 70 C1
White Pass, Canada 72 B1
White Pass, U.S.A. 84 D5
White Plains, U.S.A. 79 E11
White River, Canada 70 C2
White River, S. Africa 57 D5
White River, U.S.A. 80 D4
White Russia = Belorussia ■, Europe 24 D4
White Sea = Beloye More, Russia 24 A6
White Sulphur Springs, Mont., U.S.A. 82 C8
White Sulphur Springs, W. Va., U.S.A. 76 G5
White Swan, U.S.A. 84 D6
Whitecliffs, N.Z. 59 K3
Whitecourt, Canada 72 C5
Whiteface, U.S.A. 81 J3
Whitefield, U.S.A. 79 B13
Whitefish, U.S.A. 82 B6
Whitefish L., Canada 73 A7
Whitefish Pt., U.S.A. 76 B3
Whitegull, L., Canada 71 A7
Whitehall, Mich., U.S.A. 76 D2
Whitehall, Mont., U.S.A. 82 D7
Whitehall, N.Y., U.S.A. 79 C11
Whitehall, Wis., U.S.A. 80 C9
Whitehaven, U.K. 10 C4
Whitehorse, Canada 72 A1
Whitehorse, Vale of, U.K. 11 F6
Whitemark, Australia 62 G4
Whitemouth, Canada 73 D9
Whitesboro, N.Y., U.S.A. 79 C9
Whitesboro, Tex., U.S.A. 81 J6
Whiteshell Prov. Park, Canada 73 C9
Whitetail, U.S.A. 80 A2
Whiteville, U.S.A. 77 H6
Whitewater, U.S.A. 76 D1
Whitewater Baldy, U.S.A. 83 K9
Whitewater L., Canada 70 B2
Whitewood, Australia 62 C3
Whitewood, Canada 73 C8
Whitfield, Australia 63 F4
Whithorn, U.K. 12 G4
Whitianga, N.Z. 59 G5
Whitman, U.S.A. 79 D14
Whitmire, U.S.A. 77 H5
Whitney, Canada 78 A6
Whitney, Mt., U.S.A. 83 H4
Whitney Point, U.S.A. 79 D9
Whitstable, U.K. 11 F9
Whitsunday I., Australia 62 C4
Whittier, U.S.A. 85 M8
Whittlesea, Australia 63 F4
Whitwell, U.S.A. 77 H3
Wholdaia L., Canada 73 A8
Whyalla, Australia 63 E2
Whyjonta, Australia 63 D3
Wiarton, Canada 78 B3
Wibaux, U.S.A. 80 B2
Wichian Buri, Thailand 38 E3
Wichita, U.S.A. 81 G6
Wichita Falls, U.S.A. 81 J5
Wick, U.K. 12 C5
Wickenburg, U.S.A. 83 K7
Wickepin, Australia 61 F2
Wickham, C., Australia 62 F3
Wickliffe, U.S.A. 78 E3
Wicklow, Ireland 13 D5
Wicklow □, Ireland 13 D5
Wicklow Hd., Ireland 13 D5
Widgiemooltha, Australia 61 F3
Widnes, U.K. 10 D5
Wieliczka, Poland 17 D10
Wieluń, Poland 17 C9
Wien, Austria 16 D8
Wiener Neustadt, Austria 16 E8
Wierden, Neths. 15 B6
Wiesbaden, Germany 16 C4
Wigan, U.K. 10 D5
Wiggins, Colo., U.S.A. 80 E2
Wiggins, Miss., U.S.A. 81 K10
Wight, I. of □, U.K. 11 G6
Wigtown, U.K. 12 G4
Wigtown B., U.K. 12 G4
Wilber, U.S.A. 80 E6
Wilberforce, Canada 78 A6
Wilberforce, C., Australia 62 A2
Wilburton, U.S.A. 81 H7
Wilcannia, Australia 63 E3
Wilcox, U.S.A. 78 E6
Wildrose, Calif., U.S.A. 85 J9
Wildrose, N. Dak., U.S.A. 80 A3
Wildwood, U.S.A. 76 F8
Wilge →, S. Africa 57 D4
Wilhelm II Coast, Antarctica 5 C7
Wilhelmshaven, Germany 16 B4
Wilhelmstal, Namibia 56 C2
Wilkes Barre, U.S.A. 79 E9
Wilkesboro, U.S.A. 77 G5
Wilkie, Canada 73 C7
Wilkinsburg, U.S.A. 78 F5
Wilkinson Lakes, Australia 61 E5
Willamina, U.S.A. 82 D2
Willandra Billabong Creek →, Australia 63 E4
Willapa, B., U.S.A. 82 C2
Willapa Hills, U.S.A. 84 D3
Willard, N. Mex., U.S.A. 83 J10
Willard, Utah, U.S.A. 82 F7
Willcox, U.S.A. 83 K9
Willemstad, Neth. Ant. 89 D6
Willeroo, Australia 60 C5
William →, Canada 73 B7
William Creek, Australia 63 D2
Williambury, Australia 61 D2
Williams, Australia 61 F2
Williams, Ariz., U.S.A. 83 J7
Williams, Calif., U.S.A. 84 F4
Williams Lake, Canada 72 C4
Williamsburg, Ky., U.S.A. 77 G3
Williamsburg, Pa., U.S.A. 78 F6

Williamsburg, *Va., U.S.A.* 76 G7
Williamson, *N.Y., U.S.A.* 78 C7
Williamson, *W. Va., U.S.A.* 76 G4
Williamsport, *U.S.A.* 78 E7
Williamston, *U.S.A.* 77 H7
Williamstown, *Australia* 63 F3
Williamstown, *Mass., U.S.A.* 79 D11
Williamstown, *N.Y., U.S.A.* 79 C9
Williamsville, *U.S.A.* 81 G9
Willimantic, *U.S.A.* 79 E12
Willis Group, *Australia* 62 B5
Williston, *S. Africa* 56 E3
Williston, *Fla., U.S.A.* 77 L4
Williston, *N. Dak., U.S.A.* 80 A3
Williston L., *Canada* 72 B4
Willits, *U.S.A.* 82 G2
Willmar, *U.S.A.* 80 C7
Willoughby, *U.S.A.* 78 E3
Willow Bunch, *Canada* 73 D7
Willow L., *Canada* 72 A5
Willow Lake, *U.S.A.* 80 C6
Willow Springs, *U.S.A.* 81 G8
Willow Wall, The, *China* 35 C12
Willowlake →, *Canada* 72 A4
Willowmore, *S. Africa* 56 E3
Willows, *Australia* 62 C4
Willows, *U.S.A.* 84 F4
Willowvale = Gatyana, *S. Africa* 57 E4
Wills, L., *Australia* 60 D4
Wills Cr. →, *Australia* 62 C3
Wills Point, *U.S.A.* 81 J7
Willunga, *Australia* 63 F2
Wilmette, *U.S.A.* 76 D2
Wilmington, *Australia* 63 E2
Wilmington, *Del., U.S.A.* 76 F8
Wilmington, *Ill., U.S.A.* 76 E1
Wilmington, *N.C., U.S.A.* 77 H7
Wilmington, *Ohio, U.S.A.* 76 F4
Wilpena Cr. →, *Australia* 63 E2
Wilsall, *U.S.A.* 82 D8
Wilson, *U.S.A.* 77 H7
Wilson →, *Queens., Australia* 63 D3
Wilson →, *W. Austral., Australia* 60 C4
Wilson Bluff, *Australia* 61 F4
Wilsons Promontory, *Australia* 63 F4
Wilton, *U.K.* 11 F6
Wilton, *U.S.A.* 80 B4
Wilton →, *Australia* 62 A1
Wiltshire □, *U.K.* 11 F6
Wiltz, *Lux.* 15 E5
Wiluna, *Australia* 61 E3
Wimmera →, *Australia* 63 F3
Winam G., *Kenya* 54 C3
Winburg, *S. Africa* 56 D4
Winchendon, *U.S.A.* 79 D12
Winchester, *U.K.* 11 F6
Winchester, *Conn., U.S.A.* 79 E11
Winchester, *Idaho, U.S.A.* 82 C5
Winchester, *Ind., U.S.A.* 76 E3
Winchester, *Ky., U.S.A.* 76 G3
Winchester, *N.H., U.S.A.* 79 D12
Winchester, *Nev., U.S.A.* 85 J11
Winchester, *Tenn., U.S.A.* 77 H2
Winchester, *Va., U.S.A.* 76 F6
Wind →, *U.S.A.* 82 E9
Wind River Range, *U.S.A.* 82 E9
Windber, *U.S.A.* 78 F6
Windermere, L., *U.K.* 10 C5
Windfall, *Canada* 72 C5
Windflower L., *Canada* 72 A5
Windhoek, *Namibia* 56 C2
Windom, *U.S.A.* 80 D7
Windorah, *Australia* 62 D3
Window Rock, *U.S.A.* 83 J9
Windrush →, *U.K.* 11 F6
Windsor, *Australia* 63 E5
Windsor, *N.S., Canada* 71 D7
Windsor, *Nfld., Canada* 71 C8
Windsor, *Ont., Canada* 70 D3
Windsor, *U.K.* 11 F7
Windsor, *Colo., U.S.A.* 80 E2
Windsor, *Conn., U.S.A.* 79 E12
Windsor, *Mo., U.S.A.* 80 F8
Windsor, *N.Y., U.S.A.* 79 D9
Windsor, *Vt., U.S.A.* 79 C12
Windsorton, *S. Africa* 56 D3
Windward Is., *W. Indies* 89 D7
Windward Passage = Vientos, Paso de los, *Caribbean* 89 C5
Windy L., *Canada* 73 A8
Winefred L., *Canada* 73 B6
Winfield, *U.S.A.* 81 G6
Wingate Mts., *Australia* 60 B5
Wingen, *Australia* 63 E5
Wingham, *Australia* 63 E5
Wingham, *Canada* 70 D3
Winifred, *U.S.A.* 82 C9
Winisk, *Canada* 70 A2
Winisk →, *Canada* 70 A2
Winisk L., *Canada* 70 B2
Wink, *U.S.A.* 81 K3
Winkler, *Canada* 73 D9
Winlock, *U.S.A.* 84 D4
Winneba, *Ghana* 50 G4
Winnebago, *U.S.A.* 80 D7
Winnebago L., *U.S.A.* 76 D1
Winnecke Cr. →, *Australia* 60 C5
Winnemucca, *U.S.A.* 82 F5
Winnemucca, L., *U.S.A.* 82 F4
Winner, *U.S.A.* 80 D5
Winnett, *U.S.A.* 82 C9
Winnfield, *U.S.A.* 81 K8
Winnibigoshish L., *U.S.A.* 80 B7
Winning, *Australia* 60 D1
Winnipeg, *Canada* 73 D9
Winnipeg →, *Canada* 73 C9
Winnipeg, L., *Canada* 73 C9
Winnipeg Beach, *Canada* 73 C9
Winnipegosis, *Canada* 73 C9
Winnipegosis L., *Canada* 73 C9
Winnipesaukee, L., *U.S.A.* 79 C13
Winnsboro, *La., U.S.A.* 81 J9
Winnsboro, *S.C., U.S.A.* 77 H5
Winnsboro, *Tex., U.S.A.* 81 J7
Winokapau, L., *Canada* 71 B7
Winona, *Miss., U.S.A.* 81 J10
Winona, *Wis., U.S.A.* 80 C9
Winooski, *U.S.A.* 79 B11
Winschoten, *Neths.* 15 A7
Winslow, *Ariz., U.S.A.* 83 J8
Winslow, *Wash., U.S.A.* 84 C4
Winsted, *U.S.A.* 79 E11
Winston-Salem, *U.S.A.* 77 G5
Winter Garden, *U.S.A.* 77 L5
Winter Haven, *U.S.A.* 77 M5
Winter Park, *U.S.A.* 77 L5
Winterhaven, *U.S.A.* 85 N12
Winters, *Calif., U.S.A.* 84 G5
Winters, *Tex., U.S.A.* 81 K5
Winterset, *U.S.A.* 80 E7
Wintersville, *U.S.A.* 78 F4
Winterswijk, *Neths.* 15 C6
Winterthur, *Switz.* 16 E4
Winthrop, *Minn., U.S.A.* 80 C7
Winthrop, *Wash., U.S.A.* 82 B3
Winton, *Australia* 62 C3
Winton, *N.Z.* 59 M2
Winton, *U.S.A.* 77 G7
Wirral, *U.K.* 10 D4
Wirrulla, *Australia* 63 E1
Wisbech, *U.K.* 10 E8
Wisconsin □, *U.S.A.* 80 C10
Wisconsin →, *U.S.A.* 80 D9
Wisconsin Dells, *U.S.A.* 80 D10
Wisconsin Rapids, *U.S.A.* 80 C10
Wisdom, *U.S.A.* 82 D7
Wishaw, *U.K.* 12 F5
Wishek, *U.S.A.* 80 B5
Wisła →, *Poland* 17 A9
Wismar, *Germany* 16 B5
Wisner, *U.S.A.* 80 E6
Witbank, *S. Africa* 57 D4
Witdraai, *S. Africa* 56 D3
Witham →, *U.K.* 10 D7
Withernsea, *U.K.* 10 D8
Witney, *U.K.* 11 F6
Witnossob →, *Namibia* 56 D3
Witten, *Germany* 15 C7
Wittenberg, *Germany* 16 C6
Wittenberge, *Germany* 16 B5
Wittenoom, *Australia* 60 D2
Wkra →, *Poland* 17 B10
Wlingi, *Indonesia* 37 H15
Włocławek, *Poland* 17 B9
Woburn, *U.S.A.* 79 D13
Wodian, *China* 34 H7
Wodonga, *Australia* 63 F4
Woëvre, *France* 18 B6
Wokam, *Indonesia* 37 F8
Wolf →, *Canada* 72 A2
Wolf Creek, *U.S.A.* 82 C7
Wolf L., *Canada* 72 A2
Wolf Point, *U.S.A.* 80 A2
Wolfe I., *Canada* 70 D4
Wolfsburg, *Germany* 16 B5
Wolin, *Poland* 16 B7
Wollaston, Is., *Chile* 96 H3
Wollaston L., *Canada* 73 B8
Wollaston Pen., *Canada* 68 B8
Wollogorang, *Australia* 62 B2
Wollongong, *Australia* 63 E5
Wolmaransstad, *S. Africa* 56 D4
Wolseley, *Australia* 63 F3
Wolseley, *Canada* 73 C8
Wolseley, *S. Africa* 56 E2
Wolstenholme, C., *Canada* 66 C12
Wolvega, *Neths.* 15 B6
Wolverhampton, *U.K.* 11 E5
Wonarah, *Australia* 62 B2
Wondai, *Australia* 63 D5
Wongalarroo L., *Australia* 63 E3
Wongan Hills, *Australia* 61 F2
Wongawol, *Australia* 61 E3
Wŏnju, *S. Korea* 35 F14
Wonosari, *Indonesia* 37 G14
Wŏnsan, *N. Korea* 35 E14
Wonthaggi, *Australia* 63 F4
Woocalla, *Australia* 63 E2
Wood Buffalo Nat. Park, *Canada* 72 B6
Wood Is., *Australia* 60 C3
Wood L., *Canada* 73 B8
Wood Lake, *U.S.A.* 80 D4
Woodah I., *Australia* 62 A2
Woodanilling, *Australia* 61 F2
Woodbridge, *Canada* 78 C5
Woodburn, *Australia* 63 D5
Woodenbong, *Australia* 63 D5
Woodend, *Australia* 63 F3
Woodfords, *U.S.A.* 84 G7
Woodgreen, *Australia* 62 C1
Woodlake, *U.S.A.* 84 J7
Woodland, *U.S.A.* 84 G5
Woodlands, *Australia* 60 D2
Woodpecker, *Canada* 72 C4
Woodridge, *Canada* 73 D9
Woodroffe, Mt., *Australia* 61 E5
Woodruff, *Ariz., U.S.A.* 83 J8
Woodruff, *Utah, U.S.A.* 82 F8
Woods, L., *Australia* 62 B1
Woods, L., *Canada* 71 B6
Woods, L. of the, *Canada* 73 D10
Woodstock, *Queens., Australia* 62 B4
Woodstock, *W. Austral., Australia* 60 D2
Woodstock, *N.B., Canada* 71 C6
Woodstock, *Ont., Canada* 70 D3
Woodstock, *U.K.* 11 F6
Woodstock, *Ill., U.S.A.* 80 D10
Woodstock, *Vt., U.S.A.* 79 C12
Woodsville, *U.S.A.* 79 B13
Woodville, *N.Z.* 59 J5
Woodville, *U.S.A.* 81 K7
Woodward, *U.S.A.* 81 G5
Woody, *U.S.A.* 85 K8
Woolamai, C., *Australia* 63 F4
Woolgoolga, *Australia* 63 E5
Woombye, *Australia* 63 D5
Woomera, *Australia* 63 E2
Woonsocket, *R.I., U.S.A.* 79 D13
Woonsocket, *S. Dak., U.S.A.* 80 C5
Wooramel, *Australia* 61 E1
Wooramel →, *Australia* 61 E1
Wooroloo, *Australia* 61 F2
Wooster, *U.S.A.* 78 F3
Worcester, *S. Africa* 56 E2
Worcester, *U.K.* 11 E5
Worcester, *Mass., U.S.A.* 79 D13
Worcester, *N.Y., U.S.A.* 79 D10
Workington, *U.K.* 10 C4
Worksop, *U.K.* 10 D6
Workum, *Neths.* 15 B5
Worland, *U.S.A.* 82 D10
Worms, *Germany* 16 D4
Wortham, *U.S.A.* 81 K6
Worthing, *U.K.* 11 G7
Worthington, *U.S.A.* 80 D7
Wosi, *Indonesia* 37 E7
Wou-han = Wuhan, *China* 33 C6
Wour, *Chad* 51 D8
Wowoni, *Indonesia* 37 E6
Woy Woy, *Australia* 63 E5
Wrangel I. = Vrangelya, Ostrov, *Russia* 27 B19
Wrangell, *U.S.A.* 68 C6
Wrangell I., *U.S.A.* 72 B2
Wrangell Mts., *U.S.A.* 68 B5
Wrath, C., *U.K.* 12 C3
Wray, *U.S.A.* 80 E3
Wrekin, The, *U.K.* 10 E5
Wrens, *U.S.A.* 77 J4
Wrexham, *U.K.* 10 D4
Wright, *Canada* 72 C4
Wright, *Phil.* 37 B7
Wrightson, Mt., *U.S.A.* 83 L8
Wrightwood, *U.S.A.* 85 L9
Wrigley, *Canada* 68 B7
Wrocław, *Poland* 16 C8
Września, *Poland* 17 B8
Wu Jiang →, *China* 32 D5
Wu'an, *China* 34 F8
Wubin, *Australia* 61 F2
Wubu, *China* 34 F6
Wuchang, *China* 35 B14
Wucheng, *China* 34 F9
Wuchuan, *China* 34 D6
Wudi, *China* 35 F9
Wuding He →, *China* 34 F6
Wudu, *China* 34 H3
Wuhan, *China* 33 C6
Wuhe, *China* 35 H9
Wuhsi = Wuxi, *China* 33 C7
Wuhu, *China* 33 C6
Wukari, *Nigeria* 50 G6
Wulajie, *China* 35 B14
Wulanbulang, *China* 34 D6
Wulian, *China* 35 G10
Wuliaru, *Indonesia* 37 F8
Wuluk'omushih Ling, *China* 32 C3
Wulumuchi = Ürümqi, *China* 32 B3
Wum, *Cameroon* 50 G7
Wunnummin L., *Canada* 70 B2
Wuntho, *Burma* 41 H19
Wuppertal, *Germany* 16 C3
Wuppertal, *S. Africa* 56 E2
Wuqing, *China* 35 E9
Wurung, *Australia* 62 B3
Würzburg, *Germany* 16 D4
Wushan, *China* 34 G3
Wusuli Jiang = Ussuri →, *Asia* 30 A7
Wutai, *China* 34 E7
Wuting = Huimin, *China* 35 F9
Wutonghaolai, *China* 35 C11
Wutongqiao, *China* 32 D5
Wuwei, *China* 32 C5
Wuxi, *China* 33 C7
Wuxiang, *China* 34 F7
Wuxing, *China* 33 C7
Wuyang, *China* 34 H7
Wuyi, *China* 34 F8
Wuyi Shan, *China* 33 D6
Wuyuan, *China* 34 D5
Wuzhai, *China* 34 E6
Wuzhi Shan, *China* 38 C7
Wuzhong, *China* 34 E4
Wuzhou, *China* 33 D6
Wyaaba Cr. →, *Australia* 62 B3
Wyalkatchem, *Australia* 61 F2
Wyalusing, *U.S.A.* 79 E8
Wyandotte, *U.S.A.* 76 D4
Wyandra, *Australia* 63 D4
Wyangala Res., *Australia* 63 E4
Wyara, L., *Australia* 63 D3
Wycheproof, *Australia* 63 F3
Wye →, *U.K.* 11 F5
Wyemandoo, *Australia* 61 E2
Wymondham, *U.K.* 11 E7
Wymore, *U.S.A.* 80 E6
Wynbring, *Australia* 63 E1
Wyndham, *Australia* 60 C4
Wyndham, *N.Z.* 59 M2
Wyndmere, *U.S.A.* 80 B6
Wynne, *U.S.A.* 81 H9
Wynnum, *Australia* 63 D5
Wynyard, *Australia* 62 G4
Wynyard, *Canada* 73 C8
Wyola, L., *Australia* 61 E5
Wyoming □, *U.S.A.* 74 B5
Wyong, *Australia* 63 E5
Wytheville, *U.S.A.* 76 G5

X

Xai-Xai, *Mozam.* 57 D5
Xainza, *China* 32 C3
Xangongo, *Angola* 56 B2
Xánthi, *Greece* 21 D11
Xapuri, *Brazil* 92 F5
Xar Moron He →, *China* 35 C11
Xau, L., *Botswana* 56 C3
Xavantina, *Brazil* 95 A5
Xenia, *U.S.A.* 76 F4
Xeropotamos →, *Cyprus* 23 E11
Xhora, *S. Africa* 57 E4
Xhumo, *Botswana* 56 C3
Xi Jiang →, *China* 33 D6
Xi Xian, *China* 34 F6
Xia Xian, *China* 34 G6
Xiachengzi, *China* 35 B16
Xiaguan, *China* 32 D5
Xiajin, *China* 34 F8
Xiamen, *China* 33 D6
Xi'an, *China* 34 G5
Xian Xian, *China* 34 E9
Xiang Jiang →, *China* 33 D6
Xiangcheng, *Henan, China* 34 H8
Xiangcheng, *Henan, China* 34 H7
Xiangfan, *China* 33 C6
Xianghuang Qi, *China* 34 C7
Xiangning, *China* 34 G6
Xiangquan, *China* 34 F7
Xiangshui, *China* 35 G10
Xiangtan, *China* 33 D6
Xianyang, *China* 34 G5
Xiao Hinggan Ling, *China* 33 B7
Xiao Xian, *China* 34 G9
Xiaoyi, *China* 34 F6
Xiawa, *China* 35 C11
Xiayi, *China* 34 G9
Xichang, *China* 32 D5
Xichuan, *China* 34 H6
Xieng Khouang, *Laos* 38 C4
Xifei He →, *China* 34 H9
Xifeng, *China* 35 C13
Xifengzhen, *China* 34 G4
Xigazê, *China* 32 D3
Xihe, *China* 34 G3
Xihua, *China* 34 H8
Xiliao He →, *China* 35 C12
Xin Xian, *China* 34 E7
Xinavane, *Mozam.* 57 D5
Xinbin, *China* 35 D13
Xing Xian, *China* 34 E6
Xing'an, *China* 33 D6
Xingcheng, *China* 35 D11
Xinghe, *China* 34 D7
Xinghua, *China* 35 H10
Xinglong, *China* 35 D9
Xingping, *China* 34 G5
Xingtai, *China* 34 F8
Xingu →, *Brazil* 93 D8
Xingyang, *China* 34 G7
Xinhe, *China* 34 F8
Xining, *China* 32 C5
Xinjiang, *China* 34 G6
Xinjiang Uygur Zizhiqu □, *China* 32 B3
Xinjin, *China* 35 E11
Xinkai He →, *China* 35 C12
Xinle, *China* 34 E8
Xinlitun, *China* 35 D12
Xinmin, *China* 35 D12
Xintai, *China* 35 G9
Xinxiang, *China* 34 G7
Xinzhan, *China* 35 C14
Xinzheng, *China* 34 G7
Xiong Xian, *China* 34 E9
Xiongyuecheng, *China* 35 D12
Xiping, *Henan, China* 34 H8
Xiping, *Henan, China* 34 H6
Xique-Xique, *Brazil* 93 F10
Xisha Qundao = Hsisha Chuntao, *Pac. Oc.* 36 A4
Xiuyan, *China* 35 D12
Xixabangma Feng, *China* 41 E14
Xixia, *China* 34 H6
Xixiang, *China* 34 H4
Xiyang, *China* 34 F7
Xizang □, *China* 32 C3
Xlendi, *Malta* 23 C1
Xuan Loc, *Vietnam* 39 G6
Xuanhua, *China* 34 D8
Xuchang, *China* 34 G7
Xun Xian, *China* 34 G8
Xunyang, *China* 34 H5
Xunyi, *China* 34 G5
Xushui, *China* 34 E8
Xuyen Moc, *Vietnam* 39 G6
Xuzhou, *China* 35 G9
Xylophagou, *Cyprus* 23 E12

Y

Ya Xian, *China* 38 C7
Yaamba, *Australia* 62 C5
Yaapeet, *Australia* 63 F3
Yabelo, *Ethiopia* 51 H12
Yablonovy Khrebet, *Russia* 27 D12
Yablonovy Ra. = Yablonovy Khrebet, *Russia* 27 D12
Yabrai Shan, *China* 34 E2
Yabrūd, *Syria* 47 B5
Yacheng, *China* 33 E5
Yacuiba, *Bolivia* 94 A3
Yadgir, *India* 40 L10
Yadkin →, *U.S.A.* 77 H5
Yagodnoye, *Russia* 27 C15
Yagoua, *Cameroon* 52 B3
Yaha, *Thailand* 39 J3
Yahila, *Zaïre* 54 B1
Yahk, *Canada* 72 D5
Yahuma, *Zaïre* 52 D4
Yaita, *Japan* 31 F9
Yaiza, *Canary Is.* 22 F6
Yakima, *U.S.A.* 82 C3
Yakima →, *U.S.A.* 82 C3
Yakovlevka, *Russia* 30 B6
Yaku-Shima, *Japan* 31 J5
Yakut Republic □, *Russia* 27 C13
Yakutat, *U.S.A.* 68 C6
Yakutsk, *Russia* 27 C13
Yala, *Thailand* 39 J3
Yalbalgo, *Australia* 61 E1
Yalboroo, *Australia* 62 C4
Yale, *U.S.A.* 78 C2
Yalgoo, *Australia* 61 E2
Yalinga, *C.A.R.* 51 G9
Yalkubul, Punta, *Mexico* 87 C7
Yalleroi, *Australia* 62 C4
Yalobusha →, *U.S.A.* 81 J9
Yalong Jiang →, *China* 32 D5
Yalta, *Ukraine* 25 F5
Yalu Jiang →, *China* 35 E13
Yalutorovsk, *Russia* 26 D7
Yam Ha Melah = Dead Sea, *Asia* 47 D4
Yam Kinneret, *Israel* 47 C4
Yamada, *Japan* 31 H5
Yamagata, *Japan* 30 E10
Yamagata □, *Japan* 30 E10
Yamaguchi, *Japan* 31 G5
Yamaguchi □, *Japan* 31 G5
Yamal, Poluostrov, *Russia* 26 B8
Yamanashi □, *Japan* 31 G9
Yamantau, Gora, *Russia* 24 D10
Yamba, *N.S.W., Australia* 63 D5
Yamba, *S. Austral., Australia* 63 E3
Yambah, *Australia* 62 C1
Yambarran Ra., *Australia* 60 C5
Yâmbiô, *Sudan* 51 H10
Yambol, *Bulgaria* 21 C12
Yamdena, *Indonesia* 37 F8
Yame, *Japan* 31 H5
Yamethin, *Burma* 41 J20
Yamma-Yamma, L., *Australia* 63 D3
Yamoussoukro, *Ivory C.* 50 G3
Yampa →, *U.S.A.* 82 F9
Yampi Sd., *Australia* 60 C3
Yamuna →, *India* 43 G9
Yamzho Yumco, *China* 32 D4
Yana →, *Russia* 27 B14
Yanac, *Australia* 63 F3
Yanagawa, *Japan* 31 H5
Yanai, *Japan* 31 H6
Yan'an, *China* 34 F5
Yanaul, *Russia* 24 C10
Yanbu 'al Baḥr, *Si. Arabia* 44 F3
Yancannia, *Australia* 63 E3
Yanchang, *China* 34 F6
Yancheng, *Henan, China* 34 H7
Yancheng, *Jiangsu, China* 35 H11
Yanchi, *China* 34 F4
Yanchuan, *China* 34 F6
Yanco Cr. →, *Australia* 63 F4
Yandal, *Australia* 61 E3
Yandanooka, *Australia* 61 E2
Yandaran, *Australia* 62 C5
Yandoon, *Burma* 41 L19
Yang Xian, *China* 34 H4
Yangambi, *Zaïre* 54 B1
Yangcheng, *China* 34 G7
Yangch'ü = Taiyuan, *China* 34 F7
Yanggao, *China* 34 D7
Yanggu, *China* 34 F8
Yangi-Yer, *Kazakhstan* 26 E7
Yangliuqing, *China* 35 E9
Yangpingguan, *China* 34 H4
Yangquan, *China* 34 F7
Yangtze Kiang = Chang Jiang →, *China* 33 C7
Yangyang, *S. Korea* 35 E15
Yangyuan, *China* 34 D8

Yangzhou, *China* 33 C6
Yanji, *China* 35 C15
Yankton, *U.S.A.* 80 D6
Yanna, *Australia* 63 D4
Yanonge, *Zaïre* 54 B1
Yanqi, *China* 32 B3
Yanqing, *China* 34 D8
Yanshan, *China* 35 E9
Yanshou, *China* 35 B15
Yantabulla, *Australia* 63 D4
Yantai, *China* 35 F11
Yanzhou, *China* 34 G9
Yao, *Chad* 51 F8
Yao Xian, *China* 34 G5
Yao Yai, Ko, *Thailand* 39 J2
Yaoundé, *Cameroon* 50 H7
Yaowan, *China* 35 G10
Yap I., *Pac. Oc.* 64 G5
Yapen, *Indonesia* 37 E9
Yapen, Selat, *Indonesia* 37 E9
Yappar →, *Australia* 62 B3
Yaqui →, *Mexico* 86 B2
Yar-Sale, *Russia* 26 C8
Yaraka, *Australia* 62 C3
Yaransk, *Russia* 24 C8
Yardea P.O., *Australia* 63 E2
Yare →, *U.K.* 11 E9
Yarensk, *Russia* 24 B8
Yarí →, *Colombia* 92 D4
Yarkand = Shache, *China* 32 C2
Yarker, *Canada* 79 B8
Yarkhun →, *Pakistan* 43 A5
Yarmouth, *Canada* 71 D6
Yarmūk →, *Syria* 47 C4
Yaroslavl, *Russia* 24 C6
Yarqa, W. →, *Egypt* 47 F2
Yarra Yarra Lakes, *Australia* 61 E2
Yarraden, *Australia* 62 A3
Yarraloola, *Australia* 60 D2
Yarram, *Australia* 63 F4
Yarraman, *Australia* 63 D5
Yarranvale, *Australia* 63 D4
Yarras, *Australia* 63 E5
Yarrowmere, *Australia* 62 C4
Yartsevo, *Russia* 27 C10
Yasawa Group, *Fiji* 59 C7
Yasin, *Pakistan* 43 A5
Yasinski, L., *Canada* 70 B4
Yasothon, *Thailand* 38 E5
Yass, *Australia* 63 E4
Yates Center, *U.S.A.* 81 G7
Yathkyed L., *Canada* 73 A9
Yatsushiro, *Japan* 31 H5
Yatta Plateau, *Kenya* 54 C4
Yauyos, *Peru* 92 F3
Yavari →, *Peru* 92 D4
Yavatmal, *India* 40 J11
Yavne, *Israel* 47 D3
Yawatahama, *Japan* 31 H6
Yayama-Rettō, *Japan* 31 M1
Yazd, *Iran* 45 D7
Yazd □, *Iran* 45 D7
Yazoo →, *U.S.A.* 81 J9
Yazoo City, *U.S.A.* 81 J9
Yding Skovhøj, *Denmark* 9 J10
Ye Xian, *Henan, China* 34 H7
Ye Xian, *Shandong, China* 35 F10
Yealering, *Australia* 61 F2
Yebyu, *Burma* 41 M21
Yechŏn, *S. Korea* 35 F15
Yecla, *Spain* 19 C5
Yécora, *Mexico* 86 B3
Yeeda, *Australia* 60 C3
Yeelanna, *Australia* 63 E2
Yegros, *Paraguay* 94 B4
Yehuda, Midbar, *Israel* 47 D4
Yei, *Sudan* 51 H11
Yekaterinburg, *Russia* 24 C11
Yekaterinodar = Krasnodar, *Russia* 25 E6
Yelanskoye, *Russia* 27 C13
Yelarbon, *Australia* 63 D5
Yelets, *Russia* 24 D6
Yelizavetgrad, *Ukraine* 25 E5
Yell, *U.K.* 12 A7
Yell Sd., *U.K.* 12 A7
Yellow Sea, *China* 35 G12
Yellowhead Pass, *Canada* 72 C5
Yellowknife, *Canada* 72 A6
Yellowknife →, *Canada* 72 A6
Yellowstone →, *U.S.A.* 80 B3
Yellowstone L., *U.S.A.* 82 D8
Yellowstone National Park, *U.S.A.* 82 D8
Yellowtail Res., *U.S.A.* 82 D9
Yelvertoft, *Australia* 62 C2
Yemen ■, *Asia* 46 E3
Yen Bai, *Vietnam* 38 B5
Yenangyaung, *Burma* 41 J19
Yenda, *Australia* 63 E4
Yenisey →, *Russia* 26 B9
Yeniseysk, *Russia* 27 D10
Yeniseyskiy Zaliv, *Russia* 26 B9
Yennádhi, *Greece* 23 C9
Yenyuka, *Russia* 27 D13
Yeo, L., *Australia* 61 E3
Yeola, *India* 40 J9
Yeoryioúpolis, *Greece* 23 D6
Yeovil, *U.K.* 11 G5
Yeppoon, *Australia* 62 C5
Yerbent, *Turkmenistan* 26 F6
Yerbogachen, *Russia* 27 C11
Yerevan, *Armenia* 25 F7
Yerilla, *Australia* 61 E3
Yermak, *Kazakhstan* 26 D8
Yermakovo, *Russia* 27 D13
Yermo, *U.S.A.* 85 L10
Yerofey Pavlovich, *Russia* 27 D13
Yerólakkos, *Cyprus* 23 D12
Yeropótamos →, *Greece* 23 D6
Yeroskipos, *Cyprus* 23 E11
Yershov, *Russia* 25 D8
Yerushalayim = Jerusalem, *Israel* 47 D4
Yes Tor, *U.K.* 11 G4
Yesan, *S. Korea* 35 F14
Yeso, *U.S.A.* 81 H2
Yessey, *Russia* 27 C11
Yeu, I. d', *France* 18 C2
Yevpatoriya, *Ukraine* 25 E5
Yeysk, *Russia* 25 E6
Yezd = Yazd, *Iran* 45 D7
Yhati, *Paraguay* 94 B4
Yhú, *Paraguay* 95 B4
Yi →, *Uruguay* 94 C4
Yi 'Allaq, G., *Egypt* 47 E2
Yi He →, *China* 35 G10
Yi Xian, *Hebei, China* 34 E8
Yi Xian, *Liaoning, China* 35 D11
Yialiás →, *Cyprus* 23 D12
Yialousa, *Cyprus* 23 D13
Yianisádhes, *Greece* 23 D8
Yiannitsa, *Greece* 21 D10
Yibin, *China* 32 D5
Yichang, *China* 33 C6
Yicheng, *China* 34 G6
Yichuan, *China* 34 F6
Yichun, *China* 33 B7
Yidu, *China* 35 F10
Yijun, *China* 34 G5
Yilehuli Shan, *China* 33 A7
Yimianpo, *China* 35 B15
Yinchuan, *China* 34 E4
Yindarlgooda, L., *Australia* 61 F3
Ying He →, *China* 34 H9
Ying Xian, *China* 34 E7
Yingkou, *China* 35 D12
Yining, *China* 32 B3
Yinmabin, *Burma* 41 H19
Yinnietharra, *Australia* 60 D2
Yiofiros →, *Greece* 23 D7
Yishan, *China* 32 D5
Yishui, *China* 35 G10
Yíthion, *Greece* 21 F10
Yitiaoshan, *China* 34 F3
Yitong, *China* 35 C13
Yiyang, *Henan, China* 34 G7
Yiyang, *Hunan, China* 33 D6
Ylitornio, *Finland* 8 C17
Ylivieska, *Finland* 8 D18
Ynykchanskiy, *Russia* 27 C14
Yoakum, *U.S.A.* 81 L6
Yog Pt., *Phil.* 37 B6
Yogyakarta, *Indonesia* 37 G14
Yoho Nat. Park, *Canada* 72 C5
Yojoa, L. de, *Honduras* 88 D2
Yŏju, *S. Korea* 35 F14
Yokadouma, *Cameroon* 52 D2
Yokkaichi, *Japan* 31 G8
Yoko, *Cameroon* 51 G7
Yokohama, *Japan* 31 G9
Yokosuka, *Japan* 31 G9
Yokote, *Japan* 30 E10
Yola, *Nigeria* 51 G7
Yolaina, Cordillera de, *Nic.* 88 D3
Yonago, *Japan* 31 G6
Yonaguni-Jima, *Japan* 31 M1
Yŏnan, *N. Korea* 35 F14
Yonezawa, *Japan* 30 F10
Yong Peng, *Malaysia* 39 L4
Yong Sata, *Thailand* 39 J2
Yongampo, *N. Korea* 35 E13
Yongcheng, *China* 34 H9
Yŏngchŏn, *S. Korea* 35 G15
Yongdeng, *China* 34 F2
Yŏngdŏk, *S. Korea* 35 F15
Yŏngdŭngpo, *S. Korea* 35 F14
Yonghe, *China* 34 F6
Yŏnghŭng, *N. Korea* 35 E14
Yongji, *China* 34 G6
Yŏngju, *S. Korea* 35 F15
Yongnian, *China* 34 F8
Yongning, *China* 34 E4
Yongqing, *China* 34 E9
Yŏngwŏl, *S. Korea* 35 F15
Yonibana, *S. Leone* 50 G2
Yonkers, *U.S.A.* 79 F11
Yonne □, *France* 18 C5
Yonne →, *France* 18 B5
York, *Australia* 61 F2
York, *U.K.* 10 D6
York, *Ala., U.S.A.* 77 J1
York, *Nebr., U.S.A.* 80 E6
York, *Pa., U.S.A.* 76 F7
York, C., *Australia* 62 A3
York, Kap, *Greenland* 4 B4
York Sd., *Australia* 60 B4
Yorke Pen., *Australia* 63 E2
Yorkshire Wolds, *U.K.* 10 D7
Yorkton, *Canada* 73 C8
Yorktown, *U.S.A.* 81 L6
Yorkville, *U.S.A.* 84 G3
Yornup, *Australia* 61 F2
Yoro, *Honduras* 88 C2
Yoron-Jima, *Japan* 31 L4
Yos Sudarso, Pulau, *Indonesia* 37 F9
Yosemite National Park, *U.S.A.* 83 H4
Yosemite Village, *U.S.A.* 84 H7
Yoshkar Ola, *Russia* 24 C8
Yŏsu, *S. Korea* 35 G14
Yotvata, *Israel* 47 F4
Youbou, *Canada* 72 D4
Youghal, *Ireland* 13 E4
Youghal B., *Ireland* 13 E4
Young, *Australia* 63 E4
Young, *Canada* 73 C7
Young, *Uruguay* 94 C4
Younghusband, L., *Australia* 63 E2
Younghusband Pen., *Australia* 63 F2
Youngstown, *Canada* 73 C6
Youngstown, *N.Y., U.S.A.* 78 C5
Youngstown, *Ohio, U.S.A.* 78 E4
Youngsville, *U.S.A.* 78 E5
Youyu, *China* 34 D7
Yoweragabbie, *Australia* 61 E2
Yozgat, *Turkey* 25 G5
Ypané →, *Paraguay* 94 A4
Ypres = Ieper, *Belgium* 15 D2
Ypsilanti, *U.S.A.* 76 D4
Yreka, *U.S.A.* 82 F2
Ysleta, *U.S.A.* 83 L10
Ystad, *Sweden* 9 J12
Ythan →, *U.K.* 12 D7
Ytyk-Kel, *Russia* 27 C14
Yu Jiang →, *China* 33 D6
Yu Shan, *Taiwan* 33 D7
Yu Xian, *Hebei, China* 34 E8
Yu Xian, *Henan, China* 34 G7
Yu Xian, *Shanxi, China* 34 E7
Yuan Jiang →, *China* 33 D6
Yuanqu, *China* 34 G6
Yuanyang, *China* 34 G7
Yuba →, *U.S.A.* 84 F5
Yuba City, *U.S.A.* 84 F5
Yūbari, *Japan* 30 C10
Yūbetsu, *Japan* 30 B11
Yucatán □, *Mexico* 87 C7
Yucatán, Canal de, *Caribbean* 88 B2
Yucatan Str. = Yucatán, Canal de, *Caribbean* 88 B2
Yucca, *U.S.A.* 85 L12
Yucca Valley, *U.S.A.* 85 L10
Yucheng, *China* 34 F9
Yuci, *China* 34 F7
Yudino, *Russia* 26 D7
Yuendumu, *Australia* 60 D5
Yugoslavia ■, *Europe* 21 C8
Yukon →, *N. Amer.* 68 B3
Yukon Territory □, *Canada* 68 B6
Yukti, *Russia* 27 C11
Yukuhashi, *Japan* 31 H5
Yule →, *Australia* 60 D2
Yulin, *China* 34 E5
Yuma, *Ariz., U.S.A.* 85 N12
Yuma, *Colo., U.S.A.* 80 E3
Yuma, B. de, *Dom. Rep.* 89 C6
Yumbe, *Uganda* 54 B3
Yumbi, *Zaïre* 54 C2
Yumen, *China* 32 C4
Yun Ho →, *China* 35 E9
Yuncheng, *Henan, China* 34 G8
Yuncheng, *Shanxi, China* 34 G6
Yundamindra, *Australia* 61 E3
Yungas, *Bolivia* 92 G5
Yungay, *Chile* 94 D1
Yunnan □, *China* 32 D5
Yunta, *Australia* 63 E2
Yunxi, *China* 34 H6
Yupyongdong, *N. Korea* 35 D15
Yur, *Russia* 27 D14
Yurgao, *Russia* 26 D9
Yuribei, *Russia* 26 B8
Yurimaguas, *Peru* 92 E3
Yuscarán, *Honduras* 88 D2
Yushe, *China* 34 F7
Yushu, *Jilin, China* 35 B14
Yushu, *Qinghai, China* 32 C4
Yutai, *China* 34 G9
Yutian, *China* 35 E9
Yuxi, *China* 32 D5
Yuzawa, *Japan* 30 E10
Yuzhno-Sakhalinsk, *Russia* 27 E15
Yvelines □, *France* 18 B4
Yvetot, *France* 18 B4

Z

Zaandam, *Neths.* 15 B4
Zabaykalskiy, *Russia* 27 E12
Zabid, *Yemen* 46 E3
Zābol, *Iran* 45 D9
Zāboli, *Iran* 45 E9
Zabrze, *Poland* 17 C9
Zacapa, *Guatemala* 88 D2
Zacapu, *Mexico* 86 D4
Zacatecas, *Mexico* 86 C4
Zacatecas □, *Mexico* 86 C4
Zacatecoluca, *El Salv.* 88 D2
Zacoalco, *Mexico* 86 C4
Zacualtipán, *Mexico* 87 C5
Zadar, *Croatia* 20 B6
Zadetkyi Kyun, *Burma* 39 H2
Zafarqand, *Iran* 45 C7
Zafra, *Spain* 19 C2
Żagań, *Poland* 16 C7
Zagazig, *Egypt* 51 B11
Zāgheh, *Iran* 45 C6
Zagorsk = Sergiyev Posad, *Russia* 24 C6
Zagreb, *Croatia* 20 B7
Zāgros, Kuhhā-ye, *Iran* 45 C6
Zagros Mts. = Zāgros, Kuhhā-ye, *Iran* 45 C6
Zāhedān, *Fārs, Iran* 45 D7
Zāhedān, *Sīstān va Balūchestān, Iran* 45 D9
Zahlah, *Lebanon* 47 B4
Zaïre ■, *Africa* 52 E4
Zaïre →, *Africa* 52 F2
Zaječar, *Serbia, Yug.* 21 C10
Zakamensk, *Russia* 27 D11
Zakavkazye, *Asia* 25 F7
Zākhū, *Iraq* 44 B4
Zákinthos, *Greece* 21 F9
Zákros, *Greece* 23 D8
Zalingei, *Sudan* 51 F9
Zambeke, *Zaïre* 54 B2
Zambeze →, *Africa* 55 F4
Zambezi = Zambeze →, *Africa* 55 F4
Zambezi, *Zambia* 53 G4
Zambezia □, *Mozam.* 55 F4
Zambia ■, *Africa* 55 E2
Zamboanga, *Phil.* 37 C6
Zamora, *Mexico* 86 C4
Zamora, *Spain* 19 B3
Zamość, *Poland* 17 C11
Zanaga, *Congo* 52 E2
Zandvoort, *Neths.* 15 B4
Zanesville, *U.S.A.* 78 G2
Zangābād, *Iran* 44 B5
Zangue →, *Mozam.* 55 F4
Zanjan, *Iran* 45 B6
Zanjān □, *Iran* 45 B6
Zante = Zákinthos, *Greece* 21 F9
Zanthus, *Australia* 61 F3
Zanzibar, *Tanzania* 54 D4
Zaouiet El-Kala = Bordj Omar Driss, *Algeria* 50 C6
Zaouiet Reggane, *Algeria* 50 C5
Zaozhuang, *China* 35 G9
Zapadnaya Dvina, *Russia* 26 D4
Zapadnaya Dvina →, *Belorussia* 24 C3
Západné Beskydy, *Europe* 17 D9
Zapala, *Argentina* 96 D2
Zapaleri, Cerro, *Bolivia* 94 A2
Zapata, *U.S.A.* 81 M5
Zapolyarnyy, *Russia* 24 A5
Zaporozhye, *Ukraine* 25 E6
Zaragoza, *Coahuila, Mexico* 86 B4
Zaragoza, *Nuevo León, Mexico* 87 C5
Zaragoza, *Spain* 19 B5
Zaragoza □, *Spain* 19 B5
Zarand, *Kermān, Iran* 45 D8
Zarand, *Markazī, Iran* 45 C6
Zaranj, *Afghan.* 40 D2
Zarate, *Argentina* 94 C4
Zāreh, *Iran* 45 C6
Zarembo I., *U.S.A.* 72 B2
Zaria, *Nigeria* 50 F6
Zarneh, *Iran* 44 C5
Zarós, *Greece* 23 D6
Zarqā' →, *Jordan* 47 C4
Zarrin, *Iran* 45 C7
Zaruma, *Ecuador* 92 D3
Żary, *Poland* 16 C7
Zarzis, *Tunisia* 51 B7
Zashiversk, *Russia* 27 C15
Zaskar →, *India* 43 B7
Zaskar Mts., *India* 43 C7
Zastron, *S. Africa* 56 E4
Zavāreh, *Iran* 45 C7
Zavitinsk, *Russia* 27 D13
Zavodovski, I., *Antarctica* 5 B1
Zawiercie, *Poland* 17 C9
Zāwiyat al Bayḍā, *Libya* 51 B9
Zāyā, *Iraq* 44 C5
Zayarsk, *Russia* 27 D11
Zaysan, *Kazakhstan* 26 E9
Zaysan, Oz., *Kazakhstan* 26 E9
Zayü, *China* 32 D4
Zduńska Wola, *Poland* 17 C9
Zeballos, *Canada* 72 D3
Zebediela, *S. Africa* 57 C4
Zeebrugge, *Belgium* 15 C3
Zeehan, *Australia* 62 G4
Zeeland □, *Neths.* 15 C3
Zeerust, *S. Africa* 56 D4
Zefat, *Israel* 47 C4
Zeil, Mt., *Australia* 60 D5
Zeila, *Somali Rep.* 46 E3
Zeist, *Neths.* 15 B5
Zeitz, *Germany* 16 C6
Zelenograd, *Russia* 24 C6
Zelzate, *Belgium* 15 C3
Zémio, *C.A.R.* 54 A2
Zemun, *Serbia, Yug.* 21 B9
Zerbst, *Germany* 16 C6
Zeya, *Russia* 27 D13
Zeya →, *Russia* 27 D13
Zghartā, *Lebanon* 47 A4
Zhailma, *Kazakhstan* 26 D7
Zhangbei, *China* 34 D8
Zhangguangcai Ling, *China* 35 B15
Zhangjiakou, *China* 34 D8
Zhangwu, *China* 35 C12
Zhangye, *China* 32 C5
Zhangzhou, *China* 33 D6
Zhanhua, *China* 35 F10
Zhanjiang, *China* 33 D6
Zhanyi, *China* 32 D5
Zhanyu, *China* 35 B12
Zhao Xian, *China* 34 F8
Zhaocheng, *China* 34 F6
Zhaotong, *China* 32 D5
Zhaoyuan, *Heilongjiang, China* 35 B13
Zhaoyuan, *Shandong, China* 35 F11
Zhashui, *China* 34 H5
Zhdanov = Mariupol, *Ukraine* 25 E6
Zhecheng, *China* 34 G8
Zhejiang □, *China* 33 D7
Zheleznodorozhny, *Russia* 24 B9
Zheleznogorsk-Ilimskiy, *Russia* 27 D11
Zhen'an, *China* 34 H5
Zhengding, *China* 34 E8
Zhengzhou, *China* 34 G7
Zhenlai, *China* 35 B12
Zhenping, *China* 34 H7
Zhenyuan, *China* 34 G4
Zhidan, *China* 34 F5
Zhigansk, *Russia* 27 C13
Zhitomir, *Ukraine* 25 D4
Zhlobin, *Belorussia* 24 D5
Zhokhova, Ostrov, *Russia* 27 B16
Zhongdian, *China* 32 D4
Zhongning, *China* 34 F3
Zhongtiao Shan, *China* 34 G6
Zhongwei, *China* 34 F3
Zhongyang, *China* 34 F6
Zhoucun, *China* 35 F9
Zhouzhi, *China* 34 G5
Zhuanghe, *China* 35 E12
Zhucheng, *China* 35 G10
Zhugqu, *China* 34 H3
Zhumadian, *China* 34 H8
Zhuo Xian, *China* 34 E8
Zhuolu, *China* 34 D8
Zhuozi, *China* 34 D7
Zhupanovo, *Russia* 27 D16
Ziārān, *Iran* 45 B6
Ziarat, *Pakistan* 42 D2
Zibo, *China* 35 F10
Zichang, *China* 34 F5
Zielona Góra, *Poland* 16 C7
Zierikzee, *Neths.* 15 C3
Zigey, *Chad* 51 F8
Zigong, *China* 32 D5
Ziguinchor, *Senegal* 50 F1
Zihuatanejo, *Mexico* 86 D4
Žilina, *Czech.* 17 D9
Zillah, *Libya* 51 C8
Zima, *Russia* 27 D11
Zimapán, *Mexico* 87 C5
Zimba, *Zambia* 55 F2
Zimbabwe, *Zimbabwe* 55 G3
Zimbabwe ■, *Africa* 55 F2
Zinder, *Niger* 50 F6
Zinga, *Tanzania* 55 D4
Zion Nat. Park, *U.S.A.* 83 H7
Zipaquirá, *Colombia* 92 C4
Ziros, *Greece* 23 D8
Zitácuaro, *Mexico* 86 D4
Zitundo, *Mozam.* 57 D5
Ziway, L., *Ethiopia* 51 G12
Ziyang, *China* 34 H5
Zlatograd, *Bulgaria* 21 D11
Zlatoust, *Russia* 24 C10
Zlin = Gottwaldov, *Czech.* 17 D8
Zlītan, *Libya* 51 B7
Zmeinogorsk, *Kazakhstan* 26 D9
Znojmo, *Czech.* 16 D8
Zoar, *S. Africa* 56 E3
Zobeyrī, *Iran* 44 C5
Zobia, *Zaïre* 54 B2
Zomba, *Malawi* 55 F4
Zongo, *Zaïre* 52 D3
Zonguldak, *Turkey* 25 F5
Zonqor Pt., *Malta* 23 D2
Zorritos, *Peru* 92 D2
Zou Xiang, *China* 34 G9
Zouar, *Chad* 51 D8
Zouérate, *Mauritania* 50 D2
Zoutkamp, *Neths.* 15 A6
Zrenjanin, *Serbia, Yug.* 21 B9
Zuetina, *Libya* 51 B9
Zufar, *Oman* 46 D5
Zug, *Switz.* 16 E4
Zuid-Holland □, *Neths.* 15 C4
Zuidhorn, *Neths.* 15 A6
Zula, *Ethiopia* 51 E12
Zumbo, *Mozam.* 55 F3
Zumpango, *Mexico* 87 D5
Zungeru, *Nigeria* 50 G6
Zunhua, *China* 35 D9
Zuni, *U.S.A.* 83 J9
Zunyi, *China* 32 D5
Zuoquan, *China* 34 F7
Zurbātiyah, *Iraq* 44 C5
Zürich, *Switz.* 16 E4
Zutphen, *Neths.* 15 B6
Zuwārah, *Libya* 51 B7
Zūzan, *Iran* 45 C8
Zverinogolovskoye, *Russia* 26 D7
Zvishavane, *Zimbabwe* 55 G3
Zvolen, *Czech.* 17 D9
Zwettl, *Austria* 16 D7
Zwickau, *Germany* 16 C6
Zwolle, *Neths.* 15 B6
Zwolle, *U.S.A.* 81 K8
Zymoetz →, *Canada* 72 C3
Żyrardów, *Poland* 17 B10
Zyryanka, *Russia* 27 C16
Zyryanovsk, *Kazakhstan* 26 E9
Zyyi, *Cyprus* 23 E12

NORTH AMERICA
SOUTH AMERICA
AFRIC
4
8
68-69
72-73
70-71
78-79
82-83
80-81
84-85
76-77
86-87
88-89
74
92-93
94-95
96
12
13
10-11
18
19
22
ATLANTIC OCEAN
PACIFIC OCEAN 64-65
PACIFIC OCEAN
Arctic Circle
Tropic of Cancer
Equator
Tropic of Capricorn